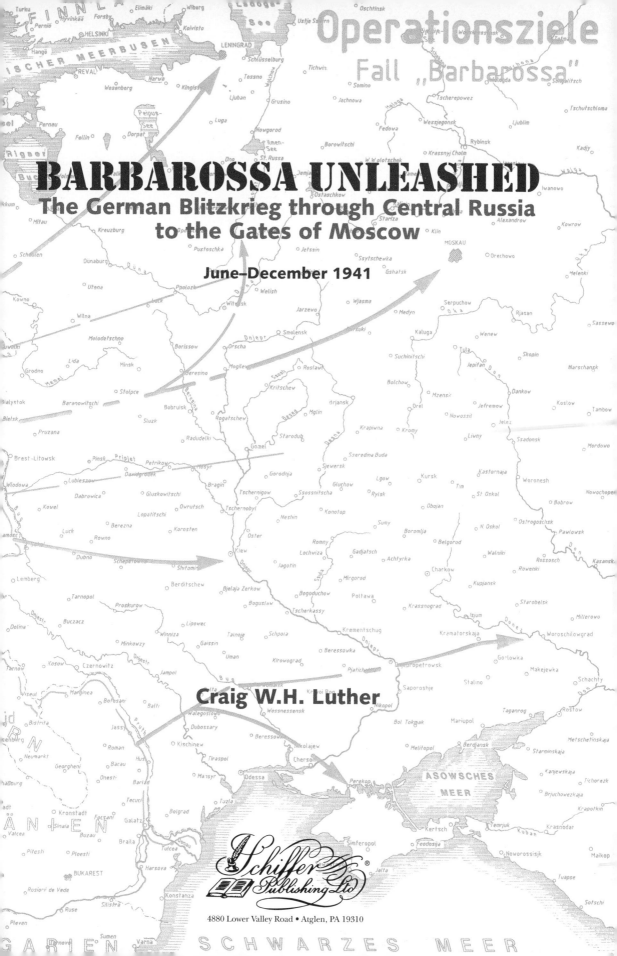

Operationsziele
Fall „Barbarossa"

BARBAROSSA UNLEASHED
The German Blitzkrieg through Central Russia to the Gates of Moscow

June–December 1941

Craig W.H. Luther

Schiffer Publishing Ltd

4880 Lower Valley Road • Atglen, PA 19310

Designed by John P. Cheek
Type set in Syntax Lt STD/ITC Garamond
ISBN: 978-0-7643-4376-6
Printed in China

Published by Schiffer Publishing, Ltd.
4880 Lower Valley Road
Atglen, PA 19310
Phone: (610) 593-1777; Fax: (610) 593-2002
E-mail: Info@schifferbooks.com

For our complete selection of fine books on this and related subjects, please visit our website at www.schifferbooks.com. You may also write for a free catalog.

This book may be purchased from the publisher. Please try your bookstore first.

We are always looking for people to write books on new and related subjects. If you have an idea for a book, please contact us at proposals@schifferbooks.com

Schiffer Publishing's titles are available at special discounts for bulk purchases for sales promotions or premiums. Special editions, including personalized covers, corporate imprints, and excerpts can be created in large quantities for special needs. For more information, contact the publisher.

Dedication

To my dearly beloved father and mother.

Epigraph

"Die Stimme des Blutes deines Bruders schreit

zu mir von der Erde." (Genesis 4:10)

Contents

PHOTO ESSAY NO. 1:
Commanders and Weapons (follows page 144)

PHOTO ESSAY NO. 2:
Vormarsch of Army Group Center through Central
Russia – Summer 1941 (follows page 352)

PHOTO ESSAY NO 3:
Battle of Moscow and Winter Battles (October 1941 –
March 1942) (follows page 592)

Notes on Style

Maps consulted in the preparation of this book were exclusively German or English in origin, no Russian-language maps were used. For consistent spellings of primary Russian cities and towns, I have relied in large part on the most recent publications on the Russo-German War 1941-45 by experts such as David Glantz or Evan Mawdsley; I have also used maps of central Russia graciously provided by Colonel Glantz. Occasionally, however, particularly in the translations of field post letters or diary entries by German eastern front soldiers, when obscure villages or towns are mentioned which could not be located on maps – and which, in many cases, were obliterated during the war, never to be rebuilt – I have used the original German spellings. For the proper names of Soviet personages (marshals, generals, etc.), I have also relied on the most common current spellings used by Glantz, Mawdsley and other experts, as well as on *The Oxford Guide to World War Two* (I.C.B. Dear, ed.).

I have sought to employ reasonably consistent protocols for German and Russian military units. German armies are spelled out, as in German "Fourth" Army, while Russian armies are always numbered, as in Soviet "31 Army." Military units, regardless of their size (or whether German or Russian), are normally referred to with the unit number followed by the type of unit, for example: 3 Panzer Group, 9 Army Corps, 24 Panzer Corps, 6 Infantry Division, 77 Infantry Regiment, etc. Sometimes shortcuts are employed, for example, 9 AK for 9 Army Corps, or 6 ID for 6 Infantry Division. In the translated German texts (letters, personal diaries, official unit war diaries, etc.), and in my own narrative, I have, in certain instances, for units below division and regimental level, elected to use abbreviated German unit designations; for example, III./PzRgt 18 (in lieu of 3rd Battalion, 18 Panzer Regiment), or 3./IR 18 (in lieu of 3rd Company, 18 Infantry Regiment). While this may appear inconsistent, it made sense on grounds of economy, while also enabling the author to retain a bit of the original German "flavor" in some of the translated materials. Readers unfamiliar with German military terminology are urged to consult the "List of Abbreviations" in this book.

Throughout the narrative I have used the dating standard common to the great majority of the world's countries – the "Gregorian Little Endian," in the sequence of day, month, and year. For example, 1.6.1941 signifies 1 June 1941, not 6 January 1941, as in American usage. For denoting distances, kilometers are generally used; in quotations where distances are given in miles, I have left them as is, and not converted them to kilometers. For denoting time, three variants are used; for example, 0315 hours, 3.15 in the morning, or 3:15 a.m.

List of Maps*
(refer to pockets on inside covers)

* Sources: K.-J. Thies, *Der Zweite Weltkrieg im Kartenbild*, Bd. 5: Teil 1.1: *Der Ostfeldzug Heeresgruppe Mitte 21.6.1941 – 6.12.1941. Ein Lageatlas der Operationsabteilung des Generalstabes des Heeres* (1); D. M. Glantz, *Atlas and Operational Summary. The Border Battles 22 June – 1 July 1941* (2); D. M. Glantz, *Atlas of the Battle of Smolensk 7 July – 10 September 1941* (3).

List of Abbreviations
(German, English & Russian)

AA	*Aufklaerungsabteilung:* Reconnaissance Battalion
AA	anti-aircraft
Abt.	*Abteilung*: branch (administrative), battalion, or unit, depending on the context employed
a.D.	*ausser Dienst:* retired
AFV	armored fighting vehicle
AK	*Armeekorps:* German army corps
Anl.	*Anlage:* enclosure
AOK	*Armeeoberkommando:* German army headquarters staff
APC	armored personnel carrier
AR	*Artillerie-Regiment*
Arko	*Artilleriekommandeur:* artillery commander
BA-MA	*Bundesarchiv-Militaerarchiv* (the German Federal Military Archives in Freiburg, Germany)
Battr.	*Batterie* (artillery)
Bd.	*Band:* volume (of book or journal)
Bf	*Bayerische Flugzeugwerke*
Btl.	battalion
Brig.	brigade
Brig.-Gen.	Brigadier General
CAS	close air support
C-in-C	commander-in-chief
d.G.	*des Generalstabes:* of the general staff
DR	*Das Reich*
DRZW	*Das Deutsche Reich und der Zweite Weltkrieg* (German quasi-official history of World War II, see "Bibliography")
FHO	*Fremde Heere Ost:* Foreign Armies East
FHq	*Fuehrerhauptquartier:* Hitler's military headquarters
Fla	*Fliegerabwehr:* air defense (anti-aircraft)
Flak	*Fliegerabwehrkanone:* anti-aircraft artillery
GAF	German Air Force
GD	*Grossdeutschland:* Greater Germany
geh.	*geheim*: secret
GenQu	*Generalquartiermeister:* chief supply officer of German Army General Staff
GenLt	*Generalleutnant* (See, Appendix No. 1, "Comparative Military Ranks (German/ American)")
GenMaj	*Generalmajor*
GenSt	*Generalstab:* German Army General Staff
GenStdH	*Generalstab des Heeres:* German Army General Staff
GFM	*Generalfeldmarschall*
GHQ	general headquarters
gK.Chefs	*geheime Kommandosachen-Chefsachen:* the highest routine security classification
GKO	State Defense Committee (Stalin's war cabinet)
GPU	State Political Directorate (Soviet Union)
GRU	Soviet Main Intelligence Directorate
HE	high explosive

Hg	*Herausgeber:* editor or publisher
HGr	*Heeresgruppe:* army group
HKL	*Hauptkampflinie:* main battle line
Hptm	*Hauptmann:* captain
HQu	*Hauptquartier:* headquarters
HVP	*Hauptverbandsplatz:* main dressing station
Ia	*Erster Generalstabsoffizier:* An operations officer responsible for operational issues at the division, army corps, army and army group levels.
Ib	*Zweiter Generalstabsoffizier:* Supply Officer responsible for supply at the division level
Ic	*Dritter Generalstabsoffizier:* An intelligence officer responsible for enemy intelligence and counterintelligence (*Abwehr*); position was clearly subordinate to that of the Ia
ID	*Infanterie-Division*
ID (mot.)	*Infanterie-Division* (motorized)
IfZ	*Institut fuer Zeitgeschichte:* Institute of Contemporary History (Munich & Berlin)
IG	*Infanterie-Geschuetz:* infantry gun
i.G.	*im Generalstab:* a member of the German General Staff
IR	*Infanterie-Regiment*
IRGD	*Infantrie-Regiment "Grossdeutschland"*
JG	*Jagdgeschwader:* fighter wing
K	*Kradschuetzen:* motorcycle riflemen
KDC	Karlsruhe Document Collection
Kdr	*Kommandeur*
Kfz	*Kraftfahrzeug:* motor vehicle
KG	*Kampfgeschwader:* bomber wing
KGr	*Kampfgruppe:* battlegroup
KIA	killed in action
Kom.Gen.	*Kommandierender General:* commanding general (army corps level)
Korueck	*Kommandant des rueckwaertigen Armeegebietes:* commandant of rear army area
Kp	*Kompanie*
KTB	*Kriegstagebuch:* war diary
KV	*Klementi Voroshilov:* for KV-1 and KV-2 tanks (Soviet)
l(e.)FH	*leichte Feldhaubitze:* light field howitzer
l(e.)Gr.W.	*leichter Granatwerfer:* light mortar
l(e.)IG	*leichtes Infanterie-Geschuetz:* light infantry gun
l(e.)MG	*leichtes Maschinengewehr:* light machine gun
Lkw	*Lastkraftwagen:* truck or transport vehicle
Lt.	*Leutnant*
Lt.-Col.	lieutenant colonel
Lt.-Gen.	lieutenant general
Maj.-Gen.	major general
MG	*Maschinengewehr:* machine gun
MGFA	*Militaergeschichtliches Forschungsamt:* Research Institute for Military History (Potsdam, Germany)
MIA	missing in action
Mot.	motorized
N	*Nachlass:* personal papers
NCO	non-commissioned-officer
NKGB	People's Commissariat of State Security (Soviet Union)
NKO	People's Commissariat of Defense (Soviet Union)
NKVD	People's Commissariat of Internal Affairs (Soviet Secret Police)
OB	*Oberbefehlshaber:* commander-in-chief
ObdH	*Oberbefehlshaber des Heeres:* Commander-in-Chief of the German Army
ObLt.	*Oberleutnant:* first lieutenant
ObstLt.	*Oberstleutnant:* lieutenant-colonel

Offz.	*Offizier*
OKH	*Oberkommando des Heeres:* High Command of the German Army
OKL	*Oberkommando der Luftwaffe:* High Command of the German Air Force
OKW	*Oberkommando der Wehrmacht:* High Command of the German Armed Forces
OODA	Observe, Orient, Decide Act ("OODA Loop")
OpAbt	*Operationsabteilung:* Operations Branch of the German Army High Command
OQu	*Oberquartiermeister:* Deputy Chief of the Army General Staff
OQu I	*Oberquartiermeister I:* Deputy Chief of Staff for Operations in the Army High Command
OT	*Organisation Todt*
Pak	*Panzerabwehrkanone:* anti-tank gun
PD	*Panzer-Division*
Pi.	*Pionier:* combat engineer
POL	petroleum, oil, lubricants
PR	*Panzer-Regiment*
Pz	*Panzer*
Pz I	Panzer 1 (tank)
Pz II	Panzer II (tank)
Pz III	Panzer III (tank)
Pz 35(t)	Panzer 35(t) (tank of Czech origin)
Pz 38(t)	Panzer 38(t) (tank of Czech origin)
Pz IV	Panzer IV (tank)
PzJg(Jaeg)	*Panzerjaeger:* anti-tank troops
PzK	*Panzerkorps*
Pz K(pf)w	*Panzerkampfwagen:* tank
PzRgt	*Panzer-Regiment*
RAD	*Reichsarbeitsdients:* German Labor Service
RD	Rifle Division (Soviet)
Rgt	*Regiment*
RH	*Reichsheer* (Denotes German Army records at BA-MA)
RL	*Reichsluftwaffe* (Denotes *Luftwaffe* records at BA-MA)
RVGK	High Command Reserve (Soviet)
SD	*Sicherheitsdienst:* Security Service (Branch of the SS)
s.FH	*schwere Feldhaubitze:* medium field howitzer
s.Gr.W.	*schwerer Granatwerfer:* medium mortar
s.IG	*schweres Infanterie-Geschuetz:* medium infantry gun
s.MG	*schweres Machinengewehr:* heavy machine gun
SP	Self-propelled
SPW	*Schuetzenpanzerwagen:* armored personnel carrier
SR	*Schuetzen-Regiment:* rifle regiment (in motorized infantry and panzer divisions)
SS	*Schutzstaffel:* elite guard of the Nazi Party
Stavka	Soviet High Command
StG	*Sturzkampfgeschwader:* dive bomber wing
StuG	*Sturmgeschuetz:* assault gun
(t)	*tschechisch:* Czech (origin)
TD	Tank Division (Soviet)
TOE	table of equipment
Uffz	*Unteroffizier:* non-commissioned officer
USAF	United States Air Force
USSR	Union of Soviet Socialist Republics (Soviet Union)
VA	*Vorausabteilung:* forward detachment
VB	*Vorgeschobener Beobachter:* forward observer (artillery)
VVS	*Voenno-vozdushnikh sil:* Soviet Air Force
WFSt	*Wehrmachtfuehrungsstab:* Armed Forces Operations Staff (OKW)

Foreword

"The result of the 1941 campaign was that Hitler's plan of operations from 18 December 1940, on which his strategy and military policy for the further course of the entire war was constructed, had failed." (*General der Panzertruppe* Walther K. Nehring, *Die Geschichte der deutschen Panzerwaffe 1916-1945*)

So wrote my father after the Second World War, after he had, in the gray morning light of 22 June 1941 – the day Adolf Hitler dispatched his battle-tested *Wehrmacht* into Soviet Russia – crossed over the German-Soviet frontier together with 2.5 million other German soldiers and, at the head of his 18 Panzer Division, hastened toward an unknown and bitter fate.

Over 60 years had passed since this world-shattering event in that fateful year, 1941, when "at the eleventh hour," and over the course of nearly a decade, a military historian from California undertook the task of questioning a very large number of former *Wehrmacht* members – who had lived through this time from June 1941 as soldiers in the USSR – about their personal views and experiences, and of examining the many personal letters, diaries, and accounts of their experiences, which were willingly placed at his disposal.

They tell of the events, circumstances, and conditions as they were experienced and preserved in the memory of the ordinary German soldier – the *Landser* (the counterpart of the American "GI" between 1941 and 1945).

Together with a group of these veterans, the author went to Russia, and they all visited the battlefields of 1941. They even met and got to know the people who live there now. During this visit, the author fell into the hands of a gang of criminals, who attacked him, and it was only by considerable good fortune and with help from the old German *Landser* that he managed to get away more or less in one piece.

This book presents the reader with the incredible harshness of the ideological struggle between two world views – that of National Socialism on the one hand, and that of a Stalinist Socialism on the other – which was carried out by both sides across the back of the ordinary soldier with unrelenting ruthlessness to the point of excess.

More wars of this kind and of this relentless nature followed after 1945 in Indochina, Algeria, Vietnam, and even still today in Iraq and Afghanistan. They have led to further bloody losses, but evidently not to any logical consequences on the part of the politicians responsible for them.

The author attempts to investigate the prevailing mood among the forces in the field and to convey this to the reader through examination of a veritable multitude of personal accounts, documents, and the written remains of participating soldiers from Army Group Center, who range from the ordinary *Landser* right up to leading generals. It is not a picture of military arrogance or of a "missionary army" that is drawn here, but rather one of obedience, of courage and of impressive bravery, of fulfilling one's duties, even when this was contrary to personal convictions.

The physical and psychological strains – or rather, excessive demands, which in very many cases overburdened ordinary mental processes – exerted on these fighters of the

German *Ostheer* are laid out in harrowing detail here. So, too, are the outstanding discipline and the perseverance of the individual, or even of the respective unit, although feelings of rage and retribution against a brutal and merciless – but also courageous – opponent meant that even these boundaries might be crossed.

There is also the ever present, almost oppressive, alienness of the Russian countryside in its breadth, emptiness, and climatic brutality, bound with wonder and compassion for the poverty – unimaginable for a German soldier – simplicity, and forbearance of the Russian civilian populace. Some of the latter in turn demonstrated overwhelming friendliness toward the German soldier as a human being, at least up until the point when the brutality of the organized partisan war on the one hand, and the start of the extermination policy enforced by Hitler and his leadership on the other, gradually turned the Russian populace against the German soldiers.

The author of this "battle panorama," however, constructs an overarching framework of events beyond all the conditions of the fighting soldier on both sides, thereby offering a near journalistic account of the larger political and strategic situation. It is presented, as it were, in a time-lapse effect, with current reports from Berlin, Moscow, London, and Washington on the one hand, and the various military headquarters – for example, Hitler's Wolf's Lair (*Wolfsschanze*) in East Prussia – on the other. This gives the reader an easy vantage point from which to discern events in three dimensions, to comprehend them, and so to assess both cause and effect.

In conjunction with this, the military expert and historian will find a wealth of substantiated sources, testament to the high academic quality of this work.

Going above and beyond all ideological standpoints, above and beyond all the prejudices, hate, and settling of accounts which this period brought the world, the author has constructed a memorial to the man who, in reality, only did and had to do that which his government – German and Soviet – ordered him to do:

To the fighter on the eastern front, who fought for his *Vaterland*:

To the soldier.

Christoph Nehring
Essen, Germany
March 2012

Preface

"Die Wahrheit ist konkret." (Georg W.F. Hegel)

"There is no abstract truth; truth is always concrete." (Vladimir Ilyich Lenin)

Reflecting on the basic mission of the guild of historians, the late Barbara W. Tuchman, no minimalist in her own prolific writings, reduced that mission to two simple words: "Tell stories," she implored. Because that's what history is – a story. Yet what is a story? E.M. Forster offered a lyrical definition: If I tell you that the king died and then the queen died, that's simply a sequence of events; but if I tell you that the king died and then the queen died of grief, that's a story – because it demands empathy on the part of the teller of the story and the reader or listener to the story. Articulated in such a way, a story brings history to life and becomes an "antidote to the hubris of the present" – the idea that all we do, and think, and feel is somehow superior to the actions, thoughts and feelings of generations that preceded us.[1]

The purpose of this book is to tell such a story – about the soldiers of a now reviled Army which, in another time and place, fought and died in a historically unparalleled conflict. The objective is three-fold. In the first place, the book explores the opening phases of Operation *Barbarossa*, Adolf Hitler's surprise attack on the Soviet Union, by following the advance of German Army Group Center across central Russia in the summer of 1941 from the vantage point of the "common" German soldier – that is, in the words of the late German philosopher, Wilhelm R. Beyer, from "below, where life is concrete:"[2] across the fields, the hills, the dense primeval forests, and the swamps which made up the main line of resistance along a bloody battlefront many hundreds of kilometers in length. Secondly, the larger tactical and operational events, as they unfolded along the central axis of the German advance, are addressed in detail. Lastly, the view from the "green table," comfortably inhabited by Hitler and his general staff well behind the lines, their battle maps swimming in red and blue arrows signifying death and annihilation, is also fully represented. While the focus is squarely on the German experience during the summer campaign (culminating in a brief account of the German push to the outskirts of Moscow in the fall of 1941 and the subsequent winter battles), the concerns, plans, and actions of Stalin and his generals are not ignored; in addition, the strategic and ideological underpinnings of Hitler's decision to strike Soviet Russia, as well as the planning by the German Army General Staff, are examined at length.

To achieve the key goal of a perspective "from below" – and, indeed, one offering many new details on the topic – I rely heavily on personal memoirs, field post letters (*Feldpostbriefe*), personal diaries, battle reports, photos, and unit histories self-published by German veterans' organizations (still active more than 60 years after the war's end). Most of this hitherto unpublished material was graciously provided by dozens of the former "*Landser*" – as the common German soldier was known in the idiom of Germany's

Wehrmacht (armed forces) – with whom I have corresponded over the years. Since late 2002, I was able to reach nearly 100 German veterans of the fighting in central Russia in 1941; now in their 80s and 90s, these former eastern front soldiers (*Ostfrontkaempfer*) dutifully completed my questionnaire, responded to my many queries, and plied me with a veritable "treasure trove" of personal materials which proved invaluable to this work. Sadly, since I began this project, dozens of these veterans have passed on, as the opportunity to gain insight into the horrors of the eastern front from the participants themselves irretrievably slips away.

I had, of course, literally waited until "five minutes before 12" to begin to reach out to the few surviving veterans of the eastern front. By the fall of 2002, most of the 17 to 18 million German soldiers who had fought in the Second World War (about 10 million of these in Russia) were gone, while the number of those still living was declining by the hundreds daily. (In the United States, we lose about 1000 of our ca. 16 million Second World War veterans each day.) And yet, as I soon discovered, among those still living were more than a few for whom the time had finally come to tell their remarkable stories. This has resulted in recent years in a most useful trickle (if not a flood) of published and unpublished personal accounts. More than one German veteran intimated to me that, with the end of life approaching, it was time to put "pen to paper" – or, better yet, in today's parlance, "finger to keyboard" – and to provide children and grandchildren with an accounting of their lives under Hitler's Third Reich and in the cauldron of modern total war.

In light of Germany's immense historical "baggage," it is, perhaps, not surprising that, for the most part, German military and social historians, as well as the German post-war military itself, have evinced little interest in personal accounts by simple soldiers of the *Wehrmacht*. To some, this state of affairs signifies a most regrettable lacuna in German scholarship and in Germany's comprehension of the Second World War. As late as 1987, more than four decades after the war had ended, Wilhelm R. Beyer vehemently pleaded for a fundamental change in how the war was studied by providing a central place for the view from "totally below" (*ganz unten*). Invoking the memory of Germany's towering 19th Century philosopher, Georg W.F. Hegel, he urged scholars to begin to assess what the poor rifleman (or as he put, the "*Schuetze Arsch*") had experienced in the Second World War:

> Consideration of all things must proceed from the "bottom," or at the very least from an equivalent position of observation … Socrates, Descartes and many other thinkers occupied the lowest ranks during their military service … He who approaches things and events *re vera* from "below" describes truth, the *objective* truth.[3]

Such voices, however, have largely remained voices in the wilderness as far as German scholarship is concerned. Indeed, Wolfram Wette, professor of contemporary history at the University of Freiburg, more recently observed (2002):

> Historical scholarship in Germany has lagged far behind that in the English-speaking countries in paying attention to the experience of ordinary servicemen. This is especially true of the majority of soldiers, meaning those who functioned obediently as cogs in the war machine and drew no negative attention to themselves …
>
> In the records of the *Wehrmacht*, the "little guy" or "average Joe" tends to exist only in anonymous form, as an unnamed statistic in reports on losses and troop strength. The logs of military units of varying sizes and other official sources generally make no mention of enlisted men by name. The same applies

to "regimental histories" written after the war and the diaries and accounts published by officers. The men under their commands remain nameless, and their ordinary hardships and battle experiences went unreported. This explains why the historical archives contain so little material on the subject. It has been estimated that the source material on enlisted men in the German [Federal] Military Archives in Freiburg amounts to less than 1 percent of the total holdings. The Library for Contemporary History in Stuttgart, by contrast, has made a priority of buying up collections of soldiers' letters and makes them available to researchers.

If one surveys the research on military history with this in mind, it becomes evident that for a long time scholars concentrated on a tiny percentage of the total military, namely, generals and admirals and their aides, the officers of the army and navy general staffs … [T]his perspective … remains overwhelmingly dominant.[4]

The attitude of the contemporary German military, the *Bundeswehr*, toward the "little guy," or "average joe," of the *Wehrmacht*, was captured succinctly by a veteran of a German World War II bomber wing:

During the last 10 years of my working life, I was the director of the cartographical department here at the German Army's Military History Research Institute [*Militaergeschichtliches Forschungsamt*], from the summer of 1978 to the summer of 1988. In this position I approached many of the Institute's historians at the time, and even the director of the Institute and the lead historian, with the suggestion that it was now imperative to talk to and write to the survivors of the war through the veterans' organizations [*Soldatenkameradschaften*], and particularly the flying units of the *Luftwaffe*, to obtain copies of flight logs, accounts of experiences, documents, etc., etc.

"No," they all said, we academics and historians deal primarily with the "upper echelons" of *Luftwaffe* leadership and planning, command structures, responsibilities, chains of command, etc., etc. – Even my proposals to the German Federal Military Archives [*Bundesarchiv-Militaerarchiv*] to task the Military History Research Institute with the matter in spite of this remained unsuccessful.[5]

The tiny silver lining in this gloomy story of German war studies is that, by the 1980s, the occasional historian, or interested party, had begun to publish works focusing on the "*Krieg des kleinen Mannes*," as Wolfram Wette called it.[6] More recently, the *Bundeswehr* has taken steps to begin a dialogue with the common soldier; for example, by soliciting information on the experiences of German soldiers supporting the ongoing NATO effort in Afghanistan. Yet it remains a tragedy that neither the *Bundeswehr* nor any university or scholarly institution in post-war Germany ever sought to systematically gather and record the experiences of their World War II veterans, whose personal stories are now lost forever. Such a failure stands in stark contrast to recent initiatives in the United States, where, for example, at the Eisenhower Center at the University of New Orleans, hundreds of former "GIs" and veterans of the Normandy invasion of June 1944 have participated in an ambitious oral history project led for years by the late historian Stephen E. Ambrose.[7]

Of course, I am well aware of the dangers of relying too heavily on such personal materials. A soldier writing home from the front, or keeping a diary, has the tiniest of perspectives – he may describe a "tree" or two with precision, but cannot begin to define the whole "forest." (And given the horrific nature of what he does see, he may not be able, or even desire, to describe it.) A memoir written after the war – indeed, one prepared 50-60 years after the events depicted – may make for a riveting and poignant read, but will likely suffer from the questionable memory of its creator. Moreover, the sometimes brutal behavior of the *Wehrmacht* in Russia, its participation in atrocities against the Soviet Union's soldiers and citizens, has no doubt resulted in a highly selective recalling of the terrible events of those days. "We must also emphasize," argues H. J. Schroeder, "that fragmentary experiences, gleaned from army post, diaries, biographical interviews, autobiographies and other historical source material, can never hope to give a total picture of the war experience of the common soldiers during the Russian campaign." Thus, it is necessary to use "complementary sources in order to prove that certain subjective, biographical experiences actually have what we call a collective historical value." In other words, the common soldier's point of view is most valuable to historical research when it is firmly imbedded in a much broader "picture" gleaned from a wide range of source materials.[8]

As Omer Bartov has written, however, a view "from below" of a historical event – even one as vast, horrific and deadly as the war in the east – must "rely to a large extent on individual experience, observation, and memory. Much as we may suspect the factual accuracy of subjective testimonies, we cannot do without them."[9] In many years of correspondence with German veterans, I often found their memories of pivotal events to be surprisingly uncluttered and precise; after all, for most of them, the crucible of combat on the eastern front forever remained the most terrible, dramatic, and meaningful period of their lives – never to be surpassed by any experience in post-war civilian life. Moreover, as a recent article on memory and the human brain observed: "Some people's memories dim and others … remain crystal bright for a lifetime … Tragedies and humiliations seem to be etched most sharply, often with the most unbearable exactitude."[10]

To supplement the veterans' materials, and to furnish this book with a scholarly foundation, I have been careful to consult the key archival repositories germane to my topic. During several visits to Germany from 2005 to 2009, I gathered pertinent archival materials at the German Federal Military Archives (BA-MA) in Freiburg, including war diaries, special reports and other documents prepared by German units operating in the central sector of the eastern front. The Library for Contemporary History in Stuttgart was "mined" for its magnificent collection of thousands of German field post letters, with additional field post located at the *Feldpost-Archiv Berlin*. The many years of research also led me to the Air Force Historical Research Agency, Maxwell AFB, AL (for its fine collection of *Luftwaffe*-related materials); the U.S. Army Military History Institute, Carlisle Barracks, PA (for its large library and copious collection of special studies produced by German officers after World War II for the U.S. Army in Europe); the Hoover Institute, Stanford University, CA; and, of course, the National Archives in Washington D.C.

I have as well perused the unrelenting flood of published primary and secondary materials germane to my topic. Due to my regrettable lack of Russian language skills, I have relied heavily on the works of retired U.S. Army Colonel David Glantz for material addressing the "other side of the hill," – that is, Stalin, the Soviet High Command, the organization, equipment and operations of the Red Army. Western scholars studying the Russo-German War 1941-45 owe a real debt of gratitude to Colonel Glantz, whose tireless efforts have brought the war to life from the perspective of the Soviet Union and her soldiers with hitherto unrivaled clarity and detail. Glantz' many works will continue to challenge and provoke, while compelling an on-going reassessment of much of the fighting on the eastern front.

A final point: Because a central focus of this book is the simple German infantryman, tank crew, or pilot, I have sought – primarily through the diaries and letters of the soldiers themselves – to offer insight into the culture of the German Army in the east (*Ostheer*) – what it believed, why it fought, how it responded to the unprecedented strain and savagery of combat on the eastern front. Reactions of German soldiers to Stalin's Russia – its land, its people, the crushing poverty, what the *Landser* sardonically characterized as the "Soviet paradise" – are also examined briefly. While no attempt is made to either glorify or denigrate the institution of the *Wehrmacht* or its fighting soldiers, the issue of "war crimes" (both German *and* Russian) is discussed in some detail in Chapter 9. My sincere hope is that the reader of this long book – and its many stories – will discover new details about the fighting in Russia in the summer of 1941 – about the ordinary *Landser* of Army Group Center as they advanced across central Russia with but a single destination in mind – Moscow!

ENDNOTES

1   D. McCullough, *"Knowing History and Knowing Who We Are,"* in: *Imprimis*, Apr 05.
2   *"Unten, wo das Leben konkret ist."* Quoted in: H. J. Schroeder, *Die gestohlenen Jahre*, 2, f.n. 4.
3   Quoted in: H. J. Schroeder, *Die gestohlenen Jahre*, 2, f.n. 4.
4   W. Wette, *The Wehrmacht*, 175-76.
5   Ltr, Hans Gaenshirt to C. Luther, 11 Jan 03.
6   In English, "War of the little man," or common soldier. See, W. Wette, *Der Krieg des kleinen Mannes. Eine Militaergeschichte von unten* (Munich, 1992).
7   Efforts by Dr Ambrose to locate and gather the experiences of U.S. Normandy veterans had begun in the early 1980s. The information was collected by means of questionnaires, cassette tapes, and, if possible, actual interviews. After Ambrose's death the mission of locating and interviewing the veterans was passed to the World War II Museum in New Orleans about 2004. Telecon Intvw, Dr Craig Luther with Michael Edwards, Eisenhower Center, 1 Mar 11.
8   H. J. Schroeder, *"German Soldiers' Experiences,"* in: *From Peace to War: Germany, Soviet Russia and the World, 1939-1941*, B. Wegner (ed.), 310-11.
9   O. Bartov, *"Von unten betrachtet: Ueberleben, Zusammenhalt und Brutalitaet an der Ostfront,"* in: *Zwei Wege nach Moskau*, B. Wegner (Hg.), 340.
10   J. Foer, *"Remember This,"* in: *National Geographic*, 44, 53.

Acknowledgments

For the preparation of this study I am deeply indebted to dozens of special people, without whose generous and patiently given support this book would not have seen the light of day. While I do so with trepidation – as certainly as night follows day I will neglect to cite a key contributor; please forgive me! – I will attempt to acknowledge some of the many whose support was vital to this effort.

First and foremost, are the dozens of veterans of the fighting along the Moscow axis in 1941, who responded to my pleas for help by offering up a truly rich tapestry of information – the intimate human details which one rarely encounters in the unit war diaries and other surviving official records. Herr Walter Vollmer, former artillerist with the 106 ID, was stalwart in his support, even arranging for me to travel with him and his veterans' group to Rzhev, Russia, in May 2005 to visit former battlefields and meet with Russian war veterans. The late Herr Heinrich Stockhoff (6 ID), furnished many useful materials and spent hours of his time transcribing *Feldpostbriefe*; it was an honor for me to get to know him and his family personally on my visits to Germany. Herr Otto Will (5 PD) provided copies of his (then-unpublished) memoirs, as well as many photographs; to this day we maintain a close friendship, talking weekly with each other on the telephone. Knights-Cross holder Ernst-Martin Rhein (6 ID) graciously provided lodging at his home in Germany and consented to a personal interview, in addition to giving me one of the few remaining copies of his fine regimental history. Many other veterans – too many to mention here – provided field post letters, memoirs, photographs and other key personal documents which greatly enriched this narrative, and to them I am deeply grateful. Sadly, many of these men have since passed on, and with their deaths the brief window of opportunity which had existed in 2002 to capture their personal narratives for posterity has forever closed.

Along with the veterans, I am eternally indebted to professional colleagues, friends and family of veterans, professional archivists, librarians, and others too numerous to mention, without whose assistance this book would not have been written. Among the professional colleagues I must begin with Dr Juergen Foerster, one of Germany's foremost military historians and a man of generous heart and spirit, who plied me with vital documents and studies, often on his own initiative without any "arm twisting" on my part. Dr Dennis E. Showalter, one of America's finest military historians, kindly volunteered many hours of his valuable time reading the manuscript and offering much-needed support and encouragement. Dr Evan Mawdsley, himself author of an outstanding recent history of the Russo-German war, provided a helping hand when needed, as did Colonel David M. Glantz. Special thanks on several counts to Colonel Glantz – for furnishing photographs of key Soviet commanders; for allowing me to use several of his situation maps of the eastern front; and, most importantly, for kindly and patiently responding to my many queries dealing with the "Other Side of the Hill." Herr Johannes Haape graciously furnished the papers of his late physician father, Dr Heinrich Haape, an eastern front veteran and author of one of the finest personal narratives ever written about the war in the east.[1] I am also deeply grateful to the German publishing house Biblio Verlag for the right to publish several of their terrific color reproductions of the daily situation maps of the German General Staff; in fact, I dare say that I could hardly have written this book were it not for these maps, whose bold, blue lines chart the "blitzkrieg" of Army Group Center along the road to Moscow. A debt of gratitude is also owed to Mr Roger Bender of Bender Publishing, for filling several lacunae in the collection of photographs used in this book.

Dr Madeleine Brook, a post-doctoral research assistant on the Medieval and Modern Languages faculty, University of Oxford, is responsible for ninety-seven percent of the German-to-English translations in this book, and I cannot praise her enough for her elegant renderings of literally hundreds of field post letters, diary entries, and other German texts in the manuscript; Ms Brook, who "doted" over my book as if she had written it herself, was also a joy to work with. Special thanks as well to Ms Jessica Guernsey, a graduate student in the Liberal Studies Program at Dartmouth College, NH, who carefully read the manuscript and saved me from acute embarrassment by catching several "bonehead" grammatical mistakes.

Not to be overlooked is the terrific staff of the library at Edwards Air Force Base, CA, who patiently responded to what must have been several hundred requests for books and articles. Mr Richard Baker, and the good folks at the U.S. Army Military History Institute, Carlisle Barracks, PA, responded time and again to my many requests for source materials, plying me with books, articles, and historical studies, without which my many years of toil would all have been for naught. The photographs in this book, many never before published, were mostly reproduced – and wonderfully so! – by the diligent and technically gifted crew at Henley's Photo, for decades an institution in Bakersfield, CA. I would be remiss if I did not also mention the German military publication "*Kameraden*," an "independent periodical for old and young soldiers," which kindly published my numerous announcements between 2002 and 2009, which, in turn, made it possible for me to contact many of the German eastern front veterans whose story I tell in this book.

Finally, no list of acknowledgements would be complete without the names of Frau Marianne Miethe, Herr Christoph Nehring, and Herr Klaus Schumann. Frau Miethe, whose late husband Erich flew his first missions as a Junkers Ju 52 pilot into the cauldron of Stalingrad in January 1943, spent hours too many to mention in the tedious work of transcribing memoirs, diaries and field post from the difficult German *Suetterlinschrift* script into readable High German. Her good cheer, intellectual curiosity and warm friendship have provided much-needed encouragement over the years. Christoph Nehring, son of the German tank general, Walther K. Nehring, has supported me from the beginning, critiquing my occasionally eccentric ideas, furnishing materials, and offering much useful guidance with his impressive knowledge of the *Wehrmacht* and its history. Klaus Schumann, whose father was killed in action fighting with Army Group North in September 1941, has also offered much needed encouragement over the years, as well as several useful primary documents he himself collected from veterans of the eastern front. I am deeply indebted to all three of these wonderful souls.

Let me end by acknowledging that, for me – and, no doubt, for many authors – the experience of writing is, most assuredly, a difficult struggle. Every sentence, each turn of a phrase, can end in paralyzing self-doubt. Did I get it right? Is that *really* what I wanted to say? Which reminds me of a wonderful epigram attributed to Voltaire: "To hold a pen, is to be at war." In times of frustration, when the right words simply didn't seem to come, I turned to Voltaire's wisdom for solace. For all errors of fact in this book – for which I alone am responsible – I turn to the bar of history, whose judgment of this work will, I hope, be kind.

ENDNOTES

1   H. Haape (in association with D. Henshaw), *Moscow Tramstop. A Doctor's Experiences with the German Spearhead in Russia* (London, 1957).

Introduction

"Why were the German planners so confident and yet, in the end, so wrong? These were not stupid men, and they possessed years of military experience and training. They believed that they had examined all the possibilities and that their conclusions were valid. In the end, though, they were actually committing one of the greatest acts of hubris in military history." (Geoffrey P. Megargee)[1]

"Our soldiers have to maintain the sort of heroism in the east that may be termed almost mythical." (Joseph Goebbels, 22 November 1941)[2]

"If ever there was a savage war, this was it." (Martin van Creveld)[3]

The German Army that plunged into the fields, forests and endless plains and steppe lands of European Russia on 22 June 1941 was perhaps the most splendid fighting force the world had yet seen. This is a bold statement. Surely, you remonstrate, the armies of Alexander the Great, the Roman Caesars, those of Napoleon, or even the ragtag, barefooted veterans of Robert E. Lee's Army of Northern Virginia – to mention but a few – must also occupy a special place in Valhalla, that mythological "hall of the slain." And such a conviction would also be correct. Yet the roughly 3.1 million soldiers that comprised Germany's *Ostheer,* the *Barbarossa* invasion force, signified something uniquely special. In terms of doctrine, training, initiative, experience, efficacy of their weaponry and success on the battlefield, modern Europe, at least, had never seen anything like them.

In barely 21 months of war – September 1939 to June 1941 – Hitler's *Wehrmacht* had registered an unparalleled string of victories. Poland fell in 37 days. France, which had fought Germany to a bloody standstill in World War I for nearly four years, was humiliated and defeated in 42 days (along with the Low Countries). In a daring display of initiative and flexibility, the Germans had conquered Norway, preempting a planned English invasion. If England had failed to submit to the *Luftwaffe's* bombing campaign in the summer and fall of 1940, to most observers this appeared but a minor setback for Hitler's victorious armies. By the spring of 1941, in a brilliant campaign planned on very short notice, the *Wehrmacht's* motorized units had rolled over Greece and Yugoslavia, securing Hitler's Balkan flank for Operation *Barbarossa.* And, in North Africa, Erwin Rommel had been set loose, while German paratroopers had conquered the strategic island of Crete. Total German killed in action (KIA) for this initial period of the war were, "by standards of [20th Century] bloodletting ... inconsiderable," amounting to about 110,000 men.[4]

By June 1941, Hitler's Third Reich dominated the European continent from the North Cape above the Arctic Circle to the Balkans in the southeast and the Mediterranean in the south. There were many reasons for the spectacular successes of the German armed forces. In the first place, it should not be forgotten that Germany, which had begun to significantly rearm by 1935-36, had clearly "stolen a march" on France, England and other potential adversaries, who were much slower to rearm. In fact, clandestine rearmament in

Germany had actually begun much earlier, during the 1920s under the Weimar Republic. In contrast, efforts of the Western powers to rebuild their armed forces were undermined by electorates that were often pacifist and in some cases even committed to complete disarmament. England and continental Europe were also slow to grasp the threat posed by Adolf Hitler.[5]

By September 1939, the German Reich had built a military machine which, for all its well-concealed shortcomings – and they were many, including, *inter alia*, serious shortages of vital raw materials, as well as aircraft and other weapons systems already bordering on obsolescence, not to mention an economy still on a peacetime footing – was better trained, equipped, disciplined and led than the armed forces of its European neighbors. The Germans had also been more successful during the inter-war period in responding to the lessons of World War I and exploiting the new technologies first introduced on the battlefields of 1914/18. The resulting successes of the *Wehrmacht* created a nimbus of invincibility, which only grew as its string of victories became ever more impressive; furthermore, in the spring of 1941, the capabilities of Germany's remaining continental foe, the Soviet Union, appeared manifestly unimpressive. Indeed, the failures of Stalin's Red Army in Poland in 1939 and, more emphatically, in Finland in late 1939 and early 1940, had led Hitler and his High Command to the fatal conclusion that little more than 10-12 weeks would be required to smash the Soviet Union to pieces. In a typical pre-*Barbarossa* assessment by the German military of their Soviet adversary, the chief of staff of Fourth Army, Colonel Guenther Blumentritt, stated on 18 April 1941 that, "there will be [14] days of heavy fighting. Hopefully, by then we shall have made it." Such thinking was, of course, fueled by the German sense of racial and cultural superiority.[6]

Hence it was with almost preternatural optimism that Hitler's eastern armies erupted into Russia in the summer of 1941. From the outset, Germany's "Fuehrer" attempted to portray the war as pre-emptive – that is, as an action to forestall or parry a threat perceived to be "imminent and overwhelming." Yet this was not so, for surviving records reveal that Hitler and his High Command hardly broke a sweat in the months preceding *Barbarossa* over the possibility of an imminent Russian attack on Germany. Nevertheless, new research into Soviet archives arguably supports the position that Hitler's attack may well have been justified as a *preventive* measure – as an action to "prevent a threat from materializing which does not yet exist," but may well exist at some time in the not too distant future.[7]

Operation *Barbarossa* commenced on 22 June 1941, and in the opening days and weeks all seemed to go like previous campaigns. The *Ostheer's* motorized spearheads sliced deep into Soviet Russia, smashing dozens of Red Army divisions with ruthless tactical precision; in the air, the *Luftwaffe* banished the Soviet Air Force from the skies, achieving air superiority and, in key sectors, absolute air supremacy. On the central front, Army Group Center, under Field Marshal Fedor von Bock, drove rapidly through Belorussia (White Russia), its two powerful armored groups executing a series of brilliant encirclement maneuvers – first at Belostok-Minsk in late June/July and then at Smolensk in July/August 1941. According to Israeli military historian Martin van Creveld, the German summer campaign in Russia signified "the greatest display of maneuver warfare in history."

> In point of preparedness, doctrine, numbers available for the offensive, and leadership, the German armed forces had peaked during the summer ... The key to this unparalleled achievement was *operativ* warfare, now waged with the aid of armored and mechanized units and honed into the blitzkrieg ... Coordinated mobility, even more than firepower, formed the key to this method of warfare ... In point of sheer operational brilliance, it has no parallel.[8]

Yet from the first hours of the campaign there were disturbing auguries. While some Red Army soldiers were more than willing to lay down their arms – particularly those recruited from Soviet-occupied Poland, the Ukraine or the Baltic States – many more resisted with courage and tenacity the Germans had hitherto not experienced. A physician assigned to 6 Infantry Division, Dr Heinrich Haape, described the opening day of the campaign in harrowing terms in an entry in his personal diary on the evening of *Barbarossatag*, 22 June 1941:

> The first day in the campaign against Russia. We have a hard day behind us! The Russians fought like devils and never surrendered, so we engaged in close combat on several occasions; just now, half an hour ago, another four Russians were struck dead with the butts of our rifles. Our regiment's losses on this single day are greater than during the entire French campaign (21 dead and 48 severely wounded). We were the focal point of the attack. Of the regiment's 6 doctors, one is KIA (shot to the head) and another injured. In addition, 4 medical orderlies are also KIA. We have pushed the Russians back along the whole line, except for a few bunkers that have not yet fallen. There is still hard fighting. – I had a lot of work to do and frequently had to bandage comrades under heavy machine gun fire. I have not yet had anything to eat today and only a very little to drink; we are cut off from our supply line![9]

As the war progressed into July and August, the Germans began to notice – with palpable unease – that the number of Red arrows on their battle maps was, in fact, multiplying; that the Red Army, far from collapsing under the weight of the *Ostheer's* "blitzkrieg," was feeding more and more resources into the battle. When one enemy army was destroyed, another took its place; when that was smashed, still another joined the Soviet order of battle. General Franz Halder, Chief of the German Army General Staff, who barely 14 days into the campaign (3 July 1941) had told his diary that the war was essentially won, would but a few weeks later, on 11 August, express amazement at the recuperative powers of the Russian "colossus," who, he admitted, had been badly underestimated.[10] Hitler, the German High Command, the generals at the front – they were becoming nervous.[11]

Far from Halder's "*gruenen Tisch*" (green table) in the dark forests of East Prussia, the German combat soldier in Russia soon realized that the war in the east – a war in which no quarter was given, and no quarter was asked – was like no other. From the outset a brutal dialectical logic of atrocity and counter-atrocity emerged. German soldiers, shocked and bewildered by Soviet combat tactics – savagely cunning and unsporting in their view – and enraged that missing comrades were often later found murdered (and often horribly mutilated) by Red Army soldiers,[12] retaliated with their own acts of brutality.

The Russo-German War 1941/45 was an existential struggle between two outlaw totalitarian states, their reciprocal hatreds stoked by racism and years of crude and vile propaganda; in this sense, the remarkable barbarism of the war in the east was foreordained. If Augustine once counseled that the sole purpose of war is to achieve a better peace,[13] Adolf Hitler, enthusiastically supported by his circle of military advisors, had other ideas: "Before a shot was fired in Russia," observes Evan Mawdsley in his recent book on the Russo-German War, "the German onslaught was planned – both at the front and the rear – to be the cruelest military campaign ever fought," with a character that was not only military, but ruthlessly imperialistic and ideological.[14] From the outset, moreover, the Soviet Union fought the war ruthlessly, and often outside the protocols of international law.

Caught in an abyss of violence and inhumanity, and trained to view their adversary as a racial inferior, many *Landser* were guilty of serious violations of the laws of war. Yet, unlike a deranged potentate in a Shakespearean play, an entire Army – much less an entire people – cannot decide to become evil; and it is my contention – supported by sound recent scholarship in Germany – that a large majority of the common soldiers on the Russian front fought with dignity and within the laws of war.[15] However, even a small fraction of perpetrators amounted to hundreds of thousands. Observes Guido Knopp:

> In recent years the question of the crimes of the *Wehrmacht* has been more carefully researched … The result is multifaceted: Numerous crimes were committed against civilians and soldiers in which *Wehrmacht* units were involved, above all at the eastern front. And time and again there were German soldiers who obeyed the voice of their conscience. It is in this area, in particular, that generalizations are not admissible. Terms such as "some," "many," or "all" leave a stale aftertaste. Many had little and few had much to answer for. However, it was at any rate "all too many" who not only knew about crimes, but also conspired to commit them. According to conservative estimates, at least five percent of *Wehrmacht* soldiers were involved in crimes. That would mean around 500,000 men at the eastern front alone.[16]

While the *Ostheer's* mobile units pressed inexorably eastward and well beyond the marching infantry, the latter, comprising more than 75 percent of the German invasion force, sought desperately to catch up to the front, marching – and marching and marching – up to 50 kilometers per day through an alien and unforgiving landscape of primitive roadways, primeval forests and swamps, all the while beset by the "unholy trinity" of the summer of 1941 – stifling heat, ubiquitous sand, and inadequate stores of life-sustaining water. Man and beast were pushed beyond the limits of endurance. Soldiers collapsed under the strain, while thousands of heavy German and western European draft horses perished along the way. Many formations were soon faced with serious logistical difficulties, an outcome of lazy German planning and an inadequate Russian road and rail infrastructure.

In less than three weeks, by 10 July 1941, total German fatal losses in the east (including 25,000 from 22-30 June), equaled or exceeded the dead *and* missing of the entire French campaign of 1940. Within eight weeks, the *Ostheer* had sustained more than 100,000 dead[17] as many as all previous campaigns combined. In the idiom of Thomas Hobbes, the life of a German soldier on the eastern front was "nasty, brutish and short." According to one source, the average life expectancy of a German *Leutnant* was 18 days; that of a company commander roughly 21 days; that of a battalion commander a little more than a month.[18] By the end of September 1941 – with Army Group Center about to begin its final, albeit abortive, push toward Moscow – the German forces in the east (all service branches) had incurred more than 185,000 fatal casualties, an average of 1830 per day.[19] To put these losses into perspective, the Germans had suffered less than 14,000 dead and missing during the Polish campaign of 1939, an average of fewer than 400 per day; and some 40,000 dead and missing during the French campaign of 1940, an average of 950 per day.[20] And these two campaigns had lasted only 35 and 42 days, respectively. In Russia, however, there was no end in sight – a war planned as a short "blitzkrieg" had become a desperate struggle of attrition, with the *Ostheer* diminished by the rough equivalent of a regiment in KIA every 48 hours of the war.

Of course this war of attrition also affected the Red Army, which sustained significantly greater losses than did the Germans in the opening phase of the war. In a matter of weeks, in fact, the Russian border armies were all but annihilated, with the Soviet Western Front – which bore the full brunt of Army Group Center's attack – suffering more than 340,000 irrecoverable losses (dead, captured, missing) through 9 July 1941.[21] In the weeks that followed the Soviet second echelon of forces was also savaged. Enjoying a pronounced tactical edge, the soldiers of the *Ostheer* maintained a remarkably positive casualty exchange rate, consistently inflicting more casualties than they sustained while crushing dozens of Soviet armies in the initial months of the war – killing, wounding, or capturing several million Red Army soldiers. Army Group Center, for example, by early August 1941, claimed well over half a million prisoners of war in the encirclement battles of Belostok-Minsk and Smolensk.[22]

Yet despite such horrific – indeed, historically unparalleled – losses, neither Stalin's rule nor the Red Army collapsed under the repeated hammer blows of Hitler's armies. What the Germans soon began to grasp, much to their dismay, was that the Soviet system, despite its brutality and inhumanity – or perhaps *because* of it – was on a much sounder footing than realized; moreover, the Soviets actually did some things extremely well. They knew, for example, how to make railroads run efficiently to shuttle newly mobilized armies of fresh recruits or reservists to the battlefront. They also operated a staggeringly successful mobilization system, which added dozens of new armies to the field throughout 1941. Another key to the ultimate ability of the Soviet Union to stop Hitler's *Wehrmacht* was Stalin's ability to make the most outrageous demands upon his people – soldiers and civilians alike. While men, women and children toiled long hours in factories beyond the Ural Mountains, in a fully mobilized economy, turning out an abundance of tanks, artillery and shells, Hitler's Germany remained on a largely peacetime footing. Such a striking asymmetry of effort on the respective home fronts played a primary role in the ultimate failure of *Barbarossa*.

Despite the *Ostheer's* spectacular victories, by mid- to late July 1941, the German advance had begun to slow. Against the solid expectations of Hitler and his High Command, the Soviet Union, far from collapsing, continued to fight with tenacity and increasing effectiveness. At this time, fundamental disagreements about strategy between the "Fuehrer" and his generals, which had been conveniently overlooked during the planning stages of the Russian campaign, burst out into the open. The story is well-known: the generals wanted to push on to Moscow, where, they argued, the Red Army would have to concentrate its forces for a final stand to protect the Soviet capital, the nerve center of Stalin's Russia; Hitler, however, thinking more in political and economic terms, looked to the flanks – toward Leningrad (and the Baltic region) in the north, the grain of the Ukraine and the industry of the Donbas region in the south.

While Hitler and his generals remonstrated, Army Group Center had, by late July and early August 1941, reverted to costly positional warfare along a front many hundreds of kilometers in length. Not until late August did Hitler make his final decision: Army Group Center was to stay put, and to dispatch an entire panzer group south into the Ukraine; Moscow could wait. While the outcome was another spectacular battle of encirclement – this time near Kiev – many historians view Hitler's decision as the turning point of Operation *Barbarossa*. Weeks of vacillation, they maintain, resulting in the "Fuehrer's" failure to move at once on Moscow after the Battle of Smolensk, forfeited Germany's opportunity to make a decisive lunge toward the Soviet capital well before the fall rainy season rendered all movement impossible. This author, however, disagrees with this perspective, for reasons explained in Chapter 11 of this book.

While the action shifted to the flanks (Army Group Center had also sent mobile forces north, to assist with the attack on Leningrad), von Bock's infantry suffered serious attrition, defending their trenches, bunkers and dugouts against repeated Red Army counterstrokes. The fighting around the town of El'nia, barely 300 kilometers from Moscow, was particularly savage, and characterized by Soviet artillery barrages reminiscent of World War I. In his diary on 24 August 1941, Dr Heinrich Haape (6 ID) captured the nature of the *Stellungskrieg* (positional warfare) along the overstretched front of Army Group Center:

24.8.1941:
Our division has to hold a line of 46 km – our battalion 4 km of this – against the constant onslaughts of the enemy. A difficult task! – We have established our

positions, proper field positions with bunkers, trenches, etc.; now just let the Russian come! The Russians did break through once in two locations – a stupid screw-up, but they were repelled again after a few hours with very heavy losses. During the counterattack, we found another 11 dead of our soldiers from 1st Batallion; they had resisted to the very last man with their MGs and rifles when the Cossacks had suddenly stormed our line with a bone-chilling "Urrah, Urrah!" Due to our superiority, they were finally overrun and killed in close combat next to their own weapons.[23]

Not until 30 September 1941 did Army Group Center begin Operation "Typhoon" (*Taifun*), the direct advance toward Moscow. Yet despite more spectacular victories, Operation *Barbarossa* had already failed. "Typhoon," in fact, was an improvised venture which should never have taken place, for the campaign was to have been decided by 30 September at the latest. In November 1941, a decimated and exhausted Army Group Center would make a last, desperate lunge for Moscow. But it was too late. A bitter cold had already descended over the battlefield; weapons suddenly refused to work, while tanks and vehicles failed to start. The *Ostheer's* system of supply, inadequate from the start, began to break down completely, leaving the soldiers without food, ammunition or winter clothing. Yet on they dutifully trudged, toward Moscow, mostly now collected in tiny combined arms battlegroups and, remarkably, despite the unparalleled hardship and suffering, with their morale still largely intact (a surprising fact corroborated by much of the surviving field post and contemporary diaries). Small groups of men actually reached the outskirts of the Soviet capital, where they watched as the city's searchlights and anti-aircraft guns sought out the small packs of German bombers which occasionally visited the city.

Yet the end had been reached, the Clausewitzian culmination point long ago crossed – Hitler's Army Group Center but a shell of the splendid fighting force which had crossed the Berezina, the Western Dvina and the Dnepr and advanced roughly 1000 kilometers to the gates of Moscow. Then, in early December 1941, disaster struck: After building up and carefully husbanding its reserves, the Red Army struck at the exposed flanks of Army Group Center just as the weather plunged to arctic depths. Caught by complete surprise in dangerously exposed conditions, the remnants of Bock's army group slowly withdrew to avoid encirclement and certain annihilation, the Red Army in rapid pursuit. By January 1942, the Soviet attack had expanded into a general offensive along the entire eastern front, while Army Group Center struggled to fend off the enveloping Soviet pincers that were closing around it. By mid-February, however, the combination of German defensive tenacity, and operational blunders made by attacking Red Army forces, resulted in an inchoate stabilization of the front 100-200 kilometers west of the high water mark of Army Group Center's advance.

While the Battle of Moscow itself and the Soviet counteroffensive are only examined briefly in this narrative, the reasons for the defeat of *Barbarossa* will be dissected in some detail. With due deference to Tolstoy, who argues in his epic novel of the Napoleonic Wars, *War and Peace*, that the real causes of historical events are not truly knowable, let me begin with a few basic observations. Foremost among them, Germany's attack on the Soviet Union in 1941 failed because it was fatally underpowered. The *Wehrmacht's* eastern armies, despite their superior training, experience, and discipline, were simply too few in number – too few men, armored vehicles, aircraft, etc. – to cope successfully with the unprecedented scope and unique challenges of the Russian theater of war. Assessing German operational and logistical planning before the campaign, one is struck by its incompleteness, superficial optimism, and the failure to prepare for the inevitable surprises, challenges and unforeseen crises that are the stuff of any and all wars. Of course, German military planners should have known better and, in fact, did know better. They were good students of history, and well aware that the elder Field Marshal von Moltke had once admonished that no battle plan survived initial contact with the enemy,[24] while Clausewitz himself had stressed the inevitable role of uncertainty and chance in armed conflict.

The shortcomings in planning, the failure to field an army adequately resourced and prepared to perform a mission characterized by unique and unprecedented challenges, were the result of that common human failing which has consigned the imperial projects of many would-be conquerors to defeat – that is, of hubris. Hitler and his military advisers, intoxicated by their spectacular victories through the spring of 1941, overestimated the capabilities of their armed forces and underestimated those of Stalin's Red Army. As they saw it, there was no task too great, no mission too daunting, for the soldiers of their undefeated *Wehrmacht*. After all, Germany's long-time nemesis, the Republic of France, which held the Imperial German Army at bay for more than four years between 1914/18, had collapsed in a mere six weeks in 1940.

Yet the mission clearly was impossible. From the beginning, too much was demanded of the German soldiers in Russia, who were regularly pushed far beyond the limits of endurance. Marooned deep inside an alien land, they fought on bitterly, garnering brilliant tactical victories and maintaining a positive casualty exchange rate to the very end, but the outcome was a matter of simple arithmetic: There were simply too many of the enemy, too many men, too many tanks, too many artillery pieces, too many aircraft. And the Russians, too, fought with great tenacity and, as the war went on, increasing tactical and operational acumen. All told, the war against the Soviet Union, which Hitler and his military advisers had expected to be over in 10 to 12 weeks, would last 1418 horrific days and claim the lives of more than four million German soldiers, including the 1.1 million who perished in Soviet captivity.[25]

As for the *Landser* of Army Group Center – they never again marched on Moscow following the failure of the 1941 campaign. For the next two and one-half years they conducted a largely successful defensive battle, until finally swallowed up and destroyed in the massive Soviet summer offensive of 1944 (Operation "Bagration"). Few survived this now all but forgotten Teutonic tragedy in the central theater of operations, which crushed German forces in Belorussia and propelled the Red Army to the very outskirts of East Prussia. Hopefully, in the narrative that follows, I have managed to bring to life the stories of the soldiers of Army Group Center who, during the decisive summer and fall of 1941, battled their way to the very outskirts of Moscow, only to be turned back in defeat.

ENDNOTES

1   G. P. Megargee, *War of Annihilation*, 26.
2   R. G. Reuth (Hg.), *Joseph Goebbels. Tagebuecher*, Bd. IV, 1708.
3   M. van Creveld, *The Changing Face of War*, 156.
4   J. Keegan, *Second World War*, 173; R. Overmans, *Deutsche militaerische Verluste*, 241. By way of comparison, by the end of 1914 – that is, after five months of fighting in World War I – total German losses had amounted to 840,000, of which roughly 150,000 were fatal losses. See, W. Hubatsch, *Deutschland im Weltkrieg*, 57-58.
5   For a useful study of Anglo-French appeasement and armament policies in the inter-war period see, J. Record, *"Appeasement Reconsidered."* According to Record, "the foundation of French appeasement was military incapacity to act against Germany," 19.
6   J. Foerster & E. Mawdsley, *"Hitler and Stalin in Perspective,"* in: *War in History*, 68-69.
7   C. Bellamy, *Absolute War*, 102. As Bellamy notes the concept of pre-emptive war has a "respectable pedigree" in international law. The concept of preventive war enjoys less "legal favor." For electrifying new research into Stalin's punctilious preparations for an eventual attack on Germany see, B. Musial, *Kampfplatz Deutschland. Stalins Kriegsplaene gegen den Westen* (Berlin, 2008).
8   M. van Creveld, *Air Power and Maneuver Warfare*, 93-94.
9   *Tagebuch* Haape, 22.6.41 (unpublished diary).

10   C. Burdick & H.-A. Jacobsen (eds.), *The Halder Diary 1939-1942*, 446, 506.

11   German historian Johannes Huerter, in his impressive work *Hitlers Heerfuehrer*, quotes from letters sent by top-level German field commanders on the eastern front to their wives in July and August 1941. The letters illustrate just how shocked were the field marshals and generals after only a few weeks of war by the Red Army's tenacious resistance and regenerative powers following catastrophic losses. It was clear to all of them from very early on that the war in the east was going to be a very different kind of war. See, J. Huerter, *Hitlers Heerfuehrer. Die deutschen Oberbefehlshaber im Krieg gegen die Sowjetunion 1941/42* (Munich, 2006).

12   Western scholarship on the Russo-German War 1941/45 – past and present – has often put significant emphasis on German war crimes in the east, the study of which in recent years has become a rather curious obsession among German military historians. Conversely, with the exception of a handful of works – the book by Alfred M. de Zayas, *The Wehrmacht War Crimes Bureau, 1939-1945*, comes immediately to mind – Soviet war crimes have traditionally been downplayed, even overlooked. An ancillary, albeit still meaningful, objective of this book is to help to set the record straight by means of a more balanced treatment of the topic of war crimes.

13   Lt.-Col. Paul Yingling, "*A failure of Generalship*," in: *Armed Forces Journal*, May 07.

14   E. Mawdsley, *Thunder in the East*, 12.

15   German historian Christian Hartmann, in his exhaustive recent study of five diverse German formations on the eastern front in 1941/42, argues convincingly that the number of perpetrators of war crimes, while significant, was relatively small. Hartmann rightly stresses the fact that most criminal activity – the shooting of civilians, plundering of property, abuse and murder of Soviet POWs, etc. – took place in sparsely occupied rear areas and not along the main battle line, where the great majority of soldiers were fully absorbed in their legitimate combat duties. See, C. Hartmann, *Wehrmacht im Ostkrieg. Front und militaerisches Hinterland 1941/42* (Munich, 2009).

16   G. Knopp, *Die Wehrmacht – Eine Bilanz*, 11.

17   R. Overmans, *Deutsche militaerische Verluste im Zweiten Weltkrieg*, 277.

18   A. Naumann, *Freispruch fuer die Deutsche Wehrmacht*, 372.

19   R. Overmans, *Deutsche militaerische Verluste im Zweiten Weltkrieg*, 277.

20   I.C.B. Dear (ed.), *The Oxford Companion to World War II*, 707; J. Keegan, *The Second World War*, 47; R. L. Dinardo, *Germany's Panzer Arm*, 109.

21   Col.-Gen. G. F. Krivosheev (ed.), *Soviet Casualties and Combat Losses*, 111.

22   According to one source, the Germans in 1941 maintained a casualty exchange rate of 11:1 in their favor, yet this figure is certainly exaggerated. See, J. Mosier, *Cross of Iron*, 181.

23   *Tagebuch* Haape, 24.8.41; K.-J. Thies, *Der Ostfeldzug – Ein Lageatlas*, "Lage am 24.8.1941 abds., Heeresgruppe Mitte."

24   As Moltke put it: "No plan of operations can look with any certainty beyond the first meeting with the major forces of the enemy ... The commander is compelled during the whole campaign to reach decisions on the basis of situations that cannot be predicted. All consecutive acts of war are, therefore, not executions of a premeditated plan, but spontaneous actions, directed by military tact." H. Holborn, "*The Prusso-German School*," in: *Makers of Modern Strategy*, P. Paret (ed.), 290.

25   R. Overmans, *Deutsche militaerische Verluste*, 265; F. W. Seidler (Hg.), *Verbrechen an der Wehrmacht*, 44; A. M. de Zayas, *The Wehrmacht War Crimes Bureau*, 305, f.n. 11; R. Traub, "*Versklavt und vernichtet*," in: *Der Zweite Weltkrieg*, S. Burgdorff & K. Wiegrefe (Hg.), 169. Some 75 percent of Germany's total fatal military losses in the Second World War were the result of the war in the east. For the most accurate estimates of total Soviet losses, which were far greater, see, Col.-Gen. G. F. Krivosheev (ed.), *Soviet Casualties and Combat Losses in the Twentieth Century* (London, 1997).

CHAPTER 1

Initial Planning and Preparations

(July-December 1940)

"Strategy is nothing more than the application of good common sense."
(The Elder Field Marshal von Moltke)

"The best strategy is always to be as strong as possible; first in general and then at the decisive point." (Carl von Clausewitz)

"The readiness is all." (Shakespeare, *Hamlet*)

1.1: Armistice at Compiègne (June 1940)

The month of June, observed American journalist and war correspondent, William L. Shirer, in his towering study of Adolf Hitler's Third Reich, was "always one of the loveliest months in the majestic [French] capital" of Paris. In mid-June 1940, Shirer had again visited Paris; this time, however, under conditions which must have torn at his heart – that is, in the wake of the German Army. On 14 June 1940, with France tottering on the brink of collapse, elements of the German 87 Infantry Division had marched triumphantly into the undefended city, while thousands of Parisians – and, for that matter, the entire world – looked on in a sublime state of shock.[1]

Although the fighting still continued, the outcome was no longer in doubt. France, until only recently the greatest military power on the European continent, was defeated. What the Germans had failed to accomplish over four long years of war between 1914/18, they had now achieved in a mere six weeks. France had declared war on Germany on 3 September 1939, two days after Hitler attacked Poland. In the months that followed, into the spring of 1940, the two sides had engaged each other in a sort of "shadow boxing" that history came to call the "Phony War." While Hitler, ever impatient, had wanted to strike France in the fall of 1939, inclement weather and the sounder judgment of his generals had prevailed. The attack was postponed until the spring of 1940, giving the Germans an opportunity to refine operational planning and better train, equip and prepare their forces.

The German western campaign, leveled against France and the Low Countries (Holland, Belgium and Luxembourg), finally began on 10 May 1940. Employing a superbly functioning combined arms team of ground and air forces – armor, mobile infantry, foot infantry, artillery, medium bombers, dive bombers, etc. – the *Wehrmacht* made quick work of its ill-prepared and sluggishly reacting opponent. On the fourth day of the campaign (13 May), the Germans, their armor sallying forth from the Ardennes Forest – an axis of advance the French had failed to anticipate – crossed the Meuse River at Sedan, achieving a decisive breakthrough. The German mechanized *Schwerpunkt*[2] then struck out rapidly to the west, making for the English Channel; by 18 May, the panzer divisions were sweeping across the battlefields of World War I, in the process reducing Hitler – who feared for the safety of his now exposed armored spearheads – to a bundle of nerves. By 20 May, elements of a panzer corps had reached the channel near Abbeville, having driven some

320 kilometers in 10 day's time. The elite units of both the French Army and the British Expeditionary Force (BEF) were now trapped in a huge pocket, their backs to the sea. Thanks in large part to Hitler's decision of 24 May, which halted the advance of his tanks just 25 kilometers from Dunkirk, the last remaining Channel port in Allied hands, the British and French were able to evacuate some 370,000 Allied soldiers, including the entire BEF, by 3 June.[3]

With British forces out of the fight, and the French now fighting alone, defeated and demoralized, all that remained for the victorious Germans were mopping up operations. Hitler's armies wheeled southward, rapidly breaching the French "Weygand Line," which, truth be told, was not much of a "line" at all. By 14 June, the Germans were in Paris; "three days later they were thronging the terrace of the Café de la Paix, happy to be sightseers in the tourist capital of the world." On 17 June, Marshal Pétain, having just formed a new French government, broadcast to the French people to inform them that negotiations for an armistice were underway.[4]

Which brings us back to Mr Shirer. On 19 June, he "got wind" of where Hitler planned to "lay down his terms" for the armistice requested by Pétain. No doubt relishing the historical irony, and clearly seeking revenge, the "Fuehrer" intended to dictate his terms on the same spot where Imperial Germany had capitulated to France and her allies on 11 November 1918: in a small clearing in the woods at Compiègne. On the afternoon of the 19th, Shirer drove out there, only to find German Army engineers "demolishing the wall of the museum where the old *wagon-lit* of Marshal Foch, in which the 1918 armistice was signed, had been preserved." By the time Shirer left, the engineers, having torn down the wall, were pulling the railroad car onto the tracks in the center of the clearing – the precise spot, they said, where it had stood at 5:00 a.m. on 11 November 1918, when the German emissaries signed the armistice.[5]

Two days later (21 June 1940), Shirer returned to the site at Compiègne "to observe the latest and greatest of Hitler's triumphs …

> It was one of the loveliest summer days I ever remember in France. A warm June sun beat down on the stately trees – elms, oaks, cypresses and pines – casting pleasant shadows on the wooded avenues leading to the little circular clearing. At 3:15 p.m. precisely, Hitler arrived in his big Mercedes, accompanied by Goering, Brauchitsch, Keitel, Raeder, Ribbentrop and Hess, all in their various uniforms, and Goering, the lone Field Marshal of the Reich, fiddling with his field marshal's baton. They alighted from their automobiles some 200 yards away, in front of the Alsace-Lorraine statue, which was draped with German war flags so that the Fuehrer could not see (though I remembered from previous visits in happier days) the large sword, the sword of the victorious Allies of 1918, sticking through a limp eagle representing the German Empire of the Hohenzollerns. Hitler glanced at the monument and strode on.[6]

Shirer studied the German dictator's face, scribbling in his diary that it appeared "grave, solemn, yet brimming with revenge." After lingering briefly – and defiantly! – at another triumphalist French monument, Hitler and his party made their way into the armistice railway car, the "Fuehrer" seating himself in the chair which Marshal Foch had occupied nearly 22 years before. Minutes later, the French delegation arrived, led by General Charles Huntziger, commander of the Second Army at Sedan. While to Shirer they "looked shattered," they retained, he thought, "a tragic dignity." As Franz Halder, the Chief of the German Army General Staff, wrote in his diary that evening, the French delegation had "no warning that they would be handed the terms at the very site of the negotiations of 1918. They were apparently shaken by this arrangement and at first inclined to be sullen … [The C-in-C of the Army] is worried that the French might not accept."[7]

Hitler and his entourage left the railway car after General Wilhelm Keitel, Chief of Staff of OKW,[8] had read out the preamble of the armistice terms to the French, leaving Keitel to preside over the negotiations, albeit with strict instructions not to depart from the conditions Hitler himself had laid down. Huntziger read them, at once informing the Germans that they – the terms – were "hard and merciless" and, in his view, much more severe than those which France had imposed on a defeated Germany in 1918. He and his delegation struck a defiant pose, argued and remonstrated, with the result that the negotiations – over issues such as French prisoners of war, the return of anti-Nazi refugees in France and her territories to the German Reich, and, most importantly, over the disposal of the French navy – dragged on into the 22nd. At 6:30 p.m., a frustrated Keitel issued an ultimatum – the French had to accept, or reject, the armistice within an hour. With no realistic alternative, the French government capitulated. At precisely 6:50 p.m., 22 June 1940, Huntziger and the OKW Chief affixed their signatures to the armistice treaty.[9]

Several days later (28 June), at 3:30 a.m., Hitler departed his headquarters at Brûly-de-Pesche and, with his personal pilot, Hans Baur, at the controls,[10] flew to Le Bourget aerodrome just outside Paris. From there, he was driven to the French capital, for what would be his first, and only, visit to the city. Arriving shortly before 6.00 in the morning, the procession of vehicles (including armed guards), drove through silent, almost deserted streets. Hitler quickly toured some of the city's most notable buildings and landmarks, among them the Arc de Triomphe, the Eiffel Tower, the Louvre, the famous opera house – whose architecture he had admired as a student – and, finally, Napoleon's tomb at the Dome des Invalides. Departing the tomb he told his entourage: "That was the greatest and finest moment of my life." During his city tour, he ordered the destruction of two World War I monuments – an order that was dutifully carried out. Leaving Paris at 8:30 a.m.[11] and returning to the local aerodrome, he ordered Baur to circle several times above the city. He then returned to his headquarters. Overcome by the joy of the moment he told his architect friend, Albert Speer: "It was the dream of my life to be permitted to see Paris. I cannot say how happy I am to have that dream fulfilled today."[12]

1.2: Reflections on France 1940

With France defeated, Adolf Hitler stood at the pinnacle of power. He – his Third Reich, his *Wehrmacht* – dominated Europe from above the Arctic Circle to Bordeaux, from the English Channel to the Bug River in eastern Poland. The former corporal and regimental dispatch runner on the western front in World War I had now become "the greatest of German conquerors."[13] His popularity among the German people was at its peak, his political position – his authority – beyond challenge. For men of the anti-Hitler resistance, those such as Colonel Hans Oster, a senior officer in German military intelligence (the *Abwehr*), the defeat of France was a devastating blow. As Oster's colleague, Reinhard Spitzy recalled, the entry of German troops into Paris had caused all critics of Hitler and his Reich to "fall silent," while the return of the victorious soldiers to Berlin was an occasion for unalloyed enthusiasm. An American journalist, Howard K. Smith, noted that, "it was the only occasion in the better part of six years that I have spent in Germany that I saw … Germans weeping and laughing from pure spontaneous joy." When Hitler finally returned to his capital in early July, he was "driven to the Reich Chancellery on a carpet of flowers. According to press reports 'the mile-long route from the Anhalter Station to the Chancellery was a perfumed avenue of greens, reds, blues and yellows flanked by cheering thousands who shouted and wept themselves into a frantic hysteria as the Fuehrer passed.'"[14]

Perhaps betraying future intentions, Hitler, in the immediate aftermath of the French campaign, informed his OKW chief: "Now we've shown just what we're capable of. Believe me, Keitel, in comparison [to France] a campaign against Russia would be little more than child's play!" (*Sandkastenspiel*)[15] Yet the victory over France, spectacular though it was, concealed some unpleasant truths – some of which have only recently come to light – about the causes of that victory and about Germany's military prowess in general. While we need not linger on these topics, they merit brief discussion.

To contemporary observers, the *Wehrmacht's* stunning success in France was another even more telling example of a new style of warfare – "blitzkrieg" or "lightning war," though Hitler himself rejected the term[16] – based on a unique combination of mechanized forces, aircraft and radio communications. The Germans had pioneered the new techniques during the 1930s, and then unleashed them on Poland in September 1939. Such was the "conventional wisdom" of the times, and it became the general view of historians for decades after the war. Of course, the French campaign was considered to be the apotheosis of blitzkrieg – its most splendid, and successful, demonstration in the course of the Second World War. And while it is true that it was on 13 May 1940 at Sedan where, for the first time in history, a battle was won, a decisive breakthrough achieved, through the massed employment of tanks and aircraft,[17] what had actually taken place was not exactly what it had seemed to be.

As more recent scholarship has revealed,[18] planning by the German General Staff for the French campaign, while clearly bold and innovative, was fundamentally cautious in approach. That the campaign would, ultimately, unfold in a blitzkrieg-like fashion was less the result of intent than of a series of fortuitous and unpredictable events, among them dramatic failures on the part of the Allies, the opportunism of a panzer general, and, of course, accident and chance. One example: By the third day of the campaign, the main German armored force found itself virtually immobilized in a massive traffic jam in the narrow corridors of Ardennes Forest, some 41,000 vehicles stretching from the Meuse all the way back 250 kilometers to the Rhein![19] While Allied air attacks could have smashed the German armor before it even joined in battle, the Allies failed to exploit the opportunity; instead, a panic by French forces (the so-called "panic of Bulson") – based on a report, apocryphal as it turned out, that German tanks had already crossed the Meuse – resulted in the French line folding up like a "house of cards" and enabled the German breakthrough at Sedan. The rapid "blitzkrieg" which followed, far from being planned, was in large part the outcome of the arbitrary and, at times, insubordinate, actions of "panzer leader" Heinz Guderian. Galvanized by the dramatic and unexpected success of his tank corps at Sedan, he at once burst out from the bridgehead with his armor and, ignoring orders of his superiors, made for the channel at breakneck speed, in the process creating – as one author put it[20] – an avalanche-like effect that pulled the other panzer units along with him. The operations thus developed a dynamic of their own, the General Staff at times even losing control over them. While it is beyond the scope of this study to delve deeper, the salient point is this: The French campaign, far from being planned and executed as a "blitzkrieg," had in the critical opening days hung from a slender reed, only to see *fortuna* smile on the Germans as a result of events which could never have been predicted or foreseen.[21]

Despite such qualifying remarks, the German victory in France was – at the risk of being redundant – a spectacular one. German losses (army and air force) had amounted to only 163,213, including 29,640 fatal casualties.[22] In fact, since September 1939, the German armed forces had only incurred about 200,000 casualties, including ca. 60,000 fatal losses. If by today's standards these figures seem exorbitant, they signify about half the losses sustained by the Kaiser's Army in a single engagement – the Battle of the Somme in 1916.[23] To cite another comparative statistic: The Imperial German Army lost more than 880,000 men between March and July 1918 in "Operation Michael," its final desperate bid to turn the tide in World War I, with 78,000 of these losses coming on the first day of the offensive, 21 March 1918.[24]

While the *Wehrmacht* was understandably proud of its successes – and the nimbus of invincibility that accompanied them – below the surface were serious shortcomings

– material and doctrinal – which would only later be revealed, with fatal consequences. Most notably, the German armed forces had not been prepared for a major war (nor was Germany's economy for that matter). They had entered hostilities in September 1939 with no serious plans for such a war; strikingly, they had no strategy whatsoever for an offensive in the west.[25] And without taking anything away from the efficacy of her armies, Germany's victories in the first 10 months had been greatly assisted by the poor preparation of her enemies.

One is struck by the fact that, by May 1940, only about 10 percent of the *Wehrmacht* was actually composed of *Schnelle Verbaende* – formations which were fully motorized and capable of "blitzkrieg;" the remainder marched on foot, moving at about the same speed as the armies of Frederick the Great or Napoleon, and were more suited to a war of position than one of rapid movement. In the pre-war period, Third Reich military planners had made the decision to build a mass army comprised mainly of traditional infantry divisions, instead of a small, elite army based on motorized units suitable for an operational war of movement (*operativen Bewegungskrieg*). Decisively influencing this decision, which illustrates that German military planners were hardly preparing for "blitzkrieg," were the still traumatic experiences of World War I and its grinding battles of attrition. After the French campaign, the Germans would double the number of armored divisions (primarily by significantly reducing the number of tanks in each division) in preparation for war with Russia; yet such formations, the "tip of the spear" as it were, still made up but a fraction of the force.[26] Moreover, the broad disparities in capability between the handful of fully motorized units and marching infantry would confront German commanders in the east with virtually insurmountable tactical dilemmas.

Nevertheless, it was with Operation *Barbarossa* in June 1941 that the Germans, for the first time, would purposely embark on a campaign based on "blitzkrieg." Seduced by the "miracle of Sedan," and the putative "lessons learned" from 1940, they fell victim to the illusion which had animated Count Alfred von Schlieffen prior to World War I – that a materially superior enemy could be quickly and decisively overcome in a rapid war of movement culminating in a decisive battle of annihilation, what the Germans were fond of calling a *Vernichtungsschlacht*.[27] In other words, to General Halder and his colleagues, the Battle of France had proven, beyond doubt, that victory in battle was simply a matter of working out the proper operational formula,[28] even against an industrial power significantly larger than Germany, like Soviet Russia. Such thinking, an outcome of the badly misconstrued lessons of 1940, exercised a pernicious influence on German doctrine and, perforce, on planning for the Russian campaign, ending eventually in defeat in the snows outside Moscow.

1.3: Strategic Considerations/Overtures to England

The *Sieg ueber Frankreich* (victory over France) was considered by most contemporaries a "colossal personal triumph" for Hitler.[29] The future course of the war – indeed, the fate of Europe – appeared in the months that followed to depend primarily on whatever decisions he was about to make. As Hitler's propaganda minister, Joseph Goebbels, penned in his diary on 12 July 1940: "Everyone waits on the decisions of the Fuehrer."[30] Yet despite such widely shared perceptions, Germany's overall strategic position in the summer of 1940 was surprisingly fragile. Many scholars of this period refer to Germany's strategic dilemma in the interregnum following the French campaign – a dilemma which, in Hitler's mind, was only resolved in December 1940, when he finally issued his *Barbarossa* directive for the attack on Soviet Russia. The crux of the matter was simple, if not the solution: How was Germany to bring the war to a successful conclusion? How was she to vanquish Great Britain and, ultimately, the U.S. and USSR, before they could bring to bear the collective weight of their material might and trap the Reich in a protracted war of attrition – a repeat, in effect, of 1914-18? A dilemma to be sure; however, one might also posit that what Germany faced that summer was a simple paradox: She was the uncontested master of most of continental Europe, yet faced certain defeat in the years ahead if her statesmen and generals failed to quickly and decisively overcome her strategic conundrum.

For Germany, the primary threats were the two great powers on the flanks – the United States and the Soviet Union. America, of course, was still neutral, but it was an increasingly hostile neutrality as President Roosevelt sought in coming months to move his country inexorably closer to Great Britain. Simply put, U.S. public opinion was of "three minds" when it came to participation in Europe's latest conflict: isolationism, interventionism and the "gray area between the two extremes." Roosevelt, however, stood squarely at the "pinnacle of the interventionist camp;"[31] hence, Hitler expected America to join the war, most likely in 1942.[32] The problem with Russia was more pressing. While few details were known – German intelligence found it virtually impossible to penetrate the Soviet Union, the consummate "counterintelligence state" – it was clear in a general sense that Russia was rearming, and doing so in a big way. Her behavior was also becoming more threatening – in June/July 1940, taking advantage of Germany's preoccupation in the west, she had occupied the Baltic states and, more disquieting to Germany, pinched off Bessarabia and Northern Bukovina from Romania, moving her borders closer to Romania's oil fields, which were vital to Germany's war effort. Moreover, after the Hitler-Stalin Pact of August 1939, relations between Germany and Russia were characterized by economic cooperation, in effect making the former's war effort dependent upon the latter's oil, grain, rubber, ores and other resources. In the long run, of course, relying on the beneficence of Stalin to "jump start" her war machine was intolerable for Germany. Hitler, in fact – ever impatient – had toyed with the idea of attacking Russia in the autumn of 1940, and "only with great difficulty [was he] persuaded to drop so risky a scheme."[33]

The final six months of 1940 witnessed a flurry of diplomatic activity, as Hitler sought to harness Franco's Spain, Vichy France and other sympathetic European nations to his various schemes. Yet this involved, for the most part, ancillary initiatives, which did not strike at the core of the problem. Indeed, Hitler had most likely concluded by the summer of 1940 that there was but one practical solution to his dilemma – and that lay in the east. To prepare for the inevitable "showdown" with America – it is surprising just how large a role the United States played in the German dictator's strategic thinking at this time[34] – he needed the oil, grain and coal of Russia. Only through the imperial conquest of the colossus in the east, and the concomitant creation of an autarkic continental base, could Hitler hope to successfully challenge the naval and air power of America and Great Britain.

I am, however, racing ahead of our story. For the immediate challenge which confronted Germany and her euphoric dictator after the fall of France was what to do about Great Britain. As is well known, the "Fuehrer" had a soft spot for the English who, after all, were an industrious people of similar racial stock. There were, Hitler thought, two alternatives: England could be enjoined to exit the war through an overarching diplomatic settlement – a *rapprochement* resolving all outstanding European and global issues – or, if recalcitrant, she could be brought to her knees through the application of military force. The latter alternative, as soon become apparent, posed real problems for Germany. Again, it was a problem of her military's force structure and doctrine. The Navy's surface fleet was much too diminutive to threaten England's survival, while the U-Boat fleet, though formidable, was also too few in number[35] and, thus, not up to the task of severing the island nation's sea lines of communication. The dreaded German *Luftwaffe*, designed in the main for tactical support of ground forces, was ill-suited for waging strategic air warfare; its two-engine bombers were short on range and bomb load, while its premier fighter, the Messerschmitt Bf 109, though a superb machine, was also deficient in range and loiter time.

Yet for Hitler, the principal option was not war but peace. He genuinely sought an arrangement with Great Britain:

> Hitler hesitated about the tactics to pursue against Britain. His objective [with the victory in the west] had been to deliver a "knockout blow" to force Britain to accept its exclusion from the continent. He still hoped his victory in the west might be enough to bring that about. He had no desire to see the break-up of the British empire which, he thought, would benefit mainly other powers – Japan, the United States and the Soviet Union. But Churchill, who became Prime Minister on 10 May 1940, was determined to continue the war. To make the point, the Royal Air Force launched bombing raids on west German cities and the Royal Navy bombarded part of the French fleet in the Algerian port of Mers-el-Kébir to prevent it falling into German hands.
>
> Hitler faced a dilemma of his own making. He did not have the naval force for a successful invasion of Britain, at least not until he had control of the air. He therefore considered every possible option for bringing Britain to accept peace. After mulling it over in his alpine retreat for a week, he made one last appeal to Britain to see reason in his victory speech to the Reichstag on 19 July … Despite the negative reaction from Britain, he continued to hope for several days that the speech would bring about a change of attitude. Only on 23 July 1940 after a broadcast by the Foreign Secretary, Lord Halifax, did he accept that the British rejection was final.[36]

The refusal of Britain to sue for peace robbed Hitler of the biggest potential political payoff of his victory in the west.[37] He now "cast around" for alternatives to force Britain to come to terms. Earlier, on 16 July 1940, he had issued a directive for preparations to be made for an invasion by the middle of August 1940. Yet he remained skeptical that his navy would be able to pull off such a venture, and it was soon pushed back to mid-September, at the earliest. He considered other options as well, such as the capture of the British stronghold of Gibraltar in cooperation with Franco's Spain, which, if successful, would close the western entrance to the Mediterranean to the British navy. In the final analysis, however, he kept coming back to Russia. Flummoxed by the fact that Britain continued to fight, desperate though her position was – from Hitler's vantage point it was "militarily hopeless" – he had suggested to Halder on 13 July 1940 that the key was Russia. As Halder wrote in his diary that day: "The Fuehrer is greatly puzzled by Britain's persisting unwillingness to make peace. He sees the answer (as we do) in Britain's hope on Russia …"[38] At a conference with his military advisors several days later (21 July), Hitler spoke of the difficulty in pulling off an invasion of Britain and of British hopes on Russia. For its part, the Army High Command began to explore the specific objectives of a campaign in the east.[39]

1.4: Initial Steps toward War with Russia (July 1940)

"Tannenberg," observed David Irving in his controversial work, *Hitler's War*, "was not one of Hitler's more attractively sited headquarters." It was nestled deep in the Black Forest, among tall pine trees, and made up of some wooden barracks and concrete blockhouses, some of them set below ground level. Hitler spent a week there in late June and early July 1940; for most of the time it rained heavily. The Italian ambassador visited him there, and Hitler made oblique references to the fact that Germany was on the threshold of "big new tasks," though he refrained from saying what those might be. He told Colonel Rudolf Schmundt, his *Wehrmacht* adjutant, that he was mulling over the problem of Russia, whether to attack or not. Hitler also appears to have brought up the topic with his foreign minister, Ribbentrop.[40]

By now, Hitler's chief military advisors were aware that he was contemplating a campaign against Russia. In response, the Commander-in-Chief of the Army, General Walther von Brauchitsch – soon to be made a field marshal along with several other top generals, their reward for the victory over France[41] – ordered his staff at OKH to "do some operational thinking" about such a possibility. In addition, "Foreign Armies East" (*Fremde Heere Ost*, or FHO), the Army department responsible for evaluating military intelligence about Soviet Russia, including analysis of her intentions and strategy, was directed to investigate the distribution of Soviet forces facing Germany. Finally, an Army High Command officer attached to the OKW Operations Staff (WFSt), Lt.-Col. Bernhard von Lossberg, began to draft a plan of attack on Russia – most likely in an effort to keep his chief at OKW, Artillery General Alfred Jodl, informed and to assess the feasibility of Hitler's intentions.[42]

By mid-July 1940, Hitler was urging Brauchitsch to examine the prospects for attacking Russia in the fall. In Berlin, on 21 July, Hitler met with Brauchitsch, Admiral Raeder (C-in-C of the Navy), and Jeschonnek (Goering's chief of staff) in the Reich Chancellery. As recorded in Halder's diary, the "Fuehrer" insisted that he "will not let the military-political initiative go out of his hand." He lectured his assembled military leaders on the need to take the requisite political and military steps to protect vital oil imports should – however unlikely – Romanian and Russian supplies somehow be threatened. The ideal strategy, he said, would be to invade Britain now and end the war; he directed Raeder to report back in a week on the prospects for an invasion, which, he said, had to be carried out by mid-September at the latest. If preparations for Operation "Sealion" (code-name for the planned invasion of England) could not be completed by the beginning of September, it would, he said, "prove necessary to ponder other plans." What Hitler meant by this was that he would postpone any decision vis-à-vis England until next spring, and move on Russia that very autumn. He had learned – just how is unclear – that his armies could regroup for the attack in as little as four to six weeks. The strategic objective, Hitler said, would be: "To crush [the] Russian army or at least take as much Russian territory as is necessary to bar enemy air raids on Berlin and Silesian industries. It is desirable to penetrate far enough [into Russia] to enable our air force to smash Russia's strategic areas."[43]

On the 26th, Hitler arrived at the *Berghof*, his mountain sanctuary on the Obersalzberg, above Berchtesgaden, in the Bavarian Alps. The future German dictator had first visited the roughly 900-1000 meter high Obersalzberg – so near to his Austria homeland – in April 1923, and was immediately enchanted by its restful quietude, meadows and forests. Following his release from Landsberg Prison in late 1924, he had returned to the mountain, where he finished the second part of *Mein Kampf*. Eventually he rented, and then purchased, the chalet "Haus Wachenfeld," which by 1936 had been refurbished and expanded into the "*Berghof*." Neither cost, nor effort, had been spared during the makeover, which included marble from Italy, elegant stone from Bohemia, and priceless wood from South America. Here Hitler would revel in his role as world statesman, entertaining some of Germany's, and the world's, most notable figures – elder statesmen, such as the former English prime minister, David Lloyd George; the Duke of Windsor (the former King Edward VIII, who had abdicated the English throne in December 1936 to marry American socialite Wallis Simpson); the boxer Max Schmeling; the famous aviatrix and Hitler admirer, Hanna Reitsch; entertainers and Nobel Prize winners; even the British historian, Arnold J. Toynbee. Here, too, before the year was out, he would sign the "Fuehrer Directive" which would "throw the switch" on Operation *Barbarossa*.[44]

But it had not yet come to that. Over the next few days, the "Fuehrer" conducted a series of meetings with Balkan leaders; the Russians, it was now known, had usurped the Romanian provinces of Bessarabia and Bukovina and placed strong forces there, including cavalry and mechanized troops. Hitler was worried by the proximity of the Russian air force to Romania's precious oil fields, so essential to Germany's ongoing war effort. In one of his conferences (28 July), he insisted: "The long-term political lineup in Europe must be straightened out. Only if one no longer has to fear being exposed to enemy bombing attack can one embark on far-reaching economic plans." One morning, following the scheduled war conference in the *Berghof's* Great Hall, Hitler asked the Chief of his OKW Operations Staff, General Jodl, about the prospect of striking at Soviet Russia in a "lightning" attack before winter set in:[45]

> He [Hitler] explained that he was perfectly aware that Stalin had only signed his 1939 pact with Germany to open the floodgates of war in Europe; what Stalin had not bargained for was that Hitler would finish off France so soon – this explained Russia's headlong occupation of the Baltic states and Romanian provinces in the latter part of June. It was now clear from the increasing Soviet military strength along the frontier on which Germany still had only five divisions stationed that Russia had further acquisitions in mind. Hitler feared Stalin planned to bomb or invade the Romanian oil fields that autumn; in such an event, Germany would be open to all manner of Soviet blackmail. Hitler would then be unable to launch a winter counteroffensive, and by spring – from all that he had heard – Russia's entire military potential would be marshaled against him. Russia's aims had not changed since Peter the Great: she wanted the whole of Poland and the political absorption of Bulgaria, then Finland, and finally the Dardanelles. War with Russia was inevitable, argued Hitler; such being the case, it was better to attack now – this autumn; postponement was only to Russia's advantage.[46]

Jodl, sober military analyst that he was, demurred; he doubted whether the *Wehrmacht* could be redeployed from the west and prepared for such a gigantic undertaking in just a few short months. Ever dutiful, however, he promised to find out. A few days later, Jodl returned to the *Berghof*, bringing with him his operations staff's analysis of the potential for an autumn offensive: "Spreading out railway maps on the large red marble table at the *Berghof*, he had to advise Hitler that for transport reasons alone it would be impossible to attack Russia that autumn."[47]

About this time, Hitler also raised the issue of an autumn invasion with the Chief of OKW, General Wilhelm Keitel. Despite his largely deserved reputation as a spineless supporter of his "Fuehrer" – "he had ambition but no talent, loyalty but no character"[48] – on this occasion Keitel asserted himself. Buttressing his subordinate Jodl's position, he noted that communications and supply facilities in the newly occupied Poland were inadequate to serve as a base of operations against Russia, and that the war might well drag on into the winter. He was, in fact, so disturbed by Hitler's intentions that he requested a "brief interview" with the dictator in August, subsequently preparing a "personal memorandum" laying out his dissenting viewpoints. A short time later, he gave the handwritten memorandum to Hitler for review. The latter was not amused and, in the confrontation that ensued, subjected his OKW chief to "savage criticism." Keitel responded by offering his resignation and requesting a front-line command. While Hitler "harshly rejected" Keitel's démarche, he had no choice but to submit to the professional judgment of his OKW advisors and abandon any hopes for an autumn offensive. He ordered the OKW to give top priority to expanding the capacity of the railways in German-occupied Poland, insisting as well that supply facilities and anti-aircraft protection in the east be improved.[49]

Hitler's meditations over a possible attack on Russia reached an initial decision point in a climactic meeting at the *Berghof* with his top military advisors on the final day of July 1940. His naval chief, Admiral Raeder, opened the conference, a detailed account of which one can follow in Halder's personal diary. Reflecting the views of his naval planners, Raeder posited that an invasion of Britain could begin no earlier than mid-September and favored postponing it until the spring of 1941. Hitler, however, wanted to keep his options open. He stated that things "will become more difficult with passing of time," and that air attacks should begin at once. If the results of air warfare were unsatisfactory, preparations for an invasion were to be stopped; on the other hand, Hitler continued, "If we have the impression that the British are crumbling and that the effects will soon begin to tell, we shall proceed to the attack."[50]

After Raeder had left the meeting, Hitler expressed skepticism about the "technical feasibility" of a landing, adding that, while air and U-boat attacks on Britain might be decisive, they would require an additional one to two years for full effect. He then got to the heart of the matter, his train of thought captured in the shorthand notes of the Chief of the Army General Staff:

> *Britain's hope lies in Russia and the United States.* [Halder's italics] If Russia drops out of the picture, America, too, is lost for Britain, because elimination of Russia would tremendously increase *Japan's power* in the Far East … *Russia is the factor on which Britain is relying the most.* Something must have happened in London! … The British were completely down; now they have perked up again. Intercepted telephone conversations. Russia is painfully shaken by the swift development of the western European situation. All that Russia has to do is to hint that she does not care to have a strong Germany, and the British will take hope … *With Russia smashed, Britain's last hope would be shattered.* Germany then will be master of Europe and the Balkans. *Decision: Russia's destruction must therefore be made a part of this struggle. Spring 1941.*[51]

The sooner Russia was "crushed," the better, Hitler went on. Moreover, the attack would only achieve its purpose if the Soviet Union was "shattered to its roots with one blow," he said – a conviction which, as it turned out, would guide German planning for the Russian campaign like a lode star, however much the operational details might change in the months ahead. Hitler then proceeded to outline the operation as he saw it unfolding, the details of which need not concern us here. He envisaged that Germany would require 180 divisions to complete its future tasks, 120 of which would be allotted to the eastern campaign.[52] The attack, as the German dictator had privately told Jodl two days before, was to begin in May 1941.[53]

None of the assembled military leaders – not Brauchitsch, not Halder[54] – "dared to make an objection or offer a strategic alternative"[55] for securing the long-term hegemony of the Reich in Europe. As historian Ian Kershaw points out, it was a "momentous decision, perhaps the most momentous of the entire war.[56] And it came just days after London had made only too clear that it had every intention of staying in the fight, revealing the causal relationship between Hitler's failure to reach a settlement with Britain and his decision to attack the Soviet Union. Yet it is supremely ironic that Hitler's decision – which at once unleashed a flurry of planning activity by concerned military staff agencies – was based on a serious misreading of his English adversary. As argued by the late German historian Andreas Hillgruber in an in-depth analysis of Anglo-American strategic planning over the period 1940/41:

> It is striking that the Soviet Union was to play no part in the long-term strategic planning [of the U.S. and Great Britain] that had been sketched out up to the victory over Germany and Japan. Therefore, the USA and Great Britain were planning to conduct a global war alone against Germany and Japan. Contrary

to what Hitler always presumed in his situation analyses, in the course of their strategic planning the USA and Great Britain, whose strengths lay in the area of sea and air power, had not in any way assumed the necessity of a "continental sword," of including the Soviet Union in the "Anti-Hitler Coalition." Up to mid-June 1941, the position of the Soviet Union was instead ... considered by the British leadership to be extremely dubious. Almost right up to the eleventh hour prior to the start of the German attack on 22 June 1941, the British side saw itself faced with two alternatives: either an attack on a Soviet Union allied with Hitler or else – very limited – support for a Soviet Union under attack from Hitler and believed unlikely to be capable of resisting the Germans for long.[57]

Hitler's basic assumption – "Britain's hope lies in Russia and the United States" – which exercised such a powerful influence on his determination to turn eastward in 1941 – was thus half wrong. While in the coming months the ties between Britain and America would grow closer, and the strategic planning become more active, Britain never looked to Soviet Russia to function as her "continental sword." This was due, certainly, to Britain's deep mistrust of the communist nation, as well as to her low opinion of Russia's prowess as a military power, points of view shared, no doubt, by military and civilian policy makers in America.

1.5: Russia – Hitler's *"eigentlicher Krieg?"*

Biographers of Adolf Hitler and historians of the Third Reich have, for decades, sought to ascertain just why he took the fatal decision to attack Russia in 1941 – a decision that culminated in the destruction of his empire and his suicide in the bunker below the Reich Chancellery in Berlin on 30 April 1945. Some focus on the exigencies of the strategic-military situation as it developed between July 1940 and June 1941; others stress racial and ideological convictions held by Hitler since at least the 1920s; while still others champion some synthesis of the two. Be that as it may, most recent scholarship has concluded that Hitler made war upon Soviet Russia because *that* was the war he had most wanted to fight all along; it was – to invoke Manfred Messerschmidt's introduction to volume four of the quasi-official German history of World War II (*The Attack on the Soviet Union*) – "Hitler's real war" (*eigentlicher Krieg*).[58] This essential perspective is supported by Ian Kershaw, who observes in the second volume of his brilliant biography of Hitler: "The war in the east, which would decide the future of the Continent of Europe, was indeed Hitler's war."[59]

Yet as Messerschmidt also states, such a perspective strongly implies that the attack on Russia signified much more than "merely an attempt to escape from a strategic dilemma."[60] A strategic dilemma there was, and we have touched on it in the narrative above. To summarize: After the fall of France and Britain's decision to fight on, Hitler needed to find a way to maintain the initiative and bring about a decision (on the continent) favorable to the Reich before America entered the conflict, most likely in 1942. To effectively challenge the Anglo-Americans – to "level the playing field" – he needed to bring the entire European continent under his control, which could only be done by subduing Russia. This would give Germany direct control of Russia's vital raw materials – her oil, ores, rubber, grain, etc. – and, perforce, a position of economic self-sufficiency (autarky) with its strong European base. Again Kershaw: "Autarky, in Hitler's thinking, was the basis of security. And the conquest of the east, as he had repeatedly stated in the mid-1920s, would now offer Germany that security."[61] Here we see the conflation of Hitler's long-standing programmatic goals (as laid out in his book *Mein Kampf*) with the strategic imperatives of the present. In more practical terms, however, given Germany's force structure and doctrine, it is evident that a land war with Soviet Russia "was the only war which Germany was equipped to fight, as was shown by its inability to launch an invasion of Britain."[62] Yet although Britain would remain a potential threat in the west (i.e., in Germany's rear), Hitler felt he had little to fear from her in 1941; hence, a "lightning" victory over Russia could be achieved without involving the Reich in a two-front war.

While such factors may seem sufficient to explain Hitler's "instinct that war with the Soviet Union was the logical next step,"[63] they do not go far enough. If one looks back to the mid-1920s, one sees strong elements of continuity in Hitler's thinking from that period up to the beginning of *Barbarossa*. In *Mein Kampf*, Hitler had said it was Germany's "mission" to conquer Russia.[64] Germany needed "living space" (*Lebensraum*) for its expanding population, whose high density, he believed, was a threat to the country; and this could only be acquired in the east.[65] By the 1930s, Hitler's thinking had become even more radicalized. On several occasions following his seizure of power, between 1933 and 1939, Hitler was surprisingly open with his generals about the ultimate aims of his policies, letting slip that they embraced violent expansion in the east with pronounced racial and ideological overtones. On one occasion shortly before the outbreak of war, in February 1939, he intimated to a gathering of officers that Germany's present *Lebensraum* was insufficient; she would have to take more. He also left no doubt about the character of the coming war: "a purely ideological war, i.e., consciously a national and racial war."[66]

Just what that meant in human terms would become frighteningly apparent after 22 June 1941. When Hitler unleashed his war on Russia, it would look more like a European colonial war of the 19th Century than a modern military conflict. German occupational policies, as they took shape before the outbreak of hostilities with Russia – and then became increasingly radicalized after the war began – called for the captured eastern territories to be ruthlessly Germanized – i.e., repopulated with Germans, or European peoples of Germanic descent (*Volksdeutsch*) at the expense of indigenous Slavic populations, millions of whom were to be left to starve to death. Millions more were to be enslaved or eliminated, while the Jews – the ultimate purveyors of "Bolshevism" – were to be exterminated. In Hitler's mind, Bolshevism and Judaism were inseparable, indistinguishable; hence, the destruction of the Soviet Russia would also signify the eradication of a key center of World Jewry. In the final analysis, Hitler conceived the war between Germany and Russia as an ineluctable confrontation – an apocalyptic struggle between two mutually exclusive *Weltanschauungen* culminating in a racial war of extermination.[67] Some 30 years ago, Andreas Hillgruber outlined the four basic – and clearly overlapping – programmatic objectives of Hitler's *Ostkriegkonzeption*, insights that remain valid to this day:

a. The extermination of the Soviet Union's "Jewish-Bolshevik" ruling elite, including its purported biological mainspring, the millions of Jews in eastern central Europe;

b. The acquisition of colonizing space for German settlers in those areas of Russia reputed to be the best;

c. The decimation of the Slavic masses and their subjugation to German authority in four "Reich Commissariats," Eastland (Belorussia, Lithuania, Latvia, Estonia), Ukraine, Muscovy, and Caucasus; however, when, in 1941, the course of the war ran counter to "schedule," only the first two were established – under the leadership of German "viceroys," as Hitler termed it, borrowing from his "ideal" model of colonial power, the role of Great Britain in India … And finally,

d. The autarky of a "large territory" in continental Europe under German authority was to be achieved which would be secure against blockades and for which the conquered eastern territories were to provide an allegedly inexhaustible reservoir of raw materials and food stuffs. This appeared to be the decisive condition for

Hitler's Reich to prevail against Anglo-American sea power in war and for it to be equal to any imaginable new "world war" in the future. It was already presupposed in the guidelines for the "*Wirtschaftsstab Ost*" [Economic Staff East] of 2 May 1941 that the aim alone of provisioning the German Army exclusively from Russia would mean that "*x*-million people" would starve.[68]

In the months preceding the Russia campaign, Hitler was careful to keep his genocidal and colonial plans mostly to himself. Not even his generals – to whom he explained his aims in traditional military-strategic terms – were made privy to the true character of the impending struggle (i.e., Germany's "Colonial tasks," requiring a "clash of two ideologies," for which the *Wehrmacht* would have to take part in a "war of extermination") until the end of March 1941, with *Barbarossa* but weeks away.[69] In any case, from this brief analysis, it is clear that Hitler's decision to attack the Soviet Union hinged on much more than the desire to vanquish Great Britain's putative "continental sword" and thereby knock the English from the war.

The proceeding discussion raises an important question, and it is this: From Adolf Hitler's vantage point, were there not practical strategic alternatives to advancing on Soviet Russia? During the latter months of 1940, several different proposals were indeed "floated" – one by Germany's foreign minister, Joachim von Ribbentrop; two by the *Kriegsmarine* – as possible alternatives to a policy of expansion in the east. Again we turn to Hillgruber:

a. Ribbentropp's political idea of creating a European-Asian "Continental Block," "from Madrid to Yokohama" (including the Soviet Union) with its barb aimed at the British Empire and the USA;

b. the basic strategic idea suggested by Raeder, the C-in-C of the German Navy, of a shift of focus in the war to the Mediterranean and the Middle East, as well as toward North West Africa, in order to gain a broad strategic and raw materials base for conducting a successful sea and air war against Great Britain and the USA in the Atlantic; and finally,

c. the stubborn demand from Doenitz, the U-Boot C-in-C, that the entire war effort immediately be concentrated on severing the sea links between Great Britain and the USA through a "total" U-Boot war so that American strength might be kept away from Europe by mastery of the Atlantic ocean routes by the U-Boats, whose numbers would have to be increased manifold in comparison to those then actually available.[70]

Hitler, however, rejected all three "options," for they failed to address what he considered the most vital challenge facing Germany at the time – the elimination of Soviet Russia. The conceptions of Hitler's naval commanders did not even consider the "Fuehrer's" programmatic eastern objectives; in effect, Hillgruber observed, the German navy – banking on Russia staying neutral, or even being an ally – wanted to fight a different war than did Hitler! Ribbentrop's concept of a "Continental Block" was also aimed at the Anglo-Americans, and embraced Russia as a potential partner. While Hitler toyed with Ribbentrop's vision for a few short weeks in the fall of 1940 for purely tactical reasons, it never entered seriously into his plans.[71] Indeed, despite such tactical maneuvering, Hitler's overarching objective – at least on the European continent[72] – always remained the destruction and enslavement of the Soviet Union; the exploitation of her people, land and resources. Hitler was acutely aware that, after the fall of France, a brief window of opportunity had opened up to settle the score with Russia. The *Wehrmacht* was at the peak of its powers, while Russia, though rapidly rearming, was not yet ready for war. To wait to strike until 1942, Hitler realized, was out of the question, for by then Russia would be ready and America most likely in the war[73] – the window slammed shut. Yet the decision to attack in June 1941 did not, in the final analysis, emerge suddenly from a pragmatic – or opportunistic – assessment of the prevailing military-strategic calculus; rather, as we have seen, it was deeply and irrevocably imbedded in Hitler's ideological worldview. In this sense, the decision – the final reckoning with the hated "Jewish-Bolshevist" enemy – signified the culmination of his life's work. The Russian war was the inevitable war. It was Hitler's war.

1.6: Military Preparations for the Russian Campaign (July – December 1940)

Even before the 31 July 1940 conference on the *Berghof*, when Hitler for the first time had announced his resolve to move against Russia in the spring, the "Fuehrer's" military planning organs had begun some preliminary planning on their own initiative. Following the conference, this activity went forth with a redoubled sense of purpose. Yet before exploring the details, a few general observations are in order. The elder Field Marshal von Moltke had combined a superior ability for organization and strategic planning with an "acute awareness of what was and was not possible in war."[74] Germany's central position in Europe, he knew, made her vulnerable to simultaneous conflicts on multiple fronts. While he wrestled with this dilemma for several decades as Chief of the German General Staff (1857-87), in the end he was unable to find a practical solution to Germany's strategic-operational quandary that would prevent a war from settling into a long, exhaustive war of attrition. He grew pessimistic about the future of war. In his final public statement, before the Reichstag in 1890, he warned prophetically that a future conflict, with popular passions aroused, could last "seven and perhaps [30] years" and smash the established social order.[75]

By mid-1940, however, German military planners had lost sight of Moltke's keen instinct for the possible, not to mention his pessimism about the future of war for a geostrategically vulnerable Germany. Of course, they remained cognizant of the danger of having to fight at the same time on more than one front, but with France defeated and England chastened, they were not overly concerned about it. Almost to a man they did not anticipate the impending battles in the east lasting more than a matter of weeks, a few months at the very most. After all, German arms were everywhere victorious, and their operational doctrine was without equal. Russia, as Hitler had assured Keitel, would simply be a matter of "child's play."

Yet this sublime, almost preternatural, confidence would exert a pernicious influence on German staff planning. To cite but one example: Virtually every assumption made by Army High Command (OKH) planners over the coming months (the size of the force structure required for the mission, the rates of fuel consumption, etc.) was highly optimistic – too optimistic. According to historian Rolf-Dieter Mueller: "Beginning with their initial operational considerations for the surprise attack on the USSR, the participants displayed a frivolous optimism [*leichtfertiger Optimismus*], which characterized the planning process to the very end."[76] Such was the level of confidence, in fact, that only minimal reserve forces were marshaled for the impending campaign; after all, reserves were hardly necessary for a short "blitzkrieg" campaign.[77] Germany's *Ostheer* would, for the most part, have to get by with whatever resources it possessed on the first day of the war.[78]

A related, ever larger issue, loomed as well: Although Clausewitz had "always stressed the subordination of strategy to policy even in war, he also emphasized the need of policy to be realistic: 'The first duty and the right of the art of war is to keep policy from demanding things that go against the nature of war.' With this statement, too, Moltke agreed completely."[79] Yet this "first duty" of a soldier was, with tragic consequences, virtually abdicated by the German General Staff. "Policy," in this case Hitler's decision to attack Russia, was far from "realistic;" the objectives, it turned out, far beyond the limited capabilities of the *Wehrmacht*. With several generations of hindsight, it is hard to conceive how German military planners could have been so blind to prevailing military-strategic realities. They never questioned Hitler's goal – neither the practicality nor morality – of swallowing up all of European Russia with a force only marginally larger than that which had brought victory in the west. The distance to Paris was only several hundred kilometers, over good, European highways; and even then too many tanks and vehicles had broken down. By comparison, the distance to Moscow from the demarcation line separating Germany and Soviet Russia was about 1000 kilometers, and the "roads" – sandy tracks for the most part – and railroads were incomparably worse. Yet because victory seemed so certain, German planners assumed that the mass of the infantry could be withdrawn from Russia in August 1941, followed by the mass of the mechanized units in September.[80] These were wild and unfounded assumptions, for which the German soldier (the *Landser*) in the east, as we will see, would pay dearly. Too much would be demanded by "policy," far too much of the German soldier. It was, in the end, a tragic moral failure on the part of the German General Staff – a failure that, in the vernacular of Clausewitz, went "against the nature of war."

Hitler would leave the military planning for the war against Russia largely to his General Staff; not until early December 1940 were the operational intentions of the Army High Command briefed to him. In July 1940, the OKH established its headquarters at Fontainebleau, some 50 kilometers southeast of Paris. The Château de Fontainebleau had once belonged to the kings of France; the history of the area reached back to the 12th Century; in all some three-dozen French sovereigns spent time there over the centuries. One of Halder's earliest discussions about how to deal with the problem posed by the Soviet Union took place at Fontainebleau, on 3 July 1940, with the chief of his operations branch, Colonel Hans von Greiffenberg. Both men proceeded from the assumption that a blow against Russia would bring an end to Great Britain's hopes of successfully remaining in the war.[81]

As first steps, Halder asked for an intelligence survey of Soviet strength and dispositions and tasked a specially selected General Staff officer – Brig.-Gen. Erich Marcks, Chief of Staff, Eighteenth Army – with preparing a strategic campaign study. Prophylactic measures to prevent any surprises on the part of the Russians were already underway, including the transfer from west to east of a number of infantry, panzer and motorized divisions (more than 20 in all), along with Eighteenth Army headquarters. While most of the planning effort was the responsibility of OKH, departments within OKW also took part, among them Brig.-Gen. Walter Warlimont's National Defense Branch (Warlimont was Jodl's deputy) and Lt.-Gen. Georg Thomas' War Economy and Armaments Branch of OKW.[82]

On 22 July, Halder began to examine the question of Russia in greater detail. Over the next few days, discussions with Greiffenberg and the chiefs of Foreign Armies East, Cartography, and Signal Communications took place. Based on such conversations he reached some – highly tentative – conclusions about potential requirements; for example, he assumed that 100 divisions would be needed for the invasion force, and that it would take four to six weeks to concentrate them. More significantly, he readily concluded that the only operational solution to the strategic problem of vanquishing Russia was to aim the Army's primary thrust at Moscow.[83] Along with its obvious political and psychological value, Moscow (and its region) was a leading industrial center – by 1941 "at least as important to the Soviet war economy as Leningrad or the Ukraine" – and the hub of Russia's railway network.[84] Throughout the planning process – and during the campaign of 1941 – the German Army General Staff would cling to the concept of a direct advance on Moscow as the *sine qua non* of victory. An internal General Staff publication just weeks before the outbreak of war put it thusly: "Central Russia is the heart of Russia, whose seizure by a very strong, armed, foreign power will paralyze all Russia and loosen the ties between all the remaining parts of the extensive Soviet empire; [its seizure] is even capable of destroying [Russia] in the long term. By far the most important objective within Central Russia is Moscow."[85]

Responding to Hitler's verbal orders of late July, efforts were soon underway to upgrade transportation and supply facilities in East Prussia and occupied Poland, a directive to this effect – entitled *"Aufbau Ost"* ("Buildup East") – having been signed by Keitel at OKW on 7 August 1940.[86] In response to the dictator's decisions of 31 July, efforts had also begun to increase the Army's force structure to 180 divisions. Factoring in the units which had already been released due to a partial demobilization following the French campaign (but would now be reestablished), this would result in a gain in the size of the Army of about 60 divisions; virtually every existing formation of the Army would be affected by this initiative, for each of the new divisions would have to be supplied with a cadre of experienced veterans. The new divisions came into being over the winter of 1940/41; among them were 10 new panzer divisions (doubling the total which had existed in May 1940) and eight additional motorized infantry divisions. (This topic is addressed in some detail in Chapter 3.)[87]

General Marcks arrived at OKH headquarters in Fontainebleau on 29 July and, after an exchange of views with Halder, got to work on his study. Completed in just five days (on 5 August), it was called: "Operational Draft East" (*Operationsentwurf Ost*). The Marcks plan was a comprehensive survey; it also "reflected fully Halder's ideas about the Russian campaign and formed the basis for more detailed staff work."[88] The Army's primary mission, as laid out in the plan, was to engage and destroy Soviet forces with a powerful thrust north of the Pripiat' Marshes[89] and then drive on Moscow – the "economic, political and spiritual center of the USSR" – whose capture would "shatter the cohesion of the Russian Reich."[90] Following the seizure of Moscow, the main force (*Schwerpunkt*) was to wheel to the south and, in cooperation with a southern force grouping, seize the Ukraine. The final stage would be an advance on a broad front at least as far as the line Rostov – Gorki – Archangel to thwart the possibility of bomber attacks on Germany. To accomplish these tasks, Marcks proposed an invasion force of 147 German divisions, among them 24 panzer and 12 motorized; these forces were to be supported by fully 44 divisions (including four panzer and four motorized) held in an OKH reserve. The time needed to conduct the campaign was estimated at nine to 17 weeks.[91]

Marcks envisaged the decisive battles taking place in the opening weeks, along and near the frontier, with the armored forces in the main role. The study posited only a slight numerical advantage for the *Wehrmacht*, albeit a pronounced superiority in training, experience and quality. Once German troops had broken through the Red Army's frontier defenses, and begun to exploit into the interior, Marcks believed the Soviet command and control system would simply collapse, enabling the Germans to destroy the enemy piecemeal.[92] That said, the almost uniformly confident assumptions in the plan were based on a paucity of real knowledge about the Soviet Union and its armed forces.[93] Moreover, while most officers agreed with Marcks' approach, Hitler did not – at least not fully. In his view, after successful execution of the frontier battles, the drive on Moscow should not take place until Leningrad in the north had been captured and the Baltic region secured. The "Fuehrer" also placed greater importance on gaining key economic targets, while the Army stressed military factors.[94] Here then, was the genesis of a serious conflict between Hitler and his Army High Command on how the war in the east should be waged; and while the conflict would be contained – or simply ignored – during the planning phase, it would burst out into the open in the summer of 1941, at a critical juncture in the Russian campaign.

The other operational plan prepared during this period was the work of Lt.-Col. von Lossberg, the OKH representative on the OKW Operations Staff (WFSt). While the origins of his study are unclear, Lossberg's draft would serve to keep his chief, General Jodl, abreast of incipient planning activities related to Russia. Despite his position as Hitler's chief military advisor, Jodl lacked the institutional resources of the Chief of the Army General Staff, General Halder, who was "incomparably better and more directly informed on the Army's problems."[95] As recently as in his memorandum of 30 June, following the victory in the west, Jodl had not even considered the prospect of an attack on the Soviet Union as a way to knock Britain out of the war. However, as a result of the discussions between Hitler and Army C-in-C Brauchitsch on 21 July, or perhaps sooner, Jodl must have become aware that a war in the east was under consideration. In any case, on 29 July, he informed his staff that Hitler planned to start a war against Russia in May 1941.[96]

Bearing the codename "Fritz," after his son,[97] Lossberg's "Operational Study East" was completed on 15 September 1940. According to David Irving, it "bore a striking resemblance to the campaign that was actually begun in the summer of 1941 ... [and] undoubtedly formed the basis of Hitler's later grand strategy against Russia."[98] Be that as it may, Lossberg's operational concepts appear to have had a discernable influence on Hitler's thinking about the coming campaign. The colonel's finished product evinced marked parallels to the study of General Marcks. Most notably, Lossberg's operational plan also envisaged the main German effort north of the Pripiat' Marshes, where a German army group was to encircle Soviet forces in the Minsk area and then advance toward Moscow; powerful tank forces were to be committed along this axis, oriented on the Minsk-Moscow highway. At this point, however, Lossberg's concept diverged from that of Marcks', for following the disruption of enemy forces at the Dnepr-Dvina line, strong mobile elements were to be shifted north to seize the Baltic coast, Leningrad, and the Soviet naval base at Kronstadt in an effort to secure deliveries of ore from Scandinavia and to protect the ongoing supply of the northern wing of the invasion force by sea. Only *after* these objectives had been secured, was the operation to capture Moscow to be continued.[99] Like Marcks, Lossberg believed the principal task of the *Luftwaffe* should be to support German ground operations along their main axes of advance; for example, by interdicting the Soviet railway network. While the final military objectives were not expressly defined, Lossberg proposed a final, distant general line from Archangel via Gorki and the Volga to the Don.[100]

Both studies were based on the firm conviction that the invading German armies would enjoy a marked superiority over the Red Army. Yet in contrast to the Marcks study, Lossberg was more open in his dismissal of the Soviet Union as a potential military opponent:

> The Russian command can only be viewed as so clumsy, the Russian railway network and the command posts' use of it as so inadequate, that every new deployment will result in considerable friction and take a correspondingly long time ...
>
> A considerable advantage that will carry weight in the operations in the south is that the Russians are expected to soon have internal difficulties in the Ukraine, which, guided by the work of our *Abwehr* II, could have an impact through disruption of the few railway lines leading there. Once the Ukraine is occupied, it is anticipated that a functioning "government" would soon be established in accordance with our wishes, which will alleviate the oversight of the expansive territory to the rear ...
>
> What, from a territorial point of view, is to be the military end goal will depend primarily on when and whether Russia will collapse from the inside after initial German successes. It seems impossible that Russia will maintain its capabilities after its west regions and its access to the seas have been lost, even if the Russian armaments region in the Urals ... is taken into consideration.[101]

On 3 September 1940, Halder appointed Maj.-Gen. Friedrich Paulus, Chief of Staff of Sixth Army, as the new *Oberquartiermeister I* (OQu I, or Deputy Chief of Staff for Operations) in OKH. In this capacity, Paulus, an acknowledged panzer specialist, would act as Halder's immediate deputy and assume responsibility for coordination of all OKH planning related to a potential campaign in the east. He was to be guided in his efforts by the studies of General Marcks and Lt.-Col. Feyerabend[102] and, working closely with the OKH Operations Branch, further develop the operational details as well as plans for the German force buildup and concentration against Russia. Paulus threw himself into his work, often engaging Halder in animated discussion well into the night. Between both men a bond of trust and friendship developed, which soon grew into social contacts between the two families.[103]

By mid-September, Paulus had already finished initial planning for the deployment of German forces in the east (*Aufmarsch Ost*). Using this as a foundation, he meticulously worked out an overall concept for conduct of the Russian campaign. He agreed with Hitler's contention that it would require no more than 128 divisions to defeat a Russian army estimated at 188 divisions, a perspective encouraged by the intelligence reports of Foreign Armies East (FHO), which estimated that the Red Army only possessed some 50 to 75 "good" divisions. (In subsequent months, FHO would continuously revise its estimation of Soviet forces upwards.) Fundamentally, however, Paulus' basic campaign concepts differed little from those of Marcks.[104]

In October, the Army High Command left Fontainebleau and moved to Zossen, some 30 kilometers south of Berlin. Here, at the former Imperial German Army training complex, OKH would stay for the remainder of the war, amidst the massive underground bunkers and Flak towers which had been finished just prior to the outbreak of war in September 1939. Accustomed to working late into the night, Paulus would often bring working papers home with him – not classified documents, of course, but maps, materials about geographical and climatic conditions in the Soviet Union, and so forth. Naturally, he was unable to keep his work hidden from his two lieutenant sons and, most importantly, from his wife, "Coca" (Constance). For Paulus, this soon led to rather uncomfortable discussions about the nature of his work. While Paulus – buried as he was in the minutiae of planning a war – wasted little time pondering potential moral questions inherent in his activities, his wife had other thoughts. Simply put, she expressed robust moral and religious objections to an attack on Russia – a prospect she found "unjust," even "disastrous." Paulus understood her protests, yet he was a soldier who carried out his orders and, in any case, was not responsible for policy. One of Paulus' sons recalled a particularly stormy encounter between the two:[105]

> At any rate, one day, in the presence of we two sons, then lieutenants, she strongly rebuked my father on this count. My father argued to the contrary that these were questions of policy, the individual was not asked for his opinion. And there were in fact important military viewpoints in support of such an undertaking. When my mother asked what would happen to our soldiers, indeed, to us, who would even survive that, my father responded that there was the possibility, the hope, that a decisive victory could be achieved as early as 1941 … It could even be the case that the campaign would be over after only 4-6 weeks. Perhaps the whole lot would tumble down like a house of cards after only the first push.[106]

On 29 October, Paulus briefed OKH about his planning to date, the results of which were combined into a staff study (*Denkschrift*) and submitted to Halder for review. In November, the planning documents were again discussed by OKH and coordination achieved with Army Supply and Administration (*Generalquartiermeister*) and long-range reconnaissance (*Fernaufklaerung*).[107] On 13 November, Paulus' study became the theme of a "Fuehrer conference;" and, on 18-19 November, Paulus again briefed his proposal to OKH – this time in the presence of Field Marshal von Brauchitsch – which was well received.[108]

By late November 1940, the OKH plan of campaign – based largely on the operational insights of Halder, as expressed initially in Marcks rough study and then refined in weeks of meticulous staff work by Paulus – was essentially complete. Paulus' biographer, Torsten Diedrich, provides details:

> In the first operational phase the bulk of the Red Army west of the Dnepr-Dvina line was to be destroyed and the retreat of combat-fit units to the east was to be prevented. There was still agreement over this point. However, "Plan *Barbarossa*" conformed to the ideas of the OKH [i.e., to Halder's ideas], according to which, in the second operational phase, the main thrust would be directed against Moscow, while the operations in the north and south would mainly aim to secure the flanks. Hitler, however, favored acquiring areas valuable to the war economy in the north and south of the Soviet Union as a material basis for rebuilding German forces. Even so, at first he approved the OKH's campaign plan.[109] The operational goal remained for the time being concentrated on reaching the Leningrad – Smolensk – Dnepr line as a result of the vast supply and provisioning problems that such a campaign entailed; every further advance was to be made dependent on the matter of provisioning and supply.[110]

Despite the largely optimistic assumptions of Marcks, Paulus, *et al.*, it was obvious that the Germans could not hope to achieve absolute numerical superiority over their, in this regard, better endowed opponent. Only by weakening some sectors could the Army hope to establish a local superiority (*Schwerpunkt*) at the points chosen for the main effort. The factor of time was also more urgent than in any previous campaign. Only the months of May to October offered conditions favorable to major military operations. By late October, the rainy season would begin, reducing roadways to muddy quagmires and paralyzing movement. And this would be followed by the dreaded Russian winter! It was "obvious that every decision and every move would be made under extraordinary pressures of time." Success, then, would hinge upon the ability of the eastern army's limited numbers of armored and motorized infantry divisions to achieve rapid, decisive breakthroughs in great depth, resulting in the encirclement and destruction of the Red Army's main forces.[111]

The many assumptions developed in the weeks and months of planning were finally put to the test in two major sets of war games (*Planspiele*), both under the direction of Paulus. The first took place on 29 November – at Zossen in the bunker complex "*Maybach* 1." Among those invited to observe was the new OKH Chief of Operations, Colonel Adolf Heusinger, a "cool, analytical thinker, fluent in Russian … and so diligent that his fellow officers called him "Little Ludendorff."[112] The second *Planspiel* followed on 3 December and addressed the operational possibilities that might unfold after attainment of the line Minsk – Kiev. The most significant insight to emerge from both games was that a major task of the army groups on the wings was to provide flank protection for the central group, which was to execute the "decisive" push along the Minsk-Smolensk axis, toward Moscow. After completing the initial stage of the advance to the Dnepr River, a three-week pause was planned to expand lines of supply and to replenish and restock the forces. The attack on Moscow was to begin on the 40th day of the campaign.[113]

On 5 December 1940, a wide-ranging conference on the future conduct of the war took place at the *Reichskanzlei* in Berlin. For the first time, OKH – Brauchitsch and Halder – briefed the Russian campaign plan to Hitler. Also present were the heads of OKW, Keitel and Jodl. Brauchitsch spoke first, among other things addressing time requirements for the Russian campaign. Hitler then held forth: "The Russian armed forces," he insisted, "were inferior to those of the *Wehrmacht* in terms of materiel and personnel, especially in leadership. The present moment, therefore, is especially auspicious [*besonders guenstig*] for an eastern campaign." It could be anticipated, he said, that "once the Russian army has incurred a serious blow, it would suffer an even greater collapse than had France in 1940."[114]

After Hitler had spoken, Halder described the operation in detail. He began by surveying the geographical characteristics of the Russian theater of war, then Soviet centers of war production (*Ruestungszentren*), the most important of which lay in the regions of Leningrad, Moscow and the Ukraine. The theater of operations, he went on, was divided by the Pripiat' Marshes into a northern and southern sector; however, the northern sector, with its better road and rail network, offered more favorable conditions for large-scale maneuver. It was apparent, he said – erroneously, as it turned out – that the Russian High Command had concentrated the bulk of its forces close to the Soviet-German demarcation line. German intentions were to prevent Russian forces from withdrawing and establishing a coherent front west of the Dnepr and Western Dvina Rivers – a decisive objective that would fall to the German armored wedges (*Panzerkeile*). Three army groups were to be committed to the offensive: Army Group North, advancing on Leningrad; Army Group Center, the strongest of the three moving from the area of Warsaw toward Moscow; and Army Group South, directed toward Kiev in the Ukraine. In all, some 105 infantry and 32 panzer and motorized divisions would comprise the German invasion force. The ultimate objective would be the line of the Volga and the area of Archangel.[115]

Hitler approved the operational plan in principle, adding that the "most important objective is to prevent the Russians from withdrawing in an unbroken front." The German advance, he said, would have to "carry far enough east so that the Russian air force is no longer able to attack the Reich, and conversely [far enough east] so the *Luftwaffe* is able to raid and destroy Russian armament centers." Hitler then expounded at length on the operational principles he wished to see applied. In doing so, he indicated that, despite his expressed agreement with the OKH plan, his operational concepts differed fundamentally from those outlined by his Army chief of staff. Simply put, he sought the decision on the flanks, with eccentric drives by the northern and southern army groups – not in the center with one concentric thrust on Moscow. In fact, after successful completion of the opening battles, the central army group, instead of moving on Moscow, was to be ready to wheel northward with strong elements to assist in encircling Red Army forces in the Baltic region.[116] In the south, a secondary thrust was to be launched toward the Dnepr near Kiev, then swing southeast to trap Soviet forces in the western Ukraine. Earlier in the conference, as Halder noted in his diary that day, Hitler had gone so far as to say that Moscow was of "no great importance."[117]

Apparently, neither Brauchitsch nor Halder raised any objections at the time, the Chief of the Army General Staff merely noting that the planned concentration of forces in the east would require about eight weeks and, from early or mid-April 1941 on, would no longer be able to be concealed from the Russians. In any case, Hitler, OKH and OKW were of one mind about the opening phase of the campaign: The mass of the Red Army was to be surrounded and annihilated west of the Dnepr – Western Dvina river barriers and the withdrawal of strong Soviet forces into the interior of Russia prevented.[118] Halder may well have thought that the emerging differences between himself and his "Fuehrer" were, in the long run, of no great consequence, for once the powerful thrust in the center had gathered momentum toward Moscow – sweeping all before it – no one would dare stop it before it had reached its objective.

The next day, General Jodl instructed his staff to codify the results of the 5 December conference in new directives, including one for the invasion of Russia based on the Army's plan and Hitler's comments.[119]

1.7: From the Battle of Britain to Berlin: Key Military, Diplomatic & Political Events (July – December 1940)

While elliptical to the main themes of this narrative, we will briefly explore several key military, diplomatic and political events from July 1940 to April 1941 that influenced Germany's impending war in the east. Two of these events – the air war over Britain and the extension of the war to the Balkans – directly affected Germany's military preparations for *Barbarossa*. Two others – the Soviet foreign minister's visit to Berlin and Roosevelt's reelection, both in November 1940 – strengthened Hitler's resolve to move against Russia.

The Battle of France, asserts historian John Keegan in his history of the Second World War, "though sensational for reasons of brevity and decisiveness, had been an otherwise conventional military conflict." To be sure, German tactical innovations – in particular their unique combined arms approach and massed employment of armor with close air support – had contributed in no small way to the *Wehrmacht's* rapid and decisive victory. Yet the outcome was attributable more to Allied "defects in strategy, military structure and readiness for war, psychological as well as material, which were buried deep in the Western democracies' reaction to the agony they had undergone in the First World War."[120]

The Battle of Britain, in contrast, "was to be a truly revolutionary conflict. For the first time since man had taken to the skies, aircraft were to be used as the instrument of a campaign designed to break the enemy's will and capacity to resist without the intervention or support of armies and navies."[121] Yet it was not to be. The German aerial assault on the British Isles – which entered the popular lexicon as the "Battle of Britain" – was to end in failure in a matter of a few short months, the inevitable outcome of deficits in force structure, doctrine and training, as well as tactical and operational blunders.

On 30 June 1940, Air Marshal Hermann Goering signed the operational directive that unleashed the air war on Great Britain. The *Luftwaffe* aerial offensive began in July, reached a climax in mid-September in a massive daylight raid on London, and gradually tailed off into night bombing raids which dragged on into the winter of 1941. None of the *Luftwaffe's* objectives were attained – neither the destruction of British Fighter Command, nor the elimination of radar facilities or vital industrial centers. Nor, ultimately, had the morale of the English people been crushed. The *Luftwaffe* had not been up to the task. Its wonderful fighter, the Bf 109, had "short legs," resulting in insufficient range and loiter time; which meant that the bombers were often inadequately protected. The bombers themselves – the masses of Heinkel, Dornier and Junkers machines roaming the skies above England – with their modest bomb loads, were ill suited for a strategic bombing campaign. The *Luftwaffe* High Command desperately sought the proper tactical and operational formulas, only to fall short. The weeks passed and losses mounted. In the words of historian Williamson Murray, aircraft losses through September 1940 "gave the impression that the Germans were running out of aircraft as well as aircrews!" On 17 September, unable to secure air superiority over the English Channel and British Isles, Hitler postponed "Operation Sealion."[122]

Luftwaffe attrition rates had, in fact, been unsustainably high. During one week alone (13-19 August 1940) the Germans "wrote off" 284 aircraft, about seven percent of their total force structure. For the entire month of August, 774 aircraft were lost from all causes, some 18.5 percent of available aircraft. Total aircraft losses from July through September (the height of the battle) were more than 1600, about 37 percent of the *Luftwaffe's* strength. More than 600 German bombers were lost during these three months, with an additional 384 sacrificed (to all causes) from October through December. Factoring in the French campaign, the German Air Force lost more than 3000 aircraft, 57 percent of initial strength, from May through September 1940.[123] And the bleeding continued through the spring of 1941, right up to the start of *Barbarossa* – the result of operations in the Balkans and against the island of Crete, whose capture decimated much of the German transport fleet.

The vital point is this: While the German Army would begin the Russian campaign largely intact after 21 months of war, the *Luftwaffe* commenced the war in the east – which, of course, signified a dramatic increase in its operational commitments – having already sustained serious losses in aircraft and irreplaceable aircrews. Because it was barely able to offset these losses through ongoing production, the *Luftwaffe*, on 21 June 1941, would possess a total force structure virtually identical to that of 11 May 1940 – 4882 versus 4782 aircraft (all types). Moreover, it would begin the Russian campaign with 200 fewer bombers.[124] Simply more proof that, in all areas, Germany began the Russian war with insufficient resources.

Despite the setbacks in the air war over England, Hitler remained optimistic about the broad course of the war. Meeting with his Italian ally, Benito Mussolini, at the Brenner Pass on 4 October 1940 (eight days later, Hitler would cancel Operation "Sealion" outright, except as a deception campaign to deflect Russian attention from his impending buildup in the east), the German dictator assured the "Duce" that "the war is won! The rest is only a question of time."[125] Three days later, German troops marched into friendly Romania – "one more step toward Hitler's goal of an unbroken eastern front against Russia."[126]

In mid-October, Hitler departed Germany for France in his special train, "*Amerika*." On 22 October, he met with the Deputy Prime Minister of Vichy France, Pierre Laval, at Montoire, in the German occupied zone. The "Fuehrer" hoped to convince Laval to agree to a more active Vichy policy vis-à-vis Great Britain, whose defeat, Hitler assured him, was inevitable. The next day, Hitler and his special train rolled southward to the French border at Hendaye, where he met with the Spanish leader, General Francisco Franco. Despite Hitler's supplications, Franco refused the offer of an alliance with Germany; moreover, he did not agree to the transit of German troops through Spain to attack the British at their Gibraltar stronghold.[127] The German dictator then returned to Montoire, furious that Franco had rebuffed him. Here he met with Marshal Pétain, whom he also pressed for closer collaboration between Vichy France and Germany – "in the most effective possible way to fight Britain in the future." Yet if the talks with Pétain were more cordial, the results were little better. Returning from his meetings with the Spanish and French leaders, Hitler told both Keitel and Jodl that war with Russia had to begin in the coming year. Several days later, he reminded his military leaders that Russia remained the "great problem of Europe," and that "we must do our utmost to be prepared when the great showdown comes."[128]

Hitler's diplomatic démarches were abruptly overshadowed when, on 28 October 1940, Italian forces suddenly invaded Greece from Albania (which they had conquered about a year-and-a-half before). The news reached Hitler on "*Amerika*," while he was underway from Munich to Florence to meet with Mussolini, who greeted him by exclaiming, "Fuehrer, we are on the march!"[129] Hitler, however, was apoplectic, regarding the Italian move as a major strategic blunder. Despite an explicit warning from their German ally in late September not to stir things up in the Balkans, the Italians had rejected the advice. Unfortunately, their Greek offensive was undertaken "with little preparation [and] no strategic planning."[130] The wily Greeks allowed the Italians to exhaust themselves in costly frontal attacks on their mountain positions; after receiving reinforcements, they counterattacked in mid-November, driving the invaders back in confusion. Although Mussolini desperately flew in reserves – some with German aircraft – by the end of the month his entire invasion force had been extruded from Greece and thrown back into Albania.[131]

Perhaps fearing impending disaster – and only days after the British had occupied Crete and the island of Lemnos in the Aegean Sea – Hitler, on 4 November, directed his OKW staff to prepare an operational plan for a German invasion of Greece via Romania and Bulgaria. Less than two weeks later (12 November) Hitler signed Directive Nr. 18, which foresaw the start of operations against Greece in January 1941;[132] a month after that (13 December), OKW issued a second directive (Nr. 20), this one outlining the Greek campaign under the code-name Operation "*Marita*" and calling for the occupation of the northern coast of the Aegean Sea by March 1941; if necessary, all of Greece was to be seized.[133]

Hitler had "good reason to fear the worst ... from a consolidation of the Greek victory over Mussolini."[134] The months following Mussolini's blunder into Greece witnessed increasingly aggressive British action in the eastern Mediterranean and North Africa, resulting in heavy Italian losses and eventual Greek consent to the dispatch of several British divisions to the Greek mainland. Hitler feared the British might seek to reestablish another "Salonika front" (1916-18), which had posed such a problem for the Germans in World War I. Eliciting even greater anxiety was the prospect of British bombers – deployed to new RAF airfields in Greece and the Mediterranean – striking at the precious Ploesti oil fields in Romania. Moreover, Hitler recognized the vital economic importance of southeastern Europe to Germany's war effort: Fully 50 percent of the Reich's grain and livestock came from the region; 45 percent of its bauxite (aluminum ore); 90 percent of its tin; 40 percent of its led; and 10 percent of its copper.[135]

The British expeditionary force would not reach the Greek mainland until March and April 1941. Adding to the tumult in the Balkans at this time was a coup in Yugoslavia (27 March 1941), engineered by a group of Yugoslav Air Force officers hostile to Germany. Hitler responded on 6 April 1941, unleashing a lightening offensive into both Greece and Yugoslavia. Before the month was out, both countries had signed armistices with Germany.[136]

The chain of events set in motion by Mussolini's October 1940 invasion of Greece would end some six months later with the Reich in firm control of southeastern Europe. While Hitler would certainly have secured the area militarily before the start of Operation *Barbarossa* (even without Mussolini's "help"), German intervention in the Balkans was to have major implications – both strategic and operational – for the Russian campaign. On the positive side (from Hitler's vantage point) the capture of Greece and Yugoslavia secured Germany's southern flank, an indispensable prerequisite to the attack on Russia. Conversely, the campaign "placed yet another drain on Germany's eroding military resources and contributed in no small measure to the mounting over-extension of the *Wehrmacht*."[137] We are, however, again peeking a bit too far ahead; hence, the impact of the Balkan campaign of 1941 on the war with Russia – including the conviction still held by many historians that it fatally delayed the start of *Barbarossa* – will be addressed in some detail in Chapter 2.

Finally, in the autumn of 1940, two events transpired which reinforced Hitler's resolve to settle accounts with the "colossus" in the east. The first was the re-election of Franklin D. Roosevelt to an unprecedented third term as U.S. president on 5 November 1940. Roosevelt garnered 55 percent of the popular vote and defeated Republican Wendell Willkie, who was critical of the President for his "hawkish" position on the war in Europe. While sharp divisions existed in the United States about potential involvement in a second European war in less than a generation, Roosevelt was clear in his convictions: It was a long-standing principle of U.S. foreign policy not to let Europe become dominated by a power hostile to U.S. interests; thus, FDR refused to abandon Great Britain and let the great island nation go the way of France. America, while technically neutral, would provide Britain, and other friendly nations, with massive material aid in their struggle against Germany and the other Axis powers. As Roosevelt put it in his famous speech on 29 December, America would become the "Arsenal of Democracy." Less than three months later (11 March 1941), he signed the Lend Lease Act, pledging support to those who resisted the Axis powers.[138]

The second pivotal event was the visit of the Soviet Commissar for Foreign Affairs, Vyacheslav Molotov, to Berlin on 12-13 November 1940. In the negotiations over this two-day period, Molotov's counterpart, German Foreign Minister Ribbentrop, sought to gain Russia's adherence to the recently signed Tripartite Pact between Germany, Italy and Japan. Molotov demurred. Direct discussions between Molotov and Hitler himself yielded no better results. Perhaps underscoring the futility of it all, a "celebratory" dinner at the Soviet Embassy on 13 November was abruptly broken off due to the arrival of British bombers over Berlin, the talks continuing in Ribbentrop's own air raid shelter. When his German interlocutor insisted that Britain was defeated – her empire ripe for partition among the Axis powers – Molotov replied: "If that is so, why are we sitting in this air-raid shelter?"[139]

The talks, then – characterized by "mutual suspicion and underlying antagonism" – went nowhere. Hitler felt "wholly vindicated in his view that the conflicting interests of Germany and the Soviet Union could never be peacefully reconciled. A clash was inevitable. Hitler saw Molotov's visit as confirmation that the attack envisaged since July could not be delayed."[140] Two days later, Hitler ordered the construction of a field headquarters deep in the forests of East Prussia, near Rastenburg.[141] On 3 December, he paid a visit to the man who, on 22 June 1941, would command his central army group, Field Marshal Fedor von Bock. "The *Fuehrer*," Bock wrote in his diary, "visited me again in Berlin to wish me a happy 60th birthday.

> He sees the bright and dark sides of the big picture calmly and clearly … The assessment of the English situation is unchanged; a landing appears to have been shelved for now. The *Luftwaffe* and the submarine arm, whose activities are to be stepped up considerably in the new year, are to shoulder the main burden of the war against England. – The eastern question is becoming acute. There are said to be contacts between Russia and America; a Russia-England link is therefore also likely. To wait for the outcome of such a development is dangerous. But if the Russians were eliminated, England would have no hope left of defeating us on the continent, especially since an effective intervention by America would be complicated by Japan, which would keep our rear free.[142]

For Hitler, the strategic picture – the future course of action it appeared to demand of him – had finally come into sharper focus. Despite alternative strategies offered up by the *Kriegsmarine* and others, there was really only one way for Germany to break free of her strategic dilemma, regain the initiative, and establish a position on the European continent formidable enough from which to challenge the industrial and military might of America; and that was by the subjugation of Soviet Russia. In his brilliant study of Hitler's strategy during the period 1940/41, Andreas Hillgruber cogently summarized these issues:

> Hitler's assessment of the overall situation had, at the turn of the year 1940/41, simplified considerably in comparison to that at the time around the end of September 1940, and had … led him to the idea of an improvised plan for a "world blitzkrieg," which alone seemed to him to promise a way out of the dilemma in which he had found himself since the end of June 1940, or rather in fact since as early as 3 September 1939. All of his attempts to decisively improve his political and strategic position in relation to the Anglo-Saxon powers, through global political combinations ("Tripartite Pact" and "Continental Block" project) or through drawing other states (Spain and Vichy France) into the war against Great Britain, had failed and had only demonstrated the futility of trying to attain such a goal in this way.
>
> The reverse of all expectations had occurred. The alliance-like relationship between Great Britain, which Hitler could not force into a "compromise" peace through either political or military means, and the now only formally neutral

USA, which could not – as had been hoped – be distracted from its political path by the "Tripartite Pact" threat of a two-ocean war, had become ever closer. The considerably greater strength potential of the two all but allied Anglo-Saxon sea powers, who had the resources of the greater part of the world at their disposal and who separated the German-dominated territory of continental Europe in the west and south from its overseas links, must in the long run and with a continuing increase in American armament inevitably lead to the war taking a turn to Germany's disadvantage. The latest point at which the Anglo-Saxon powers' superiority would not yet have a significant impact on German strategic and operational maneuverability – because American armament had only begun in mid-1940 and it would not be possible to catch up with Germany's head start very quickly, especially where equipping the Army was concerned – was around mid-1942. If Hitler was unable to bring about a radical change in the merely outwardly brilliant, but in reality uncertain, political and strategic situation in Europe by then, the European war, conducted since autumn 1939 as a series of individual German "lightning" campaigns, would take on the character of a war of resources and attrition (in the manner of the 1914/18 World War), in which the constantly increasing and finally crushing superiority of the western powers must, sooner or later, lead to Germany's utter defeat.

This evaluation by Hitler of his tricky situation in the *Westkrieg* was undoubtedly realistic. None of the suggestions brought to him by the top ranks of the branches of the armed forces, especially by the Commander in Chief of the Navy, *Grossadmiral* Raeder, in the belief – quite understandable in consideration of the limited horizons of the individual branches of the armed forces – that it would be possible to achieve a change in Germany's unfavorable overall situation through a grand-scale strategy targeting the British Mediterranean and Middle Eastern positions, promised him deliverance from the dilemma … It must be stated that a decisive blow in the war against Great Britain, let alone against both the Anglo-Saxon powers, simply could not be exacted through the instruments of power available to Hitler in the year 1940 …

This, on the whole utterly realistic, evaluation of his situation in the *Westkrieg* was diametrically opposed in Hitler to an exaggerated ideological racial-mythical misjudgment – which, at its core, was nevertheless based on widely prevalent notions – of the military possibilities for Germany in the east, an underestimation of the Soviet Union's strength potential which is difficult to comprehend in retrospect. The destruction of this Soviet strength potential appeared to provide Hitler with a – the only – way out of the dilemma in the development of the war in the west. With a "blitzkrieg" lasting only a few weeks, Hitler not only expected a radical alteration of the overall war situation, but also believed it would be possible at the same time to achieve his long striven for great aim of establishing an eastern empire on the ruins of the Soviet Union. For Hitler, the military eastern solution thus became the great "chance" to bring about the "decisive turn" and to achieve everything at a single stroke … The "alternative" for him in winter 1940/41 was not a Mediterranean strategy or a military solution in the east, nor was it a "Continental Block" or an attack on the Soviet Union, but rather the destruction of the Soviet Union as a basic precondition for a decisive turn of the war at large in his favor and for the achievement of his war aims in the east, as well as those in relation to the western powers – that is to say, "capitulation."[143]

1.8: Crossing the Rubicon: The *Barbarossa* Directive (18 December 1940)

When OKH briefed the Russian campaign plan to Hitler in Berlin on 5 December, the plan

– as in earlier references to it – still bore the original code-name of "Otto."[144] Two weeks later, when Hitler finally signed the directive for the impending operation, "Otto" had become the more imperious sounding "*Barbarossa*." Hitler alone appears to be responsible for the change in name.[145]

Frederick I, "Barbarossa" (ca. 1123-90), had become Holy Roman Emperor in 1152, the nickname a reference to his red beard. He was a "bold and skillful" commander and an "astute ruler." After participating in the Second Crusade in 1188, he had, the following year, led the greatest ever medieval crusading army back toward Palestine, only to drown crossing the Calycadnus River (in modern Turkey) in June 1190. In Germanic folklore he was to become the equivalent of the British (Celtic) King Arthur. According to legend, his body now sleeps beneath a mountain at Kyffhaeuser, on the Rhine; one day – so the story goes – Barbarossa will rise up from his resting place and, once more, take up the call to arms. It was a "brilliantly evocative and apposite code-name for the 1941 offensive, 'arrogant in its recall of medieval splendors and menacing in its hints of medieval cruelties.'"[146]

At the *Berghof* on 17 December, General Jodl, OKW Operations Chief, presented a first draft of the *Barbarossa* directive to Hitler, who rejected it outright. The document, apparently, had incorporated the primary intent of the Army High Command (OKH) – i.e., an advance by the main force via Minsk – Smolensk to Moscow – and ignored Hitler's proposal (made at the 5 December conference in Berlin) that the main thrust be directed through the Baltic toward Leningrad.[147] The directive, redrafted in accordance with the dictator's desires and retyped on the large "Fuehrer typewriter," was resubmitted to Hitler the next day, 18 December,[148] and signed by him as "Fuehrer Directive" No. 21, "Case *Barbarossa*." Only nine copies of the document – "in its top-secret cover, scarlet with a diagonal yellow line" – were made; they were to be carried "by hand of officer, only."[149]

The directive began by stating that the "*Wehrmacht* must be prepared, even before the conclusion of the war against England, to *crush Soviet Russia in a rapid campaign*" (*Sowjetrussland in einem schnellen Feldzug niederzuwerfen*). All preparations for the attack were to be completed by 15 May 1941. The bulk of the Red Army in western Russia was to be annihilated (*vernichtet*) by means of "daring operations led by deeply penetrating armored spearheads" and the enemy's withdrawal into the interior prevented. The final objective of the campaign was to "erect a barrier against Asiatic Russia on the general line Volga – Archangel." If necessary, surviving industrial areas in the Urals could be taken out by the *Luftwaffe*.[150]

As Part III of the directive ("Conduct of Operations") made clear, the document drew heavily on the plan of OKW – that is, on the study of Lt.-Col. Lossberg – and provided "bindingly for the turn of strong mobile formations from the center to the north, once the enemy had been beaten in front of the Dnepr-Dvina line:"[151]

A. *Army* (in accordance with plans submitted to me):

In the theater of operations, which is divided by the [Pripiat'] Marshes into a Southern and a Northern sector, the main weight of attack will be delivered in the *Northern* area. Two Army Groups will be employed there.

The more southerly of these two Army Groups (in the center of the whole front) will have the task of advancing with powerful armored and motorized formations from the area about and north of Warsaw, and routing the enemy forces in White Russia. This will make it possible for strong mobile forces to advance northward and, in conjunction with the Northern Army Group operating out of East Prussia in the general direction of Leningrad, to destroy the enemy forces operating in the Baltic area. Only after the fulfillment of this first essential task, which must include the occupation of Leningrad and Kronstadt, will the attack be continued with the intention of occupying Moscow, an important center of communications and of the armaments industry.

Only a surprisingly rapid collapse of Russian resistance could justify the simultaneous pursuit of both objectives.[152]

There it was in plain German: Leningrad, the Baltic region in general, and the eradication of Red Army forces operating there were codified as higher priorities than the capture of Moscow – the political, psychological and communications hub of the Soviet Union. It had also become "manifest" in Hitler's discussions with his military advisors that he considered the capture of Russia's war-essential economic centers as the "main objective of the campaign, whereas Halder considered this a dissipation of forces which would then be lacking for the decisive thrust against Moscow."[153] Yet the Chief of the Army General Staff's reaction to the directive was – once again – not to argue or remonstrate; rather he continued patiently to craft an operational plan that matched his own thinking. When his plan differed from Hitler's he simply ignored the differences and went about his business as if he and his "Fuehrer" were in complete agreement.[154] After Operation *Barbarossa* began, Halder would quietly continue to attempt to fight the war according to his own operational concepts, sometimes even engaging in subtle subterfuge vis-à-vis his "Fuehrer."

Having "turned the switch" on war with Russia, Hitler departed the *Berghof* and went off to celebrate Christmas with his soldiers along the English Channel. Something "distantly resembling the spirit of Christmas overcame Hitler.

> He instructed the *Luftwaffe* to suspend bombing missions against Britain until Christmas was over. A fortnight of aimless meandering ensued … Keitel, Halder, and much of Jodl's staff had gone on leave. Protected by extra anti-aircraft trains, Hitler set out with his personal staff on a Christmas tour of the western front. He wanted to inspect the big gun batteries which Todt's organization had installed to command the Channel coast – the sites had names like "Great Elector," "Siegfried," and "Gneisenau" – and he wanted to celebrate the holiday with the aircrews of Goering's fighter and bomber squadrons … One of Hitler's secretaries wrote to a friend: "We have not stopped moving since December 21. Christmas on the French coast – Calais and Dunkirk. As we were eating dinner in the dining car of our special train on the 23rd at Boulogne, the British came and started bombing, and our anti-aircraft guns roared back at them. Even though we were shunted into a safe tunnel" – guarded by anti-aircraft trains at each end – "I couldn't help feeling 'a bit queer.' … On New Year's Eve the mood was more than painful."[155]

Across the whole of occupied Europe, in places like Denmark, France and Poland, millions of German soldiers also enjoyed a Christmas and New Year's filled with good cheer, libations, and hope for the future. The "arch" enemy, France, had been vanquished and, in time, England would be brought to heel as well. Somehow their "Fuehrer," in whom their trust was sublimely absolute, would find a way to end the war in victory. Like thousands of German soldiers, Siegfried Knappe, an artillery officer (*Oberleutnant*) in 87 Infantry Division, had already spent months in occupied France following the great victory that spring. Wounded on the outskirts of Paris in mid-June – indeed, from a spot so close to the city he could see the Eiffel Tower – he missed the triumphant entry of his division into the French capital. In September, after several months of convalescent leave, he returned to his unit. First, however, he enjoyed a couple of days touring Paris. He attended the Opera, visited Notre-Dame, the Arc de Triomphe, and even climbed the Eiffel Tower.[156]

Knappe's battery, which he now commanded after a promotion, was quartered in the rural village of Candé-sur-Beuvron; his headquarters ensconced in a chateau, near the confluence of the Beuvron and Loire Rivers. These were idyllic times. In his post-war "reflections" Knappe recalled:

> We lived better in Candé than I had at home on convalescent leave. In Germany, everything was rationed – food clothing, gasoline, etc. But in Candé we could go to restaurants and get anything we wanted without ration cards. I was even able to go to a tailor and have riding breeches made and buy the best riding boots without a ration card ... Some of us also occasionally went pheasant hunting along the Loire River, using some of the shotguns we had confiscated from the local population ... On the weekends, two or three of us would go to Paris by train.[157]

Granted home leave, *Leutnant* Knappe spent Christmas Eve and Christmas – which all Germans celebrated with such solemn conviction – with his family. Life was good. He was "enjoying the Army in spite of its rigors and discipline." He could not, of course, foresee what the coming year, 1941, held in store: That he would again be wounded – this time, a head wound – in early December 1941, after his division had scrapped and clawed its way to the very outskirts of Moscow; that during Christmas 1941, after short stays in several hospitals, he would be home in Leipzig, visiting his mortally wounded and grievously suffering brother, Fritz – his body covered in bedsores, his pain kept at bay by morphine injections – at the local hospital;[158] that the year 1941 would end in sadness and tragedy.

Hitler had soon returned to his mountain retreat above Berchtesgaden, to begin the New Year with his mistress, Eva Braun, and his "family" of adjutants and staff. The year 1940 – having begun with such great and spectacular victories, followed by a period of stasis and uncertainty, before culminating in Hitler's decision to launch the greatest war of all time – had finally drawn to a close. In his New Year's address to the *Wehrmacht*, the dictator proclaimed that 1941 "would bring the consummation of the greatest victory in our history."[159]

1.9: German Planning Through 1940 – An Assessment

The *Barbarossa* O-Plan was, at least on paper, elegant in its clarity and simplicity of purpose: The main Red Army forces were to be enveloped, encircled and annihilated by the German armored spearheads west of two great river lines, the Dnepr and Western Dvina, in a spectacular *Vernichtungsschlacht* – a super "Cannae," whose doctrinal antecedents were to be found in the theories of Clausewitz, the elder Moltke and Schlieffen. As noted, unlike Poland (1939) and France (1940), the Russian campaign was from the start envisaged as a true "blitzkrieg," to be decided in a matter of weeks as the result of a single, devastating blow. Simply put, Hitler and his General Staff wanted to operate like Moltke on the strategic level – by isolating and defeating each opponent singly – and like Schlieffen at the operational and tactical level – by destroying the enemy in a short war through a massive battle of annihilation. By doing so, they could overcome the traditional dilemmas posed by Germany's central European position and modest human and material resources. In Schlieffen's view, argued former Israeli officer Jehuda L. Wallach, the "total destruction of the opponent is always the most advantageous because it sets the whole of the victor's forces free for other duties;" the best way to achieve this was through "encirclement and attack from the rear."[160] Hitler, Halder, *et al.*, had absorbed the lessons of Schlieffen.

Indeed, after Red Army forces west of the Dnepr-Dvina had been encircled and destroyed, the war, it was believed, would essentially be over; all that would remain would be mopping up operations and pursuit into the interior to destroy those enemy elements which had escaped destruction and to reach final geographical objectives. German planners, then, anticipated little enemy resistance after the initial battles had been fought. Their intelligence – mostly derived from top-secret high level reconnaissance flights over Soviet territory – had given them a good picture of Red Army dispositions up to a depth of several hundred kilometers from the German-Soviet frontiers; beyond that, however, little was known about potential Soviet strength and dispositions. Yet the Germans simply assumed that the mass of the Red Army was deployed near the border regions and, once these forces were eliminated, there would be little left to deal with. It was a fatal assumption.

Of course, the men responsible for working out the details of the campaign plan were not stupid men. They knew full well that, in terms of time, geography, available resources, and so forth, the Russian theater of operations would pose unprecedented challenges and they sought, as best they could, to address them. Time was limited, the campaigning season in Russia lasted from about late May – at the earliest – into September; thereafter operations, particularly those of modern mechanized forces would be seriously disrupted by rain, mud and snow. Compared to Poland or France, the theater of operations was immense. The two primary German thrusts into Poland in September 1939 had covered about 105 and 240 kilometers from East Prussia and Silesia, respectively. The depth of the longest advance in France in 1940 was about 400 kilometers (the panzer drive across the Meuse River to the Channel coast), while the length of the active front against France and the Low Countries was less than 250 kilometers. In contrast, the *Wehrmacht* would have to begin its attack on Russia along a front stretching more than 1200 kilometers.[161] Moreover, as Lossberg had pointed out, the front would expand inexorably, in the shape of a funnel, as it migrated eastward from the Russo-German frontier, resulting in the dilution of German forces over an ever-broader area[162] and complicating the operational challenge of creating a clear center of gravity.[163] This problem, of course, was inherent in *Barbarossa*, given the prodigious size of the Soviet Union; yet it would grow increasingly unmanageable should the German blitzkrieg fail to quickly knock Russia out of the war.

Despite several large rivers, broad tracks of marshland and primeval forests, the terrain itself – with the notable exception of its sheer vastness[164] – did not pose major impediments to the movements of modern armies. However, the poor road and rail infrastructure in European Russia was a truly staggering problem that would seriously complicate the movement and supply of Germany's eastern armies fighting in the depth of the country. The entire Soviet Union possessed only 82,000 kilometers of railroads – all of a different gauge than those in Germany, Western Europe and German-occupied Poland[165] – and it would have to be converted to standard gauge, a time-consuming and labor-intensive process. Of just under 1.4 million kilometers of road, 1.13 million were little more than cart tracks. There were also 240,000 km of allegedly all-weather roads, yet only 64,000 km of these possessed hard surfaces.[166] The logistical and operational headaches inherent in such statistics provide a textbook example of what Clausewitz identified as "friction," a phenomenon that would complicate and slow the German advance eastward. The often insoluble problems created by such friction will be a primary theme of the soldiers' accounts in this narrative.

The Germans grappled with all of these – and many more of the myriad challenges posed by a military campaign in Russia. In the end, however, they simply dismissed them or let themselves be seduced by the optimistic assumptions that formed the basis of all their planning. One can only marvel at the astonishing fact that, for Operation *Barbarossa*, the Germans planned to commit total forces only marginally larger than those employed in the west in 1940, during the second stage of the German offensive. In terms of space, the *Wehrmacht* was going to have to operate over some 2.6 million square kilometers (one million square miles) of terrain in the east, while victory in 1940 had been achieved in a battle space of ca. 130,000 square kilometers.[167] The underlying theme in this discussion is that Hitler and his generals dramatically overestimated the capabilities of their own forces and, conversely, dismissed the military prowess of the Soviet Union. They assumed that, once the blitzkrieg was unleashed, it would unfold according to plan and bring about a rapid decision. The Soviet Union, with all its inherent social, political and military weaknesses, would simply come crashing down when struck by the *Wehrmacht's* overpowering and ineluctable blow.

While such general observations – as far as they go – are meaningful, an analysis of German planning for war with Russia requires deeper insight into several topics. They are: a.) the failure to plan definitively beyond the initial operations; b.) over-reliance on operational planning; c.) lack of resources committed to the campaign; d.) failures of German intelligence; and, e.) failures of logistical planning. Each topic is explored briefly below.

1.9.1: Failure to Plan beyond Initial Operations

The *Barbarossa* operations plan, in accordance with Hitler's instructions, clearly stipulated that after completion of the encirclement battles beyond the frontier, strong motorized elements of the central army group were to swing north to assist in clearing the Baltic region and capturing Leningrad. Of course, Brauchitsch, Halder, and their campaign planners at OKH had other ideas, enamored as they were with Moscow, whose capture, they believed, would end the war. This fundamental disconnect between Hitler and his Army General Staff – ignored or downplayed during the planning stages – would culminate in a five-week struggle between Hitler and his generals beginning in mid-July 1941, as they argued over the center of gravity for the second phase of the campaign. In fact, one can posit that, from August 1941 onward, German operations in the east were entirely improvised:

> Many of the highest-level troop commanders reacted uncomprehendingly to the to-ing and fro-ing between the three possible centers of gravity. The commanders in chief [*Oberbefehlshaber*], as former general staff officers schooled in the operational art, no doubt saw in this vacillation an irresponsible fear of decision and squandering of the forces. Those who suffered were their troops. A campaign plan without a clear center of gravity beyond the first phase of the border battles could only be judged by the military experts as poorly conceived. Once again, it was above all the panzer generals who – because they thought in terms of rapid operations, wide spaces, and forward-looking decision-making – most criticized the debilitating altercation between Hitler and the Army General Staff.[168]

1.9.2: Primacy of Operational Planning

As we have seen, a primary lesson gleaned by the German General Staff from its victory in the west was that operational planning – sadly to the neglect of logistics, intelligence, and other aspects of the art of war – was the key to victory, a panacea of sorts. The German military, in fact, had a long tradition of overemphasizing the operational and tactical aspects of war that can be traced to the elder Moltke, while Count von Schlieffen continued the trend toward reducing the theory of war to purely military matters.[169] The *Barbarossa* directive reflected this tradition, steeped as it was in operational details without offering a comprehensive plan for the conduct of the war in general (i.e., without embracing vital political and economic factors). This is striking when one considers that it was a highest-level government planning document, signed by the head of state and commander-in-chief of the armed forces, Adolf Hitler. But the "Fuehrer" had a disturbing proclivity for obsessing over operational matters – which should have been the sole province of his General Staff – instead of working out the broader strategic picture. "If one reads Directive No. 21 carefully," observed Jehuda Wallach, "one gets the impression that this particular document ... bears the same weaknesses as the Schlieffen Plan of 1905. Instead of outlining a strategic concept, it deals merely with operational or rather tactical advice.

The real strategic issues remain untouched and undiscussed."[170]

That a directive prepared by OKW was so narrowly focused on operational concerns was, in part, the inevitable outcome of German General Staff training, which offered little insight into the larger issues of state policy as they pertained to the conduct of war. According to Israeli scholar Marcel Stein, author of a recent biography of German Field Marshal Walter Model:

> Walter Goerlitz wrote the only thorough biography of Model to date, which was first published in 1975 under the title "Model – Strategy of Defence." The title was changed in a later paperback edition to "Model – The Field Marshall and His Final Battle in the Ruhr." The first title is deceiving. Even Model's admirers would hardly describe him as a strategist. Aside from the fact that strategists were lacking in the *Wehrmacht* in the Second World War – for despite their thorough training as general staff officers, the high-ranking commanders simply lacked the necessary insight into the factors of politics and the economy, which are closely linked to strategy. Furthermore, such insight was also denied them during the war by Fuehrer Order No. 1, which limited one's knowledge strictly to his respective field. Even Model did not have a broad overview of the entire war situation.[171]

Panzer general Hermann Hoth, who would lead one of the four panzer groups into Russia, later wrote an insightful account of his operations in the summer of 1941. About the *Barbarossa* plan he stated: "It is remarkable that the directive primarily addresses operational orders, which – even if they were coordinated with him – were really the business [*Sache*] of the military leader responsible for the Russian theater of war, the Commander-in-Chief of the Army. On the other hand, in the area of strategy, it has little to say with regard to the higher object of the war."[172] Here Hoth invoked the elder Moltke's distinction between the *Kriegsobjekt* and the *Operationsobjekt*, the former concept embracing the higher objects of war (for example, a nation's capital, the power of the state), and the latter the armed forces, in so far as destroying them supported the higher objects. Hoth went so far as to pose the question: "Was it really clear to Hitler, just how he wanted to end this war?"[173]

1.9.3: Paucity of Forces Committed to the Campaign

One cannot emphasize enough that the German attack on Russia in 1941 was "seriously underpowered."[174] A brief comparison with the campaign of 1940 makes this fact only too evident. In May-June 1940, German forces deployed in the west included about 140 divisions (118 for the first phase of the offensive), 2439 tanks, 7378 artillery pieces and 3578 aircraft, of which 2589 were operational on 10 May 1940.[175] Yet in the east – to defeat the largest army in the world in an utterly immense theater of operations – the Germans would commit some 150 divisions with just 3648 tanks and assault guns, 7146 artillery pieces, and 2255 combat-ready aircraft.[176] The reader can do the calculations. Simply put, the Germans were so confident of victory – and so dismissive of their opponent – that they intended to knock Soviet Russia out of the war with a force roughly comparable in size to that of 1940.

That is not to say that the German Army had not made significant strides between June 1940 and June 1941, for indeed it had. The German infantry had been upgraded with better weapons – for example, by *Barbarossatag* it would be equipped with at least small numbers of improved anti-tank weapons, though these would still prove wanting when confronted by heavier Soviet tank models – while the armored divisions had been doubled from 10 to 20. This doubling in strength, however, had largely been achieved by greatly reducing the number of tanks in each panzer division (a topic to be explored in more detail in Chapter 3), a solution forced on the Germans by their anemic tank production. As of 1940, German factories were producing only about 2200 units per annum; in the second half of 1940, production averaged just 182 units per month. Production rose slightly to 212 units per month in the first six months of 1941, but averaged only 271 for the entire year – a figure that would not begin to keep pace with attrition at the front.[177] The manufacture of assault guns, a tank-like weapon that was of immense value to the German infantry in Russia, would only amount to 285 in the final six months of 1941.[178]

In Russia, the Germans would soon find themselves short of everything – tanks, aircraft, vehicles, fuel, munitions, but mostly, combat infantry. German infantry companies would sustain high attrition rates in the opening weeks and months of the campaign, yet the Replacement Army in Germany only had 300,000 to 400,000 replacements available on 22 June 1941; by the end of the summer, practically all of these men had been sent to the front.[179] The situation with OKH reserves was no better, the Army High Command beginning the campaign with just 28 divisions in reserve;[180] and most of these divisions had been committed by the beginning of August 1941.[181] In October 1941, Army Group Center would begin Operation "Typhoon," the advance on Moscow, with virtually no reserves at its disposal.

The *Luftwaffe* in 1941 was a "formidable force." German aircrews were far better trained and possessed more combat experienced than their Russian counterparts, while *Luftwaffe* force structure was made up of aircraft types that, in general, were markedly superior to those of the Russian Air Force.[182] Yet, as noted, it had less than 2500 combat-ready aircraft available on 22 June – less than it had possessed in May 1940 – to perform a mission that, as it turned out, proved vastly more challenging than the campaign in the west the previous year.

Faced with shortfalls in every conceivable area, the *Ostheer* was to fight a "poor man's" war in Russia. From the beginning of the campaign in the east, German Army and *Luftwaffe* operations were hampered by what soon became a catastrophic shortage of resources. Seriously exacerbating this problem was Hitler's decision to "starve" his eastern armies of desperately needed resources – new tanks, engines, vehicles and other vital weapons and equipment items were to be held back to outfit new divisions for future tasks. Indeed, Hitler, even before *Barbarossa* began, was already contemplating new offensives in other corners of the world. The *Landser* in Russia would have to do with what he had.

1.9.4: Failures of Intelligence

The Germans based their planning for war with the Soviet Union on catastrophically poor intelligence. German military intelligence had "paid scant attention to Russia"[183] after 1933, when Hitler had ordered the withdrawal of all German military personnel from the USSR. Germany still stationed a military attaché in Moscow, but the Soviets – ever paranoid – did not permit foreign military attachés to leave the city and severely restricted access to information. Moreover, the Soviet Union, unlike many countries, did not publish an annual "white paper" on their military. Thus foreign powers and, certainly, among them Germany, had no real grasp of Russia's existing military capabilities or potential.[184] Yet the situation was even worse than that:

> Probably no major campaign has ever been launched upon less intelligence. The services had furnished Hitler – to say nothing of their lower commands – with only the most inadequate information on the Russians. They were certain of only one thing: the German fighting man's inborn superiority. All else was the product of rumor, speculation, and fragile calculations.[185] Admiral Canaris [head of the *Abwehr*, German military intelligence] told Keitel the *Abwehr* had drawn a blank on Russia. Conditions for espionage were impossible. Maps were nonexistent. The

range of the army's radio-monitoring stations was strictly limited. Foreign Armies East appealed to the *Luftwaffe* to intensify photographic reconnaissance missions, as it would take eight weeks to print the maps and issue them to the troops. The Russian aircraft industry was an unknown quantity on which the veil was only gradually being lifted. Recent indications were that it was being expanded at a disconcerting speed ...

This lack of proper intelligence was the root cause of the ultimate disaster. For while Halder had confidently advised the Fuehrer on 3 February [1941] that they would oppose only a small Red Army superiority in numbers, 155 divisions, by early April that figure had been raised (as the Finns and Japanese had always recommended) to 247 divisions; and four months later, when it was too late to retreat, the Army admitted that it had now identified *360* divisions in combat with them.[186]

In the months prior to *Barbarossa*, the Germans got most of their intelligence from high-level reconnaissance over western Russia,[187] and this intelligence was reasonably accurate to a depth of several hundred kilometers beyond the frontier (beyond that, however, little was known). They also derived information about Russian strength and dispositions from the monitoring of Red Army radio traffic in the border regions; however, attempts by the *Abwehr* to conduct spying operations within the Soviet Union largely fell flat. As a general rule, the Germans tended to seriously underestimate the size and strength of Soviet forces, a nasty quirk that would continue throughout the war (although German intelligence analysis did palpably improve after Richard Gehlen took over at Foreign Armies East in the spring of 1942). By late summer 1941, the Germans found themselves facing the Red Army's "second strategic echelon," which, in turn, was reinforced by a stream of Soviet reserve divisions from the interior of the USSR. The German intelligence blunder was, by then, all too apparent; "a battle of annihilation had become a war of attrition."[188] Yet inexplicably, the outlook in OKH and Hitler's East Prussian headquarters would continue to be characterized by optimism up to the first days of December 1941,[189] when the Soviet winter counteroffensive finally shattered any remaining illusions.

1.9.5: Failures of Logistics

According to German historian Horst Boog, Hitler "fought and lost the Second World War with an inadequate understanding of logistical considerations."[190] That this was so is hardly surprising: "Logistics was never prestigious in the German Army. As early as 1848-49, the man who would become Emperor William I considered it the weakest part in the organization of the Prussian Army. Even the famous Moltke and Schlieffen treated it with disdain since it was not directly operational, an attitude that would persist among later officers, especially Rommel."[191]

By the 20th Century, the mass armies of large, industrial nations had come to depend on logistics as a vital element of warfare. Modern warfare requires prodigious quantities of fuel, ammunition, food, clothing and equipment – and all of these commodities must first be produced, purchased, transported and, finally, distributed to the armed forces at the front.[192] Despite the decisive significance of logistics to the successful prosecution of war, during 1939-45 the German armed forces considered the field the province of bureaucrats, not soldiers – a dangerous misconception that played a large role in the ultimate German catastrophe in the east.

The German attack on the Soviet Union was the largest military operation the world had ever seen. The logistical challenges inherent in the campaign were staggering; the daily requirements of the Army alone were enormous. A single infantry division consumed about 170 tons of supplies per day – food, munitions, fuel, equipment, spare parts, etc. – while the needs of a panzer or motorized division surpassed even that.[193] Across the front, from the Baltic to the Black Sea, over 3,000,000 men with some 600,000 motor vehicles and about the same number of horses would have to be supplied each day, and in climatic and geographical conditions far different from those faced previously by the *Wehrmacht*. For German field armies in the east, ensuring that this mission was carried out successfully was the daunting challenge of the OKH *Generalquartiermeister* – the Army's Deputy Chief of Staff for Supply and Administration – Brig.-Gen. Eduard Wagner, whose primary tasks embraced logistical planning for the Army and military administration of the occupied territories. Wagner was instructed on 1 August 1940 to begin his planning for the impending Russian campaign; by November 1940, his work was largely complete.[194]

The basic conclusion of Wagner's logistical planners was that the German Army's system of supply could support an advance of about 500 kilometers beyond the frontier – that is, to the Dneper-Dvina line; beyond that adequate planning could not be projected. Given the overarching operational premise of a rapid, "blitzkrieg" advance, Wagner and the Army High Command, for this first phase of the campaign, placed their trust almost exclusively in the movement of supplies by "roadbound" motorized transport, not by rail. The logic behind this was that no one could expect to be able to operate an efficient rail system inside Soviet territory in the first two weeks of the war, as it was not possible to determine with any certitude – despite the projected rapid advance – just how soon, to what extent, and in what condition Russian railway lines and rolling stock would fall into German hands.[195]

Yet the "*matérial* basis" (i.e., the motor vehicle hauling capacity) for the transport of supplies by road was "alarmingly slender," even for the first phase, necessitating "unusual and complicated solutions" in the design of the supply system by General Wagner;[196] furthermore, calculations, studies and map exercises had revealed that when the Dnepr-Dvina line was crossed, at the latest, the *Ostheer* would be dependent upon the efficient functioning of the railroads for supply because of the much greater distances involved. The Germans were aware from the outset that it would be necessary to convert captured Russian broad-gauge lines to the narrower German gauge, but hoped to keep the time consuming conversions to a minimum by relying heavily on the Soviet rail infrastructure – rail lines, locomotives and rolling stock. (Yet here, too, they were to be disappointed.)[197] In any case, it was apparent that, beyond the 500 kilometer limit, the efficient movement of supplies would only possible by a combination of motor vehicle and rail.[198]

To address the many logistical challenges of the coming campaign, Wagner improvised. For example, to outfit the three army groups with the requisite hauling capacity – the so-called "*Grosstransportraum*" or "Greater Transport Area"[199] – he stripped the marching infantry divisions of all but their most essential motorized transport and gave it to the army groups, enabling them to eventually raise the capacity of their *Grosstransportraum* to 15,880 tons in the south, 25,020 tons in the center, and 12,750 in the north.[200] For the loss of their vehicles, the infantry divisions received some 15,000 Polish *Panje* horse-drawn wagons. To boost the range of the panzer groups, their tanks were fitted with two-wheeled trailers, each carrying two 200 liter fuel tanks; some were also loaded with 20 liter fuel cans strapped to their turrets. In addition, twice the normal load of ammunition was crammed inside each tank to make them as self-sufficient as possible in the earliest phase of the fighting.[201] Because the logistical plan also foresaw the *Ostheer* living off the land to the fullest extent possible, each army group established special centers for processing captured supplies.[202]

Despite such measures, Wagner's planning suffered from the same basic defect as the High Command's operational scheme, for once again the details had been hammered out only through the first phase of the campaign; here too, then, all would be improvised after the opening weeks of operations. Complicating matters further still was the fact that efforts to supply the field armies would be affected by shortages of critical war materials, with rubber tires and fuel causing the most concern. To accumulate required stocks of fuel for the Russian campaign, the Chief of OKW, Field Marshal Keitel, had, by the autumn of

1940, imposed the strictest controls over fuel consumption by the Army. Even so, a reserve of no more than three months' consumption (with regard to diesel oil, only one month) had been stockpiled by the spring of 1941, and shortages were expected as early as July 1941. Indeed, enduring shortages of fuel, oil, spare parts[203] and other critical commodities were to become a tiresome theme of the eastern campaign, inexorably diminishing the combat power of the *Wehrmacht*.[204]

Operation *Barbarossa* – as one author puts it – was launched on a "logistical shoestring."[205] Historian David Stahel buttresses this point, noting that, "the Achilles heel upon which all else rested was logistics."[206] After 22 June 1941, the deeper the German Army drove into Russia the worse its supply situation became. Optimistic assumptions about fuel, oil, ammunition and spare parts consumption often proved hopelessly wrong, while tanks, trucks and other vehicles broke down at an alarming rate on the poor roadways of European Russia. In fact, attrition from "wear and tear" on tanks and vehicles was often greater than that caused by enemy action. The hauling capacity of the railroads, inadequate to begin with, became increasingly strained as time passed (despite Herculean efforts to convert the tracks to standard gauge and move the railheads forward); by the winter of 1941, it was to collapse altogether. Bearing the brunt of such logistical nightmares were, of course, the soldiers along the main battle line. By the fall of 1941, they were short – often desperately so – of food, ammunition, weapons, and spare parts; even basic necessities, such as clothing, razor blades and writing paper, were in short supply. Most of them had received no winter clothing, which would not arrive from depots far behind the front until early 1942, forcing them to survive in temperatures of -20, -30, -40 degrees Centigrade and below in whatever motley collection of clothing they had taken from Russian civilians or pilfered from dead or captured Red Army soldiers at the front.

Oberstleutnant Hellmuth Stieff was the chief operations officer (Ia) in German Fourth Army in late 1941. On Sunday, 7 December 1941, from his post outside Moscow, in a letter to his wife, he captured the bitterness and betrayal felt by so many German soldiers that first winter in Russia:

> Forgive me if I have become bitter! But you just *cannot* understand it. [The war] is *utterly different* to how it is portrayed to you by that preposterous propaganda. We are standing on a knife's edge every day here. That is why we feel *so* betrayed. But we will deal with that somehow – just no highfalutin words! For otherwise one could only despair and go mad …
>
> … *Every* crusade is all the same to *us*, we are fighting for our bare existence out here, every day and every hour, against an enemy who is many times more superior in *all* areas on the ground and in the air. Nothing is sent to us from the rear, quite the opposite, 3 divisions … were prematurely withdrawn, the *Luftwaffe* takes practically everything away, and our "winter equipment" is an *insult* in view of the conditions here. And our adversary can bring forward *10* new divisions from Siberia in one week, every man in felt boots, with quilted coats and trousers and fur hats (which means the prisoners now walk barefoot and die, and *our* people put the things on!), and the [enemy's] air superiority is legion (often enough during the day, [*Hauptmann*] Hobe and I end up lying flat on the ground while the bombers howl).
>
> I will stop. You will not understand me anyway. Anyway, here in front of Moscow is the meeting point for all elegant society.
>
> Heartfelt greetings and kisses,
> Your Hellmuth[207]

For his role in the German Resistance, then Brig.-Gen. Hellmuth Stieff was apprehended, tortured and tried before the notorious People's Court (*Volksgerichtshof*) following the assassination attempt on Hitler at his headquarters in Rastenburg on 20 July 1944. Stieff was sentenced to death on 8 August and hanged the same day in Ploetzensee Prison in Berlin.

ENDNOTES

1   W. L. Shirer, *Rise and Fall of the Third Reich*, 741; Internet site at: http://www.lexikon-der-wehrmacht.
2   Center of gravity, or point of main effort.
3   J. Keegan, *Second World War*, 78; I.C.B. Dear (ed.), *Oxford Companion to World War II*, 326; K.-H. Frieser, "*Die deutschen Blitzkriege: Operativer Triumph – strategische Tragoedie*," in: *Die Wehrmacht – Mythos und Realitaet*, R.-D. Mueller & H.-E. Volkmann (Hg.), 188-91; I. Kershaw, *Hitler 1936-1945: Nemesis*, 295.
4   J. Keegan, *Second World War*, 84; M. Gilbert, *Second World War*, 98.
5   W. L. Shirer, *Rise and Fall of the Third Reich*, 741-42.
6   Ibid., 742.
7   W. L. Shirer, *Rise and Fall of the Third Reich*, 742-43; C. Burdick & H.-A. Jacobsen (eds.), *The Halder Diary 1939-1942*, 213.
8   *Oberkommando der Wehrmacht*, or Armed Forces High Command. This was Hitler's personal headquarters.
9   W. L. Shirer, *Rise and Fall of the Third Reich*, 743-45.
10 In his memoirs, Baur recalled that the airfield outside Hitler's HQ was completely fogged in (*voellig im Nebel*), forcing him to make a blind takeoff. See, H. Baur, *Mit Maechtigen zwischen Himmel und Erde*, 192.
11 The times given here are Martin Gilbert's, because they appear to make sense. In his memoirs, Baur claimed that he arrived at Le Bourget at 5:00 a.m. and, within about an hour, he, Hitler and the dictator's entourage were back at the aerodrome. If Baur's account is accurate, it must have been a "whirlwind" tour – Paris in an hour! M. Gilbert, *Second World War*, 102; H. Baur, *Mit Maechtigen zwischen Himmel und Erde*, 192.
12 M. Gilbert, *Second World War*, 102; see also, C.G. Sweeting, *Hitler's Personal Pilot*, 137.
13 W. L. Shirer, *Rise and Fall of the Third Reich*, 746.
14 R. Moorhouse, *Berlin at War*, 61-63.
15 K.-H. Frieser, "*Die deutschen Blitzkriege: Operativer Triumph – strategische Tragoedie*," in: *Die Wehrmacht – Mythos und Realitaet*, R.-D. Mueller & H.-E. Volkmann (Hg.), 192.
16 On 8 November 1941, as Operation *Barbarossa* approached its climax, Hitler would tell his old guard followers (*alte Kaempfer*) in Munich, at the traditional celebration of the abortive "Beer Hall Putsch" of 1923: "I have never used the word blitzkrieg, because it is a totally idiotic [*bloedsinnig*] word. But if it is at all appropriate to describe a campaign, then it is this one. Never before has such a gigantic empire as that of the Soviet Union been smashed and beaten down in so short a time." Quoted in: M. Vogt (Hg.), *Herbst 1941 im "Fuehrerhauptquartier*," X.
17 K.-H. Frieser, "*Die deutschen Blitzkriege: Operativer Triumph – strategische Tragoedie*," in: *Die Wehrmacht – Mythos und Realitaet*, R.-D. Mueller & H.-E. Volkmann (Hg.), 190.
18 Most notably, Karl-Heinz Frieser's provocative book, *Blitzkrieg-Legende. Der Westfeldzug 1940*, published in 1995.
19 To this day, it remains the greatest traffic jam in Europe's history.
20 K.-H. Frieser, "*Die deutschen Blitzkriege: Operativer Triumph – strategische Tragoedie*," in: *Die Wehrmacht – Mythos und Realitaet*, R.-D. Mueller & H.-E. Volkmann (Hg.), 190.
21 Ibid., 188-91.
22 Precise casualty figures differ somewhat, depending on the source. These are gleaned from the *Oxford Companion to World War II*, I.C.B. Dear (ed.), 326. The Germans also suffered slightly more than 13,000 missing in the French campaign.
23 R. Moorhouse, *Berlin at War*, 65.
24 T. Weber, *Hitler's First War*, 208, 212.
25 I. Kershaw, *Hitler 1936-45: Nemesis*, 284. As Kershaw puts it: "Nothing at all had been clearly thought through. The *Luftwaffe* was the best equipped of the three branches of the armed forces. But even here, the armaments program had been targeted at 1942, not 1939."
26 K.-H. Frieser, "*Die deutschen Blitzkriege: Operativer Triumph – strategische Tragoedie*," in: *Die Wehrmacht – Mythos und Realitaet*, R.-D. Mueller & H.-E. Volkmann (Hg.), 186.
27 Ibid., 192.
28 As we shall see, the German military had a long tradition of obsessing over the operational level of war to the neglect of overarching strategic concerns. Simply put, the operational level of war – as distinguished from tactics and strategy – pertains to the movement of corps, armies and army groups on the battlefield. Operational issues would dominate German planning for Russia.
29 The words are Bernd Wegner's. See his, "*Hitlers Krieg? Zur Entscheidung, Planung und Umsetzung des 'Unternehmens Barbarossa*,'" in: *Verbrechen der Wehrmacht*, C. Hartmann, J. Huerter & U. Jureit (Hg.), 31.

30 Ibid., 31.
31 R. Kirchubel, "*Operation Barbarossa and the American Controversy over Aid to the Soviet Union*," 2 (unpublished paper).
32 P. Johnson, *Modern Times*, 375.
33 Ibid., 375.
34 As the great German historian Andreas Hillgruber observed, by late July 1940 America lay at the center of Hitler's strategic calculations: "Thus, much earlier than expected, the USA had become the pivotal factor [*Angelpunkt*] in Hitler's overall strategy." A. Hillgruber, *Der Zweite Weltkrieg 1939-45*, 45.
35 Germany began the war with just 57 U-Boats, 27 of which were ocean-going, the remainder being short range, coastal vessels. The German Navy's pre-war expansion program, the so-called "Z-Plan," envisaged construction of a fleet of 300 boats, which Karl Doenitz, the German U-Boat commander, thought a sufficient number to strangle Britain. However, he would not achieve that total until July 1942. J. Keegan, *Second World War*, 105-06.
36 J. Wright, *Germany and Origins of Second World War*, 167-68.
37 B. Wegner, "*Hitlers Krieg? Zur Entscheidung, Planung und Umsetzung des 'Unternehmens Barbarossa,'*" in: *Verbrechen der Wehrmacht*, C. Hartmann, J. Huerter & U. Jureit (Hg.), 31-32.
38 C. Burdick & H.-A. Jacobsen (eds.), *The Halder Diary 1939-1942*, 227.
39 J. Wright, *Germany and Origins of Second World War*, 167-68.
40 D. Irving, *Hitler's War*, 138-39.
41 Generals promoted to the exalted rank of field marshal also included the three army group commanders of the French campaign – Rundstedt, Leeb and Bock. Among the other promotions approved by Hitler at this time, Goering became a "*Reichsmarschall*," Halder advanced to colonel general and Jodl to full general. N. von Below, *At Hitler's Side*, 67-68.
42 H. Boog, et al., *Germany and the Second World War*, Vol. IV, 270. (Hereafter cited as *GSWW*.) Throughout the Second World War, the German military lacked unity of command. Simply put, its Armed Forces High Command (OKW) was responsible for all theaters of war with the exception of the eastern theater, which was the province of the Army High Command (OKH). Thus, Jodl, Chief of the OKW Operations Staff, needed the Lossberg study to stay informed. It should be noted, however, that all of Hitler's major directives for the war with Russia in 1941/42 were issued through OKW, which functioned as his personal military staff.
43 C. Burdick & H.-A. Jacobsen (eds.), *The Halder Diary 1939-1942*, 230-31.
44 V. Dahm, et al. (Hg.), *Die toedliche Utopie*, 53-70.
45 D. Irving, *Hitler's War*, 148-49.
46 Ibid., 149.
47 Ibid., 149.
48 The cutting remarks are those of John Wheeler-Bennett; see his, *The Nemesis of Power: The German Army in Politics, 1918-1945* (London, 1964), 429-30. (Quoted in: I.C.B. Dear, *Oxford Companion to WWII*, 508.)
49 C. von Luttichau, *Road to Moscow* (unpublished manuscript), I:17; W. Gorlitz (ed.), *Memoirs of Field-Marshal Keitel*, 121-23.
50 C. Burdick & H.-A. Jacobsen (eds.), *The Halder Diary 1939-1942*, 241-43; I. Kershaw, *Hitler 1936-45: Nemesis*, 307.
51 C. Burdick & H.-A. Jacobsen (eds.), *The Halder Diary 1939-1942*, 244.
52 Ibid., 245.
53 *GSWW*, Vol. IV, 253.
54 If both Brauchitsch and Halder were at first privately skeptical – believing from a military point of view that it was better to continue the "friendship" with Russia until England was defeated, thus avoiding a two front war – neither man rejected the idea in principle, nor thought the task of defeating Russia beyond Germany's means. J. Loeffler, *Brauchitsch – Eine politische Biographie*, 221-22.
55 J. Foerster, *Wehrmacht im NS-Staat*, 170
56 I. Kershaw, *Fateful Choices*, 68.
57 A. Hillgruber, *Der Zweite Weltkrieg*, 56-57.
58 *GSWW*, Vol. IV, 2; *DRZW*, Bd. IV, xiv.
59 I. Kershaw, *Hitler 1936-45: Nemesis*, 389.
60 *GSWW*, Vol. IV, 2.
61 I. Kershaw, *Hitler 1936-45: Nemesis*, 402.
62 See, J. Wright, *Germany and Origins of Second World War*, 169-71.
63 Ibid.
64 G. Knopp, *Die Wehrmacht. Eine Bilanz*, 88.
65 L. Yahil, *The Holocaust*, 243-44.
66 G. Megargee, *War of Annihilation*, 7.
67 R. G. Reuth, *Hitler – Eine politische Biographie*, 525; L. Yahil, *The Holocaust*, 244. Writes Yahil: "Since the entire war was perceived as a confrontation between two conflicting ideologies, with the Jews as the personification of the one that represented *the* divisive force in human society, their annihilation came to be regarded as an integral part of the war effort."
68 A. Hillgruber, *Der Zweite Weltkrieg*, 65.
69 D. Stahel, *And the World held its Breath*, 70 (unpublished manuscript). (Note: Special thanks to David Stahel for graciously providing his manuscript to this author prior to its publication as *Operation Barbarossa and Germany's Defeat in the East* (Cambridge, 2009)).

70 A. Hillgruber, *Der Zweite Weltkrieg*, 45-46.

71 Ibid., 46.

72 By the winter of 1940/41, Hitler's strategic thinking had even evolved beyond Russia, to the concept of a global blitzkrieg (*Weltblitzkrieg*) in concert with Germany's Axis allies – Italy and Japan – after Russia's rapid defeat. The objective would be to "isolate the USA in the Western hemisphere." See, A. Hillgruber, *Der Zweite Weltkrieg*, 48-49.

73 On 17 December 1940, Hitler told Jodl: "We must solve all continental European problems in 1941, for the USA would be in a position to intervene from 1942 onwards." H.-A. Jacobsen, *Der Zweite Weltkrieg in Chronik*, 34; P. E. Schramm (Hg.), *Kriegstagebuch des OKW*, Bd. I, 996.

74 See, G. E. Rothenberg, "*Moltke, Schlieffen, and the Doctrine of Strategic Envelopment*," in: *Makers of Modern Strategy*, P. Paret (ed.), 296-310.

75 Ibid., 310.

76 R.-D. Mueller, *Der letzte deutsche Krieg*, 81.

77 As German historian Horst Boog has argued, the "problem of reserves, like that of logistics, has traditionally been neglected in German military thinking … Clausewitz, Moltke, and Schlieffen did not think much of strategic reserves because they thought that the decisive battles took place at the beginning of a war." H. Boog, "*Higher Command and Leadership in the German Luftwaffe, 1935-1945*," in: *Air Power and Warfare*, A. F. Hurley & R. C. Ehrhart (eds.), 151.

78 For a detailed overview of German military planning for the Russian campaign see the pertinent sections in *GSWW*, Vol. IV.

79 G. E. Rothenberg, "*Moltke, Schlieffen, and the Doctrine of Strategic Envelopment*," in: *Makers of Modern Strategy*, P. Paret (ed.), 298.

80 A. Hillgruber, *Der Zweite Weltkrieg*, 48-49.

81 *GSWW*, Vol. IV, 244-45.

82 C. von Luttichau, *Road to Moscow*, II:1-3.

83 Ibid., I:18; II:4.

84 E. Mawdsley, *Thunder in the East*, 70.

85 *Generalstab des Heeres (Nur fuer den Dienstgebrauch!)*, "*Militaergeopolitische Angaben ueber das Europaeische Russland, Zentral Russland (ohne Moskau)*," Berlin, 15. Mai 1941, quoted in: J. Piekalkiewicz, *Schlacht um Moskau*, 16.

86 C. von Luttichau, *Road to Moscow*, I:17. The requirement for a better rail infrastructure had become urgent by July 1940.

87 B. Mueller-Hillebrand, *Das Heer 1933-1945*, Bd. II, 76-79.

88 C. von Luttichau, *Road to Moscow*, II:10.

89 Lying between Belorussia and the western Ukraine, the Pripiat' Marshes pose the greatest single natural barrier in Russia, effectively dividing the western border region into two separate compartments. In 1941, they consisted of swampland and primeval forest stretching ca. 240 km. from north to south, and more than 480 km. from west to east. The marshes began just beyond the Russo-German frontier, directly to the southeast of Brest-Litovsk, and were interlaced with numerous streams which fed the Pripiat', Dnepr and Berezina Rivers. With exception of a few man-made routes, they were virtually impassable except when frozen. The (relatively) much denser communications net (road and railroad) north of the marshes favored making the main German advance there. E. M. Howell, *Soviet Partisan Movement*, 2; C. von Luttichau, *Road to Moscow*, II:5-6; A. Seaton, *The Russo-German War*, 55.

90 The original German in the Marcks study reads: "*Seine Eroberung zerreisst den Zusammenhang des russischen Reiches*." Quoted in: W. K. Nehring, *Geschichte der deutschen Panzerwaffe*, 215.

91 C. von Luttichau, *Road to Moscow*, II:4-11; W. Murray, *Strategy for Defeat*, 77-78.

92 W. Murray, *Strategy for Defeat*, 77-78.

93 A. Hillgruber, *Die Zerstoerung Europas*, 259.

94 W. Murray, *Strategy for Defeat*, 77-78.

95 *GSWW*, Vol. IV, 270.

96 Ibid.

97 D. Irving, *Hitler's War*, 142.

98 Ibid., 142, 163. Writes Irving: "Sources differ as to Lossberg's inspiration. After the war, he himself privately claimed to have drafted the plan on a contingency basis on his own initiative and not, for example, on Jodl's instructions. But his cousin was to state under interrogation that 'in about August [1940]' Lossberg had told him the Fuehrer had commissioned the rough study from him." Ibid., 142, f.n. 5. According to Geoffrey P. Megargee, the study was ordered by Jodl. G. P. Megargee, *Inside Hitler's High Command*, 105.

99 A. Hillgruber, *Die Zerstoerung Europas*, 260; *GSWW*, Vol. IV, 273-74; G. Niepold, "*Plan Barbarossa*," in: D. M. Glantz (ed.), *Initial Period of War*, 69. According to Niepold, who, in 1941, as a young staff officer, was the personal staff officer to General Paulus, OKW presented the Lossberg plan to Hitler in December 1940.

100 *GSWW*, Vol. IV, 270-74.

101 A. Hillgruber, *Die Zerstoerung Europas*, 260.

102 Apparently, about the same time as Marcks, Halder had also directed Lt.-Col. Gerhard Feyerabend to begin his own study. Feyerabend was transferred to the OKH Operations Branch in July 1940. He was to "gather information on the Soviet Union, calculate the range of its air forces, and assess the presumable attitudes of Finland and Romania, as a basis both for map exercises and for deployment instructions for Eighteenth Army." See, *GSWW*, Vol. IV, 243-45.

103 T. Diedrich, *Paulus*, 158-61.
104 Ibid., 163.
105 Ibid., 162.
106 Ibid., 162. Paulus' hopeful comments, however, failed to convince his wife. She plied her husband with books, among them Caulaincourt's account of Napoleon's disastrous campaign in Russia.
107 In October 1940, Lt.-Col. Rowehl received a top-secret order directly from Hitler: Rowehl was to organize a long-range reconnaissance squadron capable of conducting photographic reconnaissance of western Russia from great altitudes. The secret flights began in the late winter, using specially modified Heinkel He 111s, Dornier Do 215-B2s, and Junkers Ju 88Bs and Ju 86Ps, the latter two models capable of reaching altitudes of 33,000 and 39,000 feet, respectively – sensational heights for the time. The long-range flights were "virtually the only source of really significant intelligence material for the first phase of the campaign." See, P. Carell, *Hitler Moves East*, 60.
108 T. Diedrich, *Paulus*, 158; C. von Luttichau, *Road to Moscow*, II:11.
109 Hitler approved the plan on 5 December 1940, when it was briefed to him in Berlin. See the text for details.
110 T. Diedrich, *Paulus*, 164.
111 C. von Luttichau, *Road to Moscow*, II:12-13.
112 S. J. Lewis, *Forgotten Legions*, 156, f.n. 32. Heusinger had taken over as chief of the OKH Operations Branch by 1 October 1940; the post had previously been held by Hans von Greiffenberg. *Adolf Heusinger* (Bundesministerium der Verteidigung (Hg.)), 109-10.
113 T. Diedrich, *Paulus*, 164. On 7 December 1940 a third, and final, war game took place at OKH headquarters in Zossen. Ibid., 166.
114 P. E. Schramm (Hg.), *Kriegstagebuch des OKW*, Bd. I, 205.
115 Ibid., 208-09.
116 The vital importance Hitler attached to the seizure of the Baltic area and Leningrad may have been the result of Lossberg's influence. The reader will recall that Lossberg had stressed the significance of their capture in his study. In any case, the Baltic region and Leningrad would remain *leitmotifs* in Hitler's thinking about the Russian campaign.
117 P. E. Schramm (Hg.), *Kriegstagebuch des OKW*, Bd. I, 209; C. von Luttichau, *Road to Moscow*, II:33-34; C. Burdick & H.-A. Jacobsen (eds.), *The Halder Diary 1939-1942*, 294.
118 T. Diedrich, *Paulus*, 166.
119 C. von Luttichau, *Road to Moscow*, II:34.
120 J. Keegan, *Second World War*, 88.
121 Ibid., 88.
122 W., Murray, *Strategy for Defeat*, 52.
123 Ibid., 50-55.
124 Ibid., 80.
125 M. Gilbert, *Second World War*, 130.
126 Ibid., 130-31.
127 Faced with Franco's intransigence, Hitler, in January 1941, would abandon plans to capture Gibraltar (code-name "Felix"). I. Kershaw, *Fateful Choices*, 85.
128 M. Gilbert, *Second World War*, 133-34; I. Kershaw, *Fateful Choices*, 82-83; C. Burdick & H.-A. Jacobsen (eds.), *The Halder Diary 1939-1942*, 279.
129 M. Gilbert, *Second World War*, 134-35.
130 W. Murray, *Strategy for Defeat*, 73.
131 J. Keegan, *Second World War*, 144-45.
132 Despite such Balkan distractions, Hitler kept his eye on Russia. In this context, his Directive No. 18 stated: "All preparations for the east for which verbal orders have already been given will be continued;" further directives were to follow "on this subject, as soon as the basic operational plan of the Army has been submitted to me and approved." Quoted in: M. Gilbert, *Second World War*, 141.
133 G. E. Blau, *German Campaigns in the Balkans*, 5-7 (CMH Pub. 104-4).
134 J. Keegan, *Second World War*, 146.
135 J. Keegan, *Second World War*, 146; D. Stahel, *And the World held its Breath*, 96.
136 J. Keegan, *Second World War*, 156-57.
137 D. Stahel, *And the World held its Breath*, 97.
138 R. Kirchubel, "*Operation Barbarossa and the American Controversy over Aid to the Soviet Union*," 2-3.
139 M. Gilbert, *Second World War*, 141.
140 I. Kershaw, *Fateful Choices*, 262.
141 K.-J. Thies, *Der Ostfeldzug – Ein Lageatlas*, vii.
142 K. Gerbet (ed.), *GFM Fedor von Bock, The War Diary*, 193-94.
143 A. Hillgruber, *Hitlers Strategie*, 388-92.
144 C. Burdick & H.-A. Jacobsen (eds.), *The Halder Diary 1939-1942*, 292-94. "Otto," at least, was the appellation used by Halder and his staff at OKH. The code-name employed by Lossberg and OKW was "Fritz."
145 I. Kershaw, *Hitler 1936-45: Nemesis*, 335.
146 C. Bellamy, *Absolute War*, 126.
147 H. Hoth, *Panzer-Operationen*, 30-31.
148 The 11-page document was "partly the handiwork of Jodl, a master stylist whose spoken German was very clear and simple, and party the product of Hitler's pen." D. Irving, *Hitler's War*, 190-91.

149 C. Bellamy, *Absolute War*, 126.

150 H. R. Trevor-Roper, *Hitler's War Directives*, 49. For the original German text of the directive see, W. Hubatsch (Hg.), *Hitlers Weisungen fuer die Kriegfuehrung*, 84-88.

151 G. Niepold, "*Plan Barbarossa*," in: D. M. Glantz (ed.), *Initial Period of War*, 69. According to Niepold, the directive was "based on the plan of the OKW."

152 H. R. Trevor-Roper, *Hitler's War Directives*, 50-51.

153 G. Niepold, "*Plan Barbarossa*," in: D. M. Glantz (ed.), *Initial Period of War*, 69.

154 G. P. Megargee, *Inside Hitler's High Command*, 131-32.

155 D. Irving, *Hitler's War*, 192-93.

156 S. Knappe, *Soldat*, 181-91.

157 Ibid., 191-95.

158 Ibid., 195-242.

159 M. Domarus, *Hitler – Reden und Proklamationen*, Bd. II, 1643.

160 J. L. Wallach, *Dogma of the Battle of Annihilation*, 42. Wallach's book offers provocative insight into the theories of Clausewitz and Schlieffen, and their impact on Germany's conduct of two world wars. In his view, Schlieffen exercised tremendous influence on Hitler's operational thinking.

161 E. Mawdsley, *Thunder in the East*, 41-42.

162 In France (1940), Guderian's corps frontages rarely exceeded 25 km.; in Russia, the norm for his panzer group would be 130 km. or more. In general, divisions, corps and armies in Russia would hold frontages much broader than envisaged by doctrine. D. Showalter, *Hitlers Panzers*, 160.

163 J. L. Wallach, *Dogma of the Battle of Annihilation*, 270.

164 Field Marshal Moltke himself, "despite giving preference in his deployment plans to attacking Russia first, in the event of a war on two fronts, was completely daunted by the difficulties presented by the Russian space and had no conquest of Russian territory in mind … Count von Schlieffen rejected the 'Great Eastern Deployment Plan' ('*Grosser Ostaufmarsch*') because he considered the Russian space, i.e., its vastness and its communications difficulties, as unsuitable for the achievement of a quick and decisive victory. His successor, the younger Moltke, dropped any further work on the '*Grosser Ostaufmarsch.*' . . ." In 1913, the German Great General Staff produced a secret memorandum about Russian tactics. One section of the document emphasized the problems of the terrain; these included bad road conditions, the paucity of building materials for roads and bridges, the great distances between towns and cities, vast swamps, difficult climatic conditions, and lack of accurate maps. Virtually all of these problems would adversely affect German operations in Russia in 1941. Ibid., 265-66.

165 While Germany and German-occupied Poland used standard gauge rail lines (1435mm), the Soviets continued to use wide gauge lines (1528mm), a legacy of the Czarist era. In order to receive the large quantities of foodstuffs and raw materials the USSR was obligated to deliver to Germany under the 1939 pact, Germany had to construct two special gauge conversion yards on the German-Soviet frontier. These two rail yards also became key rail centers after the start of Operation *Barbarossa*. "*Deutsche Reichsbahn*," at: www.feldgrau.com.

166 E. F. Ziemke & M. E. Bauer, *Moscow to Stalingrad*, 14.

167 J. Lucas, *War on the Eastern Front*, 3.

168 J. Huerter, *Hitlers Heerfuehrer*, 293.

169 H. Boog, "*Higher Command and Leadership in the German Luftwaffe, 1935-1945*," in: *Air Power and Warfare*, A. F. Hurley & R. C. Ehrhart (eds.), 150. Writes Boog: "[Moltke], unlike Clausewitz, separated politics from war and wanted no politician to interfere with the generals' responsibility for the conduct of war. General Schlieffen … developed an almost autonomous, mechanistic war plan, which ignored diplomacy in 1914. The famous Schlieffen Plan was not a comprehensive war plan and did not address the political and economic aspects of war." Ibid., 150.

170 J. L. Wallach, *Dogma of the Battle of Annihilation*, 271.

171 M. Stein, *GFM Walter Model*, 12.

172 H. Hoth, *Panzer-Operationen*, 33.

173 Ibid., 33-34. According to Hoth, the operational objectives outlined in the *Barbarossa* O-Plan were much too optimistic, even utopian: "Combating the armaments centers located further east was, then, to fall to the *Luftwaffe*. These were utopian ideas. The German bombers' penetration depth at that time was 1000 km. Even if the desired line Volga – Archangel was successfully reached, which was certainly not possible in a three to four-month campaign, the range of the bombers would not have been sufficient to make the Ural industrial areas … unusable for conducting war. And the world did not stop just after Sverdlovsk. It was well known that since 1928, in Siberia in the Kuznetsk region, an even mightier industrial center had developed which, together with the Ural industrial areas, comprised 12 percent of the entire area of the Soviet Union." Ibid., 35.

174 See, P. Johnson, *Modern Times*, 377-78.

175 K.-H. Frieser, "*Die deutschen Blitzkriege: Operativer Triumph – strategische Tragoedie*," in: *Die Wehrmacht – Mythos und Realitaet*, R.-D. Mueller & H.-E. Volkmann (Hg.), 185; *GSWW*, Vol. IV, 217.

176 *GSWW*, Vol. IV, 92-93, 364.

177 German tank production did not reach the figure of 400 units per month until the spring of 1942. C. Winchester, *Hitler's War on Russia*, 129; D. Stahel, *And the World held its Breath*, 81; R. L. DiNardo, *Germany's Panzer Arm*, 16; E. Bauer, *Panzerkrieg*, 113.

178 The German army in the east began the campaign with only 250 assault guns, distributed among 11 battalions and 5 separate batteries. E. Bauer, *Panzerkrieg*, 113.

179   As Halder observed on 26 August 1941: "After 1 Oct. we shall have exhausted practically all our replacements." On 1 September 1941 OKH stated: "At the moment there is such a shortage of men that it is no longer possible to offset casualties." Both quoted in: K. Reinhardt, *Moscow – The Turning Point*, 66-67, f.n. 26.

180   See, OKH Gen St d H/Op.Abtl (III), "*Kriegsgliederung Barbarossa*," Stand 18.6.41, in: K. Mehner (Hg.), *Geheime Tagesberichte*, Bd. 3.

181   D. Stahel, *And the World held its Breath*, 224.

182   R. Muller, *The German Air War in Russia*, 33.

183   S. J. Lewis, *Forgotten Legions*, 129.

184   Ibid., 129.

185   As Andreas Hillgruber pointed out: "How little of concrete value the documents were overall, on which German military planning could be based, was shown in a particularly stark way in the 'Handbook' about the 'Wartime Armed Forces of the USSR,' which the FHO [Foreign Armies East] department published on 1 January 1941. Here, it was conceded that practically nothing was known about the Soviet order of battle. Yet it was still maintained that the Red Army '[is] not suited to a modern war nor in a condition to provide decisive resistance to a boldly lead fighting force with modern arms.'" A. Hillgruber, *Die Zerstoerung Europas*, 264-65.

186   D. Irving, *Hitler's War*, 205-06.

187   While the *Luftwaffe* collected some good tactical intelligence, it did a poor job of assessing the strength of the Soviet Air Force. For example, it underestimated the number of Soviet aircraft available, and "fecklessly disregarded" major technical advances in Soviet aircraft design. The "failure of *Luftwaffe* intelligence to produce a complete assessment of Soviet capabilities was to have dire consequences on both the strategic level in the coming years and on the tactical conduct of the first campaigning season." See, R. Muller, *The German Air War in Russia*, 41.

188   E. Mawdsley, *Thunder in the East*, 85-86.

189   J. Huerter, *Hitlers Heerfuehrer*, 313.

190   H. Boog, "*Higher Command and Leadership in the German Luftwaffe, 1935-1945*," in: *Air Power and Warfare*, A. F. Hurley & R. C. Ehrhart (eds.), 142.

191   Ibid., 151.

192   "*Snapshots from History, Logistical Vignettes*," in: "*Air Force Journal of Logistics*," Vol. XXXIV, Nr. 1&2 (2010).

193   C. Hartmann, *Wehrmacht im Ostkrieg*, 39.

194   C. von Luttichau, *Road to Moscow*, II:16; D. Stahel, *And the World held its Breath*, 91; GSWW, Vol. IV, 1107.

195   K. Schueler, "*The Eastern Campaign as a Transportation and Supply Problem*," in: *From Peace to War*, B. Wegner (ed.), 208-09.

196   Ibid., 209.

197   German planners "believed that there was no reason to fear serious problems resulting from the different gauges or Soviet acts of destruction. On the contrary, in the course of planning, the Germans' disdain for their adversary had given rise to the firm expectation that they would, after a relatively short time, be able to capture much of the Russian broad-gauge railway system with only insignificant damage to the network of lines and merely minor losses of rolling stock … The Germans' expectation that they would be able to take over much of the Russian railway network and its rolling stock in a serviceable condition was thwarted at an early stage by the extensive Soviet evacuation and subsequent destruction measures, which were taken immediately after the initial element of surprise had worn off. . ." As a result, the Germans "had to convert the Russian broad gauge lines to the German standard gauge on a much greater scale than had originally been envisaged." Ibid., 210.

198   Ibid., 209.

199   The "*Grosstransportraum*" was the motor transport required to move supplies from the railheads to the divisions at the front. It was directly controlled by the army groups and is to be distinguished from the "*Kleinkolonnenraum*" ("Small Column Area"), which was organic to the divisions themselves. D. Stahel, *And the World held its Breath*, 89.

200   Wagner also "scraped together every truck he could find in Germany and the occupied territories to add to the *Grosstransportraum*." G. Megargee, *Inside Hitler's High Command*, 123. Additional trucks were accumulated from as far away as French North Africa and Switzerland. D. Stahel, *And the World held its Breath*, 90-92.

201   D. Stahel, *And the World held its Breath*, 92.

202   G. Megargee, *Inside Hitler's High Command*, 124.

203   The spare parts problem was dramatically exacerbated by the fact that German forces in Russia used some 2000 different types of vehicles. Army Group Center alone was required to stock well over one million spare parts for its bewilderingly diverse hodgepodge of vehicles. M. van Creveld, *Supplying War*, 150-51.

204   G. Megargee, *Inside Hitler's High Command*, 123; J.L. Wallach, *Dogma of the Battle of Annihilation*, 277; M. van Creveld, *Supplying War*, 150. Conversely, the conquest of France and the Low Countries had improved Germany's raw material situation, of vital importance to her panzer arm. By the end of 1941, over 105,000 tons of iron and steel and more than 910,000 tons of scrap metal had been seized in occupied France. R. L. DiNardo, *Germany's Panzer Arm in WWII*, 13.

205   R. L. DiNardo, *Germany's Panzer Arm in WWII*, 23.

206   D. Stahel, *And the World held its Breath*, 88.

207   H. Muehleisen (Hg.), *Hellmuth Stieff Briefe*, 140-41.

CHAPTER 2

Trains, Planes, Trucks and Horses: "Aufmarsch" for the Offensive

(January – May 1941)

"My dear Friedchen! We were to leave on 18.4.[41], today in fact, but the whole plan has been suspended. In all likelihood, they don't have any use for us any more. And we are having a very quiet period of duty; it's not impossible that they might send us home again very soon." (Alois Scheuer, 197 ID, 18 April 1941)[1]

"Since our arrival in the area of Rastenburg each transfer had moved us a piece further toward the east. Whoever was still not thinking about a showdown with Russia – he must have been a dreamer. We also received guidelines for the next round of training, which were already attuned to the special features of combat in Russia and the terrain conditions there. The use of Russian translators in the divisional sector also gave us pause to think. The translators were emigrés!" (H.-J. Dismer, 6 ID)[2]

"I don't believe that the war will end this year. An immense amount is being demanded of the German people in order to survive this year of German Destiny honorably. The battle to be or not to be." (Heinrich Haape, 6 ID, 1 May 1941)[3]

2.1: When did Hitler Make his Final Decision to Attack Russia?

The Barbarossa directive did not set a target date ("X-Tag") for unleashing the war against Russia; it merely indicated that all preparations for such a war were to be concluded by 15 May 1941. Does this mean that Hitler, when he put his signature to the document on 18 December 1940, had yet to reach a final decision about war with Russia? That is clearly what Halder thought – or, at least, that is what he asserted shortly after the war in his study, *Hitler as War Lord*:

> In December 1940 [Hitler] issued his order to the three Services – the "*Barbarossa*" Order – to make military preparations for an attack on Russia against the possibility of Russo-German relations undergoing a fundamental change. It was a preparatory measure, no decision had yet been taken. One must admit the politician's right to delay taking the final decision until the last moment. Precisely when Hitler did take it, can probably no longer be established … It can be assumed, however, that it was not taken until after the quick successes of the Balkan campaign, in the course of which Russia's hostility toward Hitler had been unmistakably revealed.[4]

Not surprisingly, Jodl shared a similar perspective. After the war, from his jail cell in Nuremberg in 1946, he dictated the following, which sought as well to justify Hitler's attack on Russia as pre-emptive:

> In the meantime [i.e. spring 1941], the specter of a gigantic Russian troop deployment to the German and Romanian eastern border had taken form, and

Hitler was deluding himself with the thought of playing a pre-emptive game. The world has since then heard many voices from the Nuremberg Trials that warned against this invasion.[5] All are agreed that it was Hitler's very own idea. Both are historical facts. The court may judge betwixt good and evil, world history betwixt true and false. I do not wish to concern myself with either of these judgments here, rather to ascertain that the danger from the east was seen by all soldiers and that Hitler's fear was shared, by some more, by others less. Opinions varied on whether the danger was really so acute and whether it was not to be allayed politically. We must await a later judgment on that. Here, we are only interested in Hitler's influence on the conduct of the war, and on that it must be said: The decision to conduct a campaign against the USSR, the *Plan Barbarossa*, was his and his decision alone. Nevertheless, he only finally made it on 1.4.1941. For around this time an event occurred which, while it delayed the start of the attack against the nearly fully deployed Soviet forces by around 4-5 weeks,[6] seemed to Hitler to be a beacon of light revealing to him Stalin's intentions.

That was the military putsch in Belgrade in the night following the accession of the overthrown Yugoslavian government to the Tripartite Pact. Hitler was beside himself with fury. He virtually dictated his decisions to the summoned commanders-in-chief and the *Reich* Foreign Minister. He refused to countenance any advice to clarify the political position of the Yugoslavian government through diplomatic avenues first. In his eyes they were in league with Russia, prepared to stab us in the back if we invaded Greece, and anxious to link up with the English, who had already landed in Piraeus at the beginning of March [1941]. And indeed the Yugoslavian army immediately deployed to all borders. Starting from 6 April [1941], it was overrun by the improvised deployment of German troops and disintegrated in only a few weeks.[7]

Unmoved by such "insights" from Hitler's supreme military advisors, western historians have arrived at very different conclusions. According to Ian Kershaw, the decision to attack the Soviet Union was "effectively taken on 31 July 1940," when Hitler instructed his generals to prepare for war with Russia the following spring; and if Hitler's strategic impulses in the months which followed (August-October 1940) seemed "strangely vacillating … hesitant, indecisive, weak even," he soon "returned to the chosen path from which he had never seriously wandered: attacking the Soviet Union at the earliest opportunity …"[8] Gerhard Weinberg also stresses the significance of the 31 July conference at the *Berghof*,[9] while Andreas Hillgruber and other historians considered Molotov's failed mission to Berlin in November 1940 as the watershed event. Charles von Luttichau even went so far as to maintain that Hitler made his decision sometime between 27 November and 5 December 1940, after the Russians began to behave more aggressively in the Balkans.[10] Finally, some historians have emphasized the influence of Roosevelt's re-election in early November 1940 – to Hitler an "event of peculiar ill-omen."[11]

Despite such shades of difference, the general consensus is thus that Hitler had, by late 1940, most certainly made a firm decision to strike in the east the following year, and that his Directive 21 merely confirmed a course of action he had – in his own mind – determined upon weeks or months before. The consensus is justified. Chapter 1 of this narrative touched briefly on the strategic dilemma faced by Hitler in the summer and fall of 1940, while positing that Germany's position on the European continent – to all appearances a dominant one – was actually much weaker than it seemed. This was because, as Andreas Hillgruber so insightfully demonstrated, America loomed like a specter over Hitler's "1000-Year Reich."[12] As Hitler realized, Germany's existing European base (1940) was much too fragile from which to challenge Anglo-American air and naval power in the confrontation he expected to begin as early as 1942. Hitler needed more resources for his war machine – more bread, more oil, more iron ore, more coal – and there was only one place to acquire them: Russia. Only by subjugating and absorbing the Soviet Union (or at least her European land mass) could Germany's dictator hope to attain the economic resources and self-sufficiency with which to counter America's unsurpassed industrial might.

Yet Hitler's most critical resource was time. He may have had little oil,[13] but he had even less time – which explains his half-cocked idea (following the victory in the west) of moving against the Soviet Union in the fall of 1940. Surveying the military-strategic landscape, he knew that his *Wehrmacht* – superbly trained, well equipped, experienced and, most of all, victorious – would never be stronger than it was in 1941, while the Red Army was clearly not yet ready. Yet it soon would be, most likely by 1942; and then there was America – looming. To stand pat was to lose the initiative forever; to let the narrow window of opportunity slam irretrievably shut. And that Hitler could never do, for that would signify the end of himself and of his Reich. Examined from this – that is, from Hitler's – point of view, the dictator's decision to attack Russia in the spring of 1941 – far from being "mad" or "insane" as some historians have characterized it[14] – becomes perfectly logical.[15] It offered him his only chance to compete on a global basis in what he intended to become a war for global hegemony, a *Weltblitzkrieg*.[16] Observes Martin van Creveld:

> Whether Germany was strong enough, in 1941, to defeat Russia while waging a war on two fronts may well be doubted. However, it is difficult to see what other way was open to Hitler, after his failure either to reach a political settlement with Britain or to render her harmless by military means. Risky the war against Russia may have been, but there can be little doubt that it was essential for the Third Reich's survival, even if one does not believe that a Soviet attack was imminent.[17]

To amplify Creveld's point, even had Hitler succeeded in knocking Great Britain out of the war in 1940, the requirement for the campaign in the east would not have changed. Hitler, in any case, was not without certain gifts as a strategic thinker; and he had most certainly reached such momentous conclusions by the summer or, at the latest, the fall of 1940. Which is as close as one can come to anchoring in time his final, irreversible decision to strike.

2.2: Conference at the *Berghof* (9 January 1941)

Although Halder had gone on leave,[18] Hitler, on 9 January 1941, once again assembled many of his most senior military advisors at the *Berghof*, which was now blanketed deep in the winter's snow. Those present included Keitel, Jodl, Brauchitsch and the chiefs of staff of the Navy and the *Luftwaffe*, as well as foreign minister Ribbentrop. Hitler began the "war council" by conducting a *tour d'horizon* of the general military situation. By this point, the plan for seizing Gibraltar had been effectively abandoned, for Franco had refused to support it. Yet Hitler was worried by the fact that his Italian allies were being driven back by the British in Libya and by the Greeks in Albania. While the Italian setbacks in North Africa did not concern him much strategically, he feared they could still have an adverse psychological impact. He therefore decided – reversing an earlier position – to send a small mechanized force and some air power to North Africa to shore up the Italian position – the nucleus of what later became Erwin Rommel's famed *Afrika Korps*.[19] Albania, however, posed a greater challenge, for Hitler wanted to secure the Balkans before he moved against Russia. He also feared British intervention in Greece, from where they could imperil Italy and the Romanian oil fields from the air, or even open a route to support the Russians.[20]

The "Fuehrer's" main preoccupation, however, was once again with Russia. The strategic focus for 1941, he said, was finally to be on the Soviet Union. He was convinced that Great Britain, following Russia's defeat, would simply give up or collapse. Moreover, a particularly favorable ancillary benefit of a victory over Russia, so said Hitler, would be to free Japan's rear, enabling her to turn with her powerful naval forces against the United States. Such a course of events might even compel Roosevelt's America to stay out of the European war. Never again, Hitler went on, would Russia be as vulnerable to attack as she now was: Her armed forces were leaderless, "a colossus without a head and with feet of clay." And yet, it would be a mistake to underestimate the Russians. He emphasized the need to strike with the strongest forces possible, and to not merely drive the Russians back on a broad, unbroken front, but to achieve the "most violent breakthroughs" (*brutalste Durchbrueche*).[21] The "most important task" of the campaign, he continued,

> is to rapidly cut off the region of the Baltic Sea … The distances in Russia may be great, but no greater than the distances which have already been overcome by the German *Wehrmacht*. The aim of the operation must be the destruction of the Russian army, the seizure of the most important industrial regions, and the destruction of the remaining industrial regions, above all in the area of Yekaterinburg [i.e. 2000 km east of Moscow]; furthermore, the region of Baku must be taken.
>
> Crushing Russia will mean great relief for Germany. Then, only 40-50 divisions need remain in the east, the Army can be reduced and the entire armaments industry focused on the *Luftwaffe* and *Kriegsmarine*.[22]

With Russia vanquished, Hitler said, the most vital of Germany's industries should be relocated to the east, where they would be safe from attack from the air. The Reich's position would then be "unassailable" (*unangreifbar*). The immense Russian spaces, the "Fuehrer" concluded, contained "immeasurable wealth" (*unermessliche Reichtuemer*); Germany's dominion over that wealth would enable her to wage future wars on a global scale without fear of defeat.[23]

The conference was "remarkable for Hitler's clearest expression to date of his Baltic Region first and foremost strategy."[24] (Once again, he had reduced Moscow to the status of a secondary objective.) It was also the first time he is on record making the oil rich area of Baku a primary objective. That Hitler was already looking past Russia – and to a possible confrontation with U.S. air and sea power – was evident in his stated objective to shift the *Schwerpunkt* of German armaments production from the Army to the *Luftwaffe* and the Navy after smashing the Soviet Union.

Despite Hitler's unalloyed optimism, German planners faced what were, in part, largely insurmountable obstacles in laying the groundwork for Operation *Barbarossa*. On 28 January, Chief of the Army General Staff Halder hosted a conference of senior administrators of the Army and *Luftwaffe* to discuss preparations for the impending operation. The production of trucks, critical to the motorization of the Army and its tenuous logistical apparatus, was still a low priority, despite a projected 30 percent shortfall in requirements. To eliminate this shortfall, the expropriation of French army material, as well as additional requisitions from Switzerland, appeared to offer practical solutions. Another pressing concern was the insufficient supply of tires, which caused an industrial bottleneck affecting not only new stocks but the *Wehrmacht's* entire fleet of wheeled vehicles. General Georg Thomas, Chief of the War Economy and Armaments Branch (OKW), pointed out that, while a requirement existed for 13,000 tons of rubber a month, German industry could only process 7300 tons; current stocks would be used up by the end of February 1941, their replenishment dependent on South American blockade runners and some 12,000 tons of rubber on order from Indochina. An additional 25,000 tons had been purchased from the French, but the Japanese were reluctant to release the shipment. Seriously complicating matters was the shortage of fuel stocks – a situation described as "serious" with projections showing that existing supplies could only cover the deployment of forces to the east and about two months of operations.[25] The disturbing economic indicators loomed even larger when one considers that logistics for the first phase of the operation were to be handled almost exclusively by motor transport. As Halder recorded in his diary:

Conference 28 January:

3. Mission:
a.   Commit all available units.
b.   Crush Russia in a rapid campaign.

4. Execution should evident the following characteristics:

a.   Great space (i.e., the motor transport hauling capacity) to the Dnepr = Luxembourg – mouth of the Loire.
b.   *Speed*. No stop! No waiting for the railroad. Depend on motor transport.
c.   *Increased motorization* (as opposed to 1940): 33 mobile units, motorized artillery, engineer, signal, etc.

Since the railroad (destruction, water courses, gauge) cannot be counted on for the desired tempo, the continuous operation depends on motor transport.[26]

2.3: The Deployment Order and Initial Concentrations in the East (January – May 1941)

After the basic concepts and guidelines for the conduct of the war in the east had been laid down in the *Barbarossa* directive (No. 21), the Army General Staff sought to bring its operational plans and timetables into sharper focus. In a flurry of purposeful activity, General Staff planners crafted the Army's Deployment Directive (*Aufmarschanweisung Barbarossa*), a first draft of which was issued on 22 January, with a final version submitted to Halder and dated 31 January.[27] At noon that day, Field Marshal von Brauchitsch received the three army group commanders who were to direct operations in Russia – field marshals Wilhelm Ritter von Leeb (North), Fedor von Bock (Center) and Gerd von Rundstedt (South) – together with General Halder for a discussion of the new directive. It was the first time the Army C-in-C and the Chief of the Army General Staff had met with the three Prussian field marshals for an exchange of ideas.[28]

The discussion, however, was to have at least one awkward moment. After the assertion was made that the Red Army could be engaged and defeated before the two main river barriers – the Dvina-Dnepr line – Field Marshal von Bock asked Halder just what information he had that the enemy would actually stand and fight in front of the rivers (as opposed to withdrawing into the depths of the interior). Halder, if somewhat taken aback by the question, had to acknowledge "that it might well happen otherwise,"[29] a response which could hardly have been reassuring to Bock, who was just returning from several months of sick leave and receiving his first detailed briefing on the plan of campaign. In any case, Halder, "after months of planning that he himself had overseen, was not about to be thrown off by having the whole theoretical conception called into question."[30]

Echoing the *Barbarossa* directive, the OKH deployment plan stated that the Soviet Union was to be "crushed in a rapid campaign," if necessary before ending the war with Great Britain.[31] Operations were to be conducted in such a manner that the main body of the Red Army in western Russia could be defeated by driving powerful armored wedges (*Panzerkeile*) deep through the Soviet front, enveloping and encircling the bulk of the enemy's fighting forces and preventing their intact withdrawal into the Russian interior. Despite Halder's admission to Bock, Army planners remained confident the Red Army would accept battle west of the Dvina-Dnepr line. Soviet strategy, it was assumed, would also embrace the new system of field fortifications being built along the Russo-German demarcation line, as well as the original "Stalin Line," which ran along the old Russo-Polish and Romanian borders.[32]

The primary mission of each of the three army groups was also laid out in the OKH directive. South of the Pripiat' Marshes, Field Marshal von Rundstedt's Army Group South was to break through the enemy front with strong armored units from the area of Lublin, destroying enemy forces in Galicia and the western Ukraine in cooperation with a secondary thrust from Romania. Advancing on Kiev, bridgeheads were to be seized over the Dnepr River at and below the city, enabling exploitation beyond that river barrier and deeper into southern Russia. North of the marshes, Field Marshal von Bock's Army Group Center, the strongest of the three groups, was first to annihilate the Red Army in Belorussia by means of a double envelopment closing around Belostok and Minsk; Bock's armor was then to drive eastward to capture Smolensk, less than 400 kilometers from Moscow. Once these initial (first phase) objectives were achieved, the army group was to wheel north with strong, mobile elements to support Field Marshal von Leeb's Army Group North which, in turn, was to advance out of East Prussia and through the Baltic, annihilating Soviet forces along the way and striking out in the general direction of Leningrad. German troops were to be cautioned not to anticipate the level of air support they had enjoyed during the earlier campaigns, while preparations were also to be made to combat the possibility of chemical warfare. Operational direction of the three army groups along the main front was the responsibility of OKH, while the OKW role in the eastern campaign was to be limited to the far north, where modest German forces were to secure Petsamo and advance on Murmansk.[33]

The operational intent of OKH, as expressed in the deployment plan, thus adhered closely to the guidelines set down in Directive No. 21, in that it followed Hitler's often stated preference for a main drive into the Baltic region toward Leningrad after the frontier battles had been fought. Conversely, the Army was careful to point out that, in case of a rapid and general collapse of Soviet forces, the central army group might be able to forgo a drive to the north (with von Leeb) and continue with an immediate thrust toward Moscow. The deployment directive was signed by Brauchitsch "although the Army High Command's own operational objectives remained, as ever, separate from those of Hitler.[34]

> [The OKH's] apparent acceptance was only another act of deception designed to concede only what they must ... Brauchitsch and Halder, however, knowing the limits to which their arguments and powers of persuasion could influence Hitler's reasoning, decided instead on a covert subversion of Hitler's plan. This cannot be seen in any way as an act of resistance to Hitler and his regime, rather a strictly military matter calculated to win Hitler's war in what was perceived by the army command to be a more efficient manner. This conspiracy of silence was a means to an end and was therefore in the service of the regime rather than in opposition to it. Almost certainly the plotters were restricted to the highest officers of the OKH and the extent to which any formal plan of action was developed, if indeed anything so exact was produced, is unknown ... The overriding realization of the difficulties in dealing with Hitler necessitated a patient resignation. The generals bided their time, seeking to force the issue only at the critical moment, convinced that events leading up to the secondary phase of the operations would

prove the intrinsic value of a direct assault on Moscow. Here again one identifies the overarching conviction of complete confidence in the coming campaign. The Soviet armies, in spite of their size, were believed to be so utterly inferior to the *Wehrmacht* and its relentless "Blitzkrieg" that the secondary phase of operations would have no more important goal than the immediate thrust on the Soviet capital. The certainty of a short, victorious war did not allow for dire predictions of German setbacks or troublesome Soviet counterattacks. The question was only how best to win a war that none doubted would be won. As Colonel-General Heinz Guderian later observed: "All the men of the OKW and the OKH with whom I spoke evinced an unshakable optimism and were quite impervious to criticism or objections." In a similar tone, Colonel-General Maximilian Freiherr von Weichs, who was to command Second Army in Operation Barbarossa, wrote after the war: "One began the war with an underestimation of the enemy that would be hard to surpass and an arrogance stemming from the surprisingly rapid victories of past campaigns."[35]

The OKH deployment directive also embraced an intricate timetable for assembly and concentration of German forces in the east. If the initial German advance into Russia was to rely on truck transport for logistical support, the buildup of forces for the offensive was to be handled mainly by rail – a challenge so enormous in scope it required thousands of trains to move about three quarters of the German armed forces to their new theater of operations. In October 1940, the *Wehrmacht* had issued new instructions to German rail authorities[36] for the expansion of stations, rail lines and other infrastructure of the *Ostbahn*, with the objective of more than doubling rail capacity (movement and unloading) by 10 May 1941. The entire effort came under the auspices of the "Otto" Program[37] which, in subsequent months, was to make dramatic improvements to rail lines and facilities, among them new west-east lines, new stations, platforms, signal installations, an expanded telephone net and other improvements. As a result of "Otto," the flow of trains crossing the borders of the Reich to the east increased from about 80 per day to a maximum of more than 200 per day, enabling the transport of troops, tanks, vehicles, equipment and supplies to go according to plan (*planmaessig*). Indeed, from February through mid-July 1941, well over 10,000 trains were unloaded in the east; yet, remarkably, the German and Polish rail lines were still not stretched to their utmost limit during the buildup period.[38]

The OKH deployment plan called for this vast migration of men and materiel to take place in five phases (the fifth, and final, phase beginning after the start of hostilities and consisting of the majority of the OKH reserves).[39] Simply put, most of the marching infantry divisions were to be transported in the initial phases, while the rail movement of the panzer and motorized formations was not – for reasons of security – to begin until the final few weeks before the invasion.[40] Road movements, primarily from detraining points into more forward assembly areas, were meticulously integrated into the progression of rail movements to ensure a smooth flow of men, equipment and supplies. Until three weeks before the operation was to begin, new formations arriving in the east were not to go beyond a line marked by Tarnow – Warsaw – Koenigsberg. Beyond that "invisible barrier," authority for dispositions became the responsibility of the army groups and armies. The execution of those final movements was to be carefully concealed, meaning that most of them, particularly those of armored units, were to occur only at night.[41]

The strictest security covered all phases of activity and the number of persons authorized to know about the planning was kept to an absolute minimum. To deceive the Russians, ostensible planning and preparations for the invasion of Britain were to be continued. All preparations for Russia were to be completed in time for operations to begin in mid-May 1941. So complex was the machinery of this colossal movement of men and materiel that major changes could not be made after 10 March 1941, some nine weeks prior to the anticipated "jump-off."[42]

Of course, even before the *Barbarossa* buildup began in earnest, the Germans had stationed significant forces in the east, which, by late summer 1940, were under the command of Field Marshal von Bock and Army Group B (see below, Section 2.5). These forces amounted to 23 divisions on 20 July 1940, and were slowly increased to 34 by the end of the year. Four of these divisions, however, were stationed in Austria due to the uncertain situation in the Balkans; and, in early February 1941, the Army High Command dispatched another four divisions from German-occupied Poland to the southeast, leaving Bock with just 26 divisions (there were also two divisions earmarked for *Barbarossa* in Romania). When the strategic concentration (145 divisions) for the Russian campaign commenced on 7 February, 117 divisions still had to be moved by a combination of rail and road, 22 of them twice due to the intervening requirements of the Balkan campaign.[43] The first three phases (1.-3. *Aufmarschstaffeln*) of the rail assembly in the east – Phase I: 7 February – 17 March; Phase II: 16 March – 10 April; Phase III: 13 April – 20 May – resulted in the deployment of the majority of the marching infantry divisions.[44]

One of these formations was 6 Infantry Division. After taking part in the French campaign, it had first been stationed along the demarcation line with Vichy France around Poitiers. In September 1940 it was moved to the Cotentin Peninsula in idyllic Normandy, where it secured the coastline against any eventual British landing attempt and participated in the abortive preparations for Operation "Sealion."[45] Despite the apparent lull in the war after the victory over France, the officers, NCOs and men of the division underwent tenacious and thorough training in the ensuing months, helping to make possible the division's often brilliant achievements in Russia in 1941. The area of Normandy, rich in cultural and historical tradition, offered many charming diversions, among them an inspection of the famous Bayeux tapestry by the division commander and a group of his officers. Relations with the local civilians were proper,[46] at times even cordial, and romances were not uncommon.

The pleasant period in Normandy ended abruptly on 19 March 1941, when the division began to entrain for transfer to the east. The loading was to take several days and require 71 trains. Wilhelm Buddenbohm, a soldier in the division's 37 Infantry Regiment, described the frenetic pace of the journey, as well as his dismay over the precipitous plunge in temperature as the division left the warm spring weather of Normandy and arrived in the much colder climes of East Prussia:

> The staff of 37 IR were loaded on 22.3.[41] and the route of the journey proceeded as follows: departure from Coutances via Caen and Rouen to Amiens on the same day. On 23.3. from Amiens via Albert, Cambrai, Lille, Ghent, Antwerp, Rosendal, Utrecht, Arnheim, Breda to Oldenzaal. On 24.4. it went from Oldenzaal via Salzberg to Osnabrueck to start with. Here there was a brief wait, of which 15 minutes were spent on the grounds of the central station.
>
> After this pause, the journey went via Hanover, Stendal, Berlin, Kuestrin, Schneidemuehl to Bromberg. On Wednesday, 26.3.1941, it then went via Graudenz, Marienwerder, Nieswalde, Mohrungen, Heilsberg to Rastenburg. Unloading proceeded here at 2100 hours and we took up quarters in Schmidtsdorf.
>
> The duration of this transport thus only took 4 days. Deepest winter still prevailed in East Prussia and the change in climate from the Channel coast to the new deployment area was very severe.[47]

About the same time, another soldier in 6 ID entrained in Normandy with his artillery battalion for the journey eastward. Arriving in East Prussia several days later he, too, was affected by the unpleasant shift in the weather – for him and his unit a dark harbinger of what the first winter in Russia would bring:

> Spring was already stirring when we were loaded up in Bayeux. After the staff of III./AR 6 was loaded … I went to the station officer at Bayeux to sign our transportation off. Upon returning to the station premises, my transport train had vanished; it had already departed. Without hesitating, I returned to the station officer and enquired after the next stop for taking on water. The answer was: "Next scheduled stop Caen Central Station!" I called my motorcycle messenger, who I had with me, thank God, swung myself onto the "Sozius," and roared after my transport train along the Bayeux – Caen highway. Arriving in Caen, it was in fact standing at the station and filling up on water. The motorcycle messenger and I heaved the motorcycle up the platform apron, and ran to the train, where helping hands aided the loading of our vehicle. When I reported back to my commander and I told him of my mishap in Bayeux, he nearly "convulsed with laughter." He had not even missed me yet.
>
> In the night of 21./22.03.1941, we halted in Hanover to change the engine. Leaving the train was strictly forbidden for all soldiers on grounds of security. It would, otherwise, have been easy to telephone my parents, who only lived barely 20 km away. However, military police were patrolling the station, superintending observance of the prohibition. From Hanover, the onward journey went via Magdeburg, Berlin, through the former [Polish] Corridor to Rastenburg, where we were unloaded after a nearly three-day-long train journey. I reported our arrival to the station commander and received from him a thick, top secret envelope with the field post number of my division. Inside was the division order with all the details for quartering and provisioning the arriving troops. I never experienced a more perfect preparation for relocating troops during the entire war. But after this positive experience, a bitter, negative surprise awaited us at unloading.
>
> At our arrival in East Prussia, even deeper winter prevailed there, with lots of snow and extreme cold. When we unloaded the trucks for the ration supply and baggage train, and tried to turn the motors on, these had frozen. Radiators and engine blocks had ruptured in the frost and were unusable. We were not to blame for this. During loading in France nobody had said where the journey with the train would end up. But the spare parts situation can't have been all that bad at that time either, because within a few days we had new engines for the three trucks.[48]

Despite such experiences, those German soldiers fortunate enough to spend their final weeks in East Prussia – among its friendly population and verdant, undulating countryside – before the start of the Russian campaign, had much to be thankful for – certainly when compared to those *Kameraden* stationed in areas of a largely hostile and more primitive occupied Poland.[49] Recalled Siegfried Knappe, whose 87 Infantry Division was moved from the English Channel to East Prussia – a distance of more than 1200 kilometers – in early 1941:

> France had been very pleasant, with its beautiful countryside, good food, and friendly population, and we hated to leave. But East Prussia was also nice. It was an agricultural area, hilly, with sandy soil that was good for growing rye and potatoes. The area had a lot of lakes, beautiful beaches, and forests with white beech trees. It was a prosperous horse-breeding area, with rich farms and pleasant villages.

We unloaded at Osterode and marched to Marwalde, a village nearby, about 270 kilometers from the Russian border ... From time to time while we were there, we moved out to live in the field and practice the mechanical things, such as how to secure the horses, how to put together a tent, how to camouflage the guns, how to get the guns into position, and so on. It was practically a peacetime existence, with lots of practice and maneuvers in the field. As an *Oberleutnant* and battery commander, I had two *Leutnants* and about 180 soldiers. We practiced constantly with our guns. During practice exercises, the men would take the horses to the river to water and wash them – and as often as not, to have a swim in the river. They would sing as they rode the horses to and from the river. It was a happy time for us all.[50]

Ernst-Martin Rhein, an officer in 6 ID – and one of the first of the division awarded the coveted *Ritterkreuz* (Knight's Cross) in the Russian campaign – remembered the warm reception he and his men received following their arrival in East Prussia. His post-war account, however, prefigured the conditions that were to stop the *Wehrmacht* in its tracks on the outskirts of Moscow in the fall of 1941:

At the end of March 1941, the order came to transfer the regiment. "Where," nobody at first knew. The journey was by rail transport to the east and went through Germany. Where stops were necessary, for example, for distributing rations, the train halted outside the larger stations on railway sidings. When, after two days, the regiment was unloaded in the area of Goldap in East Prussia in order, so we were told, "to protect the east border of Germany," snow still lay on the ground, it was bitterly cold. The quarters were modest, sometimes meager, and mostly unheated. But the heartiness and hospitality with which the East Prussian population took in the soldiers made up for that. Many an elderly couple vacated their own bed for the *Landser* and would not be dissuaded from doing this, even by protests.

From a letter from *Oberleutnant* Rhein ... of 7.4.41: "We have been thrust from sunny countryside, where the flowers were already blooming in the fields, into a Siberian landscape ... Our marches and night exercises in the last two weeks were accompanied by icy cold and ferocious snow storms." ...

The uninterrupted training was continued with greater intensity during those weeks, but under what conditions! "Rain and snow delight us alternately. But the paths are unimaginable, which, especially after every thaw, are 20-40 cm deep in mud, depending on their quality."[51]

The German *Landser* who suddenly found himself in occupied Poland often felt as if he bestrode an alien landscape – and certainly so when confronted by Talmudic Jews, as this field post from a soldier in 23 Infantry Division illustrates:

Finally a message!! Now you'll have an idea where we are (close to the Polish-Soviet border). In a tiny little Polish town. Every morning, the Duty Jew appears and brings us fresh rolls. We have ca. 30 in number who have been allocated to us by the mayor for artillery and vehicle cleaning work and whom I must oversee. In part they are real Talmudic Jews with fearful hangdog expressions, dirty, and flatfooted. If you address them gruffly, they spend the next five minutes toadying to you. It's likely the first time in their lives that they have really had to work, but even so, I treat them strictly, but fairly. Even though it is strictly forbidden, one evening recently I was in their street in one of their lodgings, because they had insisted on inviting me. I didn't want to snub them and they were very hospitable. Please do send me some "IA 33" [a scent by Berlin parfumier J.F. Schwarzlose] and a little bottle of Pitralon aftershave against the dreadful "odors" that waft about nearly everywhere here.[52]

The chief operations officer (Ia) of 137 Infantry Division described the disappointment he and his comrades felt when – after months of difficult training in Austria – the division was sent to Poland. The forlorn conditions there would soon be encountered again – in Soviet Russia:

> Training had progressed well, the allocation of motor vehicles, however, was not yet complete. All the speculation about the coming operational area – many were hoping for France or the Balkans – was put to an end in March 1941 with the transportation order to Poland. Great disappointment! From 24.-29.3.[1941], the division rolled by rail into the region of Litzmannstadt (Lódz) – Tomaszow – Nowe Miasto – Skierniewice; horse-drawn supply columns reached the area around Gostynin. There it came under the command of the 13 [Army Corps], in training under that of 9 Army Corps, which in turn belonged to the Fourth Army of Field Marshal von Kluge.
>
> The old veterans of the Polish campaign had already said a very great many unpleasant things about this country; for many, however, it was even worse than expected. Never-ending stretches of sand and mud for roads, an impoverished population in rundown hovels teeming with vermin was the daily scene from now on.[53]

2.4: Two Conferences – Two "Faces" of the "Fuehrer" (3 February & 30 March 1941)

2.4.1: At the *Berghof* (3 February 1941)

The OKH deployment directive of 31 January was given to Hitler the next day for his review.[54] Two days later (3 February), at the *Berghof*, the Chief of the Army General Staff – in the presence of his superior Brauchitsch – briefed the "Fuehrer" on its contents. Also present at the meeting were Keitel, Jodl, and Colonel Adolf Heusinger, the OKH Operations Branch Chief.[55]

Halder began his report with an appreciation of the Red Army forces facing the *Wehrmacht* in the east. He estimated the strength available to Soviet forces at 100 infantry (rifle) divisions, 25 cavalry divisions and 30 mechanized divisions. It was significant, he indicated, that Red Army rifle divisions were also outfitted with relatively large numbers of tanks; yet he then dismissed this observation by insisting that the Russian equipment was "poor" and rather "hastily thrown together" (*schlechtes, zusammengewuerfeltes Material*). Although the Russians possessed greater numbers of mechanized divisions, the German mobile units were "qualitatively superior." In terms of artillery, the Russians had the usual types of equipment, but even this was "inferior" in quality (*ebenfalls minderwertig*) – an assertion soon to be proven utterly false. Among the Soviet military leadership, only Marshal Timoshenko stood out as factor to reckon with. While the intentions of the Soviet leadership remained unclear, Halder noted that there were strong enemy forces along the border, and that any attempt to withdraw them would, necessarily, be limited due to the requirement to protect the Baltic and the Ukraine, regions vital to Russia's survival.[56]

The Russian forces, Halder continued, would face a total German force of some 102 infantry and 34 mobile divisions, with the mass of these forces allocated to the two army groups north of the Pripiat' Marshes (50 infantry and 22 panzer and motorized). The southern grouping was to comprise 30 infantry and 8 mobile divisions, while 22 infantry and 4 mobile divisions were to be held in OKH reserve mainly behind the central army group. The Chief of the Army General Staff went on to describe the mission of the three army groups which, in outline, was to break open (*aufreissen*) the enemy front, split it into two parts, and prevent a successful withdrawal into the depths of Russia. In reference to Army Group Center, the strongest of the three German groupings, Halder stated that its two panzer groups (each of the other army groups possessed one panzer group) were to advance on Smolensk, their first primary objective; from there, they were to cooperate with the northern army group. While Halder was undoubtedly aware that, upon reaching Smolensk, only 360 kilometers from Moscow, he would have a powerful argument in favor of Moscow, he was careful during his presentation to hew closely to the operational concepts embodied in Directive Nr. 21. Thus, once again, he sought to avoid an open conflict with the "Fuehrer." Halder also failed to bring to Hitler's attention any of the troubling economic details that had been reported to him during the conference on 28 January.[57]

Hitler agreed in principle with the operational plans as elucidated by the Chief of the Army General Staff. The "Fuehrer" remarked that the operational areas involved were immense, and that the sought after encirclement battles could only succeed if the pockets were closed tightly (i.e., and the enemy not allowed to escape). Once again, Hitler underscored the primacy of the Baltic region and Leningrad in his thinking. After a further exchange with Halder, Hitler ended the discussion about the impending campaign with a bold and ominous prediction: "When '*Barbarossa*' begins the world will hold its breath!" (*Die Welt werde den Atem anhalten, wenn die Operation "Barbarossa" durchgefuehrt werde.*)[58]

Despite Hitler's bravura, less than five months before the start of the campaign little was still known about Soviet Russia and the capabilities of her armed forces: "The fact of the matter was that the data that could be gathered on the Soviet military establishment and the intentions of the Russian leaders seemed vague and inconclusive compared to the kind of intelligence the German High Command had come to expect from earlier campaigns."[59] For example, no one knew with any precision just how many tanks the Soviet Union had, even if it was evident they had many more of them than did the Germans. In his notes made on 2 February, in preparation for the meeting, Halder had recorded the rather daunting figure of 10,000 Soviet tanks; and even if they were, as he firmly believed, markedly inferior in quality, the German Army only had about 3500 – give or take a few – to commit to the coming campaign. Guderian's 1937 book on tank warfare had also put the figure at 10,000.[60] As early as 1933, he had inspected a single Russian tank factory that was turning out 22 tanks per day; by comparison, in June 1941, German industry was still producing only about 10 tanks per day.[61] To complicate matters – and significantly so! – little to nothing was known about the Red Army's new, heavier, more powerfully armed KV-1 and T-34 tanks, which were now making their way into the Soviet force structure and which would come as a profound shock to the German Army in the east.

Three weeks after *Barbarossa* had begun, in mid-July 1941 – and after the Germans had finally gained a much more accurate picture of their adversary – Hitler would confess to Goering: "You know that never before have I had as grave doubts about a campaign as about this one, because of the uncertainty about the enemy's strength ... I don't know if I would have made the decision [to attack Russia] had I known the full strength of the Soviet Army, especially its vast complement of tanks."[62]

2.4.2: At the Reich Chancellery in Berlin (30 March 1941)

As he had consistently sought to do since the summer of 1940, when first raising the issue of war with Russia with his military advisors, Hitler had been careful throughout the conference on 3 February to speak in operational and strategic terms only. From the outset, he had argued for war with Russia as the most effective way to alter the strategic calculus in Germany's favor – most significantly by shattering Great Britain's putative continental sword (Russia) and, thus, forcing the recalcitrant island nation to sue for peace. He had, most of all, spoken a language and developed themes his generals understood well – even if some of them had not always accepted the premises. But this was all about to change. Hitler's *programmatic* objectives in a war with Russia – first conceived in the 1920s, on several occasions since 1933 at least hinted at to his top generals but, for the most part, kept in the background – were now to take center stage in his rationale for war. Now, his generals were to discover, the coming showdown in the east was no longer simply part of a strategic chess game; rather, it was to be a struggle for *Lebensraum* and a racial war of annihilation (*Vernichtungskrieg*) in which the feared and hated Bolshevist-Jewish enemy was to be – once and for all – eliminated root and branch. Every one of the 3.1 million German soldiers who made up the Russia invasion force – as well as the many millions of *Landser* who followed in their wake – would be ensnared in the whirlwind unleashed by Hitler's determination to fight what, in effect, was to be a 19th Century colonial style war of subjugation conducted outside the laws and usages of war and, in the sheer scope of its almost surreal savagery, unprecedented in the history of warfare.

Whatever parallels may have existed between Napoleon's Russian campaign of 1812 and Hitler's of 1941, the very different objectives of both men was certainly not one of them. If Napoleon had been unwilling "to damage Russia any more than was necessary," and had not wanted to destroy her as a power,[63] Hitler pursued a very different agenda, as the watershed conference in Berlin on 30 March 1941 illustrates. For it was here that he first openly revealed to his generals just what his crusade in the east held in store for them. On this day, Hitler spoke for more than two hours to a select audience at the Reich Chancellery, which included the field marshals, generals and admirals who would lead the surprise attack on the Soviet Union. Among those in attendance were the commanders-in-chief of the army groups, armies, air fleets and the naval command, as well as the commanders of the panzer groups, air groups and their chiefs of staff. Surprisingly, the OKW war diary has nothing to say about this event, other than that, at 11.00 in the morning, Hitler addressed the assembled commanders of the eastern army groups and armies.[64]

Until recently, the only account of Hitler's long speech to his generals on this day was the one recorded by Halder in his war diary. However, a second version has since come to light: Col.-Gen. Hermann Hoth, who was to lead Army Group Center's 3 Panzer Group into battle in June 1941, left handwritten notes – albeit in a difficult to decipher calligraphy – within the official files of his panzer group. While the two accounts reflect the personal needs and interests of both men – as well as their contrasting perspectives about which of Hitler's arguments were worth jotting down – taken together, they offer a more detailed picture of the "Fuehrer's" fateful remarks than has hitherto been available to historians of the period.[65]

In Halder's oft quoted version, Hitler began with an overview of Germany's strategic situation since 30 June of the previous year: It was a "mistake"[66] for the British not to seek peace when they had the chance; England was placing her hopes in America and Russia. The "Fuehrer" reviewed American capabilities ("maximum output not before end of four years"), while sharply criticizing Italy's current conduct of the war. The Reich's goals in Russia, Hitler stated, were to "crush [her] armed forces [and to] break up [the] state." The dictator also made comments about Russian tanks and, while observing that the bulk of them were "obsolete," he conceded that the Red Army enjoyed a numerical superiority in tanks and also boasted a "small number of new giant types with long 10-cm guns (mammoth models, 42 to 45 tons)."[67] Hitler's discussion about Russia – her capabilities, challenges of the theater of war, operational issues, "questions" about the Pripiat' Marshes, etc. – was far ranging. Indeed, Germany had "colossal" tasks to fulfill there. About two of his Allies in the impending war – the invasion force was to be a truly multinational one – he said that the Finns, whom he admired, "will fight bravely." The Romanians, however, were "no good at all."[68] At this point, according to Halder's notes, Hitler began to make clear that war against Soviet Russia was going to be no ordinary war:

> *Clash of two ideologies.* Crushing denunciation of Bolshevism, identified with a social criminality. Communism is an enormous danger for our future. We must forget the concept of comradeship between soldiers. A Communist is no comrade before or after battle. This is a war of extermination. If we do not grasp this, we shall still beat the enemy, but 30 years later we shall again have to fight the Communist foe. We do not wage war to preserve the enemy …

> *War against Russia*: Extermination of the Bolshevist commissars and of the Communist intelligentsia. The new state must be Socialist, but without intellectual classes of their own. Formation of a new intellectual class must be prevented … We must fight against the poison of disintegration. This is no job for military courts. The individual troop commanders must know the issues at stake. They must be leaders in this fight. The troops must fight back with the methods with which they are attacked. Commissars and GPU men are criminals and must be dealt with as such. This need not mean that the troops should get out of hand. Rather, the commander must give orders that express the common feelings of his men.

> *Embody in ObdH* [Army C-in-C] *order*. This war will be very different from the war in the west. In the east, harshness today means lenience in the future. Commanders must make the sacrifice of overcoming their personal scruples.[69]

Following Hitler's remarks, he and his guests headed for a late lunch. Later that afternoon, a "Fuehrer conference" was held, which enabled the army group commanders and several of their subordinate generals (among them, Guderian) to individually brief Hitler on their plans of operation.[70]

Panzer General Hoth's account, while generally confirming that of Halder's, does contain at least one striking difference. Hoth records Hitler's reference to a new Soviet model tank – a "heavy Russian tank with a 7.5 cm gun." Even more surprising, he noted the "Fuehrer's" respectful assessment of the Red Army as a "tenacious adversary." This signified a major shift in the dictator's thinking since the conference on 5 December 1940 when, during a discussion of the Army's operational planning for Russia, he had spoken about the Red Army in largely dismissive tones. However, as Hoth also recorded, Hitler indicated that Soviet forces were "without leadership," and that their armament capabilities were "not very good." After again invoking the importance of capturing Leningrad[71] ("[Russia's] overseas trade concentrated in St. Petersburg [Leningrad], for that reason main operational effort in these directions"), Hitler began to address his now decades old programmatic concerns:[72]

> Battle of ideologies against Bolshevism. *Criminal tendencies*. Russia is a constant hotbed of social misfits. [Necessary] to eliminate Russian-Asiatic danger … once and for all. Only then Germany gets freedom of maneuver. Russian colossus is a burden for us.

> *Conduct of war against Russia*. No pattern. Campaign against Norway different from that against Poland. Military justice too humane. Always catches the same

criminals. Protects them instead of killing them ... Crimes of Russian commissars. Everywhere. In Latvia, Galicia, Lith[uania? or] Est[onia?], they behaved in an Asiatic way. They are not to be spared. No case for military courts, but to be eliminated immediately by the troops. Not to be sent to the rear ...

Fight for our own survival. It has to be fought once. Now we have a tremendous lead on all sectors. Cannot be maintained at all times. Fuehrer feels himself responsible not to leave this task to other generation (1918: our children). Not to wait as at the end of the 19th and the beginning of the 20th Century. We have to do things for ourselves. Now scepter and sword are in one hand ... It will be an unprecedented victory. Decision was not easily made, [he] wrestled with himself for a long time. Not heavier than for Frederick the Great. [His] task insoluble. How much easier we have it today![73]

Hitler's stated intentions concerning the elimination of Soviet commissars and limiting the jurisdiction of military courts were turned into policy by OKW and OKH in the weeks and months preceding the attack on Russia. While the details need not concern us here, it should be pointed out that these and other policies promulgated by the German High Command on the eve of *Barbarossa* helped to define and shape its overtly criminal character. It is also important to note that, while much of Hitler's top-secret speech was shocking, there is no record of any official protest from his generals (even if some were privately appalled). Why this was so is explained in the German quasi-official history of the Second World War, prepared by the *Bundeswehr's* Research Institute for Military History:

> Another matter clearly documented in the present volume is concurrence between Hitler and the top military in the OKW ... and the OKH ... on the meaning of that war [against Russia]. It was to be, simultaneously, a war of annihilation and a conquest of living-space. These categories were familiar to military thinking. Even before the First World War, military leaders – and certainly not only on the German side – tended to discount the requirements of international law. Military interests, power politics, and scant regard for international law were the obverse of Wilhelminian assurance of strength and power. The Great General Staff's directive on international law of 1902 contained the statement that humanitarian requirements could only be considered to the extent permitted by the nature and objective of the war: "A vigorously conducted war cannot be aimed solely against the combatants of the enemy state or its fortifications, but will and must equally seek to destroy the entire moral and material resources of the same." Such a concept of "total war" explains the readiness to carry the war, as outlined by Hitler in 1941, to the east, especially as that opponent was the enemy *par excellence* – Bolshevism, on the disastrous influence of which the German defeat in 1918 was blamed. For that reason this war acquired a higher degree of inevitability than the war in the west, as well as a character which suppressed any moral scruples ... It far exceeded the objectives of dominion of ordinary imperialism on a Wilhelminian scale ...[74]

Yet the "concurrence" on the "meaning of that war" extended well beyond Hitler and his top military leaders. The thousands of field post perused and analyzed by this author during his years of research has led to the conclusion that the common soldiers in Russia in 1941 overwhelmingly supported the overarching objectives of the campaign. This is not to imply that most of them agreed with Hitler's genocidal policies as they played out in the east, sometimes before their very eyes. Yet the combination of years of National

Socialist propaganda, deeply ingrained cultural and racial prejudices, and not unjustified fears of Communism, had forged a generation of young men with whom the concept of a "crusade" against Bolshevism clearly resonated – a fact that will become apparent in the chapters that follow.

One must tread lightly, however, when generalizing about human behavior. Some 10,000,000 German soldiers fought in Russia from 1941 to 1944, and each of them had his own personal perspectives on the war. Moreover, recent scholarship[75] supports the conclusion that the great majority of German soldiers in Russia behaved with honor and dignity, despite participating in a savage struggle which often encouraged criminal activity; moreover, more than a few of these men ignored or thwarted the criminal orders of the German High Command. We might do well to end this section with two quotations – the first from a great military reformer in Prussian service during the Napoleonic era; the second from a tormented officer in OKH in autumn 1941. Together, they encapsulate the tragic journey taken by the Prussian-German Army from the 18th to the mid-20th Century:

1) In the Army can be found "the unification of all the moral and physical strengths of all German citizens." (Gerhard von Scharnhorst)[76]

2) "It is dreadful. How we have to sully ourselves with blood and brutality ... It is a regression of hundreds, if not thousands of years." (Georg Heino *Freiherr* von Muenschhausen)[77]

2.5: Field Marshal von Bock Takes Command

In his study of Bock's campaigns of 1941/42, Alfred W. Turney offered a vivid depiction of the austere Prussian field marshal who would lead more than one million men of Army Group Center into battle on 22 June 1941:

He was tall, thin, narrow-shouldered, ramrod straight. His sharp features, piercing green eyes, and thin-lipped expression gave him an emaciated, almost hungry appearance. He seldom smiled; his humor was dry and cynical. His arrogant, aloof manner, unbending military bearing and cold absorption in his profession foretold a determination, industry, and nerveless physical courage for which war correspondents would give him the awesome title of "master of the total assault," as he ordered hundreds of thousands of Germany's finest young men into the terrifying maw that was the final battle of Moscow in late 1941.[78]

2.5.1: His Military Career

Born on 3 December 1880 at Kuestrin, Brandenburg, Fedor von Bock was the son of a well-known general from an old military family. Perhaps predestined to become a soldier, he attended school in Wiesbaden and Berlin, thereafter joining the Royal Prussian Cadet Institute at Gross-Lichterfelde, where he was universally respected for his outstanding accomplishments. He apparently had a flair for such academic subjects as mathematics, history and modern languages; he spoke fluent French and very good English and Russian.[79]

Throughout Bock's early years, the father inculcated in his son the idea of unconditional loyalty to the state and set his professional path on a career in the Prussian military. Bock was taught that it was his life's duty as a soldier to contribute to the glory of Prussian Germany. The teachings of the father would stay with the son throughout his life. Following service as a senior NCO, in March 1898, at the age of 17, he passed the selection board and was commissioned as a second-lieutenant with the 5 Foot Guards Regiment in Berlin-Spandau. Effective 10 September 1908, he was promoted to first lieutenant (*Oberleutnant*). From 1910-12 he underwent general staff training, and was promoted to captain (*Hauptmann*) in March 1912. During this period, he joined the Army League, where he first met several of the future Third Reich's top military leaders – Brauchitsch, Halder and Rundstedt.[80]

With the outbreak of World War I, Bock saw action on both the western and eastern fronts. During the war he served in general staff positions and as a battalion commander in the field. He proved himself to be a fearless leader of men, garnering the Iron Cross First and Second Class, the Order of the House of Hohenzollern and, in April 1918, the *Pour le Mérite*. He ended the war as a major.[81]

As one of post-Imperial Germany's finest soldiers, he was taken up in the 100,000-man *Reichswehr* after the war. Over the next dozen years, he occupied important staff and field commands, rising to the rank of major general (*Generalleutnant*) in 1931. In 1933, when Hitler came to power, he commanded Military District 2 (*Wehrkreis 2*), with its headquarters in Stettin.[82] Much has been written about Bock's putative posture toward Hitler and the National Socialist movement. Suffice it to say here that he was never a Nazi. As a young officer on his staff later observed: "[Bock] found the entire business of National Socialism wholly repugnant."[83] During the war in Russia, he even tolerated the presence of a large anti-Hitler cabal among his staff; conversely, he was much too cautious, much too vain and ambitious – enticed as he was by the professional opportunities offered him by Hitler's wars – to ever make common cause with the military resistance to the Hitler's Germany. Furthermore, it appears that he – like many conservative German generals – was captivated by the "Fuehrer's" stunning successes during the 1930s and the early years of the war.

His rise in rank and stature progressed throughout the mid- and late 1930s. In 1935, he was promoted to lieutenant-general (*General der Infanterie*) and became commander of the Army Office Berlin (later Army Group 3). In October 1936, Bock married Wilhelmine Gottliebe Jenny (nee von Boddien), with whom he would have a daughter. During the *Anschluss* (March 1938), he marched into Austria at the head of Eighth Army, for which he was promoted to full general (*Generaloberst*). In November 1938, Bock replaced Gerd von Rundstedt as commander of Army Group 1 in Berlin.[84] By this point in his brilliant career, Bock appears to have made a favorable impression on Hitler. However, he was difficult to work with and could be hard on subordinates; as a man, history has judged him harshly: "Arrogant and cold-blooded, Bock's humorless, vain, inflexible, and irritating personality earned him many enemies, both in the Army and in the Party. He had nothing but contempt for all civilians and did not get along well with his subordinates."[85]

Having played a major role in the operational planning for the attack on Poland, Bock was appointed C-in-C of Army Group North for the campaign, which commenced on 1 September 1939 and unleashed the Second World War. In this first demonstration of what the world christened "blitzkrieg," Bock "proved to be a master of fast-moving operations of large formations."[86] For his role in the short campaign he was one of the first to be awarded the Knight's Cross. In October 1939, Bock was transferred to the western front; his Army Group North now renamed Army Group "B." With this army group he took part in the French campaign, albeit in a secondary role. However, he was given the honor of reviewing the military parade through Paris on 14 June 1940 at the Arc de Triomphe and was among the 12 German generals promoted to field marshal on 19 July 1940.[87]

After more than four decades serving Imperial Germany, the Weimar Republic and, now the Third Reich, the orbit of Bock's spectacular military career had finally reached its apex. Yet as this anecdote from 1941 – early in the war in Russia – reveals, even a brave and stoic German field marshal could become a bit squeamish when confronted directly with the horrors of Hitler's war in the east:

> Professor [Ferdinand] Hoff was Internal Medicine Consultant with Army Group Center … The army group's headquarters staff was stationed in Smolensk. The

army group's chief of staff, General von Greiffenberg, had suggested to Professor Hoff that he give a presentation about typhus to the entire staff and the field marshal. Professor Hoff gives an account of this:

"In the following night I was woken by heavy gunfire. I thought at first that the Russians had entered Smolensk. However, it was an outburst of panic that had occurred when a large column of Russian prisoners was being led through the town under the guard of *Landsturm* soldiers. Some prisoners had attempted to get away, the guardsmen had fired; frightened by the shots, even more prisoners took flight, now the guards had started to shoot pretty indiscriminately. This nighttime scene had then led to a bloodbath. When I went through the town in the morning, I saw around 30 Russians lying in the street. Field Marshal von Bock had gone through that street the same morning; he was horrified by the terrible sight, and had said to Greiffenberg: 'You must prevent a repetition of these horrific things at all costs!'

"When I appeared at the headquarters that afternoon with the intention of giving my presentation on typhus that evening to the field marshal and the staff, General von Greiffenberg said to me: 'Unfortunately, the presentation has to be cancelled. The *Oberbefehlshaber* was extremely upset by the sight of the dead Russians on the street … We can't now subject him to a presentation on typhus on top of that. The field marshal is a great soldier, but sometimes he is a prima donna whose nerves must be considered.'

"A general, who had led the greatest battles of World War II and could send hundreds of thousands of soldiers into the fire with the cool calculation of a chess player, had lost his equilibrium when he had seen the horrors of war directly before his eyes; this director of battles [*Schlachtlenker*] could not bear the sight of blood."[88]

2.5.2: Bock's Headquarters Transferred to the East

Following the capitulation of France, Bock and his Army Group B headquarters were assigned the task of guarding the Atlantic coast from Brest to the Spanish Frontier. The newly minted field marshal was less than enamored with this assignment, commenting caustically that his mission was simply to make sure neither the sea coast nor the demarcation line were stolen.[89] Hitler, meanwhile, was becoming more distrustful of Soviet behavior, and, on 26 August 1940, he demanded that German forces in the east be substantially augmented. As a first step, 10 infantry divisions and one panzer division were to be dispatched. Several days later, Brauchitsch, C-in-C of the Army, also proposed the transfer of Bock's Army Group B headquarters.[90] As Bock recorded in his diary, orders for the departure of his headquarters – to the city of Posen in occupied Poland – arrived on the evening of 31 August.[91] The field marshal remarked that he saw his new role – at least to begin with – as "probably nothing more than to act as a scarecrow against any sort of Russian ambition."[92]

Accommodations in Posen, however, posed a problem, as the city was teeming with troops and military agencies. As a result, and because the vital telephone links to and from Posen were not yet in place, Bock and his headquarters staff remained initially in Berlin. The headquarters finally relocated to Poland in the second half of October 1940; its main effort during the autumn months was focused on reorganization and training, as well as on the rapid construction of overland communications and of accommodations and catering for the arriving troops.[93] Another vital mission of Army Group B after its arrival in the east was to orchestrate the ongoing buildup, and, by the end of 1940, 34 divisions had been posted to the east (among them six armored divisions.)[94] In the meantime, Bock was again victimized by an old stomach problem, which, by late September, had become "down-right uncomfortable," forcing Bock to submit to bed rest. By late October, Bock's health had deteriorated to the point that he was compelled to temporarily relinquish command of his army group to Field Marshal Wilhelm List.[95]

Bock's convalescence lasted several months, and he did not to return to duty until 31 January 1941, when he took part in the OKH conference where he learned for the first time of the impending assault on the Soviet Union. It will be remembered that, during the meeting – which also included the two other field marshals earmarked for army group commands in the east, Rundstedt and Leeb – he had openly questioned the very premise of the operation – that the Red Army would stand and fight west of the Dnepr and Dvina river barriers, instead of withdrawing into the interior. On multiple occasions, in fact, Bock expressed profound skepticism about the prospect of war with Russia. In the spring of 1941, in the aftermath of the 30 March conference at the Reich Chancellery, the field marshal confided to his staff that he really did not know how such a war could be won.[96]

It is of note that, during Bock's long convalescence, Hitler appeared especially solicitous of him. Perhaps the "Fuehrer" had already selected Bock to play the primary role in Operation *Barbarossa*. On 11 November, he visited Bock in Berlin (*Helfferichstrasse*) and sat by the ailing field marshal's bed "for a good half hour." They discussed the overall military situation "at length," with Hitler intimating – perhaps disingenuously – that he was still unsure what to do about the east, but that "conditions might force us to intervene in order to head off a more dangerous development."[97] On 3 December, the "Fuehrer" was once again at Bock's side, this time to congratulate him on his 60th birthday. Now, however, the dictator insisted that the "eastern question" was becoming "acute;" yet if Russia were knocked out of the war, England would be left without hope of defeating Germany on the continent.[98]

Weeks later, with Bock once more on active duty, Hitler ordered the field marshal to report to him in Berlin on 1 February 1941. On this occasion, Bock acknowledged that it would be possible to defeat Russia – "if they stood and fought." Hitler's observations – as depicted in Bock's diary – are noteworthy for what they reveal about his thinking at the time:

> The Fuehrer … received me very warmly. He once again spoke at length on the overall situation … Conditions in France urgently require clarification; it is too early to say whether that can be achieved without an occupation of the rest of France. – England continues to be stubborn. The landing was not talked about. – The Fuehrer justified the need to prepare for the struggle against Russia by stating that this great event would very quickly divert the world from events in Africa and present it with a new situation. "The gentlemen in England are not stupid; they just act that way," and "they will come to realize that a continuation of the war will be pointless for them if Russia too is now beaten and eliminated."
>
> The implications for Japan and America he assessed as on 3 December [1940]. – I said that we would defeat the Russians if they stood and fought; but I raised the question of whether it would also be possible to force them to make peace. The Fuehrer replied that if the occupation of the Ukraine and the fall of Leningrad and Moscow did not bring about peace, then we would just have to carry on, at least with mobile forces, and advance to Yekaterinburg.
>
> "In any case I am glad," he said, "that we have continued to arm to the point where we are ready for anything. Materially we are well off and already have to think about a conversion of some factories. In terms of personnel the armed forces are better off than at the start of the war; economically we are absolutely solid."
>
> The Fuehrer sharply rejected any idea of backing down – without my having suggested it to him. "I will fight," and: "I am convinced that our attack will sweep over them like a hailstorm."[99]

On 3 February, Bock finally joined his Army Group B staff in Posen, where he was greeted with a festive reception. The field marshal's span of control included Fourth Army[100] and Eighteenth Army;[101] by May 1941, Ninth Army headquarters had also arrived (disguised initially as "Fortress Staff Blaurock")[102] followed in June by the two panzer group commands. On or about 1 April 1941, the army group was redesignated Army Group Center,[103] while Bock's staff experienced two major personnel changes prior to the war with Russia: Lt.-Col. Henning von Tresckow became the new chief operations officer (Ia), while Brig.-Gen. Hans von Greiffenberg was assigned to the headquarters as its new chief of staff.[104]

The 40-year old Tresckow, a charismatic officer of keen intellect and strong will, had served as Ia to Army Group A during the French campaign of 1940. Bock's nephew and closest confidant,[105] he was implacably opposed to Hitler and a member of the military resistance movement; during his long tenure with Army Group Center he would – in part through personnel transfers – establish a large group of conspirators on the army group's staff.[106] Shortly before the start of the Russian campaign, at the urging of Tresckow and others, Bock protested to OKH about the notorious Commissar Order of 6 June 1941, which authorized summary extrajudicial execution of Soviet political officers. While the protest proved futile, Bock took the "courageous stand" of refusing to transmit the order to his subordinate commands.[107] Nonetheless, official German military records from 1941 (war diaries, intelligence reports, etc.) indicate that it was implemented by a large majority of combat units.

A veteran of World War I and the *Reichswehr*, the 47-year-old Greiffenberg had, in the early 1930s, attended the U.S. Army's Command and General Staff School at Fort Leavenworth, Kansas. In the mid-1930s he occupied several staff and field commands, until being assigned to the Armed Forces Academy (*Wehrmachtsakademie*) in the autumn of 1937. In the autumn of 1938 he was posted to a staff position within OKH; and, on the eve of war in late August 1939, became Chief of the OKH Operations Branch.[108] Promoted to brigadier general in August 1940, Greiffenberg was posted to Twelfth Army as chief of staff during the Balkan campaign in the spring of 1941, for which he was awarded the Knight's Cross. In mid-May 1941, he was assigned to Army Group Center.[109] The appointment of Greiffenberg to the army group was apparently pushed through by Halder, and Bock was not happy to lose his "proven" chief of staff, Hans von Salmuth.[110] In any case, having his former OKH colleague attached to Bock's headquarters would enable the Chief of the Army General Staff to keep a close eye on the goings on there.

2.6: Army Group Center Prepares for War (February – May 1941)

Following his arrival in Posen, Field Marshal von Bock worked tirelessly to prepare his army group for war. His myriad activities are recorded in fulsome detail in his diary entries for this period and included: numerous meetings with army, corps and division commanders; unit inspections; observation of training exercises; and ongoing refinements to operational planning. Throughout, Bock was careful to coordinate his activities with the Army High Command. On occasion, he also played the diplomat to mollify the tender egos of disgruntled subordinates, such as Field Marshal von Kluge (Fourth Army) and General Guderian (2 Panzer Group). Relations between Bock and both subordinates were sometimes strained.[111] Excerpts from his diary offer insight into his actions and priorities through the end of May 1941:[112]

> 13.2.41:
> General Guderian … came to Posen and briefed me on a war game that he was to direct; also discussed operational questions. General [Dr Waldemar] Henrici, commander of 258 ID, reported for duty.

14.2.41:
Exercise by a rocket battalion at Schrimm, where I met several of the army group's [corps] and division commanders.

15.3.41:
Intelligence concerning Russian military measures at the border is growing stronger.

20.3.41:
Vietinghoff, Command General of the 46 Panzer Corps, reported for duty; he raised the topic of the far from complete state of equipment of the new motorized divisions; it is so inadequate that training is suffering badly as a result.

7.4.41:
Large scale "smoke exercise" [cover designation for rocket units] at the Warthelager practice grounds in the presence of numerous generals from the entire army.

9./10.4.41:
War game under my direction with the Commanders-in-Chief of the Fourth and Ninth Armies, the leaders of the panzer groups, and the [corps] commanders.

9.5.41:
Drove to 293 ID, which I saw on the march.

14.-16.5.41:
Traveled by train to the frontier in the Fourth Army's sector; on the way discussions concerning the coming missions with [corps and division commanders]. Everywhere I went the troops made a fresh, cheering impression; when I asked about their rations the answer was the same everywhere: "Good, but there could be more!"

21.5.41:
Greiffenberg, who visited the Fourth Army yesterday, advised me that Kluge is coming and that he plans to ask me to give the Fourth Army a freer hand than before; he feels that he is on too tight a rope! ... I was aware of my former Chief of Staff's ego,[113] and so far I had scrupulously avoided anything that might have injured it. My concern went so far that I recently left an exercise before the concluding conference in order to allow Kluge to speak alone. Before the war game in Posen I told him that I would direct all important questions during the game to "the Fourth Army;" it was thus left to him in every case to decide whether to answer himself or allow his chief of staff to reply. The result of all this was that at the conclusion of the exercise he took over and gave an unsolicited speech about the employment of panzer units, in which "he no doubt possessed the greatest experience!"

I swallowed this for the sake of peace. Perhaps Kluge saw that as weakness – then I will have to disappoint him.

27.-30.5.41:
Trip to the Ninth Army at Suwalki Point ... In general everything appears to be on the right path, still some details to improve. Impressions of the field units, as far as I saw, good. Countryside and population of Suwalki Point look wretched; the area appears to be dirt poor and without any culture, only the forest is good in places. – En route

came news of the sinking of the battlecruiser *Bismarck* ... A rumor is circulating at the front and at home that the Russians have made such generous offers to the *Fuehrer* that there will be no war with Russia. On the 29th the Commanding General of 5 Army Corps, Ruoff, reported that Russian soldiers had approached the border in his sector, waved over civilians and told them that there would be no war because Stalin and the *Fuehrer* had agreed on everything! Unbelievable![114]

When the strategic concentration for *Barbarossa* began in early February 1941, of the 117 divisions which still had to be moved by rail and road, 42 were earmarked for Army Group Center by the start of the campaign. Concerned army group staff officers coordinated their efforts with the German *Reichsbahn* and military rail authorities to shepherd the units to their various destinations. The movement of a complete division by rail during the first three deployment phases (i.e., through 20 May 1941) took about a week from Germany and 10 days from France. (During the final phase in June the pace would be dramatically accelerated.) After detraining, the divisions typically occupied temporary assembly areas far from the eastern frontier; in most cases, only in the final weeks before the start of the campaign, were they to begin to move – in a series of phases – to their final jump-off positions. Thus, while the railroads carried the troops as far as East Prussia or Poland, upon arrival the infantry still faced long and arduous foot marches – mostly at night for security reasons – into their final assembly areas. To ease their burden, if only slightly, the Organization Todt (OT), German Labor Service (*Reichsarbeitsdienst*, or RAD) and Army engineers labored diligently to improve roadways and reinforce bridges and culverts.[115] Yet the months of hard physical conditioning and combat training had built confidence and prepared the men well, as the following accounts – building on those earlier in this chapter – illustrate:

Lt.-Col. Wilhelm Meyer-Detring, chief operations officer (Ia), 137 Infantry Division, whose division had moved by train from Austria to Poland in late March, now faced a long march by foot – right up to the border with Russia:

> From 25.5.-2.6.[1941] the division – now completely under the command of 9 AK ... – advanced approximately 250 km further east in seven to eight nighttime marches via Warsaw into the area around Sokolov, close to the Russian border. It was a joy to see the division on the march. The regiments at full strength, equipped with new material, horses, vehicles and trucks in top condition – a magnificent image of military strength! Numerous exercises had shown what the troops had learned since the establishment of the division. A final test, the river crossing exercise across the Pilica in extreme road conditions, had made very high demands on man and animal, especially on the combat engineers, and again provided evidence that the division could look confidently to the future. What this future would look like only few in the division knew with any certainty.[116]

Dr Rudolf Gschoepf, a 40-year-old catholic priest (*Divisionspfarrer*) in 45 Infantry Division, recalled the mighty procession of men, tanks, vehicles and artillery as the units of Army Group Center advanced inexorably toward their *Barbarossa* start lines. The tinge of excitement his account betrays must have been universal at the time – the sense of power and invincibility of German arms overwhelming:

> At the end of April 1941, the transport of the division from the area around St. Quentin to the east began ... Our route cut straight across Germany. After three days, we halted in the environs of Warsaw ... During this transfer to the east, the division

suffered a heavy blow: The division commander, Brig.-Gen. Koerner, wanted to use the journey through Germany to pay his family a brief visit, but had a fatal accident en route in his automobile … He was succeeded by Maj.-Gen. Schlieper.

There now followed a couple of weeks' rest, even if a certain amount of training still had to continue. So we were back in Poland! A lot had changed here in this country since we had left it in November 1939! …

At the end of May the division began to advance further east via Siedlce up into the area around Biała-Podlaska. The former Polish barracks in the town itself offered accommodation for a portion of the troops; the greater part took up quarters in the surrounding villages … The concentrations of troops became ever more evident. Heavy movements could be observed, especially at night. Tanks, heavy artillery, anti-aircraft guns, engineering equipment, and much else besides trundled eastward toward the Russian border. A conspicuous number of discussions in the headquarters staffs; intense activity in the orderly rooms; visits from unknown and high-level commanders – all of this meant even the simplest men could clearly see that great things were imminent.[117]

The 45 Infantry Division would suffer 21 officers and 290 NCOs and men killed on Sunday, 22 June 1941, in its unsuccessful attempt to storm the Soviet citadel of Brest-Litovsk.[118]

From 6-9 April 1941, 6 Infantry Division was suddenly uprooted from its quarters in East Prussia and dispatched further to the east – right up to the frontier with Russia in the area known as the Suwalki triangle. The triangle lay east of the Masurian Lakes and beyond the historic boundaries of East Prussia; it had been made a part of Lithuania in a treaty between Lithuania and the Soviet Union in July 1920, only to see Poland grab it in defiance of that treaty. The Russo-German Secret Additional Protocol of 28 September 1939 had ceded the triangle to Germany and, in a rare act of self-restraint, the Russians made no attempt to occupy it when they seized Lithuania in June 1940. Shortly thereafter, the German government reaffirmed its intention to maintain German rights to the Suwalki triangle, refusing a Russian offer to purchase it; "if the Russians had taken decisive action earlier, they would have deprived the Germans of a vital pivot for [Operation] *Barbarossa*."[119]

The area was primitive with poor roads. The soldiers of 6 Infantry Division, accustomed to the fine, paved roads of France, struggled with "the greatest difficulties" as they marched into the triangle.[120] The town of Suwalki itself – occupied by the division's staff – with its houses of wood and straw, made a poor impression on the men compared to the clean, tidy homesteads of East Prussia.[121] Friedrich "Fritz" Belke, a 21-year-old private in 6 ID, recalled the difficult foot march of his battalion to the border with Russia in early April 1941:

> 8 April 1941. Departure in eastward direction. In night marches in stretches of 50 kilometers we move forward, weaving round the many lakes toward the old Lithuanian, now Soviet Russian, border. Through villages whose cobblestoned streets torture our feet. After a 175-kilometer march, by way of the town of Loetzen and the Rominter Heath, we reach Lake Vištytis, the locality of Seefelden. Our squad is quartered in the living room of the village blacksmith, Gustav Neumann.[122]

The hostility of local Poles in the Suwalki region was a cause for concern and, on occasion, turned deadly. Yet as this lyrical yet chilling diary entry from 6 ID's Dr Haape makes clear, the German response to such transgressions was swift and brutal:

> Outside the weather is glorious, the birds are singing and the trees are wearing the delicate green of the short, summery spring of the Polish East. You could hear

the toads in the nearby lake and the storks strut carefully through the swampy outer edges, where colorful dragonflies play, bumblebees and iridescent flies buzz around the fresh, lush flowers, and a variety of wildlife goes about its business. I am peaceful and satisfied in this magical world of a real, living peace! A strange life here; incomprehensible contrasts appear here in an ever changing, colorful game: In this moment, I think of a comrade in the Signal Corps, who lost his way a bit, stepped over the Russian border, and was immediately shot there and buried.

Two policemen had their throats cut by fanatical Poles. The next day, Poles in the population were seized; 14 of those arrested were shot immediately when they tried to escape, a further 20 were taken off for investigation. For other offenses by the Poles the punishment, for example, of flogging, is carried out with exceptional success. Every German officer must be greeted in the street. Should the Pole forget to do this, his cap will immediately be struck from his head, etc ... I could tell of even more things from this world of the east.

And so we live here completely cut off from the world, without civilized distractions, and wait patiently for the things that are coming. We'll be pleased when it all starts![123]

One of Field Marshal von Bock's primary concerns, of course, was the ongoing training of his army group. As he well knew, Soviet Russia, with its limitless expanses, primitive roadways, vast tracks of primeval forest and swamps, and general want of "creature comforts," would impose special demands on his men. Basic training in the German Army, even in peacetime, had always been tough – "long, arduous, realistic," as one author has characterized it.[124] German training programs sought to replicate combat conditions as closely as possible. Troops were trained in all types of weather and around the clock, day and night. Exercises with live ammunition – a practice employed by the pre-1914 Imperial Army during its annual summer maneuvers – were routine,[125] exposing recruits to serious injury or death. Yet German military authorities accepted the one percent fatality rate sustained during such training as the necessary price for saving soldiers' lives in combat.[126] Training was also forward-looking and thorough, with each soldier learning to perform his immediate superior's mission as well as his own, in case he had to take command. Of critical importance was the fact that all recruits – regardless of their chosen field of specialization – first received a basic infantry, or combat, training[127] – a policy which would prove of incalculable benefit during the winter of 1941/42, when rear area "comb outs" were necessary to furnish desperately needed infantry for the front. Pre-war training programs also emphasized familiarity with combined arms operations.

After the war began, training was made even a good deal more rigorous. The Army High Command was disappointed by their soldiers' performance in the Polish campaign of 1939. Chief of the Army General Staff Halder echoed complaints commonly made by field commanders that the infantry had not been aggressive enough in the attack, while the poor march discipline of mobile units – a problem again encountered at the start of *Barbarossa* – had caused traffic jams and unnecessary delays. Guderian had observed several occasions when his motorized and tank units exhibited signs of nervousness before going into action. The OKH was well aware of such concerns, having been alerted by a series of brutally honest after-action reports from unit commanders outlining deficiencies of their troops. As a result, between the Polish and French campaigns, a major effort was made to improve training and enhance efficiency.[128] Beginning in the fall of 1939, the German Army spent 17 hours a day, six or seven days a week, implementing "with precision and enthusiasm" the OKH training syllabus – a "ruthless and relentless" training program which stood in stark contrast to the generally "lackadaisical practice" of most French formations during the "Phony War" of late 1939 and early 1940.[129]

Following the French campaign, in the autumn of 1940, the OKH ordered another round of intense training, this time in preparation for a very different kind of war – that against the Soviet Union. Panzer divisions were to undergo extensive training in combined arms tactics, while motorized infantry units were to train to fight unsupported and to clear forests and villages rapidly.[130] Foot infantry were to execute long, strenuous marches to prepare for the rigors of traversing vast, inhospitable distances.[131] Yet training in the German Army for combat under Russian terrain conditions was by no means "uniform or systematic." Indeed, a truly specialized program was impossible for several reasons. Plans for war against Russia were long kept a closely guarded secret; some division commanders would – almost to the final moment – regard their transfer to, and assembly in, the east as nothing more than a precautionary measure or a bluff to extract diplomatic concessions. Other units were pulled out of the Balkan campaign in the spring of 1941, dispatched directly to the east, and given no time for special training. More importantly, there were no suitable training grounds – no places in France, the Netherlands, or central Europe where the Army could train for combat in deep forests, extensive swampland, or sandy areas. Obstacles to realistic training – particularly for tank units and motorized infantry – also resulted from shortages of fuel and vehicles. Wherever training, however much possible, was actually attuned to Russian conditions, it was done so on the initiative of individual army, corps, or division commanders.[132]

Despite such challenges, Bock and his field commanders did what they could to ready their charges for war. The training manuals issued by the commander of Fourth Army, Field Marshal Guenther von Kluge, embraced typical concerns of the army group's senior commanders, while also reflecting the still healthy respect the German Army officer corps – many of whom had fought in the east in World War I – had for the Russian Army. As Kluge understood, albeit not from personal experience,[133] any fight with the Red Army was going to be a serious affair. On 20 March 1941, Kluge ordered his subordinate commanders to step up their training efforts. The training, he demanded, should emphasize a toughening of the troops, since in Russia the soldiers would often be without even the simplest comforts. The men were to train to march great distances, while efforts were to be made to protect the troops from the possible use of chemical or biological weapons. The field marshal warned that the Red Army was likely to attack in several thick waves, with strong support from tanks and artillery; as combatants, they would be tough and disdainful of their losses. Kluge stressed that his infantry would have to effectively coordinate all of its firepower to defeat such attacks. Moreover, the infantry was to be trained for greater toughness in close combat (a specialty of the Russian fighting man) and to overcome its aversion to fighting at night. Because they could also expect to be assaulted by tanks, the infantry should be instructed to emulate Finnish and Spanish infantry by aggressively attacking enemy tanks with explosive charges. Kluge also foresaw special problems arising from the enormous scope of the Russian theater of operations, where his units would frequently be left with unguarded flanks. To address this concern, he recommended that units become accustomed to providing for adequate reconnaissance and security, paying particular attention to large forests, where Russian cavalry might lurk. Security, he admonished, must also be made more robust for German staffs; hence, all headquarters personnel were to be familiar with, and expect to use, their side arms.[134]

The Fourth Army, like all the armies deploying along the German *Ostfront*, had to prepare its own detailed deployment plans; guided, of course, by the general plan promulgated by the OKH at the end of January 1941. At their headquarters in the center of Warsaw – in the great castle from the time of August the Strong, and former home of the Polish general staff – concerned staff had hammered out their deployment order by 15 March 1941.[135] Three days later, Hans Meier-Welcker, a General Staff officer on the staff of Fourth Army, attended a conference in Zossen (OKH headquarters), just outside

Berlin, conducted by the Army's Deputy Chief of Staff for Supply and Administration (*Oberquartiermeister*); his diary entry for that day illuminates some of the trenchant problems faced by Army Group Center – and the German Army as a whole – as war crept inexorably closer:

> Berlin, 18.3.1941
> 1400 hours in the afternoon in Zossen at OKH. Discussion with the Quartermaster-Gen. and the Commander of the Training Branch about the fuel and tire situation, as well as the fuel allocation for training.
>
> Quartermaster-Gen. said: The consumption of 282,000 cubic meters of fuel per month has been calculated for the offensive in Russia. Accordingly, our fuel provisions will suffice for an offensive of not quite three months. From that point onward we will be dependent on continuous imports from Romania. If the Russians succeed in crippling or destroying the production of oil in Romania, it will have far-reaching consequences.
>
> The tire situation is even more critical. The forces (incl. *Luftwaffe*) currently have a deficit of 90,000 tires. The Qu[artermaster-]Gen. has a special reserve of 10,000 tires. Furthermore, another 70,000 tires can be allocated to the troops in the course of the operation. So after that there still remains a deficit of 10,000 tires!
>
> During the discussion, all the armies request an increase in the fuel quota for unit training, which is considerably impaired. However, it is likely that only ½ a unit of consumption will be granted in addition to the current 2½ units of consumption.[136]

After the war, Guenther Blumentritt, in 1941 chief of staff of Fourth Army, described the atmosphere that prevailed in his headquarters that spring:

> More and more divisions were moved to the east, but in order to conceal their presence from the Russians they were stationed well back from the frontier. Preparations began to be intensified and skeleton staffs of other senior commands were set up in the east. Numerous map exercises and tactical discussions took place. As it became increasingly obvious that for Hitler war with the Soviets was inevitable, preparations were intensified by staffs at all levels.
>
> A strange atmosphere prevailed during those months. In the first place we realized what this new war would entail. Many of us had fought in Russia as junior officers between 1914 and 1918, and we knew what to expect. There was uneasiness both among the staff officers and in the divisions. On the other hand duty demanded precise and detailed work. All books and maps concerning Russia soon disappeared from the bookshops. I remember that Kluge's desk at his Warsaw headquarters was usually laden with such publications. In particular, Napoleon's 1812 campaign was the subject of much study. Kluge read General de Caulaincourt's account of that campaign with the greatest attention: it revealed the difficulties of fighting, and even living, in Russia. The places where the Grand Army had fought its battles and skirmishes were on the maps before us. We knew that we would soon be following in Napoleon's footsteps. We also studied the Russo-Polish War of 1920. As Chief of Staff, Fourth Army, I delivered a series of lectures to our staff officers on this subject, illustrated by large maps.[137]

While Blumentritt's post-war recollections appear measured and sober, in the spring of 1941 he, like so many of his colleagues, had evinced a sublime optimism. Indeed, on 8 May 1941, he had said with regard to *Barbarossa*: "We should not forget the reputation and the aura of invincibility which precedes our *Wehrmacht* everywhere."[138] Nothing was impossible for the German soldier!

One area of acute concern was the potential use of gas and the possible contamination of land and water wells by Red Army forces. It is clear from contemporary accounts that the Germans genuinely feared the prospect of the enemy unleashing gas – as well as other chemical and/or biological contaminants – on their troops.[139] In general, they expected the Russians to react to the German assault with brutality and excess far exceeding earlier campaigns[140] – a foreboding which, as events soon revealed, was not without basis in fact. Only days before *Barbarossa* began, Field Marshal von Brauchitsch visited his army field commanders in the east. What he had to tell them was sobering: The Russians could be expected to use flamethrowers and gas; they would contaminate wells and stocks of supplies, while seriously threatening rear lines of communication. As he told the staff of Fourth Army on 12 June 1941, one had to be prepared for their adversary to wage "war by all possible means" (*Krieg mit allen Mitteln*).[141] As Brauchitsch predicted, the Red Army did indeed fight with virtually every means at its disposal, and often in violation of the laws and usages of war; however, despite numerous scares among German troops in the opening days of the campaign, the Russians appear to have never made use of poison gas.[142]

Training to combat potential Russian use of chemical agents included special instructional courses, as recounted by Dr Erich Bunke, in the spring of 1941 a *Leutnant* in 31 Infantry Division:

> On 25 April 1941, I was tasked by the battalion commander to drive to Rembertów near Warsaw in order to take part in a three-day training course in defense against gas attacks … The gas training introduced us to the Soviets' military regulation gas equipment … We were certain that our gas masks and the anti-gas paulin, which every soldier had to have ready to hand, would provide sufficient protection. However, negotiating contaminated terrain was practiced a great deal. Chlorinated lime had to be used in a lot of cases here. In Warsaw, they were generally convinced that the Russian campaign was imminent after Yugoslavia and Greece had been cleansed …
>
> On 30 April 1941 I went by train from Warsaw to the south. My destination was Garbatka, somewhere in a large forested area. The train had carriages for Germans and some for Poles. In a suburb of Warsaw, a young Pole entered my compartment and was very alarmed when he noticed that a German officer sat there. I let him join me and we spoke not a word until he disembarked at his home station.
>
> On 1 May, an officers' meeting took place in Garbatka that made the Russia campaign plain. It conveyed above all that the Red Army had been observed approaching the demarcation line, and had increased construction of airfields. On 8 May 41, I presented the decontamination options for terrain contaminated by chemical warfare agents to the battalion. In the meantime, the decontamination squads trained by me had been set up in the companies. An appropriate gas drill had to be completed in a night exercise on 9-10 May.[143]

No discussion of German training activities prior to the start of the war against Russia would be complete without reference to a serious lacuna in that training – the lack of special preparation for fighting in forests. As noted above, this was, in part, due to the paucity of areas available for such training. However, both Belorussia and European Russia were covered with large tracks of dense forest, and clearly more could have been done to train the German soldier for the inevitable combat in such areas – inevitable, in part, because the Russians were masters at forest fighting. World War I had demonstrated the need for such training, as early in that struggle the French *Chasseurs Alpins* had displayed their superiority over German infantry in the close terrain of the Voges forests. However, during the inter-war period, this critical technique of combat was treated as the "stepchild it has always been." (It is thus hardly surprising that both German higher and lower commands attempted – albeit unsuccessfully – to avoid forests and forest fighting during the Russian campaign.)[144] The Germans were to pay dearly for their oversight. Horst Grossmann, a commander of 6 Infantry Division, wrote after the war about the painful losses sustained by the division when clearing the enemy from a forested region at the start of the campaign:

> Two of the rest days ordered by our superiors ... provided the desired opportunity to treat marching injuries, but also brought a series of small skirmishes while combing the forest west of Prienai, with some very unpleasant losses for the infantry ... The troops had to get used to this way of fighting, where the infantry's heavy weapons were barely usable and considerable guts alone would not help at all. It would be necessary to operate like Indians against this enemy, who had such an affinity with nature.[145]

Despite such shortfalls in training, the 1.3 million soldiers of Army Group Center would begin the "crusade" against the Soviet Union well trained and equipped, their confidence buoyed and skills sharpened in the bloody crucible of 21 months of victorious battle. Among these 1.3 million men were but few who perceived the existential dangers in Hitler's wars of aggression and contemplated the gathering storm in the east with palpable trepidation. One who did was Fourth Army staff officer Meier-Welcker, as revealed in this diary entry:

> Warsaw, 7.4.1941
> An empire of war [*Kriegsreich*], such as we are currently conquering for ourselves and which we will also maintain in altered form provided there is a good outcome, cannot endure in the long term through oppression. Numerous European peoples are far too highly developed and too culturally individual for it to be otherwise. The empire of war, which is put together so heterogeneously, can only be held together, or even induced to form a community, in the long term by an overarching idea. Such an idea must be supranational and contain in itself the essence of all the nations. To destroy the independent existence of the European peoples means to rob the western world of its soul and thus also certain downfall [*sicheren Untergang*]. The sources of life lie deeper than many manifestations of politics.[146]

2.7: North Africa, the Balkans and Crete (January – May 1941)

By 1941, Germany's strategic position in southeastern Europe and the Mediterranean had become increasingly complicated as a result of Italian setbacks in North Africa and the Balkans and the British occupation of the island of Crete. In late March, the situation took a dramatic turn for the worse, when an anti-German coup toppled a Yugoslavian government which had just joined the Tripartite Pact. As a result, from January through May 1941, the Germans conducted a series of major military operations in these regions to put a stop to Italy's decline and to shore up their own southern flank prior to the invasion of Russia. Each of these interventions will be outlined below, with special attention paid to their impact – if any – on Operation *Barbarossa*.

2.7.1: North Africa

As early as 30 June 1940, General Jodl had submitted a memorandum to the "Fuehrer" in which he raised the question of German support for Italy in North Africa as a way of striking at a critical link in Britain's colonial empire. A month later, Field Marshal von Brauchitsch proposed a five-point plan which included tank support for Italy in North Africa and a direct attack on the Suez Canal; and, six weeks after that (11 September 1940), Colonel Walter Warlimont, Chief of the National Defense Branch in OKW, sent a plan to his chief, Jodl, which envisaged the employment of either a panzer corps or brigade in Africa. Hitler had, at first, vacillated, and taken no course of action. At a conference on 14 September, however, his intentions became clear: A panzer corps was to be prepared for transport to North Africa, provided the Italians were receptive to the idea.[147]

Meanwhile, events in Africa soon overtook the leisurely pace of German planning. Since Italy's declaration of war on Britain and France on 10 June 1940, Mussolini had prodded his cautious commander in Libya, Marshal Rodolfo Graziani, to move against Egypt – at that time only weakly screened by British forces. On 13 September, the long awaited Italian offensive began, with Graziani's forces crossing the Egyptian border. In three days, the Italians advanced almost 100 kilometers, but then stopped inexplicably, digging in and awaiting the arrival of reinforcements and supplies.[148]

Hitler and his advisors observed the Italians behavior with some distress. To effect closer cooperation between the two Axis powers, Hitler met with Mussolini at the Brenner Pass on 3 October. In a desultory monologue that skirted many areas of mutual concern, the "Fuehrer" renewed his offer to dispatch troops, tanks and planes to North Africa, while the "Duce" promised to renew the offensive in Egypt. True to his word, Mussolini attacked, only not in Egypt: attacking from Albania, he hurled large forces into Greece on 28 October 1940. Infuriated by the suddenly transformed strategic picture, Hitler withdrew his offer of a panzer corps for Africa.[149]

Weeks passed, but Graziani refused to budge. The British made good use of the respite to rebuild their forces in Egypt and, on 9 December, launched a counterstroke intended only as a raid to keep the Italians off balance. Disaster struck: The Italian defenses disintegrated; 38,000 startled Italians – among them four generals – marched off into captivity. By late December, the Italians were pleading for German help – in particular, for a panzer division – to prevent all of Italian North Africa from falling into enemy hands. As if to underscore their point, by 5 January 1941, the British had captured Bardia, the first town inside the Italian colony, taking tens of thousands of more Italians prisoner, and begun to press on toward Tobruk.[150]

Galvanized into action by the spectacular reversals of his Italian ally, Hitler decided on 9 January to rush a blocking force (*Speerverband*) to North Africa; two days later, his decision was enshrined in Directive No. 22, Operation "Sunflower" (*Sonnenblume*). The loss of North Africa, Hitler calculated, would not weigh heavily from a military standpoint; the psychological effect on the Italians, however, would signify a serious setback to the Axis front. Chosen to lead the small mobile force – the nucleus of what was soon to become the Africa Corps – was General Erwin Rommel. By early February, the first convoy of German troops and materiel was on its way to Libya; on 12 February Rommel arrived in Tripoli.[151]

On 14 February, the first German combat units arrived in Tripoli, to be followed by the first tank units about a month later. While Rommel agonized over the pace of his buildup, he had nothing to fear from the British, who had been forced to withdraw large forces and dispatch them to Greece, leaving only modest elements to screen Cyrenaica. Exceeding his authority, Rommel attacked suddenly and boldly in early April. He soon pushed British forces out of Cyrenaica and, by 11 April, completed the investment of Tobruk. While this first class fortress would not be captured until June 1942, the "Desert Fox" had temporarily turned the tables in North Africa.[152]

With the dispatch of Rommel and his Africa Corps to Libya, Hitler had stabilized the situation in North Africa – at least for the moment – and relieved himself of a potentially frustrating distraction which, in a worstcase scenario, might have siphoned off more forces before or after the start of *Barbarossa*.[153] As it was, North Africa would remain a strategic backwater – the number of forces committed there tiny in comparison to Russia and other theaters of war. What is intriguing, however, is a counterfactual "what if:" What if Rommel had not been sent to Africa, but had taken part in the Russian campaign? What might this tactical "artist" have accomplished on the much larger "canvas" of the eastern front?

On 19 June 1941, three days before *Barbarossa* was to set to begin, OKW issued a directive outlining Hitler's intentions for the future use and deployment of the panzer divisions. The directive indicated that the "eastern front should as much as possible live from its own materiel reserve. In case of heavy losses panzer divisions should be consolidated together. Newly established panzer divisions in Germany shall by staffed by personnel vacated due to the consolidations." The document went on to stipulate that tank losses in North Africa were to be replaced as soon as possible, leaving little in reserve for the east.[154]

2.7.2: The Balkans

German military planning to intervene in the Balkans was – in part – also a response to Italian military reversals. Mussolini, if nothing else, was consistent: His attack on Greece from Albania in October 1940 had also resulted in disaster. After some initial success, the invaders had been hurled back to their jump off positions; in the weeks that followed, Greek forces drove deep into Albanian territory, threatening the primary Italian supply port of Valona. The Greeks, in fact, would hold the initiative until March 1941, if only registering modest gains after their initial progress. On 9 March, the Italians began their spring offensive with the objective, at a minimum, of driving Greek forces out of Albania. The Italians, however, making no discernible headway, were stopped after five days.[155]

The failure of Mussolini's invasion of Greece had badly discomfited Hitler. It had, in fact, disrupted his plans to transform the Balkans into a German satellite zone by peaceful diplomacy, while also providing the British with a pretext for returning to the continent, which they promptly did in early November by transferring air units to southern Greece, thereby placing the Romanian oil fields in danger. As noted in Chapter 1, Hitler, alarmed by Britain's growing assertiveness in the eastern Mediterranean and determined to remove any threat to his Romanian oil, had, in early November 1940, directed his General Staff to work out plans for an invasion of northern Greece via Romania and Bulgaria. On 13 December, the OKW promulgated Directive No. 20, laying out plans for an operation against Greece under the code-name "*Marita*."[156] The directive envisaged the occupation of the northern coast of the Aegean Sea by March 1941 and, if necessary, the seizure of the entire Greek mainland. Meanwhile, German troops had begun to move into Hungary and Romania; by mid-February 1941, the German "army of observation" in Romania had grown to seven divisions; after Bulgaria joined the Tripartite Pact (on 1 March), the Germans were free to begin bridging the Danube into Bulgaria to prepare their attack positions for *Marita*.[157]

The advance of elements of German Twelfth Army into Bulgaria – perceived by the Allies as a clear signal of an impending invasion of Greece – elicited an immediate response from the British. On 5 March, they began Operation "Lustre," the ferrying of troops, weapons and equipment from Egypt to Greece; in the weeks that followed, more than 60,000 Commonwealth troops (several divisions) were shepherded across the eastern Mediterranean to Greece.[158] Meanwhile, on the night of 26-27 March, a group of Serb officers, infuriated by Yugoslav adherence to the German-led Tripartite Pact, overthrew the Yugoslav government and replaced Prince Paul (the regent) with the heir to the throne, 17-year-old King Peter. The new government, headed by Yugoslav Air Force chief of staff, General Dušan Simović, at once withdrew from the Tripartite Pact.[159] An enraged Hitler responded with alacrity. Operation *Marita* was at once altered to incorporate an attack on Yugoslavia as well. The same day as the coup, he issued Directive No. 25: Greece and Yugoslavia were to be attacked simultaneously; the latter, in fact, was to be smashed "militarily and as a state." To support the attack, hundreds of *Luftwaffe* planes were flown to Romania and Bulgaria from airfields along the Channel coast, as well as from Sicily and Libya.[160]

The German attack began on the morning of 6 April 1941. Prefiguring the opening hours of the Russian campaign only weeks away, most of the Yugoslav air force was destroyed on the ground, while Belgrade was ruthlessly bombed from the air, resulting in some 17,000 civilian deaths. In a brilliant display of "lightning" warfare, the Germans rapidly overran the Yugoslav army; on 17 April, Yugoslavia surrendered unconditionally and consigned more than 325,000 of her soldiers to captivity. The Greeks, and their British Commonwealth allies, fared no better. On 9 April, the attacking Germans forced the Greek defenders of the Metaxas Line to surrender; on 18 April, the Germans broke through the final defenses on the Aliakhmon Line, held by Allied troops from New Zealand. The bulk of Greek forces capitulated on 21 April. In despair, the Greek prime minister committed suicide. By 22 April, the Allied rear guard was making a desperate stand at Thermopylae – where the Spartans had died defying the Persians 2500 years before – to enable evacuation of the main body of their forces. On 27 April, the Swastika flag was hoisted over the Acropolis in Athens. By 30 April it was over – Greece firmly in German hands while 50,000 Allied forces (British, Australian, New Zealand and Polish troops) had been evacuated, mostly to Crete, leaving behind their heavy weapons, trucks and aircraft.[161]

For the Germans it was a truly spectacular feat of arms – accomplished in a mere 24 days at a cost of 151 dead, 392 wounded and 15 missing in the Yugoslav campaign[162] and some 5000 casualties (dead, wounded, missing) against Greece. To build Yugoslavia into the operation had taken some frantic last-minute staff work, as well as a shuffling of forces, yet the operation had proceeded at a breakneck pace, with tanks and motorized infantry performing well over some of Europe's most inhospitable terrain. According to one military historian: "The sheer disparity in quality between the *Wehrmacht* and its Balkan opponents … was all the explanation necessary for the catastrophe which had overcome them."[163] Once again, a great victory had contributed to the German Army's aura of invincibility – both at home and abroad.

The decisive German Balkan victory had driven the British from Greece, dramatically reducing the vulnerability of the Romanian oil fields to attack from the air; in strategic terms, by bringing both Greece and Yugoslavia within Germany's orbit, it had solidified the Reich's southern flank – a vital prerequisite to the attack on Russia. Conversely, historians have argued for decades that the Balkan campaign delayed implementation of Operation *Barbarossa* by some four to six weeks – a delay, they insist, which proved fatal to its outcome. In his magisterial study of the Third Reich published in 1960, William L. Shirer wrote:

> And though June [1941] had arrived the vast army which had been turned southeast into Yugoslavia and Greece had to be brought back great distances to the Soviet frontier over unpaved roads and run-down single-track railway lines that were woefully inadequate to handle so swarming a traffic.
> The delay, as things turned out, was fatal. Defenders of Hitler's military genius have contended that the Balkan campaign did not set back the timetable for

Barbarossa appreciably and that in any case the postponement was largely due to the late thaw that year which left the roads in Eastern Europe deep in mud until mid-June. But the testimony of the key German generals is otherwise. Field Marshal Friedrich Paulus, whose name will always be associated with Stalingrad, and who at this time was the chief planner of the Russian campaign on the Army General Staff, testified on the stand at Nuremberg that Hitler's decision to destroy Yugoslavia postponed the beginning of *Barbarossa* by "about five weeks." The Naval War Diary gives the same length of time. Rundstedt, who led Army Group South into Russia, told Allied interrogators after the war that because of the Balkan campaign, "we began at least four weeks late. That," he added, "was a very costly delay."[164]

Almost half a century later (2007), Professor Chris Bellamy, in his impressive study of Russia in the Second World War, echoed Shirer's observations: "*Barbarossa* was delayed – almost certainly with disastrous consequences for the Germans – because of the 27 March 1941 coup in Yugoslavia, and Hitler's subsequent invasion to deal with it."[165] This analysis, however, is simply false. To get it right, we turn to the venerable British military historian, Sir John Keegan:

> The Balkan campaign, often depicted by historians as an unwelcome diversion from Hitler's long-laid plan to attack the Soviet Union and as a disabling interruption of the timetable he had marked out for its inception, had been in fact no such thing. It had been successfully concluded even more rapidly than his professional military advisers could have anticipated; while the choice for D-Day for *Barbarossa* had always depended not on the sequence of contingent events but on the weather and objective military factors. The German Army found it more difficult than expected to position the units allocated for *Barbarossa* in Poland; while the lateness of the spring thaw, which left the eastern European rivers in spate beyond the predicted date, meant that *Barbarossa* could not have been begun very much earlier than the third week in June, whatever Hitler's intentions.[166]

It is true that, several days prior to commencement of the Balkan campaign, OKW had concluded that the expansion of the operation to include Yugoslavia – requiring the commitment of nine additional divisions, drawn from the German order of battle already in place for *Barbarossa* – would delay the start of war against Russia by at least four weeks – from the originally intended start date in mid-May to about mid-June 1941.[167] As matters turned out, Hitler did not settle on 22 June as the new start date for war with Russia until 30 April 1941.[168] Moreover, faced with continued uncertainty on the part of OKH as to whether even *that* deadline could be met, he did not finalize the 22 June start date until the end of May.[169]

Yet despite the added complications created by the assault on Yugoslavia – and whatever delays they imposed on the *Barbarossa* buildup – the attack on Russia, as Keegan so rightly observed, could not, in any event, have been launched much before the second half of June because of the weather. The spring of 1941 had brought unusually heavy rains to Central and Eastern Europe, while flooding rivers and dikes throughout western Russia. Until the end of May, the ground was boggy, roads and unpaved airfields virtually unusable. These adverse conditions, recalled former *Luftwaffe* general Hermann Plocher, "seriously retarded the rapid extension of German highway and road networks, the expansion of German airfields, and the construction of immense communication lines."[170] They also made operations by mobile forces – panzer and motorized divisions –

largely impossible until the rivers had ceased flooding their banks and the sodden, marshy ground had dried out. Thus, the delay in launching *Barbarossa* until well into June was "almost certainly inevitable."[171]

The primary river barrier facing Army Group Center along the German-Soviet frontier was the River Bug. It cut right across the path of the invading forces and, together with its tributaries and swampy watersheds, formed an excellent natural defensive system. The low relief of the country resulted in periodic flooding of the Bug – which was particularly severe in the spring of 1941 – while both riverbanks tended to be marshy, making the construction of approach roads a more troublesome engineering feat than actual bridging.[172] The operations officer (Ia) in Fourth Army kept a close watch on the river's gradually receding water levels right up to the time of invasion, reporting to his superiors each day in the late afternoon:

8.6.41:
Bug water level falling slowly.

9.6.41:
Bug water level falling slowly.

10.6.41:
Bug water level continues to fall.

11.6.41:
Bug water level continues to retreat.

13.6.41:
Bug water level has fallen approximately 10 cm since yesterday.

15.6.41:
Bug water level has fallen approximately 15 cm.

18.6.41:
Troop movements continue as scheduled ... Weather: very warm, dry. Roads: continue to be heavily used, but traversable throughout. Bug has fallen approximately 5 cm. Banks in parts extremely marshy.

19.6.41:
Troop movements as scheduled ... Battery 710 of the railway artillery has arrived at 7 AK. All *Heerestruppen* have arrived at Fourth Army. Weather: very humid, dry. Bug has fallen by 7 cm.

21.6.41:
Bug has fallen by 4 cm. Weather: warm and sunny. Road condition: unaltered, very dusty.[173]

Of particular note here is the entry for 18 June, which indicates that – even at this late date – the banks of the Bug were still very marshy in areas. The commander of German 47 Panzer Corps, Lt.-Gen. Joachim Lemelsen, had also kept a nervous eye on the river. In his sector of operations the riverbanks were still strongly flooded on 10 June – a situation which only added to the unbearable stress of waiting for *Barbarossa* to begin. By 17 June, however, the flooding had largely subsided, much to the general's relief. Excerpts from his personal diary for these two days – insightful on so many levels – are quoted below:

10.6.41:

The past days have been very full with work and many worries and troubles. The closer the appointed time approaches, the more nervous everybody becomes. Now all of a sudden, by order of the Commander-in-Chief of the Army in our sector, the infantry of a 7th wave division is to attack instead of our riflemen! Overturning everything again, now, so close before the appointed time? Impossible!

Very heated exchange with Guderian yesterday in Warsaw. I wish it had already started, this period of suspense is terrible.

The day before yesterday, I was at the front of the sector in extreme heat, a lot of dust, and even more mosquitoes. The Bug is still carrying a lot of water, long stretches are still flooded. The Russian is feverishly fortifying his position; new wire obstacles, anti-tank ditches, and bunkers. It is going to be a very difficult attack. The main thing is that the Bug continues to fall to its normal water level; then we'll do it alright!

The population here is shocking, only Polaks and Jews, and so dirty, miserable, and inferior, it would make you shudder; they now get only 65 grams of bread per person each day, which is, however, enough to starve; it is truly astonishing that people live on that, or better put, can decay on that.

17.6.41:

Yesterday I was at the front of our sector again. The Russian is working feverishly on constructing anti-tank ditches, and if he now has another five days' time, he'll prepare all sorts of other lousy tricks. The Bug, thank God, has fallen further, so that this concern is now eliminated.

Today, the command post of the corps headquarters is being moved forward; I will drive on with the chief of staff and Ia in the early morning, there is still too much to do here. *Generaloberst* Guderian just came by, it's his birthday today and so I had the opportunity of giving him my best wishes; he can, when he is in a good mood, be dreadfully nice and good, but if he gets a rush of blood to the head, then it's all over! You have to know him. I admire him a lot even so, because he is a total soldier.[174]

While the precious time lost was largely unavoidable because of the late spring thaw, the Balkan campaign still exacted a heavy toll on German preparations for *Barbarossa*. As historian David Stahel recently observed:

From the divisions committed to action in Yugoslavia, two-thirds were simply replaced in the line by OKH reserves and all combat divisions were on route back to the eastern border by the end of May. The forces committed to Greece, however, were a different matter. Combat losses were slight yet, as would soon be the case in *Barbarossa*, the long distances and inhospitable terrain took a much greater toll on the German panzers and motorized transports. As a result, these divisions had to make the long journey back to Germany to receive thorough overhauls and partial re-equipping. It proved a time-consuming process and meant that the 2 PD and 5 PD, as well as the 60 ID (mot.), only arrived on the eastern front well after the initial attack. The two panzer divisions were then held in the OKH reserve and did not see action until October 1941. The delay in returning motorized units to service proved an important setback given the brief window of opportunity for the success of *Barbarossa*. Compounding this was the loss of the entire Twelfth Army, which was needed to provide occupation forces and coastal defense in southeastern Europe. This complicated the already difficult task of Army Group South, which made the slowest progress of the three army groups in the opening weeks of *Barbarossa* … The Balkan campaign placed yet another drain on Germany's eroding military resources and contributed in no small measure to the mounting over-extension of the *Wehrmacht*.[175]

2.7.3: Airborne Operations in Crete

The German armed forces had one more distraction to deal with before unleashing war against Russia. The island of Crete, in the eastern Mediterranean, had been occupied by the British on 31 October 1940.[176] Possession of the island provided the Royal Navy with excellent harbors from which to threaten the Axis southeastern flank. Of even greater concern to the Germans was the fact that, from Crete, the Ploesti oil fields in Romania, which were so vital to the Reich's war effort, were within range of British bombers. Which was why Hitler decided to take the island. On 25 April, he issued "Fuehrer Directive" No. 28, code-named Operation "Mercury" ("*Merkur*"), for an airborne assault on Crete.[177]

Most of the 35,000-strong British, Commonwealth and Greek garrison had just escaped from Greece. It was, for the most part, a poorly integrated and heterogeneous force, lightly armed with little in the way of transport, artillery, and signal equipment. As of 1 May, air support – if that is the proper term – comprised a handful of Hawker Hurricanes and obsolete biplane Gladiators, all of which were to be withdrawn before the Germans arrived. The Allies, however, did have one advantage: They knew the Germans were coming. Unbeknownst to the Germans, British "ULTRA" intelligence – derived from the interception and decryption of *Wehrmacht* wireless messages encoded by their "Enigma" ciphering machine – had, in good time, revealed the details of the German plan of operation.[178]

The German offensive – the "first purposeful parachute operation in history"[179] – began on 20 May 1941. Spilling out of Junkers Ju 52 transports in groups of twelve – their parachutes opened by static line – or landing by glider, the German assault force was met by withering Allied fire. Losses sustained by the parachute battalions around Maleme airfield in the opening hours of 20 May were appalling. In fact, on the basis of the first day's operations, it appeared as if *Merkur* might end in failure, for the invaders had been unable to seize a landing strip and the survivors found themselves isolated and under intense enemy pressure. To their shock and surprise, they were also put upon by Cretan civilians, including women and children, armed with any weapons they could muster, including ancient flintlock rifles (captured from the Turks a hundred years ago), axes, even spades. Crete's thriving olive groves were soon blanketed by hundreds of dead German paratroopers.[180]

The German invasion force, however, exploiting poor Allied leadership and coordination around Maleme airfield, was soon able to capture the air base and fly in reinforcements, while air superiority gave the paratroopers vital support and prevented the Royal Navy from making its full impact felt. By 26 May, the Allied position had become untenable; the next day, permission was granted the garrison to evacuate the island. By 1 June, the Royal Navy had taken 18,000 troops off the island, despite suffering horrific losses from *Luftwaffe* air attack; thousands more were forced to remain behind, falling prisoner to the Germans.[181]

The *Wehrmacht* had garnered another great victory, yet this time the cost had been prohibitive. German losses embraced 2071 dead, 2594 wounded, and 1888 missing – more than a quarter of the total attacking force of about 22,000 men. Of the 500 transport aircraft, fully 146 were written off as a total loss, while some 150 more were damaged. Because of the frightful losses, Hitler would never again accede to a major airborne operation.[182]

One can only imagine what operational or tactical benefits German forces in Russia might have derived from the successful employment of airborne troops at critical junctures in the campaign. This, however, was not to be. The ability of the German Army in the east to re-supply its forces by air – a mission which would assume a vital significance in the fall and winter of 1941/42 – was also hampered by the losses of transport aircraft incurred during the 10-day battle for Crete.

Before the start of Operation "Typhoon," the German assault on Moscow in the autumn of 1941, Panzer General Walther K. Nehring, Commander, 18 Panzer Division, had created an air landing company (*Luftlandekompanie*) out of volunteers. Their mission was to be to seize an important road junction near Tula – a large city and armaments center more than 150 kilometers due south of Moscow – from the air and hold it until relieved by the division's armor:

> [The company] was not used. This would have been the task of the *Luftwaffe*, but it was not in a condition to do this. In his operational studies during his years with the General Staff in Berlin, Nehring had worked time and again on the collaboration between panzer troops and parachutists. Now, so he thought, the hour should have arrived for that. But there were no parachutists in the east, they had been severely smashed in Crete.
>
> Tula was to be rigorously defended. Guderian's *Panzerarmee* was unable to capture it.[183]

ENDNOTES

1 G. Scheuer (Hg.), *Briefe aus Russland. Feldpostbriefe des Gefreiten Alois Scheuer 1941-1942*, 10.

2 H.-J. Dismer, *Artillerie-Offizier im Zweiten Weltkrieg*, 41.

3 *Tagebuch* Haape, 1.5.41.

4 F. Halder, *Hitler as War Lord*, 38-39.

5 Jodl's assertion is largely negated by the facts, for a large majority of Hitler's generals supported the Russian campaign, or at least stayed silent about it. As Ian Kershaw writes, "Whatever the misgivings of some generals about the venture, Hitler's decision was neither opposed nor contested in the military leadership." I. Kershaw, *Fateful Choices*, 69.

6 As we will see, the still widely held belief that *Barbarossa* was delayed – perhaps fatally so – by the Balkan campaign is a myth.

7 P. E. Schramm, *Hitler als militaerischer Fuehrer*, 152-53.

8 I. Kershaw, *Fateful Choices*, 70.

9 G. L. Weinberg, *A World at Arms*, 187-88.

10 Specifically, the Russians were demanding, *inter alia* – as a condition for joining the Tripartite Pact – the right to conclude a mutual assistance pact with Bulgaria, which would allow the Soviet Union to set up a base for land and naval forces within range of the Bosporus and the Dardanelles. Moreover, the Russians had already taken diplomatic steps to keep Bulgaria out of the Axis camp. For Hitler, observed Luttichau, "The Russian moves in Bulgaria seem to have been the last straw." C. von Luttichau, *Road to Moscow*, I:50-51.

11 P. Johnson, *Modern Times*, 375.

12 See, for example, A. Hillgruber, "*Der Faktor Amerika in Hitlers Strategie 1938-1941*," in: A. Hillgruber, *Deutsche Grossmacht- und Weltpolitik*, 197-222.

13 In December 1940, Germany, her Axis allies and the occupied territories possessed but 4.1 percent of the world's oil refining capacity. This compared to 21.5 percent for the Allies and fully 73 percent for the neutral powers, which then included the United States and Soviet Russia. R. L. DiNardo, *Germany's Panzer Arm*, 134.

14 It should also be remembered that, after *Barbarossa* began, neither the Americans nor the British expected the Soviet Union to survive for more than a few months. For example, immediately after the war in Russia began, U.S. Secretary of War, Henry Stimson, wrote a memorandum to Roosevelt observing that, "Germany will be thoroughly occupied in beating Russia for a minimum of one month and a possible maximum of three months." R. Kirchubel, "*Operation Barbarossa and the American Controversy over Aid to the Soviet Union*," 8.

15   As noted, in December 1940 Hitler had told Jodl that Germany must solve all her "continental European problems" by the end of 1941, since America would be ready to enter the war in 1942. P. E. Schramm (Hg.), *Kriegstagebuch des OKW*, Bd. I, 996.

16   As explained by Andreas Hillgruber: "The only remaining solution … in [Hitler's] view was thus: destruction of the Soviet Union as a basic precondition for the decisive turn of the war overall in his favor and for the achievement of his war objectives in the east, as well as – then building on this – those against the western powers. Hitler staked everything on that one card: that a 'Blitzkrieg' in the east would lead to complete victory in only a few weeks and that the German Navy could then turn successfully against the west. Accordingly, planning in the winter of 1940/41 went far beyond … preparations for the military defeat of the Soviet Union. The elimination of the Red Army within four months after the start of the campaign at the latest was only the core of what could be called a 'world blitzkrieg' plan that aimed for the Tripartite Pact powers to take possession of the entire 'eastern hemisphere' of Europe-Asia-Africa, or at any rate all strategically important areas in it, within half a year in order to isolate the USA on the American twin continent." A. Hillgruber, *Der Zweite Weltkrieg*, 48.

17   M. van Creveld, *Supplying War*, 180.

18   Halder was away on leave from 25 December 1940 to 15 January 1941. C. Burdick & H.-A. Jacobsen (eds.), *The Halder Diary 1939-1942*, 310.

19   This decision was enshrined in Directive No. 22, Operation "Sunflower" (*Sonnenblume*), sent to the services on 11 January 1941. C. von Luttichau, *Road to Moscow*, III:2.

20   J. Wright, *Germany and Origins of Second World War*, 174-75.

21   P. E. Schramm (Hg.), *Kriegstagebuch des OKW*, Bd. I, 258.

22   Ibid., 258.

23   Ibid., 258.

24   C. von Luttichau, *Road to Moscow*, III:9.

25   D. Stahel, *And the World held its Breath*, 56.

26   C. Burdick & H.-A. Jacobsen (eds.), *The Halder Diary 1939-1942*, 314-15.

27   *GSWW*, Vol. IV, 285. The new chief of operations at OKH, Colonel Adolf Heusinger, played a major role in the preparation of the deployment directive. Recalled a former colleague: "It was astounding to observe how, after just a few hours in the quiet of his office, which he kept closed, the picture of the deployment took shape on his 1:1,000,000 scale maps." *Adolf Heusinger* (Bundesministerium der Verteidigung (Hg.)), 109.

28   C. von Luttichau, *Road to Moscow*, III:13-14.

29   K. Gerbet (ed.), *GFM Fedor von Bock, The War Diary*, 197.

30   D. Stahel, *And the World held its Breath*, 57-58.

31   OKH Genst. d. H. Op.Abt. (1), Nr. 051/41 g.K., *Aufmarschanweisung OKH vom 31.1.1941 "Barbarossa,"* in: *Generaloberst Halder Kriegstagebuch*, Bd. II, H.-A. Jacobsen (Hg.), 464.

32   C. von Luttichau, *Road to Moscow*, III:14-19.

33   C. von Luttichau, III:20-24; OKH Genst. d. H. Op.Abt. (1), Nr. 051/41 g.K., *Aufmarschanweisung OKH vom 31.1.1941 "Barbarossa,"* in: *Generaloberst Halder Kriegstagebuch*, Bd. II, H.-A. Jacobsen (Hg.), 464-68.

34   D. Stahel, *And the World held its Breath*, 59.

35   Ibid., 59-60.

36   These were the *Deutsche Reichsbahn Gesellschaft* (DRG, or DR) and the *Generaldirektion der Ostbahn*, or "*Gedob.*" The DR was, above all, a civilian or commercial organization, which supported the requirements of the *Wehrmacht* as ordered to do so. In war time, the DR adhered to military regulations and was placed under the direction of the German Army General Staff's Transportation Division. During the Polish campaign, the DR had been able to meet all supply and movement needs of the German Army, although the Polish armed forces had managed to disrupt large sections of the railway network as they retreated eastward. Shortly after the Polish campaign had ended, on 26 October 1939, the "*Gedob*" was established with its headquarters in Warsaw. This was a separate entity from the *Reichsbahn* and was responsible for administration of the railways in occupied Poland. "*Deutsche Reichsbahn,*" at: www.feldgrau.com.

37   As noted, the Army High Command, in general, referred to the planned invasion of Russia as "Otto" prior to promulgation of the *Barbarossa* directive in December 1940.

38   In his study of German railway operations in the eastern campaign, Hans Pottgiesser stated that rail deployment of the *Ostheer*, its equipment and supplies, took a total of 11,784 trains. (See, H. Pottgiesser, *Die Deutsche Reichsbahn im Ostfeldzug*, 21-24.) According to Alfred Philippi and Ferdinand Heim, the immense operation embraced fully 17,000 trains – a figure also cited by Charles von Luttichau, along with a total of 200,000 railcars. (A. Philippi & F. Heim, *Der Feldzug gegen Sowjetrussland*, 52; C. von Luttichau, *Road to Moscow*, IV:43.) According to yet another source, some 144 trains – traveling at an average speed of 24 km/h – headed eastward each day as part of the buildup. K.-R. Woche, *Zwischen Pflicht und Gewissen*, 97.

39   Six primary rail arteries were to be used for these movements. K.-R. Woche, *Zwischen Pflicht und Gewissen*, 97.

40   The transport of an infantry division normally required about 70 trains; that of a tank division about 90 to 100 trains. Ibid., 97.

41   C. von Luttichau, *Road to Moscow*, III:28-29.

42   Ibid., III:29-30.

43   C. von Luttichau, *Road to Moscow*, IV:34; H.-A. Jacobsen, *Der Zweite Weltkrieg in Chronik*, 35.

44   C. von Luttichau, *Road to Moscow*, IV:33; A. Philippi & F. Heim, *Der Feldzug gegen Sowjetrussland*, 52. While

the sources differ, it appears that about 60 infantry divisions had been transported to the eastern front by 20 May 1941.

45   W. Haupt, *Die deutschen Infanterie-Divisionen*, 26-27.

46   H. Grossmann, *Gesichichte der 6. Infanterie-Division*, 31-33.

47   W. Buddenbohm, *Das Leben des Soldaten Wilhelm Buddenbohm*, 39. In early April 1941, the division advanced right up to the German-Russian border, the movements taking place only at night. Ibid., 40.

48   H.-J. Dismer, *Artillerie-Offizier im Zweiten Weltkrieg*, 39-40.

49   In early May 1941, Major Meier-Welcker, a staff officer at Fourth Army headquarters in Warsaw, was transferred to 251 ID in East Prussia. After many months in Poland, the major found the change of scene, especially the hours spent horseback riding across the undulating and peaceful countryside, a time of delightful recuperation. On 24 May he wrote: "The war seems so distant from here." H. Meier-Welcker, *Aufzeichnungen*, 116.

50   S. Knappe, *Soldat*, 197.

51   E.-M. Rhein, *Das Infanterie-Regiment 18*, 43. My deepest gratitude to Herr Rhein for presenting me with his last extra copy of his fine book in May 2005.

52   K.-G. Vierkorn, *Feldpostbrief*, 20.3.41 (unpublished field post letter).

53   W. Meyer-Detring, *137. Infanterie-Division im Mittelabschnitt der Ostfront*, 14.

54   H. Hoth, *Panzer-Operationen*, 38.

55   P. E. Schramm (Hg.), *Kriegstagebuch des OKW*, Bd. I, 297.

56   Ibid., 297.

57   P. E. Schramm (Hg.), *Kriegstagebuch des OKW*, Bd. I, 297-98; H. Hoth, *Panzer-Operationen*, 38; J. Loeffler, *Brauchitsch – Eine politische Biographie*, 228-29; D. Stahel, *And the World held its Breath*, 60-62.

58   P. E. Schramm (Hg.), *Kriegstagebuch des OKW*, Bd. I, 298-300.

59   C. von Luttichau, *Road to Moscow*, III:31.

60   D. Stahel, *And the World held its Breath*, 60; H. Guderian, *Achtung Panzer!*, 153.

61   After the campaign in the west of 1940, Hitler had ordered tank production increased to 800 or even 1000 units per month. However, when the Army Ordnance Office calculated that the cost of such an expansion effort would be about two billion marks and involve the employment of more than 100,000 skilled workers and specialists, Hitler dropped the idea. H. Guderian, *Panzer Leader*, 138-44.

62   C. von Luttichau, *Road to Moscow*, III:32.

63   A. Zamoyski, *Moscow 1812*, 105.

64   P. E. Schramm (Hg.), *Kriegstagebuch des OKW*, Bd. I, 371.

65   J. Foerster & E. Mawdsley, "*Hitler and Stalin in Perspective*," 66-67. This source, for the first time, offers historians a detailed look at – and analysis of – the notes made by General Hoth on this day at the Reich Chancellery.

66   Note: All quotations are gleaned from the notes of Halder or Hoth. In some cases, they most likely represent Hitler's exact words; in others, simply the two men's interpretations of what Hitler had to say that day.

67   Comments such as these, however vague and inaccurate, make clear that the Germans, at very least, had an "inkling" about the superior new Soviet models, the KV-1 and T-34.

68   C. Burdick & H.-A. Jacobsen (eds.), *The Halder Diary 1939-1942*, 345.

69   Ibid., 346.

70   Ibid., 346-47.

71   Wrote Hoth: "Once again, Hitler stressed the significance of seizing the Baltic region." H. Hoth, *Panzer-Operationen*, 39. In his diary, Field Marshal von Bock observed: "In the afternoon a talk with the *Fuehrer* over the planned Russian operation. The *Fuehrer* went on to comment that my armored groups in particular might become decisively important in the later course of an advance on Leningrad, in order to encircle and destroy the Russian forces fighting in the Baltic region." K. Gerbet (ed.) *GFM Fedor von Bock, The War Diary*, 208.

72   J. Foerster & E. Mawdsley, "*Hitler and Stalin in Perspective*," 70-75.

73   Ibid., 75-77.

74   *GSWW*, Vol. IV, 4-5.

75   See, for example, C. Hartmann, *Wehrmacht im Ostkrieg*.

76   Quoted in: "*Handlungsspielraeume im Vernichtungskrieg*," paper presented by David Wildermuth at the German Studies Association (GSA) Conference, Oct 07. Scharnhorst, a Hanoverian by birth, saw service in the Prussian Army.

77   BA-MA N 813, *Tagebuch* Muenschhausen, Okt. 41.

78   A. W. Turney, *Disaster at Moscow*, 5-6.

79   M. M. Boatner III, *Biographical Dictionary of World War II*, 49; K. Gerbet (ed.), *GFM Fedor von Bock, The War Diary*, 13.

80   K. Gerbet (ed.), *GFM Fedor von Bock, The War Diary*, 13-14.

81   K. Gerbet (ed.), *GFM Fedor von Bock, The War Diary*, 14-15; Fedor von Bock, at: http://www.lexikon-der-wehrmacht.

82   M. M. Boatner III, *Biographical Dictionary of World War II*, 49.

83   "*Das ganze Getriebe des Nationalsozialismus war ihm innerlich zuwider.*" F. von Schlabrendorff, *Offiziere gegen Hitler*, 57.

84   Fedor von Bock, at: http://www.lexikon-der-wehrmacht; K. Gerbet (ed.), *GFM Fedor von Bock, The War Diary*, 16.

85   S. W. Mitcham, Jr., *Hitler's Field Marshals*, 148.

86   M. M. Boatner III, *Biographical Dictionary of World War II*, 50.

87   Fedor von Bock, at: http://www.lexikon-der-wehrmacht; K. Gerbet (ed.), *GFM Fedor von Bock, The War Diary*, 19.

88   K. Schneider-Janessen, *Arzt im Krieg*, 55-56.

89   S. W. Mitcham Jr., *Hitler's Field Marshals*, 150-51.

90   *GSWW*, Vol. IV, 256.

91   According to the German quasi-official history of the *Barbarossa* campaign, the order was given on 12 September 1940. See, *GSWW*, Vol. IV, 256.

92   K. Gerbet (ed.), *GFM Fedor von Bock, The War Diary*, 188-89.

93   *GSWW*, Vol. IV, 257.

94   C. von Luttichau, *Road to Moscow*, IV:33-34; *GSWW*, Vol. IV, 315. The 34 divisions were distributed among three armies, all controlled by Army Group B.

95   K. Gerbet (ed.), *GFM Fedor von Bock, The War Diary*, 192. In mid-December 1940, Field Marshal von Kluge, C-in-C Fourth Army, would take over as Bock's acting replacement. Ibid., 195.

96   K. Gerbet (ed.), *GFM Fedor von Bock, The War Diary*, 196; F. von Schlabrendorff, *Offiziere gegen Hitler*, 58.

97   The words are Bock's interpretation of Hitler's remarks to him. K. Gerbet (ed.), *GFM Fedor von Bock, The War Diary*, 193.

98   Ibid., 193-94.

99   Ibid., 197-98.

100 In the fall of 1940, Fourth Army headquarters, as well as several corps headquarters, had also been transferred to the east. Ibid. 188.

101 OKH had ordered the transfer of Eighteenth Army headquarters to the east on 26 June 1940. The headquarters would be assigned to Army Group North before the start of the Russian campaign. *GSWW*, Vol. IV, 244.

102 "*Festungs-Stab Blaurock*." 9. Armee, at: http://www.lexikon-der-wehrmacht.

103 The source for the 1 April 1941 date is Peter Hoffmann, *History of the German Resistance*, 264. Other sources say the designation did not change until 22 June 1941. The OKW war diary, however, also refers to "Army Group Center" on 1 April 1941, whereas only weeks before it was still calling Bock's command Army Group B. P. E. Schramm (Hg.), *Kriegstagebuch des OKW*, Bd. I, 373.

104 Von Tresckow had joined the staff of Army Group B in December 1940; Greiffenberg did not arrive until May 1941. D. T. Zabecki, *World War II in Europe – An Encyclopedia*, 528; also, http://www.lexikon-der-wehrmacht.

105 S. J. Lewis, *Forgotten Legions*, 153, f.n. 25.

106 In March 1943, during a visit by Hitler to Army Group Center headquarters in Smolensk, Tresckow's adjutant, Fabian von Schlabrendorff, smuggled a time bomb, disguised as bottles of cognac, aboard the aircraft which was to carry Hitler back to Germany. The bomb, however, failed to detonate. Fortunately, Schlabrendorff was able to retrieve the bomb the next day and avoid detection. On 21 July 1944, the day after the failed "*Attentat*" on Hitler at his "Wolf's Lair" headquarters in East Prussia, Tresckow, deeply implicated in the plot, drove off into no-man's land on the eastern front and committed suicide. Schlabrendorff survived the war. For a definitive account of the resistance to Hitler see, Peter Hoffmann's *History of the German Resistance*. For the role of Army Group Center in the military resistance, see, F. von Schlabrendorff, *Offiziere gegen Hitler*; also, Philipp *Freiherr* von Boeselager, *Valkyrie*.

107 R. A. Hart, *Guderian*, 71; F. von Schlabrendorff, *Offiziere gegen Hitler*, 58-59. Schlabrendorff stated, however, that through such efforts at non-compliance, it was at least possible to limit the impact of the Commissar Order.

108 FMS P-052, H. von Greiffenberg, "*Combat in Forests and Swamps*," 5.

109 Internet site at: http://www.lexikon-der-wehrmacht.

110 K. Gerbet (ed.), *GFM Fedor von Bock, The War Diary*, 211. General von Salmuth had just been made commander of 30 Army Corps. In Bock's diary on 2 May 1941 is the following entry: "Halder asked me if I agreed with General von Greiffenberg as [von Salmuth's] successor; I asked for time to think it over. He was appointed without waiting for my answer." Ibid., 211.

111 Ibid., 198-223.

112 Unit designations have been slightly altered for sake of consistency with the overall narrative.

113 The tension between the two field marshals would continue after *Barbarossa* began. A month into the campaign, Bock wrote: "Kluge was present at the meeting. While I was outside he took the opportunity to complain to Brauchitsch about interference by me in his area of command! This claim is unfounded. Always, and now as well, I have scrupulously avoided any intermixing in Kluge's area of command, because of my awareness of his ego. But such was his eloquence that Brauchitsch fell for it and asked me to leave Kluge the necessary freedom. I replied that I was sorry if Brauchitsch was bothered with quarrels between generals at a serious time; but Kluge's action forced me to set things straight. I outlined in broad strokes Kluge's strange behavior from the time in Posen, his attacks on me then, his strange behavior on the telephone on the 19th [of July 1941] etc. I told Brauchitsch that it was very hard not to wound his vanity." K. Gerbet (ed.), *GFM Fedor von Bock, The War Diary*, 258-59.

114 Ibid., 198-217.

115 C. von Luttichau, IV:34-37.

116 W. Meyer-Detring, *137. Infanterie-Division im Mittelabschnitt der Ostfront*, 15-16.

117 Dr R. Gschoepf, *Mein Weg mit der 45. Inf.-Div.*, 197-99.

118 Ibid., 208.

119 H. Grossmann, *Geschichte der 6. Infanterie-Division*, 34-35; C. von Luttichau, *Road to Moscow*, IV:10.

120 The primitive nature of the Suwalki triangle, the complete absence of paved roads, also frustrated deployment of some of the heavy weapons and equipment of 3 Panzer Group and Ninth Army. See, Chapter 5, Section 5.1.

121 H. Grossmann, *Geschichte der 6. Infanterie-Division*, 36.

122 F. Belke, *Infanterist*, 23 (unpublished memoir).

123 *Tagebuch* Haape, 2.5.41.

124 S. Hart, et al., *The German Soldier in World War II*, 8.

125 Throughout World War II, in fact, the Germans sometimes trained with live ammunition during periods of rest, refitting or rebuilding. R. L. DiNardo, *Germany's Panzer Arm*, 62.

126 S. Hart, et al., *The German Soldier in World War II*, 8.

127 Eberhard Wardin was inducted into the Army in January 1941. Before he received any training in his chosen field – radio operator in a signal unit – he first received rigorous training as an infantryman (*"eine harte infanteristische Ausbildung"*). Ltr, E. Wardin to C. Luther, 26 Jun 04.

128 R. L. DiNardo, *Germany's Panzer Arm*, 60-61.

129 W. Murray, *"May 1940: Contingency and fragility of the German RMA,"* in: *Dynamics of Military Revolution*, M. Knox & W. Murray (eds.), 166.

130 R. L. DiNardo, *Germany's Panzer Arm*, 62.

131 The training regimen of 241 Infantry Regiment (106 ID) at the troop training grounds in Wahn, Germany, included marches of up to 90 kilometers a day (135 km in two days), along with field exercises and firing practice. These long marches usually ended with a parade – for example, in front of the Opera House in Cologne. A. Meyer, *Infanterie-Regiment 241*, 8.

132 FMS T-34, K. Allmendinger, et al., *"Terrain Factors in the Russian Campaign,"* 25-26.

133 Kluge fought on the western front during World War I, and was seriously wounded at Verdun in 1918. S. W. Mitcham, Jr., *Hitler's Field Marshals*, 295.

134 S J. Lewis, *Forgotten Legions*, 131-32.

135 H. Meier-Welcker, *Aufzeichnungen*, 108.

136 Ibid., 109.

137 G. Blumentritt, *"Moscow,"* in: *The Fatal Decisions*, W. Richardson & S. Freidin (eds.), 34-35.

138 R. Steiger, *Armour Tactics in the Second World War*, 10.

139 For example, the OKH deployment directive of 31 January 1941 indicated that the troops must be prepared for the Russians to use chemical weapons, and that such weapons might even be dropped from the air: *"Auf die Verwendung chemischer Kampfmittel auch aus der Luft durch den Gegner muss die Truppe sich einstellen."* OKH Genst. d. H. Op.Abt. (1), Nr. 050/41 g.K., *Aufmarschanweisung OKH vom 31.1.1941 "Barbarossa,"* in: *Generaloberst Halder Kriegstagebuch*, Bd. II, H.-A. Jacobsen (Hg.), 465.

140 In 1929, 43 parties had signed the "Third Geneva Convention," which was actually two conventions providing protections for military personnel who fell into enemy hands – one addressing the issue of POWs, the other care of the wounded. The United States, Germany, Italy, France and Great Britain all signed them; Japan and Soviet Union did not. The USSR, however, had signed the 1925 Geneva protocol prohibiting use of poison gas and bacteriological warfare. C. Bellamy, *Absolute War*, 20.

141 J. Huerter, *Hitlers Heerfuehrer*, 231. Conferencing with the staff of Fourth Army on 12 June 1941, Brauchitsch said: "The Russians will conduct the war by all possible means: Gas, spoiling of stores, and contamination of wells." Ibid., 231, f.n. 139.

142 In this context it is fascinating to note that new research by Bogdan Musial, gleaned from Soviet archives, reveals that the Soviet Union by the end of the 1920s had begun to massively rearm with the objective of waging an ideologically based war of aggression against the West. In 1930, the future Marshal of the Soviet Union, M. N. Tukhachevsky, outlined a plan for such a conflict which envisaged the deployment of some 50,000 tanks, 40,000 aircraft, and the extensive use of chemical warfare. See, B. Musial, *Kampfplatz Deutschland*, 9.

143 Dr E. Bunke, *Der Osten blieb unser Schicksal*, 191-93 (self-published manuscript).

144 See, FMS T-34, K. Allmendinger, et al., *"Terrain Factors in the Russian Campaign,"* 50-78.

145 H. Grossmann, *Geschichte der 6. Infanterie-Division*, 43.

146 H. Meier-Welcker, *Aufzeichnungen*, 113.

147 R. Law & C.W.H. Luther, *Rommel*, 44-45.

148 Ibid., 46.

149 Ibid., 47.

150 R. Law & C.W.H. Luther, *Rommel*, 47-48; M. Gilbert, *Second World War*, 149. The fortress of Tobruk, with its 25,000 man garrison, capitulated on 22 January 1941.

151 R. Law & C.W.H. Luther, *Rommel*, 48-52.

152 Ibid., 53-70.

153 As it was, Halder confided in his diary on 30 April 1941: *"GHq. troops*: Review of need to have all forces on hand for BARBAROSSA. The 10-cm guns and siege guns sent to Libya will be badly missed. Only one 10-cm battery is to leave, while developments are watched. In case Tobruk falls, remainder will not be needed." C. Burdick & H.-A. Jacobsen (eds.), *The Halder Diary 1939-1942*, 379.

154 D. Stahel, *And the World held its Breath*, 81-82. In mid-July 1941, several weeks after *Barbarossa* began, Hitler released 85 German and the available Czech tanks to the eastern front as replacements. Despite serious attrition from all causes, by the beginning of September 1941 only 137 replacement tanks had been

allocated to the east. At Hitler's direction, most tank production at this time was being held back to equip panzer divisions intended for future tasks following Russia's defeat. P. P. Battistelli, *Panzer Divisions*, 67.

155 Internet site at: http://www.history.army.mil; M. Gilbert, *Second World War*, 162.

156 Internet site at: http://www.history.army.mil; and, http://www.lexikon-der-wehrmacht.

157 J. Keegan, *Second World War*, 134, 150-51.

158 M. Gilbert, *Second World War*, 161; Internet site at: http://www.history.army.mil.

159 J. Keegan, *Second World War*, 151-52; M. Gilbert, *Second World War*, 166.

160 J. Keegan, *Second World War*, 151-54; M. Gilbert, *Second World War*, 166.

161 J. Keegan, *Second World War*, 154-58; M. Gilbert, *Second World War*, 170-75.

162 I. Kershaw, *Hitler 1936-45: Nemesis*, 366.

163 J. Keegan, *Second World War*, 160.

164 W. L. Shirer, *Rise and Fall of the Third Reich*, 829-30.

165 C. Bellamy, *Absolute War*, 100.

166 J. Keegan, *Second World War*, 174.

167 The *Barbarossa* Directive of 18 December 1940 had only indicated that all preparations for the attack were to be completed by mid-May 1941. At some point, 15 May 1941 was selected as the initial "X-Tag" for the invasion of Russia.

168 D. Stahel, *And the World held its Breath*, 96-97; K. Assmann, *Deutsche Schicksalsjahre*, 255-56.

169 J. Loeffler, *Brauchitsch – Eine politische Biographie*, 243.

170 H. Plocher, *The German Air Force Versus Russia, 1941*. USAF Historical Study No. 153, 37.

171 D. Stahel, *And the World held its Breath*, 96.

172 E. M. Howell, *Soviet Partisan Movement*, 2.

173 K. Mehner (Hg.), *Geheime Tagesberichte*, Bd. 3, 132-48.

174 BA-MA MSg 1/1147: *Tagebuch* Lemelsen, 10.6.41, 17.6.41.

175 D. Stahel, *And the World held its Breath*, 96-97.

176 J. Keegan, *Second World War*, 134.

177 Ibid., 161.

178 J. Keegan, *Second World War*, 163-64; I.C.B. Dear (ed.), *Oxford Companion to World War II*, 213-14.

179 J. Keegan, *Second World War*, 165.

180 J. Keegan, *Second World War*, 165-66; W. Murray, *Strategy for Defeat*, 76.

181 W. Murray, *Strategy for Defeat*, 76; I.C.B. Dear (ed.), *Oxford Companion to World War II*, 215; J. Keegan, *Second World War*, 171.

182 I. Kershaw, *Hitler 1936-45: Nemesis*, 367; W. Murray, *Strategy for Defeat*, 76.

183 W. Paul, *Panzer-General Nehring*, 121-22.

CHAPTER 3

The Adversaries I: The State of the Wehrmacht

"History is said to consist of reputations; if the reputation of an Army is a measure of its quality the German Army certainly stands second to none ... The high quality of the German Army has led to its being used as a measuring rod against which other, less successful, forces can be gauged." (Martin van Creveld)[1]

"When I meet an older man [in Germany] today, then I can't help asking him if he also took part in World War II. If he says yes, then I ask: 'And how did you survive the war?' Then I usually get the answer: 'I was wounded a few times!' I have never met a Landser who survived the war unscathed – and if he did, then he certainly wasn't an infantryman." (Marianne Miethe, survivor of Hitler's Third Reich)[2]

"We followed behind the panzer and panzer grenadier divisions, because we could not keep up with the tanks and motorized infantry ... This was blitzkrieg, but not as it had been in Poland and France, where the whole front advanced quickly. In Russia, the mechanized forces were like arrows that went out ahead of the rest of us." (Siegfried Knappe, German artillery officer in 87 ID)[3]

"Whatever their images, Hitler's panzers are best described and understood as a technocracy – not merely in terms of material but of mentality. Their history during World War II is of being set tasks beyond their means, arguably more so than any other element of the Wehrmacht." (Dennis Showalter)[4]

3.1: Force Structure of the Army

On mobilization for war in September 1939, the German field army had encompassed 106 divisions, of which six were armored and eight motorized.[5] The Army underwent further expansion in the winter and spring of 1939/40, increasing in size to 169 divisions, about 140 of which were committed to the campaign in the west.[6] After toying with the idea of reducing his ground forces to a "peacetime" army of 120 divisions, Hitler, now contemplating war with Russia, decided in the summer of 1940 to expand the Army to 180 divisions. This figure again underwent revision and, by June 1941, the German Army had burgeoned to approximately 208 divisions.[7] Its force structure on the eve of *Barbarossa* embraced 152 infantry,[8] 21 panzer, 15 motorized,[9] nine security, six mountain, four "light" divisions and one cavalry division, as well as several motorized brigades/regiments. Of these divisions about 150 were part of the buildup in the east (including four divisions deployed to Finland), 38 were stationed in the western theater, eight in Norway, seven in the Balkans, two in North Africa, and one in Denmark.[10] The personnel strength of the Army had risen since September 1939 from 3,750,000 men to about 5,000,000, while the *Luftwaffe* numbered 1,700,000, the *Kriegsmarine* 400,000 and the *Waffen*-SS 150,000 men.[11]

The ca. 150 divisions earmarked for the Russian campaign signified almost 75 percent of the German Army's total force structure in June 1941; yet in terms of combat capability, the percentage was actually much higher: 19 of the 21 panzer and all 15 motorized divisions were part of the *Barbarossa* order of battle,[12] while nearly all *Heerestruppen* (formations controlled by the armies themselves and not organic to divisions or corps), including large amounts of heavy artillery, were earmarked for the east. Of those divisions *not* taking part in the eastern campaign, more than 30 had only recently been established and, in terms of training and equipment, were not ready for combat, while many of the divisions left behind in the west and the Balkans – among them some of 30 just noted – had been reduced to mere skeletons and were far from combat capable (*kampffaehig*).[13]

Despite its clearly formidable nature, the German Army of 1941 – and throughout the Second World War for that matter – possessed a force structure that was fundamentally unbalanced. As the above figures illustrate, the great majority of this Army was made up of a large unmechanized mass of "legacy" infantry divisions, marching on foot and dependent largely upon draft horses to move artillery, equipment, ammunition and supplies. Of the 208 total divisions, only 36 – a little more than 15 percent – were mobile formations (armored and motorized). The stark imbalance improves – albeit just a little – when one considers only the forces assembled for the Russian campaign: 34 mobile divisions out of 150, or less than 25 percent. The result of this "quirk" in the composition of the German Army was that it, in essence, was two separate armies – one relatively small, mobile and armored, capable of covering large areas quickly; the other large, slow, and cumbersome, and "proving not greatly more maneuverable than the Kaiser's army of 1914, or even that of Napoleon in 1812."[14] In the relatively compact theaters of war from September 1939 through the spring of 1941, this serious structural flaw had not significantly affected German ground operations; in the immense spaces of the east it would be a different matter entirely. In retrospect, one doubts whether "blitzkrieg" in Russia was even possible, given the paucity of mobile forces that made up the tip of the eastern army's spear.

Of course, neither Hitler nor anyone in his inner circle of military advisors would have entertained such doubts; they were much too preoccupied preparing for war to engage in introspection. Preparations in all areas through the spring of 1941 encompassed a large number of special initiatives to further sharpen the qualitative edge of the armies assembling in the east. These included: a.) establishment of panzer group headquarters to direct the mobile units in battle; b.) a major reorganization and expansion of the panzer divisions; c.) introduction of new – or upgrade of existing – weapons systems to boost the firepower of both infantry and mobile units; d.) improvements to combat engineers, signal and railroad troops; e.) creation of additional Flak units to protect the troops from air attack; f.) improvements in logistical support (including a significant increase in truck transport for moving food, fuel, ammunition and other supplies); and, g.) development of a new ensemble of winter clothing based on the experiences of the Finns in their winter war with Russia in 1939/40.[15]

Yet it would be false to imply that Germany's political and military leadership actually did "due diligence" in their preparations for the eastern campaign, for it is now apparent they did not – despite the unprecedented scope of the challenge presented by Operation *Barbarossa*. It is astounding to realize that Germany's overall armaments production (weapons and ammunition) in the second year of the war hardly increased at all, whereas the Soviet Union and Great Britain almost doubled their armaments production and the United States tripled theirs. Moreover, increases in production which were achieved were largely due to draconian cutbacks in the output of ammunition – cutbacks which would affect German operations in the east as early as August 1941 and seriously so in the fall and winter of 1941/42.[16] Yet even in areas where production increases were sought, such as in tanks, the gains were mostly unimpressive. As noted in Chapter I, average tank production for 1940 was less than 200 per month (all types), while in the first quarter of 1941 only 700 more left the factories.[17]

There were many reasons for these anemic production figures, among them the habitual shortages of manpower,[18] raw materials and specialized machine tools, as well as the hopelessly Byzantine nature of the Nazi regime, with its systemic inefficiencies, lack of coherent planning, corruption and stifling rivalries. Yet the underlying reason may well have been simply the conviction among the military leadership that the Russian campaign could be waged successfully with the forces and stockpiles of weapons and ammunition already on hand; thus, "additional production efforts were regarded as superfluous and, in view of the short time available, also pointless."[19] In fact, "at no time was a maximum effort even considered – an effort commensurate with the enemy's potential – because the German leadership assumed that available forces were sufficient to smash the Soviet military potential within a few weeks." As General Jodl argued, the operations in the east could be "easily conducted" with existing forces and weapons, thus no special exertions were required.[20]

If armaments production was adversely affected by such insouciance at the top levels of command, it was also undermined by the incoherent armament policies pursued since the defeat of France, a major feature of which was a shift away from production for the Army in favor of the *Luftwaffe* and the Navy. On 11 June 1941, barely a fortnight before the start of *Barbarossa*, Hitler signed Directive No. 32, submitted to him by OKW, and which began with the conceit: "*After the destruction of the Soviet Armed Forces*, Germany and Italy will be military masters of the European continent ..." It then went on to "formally direct the main industrial effort toward the [*Luftwaffe*] and the Navy," a decision which went unchallenged by Hitler and OKH.[21]

Even from this cursory analysis it is apparent that, in the critical period between July 1940 and June 1941, neither Hitler nor his military staffs were prepared to assign to their impending eastern campaign – the burden of which was to be carried by the Army – the priority it deserved. As Heinz Magenheimer has observed:

> The leadership was clearly not prepared to assign top priority to the Army, despite its enormous requirements in arms and equipment for "Operation *Barbarossa*." The acceptance of such a high risk – in the short time-span until May 1941 it was already impossible to equip the Army to the desired extent – may be explained both by the confidence inspired by the results achieved so far, and by an underestimation of the enemy. This again underlines the fact that the war against the Western powers was the real issue and the campaign against the Soviet Union was only intended to bring about a preliminary decision. It shows, too, that from the beginning of hostilities in 1939, the Supreme Command did not have an all-encompassing war plan which could have served as the basis for a well-conceived and well-founded armaments program ...
>
> Despite various improvisations, arms and munitions supply of the Army did not reach the originally planned figures. On 1 April 1941, the day set as the deadline, there were supply gaps of up to 35 per cent in the most important categories of weapons. In artillery alone, the paradoxical situation arose that in June 1941 the eastern army could only deploy 7184 guns of all calibers, whereas during the campaign in the west in 1940 there had been 7378 guns available on a considerably narrower front.
>
> Even if in certain sectors the Army was expanded and improved in quality, mainly by utilizing weapons captured so far, it is still true to say that the eastern army in June 1941 was only slightly stronger and larger than the western army had been in the spring of 1940. The equipment of the eastern army verged on

a condition that has been described as a "patchwork quilt." This unsatisfactory situation can be explained by the fact that the *Luftwaffe* was not required to accept any reduction in its arms program in favor of the Army, and only trailed the Army by 10 percent in its assignment of labor …

It is clear that during the summer and autumn of 1940 armaments control did not follow any overall long-term plan, but was more a short-term improvisation designed to serve several strategic objectives. Furthermore, the confrontation with the Soviet Union did not lead to any clear concentration of arms on the Army in order to provide it with the power that might have brought about a rapid victory. This leads to the conclusion that the campaign against the Soviet Union did not occupy the central position – neither in overall planning, nor in armaments production – that it merited, given the requirements it demanded of the *Wehrmacht*. The campaign in the east was seen merely as an intermediate, albeit important, step designed to create the conditions for the "final battle" in the west.[22]

The outcome of such myopia (and hubris) was that the German *Ostheer* thrust across the German-Soviet frontier on 22 June 1941 with "alarming shortfalls" in armor-piercing weapons, field artillery, and infantry field pieces – seriously impairing the firepower of the infantry. Some 84 infantry divisions – and several motorized infantry divisions as well – were equipped with all types foreign vehicles (mainly of French origin), while captured weapons were used to partially outfit the anti-tank units. The armored forces went into combat with hundreds of obsolete tanks, as well as large numbers of armored fighting vehicles of Czech origin. While these and other types of foreign equipment were by no means necessarily inferior to German standards, they added to the bewildering multiplicity of types[23] in the German Army, complicating already existing challenges in the areas of ammunition, spare parts and maintenance. Were it not for the use of captured material, however, it would scarcely have been possible to equip the expanded German Army of 1941 for Hitler's war in the east. Indeed, in the summer of 1940, the OKH had recognized that captured stocks of weapons, vehicles and other equipment were a "vital prerequisite" for the deployment of the eastern army.[24]

As outlined below, Germany's military leadership made significant qualitative improvements to their armed forces in the year separating the victory in the west from the beginning of *Barbarossa*. Nevertheless, the inescapable conclusion is that the order of battle assembled for war against Russia was not much more imposing than that committed to the campaign in the west in 1940, while the "patchwork quilt" of weapons, vehicles and equipment collected for the Russian campaign suggests that "Hitler's eastern army resembled a pieced-together, mismatched construction – not the imposing, purpose-built, uniformly-equipped war machine often portrayed in the immediate post-war literature."[25] Again, the proximate cause for what, in hindsight, seems scarcely comprehensible is a German military culture which – after almost two years of unbroken victories – had abandoned its professional bearings and, inexplicably, exhibited too little curiosity and concern about its future opponent in the east. To sharpen the point: The German generals' approach to *Barbarossa* reminds us "why war must be carefully planned and thoroughly researched prior to opening the latches that secure Hell's gates."[26]

3.2: The Marching Infantry

To again underscore the point: The foot infantry, depending largely on horse-drawn transport, still dominated the German force structure of 1941, comprising almost 75 percent of its 200+ divisions. Despite the "headlines" grabbed by the panzer divisions, it was the infantry that, just as in 1914/18, shouldered the primary burden on the battlefield in all theaters. The average infantryman on the eastern front lasted only a matter of weeks before being wounded or killed. Many were wounded repeatedly, only to return time and again to their units, until finally killed or taken prisoner. Yet the German infantry:

> fought with impressive tenacity and effectiveness throughout World War II, even after their units had sustained extreme losses. Statistical analyses have concluded that German troops typically inflicted 50 percent greater casualties on their opponents than they suffered in return, regardless of whether they were attacking or defending, even in the face of overwhelming Allied numerical advantages and air superiority later in the war. One of the most basic elements of this phenomenal military fighting power was unit cohesion: the ability of German soldiers to stick together and to continue operating as an integrated team despite devastating losses, long after the point where other forces would have dissolved into a mass of individuals driven by panic and the mere instinct of self-preservation. German soldiers also showed a remarkable capacity to regroup and form *ad hoc* battlegroups composed of stragglers and survivors of various units.[27]

During World War II, the German armed forces organized, trained, equipped and sent into battle 389 infantry divisions.[28] According to the German practice, these divisions were established in "waves" (*Welle*), with no fewer than 35 waves created throughout the war. As a rule, each wave evinced minor differences in armaments and equipment, while organization tended to be more standard. At full strength in 1939, a "first wave" division with highest priority for materiel possessed more than 5000 horses but fewer than 600 trucks. The "haphazard process" of rearmament from 1933-39 had precluded any attempt to expand the German automobile industry sufficiently to motorize a mass army. The High Command had responded by creating for its marching infantry a family of state-of-the-art horse-drawn wagons, outfitted with such refinements as ball-bearing wheels and rubber tires. The only fully motorized elements in German infantry divisions were the anti-tank companies and battalions, for which it was imperative to move fast enough to counter enemy armor.[29]

The total strength of an infantry division in 1941 was about 17,000 men. The core of the division was its three infantry regiments, each comprising approximately 3000 men.[30] Each regiment, in turn, broke down into three battalions, each of four companies – three rifle companies and one machine gun company. The infantry regiments were also equipped with a company of light and medium infantry guns and an anti-tank (*Panzerjaeger*) company, providing regimental commanders with substantial organic firepower. Complementing the three infantry regiments in each infantry division's order of battle were an artillery regiment, an anti-tank battalion (with the same weapons as the regimental anti-tank companies, only more of them), a reconnaissance battalion, and a combat engineer battalion, as well as signal, medical, veterinary, administrative and supply services.

Standard weapons of the rifle company included the Mauser 98K bolt-action rifle, the standard German infantry weapon throughout the war; machine pistols (normally carried by NCOs and officers); machine guns (primarily the MG 34); light and medium mortars (50mm le.Gr.W. 36 and 81mm s.Gr.W. 34); and, of course, hand grenades. The building block of the rifle company was the squad, or *Gruppe*, a 10-man unit built around its light machine gun (le.MG 34). The squad leader (NCO), originally armed with a rifle had, by 1941, been equipped with a machine pistol (MP 40) that, with a practical rate of fire of 180 rounds per minute, signified a major boost in firepower.[31] The machine gun company (actually a heavy weapons unit and always the last numbered company in a battalion; hence the 4th, 8th and 12th companies, respectively, in the three infantry battalions) was outfitted with heavy machine guns (s.MG 34) and medium mortars, giving it a good mix of flat and high-angle weapons.[32]

The infantry gun company (always the 13th company in a regiment) consisted of six 75mm light (le.IG 18) and two 150mm medium guns (s.IG 33). The anti-tank company (the 14th company in each regiment) was outfitted primarily with 37mm anti-tank guns; yet because these guns had proven ineffective against heavier Allied armor in 1940 – and, thus, were now basically obsolete – a heavier 50mm anti-tank gun had been introduced; however, by June 1941, it was only beginning to reach the forces in the field in small quantities. As a result, some divisions were also given French 47mm anti-tank weapons as a stopgap measure. Yet none of the AT weapons available to the German infantry in 1941 proved effective against the heavier Soviet KV-1 and T-34 tanks. Infantry units were thus often forced to deploy their artillery well forward in a direct-fire role to halt enemy attacks, even though this sometimes led to a heavy loss of guns due to close range line-of-sight engagements.[33]

The artillery regiment – its soldiers with their red piping arm insignia – would play an indispensable role in the fighting of 1941. A German military publication in 1943 called the artillery the "backbone of the front" (*das Rueckgrat der Front*),[34] and indeed it was. During 1941/42 alone – despite habitual shortages of shells – the German artillery in Russia would expend more than 60,000,000 rounds[35] – preparing the way for the infantry in attack and shouldering much of the burden in defense. The standard artillery regiment comprised four battalions, each of three batteries, with each battery having four guns. The first three battalions were equipped with a total of 36 105mm light field howitzers (le.FH 18), while the fourth battery normally boasted 12 150mm medium field howitzers (s.FH 18), making for 48 pieces in all.[36] The artillery was horse drawn, the regiment possessing more than 2000 horses.[37]

Whatever the shortcomings of a 1941 German infantry division, its aggregate firepower was immense. The 251 ID, a division of the fourth wave mobilized in September 1939,[38] was part of Army Group Center's order of battle for Operation "Typhoon," the assault on Moscow in October 1941. Its arsenal of weapons – typical of a German infantry division for this period – included the following in June 1941:

12,558 bolt-action rifles (*Karabiner* 98K)
405 light machine guns (le.MG)
112 heavy machine guns (s.MG)
3060 pistols (*Pistolen* 08)
800 machine pistols (*Machinenpistolen*)
87 light mortars (le.Gr.W. 36)
54 medium mortars (s.Gr.W. 34)
67 37mm Pak
6 47mm Pak (French)
20 light infantry guns (le.IG 18)
6 medium infantry guns (s.IG 33)
36 light field howitzers (le.FH 18)
12 medium field howitzers (s.FH 18)[39]

The German infantry divisions earmarked for the east would also receive fire support from several new weapon systems now entering service with the Army in significant numbers (yet not organic to the infantry divisions themselves). These included the 20mm *Vierling* Flak; the 150mm *Nebelwerfer* 41 rocket projector; 280mm and 320mm ground-to-ground rockets; and the assault gun, or *Sturmgeschuetz*. The *Vierling* Flak was an anti-aircraft gun consisting of four 20mm cannon on a single mount; with a practical rate of fire of 800 rounds per minute, it was also a devastating weapon against ground targets. The *Nebelwerfer*, a six-barreled rocket launcher, hurled a high explosive shell more than 7000 yards, also with devastating effect. The 280mm and 320mm rocket launchers fired high explosive or incendiary rockets from wooden crates which could be mounted to the sides or rear of a half-track vehicle; the shock effect of a large quantity of these rockets arriving simultaneously on their target was truly horrific. The range of the weapon – which the troops had soon christened "*Stuka zu Fuss*" ("Stuka on foot") – was about 2000 meters.[40]

For the attack on Russia the Germans were to make the first large-scale use of a highly effective new weapon – the StuG III (*Sturmgeschuetz*) assault gun.[41] By June 1941, some 375 assault guns had been produced, 250 of which were committed to the eastern campaign in 11 battalions and five separate batteries.[42] The main armament of the StuG III was a short-barreled 75mm L24 gun mounted on the chassis of a Panzer III tank. Because the weapon system had no turret (the 75mm gun was built directly into the hull) it had a low silhouette, enhancing its survivability. The assault gun had been commissioned to provide close armor support to the infantry, while also performing an anti-tank role.[43] Those infantry divisions fortunate enough to be assigned a battery or company of assault guns would come to deeply appreciate the weapon, while the Russians would come to fear it. "The *Sturmartillerie* [assault gun] is our ultimate weapon [*letzte Waffe*]," wrote an artillery officer fighting in the El'nia salient (east of Smolensk) in a letter to his wife on 30 August 1941:

> They are tanks with a gun, only they are open on top and so they shoot with the aid of a scissors telescope! The armor plating is very good! I learned to appreciate this weapon during the infantry attacks – every battalion was allocated two assault guns, they would lead the way and the infantry would advance under their protection. They use shells that are good for combating and shelling tanks.[44]

3.3: Panzer & Motorized Divisions

If the infantry dominated in numbers, the panzer and motorized divisions were to dominate on the battlefield. Although the mobile units made up but a fraction of the eastern armies, it was upon the successful outcome of their deep envelopment and encirclement operations that the Germans pinned their hopes. From 1 April 1940 to 1 June 1941 the inventory of German armored fighting vehicles (AFVs) had climbed modestly – from 3387 (all models) to 5694 (all models).[45] The latter figure, broken down by AFV type, reveals the following:

    877 Pz I
    1157 Pz II
    187 Pz 35(t)
    754 Pz 38(t)
    1440 Pz III
    572 Pz IV
    330 Armored staff cars
    377 StuG III[46]

Of these AFVs, 3648 were deployed in the east on 22 June 1941:

    281 Pz I
    743 Pz II
    157 Pz 35(t)
    651 Pz 38(t)
    979 Pz III
    444 Pz IV
    143 Armored staff cars
    250 StuG III[47]

As David Stahel correctly observes, to accurately assess the nature of the war in the east, "one must first gain a rudimentary grounding in the technical means by which it would be fought."[48] Since the primary component of the operational concept of "blitzkrieg" was clearly the tank, the technical specifications of each model in the German inventory are briefly outlined below:

Panzer I: This vehicle was the lightest, and most lightly armed, of all German tank models in use in 1941. First introduced in 1934,[49] it was intended as an interim vehicle for rapid building and training of Germany's nascent tank arm. The Pz Kpfw I[50] weighed between five and six tons, was equipped with two 7.92mm machine guns and had an armor thickness of just 13 millimeters. It had first seen action in the Spanish Civil War and, thereafter, in the early campaigns in World War II. Yet even in Spain its deficiencies – armament and protection – had become apparent and, by 1941, the tank was clearly obsolete. Nevertheless, 281 of these tanks were assigned to the *Barbarossa* strike force.[51] Only 13 days into the campaign, Brig.-Gen. Ritter von Thoma, returning from an inspection tour of 3 Panzer Group, informed Chief of the Army General Staff Halder that the Pz I had become a "burden" to the troops; that it should be removed from active service in the east and used for protection of the home front, coastal regions, and as a training vehicle.[52]

Panzer II: Because the new medium tanks the German Army required in the mid-1930s were slow to develop and produce, the Pz II was introduced as another interim AFV. First issued in 1936, it had a three-man crew, a main armament of one 20mm L/55 gun and a 7.92 MG. Several variants of the tank – which had somewhat better armored protection and was slightly heavier than its predecessor – had been introduced by 1941. More than 700 of these tanks would see duty with the four panzer groups operating in Russia in 1941 – most of them assigned to the light tank companies. Like the Pz I, the Pz II was already out of date; yet together, these two models made up more than 1000 of the tanks (28 percent) in the eastern strike force.[53]

Panzer 35(t): Following the occupation of Czechoslovakia in 1939, the Army benefited from that country's arsenal of high-grade weapons and its impressive armaments industry. The Czech tank arm was particularly valuable, for it had produced vehicles clearly superior to the early German tanks. The heavier of the two Czech tank models was redesignated the Pz 35(t) by the Germans; it boasted 25mm armor plating, a 37mm gun as main armament, and two 7.92 MGs. Unfortunately, the tank's armor was riveted, not welded like German tanks, and the rivets had the disturbing tendency to pop out under the impact of a heavy shell, sending rivet shanks swirling through the inside of the tank as secondary projectiles.[54] By June 1941, the tank was in decline, and the only unit so equipped was 6 Panzer Division, which had all 157 of them.[55] In his eastern front memoir, a former commander of 6 PD, General Erhard Raus, described the difficulties that soon arose from deployment of the Pz 35(t):

> The most noteworthy characteristic of the 6 Panzer Division at the outset of the Russian campaign was the fact that the entire division contained the equivalent of only a single heavy panzer company. [The division's] 11 Panzer Regiment consisted of three battalions of four companies each. The predominant panzer model was the light PzKw 35t, an older vehicle of Czech manufacture that was no longer in production and whose frontal armor had a maximum thickness of only 25mm. Only the 4th Company of each battalion was provided with some PzKw IVs and a few PzKw IIIs. By contrast, the 1 Panzer Division boasted an entire battalion of heavy panzers. The higher numerical strength of 11 Panzer Regiment could not compensate for its technical deficiencies. From the outset, his awareness of this weakness all but forced Major General Franz Landgraf, the division commander,[56]

to forbid the commitment of all panzers en masse and instead to employ them in conjunction with our infantry battalions. Alone our PzKw 35ts would have been grossly inferior even to the Russian tanks and anti-tank weapons about which we were already aware.

These facts require special mention because they entailed different combat methods on our part from those utilized by other panzer divisions ... Moreover, because production of the PzKw 35t had been discontinued for some time, providing spare parts became increasingly difficult. Thus the number of serviceable tanks in the division sank steadily despite only small losses due to enemy activity.[57]

By mid-December 1941, 6 Panzer Division had lost every one of its tanks and had only 350 combat soldiers remaining.[58]

Panzer 38(t): This tank was the Czech follow-on design to its Pz 35(t). While lighter than its predecessor, it was eventually outfitted with thicker armor plate. The tank's main armament was also a 37mm gun, supported by two 7.92 MGs. After seizing the Czech stocks, the Germans adapted the tank to fit a four-man crew, adding a gun loader to the driver, radio operator and commander/gunner. The tank was extremely reliable mechanically, with its durable chassis also providing a base for later variants in design, among them the tank hunters (*Panzerjaeger*) Marder III and Hetzer. Indeed, the Pz 38(t) represented "the best of all the German light tanks at this time,"[59] and 651 of them were assigned to the *Barbarossa* order of battle, the lion's share going to General Hermann Hoth's 3 Panzer Group.[60] Yet for all its attributes, the tank was still a light tank, and on the eastern front it also failed when pitted against Soviet T-34s and KV-1s and the heavier caliber artillery of the Red Army. The tank's attrition rate was correspondingly high. Such losses, avers David Stahel,

> also underline the basic weakness of the German tank force invading the Soviet Union, upon which so much of the operational plan rested. To break this down more clearly, if one adds the totals of all light tanks deployed for *Barbarossa* and takes that as a percentage of the overall total it equals 50 percent, meaning that half of the German tanks gathered for the invasion of the Soviet Union were largely obsolete for that theater.[61]

Panzer III: The first experimental models of this medium tank – disguised as a "medium tractor" – were ordered by the German Army as early as 1934, with the first few being produced by 1937.[62] The Pz III was one of the two tanks (the other the Pz IV) specifically developed for the new armored units of the *Wehrmacht*. It was envisaged as *the* main battle tank – that is, the "anti-tank" tank – of the German mobile forces, and was to be outfitted with a high-velocity armor piercing shell. However, when it first appeared, its version of the 37mm gun proved less than adequate. The weapon system experienced other "teething" problems as well in its initial iterations and, following a complete redesign of the suspension system, the "E" model (*Ausfuehrung E*) of the Pz III went into series production in December 1938. Several more series were designed and manufactured over the next few years, with a new main armament – a more powerful 50mm L/42 gun – finally becoming standard in the "G" series, 600 of which were built between April 1940 and February 1941. This model of the Pz III also had two 7.92 MGs, an armor thickness of up to 37mm, and weighed about 20 tons. It was operated by a five-man crew.[63]

The final Pz III upgrade to be undertaken before the launch of *Barbarossa* was the "J" series, which began production in March 1941 and thickened the basic hull armor to 50mm. All told, nearly 1000 Pz IIIs were allocated to the eastern strike force; of these, the majority was equipped with the "upgunned" 50mm L/42 main armament, providing the tank forces with a major boost in firepower and, in fact, "bringing the first real backbone to the panzer divisions."[64]

It should be pointed out that Hitler, apparently, had wanted the Pz III upgraded with an even longer-barreled 50mm gun, which would have had a greater muzzle velocity. As Panzer General Guderian recalled:

> On the basis of the experience gained during the western campaign, Hitler ordered a tank production of 800 to 1000 units per month. However, the Army Ordnance Office reckoned that the cost of this program would be about two milliards [billions] of marks, and that it would involve the employment of 100,000 skilled workers and specialists. In view of these heavy expenses Hitler unfortunately agreed to the abandonment of this plan for the time being.
>
> Hitler also ordered that the 37mm gun in the Panzer III be replaced by a 50mm L60. In fact it was the 50mm L42 that was used, a gun, therefore, with a considerably shorter barrel. Hitler was apparently not immediately informed of this modification to his directive on the part of the Ordnance Office; when, in February of 1941, he learned that his instructions were not being carried out even though all the technical requirements were at hand, he became extremely angry and he never forgave the responsible officers of the Ordnance Office for this high-handed act. Years later he was to refer to it.[65]

Panzer IV: This model, the final one to take part in the invasion of Russia, had first entered production in 1936. All series manufactured prior to June 1941 ("A" through "F"), were outfitted with a short-barreled 75mm L24 main gun. Originally, the Pz IV had been conceived as a close support weapon and, perforce, as a complement to the Pz III main battle tank. However, its success in the Polish and French campaigns – and later against Allied and Soviet vehicles – soon led to its active use as an "anti-tank" tank as well. The final version to enter production before the start of *Barbarossa* was the "F" series (April 1941), with generally increased armored thickness for added protection. The tank weighed about 26 tons, was operated by a crew of five, and was equipped with two 7.92 MGs as secondary armament. Various models of the Pz IV would see combat through the end of the war; with a total production run of about 9000, the Pz IV would make up the backbone of the German armored force in World War II.[66] Nearly 450 Pz IVs were assigned to the *Barbarossa* order of battle.

3.4: Reorganization & Expansion of the Mobile Forces

Even before the end of the campaign in the west in 1940, the Army High Command had contemplated a major reorganization and expansion of the panzer and motorized divisions in the Army's force structure. The initial target figure of 24 panzer and 12 motorized divisions drafted in May 1940 had, by the middle of June, been reduced to the final figure of 20 panzer and 10 motorized divisions.[67] The new divisions – 10 tank and eight motorized divisions – were established in the fall of 1940 and spring of 1941; at the same time, the existing 10 panzer divisions were reorganized and partially re-equipped. In the course of this major undertaking, the OKH was guided by the experiences of the French campaign, while also seeking to make the organization of the panzer divisions more uniform – an intent only partially realized. Before the beginning of Operation *Barbarossa*, the plan was altered only by the creation of the 5 Light Division (motorized) in early 1941, which was intended as the blocking force (*Speerverband*) for North Africa; following its arrival in Libya, it was redesignated as 21 Panzer Division on 21 August 1941.[68]

Because of the low production figures for tanks in 1940/41, the only way to double the size of the panzer force was by greatly reducing the number of tanks in each division. As a result, each panzer division now had just a single panzer regiment (of two or three tank battalions), whereas in 1940 six of the 10 existing panzer divisions had possessed two tank regiments.[69] While this measure was partially offset by phasing out hundreds of obsolete Pz Is and Pz IIs, and re-equipping the panzer divisions with more medium Pz IIIs and Pz IVs, it still reduced them to the outer limit of the minimum number of tanks needed to operate effectively.[70] In fact, the *average* number of tanks in the panzer divisions plunged from 258 in 1940 to just 196 after the reorganization and expansion, while the *actual* number of tanks assigned to the divisions ranged from a mere 147 to 299.[71]

The contraction in the number of tanks was also ameliorated by allotting each panzer division a second motorized infantry regiment, while a motorcycle battalion (*Kradschuetzen-Bataillon*) was added to each division's table of organization. In addition to the partial change out in tank models, the panzer divisions were beneficiaries of several new weapons systems and capabilities; these included the introduction of 50mm AT guns into their *Panzerjaeger* units, small numbers of 20mm *Vierling* Flak, 280/320mm rocket launchers (*Stuka zu Fuss*), as well as upgrades to artillery, signal, combat engineer and supply units.[72]

The reorganization and expansion effort had not always proceeded smoothly, with shortages in motor vehicles creating serious bottlenecks which delayed equipping the divisions and adversely affected their training. To provide even tolerable levels of motorization, the Army was forced to turn to foreign materiel (mostly French) to fully outfit both the panzer and motorized units. Some units received their vehicles so late they barely had time to become acquainted with them before being sent into action in Russia, while the bewildering diversity in types of vehicles posed problems with spare parts and maintenance. The 17 Panzer Division alone – much to its dismay – was outfitted with some 240 different types of vehicles;[73] moreover, it did not receive its full complement of vehicles until late May 1941, only weeks before *Barbarossa* began. No matter – by mid-July 1941, 17 PD – "this brave division," as Guderian called it – had destroyed 502 Red Army tanks.[74]

While it is difficult to generalize about the 1941 panzer division's order of battle – given the lack of uniformity in numbers of tanks, for example – some basic observations can be made: The personnel strength ranged from roughly 13,000 to 16,000 officers, NCOs and men; they all wore the pink (*rosa*) piping first worn by their predecessors in the motor trucking battalions (*Kraftfahrtruppen*) of the former *Reichsheer*.[75] The "typical" panzer division possessed less than 300 tracked vehicles (of which just under 200 were tanks) as well as some 3000 wheeled vehicles; if arrayed in single file on a road, this massive armada would have stretched for 130 kilometers![76] The total firepower of a panzer division encompassed some 620 automatic weapons and 260 guns of all calibers (excluding 50mm and 81mm mortars).[77] The fighting core of the 1941 panzer division's tank forces was represented by the Pz 38(t) and Pz III, which together made up 1630 of the 3250 tanks[78] assigned to Operation *Barbarossa*. Yet while the order of battle included some 600 more Pz IIIs in comparison to 1940, the number of Pz IV medium tanks allocated for the attack on Russia (444) was barely 150 more than had been available for the campaign in the west. Moreover, more than 50 percent of the German tank force (Pz I, Pz II, Pz 35(t), Pz 38(t)) was outdated and thus ill-suited for the rigors of combat in the east. Even the medium tank models were, for the most part, no match for the Soviet T-34s and KV-1s, which enjoyed a pronounced qualitative edge over all types of German tanks.[79] One can readily conclude that, while much was accomplished to augment the firepower of the German tank fleet, in terms of both quantity and quality the results fell far short of what was required to successfully confront an adversary like the Soviet Union.

Order of Battle of a German Panzer Division
(June 1941)[80]

Division HQ with Map Section (2 le.MG)

Panzer Brigade Staff with,
– Signal Platoon, Light Tank Platoon (3 Pz III command tanks, 5 Pz II)

2 Panzer Battalions[81] each with,
– 1 HQ Company (2 Pz III command tanks, 5 Pz II)
– 2 Light Tank Companies (each with 17 Pz III, 5 Pz II)
– 1 Medium Tank Company (14 Pz IV, 5 Pz II)

2 Rifle Regiments (mot.), each with,
– HQ Company (Signal Platoon, Combat Engineer Platoon,
Motorcycle Platoon, 3 l.MG)
– Two Rifle Battalions each with,
3 Rifle Companies (each with 18 l.MG, 2 s.MG, 3 le.Gr.W.)
1 MG Company (8 s.MG, 6 s.Gr.W.)
1 Heavy Company (3 37mm Pak, 2 le.IG, 4 le. MG)
– 1 Infantry Gun Company (2 s.IG, 4. le.IG)

1 Motorcycle Battalion with,
– 3 Motorcycle Companies (weapons same as rifle battalions)
– 1 Motorcycle-MG Company (same as above)
– 1 Heavy Company (same as above)

1 Medium Infantry Gun Company (Self-propelled)
– Only for 1, 2, 5, 9 and 10 PDs (6 s.IG (SP))

1 Armored Reconnaissance Battalion (mot.) with,
– Staff and Signal Platoon (2 le.MG)
– 1 Armored Scout Company (10 KwK 20mm,[82] 25 le.MG)
– 1 Motorcycle Company (18 le.MG, 2 s.MG, 3 s.Gr.W.)
– 1 Heavy Company (same as in rifle battalions)
– 1 Reconnaissance Column (3 le.MG)

1 Artillery Regiment (mot.) with,
– Staff and Signal Platoon
– 2 Light Artillery Battalions each with,
3 Light Field Howitzer Batteries (each with 4 105mm le.FH, 2 le.MG)
– 1 Medium (*schwere*) Mixed Artillery Battalion with,
2 Medium Field Howitzer Batteries (each with 4 150mm s.FH, 2 le.MG)
1 100mm Gun Battery (4 100mm Cannon, 2 le.MG)

1 Anti-Tank Battalion[83] (mot.) with,
– Staff and Signal Platoon
– 3 Anti-Tank Companies (each with 8 37mm Pak, 3 50mm Pak, 6 le.MG)
– 1 Flak Company[84] (SP) (8 20mm Flak, 2 20mm *Vierling* Flak)

1 Armored Combat Engineer Battalion (mot.) with,
– 2 Light Combat Engineer Companies (each with 9 le.MG)
– 1 Armored Combat Engineer Company (Pz I,[85] 6 SPW[86] with 280/320 rocket launchers)
– 1 Bridging Column "B" (mot.)
– 1 Bridging Column "K" (mot.)
– 1 Light Combat Engineer Column (mot.)

1 Armored Signal Battalion (mot.) with,
– 1 Armored Telephone Company (2 le.MG)
– 1 Armored Radio Company (13 le.MG)
– 1 Light Armored Signal Column

1 Field Replacement Battalion

Supply & Rear Area Services including,
– Motor Vehicle Supply Columns
– 1 Supply Company (mot.)
– 3 Maintenance & Repair Companies (mot.)
– 2 Medical Companies
– 3 Ambulance Platoons
– 1 Bakery Company (mot.)
– 1 Butchery Company (mot.)
– Military Police (mot.)
– Field Post Service (mot.)[87]

At the end of this section a few observations about the expansion of the motorized divisions: The motorized infantry were all, originally, foot infantry, numbered in the normal sequence and trained and equipped as regular infantry of the line; as such, they wore the traditional white piping of the infantry service. The only difference to the line infantry – albeit a major one – was that the motorized troops were transported to and from the battlefield in trucks or, to a much lesser degree, in armored personnel carriers (APCs). In 1939 there were four motorized divisions (2, 13, 20 and 29)[88] assigned to the 14 Motorized Corps. Early in 1940, each of these divisions was reduced from three to two regiments, while the elite motorized "Greater Germany" (*Grossdeutschland*) Regiment was established from the ceremonial *Wachregiment Berlin*.[89]

By the spring of 1941, two motorized divisions – 2 ID (mot.) and 13 ID (mot.) – had been converted to panzer divisions, while eight foot infantry divisions – 3, 10, 14, 16, 18, 25, 36, 60 – had been reorganized as fully motorized formations, making for a total of 10 motorized infantry divisions in the regular German Army. Other motorized units included the *Lehr-Brigade* 900 (Instructional Brigade 900), the Infantry Regiment *Grossdeutschland*, and several *Waffen*-SS divisions, including the SS-*Leibstandarte* "Adolf Hitler."[90]

With only two regiments of truck-born troops, the motorized division deployed just six battalions of infantry (versus nine for a typical three-regiment foot infantry division). The artillery was towed by trucks or half-tracked prime movers, while the reconnaissance units were made mobile with motorcycles and armored cars. In 1942 a battalion of self-propelled guns or tanks was added to the division's order of battle, and APCs began to appear in greater numbers. However, in 1941, these formations were essentially infantry units with greater mobility.[91]

Following the attack on the Soviet Union, the motorized infantry divisions – despite their diminutive numbers – and the mounted infantry elements of the panzer divisions were immediately recognized for their great value and saw continuous action. In fact, the physical and psychological demands placed on them were "immense." As one soldier complained: "Motorized transport is only there to make certain we poor *Panzergrenadiers* are brought up against the enemy more often than our fellows in the infantry divisions … so that we have the dubious advantage of being in action more often."[92]

3.5: The German Air Force

"At last, a proper war!" remarked *Luftwaffe* Chief of Staff Hans Jeschonnek shortly before the start of the eastern campaign.[93] After the bitter failure of aerial operations over Great Britain, the *Luftwaffe* general was no doubt anticipating with some relief the impending war in the east, where his air forces could once again return to their primary mission of providing air support to German ground forces and, thus, help to replicate the stunning victories in the west of the previous year. Yet despite Jeschonnek's observation, a student of German air operations between September 1939 and the spring of 1941 might easily conclude that the *Luftwaffe* had indeed been fighting a "proper war" all along. Certainly in the sense that it had been engaged in costly and continuous combat for the entire 21-month period leading up to *Barbarossa*, in the process sustaining serious losses in both aircraft and aircrews, while the Army had sacrificed a much smaller portion of its forces and even experienced a relative hiatus in the fighting between July 1940 and April 1941.

From the very beginning of the Second World War, the attrition experienced by the *Luftwaffe* had taken a heavy toll: In September 1939, during the invasion of Poland, Goering's air force had lost 285 aircraft, 18 percent of the operational strength committed to the campaign. Norway and Denmark (1940) cost an additional 242 aircraft, mostly transports. In France and the Low Countries (1940) the *Luftwaffe* sacrificed another 1129 aircraft,[94] while during the height of the Battle of Britain (July – September 1940) some 1600 aircraft were lost. In fact, from May to September 1940, the German Air Force lost more than 3000 aircraft, a figure equal to 57% of its entire inventory.[95] And while attrition rates thereafter ebbed and flowed, they continued right through the spring of 1941, with ongoing operations over the British Isles, in North Africa, the Balkans and Crete.

A serious outcome of the *Luftwaffe's* largely unsustainable rates of attrition was that the overall size of its force structure barely budged between the spring of 1940 and the invasion of Russia:

***Luftwaffe* Force Structure**
(May 1940 – June 1941)

5 May 1940:
335 Close Recee
322 Long-Range Recee
1356 Single-Engine Fighters
354 Twin-Engine Fighters
1711 Bombers
414 Dive Bombers
50 Ground Attack
240 Coastal

4782 Aircraft in Total

21 June 1941:
440 Close Recee
393 Long-Range Recee
1440 Single-Engine Fighters
263 Night Fighters
188 Twin-Engine Fighters
1511 Bombers
424 Dive Bombers
223 Coastal

4882 Aircraft in Total[96]

What is also striking about these figures is that the Germans began the attack on Russia with 200 fewer bombers than were available in May 1940, while the number of dive bombers – a critical ground support asset – remained virtually static, although the Russian theater of operations was an order of magnitude larger than in the west. The only significant increase between both target dates is in the number of short and long-range reconnaissance assets, but even these would prove inadequate in the endless spaces of the eastern theater of war.

All told, more than 3500 of the aircraft enumerated in the 21 June 1941 table were earmarked to take part in Operation *Barbarossa*, a force that turned out to be hopelessly inadequate – in terms of numbers at least – for the unprecedented scope of the mission. Indeed, as air power historian James S. Corum has observed: "In Russia it was a case of too much front and too few aircraft. Although the *Luftwaffe* performed brilliantly in the early stages of the campaign, it simply lacked sufficient numbers of aircraft to carry out its missions."[97]

Yet despite its modest numbers and already substantial losses, the *Luftwaffe* of 1941 remained a formidable force. Again Corum:

> By almost any measure, the *Luftwaffe* was superior to its enemies in 1939-1941. The [Bf 109] fighter was superior to most opponents, and only Britain's Spitfire could match it in combat. The Ju 88, He 111, and Do 17 medium bombers were some of the best machines of their day. In Poland, Norway, France, North Africa, and Russia, the Ju 87 Stukas proved to be fearsomely effective as close support aircraft. In addition to these combat machines, the *Luftwaffe* could field 500 transport planes, the largest air transport force in the world, and one that played a decisive role in several early campaigns.[98]

In addition to possessing aircraft types generally superior to those of the Soviet Air Force (*Voenno-vozdushnikh sil*, or VVS), *Luftwaffe* aircrews were also far better trained and enjoyed a significant edge in experience. The command organization and doctrine of the German Air Force (GAF) allowed for great flexibility, meaning air power could be shifted rapidly between sectors of the front. Moreover, an effective signal network facilitated command and control of deployed air units, enabling *Luftwaffe* field commanders to concentrate their assets at decisive points on the battlefield. These and other attributes of the GAF in 1941 would enable it to virtually sweep the Soviet Air Force from the skies in the opening days of the campaign. Conversely, in matters of logistics – supply of fuel, spare parts, ammunition, etc. – the *Luftwaffe* possessed "severe if as yet concealed weaknesses." However, in a campaign planned as a "blitzkrieg," and meant to last no more than a matter of weeks, such shortcomings did not appear particularly troublesome.[99]

The primary task of the *Luftwaffe* in Russia was to furnish the ground forces – in particular, the mobile units, upon whose success outcome of the campaign largely hinged

– with direct and indirect air support. Direct support signified the close air support (CAS) mission – i.e., attacking enemy forces at or near the "friendly" main battle line. Indirect support embraced the interdiction of roads, bridges, rail lines, supply depots, troop concentrations and other assets of value to the enemy. *Luftwaffe* field commanders were accustomed to cooperating closely with ground units and, in large part, accepted their supporting role. This attitude was exemplified by Field Marshal Albert Kesselring, commander of the air fleet operating with Army Group Center during the summer of 1941. After the war, he described his harmonious relationship with the army group and his understanding of his mission:

> It was my intention in this campaign with its many imponderables to keep in much closer touch with Army Group headquarters and to maintain constant liaison through a *Luftwaffe* General Staff officer who had previously been in the army. He had to report to my command post every evening, explain the "army situation" for the day and discuss the measures proposed for the morrow, and similarly listen to the "*Luftwaffe* situation" so that he could explain that in detail to the Army Group Command.
>
> As air commander I had a rather distant survey of the maneuvers of the army and received through the Air Groups (air service liaison) and the Flak Corps direct reports from the army front which sometimes differed very considerably from those of army headquarters. At every evening situation conference I assessed the army situation and instructed my intermediary [Lt.-Col.] Uebe to pass on my criticisms to the Army Group Command unless in urgent cases I had a telephone conversation with von Bock or my Chief of Staff rang his. Von Bock knew that I was not trying to teach him his business, but that my interference was only an understandable reaction of a partner, anxious to help a sister arm linked, for weal or woe, in a common purpose …
>
> All the same, the caption of this chapter is: exemplary cooperation between army and *Luftwaffe*. Relying on this harmony, I instructed my air force and Flak generals to consider the wishes of the army as my orders, without prejudice to their subordination to me, unless serious air interests made compliance seem impracticable or detrimental. All my commanding officers and I prided ourselves on anticipating the wishes of the army and on carrying out any reasonable requests as quickly and as completely as we could.[100]

In 1941, the mission of indirect support (interdiction) was better understood and more readily carried out than the true CAS mission. Yet although German air-ground coordination was then still in its infancy, major strides had been made in the application of close air support. When *Barbarossa* began, however, only one air corps was specifically trained and equipped to conduct CAS – a capability for which the *Luftwaffe* as a whole remained ill-prepared.[101] This was 8 Air Corps, commanded by Lt.-Gen. Wolfram Freiherr von Richthofen. One of the outstanding tactical air commanders of World War II,[102] Richthofen had fought with the "Legion Condor" in Spain from late 1936 to 1939, first as chief of staff and then as its final commander. It was here, in the Spanish Civil War, that the *Luftwaffe* had taken its first tentative steps toward developing a true CAS capability. In Poland in 1939, Richthofen led the newly created close support air corps that, by early October 1939, was renamed 8 Air Corps. In May 1940, he led his 8 Air Corps, and its fleet of Ju 87 *Stuka* dive bombers, into the campaign in the west, garnering the Knight's Cross to the Iron Cross. A brilliant tactical innovator, Richthofen applied himself between the French and Russian campaigns – while also leading his air corps in the Balkan offensive – to refining the *Luftwaffe's* close air support techniques. By June 1941, he had perfected a system with which he had experimented since 1939 – that of directing close air support from the ground using *Luftwaffe* liaisons in armored vehicles with appropriate radio sets to control the action. When the attack on Russia began, *Luftwaffe* airmen, operating directly from the front lines, were thus able to direct *Stuka* attacks on fortified enemy positions. The special CAS teams were assigned to the panzer divisions and were "enormously effective" in identifying the most valuable ground targets, while also reducing so-called "friendly fire" incidents. States Corum: "Von Richthofen's 1941 innovations made the *Luftwaffe* much more effective in supporting the German ground forces. It would be two years before the British and Americans could field similar teams to coordinate their air support for the ground armies." In Russia, Richthofen's air corps began its operations in the central sector of the front, furnishing innovative air power to Field Marshal Fedor von Bock's Army Group Center.[103]

Once the attack on Russia got underway, Richthofen's air corps and the entire eastern air fleet was committed ruthlessly to battle; air operations of all units, in fact, proceeded almost seamlessly from 22 June to the end of October 1941, when weather finally intervened to slow them. The *Ostheer*, inadequately equipped with artillery and anti-tank weapons, came to rely increasingly on air power to fill the voids in its own firepower. The mobile forces also needed air power to help them seal the outer rings of the lines of encirclement they were holding:

> The intensity of effort may be gauged by fact that during this period dive-bomber units maintained an average number of sorties per day equivalent to 75 percent of establishment aircraft, whilst fighters maintained about 60 percent and long-range bombers 40-45 percent on this basis. An average scale of effort for the whole period by the total force, averaging some 2500 aircraft, worked out in excess of 1200 sorties per day for aircraft of all types engaged on the front; in periods of great intensity, up to 2000 sorties a day or more were put up.
>
> Despite all this effort and the constant endeavor to eliminate the Soviet Air Force by attacking it at every possible opportunity, this latter aim was never success-fully accomplished, notwithstanding the fact some 20,000 Russian aircraft were claimed destroyed up to the end of October. On the contrary, it was the German Air Force itself that became seriously weakened as a result of its own immense efforts. Losses were extremely heavy, due to the enforced use of inadequately prepared and ill-equipped airfields, and especially owing to the great accuracy of Russian A.A. fire, from which both reconnaissance and long-range bomber units suffered particularly. Wastage of aircraft was such that total first-line strength … underwent a decline and dropped to approximately 4300 aircraft by the end of December 1941. Units in consequence had, in some cases, to be merged and for the first time it became apparent that the production of aircraft was inadequate to sustain a long period of heavy air operations.[104]

The discussion to this point may have left the impression that, in German air power doctrine, the *Luftwaffe* was conceived as little more than an auxiliary arm of the Army. Nothing, however, could be further from the truth. German air war doctrine, opines Richard Muller in his impressive work, *The German Air War in Russia*, as it evolved in the mid- and late-1930s, was "as ambitious and far-reaching as any developed during this heyday of air power prophesizing."[105] *Luftwaffe* theorists developed a concept they called "operational air warfare" (*operativer Luftkrieg*), which sought to integrate an independent air force into the conduct of modern "total war."[106] In other words, similar to the U.S. air power planners at the Air Corps Tactical School, Maxwell Field, Alabama, the Germans in the pre-war period also strove to work out meaningful theories on the strategic application of airpower – a perspective underscored by Dr Richard Suchenwirth in a study prepared for the U.S. Air Force Historical Division in the late-1950s:

> There are two things that make it absolutely certain that *Luftwaffe* leaders intended, from the very beginning, to utilize the newly created air arm in strategic operations in case of war.
>
> In the first place, the *Luftwaffe* Field Directive on the Conduct of Air Warfare, Section 16, treats strategic air warfare as at least as important as the other two types of aircraft employment … In Sections 143-178 and 183-185, the Directive goes on to discuss in detail all the various possibilities in strategic air warfare. In view of the fundamental importance that this Directive was to have as a basis for operational planning, it is inconceivable that the leaders of the new service branch could not have been aware of strategic air warfare as one of their three main missions.
>
> In the second place, we have seen that *Luftwaffe* leaders devoted much thought to the development of that type of aircraft that was indispensable to strategic missions. No less a personage than the Chief of the Air Command Office, Reich Air Ministry, (for all practical purposes, the first Chief of the *Luftwaffe* General Staff), General Walther Wever,[107] had openly urged the development of a four-engine bomber. The fact that this model was known as the "Ural bomber" in *Luftwaffe* circles indicates the intention to wage strategic air warfare in any future war as well as the probable enemy in any future war.[108]

Yet the so-called "Ural bomber," that indispensable prerequisite for effective strategic air operations, was not to be. On 3 June 1936, General Wever perished in an aircraft accident and work on the bomber was soon suspended. The results, in any case, had been disappointing: Two prototypes produced by the Dornier and Junkers works, the Do 19 and Ju 89, had not evinced acceptable performance; both were "underpowered, unwieldy machines"[109] and never saw active service. Shortly thereafter (1937), the Heinkel firm began development of its own long-range bomber; yet the result, the He 177, also fell far short, despite seeing a significant production run and desultory combat service in the later years of the war. A major flaw with the He 177 was the poor performance of its engines – a problem that was to plague German heavy aircraft development throughout the war.[110]

If then, in the broader scheme of things, the failure to develop the appropriate means helps to clarify why *Luftwaffe* concepts of strategic air warfare were rarely put into practice from 1939 to 1945, more germane to this narrative is that the original *Barbarossa* directive (18 December 1940) failed to even assign a strategic mission to the service for the Russian campaign – no doubt in the conviction that a short "blitzkrieg" style war hardly required one. For the attack on Russia, the role of the *Luftwaffe* was two-fold: Firstly, gain air superiority and, if possible, even total air supremacy; secondly, support the ground forces for the duration of their mobile operations. Only after the general line Volga – Archangel – Astrakhan had been reached were strategic operations to be conducted ("if necessary") by bomber forces to eliminate Russia's remaining industrial centers in the Urals.[111]

The 1941 campaign did witness a few abortive attempts by the *Luftwaffe* to conduct operations of a strategic nature. Beginning in July 1941, for example, a series of raids were conducted on Moscow; while these continued into the spring of 1942, the results were meaningless, for the means employed were thoroughly insufficient and the attacks too desultory to have any impact. Attempts were also made on occasion to strike at other centers of the Soviet armaments industry, yet such activities were clearly peripheral to primary mission of the *Luftwaffe* – support of ground forces. Not until 1943/44, when the outcome was no longer in doubt, did the *Luftwaffe* in the east make a more serious stab at a strategic air war in Russia, albeit with no better results.[112]

Once more invoking the principle that a "rudimentary grounding" in the technical means by which the war was fought is a fundamental prerequisite to accurately gauging the nature of the *Barbarossa* campaign – the details on the major German aircraft models are provided below:

Messerschmitt Bf 109: This sleek single-seat, single-engine fighter was, at its inception, probably the best fighter in the world; by early 1941, it was only outclassed by the British "Spitfire." The aircraft, which first flew in 1935 and made its public debut during the Olympics in Berlin in 1936, carried the designation "Bf" – for *Bayerische Flugzeugwerke* – even after the company became Messerschmitt AG. The Bf 109 cut its teeth in combat with the Condor Legion in the Spanish Civil War, thereafter playing an integral part in the early successes of German arms from 1939-41. Produced in many series, the first model manufactured in large numbers was the Bf 109E ("*Emil*"), which had replaced earlier iterations of the aircraft in first line combat squadrons by the autumn of 1939. The "E" model, with a top speed of about 360 mph, featured two wing-mounted 20mm automatic cannon along with two 7.92 machine guns mounted over the engine nacelle. It was followed in late-1940 by introduction of the "F" ("*Friedrich*") series that, outfitted with a somewhat more powerful engine, reached a top speed of 390 mph at 22,000 feet. Intended for precision shooting, the Bf 109F featured one nose-mounted 15mm or 20mm cannon and two 7.92 MGs.[113]

In Russia, some Bf 109s were also fitted with bomb racks to perform as fighter-bombers. Moreover, the Bf 109 employed a new weapon that marked a major increase in the *Luftwaffe's* effectiveness. This was the SD-2 fragmentation bomb (*Splitterbomb*),[114] the "first true cluster bomb," which was far more lethal than conventional munitions when used to attack ground troops or vehicles in the open:

> Since each SD-2 was a container of 96 bombs that covered an area of a few hundred meters, one aircraft dropping two or three of the canisters could effectively wipe out an entire Soviet road column. The cluster bomb was so effective in the interdiction missions against the Red Army that it was accorded top priority for German munitions production. The U.S. Air Force found the SD-2 such an effective weapon that it copied and produced the bomb after the war; the SD-2 remained in the U.S. inventory as a standard munition into the 1960s.[115]

On 22 June 1941, the majority of German fighter groups in the east were equipped with the newer, swifter Bf 109Fs, while the rest possessed the older "*Emil*" models. Both were far superior to almost anything the Soviet Air Force could bring to the fight – their only major deficiency being relatively poor endurance (flight range of about 650 km). On the eve of the campaign, the fighter *Gruppen* ranged along the eastern front registered 858 Bf 109s in their order of battle, of which 657 were fully operational (*einsatzklar*).[116] Emblazoned with their bold yellow theater markings, the Bf 109s performed magnificently during the opening months of the Russian campaign.[117] In the years ahead, more than 70 German fighter pilots – the so-called "*Experten*"[118] – would top 100 kills in the east, including two pilots with more than 200 kills and two others even surpassing the implausible figure of 300 kills.[119] By contrast, in the western theater of operations, only a handful of German fighter pilots ever reached the prestigious "century" of kills – illustrating the immense chasm that existed between conditions on the western and eastern fronts.

Messerschmitt Bf 110: This twin-engine heavy fighter and light bomber was a personal favorite of Air Marshal Goering. A "slim, rakish, low-wing cantilever monoplane," the Bf 110 equipped the so-called *Zerstoerer* (Destroyer) squadrons of the *Luftwaffe*; it represented the first serious attempt to produce a "strategic" fighter capable of escorting bomber formations and penetrating deep into enemy territory. Construction of three prototypes had commenced in 1935, with the first flown successfully on 12 May 1936. When Germany invaded Poland in 1939, 10 *Luftwaffe Gruppen*[120] were equipped with the aircraft that, owing to limited aerial opposition, served largely in a ground support role during the campaign. Some 350 Bf 110Cs took part in the invasion of France and the Low Countries in 1940, while 220 were available for the Battle of Britain. It was over the British Isles in the summer of 1940, however, where the Bf 110 more that met its match. Although heavily armed with two 20mm automatic cannon and several 7.92 machine guns, the heavy fighter's poor turning radius and slow acceleration made it easy prey for RAF fighters. The Bf 110s, in fact, suffered such a serious mauling that they were withdrawn from the Channel coast. Yet while they had largely disappeared from the western European theater by the summer of 1941, the Bf 110C/D/E variants then in service were used extensively and with success on the eastern front, where their top speed of 340 mph, varied weapons load and ability to sustain battle damage gave them a new lease on life.[121]

Dornier Do 17: Of the three twin-engine types which comprised the *Luftwaffe's* bomber fleet on the eve of *Barbarossa*, the Do 17 was the least modern and had proved the most disappointing in service. Ironically, it was first conceived as a mail plane for *Lufthanse* and as a freight aircraft for the German railways; however the Reich's Air Ministry soon requested that Dornier build a bomber variant. The Do 17 prototype first flew in the autumn of 1934. Entering service in 1937, the sleek, elegant aircraft – dubbed the "flying pencil" – was the fastest bomber in the world. Fighting with the Condor Legion in Spain in support of Franco's nationalist forces, the Do 17 was virtually immune to interception by fighter aircraft. Yet just three years later, in 1940 over England, the lightweight craft proved vulnerable to modern fighters. With its limited range, relatively small bomb load of 2200 pounds, and vulnerability to hostile fire, the Do 17 had a minimal role in Operation *Barbarossa*, being operated by two reconnaissance squadrons and three bomber groups. The *Luftwaffe* withdrew the bomber from front-line service by 1942 in favor of its replacement, the Junkers Ju 88. In the final years of the war, surviving Do 17s were used as test beds for new technologies and training schools; some were provided to allied nations.[122]

Heinkel He 111: A truly exquisite and beautifully handling aircraft, aerodynamically efficient, with an elliptical wing and a completely glazed and streamlined fuselage nose, the He 111 was one of the most outstanding airplanes of the mid-1930s – which was the problem, for by the outbreak of war in 1939 it was already approaching obsolescence. Yet because of the German aircraft industry's inability to find a suitable replacement, the He 111 was to soldier on to the end of the war, performing anti-shipping and transport roles as well as bombing. It even functioned as a launch platform for V-1 cruise missiles in 1944.[123]

The aircraft first flew in 1935. Like many of its contemporaries, the He 111 also fought with the Condor Legion in the Spanish Civil War. By September 1939, two thirds of *Luftwaffe* bomber units were outfitted with the He 111, which was to remain the backbone of the German horizontal bomber fleet throughout the war. The bomber, however, had several shortcomings; among them, an inadequate suite of defensive armament, relatively slow speed (ca. 250 mph for the He 111H-1), poor maneuverability and a bomb load (4000 lbs) too light for strategic bombing.[124] On the positive side, the He 111 was robust and reliable and able to absorb truly remarkable battle damage. Two photographs of aircraft belonging to *Kampfgruppe 100 "Wiking,"* tell the story: In the first, a Soviet "Rata" fighter has rammed an He 111, badly damaging the tail unit and fuselage and ripping a massive hole in the right wing; yet the aircraft still made it back to its airfield. In the second photograph, a He 111 has sustained a direct hit from heavy Flak, tearing a nearly two-meter wide gap in the right wing; despite the damage, the pilot flew back to base.[125]

Painted in a standard camouflage scheme – upper surfaces in shades of dark-green, undercarriage in light blue-gray – with yellow Russian campaign bands embellishing the rear portion of the fuselage, the He 111 was to be an indispensable component of the eastern campaign. According to Horst Boog, the German bomber wings (*Kampfgeschwader*) in the *Barbarossa* order of battle were equipped with 757 fully operational machines[126] on 21 June 1941, the majority of which were He 111s. During the summer of 1941, they struck at airfields and other key enemy installations; interdicted concentrations of troops; bombed rail lines, roads and bridges; launched occasional "strategic" attacks on major armaments centers (among them, Moscow); even provided close air support. During the crisis-ridden winter of 1941/42, they transported troops and supplies to the crumbling front and, on occasion, functioned as "flying artillery" on low-level missions against Red Army forces. Attrition rates were frightful, and help to explain why, in 1941, the *Luftwaffe* – just as in 1940 – lost numbers of aircraft almost equivalent to its entire force structure at the start of the year.[127]

Junkers Ju 87: Despite its slow speed and light armament – making it vulnerable to small arms fire - the Ju 87B *Stuka* was the heart of the *Luftwaffe's* close air support force for the attack on Russia. A Russian soldier fighting near the town of Rzhev, outside Moscow, in August 1942, gave this harrowing account of his introduction to the deadly German dive-bomber:

> [Our] tanks are moving forward with infantry on board. Having successfully navigated the minefields, they are now approaching the enemy's front line, moving with all their mass and firing on enemy positions – they'll fix everything; they're just about to reach the German trenches, where our infantry will toss their hand grenades, while the tanks crush the German positions.
>
> Suddenly, Stuka dive-bombers appear above the battlefield from the direction of Rzhev. Confidently and impudently they head straight for the tanks. One tank … a second … a third explodes from the direct attacks, turning into large black-and-crimson bonfires, but the remaining tanks, quickly dispersing, continue to advance on their objective. The bombers are flying in flights. The lead plane, turning on its siren, gracefully goes into a dive and, having released its bomb on its target, soars skyward again. After it, in single file, dives a second, a third, a fourth … a tenth, forming a unique carousel above the hastily scattering tanks. The bloody feast of the vultures, occurring in eyesight of the charging soldiers, causes a commotion: where are our fighters – why haven't they arrived to protect the tanks and infantry? One group of the birds of prey, having dropped its bombs, flies away, but another takes its place, and the whole grim process repeats – having arranged a merciless "funeral procession," they don't let their victims escape the fatal pocket.
>
> From that terrible day I could never bear the wild animal howling of German Stukas. The wailing they emit is head splitting; it freezes your soul, casts you into confusion, paralyzes you like the gaze of a venomous cobra, and lingers in your ears for a long, long time. Even after the war, I never once dared to visit a zoo, because I feared the wail or howl of an animal there might bring me to nervous collapse.[128]

The first prototype of the distinctive looking aircraft, with its gull wings and fixed landing gear, flew in the spring of 1935. By the late 1930s, both the original "A" model and a more powerful "B" variant had gone into serial production. A small batch of the dive-bombers (Ju 87C) was also built to serve aboard the Navy's planned aircraft carrier, *Graf Zeppelin*, whose construction was never completed. To enhance the psychological effect on enemy ground troops, the Ju 87B was outfitted with sirens operated by wooden propellers mounted on the craft's undercarriage spats; the pitch and intensity of the noise emitted by these "Jericho Trumpets" also managed to frighten many *Stuka* crews early in their training.[129]

In Poland and France, the *Stuka* showcased its ability to accomplish both the CAS and interdiction mission. In an era before precision guided munitions, the Ju 87 was a highly accurate bomber, able to strike its target in a diving attack at an angle of about 70 degrees with an accuracy of less than 30 yards. The aircraft was outfitted with special speed breaks, which reduced the speed of the steep dive from 650 to 450 k/h, making aiming easier. However, the pilots soon concluded that their attacks came off better when they did not use the breaks, which were not only cumbersome to operate but, by slowing down the duration of the dive, increased time over target and, hence, the two-man crew's exposure to enemy ground fire.[130]

The *Stuka's* reputation took a beating in the Battle of Britain, where its slow top speed of about 230 mph and lack of defensive armament (several 7.92 MGs) made it highly vulnerable to RAF Hurricanes and Spitfires. On the Russian front in 1941, however, operating in an environment of near total air superiority, it performed to great effect. All told, the *Luftwaffe* force structure in the east at the start of the campaign included 360 combat-ready Ju 87Bs, 323 of them assigned to Army Group Center.[131] The dive bombers struck a broad array of targets in the enemy hinterland, such as bridges, buildings, field fortifications, trains, railroad lines and railroad installations, as well as concentrations of troops, artillery, tanks and vehicles; as noted, they also furnished close air support for troops along the main battle line. For hard and fixed targets, 50 to 500 kg high explosive bombs were most commonly employed; for attacks on trains, the normal bomb load was one 250 kg and four 50 kg bombs; for attacks against troops and vehicles, fragmentation bombs of varying sizes were used. To increase fragmentation effect, special fuses (called Dinort sticks) were screwed into the nose caps of larger bombs, causing the bombs to detonate just above the ground.[132]

During the summer of 1941, *Stuka* pilots maintained a merciless pace of operations, receiving virtually no rest and sometimes flying multiple sorties a day for weeks on end. The physical and psychological toll taken by such ceaseless combat activity under highly stressful conditions – the noise from the sirens could shatter a crew member's eardrum – could be catastrophic, resulting in a man's complete nervous collapse.[133] For their part, the Russians would grow not only to fear, but to hate, the German *Stuka* pilots. As one pilot recalled after the war:

> Every time I was shot down behind Russian lines [he was shot down 13 times in all!] I was always prepared to shoot myself, because I never would have let them take me alive. I had seen the remains of *Stuka* fliers who had been massacred by Russian soldiers, their stomachs slit open, and so on. The Russians really hated *Stuka* crews.[134]

Junkers Ju 52: No account of the *Luftwaffe* lineup for Operation *Barbarossa* would be complete without paying tribute to the Junkers Ju 52, which saw active service both as a civilian airliner and a military transport. While one Allied pilot evaluating the aircraft shortly after the war's end called it an "aesthetically-unappealing contraption" and a "monstrosity," he nevertheless acknowledged the vital role it had played as a three-engine transport in German military operations.[135] Throughout the war, the Ju 52/3m carried thousands of troops and many tons of supplies to all combat zones, ferrying ammunition and fuel to forward airstrips and often evacuating wounded to the rear. In the western campaign of 1940, and at Crete in May 1941, the transports made paratrooper drops, losing hundreds of aircraft in the process. In 1942/43 the "*Tante Ju*" ("Aunt Ju"), as the slow and lumbering transport was known in *Landser* slang, bravely supplied friendly forces surrounded at Demiansk and Stalingrad, or isolated in Tunisia – again sustaining frightful losses.

The Ju 52 had first flown in October 1930,[136] and over the next 15 years its basic design was never altered – a measure of the farsightedness of the craft's designer, Ernst Zindel. The aircraft was used as a transport and a bomber during the Spanish Civil War, taking part in the bombing of Guernica. Although again used as a light bomber over Warsaw in September 1939, it was thereafter employed only as a transport. In that capacity, the Ju 52/3m could carry several tons of supplies distances of more than 1000 kilometers; maximum speed was about 175 mph and defensive armament was light, consisting of several 7.92 machine guns. Despite a laborious rate of climb – our Allied pilot once had the occasion to fly the aircraft up to 10,000 feet, and it "took all of 18 minutes to get there!" – the Ju 52/3m was supremely reliable, stable in flight, simple to operate (although the cockpit layout was a "mess – switches and knobs everywhere"),[137] and easy to maintain. It also had an exceptional short take-off and landing (STOL) capability and could withstand serious combat damage. Although obsolescent by the beginning of World War II, the Ju 52/3m served as the backbone of the *Transportverbaende* of the *Luftwaffe* until the end of the war.[138]

In the fall and winter of 1941/42, deteriorating weather conditions meant that Ju 52/3m *Gruppen* were often the only option for getting life-sustaining supplies to combat units at the front. The pace of their activity at this time is apparent from the operations of a single transport group in October-November 1941: Flying on the central sector of the front from airfields west and southwest of Moscow, this unit logged nearly 700 sorties during a four week period, delivering 1100 tons of fuel, munitions, equipment and replacement parts while bringing out some 600 wounded – a mission it accomplished despite frequent rainfall, low-level cloud cover and fog, sodden landing strips, and the serious threat of enemy fire from ground and air forces. On at least two occasions, the Ju 52/3m crews delivered their goods to an airfield so close to the front that they had to unload under artillery fire. Four of the transport group's Ju 52/3ms were lost during these critical missions.[139]

ENDNOTES

1   M. van Creveld, *Fighting Power. German Military Performance, 1914-1945*, 2.
2   M. Miethe, *Memoiren 1921-1945* (unpublished memoir).
3   S. Knappe, *Soldat*, 206-07.
4   D. Showalter, *Hitler's Panzers*, 376.
5   J. Keegan, *Second World War*, 174. The eight motorized divisions included four so-called "light" divisions, which also were equipped with tanks. They were soon reorganized as full-fledged panzer divisions, however. In addition to the eight motorized divisions of the Army were several *Waffen*-SS regiments (*Standarten*), which were also fully motorized. W. Keilig, *Das Deutsche Heer 1939-45*, Bd. II, Abschnitt 100, S. 6-7.
6   *GSWW*, Vol. IV, 217. Of the 169 divisions, 27 were still in the process of formation in May 1940. W. Keilig, *Das Deutsche Heer 1939-45*, Bd. II, Abschnitt 100, S. 7.
7   W. Keilig, *Das Deutsche Heer 1939-45*, Bd. II, Abschnitt 100, S. 7.
8   This figure included 15 divisions of the 15th "wave," formed in the spring of 1941 and intended primarily for occupational duties in the Balkans, Norway and the west. G. Tessin, *Verbaende und Truppen der Wehrmacht und Waffen-SS*, Bd. I, 57.
9   The 15 motorized divisions included several of the *Waffen*-SS.
10   Figures compiled from, B. Mueller-Hillebrand, *Das Heer 1933-1945*, Bd. II, 111; and, "*21. Juni 1941*:

Zahlenmaessige Uebersicht ueber die Verteilung der deutschen Divisionen und Heerestruppen," in: P. E. Schramm (Hg.), *Kriegstagebuch des OKW*, Bd. I.

11   J. Keegan, *Second World War*, 173.

12   Two of the panzer divisions earmarked for the Russian campaign were assigned to the OKH reserve, as was one Army motorized division; one *Waffen*-SS motorized division was in Finland. B. Mueller-Hillebrand, *Das Heer 1933-1945*, Bd. II, 111.

13   E. Bauer, *Panzerkrieg*, 111-12; A. Seaton, *The German Army 1933-45*, 175.

14   D. Stahel, *And the World held its Breath*, 83.

15   B. Mueller-Hillebrand, *Das Heer 1933-1945*, Bd. II, 80-81.

16   By the beginning of the eastern campaign, production of major types of ammunition had, in some cases, been reduced to a fraction of what it had been in mid-1940. For example, the monthly output of shells for light field howitzers had averaged 1,100,000 in mid-1940; in June 1941, production plunged to just 50,000 shells and, in August 1941 to the miniscule figure of 11,000. Manufacture of 81mm mortar shells, which had averaged 1,600,000 a month in mid-1940, fell to just 100,000 in June and 62,000 in August 1941. Ibid., Bd. II, 92.

17   *GSWW*, Vol. IV, 216; A. Seaton, *The German Army 1933-45*, 173.

18   Tank production alone was short of more than 6000 skilled workers in January 1941. *GSWW*, Vol. IV, 210.

19   Ibid., 212. While this quote pertains to the attitude of the *Luftwaffe* High Command, it also reflects the Army's perspective. Goering's *Luftwaffe*, moreover, by the turn of 1940/41, was already looking past *Barbarossa* and toward its future production requirements for the eventual final struggle with the United States and Great Britain.

20   Ibid., 209, 221.

21   D. Stahel, *And the World held its Breath*, 75; H.R. Trevor-Roper, *Hitler's War Directives*, 78. For the production policies pursued by Jodl and OKW in late 1940 and early 1941, which consigned the Army to third place among the three service branches, see, *GSWW*, Vol. IV, 209-11.

22   H. Magenheimer, *Hitler's War*, 65-68.

23   For example, the 18 Panzer Division was outfitted with no less than 96 different types of personnel carriers, 111 types of trucks and 37 types of motorcycles. As noted, the eastern armies began the campaign with some 2000 different types of vehicle in their inventories. R. Steiger, *Armour Tactics in the Second World War*, 127; D. Stahel, *And the World held its Breath*, 90.

24   *GSWW*, Vol. IV, 221. Of the 20 infantry divisions in the Fourth and Ninth Armies of Army Group Center, fully 11 had a complement of French anti-tank weapons; of these divisions, four were also partially equipped with French vehicles, while one other division had French vehicles (but no French anti-tank weapons). Only five of the 20 divisions – all of the first wave – were equipped exclusively with German weapons, vehicles and equipment. Ibid., 222-23.

25   D. Stahel, *And the World held its Breath*, 90.

26   "*The Wages of Short-Sighted War are Rape*," at: http://www.redstate.com/repair man jack, 24 March 2011.

27   S. Hart, et al., *The German Soldier in World War II*, 21.

28   This compares to 57 Army and SS panzer and panzer grenadier divisions established during the war. G. F. Nafziger, *German Order of Battle – Infantry*, 23.

29   G. H. Bidermann, *In Deadly Combat*, 4-5. Signal and reconnaissance units also had some motorized elements; however, the latter continued to mount some its soldiers on bicycles.

30   According to one source, an infantry regiment consisted of 75 officers, seven administrators, 493 NCOs and 2474 men. No time period, however, is given for these data. A. Buchner, *German Infantry Handbook*, 51.

31   *Handbook on German Military Forces*, U.S. War Department, March 1945, 310.

32   A. Buchner, *German Infantry Handbook*, 47-49.

33   S. Hart, et al., *The German Soldier in World War II*, 54-55.

34   E. Beinhauer (Hg.), *Artillerie im Osten*, 8.

35   Ibid., 8.

36   For technical information on German light and medium field howitzers see, A. Buchner, *German Infantry Handbook*, 88-90; see also, *Handbook on German Military Forces*, U.S. War Department, March 1945, 332-33.

37   A. Buchner, *German Infantry Handbook*, 85.

38   G. Tessin, *Verbaende und Truppen der Wehrmacht und Waffen-SS*, Bd. I, 45.

39   H. Meier-Welcker, *Aufzeichnungen*, 212.

40   A. Seaton, *The German Army 1933-45*, 173; *Handbook on German Military Forces*, U.S. War Department, March 1945, 395-99; A. Schick, *Die 10. Panzer-Division 1939-43*, 264.

41   Only six assault guns had taken part in the campaign in the West in 1940. *GSWW*, Vol. IV, 219.

42   E. Bauer, *Panzerkrieg*, 113. During the second half of 1941, German factories produced an additional 285 StuG IIIs.

43   *Handbook on German Military Forces*, U.S. War Department, March 1945, 365; D. Stahel, *And the World held its Breath*, 78.

44   Lt. J. Hahn, "*Feldzug gegen Russland*" (collection of unpublished field post letters). In one action on the central front in December 1941, two StuG IIIs assigned to 260 ID would destroy 12 T-34s and two KV-1s which had broken through the division's main battle line. Such successes were hardly uncommon on the eastern front from 1941-44. *Die 260. Infanterie-Division*, Kameradenhilfswerk und Traditionsverband der 260. ID (Hg.), 90.

45   *GSWW*, Vol. IV, 219.
46   Ibid., 219.
47   Ibid., 219.
48   D. Stahel, *And the World held its Breath*, 76.
49   Only in 1934, in fact, did the Germans introduce the term "*Panzerkampfwagen*" (literally "armored battle wagon") to describe their tanks, dropping the former designation of armored scout car ("*Panzerspaehwagen*"). W. K. Nehring, *Geschichte der deutschen Panzerwaffe*, 117.
50   Hereafter, the shortened designation of "Pz" will be used for each tank model. For example, "Pz I" in place of "Pz Kpfw I."
51   I. V. Hogg, *Armoured Fighting Vehicles*, 81; D. Stahel, *And the World held its Breath*, 76.
52   H.-A. Jacobsen (Hg.), *Generaloberst Halder Kriegstagebuch*, Bd. III, 42.
53   I. V. Hogg, *Armoured Fighting Vehicles*, 82-83; *Handbook on German Military Forces*, U.S. War Department, March 1945, 384. After production of the Pz II had been discontinued, its modified hull would still be in use late into the war as a self-propelled gun carriage, most notably for the 150mm s.IG 33 and the 105mm le.FH 18.
54   D. Stahel, *And the World held its Breath*, 77.
55   T. L. Jentz (ed.), *Panzer Truppen*, 190.
56   Raus was appointed acting commander of 6 PD in September 1941; on 29 April 1942, he officially took over the division. E. Raus, *Panzer Operations*, 352.
57   Ibid., 11.
58   K. Reinhardt, *Wende vor Moskau*, 206.
59   D. Stahel, *And the World held its Breath*, 77.
60   According to Thomas L. Jentz, more than 500 Pz 38(t)s were assigned to Hoth's 3 Panzer Group. See, T. L. Jentz (ed.), *Panzer Truppen*, 190-93.
61   D. Stahel, *And the World held its Breath*, 78.
62   W. K. Nehring, *Geschichte der deutschen Panzerwaffe*, 118.
63   I. V. Hogg, *Armoured Fighting Vehicles*, 84-86.
64   I. V. Hogg, *Armoured Fighting Vehicles*, 86; D. Stahel, *And the World held its Breath*, 78.
65   H. Guderian, *Panzer Leader*, 138.
66   I. V. Hogg, *Armoured Fighting Vehicles*, 87.
67   C. Burdick & H.-A. Jacobsen (eds.), *The Halder Diary 1939-1942*, 210.
68   W. Keilig, *Das Deutsche Heer 1939-45*, Bd. II, Abschnitt 103, S. 1; P. P. Battistelli, *Panzer Divisions*, 10.
69   T. L. Jentz (ed.), *Panzer Truppen*, 120-21.
70   E. Bauer, *Panzerkrieg*, 113.
71   B. Mueller-Hillebrand, *Das Heer 1933-1945*, Bd. II, 107.
72   For a detailed breakdown of the reorganization and expansion of the panzer divisions see, W. Keilig, *Das Deutsche Heer 1939-45*, Bd. II, Abschnitt 103, S. 1-20. For the complete order of battle of one panzer division on 22 June 1941 see, A Schick, *Die 10. Panzer-Division 1939-43*, 254-66.
73   W. Keilig, *Das Deutsche Heer 1939-45*, Bd. II, Abschnitt 103, S. 11-12.
74   H. Guderian, *Panzer Leader*, 174.
75   A. Seaton, *The German Army 1933-45*, 266.
76   One of the best equipped was the elite 4 Panzer Division. Its inventory of weapons and vehicles in June 1941 included the following: 177 tanks in its 35 Panzer Regiment (among them 105 Pz IIIs and 20 Pz IVs), 35 armored cars, 43 armored personnel carriers, 185 prime movers, 1992 trucks, 1001 cars and 1586 motorcycles. In addition to the tanks in the panzer regiment, the division's artillery regiment possessed several Pz II observation tanks (*Beobachtungswagen*), while the combat engineer battalion was equipped with a dozen Pz I and Pz II tanks. The 4 PD's anti-tank battalion was outfitted mainly with 37mm AT guns; however, just prior to the start of *Barbarossa*, it received three batteries of 50mm AT guns (all towed by half-track prime movers). See, R. Michulec, *4. Panzer-Division*, 4.
77   E. Bauer, *Panzerkrieg*, 113. In comparison, the German army corps of 1914 was equipped with only 160 77mm and 105 150mm guns.
78   The 250 assault guns, an infantry support weapon, are not included in this total.
79   As David Stahel observes: "The qualitative advantage of these Soviet tanks was enormous. In practical terms it meant that none of the German tanks regardless of armament could penetrate the armor on the T-34 at ranges above 500 meters. Indeed, only the later models of the [Pz III] equipped with 5cm L/42 main guns could effectively penetrate the armor of the T-34 at less than 500 meters. The KV-1 was simply impervious to all tank-mounted German firepower as well as the standard 3.7cm anti-tank guns issued to the infantry divisions." D. Stahel, *And the World held its Breath*, 79.
80   Note: This order of battle – simplified from Keilig – portrays a "typical" German panzer division with a tank regiment of two battalions equipped with German tanks only. There were, of course, many variations to this "normal" OOB (*Normalgliederung*).
81   Nine panzer divisions (3, 6, 7, 8, 12, 17, 18, 19, 20) had three tank battalions. W. Keilig, *Das Deutsche Heer 1939-45*, Bd. II, Abschnitt 103, S. 18.
82   These were armored cars, with a 20mm main armament.
83   Note: The actual German term, "*Panzerjaeger*," literally means "tank hunter."
84   This Flak company was not in the OOB of 3, 15, 19 and 20 Panzer Divisions.
85   No number given for tanks; however, this company in the Armored Engineer Battalion of 4 PD had a dozen Pz Is and Pz IIs. R. Michulec, *4. Panzer-Division*, 4.

86 SPW = "*Schuetzenpanzerwagen,*" or armored personnel carrier (APC). These vehicles (in German nomenclature Sd.Kfz. 250 or 251) offered significantly more protection than the typical troop transports then in service and were highly valued by the *Landser* lucky enough to ride in them. However, in June 1941, most panzer and motorized divisions possessed but a small number of these SPWs. Not uncommon was the situation of 10 Panzer Division, whose entire rifle brigade had just a single company mounted in SPWs. A. Schick, *Die 10. Panzer-Division 1939-43*, 263.

87 W. Keilig, *Das Deutsche Heer 1939-45*, Bd. II, Abschnitt 103, S. 18-20.

88 As noted, there were also four so-called "light divisions" which, at the time, were also classified as motorized divisions; however, they had all been reorganized as panzer divisions prior to the start of the French campaign of 1940.

89 A. Seaton, *The German Army 1933-45*, 264.

90 A. Seaton, *The German Army 1933-45*, 264; W. Keilig, *Das Deutsche Heer 1939-45*, Bd. II, Abschnitt 100, S. 6-7.

91 C. Winchester, *Hitler's War on Russia*, 21-22.

92 R. J. Kershaw, *War Without Garlands*, 88.

93 W. Murray, *Strategy for Defeat*, 55.

94 R. P. Hallion, "*Control of the Air: The Enduring Requirement,*" paper prepared by author, 8 September 1999.

95 W. Murray, *Strategy for Defeat*, 53-54.

96 Ibid., 80.

97 J. S. Corum, "*Defeat of the Luftwaffe, 1939-1945,*" in: *Why Air Forces Fail*, R. Higham & S. J. Harris (eds.), 217.

98 Ibid., 203.

99 R. Muller, *The German Air War in Russia*, 33-35.

100 A. Kesselring, *The Memoirs of Field-Marshal Kesselring*, 88-89.

101 R. Muller, *The German Air War in Russia*, 3.

102 "In fact," writes James Corum, "many airpower and military historians regard [Richthofen] as the best tactical air force commander of World War II. This is a fair judgment, and no hyperbole. From 1936 to 1944 von Richthofen pioneered many of the most important elements of air-ground joint warfare to include the use of air forces as flank protection for armored forces and coordination of air support for ground forces by observers on the front lines." He was also the "first major commander to employ modern precision munitions in combat." J. S. Corum, *Wolfram von Richthofen*, 4.

103 J. S. Corum, *Wolfram von Richthofen*, 4-11, 260-61; G. Huemmelchen, "*Generalfeldmarschall Wolfram Frhr. v. Richthofen,*" in: *Hitlers militaerische Elite*, Bd. 2, G. R. Ueberschaer (Hg.), 170-71.

104 Air Ministry Pamphlet No. 248: *Rise and Fall of the German Air Force*, 174.

105 R. Muller, *The German Air War in Russia*, 2.

106 Ibid., 3-15. Muller calls this concept the "central tenet of German air power theory." *Operativer Luftkrieg* "came to refer to an air force, using its unique attributes of range, speed, and surprise, striking at the sources of enemy military, economic, and moral strength (war industries, population and communication centers, and military installations) in order to achieve a strategic decision in concert with the more traditional branches of the armed service." Ibid., 11.

107 Following Germany's public recognition of its hitherto secret *Luftwaffe*, Wever was appointed chief of staff on 1 March 1935. Internet site at: http://www.lexikon-der-wehrmacht.

108 R. Suchenwirth, *Historical Turning Points in the German Air Force War Effort*, USAF Historical Study No. 189, 77-78.

109 R. Muller, *The German Air War in Russia*, 9.

110 Ibid., 4.

111 *GSWW*, Vol. IV, 802-03.

112 Ibid., 802-14. For an insightful discussion of *Luftwaffe* attempts to wage a strategic air war in Russia in 1943/44 see, R. Muller, *The German Air War in Russia*, 112-22, 149-88.

113 C. Bergström & A. Mikhailov, *Black Cross Red Star*, Vol. I, 11; Internet site at: http://www.lexikon-der-wehrmacht.

114 On 22 June 1941, three fighter groups (and only Bf 109Es) were equipped with special mounts under the fuselage to carry the SD-2 *Splitterbomben*. Yet despite the weapon's devastating effect, the suspension of the bombs under the fuselage adversely affected aerodynamic performance of the "*Emils,*" while the pilot also faced serious challenges in dropping the 96 two kilogram bomblets. Because some aircraft were lost as a result, use of the munition by the Bf 109E was soon terminated. The SD-2 was employed with more success by German bomber groups, which used it extensively during 1941. At the start of the attack on Russia, the *Luftwaffe* possessed a total inventory of 2,298,500 of the *Splitterbomben*. J. Prien, et al., *Die Jagdfliegerverbaende der deutschen Luftwaffe*, Teil 6/I, Unternehmen "Barbarossa," 34-35. For more insight into problems associated with the SD-2 fragmentation bomblets see, C. Bekker, *The Luftwaffe War Diaries*, 219-20.

115 J. S. Corum, *Wolfram von Richthofen*, 270. The SD-2 was also used against parked aircraft and airfield installations. See also, J. Prien, et al., *Die Jagdfliegerverbaende der deutschen Luftwaffe*, Teil 6/I, Unternehmen "Barbarossa," 33.

116 J. Prien, et al., *Die Jagdfliegerverbaende der deutschen Luftwaffe*, Teil 6/I, Unternehmen "Barbarossa," 28.

117 D. T. Zabecki, *World War II in Europe – An Encyclopedia*, 965; C. Bergström & A. Mikhailov, *Black Cross Red Star*, Vol. I, 11.

118   According to *Luftwaffe* expert John Weal, *Luftwaffe* fighter pilots "did not often use the dogmatic term '*As*' (ace) in relation to a specific number of victories. They preferred the more generic '*Experte*,' which was taken to mean any pilot of outstanding ability and achievement." J. Weal, *Bf 109 Aces of the Russian Front*, 7.

119   Major Erich Hartmann (52 JG) registered 352 kills, followed by Major Gerhard Barkhorn (52 JG) with 301 kills. In both cases, all of the kills took place on the eastern front. C. Shores, *Luftwaffe Fighter Units Russia 1941-45*, 46.

120   A German *Gruppe* was normally composed of about 30 aircraft of the same type; a *Geschwader* (wing) possessed some 90 aircraft at full strength.

121   C. Bergström & A. Mikhailov, *Black Cross Red Star*, Vol. I, 7, 11-12; R. Muller, *The German Air War in Russia*, 33; W. Green, *War Planes of the Second World War, Fighters*, Vol. I, 164-67.

122   D. T. Zabecki, *World War II in Europe – An Encyclopedia*, 865-66; C. Bergström & A. Mikhailov, *Black Cross Red Star*, Vol. I, 12; http://en.wikipedia.org/wiki/Dornier_Do_17.

123   D. T. Zabecki, *World War II in Europe – An Encyclopedia*, 866; Capt. E. Brown, *Wings of the Luftwaffe*, 122.

124   D. T. Zabecki, *World War II in Europe – An Encyclopedia*, 866; J. Piekalkiewicz, *Die Schlacht um Moskau*, 278.

125   U. Balke, *Kampfgeschwader 100 "Wiking,"* 54a-54b.

126   *GSWW*, Vol. IV, 364.

127   W. Murray, *Strategy for Defeat*, 103.

128   B. Gorbachevsky, *Through the Maelstrom*, 112.

129   Internet site at: http://www.lexikon-der-wehrmacht; Lt.-Col. A. J. Barker, *Stuka Ju-87*, 17.

130   Capt. E. Brown, *Wings of the Luftwaffe*, 27; Major F. Lang (a.D.), *Aufzeichnungen aus der Sturzkampffliegerei*, 6-7.

131   The remaining 37 *Stukas* were in 5 Air Fleet in Norway. *GSWW*, Vol. IV, 364. For consistency, and due to the authoritative nature of the source, this narrative relies largely on Horst Boog's *Luftwaffe* strength figures throughout (Ibid., 364). Concerning aggregate *Stuka* numbers, however, the war diary of Army Group Center states that only 276 Ju 87Bs were available to the army group on 22 June 1941. BA-MA RH 19 II/120, *KTB H.Gr.Mitte*, 22.6.41.

132   Major F. Lang (a.D.), *Aufzeichnungen aus der Sturzkampffliegerei*, 13-24; Lt.-Col. A. J. Barker, *Stuka Ju-87*, 17.

133   H. J. Schroeder, *Die gestohlenen Jahren*, 512-14.

134   J. Steinhoff, et al. (eds.), *Voices from the Third Reich*, 137-39.

135   Capt. E. Brown, *Wings of the Luftwaffe*, 132-33.

136   The initial version had only one power plant; flight testing of the Ju 52/3m with three engines began in 1932, and it was variants of this model which saw combat duty from 1936-45. Production of the aircraft ended in 1944. Internet site at: http://www.lexikon-der-wehrmacht.

137   Capt. E. Brown, *Wings of the Luftwaffe*, 134.

138   C. Bergström & A. Mikhailov, *Black Cross Red Star*, Vol. II, 28; Capt. E. Brown, *Wings of the Luftwaffe*, 134-36; W. Murray, *Strategy for Defeat*, 13-15.

139   *Geschichte einer Transportflieger-Gruppe im II. Weltkrieg*, Kameradschaft ehemaliger Transportflieger (Hg.), 107-11.

CHAPTER 4

CHAPTER 4

The Adversaries II: The State of the Red Army

"Ideologically motivated expansion was not simply one of the key features, but much rather the essential character of the first communist state, which the Bolsheviks had constructed on the ruins of the Russian Empire, and simultaneously the basis on which the identity of international Communism was established." (Bogdan Musial)[1]

"The prevailing image of the Red Army during World War II is a mass army, poorly trained and inadequately equipped, with a few exceptions, such as the T-34 tank. The general interpretation has been that this inexhaustible mass of men had overwhelmed the German Army through sheer numbers while absorbing huge losses. The true picture is more complex and deserves a closer look." (Walter S. Dunn, Jr.)[2]

" … the Soviet infantry was willing, undemanding, suitably trained and equipped, and, above all, brave and endowed with a self-sacrificing devotion to duty. The communist philosophy appeared to have become firmly rooted among the great mass of the younger people and to have made them loyal soldiers, differing much in their perseverance and performance from those of World War I." (German General Erhard Raus)[3]

The Soviet Union, observes Evan Mawdsley, "was not a normal state, and Moscow and Berlin had fateful similarities.

> Supreme authority was concentrated in the hands of a dictator. Foreign policy was highly ideological. Structures for co-ordinating the activities of different agencies and for fully rational decision-making did not exist. Joseph Stalin had consolidated sole power since the defeat of his major rivals within the Communist party in 1929-30 and the purges of tens of thousands of senior officials (and hundreds of thousands of ordinary people) in 1937-38. Among those murdered in the late-1930s were the more independently minded Soviet military commanders and diplomats. By 1939-41 fundamental issues of foreign and security policy were decided arbitrarily, not even by the party Politburo but only by Stalin and selected members of the Politburo. Especially important was the premier and foreign minister, V.M. Molotov, described as "one of the most inexorably stupid men to hold the foreign ministership of any major power this century." Stalin and Molotov were both ignorant of the outside world and, remarkably, they had little understanding of Hitler's National Socialism. As in Germany, the country's elite accepted, through conviction or fear, the radical programs of the ruling dictator.[4]

Under Stalin's uniquely brutal stewardship – propelled by his iron will – the USSR was to experience a remarkable transformation from an economic backwater into an advanced industrial and military power by the end of the 1930s. As is now, of course, well documented, this transformation was accomplished at the cost of the lives of millions of ordinary Soviet citizens, many slaughtered or starved to death during the forced collectivization, others worked to death in the factories and labor camps. Yet without its blood stained emergence into the modern world, the Soviet Union would most surely have been enslaved by Hitler's Germany. Before and during the war Soviet factories, employing modern techniques of mass production, turned out tens of thousands of guns, tanks, vehicles and aircraft, while her railroads delivered tens of millions of troops and untold tons of supplies to the front. The remarkable results of Soviet industrial policy – tethered to an equally successful system of military mobilization – enabled the Red Army to stay operationally committed for fully 88 percent of the 1418 days of warfare on the eastern front between 1941/45, while facing 65-70 percent of the total field strength of the German Army. During this time the Red Army conducted seven major defensive and 160 offensive operations, in the process destroying or disabling more than 600 Axis divisions by May 1945.[5]

Yet if Russia was only able to wage war victoriously due to Stalin's total recasting of his country in the years before 1941, how ironic is it that he had, first, to wage war on his own people? And ironic as well was Stalin's and the Kremlin leadership's second great pre-war achievement: Imbuing in the great mass of those Soviet citizens who were not among the tortured, enslaved or killed a profound sense of responsibility toward the Soviet state and a willingness to make even greater sacrifices in the Great Patriotic War of 1941/45.[6]

4.1: Buildup of the Industrial Base & Armed Forces (A Brief Overview)

The Red Army of the 1920s, while large in size, was essentially a "foot-and-hoof army: an infantry and cavalry force with very limited capability for developing tactical success into operational or certainly strategic success."[7] By the mid-1930s, however, Russia's armed forces had fully developed and implemented a concept known as "deep battle" (*glubokii boi*) while also crafting a force structure (including mechanized and airborne corps) that could begin to translate theory into practice.[8] How, specifically, did this dramatic change come about?

The leaders in the Kremlin had long viewed another internecine world war between the states of the capitalist West as inevitable, a conviction that only hardened after Hitler's seizure of power in January 1933. Such a war presented dangers – Russia might be drawn into it before she was ready – while also offering opportunities: It might enable the Red Army to intervene decisively after the western powers had worn themselves down. It is now well know that Stalin signed his spectacular non-aggression pact with Germany in August 1939 for this very reason – that is, to facilitate another war of attrition between Germany, France and England; one which would end with Soviet Russia emerging as the dominant power on the European continent. What was not known, however, is that the Kremlin leadership had assiduously been preparing their own future war of aggression against the West since at least 1930/31. That this was indeed the case has now been revealed in the pioneering research of Polish-born scholar Bogdan Musial into Soviet archives hitherto inaccessible to western scholars. As he states in the introduction to his electrifying new work, *Kampfplatz Deutschland*:

> For decades, international research has agreed that the German assault against the Soviet Union on 22 June 1941 was an ideologically motivated war of aggression, planned and executed as a war of annihilation and of *Lebensraum*. There is sufficient evidence for this, amongst other things statements by Hitler himself. Soviet wartime and post-war propaganda depicted this assault as such, yet at the same time masked the near two-year duration of the German-Soviet military alliance and, above all, their own agenda of aggression.
>
> The most recently discovered records in the Moscow archives show in particular that from the end of the 1920s, with especial intensity after 'Black Friday' (the beginning of the international economic crisis, 25 October 1929), the Soviet Union

undertook large scale and intense rearmament for an ideologically motivated war of aggression against the West. In 1930 the later Marshal Mikhail Tukhachevsky designed the concept for the war of annihilation against the West, which envisaged large-scale deployment of tanks (50,000), airplanes (40,000), as well as "massive deployment of chemical weapons."

The aim of the Soviet war of aggression was to spread Communist rule through Europe and the world by armed force. Germany was to have the key role in the Bolsheviks' plans for the world revolution, namely due to its industrial potential, the strength of its workforce, its future disciplined soldiers of the revolution, as well as its geopolitical situation in the middle of Europe. The Bolsheviks viewed Germany as the key to domination of Europe.[9]

Since at least 1924, maintains Musial, hopes of a Communist revolution in Germany had faded among the Soviet leadership. In 1925 Stalin succeeded in gaining support for the line of reasoning first expressed by Vladimir Lenin in 1915: "The first Socialist State [i.e., the USSR] shall, if necessary, advance the Communist revolution on its own through force of arms." In 1927, the Politburo approved corresponding increases in armaments production – an intent that initially went nowhere due to the underdeveloped and backward state of Soviet industry. By 1930, all of Soviet society and the entire economy had been harnessed to the preparation of a war of aggression against the West. Indeed, from the early 1930s, Stalin had pinned his hopes solely on the Red Army as a means of spreading world revolution.[10]

The rapid expansion of the Soviet war economy and the Red Army beginning in the early 1930s, along with the latter's basic restructuring and re-equipping, was supported by the purchase of modern technologies, installations and equipment, and weapons prototypes from the West; these purchases, in turn, were financed through the export of raw materials – such as wheat and wood – and even with increased sales of vodka inside Russia itself.[11] Key to Soviet preparations for war, however, was the enormous economic development initiated under the so-called Five-Year Plans, the first that got underway in 1928. Of course, whatever Stalin's and the Soviet leadership's ultimate intent,[12] they also feared a capitalist invasion before their own forces were ready; hence, much of the economic buildup was centered east of Moscow, in the Urals, Siberia and central Asia.

A few figures should illustrate the spectacular results achieved under the Five-Year Plans. The Russia Hitler had written about in *Mein Kampf* in the mid-1920s had an output of about 4,000,000 tons of steel a year, roughly what it had managed before World War I; moreover, Soviet factories produced fewer than 500 motor vehicles in 1927. By comparison, in 1940 Soviet steel production climbed to 18,300,000 tons, while industry built about 200,000 motor vehicles (mostly trucks). Of course, the dramatic increase in steel production was accompanied by an equally prodigious jump in the manufacture of weapons and shells:[13]

Soviet Weapons Production[14]
(1937-40)

	1937	1938	1939	1940
Tanks	1600	2300	3000	2800
Artillery	5400	12,300	17,100	15,100
Mortars	1600	1200	4100	37,900
Rifles	567,400	1,224,700	1,396,700	1,395,000
MGs	31,100	52,600	73,600	52,200
Aircraft	4400	5500	10,400	10,600
Munitions[15]	—	13,000,000	20,000,000	33,000,000

At the same time, while the Soviet government limited the construction of new railroad lines (of the 17,000 km of track earmarked for construction under the first Five-Year Plan, only about 5000 were actually built; even less was achieved on the second Five-Year Plan), improvements to existing tracks and other measures resulted in a four-fold increase in rail traffic between 1928-40.[16] In any case the bottom line is this: If the USSR was not yet an industrial power on the order of Germany or Great Britain – not to mention the United States – it was rapidly becoming one. A nation which, in World War I, had not been able to furnish enough rifles for its armies was outproducing most of Europe a generation later. Indeed, the Soviets had, by 1939, created one of the largest military-industrial complexes in the world.[17]

The broad increase in the production of weapons and munitions was paralleled by a concomitant expansion in the size of the Red Army. In the years prior to the outbreak of war with Germany, the Soviet General Staff studiously updated and modified its war plans, while altering the Red Army's force generation and mobilization system to reflect the new planning. From 1937-39, the Soviets increased the size and readiness of peacetime forces by converting the traditional territorial-militia force-manning system to a regular cadre system. On 1 September 1939, they enacted the Law on Universal Military Service[18] to furnish the requisite manpower for the new system to succeed. These and other measures enabled the Red Army to "creep up to war" by expanding its size from 1.5 million men in January 1938 to more than five million in June 1941; they also enabled the Army's highly efficient – albeit cumbersome – mobilization system to expand the peacetime cadre force to well beyond 500 divisions in wartime. By the time the *Wehrmacht* crossed the Russo-German frontier in the early morning hours of 22 June 1941, Red Army ground forces had swelled in size to more than two dozen armies and 300 divisions of all types, supported by dozens of fortified regions, separate engineering and artillery regiments, and other units. Nearly three million Russian soldiers stood guard in the western theater when the Germans struck.[19]

By the spring of 1941, the Red Army was the "largest and most complex fighting force in the world,"[20] endowed with larger mechanized, cavalry and airborne forces than any other nation. Yet it was also an army still in the throes of thorough and challenging reforms, including the reorganization and re-equipping of its mechanized forces. Officers and men were far from fully trained and equipped; many divisions were not yet combat ready. As will be explored in more detail below, the Red Army on the brink of war, despite its impressive achievements, was far from ready to fight.

4.2: Impact of the Purges

As one account put it bluntly: "Where Hitler had tamed his officer caste, Stalin had killed his."[21] The purges of the armed forces were part of the Great Purge of the civilian and military establishment that the preternaturally paranoid Soviet dictator had implemented in 1936. Although the Russian army had no discernable tradition of revolt or revolution – its sole attempt to usurp power, the Decembrist coup of 1825, had petered out after a day – Stalin still feared it. Obsessed that his rivals – real or imaginary – might move against him, he responded with homicidal brutality. During the height of the purges in 1937-38, more than 1.5 million people were arrested by the Soviet secret police, the NKVD;[22] of these, more than 1.3 million received some sort of sentence, while more than 680,000 were executed. The effects of the purges were felt at every level of Soviet society, from the Politburo down to ordinary citizens arrested in the streets. Among those killed were so-called "ex-kulaks," "criminal elements," "socially dangerous elements," "members of anti-Soviet parties," "former tsarist civil servants," and "White Guards." Of course, these designations were applied rather flexibly to any suspect, whether he was a Party member, member of the intelligentsia, member of the armed forces, or a simple worker.[23]

Although new scholarship has revealed that the NKVD's "*Ezhovshchina*" – "The Reign of Ezhov," a reference to Nikolai Ezhov, leader of the NKVD from September 1936 to November 1938 – had less of an impact on the armed forces than hitherto believed, its impact was nonetheless horrific. All told, some 35,000 officers were arrested or expelled from the Red Army between May 1937 and September 1938;[24] of these, about 30 percent were eventually reinstated by 1940, but more than 22,000 were either executed or their fate remains unknown. If that were not enough, a new wave of terror commenced in the fall of 1938, with the result that high-level arrests and executions of key military leaders went on – albeit at a slower pace – right up to the eve of war with Germany.[25] In the final analysis, the purges decapitated the leadership of the Soviet armed forces; among those eliminated were:

3 of 5 marshals
13 of 15 army generals
8 of 9 admirals
50 of 57 army corps commanders
154 of 186 division commanders
16 of 16 army commissars
25 of 28 army corps commissars[26]

According to Evan Mawdsley, the purges of the Soviet military had three primary outcomes, each of which was devastating: a.) indispensable trained leaders were lost during a period of rapid Red Army expansion; b.) the initiative of the officer corps was "paralyzed," and a "mental state imposed which was the very opposite of the German 'mission-oriented command system;'" and, c.) the purges convinced foreign nations – among them Hitler's Germany – that the Soviet military was nothing more than a "broken shell."[27]

Certainly, the evisceration of the Red Army's officer corps constituted one of the gravest handicaps to Soviet military effectiveness in both the Russo-Finnish conflict of 1939/40 and the initial phase of the war with Germany. As a direct result of the purges – and the rapid ongoing expansion – the Red Army's shortage of skilled specialists reached crisis proportions by 1940. Moreover, the Army faced a shortfall of 36,000 officers on the eve of the German invasion; a figure which climbed to 55,000 following wartime mobilization.[28] Only 7.1 percent of commanding officers had a higher military education (55.9 percent had a secondary education, 24.6 percent had taken accelerated courses and 12 percent of officers had received no military education at all).[29] By June 1941, 75 percent of field officers and 70 percent of political commissars had occupied their posts for less than a year.[30] Field commanders at *all* levels held "positions for which they were unqualified, lacked the practical experience and confidence necessary to adjust to changing tactical situations and tended to apply stereotypical solutions, distributing their subordinate units according to textbook diagrams without regard for actual terrain. The results were predictable."[31]

Yet if the purges had broken the back of the Soviet officer corps, they had strikingly solidified Stalin's own hold on power. From this point forward, no one dared challenge his authority on any matter pertaining to war or peace. The implications of Stalin's iron grip on the Soviet state were profound:

> The mass purges of 1937 ensured that Stalin would not be threatened, that his despotism would not be challenged, whatever his own paranoia told him. The purges also greatly weakened the position of the army's General Staff in its dealings with the political leadership, most especially with Stalin himself … Stalin – cautious, distrustful and cold-bloodedly ruthless – was increasingly told what his sycophantic and anxious subordinates thought he wanted to hear. This would play its part in the disaster of June 1941.
>
> In the vital months prior to the launch of "*Barbarossa*," therefore, decisions on all matters of importance within the Soviet Union were taken by Stalin personally. There

were discussions, sometimes lengthy and usually informal, with fluctuating groups from within the "inner circle." But those who met Stalin on a regular basis saw each other as rivals, and were, consequently, divided among themselves. They were also acutely aware that their tenure was insecure. Their dependence on Stalin was total. So, therefore, was their loyalty to him. This did not make for an open exchange of views … The reinforcement of Stalin's own views was, therefore, almost guaranteed. This would prove a major weakness, rather than a strength, as invasion loomed.[32]

Recently, some scholars[33] have concluded that even more so than the Great Purge, it was the breakneck expansion of the Red Army which was largely to blame for the decline in the Army's quality and its poor showing in the initial phases of the Russo-German war. Be that as it may, operations on the eastern front reveal that it took the Russians a good two years, perhaps longer, to begin to reach parity with the Germans on the *operational* level of war – a status they would never attain on the *tactical* level. In fact, poor small unit tactics were endemic to the Red Army in the early years of the war, as exemplified by the following example from the central front in early 1942, near the village of Olenino:

> A Russian regiment [attacked] eastward in an attempt to cut off some German units and link up with friendly forces moving in from the opposite direction. The attack methods employed by the Russian infantry showed that the troops were inadequately trained. The infantry units emerged from their jumpoff position in a disorderly manner, having the appearance of a disorganized herd that suddenly emerged from a forest. As soon as the Germans opened fire, panic developed in the ranks of the attack force. The infantrymen had to be driven forward by three or four officers with drawn pistols. In many instances any attempt to retreat or even to glance backward was punished with immediate execution. There was virtually no mutual fire support or coordinated fire.
>
> Typical of Russian infantry tactics was the tenacity with which the attack was repeated over and over again … From 27 February to 2 March, detachments, consisting of about 80 Russians each, attacked daily in the same sector and at the same time … Every one of them was unsuccessful, the attacking Russians being wiped out before they could reach the German position…
>
> During the main assault [several days later] the teamwork between Russian tanks and infantry was inadequate. In this particular engagement the Russian infantry showed little aggressiveness, and the tanks had to advance alone to break up the German defense system before the infantry jumped off…
>
> As in many other instances, the lower echelon Russian commanders revealed a certain lack of initiative in the execution of orders. Individual units were simply given a mission or a time schedule to which they adhered rigidly. This operating procedure had its obvious weaknesses. While the Russian soldier had the innate faculty of adapting himself easily to technological innovations and overcoming mechanical difficulties, the lower echelon commanders seemed incapable of coping with sudden changes in the situation and acting on their own initiative. Fear of punishment in the event of failure may have motivated their reluctance to make independent decisions.[34]

4.3: Force Structure & Dispositions on Eve of *Barbarossa*

If the expansion of Soviet armed forces accelerated in 1939/40, it became truly frantic in 1941. From January 1939 to May 1941, the Red Army added 111 rifle divisions, 12 rifle brigades and 50 tank and motorized divisions to its ballooning force structure.[35] The instability caused by such expansion (and the purges) is evident in the fact that, on two days in early March 1941, four new army, 42 corps and 117 division commanders were

PHOTO ESSAY #1

Commanders & Weapons

GERMAN

Adolf Hitler at the Wolf's Lair (*Wolfsschanze*) in East Prussia on 24 June 1941. (R. Bender)

The new Reich's Chancellery in Berlin, designed by Hitler's architect Albert Speer and completed in January 1939. (R. Bender)

General Alfred Jodl, Chief, OKW
Operations Staff. (R. Bender)

Field Marshal Wilhelm Keitel, Chief
of the German Armed Forces High
Command (OKW). (R. Bender)

Field Marshal Walther von Brauchitsch, C-in-C of the Army. (R. Bender)

General Franz Halder, Chief of the Army General Staff. (R. Bender)

Field Marshal Fedor von Bock, C-in-C, Army Group Center. (R. Bender)

General Wolfram *Freiherr* von Richthofen, C-in-C, 8 Air Corps.

Field Marshal Hans von Kluge, C-in-C, Fourth Army. (R. Bender)

Field Marshal Albert Kesselring, C-in-C, 2 Air Fleet.

General Adolf Strauss, C-in-C, Ninth Army. (R. Bender)

General Maximilian *Freiherr* von Weichs, C-in-C, Second Army. (R. Bender)

General Heinz Guderian, C-in-C, 2 Panzer Group. (R. Bender)

General Hermann Hoth, C-in-C, 3 Panzer Group (Center figure, in the field somewhere in Russia). (D. Glantz)

General Joachim Lemelsen, C-in-C,
47 Panzer Corps. (R. Bender)

Panzer I tanks in training exercise. (R. Bender)

Panzer II tank. (R. Bender)

Panzer III tank in Russia. (R. Bender)

Panzer IV tank. (R. Bender)

Assault Gun III (Stug III) near Dnepr River in Russia, taking on ammunition. (National Archives [hereafter cited as NA])

Bundesarchiv, Bild 101I-268-0185-06A
Foto: Böhmer | Oktober 1941

Panzer 35(t) tank in Russia (October 1941). (BA-MA, Bild 101I-268-0185-06A, Foto: Boehmer)

COMBAT AIRCRAFT

SB bomber, 1935

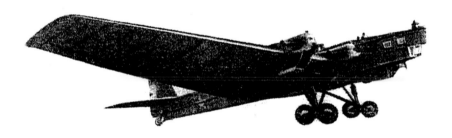

TB-3 (ANT-6) heavy bomber, 1930

Reconnaissance flying boat MBR-2

Soviet aircraft. (D.M. Glantz)

Hereafter cited as "NA."

COMBAT AIRCRAFT

Soviet aircraft. (D.M. Glantz)

Pe-2 dive-bomber

Pe-8 (TB-7) long-range bomber

Tu-2 bomber

Il-2 "Shturmovik" assault aircraft

Il-4 long-range bomber

COMBAT AIRCRAFT

I-16 fighters

MiG-3 fighter

Iak-3 fighter

La-5 fighter

Soviet aircraft. (D.M. Glantz)

76 mm divisional gun
Model 1939

122 mm howitzer Model 1938

152 mm gun-howitzer Model 1937

Soviet artillery pieces.
(D.M. Glantz)

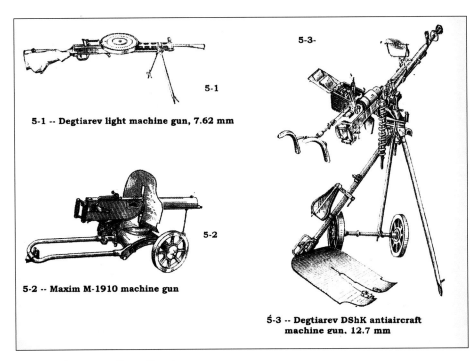

5-3-

5-1

5-1 -- Degtiarev light machine gun, 7.62 mm

5-2

5-2 -- Maxim M-1910 machine gun

5-3 -- Degtiarev DShK antiaircraft
machine gun, 12.7 mm

Soviet machine-guns. (D.M. Glantz)

4-1

4-2

4-1 -- Sudaev M-1942 (PPS-42)   4-2 -- Sudaev M-1943 (PPS-43)

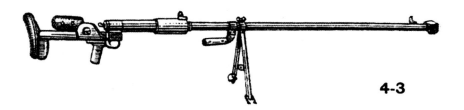

4-3

4-3 -- Degtiarev M-1941 antitank rifle, 14.5 mm

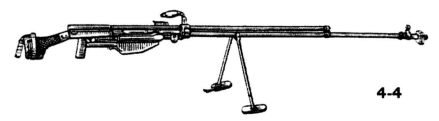

4-4

4-4 -- Simonov M-1941 antitank rifle, 14.5 mm

Soviet infantry weapons. (D.M. Glantz)

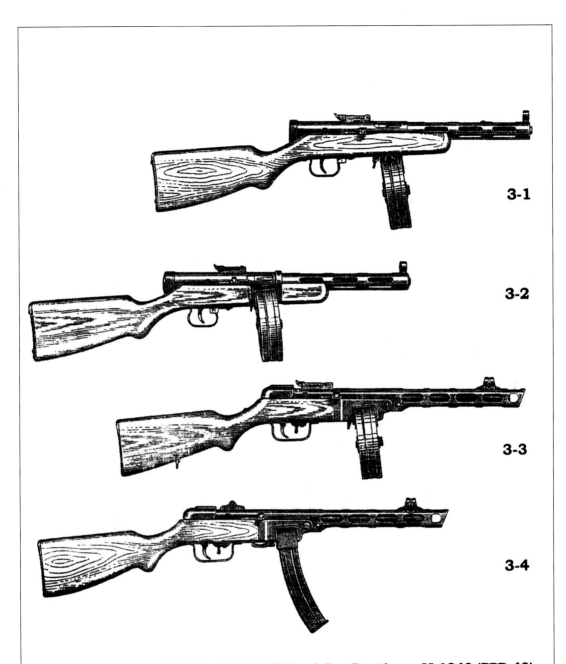

3-1

3-2

3-3

3-4

3-1 -- Degtiarev M-1934/38 (PPD-34/38)   3-2 -- Degtiarev M-1940 (PPD-40)
3-3 -- Shpagin M-1941 (PPSh-41)   3-4 -- PPSh-41 modified

Soviet infantry weapons. (D.M. Glantz)

Soviet BM-13 *Katyusha* ("Little Kate") multiple rocket-launcher in action. (D.M. Glantz)

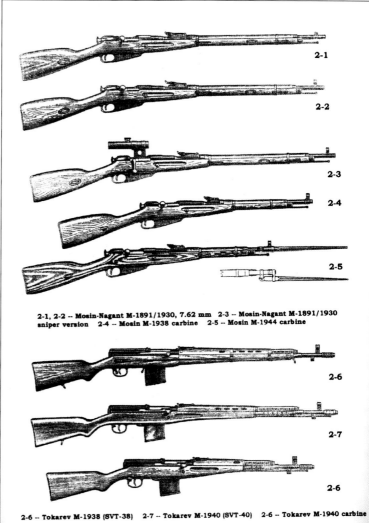

2-1, 2-2 -- **Mosin-Nagant M-1891/1930, 7.62 mm**   2-3 -- **Mosin-Nagant M-1891/1930 sniper version**   2-4 -- **Mosin M-1938 carbine**   2-5 -- **Mosin M-1944 carbine**

2-6 -- **Tokarev M-1938 (SVT-38)**   2-7 -- **Tokarev M-1940 (SVT-40)**   2-6 -- **Tokarev M-1940 carbine**

Soviet infantry weapons. (D.M. Glantz)

T-34 medium tank. (D.M. Glantz)

KV-1 heavy tank. (D.M.Glantz)

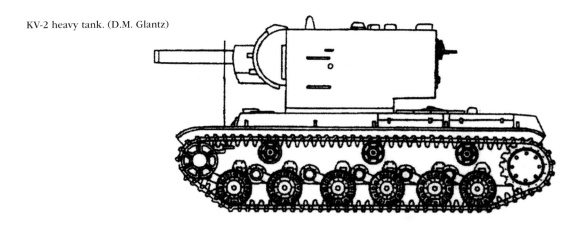

KV-2 heavy tank. (D.M. Glantz)

T-26 light tank. (D.M. Glantz)

BT-7 light tank, one of several BT models in service in 1941. (D.M. Glantz)

Soviet Marshal S.M. Budenny. (D.M. Glantz)

General K.K. Rokossovsky. (D.M. Glantz)

Soviet Marshal K.E. Voroshilov. (D.M. Glantz)

General G.K. Zhukov. (D.M. Glantz)

Д. Г. Павлов

General D.G. Pavlov, C-in-C, Soviet
Western Front. (D.M. Glantz)

Soviet Marshal S.K. Timoshenko. (D.M. Glantz)   Soviet Marshal B.M. Shaposhnikov. (D.M. Glantz)

Joseph Stalin, the ruthless Russian leader, or "*vozhd*." (D.M. Glantz)

Henschel reconnaissance aircraft with artillery observer over Russia.

Junkers Ju 88 medium bomber.

A Junkers Ju 52 transport brings supplies to trapped German troops in winter 1941/42
(BA-MA, Bild 1011-003-3445-33, Foto: Ullrich)

Bf 110 "destroyer" aircraft diving on Soviet ground positions near Smolensk.

A unit of He 111 medium bombers in flight. (BA-MA, Bild 1011-408-0847-10, Foto: Martin, 1940/41)

Bf 109 preparing for a mission. (R. Bender)

Stuka dive-bombers. (R. Bender)

Medium 81mm infantry mortar and crew. (NA)

The weapons of a German infantry company in 1941. Clockwise from upper right hand corner: *Gewehr* 98K, 12 MGs, 3 AT rifles, 3 mortars. (NA)

Stacked infantry weapons of a German advance detachment inside Russia, 24 June 1941. (NA)

Excellent photo of a MG 34, the primary German machine-gun in 1941. (NA)

German Infantryman holding MP 40 machine pistol. Propaganda company heading on the photograph – "The German infantryman: Fighter for his Fatherland and for a new world." (NA)

150mm *Nebelwerfer* Rocket
Projector battery in action
southwest of Vitebsk in July
1941. (NA)

210mm heavy howitzer outside Vitebsk in July 1941. (NA)

88mm Flak gun making change of position in Russia. (NA)

Panzer 38(t) tank in combat. (R. Bender)

150mm medium field howitzer (s.F.H. 18) in action in Russia. (NA)

appointed. They had little more than three months time to become acquainted with their new commands.[36] Observes David Glantz:

> It is clear from Soviet contemporary writings and archival materials that, by this time, fear, rather than hostile intent, was the driving force [behind the massive growth in force structure]. Soviet military assessments appearing in open and closed military journals ... were particularly candid. They show a clear understanding of superb German military performance and an unmistakable realization that the Soviet military in no way met German military standards. It is no coincidence that many of the articles that appeared in these journals during 1940 and 1941 dealt with clearly defensive themes. In short, Soviet military theorists understood what could happen to the Soviet military and the Soviet state. Politicians, including Stalin, must have known as well. This understanding provided necessary context to all that occurred diplomatically and militarily in 1940 and 1941. At the least, it explains the magnitude of the ongoing Soviet military reform program and the haste with which it was implemented. Unfortunately, for the Soviet Union, this understanding of current threats and the wholesale rearmament program that followed did not adequately prepare the Soviet military for war.[37]

Adequately prepared or not, the Soviet military had – in terms of numbers at least – transformed itself into a veritable leviathan by mid-1941. On the cusp of the greatest armed struggle she was ever to face, Russia boasted a defense establishment composed of over five million men arranged in 27 armies and 303 divisions, with 17,000 to 24,000 tanks[38] and nearly 20,000 aircraft.[39] This massive military machine – which embraced the largest number of tanks and aircraft of any nation in the world – was made up of the following ground units:

29 mechanized corps
62 rifle corps
4 cavalry corps
5 airborne corps
303 divisions
    198 rifle
    61 tank
    31 mechanized
    13 cavalry
57 fortified regions[40]
5 separate rifled brigades
10 anti-tank brigades
94 corps artillery regiments
75 RVGK (High Command Reserve) artillery regiments
34 engineering regiments[41]

Of this total force structure,[42] field forces (*Deistvuiushshaia armiia*) stationed in the western frontier zone were arranged in five fronts[43] – Northern, Northwestern, Western, Southwestern, and Southern – which were established immediately after the German invasion from the Leningrad Military District; the Baltic, Western, and Kiev Special Military Districts; and the Odessa Military District, respectively. The forces assigned to these fronts possessed a total strength of about 2.9 million men and were composed of the following formations:

16 armies
20 mechanized corps

32 rifle corps
3 cavalry corps
3 airborne corps
163 divisions[44]
    97 rifle
    40 tank
    20 mechanized
    6 cavalry
41 fortified regions
2 separate rifle brigades
10 anti-tank brigades
87 artillery regiments (52 corps/35 RVGK)
18 engineer regiments[45]

Rounding out these forces, the *Stavka* (Soviet High Command) reserve comprised five armies (14 rifle corps, 5 mechanized corps, 57 divisions) and 17 artillery regiments; while the remaining military districts and the Far Eastern Front were made up of six armies (16 rifle corps, 4 mechanized corps, 83 divisions), 16 fortified regions, three separate rifle brigades, 65 artillery regiments (29 corps and 36 RVGK), and 16 engineer regiments.[46]

In accordance with Soviet pre-war planning, Red Army forces were echeloned in great depth – extending from the "trip-wire" forces along the demarcation line with Germany back as far as the Western Dvina and Dnepr river lines. The first strategic echelon – consisting of the field forces (163 divisions) in the five western military districts (along with 8 divisions of the *Stavka* reserve physically located in the first strategic echelon, but not considered part of the field forces) – comprised three operational belts made up of 57, 52, and 62 divisions, respectively, including 20 of the 25 mechanized corps stationed in European Russia. The first operational belt (57 divisions) provided the covering forces along and near the frontier; the second belt (52) was positioned 50-100 kilometers to the rear; while the third belt (62) made up the first strategic echelon reserve, in place 100-400 kilometers from the border with Germany. Fortified regions had been established along the 1941 border, in depth along the pre-1939 Soviet-Polish border, and along approaches to major cities, such as Kiev in the Ukraine. Adding further depth to these armies was the second strategic echelon, consisting of the five armies (57 divisions) of the *Stavka* reserve and, by 22 June 1941, in the process of deploying along the line of the Dvina-Dnepr. The mission of this second strategic echelon – which was virtually unknown to German intelligence – was to carry out a counteroffensive along with the counterattacks conducted by the armies of the forward fronts. Yet when war began, neither the forward military districts nor the *Stavka* reserve armies "had completed deploying in accordance with the official mobilization and deployment plans. As in so many other respects, the German attack on 22 June caught the Soviets in transition."[47]

A striking feature of the Red Army forces assembled in the Western Special Military District (to become Western Front on the day of the German invasion) was their strong concentration far forward in Soviet occupied eastern Poland. The bulk of the Soviet troops in the Western District – even armored, mechanized, and cavalry units – was deployed in a large salient around the town of Belostok, which projected far into German held territory. As a result, these forces were already deeply enveloped by German Army Group Center in position in East Prussia and Poland. Indeed, three of the four armies of the Western Special Military District (along with three of its six mechanized corps) stood in a semi-circle around Belostok, their positions dangerously exposed.[48] Also assembling close to the frontier were Soviet Air Force units:

> Since the spring of 1941 efforts had … been in progress to set up a dense network of operational airfields in the proximity of the western frontier of the Soviet Union. This project had not been completed by the beginning of hostilities, with the result that aircraft were crowding together on those airfields which had not been completed, offering an easy target to the German Air Force. Not only had the ground and air forces been moved up close to the new state frontier, but also – in a manner now described as mistaken – supply depots, fuel stores, and mobilization supplies; these were nearly all lost at the beginning of the war. Roads, tracks, bridges, troop accommodations, and so on were massively extended, yet no attempt was made to establish rearward communication links or to set up the command centers indispensable for a defensive war. In a similar vein was the suspension of all work on the strengthening of fortifications along the old state frontier and the partial disarming of the installations; yet the large-scale fortification work planned along the new state frontier in Lithuania and in the annexed Polish and Romanian areas was making only slow progress.[49]

In other words, the Red Army found itself in a situation resembling a state of limbo, prepared neither to attack nor defend. Implicit in the paragraph above is also the fact that neither Stalin nor his lieutenants were planning on fighting a war on Soviet soil. Whenever and however the war began, the Red Army was – in accordance with Soviet military doctrine – to advance at once and aggressively into German held territory. In recent years, revisionist historians have cited these clearly offensive oriented Soviet dispositions as proof that Stalin was preparing to launch a war of aggression of his own; and, as outlined above, Bogdan Musial's ground-breaking scholarship makes the compelling case that Soviet Russia had been preparing to attack the West since the early 1930s. However, it appears more likely that, by 1940/41 – to echo David Glantz' earlier observations – whatever the Soviets may have been planning in the 1930s, they were now simply struggling desperately to ready their armies for the hammer blow about to crash down on them. The contentious issue of preventive or pre-emptive war – of who was preparing to attack whom – will be explored in Chapter 5. Before going there, however, it is necessary to take a closer look at the Soviet armed forces on the eve of *Barbarossa*, followed by a more in-depth examination of the Red Army's final plans and preparations before the German invasion.

4.3.1: Infantry & Artillery
"June is a special month all over northern Europe," reflects Catherine Merridale in her wonderful social history of the Red Army soldier:

> In European Russia and Ukraine, it is magical. Winter's bitter dark and ice are barely even memories, spring's mud and rain forgiven. Kiev's famous chestnut trees come into bloom, and so do Moscow's lilacs. Yalta's Judas trees. It is the month of the peony and the green willow, the month, in the north, of the white nights.[50]

For the Red Army soldier of 1941, the "magical" month of June was to culminate in humiliation and defeat – a meat grinder of death administered with Teutonic precision by the tanks, guns and aeroplanes of Hitler's invading armies. By early 1942, more than two million of Russia's soldiers were dead, most of them simple infantry belonging to the traditional rifle divisions which, in 1941, made up 65 percent of the Soviet force structure. The average Russian rifleman – clad in his olive green uniform, persistently short of food and kit,[51] poorly equipped and poorly led, the object of draconian discipline – had lasted in front-line duty for barely three weeks before being killed or disabled.[52]

It should not have been like this. Spurred on by the poor performance of Soviet arms during the occupation of eastern Poland in September 1939, the colossal failures in the war with Finland in 1939/40 and, perhaps most of all, by the stunning victory of the *Wehrmacht* in the west in the spring of 1940, the Soviet Union had "embarked on a crash program to reinvigorate their armed forces." The ensuing reforms, named for Commissar of War S.K. Timoshenko, were to affect virtually every facet of the Red Army. In the course of these reforms, efforts were made to expand and modernize the rifle forces, including adoption of a new rifle division establishment in April 1941, which aimed to replace the former dual peacetime manning level of the division (6000 and 12,000), increase rifle strength, and enhance firepower through "up-gunned" artillery, improved anti-tank and anti-aircraft weapons, and the addition of a light tank battalion.[53]

What emerged from these reforms was a rifle division of three rifle regiments and two artillery regiments (one gun, one howitzer regiment), as well as reconnaissance, anti-tank, anti-aircraft, engineer, signal and tank battalions. In theory, the new division's table of organization included 14,483 men, 78 artillery pieces (over 50mm), 150 mortars (50, 82 and 120mm), 54 45mm AT guns, 12 AA guns, 16 light tanks, 13 armored cars, 558 vehicles, and 300 horses.[54] In June 1941, however, most of these rifle divisions were well below their authorized strength in manpower (on average 8000 to 10,000 men, or even less), firepower, and logistics support.[55] One of the most serious deficiencies was in motorization, with each rifle division having only 10-25 percent of its prescribed number of trucks, because any new production was needed for the massive expansion of the mechanized corps. This lack of motor transport would later be identified by almost every frontline officer as the reason why the retreat that June so quickly became a rout.[56] Performance in the field was also adversely affected by the lack of an effective infantry anti-tank rifle.

In general, the Soviet 1941 rifle division was short of personnel, weapons, equipment, transport, communications equipment, and logistical support – in other words, just about everything – while also evincing weaknesses in unit and officer training. According to the late John Erickson, the rifle divisions at the beginning of the war – with their "enormous variations in strength" – equaled the equivalent of just 1/3 of a fully outfitted German infantry division.[57] Such failings "rendered the force hollow and presaged rapid Soviet defeat."[58]

The best-equipped and most thoroughly professional arm of the Red Army ground forces was the artillery. Indeed, the service had an "unbroken tradition of excellence throughout Russian history;"[59] as far back as 1810, the modernization of the Czar's artillery had made it "probably the most professional in Europe."[60] The Red Army began World War II with an excellent arsenal of artillery pieces which had been designed or upgraded in the 1930s, adding to the range, rate of fire, accuracy and destructive effect of all their artillery.[61] Soviet artillery bore a resemblance to that of the Germans, only the Red Army had a lot more of it – in 1941 more than 33,000 artillery pieces (for the entire USSR) as opposed to little more than 7000 German light and medium pieces earmarked for *Barbarossa*.[62]

The Soviet artillery park comprised a mix of guns and howitzers – some obsolete, some modern types – in 76mm, 107mm, 122mm and 152mm calibers. Like the German artillery, most of it was horse drawn, while very few of the tracked artillery pieces could operate off road.[63] Most of the heavier caliber weapons were assigned to the 94 corps artillery regiments and 75 RVGK (High Command Reserve) artillery regiments that supported the armies, corps and divisions; in fact, 92 percent of all Soviet artillery was incorporated into these 169 regiments. The standard artillery piece allotted to the rifle regiments was the short-barreled 76mm Model 1927 regimental gun; divisional artillery included 76mm guns and 122mm and 152mm howitzers.[64]

In mid-July 1941 – first at the important railroad junction at Orsha, southwest of Smolensk; then near the town of Rudnia, between Vitebsk and Smolensk – the Red Army introduced a new and highly secret weapon: the BM-13 "*Katyusha*" ("Little Kate") multiple rocket-launcher.[65] Simply put, this rather crude weapon consisted (in its initial configuration) of rails mounted on the back of truck and fired a salvo of 16 solid-fuel rockets with 132mm caliber warheads.[66] The Germans dreaded the massed fire of the "*Stalinorgel*" ("Stalin Organ"), as they called it,[67] with its infernal and distinctive scream. However, the *Landser* soon figured out that the rockets were inaccurate and the fragmentation effect poor – that they were mainly effective against personnel in the open or against lightly skinned vehicles. Yet as this account of a German battalion outside Moscow in the autumn of 1941 illustrates, initial exposure to the weapon could make for a truly terrifying experience:

> 24.10.41 1610 [hours]: Cavalry section confirms heavy enemy movements in the forest east of Dubosekovo. Battalion is being shelled for first time by Russian rocket launchers ... With a dreadful howling noise and like comets with red tails, the missiles tear through the air. On impact, they explode with a thundering crack. Their effect on morale is great, as is the effect of the sheer number of explosions in the smallest area.[68]

Throughout the Russo-German War, the Soviets would rely more on their artillery than any other major combatant. Between 1941 and 1945, they produced more than 500,000 guns and mortars, concentrating on the output of designs already in service in 1941. The destructive power of Soviet artillery – particularly in the later years of the war – often dominated the battlefield. As Dr Max Domarus, historian, archivist and editor of an anthology of Hitler's speeches and proclamations, stated in the second volume of his copious work – with more than a whiff of verisimilitude – the "successful resistance of the Soviet Union against Hitler's invasion was, exactly as in the case of Napoleon, above all the glorious work of the Soviet artillery.

> Just like the divisions and Guarde of Napoleon, in the Second World War the German Army was suddenly confronted by the immense power, precision and superiority of the Russian batteries and mortars. The Russian cannon outside Moscow in 1941, the rockets of the "*Stalinorgel*" and the 5000 firing guns of Stalingrad all belong indelibly to the picture of the great Russian war of annihilation from 1941 to 1945. And the thunder of the guns, which during the war proclaimed each new victory to the people of Moscow was, at the same time, a salute of honor to the brave and incomparable artillerymen, Russia's best arm of the service.[69]

In practical terms, a 76mm shell produced a crater one meter in diameter and .5 meters deep; a 122mm shell, a crater three meters in diameter and .7 meters deep; and a 152mm shell, a crater fully five meters in diameter and 1.8 meters deep.[70] In the static warfare that characterized the central sector of the eastern front in August-September 1941, the forces of Army Group Center suffered severe attrition at the hands of ample, well-supplied, and adroitly wielded Red Army artillery. However, similar to the other branches of the Soviet armed forces in 1941, the artillery arm exhibited serious shortcomings:

> Contemporary Soviet archival reports and after-action assessments noted several major deficiencies in artillery systems. Inspections conducted in spring 1941 indicated that regimental personnel, in particular junior and mid-range commanders, were poorly trained and unable to employ their artillery effectively in combat. Firing units experienced major difficulties in target acquisition and fire direction and were unable to coordinate their fire with that of supposedly cooperating units. The most serious deficiency found in gun artillery units was their inability to bring effective fire to bear on enemy tanks, which was one of the most critical tasks assigned to artillery units by pre-war regulations.[71]

Yet it is doubtful that such deficiencies were apparent to the hard-pressed German *Landser* who, in the El'nia salient, several hundred kilometers west of Moscow, in the summer of 1941, were hammered daily by barrages reminiscent of those of the Great War of 1914/18. A battalion clerk in an infantry regiment belonging to 292 Infantry Division recorded their ordeal:

8.8.41:
We have two rest days with the Battalion; by now, <u>1158 km</u> of pure march route have been put behind us. After this and in the following days there are long march routes in an almost northern direction toward El'nia, where heavy fighting has broken out.

El'nia Bend
The Division [292 ID] is to relieve the SS-Division *Das Reich*, and is assigned to 20 AK.

11.8.41:
After a 65 km approach march the Battalion, extremely exhausted, reaches the area of Paukova ... Here, and at Vidrina and Klematina [in the El'nia Bend], very heavy fighting takes place in the following days! After several enemy incursions into Klematina, 509 IR puts in a counterattack. Supported by artillery drumfire preparations, those Russians still sitting in Klematina incessantly charge against the regiment. Here, Ivan brings in his excellent Artillery School from Moscow, which gives us a lot of trouble. In the morning we discover that the Battalion already had 64 losses in the first attack, the highest number yet.

The baggage train is in Leonidova, we start building dugouts ... Ahead of us is the *Rollbahn* to El'nia, which leads into the narrow salient and is constantly under fire. There are losses through artillery in the baggage train as well. Parts of SS-Division *Das Reich* still remain here. They have had very heavy losses by now,[72] as the cemetery at El'nia testifies.

12.-13.8.41:
Both days brought very heavy losses.[73] Ivan used a "Stalin Organ" against us for the first time.

15.-19.8.41:
15, 16, 18 and 19 August ... are also very difficult days. Positions are under intense artillery fire for hours.[74] Well-targeted Pak and mortar fire destroys our positions and the losses are mounting from day to day. However, 45 attacks in 17 days have been repelled!

23.8.41:
Today the Battalion relieved the I./507 at Mitina, where it is supposed to be quieter. These somewhat quieter days last until 29.8.

30.8.41:
Today there is almost continuous artillery fire again. There are ferocious attacks on our regiment as well. But by evening the whole main battle line [HKL] is securely in our hands.

31.8.41:
The Russians are shooting with long-range artillery deep into the hinterland, including right up to the division command post, where there are casualties. By breaking through the neighboring corps, Russian tanks advance as far as the division CP.

2.9.41:
Ivan drives around the division CP with tanks and in Lysovka shoots into the tents of the main dressing station. Now holding the El'nia bend has become very problematic!

3.9.41:
The El'nia bend is to be evacuated!

4.9.41:
During the night, the withdrawal of the regiment proceeds according to plan. Amongst other things, the large military cemetery for the SS [*Das Reich*] was completely leveled beforehand, so as not to give any indication of our heavy losses … At 1900 hours the Russian had marched into El'nia.[75]

With the German evacuation of the El'nia salient, the Red Army had garnered its first major victory of the war.

4.3.2: Mechanized Forces

As war with Germany loomed, Soviet mechanized forces were in the middle of a massive reorganization of their force structure and change out of tanks and equipment. To ascertain why this was so, a brief introduction to Soviet doctrinal thinking as it evolved in the 1920s and 1930s is necessary. It is one of the great ironies of history that it was not the Germans but the Russians – led by the "prodigious trio" of generals, Tukhachevsky, Triandafillov and Isserson – who first introduced the concept of an "operational" level of warfare – an intermediate level of warfare falling between the Clausewitzian categories of strategy and tactics. In the process, these highly innovative thinkers devised an "entirely original doctrine" which found its fullest expression in a concept known as "deep operations." Simply stated, "deep operations" envisaged the use of robust armored and motorized forces – echeloned in depth and cooperating with infantry and artillery – to rapidly breach the enemy front and then exploit the initial success by conducting operational maneuvers far to the rear of the enemy's main deployment.[76] While at the time radically new, such thinking was clearly in line with the manifestly offensive orientation of Soviet military doctrine since the 1920s. As Geoffrey Roberts has argued, "the concept of strategic defense had no place in the doctrinal universe of the Soviet High Command at the time." Stalin as well was committed to the doctrine of offensive action. Any war fought by the Soviet Union – regardless of the posture of her foreign policy – was going to be fought on the enemy's soil.[77]

The prerequisite for transforming "deep operations" from a concept into concrete reality was, of course, the creation of a large, independent and effective mechanized force. In 1930, the Russians established an experimental mechanized (tank) brigade; by 1932, they had four such brigades; by 1936, the size of the force had expanded to four mechanized corps, as well as a host of mechanized brigades, tank regiments and tank battalions. In 1938, a Soviet tank corps (the mechanized corps of 1936 were renamed tank corps at this time) was composed of 12,710 men, 560 tanks and 118 guns; by 1939, the Soviets had five such corps in their force structure. Deep operations were also to be promoted by the formation of airborne brigades, which slowly increased in numbers and size up to June 1941.[78]

In the period before war with Germany, however, the concept of deep operations, while never completely abandoned, was significantly modified – even, it appears, forgotten for a time. In the first place, the Tukhachevsky group[79] became a victim of the purges and was liquidated in 1937. Secondly, the experiences of the Russians in Spain (1936-39), eastern Poland (1939) and Finland (1939/40) convinced the Soviet military leadership that the use of large, independently operating tank corps was not a good fit for the modern battlefield, while the tanks themselves were too prone to mechanical breakdowns and logistical problems. Thus, in late 1939, the decision was taken to abolish the five existing tank corps and replace them with smaller combined arms units with fewer tanks.[80]

This decision, however, soon collided with the reality of the German "blitzkrieg." The dramatic German victories in 1939 and 1940 "shattered Soviet confidence" that they had acted judiciously in eliminating the tank corps. As David Glantz puts it, "They looked upon German operations in Poland with wonderment and awe." Yet the real "wake-up" call was the *Wehrmacht's* stunning six-week victory over France in 1940. In a series of insightful articles appearing in late 1940 and 1941, the typical Soviet response was: "My God, they picked up on our ideas and are effectively implementing them while we have gone in the opposite direction."[81]

Finally roused to action, the Red Army leadership hastily began to reestablish a large armored force structure. In July 1940, the creation of nine new mechanized corps got underway; and, in early 1941, the Soviets began forming an additional 20 such corps. All 29 of the mechanized corps were to be partially equipped with new KV (*Klementi Voroshilov*) heavy and T-34 medium tanks. On paper, each of these corps (each with two tank divisions and one mechanized division)[82] embraced 36,080 men, 1031 tanks (including 126 KVs and 420 T-34s), 358 guns and mortars, 268 armored cars, 5165 vehicles, and 352 tractors. Yet despite frantic efforts to accelerate their formation, most of these corps were still seriously understrength in manpower, armor, equipment, and logistical support by June 1941.[83] For example, five of the six mechanized corps in the Western Special Military District – i.e., those corps facing Field Marshal von Bock's Army Group Center – had only been formed in March 1941 and were woefully understrength (unlike the one corps which had been formed in July 1940); none of these five mechanized corps had more than 518 tanks, and two of them possessed less than 100. Seriously exacerbating such shortfalls was the fact that both the officers and men who manned these corps – and their tank and mechanized divisions – were still relatively untrained.[84]

Just how far the Red Army was from equipping each of its 29 mechanized corps with more than 500 KVs and T-34s is apparent from the fact that, on the day the Germans struck, only 1861 of these marvelous tanks were in service throughout the entire Red Army; of these, 1475 were unevenly distributed to the mechanized corps in the western military districts. The corps were primarily outfitted with older, light BT and T-26 model tanks, many of which had not be adequately maintained in anticipation of their replacement by superior KVs and T-34s. In fact, as of 15 June 1941, 29 percent of the older model tanks were in need of capital repair, while 44 percent required lesser maintenance.[85]

On paper, the primary Russian tanks of 1941, the 11-ton T-26 light tank and the 14-ton light BT models (there were several) were equivalent at very least to the German Pz II, and most were outfitted with a 45mm main armament, which was similar to the Panzer III.[86] Moreover, both the T-26 and the BT tanks were available in numbers far greater than their German counterparts. Yet German tanks operated within a comprehensive radio net, while Russian tanks were equipped with few radios and hardly any below the battalion level, control being executed through the use of signal flags. As a result, it was far more difficult for Soviet mechanized forces to respond rapidly to the inexorably changing conditions on the battlefield.[87] In any case, all of these Soviet tanks were obsolete by the beginning of *Barbarossa*. On the evening of the first day of the war, the commander of Soviet 10

Army gloomily reported that his superannuated T-26 tanks were only good "for firing at sparrows."[88]

Much superior were the new tank models – the KVs and the T-34s – which were only now just starting to enter the inventory in numbers. The KV-1 was the Red Army's heavy tank; it weighed nearly 48 tons, was operated by a crew of five, protected by 75-100mm of armor, and fitted with a 76mm main armament. The KV-2 was fitted with a 152mm howitzer for demolishing enemy bunkers; the Russians, however, produced but a few of these tanks, as they were difficult to manufacture and the requirement for the heavy projectile used by the tank was limited.[89] On 25 June 1941, D+3 of the German invasion, Chief of the German Army General Staff Halder, in his diary, noted the reported appearance of two new types of Russian tanks. One of them, he observed, was said to weigh 52 tons and possess a 152mm gun. Halder was clearly skeptical that such a huge tank existed and, after listing its putative attributes, placed in parentheses the words "still questionable" (*noch fraglich*).[90]

At the front, however, along the main battle line, far removed from the High Command's "green table," German soldiers soon experienced the "shock and awe" of having to deal with such tanks without effective anti-tank and tank guns. A diary entry of an *Unteroffizier* in 17 Panzer Division from early October 1941 – most likely describing an encounter with two KV-1s – graphically portrays the havoc a couple of these behemoths could cause if left "unattended:"

> It has become bitingly cold, the first snow is falling quietly. Wind. Brief halt in a village – ask the people if German soldiers have been there already, no, only a motorcyclist drove through. Drive onward, but quickly all turn back again, have we got lost? … Huge explosions to the right, fiery glow on the horizon. Is that Briansk already? … New route. Pitch dark … Take cover in a small village, have to erect the MG behind the house, sleep in the loft, because everywhere overcrowded below, in part with refugees or men who work there …
>
> A tank officer is swearing profusely … At one point in the forest it looks dreadful; vehicles from 2nd Battalion – burned out, crushed, smashed – are lying and standing about. In the forest and on the road, 28 vehicles are destroyed, one 8.8 Flak gun and one Pak … The whole disaster was caused by two Russian. tanks, by two 50-ton tanks. One tipped over and lay on its stomach. When it tipped, it could be finished off. It had simply rolled the vehicles into the ground, driven across and over them. The Flak gun couldn't shoot, a German vehicle stood in front of it and so the tank was able to drive over both … the drivers all careered about wildly … there is said to have been one fatality and a few casualties.[91]

On a television documentary some years back, an observer characterized the T-34 as looking "like something made out of cheese by a small child with a knife."[92] An inelegant and crudely finished design it may have been, but it was also the centerpiece of Soviet efforts to modernize their mechanized forces. The medium tank weighed about 30 tons, was operated by a crew of five, carried a high-velocity 76mm main armament, had armor protection from 45-52mm, and an excellent top speed of 55 k/h. The tank's 60 percent sloping armor was revolutionary, offering significantly enhanced protection against flat trajectory AT shells, which often failed to penetrate and simply ricocheted away. Adapting the American Christie suspension system, the T-34, with extra-wide tracks and a powerful diesel engine, boasted an "enormous relative power-to-weight ratio, conferring superior mobility on the Russian vehicles." Most historians of the Second World War rate the T-34 among the top two or three tanks produced by any combatant during the war, if not the very best.[93]

Like the heavy KV models, the T-34 administered a nasty shock to the German invaders, who lacked intelligence on the tank, even though information on it should have been available to them.[94] The Russians had deployed the T-34 in August 1939 against the Japanese at Khalkin-Gol; however, there is little indication the German High Command ever paid much attention to the fighting there.[95] The standard 37mm and 50mm AT guns of the German Army of 1941 were virtually useless against the T-34,[96] which at the time was vulnerable only to the powerful German 88mm multi-purpose gun and regular artillery deployed in a direct-fire role. Only through introduction of 75mm anti-tank guns, and a more robust 75mm tank cannon, both in 1942, did the Germans begin to confront the T-34 on more equal terms. In the interim, the German *Landser* were to experience many unpleasant encounters with the tank that soon became their nemesis. In the account below, even point-blank fire from a 105mm field howitzer was incapable of disabling several attacking T-34s:

> [Kostino/January 1942]: At least five, if not six, T-34s drove out of the woods onto the road and formed a pack of tanks to attack Kostino at its western narrow side. They fired ferociously at the snow wall and the ruins of the houses in the western area. When the foremost T-34 had reached the snow wall, roughly 20 meters away from the first 37mm Pak, our Pak began to snarl. At least 20 shells bounced off the frontal armor of the T-34.[97] Then that behemoth simply drove over the Pak gun and squashed it flat, right into the snow ...
>
> Then the other behemoths approached. The 50mm [Pak] began firing as the first T-34 came level with the tanks that had been destroyed during the night. Unfortunately, the hits had no effect. The second tank immediately destroyed the 50mm gun. The gun crew were mown down with more hits. Now the next thing was the fight with the 105mm howitzer, which stood ready for firing, fully loaded with high-explosive anti-tank rounds [*Hohlraumgranaten*]. When the first T-34 came around the house ruins that were shielding the gun, exposing its entire flank, the howitzer thundered. The shell hit the T-34 squarely in the flank. The tank's driver went into reverse gear and ducked back behind the house ruins.
>
> It didn't take long before two T-34s arrived, one on each side of the house ruins. The 105mm high-explosive rounds which were now fired in quick succession hit home, but they had no impact on the Russian tanks ... The shells hadn't penetrated. They had now identified our gun and shot it to pieces with 76mm shells.
>
> Then they felt their way further forward and the tanks behind also advanced into the area ... We had fatalities and wounded. From the Russian-occupied forest edge to the south of our location the infantry now also attacked us at that point. Two T-34s drove along the road in the direction of Bolshaya and probably wanted to see whether reinforcements were approaching from the forest. They soon returned. All soldiers who no longer had a safe hide-out, or who had thought themselves watched by some of the [enemy] tank commanders, now crawled behind the large pile of straw ...
>
> Then our commander also arrived and hid behind the pile of straw with us. He had not felt safe in the command post basement any more. When yet another tank approached the pile of straw and we hid, the tank commander opened the hatch and boldly looked out under cover of fire from another tank. Then *Oberstleutnant* Ulrich confronted the tank with the commander looking out of it. We held our breath. He pulled out his 7.62mm pistol and yelled at the tank commander: "Surrender yourself!"
>
> At that, the man disappeared into the turret, the 76mm gun blazed. It obviously hit our commander directly from a 10-meter distance. Later we could only find scraps of him ... The divisional report later read: on 29 January Kostino, in the sector of 17 IR, was lost to the enemy.[98]

4.3.3: Cavalry & Airborne Troops

Unlike other branches of the Soviet armed forces, the cavalry – Stalin's favorite service branch – had not undergone the wholesale reorganization of the Timoshenko reforms and was thus more combat ready that the rifle and mechanized forces. However, because the Russian military leadership had used the cavalry forces as nuclei for the creation of new mechanized corps, total cavalry forces declined from seven corps and 32 divisions in 1937 to just four corps and 13 divisions by June 1941. The table of organization of a cavalry division called for four cavalry regiments, one tank regiment, artillery and anti-aircraft battalions and support troops; on paper, total strength was 9240 men, 68 guns, 64 mortars, 64 light tanks, 18 armored cars, 555 vehicles and 7940 horses. When war began, the Red Army's cavalry formations boasted 85-90 percent of their personnel and equipment; yet they possessed only 45-50 percent of their vehicles, did not have any AA defenses and had few tanks, since all available armor was channeled to the new mechanized forces.[99]

The truncation of the cavalry forces would be dramatically reversed in the final six months of 1941, as the cavalry proved to be a highly capable combat arm under conditions prevailing on the eastern front. Beginning in the summer of 1941, the Red Army initially established 30 new light cavalry divisions (3447 horsemen each) – a figure which had climbed to 82 such divisions by the end of the year.[100] During the winter of 1941/42, when Soviet mechanized units were often immobilized by cold and snow, the cavalry were effective at conducting long-range guerilla operations deep behind the front, cutting lines of communication, attacking German rear area installations, and, in general, supporting activities of the Red Army and partisan units. Moreover, the huge tank losses suffered by the Russians in the opening months of *Barbarossa*, and the corresponding paucity of armor in the Soviet force structure during the first winter of the war, meant that the cavalry were often the only available option for performing mobile combat operations. A German general who served on the central front that winter offered this assessment of the Russian cavalry:

> In the campaign the Russian cavalry, despite many changes in tactics and equipment, achieved a significance reminiscent of old times. In the German army, all cavalry units except one division had been replaced by panzer units. The Russians followed another course … Under conditions as characterized in Central Russia by great forest and swamp areas, muddy periods, and deep snow, cavalry is a useable arm. When the German motor failed, the Russian horse's legs continued to move. The tactical employment of cavalry forces was, however, not always suited to the situation and sometimes was even awkward. Leadership and training in the Russian cavalry were not up to the World War I standard.[101]

The airborne forces were among the most elite in the Red Army's force structure. By June 1941, the existing five airborne brigades and manpower from 11 rifle divisions had been used to create five airborne corps, each consisting of 10,400 men organized into three air assault brigades of 2634 men each and a separate light tank battalion. Each of the subordinate brigades had three parachute assault battalions, an artillery battalion, and reconnaissance and engineering companies.[102] Several of the German eastern front veterans with whom this author has corresponded have pointed to the existence of such forces – whose mission was clearly offensive, as the *Wehrmacht* itself demonstrated in 1940/41 with its airborne units – as proof of Soviet intent to wage offensive war against Germany.[103] However, the lack of fire and logistical support, coupled with the shortfall in dedicated air transport units, compelled the corps to be used as infantry in "fire brigades" after the war began. During its winter offensive of 1941/42, the Red Army did conduct several major airborne operations in support of ongoing efforts to encircle and destroy

German Army Group Center; yet these were largely desperate measures employed by the Soviets when other options could not be found, and quickly revealed the weaknesses in training and equipment of the airborne forces:

> In the night of 27.-28.1.[42] Soviet paratroopers landed in Dispersal Area B, 25 kilometers southwest of Viaz'ma, close to Asstaschevka, the location of 1./Fla 601.[104] ... This was not a jump by a few paratroopers to support the partisans, but rather an airborne operation of 3000 men targeting Viaz'ma. An amateurishly led operation without any visible success. The catastrophic airborne operation west of Kanev in summer 1943 also demonstrates that the Russians simply had no idea in this military field. Marshal Voronov wrote resignedly in his memoirs: "It is sad to have to say that we, the pioneers of the air drop, had no practicable plans for deploying these men." It seems that the technical, material and personnel problems associated with this weapon proved to be insoluble for the Red Army.[105]

4.3.4: Soviet Air Forces

With about 19,500 aircraft, the Soviet Air Force (VVS, or *Voenno-vozdushnikh sil*) was the world's largest air force in 1941. Like most of the Soviet armed forces, the VVS was also in a stage of re-equipping and expansion in the years prior to the outbreak of war with Germany, while its air forces in the western military districts – in June 1941 about 7100 planes, slightly more than 35 percent of the VVS force structure[106] – were undergoing extensive reorganization and retraining of personnel. The air force leadership labored frantically to build up its forces, including efforts to create 106 new air regiments[107] beginning in 1941; only 19 of these, however, had been formed prior to the outbreak of war, 13 of which were long-range bomber regiments. Several hundred airfields were also built or renovated (including 164 between April and July 1941),[108] the majority of them in forward areas – such as eastern Poland – where they were vulnerable to attack by the *Luftwaffe*. Yet this work, too, was unfinished by June 1941, often leaving the newly enlarged VVS units sitting on crowded airstrips or unfinished airfields, frustrating efforts at dispersal or camouflage.[109]

If there was one area where the myth of the qualitative superiority of German weaponry was no myth at all it was that of combat aircraft. The aircraft models available to the Soviet Air Force in the greatest numbers in June 1941 were antediluvian designs; these included the Polikarpov I-15 (biplane) and I-16 "*Rata*" fighters and the DB-3 and SB-2 medium bombers. *Luftwaffe* pilots had encountered most of these types in the Spanish Civil War in the late 1930s. Soviet training and operational standards also fell well short of the *Luftwaffe*, while the lack of radio equipment was a particularly serious shortcoming. With war clouds gathering on the horizon, in 1939/40 the Soviet government and Communist Party approved plans for the production and fielding of an entirely new generation of modern combat aircraft; among them were: Yak-1, LaGG-3 and MiG-3 fighters; Pe-2 and Pe-8 bombers; and Il-2 assault aircraft. Most of these new aircraft types, "were technically superior to their corresponding German counterparts;"[110] moreover, they were largely missing from *Luftwaffe* intelligence estimates and recognition manuals prior to the invasion. The Il-2 "*Sturmovik*" ground attack plane was a particularly excellent and robust design which was to wreak untold havoc on German ground forces. Unfortunately for the Soviets, these new models were only beginning to enter the inventory in June 1941, when some 80 percent of VVS aircraft were older, essentially obsolete types.[111]

If the front-line aircraft were mostly bad, VVS tactical doctrine and aircrew training were even worse. The air force's mission was limited under the 1936 regulations to close air support of ground forces, the Soviets having, for the most part, abandoned the strategic bombing mission in the late 1930s, when they disbanded their three strategic air armies and canceled production of the four-engine TB-7 bomber.[112] Like most of their aircraft, VVS air combat tactics were also obsolete, allowing for no individual initiative and proving overly cautious and inflexible.[113] Soviet fighter pilots, burdened by glaring deficiencies in equipment, organization and training, were to display an "acute sense of inferiority" vis-à-vis their German counterparts, often avoiding engagements and even turning away from unescorted Ju 52 transports (which had light defensive armament) when these were flying in close formation.[114] Such behavior, however, can hardly be attributed to cowardice; after all, many fighter pilots began the war with inadequate training, while transition training to qualify pilots for the new aircraft types proceeded at a "snail's pace" because Soviet Air Force commanders feared training accidents might result in their arrest for sabotage.[115] Consequently, in the forward areas, many fighter pilots had as few as four hours experience in the new aircraft when the *Luftwaffe* finally came calling.

In contrast to Soviet fighter pilots, VVS bomber crews displayed remarkable courage – at times, even recklessness, or at least an absence of caution – from the first hours of the war. They were at once thrown into battle in large numbers in an effort to forestall the advancing *Wehrmacht*, particularly at major river crossings; as a result, they were shot down in appalling numbers – entire formations at a time – by German fighters and anti-aircraft guns. Indeed, Field Marshal Kesselring, commander of German 2 Air Fleet supporting Army Group Center, characterized the obliteration of VVS bomber forces as "sheer 'infanticide:'"

> From the second day onward I watched the battle against the Russian medium bombers that came from the depths of the Russian territory. I thought it close to criminal that these so inept aircraft were sent out to attack in what were, in terms of air tactics, impossible formations. Thus one squadron fell after another; they approached in the same timed intervals, falling easy victim to our fighter pilots, sheer "infanticide," as I thought it then.[116]

Given the debilitating deficiencies of the VVS in almost every area, it is not surprising that the *Luftwaffe* was able to smash it in the air and on the ground in the opening hours and days of Operation *Barbarossa*. That said, it is a myth – and one stubbornly promoted over the years in many accounts of the Russo-German War – that the Soviet Air Force, because of the pounding it endured in the initial 48-72 hours of the campaign, was mostly absent from the fighting throughout the summer of 1941, only to recover at some later date. This author's analysis of literally hundreds of German primary accounts (unit war diaries, personal diaries, field post, etc.) supports the conclusion that, while the *Luftwaffe* did indeed establish air superiority in the opening stage of the war, it rarely enjoyed total air *supremacy* over the battlefield; and if total air supremacy – that desideratum of air power advocates everywhere – was achieved for short periods over certain sectors of the front in the immediate wake of the invasion, the VVS remained active, at some level, from virtually the first day of the war. The *Luftwaffe*, limited in numbers and necessarily spread thin over the staggering spaces of European Russia, could not be everywhere at once; while for its part the VVS focused its efforts, however limited, on the most dangerous component of the German *Ostheer*, the rapidly advancing motorized spearheads. Indeed, from 23 June to 10 July 1941, VVS Long-Range Bomber Aviation flew more than 2100 combat sorties against German tank and motorized columns, while the Soviets as a whole conducted more than 47,000 combat sorties,[117] even if the results were largely negligible. Although these figures (gleaned from the official Soviet account of VVS operations) may well be exaggerated, they tend to corroborate the German experience, which was that the VVS remained very much in existence despite its eviscerating losses. Moreover, by autumn 1941, it was beginning to make a remarkable recovery, even wrestling air superiority from the Germans in key sectors of the front. That the Red Air Force was able to do so signifies more than just a tribute to the courage and tenacity of its aircrews, it illustrates that the reforms begun before the war were beginning to bear fruit.

4.4: Final Strategic Planning: Failures & False Assumptions

Since the late 1930s, the Red Army General Staff had extensively refined and drilled their mobilization plans. By spring 1941, spurred by intelligence estimates of the growing German threat, the Soviet leadership had partially implemented a "special threatening military period" and accelerated "creeping up to war" by conducting a concealed strategic deployment of forces. This meant, in essence, the initial stage of a precautionary mobilization process that was to accelerate after the war began and continue into early 1942. Beginning in late April 1941, and in strictest secrecy, major forces were transferred from the interior of the country – from Trans-Baikal and the Far East, and later from the Ural and Siberian Military Districts – into the threatened western military districts. All told, four army headquarters, 19 corps headquarters and 28 divisional headquarters received orders to advance from the interior of the USSR to the western districts. In early June 1941, ostensibly for the purpose of "large scale war games," the People's Commissariat of Defense (NKO) conscripted 793,000 men to flesh out some 100 existing divisions and fortified regions. Under the General Staff's final mobilization plan (MP-41) all troops in the western districts were to be brought up to full mobilization readiness during the spring of 1941.[118] As we have seen, by 22 June 1941, the Red Army in the frontier zone (first strategic echelon) comprised 171 divisions echeloned in depth, with a further 57 divisions assembling in the second strategic echelon along the Western Dvina and Dnepr Rivers. Due to snags in the mobilization process, however, full implementation of MP-41 – which, for example, had called for assembly of 186 divisions in the first strategic echelon – had not been achieved in either strategic echelon by the time war finally came.[119]

The final dispositions of Soviet forces in the west make for interesting speculation about the motives behind Soviet strategic planning on the eve of the German invasion. What is most striking about these dispositions is that they reveal a marked concentration of Soviet forces in the Kiev Special Military District, covering the Ukraine. A total of some 60 divisions (among them 16 tank and eight motorized) were stationed in this district, far more than in any of the other military districts, with the Western Special Military District possessing the second largest number of divisions with a total of 44 (12 tank and six motorized). Soviet air regiments were also heavily concentrated in the Kiev Military District.[120]

A cursory examination of Soviet strategic planning from the summer of 1940 into the spring of 1941 reveals potential rationales behind the powerful assembly of forces on what was to become (on 22 June) the Southwestern Front – opposite German Army Group South. Beginning about July 1940, the General Staff, under the direction of Marshal Timoshenko, crafted new war plans positing that a German attack – should it come – would most likely be made north of the Pripiat' Marshes and out of East Prussia into Lithuania, Latvia and Western Belorussia (all now occupied by the Soviet Union); hence, the bulk of Red Army forces were to be stationed in the north. In October 1940, however, Soviet planning underwent a crucial revision: The main Red Army forces were not to be disposed in the north, but in the south, shielding the grain of the Ukraine and the coal and minerals of the Donbas region. The "most likely explanation" for this change, submits Geoffrey Roberts, was the "expectation" that, if war broke out, the main German forces would attack in the south, into the Ukraine. While Roberts does not say what prompted this fundamental – and wholly inaccurate – reassessment of German intentions, he goes on to indicate that, by early 1941, the Germans were carefully promoting it by means of a disinformation campaign which effectively masked their true intentions – i.e., a concentration of forces (*Schwerpunkt*) in the north, for an offensive along the Minsk – Smolensk – Moscow axis.[121]

There is, however, another interpretation of why the primary Russian concentration was in the south. Evan Mawdsley explains:

> Fear for the Ukraine was not the main reason for the concentration of the Red Army there, in the Kiev Military District. From the Russian point of view, the question was not where to defend, but *where to attack*. The alternatives lay between attacking the Germans in East Prussia and northern Poland (*out of* Belorussia), or attacking them in southern Poland (*out of* the Ukraine). The problem with the northern axis was that it meant attacking through the lakes and forests of East Prussia, which had prepared German fortifications. The Russian Army had stalled there in 1914-15; meanwhile the strength of modern field fortifications had become clear in the Red Army's 1940 attacks on the Finnish "Mannerheim Line." The southern axis, in contrast, allowed an advance into relatively open country, without long-built German fortifications, and with the attacking Red Army's left flank covered by the Carpathian Mountains. A drive into Poland, through Lublin and Kraków and Upper Silesia, would outflank the German concentration in Poland and threaten German links to the Balkans. Red Army planners looked at the options and recommended an attack along the southern axis.[122]

This plan, states Mawdsley, was approved by Stalin in October 1940, and a large force, heavy in tanks and aircraft, was subsequently deployed to the Kiev Military District. Revisionist historians have interpreted the decision by Stalin and his generals to concentrate in the south as proof that they were planning a pre-emptive strike against Germany. While Zhukov would propose just such a strike in mid-May 1941, the more logical conclusion is that the Soviets were simply acting on long-standing military doctrine, which foresaw immediate offensive action – even when under attack – to take the war to the enemy's territory. Indeed, State Defense Plan 1941 (DP-41), although clearly defensive in a strategic context, embraced many offensive features, "couched in terms of necessary and inevitable offensive reactions, that is, 'counteractions,' to potential enemy aggression."[123]

In any case, the Soviet decision to put their largest force grouping in the south, away from the main axis of the German advance, was a serious miscalculation. The decision was reinforced by the outcome of two war games conducted by the Red Army in January 1941, with the result that, by March 1941, a revised operational plan was ready which mandated that the main weight of the Soviet defenses be directed against a German attack into the Ukraine.[124] More serendipitously, as it turned out, the January war games – in which Soviet General G. K. Zhukov had participated with relative success – resulted in Stalin appointing Zhukov Chief of the Army General Staff. The games, however – both of which simulated a German offensive on different fronts and explored Red Army responses – revealed the unpreparedness of the armed forces and help to explain "Stalin's desperate attempts to postpone the war, and his cautious handling of the deployment in the months preceding the war."[125]

It should also be noted that Soviet war planning in general was based on several unfounded assumptions that, in the end, nearly proved fatal. In an "extraordinary example of strategic blindness,"[126] Soviet political and military leaders prepared for war in the mistaken belief that they would have time to mobilize and concentrate their forces prior to the start of the main fighting. They would, so they thought, be able to choose when war would begin – as had been the case with Finland in the autumn of 1939. Soviet generals failed to grasp that the Red Army, too, could be caught by surprise. Moreover, they fully expected – at least until late spring 1941 – that the Germans would require several weeks to concentrate their forces for an attack on Russia, and that such a concentration could not be carried out secretly. They also overestimated the combat capability of their border cover forces, thinking they could hold any German attack for several weeks, giving the Red Army time to mobilize and concentrate. These assumptions had begun to fall apart by May 1941, as the Soviet military leadership finally realized that the *Wehrmacht* was *already mobilized* and had assembled large forces in East Prussia and German-occupied Poland opposite the Russian border. And, yet, Stalin still directed no changes to existing plans.[127]

Soviet military planning in the months prior to the German attack was also cast into confusion by the movement of the frontier 320 kilometers to the west, after annexation of the Baltic republics, eastern Poland and Bessarabia in 1939/40. Before 1939, the Red Army had built strong defensive positions along and behind the Soviet Union's old border, fortifications the Germans christened the "Stalin Line." The Stalin Line was, for the most part, not a line at all, but a system of fortified regions (*ukreplennyi raion* – UR), each with bunkers, light artillery, machine gun positions and tank traps.[128] A German training video for the Replacement Army (*Ersatzheer*) offered a fascinating glimpse of the Soviet border defenses following their capture in July 1941: On display are tank traps (several types of them), water obstacles, wire entanglements, crisscrossed steel beams (tank obstacles), bunkers (concrete, wooden, earthen), earthworks of timber and soil, houses and barns used to conceal weapon positions, even flamethrowers with remote ignition.[129] One of the oldest fortified regions along the Stalin Line was Polotsk, which sat astride the Dvina River where the Soviet, Polish and Lithuanian frontiers came together; others at Minsk, Mozyr and Slutsk dated from the 1930s.[130]

In an effort to turn the newly occupied territories in the west into a kind of strategic *glacis*, defenses along the old 1939 frontier were stripped to provide weapons and materiel for new fortified zones along the border with Germany. The outcome was all too predictable: When the Germans struck the Stalin Line had been seriously compromised, while not nearly enough had been done to create new fortified zones along the new border. Moreover, on *Barbarossatag*, most of the divisions along the German-Soviet frontier were missing their combat engineers (they were off constructing new bunkers and obstacles), seriously degrading their combat prowess.[131] Once again, poor Soviet decision-making resulted in a Red Army that was unable to do its best in either attack or defense.

4.5: The Red Army – Ready for War?

In light of the preceding discussion, highlighting myriad Red Army deficiencies as war loomed with Germany, the reader may well find the question rhetorical in nature. The weaknesses of the Soviet armed forces were, undoubtedly, legion; and it seems apparent that, in June 1941, they were, at best, months away from being ready for war. The following list strikingly illustrates – in no particular order – the many challenges faced by the Red Army at this time:

- Conflicting doctrinal concepts; purges still underway, resulting in severe shortage of trained and experienced commanders and staff officers;
- Authoritarian concepts of combat leadership, stifling initiative on the part of junior officers and NCOs; lack of cooperation between combat arms; poor staff work;
- Massive reorganization of force structure and change-out of weapons and equipment still far from complete; in many vital spheres – tank and aircraft production, border fortifications, manpower – targets for completion set for no earlier than early 1942;
- Serious deficiencies in troop training; outmoded weapons, out of date combat aircraft; shortages of maps and equipment;
- Armed forces possessing some modern weapons, but "no indication that anyone understood how to use them;"[132] some Soviet pilots with less than four hours experience in new aircraft; cases of tanks whose main armament had not been bore-sighted before war began;[133]

- Political necessity of Red Army soldiers to defend every inch of existing frontier; many units positioned well forward in border regions and too vulnerable to German ground and air forces;
- Serious shortfalls in motorization; less than 275,000 motor vehicles in all theaters (compared to German *Ostheer's* 600,000), supplemented by ca. 200,000 mobilized from civilian economy;
- Mechanized corps near frontier with only 50-80 percent of authorized strength in combat vehicles; 208 Motorized Division (positioned near Belostok in central sector) with only 70 to 80 percent of its authorized armaments; its tank regiment with no tanks (authorized 250); situation of this division hardly out of the ordinary;
- Deficiencies in logistics bordering on the catastrophic – cases of military clothing, equipment, etc., improperly housed in military depots (clothing and materiel rotting in the open, etc.); units suffering from serious shortages of uniforms, shoes, underclothing, food, equipment; artillery shells improperly stored and rusting in the open; lack of fuel and ammunition;
- Prime movers in short supply; Russians forced to employ civilian tractors to tow artillery;
- Poor signal communications: Moscow in contact with military districts over telephone, telegraph and radio, but primarily by telephone and including use of the civilian system; communications in the field tenuous; radio networks thin;[134]
- Railroad development plan for 1941 – including 11 new lines in the western military districts – only 8 percent complete as of 1 June 1941 due to shortages of key building materials.[135]

A sobering compilation – albeit one far from complete! And, yet, the picture is more complicated than it seems. According to Albert Seaton:

> The fighting efficiency of aircraft, tanks and guns and of air and ground formations, depends largely ... on the associated fire-control, communication and auxiliary equipment, and this was woefully lacking in the Soviet Union in 1941. All in all, however, Russia went to war immeasurably better prepared and equipped than it had ever done in czarist times and, in quantitative terms, took the field with the greatest army in the world ... Stalin's failure in the opening days of the war was political rather than military, for it was the direct consequence of his own political misjudgement.[136]

There is more than a grain of truth in Seaton's words. Indeed, if Stalin had done much to cripple his country's armed forces in the years before they joined in combat with Hitler's *Wehrmacht*, and if his policy of appeasement vis-à-vis the Third Reich was inevitably doomed to failure, Stalin was, in the final analysis, largely responsible for the victory ultimately achieved. It was his policies from at least the late 1920s, however oppressive and murderous, which set the Soviet Union on its path to becoming a modern industrial state. Without the Five-Year Plans; without the creation of a second industrial infrastructure well outside European Russia; without the colossal buildup of manpower, weapons and equipment he relentlessly pursued in the years before war; and without the Communist re-education of the young he so sedulously promoted – without all these things, the Soviet Union would have collapsed in 1941. If Stalin's pre-war policies helped to bring his country to the brink of extinction in the summer of 1941, they also built the foundation that enabled the Soviet Union to emerge victoriously in 1945 and survive another 46 years. One might question whether that was a good thing, but one cannot doubt Stalin's decisive role in bringing it about. For unlike the Czar's armies in 1914, Stalin's armies had rifles; they also had tens of millions of committed soldiers and an unbroken flood of tanks, guns and planes. Together, these men and machines would ultimately smash the *Wehrmacht*, and Red Army soldiers would plant the flag of the Soviet Union above the Reichstag in Berlin on 2 May 1945.

4.6: Joseph Stalin: What did he Know and When did he Know it?

Since the topic of discussion is the Soviet dictator, another question – and perhaps a more intriguing one – must be posed: Just how well informed was Stalin in the weeks and months before 22 June about Operation *Barbarossa*, and how did he respond to what he learned? The first part of the question can be answered with relative certitude: Stalin was very well informed about the impending German invasion through several different channels. The second part, however – his reaction to what he was told – is rather more complex.

In 1811, the year before Napoleon's ill-fated invasion of Russia, a comet swept across European skies. On 25 March 1811, Honoré Flaugergues, observing the night sky from his makeshift observatory in Viviers, discovered the comet "in the now defunct constellation of Argo Navis." The next day, he noticed it again, so he began to track its flight.

> The comet was low in the south and was moving northward and brightening. On 11 April it was spotted by Jean Louis Pons in Marseille, and on 12 May by William J. Burchell in Cape Town. The comet soon became visible to the naked eye, and by the late autumn it lit up the night sky from Lisbon to Moscow. People gazed up at it, some with interest, many more with a sense of foreboding.
>
> This seemed to increase the further east one went in Europe. "As they contemplated the brilliant comet of 1811," recalled a parish priest there, "the people of Lithuania prepared themselves for some extraordinary event." Another inhabitant of the province never forgot how everyone got up from dinner and went out to gaze on the comet and then talk of "famine, fire, war and bloodshed." In Russia, many linked the comet to a plague of fires that swept the land that summer and autumn, and a blind terror gripped them as they looked on it. "I remember fixing a long look on it on an autumn moonless night, and I was struck with childlike fear," wrote the son of a Russian landowner. "Its long, bright tail, which seemed to wave with the movement of the wind and to leap from time to time, filled me with such horror, that in the days that followed I did not look up at the sky at night, until the comet had disappeared."
>
> In St. Petersburg, Czar Alexander himself became fascinated by the phenomenon, and discussed it with John Quincy Adams, the American ambassador at his court. He claimed to be interested only in the scientific aspects of the comet, and made fun of all those superstitious souls who saw in it a harbinger of catastrophe and war.
>
> But he was either being disingenuous or he was deluding himself, for the machinery of war had already clanged into gear.[137]

Joseph Stalin, of course, was not so fortunate as to have a terrifying comet to alert him to the impending arrival of the Apocalypse, yet what he did have was "perhaps the most effective intelligence apparatus of any;" and parts of it operated "right at the heart" of German decision-making.[138] Soviet spies crawled all over Europe and included, among others, Harro Schulze-Boysen (code-name "*Starshina*," or "the Elder), a German Communist sympathizer and officer in the *Luftwaffe* with access to top-secret material; and Arvid Harnack (known as "*Korsicanets*," or the "Corsican"), a lawyer who had worked in the

Economics Ministry in Berlin since 1935. Both men, who furnished a flow of excellent information to the Soviets, had been recruited in the summer of 1940 to work secretly for Soviet intelligence. They were eventually discovered and executed in 1942.[139]

There were also Soviet espionage groups operating across German-occupied Europe and neutral Switzerland, such as the so-called "Lucy" spy ring – run out of Switzerland by German refugee Rudolf Roessler. Because of the high value information provided by "Lucy," historians have speculated that the ring may have been used by the British as a covert way to pass ULTRA-based intelligence on to the Soviets. (ULTRA was the code-name for British signal intelligence derived from radio traffic which the Germans encrypted on their high-grade cipher machines, called ENIGMA.)[140] Such speculation, however, is now known to be false.[141]

Another vital source of information on German intentions was Richard Sorge (known as "*Ramzai*"), a Soviet spy embedded in the German embassy in Tokyo. In addition, British, American and other foreign governments provided Stalin and his cohorts with an abundance of intelligence, much of it highly accurate. Finally, by the spring of 1941, a plethora of tactical intelligence was flowing in to Moscow from the border military districts.[142]

In all, between late July 1940 and 22 June 1941, no less than 90 separate warnings of an impending German attack were conveyed to Stalin by his intelligence apparatus, each report first having been professionally collated, carefully evaluated and interpreted before being briefed to him. Information received in the spring of 1941 (yet by no means a complete accounting) offers insight into just what Stalin knew, when he knew it, and how he responded to it:

- April 1941: Churchill, with data derived from ULTRA indicating that elite German units are in Poland, and not in the Balkans, decides to alert Stalin with a personal message from a "trusted agent." In the margins of the report, the Soviet dictator is alleged to have scrawled, "another English provocation." He takes no action.
- 19 May 1941: Richard Sorge warns that nine German armies with 150 divisions are massing on the German-Soviet border. Stalin's response to this highly accurate report is to denounce Sorge as "a little shit who has just set himself up with some good business in Japan."
- June 1941: The German ambassador in Moscow, von Schulenburg, warns the head of the Soviet International Affairs Department: "I am going to tell you something that has never been done in diplomacy before," he says. "Germany's state secret number one is that Hitler has taken the decision to begin war against you on 22 June." Stalin's response is indignant. He tells the Politburo that, "Disinformation has now reached ambassadorial level!"
- 12 June 1941: Stalin receives information from "*Starshina*," that the decision has been taken to attack Russia. The same day, a report reaches the Foreign Ministry and Central Committee, indicating that, between 1 January and 10 June 1941, German planes had violated Soviet airspace more than 2000 times; including 91 violations in the first 10 days of June.
- Mid-June 1941: A report arrives from "Lucy," stipulating the date of the attack (22 June) and furnishing details of the German operational plan. Stalin remains in complete denial.
- 17 June 1941: Another warning arrives from "*Starshina*," indicating that all German military measures for an attack are complete and that the blow may come at any moment. Reliable reports have also been received from the German Economics Ministry, indicating an imminent attack. In the margins of the report, Stalin hisses: "You can send your source from the staff of the *Luftwaffe* to the devil. He's not a source, he is providing disinformation."

- 18 June 1941: When Army Chief of Staff Zhukov suggests that the Red Army be placed in alarm readiness, Stalin replies: "So you want a war? Don't you have enough decorations and isn't your rank high enough?"[143]

Clearly bent on avoiding war with Germany – acutely cognizant as he was of his country's lack of preparedness for such a conflict – Stalin was to cling tightly to his denials until, finally, he could cling to them no more. Early on the morning of 22 June 1941, he got a telephone call from Zhukov: A massive German assault was underway all along the western frontier, he reported; the war had begun. Deeply shaken, Stalin at first said nothing. All Zhukov could hear was his boss's heavy breathing at the other end of the line. Yet even then, the full gravity of what had happened would not become apparent to Stalin for many hours.[144]

Today, nearly three generations removed from the towering events of that summer in 1941, it seems inconceivable that Stalin could have responded so dismissively to so much good intelligence. Once again, however, the situation is more complex than it appears, and Stalin's behavior (however bizarre it may seem today) was not without a certain justification.

In the first place, much of the information that made its way to Stalin pertaining to German intentions, or their buildup in the east, was much less clear cut than the examples cited above, even contradictory in nature. Key lieutenants such as Lavrenti Beria, the sinister head of the NKVD, or F. I. Golikov, chief of military intelligence, insecure in their own positions, often simply told Stalin what he wanted to hear, confirming his own prejudices and misconceptions. In addition, the Soviet intelligence community – both civilian and military – had been badly gutted by the purges, losing many agents and analysts in the process. In his 1940 report on the state of the Red Army, Defense Commissar Timoshenko observed: "The organization of intelligence [*razvedka*] is one of the weakest sectors of the work of the Commissariat of Defense. There is no organized intelligence and systematic gathering of information on foreign armies." Golikov, moreover, who took over the GRU in July 1940, had no previous experience in the field.[145]

In assessing the Soviet dictator's failure to discern Germany's true intentions, one must not overlook the role played by the sly and effective German disinformation campaign. In June 1941, Vladimir Dekanozov, Soviet ambassador to Berlin since November 1940, passed on a report that only served to reinforce Stalin's prejudices. The report, which dealt with rumors of a possible *rapproachment* between Germany and the Soviet Union – based either on far-reaching "concessions" on the part of the latter, or on a division of territory into "spheres of influence" – was simply part of a vigorously promoted attempt by the Germans to mislead and confuse the Russians. In fact, the *Wehrmacht's* deception campaign prior to *Barbarossa* – begun in February 1941 under the codenames "shark" (*Haifisch*) and "harpoon" (*Harpune*)[146] – was the most far-reaching it ever employed. A key element of this deception was to convince the Russians that Operation "Sealion," the planned invasion of England, was still operative, and that the massed German forces in the east were simply a ruse to convince the British that "Sealion" had been cancelled. Even Stalin's firm belief that any German attack would be preceded by an ultimatum – giving him time to concede, mobilize his forces, or even act pre-emptively – was based on German deception.[147]

Yet the crux to Stalin's calculations can perhaps best be understood as a kind of "mirror imaging." The Soviet leader "took it for granted that Hitler employed the same calculus of power that he did, and would never attack in the east until he had settled with Britain."[148] This bedrock conviction that Hitler – like Stalin himself – was much too rational to risk a two-front war – goes furthest to explain Stalin's inability to grasp the reality of *Barbarossa*. As he reportedly told Zhukov only days before war began, "Germany is involved up to its ears in the war in the west, and I believe Hitler will not risk creating a second front for himself by attacking the Soviet Union."[149] Yet Stalin was far from alone in assuming this. Even the British Joint Intelligence Committee had been "ambivalent in its conclusions until the end of May 1941 and only confirmed the Germans' final intention to invade in early June."[150]

Finally, Stalin's assessment of the German power structure may have also contributed to his wishful thinking. Opines Evan Mawdsley:

> Stalin may well have believed that the leaders of the Third Reich were divided between those who wanted immediate war with the USSR and those who did not, and he may well have placed Hitler in the latter group. Stalin's key assumption was perhaps that German policy was undecided, but that rash Soviet action could bring about an unnecessary, or at least premature, war with the Reich. Such action would include precipitate mobilization and concentration of the Red Army or changes in the propaganda line toward Nazi Germany. This was also the reason for the harmful military decision not to man the security zone (*predpol'e*) immediately adjacent to the border; indeed the NKVD was instructed to insure that Red Army units obeyed this directive.[151]

Examined in this context, Stalin's stubborn refusal to acknowledge and respond robustly to the threat of invasion becomes (at least partially) comprehensible. And it helps to explain his virtual obsession with avoiding any action which the Germans may have interpreted as a provocation and, hence, as a potential *casus belli*. Furthermore, it clarifies his careful adherence to a policy of appeasement vis-à-vis Germany. Indeed, even as the Germans fell further behind in their deliveries of finished goods to the Soviet Union, the Soviets were careful not only to meet but to surpass their quotas in shipments of raw materials to Germany; by 22 June 1941, they had delivered 2.2 million tons of grain, one million tons of oil, and 100,000 tons of cotton. These deliveries – particularly those of oil – were to prove essential to the *Wehrmacht's* conduct of Operation *Barbarossa*.[152]

Of course, Stalin's "willful blindness" to German intentions was, as often as not, the outcome of his own inveterate paranoia and suspicion, for his "own profound cynicism went much further than healthy skepticism. It led him to disbelieve all information, however compelling and however well placed the source, which contradicted his own analysis of German intentions."[153] This was particularly the case concerning information derived from British sources, even from Churchill himself. As Antony Beevor argues, the Soviet dictator was convinced that "every warning of Operation *Barbarossa* was a provocation from British intelligence. It was all part of a plot by Churchill to trick the Soviet Union into war with Germany."[154] As early as July 1940 Churchill had written a personal note to Stalin, warning him of Hitler's intentions. Stalin, however, simply dismissed the note as a feeble attempt to entice Russia prematurely into war in the wake of the British debacle at Dunkirk.[155]

As Marshal Zhukov told Soviet writer Konstantin Simonov, it was in the spring of 1941, when reports of German troop concentrations in Poland began to increase alarmingly, that Stalin, seeking an explanation, decided the time had come to write a personal note to Hitler. In his "confidential" reply, the "Fuehrer" informed the Soviet dictator that large German forces were indeed stationed in Poland:

> But being confident that it would go no further than Stalin himself, Hitler was duty bound to make it clear to him that the formations in Poland were not directed at the Soviet Union. He said that the territories of west and central Germany were being subjected to heavy British bombing; hence the reason for removing a

considerable part of his troops and placing them in Poland. Stalin believed that the *Fuehrer* intended to adhere strictly to the Pact, which had been guaranteed by the very honor of the head of government. It appears, said Zhukov, that Stalin believed in Hitler's argument.[156]

It is supremely ironic that, as war bore inexorably down on him, there was, it seems, only one man whom the paranoid Soviet dictator now professed to believe – and that man was Adolf Hitler. And yet it is hard to believe that Stalin was not plagued by "hidden doubts about his own convictions. He must, in solitary moments, have wondered whether he had not for months been outbluffed by Hitler."[157] Alarming reports were now pouring in from all sides; still, Stalin "seemed to be suppressing all thoughts of war." His behavior, however, betrayed to Nikita Khrushchev and others that he was "restless and seriously worried.

He now took to heavy bouts of drinking, to which he also subjected his entourage. Moreover, unlike his usual habit he sought constant company, which seemed to banish from his mind the nightmarish thoughts of an imminent war. Prolonged dinners and gatherings at his dacha replaced the working sessions in the Kremlin which had previously characterized his routine. Up to the very last minute Stalin continued to believe that the German army was trying to provoke the conflict. As Kollontai[158] admitted on the day of the invasion, Stalin "certainly hoped and believed that a war would not break out without prior negotiations during which a solution to avoid war would be found." He had, however, lost the initiative and was practically paralyzed.[159]

ENDNOTES

1   B. Musial, *Kampfplatz Deutschland*, 463.
2   W. S. Dunn, Jr., *Stalin's Keys to Victory*, 3.
3   E. Raus, "*Russian Combat Methods in World War II*," in: *Fighting in Hell. The German Ordeal on the Eastern Front*, P. G. Tsouras (ed.), 34.
4   E. Mawdsley, *Thunder in the East*, 12-13.
5   J. Erickson, "*Soviet War Losses*," in: *Barbarossa. The Axis and the Allies*, J. Erickson & D. Dilks (eds.), 256.
6   As German officers recalled in a post-war study, the very first days of the Russian campaign revealed the fact that the "Red Army soldier bore little resemblance to the Russian soldier of 1914-17. The Bolshevist regime had certainly understood how to imbue the Soviet soldier with a new spirit over the course of 20 years. This revelation was another of the surprises of the Russo-German war. The Russian soldier had always been brave and steadfast. But the new masters of Russia have succeeded in rousing the soldier from his passive stupor, in giving him a strong sense of responsibility toward state and nation, and even in turning him into a fanatic." FMS T-34, K. Allmendinger, et al., "*Terrain Factors in the Russian Campaign*," 64-65.
7   D. M. Glantz (ed.), *Initial Period of War on the Eastern Front*, 2.
8   Ibid., 4-5.
9   B. Musial, *Kampfplatz Deutschland*, 9.
10   Ibid. 450, 463-64. Musial sees a strong continuity in Soviet Russia's preparations for a war of aggression against the West since at least 1931.
11   Ibid., 464.
12   By 1940, at the latest, in view of the dramatically transformed strategic situation in Europe, the Soviet military buildup was driven less by any immediate or future aggressive intent than by fear of an impending German invasion.
13   E. Mawdsley, *Thunder in the East*, 48. According to Walter S. Dunn, after eight years of developing their heavy industry, the Soviets switched to weapons production in 1937. See, W. S. Dunn, Jr., *Hitler's Nemesis. The Red Army 1930-45*, xv.
14   E. Mawdsley, *Thunder in the East*, 43.
15   Munitions = shells and mines.
16   J. N. Westwood, *A History of Russian Railways*, 242-43.
17   American engineers played an integral part in helping the Soviets reach their economic objectives. During the 1920s and 1930s, they instructed the Russians in the techniques of low-cost mass production and planned

obsolescence. "Planned obsolescence," avers Walter S. Dunn, "by cutting tolerances, that is, increasing the margin of error, the acceptable variation from the ideal measurement, reduced the number of hours and degree of skill required to complete a product but at the same time reduced the life span of the engine or weapon. However, the determining factor of the life expectancy of a weapon on the eastern front was not its degree of perfection but shells from a German anti-tank gun." During the 1930s, American engineers also designed and constructed *all* of the Russian tank factories and many other factories for mass production. "Many were improved copies of the most efficient American plants. The Germans could not adopt the American philosophy because their factories were smaller and not designed for mass production." W. S. Dunn, Jr., *Stalin's Keys to Victory*, 24-26.

18 Compulsory military service was a major feature of Soviet military policy between the wars, providing the Red Army with an immense pool of trained men. Ibid., 5.

19 D. M. Glantz, *Red Army Ground Forces in June 1941*, 1-3.

20 Ibid., 48.

21 P. Calvocoressi & G. Wint, *Total War*, 168.

22 NKVD = People's Commissariat for Internal Affairs.

23 S. Courtois, et al., *The Black Book of Communism*, 184-90.

24 According to Russian scholar Dmitri Volkogonov, whose own father was arrested and shot during the purges, between May 1937 and September 1938, 36,761 men were purged in the army and more than 3000 in the navy. D. Volkogonov, *Stalin*, 368.

25 S. Courtois, et al., *The Black Book of Communism*, 184, 198; I. Kershaw, *Fateful Choices*, 247.

26 S. Courtois, et al., *The Black Book of Communism*, 198.

27 E. Mawdsley, *Thunder in the East*, 21. Mawdsley, however, offers somewhat different figures for top-level Red Army leaders executed in the purges, compared to those listed in the *Black Book of Communism* (and cited above).

28 C. Merridale, *Ivan's War*, 70-71.

29 D. Volkogonov, *Stalin*, 368.

30 I. Kershaw, *Fateful Choices*, 247-48.

31 D. M. Glantz, *Barbarossa*, 62.

32 I. Kershaw, *Fateful Choices*, 249-50.

33 For example, writes Robert Kirchubel: "Massive Soviet military expansion, especially following 1938, had far more impact on the decline of the army's quality" than did the purges. See, R. Kirchubel, *Operation Barbarossa 1941 (3), Army Group Center*, 25.

34 Dept. of Army Pamphlet No. 20-269, "*Small Unit Actions during the German Campaign in Russia*," 32-37. (Note: The authors of this document are German veterans of the eastern front; however, they are not mentioned by name.)

35 R. Kirchubel, *Operation Barbarossa 1941 (3), Army Group Center*, 25.

36 J. J. Kiršin, "*Die sowjetischen Streitkraefte am Vorabend des Grossen Vaterlaendischen Krieges*," in: *Zwei Wege nach Moskau*, B. Wegner (Hg.), 390.

37 D. M. Glantz, *Red Army Ground Forces in June 1941*, 48.

38 The figure of 17,000 is derived from Glantz; the figure of 24,000 is cited by both Joachim Hoffman and Jurij J. Kiršin. See, D. M. Glantz (ed.), *Initial Period of War on the Eastern Front*, 33; J. Hoffmann, "*Die Angriffsvorbereitungen des Sowjetunion 1941*," in: *Zwei Wege nach Moskau*, B. Wegner (Hg.), 369; and J. J. Kiršin, "*Die sowjetischen Streitkraefte am Vorabend des Grossen Vaterlaendischen Krieges*," in: *Zwei Wege nach Moskau*, B. Wegner (Hg.), 390.

39 D. M. Glantz, *Red Army Ground Forces in June 1941*, 3; D. M. Glantz, *Barbarossa*, 27.

40 A fortified region was a "defensive formation designed to create a strong defensive barrier and help canalize attacking enemy forces into regions where they could be destroyed by counterattacking mechanized forces." The 57 fortified regions in the force structure on 22 June 1941 (41 of them in the west) included more than 190,000 men organized into seven regiments and 160 artillery and MG battalions outfitted with 1700 guns/mortars and 9800 light and heavy MGs. They were deployed in prepared positions along the frontier and in depth near the old 1939 border, as well as on the approaches to major cities. D. M. Glantz, *Red Army Ground Forces in June 1941*, 34.

41 Ibid., 3.

42 For the complete Red Army order of battle on 22 June 1941 see, D. M. Glantz (ed.), *Atlas and Operational Summary. The Border Battles*, 32-36. For a complete order of battle for Western Front see, Appendix 5 of this history.

43 A Soviet "front" was roughly equivalent to a German army group. After 1941, the Red Army increased the number of fronts yet reduced them in size, making them about equal to German armies. D. M. Glantz, *The Soviet-German War: Myths and Realities*, 15, f.n. 1.

44 The number and type of divisions assigned to each of the five fronts was as follows (the first figure is total divisions, followed by rifle, tank, motorized and cavalry divisions): Northern Front (21: 15, 4, 2, 0), Northwestern Front (25: 19, 4, 2, 0), Western Front (44: 24, 12, 6, 2); Southwestern Front (58: 32, 16, 8, 2), Southern Front (22: 13, 4, 3, 2). H. Magenheimer, *Hitler's War*, 76; H. Seidler, *Images of War. Operation Barbarossa*, 171; D. M. Glantz, *Barbarossa*, 16. According to Evan Mawdsley, the Kiev Military District (Southwestern Front) possessed 60 divisions (including 16 tank and 8 motorized) on 22 June 1941. E. Mawdsley, *Thunder in the East*, 40. (*Note*: The above figures include the 163 divisions of the Soviet field forces, plus 8 divisions of the *Stavka* reserve that were physically located in the first strategic echelon of forces, with one division unaccounted for.)

45   D. M. Glantz, *Red Army Ground Forces in June 1941*, 3; H. Magenheimer, *Moskau 1941*, 25; C. Bellamy, *Absolute War*, 175; E-mail, D. M. Glantz to C. Luther, 6 Nov. 2013.

46   D. M. Glantz, *Red Army Ground Forces in June 1941*, 3.

47   D. M. Glantz, *Red Army Ground Forces in June 1941*, 3; D. M. Glantz, *Barbarossa*, 16.

48   *GSWW*, Vol. IV, 85. According to this quasi-official German history, 170 divisions were stationed in the western frontier zone; of these, 48 divisions were deployed 10-50 km., 64 divisions 50-150 km., and 56 divisions 150-500 km. east of the Russo-German demarcation line.

49   Ibid., 86.

50   C. Merridale, *Ivan's War*, 82.

51   The Soviet Union endured severe food shortages throughout the war, particularly during 1941/42. After the launch of *Barbarossa*, the Red Army's logistical system collapsed, consigning its soldiers to "severe and persistent food deprivation." D. M. Glantz, *Colossus Reborn*, 555.

52   C. Merridale, *Ivan's War*, 16.

53   D. M. Glantz, *Red Army Ground Forces*, 13. However, as war loomed, most divisions in the internal military districts had yet to make the transition, or were in the process of doing so.

54   Ibid., 13.

55   D. M. Glantz, *Barbarossa*, 24.

56   C. Bellamy, *Absolute War*, 176; C. Merridale, *Ivan's War*, 100.

57   J. Erickson, "*Soviet War Losses*," in: *Barbarossa. The Axis and the Allies*, J. Erickson & D. Dilks (eds.), 267.

58   D. M. Glantz, *Red Army Ground Forces*, 19.

59   C. Bellamy, *Absolute War*, 176.

60   A. Zamoyski, *Moscow 1812*, 116.

61   W. S. Dunn, Jr., *Stalin's Keys to Victory*, 28.

62   E. Mawdsley, *Thunder in the East*, 26.

63   Ibid., 26.

64   D. M. Glantz, *Red Army Ground Forces*, 29; D. M. Glantz, *Red Army Weapons and Equipment*, 11.

65   M. Foedrowitz, *Stalin Organs*, 11; A. Werth, *Russia at War*, 172.

66   The rocket launchers were first demonstrated to the Soviet military on 15 June 1941: "Minister of Defense Timoshenko wanted a demonstration of new artillery armaments to be conducted at the firing range ... The demonstration of the rocket weaponry was the last item on the schedule. The effect of the drumfire and the howling of forty-eight flying projectiles made a staggering impression on the marshals and generals. Clouds of dust rose up and flames raged in the area of the target. It seemed that nothing living could have withstood such an artillery strike ... Twenty-four hours before Nazi Germany attacked, a resolution was issued, signed by Stalin, for the series production of rockets and launchers." B. Chertok, *Rockets and People*, Vol. I, 167-71.

67   Apparently, the length of the rockets reminded the Germans of organ-pipes. D. Peeters, *Vermisst in Stalingrad*, 13.

68   A. Gutenkunst, *Geschichte der 3. Kompanie des Infanterie-Regiments 109*, 255.

69   M. Domarus, *Hitler. Reden und Proklamationen 1932-1945*, Bd. II, 1742-43.

70   W. S. Dunn, Jr., *Stalin's Keys to Victory*, 29.

71   D. M. Glantz, *Red Army Ground Forces*, 29.

72   By 2 August 1941, *Das Reich* had sustained nearly 3000 casualties in the El'nia salient, with company strengths in some cases down to 60-70 men; two days later, company strengths had plunged to as few as 20 combatants. D. Stahel, *And the World held its Breath*, 223.

73   On 12-13 August 1941, 292 ID incurred more than 400 casualties. G. Nitz, *Die 292. Infanterie-Division*, 52.

74   As the division historian noted, in a 10-day period in mid-August 1941, Soviet artillery had fired into the division's sector from 263 different gun positions, at least 40 of which were permanently manned by the Russians. Ibid., 53.

75   Ofw. Jakubowski, *Tagebuch I./I.R. 509 – I./I.R. 507* (unpublished diary).

76   G. Gorodetsky, *Grand Delusion*, 115-17.

77   G. Roberts, *Stalin's Wars*, 70-71, 80. "The Soviet High Command," avers Roberts, "intended to fight the next war by taking the battle to the enemy, by launching attacks and counterattacks and by the deep penetration and invasion of the opponent's territory."

78   D. M. Glantz (ed.), *Initial Period of War on the Eastern Front*, 10-11.

79   Marshal of the Soviet Union Tukhachevsky was put on trial and executed in June 1937. Triandafillov had perished in an airplane accident in 1931. Isserson was arrested in 1942 and spent 14 years in labor camps and internal exile. He died in 1976.

80   D. M. Glantz (ed.), *Initial Period of War on the Eastern Front*, 13-16. Writes Glantz: "The Soviets generally concluded, as a result of combat in Spain, that armored forces were indeed fragile on the battlefield unless they were fully integrated into a well articulated combined arms force. Tanks proved very vulnerable to artillery fire, and when their supporting infantry was stripped away they were very vulnerable to destruction by enemy infantry as well. When they returned from Spain, many Soviet military leaders recommended the creation of smaller armored units of more balanced combined arms nature." Apparently, the miserable state of Red Army logistics contributed significantly to the decision to do away with the tank corps. According to the late German historian Joachim Hoffmann, the Soviet decision was also influenced by the fighting against the Japanese at Lake Khazan in July-August 1938, and on the Khalkin-Gol River in May 1939. See, *GSWW*, Vol. IV, 72.

81   D. M. Glantz (ed.), *Initial Period of War on the Eastern Front*, 16.

82   The TOE for a tank division was roughly 11,000 men, 60 guns and mortars, and 375 tanks; in theory, the motorized division possessed 11,650 men, 98 guns and mortars, 275 light tanks, and 49 armored cars. D. M. Glantz, *Red Army Ground Forces*, 20.

83   The Soviet intent was to complete the creation of these immense new mechanized corps by the summer of 1942. Ibid., 20.

84   Ibid. 20-21.

85   Ibid., 20.

86   E. Mawdsley, *Thunder in the East*, 26.

87   R. J. Kershaw, *War Without Garlands*, 70.

88   C. Merridale, *Ivan's War*, 87.

89   W. S. Dunn, Jr., *Stalin's Keys to Victory*, 93.

90   H.-A. Jacobsen (Hg.), *Generaloberst Halder Kriegstagebuch*, Bd. III, 14.

91   MS 506 (IfZ), *Tagebuch Uffz. R. Rupp*, 6.10.41.

92   *"Top Ten Tanks,"* Military Channel documentary, Oct 05.

93   W. S. Dunn, Jr., *Stalin's Keys to Victory*, 92-93; R. J. Kershaw, *War Without Garlands*, 69.

94   Steven Zaloga, who has written extensively on the T-34, doing research in both Russian and German sources, argues that the German Army was not "totally unaware" of the new Soviet tank: "Documents in the archives in Washington identify it by the prototype number T32. So German intelligence did know the Soviets had a new medium tank T32, but they did not know the significance of it." According to Zaloga, a German study of the Soviet war industry shortly before the outbreak of war with Russia even identified – correctly – that the T32 prototype was in production at a factory in Khar'kov. Remarks by Steven Zaloga in: D. M. Glantz (ed.), *Initial Period of War on the Eastern Front*, 452.

95   G. P. Megargee, *Inside Hitler's High Command*, 114.

96   According to a *Wehrmacht* training video, the rear and flanks of the T-34, where the armor was thinner, along with the turret ring, were the most vulnerable areas of the tank. *Frontschau Nr. 5/6*, in: *Die Frontschau*, distributed by International Historic Films.

97   Statistical research conducted by the Soviets' NII-48 (Scientific Research Institute 48) in the autumn of 1942, concerning battle damage to T-34 tanks then in repair in maintenance workshops in Moscow, revealed that out of 109 hits on the upper front part of the tanks 89 percent had had no effect; however, destructive penetrations had been achieved by guns of 75mm caliber or greater. In the early period of the war, most hits were to a tank's hull, the same research concluding that 81 percent of hits were to the hull (and only 19 percent to the turret); however, most of the hits proved harmless (non-penetrating or only partially penetrating). Fully 89 percent of hits on the upper front portion, 66 percent on the lower front portion, and roughly 40 percent of hits on the sides of the hull failed to penetrate. Conversely, the turret was pierced with relative ease, "its softer cast armor providing poor resistance even to the 37 mm shells of automatic AA guns." These findings supported those of the Germans as explained in the footnote immediately above. A. Drabkin & Oleg Sheremet, *T-34 in Action*, 23, 27.

98   Dr E. Bunke, *Der Osten blieb unser Schicksal*, 545-50.

99   D. M. Glantz, *Red Army Ground Forces*, 28.

100   D. M. Glantz, *Barbarossa*, 65.

101   E. Raus, *"Russian Combat Methods in World War II,"* in: *Fighting in Hell*, P. G. Tsouras (ed.), 40-42.

102   D. M. Glantz, *Red Army Ground Forces*, 28-29.

103   In doing so, however, the German veterans have a tendency to dramatically overestimate the numbers of Soviet airborne forces available in June 1941. For example, a pamphlet prepared by two German eastern front veterans in the 1990s contends that the Red Army on 22 June 1941 included more than one million parachutists distributed over 10 air landing corps – a figure apparently gleaned from the works of Russian revisionist historian Vladimir Rezun (pseudonym of Viktor Suvorov). E. Wardin & H. Drenger, *Ich hatt' einen Kameraden*, n.d.

104   This unit was the 1st Company of Army Flak-Battalion 601. A typical Army Flak company at full strength (1941/42) was composed of 12 20mm Flak 30 or Flak 38 guns, or eight 20mm Flak 30/38 and two 20mm Flak 38 *Vierlingen* (weapons with four 20mm guns). Ltr, F.-K. Scharffetter (Fla-Kameradschaft) to C. Luther, 29 Nov 02.

105   H. Freter, *Fla nach vorn*, 445.

106   D. M. Glantz, *Barbarossa*, 27-28.

107   A Soviet air regiment on the eve of war was roughly equivalent in size to a German *Gruppe*, possessing about 30 aircraft. E. Mawdsley, *Thunder in the East*, 25.

108   M. N. Kozhevnikov, *The Command and Staff of the Soviet Army Air Force*, 14-18. "Extensive measures were implemented to prepare the theater of military operations," states Kozhevnikov. "Runway construction, expansion, and reconstruction at more than 250 airfields assumed broad scope in spring 1941. A significant number of airfields was built in the new border zone formed due to the annexation of western Belorussian and Ukrainian regions [i.e., eastern Poland] and admission of new republics – Latvia, Lithuania, and Estonia – into the USSR ... One hundred airfield construction battalions were formed to accelerate airfield construction previously begun. In addition, 25,000 laborers were transferred at the end of March from railroad construction projects to construction of airfields. In western border military districts, where new types of planes were to be based, the runways were lengthened and paved with concrete, and fuel and ammunition dumps and airfield control posts were built at many existing airfields.

Owing to this, new types of aircraft could not operate from these airfields temporarily, while the use of obsolete aircraft was restricted." Ibid., 18.

109　D. R. Jones, *"From Disaster to Recovery: Russia's Air Forces in the Two World Wars,"* in: *Why Air Forces Fail*, R. Higham & S.J. Harris (eds.), 275.

110　D. M. Glantz, *Red Army Weapons and Equipment*, 47.

111　R. Muller, *The German Air War in Russia*, 40-41.

112　R. Kirchubel, *Operation Barbarossa 1941*(3), *Army Group Center*, 28.

113　V. Hardesty, *Red Phoenix*, 26; C. Bergström & A. Mikhailov, *Black Cross Red Star*, Vol. II, 36-37.

114　V. Hardesty, *Red Phoenix*, 61; A. Seaton, *The Battle for Moscow*, 82.

115　On 12 April 1941, Timoshenko and Zhukov complained that two or three aircraft were being lost each day to training accidents and demanded removal of several senior VVS officers. D. M. Glantz & D. House, *When Titans Clashed*, 37-38.

116　A. Kesselring, *Soldat Bis Zum Letzten Tag*, 120.

117　R. Wagner (ed.), *The Soviet Air Force in World War II*, 44.

118　In accordance with order No. 008130 of 26 March 1941, promulgated by the war council of the Western Special Military District, all units of that military district were to be at full mobilization readiness by 15 June 1941. *GSWW*, Vol. IV, 84.

119　D. M. Glantz, *Red Army Ground Forces*, 1-2; D. M. Glantz, *Barbarossa*, 16; see also, *GSWW*, Vol. IV, 84.

120　E. Mawdsley, *Thunder in the East*, 40; H. Magenheimer, *Hitler's War*, 76-77.

121　D. M. Glantz, *Barbarossa*, 16; G. Roberts, *Stalin's Wars*, 73-74. According to Roberts: "From spring 1941 onward Soviet intelligence reports [erroneously] emphasized that if the Germans did attack it would be mainly in the south ... The decision to plump for a southern concentration of the Red Army was a fateful one, which Zhukov and others were keen to explain away in their memoirs. In their version of events the decision was made by Stalin who believed that Hitler wanted to seize the economic and mineral resources of the Ukraine and southern Russia, including the oil of the Caucasus. While it is true Stalin thought that the struggle for raw materials would be crucial in the coming war, there is no direct evidence that the decision to concentrate forces in the south was specifically his, although he must have gone along with it."

122　E. Mawdsley, *Thunder in the East*, 40.

123　D. M. Glantz, *Barbarossa Derailed*, Vol. I, 21. Mandated by Stalin, State Defense Plan 1941 had been prepared by G. K. Zhukov in early 1941, following his appointment as chief of the General Staff in January 1941. The document envisaged the Red Army beginning "military operations in response to an aggressive attack." Apparently, Zhukov's May 1941 contingency plan for a pre-emptive strike was an outgrowth of DP-41. In general, DP-41 was to be carried out in harmony with the Red Army's mobilization plan (MP-41).

124　I. Kershaw, *Fateful Choices*, 268.

125　G. Gorodetsky, *Grand Delusion*, 129-30. "The games," concludes Gorodetsky, "shook the confidence displayed at the conference [of the Red Army High Command convened by Stalin in late December 1940] and exposed the vulnerability and deficiencies of the defense. The umpires of the games drew unflattering conclusions about the performance of the army." Ibid., 128.

126　E. Mawdsley, *Thunder in the East*, 37.

127　Ibid., 37.

128　"Rather than a line like the Maginot [line]," observes David Glantz, the Stalin Line "was a series of contiguous and noncontiguous fortified regions covering the most important axes of the enemy advance." In 1938, there were 13 fortified regions along the old Soviet border manned by 25 machine gun battalions totaling 18,000 men. Late in 1938 and early 1939, the Soviets added eight new fortified regions to the existing structure. In 1940/41, following the incorporation of eastern Poland and the Baltic States, the Soviets built 20 fortified regions along the new border – each consisting of two defensive belts to a depth of 15-20 kilometers. These new defensive zones, however, were only partially completed by June 1941. E-Mail, D. M. Glantz to C. Luther, 12 Jul 11; D. M. Glantz, *The Military Strategy of the Soviet Union. A History*, 75.

129　*Frontschau Nr. 2*, "Russischer Stellungsbau," in: *Die Frontschau*, distributed by International Historic Films.

130　R. Kirchubel, *Operation Barbarossa 1941* (3), *Army Group Center*, 27. For a detailed study of the Stalin Line see, S. Wetzig, *Die Stalin-Linie 1941*; for an examination of Soviet field fortifications in general see, G. L. Rottman, *Soviet Field Fortifications 1941-45*.

131　R. Kirchubel, *Operation Barbarossa 1941* (3), *Army Group Center*, 27.

132　J. Mosier, *Rise and Fall of German War Machine*, 174.

133　In one incident in the north at beginning of *Barbarossa*, 6 Panzer Division fought a two-day battle with a group of Soviet KV tanks. The tanks eventually became immobilized and were systematically destroyed with satchel charges, after which the Germans discovered that the tanks' main armament had not been bore-sighted. D. M. Glantz, *Red Army Group Forces in June 1941*, 27.

134　The massive amounts of weapons and equipment captured by the Germans in 1941 included just 150 radio sets. In their memoirs, Zhukov and other high ranking officers acknowledge that they were often out of touch with subordinate units. (E. F. Ziemke & M. E. Bauer, *Moscow to Stalingrad*, 12.) According to David Glantz, "the Soviets did have an aversion to radios early on, first, because of the paucity of reliable radio sets and, second, because of the likelihood of German 'listening,' especially when inexperienced Soviet commanders had difficulties using codes. Therefore, they relied on telephone, even commercial at times, and field telephones, even though wire proved highly tentative in mobile warfare. In addition, the most sensitive orders and information, in particular, at the *Stavka* ... and front and army levels, went by BODO, enciphered radio-teletype, a sort of telegram. And many commanders also relied on liaison officers and couriers, both airborne and ground. Of course, changes occurred in 1942 with more widespread use of radios." E-Mail, D. M. Glantz to C. Luther, 20 Aug 10.

135 Other sources for this list include: B. Musial, *Kampfplatz Deutschland*, 442-43, 452-54; I. Kershaw, *Fateful Choices*, 264-65; E. Mawdsley, *Thunder in the East*, 26; D. M. Glantz, *Barbarossa*, 22-24; *GSWW*, Vol. IV, 89.

136 A. Seaton, *Stalin as Military Commander*, 270.

137 A. Zamoyski, *Moscow 1812*, 78-79.

138 J. Erickson, *Road to Stalingrad*, 340.

139 I. Kershaw, *Fateful Choices*, 272-73.

140 The British Government Code and Cipher School at Bletchley Park, England, was responsible for deciphering, analyzing, and evaluating the intercepted German wireless communications, and then for passing them on to concerned military and civilian agencies. The German Navy had begun to use ENIGMA in 1926, the Army in 1928, and the *Luftwaffe* in 1935. The Germans, of course, were well aware that their enemies were listening in on their radio traffic; however, they "placed absolute trust in ENIGMA," being quite convinced that their messages were undecipherable. ULTRA, the major Allied intelligence coup of the Second World War, was to remain a well-guarded secret until the early 1970s, with some aspects of the project concealed even into the 1980s because of their impact on operations against Soviet codes. D. T. Putney (ed.), *Ultra and the Army Air Forces in World War II*, ix-x; P. Johnson, *Modern Times*, 399.

141 See, for example, the comment by John Somerville (Wells, England) in: J. Rohwer & E. Jaeckel (Hg.), *Kriegswende Dezember 1941*, 221.

142 I. Kershaw, *Fateful Choices*, 274.

143 Sources for this compliation are: J. Hughes-Wilson, *Military Intelligence Blunders*, 47-57; I. Kershaw, *Fateful Choices*, 284; B. Musial, *Kampfplatz Deutschland*, 432-33; and, R.-D. Mueller, "*Duell im Schnee*," in: *Der Zweite Weltkrieg*, S. Burgdorff & K. Wiegrefe (Hg.), 114.

144 I. Kershaw, *Fateful Choices*, 286.

145 E. Mawdsley, *Thunder in the East*, 32.

146 On 21 February 1941, General Jodl, Chief, OKW Operations Staff, had tasked Colonel Hasso von Wedel, Chief, OKW Propaganda Branch, with carrying out the deception campaign, which even helped to spread false rumors among the German troops massing in the east. See, O. Buchbender & R. Sterz (Hg.), *Das andere Gesicht des Krieges*, 63-64.

147 J. Hughes-Wilson, *Military Intelligence Blunders*, 52-53; I. Kershaw, *Fatal Choices*, 272; D. Volkogonov, "*The German Attack, the Soviet Response, Sunday, 22 June 1941*," in: *Barbarossa. The Axis and the Allies*, J. Erickson & D. Dilks (eds.), 82. At the end of May 1941, German propaganda minister Goebbels directed that rumors be spread of an impending cross-channel attack on Great Britain. To add credibility to the rumors, Goebbels even directed the composition of an invasion song and new fanfares! R. G. Reuth, *Goebbels*, 476-78.

148 D. Pryce-Jones, "*Turning Points*," (book review of Ian Kershaw's *Fateful Choices*), in: *National Review*, 30 July 2007, 50-51.

149 E. Mawdsley, *Thunder in the East*, 35-37.

150 J. Hughes-Wilson, *Military Intelligence Blunders*, 58.

151 E. Mawdsley, *Thunder in the East*, 35.

152 W. Murray & A. R. Millett, *A War to be Won*, 111.

153 I. Kershaw, *Fateful Choices*, 272.

154 A. Beevor, *The Mystery of Olga Chekhova*, 159.

155 J. Hughes-Wilson, *Military Intelligence Blunders*, 51-52.

156 D. Volkogonov, "*The German Attack, the Soviet Response, Sunday, 22 June 1941*," in: *Barbarossa. The Axis and the Allies*, J. Erickson & D. Dilks (eds.), 81-82.

157 I. Kershaw, *Fateful Choices*, 283.

158 Alexandra Kollontai, the Soviet ambassador to Sweden.

159 G. Gorodetsky, *Grand Delusion*, 307.

CHAPTER 5

The Eve of War: Final Preparations
for the Russian Campaign

(May – June 1941)

"I have the sort of feeling that tomorrow or the day after tomorrow things are going to happen that will make the world sit up and take notice. And I also have the feeling that these things will not pass me by without leaving their mark. Hopefully, the time to come will bring us a good step closer to final victory." (Uffz. E.N., 6 ID, 21 June 1941)[1]

"It is profoundly peaceful everywhere, the cows and horses are in the field and the Panje-horses are raking the potatoes, and what will it look like tomorrow morning? The bombs and shells will explode everywhere and the houses will burn, the residents flee. The contrast is too unreal." (Panzer General Joachim Lemelsen, 21 June 1941)[2]

"The talk with Field Marshal von Bock ... could be kept brief; we understood each other and were in agreement about the solution to the problems of the attack. When I called on him again in the evening of 21 June 1941 to discuss a few doubts or requests which had arisen in the meantime, I found him, in contrast to how he had been in the closing meetings for previous campaigns, somewhat downcast – a thoughtfulness which dignifies every responsible leader before the start of a fateful, large-scale operation." (Field Marshal Albert Kesselring, 21 June 1941)[3]

5.1: German Assembly in the East Completed (May – June 1941)

5.1.1: The Ground Forces:

By the spring of 1941, the flow of troop trains crossing the borders of the Reich to the east, and carrying the soldiers, tanks, guns, vehicles and equipment of the *Ostheer*, had increased to as many as 220 a day. As briefly described in Chapter 2 (Section 2.3), the rail movements (*Eisenbahnaufmarsch*) were conducted in five phases, beginning in early February 1941; by 20 May 1941 (end of the third phase) the majority of the marching infantry divisions in the *Barbarossa* order of battle had been deployed in the east. Initially, most formations were kept well back from the German-Soviet frontier; however, during the final 10 days of May, entire divisions began to close up to the frontier in a series of night marches – all movements carried out under painstaking security and with disinformation measures to conceal their actual intent from the Soviets. At the end of May and beginning of June, with the offensive barely weeks away, the Germans began to flood the border zones of occupied Poland and East Prussia with as many as two or more divisions per day. Meanwhile, the fourth (and final) phase of the pre-war rail deployments was split into two segments: 23 May – 2 June (9 infantry divisions from the west) and 3 – 23 June (12 panzer and 12 motorized divisions from the Reich, the west and the Balkans). For reasons of security, the deployment of these 24 mobile divisions – which embraced the backbone of the German invasion force – was thus conducted at the last possible moment before the start of the campaign.[4] Also from 3-23 June the "super heavy" rail-borne artillery was brought up from the Channel coast and assigned to the eastern army groups: Four "K5" pieces, each with 90 rounds of ammunition to Army Group South; eight "K5" guns and two of type "*Karl*" to Army Group Center; and four guns, type "*Bruno*" (short), with 300 rounds to Army Group North. Understandably, the transport of these guns and the construction of gun positions was a "major effort."[5]

The short nights in June complicated efforts to complete the final concentration of forces, while the troops were discomfited by a plague of mosquitoes "of biblical proportions," the result of unusually wet spring weather. Transportation and assembly schedules were encumbered by a number of unanticipated challenges, including the last-minute decision to move 8 Air Corps ground elements across the east-west lines of communication to East Prussia – its 8000 motor vehicles threatening to tie up every main artery from the Reich to the eastern front. Facing the prospect of a nasty traffic jam, Army Group Center solved the problem by appointing a special road communications staff commanded by a general, who enforced strictest control and march discipline. German headquarters also fretted over the possibility of forest fires, which the Russians could have easily started by dropping incendiary bombs, potentially causing havoc among the many fuel and ammunitions dumps scattered throughout the forests. The Russian air force, however, did not interfere with the German preparations.[6]

Improvements to roads and the reinforcement of bridges and culverts went forward to the last minute, the Organization Todt (OT), Reich Labor Service (*Reichsarbeitsdienst*) and Army engineers all cooperating in these efforts. Some of the biggest "headaches" occurred in the primitive Suwalki triangle – the salient where 3 Panzer Group was to concentrate – due to the complete absence of paved roads. Lacking heavy construction equipment, the Germans were unable to sufficiently reinforce the roads in this backwater region, with the result that the roads were not strong enough to handle some of the heavy weapons – such as the 300mm mortars – which Ninth Army wanted to commit to "crack the big bunkers of the Soviet border defense line."[7] Despite such challenges, by 22 June 1941, via the combination of rail and road movements outlined here and in Chapter 2, 126 divisions (along with *Heerestruppen* and supply services) had been deployed to the eastern front (the initial assault wave of 117 divisions and 9 OKH reserve divisions). The final 19 reserve divisions would be dispatched to the east by mid-July 1941, during the final phase of the German rail *Aufmarsch*.[8]

One of the mobile corps arriving in Poland in early June 1941 was General Joachim Lemelsen's 47 Panzer Corps. Its 17 Panzer Division, moving by road and rail, crossed the German border, detrained, and continued on to Warsaw, which it reached on or about 11 June. The division then occupied a temporary assembly area outside the Polish capital. At the same time, General Lemelsen's 18 Panzer Division and 29 Motorized Infantry Division – the other two mobile divisions of his corps – were assembling southeast and south of Warsaw. In a post-war study addressing the initial attack of 17 Panzer Division, the author, a former commander of the division's 39 Panzer Regiment, outlined the elaborate efforts of his regiment in the days before 22 June to conceal its preparations for war with Russia. For example, regimental insignia on uniforms, standards, and unit symbols on motor vehicles had been removed prior to entraining for the journey eastward. In addition, a news blackout was imposed and all outgoing mail restricted. To prevent detection by Russian listening posts, all radio traffic was prohibited, while movements during daylight hours were (for the most part) forbidden in order to frustrate potential aerial reconnaissance. Motor vehicles, in particular armored fighting vehicles, were carefully camouflaged. To provide an added increment of security, the comings and goings of local inhabitants were restricted to limited areas around the German occupied villages and to certain hours of the day. Headquarters, as well as military and regular police units, had special authority to enforce and supervise the strictest secrecy as well as requisite camouflage measures.[9]

A history of 40 Rifle Regiment, a primary component of 17 Panzer Division, offers detailed insight into this final, pre-war phase of the German *Ostaufmarsch*, while also underscoring the confidence of the German invaders:

> On 3.6.41, the advance party departs for their new quartering area near Warsaw, which is reached in a three-day march; on 4.6., the division order arrives for the regiment itself to depart. Inspections and loading exercises proceed in uninterrupted succession until we depart on 6.6. in motorized march in the direction of Auerbach – Plauen – Reichenbach – Zwickau – Glauchau. On 7.-8.6., the Elbe River near Senftenberg is reached via Chemnitz – Dresden. From here, the transport continues by train toward Cottbus, across the Oder River to Poland. The traces of the German-Polish war of 1939 are still visible everywhere. After unloading at Kalisz and Litzmannstadt [Lódz, southwest of Warsaw], the motorized march continues through Warsaw on poor, dusty roads. On 11.6. is a rest day. In the afternoon of 16.6., the march continues into the temporary assembly area to Siedlce – Konstantinov. The regimental staff has already driven ahead toward Wiśniew in trucks ...
>
> Positioning and assembly for attack are completed without a hitch. The Russians notice barely anything of our intentions to attack. On 16.6.41, the divisional order arrives for the regiment to move into the assembly area at Derlo – 15 kilometers north of Brest-Litowsk ... Parts of 3 Company take over surveillance and security along the Bug River, after men from our regiment, disguised in customs uniforms, have carried out reconnaissance and soundings on the Bug beforehand. Firing positions and observation posts for the heavy weapons are determined. Frequent discussions have taken place concerning the method of carrying out the attack. The remaining elements of the regiment arrive in the staging area by the evening of 21.6 ...
>
> Since there is sufficient time available, the attack is thoroughly prepared. The surveillance of the enemy riverbank provides a clear picture of the enemy. The favorable terrain permits a move under cover into the staging area. Officers Bapst and Steiner swim across the Bug repeatedly and tap the Russian telephone lines. The sand on the Russian riverbank is regularly smoothed over in order to detect any footprints.
>
> In view of our superiority of personnel and materiel (240 guns have been positioned in a sector of approximately 8 km), we are certain that our mission will lead to success.[10]

Only the final four nights before the attack was to begin – from 18-21 June 1941 – were the mobile divisions permitted to advance – as stealthily as possible – into their final assembly areas adjacent to the border with the Soviet Union.[11] Among the mechanized mass of panzer and motorized units moving up to the frontier was General Hermann Hoth's 3 Panzer Group. A report in the panzer group's official records describes the movements of its four armored and three motorized divisions into the Suwalki triangle, an area dotted with forests and lakes and the group's final concentration area for the attack:

> The deployment of 3 Panzer Group in the Suwalki triangle proceeded according to plan from 19.-22.6.[41]. The three short nights that were available, as well as the availability of only two roads for moving up the troops, made it necessary to move elements into the assembly areas during the day. This disadvantage was consciously taken into account, so that the bulk of the divisions might make their appearance at the frontier at the latest possible time. Despite this, secrecy was maintained, as the later attack demonstrated.

All deployment movements proceeded smoothly amid good traffic discipline. Disruption through SS units could be eliminated through the intervention of Ninth Army headquarters. The strict separation of combat vehicles and vehicles which were to follow had proved its worth. All vehicles required for combat, as well as those extensively equipped with bridging columns, reached the designated areas on time along poor roads. The strict separation of the sectors assigned to the panzer corps and infantry corps for their movement, repeatedly requested by the *Panzergruppe*, had already borne fruit for the deployment.

The divisions, well camouflaged, prepared for the attack under the protection of the artillery, heavy weapons and Flak. At 0200 hours on 22.6.[41], the assembly was completed without disruption, which in itself was an achievement, since a Russian attack into our troop movements and assembly areas could have caused a difficult situation.[12]

On 16 June, panzer soldier Erich Hager, a tank radio operator in 17 Panzer Division, scribbled in his diary that things were "gradually getting serious." By 20/21 June, he and his entire division – a key component of General Guderian's 2 Panzer Group, a fact apparent from the white "G" emblazoned on the stern of all tanks and vehicles as a tactical identification sign – had reached their final concentration area, a large pine forest just a few kilometers from the Russian border.[13] Paul Carell, in the opening paragraphs of his immensely popular account of Operation *Barbarossa*, *Hitler Moves East*, described the situation of Hager and his fellow tankers only hours before war with Russia was set to begin:

> For two days they had been lying in the dark pinewoods with their tanks and vehicles. They had arrived, driving with masked headlights, during the night of 19-20 June. During the day they lay silent. They must not make a sound. At the mere rattle of a hatch-cover the troop commanders would have fits. Only when dusk fell were they allowed to go to the stream in the clearing to wash themselves, a troop at a time …
>
> 39 Panzer Regiment, which formed part of 17 Panzer Division … had been moved first to Central Poland and then brought here into the woods of Pratulin. Here they were, less than three miles from the river Bug, which formed the frontier, almost exactly opposite the huge old fortress of Brest-Litovsk, occupied by the Russians since the partition of Poland in the autumn of 1939.
>
> The regiment was bivouacking in the forest in full battle order. Each tank, moreover, carried 10 jerry cans of petrol strapped to its turret and had a trailer in tow with a further three drums … In the dense pinewoods of Pratulin the hot day was drawing to its end. The pleasant smell of resin and the stench of petrol hung in the air.[14]

5.1.2: The Logistical Buildup:

Of course, the jerry cans and drums of fuel carried by the tanks of 39 Panzer Regiment represented but a tiny fraction of the fuel which had been stockpiled for months – along with rations, ammunition, spare parts, etc. – as part of the logistical buildup for the Russian campaign. Each of the three army groups – North, Center, South – was supported by a supply district (*Versorgungsbezirk*) which accumulated tens of thousands of tons of supplies in multiple depots in the weeks and months leading up to 22 June 1941. By way of example, Supply District Center (supporting Army Group Center) distributed its massive tonnage of supplies over 13 ammunition, 11 fuel and 14 ration depots. As of mid-February 1941, Supply Districts North, Center and South had built up stocks of ammunition amounting to 42,560 tons, 87,460 tons and 42,300 tons, respectively. By 20 June, these stockpiles had climbed to 68,000 tons, 127,000 tons and 84,000 tons, respectively. Before the start of the campaign, each division was allotted a full initial load (*Erstausstattung*) of ammunition,[15] while those divisions taking part in the opening attack were allocated an additional half load of ammunition to support the initial breakthrough of the Soviet border defenses. Army Group Center, the largest of the three groups, required roughly 30,000 tons of ammunition to furnish its 50 divisions with a full initial load (excluding all elements organic to the army group, its armies or corps, or assigned temporarily to them, including combat engineer and artillery units).[16]

The quantities of fuel and rations assembled for the armies of Hitler's *Ostheer* were just as impressive. Supply District Center alone possessed 52,000 tons of fuel and 45,800 tons of rations in its depots on 22 June 1941. This amounted to 13 *Verbrauchsaetze*, or units of consumption (a measurement of fuel),[17] and enough rations to support the army group for some 20 days.[18] One unit of consumption for the divisions of Army Group Center (again, excluding elements assigned directly to the army group, its armies or corps) amounted to about 3500 tons of fuel, while the daily ration requirement (*Tagessatz*) was roughly 2400 tons. Each division of the army group began *Barbarossa* with a full load of fuel as well as enough food to last – if stretched – for about two weeks. To ensure adequate mobility for the first two weeks of operations, panzer and motorized divisions carried an additional allotment of fuel in their organic transport. Finally, the two panzer groups assigned to Army Group Center were each supported by a supply dump filled with some 400 tons of tank replacement parts.[19]

Despite such in-depth preparations – which were, of course, accomplished by all three of the army groups in the *Barbarossa* order of battle – shortages of all kinds would affect German operations virtually from the start of the invasion, the result of the speed and depth of the advance (particularly of the mobile formations, which had soon pushed well beyond their initial supply points), the Soviet Union's poor road and rail infrastructure, Red Army destruction of bridges, railroads and rolling stock (and the overly deliberate pace of German conversion of the railroads to the European standard gauge), an inadequate German motor transport pool, and other factors. In some cases, supplies even had to be flown to armored units stranded hundreds of kilometers beyond the Russo-German frontier without ammunition or fuel.

5.1.3: The *Luftwaffe*:

The *Luftwaffe* had completed its plans for the eastern campaign in late February 1941, issuing sealed orders to aircrews that were not to be opened until eight hours before "H-hour."[20] The construction of airfields, the provision of accommodations and other preparatory activities had begun in the fall of 1940, continued through the winter of 1940/41, and accelerated in March 1941 as the weather improved. However, it was only in April/May 1941 that actual preparations for the arrival of the flying units began to go forward in occupied Poland, including the establishment of administrative and supply units, aircraft maintenance shops and equipment issuing stations. Once again, all these initiatives proceeded as unobtrusively as was possible, with every conceivable security precaution.[21]

To preclude possible detection, the transfer of *Luftwaffe* units to the east was delayed to the last possible moment. Motorized elements of the *Luftwaffe* ground organization, including anti-aircraft and signal units, were deployed by rail and road – movements they had largely completed by 15 June 1941. The assignment of flying units to the eastern front was accomplished in its entirety in a period of just three weeks by 20/21 June 1941. Gradually, under conditions of strictest secrecy, supported by radio deception measures, *Luftwaffe* units were pulled out of operations against Great Britain. The first to be withdrawn were the fighter formations, which were not required for the night air offensive; the last were the bombers, which had conducted that offensive. As much as possible, the flying formations were first shifted to their home bases for a brief period of rest and rehabilitation; from there, the aircraft were brought up to their prepared air fields in the east in individual flights or in small formations of several planes (*Ketten*), avoiding larger urban areas as a security precaution. The deployment of the *Luftwaffe* to the east, however, did not remain hidden from British radio intelligence, which, through ULTRA, was able to read the German Air Force's code.[22]

One of the last air elements to deploy was Lt.-Gen. Wolfram *Freiherr* von Richthofen's 8 Air Corps, one of two air corps assigned to Field Marshal Albert Kesselring's 2 Air Fleet, responsible for air support to Army Group Center. The 8 Air Corps had been heavily committed during the Balkan Campaign that spring, and now it was about to begin an even greater challenge with little time to rest and refit, as Richthofen complained in his diary. Only on 19 June did it finally deploy to East Prussia from deep inside Germany, where it had replenished its supplies and taken on new aircraft and aircrews. Still, 8 Air Corps would begin *Barbarossa* short some 600 motor vehicles, 40 percent of its aircraft, and vital spare parts and communications equipment.[23] Despite such challenges, the air corps – the only dedicated close air support unit in the *Luftwaffe* – would be ready to accomplish its mission, and would do so to great effect.

Field Marshal Kesselring did not leave the Channel Coast – from where he had led the German air campaign against Great Britain – until 12 or 13 June, heading first to Berlin for the final pre-*Barbarossa* conference; according to official German pronouncements, however, he was still with his bombers in the west, where bogus German wireless transmissions throughout the first days of June sought to convey the impression that certain *Luftwaffe* formations were still operating against England, instead of redeploying to the east. Several days later Kesselring flew on from Berlin, landing at an airfield outside Warsaw, joining his headquarters staff, and throwing himself into his final preparations for the impending air campaign.[24]

5.1.4: Total Forces in the East:
By 20/21 June 1941, the largest invasion force the world had ever seen – and, most likely, ever will see – had lurched finally into place. In its entirety the German *Ostheer* embraced the following:

3,050,000 men
3600 tanks and assault guns
600,000 vehicles
625,000 horses

Artillery:
4760 light guns
2252 medium & heavy guns
104 Army Flak guns (88mm)
30 super-heavy high-/low angle guns[25]

This extraordinary mass of men and materiel was organized into 145 divisions, including 28 of the OKH reserve:

103 infantry
19 panzer
13 motorized (+3 brigades/regiments (mot.))
6 security
2 mountain
1 cavalry[26]

Deducting the OKH reserve, 117 divisions were (as noted) earmarked for the first assault wave. Of the panzer divisions, two belonged to the OKH reserve, leaving 17 for the initial attack. The motorized formations included four *Waffen*-SS divisions and several motorized brigades/ regiments, among the latter the elite Infantry Regiment *Grossdeutschland*. The final mobile unit, 1 Cavalry Division, was the only cavalry division remaining in the German Army inventory.[27]

In addition to the primary force structure outlined above, the German Army of Norway deployed several divisions (67,000 men) in northern Finland. Among the allied contingents were about 500,000 Finnish troops, distributed over 14 divisions and several brigades; 150,000 Romanian troops in 14 under strength divisions and several brigades; and smaller levies from Hungary and Slovakia. In addition, Italy would dispatch a small expeditionary force of several divisions to the east in August 1941. However damning history's verdict may be of Hitler's decision to wage a war of annihilation against Soviet Russia, the German dictator cannot be accused of "going it alone!" His *Ostheer* was truly a "multicultural" army.[28]

Providing the "vertical envelopment"[29] was a *Luftwaffe* force structure in the east comprising nearly 3000 aircraft, of which 2255 were combat ready. On 22 June, this force included 757 bombers (mostly He 111s), 360 Ju 87 *Stuka* dive-bombers, and 657 single-engine Bf 109 fighters fully operational. The eastern air forces also encompassed short-and long-range reconnaissance aircraft under tactical control of the Army; these included 111 long-range and 358 short-range aircraft that were fully operational. All of these aircraft (*Luftwaffe* and Army-controlled) were apportioned over four air fleets (1, 2, 4, 5).[30]

To replenish the advancing armies, the German High Command had made provisions for replacement personnel; these plans, however – just like the strategic, operational, and logistical plans for Operation *Barbarossa* – were based on the erroneous assumption of a short 8-12 week campaign. On 20 May 1941, the head of the Replacement Army, General Friedrich Fromm, reported to Chief of the General Staff Halder on the results of the plans. All told, 90,000 men had been assembled for the field replacement battalions, and these were being transferred to the front-line units. This left the Replacement Army with 475,000 men; the *Luftwaffe*, however, claimed 90,000 of these men, leaving only 385,000 as replacements for the *Ostheer*. Losses during the frontier battles (through August) were projected to be about 275,000 men, with an additional 200,000 casualties anticipated for September – meaning that the Army's trained reserves would be exhausted by October. Simply put, "there was no room for serious setbacks [during the course of *Barbarossa*], any more than for an extension of the planned duration of operations into the winter. For neither of these contingencies were there any preparations prior to 22 June 1941."[31]

5.1.5: The Army Groups: Orders of Battle and Missions:

In assessing the orders of battle of the three German army groups, what is at once apparent is that only Army Group Center was in possession of two panzer groups, while the army groups on the wings had just one each. The result was that only in the middle of the Russo-German front, along the Belostok – Minsk – Smolensk axis, were the Germans largely successful in meeting the basic objective – as outlined in the original *Barbarossa* directive (December 1940) – of encircling and destroying the bulk of Red Army forces west of the Dvina-Dnepr river lines. While army groups North and South also advanced deep into Soviet territory, destroying large chunks of the Soviet forces facing them, they only managed to push the enemy back without, for the most part, destroying his cohesion as a fighting force. The implications of this failure for the outcome of *Barbarossa* were, of course, profound.

Army Group North: This army group, on the left wing of assembled German forces and the smallest of the three, was commanded by 65-year-old Field Marshal Ritter von Leeb. It comprised 20 infantry, three panzer, and three motorized divisions – 26 in all, organized into two armies (16 and 18) and the 4 Panzer Group[32] – deployed in East Prussia along a narrow, ca. 300 kilometer front. Commanded by Panzer General Erich Hoepner, 4 Panzer Group had approximately 600 tanks[33] divided among its three armored divisions. The mission (*Auftrag*) of Army Group North, as laid out in the final, definitive version of the OKH deployment directive, dated 8 June 1941,[34] was to eliminate enemy forces in the Baltic region, occupy the Baltic ports and, ultimately, to deprive Soviet naval forces of their key bases by seizing Kronstadt and Leningrad. To support the mission of Leeb's army group, mobile forces were eventually to be brought up from Army Group Center. Providing air support for Army Group North was the relatively tiny 1 Air Fleet, with only 211 operational bombers and 167 combat-ready fighters.[35] As John Keegan has pointed out, this army group's axis of advance was to take it through territory which had been Germanized by the Teutonic knights and the Hanseatic traders for 500 years; moreover, from the Baltic region had come many of the families which had "officered the Prussian and German armies throughout their history. Manstein and Guderian, who were to win Hitler his greatest eastern victories, descended from landowners of those parts."[36]

Army Group South: Situated on the right wing, from southern Poland to Romania, this army group was commanded by 65-year-old Field Marshal Gerd von Rundstedt. At its disposal were 29 infantry divisions (including four so-called "light" divisions), five panzer, three motorized, three security and one mountain division – 41 divisions in all, arranged in three armies (6, 11, and 17) and the 1 Panzer Group.[37] Commanding the panzer group was General Ewald von Kleist, with more than 700 tanks between his five armored divisions.[38] With its *Schwerpunkt* on the left wing – two infantry armies and the Kleist's panzer group – Army Group South was to break through the Red Army defenses covering the Ukraine and, advancing by way of Berdichev and Zhitomir, gain the line of the Dnepr River at and below Kiev. 1 Panzer Group was then to turn southeast and continue the advance along the Dnepr, preventing the enemy from withdrawing beyond the river and defeating him in battle with an inverted front in cooperation with the advancing infantry. On the far right wing of Rundstedt's army group, Eleventh Army, operating out of Romania, was to tie down enemy forces and prevent their orderly retreat into the interior of Russia. Operations of Army Group South were supported by 4 Air Fleet, whose order of battle embraced 307 operational bombers and 272 combat-ready fighter aircraft. Also assigned to 4 Air Fleet was 2 Flak Corps, its complement of 88mm guns highly effective in both an air and ground support role. Cooperating with the air fleet were several hundred Romanian aircraft and, after 27 June, a small contingent of Hungarian planes.[39]

Army Group Center: Since subsequent chapters will follow the 1000 kilometer advance of this army group – along the route taken by Napoleon in 1812, running through the ancient cities of Minsk and Smolensk to the outskirts of Moscow – its order of battle and *Barbarossa* mission will be outlined in more detail. Commanding Army Group Center, the largest of the three, was 60-year-old Field Marshal Fedor von Bock, with whom the reader has already become familiar.[40] Deployed along a 500 kilometer front from Suwalki in the north to below Brest-Litovsk in the south, the army group was composed of the following forces on the eve of war with Russia:

1,308,730 personnel

50.5 divisions
    31 infantry
    9 panzer
    6½ motorized
    3 security
    1 cavalry

Artillery:
421 light batteries
329 medium & heavy batteries[41]

_____

750 total batteries

The ground forces were organized into two armies (4 and 9) and two panzer groups (2 and 3). Among the artillery assigned to the army group were 17 210mm heavy howitzer (*Moerser*) battalions and four 150mm rocket projector (*Nebelwerfer*) battalions (out of seven on the entire eastern front). Bock's army group also boasted six of the 11 assault gun battalions in the *Barbarossa* order of battle. 2 Panzer Group, commanded by General Heinz Guderian, was the largest of the four tank groups in the east, with a complement of about 930 tanks distributed among five panzer divisions. 3 Panzer Group, led by General Hermann Hoth, possessed about 900 tanks in its four armored divisions. In total, the army group had more than 1800 tanks, considerably more than the other two army groups combined. Resources assigned to the armies and armored groups of Army Group Center also included large numbers of combat engineers (such as units for repair and construction of bridges), 35 construction battalions, 11 battalions dedicated to road repair, as well as units from the Organization Todt and the Reich Labor Service (*Reichsarbeitsdienst*).[42]

This vast armada of men and machines on the ground was supported by Field Marshal Kesselring's 2 Air Fleet, the largest of the three air fleets earmarked for the eastern campaign:

Operational Aircraft (2 Air Fleet):

222 bombers
323 dive bombers
60 destroyers
284 fighters
69 transport
36 other

_____

994 total aircraft (operational)[43]

The 2 Air Fleet was composed of two air corps – 2 Air Corps under Lt.-Gen. Bruno Loerzer in the Warsaw – Brest-Litovsk – Deblin area; and 8 Air Corps under Lt.-Gen. von Richthofen in the Suwalki triangle. Together, they possessed (as noted) 994 combat-ready aircraft; added to these were some 200 operational reconnaissance and liaison aircraft (tactically controlled by the Army). Nearly all of the Ju 87 *Stuka* dive-bombers assembled in the east were massed under this air fleet, with the majority of them (5 1/3 *Gruppen*) assigned to 8 Air Corps (versus 3 *Gruppen* in 2 Air Corps). In addition, three bomber, one dive bomber, one destroyer and two fighter *Gruppen* of 8 Air Corps were outfitted with dropping devices for 2-kg anti-personnel SD-2 fragmentation bombs for close combat. As Bock's army group advanced on Moscow, Loerzer's air corps was to support Fourth Army and, more particularly, Guderian's 2 Panzer Group, while Richthofen's air corps cooperated with Ninth Army and the panzer spearheads of Hoth's 3 Panzer Group. Also controlled by Kesselring's air fleet was 1 Flak Corps, which was to cooperate with both armored groups during their penetration of the frontier fortifications and in subsequent operations.[44]

The plan of attack called for Army Group Center to destroy opposing Soviet Western Front forces in Belorussia by means of a deep double envelopment directed toward the Belorussian capital of Minsk, roughly 250 to 300 kilometers beyond the German-Soviet frontier.[45] This was to be accomplished by the two panzer groups, with Hoth operating north of the Belostok salient from the Suwalki triangle, which projected deep into Russian territory; and Guderian attacking south of the salient, out of the German controlled General-Gouvernement of Poland, on either side of Brest-Litovsk, via Slutsk toward Minsk. A shorter double envelopment – inside the pincers of the armored forces – was to be made by General Adolf Strauss' Ninth Army on the northern wing and Field Marshal Guenther von Kluge's Fourth Army in the south, with the objective of encircling Western Front forces inside the Belostok salient. When these objectives had been secured, the tanks and motorized infantry of 2 and 3 Panzer Groups were to push on rapidly to the east – preventing whatever Western Front forces remained from reestablishing solid lines of resistance along the Dvina-Dnepr river lines, fording both of the river lines, and linking up again near Smolensk – some 600 kilometers from the start line and for Bock's army group the first operational objective of the campaign.[46]

As stipulated in the original *Barbarossa* directive, after the Red Army had been routed in Belorussia, Army Group Center was to send "strong mobile forces" northward to assist the drive of its northern neighbor through the Baltic toward Leningrad. Only after the attainment of key objectives in the north – such as the occupation of Kronstadt and Leningrad – was the attack to be continued toward Moscow, "an important center of communications and of the armaments industry."[47]

5.2: The *Ostheer* – A "First Strike" Capability? (*Erstschlagkapazitaet?*)

In the idiom of nuclear war, a "first strike" capability denotes the ability of one nuclear armed power to conduct a devastating surprise attack – perhaps pre-emptive or preventive in nature – against another nuclear power, rendering it unfit to respond effectively and compelling it to admit defeat. Although the German Reich was armed only with an arsenal of conventional weaponry, its objective in Operation *Barbarossa* was fundamentally the same – to inflict a single blow so powerful, so devastating (and perhaps also pre-emptive, or at least preventive), it would be sufficient to crush the Soviet Union in a short campaign of just two to three months duration.

On 22 June 1941, however, Hitler's *Wehrmacht* enjoyed no advantage over its Red Army opponent in terms of total numbers of personnel or quantities or quality of its weaponry. The only exception in this context would have to do with the German air forces, whose machines were palpably superior – in quality if not in numbers – to the majority of those in the Soviet Air Force order of battle. Conversely, Red Army artillery and its latest tanks, now moving off the assembly lines in significant numbers, were equal or superior to those of the German *Ostheer*, as were several of the primary Soviet small arms, such as their excellent sub-machine guns.

As English historian Paul Johnson has argued, Operation *Barbarossa* was "seriously underpowered in terms of the magnitude of its objectives;" and, eventually, "the Germans found themselves fighting a Forties war with late-Thirties weaponry, and not enough even of that."[48] Certainly, as this account has made clear, German ground and air forces committed to the war in the east were manifestly inadequate. There was simply too little of everything – from combat infantry to armored fighting vehicles to bomber and fighter aircraft; and much of what the Germans *did* have often proved ill-suited for the harsh conditions of combat on the eastern front. As noted, Army Group Center, the center of gravity of the initial German attack, had to advance along a 500 kilometer front, but to do so it had barely 1800 tanks and 1000 operation aircraft – or a ratio of about 3.6 tanks and two aircraft per kilometer. Of course, these forces could – and would – be concentrated at critical points; however, the serious disconnect between means and ends is evident nonetheless. A revealing anecdote in the memoirs of Field Marshal Kesselring further underscores this point:

> At the beginning of 1941, I flew to Warsaw to confer with the commander-in-chief there, Field Marshal von Kluge, and to issue supplementary instructions about expanding the ground organization in that area. I went back again in May 1941 to patrol the deployment base for my air fleet in the east, and found that the work could not be completed before the beginning of June (primarily due to weather and ground conditions), but still with enough time for the rescheduled *X-Tag* (22 June) to be met. The operational and tactical inspections revealed that the attack by Army Group Center could not be supported to the best possible extent with the forces allotted me by the Commander-in-Chief of the *Luftwaffe*. In a heated exchange in Goering's command train north of Paris, and with the support of my dear Jeschonnek (Goering's Chief of Staff), I succeeded in pressing my case and I was promised the minimum reinforcements of aircraft and Flak troops that had been requested.
>
> I could sympathize with the irate *Reichsmarschall* when he said that I was not the only one making demands, that England still had to be fought. But I had to insist that he appreciate my point of view that an attack should not be started if the forces necessary for it could not be assembled.[49]

And, yet, still only two aircraft per kilometer (and 3.6 tanks) to support Army Group Center when war began! By way of comparison, the Soviet offensive in January 1945, on the Berlin front alone, encompassed 6250 tanks, 7560 aircraft and no fewer than 41,600 guns.[50] How, then, did the *Ostheer* manage to conduct such a brilliant campaign in the summer and fall of 1941 – seizing hundreds of thousands of square kilometers of European Russia,[51] advancing to the gates of Leningrad and Moscow, and occupying the Ukraine, while annihilating virtually the entire peacetime Soviet army – and then some! – in the process? To put a finer point on it: In Belorussia, during the frontier battles from 22 June to 9 July 1941, opposite Army Group Center, the Red Army sustained average daily losses of 23,207 personnel, 267 tanks, 524 guns and mortars and 99 aircraft. During the final six months of 1941, the Germans inflicted an aggregate of 4,308,094 casualties on the Red Army, including nearly 3,000,000 irrecoverable losses (dead, captured and missing).[52] By 31 December 1941, Red Army's staggering equipment losses across the eastern front included 24,400 artillery pieces, 60,500 mortars, over 20,000 tanks and almost 18,000 aircraft.[53]

Perhaps an equally germane question would be: How was the Red Army able sustain such a shellacking yet still manage to assemble the resources for a successful "counterstrike" strategy, which inexorably wore down and eventually stopped the *Wehrmacht* well short of its *Barbarossa* objectives? That duly noted, the answer to our original query is not to be found in the material trappings of the German armed forces but in several vital intangibles – most important among them those of surprise, training and experience; the concept of *Schwerpunkt*; and the doctrinal underpinning of "mission tactics." In the first place, tactical surprise was achieved along the entire 1200 kilometer front between the Baltic and the Black Sea, giving the Germans a significant opening advantage they were quick to exploit. Secondly, the German eastern armies were able to leverage their superior training and 21 months of combat experience into major force multipliers; indeed, no matter how technically capable some of the new Soviet weapons may have been, that hardly mattered if Soviet tank crews had

had little time to operate their tanks or pilots to fly their aircraft. German shortfalls in men and materiel were also partially offset by massing their forces – particularly the mobile units – at certain points, thereby creating force ratios strongly in their favor at key sectors of the front. For the opening attack, Army Group Center's 2 Panzer Group (Guderian) was able to deploy its armor along a 70 kilometer front, while the frontage of 3 Panzer Group (Hoth) was even narrower (50 kilometers). Similar or even superior *Schwerpunkte* would be achieved in the Ukraine in September 1941, and for Operation "Typhoon," the assault on Moscow," in October.[54]

No explanation of the reasons behind the *Wehrmacht's* successes in Russia in 1941 – and, indeed, throughout the period 1939-42 – would be complete without addressing the German military's doctrinal imperative of "mission tactics" and its incomparable value as a force multiplier. German military traditions – from Frederick the Great to Scharnhorst, Gneisenau, and the elder Moltke – had taught Prussian and German officers how to resolve tactical and operational problems with originality, insight and initiative. Moreover, while most of Clausewitz's theory had faded away by the early 20th Century, one of his lasting legacies to German military thought was his concept of imponderables: The chaos of war inevitably caused unforeseen events; not to be overwhelmed by such events required flexibility of thought and action in all aspects of war – from grand strategy to small-unit tactics. One outcome of this insight was the doctrine of "mission tactics" (*Auftragstaktik*), which can be defined as the practice of promulgating orders and directives which, while laying out the overall intentions of the higher command, were careful to leave a high degree of initiative and the issuance of specific orders to the subordinate commands:[55]

> At the heart of German training was the inculcating of a progressive, universally taught doctrine: a set of basic assumptions, beliefs and operating instructions that all German troops, irrespective of service, learned and were expected to follow. Adherence to this modern, uniform and realistic doctrine, enshrined in the 1936 *Truppenfuehrung* (Troop Leadership) manual, was one of the great strengths of the German Army. Developed in the early-1930s by some of the Army's best minds, it avoided the parochialism inherent in individual service doctrines and represented a holistic set of procedures for the Army as a whole. The soundness and forward-looking nature of this doctrine made a significant contribution to the military triumphs Germany achieved in the early years of World War II.

> Among the basic principles of German doctrine was due emphasis on individual leadership and initiative. The *Truppenfuehrung* emphasized what the Germans termed mission-oriented tactics. That is to say, doctrine expected senior commanders to give subordinates broad orders but to leave the actual implementation of those orders to the discretion and experience of subordinates. Such an approach provided maximum flexibility and initiative. Junior officers did not simply learn "school" solutions to the problems they might encounter but were instead taught to think for themselves, to apply their military knowledge and expertise, to have confidence in their own decisions, and to act upon them.[56]

Colonel Dr Alfred Durrwanger, a former *Bundeswehr* officer and company commander in Russia in the summer of 1941, described an incident from the opening days of the war that encapsulated the mission tactics "mind set:"

> My regiment, after being detained by the resistance of crack Soviet units during the border battles, subsequently followed the two other regiments of my division and gradually approached the wide Neman River, about 90 kilometers away from

the German border. During the night and the early morning of 28 June [1941] the units of the regiment reached the little village of Holynka, about 10 kilometers distant from the Neman. The regiment was the reserve of the division behind the two other regiments, which were now involved in combat with the Soviets.

I would like to draw attention now to one element of German warfare that had great success, especially in Soviet Russia, the so-called *Auftragstaktik* … Let me give you a practical example of *Auftragstaktik*. After having arrived at that little village during the night, the regimental commander ordered me in the early morning, and also the commander of the 14th Company, to contact the other regiments of our division in the frontline. We were to explain to the other regimental commanders the situation in our regiment and ask for their respective situations. My regimental commander had acted according to his own decision that it would always be good to be informed concerning the present situation although not being in the front line: *Auftragstaktik!*[57]

Riding on a motorcycle with a side-car, and accompanied by his small company staff, Durrwanger located the neighboring regimental commander, who proceeded to explain the situation of his regiment, which had faced serious enemy opposition since the day before. Durrwanger immediately passed on what he had learned to his regimental commander, and then pondered his next move. It was a bright, sunny day, and the morning was hot; however, at the moment, there were no sounds of battle – nothing but the "warbling of some birds." He finally decided to approach closer to the Neman River with his staff (three or four men) and conduct his own reconnaissance. After informing the regimental commander of his intention, Durrwanger requested that the regiment send him, as soon as possible, a platoon of infantry and a platoon of light infantry guns from his own company.[58]

After lodging this request, Durrwanger and his small group continued their dangerous journey, cautiously approaching a village near the banks of the Neman along a major road. Before reaching the village, they noticed a Soviet anti-tank gun positioned at the first house; clustered around it were several dead Red Army soldiers. Moving forward gingerly, they soon discovered that the village, occupied the night before, had since been abandoned by the Russians. Climbing atop an observation tower adjacent to the river, they observed what appeared to be a "sturdy bridge" over the 70-80 meter wide Neman, leading out of the village and across the river. The bridge appeared to be intact, but was not marked on Durrwanger's "poor and inaccurate maps," a nearly universal problem for the Germans in the opening stages of *Barbarossa*. Finally approaching the bridge, whose capture intact would be of great benefit to their division, they discovered it had not been prepared for demolition:[59]

> Immediately, I sent another report to my regiment telling all what we had found and how favorable it would be to have some reinforcements in order to take the bridge and create a bridgehead on the south side of the river. After a short period the requested reinforcement arrived and we briefed them on the situation and told them how to proceed. My regimental commander himself arrived with these soldiers. He told me that he had mobilized a whole battalion to profit from this situation and to gain, if possible, the other side of the river. Meanwhile, the Soviets on the opposite side of the river began to realize what had happened and started to shoot across the bridge. The regimental commander was the first to shoot from our anti-tank gun, positioned to shoot near the bridge.
>
> The bridgehead on the other side of the Neman River was established by our regiment in the course of the afternoon. The little resistance we faced was probably from the enemy rearguards. Possession of the bridge, of course, provided

an enormous advantage for the quick advance of our division. The regimental commander had pushed his units forward without any direct or specific order of the division, but only motivated by the will to make use of that recently discovered weakness on the Soviet side. That is the essence of *Auftragstaktik*.[60]

In June 1941, the *Wehrmacht* was at the very peak of its efficiency, and its ability to respond to the inevitably fluid and ever-changing situations on the battlefield with imagination, insight and initiative, was unparalleled. Long before the summer of 1941, however, new technologies, such as the radio, and the growing necessity for ground commanders to coordinate their actions with air power, had begun to bring an end to the commander's independence on the battlefield.[61] The exercise of mission tactics was to suffer another blow in December 1941, following Hitler's assumption of direct command of the Army (after Field Marshal von Brauchitsch's retirement for health reasons) and, in general, as a result of his increasingly iron grip over its operations. In late December 1941, a nervous "Fuehrer" would pass many hours on the telephone with the new C-in-C of Army Group Center, Field Marshal von Kluge, often insinuating himself into the most minute tactical details of the army group's operations. The German front-line soldier, however, would never completely lose his reflex for independent thought and action, as this author's study of the operations of a *Waffen*-SS division in Normandy in 1944 make abundantly clear.[62]

The intangibles outlined above – surprise, training and experience, *Schwerpunkt*, mission tactics – were largely responsible for the *Wehrmacht's* impressive surge from the Russo-German border to the suburbs of Moscow 1000 kilometers to the east in less than six months time. And yet, despite such a brilliant feat of arms,[63] *Barbarossa* was to end in dismal failure. Did the German Army in the east possess a first-strike capability in June 1941? Given that we know the outcome, the answer to this question is obvious: No, it did not possess such a capability. In the final analysis, however, this was only because the Soviet state, and its people, played by a much different set of rules than did the Western democracies. In 1940, the death of 90,000 French soldiers[64] was enough to force France to capitulate. By way of comparison, the Soviet people suffered an average of more than 20,000 civilian and military deaths each and every day of the war for 1418 days. In other words, in less than a single week's time, the Russians sustained significantly more fatal losses than did the French during the entire campaign of 1940, and yet they continued to fight (and to die in numbers utterly inconceivable by today's standards). That they *could* do so was, in part, due to their country's prodigious size, and the strategic depth it provided, which bought them time. That they *did* do so was, in large measure, the end result of the brutality of Stalin's regime – by 1940/41, it had broken the back of the opposition through its war on the peasantry (force collectivization), the purges, etc. – coupled with their implacable response to the oppressive and genocidal policies of the German invaders. Indeed, it was the incomparable tenacity of the Soviet people and their willingness – coerced or otherwise – to endure such a horrific blood letting which, ultimately, decided the outcome of the war with Germany. Without such a willingness, the savage initial blow inflicted by the *Wehrmacht* in the summer of 1941 would have surely sufficed.

5.3: Rumors of War in Far Away Places

On 2 September 1941, *Leutnant* Jochen Hahn, a forward observer in 292 Artillery Regiment (292 Infantry Division), wrote a letter to his wife from the bloody El'nia salient east of Smolensk:

> We have been living in our dugout for over three weeks now – no sun, little daylight, constant shooting from the Russians. It could often drive you mad. But hopefully this, too, will all blow over. Another telephone operator was injured

yesterday while locating a disturbance in the line. People are got like this almost every day, but only few replacements arrive. We now have 37 vacant posts ... You wrote recently about troop transfers to the west: we've also been hearing that watchword here, too, that we're to go west ... Keep your fingers crossed that we'll go to the west, since we've been here for three weeks in tough defensive combat. We horse-drawn artillery will never be considered for England, unless we were to be motorized. But at any rate, the main thing is to get out of this shit. It's a witch's brew out here.[65]

Leutnant Hahn can be forgiven for hoping to make a sudden escape from the Russian Front. After all, after three weeks in the meat grinder of the El'nia salient, the prospect of fighting against the "Tommies" must have seemed like a salvation of sorts in comparison. Yet, alas, it was not to be. It was simply a rumor. And, like rumors too many to count which swirled through the ranks of the millions of *Landser* on the eastern front, it soon faded away and was forgotten.

It has been remarked, perhaps with glibness in mind, that the lot of the soldier in wartime is one of interminable boredom punctuated by moments of visceral fear. Yet it was also the fate of the vast majority of soldiers – at least before the advent of modern satellite- and computer-based communications – to have little awareness of what took place on the battlefield beyond what they could touch, smell or observe with their own eyes. They may have known the enemy on the patch of ground before them intimately, but beyond that they knew little to nothing. Such enforced isolation in a time of heightened senses and emotions – and fear – led, ineluctably, to half-baked speculation about what the days ahead might hold.

Such was surely the case that winter and spring of 1941, when several millions of German soldiers – from Germany, France, the Balkans and other regions of occupied Europe – took part in the gigantic secret troop movements toward the eastern frontier. After the fall of France in June 1940, many had hoped for a swift end to the war and a return to their families and civilian life. Yet Great Britain held out and the war dragged on. Now, suddenly, the great bulk of the German Army was rolling eastward, across the Elbe and Oder; and as their troop trains trundled across the borders of the Reich, they wondered where they were going and why they were going there. They knew nothing, of course, about *Barbarossa*; in fact, most of these soldiers did not learn about the Reich's impending attack Russia until the final hours before the attack began, when officers and NCOs read out to them their "Fuehrer's" proclamation "To the Soldiers of the Eastern Front!" Yet in the weeks and months before that watershed moment, they were undoubtedly aware that they were participating in an extraordinary undertaking; that something big, very big, was in the air.

Just what that might be, however, was unclear, as surviving diaries and field post of German soldiers illustrate. With the luxury of hindsight, it may seem odd that the answer wasn't patently obvious at the time – that is, that Germany was about to attack Russia! Yet in the spring of 1941, Germany was at war with England and at peace with Russia. Indeed, the Reich and the Soviet Union had – on the surface of things at least – enjoyed good relations since late August 1939, when Hitler's Foreign Minister Ribbentrop had flown to Moscow and put his signature to the non-aggression pact between the two countries which stunned the world. Moreover, since that time, the peaceful relations between Germany and Russia had been expanded through growing economic cooperation.[66] Besides, England had yet to be vanquished, and the "Fuehrer's" own experience in World War I had taught him well the folly of allowing the Fatherland to be ensnared in a war on two fronts. To be sure, many *Landser* still managed to see the *Aufmarsch* in the east for what it was. Yet many did not, and often took refuge in flights of fancy to explain the mighty war machine metastasizing along the frontier with Soviet Russia. Simply put, the "rumor mill" ran amuck, as the following first hand accounts demonstrate:

Leutnant H.H. (258 ID) – 20 May 1941
The craziest rumors about Russia are making the rounds here. Some are saying that we've leased the Ukraine for 90 years and received permission to march through Turkey and Iraq. Others claim that the threat of war has been averted by Stalin's stance, etc. Every latrine rumor is closely followed by another. I'd be quite happy if it didn't come to war. That bogland and its vermin would hold no attraction for me. And all that time I've invested in learning Russian might just as well be wasted, too, for all I care.[67]

Officer (SS *Das Reich* Division) – June 1941
At the beginning of May 1941, the peacetime atmosphere in which we had been living suddenly changed. All unit commanders in the Division were called to a conference at Gmunden am Traunsee, to be briefed on the coming war against Soviet Russia. There were no enthusiastic cries of "Sieg Heil!" at this announcement for there was none of us who did not have some concern at the size of the landmass in which we were soon to operate. The rank and file were not put in the picture at that time so that when the eastward movement began in June the wildest rumors spread – including one about a march through Russia and into India.[68]

R. Hertenstein (13 PD) – June 1941
They transferred us to the southern part of Silesia which was a German province until the end of World War II. We got there around the late spring of 1941, and around June we slowly moved further east toward the Soviet/German demarcation line in Poland. We were in the area where we had fought in 1939, northwest of Lemberg.
    At that time there were all kinds of rumors going around as to what would happen next. One rumor was that we would go through the Ukraine and the Caucasus mountains down into Persia to cut off the British oil sources there. The Russians would permit us to do it. There was a second rumor that we would go through the Caucasus, Turkey, and Palestine, and go west from there to cut off the Suez Canal. Rommel with his *Afrika Korps* would then advance toward the canal from Libya.[69]

Gefreiter (Unit unknown) – 2 June 1941
Yesterday somebody was saying we had got three roads and two railway lines from Russia for the march through. Why do you lose hope for an early end to this? Now that the business with Russia is hunky-dory [*so in Butter ist*], I am increasingly hopeful. Because of course Russia is much more important than, perhaps, America. Because, if America were really to step in – which I don't believe any more – and in the meantime we've got all the English bases up to the Indian Ocean, the Americans would be over a barrel. Of course they know that, too, in America.[70]

Unteroffizier W. P. (167 ID) – 8 June 1941
We've been packing all day today, because we're moving onwards. Where, we don't know of course! Either east (Russia) or to the southeast, Syria, Iraq, etc. In any case, it will mean the deployment we were promised back home. Of course, I can't and mustn't tell you about anything else. We are all very curious about all the days to come ourselves, because everything in the future is so vague.[71]

Otto Skorzeny (SS *Das Reich* Division) – mid-June 1941

In mid-June 1941 our division was transferred by rail to Litzmannstadt (Lódz) in Poland. After all vehicles and supplies had been loaded onto the flat cars, we boarded our passenger cars and enjoyed the journey without worry.

For hours we speculated about our next military objective, but none of us envisioned that we would soon embark on a war against Russia. To the contrary, the most persistent rumor was that our objective would be the oil fields of the Persian Gulf. Russia would grant the German Army free passage and we would march across the Caucasus into Iran. We discussed the possibility of winning over the Islamic world, and, by doing so, securing access to trade and raw materials that could prove decisive to the outcome of the war.

Another rumor was that we would march via Turkey into Egypt and surround the English Near-East Army in a pincer action. As a result of this conjecture I took along the book *The Seven Pillars of Wisdom*, by T.E. Lawrence. The tempting Orient provided us with many hours of conversation while we were transported in a wide arc around Bohemia and Moravia to reach Poland via Upper Silesia ...

We soon discovered that our speculation about our next move had been completely off base, as our orders pointed to an imminent offensive against the Soviet Union. This option had not occurred to us, although we had assumed the non-aggression pact between Germany and Russia could not last forever.[72]

H.-G. Alvermann (110 ID) – 20-22 June 1941

Early in June we were made aware of an imminent departure. I was fortunate enough to find myself in my home area and so had a few advantages over my other comrades. But even then, saying farewell is not exactly easy: on 20 June 1941, I said goodbye to my parents.

Sometime that evening, our block warden came by – in the Party that was something like a lance-corporal in the *Wehrmacht*. He was employed with the camp command staff and, in his position, naturally "knew" something about the secret affairs of the Army: our unit was to be transferred to India to stir up trouble for the English in their imperial colonies. So I returned to our quarters, a cantonment, with this secret knowledge, but didn't tell anyone about it.

Our transport began the following morning with a train via Hamburg – Mecklenburg – Pommerania. On 22 June, we had a roll call on the station platform in Neustettin, where the news of the war with Russia was revealed to us. We were astonished because of course our government had sealed a non-aggression pact with that country in [August] 1939. So nothing was going to come of that trip to India. We couldn't do anything about it; our tickets could not be exchanged.[73]

F. Belke (6 ID) – 21 June 1941

We get an injection in our chest against dysentery, a vaccination that you can really feel for some time. Otherwise it's an off-duty day. Our bare upper torsos bask in the warm sun – consequence: sunburn that will cause us additional agonies in the coming days. During the course of the day it becomes crystal clear: we're going up against the Soviet Union! The rumors of a march through Russia and being deployed against the Brits in the Middle East or in India have exploded. Calm, but earnest and tense, we look the issues squarely in the eye. I am now located in the same sector in which my father fought in June 1915, exactly 26 years ago, against the Russians.[74]

G. W. Schrodek (11 PD) – 22 June 1941
Right up to late in the evening of the previous day we cherished the delusional hope of staying in eastern Poland and just waiting for Stalin's permission to march across Russia to Syria (!). Until then, really nobody had considered a war against Russia.[75]

These accounts provide a representative sample of the kinds of rumors that circulated among the *Landser* on the eve of war with Russia. What fascinates about them is how focused they are on possible strategies for defeating Great Britain; and they make more understandable the failure of so many to comprehend the real purpose behind the buildup in the east, for their "Fuehrer" – in whom the average German soldier had implicit faith and trust – would never begin a war with the Soviet Union before he had finished with England. Ironically, their thinking ran roughly along the same lines as that of Joseph Stalin! For like Stalin, it appears that they were also purposely misled by Germany's disinformation campaign, which had begun in February 1941. (See Chapter 4, Section 4.6)

It should be pointed out that it was not only rank-and-file soldiers who failed to grasp the Nazi leadership's true intentions. General Erich Hoepner, commander of 4 Panzer Group, also found the prospects of war against Russia virtually inconceivable, as his biographer explained:

Among his family, on the evening of 30 March 1941, Hoepner expressed the hope that this new campaign could be averted. This hope is also echoed once again, although diminishing, in a short letter to his mother from 26 May 1941: "Nothing will happen here before 20.6. The question of whether it is even going to occur is also being asked here constantly. A 99-year lease of the Ukraine is even being spoken of. On the one hand, I can hardly believe that the USSR would risk this loss of prestige. On the other hand, our demands would not be satisfied by that …" Moreover, his *Ordonnanzoffizier* 03, responsible for military intelligence, who for three years was among his closest confidants, later stated: "Hoepner believed a war against the Soviet Union to be out of the question and the whole deployment to be a bluff … It is utterly impossible that Hoepner could ever have considered war against the USSR to be unavoidable, or to be a fight for survival which had been imposed on us. Three or four days before the attack on the Soviet Union he said to me: 'This cannot be true, this is our hara-kiri!'"[76]

In the late autumn of 1941, the surviving remnants of Hoepner's 4 Panzer Group were to come closest to Moscow of all German forces. Less than three years later, on 8 August 1944, Hoepner was hanged in Ploetzensee prison in Berlin for his role in the anti-Hitler resistance.

5.4: Final Meeting at the Reich Chancellery (14 June 1941)

On 14 June 1941, a mere eight days prior to the launch of Operation *Barbarossa*, Hitler assembled the commanders of his eastern army groups, armies, *Panzergruppen* and air fleets at the new Reich Chancellery in Berlin for a final conference to discuss the impending campaign.[77] On direct orders from Hitler, the new *Reichskanzlei* had been designed by Albert Speer and the extraordinary project completed in less than a year's time in January 1939 by some 8-9000 artisans, craftsmen and workers.[78] The imposing structure – with its harsh granite facade, sumptuous marbled floors, lush mosaics and tapestries, elegant windows and doors – sprawled along the *Voss Strasse* from the *Wilhelmplatz* to the *Tiergarten* and was a fitting symbol of the growing power and influence of the German Reich, as, of course, it was meant to be.[79] Soon after the war had ended in 1945, what remained of Hitler's Chancellery would be removed by the Russians; the stone and marble providing materials for their war monument in Berlin-Treptow.[80]

Because secrecy was essential, a "strict agenda of arrival routes, times and car parking was enforced,"[81] with the participating general staff officers assigned different street entrances by which to reach the Chancellery complex – prophylactic measures to conceal from curious Berliners that something – something very big – was being set into motion. Yet if the average citizen knew nothing about the sinister and world-historical events about to unfold along the eastern frontier, the same cannot be said of the generals slipping discreetly behind the tall granite walls of the Chancellery. By now, just days before the war was to begin, the Army and *Luftwaffe* generals set to lead the surprise attack on Russia were fully aware of the uniquely thuggish underpinnings of the colonial-style campaign the German Reich planned to unleash – not only upon the Red Army but the Russian people as well.

Beginning in mid-May 1941, the German High Command had ordered promulgation of three notorious measures which were to shape German policy toward Soviet prisoners and civilians in the occupied territories: a.) the Decree on Military Jurisdiction (*Gerichtsbarkeitserlass*) of 13 May 1941, which, *inter alia*, exempted *Wehrmacht* soldiers from prosecution for a broad array of criminal acts committed against civilians;[82] b.) the so-called "Guidelines for the Conduct of Troops in Russia," distributed on 19 May 1941, which demanded "ruthless and energetic action against *Bolshevik agitators, guerillas, saboteurs, Jews* and the complete liquidation of any active or passive resistance;"[83] and, most notorious of all, c.) the Commissar Order of 6 June 1941, which, in flagrant violation of international law, stipulated that Red Army commissars were not to be regarded as soldiers (which they clearly were) under the Geneva Conventions, but eliminated outright.[84]

One wonders if any of the *Barbarossa* generals making their way to the Chancellery that late spring morning paused, perhaps for just a moment, to consider the implications of the war of annihilation they were about to begin. Most likely they did not, wrapped up as they must have been in final thoughts and preparations for their important presentations before the "Fuehrer." The conference began at 11.00 in the morning, with Hitler addressing a few words of welcome to his assembled lieutenants. He then invited each of them to report on his intentions for the opening phase of operations in his sector of the front. The commanders in Army Group South went first, followed by those in Army Group North and Army Group Center in the late afternoon. According to Hitler's *Luftwaffe* adjutant, Nicolaus von Below, the "Fuehrer" for once rarely interrupted, but rather listened attentively to the various reports being made. These provided an overview of the strength of the forces, the numbers of tanks, aircraft and the like; overall, the picture presented was of an enemy who, while admittedly superior in numbers, was markedly inferior in quality to the forces arrayed against him. The generals' tone, then, was decidedly optimistic, and they continued with their reports until about 6.30 in the evening.[85]

In the midst of these recitations, at 2:00 p.m., Hitler broke for lunch, which he took sitting at a long, oval-shaped table with more than two-dozen of his top commanders.[86] About an hour later, Hitler called for silence and began to lecture his distinguished audience about his reasons for attacking Russia. The gist of the "Fuehrer's" remarks – what Halder characterized as a "comprehensive political address" (*umfassende politische Rede*)[87] – was recorded by a number of onlookers that day. Hitler again laid out the reasons, and justifications, for his decision to attack the Soviet Union. He stressed the preventive character of the impending conflict, intimating that the more he had thought about his decision, the more determined he had become to eliminate the "grave threat" that Russia posed to Germany's back.[88] He repeated his often made argument that the collapse of Stalin's Bolshevik state would compel England to lay down its arms. But the fight would be difficult, he said, for the Russian soldier would offer tough resistance. Heavy air raids were to be expected, and measures needed to be taken to protect the Reich by building up strong air defenses. The *Luftwaffe* would gain rapid successes and thereby facilitate the advance of the three army groups toward their objectives. While Hitler estimated that the worst of the fighting would be over in about six weeks' time, every soldier still needed know just what he was fighting for: the destruction of Bolshevism. He spoke in "bitter tones" about Great Britain, which preferred an understanding with Russia to one with Germany: these were the politics of the 19th not the 20th Century, he insisted.[89]

That afternoon, Hitler had further discussions with the commanders of Army Group South. The mass of the Red Army, he said, was expected on the front of Army Group Center; once it had been eliminated, Army Group South could expect to be reinforced from von Bock's central army group. Brauchitsch and Halder both listened but said nothing.[90] At some point, Hitler also emphasized the operational objective which had become an *idée fixe* of sorts – the capture of Leningrad, which he called the "cradle of Bolshevism," and which held a particular fascination for him as the former St. Petersburg of the czars and the symbol of Russia's claim to great power status.[91] In his memoirs General Guderian stated that, at some point that afternoon during the military discussions, he was asked – he does not say by whom – how long it would take his panzer units to reach Minsk. To this question, the only one he was asked, he replied: "Five to six days." As matters turned out, Guderian was right on the mark, for his spearheads would reach the Belorussian capital on 27 June, the sixth day of the campaign.[92] Unfortunately for the German invaders, Hitler's prognostication of six weeks of hard fighting was rather wide of the mark.

5.5: Operation *Barbarossa* – Pre-emptive or Preventive War?

From the outset Adolf Hitler sought – disingenuously to be sure – to justify his decision to attack the Soviet Union as the only option left to him to thwart the imminent and existential threat of a Soviet attack on Germany. As we have seen, he emphasized the prophylactic aspect of Operation *Barbarossa* in his address to his generals at the Reich Chancellery on 14 June 1941. He did so again in his proclamation to the soldiers in the east, which was read out to them on the night of 21/22 June, and in which he referred to the increasingly threatening concentrations of Soviet offensive forces (armored and paratroop units) close to the frontier, stating ominously that some 160 Russian divisions were now poised along the border with Germany, and that only days before, for the first time, Russian patrols had even crossed into territory of the Reich and were only turned back after a prolonged firefight.[93]

On the morning of 22 June, in the diplomatic note handed to Soviet Foreign Commissar Molotov by the German ambassador, the attack was also justified as a response to the "steadily growing concentration of all available Russian forces on the long front from the Baltic to the Black Sea;" moreover, the note charged that reports "received in the last few days eliminated the last remaining doubts as to the aggressive character of this Russian concentration …" Later that day, in his radio address to the German people, Hitler again alluded to the sinister buildup of Red Army forces along the border with Germany, and described the task of the Reich and her Axis allies as the "defense of the European continent."[94] Five days into the campaign, on 27 June, the German High Command got into the act, announcing that the large concentrations of enemy forces in the border areas, particularly in the salients around Belostok and Lemberg, had prefigured an impending Red Army assault on central Europe.[95] By early July 1941, Hitler, no doubt influenced by front-line reports revealing the stunning numbers of Red Army forces in the frontier districts, had even convinced himself that the cynically promoted fiction of *Barbarossa* as a preventive action was in fact real, as this diary entry of Propaganda Minister Joseph Goebbels illustrates:

9 July 1941:

Yesterday: ... At midday, around 1200 hours, we land at an airfield close to Rastenburg. The heat is scorching. The entire area is teeming with swarms of mosquitoes, which have a most unpleasant effect ... A half-hour car journey and we arrive at the headquarters ... Then the *Fuehrer* arrives from the military discussions. He looks unexpectedly well, and he makes a thoroughly optimistic and encouraging impression. He describes, at first in short bursts, the military situation to me, which he views surprisingly positively. According to his certain and proven documents, two thirds of the Bolshevik military force is already destroyed or severely crippled. Five sixths of the Bolshevik air and tank forces can also be deemed destroyed. Thus the major thrust which the Bolsheviks had planned to make into the Reich may be considered defeated ...

There is no longer any doubt that the Russians had assembled their entire striking power along their western border and that this threat, at a time of crisis, which could have befallen us in the course of the war, would have been fatal for us ... The *Fuehrer* is righteously angry with the Bolshevist leadership clique, which deluded itself with the idea of attacking Germany, and thus Europe, and, at the final moment, when the Reich was weakened, attempting to carry out the bolshevization of the continent after all, which had been planned since 1917 ... Now all the broad social strata of the *Volk* can see that the conflict with Bolshevism was necessary, that, once again, the *Fuehrer* had made the right decision at the right moment ... The *Fuehrer* emphasizes to me once more that the experiences of the military up to the present also forcefully demonstrate that it was high time that he went forward on the attack in the east ... Preventive war is still the surest and most benign way when you are certain that your enemy will attack at the first good opportunity anyway; and that was the case with Bolshevism.[96]

In the coming months, Hitler time and again returned to the theme of *Barbarossa* as a preventive,[97] indeed pre-emptive,[98] measure. In mid-September 1941 he told his entourage: "It needed the greatest strength to take the decision last year for the attack on Bolshevism. I had to reckon that Stalin would go over to the attack in the course of this year. It was necessary to move as soon as at all possible. The earliest date was June 1941."[99] In October 1941, while inaugurating an appeal for winter clothing for the eastern front, Hitler explained that, only months before, in May, "the situation was so threatening that there could no longer be any doubt that Russia intended to fall upon us at the first opportunity." In May 1942, once more justifying his decision to move against Russia, he insisted that, if he "had listened to his badly informed generals and waited, and the Russians, in accordance with these plans of theirs, had stolen a march on us, there would have been hardly a chance of stopping their tanks on the well-constructed road system of Central Europe."[100]

Hitler, in fact, with what degree of verisimilitude one can only venture to guess, would maintain the pretext of preventive, or pre-emptive, war until the very end of his life. In February 1945, with the Reich in ruins and Russian troops and tanks poised along the Oder River, on the threshold of Berlin, Hitler dictated his political testament to his deputy, Martin Bormann; in it, he explained that he had attacked Russia in an effort to eliminate Great Britain's sole remaining ally on the continent and, in this manner, induce the English to make peace. Yet there was, he said, a "second compelling reason [for invading Russia], which would have been enough on its own: that from the very existence of Bolshevism there was a threatening danger. From this side one day must inevitably come an attack."[101]

Is there so much as a scintilla of truth to the notion that *Barbarossa* was pre-emptive or, at least, preventive, in nature? The first part of the question – was the war pre-emptive – can be dismissed out of hand. Although the war in the east was, from the start, presented to the German people as an effort to ward off an imminent and existential threat,[102] this was merely Goebbels' propaganda at work. As Ian Kershaw has argued, Hitler's decision to attack Russia was "a momentous decision, perhaps the most momentous of the entire war." Yet the decision was "freely taken. That is, it was not taken under other than self-imposed constraints. It was not taken in order to head off an immediate threat of attack by the Soviet Union. There was no suggestion at this time [second half of 1940] – the justificatory claim would come later – of the need for a pre-emptive strike."[103] From the beginning, German planning for Operation *Barbarossa* had "completely overlooked the magnitude of the undertaking and arrogantly underestimated the capabilities of the opponent;"[104] indeed, as we have seen, Hitler had assured OKW Chief Keitel in the immediate aftermath of the French campaign, that war with Russia, by way of comparison, would be "little more than child's play!" In other words, Hitler and his General Staff "*a priori* ruled out the possibility of a Russian pre-emptive strike." General Erich Marcks, who had drawn up the initial outline of an operational plan in the summer of 1940 for the Army High Command, had even lamented the fact that the Red Army would not do the Germans "the courtesy of attacking."[105]

If Hitler and his generals in the weeks before 22 June were occasionally discomfited by the accelerating pace of Soviet war preparations,[106] there are absolutely no indications – neither in contemporary documents nor memoirs – that anyone was unduly concerned about the prospect of *Barbarossa* being pre-empted. German military intelligence (Foreign Armies East) offered no indications of an impending Soviet attack,[107] while Halder at OKH, in June 1941, characterized the Red Army's dispositions along the border as "purely defensive" (*rein defensiv*) in nature and rejected the notion of a Soviet attack as "nonsense"(*Unsinn*).[108] German thought processes at the time are neatly summed up by German historian Juergen Foerster:

> Since Stalin was not presumed to harbor aggressive, but rather defensive, intentions, Hitler and his military command were not alarmed by the capacity of the Red Army for war. Its concentration in the advance areas around Lemberg and Belostok was actually quite convenient for them. The greater concern for Hitler was rather that Stalin might spoil his bellicose idea with a political gesture of good will.[109]

Turning to the question of a possible justification for a preventive war, the answer becomes rather more complex – in large part due to new, and decidedly different, interpretations of Soviet behavior in the years prior to and at the beginning of the Second World War. While the significance of *Barbarossa* as an ideologically and racially motivated war of annihilation has remained relatively constant in post-war historiography, the national security policy of the Soviet Union under Stalin has been subject to a broader range of interpretations. For many years, for example, the historical consensus was that Stalin's Russia, in the period between the summer of 1939 and June 1941, was a largely passive force; and while it may have made gains at the expense of its weaker and smaller neighbors (Poland, the Balkans, Romania), and was engaged in an extensive military buildup, these actions were generally rationalized as defensive responses to the growing German threat.[110]

In the 1980s and 1990s, however, new lines of interpretation began to emerge, suggesting that Stalin's intentions throughout this period were much more sinister than previously thought and, indeed, "on par with those of Hitler."[111] Most notable among the revisionist historians is the Russian émigré and former officer in the Soviet Main Intelligence Directorate (GRU), who goes by the pseudonym Viktor Suvorov (née Rezun). Simply put, Suvorov, and other revisionists, argued that the Soviet dictator was an ambitious revolutionary with the long-term strategic goal of advancing the cause of Communism, in part by means of military conquest. To this end, Stalin had signed the notorious pact with Hitler in August 1939, hoping to use his unwitting National Socialist counterpart as an "ice breaker" to weaken the western democracies – and Germany as well – before Stalin himself overran Europe. According to Suvorov, by 1941, Stalin was ready to proceed to the final stage of his plan, which was to begin with the conquest of Germany. Suvorov even professed to know the date the Soviet attack was to set to begin – 6 July 1941.[112]

It is, of course, beyond the scope of this narrative to "fight" the academic battles that followed in the wake of Suvorov's "revelations." Suffice it to say that the more traditional historians – among them, the late John Erickson, Gabriel Gorodetsky and David Glantz – pushed back hard against Suvorov and other revisionists with related perspectives. They pointed out that, in 1941, the Soviet Union was much too weak to undertake offensive action against Hitler's Germany and that Stalin was well aware of this, which explains his appeasement policies vis-à-vis the Reich as well as his obsession with not provoking Hitler or his generals. While the rebuttals of the traditionalists are firmly grounded, the general line of Suvorov's thesis is supported by Bogdan Musial's extraordinary new book, *Kampfplatz Deutschland*, to which the reader was introduced in Chapter 4 (Section 4.1). If Musial rejects outright Suvorov's dramatic claim that Stalin was set to attack Germany on 6 July 1941, he also holds that insights gained from recently opened Soviet archives largely uphold Suvorov's interpretation of Stalin's basic designs:[113]

> What is undeniable is that in spring 1941, Stalin was in the process of building up the largest invasion force of all time along the German-Soviet border in order to attack his German ally at the right moment. This intention was not the result of the fear that Germany would soon attack the Soviet Union, but rather of the Communist ideology of world revolution. The aim was to implement the next and decisive stage of the world revolution, to sovietize Central and West Europe, indeed the whole of Europe. For a victory over Germany would then have meant mastery of all Europe. The German attack on 22 June 1941 caught this invasion force off guard in the midst of its preparations.[114]

In other words, not only was Hitler preparing a war of aggression, but Stalin was as well. Once this fundamental – yet paradigm altering – fact is accepted, convoluted arguments over who planned to attack whom tend to forfeit their meaning, trumped as they are by the overarching reality that each dictator was preparing to strike the other! To employ the vernacular of revisionist historian Heinz Magenheimer, it thus makes more sense to consider the war between Germany and Russia as a "war between two attackers" (*Krieg zweier Angreifer*).[115] To underscore this point, more needs to be said about Soviet preparations for war in the spring of 1941. In Chapter 4 the author examined in some detail the Soviet buildup along the western frontier prior to the German attack. It was noted that this buildup, while still incomplete on 22 June, could be interpreted as offensive in nature. However, it was also pointed out that, by 1940/41 – and certainly for the period following the *Wehrmacht's* convincing victory over France in June 1940 – Soviet military preparations were more likely driven by fear of an impending German invasion, rather than by aggressive intent.[116] Yet while this may be so, it does not explain Stalin's longer-range and, ultimately, expansionist intentions. To gain more insight into those intentions we turn to another of the revisionist historians, the late Joachim Hoffmann.

In an essay first published in 1991, Hoffmann stated that, shortly after *Barbarossa* began, the Germans discovered "concrete evidence" of Red Army offensive preparations. For example, at several locations near the border, but also deep inside the Soviet Union, German troops captured military maps which displayed areas far to the west of Russia's borders and even into Germany itself; the invaders also seized "comprehensive reconnaissance documentation about Germany." These materials were found at Kobrin, Dubno, and Grodno, among other locations. On 1 July 1941, 48 Panzer Corps reported that, in the citadel of Dubno, they had discovered "sets of maps packed ready for combat use … They were maps showing only the area west of the Reich border up to the Cracow area."[117] A report prepared by 28 Army Corps on 16 July 1941 stated that, at a training area (location not given), "Red Army mobilization maps [were found], which showed exclusively southern Lithuania, the former Polish areas and parts of East Prussia. From these maps we once more became certain of the Red Army's intentions of invading the German Reich."[118] Months later, in October 1941, 24 Panzer Corps found a map of Lithuania – "what seemed to be an operational-level study for an attack on East Prussia."[119]

To such details, argued Hoffmann, must be added the fact that the Red Army "lacked the necessary maps when the war unexpectedly took place east of the Soviet border." Hoffmann continued:

> The (recently deceased) Professor of Eastern European History at the University of Mainz, Dr Gotthold Rhode, at that time interpreter and *Sonderfuehrer* (K) (specialist grade) on the staff of the German 8 Infantry Division, found, on 23 June 1941, in the headquarters building of the Soviet 3 Army in Grodno, as he wrote in his diary, "in one room piles of maps of East Prussia, excellently printed, on a scale of 1:50:000, much better than our own maps. The whole of East Prussia was covered." … Maps of East Prussia were the basis for the preparations made by [Soviet] 16 Infantry Division "Kikvidze" in Estonia, according to Lieutenant O.A. Krasovsky. On 23 July 1941, Captain N.S. Bondar, Chief of Staff of 739 Infantry Regiment, also stated that, "the Red Army had prepared itself for an attack on the *Generalgouvernement* rather than for defense." Thus the regiments within 213 Infantry Division "had already been given maps covering an area including Cracow, as had other Red Army elements."[120]

Such evidence, of course, is far from conclusive proof of aggressive Soviet designs; after all, Red Army doctrine was almost obsessively offensive in nature, meaning that *any* war, however it was to begin, was to be fought on the enemy's soil. Yet as Hoffmann pointed out, suspicions of "Soviet attack intentions become even clearer" when one also considers the large-scale, comprehensive propaganda campaign, begun at Stalin's behest, which was underway by the spring of 1941. Simply put, its objective was to instill a revolutionary warlike and anti-German fervor in Red Army officers and men, convincing them that war with Germany was inevitable and that they would have to deliver the first blow. During the opening days of the war in the east, German troops also became privy to this revealing Soviet propaganda:

> German troops got hold of important files in the headquarters building of the Soviet 5 Army in Luck on 4 July 1941. Among this material was a "Plan for the Political Security of Army Offensive Operations." In this plan the 5 Army's Head of Political Propaganda, Uronov, who was fully cognizant of Stalin's intentions via the [Red Army's] Main Administration [for Political Propaganda], gives detailed instructions on the politico-propaganda preparations and execution of a surprise attack on the German *Wehrmacht* … "It is necessary," the plan [states], "to deal the enemy a very strong, lightening blow, so as swiftly to shatter the soldiers' moral resistance."[121]

That Soviet Russia was planning to wage aggressive war on Germany is, according to revisionist historians, also underscored by Stalin's famous speech in Moscow of 5 May 1941, before new graduates of the Frunze Military Academy, the country's "most prestigious staff or war college, attended by promising captains and majors."[122] All told, 1500-2000 people[123] – hundreds of academy graduates, the elite of the Red Army, representatives of the Defense Commissariat and General Staff, and senior government officials – listened to Stalin speak for about 40 minutes. In calm and measured tones, he talked about the great advances which had been made in modernizing and building up the Red Army, marshalling an array of impressive figures outlining the huge improvements made in the size and combat capability of the armed forces, as well as in its weaponry. He also analyzed the reasons behind the great German victories since September 1939, while being careful to insist that, despite such victories, Hitler's *Wehrmacht* was far from invincible. After his speech, in the reception that followed, Stalin gave three short toasts:

> In the third, he corrected an officer who wanted to toast his [Stalin's] peace policy. The peace policy had served the country's defenses well, Stalin said. It had been pursued until the army had been rebuilt and given modern weaponry. But now, he declared, the Soviet Union had to move from defensive to offensive operations. "The Red Army is a modern army," he ended, "but a modern army is an attacking army."[124]

Revisionist historians have seized upon these remarks to anchor their claims that Stalin was now preparing his armed forces for an impending attack on Germany. "The speech," affirmed Hoffmann, " … is an important pointer to the fact that the Soviet Union was preparing for an offensive war in 1941;" and, again: "[Stalin] considered a German-Soviet war inevitable, and on 5 May 1941 at the latest he let it be known that he had decided to take the initiative himself and begin a "revolutionary war of liberation."[125] Traditionalists, however, claim that Stalin's speech was, at best, ambiguous in meaning,[126] while his toast may have simply been an attempt at boosting morale. Furthermore, these brief remarks of Stalin, "offered no more than a terse restatement of the long-standing military strategy of converting defense into devastating attack, though it is certainly true that they presented, and were seen to present, a new emphasis upon offense."[127]

What appears more certain is that Stalin's 5 May speech motivated the Red Army High Command to put together a proposal for a pre-emptive strike, for 10 days later, on 15 May 1941, General Zhukov, Chief of the Red Army General Staff, forwarded just such a proposal to Stalin. The existence of this plan, states Gabriel Gorodetsky, "is of course a centerpiece in the case produced by the 'revisionists.' They assume that the plan had originated with Stalin himself and was 'appropriately signed,' thus proving Soviet strategy to be 'offensive,' that is aggressive." Yet the pre-emptive war plan was rejected by Stalin and, in any case, it was conceived "not as a springboard toward the seizure of the heart of Europe, but as a limited operation aimed at disrupting the German build-up and therefore of a defensive nature."[128] Indeed, in view of the cascading streams of intelligence now reaching Stalin and his military from all sides, and pointing to an imminent German assault, such a pre-emptive strike would have been fully justified as an act of self-defense.

What then, can be reasonably concluded about the original query at the beginning of this section – that is, can Hitler's June 1941 attack in any way be considered pre-emptive or preventive in nature? The first part of the question was dealt with summarily and answered in the negative: Germany did not wage pre-emptive war because Russia was far from ready to attack in the summer of 1941; moreover, Hitler and his High Command had no fear of an imminent Soviet attack. In this context, one can also dismiss the weaker arguments of the revisionists – those pertaining to Stalin's speech of 5 May and the pre-emptive war plan which followed in its wake.

Was *Barbarossa* a preventive war? As we have seen, the Soviet Union had been arming itself for a war of aggression against Germany and the West since the early 1930s. The

USSR's spectacular military buildup, as well as its foreign and defense policy from the summer of 1939 onward, can thus be reasonably understood as an effort to bring about a positive "correlation of forces," one which would enable the Communist state, at a time of its choosing, to vanquish Germany through an offensive war, culminating in domination of the entire European continent. In this author's view, the fact that Stalin's plans for the domination of Europe were thrown off kilter by Germany's stunning defeat of France in 1940 – and, hence, by the sudden and foreboding prospect of having to face the full might of the *Wehrmacht* at the height of its powers – in no way alters the fact that Soviet Russia under Stalin was a revolutionary state pursuing expansionist goals; and, since the early 1930s, Stalin was pinning his hopes on the Red Army as the sole means of spreading revolution to Germany and the West.

Such was the very essence of Communism under the "*vozhd*," as the Soviet leader was called. Stalin, like Hitler, viewed war as inevitable; and if the German Reich had not struck in 1941, Stalin would have most likely done so himself in 1942, when his army and air force were finally equipped with the thousands of new tanks (the superior T-34s and KVs) and aircraft on which he was waiting. Indeed, the conviction that Stalin may well have attacked in 1942[129] is a perspective that has gained increasing acceptance (or at least legitimacy) among historians in recent years. If the Russian archives have yet to reveal a "smoking gun," the basic objectives of Stalin's Russia, its foreign and defense policies in the years prior to June 1941 – as well as the intrinsic nature of the Communist state and its incompatibility with National Socialist Germany – lead to the reasonable conclusion that Hitler's attack on the Soviet Union, while hardly planned as such, served a preventive function. As we will see, the German *Landser* who poured into Russia in the opening days of the war were often stunned by the massive concentrations of Red Army troops, tanks and equipment they encountered, leading many of them to conclude – however erroneously – that they had indeed just barely averted the disaster of a Russian attack.

5.6: Final Days & Hours before "X-Tag"

5.6.1: Berlin (An Anxious "Fuehrer")
By the spring of 1941, Berlin's roughly 4,000,000 inhabitants were becoming used to the hardships of war. They had been living with rationing and blackouts since the beginning of the war. Rationing, in fact, had been introduced on 27 August 1939, a few days before the attack on Poland; from that point forward, the distribution of most foods, clothing, footwear and coal was strictly controlled.[130] The first British air raid over the Reich's capital, a rather trifling affair, had taken place on 26 August 1940. By the autumn of that year, however, the raids had become a regular occurrence; and, following a brief hiatus in the first months of 1941, had resumed again in March with desultory attacks over the central areas of the city. While the damage from the RAF bomber "offensive" was normally slight at this time, a heavy raid on 10 April caused serious damage to the State Opera House and other key buildings, eliciting outrage from Hitler and a furious argument with Air Marshal Goering.[131]

As the days marched on through May and into June, Berliners began to talk more and more about a possible war with Russia. By mid-June 1941, such talk had exploded into a flood of rumors about what the days ahead held in store for German-Soviet relations. Some deluded themselves with wishful thinking; for example (like Panzer General Hoepner, see above), with the notion that Stalin had agreed to cede the Ukraine to Germany for 99 years, or that Russia was about to adhere to the Tripartite Pact, or even that the Soviet dictator was headed to Berlin to arrange a deal with Hitler. Yet others – if only a minority, according to reports of the SS Security Service (*Sicherheitsdienst*), which regularly monitored the mood of the German people – were convinced the immense buildup of German forces in the east meant that war with Russia was imminent.[132]

At the Reich Chancellery in Berlin, Hitler passed the final days before the launch of *Barbarossa* in a condition of growing agitation. As his *Luftwaffe* adjutant observed, the "Fuehrer" seemed "increasingly nervous and troubled. He was garrulous, walked up and down continuously and seemed to be waiting anxiously for news of something."[133] According to David Irving:

> The old familiar bouts of insomnia began to attack him as the last days before "*Barbarossa*" dragged by. By night he lay awake and asked himself what loopholes in his grand design the British might yet exploit. He believed he had plugged them all ... Yet Hitler could still only go to sleep with sedatives, even after staying up until three or four each morning discussing Turkey, Russia, war, and warfare with dutiful but weary henchmen like Himmler, Ley, Hewel, Ribbentrop, and Seyss-Inquart.

> On June 18, with the newspapers of every country but Germany openly asking when Hitler's attack on the Soviet Union would begin, the Russians unwittingly caused him his most anxious hours ever when the Soviet ambassador in Berlin, Dekanozov, asked for an interview with Ribbentrop's state secretary, Baron von Weizsaecker. Hewel, at Hitler's Chancellery, wrote an agitated note in his diary: "Big problem: Dekanozov has announced he is to see the state secretary. What is he bringing? Is Stalin going to bring off a major coup even now? A big offer to us, etc. etc.? ... The Fuehrer and foreign minister will have to vanish – so they can't be reached ..." The next evening, however ... Ribbentrop telephoned that Dekanozov had called on his state secretary at 6 P.M., had discussed purely routine affairs, and had left after cracking a few jokes.[134]

If Hitler had dodged a last minute diplomatic bullet, he still had much to be anxious about, had he only known it. As outlined in Chapter 1, German intelligence prior to the start of the Russian campaign was woefully inadequate. Through aerial reconnaissance, analysis of radio traffic and other means, the Germans had acquired a reasonably accurate picture of Red Army concentrations in the frontier regions; however, they still managed to overestimate the number of Russia divisions in the border districts, while remaining oblivious to the second echelon of forces assembling along the Western Dvina and Dnepr river lines. Moreover, the Germans were "totally ignorant" of the Red Army's gigantic mobilization capabilities.[135] Just how ignorant the Germans were of their opponent is illustrated by a handbook on the Russian military issued by the Army High Command's Foreign Armies East (FHO) on 1 January 1941, in which it was admitted that little was actually known about the Soviet order of battle.[136] Even maps prepared for the Russian campaign were far from adequate, particularly when it came to determining which roads and bridges could support tanks and other heavy vehicles.[137] In general, the overall assessment of the Red Army by FHO can only be described as "incomplete and inaccurate;" hence, it offered "no corrective to the erroneous *Russland-Bild* that informed German military thinking."[138] This is hardly surprising, because the agency was headed by Colonel Eberhard Kinzel, a man with no special training in intelligence, who neither spoke Russian nor possessed any special knowledge of the Soviet Union and its armed forces.[139]

Yet Hitler – a man of superior intellect and keen instincts – must surely, at some level, have been aware of the extraordinarily brittle foundation upon which *Barbarossa* was built. Such an awareness explains – in part at least – his anxious behavior in the days prior to the outbreak of war. During the daily coffee break with his female secretaries, on or about 20 June, Hitler told them that there was something "sinister" (*unheimlich*) about

Russia – something which reminded him of the "ghost ship" (*Gespensterschiff*) in *The Flying Dutchman*. When *Fraeulein* Schroeder, "a clever, critical, and often dangerously outspoken" 33-year-old stenographer, asked him why he continually stressed that the decision to attack Russia was his toughest yet, the "Fuehrer" replied: "Because we know virtually nothing about Russia. It could turn out to be a big soap-bubble, or it might be something quite different."[140] On 20 June, Walther Hewel, Hitler's diplomatic liaison officer, wrote in his diary:

> A long conversation with the Fuehrer. Expects a lot of the Russian campaign. Wishes he was 10 weeks on from hence. After all there must always be a big element of risk. We are standing outside a locked door. [Will we run into] secret weapons? The tenacity of the fanatic? He now has to take sleeping pills to fall asleep … He told me that this morning he again pored over every minute detail, but found no possibility for the enemy to get the better of Germany. He thinks Britain will have to give in – and he hopes it will be before the year is over.[141]

Hitler's activities in the final days before Sunday, 22 June 1941, can now be briefly summarized. On 17 June, he dispatched a telegram to Admiral Horthy, the Regent and head of Hungary, congratulating him on his birthday. The next day (18 June), in another attempt to secure Germany's southern flank, a treaty of friendship was signed between Germany and Turkey, resulting in an exchange of telegrams between Hitler and the Turkish head of state on the 18th and 19th. On 19 June, Hitler greeted Field Marshal List, fresh off his victories in the Balkans, at the Reich Chancellery.[142]

By now, Hitler was busy dictating his proclamation "To the Soldiers of the Eastern Front" (*Tagesbefehl an die Soldaten der Ostfront*), an effusive and self-serving document which sought to justify the attack on the Soviet Union as a pre-emptive measure, while providing a *tour d'horizon* of German foreign policy since September 1939. The proclamation was then printed in the hundreds of thousands and issued secretly to the armed forces.[143] On Friday evening, 20 June, on Hitler's orders, General Jodl released the prearranged codeword, "*Dortmund*," notifying all service branches that Operation *Barbarossa* was to go forward as planned.[144]

On Saturday, 21 June, Hitler finally composed a long letter to his chief ally, Benito Mussolini, belatedly explaining his reasons for striking out against Russia to the Italian dictator. (Much to his annoyance, Mussolini did not receive the letter until 3.00 the next morning, just minutes before German troops crossed the border.)[145] That evening, Hitler summoned Goebbels to him in the Reich Chancellery. Although Hitler appeared exhausted, he soon became carried away by his remarks about the war about to break. For three full hours, the two men marched, back and forth, inside the cavernous building. For an hour or so, they tried out the new fanfares to be used for the Russian campaign. Gradually, Hitler began to unwind a little. "The Fuehrer is freed from a nightmare the closer the decision comes. It's always so with him," confided Goebbels to his diary. At 2.30 in the morning, with the start of *Barbarossa* less than 40 minutes away, Hitler finally retired to bed.[146]

It was not until an hour later that Goebbels, after returning to his ministry through the blacked-out streets of Berlin, and putting his waiting staff in the picture, withdrew to his room. By then, "the most destructive and barbaric war in the history of mankind" had begun.[147] In his diary Goebbels wrote:

> Now the artillery is thundering. God bless our weapons! … I pace restlessly up and down in my room. I can hear history breathing. Great, wondrous time in which a new *Reich* is being born. In pain, it is true, but it rises upwards to the light.[148]

5.6.2: Headquarters, Army Group Center

In the final days before "X" Tag, Field Marshal von Bock, Commander, Army Group Center, drove frequently to the eastern frontier,[149] meeting with front line commanders and coordinating last minute details or changes of plan. His powerful army group, the largest of the three, comprised 51 divisions, 1.3 million men, and more than 1800 tanks; as noted, its mission was to envelop, surround and destroy the forces of Soviet Western Front in Belorussia before moving on its first operational objective, the city of Smolensk some 600 kilometers beyond the German-Soviet demarcation line. After achieving these initial successes, the *Barbarossa* directive and OKH deployment plan called for strong mobile elements of Army Group Center to be shifted northward, to support the German advance through the Baltic and on Leningrad. Like Halder, however, Bock secretly hoped that the momentum of his initial plunge eastward would render such requirements null and void and enable his forces to continue their drive all the way to Moscow, whose capture, he believed, would be decisive.

Facing the field marshal's army group along the eastern frontier was the Soviet Western Front. Commanded by General D.G. Pavlov, its four armies (3, 4, 10, and 13) comprised 671,165 men, 2900 tanks, 14,171 guns and mortars, and over 1500 combat aircraft.[150] Despite its impressive size (and numerical superiority in tanks, artillery and aircraft to Bock's army group and supporting air fleet), Pavlov's front was not the center of gravity of the Soviet deployment, for significantly larger forces were positioned further south, covering the Ukraine and ready for offensive operations directed at southern Poland. Moreover, the mass of Pavlov's forces, including three of his six mechanized corps, were deployed far forward, in the Belostok salient. The enemy's vulnerable configuration, Bock knew, would make his operational mission far easier, for his armies and panzer groups already enveloped Pavlov's forces on both flanks.[151]

Since October 1940, Bock's headquarters had been located in the city of Posen, in occupied Poland. By 21 June 1941, however, he had transferred his headquarters much farther to the east, to the village of Rembertov on the eastern outskirts of Warsaw, the Polish capital.[152] It was here, only hours before "X" Tag, that Alexander Stahlberg, an officer in 12 Panzer Division, ran into his cousin, Colonel Henning von Tresckow, chief operations officer (Ia) of the army group. Their fascinating and insightful discussion is recounted in *Hauptmann* Stahlberg's memoirs:

> The closer we came to the Russian frontier, the more densely the regiments massed. The numbers of troops now mustering exceeded anything we had seen before.
>
> Radio silence was imposed, as usual before an offensive, so that the enemy reconnaissance could not pick us up. But of course there were other types of reconnaissance, such as observation from the air, or espionage. Our approach could not remain hidden from the Russians – unless they were asleep …
>
> On 21 June we drove through a village, where I noticed beside the entrance to a farmyard the insignia of an Army Group headquarters, which could only mean the Headquarters of Army Group Center, to which we belonged. When we had already left the village, it occurred to me that this might be an opportunity to find out if my cousin Henning von Tresckow was there …
>
> I took one our new BMW motorbikes and drove back along the column. On the first floor of the farmhouse I quickly found the door marked Ia and knocked. Henning received me in his usual extraordinarily affectionate manner, like an old friend …
>
> I asked him if he thought the Russians could possibly have missed our troop concentrations. Instead of answering, he led me to the big situation map of the Army Group, with its armies, corps and divisions, which I was seeing for the first time. The enemy units were also plotted, on the far side of the frontier. I was astonished at the huge number of Russian units – the Soviets had evidently mustered against us

in great strength – but their positions did not reveal whether the Red Army knew of our attack, planned for the next morning. Henning explained it all to me in detail …

When I asked what he thought of our chances in this campaign, he said he saw an opportunity for us to bring about the seizure of the whole of the Soviet Union, but only on condition that Army Group Center had first won the battle of Moscow and occupied the city before the coming of winter. If we succeeded in destroying the centers of Soviet government, the administration, economic control, transport and intelligence, we could expect Russia to collapse. But if we had not succeeded by the onset of winter, he was convinced that our prospects were dismal. Everything therefore depended on the rapid and sweeping success of Army Group Center …

Still standing before the big situation map, I asked what the neighboring Army Groups North and South were to do. Army Group North was to take Leningrad and establish contact with the Finns, he said, while in the South the Ukraine was to be conquered for its huge agricultural acreage, its mineral wealth and its oil. Since the three Army Groups were consequently divided geographically, we would in fact have three mutually independent theaters of war in Russia, which meant that the plan of this campaign was contrary to all the rules of warfare. Our only chance of winning was to strike at the "heart" of the Soviet Union, Moscow …

For me, personally, Henning Tresckow's assessment of the situation was the first I had heard on this scale, which is why it is imprinted on my memory. We would often have reason to remember it later. I asked him other questions, especially what was known of any Russian reserves deep in the hinterland. "Largely *terra incognita*," he replied …

Then Henning suddenly asked me whether we had yet been informed about the treatment of Soviet political commissars. I admitted my ignorance and he went on: "An order came through recently that all Red Army commissars … are to be shot on capture." I was appalled. "That would be murder!" "The order is just that," he replied. "And for that reason we are not allowed to give it to the troops in writing, but you will receive it by word of mouth before the attack beings and will have to pass it on by word of mouth to the companies." Still half incredulous at this atrocity, I asked from whom the order came, and he replied – I have never forgotten it – "From the man to whom you gave your oath.[153] As I did," he added, with a penetrating look.[154]

Stahlberg's anxieties about the security of the buildup – whether or not the Russians were now privy to what was about to break over them – were widely shared by the field commanders and their staffs. As then chief of staff of Fourth Army, Colonel Guenther Blumentritt, later wrote:

> Tensions rose steadily on the German side. By the evening of the 21st we assumed that the Russians must have realized what was happening, yet across the River Bug on the front of Fourth Army and 2 Panzer Group … all was quiet. The Russian outposts were behaving quite normally. At a little after midnight, when the entire artillery of the assault divisions and of the second wave too was already zeroed in on its targets, the international Berlin-Moscow train passed without incident through Brest-Litovsk. It was a weird moment.[155]

Discussing his final activities prior to the impending assault, General Heinz Guderian, Commander, 2 Panzer Group, noted that:

> On the 20th and 21st I visited the forward units of my corps to make sure that all preparations for the attack were satisfactorily completed. Detailed study of the behavior of the Russians convinced me that they knew nothing of our intentions.

We had observation of the courtyard of Brest-Litovsk citadel and could see them drilling by platoons to the music of a military band. The strong points along their bank of the Bug were unoccupied. They had made scarcely any noticeable progress in strengthening their fortified positions during the past few weeks. So the prospects of our attack achieving surprise were good ...

On the fateful day of [22 June 1941], I went at 0210 hrs. to my Group command post which was located in an observation tower south of Bohukaly, nine miles northwest of Brest-Litovsk. It was still dark when I arrived there at 0310 hrs. At 0315 hrs. our artillery opened up.[156]

Conversely, Panzer General Lemelsen, Commander, 47 Panzer Corps, was convinced that the Russians had long ago put "two and two" together:

Saturday, 21.6.41 (B-1 Day)
The days have passed quickly; on Wednesday we changed position to [B.] and moved into a really charming little chateau that doesn't really fit with Poland at all ...

It really is a strange state of affairs: the *Panje*-horses are still running around everywhere here right up to the Bug and they haven't been evacuated, but no doubt it is to preserve the element of surprise as much as possible. Even so, we are certain that the Russians have known for some time about what is going on here. They are working further forward, but it seems as if they have left only the weaker forces up front in order to fight with the bulk of the army further back. That would not be very pleasant for us. At this time tomorrow we shall know more ...

It is profoundly peaceful everywhere, the cows and horses are in the field and the *Panje*-horses are raking the potatoes, and what will it look like tomorrow morning? The bombs and shells will explode everywhere and the houses will burn, the residents flee. The contrast is too unreal.

Tonight we will move our command post from the chateau, which would naturally only fall victim to enemy fire, out to a wood, and in the early morning at 0200 hours, I will set off to witness the start of the great new campaign at the front line with the attacking troops.[157]

Meanwhile, the final preparations were being brought to a close, including the checking out of communication links between Hitler's new headquarters in Rastenburg, East Prussia, and Bock's army group, while signal troops completed installation of telephone trunk lines from higher headquarters to ground and air units along the forwardmost line.[158] The pressures on commanders and their staffs, the weight of their responsibilities, must have been immense in these final days before the onset of war. At least one superior and trusted officer, Dr Dr Seidel, chief intelligence officer (*Luftflotten-Nachrichtenfuehrer*) in Kesselring's 2 Air Fleet, broke down under the strain and took his life. Kesselring himself made numerous flights in his twin-engine Fw 189 tactical reconnaissance aircraft, from south of Brest-Litovsk to the border of East Prussia, to become better acquainted with the deployment areas of his wings, groups and squadrons. One of his last acts before the onslaught was to visit Field Marshal von Bock on the evening of 21 June. He found the army group commander, in sharp contrast to their final meetings before earlier campaigns, downcast and pensive – no doubt weighed down by the solemn responsibility he alone shouldered for more than one million men.[159]

5.6.3: The Soldiers at the Front
Along with checking weapons and equipment and performing necessary maintenance, some soldiers in the east marked their final days before "X-Tag" with soccer games and

equestrian competitions.[160] Tank and motorized units, before slipping into their final assembly areas, carefully reconnoitered their approach routes, as well as the assembly areas themselves, which, as much as possible, were concealed in forested regions. Once in their assembly areas, the mobile assault formations rapidly made ready for combat, which included clearing all barriers and obstacles – such as barbed wire entanglements – along their attack frontage.[161] Radio silence was strictly enforced by all units, ammunition was quietly brought forward, and extra containers of fuel were hung on tanks and vehicles. Artillery and other heavy weapons were shepherded into their firing positions. Telephone wire was laid between the gun batteries and the forward observation posts. Dr Alfred Opitz, then a 30-year-old *Obergefreiter* in 18 Panzer Division, recalled after the war:

> On 21 June the noise of motors and vehicles began to roar and drone in the broad extent of forest to our rear. Tanks and heavy artillery seemed to be moving up from there. Now and then a reconnaissance aircraft circled over the river terrain. The air was thick enough to stifle, it smelled of something horrendous.[162]

Last minute reconnaissance of terrain and enemy forces beyond the frontier was carried out, some of the reconnaissance teams going forward to inspect border regions disguised as local hunters and farmers, and even carrying farm implements to complete the deception. Liaison was established with supporting combat and combat-support units, and front-line commanders were briefed on their missions. In the final hours, chocolate and cigarettes were distributed to troops, while some were fortunate enough to receive an allotment of *Schnapps*, one bottle for each four men.[163]

Last-minute briefings were held once the troops had finally learned what their mission was to be – a surprise attack on the Soviet Union. During the night of 21 June, Hitler's proclamation was read out to the more than three million men assembled along the eastern frontier from the Baltic to the Black Sea, ending weeks and months of agonizing uncertainty about what the future was to bring. The proclamation included the following passages:

Soldaten der Ostfront!

> Troubled by deep concerns, condemned to months of silence, the hour has finally arrived in which I may speak to you, my soldiers, openly …
>
> At this very moment, Soldiers of the Eastern Front, a concentration of forces is underway which, in its extent and scope, is the largest the world has ever seen … When this greatest front of world history now advances, then it will not only be to secure the conditions for the final conclusion of this great war in general, or to protect those countries affected at this moment, but rather to save the entire European civilization and culture.
>
> German soldiers! You are thus entering into a struggle that is both difficult and laden with responsibility. For:
>
> The fate of Europe, the future of the German Reich, the existence of our *Volk* now lie in your hands alone.
>
> May the Lord God aid us all in this struggle!

Adolf Hitler
Fuehrer and Supreme Commander of the *Wehrmacht*[164]

While it is problematic at best to generalize about human behavior – much less the behavior of some three million men – it is apparent from surviving field post letters and diaries that most of the *Landser* – even those who were not convinced National Socialists – welcomed war with Russia,[165] convinced as they were of the necessity to eliminate once and for all the growing threat posed by the sinister and secretive Bolshevik state.[166] A notation of a regimental adjutant (45 Infantry Division) in his diary is, in this sense, instructive:

> Today [16 June 1941] the order came. So it is getting serious. The *Fuehrer* has decided, after the collapse of the peace efforts with England, to first overthrown Russia. Only the How and When still present us with a conundrum. With no declaration of war? But: it will be war against the archenemy [*Erzfeind*] of our idea, Bolshevism. And we will know how to conduct it, grimly and resolutely.[167]

Of course, what is also quite true is that a large majority of German soldiers were imbued with a sublime sense of superiority vis-à-vis their Russian opponents, despite knowing little about them, which also shaped their thinking about a war with Russia. "Most of us are awfully pleased, that it's finally come to blows again," noted an officer of 4 Panzer Division in his diary on 22 June.[168] In 296 Infantry Division, the feeling was that the Soviet Union would collapse after some three weeks of fighting. "It'll go quite fast with the Russians, even if many of us will 'bite the dust'" (*wenn auch mancher "ins Gras beissen muss"*), wrote a soldier in 296 ID on that fateful Sunday. "But it won't be in vain, it will be for Germany's future," he added.[169] On the eve of battle, SS-General Paul "Papa" Hausser, Commander, SS Division *Das Reich*, addressed his assembled officers; exuding optimism, he told them that, "in a few weeks we want to conduct a victory parade in Moscow."[170]

The Sunday before *Barbarossa* began (15 June), the soldier in 296 Infantry Division had written: "Our *Fuehrer* knows only too well, that the German soldier will do his duty, and that he can be relied upon."[171] Without question, the profound and implicit trust the average German soldier placed in his "Fuehrer," and in Hitler's military leadership in general, outweighed any second thoughts he may have had about the new campaign.[172] And it would take many defeats, many unanticipated and shocking setbacks in the months ahead, to even begin to shake that confidence.

The night of 21/22 June was dark, with only a "faint crescent of the waning moon."[173] Concealed in forests, farmsteads, and fields along the frontier, the "Soldiers of the Eastern Front" waited. Heavily armed and equipped, their weapons *schussbereit*, their hand grenades armed, taking their last, slow draws on their cigarettes, they waited – waited in growing and almost unbearable tension as the final hours, minutes, seconds, ticked irretrievably away. Last minute preparations kept many of the men busy, and few but the most seasoned veterans were able to snatch a few hours of sleep before the "big show" began. What, they wondered, would they encounter beyond the border? Were the Russians waiting for them, or were they still largely in the dark about the firestorm about to break – about the hecatombs of Red Army dead (and their own, had they known it) which were to follow in its wake?

Below is a sampling of accounts – contemporary and post-war – that offer further insight into the final days and hours of the German *Landser* before the start of Operation *Barbarossa*. The majority of these accounts issue from soldiers belonging to Army Group Center; their diversity illustrates the futility of attempting to reduce human thought and action to a common denominator:

Leutnant Erich Bunke (31 ID) – 19/20 June 1941
In Brest[-Litovsk], at least three [Soviet] tank brigades were thought to have been positioned at the exit route of the town, and we, of course, were to await their counterattack … We also heard that it was very important for the battle for Brest-Litovsk to preserve the good condition of the railway bridge …

In the night of 19/20 June we remained in our positions. We fortified them and supplied them with ammunition so that only our anti-tank guns needed to be brought forward. These tasks were carried out quickly and then we lay in our foxholes and listened into the night for sounds from over there. Peace reigned there, nothing was happening. Now we could even identify our targets in the darkness. It was a bright moonlit summer's night. Suddenly, a flare shot up opposite us. It proved that there were Russian listening posts on the far-lying bank.

I spoke with a *Leutnant* platoon leader from the 12th [MG] Company of 82 IR … He also believed, as did I, that this hustle and bustle and this deployment could surely not have remained hidden from the Russians, and we expected a fiery passage in our battle for Brest-Litovsk. Then I went over to Hans Bachmann, over by the railway embankment. The large railway bridge spanned the unregulated riverbed of the Bug in five arches … Three arches of the bridge belonged to Germany and two arches to the Russians. In the middle, at the demarcation line, there was a thick red line. The agreement stipulated that each side had only two guards patrolling on the bridge and that they could be relieved on the bridge.

Until now, the guards had been relieved at 0200 hours in the morning. A week previously, however, this had changed. Since the attack was to start at 0315 hours, the time to change the guard was now at a few minutes before 0315 hours, so that then four guards from the German side would be present on the bridge, thus guaranteeing that these four German soldiers could overpower the two Russians. The little house to the left of the railway embankment, on the other side of the river, had to be shot at because the detonation controls for the bridge were installed here. "Crazy times, don't you think, Hans," I said; "Yeah, yeah," he answered, "it'll be a real ambush." Well, the Bolshevists should be beaten with their own weapons after all, because in Finland they went up against that country without any declaration of war.

I went back. We lay for hours in our foxholes and listened into the cool, still June night … The day after tomorrow things would get serious and kick off again. I was ready.[174]

Oberfeldwebel Albert Blaich (3 PD) – 20-22 June 1941

In the two nights prior to the start of the attack the regiment's battalions were brought forward to the front. On the evening of 21 June 1941, 6 Panzer Regiment was located about three kilometers west of Koden on the Bug, equipped with [more than 200 tanks]. They all stood ready for their greatest test, although even now nobody could really believe that a new war was imminent.

From midnight, calm set in and the land was as peaceful as ever, or so it seemed to the men. It was June and already rather light. Even in the hours around midnight a pale glimmer stood in the sky. But the nights before an attack were always short. The tension built up too much in every soldier and robbed him of sleep. Only the most hardened and battle-experienced men succeeded in napping.

Suddenly the silence was disturbed by quiet sounds. Weapons clinked, machine guns, carbines, and munition boxes were readied. In front of the river, combat engineers cut through the wire in the riverbank barriers. Something cracked in the bushes, getting ever louder. Assault boats were brought forward and pneumatic boats inflated.

… The day of the attack was a Sunday this time, 22 June 1941, the time of the attack was 0315 hours. There was another 30 minutes until then. The soldiers fastened their helmet straps tighter. They didn't yet know whether the other bank was fortified, whether there were dugouts over there. Nothing could be seen. The riverbank was overgrown, as it was almost everywhere along the Bug. Tall reeds, undergrowth, and trees blocked the view.

The soldiers glanced at their watches with increasing frequency. It seemed to them as if the hands of their watches moved ever faster. The tension was ratcheted up to its highest point, the men could even hear their own heartbeats. The final minute before the campaign against the Soviet Union began to count down.[175]

Dr Heinrich Haape (6 ID) – 21 June 1941
It all starts in a few hours! – The Germans are facing what must be an enemy force three times more superior in number; our regiment is positioned at the very front line. The resistance must be broke, despite bunkers, hordes of men, and any amount of devilry. It is a war for Germany's greatness and future.

Until now I have been completely calm; the world seems to me to be peaceful and unconcerned, and right now I feel that peace in nature twice as deeply. And even though a lot, a very great lot of our forces have marched up to the frontier, you can't see any soldiers!

The weather is wonderful, the birds are singing, and the trees are clothed in fresh green. There is a magnificent lake close by and the same atmosphere exists that I had already described to you on Whit-Sunday. [It is] a magical world of a real, living peace. Just before the storm that will make the earth tremble, with all its consequences![176]

Hauptmann Herbert S. (292 ID) – 21 June 1941
By the time this letter gets to your hand, you'll have read all sorts of news in the newspapers. You may, however, have to accept that sometimes a message from me takes a few days. That will be because of the mail or the conditions. You don't need to worry because of that. God will be with us,[177] just as He has been with us until now.[178]

Bernard Haering (Medic and Catholic Priest) – 21 June 1941
The evening before the war with Russia began, we were all quite aware of its imminence. I was called by the official chaplain of the division and asked if I would hear the confessions of soldiers in one of the nearby churches of Eastern Catholics. A great many soldiers made their confessions that evening ... On the way back to the barracks, I was accompanied by my best friend, Brother Fichter, a Jesuit student, a wonderfully good and gifted man. Knowing that the war against Soviet Russia would begin within a few hours, we talked very seriously about the prospects of the Church and the world.[179] I expressed my dismay about the insane war and my readiness to give my life as a prayer that men might free themselves from the age-old slavery of hatred and war. I saw no bright future, I said, for people like us. My friend, on the contrary, insisted, "I do not want to lose my life in this senseless business; I want to spend it for something worthwhile. When the war is over, there will be a great task ahead of us, as ministers of the Church, to serve people and to work for a better, freer world.

Toward midnight, everyone knew that only a few hours remained before we would go into battle. I invited my friends to a prayer service. Crowds of soldiers, including officers of the whole regiment, assisted at the penance service, the general absolution, and the Eucharistic celebration. No distinction was made between Catholics and Protestants. I celebrated without altar and altar stone. It was one of the most moving experiences of my priestly life. Everyone knew what it meant to receive the assurance of peace with the Lord, and the body of Christ as a promise of everlasting life.[180]

Gerd Habedanck (War Correspondent with 45 ID) – 21/22 June 1941
We came from Warsaw through heat, dust and jam-packed roads to the Bug. We passed tracts of woodland bristling with vehicle parks, artillery batteries in villages and radio relay stations and headquarters staffs under tall fir trees. Silently, absolutely silently we crept up to the edge of the Bug. Sand had been strewn across the roads so that our hob-nailed boots made no sound. Assault sections already grouped moved along the road edges in mute rows. Outlines of rubber dinghies were discernible as they shuttled along, raised up against the light of the northern sky.[181]

Oberleutnant Juerg v. Kalckreuth (6 ID) – 21/22 June 1941
The tension is immeasurably high. Everything is being feverishly prepared. And yet there are still a few who believe that the whole affair is just a bluff … It is incredible that the paper war [*Papierkrieg*] could flare up again now, of all times. New orders arrive all the time with deadlines, mostly for "immediately." Many a piece of paper ends up unheeded in a large file marked "outstanding." It can wait until the baggage train moves up again, perhaps only after weeks – already deep in Russia … The 18 IR is to be the "point of main effort." [*Schwerpunkt-Regiment*] (Now I can write to you about this, because everything will already be well under way long before this letter reaches you) … The division's evening messenger brings an entire motor car full of paper, including 20 "secret" messages. Crazy! – Amid this are all the various visitors, for whom I only have a few seconds' time: Graminsky, the division physician, *Leutnant* Mohn, and a war correspondent who wants to come with us at the start of the attack and make reports. – At 2400 hours I lie down for an hour-and-a-half.

At 0130 hours, we get ready at the command post in order to go to the observation post, where the commander – in his tent – awaits us. With me is *Leutnant* Sengelhoff. – A deathly calm lies over the frontier area. Everybody around us and immediately in front of us moves inconspicuously and quietly forward, to the frontier. – The telephone jangles: the units report that they've all completed their preparations. A scouting party receives rifle fire from the direction of Hill 220, no casualties. – Around 0215 hours it begins to dawn; the sky reddens in the east and announces a clear day.[182]

Obergefreiter August Freitag (6 ID) – 21/22 June 1941
At a company briefing on the morning of 21 June 1941 we were informed that it would all start the following day. Naturally, tension was now high. For a great many of us, like me, had not yet seen anything of the war. But the Russian was a new and completely unknown enemy even for those who had already taken part in the French campaign. The vehicles were checked once more, so that no unnecessary baggage was dragged along. Provisions, oats, and ammunition were also taken on; and everything was carefully prepared for the following morning.

Then the afternoon was free to carry out our private affairs. We had spread out our ground sheets and, dressed only in shorts, we soaked up the sun. Very few of us could sleep now. Everybody talked about what might happen the next morning. I wrote another letter, for who knew when I would be able to write again.

In the afternoon our commanders, from platoon leader to the regimental commander, dressed in cotton-twill overalls as laborers with a shovel or a pickax over their shoulders, went to the frontier to locate positions and to finalize the attack plan. The evening slowly declined to a balmy summer's night, the night of the summer solstice.

After we had tended properly to our horses, we began to get ready to move the last two to three kilometers to our assembly area. We crept even more quietly than usual to within a few hundred meters of the frontier. Here, we unlimbered our guns, unloaded the ammunition, and withdrew with the empty limbers about 200 meters back to a depression by a stream. I looked at my watch; it was just approaching 0100 hours. So it had worked. By 0100 hours the deployment was supposed to be complete.

We unbridled the horses, loosened the harnesses, and let the horses tuck into the dewy fresh grass again. We had plenty of time until half past two. A glorious Sunday morning heralded the beginning of summer. Secretly, the thought skulked in the back of our minds: "Will we all still be alive this evening?" And several quietly prayed with me: "God, grant me a good guardian angel" [*Schutzengel*].

At half past two, we readied our horses, put our steel helmets on, and silently loaded our guns. Then we checked over everything again and waited tensely in the last half an hour for the events to come. Tension was high, and while we had not slept, we were awake in a way we had rarely been before.[183]

Helmut Martin (14 ID (mot.)) – 22 June 1941
On this morning, the light of a radiant rising sun flooded the broad, gentle hills of the East Prussian countryside. A June Sunday dawned and it could not have been any more beautiful, a real feast day, if only it had not brought war with Soviet Russia from 0305 hours.[184]

I spent the spare time until orders were issued at midday in the vicinity of our quarters … Thoughts whirled, driven round by stormy waves of inner turmoil, only to be inundated shortly after by the expectation of coming events, for suddenly it was there, the big adventure that made the blood pulse more strongly in my veins and for which I had always thirsted. The yearning for it had caused me many a moment of frustration in my day-to-day life, had made me unhappy, even angry – sitting inactive in school while outside great battles were going down in history. Success everywhere, but I was stuck at home. There was nothing I could do except stick blue pins into the maps to mark the spearheads of the armies in Poland and later in France. – And now, suddenly overnight, on this Sunday morning, my wish had become reality. The war was now also beginning for me, when only a few months before, I had thought I had arrived too late.[185]

Ekkehard Maurer (23 ID) – 22 June 1941
On 22 June, at 0300 hours in the morning, my [battalion] commander called over to me: "Make a note of this date, 22 June, 0315 hours in the morning. But you really won't need to memorize it, because you won't forget it your whole life long anyway. This is the moment when the greatest catastrophe of German history starts."[186]

Unteroffizier Eberhard Krehl (Art. Cdr. 121) – 22 Juni 1941
Two days before the attack against Russia, we were transferred to Suwalki … Shortly before daybreak on 22 June 1941, *Oberleutnant* Wieland turned up in our quarters with the words: "It's all kicking off against Russia. I've just come from a meeting with the generals of the panzer units. One declared, 'In five weeks I'll be in Moscow,' then the next: 'I'll be there in four at the latest,' then the last retorted: 'I'll make it in three.' So it's going to go very quickly."[187]

Siegfried Risse (18 PD) – 22 June 1941

0300 hours:

It was still dark. The summer night lay over the banks of the River Bug. Silence, only now and then a brief clanking somewhere. Over by the water, the frogs croaked. Anyone who was there in an assault detachment, or who was among the attack spearhead in the Bug meadows up front that night of 21-22 June 1941, will never forget the creaking courting calls of the Bug frogs. Watches ticked. Clock hands slipped over the luminous dials.

0312 hours:

Many had raised their watches to their eyes. Everyone had a strange feeling in their throat; felt their heartbeat right up into their collar bind. The silence became simply unbearable.

0313 hours:

Everything could still be put back together. Nothing was yet past recall. But with the progress of the clock hand, the war against the Soviet Union, which lay over there in peaceful darkness, crept ever more irrevocably closer.

0314 hours:

The morning dawned weakly on the horizon. Deathly silence still prevailed across the front. Sleepy fields, silent forests. Didn't they notice, over there, that armies were gathered in the villages and forests? Ready to pounce, division by division, along the entire border. Then the precisely synchronized watches started up:

0315 hours:

As if they had set off a charge, at the same moment, a gigantic bolt of lightning flashed through the night. The muzzles of all gun calibers opened up. Light trails from the Flak shells arced across the horizon. The front at the Bug was lit up by shell fire as far as the eye could see. Then the rumbling thunder rolled like a barrel over the river. Mingled with this was the nightmarish howling of rocket projector batteries. Beyond the river, a sea of smoke and fire seethed up. The slender sickle moon hid behind a rising shroud of smoke. The war took its first, terrible, baleful breath.

Peace was dead [*der Friede war tot*].[188]

ENDNOTES

1   O. Buchbender & R. Sterz (Hg.), *Das andere Gesicht des Krieges*, 68.
2   BA-MA MSg 1/1147: *Tagebuch* Lemelsen, 21.6.41.
3   A. Kesselring, *Soldat Bis Zum Letzten Tag*, 117.
4   W. Murray & A. R. Millett, *A War to be Won*, 118; A. Philippi & F. Heim, *Der Feldzug gegen Sowjetrussland*, 52; H.-A. Jacobsen, *Der Zweite Weltkrieg in Chronik*, 35; *GSWW*, Vol. IV, 316; C. Burdick & H.-A. Jacobsen (eds.), *The Halder Diary 1939-1942*, 378; C. von Luttichau, *Road to Moscow*, IV:33.
5   *GSWW*, Vol. IV, 316; *DRZW*, Bd. IV, 269.
6   C. von Luttichau, *Road to Moscow*, IV:36-37.
7   Ibid., IV:37.
8   A. Philippi & F. Heim, *Der Feldzug gegen Sowjetrussland*, 52.
9   FMS D-247, C. Cuno, "*German Preparations for the Attack against Russia*," 1; D. Garden & K. Andrew (eds.), *The War Diaries of a Panzer Soldier*, 28-29.

10   J. Dinglreiter, *Die Vierziger. Chronik des Regiments*, 39-40.

11   A. Philippi & F. Heim, *Der Feldzug gegen Sowjetrussland*, 52; FMS P-190, R. Hofmann & A. Toppe, "*Verbrauchs- und Verschleisssaetze waehrend der Operationen der deutschen Heeresgruppe Mitte vom 22.6.41 – 31.12.41*," 11.

12   BA-MA RH 21-3/732, "*Gefechtsberichte Russland 1941/42.*"

13   D. Garden & K. Andrew (eds.), *The War Diaries of a Panzer Soldier*, 30.

14   P. Carell, *Hitler Moves East*, 11-13.

15   A full initial load of ammunition was the TOE-prescribed number of rounds for all weapons in a division and was to be carried in a division's organic transport. It amounted to some 600 tons for infantry and motorized divisions and 750 tons for armored divisions. Under a typical combat scenario, one load of ammunition was expected to last for 4-5 days; the initial attack, however, might consume 1/3 to ½ of a load. For the start of *Barbarossa* there were, at a minimum, three full loads of ammunition available – one with each division, and two in supply dumps (with a fourth load in the depots for tank guns and special weapons, such as rockets and AT guns). FMS P-190, R. Hofmann & A. Toppe, "*Verbrauchs- und Verschleisssaetze waehrend der Operationen der deutschen Heeresgruppe Mitte vom 22.6.41 – 31.12.41*," 94-95; C. von Luttichau, *Road to Moscow*, IV:41-42.

16   *GSWW*, Vol. IV, 298; FMS P-190, R. Hofmann & A. Toppe, "*Verbrauchs- und Verschleisssaetze waehrend der Operationen der deutschen Heeresgruppe Mitte vom 22.6.41 – 31.12.41*," 77-78; C. von Luttichau, *Road to Moscow*, IV:41-42.

17   A unit of consumption (*Verbrauchsatz*) was the amount of fuel required by a division to move 100 kilometers. This was roughly 25 tons for an infantry division (sufficient for about two days' operations), and 150-200 tons for a panzer division. C. von Luttichau, *Road to Moscow*, IV:42.

18   Ration requirements for all types of divisions were ca. 20 tons a day. However, infantry divisions required about 20 tons of hard feed (oats) for their 5000+ horses and another 20 tons of roughage. Since the roughage was not consistently supplied, the average daily ration supply of an infantry division was about 50 tons – that of a panzer or motorized division 20 tons. OKH had mandated that a supply for 20 days be stored in the assembly areas. The troops themselves were issued three days' field rations, while five days' standard field rations were to be held ready near the border in division supply dumps. The troops also carried four days' iron rations. Ibid., IV:41.

19   FMS P-190, R. Hofmann & A. Toppe, "*Verbrauchs- und Verschleisssaetze waehrend der Operationen der deutschen Heeresgruppe Mitte vom 22.6.41 – 31.12.41*," 75-79; C. von Luttichau, *Road to Moscow*, IV:42.

20   R. Kirchubel, *Operation Barbarossa 1941* (3), *Army Group Center*, 13.

21   Air Ministry Pamphlet No. 248: *Rise and Fall of the German Air Force*, 162.

22   H. Plocher, *German Air Force Versus Russia, 1941*, 32-33; Air Ministry Pamphlet No. 248: *Rise and Fall of the German Air Force*, 162; *GSWW*, Vol. IV, 361.

23   D. Stahel, *And the World held its Breath*, 88; J. S. Corum, *Wolfram von Richthofen*, 267; W. Murray, *Strategy for Defeat*, 81.

24   A. Kesselring, *Soldat Bis Zum Letzten Tag*, 112, 116; Air Ministry Pamphlet No. 248: *Rise and Fall of the German Air Force*, 165.

25   *GSWW*, Vol. IV, 318; *DRZW*, Bd. IV, 270. Figures for tanks and assault guns, vehicles and horses are approximate.

26   OKH Gen St d H/Op.Abt. (III), "*Kriegsgliederung Barbarossa*," *Stand 18.6.41*, in: K. Mehner (Hg.), *Geheime Tagesberichte*, Bd. 3. The same compilation can be found at the very back of, P. E. Schramm (Hg.), *Kriegstagebuch des OKW*, Bd. I. See also, W. Keilig, *Das Deutsche Heer 1939-45*, Bd. II, Abschnitt 100, S. 6.

27   *GSWW*, Vol. IV, 318.

28   H.-A. Jacobsen, *Der Zweite Weltkrieg in Chronik*, 36; E. F. Ziemke & M. E. Bauer, *Moscow to Stalingrad*, 7. According to Ziemke and Bauer, the actual number of German ground troops committed to operations in the east by the first week of July 1941 was 2.5 million.

29   A term used by Richard Muller to describe the *Luftwaffe's* 1941 campaign in Russia. See his, *German Air War in Russia*, 27.

30   *GSWW*, Vol. IV, 364; J. Prien, et al., *Die Jagdfliegerverbaende der Deutschen Luftwaffe*, Teil 6/I, *Unternehmen "Barbarossa,*" 28.

31   *GSWW*, Vol. IV, 317.

32   OKH Gen St d H/Op.Abt. (III), "*Kriegsgliederung Barbarossa*," *Stand 18.6.41*, in: K. Mehner (Hg.), *Geheime Tagesberichte*, Bd. 3.

33   Figures on tank strength differ slightly from source to source. According to Eddy Bauer, 4 Panzer Group had 570 tanks on "Tage X." See, E. Bauer, *Der Panzerkrieg*, Bd. I, 115. Thomas Jentz offers the figure of 602 tanks for the panzer group. T. L. Jentz (ed.), *Panzer Truppen*, 190-91.

34   Apart from "minor amendments," however, the assignments of all three army groups closely adhered to Directive No. 21 of 18 December 1940. *GSWW*, Vol. IV, 290.

35   Ibid., 290-91, 364.

36   J. Keegan, *The Second World War*, 182.

37   OKH Gen St d H/Op.Abt. (III), "*Kriegsgliederung Barbarossa*," *Stand 18.6.41*, in: K. Mehner (Hg.), *Geheime Tagesberichte*, Bd. 3.

38   Bauer provides a figure of 750 tanks; Lenz, however, only 726. E. Bauer, *Der Panzerkrieg*, 117; T. L. Jentz (ed.), *Panzer Truppen*, 191-92.

39   *GSWW*, Vol. IV, 290, 362-64; W. K. Nehring, *Geschichte der deutschen Panzerwaffe*, 219.

40   See Chapter 2, Section 2.5.

41   BA-MA RH 19 II/120, *KTB H.Gr.Mitte*, 2.10.41.

42   OKH Gen St d H/Op.Abt. (III), "*Kriegsgliederung Barbarossa*," Stand 18.6.41, in: K. Mehner (Hg.), *Geheime Tagesberichte*, Bd. 3; BA-MA RH 19 II/120, *KTB H.Gr.Mitte*, 2.10.41; E. Bauer, *Der Panzerkrieg*, 116; T. L. Jentz (ed.), *Panzer Truppen*, 190-93. Figures on tank strength for both Guderian's and Hoth's panzer groups exclude command tanks. For a complete breakdown of tank strength by division for both panzer groups see, Appendix 4.

43   *GSWW*, Vol. IV, 364. Figures on the numerical strength of the *Luftwaffe* order of battle for *Barbarossa* differ significantly from source to source. The figures used here, however, gleaned from the German quasi-official history of World War II, are drawn from several key *Luftwaffe* and OKH documents, hence one can be relatively confident of their accuracy.

44   Ibid., 366-67.

45   Minsk was roughly 250 kilometers to the east (as the crow flies) of 3 Panzer Group in the Suwalki region; from the sector of 2 Panzer Group, on the right wing of Army Group Center, the city was more than 300 kilometers distant.

46   A. Seaton, *The Battle for Moscow*, 38; *GSWW*, Vol. IV, 290; H. Guderian, *Panzer Leader*, 146-47.

47   H. R. Trevor-Roper, *Hitler's War Directives*, 50.

48   P. Johnson, *Modern Times*, 377-78.

49   A. Kesselring, *Soldat Bis Zum Letzten Tag*, 111-12.

50   P. Johnson, *Modern Times*, 377.

51   According to official Soviet estimates, the Germans had occupied ca. 1.8 million sq.km. (693,000 square miles) of Russia territory by November 1942. E. Mawdsley, *Thunder in the East*, 45.

52   Col.-Gen. G. F. Krivosheev (ed.), *Soviet Casualties and Combat Losses*, 101, 111, 260.

53   E. Mawdsley, *Thunder in the East*, 47.

54   E. Bauer, *Der Panzerkrieg*, 122; *DRZW*, Bd. IV, Beiheft (maps); K.-J. Thies, *Der Ostfeldzug – Ein Lageatlas*, "Aufmarsch am 21.6.1941 abds., Heeresgruppe Mitte."

55   P. Paret, "*Clausewitz*," in: *Makers of Modern Strategy*, P. Paret (ed.), 212; see also, H. Holborn, "*The Prussian-German School: Moltke and the Rise of the General Staff*," in: *Makers of Modern Strategy*, P. Paret (ed.), 281-95. Writes Max Boot about the campaign in France in 1940: "The German leadership advantage extended to the lower ranks, which, in the best Moltkean tradition, were taught to exercise their own initiative. German commanders continued to issue spare *Auftragstaktik* (mission-type orders) and push authority down to the lowliest NCO, while the French forces relied on a more centralized style of command that made it difficult for them to deviate from elaborate plans prepared before the start of the fighting. Contrary to cultural stereotypes, the soldiers of the Nazi regime often displayed more individual initiative than the soldiers of the liberal democracies." Boot's analysis, of course, holds true for the war in Russia as well. M. Boot, *War Made New*, 224.

56   S. Hart, et al., *The German Soldier in World War II*, 8-9.

57   Col. Dr A. Durrwanger, "*28th Infantry Division Operations*," in: *Initial Period of War on the Eastern Front*, D. M. Glantz (ed.), 235-36.

58   Ibid., 236.

59   Ibid., 236-37.

60   Ibid., 237.

61   R. Citino, *The German Way of War*, 303.

62   See, C. Luther, *Blood and Honor: The History of the 12th SS Panzer Division "Hitler Youth,"* 1943-1945 (San Jose, 1987).

63   It has been argued that the extraordinary German successes in the first half of 1941 were as much the result of Soviet incompetence at all levels as they were of German operational brilliance. This author agrees with that assessment.

64   J. Keegan, *The Second World War*, 87.

65   Lt. J. Hahn, "*Feldzug gegen Russland.*"

66   The original non-aggression pact of 23 August 1939 had led to trade agreements between Germany and the Soviet Union in February 1940 and January 1941. See, M. Zeidler, "*Deutsch-sowjetische Wirtschaftsbeziehungen im Zeichen des Hitler-Stalin-Paktes*," in: *Zwei Wege nach Moskau*, B. Wegner (Hg.), 93-110.

67   O. Buchbender & R. Sterz (Hg.), *Das andere Gesicht des Krieges*, 67.

68   J. Lucas, *Das Reich*, 56.

69   "*The Experiences of a World War II German Panzer Commander*," interview conducted by R. Mulcahy, 24 February 1992.

70   O. Buchbender & R. Sterz (Hg.), *Das andere Gesicht des Krieges*, 67.

71   Ibid., 67.

72   C. Luther & H. P. Taylor, *For Germany. The Otto Skorzeny Memoirs*, 92-93.

73   H.-G. Alvermann, "*Erlebnisbericht*," in: "*Jahresbrief 2007*," *Traditions-Verband der 110. Infanterie-Division.*

74   F. Belke, *Infanterist*, 24.

75   G. W. Schrodek, *Die 11. Panzer-Division*, 116.

76   II. Buecheler, *Hoepner. Ein deutsches Soldatenschicksal*, 130-31.

77   Also present for the conference were the C-in-C of the Army, Field Marshal von Brauchitsch; Chief of the Army General Staff, General Halder; the OKH *Generalquartiermeister*, Brig.-Gen. Wagner; and Chief of the OKH Operations Branch, Colonel Heusinger. P. E. Schramm (Hg.), *Kriegstagebuch des OKW*, Bd. I, 415.

78   According to Speer, Hitler had characterized the Chancellery into which he had moved on 30 January 1933 as "suited for a soap company" (*einem Seifenkonzern angemessen*); hence, it would hardly do as the headquarters (*Zentrale*) of the now powerful German Reich. A. Speer, *Erinnerungen*, 116.

79   L. Krier (ed.), *Albert Speer Architecture 1932-1942*, 125.

80   A. Speer, *Erinnerungen*, 130.

81   N. von Below, *At Hitler's Side*, 101.

82   B. Wegner, "*The Road to Defeat*: The German Campaigns in Russia 1941-43," in: *The Journal of Strategic Studies*, March 1990, 108.

83   C. Bellamy, *Absolute War*, 25; K. Latzel, *Deutsche Soldaten – nationalsozialistischer Krieg?*, 48.

84   C. Bellamy, *Absolute War*, 25-26.

85   N. von Below, *At Hitler's Side* 101-02; D. Irving, *Hitler's War*, 266; H.-A. Jacobsen (Hg.), *Generaloberst Halder Kriegstagebuch*, Bd. II, 455.

86   D. Irving, *Hitler's War*, 266.

87   H.-A. Jacobsen (Hg.), *Generaloberst Halder Kriegstagebuch*, Bd. II, 455.

88   K. Gerbet (ed.), *GFM Fedor von Bock, The War Diary*, 220-21. In addition, Field Marshal Kesselring, commander of Army Group Center's air power, wrote in his memoirs: "Hitler had explained earlier, and did so again in his final address to the generals on 14 June 1941, that the eastern campaign was unavoidable; that we had to attack now in order to avoid an untimely Russian attack [on Germany]." A. Kesselring, *Soldat Bis Zum Letzten Tag*, 113. Recalled Guderian, perhaps disingenuously: "[Hitler's] detailed exposition of the reasons that led him to fight a preventive war against the Russians was unconvincing." H. Guderian, *Panzer Leader*, 150.

89   N. von Below, *At Hitler's Side*, 102.

90   Ibid., 102.

91   R.-D. Mueller & G. R. Ueberschaer, *Hitler's War in the East – A Critical Assessment*, 104.

92   H. Guderian, *Panzer Leader*, 150.

93   M. Domarus, *Hitler – Reden und Proklamationen 1932-1945*, Bd. II, 1726-32; Dr E. Bunke, *Der Osten blieb unser Schicksal*, 208-09.

94   E. Mawdsley, *Thunder in the East*, 8.

95   K. Knoblauch, *Zwischen Metz und Moskau*, 156.

96   R. G. Reuth (Hg.), *Joseph Goebbels Tagebuecher 1924-1945*, Bd. IV, 1622-25.

97   Preventive war – defined as "acting to prevent a threat from materializing which does not yet exist." C. Bellamy, *Absolute War*, 102.

98   Pre-emptive war – defined as "action to forestall or deflect a threat which is 'imminent and overwhelming.'" Ibid., 102.

99   I. Kershaw, *Hitler 1936-45: Nemesis*, 944, f.n. 39.

100   G. Gorodetsky, *Grand Delusion*, 86-87.

101   E. Mawdsley, *Thunder in the East*, 7-8.

102   For example, Goebbels, in one of his "Total War" speeches which followed on the heels of the Stalingrad disaster, declared on 18 February 1943 that, for Germany in June 1941, "it was two minutes before twelve!" Ibid., 8.

103   I. Kershaw, *Fateful Choices*, 68.

104   G. Gorodetsky, *Grand Delusion*, 86.

105   Ibid., 86.

106   In his book, *Hitler's War*, David Irving offers a long list of Soviet war preparations to which German intelligence had become privy. These included details of the ongoing assembly of Russian forces along the frontier and disturbing indications that the Soviet air force "was a far greater menace than Hitler had bargained for – both in size and aircraft performance." See, D. Irving, *Hitler's War*, 236-37.

107   As Field Marshal Paulus admitted after the war, "no preparations whatever for an attack by the Soviet Union had come to our attention." G. Gorodetsky, *Grand Delusion*, 87.

108   Halder, however, had noted in his diary weeks earlier, on 7 April 1941 that, "disposition of the Russian forces gives food for thought … one cannot help admitting that their troop dispositions are such as to enable them to pass to the offensive on shortest notice. This might become extremely unpleasant for us." C. Burdick & H.-A. Jacobsen (eds.), *The Halder Diary 1939-1942*, 354.

109   J. Foerster, *Die Wehrmacht im NS-Staat*, 172.

110   J. Foerster & E. Mawdsley, "*Hitler and Stalin in Perspective*," in: *War in History*, 78; H. Magenheimer, "*Krieg zweier Angreifer*," in: *Junge Freiheit*, 20 Jun 08.

111   J. Foerster & E. Mawdsley, "*Hitler and Stalin in Perspective*," in: *War in History*, 78.

112   J. Foerster & E. Mawdsley, "*Hitler and Stalin in Perspective*," in: *War in History*, 78-79; C. Bellamy, *Absolute War*, 102.

113   B. Musial, *Kampfplatz Deutschland*, 12.

114   Ibid., 456. Musial, however, soundly rejects the "*Praeventivkriegsthese*" – the notion that Hitler's attack on Russia was in any way pre-emptive. As he thoroughly demonstrates, Russia was not ready for war in the summer of 1941; moreover, the Germans, he points out correctly, were largely in the dark about the true strength of the Soviet armed forces, and about ongoing Soviet preparations for their own war of aggression, which were "in full swing" (*auf Hochtouren*).

115   H. Magenheimer, "*Krieg zweier Angreifer*," in: *Junge Freiheit*, 20 Jun 08.

116   Following the German defeat of France in June 1940 Stalin is said to have remarked, "The Germans will now turn on us, they will eat us alive." J. Erickson, "*Barbarossa June 1941: Who Attacked Whom?*," in: *History Today*, Jul 01.

117   BA-MA RH 24-48/198, 1.7.41, quoted in: J. Hoffmann, *"The Soviet Union's Offensive Preparations in 1941,"* in: *From Peace to War*, B. Wegner (ed.), 373.

118   BA-MA RH 24-28/10, 16.7.41, quoted in: J. Hoffmann, *"The Soviet Union's Offensive Preparations in 1941,"* in: *From Peace to War*, B. Wegner (ed.), 373-74.

119   Ibid., 373.

120   Ibid., 374.

121   Ibid., 375. Hoffmann quoted a captured Red Army commissar who, in August 1941, stated that, since May 1941, "anti-German agitation had again been openly carried out everywhere."

122   C. Bellamy, *Absolute War*, 115.

123   Ian Kershaw gives a figure of "around 1500," while Evan Mawdsley states 2000 were in attendance. See, I. Kershaw, *Fateful Choices*, 277; also, J. Foerster & E. Mawdsley, *"Hitler and Stalin in Perspective,"* in: *War in History*, 79.

124   I. Kershaw, *Fateful Choices*, 277.

125   J. Hoffmann, *"The Soviet Union's Offensive Preparations in 1941,"* in: *From Peace to War*, B. Wegner (ed.), 365-66, 380.

126   See, for example, J. Foerster & E. Mawdsley, *"Hitler and Stalin in Perspective,"* in: *War in History*, 78-103.

127   I. Kershaw, *Fateful Choices*, 277-78.

128   G. Gorodetsky, *Grand Delusion*, 322. Zhukov's plan had called for an *"udar,"* or a limited strike deep into the rear of the German force concentrations.

129   Revisionist historian Heinz Magenheimer, however, argues that Stalin would have struck in 1941. He estimates that the gigantic Red Army deployments would have been complete by 15-20 July 1941. Furthermore, he states that, "even if there is no documentary proof for the exact date of a Soviet attack, the circumstances of the deployment itself, and the pressures of time on deployment, logistics and mobilization, all indicate a deadline in the latter half of the year, no later than the beginning of autumn." While Magenheimer's argument is intriguing, it is difficult for this author to imagine how the Red Army could have been ready for offensive war before the spring of 1942 at the earliest, so great were the shortfalls in training and equipment in the summer of 1941. H. Magenheimer, *Hitler's War*, 51-53; see also, H. Magenheimer, *Moskau 1941*, 32-33.

130   By the spring of 1941, American correspondent in Berlin Harry W. Flannery was even noticing shortages of beer in the German capital, while cigarettes "also became harder to buy." H. W. Flannery, *Assignment to Berlin*, 259-60.

131   R. Moorhouse, *Berlin at War*, 81, 136-44; N. von Below, *At Hitler's Side*, 93. See also, H. W. Flannery, *Assignment to Berlin*.

132   R. Moorhouse, *Berlin at War*, 68; S. Risse, *"Das IR 101 und der 2. Weltkrieg"* (unpublished report). On 24 May 1941, 24-year-old White Russian émigré, Marie Vassiltchikov, wrote in her secret Berlin diary that people were speaking more and more of troop concentrations along the border with Russia, and that "nearly all the men we know are being transferred from the west to the east. This can only mean one thing." On 10 June 1941, she observed: "Most of the German army seems to be massing on the Russian border." M. Vassiltchikov, *Berlin Diaries*, 52, 54.

133   N. von Below, *At Hitler's Side*, 103.

134   D. Irving, *Hitler's War*, 267-68.

135   D. M. Glantz, *Barbarossa Derailed*, Vol. I, 20.

136   A. Hillgruber, *"Das Russland-Bild der fuehrenden deutschen Militaers vor Beginn des Angriffs auf die Sowjetunion,"* in: *Die Zerstoerung Europas*, A. Hillgruber, 264-65.

137   Recalled Panzer General Hermann Hoth: "Only gradually, beginning in January 1941, did the army and corps commanders become familiar with their tasks in the eastern campaign ... Only now were military-geographic descriptions of the terrain and maps prepared. These were based, in part, on meticulous work done in the years before World War I and were now outdated and insufficient. From the maps we were given we could only seldom determine which roads and bridges were useable for motor vehicles and tanks. Frequently, roads had to be assigned without knowing if they were actually passable, leaving it up to the units themselves to deal with whatever problems arose." H. Hoth, *Panzer-Operationen*, 44.

138   D. Thomas, *"Foreign Armies East and German Military Intelligence in Russia 1941-45,"* in: *Journal of Contemporary History*, 275.

139   G. P. Megargee, *Inside Hitler's High Command*, 111. "The fact that the Germans," observes Megargee, "would entrust such a man with a task of such importance speaks volumes." One again, the Germans would pay dearly for their underestimation of the vital importance of such fields of warfare as intelligence and logistics, while overemphasizing the operational art of war.

140   *"Weil man so gar nichts ueber Russland wisse, es koenne eine grosse Seifenblase sein, es koenne aber auch ebensogut anders sein."* Quoted in: C. Schroeder, *Er war mein Chef*, 113; see also, D. Irving, *Hitler's War*, 271.

141   Quoted in: D. Irving, *Hitler's War*, 269.

142   M. Domarus, *Hitler – Reden und Proklamationen 1932-1945*, Bd. II, 1724.

143   D. Irving, *Hitler's War*, 268.

144   D. Irving, *Hitler's War*, 269; P. E. Schramm (Hg.), *Kriegstagebuch des OKW*, Bd. I, 408; G. R. Ueberschaer, *"Das Scheitern des Unternehmens 'Barbarossa.' Der deutsch-sowjetische Krieg vom Ueberfall bis zur Wende vor Moskau im Winter 1941/42,"* in: G. R. Ueberschaer & W. Wette (Hg.), *"Unternehmen Barbarossa." Der deutsche Ueberfall auf die Sowjetunion 1941*, 145.

145 By attacking Soviet Russia, Hitler had once again confronted his Italian partner with a *fait accompli*. Mussolini's response upon learning of Operation *Barbarossa* was to tell his foreign minister Ciano: "I hope for only one thing, that in this war in the east the Germans lose a lot of feathers." W. L. Shirer, *Rise and Fall*, 851.

146 R. G. Reuth, *Goebbels*, 479-80; I. Kershaw, *Hitler 1936-45: Nemesis*, 386-87.

147 The words are Ian Kershaw's. I. Kershaw, *Hitler 1936-45: Nemesis*, 388.

148 R. G. Reuth, *Goebbels*, 480.

149 L. Besymenski, *Die Schlacht um Moskau 1941*, 32.

150 Of the Western Front tanks, 2192 were operational on 22 June 1941; of these, most were obsolete older models, but several hundred were new KVs and T-34s. Special thanks to David Glantz for Soviet Western Front strength figures. E-Mail, D. M. Glantz to C. Luther, 16 May 12.

151 K.-J. Thies, *Der Ostfeldzug – Ein Lageatlas*, "Aufmarsch am 21.6.1941 abds., Heeresgruppe Mitte."

152 K. Gerbet (ed.), *GFM Fedor von Bock, The War Diary*, 223; K.-J. Thies, *Der Ostfeldzug – Ein Lageatlas*, "Aufmarsch am 21.6.1941 abds., Heeresgruppe Mitte."

153 On 2 August 1934, all members of the *Wehrmacht* had taken a personal oath of loyalty to Adolf Hitler. L. L. Snyder, *Encyclopedia of the Third Reich*, 257.

154 A. Stahlberg, *Bounden Duty*, 156-59. See also, B. Scheurig, *Henning von Tresckow. Ein Preusse gegen Hitler*, 118.

155 G. Blumentritt, "*Moscow,*" in: *The Fatal Decisions*, W. Richardson & S. Freidin (eds.), 46.

156 H. Guderian, *Panzer Leader*, 153.

157 BA-MA MSg 1/1147: *Tagebuch* Lemelsen, 21.6.41.

158 D. Volkogonov, "*The German Attack, the Soviet Response, Sunday, 22 June 1941,*" in: *Barbarossa, The Axis and the Allies*, J. Erickson & D. Dilks (eds.), 84; A. Kesselring, *Soldat Bis Zum Letzten Tag*, 117.

159 A. Kesselring, *Soldat Bis Zum Letzten Tag*, 116-17.

160 R. Kirchubel, *Operation Barbarossa 1941* (3), *Army Group Center*, 32.

161 W. Schneider, *Panzer Tactics*, 5.

162 A. Opitz, "*Die Stimmung in der Truppe am Vorabend des Ueberfalls auf die Sowjetunion,*" in: *Der Krieg des kleinen Mannes*, W. Wette (Hg.), 236.

163 W. Schneider, *Panzer Tactics*, 5; C. G. Sweeting, *Hitler's Personal Pilot*, 155; R. J. Kershaw, *War Without Garlands*, 10.

164 Quoted in: Dr E. Bunke, *Der Osten blieb unser Schicksal*, 208-09.

165 This, of course, is a large generalization, which was far from always true. Dr Alfred Opitz wrote after the war that, in his company, news of the impending war with Russia – as well as the officially proffered justifications for it – which they received on the afternoon of 21 June, was met with "very mixed feelings." (A. Opitz, "*Die Stimmung in der Truppe am Vorabend des Ueberfalls auf die Sowjetunion,*" in: *Der Krieg des kleinen Mannes*, W. Wette (Hg.), 236-37.) In the recollections of another German veteran, Emanuel Selder (62 IR/7 ID), the response to Hitler's dramatic proclamation "fluctuated … between dismay and elation." E. Selder, *Der Krieg der Infanterie*, 25.

166 C. Hartmann, *Wehrmacht im Ostkrieg*, 247-48. Observes Hartmann, "Much of the evidence indicates that most of the soldiers (even those who had little to do with NS-ideology) were convinced of the necessity for such a war."

167 Ibid., 248.

168 "*Die meisten,*" wuerden sich "*maechtig*" freuen, "*dass es endlich wieder einmal kracht.*" BA-MA MSg 1/3268: Fritz Farnbacher, *Tagebuch*, 22.6.41, quoted in: C. Hartmann, *Wehrmacht im Ostkrieg*, 247.

169 BfZ, Slg. Sterz (04 650), *Brief L.B.*, 22.6.41, quoted in: C. Hartmann, *Wehrmacht im Ostkrieg*, 248. (Note: BfZ = *Bibliothek fuer Zeitgeschichte*, Stuttgart. Hereafter cited as "Collection BfZ.")

170 C. Luther & H. P. Taylor, *For Germany. The Otto Skorzeny Memoirs*, 93.

171 Slg. Sterz (04 650), *Brief L.B.*, 15.6.41, Collection BfZ, quoted in: C. Hartmann, *Wehrmacht im Ostkrieg*, 248.

172 C. Hartmann, *Wehrmacht im Ostkrieg*, 248.

173 R. Kirchubel, *Operation Barbarossa 1941* (3), *Army Group Center*, 32.

174 Dr E. Bunke, *Der Osten blieb unser Schicksal*, 211-14.

175 H.-J. Roell, *Oberleutnant Albert Blaich. Als Panzerkommandant in Ost und West*, 41-42.

176 Ltr, H. Haape to fiancée, 21.6.41.

177 Emblazoned on the field belt buckle (*Koppelschloss*) of every German soldier was the Prussian motto, "*Gott mit uns*" (God is with us). The phrase, however, was not stamped onto the belt buckles of *Luftwaffe* or SS soldiers. A. Sáiz, *Deutsche Soldaten*, 89.

178 Hptm. Herbert S. (00 401), Collection BfZ.

179 On 26 June 1941, in a pastoral letter, the German catholic bishops hailed Operation *Barbarossa* as a "service to the fatherland" (*Dienst am Vaterland*). Four days later (30 June 1941), an official agency of the German protestant (*evangelisch*) church, in a telegram to Hitler, approved the war as a struggle "against the mortal enemy of all order and western Christian culture." W. Schneider (Hg.), *Alltag unter Hitler*, "*Chronik 1941.*"

180 B. Haering, *Embattled Witness*, 4-6.

181 G. Habedanck, "*Bei Brest-Litovsk ueber die Grenze,*" *Die Wehrmacht, 1941*, 233; quoted in: R. J. Kershaw, *War Without Garlands*, 29.

182 D 107/56 Nr. 4, "*Aus Briefen des Adjutanten Inf.Rgt. 18, Oberleutnant Juerg von Kalckreuth,*" Staats- und Personenstandsarchiv Detmold. *Oberleutnant* Kalckreuth was on the staff of 18 Infantry Regiment (6 ID). The first paragraph is from a letter to his wife, Gisela; the second was gleaned from his personal diary.

183 A. Freitag, *Aufzeichnungen aus Krieg und Gefangenschaft*, 50-51.

184 German Ninth Army and 3 Panzer Group attacked at 0305 hours, in synchronization with Army Group North; Fourth Army and 2 Panzer Group began their attack 10 minutes later (0315 hours) along with Army Group South. C. von Luttichau, *Road to Moscow*, VI:9.

185 H. Martin, *Weit war der Weg*, 13.

186 Quoted in: G. Knopp, *Die Wehrmacht. Eine Bilanz*, 79. See Chapter 6 (Section 6.2.2) for his battalion commander's (Major Werner Heinemann's) somewhat different, albeit largely confirming, recollection of this event.

187 E. Krehl, *Erinnerungen eines 85 Jahre alten Mannes*, 42 (self-published memoir). Krehl served on the staff of Artillery Commander 121 (Arko 121), which was assigned to 57 Panzer Corps. OKH Gen St d H/Op.Abt. (III), "*Kriegsgliederung Barbarossa*," *Stand 18.6.41*, in: K. Mehner (Hg.), *Geheime Tagesberichte*, Bd. 3.

188 S. Risse, "*Das IR 101 und der 2. Weltkrieg*."

CHAPTER 6

BARBAROSSA Unleashed: Army Group Center Goes to War

(Sunday, 22 June 1941)

"War is ... an act of force to compel our enemy to do our will." (Clausewitz, *On War*)[1]

"It is not necessary that I should live; it is, however, that I should do my duty and fight for the fatherland." (Frederick the Great)[2]

"At exactly 0310 on 22 June 1941 we were ready to fire ... At 0315 a lightning bolt of gigantic dimensions tore through the night. Thousands of artillery pieces shattered the silence. I will never forget those seconds." (*Leutnant* Heinz Doell, 18 PD)[3]

"On this morning, the light of a radiant rising sun flooded the broad, gentle hills of the East Prussian countryside. A June Sunday dawned and it could not have been any more beautiful, a real feast day, if only it had not brought war with Soviet Russia from 0305 hours." (H. Martin, 14 ID (mot.))[4]

"And now at 0330 hours it all began, perhaps not as abruptly as it had in the west and not on the scale that it had in the world war, but a quarter of an hour later the first Luftwaffe air wings roared back, and now squadron after squadron travels eastward. And all the while the sun shone ... .You now know more than we do, because there is now no opportunity to listen to the radio, and everything will happen at once, and the spaces will be so vast that you can even find them on our wall map. We have maps that reach a long way to the east, and if you remember Napoleon's army did that on foot, but we're motorized and we'll get it done in 14 days." (*Oberleutnant* Richard D., 7 PD)[5]

Sunday morning, 22 June 1941, followed the first day of summer and the shortest night of the year, known as "white nights" in northern Russia, because the sun never really sets.[6] As the first slivers of light emerged tentatively above the horizon far to the east, the first wave of more than three million German soldiers swarmed across the frontier from the Baltic Sea in the north to the Prut River in the south. As virtually all contemporary accounts confirm, complete tactical surprise was achieved along the entire front of more than 1200 kilometers, enabling the German assault teams to capture all bridges intact – most importantly, those over the Bug River in the sector of Army Group Center.[7] Within a few short hours, the attackers had shattered the Soviet border defenses and, rapidly exploiting the nearly universal confusion in their enemy's ranks, begun to drive eastward.

Yet if the day was crowned with spectacular victories for the German invaders, it also brought – as every war does – more than its share of challenging, traumatic, even shattering experiences in its wake, as a brief follow up to the accounts at the end of Chapter 5 illustrates:

Leutnant Erich Bunke began the war as a platoon leader in a *Panzerjaeger* company in 31 Infantry Division; by 7.00 that morning, his company commander was dead – shot through the head, most likely by a Russian sniper. After helping to retrieve the body, *Leutnant* Bunke, still shaken by the death of his *Chef*, *Oberleutnant* Becks – and clearly stunned by the tenacity and bravery of the enemy facing his unit outside the Soviet fortress of Brest-Litovsk – suddenly found himself in temporary command of the company.[8]

Bernard Haering, a Catholic priest, had been assigned as a medic to a German division stationed near Bayeux, France, in the autumn of 1940. Here he had conducted a regular – albeit unofficial[9] – Sunday mass in the beautiful medieval cathedral at Bayeux for German soldiers stationed in the area. In early May 1941, his division was moved to Poland as part of the *Barbarossa* buildup; on 22 June, it too crossed the frontier into Soviet occupied territory. Recalled Haering:

> At the first sign of dawn, our company passed the boundary line and came under attack. And the first man who needed my help – as priest, for he was beyond medical help – was my dear friend and brother who had been so vitally alive only a few moments before, and so anxious to survive in order to rebuild a world gone mad. Brother Fichter had been struck by a shell. His head was shattered and his brains spilled out like water, even while his body was still alive and wrestling against death.
>
> I was utterly overwhelmed, and cried bitterly. It was the first and the last time I wept during the war. Very soon things became so difficult that, if one were to survive, one could not give in to his feelings.[10]

Assistenzarzt (2nd Lt., medical) Heinrich Haape (6 Infantry Division), after crossing into Russia from the Suwalki triangle with his battalion, was busy treating wounded German soldiers and hanging casualty cards around their necks. He soon learned of the first dead officer in his battalion – it was *Leutnant* Stock, his life snuffed out by a sniper's bullet, his body "lying in a trampled cornfield." A hole was quickly shoveled out of the ground and Stock's body lowered into the earth. The helmet and identity disc festooned to the rough birch cross – hammered into the ground with trench-spades – revealed that the dead second lieutenant was barely 21 years of age. "But there was nothing," Haape wrote in his splendid war memoirs, *Moscow Tram Stop*, "to say that this sensitive lad had been a brilliant pianist; that he had been able to make me forget everything when I listened to him play the 'Moonlight Sonata' in the mess at Littry la Mine before we left Normandy."[11]

Later that day, Haape lost one of his dearest companions, also a front-line doctor – shot down by the Russians despite his Red Cross flag and armband: "It was too much – too much for the first day of a war against a new foe, whose ways we had hardly begun to gauge. My overtaut consciousness half-refused to accept Fritz's death."[12] By the end of this day, Sunday, 22 June 1941, 18 Infantry Regiment, Haape's regiment, had sustained more losses (21 dead, 48 badly wounded) than it had suffered during the entire French campaign of 1940. "It has been a most difficult day," he jotted in his diary that night. "The Russians fought like devils and never surrendered, so we engaged in close combat on several occasions; just now, half an hour ago, another four Russians were struck dead with the butts of our rifles."[13]

Gerd Habedanck, the war correspondent with 45 Infantry Division, observed the start of the "great day" from a battalion headquarters bunker close to the Bug River, opposite the fortress of Brest-Litovsk. It was crowded inside the bunker, and as the final seconds crept up to 0315 hours and the start of the artillery bombardment, there was a "profusion of shoving, steel helmets, rifles, the constant shrill sound of telephones, and the quiet voice of the *Oberstleutnant* drowning everything else out. 'Gentlemen, it is 0314 hours, still one minute to go.'" Habedanck peered through the bunker vision slit; nothing to see – not yet. He suddenly recalled the battalion commander's comment from the day before, about the opening bombardment: "It will be like nothing you have experienced before," he had assured Habedanck.[14] And, indeed it was. Yet by the end of this fateful Sunday, 22 June, more than 300 men of 45 ID had died in their desperate attempts to capture the bunkers, casemates and forts inside the fortress of Brest-Litovsk.[15]

6.1: 0305 & 0315 Hours – The Artillery Preparation

The launch of Operation *Barbarossa* was preceded by several preliminary actions of note. In the final hours before the outbreak of war, German special operations forces, belonging to 800 Regiment – the so-called "*Brandenburgers*" – many of them Russian speaking, infiltrated or were dropped from aircraft inside Soviet held territory. Once behind Soviet lines, they proceeded to blow up or otherwise incapacitate power and signal stations, activate German agents, seize bridges vital for German operations (and secure them from demolition), cut telephone lines, and, in general, foment alarm and confusion. Wearing Red Army uniforms, the *Brandenburgers* made for the fortress of Brest-Litovsk or for the bridges over the Bug. Some of the men, secreted across the frontier the day before on goods trains, or concealed beneath loads of gravel in rail trucks, hid out in the town of Brest for many hours before the attack began. At 0220 hours, barely 45 minutes before the start of the German bombardment, Soviet 4 Army, having interrogated yet another German deserter, attempted posthaste to circulate this latest confirmation of the imminent attack. The news, however, never got out: German special forces had already severed the telephone lines.[16]

At precisely 0300 hours, 30 Heinkel He 111 and Dornier Do 17Z medium bombers, elements of several bomber wings, droned across the German-Russian demarcation line at high altitude. The vanguard of the *Luftwaffe's* eastern air fleet, the clutch of bombers – their hand-picked crews with many hours of night flying experience – set out, in groups of threes, to strike fighter bases between Belostok and Minsk and at other locations behind the central front. The bombers flew over sparsely populated regions of marsh and forest, their aircrews scanning the still darkened terrain for navigational clues, while ahead of them the first yellow and red hues of a new day marked the eastern horizon. As the aircraft approached their targets – still undetected – they began their decent. By 0315 hours they were roaring in at low level, ready to disgorge hundreds of small SD-2 fragmentation bombs from their open bomb bays.[17]

On the ground, in the sector of Lt.-Gen. Geyr von Schweppenburg's 24 Panzer Corps, the highway bridge across the Bug River at Koden, 40 kilometers south of Brest-Litovsk, was vital to the deployment and advance of the corps' armor. As a result, a *ruse de guerre* was concocted to seize it. The Russian frontier guards were summoned by their German counterparts with shouts of "important business." As the Russian guards approached, they were machine gunned by the German assault party, which had seized the bridge by 0310 hours, five minutes before the artillery preparation was to begin. To Guderian's "immense relief," Geyr had thus gained a bridgehead that would ensure his tanks access to Panzer Route 1 – the *Panzerstrasse* leading via Kobrin and Slutsk to Bobruisk.[18]

As the final minutes ticked away, senior German officers assembled at observation points along the front to observe the spectacle about to begin. General Guderian, Commander, 2 Panzer Group, after all his subordinate corps had reported their troops ready for action,[19] made off at 0210 hours for his CP – located in a wooden observation tower south of Bohukaly and overlooking a bend in the Bug River – arriving there an hour later, at 0310.[20] From the tower, Guderian could observe the lights of the city of Brest-Litovsk, 15 kilometers to the southeast. The formidable citadel of Brest-Litovsk, however, "with its forts and casemates pointing at the German line like an anchored battleship, lay in darkness."[21] General Lemelsen, 47 Panzer Corps, drove down to the Bug River with his escort officer to watch his riflemen and combat engineers in their assembly areas.[22] Field Marshal von Kluge, Commander, Fourth Army, and his staff were in the sector of 31 Infantry Division, also close to Brest-Litovsk and just a few kilometers from the Bug. As Kluge's chief of staff, Colonel Guenther Blumentritt, recalled,

"We watched the German fighter planes take off and soon only their tail lights were visible in the east … As [zero hour approached], the sky began to lighten, turning to a curious yellow color. And still all was quiet."[23]

Suddenly, at 0305 hours, thousands of German guns opened fire on the left wing of Army Group Center (Ninth Army and 3 Panzer Group) and along the front of Army Group North. Ten minutes later (0315 hours), thousands of guns began to bellow on the right wing of Army Group Center (Fourth Army and 2 Panzer Group) and along the front of Army Group South.[24] For the preparatory bombardment, Field Marshal von Bock had assembled more than 60 battalions of *Heeresartillerie* (GHQ artillery), including 15 100mm cannon battalions (*Abteilungen*), 16 150mm medium field howitzer battalions (s.F.H. 18), 17 210mm heavy howitzer (*Moerser*) battalions, and four 150mm *Nebelwerfer* rocket projector battalions. All told, the army group bristled with some 750 batteries of light, medium and heavy artillery, massing its several thousand guns along a 500 kilometer front.[25]

Although the opening artillery barrage was of relatively short duration (in many cases lasting no longer than several minutes), no one who took part in it – or witnessed it – was ever to forget it. To Dr Heinrich Haape (6 ID), waiting to provide first aid to the assault troops of his battalion, the barrage resembled a "mighty clap of thunder," the flashes from the guns turning "dawn into daylight."[26] Artillery of every caliber fired point-blank at known or suspected Russian field positions and fortifications, while shells from mortars and other high-angle fire weapons traversed the dawn sky in arc-like orbits as they sought out their targets beyond the frontier. To Colonel Blumentritt it seemed as if "a miracle" had happened, when the Russian artillery, for the most part, failed to respond: "Only very rarely did a gun open fire from the far bank."[27] *Soldat* Franz Frisch, an artillerist in a motorized *Heeresartillerie* battalion (100mm cannon), took part in the cannonade, recalling that the sustained "drumfire," as it swelled to an infernal roar, created a level of noise that he found "incredibly uncomfortable."[28] "The thunder of guns awakened us at 0315 in the morning," wrote a soldier from Berlin:

> 34 batteries are firing. We can see the barrage from the edge of the forest, since we are merely 7 kilometers away from the frontier (Bug). Soon towns are burning, white flares shoot up, the front rages like a storm. When there is Flak fire, gray streaks rise into the sky, slowly drifting away. A plane goes down burning. The sky, at first clear and red, gradually turns purple mixed with green. There is a gigantic smoke cloud behind the low silhouette of the horizon and it drifts leadenly to the right.[29]

Oberleutnant Siegfried Knappe, an artillery officer in 87 Infantry Division, was struck by the pungent odor of pine needles as he wandered among the 180 men of his battery to conduct final checks. The men, he knew, were supremely sure of themselves. "Their confidence was total, like that of a diamond cutter taking a chisel to a priceless gem … I was confident the world had never seen anything like them," he later wrote. Knappe checked the forward observation post. Then, at the designated time, his battery opened fire on a small village across the frontier:

> I was not in the front line with the infantry but at a little hill about a half kilometer away, which I thought would be a good place from which to watch the effectiveness of our fire. I could see our shell bursts clearly from my observation post, as well as the oily black-and-yellow smoke that rose from them. The unpleasant, peppery smell of burnt gunpowder soon filled the air as our guns continued to fire round after round. After 15 minutes we lifted our fire, and the soft pop-pop-pop of flares being fired replaced it as red lit up the sky and the infantry went on the attack.[30]

A veteran of 19 Panzer Division and prolific military historian, the late Rolf Hinze was struck by the peculiar juxtaposition of the gunfire with dance music wafting from the radios of some of the armored fighting vehicles:

> The tension became unbearably high. Nerves seemed to vibrate ... A few minutes before 0300 ... the hum of the motors in the west made the presence of the first German bombers felt. At exactly 0300 hours, they crossed the frontier. [At 0305 hours] the artillery fire began abruptly from all gun barrels positioned along the front line. The all-encompassing tension like that before a storm was discharged in a thundering artillery barrage at the start of the attack. Everyone felt this deafening declaration of intent by a great Army to be a powerful event which would never be forgotten by any participant, regardless of its damaging impact on the peace of nations. We were proud to take part in such an event as a small cog in the vast Army machinery – an event which would later be regaled by the history books. The relentless forward movement of all units, whether horse-drawn, on foot, motorized, or in the air, this imposing demonstration of numbers, triggered a veritable mass frenzy, all rushing forward. If, in this strange atmosphere, this electrically charged mood, you could even hear dance music from some of the tanks, this produced a rather incongruous atmosphere. The German radio station broadcast dance music all night with rolling news bulletins, for which everyone waited eagerly.[31]

Along the front of 17 Panzer Division, northwest of Brest-Litovsk, some 60 batteries (240 guns) were assembled on a front of eight kilometers. At precisely 0315 hours, the division unleashed a hurricane of fire across the Bug – 80-90 meters wide in this sector – against known Russian field positions and bunkers. A post-war history of 40 Rifle Regiment, a component of 17 PD, graphically portrayed the regiment's role in the bombardment:

> The air roars. Commands can barely be understood. Our infantry guns fire 60 rounds per gun in 10 minutes. Flak guns finish off the bunkers along the enemy bank. Soon, fires on the other side of the Bug can be seen. At 0340 hours, the bombs from the *Stukas* strike the enemy positions. From 0415 hours, the transport [of troops and weapons] across the river begins.[32]

In the sector of 18 Panzer Division, 50 batteries of all calibers disgorged a furious cannonade and a protective smoke screen.[33] *Leutnant* Georg Kreuter contributed to the opening barrage with his two 150mm medium infantry guns (s.IG 33). Because the guns' shellfire merged with the general bombardment, it was impossible for him to discern its effect on the far side of the Bug. What he did clearly observe, however, was an unfortunate Ju 87 *Stuka* dive-bomber, which dove into the ground after being struck by a shell from a German gun. Such "friendly fire" incidents were far from uncommon on this day, or any other day on the eastern front.[34]

One of the salient characteristics of warfare in the first half of the 20th Century was the progressive blurring of distinctions between soldiers and civilians, with the latter all too often becoming its innocent victims. In this account from *Obergefreiter* August Freitag (6 Infantry Division), civilians begin to prepare themselves for an uncertain and perilous future:

> At 0300 hours, we saw and heard the first *Stuka* units approaching. At precisely 0305, the first bombs fell ... Immediately afterwards, the artillery also started up. The atmosphere had broken and we could breathe freely again. Then we also heard the first MGs firing. The civilians emerged from their houses, alarmed by this

night-time disruption. But they soon realized what was going on. They hurriedly ran back into their houses to fetch things like beds, clothes, chairs, tables, and the like, to hide them in the garden behind the bushes or in the rye fields.

At about 0320 we also received the order to move our position forward ... Now it was time to quickly limber up the guns and load the ammunition in order to reach the rifle companies, whom we were, of course, there to support. Shortly after 0330 we passed through the frontier. To our left, right, and ahead of us, white Very signal lights bore witness to the unstoppable advance of the German infantry.[35]

The 10 Panzer Division, a component of 46 Panzer Corps (2 Panzer Group), was held in reserve on 22 June and, thus, did not participate in the opening attack; its artillery, however, was assigned to 18 Panzer Division (47 Panzer Corps) for the opening barrage (*Feuerschlag*). An excellent unit history, published by the 10 PD veterans' organization (*Traditionsgemeinschaft*) in 1993, offers a vivid picture of the preparations required for the artillery barrage, as well as of the barrage itself:

In the late afternoon of 21.6.[41], the observation posts are manned, the computing units move into the firing positions. When evening falls, the *Fuehrer's* proclamation is read out, which begins with the words: "Soldiers of the Eastern Front!" And suddenly all the guessing games that had been going on are at an end, everybody knows that the weapons will be doing the talking once again ...

Weather reports, known as "Barbara Reports" by the artillerymen, have been coming in every two hours since evening at the batteries' computing section posts. The trajectory of the shells is, of course, influenced by various factors, such as temperature, air pressure, humidity, wind direction, and wind force. When firing blind, these variables have to be taken into account, and so every two hours the computing units calculate all the firing commands for the planned *Feuerschlag* anew. And then the X-hour is announced: 22.6., 0315 hours!

At 0300 hours, the firing commands are adjusted for the last time, there is nothing more for the computing units to do. The guns are aimed and loaded, the battery officers have the handset of a field telephone to their ear; they look at their watches. The artillery commander has reserved for himself the order to open fire. Over on the horizon, a pale light, just a narrow sliver, is very weakly discernible. A quiet shiver, more like a thrill, takes hold of the soldiers standing in the night. The battery officer repeats the words which are coming out of the telephone: "10 minutes more." – "5 minutes more." – "1 more minute." – "30 seconds more." – "15 seconds more, – and 10 seconds, – 8, 7, 6, 5, 4 – battery ..." He raises his arm and thrusts it down, the command "Fire!" erupts from his mouth like thunder and lightning – a single bolt of lightning flashes across the whole sky, a deafening crash tears through the silence. And then shell after shell speeds across the Bug, rising to a drum fire due to the sheer numbers of batteries standing to the left and right.

Over there, a wall of dense smoke and dust rises sluggishly, blotting out the pale slivers on the horizon. Then suddenly German rocket projector batteries join the fray: howling and whining, whole series of rockets with long trails of fire and smoke sweep across into the inferno. The first rays of sun light up the edges of the clouds and the wall of smoke in a bloody red. And with the first light come the *Stukas*, seeking out their targets, positioning themselves in a row, circling and plunging earthward, dropping their bombs and pulling up again. And behind them, black smoke pours up into the sky again ...

When day has come and the rolling barrage has ended at the limit of the artillery's range, as the gunners from 90 Artillery Regiment collect the empty cartridges and the ammunition boxes and the sounds of combat across the advancing front rumble like a receding storm, suddenly Russian bombers appear above the German positions, approaching in strict formation, as if on maneuvers.[36]

Nimble German fighters, Bf 109s, from the air field at Biala Podlaska, rose to challenge the enemy bombers, pouncing on them suddenly from behind. Firing short bursts from their 20mm cannon, they summarily shot down one of the intruders; a second bomber was soon hit and broke apart in mid-air. None of the Russian bombers made it through to their objective that day.[37]

6.2: The Ground Attack – Initial Contact with the Red Army

Among the surviving photographs taken on the early morning of 22 June 1941 is one of a clutch of German infantry and combat engineers, somewhere along the eastern front, tucked behind a sheltering railway embankment and awaiting the signal to begin their assault. While the first rays of sunlight wash over the railroad and telegraph lines in front of them, the men themselves are enveloped in darkness and shadows, the morning sun glinting off of their steel pots. Some of the men are still sleeping, while a group of them is peering off to the left, their attention captured by what we do not know. Perhaps they are observing the disciplined formations of German fighters and bombers as they droned on toward their targets away to the east. The troops are loaded down with weapons and equipment – rifles, machine pistols, hand grenades, mess kits, water bottles, entrenching tools and the like. What appear to be ammunition boxes are discernable, as are several of the steel gasmask containers (*Tragbuechse*) strapped to the backs of the men.[38] One can only wonder what thoughts were racing through the minds of these soldiers, minutes away from rushing across the embankment and into battle against an enemy about which they knew so little. Some, no doubt, prayed; others thought of their wives and families; others still were likely struck by the profound historical significance of the war about to break. Disciplined soldiers that they were, they also engaged in purposeful last minute checks: Were rifles loaded and safety catches on? – Were helmet straps adjusted properly and uniforms buttoned up? – Were hand-grenade arming mechanism screws easy to adjust?[39]

Beginning at 0305 or 0315 hours, the anonymous assault party captured in the photograph, and hundreds more just like it, poured across the frontier under cover of protective artillery barrages (and artificial smoke) and began their deadly journey into the unknown. On the right wing of Army Group Center (Fourth Army and 2 Panzer Group), where the frontier meandered along the Bug River for more than 200 kilometers,[40] the assault parties crossed in rubber dinghies or assault boats (*Sturmboote*), while armored fighting vehicles, artillery and motorized infantry were soon advancing across the captured Bug bridges. At many other points along the river combat engineers labored furiously to build additional bridges to shepherd troops, weapons, vehicles and equipment to the far bank. In other instances, weapons and equipment were ferried across the Bug, while in the sector of 18 Panzer Division, just above Brest-Litovsk, a battalion of tanks, specially outfitted for the purpose, plunged right through the four-meter deep river and crawled up the eastern bank.[41]

On the left wing of Army Group Center (Ninth Army and 3 Panzer Group), armor and infantry burst forth from the Suwalki triangle through heavily wooded and almost trackless sandy terrain. Here the "roads" running east into Lithuania were little more than narrow sandy tracks, many of which had never been crossed by a motor vehicle before; in fact, the terrain was often so inhospitable that enemy resistance, however slight, could not be countered by deployment off the roads. The result was that the long columns of men and vehicles were repeatedly forced to halt, with the many forest fires also contributing to the confusion.[42]

Despite such difficulties, tactical surprise was achieved along the entire front. As Field Marshal von Bock recorded laconically in his diary, "Everything began according to plan."[43] Indeed, enemy resistance was, at first, desultory or even non-existent. As noted in the OKW war diary, the Russian border defenses, during the morning hours, were penetrated to a depth of four to five kilometers along the entire front;[44] by the end of the day, German mobile units on both wings of Army Group Center had advanced well beyond the frontier. Many Polish and Lithuanian peasants, glad to be rid of their Soviet oppressors, greeted the invaders with gifts of salt and bread, the traditional gifts for travelers.[45]

Conversely, some of the NKVD border units, and troops assigned to local fortified regions, fought with great tenacity to the last man – a harbinger of what was to come in the days and months ahead.[46] As the day went on, and the Red Army began to recover from the shock of invasion, resistance began to stiffen, with the most horrific combat taking place inside the Soviet fortress of Brest-Litovsk (see directly below, Section 6.2.1). Red Army mechanized units even managed to pull off several ill-coordinated counterthrusts. In the ensuing narrative, a more detailed look will be offered into the experiences of the soldiers of Army Group Center on this first day of the war. As is wont to do, the "action" will proceed from right to left, beginning with the activities of General Heinz Guderian's 2 Panzer Group.

6.2.1: 2 Panzer Group

The opening attack of Army Group Center struck the left flank of Lt.-Gen. V.I. Morozov's 11 Army of Soviet Northwestern Front and the entire span of General D.G. Pavlov's Western Front. The mission of Bock's powerful mechanized forces (9 panzer and 6 motorized divisions) was to pierce Soviet defenses on both flanks of the Belostok salient and, advancing along the Minsk-Smolensk axis, envelop, encircle and annihilate Russian forces west of the Western Dvina and Dnepr river lines. For Guderian's assault formations, the war began at 0315 hours, supported by an artillery barrage of 30 minutes duration. In an order to his subordinate divisions, the brilliant panzer general had let it be known just how much he expected of his men:

> Our panzer group, on the right wing of the army[47] and advancing ahead of it, is to break through the frontier positions on both sides of Brest[-Litovsk] and strike out along *Panzerrollbahn*[48] 1 and 2 toward Slutsk and Minsk, and then into the area of Smolensk, in order to destroy the cohesion of the enemy army. After breaking through, it is of decisive importance to advance as far as the gasoline will take us, at full throttle, without pause or rest, marching day and night, without consideration for any threat to the flanks … The main thing is to advance far, and to shoot little. [*Es kommt darauf an, viel zu fahren, wenig zu schiessen.*][49]

There was "little finesse" to the panzer group's opening moves, as it simply struck the center of Lt.-Gen. A.A. Korobkov's 4 Army.[50] The group's two forward panzer corps,[51] 47 and 24 Panzer Corps, echeloned in depth,[52] crossed the Bug on both sides of Brest-Litovsk. The fact that they attacked immediately, in the forwardmost line, was because Guderian had prevailed over his superior, Field Marshal von Kluge, C-in-C Fourth Army, in a tactical dispute prior to the start of the campaign. Kluge had argued that his infantry should make the initial penetration to preserve the armored forces, which would then exploit the breakthrough. Guderian demurred, insisting instead that his tank units be committed at once to smash through the front and exploit resultant breakthroughs without loss of time. The panzer leader appealed to Bock, and the field marshal came down on Guderian's side, allowing him "much freedom to execute operations as he saw fit and to commit his armor immediately as he desired."[53]

Within minutes (0324 hours), the first riflemen of 3 Panzer Division (24 Panzer Corps) were across the river, while heavy weapons also began to move across the bridge at Koden. A minute later, one of the division's assault units (*Gruppe Kleemann*) reported that the enemy had yet to show himself; only a single round of artillery had been fired near the bridge. Fifteen minutes later, *Oberst* Kleemann reported that two of his companies were across the river; and, by 0350, the first tanks of the division were rolling across the bridge.[54] Forming the spearhead was the third battalion of 3 Panzer Division's 6 Panzer Regiment. In one of the battalion's Panzer IV tanks rode *Oberfeldwebel* Albert Blaich, a platoon leader in 12th Company:

> The enemy defensive fire was weak, and after only a few hours the soldiers of 3 Panzer Division had cleared the enemy riverbank and the town of Stradecz. At 1000 hours, the main body of the panzer regiment could begin to advance, while the 3rd Battalion, advancing in the lead, fought the first nests of resistance.
>
> In the afternoon, the heavy Panzer IVs of 12th Company set off again. *Oberfeldwebel* Blaich stood at the open turret of his tank and looked through his field glasses at the flat terrain dotted with bushes and many swamps. But his attention was fixed on the small town of Przyluki.
>
> After only a few meters, the first shots popped. There was a crackling in the headphones, then the voice of the battalion commander sounded:
>
> "Blaich platoon, sheer off to the right ahead of the town and then attack from the flank!"
>
> "*Panzer marsch!*"
>
> Albert Blaich shouted the order into the throat microphone, then he closed the hatch. Shortly after that, 12th Company found itself in a difficult fight with Russian anti-tank guns. Bent over the observation slit, Blaich observed the houses of the small town. His commands then followed. The tank slid off the road and rolled through open meadow land. Beside it rolled the tanks from the same platoon. In a wide formation 12th Company now attacked the village; resistance became more intense. The muzzle flash of an anti-tank gun flared in front of a white painted house.
>
> "Turret 11 o'clock – distance 800 meters – armor piercing shells!"
>
> The gunner, *Unteroffizier* Engel, and the loader, *Gefreiter* Greiner, were ready. The turret was already swinging in the indicated direction; the shell was already in the barrel. The gunner had the target in his sights. Blaich looked through the eyepiece once more. There was another flash over there. Missed! The next shot would be theirs.
>
> "Fire at will!"
>
> *Unteroffizier* Schulz abruptly stopped the tank. Milliseconds later, the shot cracked. The men involuntarily ducked their heads as the reverberations of the gun discharge made the tank shake.
>
> "Forward!"
>
> At the moment the tanks began to advance again, a tall, fiery glow flared up over by the AT gun. Then, only billows of smoke could be seen.
>
> "Bulls-eye!"
>
> The tanks rolled at high speed into the town. About 50 meters away from them another AT gun exploded and flew into the air. It hit the tank of *Feldwebel* Kuehn, the second tank in Blaich's platoon. Ahead of them a house went up in flames: everywhere the picture was the same. Gradually the Russian defensive fire abated.

"Blaich, go through the town with your platoon immediately and take possession of the *Rollbahn*," came the voice of *Hauptmann* Schneider-Kostalski [the battalion commander] through the headphones.

Blaich shouted his orders into the throat microphone again. Then the four Panzer IVs rolled on. Through the observation slit Blaich saw a destroyed AT gun, its protective shields smashed and twisted. The barrel projected almost vertically into the sky and the gun crew lay dead on the ground beside it.

"Keep going – just keep going!" bellowed Blaich. "We have to get through the town!"

Przyluki was traversed at high speed. To the north, Blaich saw a fiery glow and thick clouds of smoke on the horizon – that must be where Brest-Litowsk, which the Russians had turned into a fortress, was burning.[55]

24 Panzer Corps' other tank unit, 4 Panzer Division, also met little resistance as it crossed the Bug. "The first assault detachments crossed in assault boats and rafts," recalled Hans Schaeufler, a signal officer in the division:

> At 0400 hours, we moved to a staging area in a patch of woods right on the river [Bug]. The resistance across the way was slight. At 1200 hours, we crossed the river on pontoon ferries with our radio vehicles. The tanks still had to wait, because the crews manning the bunkers at the bridges were still firing. Our vehicles wormed their way through the knee-deep sand of the Bug lowlands. The civilians, former Poles, were very friendly. They cooked eggs and milk for us.[56]

Soviet resistance throughout the morning was predominantly light; by late afternoon, the forwardmost elements of 24 Panzer Corps – the tanks encrusted with dust, obscuring the large white "G" adorning their hulls[57] – had advanced 18 to 30 kilometers beyond the Bug and were heading east unhindered along the *Panzerstrasse* (Panzer Route 1) toward Bobruisk.[58]

Northwest of Brest-Litovsk, Lemelsen's 47 Panzer Corps (two panzer, one motorized infantry, one regular infantry division) also made its way swiftly across the Bug. By 0355 hours, the riflemen of both 17 and 18 Panzer Divisions were on the eastern bank, having met little resistance and no enemy artillery fire. Less than an hour later (0443), the 80 "submarine" tanks (Pz IIIs and Pz IVs) of I./PzRgt 18 (18 PD) began to ford the Bug by wading directly through the river.[59] The special tanks, originally intended for Operation "Sealion" (invasion of Britain), had all openings sealed and were outfitted with air intakes and exhaust snorkel pipes. The specter of "swimming" tanks caused something of a sensation and, in one instance at least, more than a little skepticism: "The artillerymen told me about an unbelievable experience," wrote an officer in 18 Panzer. "At our crossing point, they said, tanks dived into the Bug like U-boats and then reappeared on the east bank. Must be pretty strong tobacco they're smoking, I thought to myself, but it was true."[60]

His tanks having made military history by wading across the Bug, General Walther K. Nehring, Commander, 18 Panzer Division, climbed into one of the assault boats of his combat engineers and crossed the river. After the vehicles of his tactical headquarters[61] were sent over on pontoon ferries, Nehring joined his tanks as they rolled into Soviet territory, accompanied by several of his staff and the commander of the tank battalion, Major Graf Manfred von Strachwitz. Commencing their "panzer raid" into Russia, they made for Pruzhany, racing far beyond the wheeled elements of the division. As soon as his command car and two radio communications vehicles were ferried across the river, Guderian also struck out for Nehring's tanks.[62]

Along the front of 2 Panzer Group, nine bridges were in use by midday, three of them newly constructed by engineers.[63] In his diary, General Lemelsen (47 Panzer Corps) registered his satisfaction with the opening act of the campaign:

> It was certainly a pretty grand experience, that start to the attack … At 0315 hours precisely … the hellish concert of the artillery let rip and, at the same time, the riflemen plunged into the water with pneumatic boats and made the crossing with those and assault boats. Contrary to expectations, the reaction of the enemy was extremely limited, which meant that construction of the bridge could start very quickly; astonishingly, neither did enemy artillery open up nor did their planes drop bombs. All the bunkers that had been located through weeks of observation were incomplete and unmanned. The greatest difficulties were caused by the very wet terrain on the other side of the Bug before you could get to a solid pathway. I soon crossed over the river in my command tank and accompanied the forward elements of 18 Panzer Division. Then we went inexorably onward along the Bug, at first straight to the east – the enemy had not thought of that – and then to the northeast across the Lesna. All the bridges were intact – our greatest concern – a sign that the Russians had been taken completely be surprise.[64]

Like his panzer general colleagues, Lemelsen also led from the front, which could – and often did – result in sudden and unpleasant contact with the enemy. His account continues as follows:

> I got into a really sticky situation during the afternoon: I was standing with my armored command vehicle at a crossroads, completely on my own … when suddenly there were loud bangs from all directions. We subsequently apprehended 14 Russians who had been hiding in the cornfields; they had leapt up, fired their pistols, and fled again into the cornfield; they were all shot while trying to escape. And then suddenly there were shots from a sewage pipe beneath the road. Shooting and throwing hand grenades into the opening had no effect; it was only after the second hand grenade was thrown in that four Bolsheviks, all wounded, emerged with raised hands. The Russian soldier is a spirited and wily fighter; he has doubtless been told that he would be slaughtered if he fell into German hands, this is the only way to explain their dogged all-or-nothing defense.[65]

The armored vanguard of 18 Panzer Division reached the Lesna River, just beyond the Bug, later that morning, and crossed over on the still intact bridge. Nehring's tanks rumbled on along the *Panzerstrasse* (Panzer Route 2) toward Pruzhany, continuing their pursuit of the still shaken enemy without regard to their flanks, or the fact that the main body of the division's armor was still to the rear.[66] 18 Panzer encountered its first serious opposition that afternoon, when it was counterattacked by Soviet 14 Mechanized Corps, the armored reserve of 4 Army. In the ensuing three-hour *Panzerschlacht*, 36 enemy tanks were destroyed; within 48 hours, the Soviet mechanized corps had lost half of its 500 tanks, while battling in vain against the superbly trained and experienced panzer troops.[67]

Of all the operations along the front of 2 Panzer Group this day – indeed, along the entire eastern front – none was more savage, and more costly, than the attempt to capture the Soviet fortress of Brest-Litovsk. The Germans had hoped to seize the fortress in a *coup de main* – as one author put it, Field Marshal von Kluge "hoped to capture the fortress before dinner"[68] – but would be bitterly disappointed by the outcome of the day's fighting. In fact, Soviet resistance within the fortress's many strong points would continue for days and, in the words of the late professor and Red Army expert, John Erickson, "became a ghastly but epic illustration of how Russian infantrymen could fight in traditionally ferocious style."[69]

Built by Russian engineers after the War of 1812, the fortress of Brest-Litovsk sat at the confluence of the Bug and Muchaviec rivers, whose waters had been used to form four partly natural and partly artificial islands. The center island (Citadel Island), the smallest of the four, was the heart of the fortress, and was ringed by the three other islands to the south, west and north; together, they formed the four fortified blocks that made up the massive citadel. It was surrounded on all sides by earthworks almost 10 meters high and stretching for eight kilometers, while deep moats filled with water posed another daunting obstacle. The four islands themselves bristled with strong points of all kinds – massive underground casemates, armored cupolas, and dug in tanks, among others, all concealed among thick undergrowth and clumps of tall trees. Even the barracks, which could hold 12,000 troops, were reinforced with walls 1½ meters thick which could withstand fire from all but the heaviest caliber artillery.[70]

The Soviet garrison, however, was far from full strength. Some of its troops, artillery and tank forces were off at camps in the surrounding countryside, taking part in summer training activities. On 22 June, only seven undermanned battalions of infantry, belonging to 6 and 42 Rifle Divisions, augmented by an NKVD border guard detachment and an independent NKVD battalion, were inside the fortress – in all, about 3500 men out of a possible 8000. Some of the troops did not even have weapons and many officers, spending the weekend at home, were also absent.[71]

As we have seen, Guderian's two panzer corps launched their attacks on either side of the citadel, whose two rivers and water-filled ditches made it, in the panzer commander's view, "immune to tank attack."[72] As a result, an infantry corps, the 12th, was placed under his command and assigned the task of assaulting the fortress and protecting the inner flanks of the panzer corps as they crossed the frontier. The mission of capturing the fortress fell to 12 Army Corps' 45 Infantry Division, commanded by Maj.-Gen. Fritz Schlieper. In addition to seizing the citadel, the mostly Austrian division was to capture the four-span railway bridge over the Bug (at a point directly northwest of the fortress) and the five bridges spanning the Muchaviec south of the town of Brest, while securing the high ground immediately beyond the town. If successful, this would clear the way for the advance of Guderian's armor along Panzer Route 1, the route toward Kobrin assigned to 24 Panzer Corps.[73]

With German *Wochenschau* newsreel cameramen on hand to record the spectacle, the assault began precisely at 0315 hours. Opening up on the citadel in a five-minute preparatory barrage were the nine light and three medium batteries of 45 ID, along with nine heavy 210mm howitzers, two mighty 600mm "*Karl*" siege guns, and the 4 Rocket Projector Regiment, whose nine batteries dropped 2880 missiles on the fortress in rapid succession. Artillery of the neighboring 34 and 31 Infantry Divisions (12 Army Corps) also contributed to the fire plan.[74] Rudolf Gschoepf, a chaplain in 45 ID, later compared the bombardment to a "hurricane," which "broke loose and roared over our heads, the likes of which we had never experienced before and never would again."[75] To *Leutnant* Erich Bunke, observing in awe in the sector of the adjoining 31 ID, it was as if the "jaws of hell" (*Schlund der Hoelle*) had opened, while the thousands of shells arcing across the dawn sky made the "air vibrate."[76]

After the initial *Feuerschlag* had ceased, swarms of *Stuka* dive-bombers appeared over the fortress, lunging earthward and loosing their bombs. German combat engineers and infantry emerged from the thickets lining the Bug, crossed the river in rubber dinghies and assault boats, and began their attack on the citadel. A group of nine assault boats, a mixed force of combat engineers and infantry, was assigned the task of seizing several of the bridges over the Muchaviec; four of the boats, however, were immediately put out of action: After barely reaching the water they were struck by "friendly" artillery falling short, leaving 20 men dead and wounded. The survivors reorganized and motored up the river, but soon lost two more boats to enemy fire. Pressing on with the remaining three boats, they secured the first two bridges by 0355 hours, with support from other infantry forces; at 0510, the assault group captured the third "Wulka" bridge, its final objective. Attempting to raise a swastika battle flag over the bridge, the elated commander of the assault party was cut down by a sniper's bullet. With troops from 130 Infantry Regiment attacking south of the fortress and town of Brest-Litovsk, all five of the still intact bridges over the Muchaviec were soon in German hands. The Russians counterattacked with armor but were rapidly repulsed, 130 IR destroying 12 Russian tanks in the course of these attacks.[77]

On the northern axis of the attack, assault troops belonging to 135 Infantry Regiment secured the vital railway bridge in less than 15 minutes. German armored cars began to roll across immediately; by 0415 hours, assault guns of the neighboring 31 Infantry Division were also rumbling over the bridge. Initial progress against the citadel itself also appeared to be good, with the attacking battalions forcing their way deep into the fortress in some locations. Both 12 Army Corps and 45 ID were encouraged by the early results, with the latter reporting at 0625 hours that "the division believes it will soon have the citadel firmly in hand."[78]

Then the "worm began to turn." By 0730, 45 ID was reporting for the first time that strong elements of the garrison were now firing from behind on the forward assault parties. Moreover, the attacking Germans, ensconced among the bushes, trees, buildings and ruins of the fortress, were now so intermingled with the citadel's defenders that artillery support could no longer be provided. Russian sharpshooters, hidden in trees or firing from roof top outlets, began to take a heavy toll, particularly of German officers and NCOs. Others shot at the Germans from buildings, cellars or sewers; even while hidden in garbage cans or behind piles of rags. Among the officers of 45 ID to perish this day were three battalion commanders – two belonging to 135 Infantry Regiment and one to 1st Battalion, 99 Artillery Regiment.[79]

Confidence among the attackers soon began to fade, giving way to a growing pessimism. In an effort to stem the tide, reserves were committed to battle by early afternoon. Infantry guns, anti-tank guns, and light field howitzers were brought forward to engage strong points in direct fire, while a battery of assault guns passing by was commandeered by the commander of 135 IR and thrown into the fight – all with little impact on the impervious fortifications of the citadel. Some of the assault parties had also become cut off, with one group of 70 men pinned down in the very heart of the fortress, in the church in the center island.[80]

At 1350 hours, General Schlieper, observing the faltering attack from the vantage point of the northern island, finally reached the only conclusion possible: The citadel of Brest-Litovsk was not to be taken by infantry close combat alone. Field Marshal von Bock, who had visited the command post of 12 Army Corps less than an hour before, reached the same conclusion. Thus, at 1430 hours, Schlieper decided that he would withdraw the infantry from the citadel under cover of darkness. The fortress was to be tightly encircled and subjected to withering and unremitting artillery fire to wear down and destroy the defenders. Early that evening, Field Marshal von Kluge arrived at the CP of 45 Infantry Division. He strongly supported Schlieper's decision, indicating that the fighting for the fortress was now of little more than local significance, for the key bridges had all been captured and traffic across the railway and along Panzer Route 1 was now possible. As a result, unnecessary losses were to be avoided; instead, Kluge said, the enemy was to be starved into submission.[81]

In a publication released by the German Armed Forces High Command (OKW) in 1943, a participant in the fighting at Brest-Litovsk recorded his initial impressions of the Red Army:

> The battles on the islands extremely difficult. Complex terrain: groups of houses, clusters of trees, bushes, narrow strips of water, plus the ruins, and the enemy is everywhere. His snipers are excellently camouflaged in the trees.

Camouflage suits made of gauze with leaves attached to them. Superb snipers! Shooting from hatches in the ground, basement windows, sewage pipes …

First impression: the Bolshevist fights to his very last breath. Perhaps because of the threat of the commissars: those who fall into German captivity are shot. (According to statements by the first prisoners.) At any rate: no slackening of fighting power, even though resistance futile since citadel is surrounded.

Silent night. We dig the first graves.[82]

Under cover of darkness, the German assault troops were withdrawn from the citadel and organized in the encirclement ring, with the exception of the exhausted and, in some cases, wounded men trapped inside the citadel church.[83] The abandoned positions were immediately reoccupied by the surviving Russian defenders. The bitter, and unexpected, fighting on this day had cost 45 Infantry Division 311 dead – 21 officers and 290 NCOs and enlisted men.[84] Organized Russian resistance inside the fortress would not be broken until the end of the month, by which time 45 ID had lost about as many men as it had during the entire French campaign of 1940.

6.2.2: Fourth Army

Adjoining 2 Panzer Group on the left, Field Marshal Guenther von Kluge's Fourth Army struck the southern face of the Belostok salient with several infantry corps along a front of more than 100 kilometers.[85] The army recorded in its war diary that, by 0420 hours – in other words, in little more than one hour – all of the attacking divisions were across the Bug and reporting little to no resistance.[86] Almost immediately after the attack began, the army's signal intercept service listened in on a Russian message that graphically reflected the confusion in the enemy's ranks: "We are being fired upon. What shall we do?" The senior Soviet headquarters to whom the frantic query was directed responded contemptuously: "You must be insane. And why is your signal not in code?" As Fourth Army Chief of Staff, Colonel Blumentritt, recalled after the war, "all went according to plan."[87]

On the left wing of Fourth Army, the assault parties of 23 Infantry Division stormed across the frontier. One of them was led by *Feldwebel* Becker. Exploiting the cover of the opening barrage, and clutching his 9mm Walther P38 pistol in his right hand, he rushed forward toward a railway embankment, motioning for his men to follow; together, and to their astonishment, they reached the embankment without any discernable reaction from the Russian border troops. Instinctively bent over for protection, the men climbed up the embankment, crossed the tracks and pressed on, the enemy opposite them now responding with isolated fire. On his right, out of the corner of his eye, Becker noticed a German motorized column moving along a road; as far as he could see in either direction German troops, widely dispersed and recognizable by their field gray uniforms, were advancing briskly. The tension drained from Becker's body. The start of the attack had gone smoother than anticipated; he had not lost a man.[88]

For *Gefreiter* Kredel, another infantryman in 23 ID, this Sunday, 22 June, was unforgettable for many reasons, most significantly because it was his first day ever in action – his "baptism of fire." At precisely 0315 hours, he leaped forward and began to run as fast as his legs could carry him, his machine gun cradled on his shoulder. To ease his anxiety, a veteran had assured him that the first wave, exploiting the surprise of the attack, usually made it through unscathed, while those coming after bore the brunt of the enemy's reaction. As he ran, he noticed that bullets were whistling passed his helmet; they made an odd sound, he thought. He watched as a wooden observation tower on the far side of the river, struck by a German anti-tank shell, suddenly disintegrated, sending fragments of wood along with Russian soldiers hurtling though the air. *Panzerjaeger* in open vehicles (*Kuebelwagen*) roared passed him, their light 37mm anti-tank guns in tow. In the next moment, German artillery fire began to drop short among the assaulting troops, evoking cries and curses from the wounded. Providently, the "friendly" artillery abruptly shifted its fire forward.[89]

42-year-old Major Werner Heinemann, a decorated World War I veteran and battalion chief in 67 Infantry Regiment (23 ID), approached this first day of the war with palpable foreboding. A committed anti-Nazi, Heinemann had been placed under house arrest in 1934 and, following his own petition, was released from active service in the *Wehrmacht*. In 1940, he had been put back on active duty and took part in the French campaign, as both a company and battalion commander. Now, in the final hours before war with Russia, on the warm summer night of 21/22 June, his men were quietly moving up to the frontier and assembling for the attack. They had their work cut out for them: Thickets of barbed wire, some 15 rows of them, one after the other, lined the border. Heinemann's assault units would have to cut through this wire before they could begin their attack; to perform this task, an abundance of wire cutters were on hand.[90]

With the final minutes of peace slipping away, Heinemann's thoughts suddenly turned to his experiences in Russia as a young soldier in the Great War. His heart was troubled. He recalled the country's seemingly endless expanses and the difficulties encountered there because of the terrain. More than most, he recognized the gigantic task now facing the German Army. And while he knew that his men were, at this very moment, in their highest state of readiness and strength, he could not shake lose from the thought that this imminent attack on Russia was an inconceivably irresponsible enterprise, not to mention a breach of the non-aggression pact which had been in place for the better part of two years.[91]

As the final shadows of the shortest night of the year dissolved into sunlight, the artillery opened up along the front of 23 Infantry Division. Minutes later, Heinemann's two lead companies stirred into action, cutting through the thickets of wire and advancing in open order (*entfaltet*) toward their first objective – a village on the far side of the frontier. Above them, squadrons of German bombers in tight formations winged eastward toward their targets. On the ground, the artillery barrage was coming to an end, with the exception of several heavy howitzers. Yet here, too, the big guns fired short, their 210mm shells dropping among the forwardmost German infantry who had just skirted passed the frontier, sending impressive columns of dirt and smoke into the air. Very signal lights soon filled the dawn sky with bright red bursts: "The artillery is firing short! Lift your fire!" (*Artillerie schiesst zu kurz! Feuer vorverlegen!*) Yet the damage had been done, the battalion sustaining several wounded and its first dead soldier of the Russian campaign (a radioman in its signal section)[92]

After the initial assault groups had forced their way through the lanes cut in the wire, Major Heinemann, at the head of his tactical operations staff, set out for the frontier – a moment he recalled in his memoirs (in third person):

> Later, only many months later, his adjutant, Ekkehard Maurer, confided in him that he [Heinemann] had, back then, turned around at the entry point through the cut barbed wire entanglements and, to his adjutant and the special-missions staff officer, Zitelmann, who were following close behind him, said with an expression and tone more serious than any his long-trusted subordinates had ever seen in him: "Always remember this moment! It is the beginning of the end!"[*Es ist der Anfang vom Ende!*]
>
> At that time, those words, which were even utterly forgotten by the commander, hardly penetrated the consciousness of his subordinates. In any case, they were young and more carefree than the "Old Man," and it seemed even to him that the deeply serious statement had arisen out of the unconscious of his heavy thoughts.

But it happened just as it is described here and that is why it is reported, in order to show how the clash of arms back then was approached with the most insightful and grave misgivings.[93]

Lt.-Col. Meyer-Detring, chief operations officer (Ia) of Fourth Army's 137 Infantry Division, described the initial experiences of his division as they crossed the Bug in a sector some 100 kilometers northwest of Brest-Litovsk and north of the Polish town of Siedlce:

> After careful preparations, in the night of 21.-22.6.[41] the regiments' assault companies had advanced to the west bank of the Bug. Pneumatic boats and assault boats for the crossing lay ready. Shortly after 0300 hours, General Bergmann arrived at the advanced division command post on the river embankment of the Bug. The telephone operator at the switchboard in the cramped dugout recalled:
> "The matter was made more difficult because in the excitement we had forgotten the portable switchboard and now had to construct our own switchboard relay. We had connected both neighboring divisions, Artillery Commander 44 and 9 Army Corps. For me, the humble soldier, the following hours were unforgettable. The general's calm, kind manner had impressed me deeply. That day was also a great experience for me from a military perspective, because the corps commander and the artillery commander came to the dugout later."
> The attack began in the early morning hours of the 22.6.[41] – 0315 hours – with a barrage from all weapons and calibers lasting one minute. Under cover of this fire from around 200 barrels of between 100 and 210mm, the first infantry formations embarked across the river and everywhere reached the opposite bank without a fight. Somewhere, a village was burning. Our own artillery then continued its incessant firing, now striking target areas located farther back, in line with the tactical plan of fire, and after 25 minutes transitioned to observed fire. Large elements of the infantry were already on the opposite bank, and still nothing stirred on the enemy side. The surprise had succeeded flawlessly! Approximately one hour after the start of the attack, the first isolated pockets of resistance flared up in the bunkers, but were immediately quelled through rapid and ruthless action. Contrary to expectations, the enemy artillery also remained silent, so that the construction of the bridge could begin immediately. Eight hours later, the division's heavy weapons were already rolling across the completed bridge.[94]

Despite the good beginning, 137 ID was to sustain serious losses on this day, fighting in the forests and border villages against an enemy who often resisted with determination. Divisional records show that its casualties amounted to 345 men (73 killed, 262 wounded 10 missing) on the first two days of the war.[95]

Like many other German headquarters, Fourth Army was also astonished by the virtual lack of enemy artillery fire (*ganz geringe Artillerie-Taetigkeit*) encountered in the initial hours of the attack. At 0900 hours, Kluge returned to his headquarters following a visit to 2 Panzer Group. The army had, by now, identified six Russian divisions opposite a narrow sector of its front. Nevertheless, Kluge was convinced that the main enemy forces were not along the border, but further back in the interior. Fourth Army had earlier requested (about 0800) that 2 Air Fleet fly reconnaissance well behind the front to locate Red Army forces astride the army's axis of advance. By late afternoon, however, long-range aerial reconnaissance (*Fernaufklaerung*) had revealed no signs of major defensive preparations farther to the rear.[96]

Despite the mostly smooth going, by late morning, reports were beginning to trickle in to Kluge's headquarters indicating that enemy resistance – while still largely desultory in nature – was stiffening. At several points, the Russians had fought with real tenacity (*hartnaeckig*); they had also conducted several minor armored thrusts, which were easily repulsed.[97] Moreover, here and along the rest of the front, many of the Soviet frontier units, facing a crushing local German superiority of forces, had simply melted away into the forests, marshes and cornfields; after the main German assault columns had passed by, they often emerged from their hiding places to fall on German supply troops, medical personnel, motorcycle messengers and other easy targets,[98] or they simply shot at German soldiers from concealed positions. In innumerable contemporary German accounts – field post, personal diaries, war diaries – a word suddenly began to appear with disturbing frequency – *Heckenschuetze*, or sniper. Indeed, from the first hours of the war, the German *Landser* faced a tenacious and deadly adversary who was to torment him unremittingly – the Russian sniper.

6.2.3: Ninth Army

German Ninth Army, commanded by the 61-year-old General Adolf Strauss,[99] advanced on a broad front against the northern face of the Belostok salient, its attack striking Lt.-Gen. V.I. Kuznetsov's Soviet 3 Army. The *Schwerpunkt* (point of main effort) of Strauss' attack was on his left, where the three infantry divisions of his 8 Army Corps burst out of the Suwalki triangle from a start line east of Augustovo and smashed into Soviet 56 Rifle Division covering Grodno.[100] Kuznetsov's army, short of ammunition and lacking proper reserves, its telephone lines cut and radio communications disrupted by German saboteurs or the tenacious *Luftwaffe* bombing, soon found itself in a perilous predicament.[101]

The mission of 8 Army Corps (8, 28, and 161 ID) was to protect the southern flank of 57 Panzer Corps (3 Panzer Group) by seizing the border defenses southeast of the Suwalki triangle and securing crossings over the Neman at and above the ancient fortress of Grodno. 8 Infantry Division, on the corps' right flank, had Grodno directly within its attack sector. The fighting was ferocious:

> The bunker line on the border consisted of more than a dozen works clustered around Hill 150 which commanded the secondary road to Grodno. Under cover of an artillery barrage by 29 batteries, 38 Infantry Regiment, 8 Infantry Division, attacked the position. An engineer assault company, reinforced by an anti-tank platoon and an 88mm anti-aircraft section, was attached to the regiment with the task of destroying the bunkers. The first resistance was encountered less than a mile from the border. A dug-in tank covered an anti-tank ditch, behind which stood groups of bunkers on both sides of the road. The preparatory fires had not silenced them. Anti-tank guns and machine guns concentrated their fires on the embrasures.
>
> The engineer assault teams worked their way through wheat fields, fortunate to find cover in them and then behind earth mounds near the bunkers. Blinding the apertures with flamethrowers, individual engineers charged up to the bunker walls and with extension ladders scaled them. From the relative safety of their perches, they lowered explosive charges to the apertures, blasted holes into ventilation and periscope shafts, then poured gasoline into them followed by smoke grenades and chain charges. Meanwhile, other demolition teams blasted the often hidden entries to the bunkers.
>
> In some of the storied bunkers, each level had to be destroyed in this manner, down to the basement. Rarely did the Russian crews, which numbered from 20-50 men, surrender, and most of the defenders fought to the death. In some instances survivors believed to be dead came to after hours and resumed the fight, requiring the same position to be neutralized all over again.[102]

Farther west, Strauss' 129 Infantry Division (42 Army Corps) quickly reached its initial objectives that morning.[103] By 0445 hours, the first Soviet prisoners were being marched to the division CP for interrogation:

> The prisoners give the impression that they had been taken completely by surprise by the attack. Some say that they had had neither weapons nor ammunition at hand; others claim they were surprised in their sleep (as a result, some of them appear without boots or socks). The prisoners are willing to make statements, but are, however, not apprised of the intentions of their commanders (e.g., they do not even know the orders for the platoons or companies, or whether frontier positions should be held or not).[104]

During the course of its advance 129 Infantry Division was at first unable to clear rear areas of all Soviet troops (an almost universal problem in the opening days of the war). Dispersed enemy elements often emerged from their hiding places to attack the division's supply troops as they moved up behind the assault groups. From one farmstead captured by the advancing infantry early that morning, Soviet troops suddenly opened fire on German baggage train vehicles hours later. The Germans responded by pulverizing the farmstead with artillery fire, leaving behind 14 dead and seven wounded Russians. In a similar incident, this one in late afternoon, troops of 129 ID at the railroad station at Grajewo (captured that morning), were fired upon by Red Army soldiers concealed in a farmstead. A platoon from the division's replacement battalion (*Feldersatz-Btl.*) quickly cleared out the enemy, losing two men in the process. From the papers of a dead Russian officer it was discovered that Soviet battlegroups had been ordered to let the German combat troops pass by, and then fall upon their supply traffic circulating on the roads behind the front. Such skirmishes, so typical of Red Army tactics, were to continue for days.[105]

The experiences of Ninth Army's 256 Infantry Division (20 Army Corps) were also typical. The division attacked with all three infantry regiments up front, debouching from the Suwalki triangle in a southeasterly direction. While key terrain features and villages in the path of the advance were rapidly secured, the attacking battalions, on more than one occasion, were forced to clear tenaciously resisting Red Army troops from bunker positions. Moreover, a major axis of advance (*Vormarschstrasse*) taken by the division, as it pushed into Soviet held territory, turned out to be little more than a "sea of sand," as registered in the divisional war diary:

> The division's *Vormarschstrasse* via G. Haczitowka to Kuryanka is in a very poor condition. On this side of the frontier it was alright, but immediately after crossing over the frontier, the road went through a sea of sand. Many vehicles got stuck and could only be put back to rights with the help of others. In addition to that, the bridge across the stream along the border collapsed after a short time as a result of the great strain and heavy use it was subjected to by the GHQ artillery and the assault guns, and it could only be used again after a lot of intense work.[106]

Despite such difficulties – typical of those encountered up and down the front by the attacking German formations – the combat infantry of 256 ID pushed on impetuously toward their objectives. By 1230 hours, lead elements of 481 Infantry Regiment reached an airfield several kilometers north of the small town of Novy Dvor, just as a large group of Red Army aircraft were frantically trying to get airborne. The German infantry unleashed a torrent of heavy machine gun fire; supported by a battery of 75mm assault guns from 210 *Sturmgeschuetz* Battalion,[107] they shot up 38 of the Soviet planes on the ground, along with several hangars in which other planes were housed. By 1315, the town of Novy Dvor itself, with its thriving Jewish community dating back to the early 16th Century, was in German hands. Only six of the town's Jews would survive the war, three of them in the partisan movement.[108]

6.2.4: 3 Panzer Group

Panzer General Hermann Hoth's 3 Panzer Group began their attack at precisely 0305 hours, supported by the fighter, ground attack, dive bomber and bomber squadrons of Richthofen's 8 Air Corps. It was a starlit night, and Hoth and his two panzer corps commanders, Generals Rudolf Schmidt (39 Panzer Corps) and Adolf-Friedrich Kuntzen (57 Panzer Corps), watched from forward command posts as their armor and motorized infantry (along with two corps of marching infantry) headed due east out of the Suwalki triangle into Soviet occupied Lithuania. The Red Army border defenses on 3 Panzer Group's front were relatively weak, while many of the field fortifications were not even occupied; Soviet artillery was largely a non-factor. Facing Hoth was V.I. Morozov's 11 Army, which anchored the left wing of the Soviet Northwestern Front. Morozov's army was no match for Hoth's seasoned troops, and soon the Red Army defenders were disappearing into the woods in the face of the unrelenting German onslaught.[109] Where the enemy did put up a fight, he acquitted himself well, often fighting to the death. Few prisoners were taken.[110]

While Hoth's tank group attacked along a "dry" front, and thus did not have to contend with a major river barrier, it still had its own terrain challenges to contend with; particularly the thick belts of woodland and roads which were no more than sandy tracks, hardly suited for tanks and vehicles weighing many tons. The forward motion of the mobile units was also affected by the poor march discipline displayed by some units, while the armor of 57 Panzer Corps was slowed by numerous physical barriers placed in its path and stoutly defended by the enemy.[111]

The initial objective of 3 Panzer Group was to reach the Neman River on a broad front, cross over the river, and establish bridgeheads beyond it. The first to accomplish this goal was *Oberst* Karl Rothenburg's 25 Panzer Regiment of 7 Panzer Division (39 Panzer Corps). By midday, the tanks of Rothenburg's reinforced panzer regiment had thrust over 50 kilometers into enemy territory and, in a daring *coup de main*, seized intact the bridge spanning the river at Olita (Alytus), as well as a second bridge a short distance to the east. A captured Red Army engineer officer explained that he had been given orders to destroy both bridges at 1700 hours; adhering strictly to those orders, he had made no attempt to blow them up before the Germans arrived.[112]

The highly decorated Rothenburg, holder of the *Pour le Mérite* (World War I), and the *Ritterkreuz* (World War II), immediately pushed on across the river at both points before the defenders could react. Within an hour, however, the Soviets were furiously counterattacking with armor, buttressed by infantry and artillery. In the ensuing six-hour tank-on-tank engagement, pitting Soviet 5 Tank Division against 25 Panzer Regiment, 80 Russian tanks were knocked out, while Rothenburg's *Panzermaenner* clung tenaciously to their fragile bridgeheads. Yet the panzer regiment also suffered heavily: If only a handful of its tanks became permanent losses in the tank battle, many had been destroyed along the approach routes leading into Olita – victims of Soviet T-34s in good, hull-down fighting positions. Some of the German tanks – mostly light Pz 38(t)s of Czech design[113] – had their turrets blown clean off their hulls.[114]

If the Russians had gotten the worst of the tank duel on the eastern bank of the Neman, they had also fought with tenacity and courage. Reflecting on the furious combat this day, Rothenburg called it the "toughest battle of his life."[115] Only days later, the splendid panzer leader would be dead.[116]

One of the infantry units assigned to Hoth's armored group for the opening assault was 35 Infantry Division (5 Army Corps), affectionately referred to by its soldiers as the

"Fish Division" – its symbol a smiling fish – in a not so oblique reference to its commander, Maj.-Gen. Fischer von Weikersthal. Following the artillery preparation, *Gefreiter* Gerhard Bopp, a radio operator in the division's reconnaissance battalion (35 AA), moved out with his unit at 0330 hours; a half hour later (0403), they reached the border – here only discernable by bundles of straw – and advanced into Lithuania, moving through largely open and undulating terrain. In his personal diary, Bopp recorded the first hours of the campaign as they unfolded in his sector:

> All along the horizon columns of smoke from burning houses. The populace (Lithuanians) greets us joyfully, some with tears in their eyes. The girls and children throw flowers at us and all the vehicles are decked out with lilac blossoms, like in maneuvers … if there were no war.
>
> Around 0700, the first prisoners, shaven bald heads, Mongol faces, etc. Then the first fatalities … dead horses, etc. – through artillery fire before reaching the Kirsna River in the Didžioji region. Shells strike to the left and right of the road, but at great distances away. We get through unscathed. We capture the bridge over the Kirsna intact. After a brief stop, we continue to [a location] where there has been intense enemy resistance since midday, which is only broken that evening. There, bivouac and provisions are in short supply, because the roads are sandy and in poor condition, and so the field kitchen can barely get through. There is only a little warm food and coffee.[117]

The assault teams of 6 Infantry Division (6 Army Corps) went forward at 0305 hours, decamping from the Suwalki triangle in a thick fog, which severely limited visibility. They cut lanes through the enemy's wire entanglements, spread over the meadows and cornfields, and slipped across the frontier. A flight of gull-winged *Stukas* peeled off and dived on the border town of Kalvaria, where a Russian staff was thought to be quartered, leaving it enveloped in smoke and flames. The division advanced with two regiments in the line (18 and 58 IR) and one in reserve (37 IR).[118] The attackers, meeting negligible resistance, rapidly gained their initial objectives; by late morning, however, a battalion of 18 Infantry Regiment, supported by artillery and combat engineers, was abruptly halted by a cluster of concrete bunkers near Akmenynai. The bunkers were savagely defended by their occupants, the battalion sustaining serious casualties. Here resistance would not be broken until the next day, and only then with the support of Flak artillery and flamethrowers.[119]

Soon the first prisoners were being shepherded to the rear. "We gazed at them eagerly," recounted *Assistenzarzt* Heinrich Haape. "They were about a platoon strong and wore shabby khaki-yellow uniforms, loosely-flapping, unmilitary looking blouses and had clean-shaven heads. Their heavy faces were expressionless." As the sun rose in the sky, the day grew hot. Haape continued: "As the men marched the dust rose, until we were all covered in a light yellow coating – battledress, rifles, faces and hands. Men and vehicles assumed ghostly outlines in the dust-laden air. I wet my dry lips with a little water from my bottle and was glad when the order was given to halt. It was noon, and we rested in a small wood." Suddenly, Haape craned his neck skyward, his attention riveted on a formation of Russian bombers approaching from the east:

> They circled to make sure of their target. But this time they had to reckon with the Messerschmitts. The 109s swooped like hawks into a flight of pigeons. They attacked from the sun, firing as they dived. Breaking off the attack they zoomed to regain height for another attack and one by one the bombers were picked off. One Russian burst into flames, a second followed, and like torches they sank toward the ground. It surprised me to see how slowly they fell. A wing broke off another

bomber and the plane spun earthward. I noticed two parachutes drifting gently above it. Our fighters continued the attacks until every bomber had been shot down. The action had taken 10 minutes at most.[120]

A dispatch rider came roaring up to Haape on a motorcycle. One of the bombers had crashed and exploded among the staff of an artillery battalion, engulfing many of the men in a wall of flame. Extra medical help was urgently needed. By the time Haape arrived, 15 of the artillerymen were already dead; behind a hedge lay nine more wounded men, five of them so badly burned he held out no hope of their survival beyond a day or two. The conscientious doctor did what he could, most importantly sending for a field ambulance. Two hours later Haape was again underway, looking for his battalion, with which he had broken contact.[121]

By early afternoon matters were deemed well enough in hand for corps headquarters to issue orders to 6 ID to begin a general pursuit of the enemy. With Russian resistance largely shattered, the division's infantry marched on eastward, along two axes of advance (*Vormarschstrassen*) in the direction of the Neman River, more than 70 kilometers beyond the frontier. By late afternoon, the 6 ID's improvised reconnaissance battalion,[122] led by Cavalry Captain (*Rittmeister*) Georg *Freiherr* von Boeselager, had already covered more than 50 kilometers. Pushing on through endless tracks of forest and marsh, Boeselager then made out for the bridge over the Neman at Prienai, only to be stopped abruptly by a well-organized and superior enemy defense, which inflicted considerable losses on the squadron. The capture of Prienai, the crossing of the Neman, would have to wait until the following day.[123]

On the far left flank of 3 Panzer Group, abutting the boundary with Army Group North, 26 Infantry Division (6 Army Corps) attacked alongside its neighbor to the south (6 ID). The 1st Battalion of the division's 77 Infantry Regiment quickly reached its initial objective, the opposing high ground, with no enemy contact; 2nd Battalion, after eliminating several Russian combat outposts (*Gefechtsvorposten*), also advanced successfully. Only the regiment's 3rd Battalion, its companies echeloned behind the 2nd Battalion, encountered stiff resistance – from an NKVD border strongpoint that fought to the end, punishing the attackers with painful losses.[124]

Following capture of its initial objectives, 77 IR sent out well-armed patrols to reconnoiter, but they reported no contact with the enemy, who had apparently withdrawn. By late morning, the regiment's battalions had reassembled and were ready to begin their pursuit march.[125] It was a march which they – along with 35 ID, 6 ID, and dozens more of the foot infantry divisions – would continue for weeks, behind the tanks and mobile infantry motoring far beyond them to the east. For hundreds of kilometers they would march, in insufferable heat along sandy tracks – their boots kicking up clouds of fine dust which engulfed uniforms and equipment and filled every pore – across desolate terrain and through belts of primeval woodlands; all the while maintaining constant combat readiness because of the threat posed by dispersed Red Army units, which lingered in the forests, marshes and cornfields, prepared to fight it out rather than to surrender. The days and weeks ahead would often push the *Landser* to the limits of their physical and psychic endurance, and sometimes well beyond. A vitally important story, but a story to be told later on.

6.3: Berlin, Germany, and the Start of the War

Hitler had withdrawn to his chambers at 2.30 in the morning on Sunday, 22 June, with the beginning of Operation *Barbarossa*, the war which he – and he alone – had willed into existence, just minutes away. In the days prior to the start of the campaign, the "Fuehrer" had grown increasingly anxious, as if tormented by some dreadful harbinger of what might lay before him and his 1000-year Reich. And yet, like the soldiers at the front, whose conscious fears dissolved into purposeful action as they poured across the frontier into Russia, Hitler's anxieties seemed to give way now that the die had finally been cast. According to his diplomatic liaison, Walther Hewel, a "tranquil, self-possessed mood" seemed to overcome the Chancellery in Berlin on this "morning of tumultuous events." According to David Irving:

> It was almost like any other Sunday, except that Hitler and Ribbentrop fell fast asleep after lunch. The foreign minister had summoned the Soviet ambassador at 3.30 that morning to break the grim news to him, and then in rapid succession he summoned the representatives of Germany's allies – Italy, Japan, Hungary, Finland and Romania. At 5.30 Dr Goebbels had spoken, and at 6.00 Ribbentrop had addressed the press, surrounded by his assembled staff. Many of Hitler's adjutants, wilting under the Central European sun, went swimming.
>
> By the time Hitler awoke late that afternoon, his armies were already many miles inside the Russian frontier, and the first reactions of the world were being monitored. Italy had honored her obligations with notable speed: at 3:00 p.m. Rome had cabled that Italy regarded herself as at war with Russia since 5.30 that morning. Romanian troops had cross the Prut and were fighting in the provinces invaded by Russia 12 months before. Madrid telephoned that a Spanish volunteer legion was being recruited to join the crusade. An ecstatic Admiral Horthy exulted at the "magnificent" news and told the German ambassador that this was a day of which he had dreamed for 22 years – mankind would thank Hitler for this deed for centuries to come. Hungary dutifully broke off diplomatic relations with Moscow before Hitler retired to bed, but this was as far as it would go. At 6:00 p.m. a disappointed General Jodl telephoned his liaison officer in Budapest to remind the Hungarians of the historic importance of the hour.[126]

As was his custom, Hitler sat up late with his staff, monitoring the military reports pouring in from the east. The *Luftwaffe* had struck Kiev, Kovno (Kaunas), Sevastopol, Murmansk, Odessa and other cities in European Russia, while dozens of Soviet forward air bases had been smashed and more than a thousand Red Army aircraft destroyed on the ground and in the air. Good news also arrived from North Africa, where Rommel's *Afrika Korps* was on the move. Earlier that day, the first of 1418 days of war between Russia and Germany, which would visit untold suffering and death upon so many millions, and bring catastrophe to Europe overall, Hitler had sent a telegram to Lt.-Col. Werner Moelders, Commander, 51 Fighter Wing, congratulating him on his 72nd aerial victory and awarding him the Swords to the Knight's Cross with Oak Leaves. A week later, Moelders, while supporting the operations of Guderian's panzer group with his Bf 109s, would become the first fighter pilot of any belligerent nation to record 80 kills during the Second World War, tying him with the total attained by Manfred von Richthofen in the First World War.[127]

Propaganda Minister Goebbels, who had been at Hitler's side in the Reich Chancellery during the final anxious hours before war with Russia began, recorded his impressions of this apocalyptic Sunday in his diary:

23 June 1941:
Yesterday: an oppressively hot day. Our troops won't have it easy in battle. Molotov gives a speech: a crazed rant, and an appeal to patriotism, maudlin complaints, the fear can be seen between the lines: "We will prevail," he says. The poor man! ... All Europe is experiencing a wave of anti-Bolshevism. The *Fuehrer's* decision is the greatest sensation ever imaginable. Our air assault begins in grand style ... On Russian towns, including Kiev ... and airfields ... The Russians are already experiencing very heavy aerial losses. During an attack on Tilsit [now Sovetsk], they lost 22 out of 73 attacking planes.

The operations are going to plan ... The Russian troop concentrations ... will suffer the same catastrophe [as the French in 1870]. The Russians are only putting up modest resistance for the time being. But their air force has already suffered terrible losses: 200 shot down, 200 destroyed on the ground, and 200 damaged. Those are pretty serious losses.

We will succeed soon. We simply have to succeed soon. Morale in the population is a bit low. Although the people want peace, they do not want it as a result of defeat; but the initiation of every new theater of war makes them worried and anxious. . .

New reports arrive nearly every minute. Generally very positive. Up to this time 1000 Russian planes destroyed. That's a nasty shock ... All of the day's objectives are achieved. No complications so far. We rest completely assured. The Soviet regime will go up like tinderwood ... Once again it has become very late. Sleep has become a luxury for us in recent days.[128]

If Hitler and Goebbels were ecstatic about the magnificent successes of the opening hours of the campaign,[129] their generals were no less carried away by the initial victories of their armed forces. An event that day at Army High Command (OKH) headquarters in Zossen, south of Berlin, graphically underscores this point: Deputy Chief of Staff for Operations (*Oberquartiermeister I*), Maj.-Gen. Friedrich Paulus, the man who, more than any other, had been responsible for developing and refining operational war plans for Russia, briefed Field Marshal von Brauchitsch, C-in-C of the Army, on the first reports coming in from the front. The reports were auspicious. Brauchitsch asked Paulus how long he thought the war against Russia would last. Paulus, the consummate general staff officer, and normally sober judge of events, predicted the war would last only six to eight weeks. "Ja, Paulus, you are certainly correct," replied the field marshal. "We will need about eight weeks for Russia."[130]

At 5.30 that morning, the new Russian fanfare, based on a symphonic theme from Franz von Liszt, had reverberated for the first time over all German radio stations. In sonorous tones, befitting the breathtaking reality of the moment, Dr Goebbels read out Hitler's "Proclamation to the German People" from his office in the Reich Ministry for Propaganda. "It was," writes Roger Moorhouse in his fine history of Berlin during the war years, "a strange document."[131] "German People! National Socialists!" it began: "Troubled by deep concerns, condemned to months of silence, the hour has arrived in which I may finally speak openly." What followed was a long, meandering attack on Great Britain, which took up fully half of the proclamation. Hitler then turned to Russia, offering a point-by-point refutation of Soviet claims and demands, and justifying the new German front in the east as a pre-emptive measure. The proclamation ended as dramatically as it had begun:

> *Deutsches Volk!* At this very moment a concentration of forces is underway which, in its extent and scope, is the largest the world has ever seen. The fighters of the victor of Narvik at the Arctic Ocean stand allied with our Finnish comrades ... The formations of the German *Ostfront* extend from East Prussia to the Carpathian Mountains. At the Prut River, at the lower reaches of the Danube to the shores of the Black Sea, German and Romanian soldiers are united under [Romanian] head of state Antonescu.
>
> The task of this front is thus no longer the protection of individual countries, but the safeguarding of Europe and with that the salvation of all.
>
> I have, therefore, today decided to place the destiny and future of the German *Reich* and our *Volk* in the hands of our soldiers.
>
> May the Lord God aid us in this very struggle!

Adolf Hitler[132]
Berlin, 22 June 1941.

Public reaction to the sudden outbreak of war with Soviet Russia was mixed. In Berlin, the official public response was stoical, demonstrating "complete trust in our *Wehrmacht*" and "facing the coming events with calmness and martial determination."[133] The reality was rather different. Many people, particularly those who had not seen it coming, reacted with a profound sense of shock.[134] Marie Vassiltchikov, a young White Russian émigré fortunate enough to have landed a minor position in the German Foreign Office due to her language skills, *had* seen the war coming, but was still "thunderstruck" by the news.[135] Marianne Miethe, a 20-year-old employee in an accountancy firm in Hirschfelde, greeted the start of Operation *Barbarossa* with dread, and a dire prediction from her father-in-law:

> How happy we were about the non-aggression pact between the German Reich and the Soviet Union, and we had no inkling that this was merely a clever move on the part of both the dictators, Hitler and Stalin, in particular to carve up Poland and win time before the outbreak of war. We thought that the non-aggression pact between the German Reich and the Soviet Union could pave the way for a peaceful solution to the whole conflict.
>
> The special announcement about the entry into war with the Soviet Union hit us like a bolt from the blue and we thought with dread back to Napoleon's Russian campaign. The critics, among them my father-in-law, said: "Now we have lost the war." We hoped that these fears would not come to pass and had no idea of the suffering that lay ahead for humanity.[136]

Yet there was also a profound sense of liberation among many ordinary Germans, as the weeks fraught with speculation and rumor were finally over and "Germany could at last engage with what many of them regarded as their country's most dangerous opponent. Even the less ideologically committed would have absorbed the vehement anti-Soviet rhetoric of the early 1930s and adjusted only with difficulty to the tactical alliance with Moscow which had opened the war."[137] The thoughts of Frau "A.N." on this day were far from atypical:

> Well, I had just turned the radio on and heard this: the latest reports from the *Ostfront*, and this brings me straight to the thing that no doubt concerns every German the most today. When I switched on the radio this morning and then, totally unsuspecting, heard the *Fuehrer*'s proclamation, I was totally speechless at first. And yet, I don't know, I don't think anybody really took the friendship between the USSR and the German Reich very seriously. We all had our doubts about whether this would go well and we didn't trust the Russians.
>
> What it must have cost the *Fuehrer* to have to associate with Stalin at all and to go into a friendly relationship with him! Today I came to realize with complete clarity the full extent of his diplomacy. This whole matter has been of great concern to him. You can just sense that. And when you just think about it, you feel really quite humble.
>
> What is our little bit of suffering, our cares, and the tiny sacrifices that have to be made in this wartime economy? But that's the way we are, really we don't reflect enough, and then we just get so wrapped up in personal matters, and life just goes by.
>
> At any rate, the struggle will surely be tough, and yet many will breathe a sigh of relief after the long weeks of suspense. For, at the end of the day, a proper soldier longs for battle and victory so that he may again go about his normal tasks.[138]

Harry Flannery, an American journalist in Berlin, in his book *Assignment to Berlin*, published in 1942, recorded the mood in the German capital on this clear, bright early summer day:

> Within a few hours the first extra editions of the papers were on the streets. As usual, all were single sheets. The *Voelkischer Beobachter* headlines were typical: "War Front from North Cape to Black Sea in Bringing to Reckoning of the Moscow Traitors. Two-faced Jewish Bolshevist Rulers in the Kremlin Lengthen the War for the Benefit of England."
>
> The people bought the extras almost as fast as they appeared. For the first time since the war began, there was momentary enthusiasm among the German populace. The war against Russia was the first popular campaign that had been launched. None of the Germans had ever been able to understand why a treaty should have been made with the Soviets, after they had been the main object of denunciation since 1933. Now they had a sense of relief, a feeling of final understanding. I listened to their conversations around the newsstands and on the subways. I talked with a number of them. For the first time they were excited about the war.
>
> "Now," they said, "we are fighting our real enemy."[139]

That most of the three million *Landser* now advancing the boundaries of the Greater German Reich further to the east also shared such sentiments about Bolshevist Russia is hardly surprising. For what is a modern, mass military organization if not an organic outgrowth of the society that creates it?

6.4: Stalin & Soviet Western Front Respond

The winter of 1941 had been unusually long in Moscow. Snow was falling there as late as the second week of June.[140] On Saturday, 21 June 1941, a warm sun finally broke through and throngs of people made out for the city's parks. Despite the disquieting rumors of impending war with Germany, the official mood in Stalin's capital was one of robust confidence. Only a week before, on 14 June, the Tass news agency had released its now infamous communiqué, insisting that rumors of Germany's intention to tear up the non-aggression pact and attack Russia were "without any foundation." The communiqué also attempted to explain away the now obvious German buildup taking place along the Soviet Union's western frontier, stating that the German troop movements were, "one must suppose, prompted by motives which have no bearing on Soviet-German relations."[141] In reality, however, the Soviet political and military leadership were, by now, seriously worried, even panicked, over the burgeoning possibility of an imminent German attack.

In Berlin, the day (21 June) was also pleasantly warm, and most members of the Soviet embassy staff were resting or swimming in the halcyon surroundings of the Potsdam and Wannsee parks. But appearances can be deceiving, for frenetic efforts had been underway for days at the embassy to open a dialogue with their German counterparts, the aim of which was to gain direct access to Hitler. Yet all attempts to make contact with the German Foreign Office were futile now: Hitler's foreign minister, Ribbentrop, had deliberately departed Berlin early that morning, leaving instructions with his staff to hold the Russian ambassador at bay.[142]

Rebuffed in Berlin, the Soviets turned frantically to the German ambassador in Moscow, Schulenburg, rushing him to the Kremlin at 6:00 p.m. A clearly agitated Molotov complained about the ongoing violations of Soviet airspace by German military aircraft; furthermore, he wished to know why members of the German embassy staff, along with their wives, had suddenly left the country, resulting in rumors of imminent war. Why had the German government not responded to the "peace loving" Tass communiqué? What was behind the German discontent – "if it actually exists" – with the Soviet Union? Schulenburg's replies failed to allay the Soviet foreign minister's anxieties. The German ambassador did, however, drop "his final hint about the German intentions, which obviously he did not report home. He admitted that 'posing those issues was justified,' but unfortunately he was in no position to answer, as Berlin 'kept him entirely in the dark.' Rather pathetically, Molotov whined that 'there was no reason for the German government to be dissatisfied with Russia.'"[143]

Stalin had arrived at the Kremlin late that Saturday, in the early hours of the afternoon. The massive fortress, one of the largest structures in Europe, was now more than four-and-a-half centuries old, and its massive, red brick walls and tall towers loomed menacingly over the city.[144] By now, the Soviet dictator was well aware that events were rapidly slipping from his grasp. That evening, beginning around 7:00 p.m., Stalin met with many of his closest associates, among them Molotov, Beria, and his top generals, Timoshenko and Zhukov. Since the beginning of June, Stalin had been subjected to an unremitting stream of warnings about Germany's nefarious intentions, but he had tended to fob them off as "provocations." Now he learned that a German defector had crossed the border and told the local Russian commander that war was to begin on 22 June – in other words, in a few hours.[145]

Although he was now worried, Stalin, still unable to face head on the disaster about to strike, flirted with the idea that the German generals had deliberately sent the defector "to provoke a conflict." Nevertheless, after lengthy discussions in his study with both his Commissar (Minister) of Defense, Timoshenko, and Chief of Staff, Zhukov, present, Stalin was finally stirred to issue a directive alerting the armed forces. Directive No. 1, as it was called, was issued by the Main Military Soviet. It read in part: "In the course of 22-23 June 1941, sudden attacks by the Germans on the fronts of Leningrad, Baltic Special, Western Special, Kiev Special and Odessa Special Military Districts will be possible. The task of our forces is not to yield to any provocations likely to prompt major complications."[146] Diffident and confusing in its content, the order went on to stipulate that, during the early morning of 22 June, the "firing positions of the fortified regions on the state border are to be occupied secretly," while all aircraft were to be "dispersed and carefully camouflaged" and "all units … put in a state of military preparedness without calling up supplementary troops."[147]

After the order had been encoded, it was dispatched to the headquarters of the military districts sometime after midnight.[148] "Discreetly and effectively blockaded by German saboteurs … the Red Army frontier units never received Stalin's directive. Their inland headquarters did – but not until 3.00 o'clock in the morning. As Zhukov and Timoshenko had predicted, the directive caused immense confusion. What should the commanders expect – border clashes or war? If they were not supposed to yield to provocations, should they react at all?"[149]

Having done what he could – or, at least, what he was willing to do – the *vozhd*, after final discussions with Molotov and Beria, felt confident enough to return to his dacha outside Moscow at 11:00 p.m. Timoshenko and Zhukov, however, hardly propitiated by the general warning to the troops, returned to the Ministry of Defense, where they remained on alert. About midnight, they learned of a second deserter: A soldier from a German infantry division had swum across the river and informed the NKGB border police that the attack would start at 4.00 in the morning. Stalin, although promptly notified at his dacha, was unmoved. He retired to bed.[150]

Meanwhile, Soviet headquarters charged with protecting the western border, were growing increasingly agitated due to the ominous and burgeoning level of activity now unfolding along the German side of the frontier. The chief of staff of the Baltic Special

Military District reported that: "The Germans have finished the construction of the bridges across the [Neman] ... The civilians have been advised to evacuate to a depth of 20 kilometers from the frontier." Another report, from the C-in-C of Soviet 3 Army, Lt.-Gen. V.I. Kuznetsov, indicated that the Germans had cleared barbed wire barriers at one of the border crossings, and that the roar of many engines was heard from the woods in that region. These reports, and many others like them, were dutifully passed on to Stalin that evening, before he returned to his dacha.[151]

Not everyone, however, shared such concerns. General D.G. Pavlov, commander of what, in a few hours, was to become Western Front, was 250 kilometers east of the frontier, attending a play, a patriotic musical at a theater in Minsk. Despite the growing buildup of German forces along the border and the continued violations of Soviet airspace by German reconnaissance planes, Stalin had ordered his commanders not to worry, and Pavlov considered it his duty to showcase his *sangfroid*. Just before midnight, Pavlov's chief of intelligence visited his superior's box, whispering that the Germans were bringing more troops up to the frontier. Intent on avoiding a potential German provocation, Pavlov brusquely dismissed the warning: "Nonsense," he said, "This simply cannot be."[152] And yet: While General Pavlov enjoyed the show, German commanders were reading Hitler's proclamation to their men, "huddled in small groups around them, by the dim illumination of shielded flashlights."[153]

The commander of Pavlov's 4 Army, Lt.-Gen. A.A. Korobkov, was at a theater in Kobrin, attending a popular operetta, *The Gypsy Baron*. He knew that his superior wanted everyone to stay calm, and Korobkov was nothing if not a dutiful soldier: If Pavlov went to the theater, he would do so as well. Still, he was distracted and unable to enjoy the entertainment. In the early evening, Korobkov had telephoned Maj.-Gen. Klimovskikh, Chief of Staff, Western Special Military District, and reported that the Germans had moved closer to the border. He asked for permission to order his troops to occupy their battle stations:

> Klimovskikh said that that was impossible. To Korobkov's immense relief, he was able to leave the theater early. At about 11.00 o'clock, Klimovskikh called and told him to go to headquarters immediately and remain alert throughout the night. Unlike their carefree and trusting boss [i.e., Pavlov], Klimovskikh had a sharp mind. Having smelled a rat, he was now taking his own quiet precautions.
>
> Still forbidden to communicate anything to his troops, Korobkov sent for his staff officers. In the headquarters, the officers wandered from one room to another, discussing the situation in whispers and trying to determine whether the sudden summons meant war. All divisions stationed at the frontier as well as the border guards kept reporting abnormal activity on the German side of the Bug River.[154]

At 2.00 in the morning, Korobkov received a call from the border city of Brest-Litovsk. The power, it seemed, was out, and there was no running water. Minutes later, the town of Kobrin, site of 4 Army headquarters, also went "dark." Thirty minutes after that, the general became aware that all communications with Pavlov's headquarters and with his troops along the border had been cut.[155]

At 3:30 a.m., the coded telephones at the Ministry of Defense began to jingle, bringing reports of heavy German shell fire along the entire frontier. Zhukov immediately telephoned Stalin at his dacha. The *vozhd* said nothing at first. Only his heavy breathing was audible. In spite of Zhukov's remonstrations, Stalin refused to sanction countermeasures. Within an hour, both Zhukov and Timoshenko were rushing to the Kremlin; when they arrived there, they encountered a "very pale" Stalin, "sitting at the table clutching a loaded unlit pipe in both hands."[156] With him were Molotov, NKVD Chief Beria, and Marshal K.E. Voroshilov, the former People's Commissar of Defense who had made dancing lessons mandatory for officers of the Red Army.[157] Stalin, while clearly "bewildered," desperately refused to let go of the thought that it all might only be "a provocation of the German officers." He was, writes historian Gabriel Gordetsky,

> little moved by Timoshenko's attempts to bring him down to earth, and ignored the Marshal's insistence that rather than being a local incident this was an all-out offensive along the entire front. Stalin simply dug in his heels, suggesting that, "if it were necessary to organize a provocation, then the German generals would bomb their own cities." After some reflection he added, "Hitler surely does not know about this."[158]

Even after Molotov had met with Schulenburg, who informed the Soviet foreign minister, "with the deepest regret," that his government had felt it necessary to take "military measures" to counter Soviet troop concentrations along the eastern frontier, Stalin refused to exclude the possibility that Germany was simply trying to submit Russia to political blackmail. Not until 7.15 that morning were the Soviet armies in the west directed to "destroy the enemy forces" at once through the execution of "deep operations," in which the Soviet Air Force was to play a decisive role by disrupting German ground and air forces to a depth of 100-150 kilometers beyond the frontier. But the Soviet Air Force was already undergoing its destruction at the hands of hundreds of German bombers, fighters and destroyer aircraft, operating with surgical precision. Thus the orders (Directive No. 2) were never carried out.[159]

In his fascinating account of the "tragic first ten days" of Operation *Barbarossa* from the Soviet perspective, Russian historian Constantine Pleshakov trenchantly depicts the way the war sounded, looked and felt to the Russian people – civilians and military alike – in its terrible first moments:

> The war first reached people in sounds. Up and down the western border, people were woken at dawn by ferocious deafening blasts that went on and on, making the ground and the buildings shake. Some thought it was an earthquake. The mistake was understandable – most men and women hastily putting on their clothes had never experienced an earthquake or, for that matter, war.
>
> Other sounds followed – ones that definitely could not be caused by an earthquake. Buglers' horns trumpeted; officers yelled, "Alarm! Alarm!" and "Out! Quick!;" and an occasional hysterical voice wailed, "It's war!"
>
> The soldiers were met with a different kind of sound as soon as they left their barracks or tents and ran outside. The noise was very close, very difficult to describe, but unmistakably deadly: the humming of shrapnel whizzing by. The invisible pieces of steel sounded almost alive, like a swarm of locusts, perhaps. "Something buzzing flew by," a young lieutenant wrote, "and, having hit the sand, went quiet."
>
> After the soldiers adjusted to the sounds, they noticed the fires. In the dim light, flames dotted the horizon, leaping, flaring, blinking, and spreading. They looked particularly sinister in the woods, though in the cities they did more damage.
>
> The German planes were faintly visible in the dawn air. Tight black packages – the bombs, or "lead hail," as many on the ground put it – separated from their fuselages. Boys climbed the trees to see the assaulting aircraft more clearly, but that didn't make the sight more realistic; it was "like watching a movie," one recalled.
>
> When the sun rose, it subdued the glare of the fires, and pitch-black plumes of thick smoke dominated the landscape. The sun unveiled the devastation: corpses

lying on the ground, buildings turned into smoking piles of rubble, burned-out cars littering the streets, craters bored by bombs. Parents hastily escorting their children out of town shielded their eyes, wanting to protect them from seeing the carnage. Most of the frontier ran near a river, and some people felt as if the water had turned brown with blood, although this might have been just their imagination.

Almost everyone noticed a strange byproduct of the shock: many people were worrying about a trivial loss or an insignificant problem. A border guard who had been showered with German shrapnel as he crossed the Bug River loudly lamented the loss of his service cap. Another soldier, trapped in a fort on the border, suddenly reached for his Komsomol membership card[160] and complained that it had no stamp indicating that he had paid his dues in June. Often people found themselves absorbed by something totally irrelevant to their own survival, like a flock of rooks circling some felled trees that had once contained their nests.[161]

At Soviet 4 Army headquarters in Kobrin, the soldiers sent to repair their communications reported that hundreds of feet of telegraph wire were cut. At 3:30 a.m., Korobkov finally made contact with Western Front headquarters in Minsk, receiving instructions to place his troops on combat alert. Huddled with his staff in the headquarters' basement, Korobkov, by the faint light of kerosene lamps, struggled to contact his units to order them to their battle stations. Before he could do so, 42 Rifle Division reported that Brest was under attack. Fifteen minutes later (4:30 a.m.), the commander of an air force division burst into the headquarters, yelling that German bombers were obliterating his airfields. Before he could say more, an explosion rocked the building, followed by the drone of aircraft engines. Officers who had served in Spain at once recognized the sound for what it was – the unmistakable roar of Junkers bombers. After the planes had loosed their bombs, Korobkov ordered the immediate evacuation of the building. But before the headquarters staff had finished extricating the important documents from the safes, the *Luftwaffe* struck again. Seconds later, 4 Army headquarters was enveloped in smoke, fire and dust – the surviving Soviet officers hiding in ditches.[162]

Shortly before the destruction of 4 Army headquarters, General Pavlov, in Minsk, received a disconcerting telephone call from Lt.-Gen. V.I. Kuznetsov, the commander of Soviet 3 Army. The Germans, he said, were bombing Grodno, a major city at the northern end of the Belostok salient. The army's communications were destroyed, and Kuznetsov could no longer contact his troops. Pavlov was flummoxed – "I don't understand what's going on," he replied.[163]

And so it was throughout this terrible Sunday, 22 June 1941. Confronted by the overwhelming onslaught of Field Marshal von Bock's Army Group Center, Pavlov's Western Front experienced an almost immediate paralysis of its command and control. The headquarters of Korobkov's 4 Army, destroyed in the opening hours of Operation *Barbarossa*, was never able to establish reliable contact with headquarters above and below it; and even though Kuznetsov's 3 and Golubev's 10 Armies "were in tenuous radio communications with Pavlov's headquarters, they were hardly more functional as command elements."[164] Adding to the problem was the fact that the Soviet officer corps did not trust wireless communications, "which seemed to them too vulnerable in a society obsessed with control.

As a result of that distrust, the military districts were acquiring radios slowly and were hesitant to put them to use. Of course each radio network was to have special operational and reserve airwaves, each radio its own call sign. The wartime airwaves and call signs were different from the ones normally used, and the military staff knew that it would take about a week to introduce them to every army unit down to battalion level. It was decided that, for "security reasons," the call signs couldn't be communicated to the troops earlier, which meant that on June 22 the Red Army radios were not used.

Cable communications were mistakenly believed to be more reliable. In fact, only the last few miles of cable, in the immediate vicinity of front headquarters, ran underground. Most of the hundreds of miles of telegraph wires hung on poles lining the country's highways and railroads – an obvious and easy target for Hitler's commandos. All a saboteur had to do to disable a division was to cut out 100 feet of cable at the highway nearest its headquarters.

In something approaching criminal negligence, the telegraph lines had been left unprotected on the night of June 21. Neither the army nor the police, Zhukov nor Beria, the local field commanders nor the police chiefs had bothered to take the most obvious precautions.[165]

General Pavlov was not a man endowed with strategic vision. He had no idea what Bock's ultimate designs were and "spent the day of June 22 in anguish, shuttling between different units and vainly trying to figure out what was going on."[166] But with his communications knocked out by the German attack, he was unable to reach most of his generals. What he did know was that his supporting air forces were all but gone – for the most part obliterated on their airfields in the opening German strikes. In the first hours of the war, Western Front had lost hundreds of aircraft and the *Luftwaffe* now had firm control of the skies.

In an effort to gain some control over his tottering front, Pavlov ordered his deputy, Lt.-Gen. I.V. Boldin, to fly to 10 Army headquarters near Belostok and organize a counterattack. Flying through airspace swarming with German planes, Boldin somehow managed to reach Golubev's headquarters – two tents in a small wood by an airstrip. The 10 Army commander had been struggling to put up resistance despite shattered telephones, constant radio jamming and general chaos resulting from teams of German *Abwehr* (intelligence and counterintelligence) agents active at his rear. Not until 23 June did he try to attack with his mechanized corps in adherence to prewar plans; within days his army would cease to exist, except for stragglers struggling to break out of German encirclements.[167]

If Pavlov knew little about the actual extent of the catastrophe unfolding along his front, in Moscow they knew even less. In fact, the situation was far worse than anyone at the Kremlin or the Ministry of Defense believed, resulting in a series of hopeless orders for counterstrokes with formations that no longer existed. At 2115 that evening, Stalin and Timoshenko issued Directive No. 3, calling for a general counterattack along the entire eastern front. Specifically, Northwestern and Western Fronts were to attack, encircle and destroy Army Group North, while Southwestern Front was to execute the same mission against Army Group South. Western Front was also ordered to contain the advance of Bock's Army Group Center along the Warsaw-Minsk axis. "This directive," argues historian Geoffrey Roberts:

> was broadly in line with prewar plans for Red Army counter-offensive action in the event of war. It indicates that Stalin and the High Command fully expected the Red Army would be able to cope with the German attack and to carry out its own strategic missions, including mounting an effective counter-invasion of German territory. Indeed, according to the third directive, the Red Army was expected to achieve its initial objectives in East Prussia and southern Poland within two days.[168]

On the evening of 22 June, Pavlov and his chief of staff reported to Moscow that their 3 and 10 Armies had been pushed back, but only negligibly. 4 Army, they assured their superiors, "is fighting, it is estimated, on the line Mel'nik – Brest-Litovsk – Vlodava." Basically unaware of the situation, having lost control over his armies, Pavlov was now reporting "estimates."[169]

The night brought temporary respite to elements of the Soviet border commands. It also brought the first operational digest (*svodka*) from the Soviet General Staff, completed by 2200 hours. "Of the urgency of the situation," writes the late John Erickson, "it contained not the slightest trace. Blatant with complacency and swelled with ignorance, it read:

> Regular troops of the German Army during the course of 22 June conducted operations against frontier defense units of the USSR, attaining insignificant success in a number of sectors. During the second half of the day, with the arrival of forward elements of the field forces of the Red Army, the attacks by German troops along most of the length of our frontiers were beaten off and losses inflicted on the enemy.[170]

Early that afternoon, Stalin, convinced that his commanders were simply "not up to it" – "our front commanders ... have evidently become somewhat confused" – had decided that several very senior officers, acting as representatives of the High Command, should be sent to the fronts to find out what was going on and to offer assistance. Late that evening, the chosen officers (Zhukov among them) began to set out from Moscow for their separate destinations, where they were to observe first hand just what the Germans' "insignificant success" had amounted to:

> Even the brash and bumptious Kulik[171] was aghast at what he found at the battlefront. General Zhukov, however, had few illusions: now with the South-Western Front, having fed on the tea and sandwiches the aircrew scraped up for him during his flight to Kiev, he learned from Vatutin[172] (now placed in charge of the General Staff) on the evening of 22 June that the General Staff lacked "accurate information" about either Soviet or German strengths and movements, that no information was to hand about losses and that there was no contact with Kuznetsov[173] or Pavlov in the Baltic and Western theaters. In spite of this, Stalin was sticking grimly to *Directive No. 3* and ordered that Zhukov's signature be added to the document even in his absence.[174]

Over the next few days, Stalin and Timoshenko stubbornly insisted that Directive No.3 be carried out,[175] although it had long been consigned to irrelevance by a situation shifting much too rapidly for them to grasp. Except on the Southwestern Front, where Zhukov's skill and experience – as well as his brutality – weighed in the balance, contributing to the initial success of the massive Soviet armored counterthrusts on this front, the outcome was to be "uniformly disastrous." By 23 June, the dangerous gap between Northwestern and Western Fronts, ripped open by the advancing German armor, had already widened to well over 100 kilometers.[176] The Soviet armies protecting the frontier were being routed, enveloped, and destroyed. Within six days, German tanks would be rumbling into Minsk, more than 250 kilometers beyond the frontier. Of all the disasters that befell the Red Army in the initial days of Operation *Barbarossa*, it was the break up and disintegration of Pavlov's Western Front that "reduced Stalin to wild, if impotent, fury."[177] He would soon settle accounts with the men he held responsible for the disaster.

6.5: The *Luftwaffe* has a Field Day

At 0315 hours, the first wave of the *Luftwaffe* assault, 30 He 111 and Do 17Z bombers flown by hand-picked crews, began their low level attacks on selected Soviet fighter bases beyond the front of Army Group Center, striking them with hundreds of small SD-2 fragmentation bombs. The two-kilogram bombs burst among the rows of Soviet aircraft, arranged wingtip to wingtip on their airfields, with personnel tents located nearby. After all, it was peacetime, and the Russian planes were neither camouflaged nor had they been dispersed. Multiple explosions soon engulfed the rows of aircraft; airframes were lacerated and fuel tanks punctured, the latter causing multiple fireballs that tossed columns of dense black smoke into the dawn sky. In the resulting chaos dazed ground crews struggled desperately to combat the fires but were frustrated by delayed-action explosions. With no instructions from superior headquarters, each base coped as best it could.[178]

As the sun rose, these initial attacks were followed by the main body of the *Luftwaffe's* strike force, consisting of hundreds of medium bombers, dive-bombers, fighters and destroyer aircraft.[179] The weather was virtually ideal – warm and sunny with hardly a cloud in the sky. On the central front, the aerial assault was conducted by Field Marshal Kesselring's 2 Air Fleet, with its 2 Air Corps operating from the Warsaw – Brest-Litovsk – Deblin area, and 8 Air Corps out of the Suwalki triangle; together they possessed nearly 1000 operational combat aircraft. In a post-war study prepared for the U.S. Air Force, a former chief of staff of 8 Air Corps, *Oberst* Lothar von Heinemann, described the operations in his sector:

> The initial start of the attack proceeded without delay. The weather conditions were clear, isolated patches of fog did not hinder any of the units. And it was only a little more misty in lower lying areas. In the initial stages of the attack, towns and villages were encountered lit up as if for peacetime, which made locating targets a great deal easier. Work on the [enemy] airfields was being done in part under floodlights. The element of surprise was total. Enemy defensive action barely had any appreciable effect and where it did, then only at a point when the main attacks had already been carried out.[180]

While the *Luftwaffe's* primary objective was the destruction of enemy air forces and the establishment of air superiority across the entire front, many types of targets were struck in the opening assault. Along with at least 31 airfields, these targets included: Trains and railroad cars (the Germans using incendiary bullets to destroy cars filled with fuel), gasoline and grain warehouses, fuel dumps, barracks and bunkers. Suspected locations of senior Red Army staffs were also blasted from the air, including the headquarters of Soviet 4 Army, taken out little more than an hour after the attack began. *Stuka* dive-bombers attached to 8 Air Corps made precision attacks on tanks, motor vehicles, bridges, fieldworks, artillery and anti-aircraft sites, while German bombers operating along the central axis dropped their loads on Belostok, Grodno, Lida, Volkovysk, Brest-Litovsk and Kobrin (site of 4 Army headquarters).[181]

Leutnant Heinz Knoke, a Bf 109 fighter pilot in 52 Fighter Wing (52 JG), had flown four missions by noon, dropping SD-2 fragmentation bombs from a rack slung under the belly of his *"Emil"* and strafing enemy positions from as little as six feet above the ground. Knoke and his comrades were enthusiastic about the opportunity to finally destroy the hated Bolshevik enemy, and duly impressed by the sinister designs they attributed to the massed Soviet columns they encountered:

> The Chief sees smiling faces all round when the pilots report. At last the spell is broken. We have dreamed for a long time of doing something like this to the Bolshevists. Our feeling is not exactly one of hatred, so much as utter contempt. It is a genuine satisfaction for us to be able to trample the Bolshevists in the mud where they belong ...

New operation orders have arrived. Russian transport columns have been observed by our reconnaissance aircraft retreating eastward along the Grodno – Zytomia – Skidel – Szczuczyn highway, with our tanks in hot pursuit. We are to support them by bombing and strafing the Russians as they retreat.

Take-off at 1007 hours [this was sortie number four for *Leutnant* Knoke], accompanied by *Stukas*. They are to dive-bomb the Russian artillery emplacements in the same area.

We soon reach Grodno. The roads are clogged with Russian armies everywhere. The reason gradually dawns on us why the sudden surprise attack was ordered by our High Command. We begin to appreciate the full extent of the Russian preparations to attack us. We have just forestalled the Russian timetable for an all-out attack against Germany for the mastery of Europe.[182]

Stuka pilot Hans-Ulrich Rudel, flying with 2 *Stuka* Wing (2 StG), the "*Immelmann*" Wing, was also struck by the "preventive" nature of Operation *Barbarossa*. "On my very first sortie," he later observed,

I notice the countless fortifications along the frontier. The fieldworks run deep into Russia for many hundreds of miles. They are partly positions still under construction. We fly over half-completed airfields; here a concrete runway is just being built; there a few aircraft are already standing on an aerodrome … Flying in this way over one airfield after another, over one strongpoint after another, one reflects: "It is a good thing we struck." … It looks as if the Soviets meant to build all these preparations up as a base for invasion against us. Whom else in the West could Russia have wanted to attack? If the Russians had completed their preparations there would not have been much hope of halting them anywhere.[183]

Rudel flew four sorties on this first day of the war, between Grodno and Volkovysk on the central front. He would end the war having flown more than 2500 operational missions, and with credit for destroying 519 Red Army tanks (one-third of a month's production, according to Foreign Armies East calculations of November 1943) along with the Soviet battleship *Marat* in its harbor outside Leningrad.[184]

Initially, Soviet fighter aircraft evinced little desire to engage in aerial combat, and often turned away at considerable range if fired upon.[185] Soviet bomber forces, however – at least what was left of them after the first German strikes – often demonstrated remarkable courage in the face of hopeless odds. Many German accounts of this day – and in the days which followed – report streams of VVS bombers heading west, in rigid tactical formations[186] and without air cover, to attack German positions. Squadron after squadron of these hapless planes was decimated by the packs of Bf 109s that rose to challenge them, or by well-placed anti-aircraft fire. Kesselring, who observed the slaughter first hand, called it "sheer infanticide."[187] German soldiers watched in awe and fascination as the Soviet bombers tumbled from the sky. Typical of German accounts is the following from Lt.-Col. Meyer-Detring, chief operations officer (Ia) of Fourth Army's 137 Infantry Division:

The air wings of the German *Luftwaffe* had started off for the east together with the first German infantrymen. The first enemy bomber squadron appeared around midday. It slowly approached the bridge, was intercepted in an instant by our fighters or by all calibers of our Flak guns! No machine escaped its fate, one after another plunged burning to the ground – the first convincing evidence of German superiority.[188]

Observing the German attack on the fortress of Brest-Litovsk, Chaplain Rudolf Gschoepf (45 ID) also witnessed the destruction of a Soviet bomber formation, as well as the fanaticism of an enemy crewmember:

> It had become lively in the air as well in the early morning hours. Russian planes approached the frontier region in large numbers, but were intercepted by our fighters – which already held complete sway over the air – with such speed that the parachutes of enemy pilots who had been shot down now floated through the blue skies in their dozens. One small incident illustrates the fanaticism with which even the Russian pilots tried to fight. A Russian went down with his parachute approximately 100 meters ahead of the battalion dressing station, where I found myself. Since he did not get up, we assumed that he was wounded. Two of our medics tried to get to our opponent with a stretcher to help him, but as they approached him, they were shot at with a machine pistol and forced to take cover. Holding his weapon in his hand, the Russian pilot had refused our medical services.[189]

By midday, the Germans were claiming the destruction of 890 Soviet aircraft across the front – 222 of them in aerial combat or to AA fire and 668 on the ground – with a loss of only 18 *Luftwaffe* planes.[190] Late that afternoon, the commander of the Western Front's air forces, Maj.-Gen. Ivan Ivanovich Kopets, overcome by the burgeoning catastrophe, committed suicide. In a telegram dispatched to Moscow, to the Main Office of Political Propaganda, Kopets' suicide – that is, his "faint-heartedness" – was attributed to "private failure and comparatively heavy losses in aviation."[191]

Perhaps there is no better illustration of the chaos caused by the German aerial assault on this first day of the war than the harrowing account by journalist Alexander Werth, in his classic study, *Russia at War 1941-1945*, of General I.V. Boldin's frantic attempts to reach 10 Army headquarters outside Belostok. As mentioned, General Boldin, Pavlov's deputy at Western Front, had been ordered to fly to army headquarters to help its commander, General Golubev, organize a counterstroke. On the flight there, Boldin's plane absorbed 20 bullets from a Bf 109, but managed to land safely on an airfield about 30 kilometers east of Belostok. Minutes later, nine German planes were over the airfield and dropping bombs with impunity, for there were no anti-aircraft guns to fire back at them. Several vehicles and Boldin's plane were destroyed.[192]

The general commandeered a small truck and, together with some officers and men, got in and drove off – Boldin taking the seat next to the driver. After what must have seemed an eternity, they finally reached the main road to Belostok. Through the windscreen he could see 15 German bombers approaching from the west: "They were flying low," he recalled, "with provocative insolence, as though our sky belonged to them. On their fuselages I could clearly see the spiders of the Nazi swastika." Shortly thereafter, he stopped a crowd of workers making off in the opposite direction:

> "Where are you going?," I asked.
> "To Volkovysk," they said.
> "Who are you?"
> "We had been working on fortifications. But the place where we worked is now like a sea of flames," said an elderly man with an exhausted look on his face.
> These people seemed to have lost their heads, not knowing where they were going and why.
> Then we met a few cars, led by a Zis-101. The broad leaves of an aspidistra were protruding from one of the windows. It was the car of some local top official. Inside were two women and two children.

"Surely," I said, "at a time like this you might have more important things to transport than you aspidistra. You might have taken some old people or children." With their heads bent, the women were silent. The driver, too, turned away, feeling ashamed.[193]

Then the ubiquitous *Luftwaffe* arrived, pumping several volleys of machine gun fire into Boldin's truck:

The driver was killed. I managed to survive, as I jumped out just in time. But with the exception of my A.D.C. and a dispatch rider, all were killed … Nearby I noticed the same old Zis-101. I went up to it. The women, the children, the driver were all killed … Only the evergreen leaves of the aspidistra were still sticking out of the window.[194]

Arriving in Belostok, he encountered a scene reminiscent of Dante's *Divine Comedy*, or some other allegory of hell. The town was in total chaos. At the railway station a train filled with evacuees, women and children, was struck by bombs; hundreds were killed. Toward evening, Boldin reached 10 Army headquarters – two tents, a table and some chairs in a little wood outside of Belostok. General Golubev, Boldin learned, had been unable to reach front headquarters in Minsk, for the telephone lines were all destroyed and radio communications were under constant jamming. The 10 Army commander was profoundly shaken by the events of the day. To prevent being outflanked in the south, he informed Boldin, he had deployed his 13 Mechanized Corps along the Kuretz River: "But as you know Ivan Vasilievich, there are very few tanks in our divisions. And what can you expect from those old T26 tanks – only good enough for firing at sparrows."[195]

Golubev went on to say that both the aircraft and anti-aircraft guns of the army corps were now out of action, smashed by the German aerial onslaught. Moreover, through spies, the Germans had apparently been informed of the locations of the army's fuel dumps, all of which were destroyed during the first hours of the invasion by *Luftwaffe* bombing. Then General Nikitin, Commander, 6 Cavalry Corps, arrived, reporting that his men, after repelling the initial German assaults, had been practically exterminated by air attack, the survivors withdrawing into a patch of forest northeast of Belostok.[196]

Finally, communications were restored with front headquarters in Minsk. General Pavlov, Commander, Western Front, spoke with Boldin, peremptorily demanding that the counterstroke proceed that very evening. Boldin demurred, indicating that 10 Army was already all but shattered. For a moment, Pavlov appeared to hesitate, but soon caught himself: "These are my orders. It's for you to carry them out." The counterstroke did not come off that night.[197]

Depending on whether the attacking formations consisted of bombers, dive-bombers or fighters, *Luftwaffe* units flew between four to eight missions on this day, an extraordinary operational tempo that German flyers were to maintain in the days and weeks ahead. These were "astonishing figures," notes Martin van Creveld, "attributable to the simplicity of the machines, the often short distances that had to be covered, the excellence of the ground organization (including a specially developed apparatus that allowed nine aircraft to be refueled simultaneously), and the unparalleled determination of the crews."[198] Thus even by conservative estimates, Kesselring's 2 Air Fleet, with nearly 1000 operational aircraft, must have flown a minimum of 4000 sorties alone on 22 June.

The outcome surpassed the *Luftwaffe* leadership's most ardent expectations. Brig.-Gen. Otto Hoffmann von Waldau, Chief, *Luftwaffe* Operations Staff, recorded in his diary that "complete tactical surprise" had been achieved, and that he expected "an outstanding success."[199] Indeed, by midnight, the Soviet Air Force (VVS) had lost an astounding 1811 aircraft according to official German estimates. Of these, 322 had been destroyed in the air or by anti-aircraft fire, and 1489 on the ground.[200] More than 900 of the VVS losses were attributed to the operations of 2 Air Fleet;[201] and, as a result, the *Luftwaffe* succeeded in gaining complete air superiority in the sector of Army Group Center on this first day of the war.[202] By the end of the second day, with another 800 Soviet aircraft reported destroyed, complete air supremacy, or at least superiority, had been won along the entire 1200+ kilometer eastern front.[203]

As historian Williamson Murray correctly observes, whether or not the *Luftwaffe* actually destroyed that many aircraft misses the point – which is that a "defeat of immense proportion had overtaken the Red Air Force – a catastrophe overshadowed only by events on the ground."[204] The significance of this brilliant aerial victory was explained by Kesselring in his memoirs:

> Thanks to the tactical air planning and to the indefatigable dedication of the air units, it was possible, by virtue of the excellent aerial photographic reconnaissance, to gain "air supremacy" [*Luftherrschaft*] within two days. Reports of aircraft shot down in the air and destroyed on the ground reached approximately 2500 planes, a figure that *Reichsmarschall* Goering at first refused to believe. When, after the area had been secured, he had the figures verified, he had to tell me that the real figures were around 200-300 higher. Without running the risk of coming to the wrong conclusion, I believe I can safely say that, without this prelude, the ground operations [*Heeresoperationen*] would not have proceeded so rapidly or so successfully.[205]

Yet the *Luftwaffe's* unparalleled accomplishments of 22 June – "the greatest numerical success ever achieved in a 24-hour period in the battle between two air forces"[206] – had exacted a heavy toll. Historians have traditionally maintained that only 35 or 36 German planes were lost to all causes on this day.[207] However, a well-documented study of German fighter units on the eastern front in 1941, published in 2003, offers convincing evidence that the actual number of *Luftwaffe* aircraft lost on 22 June was more than twice that number – 78 to be exact. Citing a detailed internal *Luftwaffe* report,[208] the authors of the study provide the following breakdown of aircraft lost (i.e., those "written off" with 60 to 100 percent damage):

German Aircraft Losses[209]
(22 June 1941)

Bf 109	24
Bf 110	7
Ju 88	23
Ju 87	2
He 111	11
Do 17	1
Other	10
	78

Of these, 61 planes were lost to enemy action (*Feindeinwirkung*) and 17 to "other causes." Personnel losses among aircrews were also considerable, including 113 dead or missing, four men taken prisoner, and dozens more wounded. In addition, 89 aircraft sustained levels of damage ranging from 10-59 percent.[210] When considering that the eastern air fleets began *Barbarossa* with only 2255 operational machines, the losses of 22 June signified serious attrition. Total losses, in fact, amounted to more than three percent of the combat-ready force; numerically, they represented the greatest single day's loss since the start of the war in September 1939.[211] It is remarkable, however, that of 360 operational Ju 87 *Stukas*, which flew multiple sorties – indeed, as many as seven or eight per machine![212] – only two were lost on 22 June.

6.6: Midnight, 22 June 1941 – the First 21 Hours

The terrible and murderous forces unleashed across the Russo-German frontier on this Sunday, 22 June 1941, would, in the end, decisively shape world history for decades to come. Yet for the tens of millions of soldiers and civilians suddenly engulfed in the maelstrom of war, concerns were, necessarily, more immediate and parochial. In his personal diary, General Franz Halder, Chief of the German Army General Staff, recorded the results of the day not only with considerable satisfaction, but with real insight as well:

The *overall picture* of the first day of the offensive is as follows:

The enemy was surprised by the German attack. His forces were not in tactical disposition for defense. The troops in the border zone were widely scattered in their quarters. The frontier itself was for the most part weakly guarded.

As a result of this tactical surprise, enemy resistance directly on the border was weak and disorganized, and we succeeded everywhere in seizing the bridges across the border rivers and in piercing the defense positions (field fortifications) near the frontier.

After the first shock, the enemy has turned to fight. There have been instances of tactical withdrawals and no doubt also disorderly retreats, but there are no indications of an attempted operational disengagement.

Such a possibility can moreover be discounted. Some enemy Hq. have been put out of action; e.g., [Belostok][213] and some sectors are deprived of high-echelon control. But quite apart from that, the impact of the shock is such that the Russian High Command could not be expected in the first few days to form a clear enough picture of the situation to make so far-reaching a decision. On top of everything, the command organization is too ponderous to effect swift operational regrouping in reaction to our attack, and so the Russians will have to accept battle in the dispositions in which they were deployed.

Our divisions on the entire offensive front have forced back the enemy on an average of 10 to 12 km. This had opened the path for our armor.[214]

In the area of Army Group North, Field Marshal Ritter von Leeb's assault divisions had also achieved complete tactical surprise. Which was "all the more astonishing" because it had been impossible to conceal the masses of German troops, tanks and vehicles crossing the lower course of the Neman to reach their assembly areas, much less the "conspicuous" bridge-building activity.[215] Advancing on a narrow front with one panzer group and two infantry armies, Leeb's forces ripped through the partially defended Soviet positions and penetrated deep into enemy territory, frustrating Red Army defensive plans and everywhere spreading chaos. In the van was 56 Panzer Corps, commanded by brilliant *Panzergeneral* Erich von Manstein. Its tanks crossed the East Prussian frontier at dawn and plunged into Lithuania; by late afternoon, northwest of Kaunas, Manstein's 8 Panzer Division had reached the Dubissa River and captured the vital Airogola road viaduct across it – an advance of more than 80 kilometers and the deepest drive made by any German unit on 22 June.[216]

On the right wing, in the sector of Field Marshal Gerd von Rundstedt's Army Group South, the armor of General Ewald von Kleist's 1 Panzer Group rumbled across the Western Bug, rapidly breaking through along the boundary of Soviet 5 and 6 Armies in the direction of Rovno. The fighting in the south, however, was to be tenacious and difficult: Col.-Gen. M. P. Kirponos, Commander, Soviet Southwestern Front, had deployed his armies in depth and in positions bristling with well-camouflaged pillboxes, heavy field artillery and devious obstacles. Because the Soviets had expected the main German attack into the Ukraine – to seize its grain and, eventually, the coal of the Donbas and oil of the Caucasus region – the Southwestern Front order of battle included eight mechanized corps with almost 4300 tanks, among them more than 750 new KV and T-34 models. In the days ahead Kirponos, in an effort to bring off the major counterstroke mandated by Stalin's Directive No. 3, would commit this mammoth armored armada with some skill against Kleist's panzers, resulting in the greatest tank battle of the Second World War to date.[217]

In the center, the attacking forces of Field Marshal von Bock's Army Group Center had breached the Soviet frontier defenses all along the 500 kilometer front, with mobile advance detachments pushing up to 40 kilometers and, in some cases, even beyond, into Soviet territory. The greatest gains were made on flanks, by 2 Panzer Group on the right wing and 3 Panzer Group on the left wing of the army group. The armored spearheads of both panzer groups advanced rapidly, ignoring the enemy on their flanks and, ably supported by the *Luftwaffe*, inaugurated the envelopment of Soviet Western Front in eastern Poland and Belorussia.[218] By 2200 hours, as darkness descended upon the battlefield, the spearheads of Guderian's 2 Panzer Group, having smashed Soviet 4 Army, were fighting around Maloryta, Kobrin, and Pruzhany.[219] Specifically, the lead tanks of 3 Panzer Division (24 Panzer Corps) were approaching Kobrin, more than 30 kilometers beyond the frontier; on Guderian's left wing, 18 Panzer Division (47 Panzer Corps), chasing down Panzer Route 2, was only 20 kilometers southwest of Pruzhany.[220]

On the left flank, Hoth's 3 Panzer Group had, by nightfall, pulverized Soviet 11 Army, pried open a dangerous gap north of Grodno between Soviet Northwestern and Western Fronts, and begun the envelopment of the latter's 3 Army. In doing so, Hoth's armor had dashed 40 to 50 kilometers and seized all three bridges over the Neman – two at Olita by midday (7 Panzer Division) and one at Merkine that afternoon (12 Panzer Division). Moreover, elements of an infantry division of Hoth's 5 Army Corps, advancing between his two armored corps, had, despite tough resistance, crossed the Neman that evening between Merkine and Olita, while infantry of 8 Army Corps (Ninth Army) forded the river on a broad front north of Grodno.[221] It was, Halder commented in his diary, "quite a remarkable success ... Full operational freedom of movement appears to have been achieved in [3 Panzer Group's] sector."[222]

These successes were all the more remarkable in view of the fact that, across the front, forward movement of both armor and infantry was severely inhibited by multiple terrain factors, including dense, almost primeval forest, marshes, and roadways which rapidly deteriorated under the strain of the thousands of tracked and wheeled vehicles moving across them. Once German units crossed the frontier, they discovered that the roads often turned to primitive sandy tracks in which vehicles became stuck, leading to serious congestion, stalling movement and multiplying fuel consumption. The few bridges leading across the Bug and other river lines became frustrating bottlenecks, a problem often exacerbated by poor march discipline.[223] In some cases, German units reported that difficult terrain and poor roads had caused them more difficulties than had Soviet resistance.[224]

Conversely, the impressive accomplishments of Army Group Center – and along the entire eastern front – were greatly facilitated by the lack of Soviet leadership at both the tactical and operational levels, while individually the Russian soldier often fought with laudable courage. Illustrative of the analyses found in German field reports are these observations by 3 Panzer Group:

> Enemy aerial attacks did not take place on 22.6. No kind of general, orderly leadership could be discerned. There was resistance only through unconnected groups, the many field fortifications were either unmanned or only poorly manned.
>
> Where the enemy did stand his ground, he fought doggedly and bravely to the death. No position reported any deserters or surrenderers. This made the fight tougher than in Poland and in the western campaign …
>
> The teamwork with 8 Air Corps was particularly close and lively … Control of the air was almost totally achieved on the first day of the attack … Just as in Poland, our air assaults drove the enemy into the forests, from where he successfully harassed our rearward elements and columns. This may also be viewed as a reason for the initially surprisingly low numbers of enemy forces which appeared …
>
> Higher level [Russian] leadership did not make an appearance at all during the first days. Lower level leadership was inert, mechanical, and lacked resolve in adapting to the situation as it developed. Orders were found which, despite knowing about German progress in the morning, demanded that a defensive line be occupied in the evening which we had already reached in the afternoon … Their methodical training was no match for the huge impact of the surprise.
>
> The individual fighter was tougher than the fighter of the World War, no doubt a result of the Bolshevist concept, but also incited by the political commissars (who, for their part, had carefully taken off their insignia and wore ordinary soldiers' uniforms), and by 20 years of a Soviet rule which had no consideration for human life and was filled with a veritable contempt for life [*Lebensverachtung*].[225]

Despite Halder's conviction that Russian forces in the frontier regions had offered "no indications of an attempted operational disengagement" – and indeed, were now incapable of such a response – German front commands were much less certain about Soviet intentions. In an early evening conference at Guderian's headquarters, Field Marshal von Kluge expressed the opinion that Russian forces were conducting a planned withdrawal (*planmaessig ausweicht*) and intended to put up "strong organized resistance" in positions further to the rear. Guderian disagreed, pointing out that the enemy had been badly shaken by the initial German assault and was only capable of offering weak local resistance.[226] What *was* certain, however, was that German forces, in particular the mobile troops, needed to rapidly and unmercifully exploit the confusion in the enemy's ranks by building on the day's successes and thwarting Russian attempts to reestablish a stable front line in the interior. "In the staff of 3 Panzer Group there was no doubt," recalled Hermann Hoth after the war, "that the advantages gained through surprise needed to be exploited the next day with every means at our disposal. The panzer corps had to advance far to the east."[227]

ENDNOTES

1   Quoted in: J. L. Wallach, *Dogma of the Battle of Annihilation*, 16.
2   *Deutscher Soldatenkalender 1961*, 30.
3   W. Kempowski (Hg.), *Das Echolot*, 23.
4   H. Martin, *Weit war der Weg*, 13.
5   Oblt. Richard D. (35 232), Collection BfZ.
6   F. Frisch & W. D. Jones, Jr., *Condemned to Live*, 69.

7   Chief of the Army General Staff Franz Halder recorded in his diary on 22 June that, "the enemy has apparently been tactically *surprised* along the entire line. The Bug River bridges, and those along the entire river frontier, were undefended and have fallen into our hands intact." H.-A. Jacobsen (Hg.), *Generaloberst Halder Kriegstagebuch*, Bd. III, 3.

8   Dr E. Bunke, *Der Osten blieb unser Schicksal*, 223-25.

9   "It must be understood," recalled Haering, "that in the German army at that time it was absolutely illegal for priests who were medical aides – not chaplains – to engage in any pastoral care for soldiers or lay people, or to conduct any religious service." B. Haering, *Embattled Witness*, 2.

10   Ibid., 1-6.

11   H. Haape, *Moscow Tram Stop*, 16-18.

12   Ibid., 27.

13   *Tagebuch* Haape, 22.6.41.

14   G. Habedanck, *"Bei Brest-Litovsk ueber die Grenze,"* *Die Wehrmacht*, 1941, 233; quoted in: R. J. Kershaw, *War Without Garlands*, 31.

15   Dr R. Gschoepf, *Mein Weg mit der 45. Inf.-Div.*, 208.

16   J. Erickson, *The Road to Stalingrad*, 109.

17   R. J. Kershaw, *War Without Garlands*, 31; D. M. Glantz, *Barbarossa*, 35.

18   24 Panzer Corps reported the capture of the bridge at Koden to its superiors at 2 Panzer Group at 0345 hours that morning. BA-MA RH 21-2/927, *KTB Panzergruppe 2*, 22.6.41. The German assault party belonged to 3 Panzer Division. W. Haupt, *Army Group Center*, 26-27. See also, C. von Luttichau, *Road to Moscow*, VI:8.

19   BA-MA RH 21-2/927, *KTB Panzergruppe 2*, 22.6.41. By 0030 hours, 22 June, all corps had passed on the codeword *"Kyffhaeuser"* to panzer group headquarters, signifying that all units had completed their concentration (*Bereitstellung*) for the attack.

20   H. Guderian, *Panzer Leader*, 153.

21   C. von Luttichau, *Road to Moscow*, VI:8.

22   BA-MA MSg 1/1147: *Tagebuch* Lemelsen, 25.6.41.

23   G. Blumentritt, *"Moscow,"* in: *The Fatal Decisions*, W. Richardson & S. Freidin (eds.), 46-47.

24   Apparently, the reason for the staggered start times was that sunrise occurred minutes earlier farther north, in the sectors of Army Group North and the left wing of Army Group Center. M. Graf v. Nayhauss-Cormons, *Zwischen Gehorsam und Gewissen*, 130. In his diary, Bock insisted that, despite his concerns about the staggered times for beginning the bombardment, Field Marshal von Leeb, Commander, Army Group North, was adamant about beginning the artillery preparation at 0305 hours. "So I'm the one who has to suffer and have to attack with my right wing at Rundstedt's time and with my left wing at Leeb's time," Bock wrote in his diary two days before the attack. K. Gerbet (ed.), *GFM Fedor von Bock, The War Diary*, 222.

25   OKH Gen St d H/Op.Abt. (III), *"Kriegsgliederung Barbarossa,"* Stand 18.6.41, in: K. Mehner (Hg.), *Geheime Tagesberichte*, Bd. 3; BA-MA RH 19 II/120, *KTB H.Gr.Mitte*, 2.10.41.

26   H. Haape, *Moscow Tram Stop*, 15.

27   G. Blumentritt, *"Moscow,"* in: *The Fatal Decisions*, W. Richardson & S. Freidin (eds.), 47.

28   F. Frisch & W. D. Jones, Jr., *Condemned to Live*, 69.

29   I. Hammer & S. zur Nieden (Hg.), *Sehr selten habe ich geweint*, 226-27.

30   S. Knappe, *Soldat*, 203-05.

31   R. Hinze, *19. Infanterie- und Panzer-Division*, 125-26.

32   J. Dinglreiter, *Die Vierziger. Chronik des Regiments*, 39.

33   C. von Luttichau, *Road to Moscow*, VI:10.

34   *Tagebuch* Kreuter, 22.6.41 (unpublished diary). The *Stuka* mentioned by Kreuter was apparently one of only two Ju 87s lost on this first day of the war. See, Section 6.5.

35   A. Freitag, *Aufzeichnungen aus Krieg und Gefangenschaft*, 51. Corporal Freitag served principally as a limber driver (*Protzenfahrer*) in the infantry gun company (13) of 18 Infantry Regiment, one of the three infantry regiments of 6 ID.

36   A. Schick, *Die Geschichte der 10. Panzer-Division*, 270-71.

37   Ibid., 271.

38   As addressed in Chapter 2, the Germans fully expected the Russians to use chemical or biological agents against their troops. In fact, by the start of World War II, the Soviet Union possessed some 77,000 tons of mustard gas. A. Sáiz, *Deutsche Soldaten*, 95.

39   For the photograph see, J. Keegan, *The Second World War*, 185.

40   K.-J. Thies, *Der Ostfeldzug – Ein Lageatlas*, "Aufmarsch am 21.6.1941 abds., Heeresgruppe Mitte."

41   R.-D. Mueller, *"Duell im Schnee,"* in: *Der Zweite Weltkrieg*, S. Burgdorff & K. Wiegrefe (Hg.), 114.

42   A. Seaton, *The Russo-German War*, 118.

43   K. Gerbet (ed.), *GFM Fedor von Bock, The War Diary*, 224.

44   P. E. Schramm (Hg.), *Kriegstagebuch des OKW*, Bd. I, 417.

45   That the Germans were often greeted in the border regions as liberators is confirmed by contemporary accounts too many to mention. The reference here is from, R. Kirchubel, *Operation Barbarossa 1941 (3)*, *Army Group Center*, 32.

46   D. M. Glantz, *Barbarossa*, 35.

47   Guderian is referring to Kluge's Fourth Army, to which his panzer group was subordinated for the initial attack. W. Keilig, *Das Deutsche Heer*, Bd. I, Abschnitt 34, S. 7.

48   A *Rollbahn*, or *Panzerstrasse*, was a road designated as a main axis of advance for motorized formations. Normally, marching infantry divisions were barred from using these "good" roads, which were vital to the forward progress of the mobile units. J. Steinhoff, et al., *Voices from the Third Reich*, 535; FMS T-34, K. Allmendinger, et al., "*Terrain Factors in the Russian Campaign*," 52.

49   Quoted in: J. Dinglreiter, *Die Vierziger. Chronik des Regiments*, 38.

50   R. Kirchubel, *Hitler's Panzer Armies*, 63.

51   The panzer group's third tank corps, 46 Panzer Corps (10 PD, SS *Das Reich*, Inf.-Rgt. *Grossdeutschland*) was well back from the front in reserve. K.-J. Thies, *Der Ostfeldzug – Ein Lageatlas*, "Aufmarsch am 21.6.1941 abds., Heeresgruppe Mitte;" W. Keilig, *Das Deutsche Heer*, Bd. I, Abschnitt 34, S. 7-8.

52   H. Magenheimer, *Moskau 1941*, 38-39.

53   R. A. Hart, *Guderian*, 71. See also, H. Guderian, *Panzer Leader*, 146-47. According to Hart, "Guderian's squabble with von Kluge was both personal and professional. Von Kluge saw Guderian as a dangerous, impetuous innovator. Guderian saw von Kluge as intolerant, deceitful, and doctrinally opposed to maneuver warfare. He thus disliked von Kluge from the beginning and became even more distrustful, his suspicion ultimately burgeoning into hatred. Von Kluge tried repeatedly to patch up their relationship, but was rebuffed each time by Guderian. Their squabble was a fundamental clash between two different types of commanders – a calculating risk-taker versus a prudent, yet equally distinguished, commander."

54   BA-MA 27-3/14, *KTB 3. Pz.-Div.*, 22.6.41. See also, *Geschichte der 3. Panzer-Division*, Traditionsverband der Division (Hg.), 108-09.

55   H.-J. Roell, *Oberleutnant Albert Blaich. Als Panzerkommandant in Ost und West*, 42-43.

56   H. Schaeufler (ed.), *Knight's Cross Panzers*, 72.

57   The "G," about 30 centimeters in height, identified the tanks as belonging to Guderian's panzer group. *Geschichte der 3. Panzer-Division*, Traditionsverband der Division (Hg.), 107.

58   BA-MA RH 21-2/927, *KTB Panzergruppe 2*, 22.6.41; R. Kirchubel, *Hitler's Panzer Armies*, 63. As noted, Panzer Route 1 led via Kobrin and Slutsk to Bobruisk.

59   BA-MA RH 27-18/20, *KTB 18. Pz.-Div.*, 22.6.41.

60   *Leutnant* H. Doell, quoted in: *Das Echolot*, W. Kempowski (Hg.), 23.

61   According to one of General Nehring's staff officers, these included: An armored personnel carrier (Nehring's command vehicle), two Panzer III command tanks, two self-propelled Flak guns, a vehicle which served as the general's living quarters, and some 30 motorcycles. G. A. Schulze, "*General der Panzertruppe a.D. Walther K. Nehring. Der persoenliche Ordonnanzoffizier berichtet von der Vormarschzeit in Russland 1941-1942*" (unpublished manuscript).

62   W. Paul, *Panzer-General Walther K. Nehring*, 118; C. von Luttichau, *Road to Moscow*, VI:10; P. Carell, *Unternehmen Barbarossa*, 24.

63   C. von Luttichau, *Road to Moscow*, VI:10. According to von Luttichau, "Lemelsen's 47 Panzer Corps had no Bug bridges to capture. It had to build them … The axis of advance was to be Panzer Route Two, an arbitrary link between the towns of Pruzhany, Slonim, and Minsk." Ibid., VI:9.

64   BA-MA MSg 1/1147: *Tagebuch* Lemelsen, 25.6.41.

65   Ibid., 25.6.41. Lemelsen's account of his encounter with Russian stragglers follows immediately on the heels of his discussion of events on 22 June 1941. My assumption is that this encounter also took place on 22 June; however, it may have occurred on the 25th. Regardless, it is indicative of the dangerous situations often faced by German tank generals – with their penchant for leading from the front – from the very first day of the war in the east. The impetuous Guderian also had several close scrapes with the Russians in the opening days of the war. See his, *Panzer Leader*, 154-56; also, Chapter 8, Section 8.2.2.

66   18 PD began the campaign with 6 Pz I, 50 Pz II, 114 Pz III, 36 Pz IV and 12 command tanks – 218 tanks in all. T. L. Jentz (ed.), *Panzer Truppen*, 192.

67   BA-MA RH 27-18/20, *KTB 18. Pz.-Div.*, 22.6.41; W. Paul, *Geschichte der 18. Panzer-Division*, 17; R. Kirchubel, *Hitler's Panzer Armies*, 63; A. Seaton, *The Russo-German War*, 120.

68   A. Axell, *Russia's Heroes 1941-45*, 24.

69   J. Erickson, *The Road to Stalingrad*, 120.

70   A. Axell, *Russia's Heroes 1941-45*, 23-24; R. J. Kershaw, *War Without Garlands*, 29-30; Dr R. Gschoepf, *Mein Weg mit der 45. Inf.-Div.*, 206-07.

71   C. Bellamy, *Absolute War*, 185; J. Erickson, *The Road to Stalingrad*, 119-20. After the start of hostilities, the Soviet garrison was reinforced by troops falling back on the fortress, which helps to explain the much larger number of Russian prisoners (more than 7000) captured there by the end of June. (See, Section 7.2.3.)

72   H. Guderian, *Panzer Leader*, 147.

73   Dr R. Gschoepf, *Mein Weg mit der 45. Inf.-Div.*, 202-03.

74   Dr R. Gschoepf, *Mein Weg mit der 45. Inf.-Div.*, 204-05; R. J. Kershaw, *War Without Garlands*, 47. Despite the powerful artillery assembled for the preliminary barrage, the commander of 45 ID found it inadequate for the task at hand. According to an after-action report prepared by the division: "The plan of attack for the artillery was based less on its actual physical impact [*tatsaechliche Wirkung*] than on its surprise effect on the enemy. This was because the available artillery, despite repeated requests of the division, was insufficient." BA-MA RH 20-4/192, "*Gefechtsbericht ueber die Wegnahme von Brest Litowsk.*"

75   Dr R. Gschoepf, *Mein Weg mit der 45. Inf.-Div.*, 204.

76   Dr E. Bunke, *Der Osten blieb unser Schicksal*, 218.

77   Dr R. Gschoepf, *Mein Weg mit der 45. Inf.-Div.*, 206; R. J. Kershaw, *War Without Garlands*, 48; BA-MA RH 20-4/192, "*Gefechtsbericht ueber die Wegnahme von Brest Litowsk.*"

78   BA-MA RH 26-45/20, *KTB 45. Inf.-Div.*, 22.6.41.

79   BA-MA RH 26-45/20, *KTB 45. Inf.-Div.*, 22.6.41; Dr R. Gschoepf, *Mein Weg mit der 45. Inf.-Div.*, 207.

80   BA-MA RH 20-4/192, *"Gefechtsbericht ueber die Wegnahme von Brest Litowsk;"* C. von Luttichau, *Road to Moscow*, VI:11.

81   BA-MA RH 20-4/192, *"Gefechtsbericht ueber die Wegnahme von Brest Litowsk;"* BA-MA RH 26-45/20, *KTB 45. Inf.-Div.*, 22.6.41; R. J. Kershaw, *War Without Garlands*, 50.

82   *"Die ersten acht Tage,"* in: *Kampf gegen die Soujets*, Oberkommando der Wehrmacht (Hg.), 37-38.

83   Not until noon, two days later, did an assault group from 133 IR break through to the men trapped inside the church and rescue them. Dr R. Gschoepf, *Mein Weg mit der 45. Inf.-Div.*, 210; BA-MA RH 20-4/192, *"Gefechtsbericht ueber die Wegnahme von Brest Litowsk."*

84   Dr R. Gschoepf, *Mein Weg mit der 45. Inf.-Div.*, 208.

85   K.-J. Thies, *Der Ostfeldzug – Ein Lageatlas*, "Aufmarsch am 21.6.1941 abds., Heeresgruppe Mitte;" BA-MA RH 20-4/188, *Die Kaempfe der 4. Armee.*

86   BA-MA RH 20-4/1199, *KTB AOK 4*, 22.6.41.

87   G. Blumentritt, *"Moscow,"* in: *The Fatal Decisions*, W. Richardson & S. Freidin (eds.), 47. This incident (and another like it) was also recorded in the Fourth Army war diary. BA-MA RH 20-4/1199, *KTB AOK 4*, 22.6.41.

88   M. Graf v. Nayhauss-Cormons, *Zwischen Gehorsam und Gewissen*, 131.

89   Ibid., 131-32.

90   W. Heinemann, *Pflicht und Schuldigkeit*, 255.

91   Ibid., 256.

92   Ibid., 256-57.

93   Ibid., 257.

94   W. Meyer-Detring, *Die 137. Infanterie-Division im Mittelabschnitt der Ostfront*, 19. According to the war diary of 137 ID, combat engineers had completed a bridge across the Bug by 1230 hours, while assault guns, light 100mm howitzers and heavy weapons of the infantry were ferried across the river. BA-MA RH 26-137/4, *KTB 137. Inf.-Div.*, 22.6.41.

95   BA-MA RH 26-137/5, *"Verlustliste der 137. Inf. Division."*

96   BA-MA RH 20-4/1199, *KTB AOK 4*, 22.6.41.

97   Ibid.

98   292 Infantry Division (9 Army Corps, Fourth Army) noted in its war diary that morning occasional fire fights (*Schiessereien*) with Russian elements in the forests and cornfields. BA-MA RH 26-292/7, *KTB 292. Inf.-Div.*, 22.6.41.

99   J. Huerter, *Hitlers Heerfuehrer*, 664.

100 K.-J. Thies, *Der Ostfeldzug – Ein Lageatlas*, "Aufmarsch am 21.6.1941 abds., Heeresgruppe Mitte" & "Lage am 22.6.1941 abds.;" J. Erickson, *The Road to Stalingrad*, 129.

101 At the same time, the advance of Hoth's 3 Panzer Group out of the Suwalki triangle was threatening Soviet 3 Army with envelopment. J. Erickson, *The Road to Stalingrad*, 129.

102 C. von Luttichau, *Road to Moscow*, VI:16-17.

103 For details see, H. Boucsein, *Halten oder Sterben*, 16-17.

104 BA-MA RH 26-129/3, *KTB 129. Inf.-Div.*, 22.6.41.

105 Ibid., 22.6.41.

106 BA-MA RH 26-256/12, *KTB 256. Inf.-Div.*, 22.6.41.

107 H. Wijers (Hg.), *Chronik der Sturmgeschuetzabteilung 210*, 3. The assault gun battery also destroyed 11 Soviet tanks on this first day of the war.

108 BA-MA RH 26-256/12, 22.6.41; Internet sites at: http://www.shtetlinks.jewishgen.org/lida-district/now-encyc.htm, and, http://www.jewishvirtuallibrary.org. In 1921, there were 402 Jews in Novy Dvor, about one-third of the town's population. In October 1941, the Jews of Novy Dvor were transported to the ghetto at Ostryna and, in the spring of 1942, to the ghetto in Sukhovolia. From there they were sent to the extermination camp at Auschwitz. No Jews returned to Novy Dvor after the war.

109 K.-R. Woche, *Zwischen Pflicht und Gewissen*, 100; R. Kirchubel, *Hitler's Panzer Armies*, 97. With the help of sympathetic Lithuanians on both sides of the border, 3 Panzer Group was able to develop good intelligence about Soviet dispositions.

110 As recorded in an official account of 3 Panzer Group: "The fighting was … tougher than in Poland and the western campaign." (*Der Kampf wurde … haerter als in Polen und im Westfeldzug.*) BA-MA RH 21-3/732, *"Gefechtsberichte Russland 1941/42."* Hermann Hoth, in his post-war study of the operations of his panzer group in the summer of 1941, also emphasized the vigorous resistance put up by some Red Army units. H. Hoth, *Panzer-Operationen*, 53-55.

111 H. Hoth, *Panzer-Operationen*, 53.

112 BA-MA RH 21-3/788, *KTB Panzergruppe 3*, 22.6.41; BA-MA RH 27-7/46, *KTB 7. Pz.-Div.*, 22.6.41; K.-R. Woche, *Zwischen Pflicht und Gewissen*, 100.

113 On 22 June 1941, 7 Panzer Division possessed 53 Pz II, 167 Pz 38(t), 30 Pz IV, and 15 command tanks in its three tank battalions. T. L. Jentz (ed.), *Panzer Truppen*, 190.

114 BA-MA RH 27-7/46, *KTB 7. Pz.-Div.*, 22.6.41; BA-MA RH 21-3/788, *KTB Panzergruppe 3*, 22.6.41; K.-R. Woche, *Zwischen Pflicht und Gewissen*, 100; H. v. Manteuffel, *Die 7. Panzer-Division*, 49; R.H.S. Stolfi, *German Panzers on the Offensive*, 17; R. Kirchubel, *Hitler's Panzer Armies*, 97.

115 Even the war diary of 3 Panzer Group acknowledged that "our own 7 Panzer Division has won its most difficult battle since the beginning of the war, in the process destroying 80 enemy tanks." BA-MA RH 21-3/788, *KTB Panzergruppe 3*, 22.6.41.

116 F. Kurowski (Hg.), *Hasso von Manteuffel*, 213; Internet site at: http://www.lexikon-der-wehrmacht.de. For the circumstances of Rothenburg's death see, Section 7.2.2.

117 G. Bopp, *Kriegstagebuch*, 72.

118 One battalion of 37 IR participated in the opening attack to seize a commanding terrain feature, which would have adversely affected the advance of 18 IR. The battalion had successfully completed this mission by 0310 hours. BA-MA RH 26-6/8, *KTB 6. Inf.-Div*, 22.6.41.

119 BA-MA RH 26-6/8, *KTB 6. Inf.-Div.*, 22.6.41; H. Grossmann, *Geschichte der 6. Infanterie-Division*, 40-41.

120 H. Haape, *Moscow Tram Stop*, 20.

121 H. Haape, *Moscow Tram Stop*, 20-21; H. Grossmann, *Geschichte der 6. Infanterie-Division*, 41. According to Haape, a flight of eight Russian bombers took part in the attack, while Grossmann mentioned 20 Soviet "aircraft."

122 Most of the 6 ID's reconnaissance battalion (6 AA) had been assigned directly 6 Army Corps, to serve as an advance detachment (*Vorausabteilung*) for the corps. All that was left of the battalion to 6 ID was a cavalry and a cycle squadron, reinforced by a mortar battery, a heavy MG battery, and an AA battery. These units were assembled under Boeselager's command. P. *Freiherr* von Boeselager, *Valkyrie*, 38; H. Grossmann, *Geschichte der 6. Infanterie-Division*, 39.

123 BA-MA RH 26-6/8, *KTB 6. Inf.-Div.*, 22.6.41; H. Grossmann, *Geschichte der 6. Infanterie-Division*, 41-42.

124 W. Knecht, *Geschichte des Infanterie-Regiments 77*, 53-54.

125 Ibid., 55.

126 D. Irving, *Hitler's War*, 273.

127 D. Irving, *Hitler's War*, 273; M. Domarus, *Hitler – Reden und Proklamationen 1932-1945*, Bd. II, 1739; J. Prien, et al., *Die Jagdfliegerverbaende der Deutschen Luftwaffe*, Teil 6/I, *Unternehmen "Barbarossa,"* 207.

128 R. G. Reuth (Hg.), *Joseph Goebbels. Tagebuecher*, Bd. IV, 1611-13.

129 Shortly after the war began, Hitler told his former ambassador to the Soviet Union, Friedrich Werner Graf von der Schulenburg, that he expected to be in Moscow by mid-August 1941, and to finish the entire war by 1 October. D. Stahel, *And the World held its Breath*, 197.

130 According to Maj.-Gen. Gerd Niepold, who worked with Paulus for most of 1941, Brauchitsch said: "*Ja, Paulus, Sie werden Recht haben, acht Wochen werden wir wohl fuer Russland brauchen.*" See, Georg Meyer, *Adolf Heusinger*, 151, 850 (f.n. 23).

131 R. Moorhouse, *Berlin at War*, 70. It was also, for the most part, the same proclamation Hitler had already issued to his troops in the east, only both had slightly different endings tailored to their audiences. For the complete text of Hitler's "*Proklamation an das deutsche Volk,*" see, M. Domarus, *Hitler – Reden und Proklamationen 1932-1945*, Bd. II, 1725-32.

132 M. Domarus, *Hitler – Reden und Proklamationen 1932-1945*, Bd. II, 1725-32.

133 *Voelkischer Beobachter*, 24.6.41, 2. Quoted in: R. Moorhouse, *Berlin at War*, 71.

134 R. Moorhouse, *Berlin at War*, 71.

135 M. Vassiltchikov, *Berlin Diaries*, 55.

136 M. Miethe, *Memoiren 1921-1945*.

137 R. Moorhouse, *Berlin at War*, 71.

138 O. Buchbender & R. Sterz (Hg.), *Das andere Gesicht des Krieges*, 70.

139 H. W. Flannery, *Assignment to Berlin*, 365.

140 G. Gorodetsky, *Grand Delusion*, 309.

141 A. Werth, *Russia at War*, 125-26.

142 G. Gorodetsky, *Grand Delusion*, 309. The Soviet ambassador, Dekanozov, finally received an audience with State Secretary Ernst von Weizsaecker at 9.30 that evening, and "handed him a note, similar to the one Schulenburg had received in Moscow, specifying some 180 cases of German reconnaissance flights over Soviet territory since the latest Soviet complaint in April … Weizsaecker gained time by proposing that Dekanozov await the official response." Ibid., 310.

143 Ibid., 309.

144 C. Pleshakov, *Stalin's Folly*, 23-24.

145 C. Pleshakov, *Stalin's Folly*, 24; G. Gorodetsky, *Grand Delusion*, 310-11.

146 D. Volkogonov, "*The German Attack, the Soviet Response, Sunday, 22 June 1941,*" in: *Barbarossa, The Axis and the Allies*, J. Erickson & D. Dilks (eds.), 86.

147 G. Gorodetsky, *Grand Delusion*, 310-11.

148 D. Volkogonov, "*The German Attack, the Soviet Response, Sunday, 22 June 1941,*" in: *Barbarossa, The Axis and the Allies*, J. Erickson & D. Dilks (eds.), 86.

149 C. Pleshakov, *Stalin's Folly*, 98. According to Rodric Braithwaite, the directive reached Pavlov's Western Special Military District headquarters "just before 1:00 a.m. on 22 June," and was "passed on to subordinate units only at 2:30 a.m." In any case, as Braithwaite correctly observes, "it did not matter. The message was far too late." R. Braithwaite, *Moscow 1941*, 67.

150 G. Gorodetsky, *Grand Delusion*, 311; C. Pleshakov, *Stalin's Folly*, 97. According to Pleshakov's account, Zhukov called Stalin at 0:30 a.m. Stalin asked him if he had sent the directive to the military districts. Zhukov replied that he had, and that was the end of the discussion.

151 D. Volkogonov, "*The German Attack, the Soviet Response, Sunday, 22 June 1941,*" in: *Barbarossa, The Axis and the Allies*, J. Erickson & D. Dilks (eds.), 85; E. P. Hoyt, *Stalin's War*, 25.

152 C. Pleshakov, *Stalin's Folly*, 99-100.

153 C. von Luttichau, *Road to Moscow*, VI:3-4.

154 C. Pleshakov, *Stalin's Folly*, 100-01.

155 Ibid., 101.
156 G. Gorodetsky, *Grand Delusion*, 311.
157 R. Braithwaite, *Moscow 1941*, 35.
158 G. Gorodetsky, *Grand Delusion*, 311.
159 G. Gorodetsky, *Grand Delusion*, 312-13; C. Pleshakov, *Stalin's Folly*, 110.
160 The Komsomol was the Communist youth organization.
161 C. Pleshakov, *Stalin's Folly*, 104-05. For an account of how the citizens of Moscow responded to the news of war see, R. Braithwaite, *Moscow 1941*, 73-79.
162 C. Pleshakov, *Stalin's Folly*, 106.
163 Ibid. 106.
164 D. Glantz, *Barbarossa*, 38.
165 C. Pleshakov, *Stalin's Folly*, 111-12.
166 Ibid., 126.
167 D. Glantz, *Barbarossa*, 38-39; D. Glantz, *Barbarossa Derailed*, Vol. I, 31.
168 G. Roberts, *Stalin's Wars*, 93.
169 D. Volkogonov, "*The German Attack, the Soviet Response, Sunday, 22 June 1941*," in: *Barbarossa, The Axis and the Allies*, J. Erickson & D. Dilks (eds.), 89.
170 J. Erickson, *The Road to Stalingrad*, 134.
171 Marshal G. I. Kulik, a Soviet artillery specialist, was sent to Western Front, along with Marshal Shaposhnikov. As noted by John Erickson: "Kulik was a nonentity. His prime qualification was that Stalin had known him during the days of the defense of Tsaritsyn [Stalingrad] in 1918. It was this which ultimately transformed him, in 1937, into the overlord of Soviet artillery, head of the Main Artillery Administration, Deputy Defense Commissar." Ibid., 17. Writes Simon Montefiore: "The boozy buffoon, Marshal Kulik, whose war was to be a chronicle of tragicomical blunders, outfitted himself in a pilot's fetching leathers, cap and goggles and arrived on the Western Front like a Stalinist Biggles on the evening of 23 June. Bewildered by the rout of 10 Army, he was cut off, surrounded and almost captured." S. S. Montefiore, *Stalin. The Court of the Red Tsar*, 369-70.
172 General N. F. Vatutin. According to Evan Mawdsley, Vatutin, Zhukov's deputy, was sent to oversee the Northwestern Front. E. Mawdsley, *Thunder in the East*, 65.
173 Col.-Gen. F. I. Kuznetsov, Commander, Northwestern Front.
174 J. Erickson, *The Road to Stalingrad*, 126, 134.
175 D. Glantz, *Barbarossa*, 39.
176 J. Erickson, *The Road to Stalingrad*, 134-35.
177 S. S. Montefiore, *Stalin. The Court of the Red Tsar*, 369.
178 R. J. Kershaw, *War Without Garlands*, 31-33; D. Glantz, *Barbarossa*, 35.
179 Accounts differ as to the number of German aircraft committed to the initial attacks. David Glantz cites figures of 500 bombers, 270 dive bombers and 480 fighters. Martin van Creveld states the first strike was conducted by 637 bombers (and dive bombers) and 231 fighters. The quasi-official German history (*GSWW*, Vol. IV) does not appear to provide figures. D. Glantz, *Barbarossa*, 35; M. van Creveld, et al., *Air Power and Maneuver Warfare*, 69.
180 L. von Heinemann, "*Erste Kaempfe vom 22.6. bis ca. 3.7.41*," in: Karlsruhe Document Collection. (Hereafter cited as "KDC.")
181 *GSWW*, Vol. IV, 764; E. P. Hoyt, *Stalin's War*, 28-30; H. Rudel, *Stuka Pilot*, 17; M. van Creveld, et al., *Air Power and Maneuver Warfare*, 69; J. Erickson, *The Road to Stalingrad*, 118.
182 H. Knoke, *I flew for the Fuehrer*, 46-47. *Leutnant* Knoke lifted off on his sixth, and final, sortie of the day at 2000 hours: "There has been no sign of the Russian Air Force the entire day, and we are able to do our work without encountering opposition." Ibid., 48.
183 H. Rudel, *Stuka Pilot*, 17.
184 H. Rudel, *Stuka Pilot*, 16; R. Muller, *The German Air War in Russia*, 122-23.
185 Once again, however, one must be careful when generalizing about human behavior. On 22 June 1941, 15 Soviet fighter pilots displayed the indomitable courage to ram German aircraft in flight. Because most Soviet fighters "were light and slow, a ram wasn't necessarily fatal for the desperate crew if they had their parachutes ready; if they didn't damage the fuel tank, they could leap from the flaming plane. Nonetheless, instant death was probable." C. Pleshakov, *Stalin's Folly*, 140.
186 D. M. Glantz & J. House, *When Titans Clashed*, 38. Write Glantz and House: "Both in Spain and in the opening battles of 1941, Red Air Force tactics tended to be very rigid. Throughout the disastrous summer of 1941, Soviet bombers stubbornly attacked at an altitude of 8000 feet, too high to ensure accurate bombing but low enough for German fighters to locate and attack them."
187 A. Kesselring, *Soldat Bis Zum Letzen Tag*, 120. In fact, in the opening days of the war, the Soviet bomber fleet was "practically eliminated and hardly made its presence felt during the following months, even though it still undertook sporadic, ineffective, and costly attacks against the German rear area." *GSWW*, Vol. IV, 766.
188 W. Meyer-Detring, *Die 137. Infanterie-Division im Mittelabschnitt der Ostfront*, 20.
189 R. Gschoepf, *Mein Weg mit der 45. Inf.-Div.*, 206.
190 *GSWW*, Vol. IV, 764.
191 D. Volkogonov, "*The German Attack, the Soviet Response, Sunday, 22 June 1941*," in: *Barbarossa, The Axis and the Allies*, J. Erickson & D. Dilks (eds.), 91.
192 A. Werth, *Russia at War*, 151-52.

193   Quoted in: A. Werth, *Russia at War*, 152.
194   Ibid., 152-53.
195   Ibid., 153.
196   Ibid., 153.
197   Ibid., 154.
198   M. van Creveld, et al., *Air Power and Maneuver Warfare*, 69; *GSWW*, Vol. IV, 764.
199   BA-MA RL 200/17, Hoffmann von Waldau, *Tagebuch*, 22.6.41. Wrote von Waldau: "*Im Grossen ist mit durchschlagendem Erfolg zu rechnen.*"
200   *GSWW*, Vol. IV, 764; "*Der Luftkrieg im Osten gegen Russland 1941. (Aus einer Studie der 8. Abteilung 1943/1944.)*," KDC.
201   "*Der Luftkrieg im Osten gegen Russland 1941. (Aus einer Studie der 8. Abteilung 1943/1944.)*," KDC.
202   Ibid.
203   *GSWW*, Vol. IV, 766.
204   W. Murray, *Strategy for Defeat*, 82.
205   A. Kesselring, *Soldat Bis Zum Letzen Tag*, 119-20.
206   J. Prien, et al., *Die Jagdfliegerverbaende der Deutschen Luftwaffe, Teil 6/I, Unternehmen "Barbarossa,"* 12.
207   Even some official German accounts posit these figures. See, for example, "*Der Luftkrieg im Osten gegen Russland 1941. (Aus einer Studie der 8. Abteilung 1943/1944.)*," KDC. The quasi-official German history of Operation *Barbarossa*, citing a *Luftwaffe* situation report, also gives the figure of 35 German aircraft lost on 22 June 1941. See, *GSWW*, Vol. IV, 764.
208   BA-MA RL 2/1185, "*Verluste lt. Meldungen des GQM, 6. Abt.*" No date is provided for this report.
209   J. Prien, et al., *Die Jagdfliegerverbaende der Deutschen Luftwaffe, Teil 6/I, Unternehmen "Barbarossa,"* 12-13.
210   Ibid., 13.
211   On 18 August 1940, at the height of the air war over England, the *Luftwaffe* had suffered a loss of 77 aircraft. Ibid., 13.
212   *GSWW*, Vol. IV, 764.
213   The reference here is to Soviet 10 Army. H.-A. Jacobsen (Hg.), *Generaloberst Halder Kriegstagebuch*, Bd. III, 5.
214   C. Burdick & H.-A. Jacobsen (eds.), *The Halder Diary 1939-1942*, 412-13.
215   *GSWW*, Vol. IV, 539.
216   *GSWW*, Vol. IV, 539; J. Erickson, *The Road to Stalingrad*, 128; D. M. Glantz, *Barbarossa*, 43; A. Clark, *Barbarossa*, 49.
217   A. Seaton, *The Russo-German War*, 135; P. Carell, *Hitler Moves East*, 37; D. M. Glantz, *Red Army Ground Forces*, 25; E. Mawdsley, *Thunder in the East*, 76-77.
218   W. Haupt, *Sturm auf Moskau 1941*, 23; *GSWW*, Vol. IV, 526-27.
219   H. Guderian, *Panzer Leader*, 154.
220   BA-MA RH 27-3/14, *KTB 3. Pz.-Div.*, 22.6.41; BA-MA RH 21-2/927, *KTB Panzergruppe 2*, 22.6.41; C. von Luttichau, *Road to Moscow*, VI:11-12.
221   H. Hoth, *Panzer-Operationen*, 53-54; C. von Luttichau, *Road to Moscow*, VI:15; K.-J. Thies, *Der Ostfeldzug – Ein Lageatlas*, "Lage am 22.6.1941 abds., Heeresgruppe Mitte."
222   C. Burdick & H.-A. Jacobsen (eds.), *The Halder Diary 1939-1942*, 413.
223   W. Haupt, *Sturm auf Moskau 1941*, 22-23; R. Kirchubel, *Operation Barbarossa 1941 (3), Army Group Center*, 33.
224   In its evening report to corps headquarters, 3 Panzer Division reported that the challenges of navigating difficult terrain had been greater than those caused by the enemy on this day. BA-MA RH 27-3/14, *KTB 3. Pz.-Div.*, 22.6.41.
225   BA-MA RH 21-3/732, "*Gefechtsberichte Russland 1941/42.*"
226   BA-MA RH 21-2/927, *KTB Panzergruppe 2*, 22.6.41.
227   H. Hoth, *Panzer-Operationen*, 55.

CHAPTER 7

Vormarsch I: The Frontier Battles
(The Encirclement Battles of Belostok – Minsk)

(23 June – 9 July 1941)

"We have been speaking about a total victory – that is, not simply a battle won ... Such a victory demands an enveloping attack or a battle with reversed fronts, either of which will always make the result decisive." (Carl von Clausewitz)[1]

"The fighting increased in intensity [Haerte] from day to day, as Red Army resistance began to coalesce ... What was certain was that we were striking an assembled Red Army directly inside the frontier area." (*Leutnant* Heinz Doell, 18 PD, 1 July 1941)[2]

"The Russian now fights fanatically and is even ruthlessly deploying his air force, despite heavy losses. On the ground, the General himself is driving everyone forward ... There is enemy resistance at many points. We are not only receiving fire from the front, either. There is shooting from our right, our left, and behind us, which has led to this verse: 'Russians to the right, Russians to the left, shooting from the front and shooting from behind.'" (*Offizier* Hans Hertel, 39 Panzer Corps, 1 July 1941)[3]

"There is no news from the east ... The big and utterly unanswered question still remains: have we really struck at the critical core of the Russian army? Today's report explicitly states that the Russians 'are withstanding even rolling Stuka attacks.' Until now, only the British managed that. Even the fact that more than half of the forces fought at Belostok had to be crushed in combat and only those remaining surrendered is eloquent testimony to the quality of the Russian Army." (Helmuth James von Moltke, 4 July 1941)[4]

7.1: A New Kind of War

From the very first hours of the Russian campaign, German soldiers began to experience disturbing and unanticipated challenges – and, in some cases, viscerally shattering events – which, as they inexorably accumulated over days and weeks, soon convinced the average *Landser* that the war in the east bore little resemblance to previous campaigns in Poland, France, and the Balkans. As outlined in the preceding chapter, even prior to entering combat the poor roadways and rough terrain beyond the Russo-German frontier posed unexpected problems, as vehicles broke down, fuel consumption increased and forward progress stagnated. Field maps furnished to combat units were often marred by inaccuracies, causing added frustrations for tactical commanders as they sought to carry out their missions. The inhospitable Russian climate; the immense distances to be overcome; the constant forced marches for days on end, often without adequate rest, provisions or drinking water, while being tormented by heat, sand and insects – all placed immense physical and psychological burdens on the men, as revealed by countless field post letters and personal diaries.

Shortages of food, water, ammunition, clothing, fuel, spare parts, medical care, and other vital components of modern warfare are, of course, common to periods of prolonged combat; in Russia, however, such shortages tended to be the rule rather than the exception, as inadequate German preparations, coupled with the primitive road and rail infrastructure of European Russia, and a nascent but rapidly expanding partisan threat, conspired to seriously complicate the *Ostheer's* logistical arrangements. Indeed, in assessing the characteristics of wartime daily life for the German soldier in Russia in the summer of 1941, "it is clear that, on the whole, the hardships faced by the majority of the soldiers from the start of the Russian campaign were extreme in nature and cannot be seen simply as 'normal for wartime.' It is doubtful whether the political leadership and the generals, prior to 22 June 1941, fully understood just what they were asking of the troops by ordering them to attack the Soviet Union."[5]

Yet for the German soldier the Russian campaign's most staggering revelation was, far and away, the atavistic cruelty that, from the outset, was to become its most defining feature. As John Keegan keenly observes, the frontier battles were "fought with a brutality and ruthlessness not yet displayed in the Second World War, perhaps not seen in Europe since the struggle between Christians and Muslims in the Ottoman wars of the 16th Century."[6] If not always, Red Army soldiers often enough fought with a tenacity, courage, and a savage cunning that clearly startled, even enraged, their German adversaries. And if the German political and military leadership had set the tone by unleashing a war of annihilation, the Russians often responded in kind: The rampant killing of captured German soldiers, sometimes preceded by their ghastly mutilation; the failure to observe the laws and usages of war as they pertained to German military doctors and other medical personnel; the use of ammunition proscribed by international law (such as so-called "dum-dum" bullets);[7] the conduct of partisan warfare[8] in a manner often characterized by an almost preternatural barbarism – all became hallmarks of the "Russian way of war" from 22 June 1941 onward. While these topics will be explored in greater detail later in the narrative,[9] several historical vignettes from the first days of the Russo-German War will help to highlight its savage and uncompromising character:

Attacking on *Barbarossatag* on the far left flank of Hoth's 3 Panzer Group, 77 Infantry Regiment (26 Infantry Division) learned a bitter, and costly, lesson – the Russian soldier was not to be compared with previous antagonists:

> "X-hour" has arrived. Whistles sound. Rifle squads leap up and storm forward across the frontier. Only quickly overcome the uncertainty! The nervousness subsides. Our soldiers are filled with resolve.
>
> 1st Battalion, on the right, has been tasked with pushing through to the hills directly in front of it and, after taking possession of them, to hold that position for the time being. 2nd Battalion, on the left, has the same mission, while the 3rd Battalion is to follow 2nd Battalion at staggered intervals and cover the Russian frontier posts identified to the north of the attack sector and to neutralize these in the course of the further attack.
>
> While 1st Battalion reaches its objective in the shortest possible time without enemy contact, the 2nd Battalion first has to overpower a few Russian outposts, which had evidently been advanced there by the Russian border guards to the north.
>
> The dogged fighting style of the Russians was evident, even in these early moments. Only by jumping quickly aside at the last minute did the commander of 2nd Battalion evade the detonation of a hand grenade, which a dying Russian, who had been shot down, had thrown between his legs. The 3rd Battalion had its first serious contact with the enemy. After reaching the NKVD frontier post, it did not, unfortunately, await the deployment and support of the heavy weapons, but instead swung into an attack against the outpost.

The officers and men were, no doubt, still overly influenced by the previous, relatively easy days of battle in France. This was to have dire consequences. The Russian NKVD garrison hadn't the slightest intention of surrender or flight. They opened fire with machine guns and rifles, and fought tenaciously to the very last man. When the outpost was taken, 3rd Battalion had the lives of six officers, 12 NCOs and soldiers to mourn. Three officers and 46 NCOs and soldiers were wounded. A sad result.[10]

Hans Hertel, a staff officer attached to 39 Panzer Corps, described the "Russian way of war" as it unfolded on 22 June 1941, and how the *Landser* responded with equal determination and toughness:

When we crossed over the Soviet frontier at 0315 hours on the morning on 22 June 1941, we were aware that this campaign would defy comparison to any previous operations. Even the campaign in the Balkans had proceeded at lightning speed. But, from the outset, the strength of the Red Army and the vastness of the Russian territory made a much tougher and longer fight necessary. Above all, the Red Army soldier was a different soldier to any of our previous opponents. We could already see that in the first hour. Our cries of "*ruki wjerch!*" (hands up!) were completely ignored. Here, they all fought, even in the most hopeless of situations. We experienced Red Army soldiers who lay "wounded" or "dead," let us pass by, and then suddenly shot at us from close behind. What protection is there against a fighting style like that? Only steely ruthlessness. Thus the campaign in the east wore a grim mask from the first hour on. The Soviet soldiers fought with a death-defying determination [*Todesverachtung*] that we had never encountered in any western opponent.[11]

Unteroffizier Fritz Huebner, making contact with the enemy west of Belostok, recalled his shock and consternation – and that of his comrades – when confronted with gruesome atrocities perpetrated by Red Army soldiers. His account also amplifies the insidious dialectic that would result in an ever-expanding universe of brutality and barbarism on the part of both antagonists:

[On 22 June] at 0400 the [artillery] fire ended and the attack began. The enemy may have been pushed back by the force of the blow, but with what tenacity did these Russian soldiers fight back! Indeed, we had the misfortune to stumble upon some disciples of Stalin on the first day: they were real budding officers and *politruks* who wouldn't surrender, but fought instead to the last man, preferring to be shot or beaten to death in their foxholes.

The way of waging war had fundamentally changed; it was completely unfamiliar to us. We soon found the first reconnaissance patrols that had fallen into Russian hands. They had had their genitals cut off while still alive, their eyes gouged out, throats cut, or ears and noses cut off. We went around with grave faces, because we were frightened of this type of fighting. Inevitably, we, too, developed an unnatural ruthlessness [*unnatuerliche Haerte*] that had not been instilled in us during training.[12]

Soldat Erwin Wagner, a 19-year-old radio operator in 263 Artillery Regiment (263 Infantry Division), saw no combat on 22 June, marching with his unit in rapid tempo across the Bug River and, by evening, reaching the front near the village of Bransk, 40 kilometers inside Soviet occupied Poland. The next morning, 23 June, he was ordered to the command post of the artillery regiment's 1st Battalion, located on the far outskirts of Bransk, where he and a comrade were to establish radio contact with regimental headquarters. The village was already in flames, while the road leading into it was being swept by Russian machine gun fire. Enemy armor sought doggedly to push down the road, both sides of which were lined with burnt-out enemy tanks; and inside them the carbonized bodies of their crews. "That was my first disturbing exposure to the war," Wagner recalled, "and it turned my stomach." Evading the hostile MG fire, he worked his way through a ditch alongside the road, the radio perched on his back, reaching the battalion CP at 7.00 that morning. At this point, the dreadful "dance" began. It was to be a horrific baptism of fire:

> We had set up our radio equipment in the courtyard of a shell of a building that was still under construction and established radio contact between the regiment and the battalion command post. We soon noticed that our infantry spearhead had come up against serious resistance for the first time. In addition, there were incoming shells, which, though still isolated and scattered, gradually became more focused on our positions and struck more accurately. The Russian artillery, with its 150mm long barrel guns, was homing in. And it didn't take very long for a multitude of shells to hail down on us.
>
> A bicycle troop was just proceeding past us toward the front. There was no escape for them when a few artillery rounds struck in the middle of their column. It was a gruesome scene that greeted us: body parts, heads, arms, legs, and pieces of flesh whirled through the air; the ground was drenched in blood. This, then, was what war looked like in all its grim reality! Ike [his comrade] and I just had time to find safety in a potato cellar from the shrapnel zipping past. I saw and witnessed the dead and wounded for the first time; the groaning of those in the throes of death – I have never forgotten it to this day. After this interlude, my initial enthusiasm for war had understandably plummeted to zero, and I was convinced that the war could well end for me on the very first day of operations.[13]

Young Wagner, however, had little time for existential contemplation, for no sooner had one crisis ended than another began: Russian tanks had broken through and were bearing down on the command post. In clear, he radioed regimental headquarters, urgently requesting support:

> And then they were there already, the Russian tanks, two, three, four, and five, coming directly toward us. Although they were small – and as we later found out – training tanks from a Russian cadet school; but they shot wildly from light machine guns. They came ever closer, closing to only 10m away from our radio station; my heart was palpably in my mouth. Luckily, somebody had put a small Pak gun into position around 3m away from us. We fired with our armor-piercing rifle ammunition, but most of the tanks were repelled by the defensive fire of our Pak gun, they turned round or stood where they were, burning.
>
> One tank, however, was bold enough to come directly toward our radio station, to within approximately 2m, and subjected us to frenzied machine gun fire; then he drove round our flank and advanced toward us from behind. Our spirits hit rock bottom again, and for the second time on that day, 23 June 1941, we thought that the Last Judgment had arrived. But the Pak gun crew positioned next to us succeeded through its cold-blooded reactions in immobilizing the tank with a single, targeted shot. We breathed a sigh of relief and thought the danger was over, when suddenly the tank gunner jumped out of the tank and opened fire again with a machine pistol, then leapt back into the tank and activated the machine gun. But now our Pak had an immobile target in its sights and a single shot sufficed: a high-explosive shell blew the tank and those inside sky high with a thundering crack.[14]

Eventually, the desperately needed reinforcements arrived – fresh assault battalions that relieved the exhausted infantry in the line and, by evening, restored the precarious situation. All told, Wagner and his comrades were on the receiving end of *seven* separate tank attacks this day, the Russians coming at them with remarkable and disturbing tenacity. "Thus did my first combat in this war, which could have been my last, come to an end," wrote Wagner. "Lost in thought, after a short night spent under an open sky, we marched on further to the east. One thing was already clear to me: This war against Russia was not going to be a stroll in the park!" (*Ein Spaziergang wird dieser Krieg gegen Russland bestimmt nicht werden.*)[15]

As the German mechanized units pushed on deeper into Russian territory, leaving the marching infantry behind and spreading chaos and confusion among the enemy, they sometimes became intermingled with retreating Red Army units, or temporarily cut off from friendly forces. On the night of 24/25 June, the forward CP of 18 Panzer Division, located not far from the town of Slonim, suddenly found itself isolated and enmeshed in a wild and violent skirmish which can only be characterized as surreal. The unsettling incident was recorded by *Leutnant* Georg Kreuter, 101 Rifle Regiment (18 PD), in his personal diary:

24.6.41:
At 2200 hours, I am summoned to the division. I take another five motorcycle messengers with me. The road is blocked by vehicle columns; it takes a long time for me to get through. At the head of the column, I discover that the division [CP] is surrounded. I continue on alone. It is pretty dark. Now and then, I come across one of our soldiers. Russian tanks may be attacking? I establish a hedgehog position with a few hastily organized people.

When a rifle company continues ahead, I join them. We meet the commander of the combat engineer battalion, Major Rahl. He seems to think that there are absolutely no Russians there at all and that we are simply shooting at each other. When I continue onward, I meet my chief, who is going to get help. I go with him to the division command post. We can't go along the road and must take a long detour.

A crazy shoot-out [*tolle Schiesserei*] is underway and there's nothing to be seen. Close to the location of the command post, we come across some Russians, who are lying ahead of us in the grass … It looks like everything has gone berserk at the command post. A Russian column coming from the west had thrust directly onto our march route. They probably wanted to get out of the cauldron. A few trucks were shot into flames by a tank that just happened to be standing by for repairs. The enemy dismounted from the rest and attacked.

It was a strange group of people. There were even a few German Communists among them. Most of them were in civilian clothes! Even women and children were there. They wore steel helmets, too, and shot at us. Everything around us was in flames. Russian trucks and German gasoline trucks! If only day would come so that we can get some help. The shooting is coming from everywhere! … My chief now has command here. The division commander [Nehring] isn't here, but with reconnaissance.

25.6.41:
Even the longest night finally comes to an end! Now we can see clearly! Russians are still being pulled out of the trucks, some of them are hidden under the axles; there are even some in our [vehicles]. It is quite a considerable number coming together here. The woman who wailed so madly through the night has now become quieter. She has an infant with her. Her wailing made everyone nervous

all night long; she must be mad, because she pounds away and talks as if making a grand speech.

Around 20 of the worst renegades and those who have passed themselves off as German soldiers are executed. And the woman is among them! I am pleased that this chapter is closed. If it is to go on like this, then we'll have to receive fresh supplies of nerves![16]

The war diary of 18 Panzer Division also chronicled the harrowing encounter at the division CP that night, noting that "robust small arms and MG fire was punctuated by the wailing of Russian female partisans [*Flintenweiber*], drunken Bolshevists and the cries of wounded German soldiers. It was an unforgettable night of terror [*Schreckensnacht*] and a black day for the divisional staff." Early the next morning (25 June) the Germans were finally able to repulse the surprise Russian attack, having inflicted serious losses on the enemy, beside whose burnt-out trucks were the charred corpses of Russian children. German losses were also prohibitive – seven dead (among them six officers) and 45 wounded, including 11 from the headquarters staff. Breathing a collective sigh of relief, and shaking off the macabre and dreadful events of this "horrible night," the men of 18 Panzer continued their drive eastward, toward Minsk, still confident in the conviction that victory would soon be theirs.[17]

7.2: Forging the Pockets

As historian Dennis Showalter argues in his recent book, *Hitler's Panzers*, one can make the case that the "relative tactical and operational superiority" of the German Army's mobile forces over their adversaries was never greater than at the beginning of Operation *Barbarossa*.[18] In fact, with regard to leadership, training and experience, the *Wehrmacht* as a whole was at the peak of its powers in June 1941, while facing an opponent, the Red Army, which, for all the reasons adumbrated in this narrative, and many others as well, was anything but fully prepared for war. Thus it was hardly surprising that Army Group Center, its armor and motorized infantry advancing swiftly on both flanks, was able to envelop and encircle the armies of Soviet Western Front in several pockets (*Kessel*) between Belostok and Minsk in a mere seven day's time, thereby trapping some 30 Red Army divisions. "It was," avers historian Evan Mawdsley, "the 'Cannae' operation – inspired by Hannibal's 216 BC battle of encirclement and annihilation – that classically educated Prussian staff officers had dreamed of since the time of Field Marshal von Schlieffen."[19]

Ably supported by the air corps of Kesselring's 2 Air Fleet, the pace of the German assault through Belorussia was so spectacular, the chaos and disruption visited upon the Russians so catastrophic, that command and control of Red Army units collapsed from the outset. Unable to operate on a level even approaching the lighting tempo displayed by Hoth's and Guderian's panzers, Soviet commanders reacted sluggishly and ineffectively along the key axes of the German advance. To put a finer point on it, the field-gray invaders were able to get inside the Red Army's "OODA Loop" – a concept invented by the late USAF fighter pilot and strategist John Boyd,[20] and standing for "Observe, Orient, Decide, Act" – and, thus, to palpably disrupt their decision-making cycle. Unable to parry Army Group Center's mechanized spearheads, surrounded and systematically dismantled by German armor, infantry, and air forces, Pavlov's Western Front had practically ceased to exist by 30 June.[21]

Yet the unprecedented victory of Field Marshal von Bock's army group was not without its flaws, nor the Red Army defeat – from the Soviet perspective – without its positive angles. Given the very different marching tempos of the German mobile units and foot infantry, the latter rapidly fell behind the thrusting panzer spearheads, creating dangerous gaps along lines of communication – gaps which Red Army stragglers roamed at will, and which German motorcycle messengers and supply columns navigated at their peril.

Furthermore, although Bock had some 50 divisions at his disposal (among them 31 infantry and 15½ mobile formations), these forces, given the tremendous distances involved, were not enough to hermetically seal off the pockets or thwart every desperate Russian breakout attempt. The result was that significant numbers of Red Army troops – having abandoned their heavy equipment – were able to elude capture, either by successfully reaching Red Army lines to the east, or slinking away into the forests and swamps behind German lines, where their presence as partisans was soon felt. Because Soviet resistance in the pockets was protracted (the *Kessel* were not completely cleared until the first week of July), and because the marching infantry were unable to rapidly relieve mobile units holding down the easternmost encirclement line near Minsk, large elements of 2 and 3 Panzer Groups remained tied down and unable to resume the advance eastward in timely fashion.[22]

In the narrative below, the operations of both panzer groups – and the creation of the outer pocket – will be outlined initially. This will be followed by a brief accounting of the formation of the inner pocket by Army Group Center's two infantry armies closer to the Russo-German frontier. Once again, the narrative will focus extensively on the personal experiences of those – generals, officers, NCOs and common soldiers alike – who fought these battles in the east in the summer of 1941, as illustrated through their personal diaries and letters, official unit war diaries, and accounts prepared by or about them after the war.

7.2.1: 2 Panzer Group

Ignoring enemy units on their flanks – those could be dealt with by the marching infantry later – the two tank corps of Guderian's *Panzergruppe* advanced from the Bug River on either side of Brest-Litovsk, striking out, rapier-like, to the east and northeast for Slonin, Baranovichi and Slutsk. The detailed situation maps prepared daily by the Operations Branch of the German Army General Staff show the panzer divisions – represented by blue ellipses – rapidly and inexorably slipping around the southern flank of Soviet Western Front, forging one arm of Army Group Center's larger outer encirclement.[23] Operations on the ground were greatly facilitated by Loerzer's 2 Air Corps, which was responsible for assisting Guderian's panzer group. In action on 23 June, Bf 109Fs of 51 Fighter Wing, led by the brilliant 28-year-old fighter ace Lt.-Col. Werner Moelders, and operating from a cluster of air fields east of Warsaw, used their 20mm cannon to knock out at least 25 Soviet tanks near Pruzhany. By the end of the day, 2 Air Corps had run its total of Russian aircraft destroyed (in the air or on the ground) to the improbable figure of 716, while losing just 12 planes itself.[24]

Proceeding along two axes – 24 Panzer Corps on the right and 47 Panzer Corps on the left – Guderian's armor made rapid progress on 23 June against faltering Soviet opposition. Lemelsen's 17 and 18 Panzer Divisions (47 Panzer Corps), pushing aside remnants of Soviet 14 Mechanized Corps, advanced on Baranovichi, nearly 200 kilometers beyond the frontier as the crow flies. Further south, Geyr's 3 and 4 Panzer Divisions (24 Panzer Corps), attacking in tandem, shattered Red Army resistance west of Kobrin and drove the defending Soviet task force from the city. 14 Mechanized Corps, the armored reserve of Soviet 4 Army, sought desperately to defend against Guderian's juggernaut but, by day's end, what remained of the corps was forced to beat a rapid retreat eastward. The corps, which had entered battle with about 500 tanks, had been reduced in strength to just 250; two days later, it had but 30 tanks ready for battle. As noted by eminent eastern front historian David Glantz, such a catastrophic attrition rate was typical for Soviet mechanized units during the initial engagements near the frontier.[25]

The spectacularly successful encounters with Soviet 14 Mechanized Corps on 22/23 June not only buoyed the confidence of the tankers of 18 Panzer Division but, as this entry in the divisional war diary reveals, strongly reinforced their feelings of superiority vis-à-vis their Russian adversary:

23.6.41:

0630: The operations group is ordered to decamp from the assembly area to the Bug crossing ... A staff officer is sent ahead to report the reason for the long absence of Operations Group I to the division commander.

On his arrival, the report reaches the division commander that III./PzRgt 18 reached the Jasiolda sector at 0730 hours without any particularly heavy enemy action and that they have created a small bridgehead there. Many tanks were destroyed by the II. and III./PzRgt 18 during their advance to the Jasiolda – once more demonstrating the superiority of the German over the Red tank force. Despite the fierce battles, 18 Panzer Regiment has suffered hardly any losses from enemy fire. Renewed evidence for the absolute superiority of German panzers ...

The morale in the panzer brigade is particularly strong thanks to the kill rate that it has achieved, since nobody reckoned with such great success and such clear superiority right from the first days of the campaign. The Bolshevist as an individual fighter [*Einzelkaempfer*] is extraordinarily tenacious and dogged. Since he has been incited against the Germans, he expects the worst if he is taken prisoner. On many occasions he tenaciously defends himself to the last round to avoid capture at all costs.[26]

The swift dismantling of 14 Mechanized Corps by Guderian's armor, however, was due in part to the fact that it had no new medium or heavy tanks (T-34s or KVs) in its inventory, only older tanks;[27] as the following entry in the war diary of German Fourth Army illustrates, these tanks failed to impress Fourth Army Commander, Field Marshal Hans von Kluge:

> At 1915 hours [Kluge] tells the chief of staff from Pruzhany that he has been with *Generaloberst* Guderian ... The C-in-C also reports that around 100 shot up Russian tanks are lying on the road leading from the south to Pruzhany; a "tank fright" [*Panzerschreck*] is really unnecessary, because these were "virtually ridiculous things." On the other hand, the Russians have to a certain extent put up a brave fight: they had leapt onto the German panzers and shot into the hatches with pistols.[28]

The most spectacular initial advance along the front of 2 Panzer Group was made by Maj.-Gen. Walter Model's battle-tested 3 Panzer Division, the *"Berliner Baerendivision"* ("Berlin Bear Division"). Model, the monocled 50-year-old Prussian general and future field marshal, who was soon to develop a "solid reputation as an energetic commander and brilliant tactician,"[29] had, within 48 hours, pushed his vanguard more than 150 kilometers into Soviet battlespace. The lightning thrust of 3 PD along Panzer Route 1 on 23 June is vividly portrayed in a divisional history published in 1967 by the division's veterans' organization – an account which brings into bold relief the superior training and experience of the German tank forces at the start of the campaign vis-à-vis their Russian counterparts:

> 6 Panzer Regiment rises at 0430 hours because the supply train with the precious fuel has arrived. Immediately after refueling, the tanks rattle on ahead. III./PzRgt 6 drives at the head of the column. The road is heavily choked with sand and the tanks can only get through slowly. In spite of this, the lighter vehicles of the advance detachment make progress and are soon in front of Kobrin, which the Russian is defending.
>
> III./PzRgt 6 arrives shortly after 1100 hours and resolutely comes to grips with the nests of enemy resistance at the western edge of the town, destroying them. While pushing into the town, light Russian tanks turn up and are destroyed without exception. High-explosive shells also crash into the houses from which Russian machine gun fire flares up. After a quarter of an hour the detachment has extinguished all resistance ...

Soon the regiment has got through the town and all elements have reached the road heading east ... A journey begins which will be significant for this day, 23 June 1941.

The tanks of 3 Panzer Division push ahead unrelentingly along the wide road. Movement off the road is impossible because impassable marshland stretches out to the left and right. The Russians have been driven from the road; only the abandoned vehicles, guns, discarded weapons and equipment are a reminder that the enemy is hastily withdrawing. Sometimes our panzers find it difficult to maneuver past the enemy vehicles that often lie across the roadway. The Soviet infantry have fled into the high cornfields and from there are shooting at the German columns following in their open all-terrain vehicles. The troops have to disembark from their vehicles and repulse the Russians at bayonet-point [*mit der blanken Waffe*].

I./PzRgt 6 unexpectedly happens upon Russian tanks at Buchowiecze at 1540 hours. The enemy tanks have suddenly broken out of the nearby forest and taken the German columns under fire. Major Schmidt-Ott immediately put all his companies into action and, in an envelopment maneuver, destroys 36 Russian tanks, type "T-26;" 2./PzRgt 6 (*Oberleutnant* Buchterkirch) alone manages to dispose of 12 tanks in only a few minutes. Polish farmers direct the attention of passing German panzer crews to hidden Russian defensive positions. The light platoon from 6 Panzer Regiment (*Leutnant* Jacobs) is directed toward the small village of Podberje, away from the march route. Here, the tanks come across 6 heavy guns and tractors. The Russian gunners are so surprised by the appearance of the Germans that they give themselves up. Reinforced by medium tanks, 7./PzRgt 6 is ordered forward to join III./PzRgt 6 to support the battalion in its fairly sizeable skirmish with fleeing Soviet columns.

The advance detachment has reached the main district town, Bereza-Kartuska, along the rail line to Minsk, and broken initial resistance with its own forces prior to arrival of 6 Panzer Regiment ... The advance detachment and the panzer regiment are far ahead. The rifle brigade can only follow slowly, as the only road is more than a little jammed ...

The division command post has been transferred to Kobrin via Zabinka on this day. The operations group moves into the church to the east of the bridge. The population is predominantly friendly to the Germans and caters to the soldiers in the rear baggage train and supply columns. A lot of valuable material from the Soviet 4 Army, which had its headquarters in Kobrin, falls into the hands of intelligence staff (Ic) here ...

Despite this success, *Generalleutnant* Model does not grant his soldiers any rest. He himself has arrived in Bereza-Kartuska[30] and orders that the fleeing enemy be pursued without respite. Major Beigel, Commander, Combat Engineer Battalion 39, quickly regroups the advance detachment and immediately continues the advance. The tanks and motorcycles push unrelentingly along the road without regard for withdrawing enemy groups. They drive through villages and forests, cross bridges over the many small river courses, and quickly quell resistance that flares up at their flank. At the railway crossing southwest of Byrten the Russian resistance increases. The light scout vehicles [*Spaehwagen*] fire from all barrels. Soon the wooden freight station goes up in flames. Then the first panzers arrive.

Suddenly well-aimed artillery fire strikes the road. But there is no way of eluding it. So the tanks, followed by the motorcycle riflemen, clatter onward. The journey goes on for 3 km through the night, through the dark forest and the Soviet artillery fire. At 2200 hours the lead platoon of 7./PzRgt 6 (*Leutnant* Ruehl) arrives at the bridge across the initial sector of the Shchara River. The tanks roll unmolested across the wooden bridge and advance a few kilometers beyond it. The motorcycle riflemen and combat engineers take over the defense of the small bridgehead. The tanks then return in the darkness to rest.[31]

By nightfall, 23 June, 3 Panzer Division had rendered 107 Soviet tanks *hors de combat* (bringing its total of destroyed enemy tanks for the first two days of the war to 197) and destroyed or captured several hundred Soviet artillery pieces of different calibers.[32] For his accomplishments on this day, Major Beigel, who led the advance detachment (*Vorausabteilung*), became the first officer of the division to be awarded the Knight's Cross. His official award document read in part: "the capture of a vital bridge over the Shchara succeeded through lighting-quick action [*blitzschnelles Zugreifen*], creating the conditions for the rapid advance of a *Panzerkorps*."[33] At the moment, however, elements of Model's division, rear services mostly, were strung out all the way back into occupied Poland, and did not begin to cross the border until the following day, 24 June. General Model, moreover, barely escaped death on the 24th, when a direct hit by Soviet artillery blew apart the eight-wheeled armored car (killing the four-man crew) in which he had been riding moments after he dismounted the vehicle.[34]

By the evening of 24 June, organized Soviet resistance east of Brest-Litovsk, along the axis of 2 Panzer Group, had largely ceased. While remnants of several Red Army units (among them two tank divisions) were conducting a slow delaying action as they fell back to the east, toward an area south of Slutsk and Bobruisk, the entire southern flank of Soviet Western Front had, in fact, begun to collapse.[35] By 25 June, 47 Panzer Corps had cleared Slonim – where 17 Panzer Division, "running the gauntlet" between Russian units streaming out of the forming pocket and fresh Soviet forces assembling around Baranovichi, had been temporarily encircled the night before[36] – while forward elements of the corps' 18 Panzer Division were fighting for Baranovichi. Directly to the south, Model's 3 Panzer Division (24 Panzer Corps) was bearing down on Slutsk, nearly 300 kilometers from the frontier.[37] At this point, Guderian dispatched his 29 Motorized Division (47 Panzer Corps) to the northwest, toward Volkovysk, and into the rear of Soviet 10 and 3 Armies. Volkovysk was a "particularly important target, for its road network controlled all Soviet lateral and forward movement, as well as resupply between Belostok and Minsk."[38] By now, the remnants of Red Army units from southeast of Belostok to Pruzhany had withdrawn into the forests, with German infantry in rapid pursuit.[39]

While the *Vormarsch* progressed at a rapid pace, the Soviet Air Force demonstrated that, despite its catastrophic losses, it still remained active, at least along the most dangerous axes of 2 Panzer Group's advance, as underscored by two accounts involving 3 Panzer Division on 24 and 25 June, respectively:

24.6.41:
All at once the Soviet Air Force is there! Nobody had reckoned on their still being active, since no Russian planes had been observed in the first couple of days. From 1345 hours the enemy fighter and bomber aircraft strike the road in rolling attacks, bringing the advance to a halt. The operations group of 3 Panzer Division, which is following the panzer brigade to Niedzwiediewa, is also attacked several times.[40]

25.6.41:
On [this day], due to lively enemy air activity, the main body of 6 Panzer Regiment took cover in a few forested areas at either side of the route of advance [*Vormarschstrasse*]. Only the 2nd Battalion with the 5th Company, under *Oberleutnant* Jarosch von Schweder at the vanguard of the division, pushed further on across the initial sector

of the Shchara River. In the meantime, the Soviets sought to halt the German advance with intense bombing attacks, which affected the regimental staff in particular. There were several dead and wounded, while four wheeled vehicles were completely destroyed and two Flak guns suffered direct hits.[41]

Yet neither delays caused by Soviet air attacks, nor by Red Army engineers blowing the bridges along the routes of advance succeeded in significantly slowing Guderian's tanks, which continued to tighten the noose around the Soviet Western Front from the south; Guderian also dispatched strong mobile forces due east, toward the critically important crossings of the Berezina River. On 26 June, Model's 3 Panzer Division, continuing its furious drive, captured Slutsk, about 110 kilometers from Bobruisk and the Berezina, the last major river barrier before the Dnepr. On the morning of 27 June, 47 Panzer Corps, on the left flank of the panzer group, captured Stolpce, less than 75 kilometers from Minsk, despite coming under repeated attack from Red Army units migrating southeast from the Belostok – Novogrodek sectors in an effort to escape encirclement.[42]

On 28 June, at 0000 hours, Guderian's subordination under Kluge's Fourth Army was finally lifted and 2 Panzer Group placed under the direct control of Army Group Center – this in recognition of the fact that Guderian and his armor had achieved complete operational freedom.[43] The panzer general was no doubt relieved to no longer be under Kluge's nominal control – at least for the time being. Relations between the two men had long been strained, and had continued to deteriorate after the start of *Barbarossa*, no doubt in part because of Guderian's ongoing acts of subterfuge, if not outright insubordination.[44]

Yet regardless of formal command arrangements, Guderian had his own ideas about how the campaign was to be fought and he was not about to be deterred from implementing them. Simply put, his immediate objective was the Dnepr River line, far to the east, and he was determined to get there, even if it meant violating his orders: On 26 June, with the spearheads of Hoth's 3 Panzer Group barely 30 kilometers from Minsk, Army Group Center had directed Guderian to wheel northward with the bulk of his group and to close the outer pocket by linking up with Hoth at Minsk; by 30 June, however, only two of Guderian's divisions (17 PD and 29 ID (mot.)) were in position along the eastern and southern walls of the pocket, while seven divisions were continuing to push on to the east. In Guderian's defense, he had been granted permission to advance toward the Berezina (and the Dnepr), yet by leaving only the thinnest of screens to hold the pocket, he was, at a minimum, violating the spirit of his orders.[45]

On 28 June, 3 Panzer Division took Bobruisk. Model then ordered his exhausted infantry to seize a bridgehead over the Berezina – the "River of Birches" – without regard to losses. With the bridge demolished by the Russians, and no armor available for support, the men of II./SR 394 crossed the river in pneumatic rubber boats while under heavy fire and built a modest bridgehead on the eastern bank. Only robust artillery support and air support from Moelders' 51 Fighter Wing saved them from being crushed by Red Army counterattacks during the next 24 hours.[46] An entry in the 3 PD war diary (2100 hours, 29 June) described the fighting:

> The Russians have attacked our right flank – in cases "in droves," penetrating our forwardmost elements amid cries of "Urrah" – but were driven back and have withdrawn under cover of suddenly descending ground fog, hiding in foxholes from which they only occasionally rattle off well-targeted rifle and machine gun fire at [our] riflemen. The result of this is a number of losses (fatalities and wounded). In the main, they have established their position on either side of the railway embankment and at the tip of the forest, 3 km southeast of Bobruisk. An arc of disruptive fire comes from 75 AR on a level with Titovka. Enemy artillery fire is only very isolated and untargeted. As soon as darkness falls, the fire suddenly

picks up again; the Russian also begins to attack again from the left of the road and after firing flares. But this attack also slackens once more and the regiment manages to hold the small bridgehead, while a platoon of anti-tank guns is deployed for reinforcement.[47]

Despite heavy casualties, Model's reconnaissance units were soon probing further east, beyond the river, toward the Dnepr.[48] In just seven days, his division had dashed some 400 kilometers beyond the Russo-German frontier.

By now, both flanks of Soviet Western Front were in a state of collapse. Hoth's 3 Panzer Group, operating on the left wing of Army Group Center, reached the high ground around Minsk on 27 June and seized the flaming city the next day, while Guderian's 17 Panzer Division reached its southern outskirts.[49] A city of about 250,000 inhabitants, Minsk had been badly disfigured by a series of savage *Luftwaffe* raids. Those Red Army forces that had retired eastward through the city "saw not a city but a bonfire.

> Even the parks were in flames. The capital of Belorussia was shrouded in smoke, and blasts shook the air. One wave of German bombers after another rolled over the city, turning it into rubble. Thousands of refugees streamed east, only to be massacred by German pilots on blocked roads ...
>
> German pilots looked at Minsk as one huge target and dropped bombs indiscriminately, making no distinction between Western Front headquarters and a grocery store. Many citizens in Minsk had lived through the devastation of the revolution and the civil war, but no one had ever before seen a blazing park or a city block turned into dust, and no one had thought that such destruction was in the power of humans.
>
> About 40,000 people left their homes, but no one knows how many died on the way to supposed safety, killed by collapsing walls or friendly fire or mowed down by a machine gun burst from a Messerschmitt. What is known is that about 200,000 stayed. Some had already heard the horrifying accounts of the first wave of refugees that had descended on Minsk from Brest, Baranovichi, and Molodechno, reporting clogged roads, indifferent army officers, deserters in the woods, and ferocious *Luftwaffe* strikes.[50]

Reaching Minsk in early July 1941, days after the fighting there had ceased, soldiers of 137 Infantry Division marveled at the destruction wrought by the *Luftwaffe* on this important road and rail junction:

> In the city center, smoke-blackened chimneys revealed that wooden houses had stood here. The ruins of a few formerly stately, but now burned out Red Army buildings, and the Party buildings of the Soviets, appeared disconsolate in contrast. It looked particularly bad in the area around the train station. Here, the *Stukas* had virtually ploughed the ground over; burned out trains, ripped up rail carriages, and chaotically twisted rails jutting up into the air embodied a picture of total destruction. Mighty iron posts of the rail system had snapped like matchsticks. In multitudes the civilian population migrated into the countryside. A sack slung over the shoulder contained all the possessions which these people had been able to retrieve from the chaos.[51]

Meanwhile, with the headstrong Guderian intent on driving eastward and less concerned with sealing the pocket, the Soviets were given at least a 24 hour reprieve, enabling some of their units to slip from the looming trap. Finally, on 29 June 1941, the tanks of

Nehring's 18 Panzer Division, racing up to Minsk from the south, linked up with elements of 3 Panzer Group.[52] The outer wall of the encirclement ring around Soviet Western Front was now complete. Thus, by the end of June, the remnants of four Soviet armies (3, 4, 10, 13) were trapped in several pockets stretching from Belostok through Novogrodek to Minsk. Western Front had "virtually ceased to exist as an organized force."[53] Fierce fighting, however, was to go on for days, as the Soviets struggled tenaciously to break out to the northeast, east and southeast. During one five-day period (26-30 June), 71 Infantry Regiment (29 Motorized Division) was alone responsible for taking 36,000 prisoners – "proof," stated Guderian, "of the massive scale of the Russians' attempts to break out."[54]

On 30 June, Guderian flew in a bomber to the command post of 3 Panzer Group to meet with General Hoth and discuss "the future coordination of our activities."[55] Both panzer commanders chafed under the restrictions placed on their movements by Hitler and the Army High Command (OKH); both were convinced that the mobile units tied down along the *Kesselfront* needed to be replaced by marching infantry, so the panzer groups could strike out in force for the Western Dvina and Dnepr River lines and prevent the Red Army from reforming a coherent defensive front behind these formidable geographical barriers. The matter, moreover, was becoming urgent, for German aerial reconnaissance had revealed that the Russians were assembling fresh armies in the Smolensk – Orsha – Mogilev area.[56]

Deus ex machina, an order arrived that very day from General Halder, Chief of the Army General Staff, instructing Hoth and Guderian to prepare to advance against both rivers along the line Rogachev – Mogilev – Orsha (Dnepr) – Vitebsk – Polotsk (Dvina). The new operation, which Halder deemed of decisive importance, was to begin as soon as possible (at the latest, by 5 July);[57] its successful execution would create favorable conditions for the capture of the area around Smolensk, including the vital landbridge west of that city, which stretched from Orsha to Vitebsk, along the watershed between the two rivers. As Halder, Bock, and the panzer generals were fully aware, possession of this area was a pivotal prerequisite to the capture of Moscow.[58]

Meanwhile, no sooner had 18 Panzer Division reached the southern outskirts of Minsk than Guderian ordered it to advance at once on Borisov, on the Berezina. In response, at daybreak on 30 June, Nehring's tankers rumbled east over surprisingly good roads, striking out for the Minsk – Smolensk – Moscow *Autobahn*. After days of struggling along wretched roadways, the tank commanders "were beaming;"[59] they began a brilliant *Panzeraid* which was to take them over 100 kilometers into the rear of Soviet forces and culminate in the capture of the town and a vital bridgehead over the Berezina. Observing their advance from high overhead was General Lemelsen, Commander, 47 Panzer Corps:

> 1.7.41:
> We are still located in Stolpce with the staff, because the threat to our flanks continues to be considerable. But 18 Panzer Division has already begun advancing to Borisov today and at midday had already reached the Berezina River. Hopefully they will pull off the historic crossing as successfully as did Napoleon. I flew in the *Storch* this morning to the division in Sinoleviza, approximately 130 km (the distances here are enormous), and could observe the entire advance of the division from the air. March discipline is, thank God, improving from day to day.[60]

In an article published in 1961, General Nehring recalled the dramatic events of 30 June and 1 July 1941:

> The panzer spearhead reached Minsk amid constant fighting on the evening of 29 June via Stolpce … Here 18 Panzer Division received the order to advance on the *Autobahn* alone to Borisov on the Berezina River, while skirting Minsk to

the south. The continued advance of Guderian's *Panzergruppe* was to be ensured by gaining a bridgehead there and holding it open – an undertaking which closely resembled a suicide mission [*Himmelfahrtskommando*] since it led around 100 km deep into enemy-occupied territory, into which fresh Russian forces were continually being brought. The two other divisions of the [47 Panzer] Corps remained tied to the encirclement front at the Belostok cauldron. Hence the solo run!

Early on 30 June, we start off for Borisov on very good, new roads that were at that time not entered on our extremely inadequate maps of the Russian terrain. This situation only improved after reprinting captured Russian maps, which were excellent. In the Ussa sector near Kolodniki there is serious resistance, which can only be broken during the course of the night. Immediately, in the early morning of 1 July, an advance detachment is formed which is to strike ahead at greater speed. The core of this: 2nd Battalion, 18 Panzer Regiment, under Major Teege, plus 18 Motorcycle Battalion mounted on the tanks, plus Major Teichert's artillery battalion. The rest of the division is to assemble after the battle and to move up quickly.[61]

Shortly after dawn, 1 July, 18 Panzer resumed its blistering advance, with the tanks of Major Teege and the rest of the advance detachment in the lead. By 0900 hours, after clearing a large wooded area, they reached the *Autobahn*, where they swept aside the Soviet defenders and raced on toward Borisov; by noon, they were approaching the outskirts of the town. As so often before, the Russians were caught off balance by the speed of the German advance and were unprepared. Yet just as it seemed the town might be secured without major opposition, German aerial reconnaissance reported about 100 Russian tanks approaching from the east.[62] At this point, the war diary of 18 Panzer Division picks up the story:

At 1400 hours the armored spearhead is in the midst of a firefight with around 20 enemy tanks, which, in camouflaged positions on either side of the *Autobahn*, are destroyed, one by one, without our incurring any losses; one after another they go up in flames. Attacking immediately, 3./K 18 to the right and I./SR 52 to the left of the highway succeed in clearing the forested area on both sides of the road during the first onslaught, though suffering <u>serious</u> losses. On the left in particular, the enemy is successfully removed from his excellent fortifications in close combat, at the point of a bayonet, and the open terrain west of Borisov reached. Through the relentless action of the advance detachment, complete exploitation of the element of surprise, and the responsible intervention by the commander of II./PzRg 18, a favorable jump-off position for crossing the Berezina River is won.

An unexpected and powerful advance by 18-20 enemy tanks in two rows on the highway from the direction of Borisov into the position of 18 Panzer Division, and almost reaching the division command post, also ends with the total destruction of these enemy tanks. This attack, which ignored all the usual prerequisites for an armored attack, was conducted with admirable élan and the greatest audacity. The attackers were elements of the 1 Moscow Proletarian Division.

Before nightfall, the division [18 PD], striking out boldly to the left with 52 SR and II./PzRg 18, continues its attack, crossing the bridge over the Berezina north of the railway bridge and establishing an operationally valuable bridgehead on the east bank of the Berezina while under heavy enemy artillery fire and again suffering serious losses ... The formation of the bridgehead across the Berezina along the highway can be reported at 2150 hours.[63]

Throughout the night, the units of 18 Panzer in the bridgehead, in open terrain offering no protection, were pounded by Soviet artillery, resulting in more casualties. But the bridgehead was held. Through 18 PD's spectacular *coup de main*, and the earlier successes of Model's 3 Panzer Division, the prerequisites for an advance to the Dnepr were rapidly falling into place.[64]

7.2.2: 3 Panzer Group

The four panzer and three motorized infantry divisions of Hermann Hoth's 3 Panzer Group made up the northern prong of Army Group Center's outer envelopment operation. On 22 June, Hoth's armor had broken through the main Soviet defensive belt and driven a deep wedge north of Grodno between Soviet Northwestern and Western Fronts, while also capturing intact the three bridges over the Neman River at Olita and Merkine, an essential prerequisite for the fulfillment of the panzer group's mission. Within 48 hours, Field Marshal von Bock, in acknowledgement of Hoth having achieved operational freedom, released his group from Ninth Army control and subordinated it directly to Army Group Center.[65]

On 23 June, however, as 3 Panzer Group continued its advance through Lithuania and into Belorussia, it was confronted by unexpected delays due more to challenges posed by the terrain than by enemy resistance. Hoth's armor and vehicles had to navigate the primitive sandy tracks through the Rudnicka Forest (Puszcza Rudnicka) – a dense, primeval woodland of pine, black alder and birch which, as Hoth himself recalled, "had probably never before seen a motor vehicle."[66] Wheeled vehicles broke down, or became stuck in the deep sand, blocking the routes and causing serious delays; the wooden bridges which crossed the network of streams first had to be strengthened by German pioneers to support tanks and other vehicles, resulting in further delays. Movement was also slowed by the presence of Red Army stragglers on the flanks or in the rear of the marching columns, while wildfires caused by the fighting, or perhaps set intentionally by the withdrawing Russians, posed an additional concern. As the marching columns became strung out, the long distances disrupted communications by telephone, while radio vehicles of French origin, unable to withstand the rigors of the march on the poor roads, rapidly broke down.[67] Adding gratuitously to the general disruption was the poor march discipline of infantry and *Luftwaffe* units, which strayed from their assigned routes to join the "faster" routes taken by 3 Panzer Group:

> At von Brauchitsch's insistence, some routes had been allocated to infantry formations, but there were in fact too few routes for either armor or infantry. A marching infantry division allotted the use of a single route occupied 22 miles of track and took a whole day to pass a point, and when in danger of being left too far behind by the panzer formations, infantry horse-drawn transport and guns frequently disobeyed orders and left the allotted route to join the axes of the panzer troops, where they often blocked or slowed down motorized movement. 19 Panzer Division was halted for hours by a column of nearly 2000 *Luftwaffe* lorries,[68] many of them loaded with telegraph poles, which had ignored the vehicle march table, and Ninth Army, forgetful of its own orders, began to drive the infantry divisions forward, urging them to form mobile detachments by centralizing their limited number of motor vehicles. These motorized elements took to the panzer axes as there were no other fast routes available to them.[69]

Delayed by fuel shortages resulting from the hopelessly inadequate and overburdened road net, 7 Panzer Division, the spearhead of General Rudolf Schmidt's 39 Panzer Corps, did not get moving again until 0900 hours on 23 June, a warm and sunny early summer's day. 7 Panzer's tanks and support vehicles struggled to move through the deep sand of the few tracks leading out of the Rudnicka Forest as they left their bridgehead southeast of Olita and struck out for the former Lithuanian capital of Vilnius (Vilna), some 75 kilometers to the east. By afternoon, elements of the division's 25 Panzer Regiment had cleared the forest and, despite some fierce enemy opposition, reached Vilnius and the high ground east of the city by the evening of the 23rd. Decamping from its bridgehead over the Neman at Merkine, General Adolf-Friedrich Kuntzen's 57 Panzer Corps, also slowed by the primitive pathways, made more modest gains; by day's end, however, its forwardmost units had motored 70 kilometers to Voronov on the Lida-Vilnius road. Through its advance on this second day of the war, Hoth's armor had widened the gap between Soviet Northwestern and Western Fronts to well over 100 kilometers and further enveloped the latter's 3 Army.[70]

The next day, 24 June, also broke clear and sunny. At first light, Brig.-Gen. Hans *Freiherr* von Funck's 7 Panzer Division resumed its march. Supported by tanks of the panzer regiment, the division's motorcycle borne infantry stormed into Vilnius and, after disposing of light opposition, occupied the city later that morning, having earlier seized the adjacent airfield and 25 intact Red Army aircraft. In anticipation of the German capture of Vilnius, local officials had adorned the city in traditional colors, while the inhabitants enthusiastically received their "liberators" with flowers and wine. The withdrawing Russians had a rather different reception in mind: According to the war diary of 7 PD (0630 hours), the troops were to be alerted at once because the local wells had all been poisoned (*vergiftet*).[71]

Also operating in the Vilnius sector was Schmidt's other tank division, 20 Panzer, led by Maj.-Gen. Horst Stumpff. A divisional history – another by the prolific German author and eastern front veteran, Rolf Hinze – offers an insightful glimpse into the nature of the advance along the front of 3 Panzer Group:

> On 24.6.[41], 21 Panzer Regiment crossed over the Warka River and pushed enemy tanks back toward Vilnius. The regiment secured the area to the east and north beyond the Warka. The unbelievably poor roads meant increased gasoline consumption. Since the fuel trucks could not yet get through, due to the impeded roads, the forces lacked fuel supplies. In the summer heat, the slow-moving elements of the division moving up along the route of advance churned up dust clouds on the dry and unsurfaced roads, which, visible from a great distance, provided ideal targets for attacking bombers ...
>
> The division then received the order to cut Vilnius off from the west and southwest, joining up on the right with 7 Panzer Division. So the artillery took up position in front of the city, while 59 SR pushed into Vilnius from the southwest ... During the combat on 23.-24.6., the division destroyed 26 enemy tanks, of which 18 were destroyed by III./PzRgt 21 ...
>
> The poor roads in the forest terrain to the west of Vilnius, which, in their condition, could not cope with the heavy traffic, and the lack of fuel delayed the division's ability to close ranks, meaning that only 112 SR, as well as a light battery from 92 AR, and a light Flak battery, were available for further action on the high ground around Losk, while the heavy elements continued to drag – or push – themselves along the forest tracks to the west of the Warka. The poor cross-country mobility of the commercial French vehicles was extremely noticeable here. As a result of these difficulties, the forces failed to meet all of the division's time schedules by several hours.[72]

The rigors of the *Vormarsch* are described in the memoirs of Helmut Martin, in 1941 a young anti-tank gunner in the *Panzerjaegerabteilung* of 14 Motorized Infantry Division

(39 Panzer Corps), which began the eastern campaign in reserve, moving up behind the panzer corps' armored vanguard. Martin's experiences in the first days of the war, in "this alien land" (*dieses fremde Land*), were almost universally shared by the *Landser* in the summer of 1941. His story also reveals that he – like many young German soldiers – approached the war as a stirring adventure and an opportunity to escape the often stultifying cadence of civilian life:

> In early morning on the 25 June, we continued on. We rolled back to Kalvaria and turned onto the road to Vilnius. On this road, we passed a small town … of which only the large, wide, crumbling ovens with their high chimneys still remained, looking like long, charred, shrivelled fingers towering up into the blue sky. The wooden house walls had all burned down … Not a soul could be seen any more. At the far end of the village lay a two-wheeled cart with the bloated corpse of a horse lying in the ditch by the roadside. Huge dust clouds, churned up by the vehicles driving ahead of us, cloaked this town of destruction in a gray fog.
>
> From now on, we put huge distances behind us every day. Sometimes we branched off the *Rollbahn* and would drive onward on dirt tracks or forest paths. Beginning the advance as a reserve unit was welcome to me, since it allowed me to gradually get a feeling for battle, whereby I hoped to be able to gather good experiences. It wasn't simply the journey into this foreign land that excited me, but also the opportunity to lay under the birch trees in the tall grass, far away from the dreariness of school, cramped classrooms with stale air and irritating studying. This yearning for faraway places, for the unknown, had a relentless grip on me, and the war, which promised me something, as it were, athletic, noble, provided me with the means to satisfy it …
>
> On the morning of 26 June, at a brisk pace, the company traversed the relatively undamaged outlying districts of the city of Vilnius and at midday, after well over 100 kilometers of distance traveled, moved into Gierwiadi, where vehicles were checked and refueled. The *Landser* were also in need of some maintenance, since due to the poor road conditions, enormous clouds of dust had rained down on the column. Faces and uniforms were coated in several millimeters of dirt. Droplets of sweat had forged deep rivulets and we hardly recognized each other when we saw each other at the resting place.
>
> This was located next to a church, which was built of stone and whose white paint was visible from far away, gleaming out from among the inhabitants' wooden houses. As we drove through Russia, we came across this characteristic scene time and time again. During this rest, I took the opportunity of looking more closely at the wooden huts, though I avoided spending much time in them, in order to spare myself the acquaintance with any lice, bugs, or fleas … On our journey thus far, I had noticed that there were no stone buildings in the villages except the church. Only in the larger towns were houses in the center constructed of solid materials.[73]

It will be recalled that, on 22 June, Lt.-Gen. I.V. Boldin, Deputy Commander, Soviet Western Front, had flown through airspace teeming with German planes to 10 Army headquarters in a futile attempt to organize a counterstroke. Two days later (24 June), Boldin, on Pavlov's orders, finally managed to launch a counterattack with two mechanized and one cavalry corps, striking northward toward Grodno in an effort to parry Hoth's steel juggernaut and stave off the impending encirclement of Red Army formations around and north of Belostok. Without effective communications, air cover, logistical support or sufficient numbers of modern tanks, Boldin's attack was "doomed from the start."[74] Decimated by the *Stukas* of Richthofen's 8 Air Corps, his forces arrived in the Grodno region long after

3 Panzer Group had pushed well beyond the frontier to Vilnius. Boldin's surviving armor, infantry and cavalry thus engaged units of Strauss' Ninth Army, which finished off the attacking Russians by means of a devastating infantry and anti-tank ambush.[75] (Note: A more detailed account of this action can be found in Section 7.2.3.)

The advance of Hoth's panzer group had also entrapped large numbers of Red Army soldiers in the Rudnicka Forest,[76] while others had fled into its dense woodlands and swamps to escape the merciless strafing and bombing by German aircraft. From the relative protection of the forest, Russian stragglers conducted what the Germans called a *"Kleinkrieg"* (guerilla warfare) against supply columns, medical units, and other rear services, sometimes causing serious disruptions. Late that afternoon (24 June), 3 Panzer Group appealed to Ninth Army for additional infantry to assist with clearing the Russians from the forests, a mission which in the days ahead was to be handled by the divisions of 5 and 6 Army Corps.[77]

His armored group having reached Vilnius, Hoth prepared to move on Vitebsk on the Western Dvina, more than 300 kilometers to the east. From the panzer commander's perspective, such a move was in accordance with his overarching mission of preventing the enemy's retreat across the Dvina-Dnepr River lines; moreover, he did not anticipate meeting significant resistance along this axis of advance. Hoth informed Army Group Center of his intentions, while his staff worked out the requisite details for the drive to Vitebsk. Shortly thereafter, however, a radio message arrived from army group, stating that OKH had rejected Hoth's proposal; instead, 3 Panzer Group was to attack southeast, in the direction of Minsk and, in close cooperation with Guderian's group, seal the pocket around the Soviet frontier armies.[78] In his post-war study of the 1941 summer campaign, Hoth recalled his reaction to the OKH directive:

> This order had a devastating effect in the headquarters of 3 Panzer Group, which was attempting to shift its command post from Olita to Voronov. All efforts by the forces in the previous days – "racing on ahead of the army group's left wing" – to gain the Orsha-Vitebsk landbridge before the enemy seemed to have been in vain.[79]

As yet unwilling to accept the rejection of his operational plan, Hoth went so far as to send his OKH liaison officer, an "obliging and judicious" lieutenant-colonel, back to OKH headquarters in East Prussia to argue his position. Hoth's envoy met with Chief of the Army General Staff Halder, who rejected the "big solution" (*groessere Loesung*) – a solution also favored by Field Marshal von Bock – of an advance all the way to the Dvina-Dnepr river barriers. Fearing the panzer corps could become separated and defeated in detail if they continued toward the rivers, Halder persuaded Army C-in-C Brauchitsch to direct the army group to implement the smaller solution (i.e., closing the ring at Minsk). As Halder conceived the operation, it was imperative "to form an inner encirclement ring with infantry corps south of the confluence of the Shchara and Neman Rivers [near Mosty], while the Panzer Groups Guderian and Hoth, converging on Minsk, closed an outer ring."[80]

Like Guderian a brilliant panzer leader, yet unlike his colleague a more dutiful one, Hoth at once turned his tanks southeast toward Minsk. While Vilnius was to be the northern shoulder of Hoth's advance, the town of Lida, 100 kilometers to the south, was to be the pivot. Brig.-Gen. Josef Harpe's 12 Panzer Division (57 Panzer Corps) now took the lead; by nightfall, 24 June, it was approaching the Belorussian capital. The colorful situation maps of the Army General Staff's Operations Branch illuminate the dramatic tempo of the advance, as Hoth's four panzer divisions wheeled into line and rumbled on toward their destination. The armored columns tossed up clouds of dust. The heat was insufferable. The "good" roads, marked on the German General Staff maps in primary red, were, more often than not, little more than tracks of sand. The terrain tore up the vehicles, which consumed fuel and oil filters at a rate much greater than anticipated by the Army's logisticians prior to the campaign. Enemy resistance increasingly made itself felt and was becoming more coherent in its application.[81]

With support from 8 Air Corps temporarily interrupted – its ground organization was struggling to keep pace with the advance of the panzer group and shift its bases forward – the Soviet Air Force was able to operate with some effectiveness against the German spearheads. For example, on 26 June, 7 Panzer Division, lacking fighter protection, suffered serious losses in men and vehicles when struck by rolling bomber and low-level attacks.[82] A *Luftwaffe* General Staff study prepared later in the war acknowledged the problem:

> Already in the initial days, the operations of the fighter planes formed … their point of main effort above the *Panzerrollbahnen* and armored spearheads, which were heavily attacked by the Soviet bomber formations. With the rapid advance of Army Group Center's armored spearheads, it was frequently very difficult to bring the fighters' ground organization forward quickly enough, thus their range was sometimes not sufficient to guarantee fighter protection for the foremost armored units.[83]

Yet in spite of such challenges, the impetus (*Vorwaertsdrang*) of the German drive was ineluctable.

Once again experiencing fuel shortages, 7 Panzer Division serendipitously discovered a Soviet fuel dump with satisfactory octane gasoline, enabling it to set out for Minsk on the morning of 25 June – a mixed battlegroup (*Kampfgruppe*) based on its 6 Rifle Regiment leading the way. Moving swiftly to the southeast, along the road from Vilnius via Molodechno to Minsk, the division overran all Russian resistance, parried repeated Soviet attacks with armor – 25 Panzer Regiment destroying large numbers of tanks and other armored vehicles – skirted past the still unoccupied bunkers of the Stalin Line east of Molodechno (along the former Polish-Russian border) and, the next day (26 June), reaching out behind Minsk, cut the highway and rail lines linking the city with Moscow.[84]

Also on 26 June, Harpe's 12 Panzer Division broke through the Stalin Line at Rakuv (Rakow), northwest of Minsk and, by nightfall, was nearing the outskirts of the burning city. Indeed, by evening, both 12 and 20 Panzer Divisions were bearing down on Minsk, while 7 Panzer was ranging far to the northeast, toward the Berezina River[85] – its elated panzer regiment reporting "victory along the entire line" (*Sieg auf der ganzen Linie*), despite some heavy losses.[86] The next day (27 June), 20 Panzer Division fought its way into the now fully manned bunkers, barbed-wired entanglements, tank traps, and other obstacles of the Stalin Line;[87] bitter close combat among the bunkers dragged on into the 28th, the division sustaining serious losses and counting among its dead one regimental commander and eight other officers.[88] That night, however, 20 Panzer Division was only 14 kilometers north of Minsk.[89] Meanwhile, along the front of Guderian's 2 Panzer Group, lead elements of 47 Panzer Corps, pushing past Baranovichi, were closing on the city from the southwest. The jaws of the trap were about to snap shut around Pavlov's Western Front.[90]

Having reached the Stalin Line meant that Hoth's divisions were now crossing the borders of the Soviet Union as they had existed prior to start of the Second World War in September 1939. If in Lithuania and Soviet-occupied eastern Poland the German invaders had often been greeted as liberators, they now needed to brace themselves for a singularly less enthusiastic reception, as addressed in the war diary of 3 Panzer Group on 28 June: "The troops are being informed that the actual Bolshevik-Soviet territory starts at Minsk. In contrast to the mostly friendly populations hitherto encountered, we can now anticipate increased incitement of the population against us, sabotage and guerilla warfare [*Bandenkrieg*]."[91] This was not, however, the only disturbing passage in the group's war diary this day:

> 57 Panzer Corps reports that the Russians have appeared in great numbers during the attacks on the morning of the 28th. The fight against these human waves has given our soldiers a certain feeling of superiority. The Russians had also reportedly deployed heavy tanks (4), which our 50mm Pak guns have not been able to penetrate.[92]

As was hardly atypical for central European Russia at this time of year, 28 June brought thundershowers along the front of 3 Panzer Group. The defenders of Minsk, however, had a more ominous and deadly thunder to contend with, as German mechanized columns crashed down upon them from the north. By 0925 hours, lead elements of 12 Panzer Division were but 10 kilometers northwest of Minsk and attacking toward the city; by 1600 hours, Minsk was in Harpe's hands. It was a great victory, marred only by the painful loss of the valiant commander of 7 Panzer Division's 25 Panzer Regiment, *Oberst* Karl Rothenburg; after being wounded, and while being transported to a dressing station in the rear through territory still occupied by the Russians, his small convoy was ambushed, resulting in his death. To honor his memory, 25 Panzer Regiment was now to be known as "Panzer-Regiment Rothenburg."[93]

Elements of Stumpff's 20 Panzer Division, entering Minsk soon after 12 Panzer had done so, fought fierce street battles in the southern parts of the city. A soldier in the division's *Kampfgruppe Bismarck* offered this impression of the now badly defaced Belorussian capital:

> At first glance, Minsk seemed rather village-like. The small wooden houses at the northern edge of the city, with their dilapidated garden fences, resembled the Polish and Belorussian villages we had gone through. To the left, a barracks rose up, in part just bare brickwork, but at least made of red brick. While we slowly rolled by the main gate, civilians dragged boxes and bags out the rear exits of the barracks. Nobody gave them a second glance.
>
> Between the low, old wooden houses, the high facades of large buildings suddenly sprang up, partially also bare brickwork, some complete. The attempt to construct prestigious buildings was discernible here. None of the buildings were accomplished or architecturally pleasing. Looking closer, we could see the cheap schematic nature of the buildings. Whitewashed outer walls instead of striking facades, cheap plaster impressions with silver or gold-bronze leaf confirmed our impression of uniform mass production.
>
> The *Luftwaffe* must have visited a major attack on Minsk one or two days previously; leaving only ruins behind. All the Party buildings, schools, tenement blocks, and state grocery stores were destroyed, with the exception of the large Party building by the Lenin monument. Dead Red Army soldiers lay along the edges of the streets. Nobody bothered about them. The apathy and dullness of the populace could not be characterized more fittingly than through this attitude to their own dead. Instead, the rabble appeared assiduously concerned with salvaging useful things from the ruins, especially foodstuffs and items of clothing from the warehouses. Women with huge bundles, under whose weight they nearly collapsed, stole away into the side streets.[94]

On 29 June, elements of 2 Panzer Group's 18 Panzer Division, coming from the south, linked up with Hoth's forces near Minsk; on 30 June, a battalion of 18 Panzer pushed directly into the city.[95] The outer encirclement ring was now complete, sealing the fate of several hundred thousand Red Army soldiers. In accordance with his orders, Hoth distributed his divisions along the northern edge of the pocket, from an area north of Lida through Volozhyn to Minsk – a defensive front more than 150 kilometers in length.[96] It was a strongly held front, less porous than Guderian's more thinly held line to the south. In the days which followed Hoth's sector would hold – nothing but prisoners would get through to the rear – while the divisions of his panzer group were gradually relieved by the infantry of Ninth Army arriving on the battlefield, freeing the panzers again for mobile operations.[97]

As mentioned above (Section 7.2.1), on 30 June, Guderian flew to Hoth's headquarters to discuss future operations. Some historians have speculated that the two generals used their meeting to conspire to renew their eastward drive without waiting for orders from higher headquarters (OKH or Army Group Center).[98] In the German quasi-official history of the Second World War (Vol. 4, *The Attack on the Soviet Union*), Ernst Klink argues that, "as an undesirable consequence of the protracted resistance in the pockets, mobile units remained tied down there and were delayed in resuming their advance eastward. Not surprisingly, under these circumstances the commanders of the armored units were suspected of wishing to evade tight control of their movements and, notwithstanding their task of destroying enemy forces, continued to advance as fast as possible."[99] To make such a claim *writ large*, however, is unfair to Hoth, who appears, albeit reluctantly, to have complied faithfully with his orders; in fact, on 29 June, five of his seven divisions were manning the encirclement ring,[100] while most of Guderian's divisions were already heading east despite the clear priority assigned to compressing and destroying the pockets.[101]

In any case, before the eastward push of the panzer groups could be resumed at full strength, there was some serious and costly fighting to finish along the encirclement ring, for the Russians were not going gently into captivity:

> The Russians trapped within the pocket did not, however, lay down their arms and surrender, nor did they wait passively in defensive positions for the German infantry divisions marching through the dust of the panzer spearheads. Unit after unit of the Red Army marched resolutely out to attack its way out of the encirclement. There was little coordination or finesse involved in these attacks, but the Russians heavily outnumbered the handful of German divisions blockading their route to freedom.[102]

7.2.3: Fourth & Ninth Armies

The Belostok-Minsk cauldron envisaged by General Halder was enormous in size, forming an oval-shaped pocket more than 300 kilometers long and about 100 kilometers wide at its widest point. Moving clockwise, the pocket stretched roughly from Belostok across Grodno, Lida, Rakuv, Minsk, Stolpce, Baranovichi, Slonim, Pruzhany to Bielsk. The Belostok-Volkovysk inner encirclement ring (the responsibility of Bock's infantry) measured about 100 kilometers in length. To avoid impending annihilation, Soviet Western Front had only two primary escape routes: in the north, via Mosty to Novogordek and, ultimately, Minsk; and in the south by way of the Belostok-Volkovysk-Slonim road to the communications hub of Baranovichi, Grand Duke Nicholas' Stavka headquarters site at the start of the First World War.[103]

Possessing between them some two dozen foot infantry divisions, Army Group Center's two infantry armies, Field Marshal Hans von Kluge's Fourth Army in the south, and General Adolf Strauss' Ninth Army in the north – operating on the inner flanks of 2 and 3 Panzer Groups, respectively – sought to seal off these enemy escape routes in the areas of Mosty and Volkovysk. The marching infantry – plagued by heat, dust, mosquitoes and flies; often pushed to the limits of endurance by forced marches of 40-50 kilometers a day and more; at times facing ferocious Red Army resistance; at times cut off from support units to the rear – advanced through the dense forests and marshlands of the border zone and curled ominously around the flanks of Western Front. The mission of Kluge's and Strauss' infantry was made easier by the fact that three of the four armies of Pavlov's Western Front (along with three of his six mechanized corps) were crammed into the large salient around the border town of Belostok – itself a strategically significant rail hub – which jutted deep into German-occupied Poland. The salient was some 130 kilometers deep and 200 kilometers wide, and even a glance at the situation map of the German Army General Staff's Operations Branch for 21 June 1941 reveals the dangers it posed for its defenders – with Field Marshal von Bock's infantry armies and panzer groups poised on the northern and southern shoulders of the salient and, hence, already enveloping Western Front forces before a shot had been fired. Exploiting the serendipity of geography – as well as the injudicious disposition of Pavlov's armies – German Fourth and Ninth Armies trapped large portions of the Western Front in the inner Belostok-Volkovysk cauldron, then held on for dear life in the face of massive, desperate and, at times, overwhelming Red Army breakout attempts.[104]

On 22 June, the infantry divisions of Fourth and Ninth Armies had pierced the Red Army border defenses and, in some cases, advanced as far as 30-40 kilometers beyond the frontier; Red Army resistance, at times tenacious – e.g., at Grodno in the sector of Ninth Army and at the Fortress of Brest-Litovsk on the front of Fourth Army – had, for the most part, been desultory and disconnected, if becoming more vigorous as the day had progressed. The next day (23 June), Kluge's infantry corps continued to lance deeper into Soviet defenses south of Belostok, seizing key bridgehead positions across the main Soviet river defense line; in its war diary, Fourth Army noted that Russian resistance was, in places, "extreme;" and, in one example, 9 Army Corps' 263 Infantry Division repulsed seven separate tank attacks in the area of Bransk (nearly 50 kilometers southwest of Belostok).[105] Units of Fourth Army were also complaining about the sudden appearance of enemy snipers. Along Strauss' Ninth Army front, 8 Army Corps captured Grodno, while further west lead elements of 42 Army Corps made their way into the Hajnowka Forest, severing communication links between Soviet forces operating in the Belostok and Brest-Litovsk sectors; within 48 hours, the formations of Soviet 10 Army had abandoned attempts to defend and retired into the forest. Thereafter, it became "a difficult task for the Germans to root them out of this swampy, heavily wooded, and generally nasty region."[106]

Already on this second day of the war, some German units were observing improvements in Soviet combat technique. One of these was 6 Infantry Division,[107] commanded by 54-year-old Maj.-Gen. Helge Auleb and deployed on the far left wing of Army Group Center. The division had suffered heavy losses on 22 June (54 dead, 106 wounded, and 19 missing in action) in its push across the frontier. The next morning, its advance detachment, with orders to seize the bridge over the Neman at Prienai as fast as possible, was held up for hours by a well-prepared and numerically superior opponent who exhibited "skillful conduct in battle and superior exploitation of the terrain" (*geschickte Kampffuehrung und vorzuegliche Gelaendeausnuetzung*). As a result, the "VA" (advance detachment) did not reach the large track of forest outside Prienai until early afternoon; as its lead vehicle was approaching the Neman (barely 400 meters away), the bridge blew into the sky, demolished by Russian engineers. Without delay, the detachment crossed the river in pneumatic boats, establishing a bridgehead on the far bank despite vigorous enemy resistance.[108]

Two accounts of this day – from the personal diaries of Heinrich Haape and Hans Lierow, respectively (both doctors with 6 ID) – provide insight into the hardships faced by the marching infantry of 6 Infantry Division:

23.6.[41]:

These two days were hard, really hard! Today we had only a few wounded and no fatalities – but still no contact with the [supply train]. In the last couple of days, I have eaten only 2 slices of bread and had only a little to drink. The dust mixes with sweat and sticks to the skin, and then eats away into it. My lips are swollen and have dry cracks in areas. It is hot and the sky is blue.

The war is bloodier than I had thought, but we are getting along alright and know no mercy. Death is having a rich harvest. The battle yesterday was harder than that today. Yesterday our soldiers suffered several bombing attacks. We were depressed about the loss of our dear comrades and wondered what will happen if this all continues in this way. There is shooting from out of every cornfield, every farmstead. When I was patching up yet another Russian, those "pigs" shot at me continually with their machine guns …

It is all for the greatness of Germany and her future, and I can only say that at this moment I would not want to be anywhere other than here. I am in very good health, so I am able to cope with the greatest strains.

During the few hours of peace at night we will sleep in the forest. For days already my gas mask has been my pillow, on which I lay my garrison cap. And how wonderfully I sleep on that – better than in the nicest bed! That's due to good, honest exhaustion![109]

23.6.1941:

Decamp at 0700, bright day. Dust and yet more dust. March casualties begin to mount. It is 1100 hours, the sun beats down. At least a fresh breeze. Even so, many exhausted men. The acting medical officer and the ambulance haven't got through to the troops yet. The companies must use their own resources. Officers and enlisted men are able to ride on requisitioned *Panje*-carts. Now that 18 km have already been done, there are still approximately another 50 km to march today.

The great event of the day is not a particularly warlike event, but just a stupid sand track – many kilometers long through a large forest – through which man, horse, and vehicle must plough, having to make the most incredible exertions. Many cases of heat stroke [*viele Hitzeschlaege*] with loss of consciousness. No acting medical officer, who should now be 5 km behind us. Insufficient evacuation transport. Eventually, the units drive the heatstroke victims in *Panje*-carts …

The populace is flying Lithuanian colors. They have placed drinking water in buckets along the road. The anti-tank troops were greeted with cheers. Masses of lilacs were strewn across their vehicles … The village inhabitants and their clerics cheered and prayed for God's blessing on the German colors.

The day stays hot. Teams of horses pull the carriages of the infantry and the artillery; the sweat runs rivulets through the thick dust on the soldiers' faces. On the second day of war, in the evening at 2100 hours, we reach the Neman River at Primar-Preny.[110]

A third account, posted by an officer in the division's 18 Infantry Regiment on 24 June, ended with a dark prediction:

> Review of the first two days: A complete success. Breach of the frontier fortifications. The enemy is retreating along the entire front. The regiment has suffered the following losses: 2 officers and 29 NCOs and enlisted men fallen; 1 officer, 57 NCOs and enlisted men wounded; 3 NCOs and enlisted men missing.

The high percentage of dead is doubtless the result of the underhanded way of fighting [*hinterlistige Kampfesweise*] of the numerous snipers and partisans. This will be "no humane" war.[111]

On the third day (24 June), as logged in the war diary of Ninth Army, operations were running "according to plan."[112] The "Situation East" (*Lageost*) map of the General Staff's Operations Branch shows the infantry divisions of Army Group Center gnawing their way deeper into the flanks of Soviet Western Front, which had yet to fully recognize the looming disaster.[113] As noted, it was on this day that Pavlov attempted to undertake a "planned and coordinated counterattack"[114] in an effort to restore the situation on his right. Although the Soviet attacks were not particularly well coordinated, they were indeed heavy, as confirmed by German sources; furthermore, they came as a complete surprise, for German aerial reconnaissance, focused on long-range missions, had failed to detect the closer concentration of hundreds of Russian tanks. Supported by infantry and cavalry, they began to rumble northward toward Grodno, with the ultimate objective of Augustovo more than 50 kilometers to the northwest and just beyond the frontier. The Soviet "shock group," was composed of 6 and 11 Mechanized Corps and 6 Cavalry Corps. The most powerful of these formations was 6 Mechanized Corps, whose order of battle embraced more than 1000 tanks, about half of them T-34 and KV models. These modern tanks, however, had only been received about a month before, giving their crews little time to train and become familiar with them.[115]

Led by Pavlov's deputy, Lt.-Gen. I.V. Boldin, this massive armored armada – having missed its intended target, Hoth's panzer group – struck Lt.-Gen. Friedrich Materna's unsuspecting 20 Army Corps (Ninth Army), which had been following behind 8 Army Corps, echeloned to the latter's right rear.[116] Materna's two infantry divisions (162 and 256 ID), engaged by the Russians on three sides, were forced onto the defensive. In his unfinished manuscript, *The Road to Moscow, The Campaign in Russia – 1941*, the late Charles V.P. von Luttichau, former U.S. Army historian (and German eastern front veteran), described what happened next:

> The [German] infantry lacked anti-tank weapons in numbers sufficient to deal with so massive an attack. The grenadiers nevertheless knocked out 50 Soviet tanks before running out of ammunition. More had to be airdropped. Then the *Luftwaffe* came to the rescue with heavy Flak and 200 *Stukas*. In rolling attacks the *Stukas* broke up Boldin's tank formations. The "eighty-eights" [88mm Flak guns] proved they could crack the massive armor of the heavy KVs where the smaller 37mm and 50mm anti-tank guns had failed. In self-defense the field artillery successfully applied direct fire, often at distances of less than 100 yards.
>
> The dramatic climax came at 2110, when the point of Boldin's counterattack penetrated almost the heart of Grodno. One mile short of its objective, the assault faltered. Plumes of smoke from more than 100 tanks rose over the battlefield. The remaining tanks had run out of fuel. Boldin desperately tried to have fuel flown in from Minsk. The two planes he sent to Pavlov with his plea were shot down.[117]

By the end of 24 June, 256 Infantry Division, defending a bridgehead around Kuznika, southwest of Grodno, and buttressed by a battalion of Flak guns, had weathered repeated Soviet attacks and knocked out 80 tanks.[118]

Despite prohibitive losses, the next day (25 June) Boldin again drove his forces forward to attack. Ninth Army, meanwhile, bolstered 20 Army Corps' defenses by allocating it another infantry division (129 ID)[119] along with more Flak and anti-tank guns. These new resources arrived just in time to confront the renewed onslaught by Maj.-Gen. M.G. Khatskilevich's 6 Mechanized Corps. Richthofen's 8 Air Corps, shifting its support from 3 Panzer Group, again swarmed over the battlefield, smashing the Soviet armored spearheads.[120] 256 Infantry Division once more found itself hard-pressed – at one point its 456 Infantry Regiment was attacked by 150-200 tanks – yet managed to hold firm while destroying large numbers of tanks.[121] Later that day, Khatskilevich arrived at the command post of 10 Army, nestled in a small wood outside Belostok, where Boldin had been since the first evening of the war. In a "state of great agitation," Khatskilevich informed his superior, "We are firing our last shells. Once we've done that, we shall have to destroy the tanks." Boldin, however, could offer no support, only understanding. Hours later, Khatskilevich died at the front.[122]

By the close of 25 June, 6 Cavalry Corps had sustained over 50 percent casualties, mostly from air attack; one of Boldin's tank divisions had run out of ammunition, while another had only three tanks left. 11 Mechanized Corps had lost all but 30 of its 400 tanks, while its personnel strength, roughly 32,000 on 22 June, had also disintegrated (only 600 men remained). Materna's army corps, deploying its anti-tank screens with tactical deftness, had accounted for 322 Russian tanks destroyed, while the *Luftwaffe* had knocked out the rest.[123]

The next morning, with little more than infantry remaining, the Soviet counterstroke petered out for good, having carried almost to the Grodno bridges over the Neman. The collapse of the Red Army attacks meant that the most credible threat to the German northern infantry prong had also ended. What remained of Boldin's group fled into the forests, seeking to escape eastward in small groups. After a harrowing 45-day trek, Boldin and some 2000 men managed to cross the front east of Smolensk and rejoin the main Red Army forces.[124]

With any prospects for a successful counterstroke now dashed, Western Front headquarters finally issued a general order on 26 June to all its forces to withdraw. In doing so, Pavlov hoped to use the remnants of his battered mechanized formations to help clear an escape route to the east. Yet even this hope, writes David Glantz, "was frustrated by the German 29 Motorized Division's seizure of the highway east of Volkovysk. This left in Soviet hands only a small corridor running westward along the southern bank of the Neman River, by the village of Mosty. Even this corridor was threatened as German 8 Army Corps' 28 Infantry Division was pushing Soviet 56 Rifle Division remnants south toward the river."[125] By the evening of 26 June, 28 Infantry Division had almost reached the village.[126]

While Pavlov's tanks and cavalry were attacking in the north, Field Marshal von Kluge and his Fourth Army had been making progress along the southern axis of the German infantry advance. On the morning of 25 June, Kluge directed General Gotthard Heinrici's 43 Army Corps (131, 134, 252 ID) to wheel to the northeast from Pruzhany and into the rear of Western Front at Volkovysk. To carry out his orders, Heinrici immediately reinforced his advance detachments and brought up infantry in trucks.[127] Later that morning, Colonel Guenther Blumentritt, Fourth Army Chief of Staff, spoke with Field Marshal von Bock. In the course of their discussion, Bock pointed out that Hoth's 3 Panzer Group was rapidly approaching Minsk, and that the infantry corps were urgently needed further east, to assist the panzer spearheads.[128] Kluge knew he had to finish off the inner pocket without delay.

To contain and compress the pocket, Kluge's operational intent was to position his infantry corps in a vast semi-circle extending from the area west of Belostok, across Porozovo and Pruzany to Ruzhany – a sector more than 150 kilometers in length.[129] In addition, with his *Schwerpunkt* on the right wing, he strove to join forces with Strauss' Ninth Army to complete the encirclement; with this in mind, at 1800 hours on 25 June, Kluge issued a general order (*Armeebefehl Barbarossa Nr. 1*), calling for strong forces to advance into the area of Slonim and Volkovysk.[130]

The German *Lageost* map offers a "snapshot" of the positions reached by Fourth Army by the evening of the 25th. Kluge's 7 and 9 Army Corps, squeezing the southern edge of the pocket, were pushing north/northeast from positions directly above the line Bransk-Bielsk. Further east, Heinrici's 43 Army Corps, in adherence to Kluge's morning order, had swung sharply northeast, sending advance detachments of its 131 and 134 Infantry Divisions toward Volkovysk (these were soon stopped by massive Russian counterattacks). To the rear, 13 and 53 Army Corps, forming the army's second echelon, were beginning to move up. Meanwhile, 12 Army Corps, still assigned to Guderian's 2 Panzer Group[131] (and with its 45 ID still locked in bitter fighting for the fortress of Brest-Litovsk), was straining to fill the gap between Ruzhany and Slonim, while the reinforced 29 Motorized Division (47 Panzer Corps) was now in position astride the road from Slonim to Volkovysk, blocking a major Soviet escape route.[132]

Over the next several days, while Guderian's tanks were dashing for Minsk, Kluge's furious attempts to seal off the inner ring, while ultimately successful, were beset by frustration and crisis, which, in the words of his chief of staff, "defied the lucid solutions of a map exercise."[133] In the first place, Kluge's infantry corps were consigned largely to wretched trails – the tank units having exclusive rights to the two good roads (Panzer Route 1 and 2) – where they labored through the deep sand at one to two kilometers an hour, pushing and pulling guns and vehicles along with increasingly worn out teams of horses. Every road and trail was overloaded, and when vehicles or guns became stuck, traffic jams ensued. No one was exempt from the "hardships and hazards"[134] of the road: Simply to reach 7 and 13 Army Corps, barely 100 kilometers from the frontier, the Army Group Center commander endured a "12-hour drive in great heat, awful dust and terrible roads."[135]

The travails of the marching German infantry along the front of Fourth Army are brought to life by the following *Landser* accounts:

Soldat S. K. (78 ID) – 25 June 1941
For the time being, our division is advancing in the second wave behind the fighting troops, distance approximately 30 km. Since yesterday, we stopped advancing to the east and are now marching in a more northerly direction. Today, the noise of battle in front of us is very loud; one comrade thinks it is from the fortress of *Belostok*. According to the map, that could be right. We generally get our tramping done at night; thank God, I have no foot problems, and generally I can't complain about anything. Today, incidentally, we had to really put our backs into our combat vehicles: the horses couldn't manage it alone any more.[136]

Wm. Josef L. (129 ID) – 27 June 1941
For the last 10 days I have been unable to write to you. Correspondence restrictions are still in place; I don't know when this letter will make its way to you. The last few days were filled with forced marches, defensive battles, and advances through enemy lines and fortifications ... Only someone who went through everything in the last Great War can tell you what it's like to march for hour upon hour in swampy terrain, in never-ending flatlands, through dust and beating sun.[137]

Of course, the conditions which prevailed in the Fourth Army sector were also encountered by the infantry of Strauss' Ninth Army. Ernst-Martin Rhein, in June 1941 a company commander in 6 Infantry Division, recalled the conditions along the march route of his regiment:

During the course of the march, elements of the regiment continually comb the terrain on both sides of the route of advance for dispersed enemy forces, which are ambushing and inflicting severe losses on the infantry, who are without heavy weapons. The hazy, humid, very hot weather and extraordinary terrain difficulties (poor roads, destroyed bridges), along with being overtaken by support columns of the panzer divisions, which are fighting far to the front, cause stoppages and delay the advance. Isolated thunder showers on 28.6. bring some welcome coolness and dampen the horrendous clouds of dust.[138]

In spite of such hardships – or "*Strapazen*," as the Germans called them – morale remained high, as this letter from *Oberleutnant* Rhein to his parents on 27 June 1941 illustrates:

Dear parents!
Since the six-day long mail ban will be lifted tomorrow, I wanted to send you a quick word. I am very well, the leaden exhaustion of the last few days and nights has been thoroughly overcome by an extended day of rest, and this evening we have our sights set on new objectives.

The last five days brought some great moments and many valuable experiences. The company proved itself just as I had hoped it would. The most pleasing thing is that I had only 6 casualties in the company, despite tough fighting …

The Russian soldier fights courageously and doggedly, with much more spirit than the Frenchman. On the other hand, their leadership seems to be rigid and lacking any particular initiative … Here in Russian-occupied Lithuania we have seen the most alarming examples of the effects of Communism, which destroys property and wealth. The populace continually pleads with us to protect them against the communist gangs, which ruthlessly shoot dead any nationalistically minded people.

For days now, the heat has been oppressive. Our constant companions are dust, sweat, and thirst. Despite the frequently very primitive conditions in which we are living, the stresses, and the immense heat – not to mention the dusty tracks and roads, often covered in sand 20 cm deep – to a man our mood is marvelous … You should see my boys, how their eyes light up in their dust-encrusted, pinched faces when it is time to go to battle.[139]

The slow progress of the foot infantry troubled Hitler. At Army Group Center headquarters at Rembertov, due east of Warsaw, Bock conferred with the Army C-in-C, Field Marshal von Brauchitsch, about how to assist Kluge in closing the pocket. The solution, reluctantly accepted by Bock, was to assign Guderian's 29 Motorized Infantry Division to Fourth Army and, if necessary, to offer Kluge elements of 10 Panzer Division,[140] which was now rumbling east on Panzer Route 2 in the van of Guderian's reserve – Lt.-Gen. Heinrich-Gottfried von Vietinghoff's 46 Panzer Corps. Through such measures, Bock hoped to emphatically tighten the ring around those forces of Soviet Western Front – now thought to be quite considerable[141] – trapped between Belostok and Volkovysk and then resume the drive eastward – a task which proved easier said than done.[142]

On 26 June, Kluge shifted his command post to a location just south of Pruzhany, where he could better lead from the front.[143] However, a breakdown in Fourth Army signal communications precluded him from taking effective control. Signal troops fell behind in laying cable to subordinate command posts; radio channels became hopelessly overloaded, often delaying the transmission of vital orders for hours, while atmospheric conditions frequently caused blackouts. Kluge and his staff tried to work around such problems by dispatching aides by car and plane to corps headquarters – a poor substitute at best.[144]

Of course, the most serious crises were not caused by geography or poor atmospherics, but by the Russian units desperately trying to escape from inside the slowly – albeit irrevocably – coalescing pocket. During the final days of June 1941, wave after wave of frantic Red Army soldiers washed against the German defensive lines which, for the most part, were manned by thin screens of infantry armed with machine guns and mortars, and backed up by anti-tank weapons and artillery. Most of the Soviet breakout attempts were smashed by concentrated German defensive fire, causing horrific losses for the attackers; yet on occasion they rolled over the defenders (an outcome which could end with the wiping out of an entire German platoon or company) and escaped – if only temporarily, in view of the outer panzer ring taking shape west of Minsk – to the northeast, east, or southeast. By 27 June, the pressure exerted by these frenetic, if largely uncoordinated attacks, had become intense, precipitating a series of local crises that day for Fourth Army:[145]

> These attacks separated 9 and 43 [Army] Corps, slowed down the 12 [Army Corps], and temporarily cut off advance units of all three corps. Russian tanks and infantry repeatedly struck Panzer Route Two and were reported "roaming the field near Slonim."
>
> From forward [air] fields at Pruzhany, *Stukas* went into action against Russian columns and targets of opportunity, even as their runways were in danger of being overrun. Other critical spots developed at Porozovo, Ruzhany, and near Zelva. The situation got so confused that Fourth Army was unable to get a clear picture of what was happening. Constantly with the forward troops, often using his revolver in close encounters, Kluge tried to patch up his front as best he could.[146]

The desperate Russian breakout attempts, in some cases with tanks, went on through the night and into 28 June, striking, from east to west, the thin defensive lines of 12, 43, 9 and 7 Army Corps.[147] Behind the front the situation was equally chaotic, as Field Marshal von Bock observed in his diary:

> Our losses are not inconsiderable. Thousands of Russian soldiers are sitting in the forests, far behind the front, some in civilian clothes. They will eventually come out when they get hungry. But catching them all is impossible given the tremendous size of the area. 100 km behind the front, at Siemiatycze, the 293 Infantry Division is still fighting for a row of strongly fortified bunkers, which have to be taken one at a time. In spite of the heaviest of fire and the employment of every means the crews refuse to give up. Each fellow has to be killed one at a time.[148]

From the "green table" (*gruener Tisch*) in distant East Prussia, however – that is, from the headquarters of Army High Command – the situation on the ground seemed much less troubling. Indeed, on 27 June, Halder told his diary that, in the sector of Army Group Center, "everything is going as anticipated." The next day (28 June), he admitted that the repeated Russian attempts to break out of the Volkovysk and Novogrodek pockets were causing "many tight situations;" still, he remained confident the situation was developing "as anticipated" (29 June).[149]

By midday, 28 June, the situation along most of Fourth Army's front had palpably improved. At 9.50 that morning, the army's war diary indicated that the Russians were suffering from shortages of food, and were beginning to surrender when offered bread. At 1000 hours, Blumentritt reported to his counterpart at Army Group Center, Brig.-Gen. Hans von Greiffenberg, that "the army now views the situation as a whole as less tense" (*weniger gespannt*). At 1040 hours, 43 Army Corps reported that its front was currently calm, that the corps now occupied a cohesive front, and that it was now judging the situation "confidently" (*zuversichtlich*). Ten minutes later (1050), Blumentritt reported to Bock that the sectors of both 43 and 9 Army Corps were no longer a cause for concern; and, finally, at 1210, Blumentritt told the 2 Panzer Group chief of staff that, while the day before had been difficult (*Gestern heisser Tag*), the situation was "now beginning to solidify."[150]

The period from 27 to 28 June had indeed brought several critical developments along the front of both Kluge's Fourth and Strauss' Ninth Army, finally tipping the outcome in their favor. In the north (Ninth Army sector), on 27 June, 20 Army Corps began to push southward from Grodno,[151] beyond the burnt-out hulks of hundreds of Red Army tanks. On its left flank, elements of German 28 Infantry Division (8 Army Corps), crossed the Neman River and captured the vitally important town of Mosty. In doing so, 28 ID, along with lead elements of the newly arrived 5 Infantry Division (5 Army Corps), cut the final Soviet withdrawal route from the Volkovysk pocket.[152] To the south (Fourth Army sector), German infantry (7 Army Corps) emerged from the Hajnowka Forest, stormed the ruins of Belostok, and "pressed against Soviet forces in the [inner] pocket, now numbering over 100,000 men."[153] Infantry of both 7 and 9 Army Corps cut the road from Belostok to Volkovysk.[154] As this was occurring, Soviet forces inside the ring streamed eastward; indeed, on the afternoon of the 26th, the Germans had observed a mixed Russian column (motorized and horse-drawn vehicles) some 50 kilometers in length migrating from Belostok toward Volkovysk. Richthofen's *Stukas* lifted off their airfields to attack it.[155]

Throughout 28 June, Russian units trapped in the forests around Belostok and in the area of Volkovysk sought repeatedly to break through the tenuous defensive screens of Ninth and Fourth Armies. Perhaps betraying a glimmer of admiration, the daily report (*Tagesmeldung*) of the OKH Operations Branch noted that the enemy was fighting with "exceptional tenacity and bravery."[156] Yet the ring continued to tighten. At 1010 hours, 137 Infantry Division (9 Army Corps), which was approaching Volkovysk from the southwest, got orders to seize the town. To carry out this mission, the division assembled a strong advance detachment, which was set in motion by late afternoon. The attackers, after brushing aside forays by Russian tanks and destroying a charging Red Army cavalry unit, entered Volkovysk at exactly 2023 hours.[157] The Soviet 10 Army had its command post there, but General Golubev, the commander, had fled – the Germans seizing only his cook and some of the army's papers. As for the town itself, little remained, as recorded in this German primary source:

> Volkovysk, in peacetime a small town with around 20,000 inhabitants, a little machine industry, and a few tanneries and canning factories, had suffered severely under the impact of the war. Already in the days before, waves of German dive-bombers had attacked concentrations of troops in this town with devastating results. Hardly a house was left standing in the center of the town. For the first time, the soldiers of the division had the opportunity to gauge the effects of aerial attacks on towns. Nobody had any idea that German towns would not be spared this fate.[158]

With the capture of the towns of Mosty and Volkovysk, the inner ring around Soviet Western Front, if not airtight, was, for all practical purposes, sealed.[159] Inside the pocket – by now, as the Germans chopped up and liquidated Western Front troops between Belostok and Volkovysk, multiple pockets were starting to emerge – remnants of Golubev's 10 Army were being finished off north of Belostok, while Kuznetsov's 3 Army was in its death throes in the thick and expansive forests of western Belorussia.[160] Yet the process of breaking up and destroying Soviet units, and clearing Red Army stragglers from forests and swamps, was costly,[161] and took time; and with each passing day, the German armored spearheads moved further away from the marching infantry.

While the Soviet defenders inside the pocket were being methodically destroyed, most of them were far from ready to capitulate. An example of the bloody combat along the edges of the encirclement ring took place near the village of Zelva, west of Slonim. In this sector, by 25 June, 29 Motorized Division had taken up positions covering the road leading out of the pocket from Volkovysk; perforce, it found itself in the path of a series of furious Russian breakout attempts from 27-30 June 1941. The division, known as "the Hawks" due to its tactical sign, was commanded by 51-year-old Brig.-Gen. Walter von Boltenstern; its lengthy front, near the little Zelvianka River, formed a wedge-shaped line pointing at Zelva. Providing support during the engagement was Machine Gun Battalion 5, a battalion of 210mm heavy howitzers (II./AR 109), and elements of 10 Panzer Division and 12 Army Corps. Air support from *Stuka* dive-bombers added additional backbone to the defense.[162]

As outlined in a divisional enemy intelligence report (*Feindnachrichtenblatt*), Russian forces encountered in this battle belonged mainly to 10 Army. These forces, in the face of German pressure, had been withdrawing eastward through the pocket in an effort to escape toward Minsk; on 27 June, they slammed into the defensive front of 29 ID (mot.).[163] In the ensuing four-day battle, the Russians attacked in wave after wave; after each failed assault, they formed up again – tanks, infantry, artillery, cavalry – and kept coming. German machine gunners mowed them down, but they refused to let up. At one point, Russian tanks penetrated to within 1.5 kilometers of the division's command post. Some German units were temporarily encircled; they pleaded for support, lest they be wiped out. At times, the German defenders suffered from a lack of ammunition and fuel; even maps were in short supply. Every available body was thrown into the fight, including members of the divisional staff.[164] The following account explicitly portrays the action on 28 June 1941:

> The men of the 15 [Motorized Infantry] Regiment could not believe their eyes. Out of the ground rose seemingly endless ranks of earth-brown shapes arm-in-arm, four ranks deep, their bayonets gleaming, a moving wall. "Hold you fire," ordered Captain Schmidt of the 1st Battalion. Then his men heard the blood-curdling battle cry, "Urrä, Urrä." At last the command, "fire," and every weapon went into action. The first Russian wave collapsed, then the second. The third wave staggered, then fell back in confusion. Mounds of bodies covered the open field. [German] ammunition ran short. In places, the human sea lapped over the dams. General Boltenstern's staff had to fight for its life.
>
> At night the Russians renewed the attack. This time, an armored train spearheaded the assault. Cavalry flanked it on the left and tanks on the right. The 29th Engineers blew up the railroad tracks and anti-tank guns set the armored train ablaze. In the eerie illumination, other anti-tank guns blasted the approaching tanks, while heavy machine gun volleys broke up the charge of the [cavalry]. Never before had the troops of the [division] witnessed such slaughter. Yet there were no surrenders.[165]

The spectacular decimation of the Russian cavalry charge is chronicled by the late Paul Carell, in his popular history of Operation *Barbarossa*:

> Simultaneously, two squadrons of cavalry were charging on the left of the rail track ... The cavalry charge collapsed in the machine gun fire of 8th Company. It was the most terrible thing the men had experienced so far – the screaming of the horses. Horses howling with pain as their torn bodies twisted in agony. They rolled on top of one another, and, sitting up on their lacerated hindquarters, flailed the air with their forelegs like beasts demented.[166]

The German defenders had no choice but to machine gun the dying horses to put a stop to their suffering.[167]

At Zelva, the Russians did not break out (one regiment of 29 ID (mot.) was alone responsible for taking 36,000 prisoners),[168] although Boltenstern's men paid for their victory with dreadful losses, among them 47 officers.[169] Further to the southwest, however, about Ruzhany and Porozovo, the Russians managed to do just that.[170] Whenever and wherever they located a gap in the German lines – and there were many – they filtered out of the pocket. Many – perhaps most – of them were later caught again, for they were now 200-300 kilometers behind their receding front lines; others joined up with partisan units and went on fighting against the fascist invaders.

By 29 June 1941, some two-dozen divisions (nine army corps) of Fourth and Ninth Armies were occupied along the Belostok-Volkovysk encirclement ring. Despite ongoing local crises – e.g., on the still tenuous front of 12 Army Corps in the southeast, where the "badly shaken" corps commander estimated that 7000 dead Russians and 100 destroyed tanks lay before his front line[171] – the worst had been overcome. The next day, 30 June, "brought the climax."[172] While German infantry continued to squeeze the pocket and sweep the forests of enemy stragglers,[173] the Russians began to give up in large numbers, some of them displaying to their captors leaflets the German Armed Forces High Command (OKW) had ordered dropped by plane over the vast tracks of forest and fields. Immense quantities of weapons and equipment of all types were also falling into German hands.[174] In the sack were fragments of Soviet 3, 10 and 13 Armies, while Soviet 4 Army was a "mere shell of its former self;" moreover, most of Western Front's mechanized corps had ceased to exist.[175] Indeed, "the time had come for mopping up and tallying the results."[176]

Yet "mopping up" on the eastern front was an uncommonly deadly endeavor. The Red Army soldier was unlike any the *Landser* had hitherto encountered – cunning, brutal, even beastial at times – a point pressed home by these field post letters of Major Werner Heinemann, a battalion commander in 23 Infantry Division:

25.6.41:
The advance continues with disruptions, we're already deep inside Russia; but the Russian fights doggedly, bravely, and with extraordinary cunning [*ausserordentlich verschlagen*].[177]

30.6.41, In the field:
The field kitchen is steaming, and all around the horses are tucking in to plentiful supplies of seized oats, the *Landser* are sitting in the corn and cleaning their gear for the first time in 8 days. It is a profound image of peace, only the continual appearance of Russians from out of the cornfields and the bushes is a reminder of the collapse of the two huge Belostok armies. Whenever possible, they are shot dead, because they have murdered Germans who fell into their hands in the most bestial manner. But we can't always bring ourselves to do that when these utterly shell-shocked, half-starved, and parched half-animals come crawling out of the cornfields.

The never-ending crack of snipers is also dying away, they too are exhausted. But many a motorcyclist or other messenger or ration carrier still meets with danger in the rear areas; one of my motorcycle messengers lay behind his machine in the forest for 3 hours receiving fire from all directions, after we had already marched along that same route several hours previously without any contact with the enemy. It's a truly barbaric war [*asiatischer Krieg*], but with time we can learn to deal with this, too.[178]

On 30 June 1941, Lt.-Gen. Richard Ruoff, Commander, 5 Army Corps – who, the day before, was himself awarded the Knight's Cross[179] – issued an order of the day praising his troops for their role in the great victory now taking shape. The order was, no doubt, typical of many promulgated at this time:

> A great operational success is underway in the wide cauldron of Belostok and beyond it to the east. The soldiers of the corps are playing a crucial part in this decisive blow against the Russian army. Through the rapid breakthrough across the Neman River and strenuous forced marches on poor roads, in particular as the corps turned south, the corps has sealed the encirclement ring in the north. The extraordinary efforts of man and horse have found their reward in this. The Commander-in-Chief of the German Army and the Commander-in-Chief of the [Ninth] Army have expressed their special appreciation for the corps' exceptional achievements to me.
>
> I am proud of the achievements and the decisive initial successes of the corps and I am convinced that every soldier will continue to do his duty in the certain knowledge of victory.
>
> Corps Commander
> Sgd. Ruoff [180]

The end of June 1941 also brought closure to the merciless battle for the fortress of Brest-Litovsk, back at the former Russo-German frontier. For days the Soviet defenders had resisted heroically, only to be worn down by the Germans' remorseless application of heavy, bunker-busting howitzers, flamethrowers, and air power, as well as by their own sheer exhaustion from the bitter combat at close quarters. By 29 June, the eighth day of the siege, the survivors were still clinging to the so-called "East Fort" (*Ostfort*) on the fortress' North Island.[181]

That morning (0800), the *Luftwaffe* struck the fort for the first time with 500 kilogram bombs, but the effects were negligible; that afternoon, a second attempt with 500kg bombs also failed to dislodge the fort's defenders. The German infantry besieging the fort – mostly Austrians of 45 Infantry Division – prepared for a close-in ground attack the next day, to be conducted with the help of incendiary devices. Barrels and bottles were filled with a nasty mixture of gasoline, oil and fat; these were to be rolled into the trenches in front of the fort and set aflame with hand grenades and Very pistols in an attempt to smoke out the defenders. Yet 45 ID had already incurred brutally heavy losses, and no one relished the impending assault. Fortunately, the *Luftwaffe* still had a final card to play.[182]

Late in the afternoon, a lone *Luftwaffe* bomber droned overhead and headed for the *Ostfort*. Soldiers moving through the devastation of the surrounding parkland and along the battered walls of the citadel gazed curiously up into the sky, while cameras whirred to capture the moment on film. Headquarters staff of 45 ID, like spectators at a sporting event, assembled on the roof of a close-by building to watch. Circling above, the lone bomber precisely executed its bombing run, disgorging a solitary 1800 kilogram bomb from its undercarriage. The malevolent, black, cylindrically shaped object plunged earthward, until it finally struck the corner of the fort's massive wall. A mighty crack and a shockwave reverberated through the streets of the town of Brest; windows disintegrated, and the townspeople stared at the massive plumes of smoke rising up from the stricken fort. This time, the effect was devastating – Russian soldiers, women and children among them, began to drift out from the fort. By 2000 hours, nearly 400 men had surrendered. A laconic entry in the war diary of 45 ID encapsulated the results produced by the lone, massive bomb: "With that, the situation at the citadel is finally resolved."[183]

Even then, however, individuals and small groups of men would go on resisting for weeks, with a handful of the defenders surviving until late July 1941. According to some reports, individual Soviet officers and men, as well as small groups of men, held out until August 1941, when the Germans finally flooded the cellars of the fortress to eliminate them. The final survivor of the fortress of Brest-Litovsk may have held out until April 1942.[184]

Throughout the early morning of 30 June, the *Ostfort* was thoroughly searched and cleared of Russian wounded, while the bodies of German soldiers, which lay for days among the detritus of the fort, were finally recovered. German flamethrower teams sought to incinerate likely hiding places of Russian soldiers, rather than risking life and limb by looking inside. All told, the Germans had captured more than 7000 Red Army troops (among them 100 officers) in the *Zitadelle*; booty taken included 14,576 rifles, 1327 machine guns, and dozens of anti-tank guns, artillery pieces, and other weapons. Some 2000 dead Russians were found in and about the citadel, but as many as 3500 may have perished in the fighting there.[185] Yet the cost to the Germans had been prohibitively high: 32 officers, 421 NCOs and men dead or missing; 31 officers, 637 NCOs and men wounded.[186] In fact, the losses of 45 Infantry Division may well have been larger than those sustained by *any* other German division along the entire eastern front in the first week of the war.[187]

The dead were laid to rest in the division's first cemetery of the war with Russia – built in a park outside a Russian Orthodox church in the southern part of the town of Brest-Litovsk.[188]

7.3: Hitler and the German High Command

At midday, 23 June 1941, Hitler boarded his special train at Anhalt station in Berlin and set out for East Prussia. Throughout the afternoon and evening, the train's twin-locomotives shepherded the "Fuehrer" and his staff across Pomerania, past cities and fields "liberated" from the Poles in September 1939. Sometime after midnight Hitler, and the procession of vehicles making up his entourage, slipped past the cordon of sentries guarding the entrance to his new military headquarters; at 1.30 a.m., Hitler finally entered the compound. During the long train journey, Hitler had decided to call it "*Wolfsschanze*," or "Wolf's Lair." As he explained to one of his secretaries, Wolf had been his code name during the Years of Struggle.[189]

Tucked deep inside a region of lakes, marshes, and dense forests of pine, spruce, beech and oak, the *Wolfsschanze* sat astride the Rastenburg-Angerburg railroad (8 kilometers east of the town of Rastenburg). Constructed by the Todt Organization, the austere and gloomy installation consisted of assiduously camouflaged concrete buildings and bunkers and prefabricated barracks, sealed off from the outside world by layers of barbed wire, mines, steel fences, palisades and earthworks. Hitler lived and worked with his closest military and political advisors in one compound; another, close by, housed a contingent of the OKW Operations Staff and a signal center. Some 20 kilometers away, and also astride the railroad – which was closed to general traffic – the OKH was ensconced in a compound in the Mauerwald just beyond Angerburg.[190] "Elaborate as they were, the *Wolfsschanze* and the Mauerwald compound could only accommodate fractions of the OKW and OKH staffs; the rest stayed in and around Berlin and kept in contact with the *Wolfsschanze* by air and courier train."[191]

General Alfred Jodl, Chief, OKW Operations Staff, would later refer to the new *Fuehrerhauptquartier* as "a mixture of cloister and concentration camp."[192] Hot and humid in the summer, cold and damp in the winter, the environment was also physically unhealthy and hardly conducive to good work. Only days after his arrival at the *Wolfsschanze*, Helmuth Greiner, the OKW war diarist, complained about conditions there in a letter to his wife:

> We are being plagued by the most awful mosquitoes. It would be hard to pick
> on a more senseless site than this – deciduous forest with marshy pools, sandy
> ground and stagnant lakes, ideal for these loathsome creatures. On top of that we

have cold, damp bunkers, in which we freeze to death at night, can't get to sleep because of the humming of the electric air conditioning which makes a terrible draft as well, and then wake up in the morning with a headache. Our underwear and uniforms are always cold and clammy.[193]

Christa Schroeder, one of Hitler's young female secretaries, had also accompanied the "Fuehrer" to his new headquarters. She recorded her first impressions in a letter to a friend on 28 June 1941:

> Now that we have been in our quarters for 5 days I can give you a bit of an update on the mood here … The bunkers are scattered throughout the forest, divided according to the type of work. Every department has one just for itself. Our sleeping bunker is the size of a railway compartment and has a friendly cladding of light wood. It has a concealed washstand with a mirror above it, a small Siemens radio, with which we can still listen to a great many stations. The bunker area even has electric heating, although it isn't switched on, has elegant lights on the wall, and a narrow, hard bed filled with sea grass. The space is tight, but, all in all, after I had hung some pictures on the bunker wall, it makes a pleasant impression.
>
> Mixed shower rooms are also available, but we haven't used these yet. At first there was no hot water and then of course we always sleep in to the very last minute! Because the noise of the bunker's ventilator kept us awake and the draft constantly blew across our heads – which I was particularly anxious about since I've had rheumatic pain so often – we had it switched off over night, which meant that we now sleep in rather poorer quality air and consequently have a heavy, leaden feeling in our limbs all day long.
>
> Even so, everything is lovely, with the exception of a blasted plague of mosquitoes. My legs have already been bitten all over and are covered in large red welts. The mosquito repellents we have been given are unfortunately only effective for a short time. With their high leather boots and thick uniforms, the men are much better protected than we are from these abominable bites. Their only vulnerable spot is their neck – so some constantly go about with a mosquito net round them. I tried it for an afternoon, but found it irritating to wear for a long period. The little beasts aren't so bad indoors. Wherever a mosquito shows itself, a frenzied hunt immediately ensues.[194]

As historian Geoffrey Megargee correctly argues, Hitler's isolation in such a remote headquarters "allowed him to fully understand neither events at the front nor developments in the homeland … He was in fact the only head of state in the Second World War to isolate himself in such a way."[195] Yet it was here – far from Berlin, in a mosquito-infested marshland and forest – where the leader of the German Reich was to conduct his final reckoning with Bolshevik Russia. Assailed by an unhealthy climate, increasingly troubled by the uncertainties of the eastern campaign, Hitler would, in the weeks ahead, become seriously ill, with unfortunate consequences for his conduct of the war.

Hitler quickly settled into his normal routine. With the help of gold-rimmed reading glasses, he carefully studied the dispatches from along the front; perused the great General Staff maps, which were printed twice daily; and issued his orders and directives. Uncomfortable rendering quick decisions, he shunned the telephone, and came to rely on the "colored briefings" by Jodl and a handful of other key assistants. Like a "young boy playing at war," he was passionate about moving the multi-colored unit symbols about the large battle maps – toward their far-flung objectives across the eastern front.[196]

In his memoirs, Nicolaus von Below, Hitler's *Luftwaffe* adjutant, outlined the "Fuehrer's" daily routine at his East Prussian headquarters:

> Each day at twelve Hitler would make his way to Keitel's bunker for the main situation conference, which would normally last about 90 minutes. Once or twice a week, Brauchitsch, Halder and Heusinger would attend these briefings. In the afternoons Hitler would have conversations and dealings with non-military callers, but the subject was always to do with the war. The evening situation conference, chaired by Jodl, followed at six. Hitler usually ate punctually at two in the afternoon and at seven-thirty. If no special visitors were expected, he would take his time at table – often up to two hours … Meals were *Wehrmacht* catering and consisted of soup, meat and a dessert. Hitler had his own vegetarian menu that he drew up at breakfast time.[197]

As accounts by Christa Schroeder[198] and other observers illustrate, Hitler was in high spirits at the start of the campaign. He eagerly followed the advance of the troops and marveled at their early victories – in particular the spectacular progress made by Army Group Center and the success of the *Luftwaffe* which, in the first week alone, destroyed more than 4000 Soviet planes.[199] During these first days, Hitler had forbidden the release of *Wehrmacht* bulletins to the German people. But on Sunday, 29 June, beginning at 11.00 in the morning, the OKW broadcast 12 "special announcements" (*Sondermeldungen*); one after the other – and each introduced by the new Russian fanfare, based on Liszt's "Hungarian Rhapsody" – they trumpeted the capture of this or that city, the securing of this or that objective. If the public reception was less enthusiastic than hoped – people soon tired of the special announcements, and suspected they were colored by propaganda[200] – the "Fuehrer" himself was scenting victory. On 2 July, he was handed a decoded Turkish report, revealing that both Stalin and Marshal Timoshenko had privately admitted to foreign diplomats that Leningrad, Minsk, Kiev, perhaps even Moscow, had already been "written off."[201] Two days later (4 July), Hitler said, "I am always trying to put myself in the situation of the enemy. He has practically lost this war already. It is a good thing that we destroyed their tanks and aircraft right at the start. Now the Russians won't be able to replace them."[202] In a "breezy mood, Hitler often lingered until 2.00 or 3.00 a.m. talking with his staff about the future – and above all about his plans for colonizing Russia for the Germans. 'I will go down in history as the destroyer of Bolshevism,' he bragged."[203]

On 6 July, Hitler, for the first time, declared that the final geographical objective of the war in the east was no longer the line Archangel-Astrakhan, as formulated in the original *Barbarossa* directive (December 1940); rather, the new objective was hundreds of kilometers beyond, extending all the way to the natural border between Europe and Asia – the Ural Mountains. Unaware of his "Fuehrer's" fantasy, Major Hans Meier-Welcker, Chief Operations Officer (Ia), 251 Infantry Division, could not have conceived of the splendid irony in his diary entry that day, as he and his comrades plodded painstakingly, by fits and starts, through the northernmost tip of Poland:

> The artillery is causing us concern because the horse teams can't cope with the marching distances on these poor roads. The horses are falling out at an alarming rate. The trouble began with the heavy artillery, but now even the light artillery is barely able to keep up.[204]

Meier-Welcker went on to note that the rate of advance of the horse-drawn components had sunk to below two kilometers an hour. Three quarters of Hitler's *Ostheer* was made up of just such foot slogging infantry.[205]

For the Reich's dictator, on the cusp – so it seemed – of his greatest victory, the rapid pace of the *Vormarsch* into Russia – at least of the eastern army's mobile components – brought anxiety as well; and, much to Halder's chagrin, Hitler soon began to intervene in operational, even tactical, affairs which should have been the sole province of OKH. On 24 June – that is, on the third day of the campaign – Hitler told Brauchitsch that he feared the encirclement at Belostok was not tight enough. The next day (25 June), fretting that the tanks of both Army Group Center and South were pushing ahead too fast, he dispatched his chief Army adjutant, Colonel Rudolf Schmundt, to Field Marshal von Bock's headquarters, with the nervous suggestion that the cauldron (*Kessel*) be closed well short of Minsk, at Novogrodek – a proposal Bock managed to parry "with all the eloquence at his command."[206] On 27, 29, 30 June, and again on 2-3 July 1941, Halder recorded in his diary more anxious queries or interventions by Hitler in operational and tactical details. "The same old song" (*das alte Lied*), noted Halder in obvious frustration (25 June) – no doubt a reference to Hitler's disquieting behavior early in the French campaign of the previous year.[207] Yet so far at least, with operations proceeding according to plan, the inchoate tension between the Nazi dictator and his generals seemed of little concern.

Like Hitler, the German General Staff reacted with euphoria to the swift progress of their field armies in late June and early July 1941. On 25 June, Colonel Adolf Heusinger, Chief, OKH Operations Branch, in his first letter from the Mauerwald to his wife, gushed that the initial victories were "once again fabulous" (*mal wieder maerchenhaft*); yet he also conceded that the enemy was "tenacious and willing to fight" (*zaeh und kampfwillig*), adding that the battles now being fought were "surely the most difficult battles" of the war. Two days later (27 June), he wrote of "unimaginable" successes, attributing them to the "towering superiority" (*turmhohe Ueberlegenheit*) of German leadership over that of their opponent; everything, he assured his wife, was going "as smoothly as possible."[208]

Heusinger's boss, General Halder, had at first feared that the Russians might rapidly withdraw from the frontier, complicating German efforts to encircle and destroy them west of the Dvina-Dnepr River lines; however, he was soon able to a breathe a sigh of relief – the Russians were standing and fighting, even shifting reserves toward the border areas. As he jotted in his diary on 24 June, "In general, it is now clear that the Russians are not thinking of withdrawal, but are throwing everything they've got against the German invasion."[209] Four days later (28 June) he observed that the trap near Belostok (inner ring) was closing, while the outer ring at Minsk had yet to be sealed. Brig.-Gen. Walter Buhle also brought what appeared to be good news that day, informing Halder that total casualties for the first week of the war, compared to those of World War I, had been negligible (*gering*).[210]

On 2 July 1941, the OKW reported that the battle of annihilation (*Vernichtungsschlacht*) across the front of Army Group Center, now nearing its completion, signified a victory of "world-historical dimension." The report went on to state that an "unimaginable chaos" had befallen the Soviet armies, which had been poised along the frontier "to fall on Germany's back and carry the torch of Bolshevism into Europe."[211] The overall assessment of the *Barbarossa* campaign by OKW and OKH, however, after two weeks of fighting, was most clearly expressed by Halder in his diary entry of 3 July. After pointing out that the pocket near Novogrodek had been "further contracted and sealed," and that Hoth and Guderian, in accordance with their orders, had started their advance toward the Dvina-Dnepr River barriers, he summarized the results to date as seen through the eyes of the General Staff:

> On the whole, then, it may be said even now that the objective to shatter the bulk of the Russian army this side of the Dvina and Dnepr has been accomplished. I do not doubt the statement of the captured Russian corps [commander] that east of the Dvina and Dnepr we would encounter nothing more than partial forces, not strong enough to hinder realization of German operational plans. It is thus

probably no overstatement to say that the Russian campaign has been won in the space of two weeks.

Of course, this does not yet mean that it is closed. The sheer geographical vastness of the country and the stubbornness of the resistance, which is carried on with all means, will claim our efforts for many more weeks to come.[212]

Halder, however, was wrong – the "bulk of the Russian army" had not been annihilated west of the two great rivers. To be sure, Soviet forces in the western theater – and, particularly, those fighting along the central axis of the German advance – had sustained shattering blows by the beginning of July 1941. Dozens of divisions had been destroyed; hundreds of thousands of men lost, along with thousands of tanks, vehicles, aircraft and other equipment. Yet in the areas of both Army Group North and South, where the Germans were operating with but a single panzer group along each axis, the Russians, while relinquishing large tracks of territory, had managed to avoid encirclement and complete destruction. Moreover, what Halder did not know – because German intelligence did not know it – was that the Soviets were rapidly raising new armies, many of them, behind the front, and beginning to deploy them – most significantly, in depth from Smolensk to Moscow. In July and August 1941, these armies would conduct a series of major counteroffensives that, despite their operational and logistical failings, blunted the drive of Army Group Center toward Moscow. Only at that point did it begin to dawn on the Germans just how badly they had underestimated the resilience and regenerative powers of the Red Army.

The *Vormarsch* of Army Group Center would also be disrupted by the eventual outcome of still latent disaccord between Hitler and his generals about what to do with the tanks of Hoth and Guderian after completing the first phase of *Barbarossa* – that is, after piercing the two mighty river lines and capturing the Orsha-Vitebsk corridor and Smolensk. As early as 26 June, Hitler began to consider the next phase of the campaign; on 27 June, he again emphasized that not Moscow, but the destruction of the Red Army, was the most critical objective. Two days later (29 June) he was leaning toward turning elements of Bock's army group northward, toward Leningrad – in accordance with operational planning as outlined in the original *Barbarossa* directive – and eliminating the Soviet Baltic Sea Fleet, which posed a threat to iron-ore shipments from Sweden.[213] At the same time, Hitler stressed the importance of the Ukraine, the Donbas,[214] and the oil of the Caucasus region. In any case, he realized that, whatever decision he made – to turn north or to turn south with the mobile units of Army Group Center – it would be the "most difficult decision of the war" (4 July).[215]

The generals, of course – Brauchitsch and Halder; and the field commanders, Bock, Hoth, and Guderian – all looked to the capture of Moscow as the decisive act of the campaign; one which would not only destroy the bulk of the remaining Russian forces, but also eliminate the primary rail hub and political heart of the Soviet Union. They were acutely aware that, should Hitler decide to shift the armor of Army Group Center north or south – or perhaps in both directions – this would bring a temporary, perhaps fatal, halt to the drive on Moscow; after all, the traditional campaigning season in Russia ended by late September.[216] In early July, however, with the frontier battles still in progress, a decision about the next set of operational priorities was hardly urgent, and would only become so several weeks later, at which time the fundamental differences between the "Fuehrer" and his generals on how to deploy the panzers finally burst out into the open, disrupting the decision-making process until late August.

Once again, it is important to point out that the overarching problem was one of resources. The Germans were moving along three axes; as they drove deeper into Russia, its funnel-shaped geography meant that the front was expanding rapidly. Because their resources were limited (e.g., only four modestly equipped panzer groups to support the three attacking army groups, South, Center and North) they would soon no longer enjoy the luxury of advancing simultaneously in all three directions – toward Leningrad, Moscow, and into the Ukraine. Decisions would have to be made, *Schwerpunkte* assigned, while other units temporarily halted their advance; and all the while the lines of communication and supply were becoming longer and more tenuous. The Clausewitzian culmination point had not yet been reached, but the Germans were already inching closer to it.

7.4: Stalin & Soviet High Command Respond

As this account has consistently sought to emphasize, Operation *Barbarossa* caught the Soviet Union by surprise and in a state of partial unpreparedness. The initial German blows were devastating in their effects; moreover, their impact was amplified by the ineptness of Red Army commanders at higher levels, which was only partially offset by the stoicism, tenacity and bravery of junior officers and troops.[217] As David Glantz recently observed, "the post-war Soviet leadership often boasted that, during the initial days of its Great Patriotic War, the Soviet Union and Red Army experienced the equivalent of a nuclear first strike, yet survived. While overstated a bit, this claim is not far from the truth."[218]

In this section, the narrative will explore developments during the opening phase of war from the "other side of the hill." No attempt will be made to again "fight" the battles which raged along the central sector of the front, culminating in the encirclement and destruction of Soviet Western Front armies in the Belostok-Minsk cauldron (for the final outcome of these battles, and the German drive to the Dvina-Dnepr River lines, see below, Sections 7.5 and 7.6). Instead, the focus will be on the overarching policies of the Soviet Union (strategic, organizational, economic, etc.) in response to Operation *Barbarossa*. Simply put, if the Soviet political and military leadership reacted in "wooden fashion" to Germany's surprise attack, they still managed to do "what was prudent and necessary under the circumstances."[219] Indeed, as the "fiery avalanche of war [sped] eastward, the country and its leaders began to act."[220]

7.4.1: Immediate Measures taken by Soviet Leadership

On 22 June 1941, in the immediate aftermath of invasion, martial law was declared throughout the western Soviet Union. Several days later (26 June), the workday for civilians was extended by a mandatory three hours, while all leave and public holidays were cancelled. Another measure implemented at the start of the war was a labor conscription law, which "compelled all men between 18 and 45 and all women between 18 and 40 to work eight hours a day constructing rudimentary defenses. In all weathers, hour after hour, the conscripts dug anti-tank traps, trenches, and artillery emplacements."[221]

The Soviet people responded with enthusiasm, and in a remarkable spirit of self-sacrifice, to the terrible challenges of what was soon to become a war for their very survival. In the first flush of war, hundreds of thousands of Soviet citizens – often entire families – joined the militia in their cities, towns and villages. In Moscow, thousands of Soviet youth, "motivated by the highest feeling of patriotism," "came to the induction stations without being called, expressing a fierce desire to stand in the ranks of the military defenders of the Motherland." In Leningrad, 32,000 girls and women volunteered for service at the front as nurses and medical auxiliaries; many others went to work in the factories, replacing the men called to arms. Even pensioners volunteered for duty, returning to their factories and offering their experience to the newcomers – the wives, brothers and sisters of soldiers at the front.[222] It was this collective, indomitable will which, when on display at the front, so shocked the German invaders.

To replace losses at the front, efforts to raise strategic reserves in the interior of the USSR began posthaste, the Soviet High Command drawing from its mobilization pool of more than 10,000,000 men. Through the mobilization decree of the Supreme Soviet

Praesidium of 22 June 1941, all persons belonging to the classes of 1905 to 1918, and liable for active service, were mobilized throughout the country's military districts, with the exception of the Central Asian, Trans-Baikal, and Far Eastern Military Districts. By 30 June, 5.3 million reservists, all with previous military training, had been called to the colors. During July, mostly from reservists (but also from new inductees), the Soviets created 109 new divisions (among them, 34 rifle divisions formed in the Moscow Military District). In sum, 156 new divisions were raised in June and July 1941. Put another way, eight armies were mobilized in late June and a further 13 new field armies in July 1941. (A Russian army was about the size of a German corps.) In the weeks and months which followed, most of these armies – and many more raised later that summer – were dispatched to Soviet fronts operating on the central (Moscow) axis against German Army Group Center.[223]

"In planning *Barbarossa*," write historians Williamson Murray and Allan R. Millett, "the Germans had assumed that after the initial onslaught and the destruction of the Red Army along the frontier, the Soviets would not be able to field substantial reserve forces – certainly not in any coherent fashion. In late July and August the Germans learned the folly of such ill-founded optimism."[224] In fact, the most egregious blunder by German intelligence lay in underestimating the Red Army's ability to rebuild destroyed units and create new ones from scratch. To be sure, the pre-war Soviet divisions "were not interchangeable" with those mobilized after 22 June: "For all their shortcomings, the divisions lost in the first weeks of battle were far better trained and equipped than their successors. The later units lacked almost everything except rifles and political officers. Perhaps most important, they had little time to train as units."[225] Yet ready or not the new armies and divisions were flung in wave after wave against the German spearheads, which systematically obliterated them, by the dozen; yet they fought, and in doing so, they contributed to the gradual erosion of German strength and helped to blunt the progress of the "blitzkrieg." Thus, it is not too much to assert that it was the Soviet mobilization system which, despite its many flaws, "ultimately saved the Soviet state from destruction."[226]

In addition to the massive mobilization program, the Soviets began to relocate their factories in western Russia to locations much further east, where they would be safe from seizure by the advancing German Army. Prior to 22 June 1941, the great majority of Soviet manufacturing capability was situated in the western part of the country and heavily concentrated around major industrial centers, such as Leningrad, Moscow and the eastern Ukraine. By 24 June, Soviet leadership had established a Council for Evacuation to orchestrate relocation of hundreds of industrial plants eastward, to the Volga River, Siberia, and Central Asia. Before the end of 1941, in an undertaking of staggering dimensions, more than 1500 factories – among them, 1360 related to armaments production – were transferred to these areas, along with millions of workers and their families.[227]

Nonetheless, the Council for Evacuation was unable to evacuate everything of value. For example, in the case of the Donbas mines, which produced 60 percent of the Soviet Union's coal supply, evacuation was impossible; the mines could only be destroyed.[228] Conversely, the successful relocation of the Soviet railroads (engines and rolling stock) meant that the Germans were forced to commit much larger numbers of their own locomotives (already in short supply) and railcars than they had anticipated to sustain the war in the east;[229] signifying, in turn, that the Germans had no choice but to convert large swaths of the captured Soviet rail network from the broader Russian gauge to their own, narrower gauge. The success of the Soviet leadership in evacuating or destroying so much of its industrial infrastructure frustrated German economic planners, who had intended to exploit Soviet resources to meet Germany's military and civilian production goals.[230]

The stubborn Soviet resistance during the summer of 1941, and the terrible casualties sustained, must be viewed in the context of the evacuation effort: The front had to hold long enough to complete the dismantling and relocation of the industries essential to

Russia's continued existence. The migration of so much industrial material and equipment eastward severely strained the railroads, making the transport of military reserves to the front – already under attack from the *Luftwaffe* – that much more difficult. In addition, the evacuations severely disrupted Soviet production for a considerable period of time – well into 1942, in fact – with the result that the battles of 1941 were waged in large part with existing stockpiles of weapons and ammunition, augmented by modest numbers of new tanks and guns, which often went into battle straight from the factory, before they had even been painted.[231]

Of course, to effectively fight and survive a war, a nation needs an efficient system of command and control (C2), yet the pre-war Soviet system was far from adequate to cope with the existential crisis unleashed by *Barbarossa*. No *Stavka* or High Command, nor any strategic system of command posts (CPs) or communications centers, were present in peacetime. Strategic leadership was also undermined by constant changes in top-level personnel, while operational C2 organs were inadequately prepared for war, both in terms of their organizational structure and with regard to training and readiness. Furthermore, most Soviet fronts, armies and corps did not have complete operational plans (OPLANS) or command communication nets; following the German attack, they had little choice but to improvise against Europe's most experienced and professional armed forces, with catastrophic results.[232]

The Soviet leadership began to remedy these serious shortfalls on the second day of the war (23 June). At this time, Stalin activated the *Stavka* (general headquarters) of the Main Command (*Stavka Glavnogo Komandovaniia* – SGK) as a war council signifying the "highest organ of strategic leadership of the Armed Forces of the USSR."[233] Chaired by Defense Commissar Timoshenko, the *Stavka* membership included Stalin, V. M. Molotov (People's Commissar for Foreign Affairs), Chief of the General Staff G. K. Zhukov, Marshal S. M. Budenny, Marshal K.E. Voroshilov, and Admiral N. G. Kuznetsov (People's Commissar for the Navy).[234] While the presence of Kuznetsov on the new war council made it an armed forces headquarters, it "did not resolve the ambiguity as to where the supreme authority really lay. As Zhukov later put it, there were two commanders-in-chief, Timoshenko *de jure* and Stalin *de facto*, since, 'Timoshenko could not make any fundamental decisions without Stalin anyway.'"[235] This anomalous situation was rectified on 10 July, at which time the *Stavka* was reorganized and placed under the direct control of Stalin, who, only weeks later, was made supreme commander of the Soviet armed forces.[236]

A second major step in creating a more responsive national command structure was taken on 30 June 1941, with Stalin's decree establishing a State Defense Committee (GKO, or *Gosudarstvennyi Komitet Oborony*). The GKO would "stand at the pinnacle of Stalin's decision-making system during the war."[237] Chaired by Stalin, it was a political body responsible for directing and controlling all facets of the Soviet war effort; among the initial members were: Molotov, security chief Lavrenti Beria, Politburo member G. Malenkov, and Marshal Voroshilov, "Stalin's long-time military crony." While the Politburo "continued to exist and function in a formal sense during the war, it rarely met as a body and the GKO in effect took its place as the highest collective body of the Soviet leadership."[238] Simply put, the GKO directed the activities of all government agencies, ministries, and state planning bodies, including those of the *Stavka* and the General Staff.[239]

Completing the top-level Soviet command structure was the People's Commissariat of Defense (NKO, or *Narodnyi Kommissariat Oborony*);[240] and, on 19 July, Stalin was appointed People's Commissar for Defense. The NKO was composed of a grouping of directorates – among them, Artillery, Armor, Airborne, Air Defense, Communications, Reserve Forces, Military Intelligence, and Propaganda – which functioned as organs of the GKO.[241]

The outcome of these initiatives was to provide the Soviet Union with a rational and unified system of command that, in the long run, functioned much more effectively than Nazi Germany's fragmented and compartmentalized command organs.[242] Another result of the reorganization was "formally to unify in the person of Stalin the control and direction of the entire Soviet war effort. Stalin's personal control over his country's war effort was more extensive and more complete than that of any of the other warlords of the Second World War."[243] Like Hitler, Stalin was not a military man – as Zhukov once said, "He was a civilian, and a civilian he remained"[244] – yet unlike Hitler, he would slowly begin, through trial and error, through the "bloody empirical process" of war, to direct his armed forces with a certain rational (if incomparably brutal) efficiency.[245] But the learning process would take time; and in the summer of 1941, his constant meddling in matters better left to his generals was to have disastrous results.[246]

7.4.2: Stalin's Behavior in Wake of the German Attack

In attempting to understand Soviet dictator I. V. Stalin's behavior and actions at the start of the German attack one salient fact must be considered: During the first few days of war – with communications disrupted between Moscow and the front – he had virtually no idea of the scope of the disaster which had overtaken his armed forces and his country.[247] His near total ignorance of actual developments along the western frontier helps to explain his initial optimism,[248] as well as his decision to again and again order the frontier armies forward to conduct suicidal counterstrokes which, on the central front at least, only propelled them deeper inside the enveloping jaws of the German panzer groups. When, after several days, the state of near total confusion began to lift, it was too late to restore the crumbling positions of Soviet Western Front in the fields and forests of Belorussia.

In spite of Stalin's many missteps in the wake of the German invasion, it is *not* true that he suffered a psychological breakdown of sorts on 22 June 1941. This is a myth, albeit a persistent one which managed to survive for decades in the historiography of the Russo-German War. In February 1956, at the 20th Party Congress of the Soviet Union, Nikita Khrushchev told the delegates that Stalin had broken down after the war began and "for a long time ... actually did not direct military operations and ceased to do anything whatever."[249] The truth however, is rather different. Historians now know, through the discovery of Stalin's appointments diary, that he was fully engaged from the beginning in meetings with generals and party leaders during the week of 22-28 June.[250] Still, he was devastated as he gradually became aware, in bits and pieces, of the singular catastrophe unfolding at the frontier. Particularly disturbing to him was the massive defeat taking shape along the central axis, as the tanks of Hoth and Guderian raced round the flanks of Western Front and on to the Belorussian capital of Minsk. "Unable to come to terms with the staggering retreat in the west," writes Russian historian Constantine Pleshakov, "he sank into depression, which was occasionally interrupted by fits of uncontrollable rage."[251]

On 26 June, Stalin, finally privy to the desperate situation developing in the center, along and behind Pavlov's Western Front, telephoned Zhukov at the command post of Southwestern Front at Ternopol in the Ukraine.[252] German tanks were approaching Minsk, Stalin told him, and Pavlov was in a state of total confusion. (Reaching Western Front headquarters several days later, General A. I. Eremenko discovered Pavlov "in the incongruous state of being hopelessly in the dark regarding the *front's* situation and calmly having breakfast.")[253] Stalin ordered his chief of staff to return to Moscow at once. Arriving in the Soviet capital, Zhukov was taken straight away from the airport to Stalin at the Kremlin:

> In Stalin's office I saw Marshal Timoshenko and Lieutenant-General Vatutin, my First Deputy, standing stiffly at attention. Both of them were pale and drawn, their eyes red from lack of sleep. Stalin was not in his best mood.
>
> With a brief nod, he said, "Put your heads together and tell me what can be done in this situation." And he flung on the table a map showing the situation on the Western Front.

I told him we would need about 40 minutes to analyze the situation. "Very well. Report to me in 40 minutes."

We went out into an adjoining room and began to discuss the situation and our capabilities on the Western Front.[254]

Admitting they could find no definitive solution to the grave problems confronting Western Front, the generals suggested building a defense in depth along the approaches to Moscow; they also proposed the urgent establishment of several new armies from Moscow militia formations. After checking the German advance, a counteroffensive was to be organized, using troops drawn from the Far East and new units. These proposals were at once approved by Stalin.[255] (See the following Section, 7.4.3, for a more detailed explication of these issues.)

The first unconfirmed reports that Minsk had fallen reached the Kremlin on the morning of 29 June (mobile units of Hoth's panzer group had captured the city the previous afternoon). Pleshakov describes what happened next:

Upon hearing the news, Stalin became flushed with rage. Minsk didn't amount to much strategically, but in a country of false pretenses it had been upgraded to a glorious metropolis, because it was the capital of a Slavic Soviet republic, Belorussia. (Stalin promoted Slavs as the ethnic core of the empire, just as the czars had, though he himself was a Georgian.) No matter how cynical Stalin was, he had a dangerous habit for a dictator, which was believing his own propaganda. Now, instead of bemoaning the loss of Minsk as he had bemoaned the loss of Kaunas in Lithuania and Lvov in the Ukraine … he regarded the loss of Minsk as a major strategic setback and angrily called Timoshenko. "What happened to Minsk?" he demanded.[256]

Timoshenko did not have an answer; besides, Pavlov had yet to verify the loss of the city. Stalin reproached his defense minister and hung up. Molotov, Malenkov, Mikoyan and Beria had all been present during the conversation. After a period of awkward silence, Stalin said, "I don't like this uncertainty. Let's go to the General Staff and check the reports from the front ourselves."[257]

Minutes later, the "five most powerful men in the country were entering the heavy brass-laden doors of the General Staff building" (the Commissariat of Defense). Stalin found Timoshenko and Zhukov, along with a clutch of officers and generals, arguing over the war maps spread out on the tables. Stalin at first said nothing. Slowly walking by the tables, he located the map of Western Front and examined it closely; then he demanded to know just what the situation was. When it became apparent to him that no one knew for sure (Timoshenko: "Comrade Stalin, we haven't had time to process the information yet. Many things still have to be confirmed. The accounts are ambiguous. I am still not ready to report."), a stormy encounter ensued. As Stalin raged against his generals, Zhukov became so distraught that he fled the room in tears. With nothing left to accomplish, Stalin left the building, but before he did he remarked, "Lenin left us a great legacy, and we have fucked it up."[258]

For Stalin it was the last straw. The fall of Minsk, the collapse of Western Front, the total breakdown of communications with Pavlov's CP – the full magnitude of the disaster bearing down on his country, on him, had finally become apparent. Stalin responded by withdrawing in despair to his dacha outside Moscow, in the forest of Poklonnaia Gora; the next day (30 June), he failed to show up at his office in the Kremlin, and refused to pick up the telephone. Frightened by their dictator's behavior, Molotov, Beria and others in the *vozhd's* inner circle decided to go to him and "coax him back to the Kremlin."[259] The story of their meeting with Stalin has often been told, and need not be recounted here. Suffice it to say that, despite Stalin's obvious responsibility for the catastrophes piling up along the front – in a week, more territory had been lost than Czar Nicholas II had lost in 1914-17 – no one dared to hold him accountable. Rather, they pleaded with him to return to work – and this time with all power concentrated in his hands as chairman of a new emergency organization, the State Defense Committee (GKO). Stalin, who had expected a rather different outcome, readily agreed.[260]

On 1 July, Stalin was back in the Kremlin; having finally steadied himself and adjusted to the crisis, he was, once again, in complete control.[261] There are, however, credible indications that he, Molotov, and Beria, at the end of June, sought to put out peace feelers to determine what price Hitler might exact to bring his attack to a halt. Their intention, it seems, was to offer Germany large chunks of the western Soviet Union, including the Baltic States, the Ukraine, and Bessarabia, while also asking for a cease-fire. The attempt was to be made using a trusted intermediary, the Bulgarian ambassador to Moscow, as a mediator. Molotov, in particular, is said to have supported the initiative, which he characterized as a second Brest-Litovsk – a reference to the draconian treaty with Germany of March 1918, which enabled Russia to withdraw from the Great War in exchange for cessation of large tracks of territory. The highly secret meeting with the Bulgarian ambassador did indeed take place (in a Moscow restaurant), yet nothing came of it, and the matter was quietly dropped.[262]

At the beginning of July 1941, Stalin appointed Marshal Timoshenko to the command of Western Front, while also reinforcing the front with several reserve armies.[263] As for the hapless General Pavlov, he had been recalled by Stalin to Moscow. So changed was the general's physical appearance – as a result of the ordeal suffered during the first week of war – that he was now barely recognizable. Needing a scapegoat for the failures along the front, Stalin had Pavlov, along with several members of his staff, tried and executed. General of the Army Dmitrii Pavlov was just 44 years of age when he was shot.[264] Explains Evan Mawdsley:

> Interrogated on 7 July, Pavlov refused to accept any personal responsibility for the debacle, although he did criticize defecting Lithuanian units on the border with Northwestern Army Group, and he accused his own 4 Army Commander of panicking (the 4 Army had been rolled over by the Germans, and its commander would also be executed). Above all, Pavlov complained about the "huge advantage of enemy tanks, his [the enemy's] new equipment, and the huge advantage of the enemy air force." He complained, too, that Soviet forces in the Ukraine had been given more personnel and equipment than he had.[265]

Meanwhile, nearly two weeks into the war, Stalin had yet to make a public statement to the Soviet people, his sudden and unexplainable absence at so critical a time eliciting whatever wild rumors and speculations were conceivable in the fertile minds of Moscovites. One rumor was that Stalin was already under arrest and condemned for his crimes, and that Leon Trotsky, Stalin's banished former rival, was on his way to assume the mantle of leadership.[266] Trotsky, of course, was long dead, having been bludgeoned to death with an ice pick in August 1940 (while in exile in Mexico) by an undercover NKVD agent.

Immediately following the German attack, Stalin had let his Foreign Minister, Molotov, speak to the Soviet people. Now, at last, on 3 July 1941, Stalin made his first wartime address to the nation:

> He was obviously under strain. His voice was dull and slow. He sounded tired, and he could be heard pausing to drink water as he talked. Calling the listeners

"brothers and sisters" and "friends," he told them for the first time, after two and a half weeks in which government communiqués had depicted the fighting as being confined to the border, that Soviet territory had been lost and that the Germans were advancing. Reiterating instructions given to all party offices four days earlier, he called for evacuation and a scorched earth policy in threatened areas and partisan warfare in enemy-occupied territory. He asked the peasants to drive their cattle eastward ahead of the Germans and the workers to organize *opolcheniye* (home guards) "in every town threatened with invasion." The speech emphasized the national rather than the ideological nature of the war and characterized Great Britain and the United States as "trustworthy partners" in a common struggle for "independent and democratic freedom."[267]

A few days prior to Stalin's address, Lt.-Gen. Eremenko had arrived at Western Front headquarters – since 27 June, hidden in a hilly pine forest in the fortress town of Mogilev, on banks of the Dnepr River – to replace Pavlov. Eremenko would only lead the front for a couple of days, until replaced by Timoshenko, who he would then serve as deputy front commander. The situation encountered by Eremenko was almost indescribably bad. Pavlov complained of "stupefying strikes" by the Germans, which had caught his troops by surprise; losses of men, aircraft, artillery and tanks were enormous. Eremenko did learn of one positive development, however: Despite the incomparable chaos, the evacuation of Belorussia had been a success, with 13,000 machines, 4000 tractors, 842 tons of rare metals, and 600,000 head of cattle being shipped eastward; in addition, of 150,000 tons of Belorussian grain, 44,000 tons had been salvaged and 42,000 destroyed. Yet positive statistics about tractors, cattle and grain could not conceal the grim reality of the moment. Having taken Minsk, German Army Group Center was pushing further east, toward Smolensk and Moscow, and seeking to encircle and destroy the tattered remains of Western Front.[268]

7.4.3: Military Developments: First 18 Days from the Soviet Perspective

During the 18-day battle of the frontier (22 June – 9 July 1941) the average daily losses of Western Front forces facing Army Group Center in Belorussia amounted to: 23,207 men, 28,900 small arms, 267 tanks, 524 guns (artillery) and mortars, and 99 combat aircraft.[269] It was losses such as these, coupled with the huge swaths of territory relinquished by the Red Army in the summer of 1941, which has led many scholars to depict *Barbarossa* as a "virtually seamless *Wehrmacht* march from the Soviet Union's western frontiers to Leningrad, Moscow, and Rostov."[270] The irresistible German *Vormarsch*, we are further assured, was not checked primarily by Soviet resistance, but by the mud and snow of the fall, which stopped the *Ostheer's* mechanized units, literally, in their tracks.

While it is true that the German air fleets and panzer groups practiced a new kind of warfare – one which temporarily overwhelmed the Red Army and for which it was completely unprepared[271] – it is far from true that the German advance resembled a "cakewalk" of sorts. As this narrative has repeatedly sought to emphasize, from the outset the Germans faced an adversary who fought with a tenacity, ruthlessness, and readiness to die virtually unknown in earlier campaigns. Evidence gleaned in recent years from Soviet archives underscores this point: It is now known that, from the very first days of the war – in accordance with pre-war Soviet doctrine and operational planning – Stalin, *Stavka* and the Soviet General Staff strove to drive back the German invaders through a series of coordinated counterstrokes which went on unabated through early September 1941.

The objective of this offensive strategy, as implemented on 22 June 1941, was to carry the war away from Soviet borders and onto the territory of Nazi Germany. The initial counterstrokes, however, awkwardly executed and undertaken with little awareness of actual conditions at the front, succeeded only in grinding up large chunks of the Soviet first strategic echelon of forces; within days, moreover, the Soviet military leadership became aware that it had grossly underestimated the weight of the German attack, while seriously overestimating the prowess of their own attacking forces. As Zhukov explained in his memoirs:

> We did not foresee the large-scale surprise offensive launched at once by all available forces which had been deployed in advance in all major strategic directions. In short, we did not envisage the nature of the blow in its entirety. Neither the People's Commissar, nor myself or my predecessors – B.M. Shaposhnikov, K.A. Meretskov nor the General Staff top officers – expected the enemy to concentrate such huge numbers of armored and motorized troops and, on the first day, to commit them to action in powerful compact groupings in all strategic directions with the aim of striking powerful wedging blows.[272]

In late June 1941, the Soviet High Command began to adjust its strategy. While the counterattacks continued – usually with the same dismal results – the Red Army, on the basis of Zhukov's proposals, began to implement a two-prong policy of active strategic defense coupled with defense in depth. Along the central axis, in particular, the Soviets began to build multiple lines of defense, manned by new groupings of forces, in an effort to wear down and delay the German juggernaut. Soon recognizing a basic weakness in the German attack – i.e., the growing separation of the panzer forces from the marching infantry following far behind[273] – the *Stavka* began to lash at the unprotected flanks and rear of Hoth's and Guderian's armored groups. These attacks – prohibitively costly and, for the most part, unsuccessful – did manage to create breathing space, giving the Russians time to deploy their reserves and solidify their defenses. All, of course, in preparation for the envisaged massive counterblow, which, it was hoped, would drive the Germans in defeat from sacred Soviet soil.

In the remainder of this section, key events of the first 18 days of war – the period of the border battles – are outlined in chronological order to provide further insight into the start of the war from the Soviet perspective.

25/26 June 1941:

With his Grodno counterstroke a dismal failure, General Pavlov, his forces faced with impending envelopment, ordered a general disengagement and pull back of Western Front forces. The new line earmarked for defense was along the Shchara River, near Slonim. Yet with the front's communications still in shambles, most of the units did not receive the order to withdraw; those that did were, generally, unable to effectively break contact with the aggressively pursuing forces of Army Group Center. Having already lost much of their fuel, motor transport (in short supply to begin with) and air support, elements of Western Front streamed eastward in utter disarray, on foot and under remorseless attack from the air. Further east, German forces ambushed the command post of Lt.-Gen. P.M. Filatov's 13 Army, Pavlov's second echelon army, which was trying to deploy its divisions forward, and captured classified documents outlining Red Army defense plans.[274]

28 June 1941:

By late June, records from all operating Soviet fronts revealed significant shortages of personnel and equipment, as well as unit and officer training shortfalls. On 28 June, as Hoth's armor converged on Minsk, Maj.-Gen. A. N. Ermakov, Commander, 2 Rifle Corps, submitted the following report:

> At the present moment the corps' position is rather difficult:

a)   no ammunition;
b)   no fuel;
c)   no food;
d)   no transport for resupply or evacuation;
e)   no communications with the 161 Rifle Division, and the corps separate signal battalion is greatly understrength;
f)   no hospitals (the corps hospitals were not mobilized).[275]

Meanwhile, Soviet troop trains, rolling toward the front in an unremitting stream, were experiencing challenges of their own. Recalled S. M. Shtemenko, then an officer on the Soviet General Staff:

> We, operations officers, had to keep in touch with [all key] departments, particularly with Military Communications, since troop movements from the interior districts to the front line required constant supervision ... One or another of us was always being sent to a station where troops were being detrained. The complexity and uncertainty of the situation often made it necessary to stop detrainment and send the train on to another station. Sometimes the commanders and staff of a division would be detrained in one place and their regiments, in another, or even in several places considerable distances apart. Instructions and directives addressed to the troops sometimes went out of date before they reached their destination. An operations officer had to keep watch on all this and take suitable action.[276]

"These and many similar reports," affirms David Glantz, "explain why the German attack utterly collapsed the Western Front in a matter of only days."[277]

Late June – July 1941:

By 27 June, the Soviet military leadership, with Zhukov playing a key role, had crafted a new strategy for stopping the German advance in center, along the road to Moscow. Hence, the *Stavka*, by early July, began to deploy its strategic reserves, hurriedly brought up from the interior of the country, on a new defensive front covering the approaches to the Western Dvina-Dnepr Rivers, and along the river lines themselves. The Soviet 19, 20, 21 and 22 Armies, all from Marshal S.M. Budenny's Front of Reserve Armies (and now assigned to Western Front), were to occupy and strengthen defensive positions on a line running roughly along the Dvina from Drissa via Polotsk to Vitebsk, then across the landbridge between the two rivers (some 75 kilometers in length, and the most heavily fortified sector of the Stalin Line),[278] and finally along the Dnepr from Orsha to Mogilev and Zhlobin, to an area further south around Gomel. In addition, a second defensive layer was formed further east, in the Viaz'ma – Spas Demensk regions east of Smolensk; this was occupied by troops of 24 and 28 Armies, the first two Soviet armies mobilized since 22 June 1941. Soon thereafter, other newly raised armies were distributed along a front extending from Staraia Russa in the north to a point southeast of Viaz'ma, erecting yet another defensive barrier before Moscow.[279] In this way, the Soviet High Command sought to ensure that "a breakthrough in the direction of Moscow could be contained in a deeply echeloned defensive system."[280]

July 1941:

At the beginning of July, all Soviet armies, corps, and divisions were beset by severe shortages of tanks, anti-tank weapons, anti-aircraft guns, and communications gear. During the first half of the month, the *Stavka* assigned six new mechanized corps from the interior military districts to Timoshenko's Western Front to replace the mechanized corps eliminated during the frontier battles.[281] At the same time, in response to the hard lessons learned since 22 June, the Soviet High Command decided to undertake a major reorganization of its force structure. Because the large mechanized corps (two tank divisions and one motorized division) had proven too unwieldy to be effectively led in combat (by their still inexperienced commanders and staffs), these were to be broken up and the tank divisions put directly under army-level command. The motorized divisions were to be converted to regular rifle divisions and their motor transport assigned to army-level transport battalions. Along with these changes, light cavalry divisions were to be formed to harass German rear areas and lines of communication, now stretched dangerously over hundreds of kilometers, and often running through wooded regions that had yet to be secured. In general, to reduce commanders' span of control, armies were to be reduced in size to a maximum of six divisions, with no corps echelon. For the same reasons, Soviet Air Force units – the large air corps and air divisions – were also to be broken up into smaller, more manageable formations. The Russians, it seems, were learning.[282]

6-9 July 1941:

In early July, the mobile units of Hoth and Guderian (2 and 3 Panzer Groups) began their drive toward the Dvina-Dnepr River barriers. As German mobile forces moved closer to the "Smolensk gate" (i.e., the Vitebsk-Orsha landbridge), Russian counterstrokes began to increase in scope. On 6 July 1941, hundreds of tanks belonging to Soviet 5 and 7 Mechanized Corps, slashed at the southern flank of 3 Panzer Group as it reached the upper Dvina east of Lepel. The attacking Red Army forces, however, suffered from a paucity of air cover and too few anti-aircraft guns. The two mechanized corps, hit by waves of *Stukas*, sustained serious losses; they were then worked over by both Hoth's and Guderian's panzer groups. In a mere four days, the Soviet armored grouping was utterly smashed, losing over 800 tanks.[283] In its application of operational-level warfare, the Red Army was simply too far behind at this point to emerge victorious from such engagements. Yet each such battle, whatever the outcome for the attacking Red Army forces, attrited and slowed the advancing Germans. (For a detailed account of this Soviet counteroffensive, see below, Section 7.6.)

9 July 1941:

Another myth which has managed to endure for decades is that the Soviet Air Force (VVS), as a result of the pounding sustained at the start of the war, was largely out of action through the remainder of 1941. Typical of this false narrative is a statement by Earl F. Ziemke: "Having committed the irreversible error of basing its main forces close to the border in anticipation of an offensive mission, the Red Army Air Force was largely demolished on the ground and in the air by nightfall on 22 June and would not recover significantly before the end of the year."[284]

While it is certainly true that the VVS, like many Red Army ground units, was largely eviscerated during the first few days of the campaign, many German accounts[285] support the position that the Soviet Air Force made a surprisingly rapid recovery from the unprecedented catastrophe it had experienced. A contributing factor was that the German Air Force, few in number and operating over much too broad a front, was unable to maintain requisite pressure on Soviet air forces (the air superiority mission) while simultaneously meeting the growing demands of the armored spearheads as they plunged further eastward.[286] As early as 4 July, Kesselring's 2 Air Fleet reported that, in spite of the heavy VVS losses, the number of Russian aircraft had hardly declined, while the Army began to complain that, in certain sectors, the Soviets had even regained air superiority.[287]

That the VVS remained active throughout the summer of 1941 is also underscored by statistics of sorties flown through 9 July 1941 across the entire eastern front. According to the Soviet official history of the air war, more than 47,000 sorties were registered over this 18-day period, or in excess of 2500 per day; of these, 47 percent were in support of ground troops. Weapons employed included high-explosive and fragmentation bombs, along with machine gun fire and rockets. The primary targets of VVS attacks were "tanks, artillery, and mortars in firing position, tank and motorized columns, vehicle concentrations, river crossings, reserves, and troops on the battlefield."[288] Starting in July, Red Army air units also began to actively strike German airfields; in one such attack, at dawn on 8 July, the air force of Western Front destroyed or damaged 54 German planes.[289]

Combat sorties flown during the frontier battles included 2112 by Soviet Long-Range Bomber Aviation, mostly against German tank and motorized columns along the main axes of advance. "On the whole, however," as another Soviet source openly acknowledges, "the actions of Soviet aviation against enemy troops did not have a noticeable influence" on the battlefield during the initial period of the war. VVS efforts were, "often dispersed, planes were not massed adequately in the main sectors, the weapons selection and the methods and altitude of bomb strikes were not always appropriate, and the tactics of bomber and ground attack aviation did not fit the situation."[290] As a result of such faulty methods, Soviet air strikes, it seems, were not always taken seriously by Germans on the receiving end, as the recollections of an officer in 7 Panzer Division demonstrate:

> It soon became clear that the Russian air force had only obsolete machines at its disposal, but above all that the pilots did not function nearly as well as our fighter and dive bomber pilots, or the pilots of our Western opponents. This was naturally a great relief to us, and when Russian aircraft appeared, we hardly bothered to take cover. We often had to smile, in fact, when, for want of bombs, thousands of nails rained down on us from their bomb bays. We soon came to realize that neither war at sea nor war in the air was suited to the Russian mentality.[291]

Yet it would not always be this way, for, once again, the Russians were learning quickly how to fight.

7.5: Final Destruction of the Belostok-Minsk Pockets

By 2 July, the fighting between Belostok and Volkovysk was largely over, the OKH *Lageost* map for that day showing no Soviet forces left in the region.[292] Serious fighting, however, continued further east, in the pocket west of Minsk, centered on Novogrodek. Yet even here, Russian soldiers – "disorganized, disheartened, and starving"[293] – were beginning to give up *en masse*. In the sector of 12 Panzer Division, directly northwest of Minsk, 52,000 surrendered on a single day. "Suddenly, taking prisoners was less of a problem than feeding them and shipping them to the rear. If thousands were filing into stockades, thousands more were still on the loose wandering about in the vast areas the Germans had conquered, yet found near impossible to administer."[294] It would be left to the German infantry to mop up these Russian stragglers as best they could from the forests and swamps of Belorussia.[295]

Even now, with the Germans applying merciless pressure, systematically compressing and breaking apart what was left of the pocket, the Russians often put up stout resistance. A soldier with the elite motorized Infantry Regiment *Grossdeutschland* recalled a grim encounter near Stolpce, on 5 July:

> *Rollbahn*; enemy in the woods to the left. *Sturmgeschuetze* [assault guns] are under Lieutenant Franz, with whom we coordinate and make plans to destroy the enemy. As they are still 400 meters in front of the grain field, the company

advances across a broad front. When we get to the edge of the woods a platoon goes in. Then: "Urrah!" the Russians attack with total surprise. Wild explosions, ricochets, panic. A few men run back to the road embankment. We build a new holding line here – that was quite a shock. One half hour later, accompanied by a 50mm PAK, the company pushes into the woods again to save our wounded comrades. There were 5-6 men … Finally we reach them. There they lay, wickedly mutilated, bestially disfigured – all dead! That was quite a shock that all the men carried with them: everyone knew what it meant to fall into Russian hands.[296]

Fighting in the Novogrodek-Minsk region continued until 8/9 July 1941, when organized Red Army resistance finally collapsed. In his diary on 8 July, Field Marshal von Bock estimated that his forces had destroyed 22 rifle divisions, seven tank divisions, six motorized brigades and three cavalry divisions; as of 7 July, Bock noted, 287,704 prisoners had been taken (among them several corps and division commanders) – a figure which, according to German estimates, was to rise to 324,000 over the next few days.[297] The material booty was also tremendous, and amounted to more than 3300 tanks and 1800 guns destroyed or captured, along with the seizure of immense quantities of fuel, ammunition and rations.[298] "With the fuel we have captured, we'll get to Moscow," exulted the keeper of Fourth Army's war diary. Actually, the truth was rather more mundane, for the captured stocks met only one third of German fuel requirements, which were amounting to 11,500 cubic meters per day (the equivalent of 28 trainloads), or about 350,000 cubic meters per month – roughly 25 percent higher than German logisticians had estimated.[299]

While German figures for Soviet prisoners are most likely inflated (through inadvertent inclusion of civilians),[300] Belostok-Minsk was, by any measure, an unprecedented victory – one which, in the west, would have yielded decisive results. According to authoritative Russian figures published in the 1990s, Western Front suffered 417,729 casualties, including 341,012 "irrecoverable losses" (i.e., dead, captured, and missing), through 9 July 1941 – out of a total force of almost 675,000 men.[301] Western Front also lost 4799 tanks (many having simply run out of fuel), 9427 guns and mortars, and 1777 combat planes (most of which were destroyed on the ground) during 18 days of fighting in the western frontier regions from 22 June to 9 July 1941.[302]

Any major corporate body is susceptible to inflating its own successes and minimizing its failures, the German General Staff being no exception to this truism. Thus, it is not surprising that, in the wake of the first dramatic victories, the Germans exaggerated the predicament – admittedly dire – of the Red Army. At Rastenburg on 8 July 1941, Brauchitsch and Halder, using data provided by Foreign Armies East, informed Hitler that, of 164 identified Soviet rifle divisions, 89 were now destroyed, 46 still active on the main fronts, and 18 tied down in secondary theaters of war (mostly on the Finnish Front); 11 more divisions were most likely in reserve. Of 29 Soviet armored divisions hitherto identified, 20 had been shattered, and only nine still retained full combat capability.[303] "The enemy," Halder confided in his diary (8 July),

> is no longer in a position to organize a continuous front, not even behind strong terrain features. At the moment the apparent plan of the Red Army High Command is to check the German advance as far to the west as possible by draining our strength with incessant counterattacking with all available reserves. In pursuing this policy they evidently have grossly overestimated German losses.
>
> Meanwhile we must reckon with the attempt to activate new units with which they might eventually stage an offensive. The plan of a large-scale disengagement is nowhere discernible.

Activation of new units, certainly on any larger scale, will fail for lack of officers, specialists, and artillery materiel. This holds particularly for their armor, which even before the war was sadly lacking in officers, drivers, and radio operators, as well as signal equipment.[304]

That the German assessment of Soviet strength was grossly inaccurate can be gauged from the fact that Timoshenko alone, on Western Front, commanded 66 divisions in the first week of July; of these, 37 had taken up positions defending along the main axes of Army Group Center's advance toward the Dvina-Dnepr Rivers.[305] Three days later (11 July) Halder noted that the Soviets had "no more reserves left" behind the central front, and "cannot hold much longer."[306] In fact, the *Stavka* was assembling reserves which "the [German High Command] could only envy."[307]

With the pocket battles over, the infantry divisions of Army Group Center began to press on eastward, in a series of brutal forced marches, in an effort to regain contact with the armored spearheads. Stifling heat and dust, punctuated by occasional heavy rains and thundershowers, marked the line of advance. Average daily marches of 30, 40, 50 kilometers and more – down narrow forest tracks, across marshy ground, often without warm food and with scant drinking water, weighted down by weapons, ammunition, and equipment – were not uncommon, and a trial for man and beast. Remembered one veteran, an artillerist with 106 Infantry Division: "On the advance through Russia it was very hot at times. Many comrades simply collapsed in the heat. The machine guns, ammunition boxes, mortar parts and heavy radio equipment were an enormous burden."[308] "On the German side," wrote Albert Seaton,

> ... particularly in Army Group Center, there was unbounded confidence and this was notably strong in the marching infantry formations. Success at this time was measured by stamina and marching ability ... As the long marching days stretched into weeks the men became harder and fitter and less tired, but not so the horses which, unstirred by patriotism and careless of the impetus of victory, grew resentful at the loss of the weekly rest day. Thirty miles a day were frequently covered, sometimes more, the troops marching through thick clouds of dust which rose as high as a house, hanging over the forested march routes in the hot windless air, since the high trees on either side of the tracks were like walls, cutting off any breath of wind. Even the trees were gray, there being no trace of green to be seen anywhere. Faces were covered with a thick gray mask. Men and clothing were sweaty and filthy with no time or opportunity for bathing or washing. The marching infantry, but not its transport, greeted the occasional thunderstorms and torrential rains with delight, as a relief from the insufferable heat and all-pervading dust.[309]

To expedite the march, some divisions formed mobile advance detachments by combining divisional components with available motor transport.

7.6: The Race to the Rivers – Drive to the Dvina-Dnepr River Lines

It will be recalled that, on 30 June, OKH had ordered Hoth and Guderian to begin their all-out drive for the Dvina-Dnepr Rivers as soon as possible; the day finally agreed upon for a formal resumption of the advance was 3 July. By 2 July, 2 Panzer Group, on its right wing (24 Panzer Corps), had already breeched the Berezina, sending advance detachments of 3 Panzer Division on toward the Dnepr. In the center of Guderian's group, 46 Panzer Corps (10 Panzer Division and the motorized SS *Das Reich*) was approaching the Berezina, while on the left wing, General Nehring's 18 Panzer Division (47 Panzer Corps) had reached the river at Borisov. Guderian's 17 Panzer Division, 29 Motorized Infantry Division, Motorized Infantry Regiment *Grossdeutschland*, and Machine Gun Battalion 5, were still tied down along the south and southeastern shoulder of the Novogrodek-Minsk cauldron. Hoth's 3 Panzer Group, with 39 and 57 Panzer Corps, had reached the line Okolovo – Glubokoe, from where it was to continue its push toward the Dvina; two divisions of Hoth's group, 12 Panzer Division and 14 Motorized Infantry Division, were still holding the sector of the pocket directly west and northwest of Minsk.[310]

As of 4 July, having been reinforced by OKH reserves, Army Group Center consisted of 59 divisions (among them nine panzer, five motorized and one cavalry division), one motorized "instructional" brigade (*Lehr-Brigade* 900), and one motorized infantry regiment (*Grossdeutschland*). Included in this mighty force were more than 1000 combat-ready tanks and 6600 guns, supported by 1500 combat aircraft. Thirty-nine of Bock's divisions were in action with 15 first echelon army corps and panzer corps, while 28 divisions were deployed along the forward edge of battle. The vanguard of this powerful grouping, the five panzer corps of 2 and 3 Panzer Groups, advancing toward the river barriers, was operating across an extended front of more than 300 kilometers,[311] with virtually nothing in reserve – their movements impeded by heavy summer rains, which transformed the sandy roads and tracks into a bottomless sludge.[312] Meanwhile, German aerial reconnaissance indicated that the Soviets were rushing new formations to the front to shore up their defenses along the river lines.[313] Hoth and Guderian would have to move quickly!

Only a few days into the campaign, the OKH and Army Group Center had begun to contemplate how to manage these new operations.[314] As a result, they "did something in common with many organizations (military and otherwise) that often pays minimum dividends at a steep cost: [they] reorganized."[315] Field Marshal von Kluge's Fourth Army headquarters was converted into Fourth Panzer Army, and given control over both Hoth's and Guderian's panzer groups; as a result, Kluge turned over most of his infantry divisions to the newly activated headquarters of Second Army (General Maximilian *Freiherr* von Weichs), which assumed responsibility for operations along the encirclement ring. Simply put, the reason for the move was to "make von Bock's job easier and both to coordinate better and somewhat rein in Hoth and Guderian by placing them under an intermediate headquarters."[316] In part, at least, the initiative was likely an attempt – once again! – to assuage Hitler's anxiety about the tanks pushing ahead too far too fast. Basic technical considerations also played a role: The encirclement maneuvers had created a "massive tangle of units," which needed to be sorted out before the next phase of the campaign could begin; also, the mobile units had now pushed so far ahead that armor and marching infantry could "no longer be bound together in mutually supporting roles." Perforce, OKH felt it necessary to alter command and control, so the army group could better control its forces.[317]

Regardless of the reasons for it, the reorganization worked out poorly (it went into effect at 0000 hours on 3 July).[318] Kluge's headquarters was set up to control infantry forces; thus, it lacked the radio communications, cross-country mobility, and liaison aircraft needed to manage mechanized forces effectively. The new command arrangement also made personality clashes between Kluge, Guderian and Hoth virtually inevitable. In fact, Guderian, when he first got wind of the plan, had even threatened to resign. As for Kluge – a gifted commander, but one uncomfortable with the slashing and chaotic operations of a "blitzkrieg" – he was hardly suited for leading a large armored force, while Bock feared his control over his tank commanders might be seriously compromised. As matters turned out, Kluge had difficulty managing Hoth and Guderian, in part because of frequent breakdowns in communication. Both OKH and Bock soon grew frustrated with Kluge's less aggressive style of leadership, and Bock, concerned that the panzer units were being dispersed across too broad a front, urged Kluge on 6 July to concentrate his forces: "make a fist somewhere."[319]

7.6.1: 2 Panzer Group

Along the front of Guderian's 2 Panzer Group, it was 3 Panzer Division that was first to reach the Dnepr – at Rogachev, on the far right wing of Geyr's 24 Panzer Corps. Model's men had had little rest or sleep for days; his French- and Czech-manufactured trucks were starting to break down (from the pounding they'd taken on the wretched roads) and tank strength was declining, more due to the fine, ubiquitous dust, which cut the life expectancy of tank engines in half, than to enemy action. Yet the dynamic division commander, despite objections from his more conservative subalterns, had pushed his men onward without respite – success now would save lives later, he reasoned.[320]

Spearheading the advance of 3 Panzer Division on 3 July was a battalion of submersible tanks (originally intended for Operation "Sealion," the invasion of Great Britain) of 6 Panzer Regiment. Crossing the Drut River, they rumbled eastward another eight kilometers, reaching the Dnepr northeast of the already burning city of Rogachev by nightfall. While this action was underway, infantry and combat engineers of the division burst into the city, only to be met by "murderous" fire from the Russians defending in the houses and buildings. German anti-tank crews struggled to manhandle their guns into position, taking the enemy strongpoints under direct fire. Slowly, deliberately, the battalions of 3 and 394 Rifle Regiments "chewed" their way into Rogachev, the combat engineer platoon of *Leutnant* Moellhoff being the first to reach the church in the city center. At several points, the infantry reached the Dnepr, giving rise to intense machine gun and artillery fire from the far bank and forcing them to seek cover. Yet just outside the city, several small infantry *Kampfgruppen* of 3 Rifle Regiment managed to form a tiny bridgehead on the far (eastern) bank of the river. The Russians, however, had demolished all bridges over the Dnepr.[321]

Throughout the night, a hurricane of artillery fire – from 36 batteries (up to 150mm) in position along the far bank, southeast of Rogachev – pounded German positions. Savage street fighting went on as well – with Russian resistance particularly robust in the southern part of the city – and German losses mounted by the hour: *Oberleutnant* Spillman (6./SR 394) – killed in action, along with many of his men; Major Zimmermann (II./SR 3) – wounded (for the third time); *Oberleutnant* von Becker (8./SR 3) – badly wounded, his unit suffering serious losses; *Leutnant* Fritze – killed in action; *Leutnant* Gleitz, leader of the combat engineer assault team – killed in action, along with three of his men. Bowing to the intense enemy pressure, the bridgehead was withdrawn.[322]

The next day (4 July), the battle for the bridgehead continued unabated. After a swarm of *Stukas* sought to silence the heavy Russian artillery fire, albeit without success, 3 Panzer Division launched a set piece assault to take it across the Dnepr. The infantry of 2nd Battalion, 3 Rifle Regiment, debouching directly from Rogachev, soon faltered in the withering enemy fire (in two days, the battalion saw one of its companies wiped out, while the remaining four sustained 146 casualties). To the north, however, another battlegroup (II./SR 394, elements of 6 Panzer Regiment and anti-tank units) was more successful. Here, three submersible Panzer IVs[323] plunged through the Dnepr, barely 100 meters wide at this point,[324] and emerged on the other side. While one of the tanks was blown apart by Russian fire, its crew perishing, the remaining two provided supporting fires long enough to enable the infantry to get across as well. Thus had a second small bridgehead been established; it was, however, soon sealed off from the rest of 3 Panzer Division by a curtain of Russian artillery fire, and fighting for its life against waves of Russian infantry.[325]

Fifty kilometers upstream, at Stary Bychov, Geyr's 4 Panzer Division also crossed the Dnepr on 4 July. Yet the fighting in this sector was severe, too. The garrison town was well defended and protected by a stout anti-tank ditch. "In spite of contemporary military intelligence," argues U.S. Army Lieutenant Colonel (retired) Robert Kirchubel, "(and subsequent military history) to the contrary, from what the Germans on the scene could tell, the so-called Stalin Line was very real."[326] In fact, 4 Panzer Division's 35 Panzer

Regiment, which led the assault on Stary Bychov, suffered its most severe single day's losses since the beginning of the war: 18 dead, 10 wounded and six missing. In one engagement at Stary Bychov, the tank regiment lost several tanks in swift succession, knocked out at point-blank range after being ambushed by a dense Russian screen of well-concealed anti-tank and anti-aircraft guns and artillery firing over open sights. Forty-eight hours later, the panzer crews, given up for dead, made their way back to the regiment, having swum across the Dnepr.[327]

By now, it was becoming apparent that Guderian, at least on his right wing, may indeed have "pushed too far too fast."[328] (Hitler knew his tank commanders, and his instincts were often quite good.) Despite 3 Panzer's slender bridgehead over the Dnepr, the rest of Model's division was strung out across muddy roads as far back as the Berezina; elements of 4 Panzer Division were struggling along the road from Slutsk to Mogilev; 10 Motorized Infantry Division was precariously spread out over many kilometers near Zhlobin; and 1 Cavalry Division was still tramping across the outer fringes of the Pripiat' Marshes. The closest supporting units, those of 46 Panzer Corps, were astride the Berezina, far to the northwest. Put another way, Guderian's spearheads "stood poised on the brink of victory and disaster at the same moment, and not a few German officers began to realize viscerally just how large the Soviet Union was."[329]

Perhaps aware of the exposed and vulnerable position of Guderian's right wing, on 6 July, the Russians went over to the offensive. Lt.-Gen. V. F. Gerasimenko's 21 Army began a series of counterstrokes that "threw the 24 Panzer Corps into its first major crisis of the campaign."[330] While the army's 63 Rifle Corps (three divisions) attacked Model's Dnepr bridgehead, 66 Rifle Corps, supported by tanks, crossed the river at Zhlobin and struck Loeper's 10 Motorized Infantry Division just as it was assembling for its own attack. Although, once again, the Soviet assaults were poorly coordinated, Geyr's panzer corps was deployed for pursuit, and lacked so much as a small tactical reserve. Penetrating rapidly, and with tactical surprise, into Pobolovo, the Soviets wiped out elements of 10 ID (mot.).[331]

Having already dispatched 1st Battalion, 6 Panzer Regiment, to Loeper's division as a precaution on 5 July (ground reconnaissance had reported strong Russian forces to the south, in the vicinity of Zhlobin), Model now had no choice but to send more of his forces to the aid of his hard-pressed neighbor – this time a powerful battlegroup, including more tanks (II./PzRgt 6) and several batteries of anti-tank guns. At the same time, trying to keep up pressure at Rogachev, Model finally managed to reinforce his shaky Dnepr bridgehead with additional infantry. Being forced onto the defensive for the first time since the start of the campaign administered an adrenal shock to the division; as a post-war history put out by former division members recalled: "After the intoxicating victories of the first days of the war, no one had counted on the Russians gathering the strength to put up such strong resistance on the Dnepr, even though the so-called Stalin Line was at the river."[332]

Reacting to the threat, 10 Motorized Infantry Division, without waiting for the additional reinforcements from Model to arrive – and without notifying the commander of 3 Panzer Division of its intent – at once committed I./PzRgt 6 to battle against the advancing Soviet forces. The bloodletting was costly, particularly for the battalion's unfortunate 4th Company:

> 4./PzRgt 6 (*Oberleutnant* von Brodowski) is advancing at top speed directly toward Zhlobin on a road not marked on any map. The company breaks through an anti-tank front in close order, since it is not possible to leave the road. So now tank after tank is rolling toward Zhlobin, into the increasingly intense enemy defensive fire. The Russian guns can hardly be seen, and a few tanks[333] have concealed themselves so well in the high cornfield that their fire strikes into 4./PzRgt 6 at very close range. The first German tank gets stuck, the second runs over a mine,

the following 3 are destroyed by Russian tanks. The infantry has lagged behind and their advance is disrupted by the enemy's long-range artillery. The Soviets concentrate their defensive fire on those tanks of 4./PzRgt 6 which have rushed forward. At the start that morning, the company had 13 tanks. Now, one after the other, they lie shattered amid fire and smoke. *Leutnant* von Wedel falls, shortly thereafter also *Leutnant* Busse. The company commander is seriously wounded. *Oberleutnant* von Brodowski dies a few days later from his burns. 22 other NCOs and enlisted men fall alongside him, while 36 men are wounded, many seriously. Only 3 of our own tanks return from this death march of 4./PzRgt 6!

Major Schmidt-Ott orders his 1st Company forward, which also suffers many losses. 1./PzRgt 6 provides sufficient covering fire that the remnants of 4th Company can extricate themselves from the enemy … By midday on this "black" day, I./PzRg 6 has lost 22 of its tanks, half of its strength. This loss cannot be compensated for by the capture or destruction of 19 Russian tanks, 21 artillery pieces, 2 Flak guns and 13 anti-tank guns. Major Schmidt-Ott will be mentioned in the honor roll of the German Army [*Ehrenblatt des Heeres*] for the sacrifices made by his battalion in this operation.[334]

In two days of bitter fighting, and despite heavy losses, the Germans succeeded in throwing back the Russians around Zhlobin. (By 9 July, 3 Panzer Division's tank strength had fallen to 153, from 215 on 22 June.) Yet it was now abundantly clear that the enemy position around Rogachev was simply too strong; hence, on 7 July, 3 Panzer evacuated its Dnepr bridgehead, the infantry of 394 Rifle Regiment and supporting elements withdrawing back across the river on pneumatic boats under cover of darkness.[335] "Small as it was," writes historian Steven Newton, "Gerasimenko's counterattack had delivered the first check to Guderian's impetuous plunge toward Moscow." That same day (7 July), the Red Army registered another tactical victory, when 46 Panzer Corps was unable to capture the bridges around Mogilev, while further south, 4 Panzer Division had yet to move beyond Stary Bychov.[336]

On Guderian's left wing, 18 Panzer Division made slow but steady progress toward Orsha after resuming its advance on 3 July, while 17 Panzer Division (both 47 Panzer Corps), having extricated itself from the encirclement ring at Minsk, was soon moving up on 18 Panzer's left, toward Senno.[337] Here, too, German forces closing on the Dnepr were challenged by bad weather and difficult terrain; yet these were far from the only frustrations faced by General Lemelsen, Commander, 47 Panzer Corps. On 6 July, he confided in his diary:

> It is raining; this is seriously impeding all movements, because the roads immediately dissolve; in any case, they usually go through marshes and are only just traversable during the dry season. So we are currently struggling step by step through the most difficult terrain and are so eager to cross the Dnepr at Orsha, but our forces available for this have been considerably weakened, because 29 ID (mot.) was held back at Minsk. The *Fuehrer* wants to clean out the cauldron at Belostok first and only continue onward after that. So he has ordered all forces to be left at Minsk. But if we want to advance farther east at all, then we will have to be quick about it, before the Russian brings more strong forces to the Dnepr line, or else it will cost us a lot of blood. That is why we had permission from the *Panzergruppe* to punch our way ahead east to the Dnepr with both panzer divisions, but we will gradually run out of steam if 29 ID (mot.) doesn't rejoin us from behind.
>
> The advance of 17 Panzer Division from Minsk has had serious consequences after all. I had Guderian with me yesterday evening, and he was very depressed.

He has thus been accused of disobeying an order and there was a heated exchange between him and von Kluge, in which the latter threatened him with court martial.[338] Very, very unfortunate if the forces, in their urge to advance, are encumbered by a leaden weight at their back. That will be debilitating. As a result, the mood today has sunk to absolute zero, exacerbated, of course, by our not really advancing in the way we want, and by the cold and wet weather, which is really putting the brakes on us. Well, after rain comes sunshine. Let's hope so, anyway![339]

By early July 1941, the tankers and panzer grenadiers of 18 Panzer Division – whose early successes against obsolete Soviet armor had so buoyed their confidence – had been unceremoniously introduced to the newer, heavier, and deadlier Russian KV and T-34 tanks. Against these well-armored leviathans, the German tanks and anti-tank guns were largely ineffective, forcing the *Landser* to turn to more radical measures in an effort to neutralize them. *Leutnant* Georg Kreuter, a company commander in 18 PD, described one such encounter – most likely with a KV-1 – on the road to Orsha, in his personal diary:

7.7.41:
We attempt to envelop and defeat the enemy on and along the highway ... We push ... ahead on dreadful roads. We meet Red tanks everywhere. They appear to be very badly led. Many of them and a few trucks are destroyed. The enemy draws many forces into the encircled area. We are stuck in a forest area – the regiment with its staff, the 2nd Battalion, and I with my platoon headquarters group, with no guns. The commander of the panzer battalion (Teege) with 20 tanks is also with us. Who is encircling whom here??? That's the question!

We are cut off by tanks to the rear. Messengers can only get through occasionally. Russian tanks attack us! The second heaviest type among them![340] Our Pak, even the 50mm, can only penetrate at the weakest points. One heavy and 4 light tanks are put out of action. One heavy tank has driven into our forest, another on the road around the forest. Since the anti-tank guns cannot reach them – and have no effect in any case – I receive the order from the regiment to destroy them. Our tanks were just as powerless and kept very quiet when they drove past, only a few meters away. I try it with hand grenades that I have adapted into concentrated charges. It's useless. Only a hand grenade down the barrel brought the interior to explode.[341]

By 7 July, Nehring's 18 Panzer Division, moving east along the highway from Minsk to Smolensk, and having reached Tolochino (less than 50 kilometers from Orsha), was bearing down on the Dnepr. The 17 Panzer Division, now commanded by Brig.-Gen. Karl Ritter von Weber,[342] stood at Senno (50 kilometers northwest of Orsha),[343] where it was struck by powerful Red Army mechanized forces (the Soviet Lepel counteroffensive, see below, Section 7.6.2). "The last few days have again been most difficult," wrote Lemelsen on 10 July.

The sunshine may have returned, but despite the roads drying off, intense enemy resistance meant any advance was difficult. The 18 PD is just too battle-weary now, it lacks the right fighting spirit, which in any case can't be expected of the Saxons. There were tough battles around Tolochino for 18 PD and very severe crises for 17 PD at Senno. The 17 PD, which is about 50 km away from us, was very heavily attacked the day before yesterday at Senno by at least one Russian armored division. I flew in a *Storch*[344] to them at Tolpino and found a critical situation there. Tolpino was under heavy enemy artillery fire, the houses were burning, and the Russian was attacking from the north and south in massive waves with countless tanks. Our riflemen fell back, batteries were overrun by the Russians – things looked bleak.

I flew back at once to my command post, which in the meantime had been transferred to the area of Natscha, and directed *Stukas* to attack this strengthening enemy, who was continually drawing reinforcements from Orsha. This provided relief and by the evening, 17 PD was again in control of the situation. It could have gone very badly. And Russians with tanks are still swarming between the individual groups of this division.

Over 100 [enemy] tanks were destroyed on this day during the battles of both divisions, burning tanks could be seen everywhere. The 17 PD needed a very long time to reorganize itself, to rearm, and refuel, especially since the supply columns were cut off from the division at Tscheriza and had to be rescued by tanks first.[345]

Despite such bitter enemy resistance, all three of Guderian's tank corps (24, 46, and 47) were now closing on the Dnepr.[346] At this point, however (7 July), Guderian, having failed in his initial attempts to puncture the river barrier at Rogachev and Mogilev, decided to regroup his panzer forces and shift the *Schwerpunkt* of his assault. Yet he also faced another critical decision:

> Was I to continue my advance as rapidly as heretofore, to cross the Dnepr with panzer forces only, and attempt to reach my primary objective [i.e., the area Smolensk – El'nia – Roslavl] as quickly as possible according to the original plan of campaign? Or should I, in view of the measures that the Russians were taking to construct a defensive front along the line of the river, break off my advance and await the arrival of the infantry armies before launching the battle for the river?[347]

During the Belostok-Minsk pocket battles, the infantry of Fourth (later Second) and Ninth Armies had fallen as much as 250 kilometers behind the surging panzer divisions. On 7 July, the infantry of 7, 9, 12, 13 and 53 Army Corps were still bunched up between Baranovichi and Minsk, 200 kilometers and more from the Dnepr, with other infantry units even further to the rear.[348] In his post-war recollections, Guderian stated – rather overstated – that the marching infantry would require 14 days to reach the Dnepr,[349] by which time the Russian defenses, now in the process of being built up, would be considerably stronger. "Whether the infantry," Guderian wrote, "would then be able to smash a well-organized river defensive line so that mobile warfare might once again be possible seemed doubtful …

> I was well aware of the importance of the decision to be taken. I calculated the dangers of heavy counter-attacks against the open flanks of all three panzer corps once they were across the river. On the other hand I was so convinced of the vital importance and of the feasibility of the task assigned to me, and at the same time so sure of the proved ability and attacking strength of my panzer troops, that I ordered an immediate attack across the Dnepr and a continuation of the advance toward Smolensk.
>
> I therefore ordered that the battles on either flank – at Zhlobin and Senno – be broken off, and that the commanders responsible be satisfied with keeping the enemy there under observation.[350]

Guderian's decision was bound to bring him into conflict – again – with his more conservative superior, Field Marshal von Kluge, and, according to the panzer general, it soon did. On the morning of 9 July, Guderian later recalled, Kluge appeared at his (Guderian's) command post in Borisov,[351] where an "exceptionally heated conversation" ensued. Kluge's position, perhaps influenced by the failures at Rogachev, Mogilev and Stary Bychov, was that the armor, on its own, was not strong enough to push through the defenses of the Stalin Line along the Dnepr; because he believed significant infantry support would be required, the crossings should not be attempted until such support became available. Guderian defended his contrarian views "with obstinacy," informing Kluge that his (Guderian's) preparations for the assault "had already gone too far to be cancelled." The troops of 24 and 46 Panzer Corps, he insisted, having regrouped, were now ready to jump off – to leave them massed in their assembly areas would simply make them targets for attack from the air. Furthermore, Guderian was optimistic his renewed attack would not only succeed, but be decisive. ("I expected that this operation would decide the Russian campaign this very year, if such a decision were at all possible.")[352] Confronted with Guderian's persuasive arguments, Kluge relented. The operation would begin the next day, 10 July. Still, the unhappy Kluge got in the final word: "Your operations always hang by a silk thread!" he said. (*Ihre Operationen haengen immer an einem seidenen Faden!*)[353]

7.6.2: 3 Panzer Group

On the left wing of Army Group Center, Hermann Hoth's 3 Panzer Group resumed its drive toward the Western Dvina River on 3 July.[354] To more effectively exploit the meager road net and avoid the swamps and marshes along the upper reaches of the Berezina, Hoth elected to advance on a broad front. On his left, Kuntzen's 57 Panzer Corps was to cross the Dvina at Polotsk, while well to the southeast Schmidt's 39 Panzer Corps seized a river crossing at Vitebsk. Kuntzen was then to press on to the northeast, toward Rudia and Nevel (near the boundary with Army Group North), while Schmidt skirted Smolensk to the north and headed for Iartsevo, far to the rear of Timoshenko's Western Front. The objectives assigned to the two corps – some 160 kilometers apart – placed them on diverging trajectories and precluded mutual support; Hoth, however, accepted the risk, for he expected to encounter little or no enemy resistance along the route of advance.[355] Hoth also assumed the few available roads were "trafficable," and that dry weather would persist.[356]

As matters turned out, all three of Hoth's assumptions were wrong. Both of his panzer corps encountered vigorous opposition, particularly 39 Panzer Corps as it advanced on Vitebsk. Hoth's tanks and motorized infantry were also slowed by heavy thunderstorms, which lasted for days, turning the tracks and trails leading east into bottomless pits of mud and raising water levels of the rivers, streams, lakes and swamps which dotted 3 Panzer Group's attack frontage in great profusion and proved more difficult than anticipated to negotiate. The many wood bridges along the axes of advance, not built to withstand the pounding of a modern, mechanized army, collapsed under the weight of the heavy vehicles, and had to be rebuilt or replaced by overworked combat engineers.[357] The roads, which seemed to become worse the further east one went, also took a heavy toll, causing mechanical breakdowns of tanks and vehicles – so many, in fact, that, on 4 July, Hoth reported his combat strength at barely 50 percent.[358] Yet despite such serious obstacles, Hoth would fulfill his mission, and, along with Guderian's operations to the south, help to create the operational conditions for a second great battle of annihilation, near Smolensk, beginning in mid-July 1941.

One of the major advances registered by Hoth's forces over 3/4 July was by Maj.-Gen. Otto von Knobelsdorff's 19 Panzer Division (57 Panzer Corps). Effectively supported by *Stukas* of Richthofen's 8 Air Corps, and using a decent road, the division lunged nearly 100 kilometers in 24 hours, its motorcycle riflemen (*Kradschuetzen*) capturing Disna on the Dvina on the evening of 4 July, after tough house-to-house fighting, and helping to secure a bridgehead across the river.[359] On 19 Panzer's right, 18 Motorized Infantry Division encountered stout resistance from Soviet bunker positions on the approaches to Polotsk, thwarting a crossing there; by day's end (4 July), however, the division was within five kilometers of the city,[360] where it was to remain, held in check by Lt.-Gen. F. A. Ershakov's 22 Army. At Disna, by late 6 July, 19 Panzer Division (reinforced by elements of 18 ID (mot.)) was also under attack from Soviet 22 Army, which, in an (ultimately unsuccessful) effort extending over several days, sought to crush Knobelsdorff's Dvina bridgehead. In this sector then, after a promising start, the operations of 3 Panzer Group were temporarily stalemated.[361]

To the south, Schmidt's 39 Panzer Corps also made off for the Dvina with two divisions (7 PD and 20 PD). Operating on the corps' left, Maj.-Gen. Stumpff's 20 Panzer Division closed up to the river at Ulla (ca. 70 kilometers due west of Vitebsk) with its vanguard on 4 July. The mass of Stumpff's division, however, was still far behind, near Lepel, its progress disrupted by serious traffic congestion (both 7 PD and 20 PD were sharing the same road) and bridge failures. The next day (5 July) 20 Panzer's tank regiment crossed an emergency bridge (*Behelfsbruecke*) erected by the combat engineers at Lepel and rumbled east. While the initial plan had been to attempt an immediate crossing at Ulla with 20 PD's advance detachment, reinforced by artillery and a combat engineer battalion of 39 Panzer Corps, this intent was soon dropped in favor of a more deliberate attack. Yet this would take time to prepare, as thundershowers now rendered the road of advance virtually unusable in places, further hampering movements of the main body of 20 Panzer Division as it approached Ulla.[362]

Schmidt's other tank unit, Brig.-Gen. *Freiherr* von Funck's 7 Panzer Division, headed for Vitebsk, advancing east along the road from Lepel. On 5 July, its lead elements were visited by a swarm of heavily armored Il-2 *Sturmovik* ground attack planes, which, despite taking as many as 200 hits from German fire, did not suffer a loss. Despite furious Russian resistance, 7 Panzer continued its push; by evening, 6 July, it was just 30 kilometers southwest of Vitebsk.[363]

The stiff resistance experienced by Funck's tankers and panzer grenadiers was the result of the Red Army's Lepel counteroffensive, which began early on 6 July. Several days before, Marshal Timoshenko, Commander, Western Front, had received a new directive from *Stavka*, ordering him to hold off "3 and 2 Panzer Group's onslaughts, organize a reliable defense along the line of the Western Dvina and Dnepr Rivers and, after concentrating reserves arriving from the depth of country, deliver a series of counterstrokes along the Lepel, Borisov, and Bobruisk axes."[364] In response, late on 4 July, Timoshenko ordered Lt.-Gen. P.A. Kurochkin's 20 Army, along with two fresh mechanized corps (5 and 7) – both drawn from Stalin's "Palace Guards" in the Moscow Military District – to attack toward Lepel and Senno; other forces were to recapture the crossings over the Berezina at Borisov. While the 5 and 7 Mechanized Corps order of battle (on paper at least) showed a combined strength of more than 1500 tanks, the great majority were superannuated BT, T-26, and T-37/38 models (only 80 were modern KVs and T-34s). Both corps, moreover, had to make long approach marches, during which they suffered losses to German air strikes and mechanical breakdowns caused by failures of tank engines and drive trains.[365]

The two mechanized corps launched their assault at 1000 hours, 6 July. Over the next four days (6-9 July 1941), an enormous tank battle took place south and southwest of Vitebsk, between Lepel and Senno. Drawn into the fighting on the German side were 7 Panzer Division (39 Panzer Corps) and 17 and 18 Panzer Divisions (47 Panzer Corps), with Brig.-Gen. Harpe's 12 Panzer Division providing additional support near the end of the battle.[366] Exploiting their experience and superior tactical skill, the German tank crews destroyed hundreds of Soviet tanks; others were decimated by waves of German dive-bombers and destroyer aircraft. Typical of the Soviet experience is the following account involving 7 Mechanized Corps:

Late in the day [6 July 1941], [Maj.-Gen. V.I.] Vinogradov's two tank divisions ran straight into the defenses of Funck's 7 Panzer Division on the northeastern approaches to Senno, beginning two days of heavy fighting, during which Vinogradov perished … During the assault, Colonel Ivan Dmitrievich Vasil'ev's 14 Tank Division, which had marched unimpeded 116 kilometers from the region south of Vitbesk, attacked toward Lepel without any air cover and with inadequate maps through difficult heavily wooded terrain against an unknown enemy force. As the former chief of the division's political department later reported, "Unfortunately, we had to operate practically 'on the off-chance.' We did not know who was in front of us – a battalion, regiment, or corps. There was no advanced reconnaissance."[367]

Attacking at first against light German resistance, Vasil'ev's tanks pushed back reconnaissance parties of 7 Panzer Division. In the hours that followed, however, the 14 TD commander received a series of conflicting orders from Vinogradov, the cumulative effect of which was to disperse his division over a wide area, diluting its firepower. Still, the division continued its advance toward Beshenkovichi on the Dvina, while doing so squandering precious hours as its tanks struggled to negotiate the swampy ground. As Vasil'ev dutifully carried out his orders, Funck's forces were building a powerful screen of anti-tank guns along the river's western bank. When Vasil'ev finally attacked early the next day (7 July) at Vinogradov's insistence, his division was taken apart by murderous anti-tank fire, losing more than half of its tanks, many of which became stuck in the bed of the river.[368]

Although the Germans had tapped the Russian telephone lines, and, thus, were privy in advance to Timoshenko's intentions,[369] they were, nevertheless, hard-pressed at times by the poorly orchestrated, albeit zealous Soviet assaults. As noted above, General Lemelsen (47 Panzer Corps), on 10 July, referred in his diary to the "very severe crises" at Senno, in the sector of Weber's 17 Panzer Division.[370] By 9 July, however, Hoth's and Guderian's armor, once again effectively supported by 8 Air Corps, had largely destroyed the Soviet 5 and 7 Mechanized Corps, which suffered a combined loss of 832 tanks. Both tank corps – what remained of them at least – retired across the Dnepr River "in considerable disorder." "The only appreciable end the futile attacks achieved," concludes David Glantz, "was delaying [47 Panzer Corps'] capture of Orsha and [39 Panzer Corps'] seizure of Vitebsk."[371]

While the tank battles flared along the southern flank of 39 Panzer Corps, to the northwest, at Ulla, Stumpff's 20 Panzer Division breached the Soviet defenses on the Dvina and, in a deft flanking maneuver, advanced on Vitebsk. On the night of 6/7 July, under cover of rainfall, the Soviet defenders had strengthened their positions around Ulla, bringing up additional artillery and anti-tank guns. At 1445 hours on 7 July, *Stukas* struck the stout Soviet defensive positions on the eastern bank to good effect. Following a brief preparatory barrage by 20 PD's artillery, augmented by *Heeresartillerie* assigned to the division to support the breakthrough, the panzer grenadiers of 59 and 112 Rifle Regiments poured across the river in assault boats on either side of Ulla. The next morning (8 July), after combat engineers had built a bridge over the river, *Kampfgruppe von Bismarck* (tanks, infantry, engineers; anti-tank, Flak and artillery units) crossed the Dvina and began to roll toward Vitebsk. Capitalizing on 20 Panzer's powerful assault, Brig.-Gen. Hans Zorn's 20 Motorized Infantry Division crossed the Dvina at Beshenkovichi, 25 kilometers southeast of Ulla, and advanced toward Vitebsk along the Dvina's northern bank. Together, by late 9 July, Zorn's infantry and von Bismarck's *Kampfgruppe* had seized the flaming city of 200,000, which had been set on fire by the Russians before they withdrew. Demolition squads were still setting off charges as the Germans entered the city.[372] (Later in July, when elements of 129 Infantry Division marched through Vitebsk, they were greeted by scenes of utter devastation. Across large stretches of the city, all that remained of the wooden domiciles were the stone chimneys, which pointed skyward like boney fingers.)[373]

By establishing secure bridgeheads across the Dvina at Ulla and Beshenkovichi, and capturing Vitebsk, Hoth's 3 Panzer Group, as the OKH Operations Branch recorded in its daily report on 9 July, "had essentially cracked the enemy defensive front along the upper Dvina."[374] In fact, with the collapse of his right wing, Timoshenko's efforts to hold firm along the Dvina-Dnepr River lines – as he had been ordered to do so – had been fatally compromised. Still, Timoshenko was determined to stay put, setting the stage for a second Soviet catastrophe on the central front – this time in the forests, fields, and steppelands west of Smolensk.

Postscript: For his decisive contribution to the operations along the Dvina, General Schmidt, Commander, 39 Panzer Corps, was awarded the highly prestigious Oak Leaves to the Knight's Cross. On 12 July 1941, a special courier from Germany arrived at the command post of General Schmidt. In his possession was a telegram from Hitler, awarding Schmidt the Oak Leaves, effective 10 July 1941, as the 19th soldier of the *Wehrmacht*. While Schmidt thus became the first general on the eastern front to earn the distinction, one can only speculate what crossed his mind – outside of professional pride – upon notification of the award, for "Papa" Schmidt, as his men called him affectionately, was a "hostile critic"[375] of Hitler's regime.[376] Schmidt's biographer, Klaus-R. Woche, recounts a telling incident a short time later:

> One day, between the encirclement battles of Minsk and Smolensk, the *Fuehrer's Wehrmacht* adjutant, *Oberst i.G.* Schmundt, appeared at the corps' command post and presented General Schmidt with the Oak Leaves to the Knight's Cross. As Hans Hertel [staff officer with 39 Panzer Corps] reported, General Schmidt now used the opportunity to tell *Oberst* Schmundt about the evident lack of coordination in the military operations so that this could be communicated to the *Fuehrer*.
>
> [Schmidt] also aired his thoughts on the political conduct of the war in Russia. *Oberst* Schmundt explained the official view of the OKH: "*The book on the Russian campaign is already closed!*" He himself did not share this view, and General Schmidt declared that one look at a map of Russia would surely prove that it was only the first page of the book on Russia that had just been written. OKH evidently had no idea of the actual events at the front, thus "*many pages more*" would have to be written.[377]

7.7: Food, Fuel, Munitions – Supplying Army Group Center

The German Army which invaded in the Soviet Union in June 1941 comprised over three million men, more than 600,000 horses, and 600,000 vehicles of all types. Like all modern armies, it depended on the timely delivery of enormous quantities of food, fuel, ammunition, spare parts and other necessary supplies for the successful execution of its mission, indeed for its very survival. As one German general put it shortly after the war: "In modern mobile warfare the main thing is no longer tactics. The deciding factor is the organization of supplies in order to keep things moving."[378] And, as psychiatrist Dr Jonathan Shay more recently averred: "The mortal dependence of the modern soldier on the military organization for everything he needs to survive is as great as that of a small child on his or her parents."[379] One cannot put too fine a point on it: In modern, mechanized warfare, logistics are decisive.

The armies of the *Ostheer* received their supplies from depots behind the front by means of road or rail (and, infrequently, by air). Prior to the start of the campaign, German logistical planners had concluded that the Army's supply system could sustain an advance of up to 500 kilometers beyond the frontier, to the line of the Western Dvina and Dnepr

Rivers; beyond that point, however, requirements could not be projected. Because it would take time to bring rail lines inside Soviet territory into working order, the delivery of supplies during this first, decisive phase of operations was to depend mostly on motor (truck) transport across Russia's thin road net. Yet as calculations, studies, and map exercises had revealed, upon reaching the Dvina-Dnepr line at the latest, the *Ostheer* would be dependent on the smooth functioning of the railroads for resupply.[380] In general, German logisticians, like their counterparts on the operational side, fell victim to facile and dangerously optimistic assumptions – in this case about their ability to successfully supply the armies in the east. After all, even if *Barbarossa* was launched on a "logistical shoestring,"[381] this was of little concern, for the "blitzkrieg" would be over in a matter of weeks.

Yet as Clausewitz admonished in *On War*, "these arteries [of supply] … must not be permanently cut, nor must they be too long or difficult to use. A long road always means a certain waste of strength, which tends to cripple the army."[382] While the *Wehrmacht* in Russia experienced no crippling logistical problems in the opening weeks of the campaign, it did encounter challenges – some anticipated, some not – which upset the pre-campaign calculations of the German General Staff and, in their cumulative impact, began to adversely affect troop operations and resupply.

As German forces pressed deeper into Soviet territory, their lines of supply, particularly those of the mobile units, rapidly lengthened, placing added strain on the supply organization. The transportation companies ran into difficulties from the start because of the lack of roads; still, many of them managed to accumulate an astounding total mileage as they shuttled back and forth between the depots, the railheads, and their forward bases. For example, in one eight-week period, the supply vehicles of a single panzer division traveled 303,982 kilometers hauling ammunition, 199,385 hauling fuel, and 63,073 kilometers hauling spare parts.[383]

The outcome of such Herculean efforts was that many of the supply trucks, particularly civilian transport drawn from captured enemy stocks or ongoing Western European production, simply disintegrated on the primitive Russian roadways. By 10 July 1941, the hauling capacity of the *Grosstransportraum* (the motor transport directly controlled by the three army groups) had declined by 25 percent; 10 days later (20 July), the number of broken-down vehicles in Army Group Center (including those lost to enemy action) had risen to more than 30 percent.[384] The problem is accurately assessed by historian Rolf-Dieter Mueller:

> Much of the damage sustained by the motor-vehicles could have been avoided if there had been enough time and fuel to prepare the drivers for the extraordinary conditions they would meet in Russia, and the special driving skills they would require. A shortage of maps also necessitated travel in convoy, causing considerable loss of time in the event of a major breakdown. Many of the civilian vehicles used by the troops, especially the motor-cars, proved to be unserviceable because of their low ground clearance. In summer they bottomed out on sandy and sodden tracks, and in winter they were stuck in snowdrifts. As a result, these vehicles frequently suffered irreparable damage to their oil-sumps and transmission. During the advance, many breakdowns were also caused by broken suspensions. Stocks of spring steel in the replacement-part depots, provided on the basis of demand during the French campaign, were exhausted after a short period, compelling the armies to use their own lorries to fetch small amounts of spring steel from Koenigsberg and Elbing, or from Stuttgart and Ulm. Tires proved unable to withstand the abrasion of the sandy tracks, but could be replaced only infrequently. On 10 July 1941, Army High Command informed the armies that no more tires at all would be supplied.[385]

"Under such conditions," argues Israeli historian Martin van Creveld, "the actual capacity of the *Grosstransportraum* fell far below that which had been expected, and it became difficult to supply the operation every time the front was more than [100 kilometers] removed from the railways."[386] Despite the vital importance of the motor transport during the first phase of operations, when movement of supplies occurred mainly by road, few replacement vehicles were made available; in fact, through July 1941, only about one in 10 of the lost vehicles was replaced; after that, the Army High Command refused to provide replacement vehicles because of the shortage of trucks, and because the vehicles were needed to form new divisions.[387]

Like the motor vehicles, the horse-drawn vehicles of the marching infantry divisions also suffered numerous breakdowns. The rubber tires with which they were typically outfitted were "rapidly worn to shreds, and had to be replaced with wooden wheels clad with iron hoops."[388] The large German and western European draft horses suffered terribly due to the unending demands placed on them. The heavy columns and field howitzer batteries, in particular, often became stuck in the deep, loose sand, and had to be pulled free by teams of straining soldiers. The numbers of horses falling out due to exhaustion rose inexorably, confronting some infantry formations with the prospect of leaving their heavy artillery behind. Many units attempted to address such challenges through improvisation. For example, 167 Infantry Division "maintained its mobility and fighting strength by leaving its 'heavy baggage,' vehicles, and equipment in a divisional camp at Slonim, together with 200 men who lived independently under military administration and did agricultural work."[389]

As this narrative has shown, the tenuous lifelines of supply were also vulnerable to disruption, as they often ran through regions teeming with Soviet stragglers, or beset by nascent partisan activity. On the second day of the campaign, 3 Panzer Group reported: "There was an increase in resistance by enemy stragglers in some areas in the rear of the Panzer Corps."[390] On 3 July 1941, 57 Panzer Corps informed 3 Panzer Group that, "In the rear area there are unknown numbers of Russians lurking in the woods, who cannot be captured by the Corps with its present manpower, but who pose a serious threat to supply convoys."[391] Indeed, given German manpower shortages, adequate security along roadways behind the front was often impossible to obtain.

The mostly unmetalled roads and the weather (early July brought heavy rainfall) also played havoc with the tank units, which often incurred more attrition from such factors than from enemy action. Of course, there was, first of all, the dust, which not only plagued man and beast, but tanks and vehicles as well. On 16 July 1941, 10 Panzer Division reported to 46 Panzer Corps:

> During the last 100 kilometers, 24 tanks have broken down, their engines irreparable, because of a build-up of dust which has sprung up from nowhere. This dust, which cannot be kept out by air filters, has such an abrasive effect, in conjunction with motor oil, that there is a sharp drop in power and the engines are no longer able to propel the tanks forward.[392]

Worse still was the situation of Nehring's 18 Panzer Division. Having begun the campaign with 218 tanks, by 20 July, the division had incurred 37 total losses, while 126 tanks were in need of repair.[393] Hoth's 3 Panzer Group, which began *Barbarossa* with about 900 tanks, had, by 9 July 1941, total losses amounting to 154 tanks, with 264 tanks (nearly 30 percent) awaiting repairs.[394]

Because the supply system was unable to keep up with the demand for spare parts, more and more tanks became temporarily immobilized. Palpably exacerbating the problem was the fact that facilities for making major repairs had not been brought forward, but left far to the rear in Germany. This was because the German Army's "essentially centralized system of tank maintenance"[395] required all major repairs and refurbishment to be done at manufacturing plants in the Reich. Therefore, disabled tanks (vehicles as well) had to be loaded onto railroad flatcars and shipped to Germany, then back to the front, further stressing an already overstressed rail system. Replacement tanks were also hard to come by: As of 1 July, tank parks in Germany had only 85 tanks on hand, with another 210 to be manufactured by the end of the month – figures which were inadequate to satisfy the replacement needs of a single panzer group, much less four.[396] Hitler, moreover, convinced as he was of impending victory, would soon tell his Army C-in-C to send no more tanks to the eastern front.

By early July it was also apparent that, as a result of the appalling road conditions, tanks and vehicles were burning up fuel at a rate far greater than anticipated by German logistical planners. As noted above (Section 7.5), while OKH had reckoned consumption for the *Ostheer* at about 9000 cubic meters (2,621,049 gallons) per day, the actual figure was 11,500 cubic meters (3,348,800 gallons) per day; or, as Halder jotted in his journal on 1 July, "considerably higher than expected."[397] Thus, instead of a daily allotment of 22 tank car trains, 28 would be needed to fulfill fuel requirements.[398] Measured another way, the amount of fuel required for 100 kilometers under normal terrain conditions (i.e., a typical unit of consumption, or *Verbrauchsatz*), was adequate for just 70 kilometers in the Russian countryside.[399] Fortunately, the panzer groups had been able to supplement their regular fuel supplies with captured Soviet stocks, 3 Panzer Group alone seizing 30,000 tons of fuel by 2 July 1941.[400]

Oil was also consumed at a rate far greater than expected, with an equally inimical effect on operations. During 4 Panzer Division's drive toward Kiev (later in the summer of 1941), about 50 percent of the tanks were put out of action simply because of insufficient deliveries of oil.[401] At the beginning of July 1941, 30 Pz III and four Pz IV tanks of 2 Panzer Group broke down from engine damage caused by the use of captured Russian oil.[402] Due to the difficult terrain, tanks had to be driven in first gear, often for days on end, with the result that the "engines began to 'drink' oil!"[403] On 6 August 1941, 57 Panzer Corps reported that many vehicles were burning 20-30 liters of oil per 100 kilometers, instead of the normal ½ liter![404]

Expenditures of ammunition during the first few weeks of the *Russlandkrieg*, although well above levels experienced in France in 1940, were actually less than envisaged by German planners.[405] Average daily consumption amounted to 2,840 tons, compared to 2,057 tons per day over 43 days in 1940. Specifically, by 31 July 1941, a total of 113,458 tons of ammunition had been consumed in the east, requiring 252 supply trains hauling an average of 450 tons. Nevertheless, temporary shortages were not uncommon – for example, as a result of mechanized units outrunning their supply lines, or becoming temporarily cut off – and, by August 1941, Army Group Center was experiencing a full-blown ammunition crisis. Even before the attack on Russia, however, the Germans were already looking ahead to post-*Barbarossa* campaigns and throttling back ammunition production for the Army; particularly hard hit was production of artillery and mortar shells, which was dramatically reduced. (See Chapter 3, Section 3.1: "Force Structure of the Army.") Such miscalculations were to have serious consequences for the *Ostheer* by the end of the year[406]

With each passing day, as the German armored spearheads raced deeper into Russia, across the Berezina and toward the Dvina-Dnepr River barriers, the significance of the Soviet rail net increased. Once again, however, the assumptions of German planners proved hopelessly optimistic – in this case, that they would capture intact extensive chunks of the rail infrastructure in European Russia, thus enabling the Germans to operate them unaltered with captured locomotives and rolling stock, while reducing to a minimum conversion efforts from the Russian broad gauge to the narrower German gauge. Yet damage to rail lines, water stations, signal equipment, rolling stock, telephone lines, bridges, engine sheds, etc. – either by deliberate Russian action or as a result of ground combat or *Luftwaffe* bombardment – was greater than anticipated, while the Russians managed to evacuate most of their locomotives and rolling stock, compelling the Germans to commit massive resources of their own in an effort to restore the rail system to a functioning state.[407]

During World War I, from 1914 to 1916, German armies in the east had also converted Russian rail lines to the narrower German gauge. At that time, however, these efforts had only extended to parts of Russian-occupied Poland, the Baltic States and the western portion of Belorussia (in the Ukraine and southern Russia such work was not required, for sufficient quantities of locomotives and rolling stock were seized there). By comparison, during 1941/42, the scope of conversion activities was to cover an area more than three times as large – and extending all the way to the Caucasus region in the south – and a rail net four times as dense. All told, some 35,000 kilometers of the Soviet railway would be converted,[408] at a rate of 10 to 12 kilometers a day by a company of German railway troops (*Eisenbahntruppen*) outfitted with the most advanced tools and techniques.[409]

Efforts to convert the rail lines, and operate them with German equipment, were not only enormous, but much more difficult than foreseen. For example, the bed of the Russian tracks was normally so weak, and the load-carrying capacity of the rails so deficient, that the only German engines they could support were light models built before World War I.[410] Because Soviet locomotives were larger, water stations were fewer and further apart; in addition, Russian coal, it was soon discovered, could not be burned efficiently in German engines without German coal or fuel additives, while the transfer points (*Umschlagstellen*) between German and Russian railway gauges formed time-consuming logistical bottlenecks.[411]

While the railroad troops labored feverishly to convert the rail lines and, thus, move the railheads forward, their efforts suffered from critical shortages of manpower and materials, rendering rapid progress impossible. Not being combat formations, they ranked at the bottom of priorities for the three army groups, upon which they depended for their supply of fuel. Moreover, only one-sixth of the railway units were fully motorized, while two-thirds had to operate with no vehicles at all. All told, only about 1000 vehicles were allocated to the *Eisenbahntruppen* across the entire eastern front, and these were mostly inferior French and British types. In addition, the railroad troops had not been adequately trained and their numerical strength "proved hopelessly inadequate;" thus, by July 1941, it had become necessary to supplement their units with men taken from the civilian *Reichsbahn*.[412]

Yet despite these – and many other – challenges, the main problem remained the conspicuous shortfall of railroads within the Soviet Union. In contrast to European standards, where a field army would normally control one double-tracked rail line, Army Group Center began the Russian campaign with only *one* such main line to support its three armies and two panzer groups. Working around the clock, the railroad engineers and their troops had soon restored the Brest-Litovsk – Minsk rail line as far as Baranovichi (200 kilometers), causing Field Marshal von Bock to note in his journal (3 July) that the "railroad is keeping up surprisingly well."[413] One track of the rail line was operational in the German gauge, while the other was hauling war materiel and supplies on the wider Russian gauge. The latter track was functioning as far as Minsk by 4 July.[414]

Meanwhile, the tracks leading from the Grodno area to Molodechno, and that were earmarked to support Ninth Army and 3 Panzer Group, were also being rebuilt. In the sector of Strauss' Ninth Army, however, the performance of available lines in early July was so far below requirements that the army complained it was receiving but a third of the daily allotment of trains to which it was entitled, and the situation only got worse: After 8

July, the railway only hauled supplies to sustain Hoth's panzer group, while Ninth Army had to make do with the *Grosstransportraum*, even though the distance from their supply base was now almost 400 kilometers and the intervening roads in wretched shape.[415]

Despite the strains on the supply system, Chief of the Army General Staff Halder, and OKH *Generalquartiermeister*, Brig.-Gen. Wagner, sought to shift the supply bases forward to support the ongoing advance and prepare for future operations. Supply District Center, which supported the operations of Bock's army group, had been established before start of the campaign in the Warsaw – Suwalki region. After the first days of war, the army group, in an effort to shorten supply routes, had begun to move its bases eastward, onto the line Olita (Alytus) – Voronovo – Lesna. Each supply base was made up of ammunition, fuel and foodstuffs depots, field hospitals, maintenance and repair workshops, bakers' and butchers' companies, a spare-parts detachment, and a supply battalion or personnel from the Reich Labor Service (RAD), as well as a Vehicle Transportation Detachment.[416]

At the end of June, preparations began to build a new set of bases, starting on the line Molodechno – Minsk – Slutsk.[417] By mid-July 1941, as the railroads were slowly converted to German gauge – and by which time Guderian's tanks were across the Dnepr and racing for Smolensk and beyond – the bases were pushed forward yet again – this time to the line Polotsk – Lepel – Borisov – Bobruisk. This new backbone of supply depots, the Dnepr Supply District, was intended by Halder and Brig.-Gen. Wagner, the Army High Command's chief logistician, to sustain the drive of the tank forces all the way to Moscow.[418]

7.8: The Frontier Battles in the Balance

By 9 July, 18 days after the start of Operation *Barbarossa*, the frontier battles had come to close and the *Ostheer* was racing toward distant objectives along three axes of advance. From the perspectives of Adolf Hitler, the German High Command, and the *Oberbefehlshaber* of the army groups, armies and panzer groups, a decisive victory was taking shape, one which would make the German Reich the undisputed master of the European continent from the English Channel to the Ural Mountains. Along the front of Army Group North, the six mobile divisions (three panzer, three motorized) of General Erich Hoepner's 4 Panzer Group had rapidly occupied Lithuania and, by 30 June, seized bridgeheads across the lower reaches of the Western Dvina River. Although impeded from the outset by lakes, impenetrable forests and rivers, Hoepner's tanks trundled on toward the northeast, capturing Ostrov, on Latvia's pre-1940 frontier with Russia, and piercing the Stalin line by 5 July; several days later, 41 Panzer Corps stormed into Pskov, at the southern tip of Lake Peipus and barely 300 kilometers from Leningrad. By 10 July 1941, Hoepner had – so he believed – satisfied all preconditions for a final thrust on Leningrad.[419]

While the going had been tougher for Army Group South, General Ewald von Kleist's 1 Panzer Group (five panzer, four motorized divisions) was now driving deep into the Ukraine. After shattering the mechanized corps of Soviet Southwestern Front in a series massive tank-on-tank engagements in late June, Kleist's armor broke through the Stalin line astride Novograd-Volynskiy on 6/7 July, capturing Berdichev (7 July) after costly fighting and creating the operational prerequisite for an advance on Kiev and into the great Dnepr bend to the southeast. By 10 July, Zhitomir had fallen – the vanguard of 3 Panzer Corps now barely 75 kilometers from Kiev and awaiting arrival of the marching infantry, still far to the rear.[420]

In the center, the successes of Field Marshal von Bock's army group were even more remarkable. By 1 July, 10 days into the campaign, its forces had advanced more than 400 kilometers into Russian territory,[421] encircling and destroying the armies of Soviet Western Front; by 9 July, Red Army resistance in the huge cauldron between Belostok and Minsk had finally flickered out. Hundreds of thousands of Soviet troops trudged into captivity, the Germans also seizing huge quantities of war material. Having registered a "decisive" victory at the frontier, the armor and motorized infantry of Hoth's and Guderian's tank groups had pressed on eastward, to the Dvina-Dnepr River barriers and the strategically vital Smolensk gate – to be followed, they fervently hoped, by an all-out advance on Moscow itself. The month of July would be a good one for the field captains of Army Group Center: Lemelsen (47 Panzer Corps), Geyr (24 Panzer Corps), Nehring (18 Panzer Division) and Model (3 Panzer Division) all garnering the Knight's Cross, while Hoth (3 Panzer Group), Guderian (2 Panzer Group), Schmidt (39 Panzer Corps) and Richthofen (8 Air Corps) were awarded the even more prestigious Oak Leaves to the Knight's Cross.[422]

Carried away by the moment, Adolf Hitler, on 8 July 1941, announced his final plans for both Moscow and Leningrad. These great, historic cities were, he informed his military staff, to be "razed to the ground."[423] As Halder noted laconically in his diary that day, this would render the cities "uninhabitable, so as to relieve us of the necessity of having to feed the populations through the winter. The cities will be razed by the *Luftwaffe*. Tanks must not be used for the purpose."[424] Also on 8 July, Hitler instructed Brauchitsch not to dispatch any new tanks to the eastern front, as these were needed for future campaigns; furthermore, the panzer divisions in the east were to be reduced in number, and idle tank crews returned to Germany to train crews for new divisions. The "Fuehrer" was already thinking well beyond *Barbarossa*.[425]

So profoundly convinced were the Germans of their impending triumph that, later in July, Senior SD leader and SS-Colonel (*Standartenfuehrer*) Dr A.F. Six, and his "Advanced Detachment Moscow" (*Vorkommando Moskau*), anxious to reach the Soviet capital on the heels of the fighting troops, arrived at the command post of Kluge's Fourth Panzer Army. Once inside Moscow, the SS-colonel and his men intended to take over "security police duties" in the city, while also securing Soviet archives, art, cultural artifacts, and other objects of use to the Germans.[426]

And yet, at the highest levels of command, a vague, incipient feeling of unease was beginning to stir among a few more thoughtful souls. In a missive to his wife on 3 July 1941, Colonel Heusinger, Chief, OKH Operations Branch, again radiated confidence, but added, "in the long run the world cannot endure" based on wars of aggression. He consoled himself with the thought – the hope – that History would have a short memory; besides, surprise attacks like *Barbarossa* were "hardly unique" (*keine Seltenheit*). Still, he was troubled by how far removed things had become from the "humanity of the last century." In a startling admission, he added: "We are acting like Genghis Khan of old." Heusinger also intimated that the distances still to be covered – to Moscow, Leningrad and the Baku oil fields – were "crazy" (*irrsinnige Wege*); in fact, he told his wife on 8 July, it made him shudder to think "how far we still have to go until we've eliminated the Russian threat once and for all."[427]

Far beyond the OKH Mauerwald compound, and the dark forests of East Prussia, Maj.-Gen. Bogislav von Studnitz, Commander, 87 Infantry Division, wrestled with similar forebodings. For most of July 1941, Studnitz' division was far behind the battle front, in the area around Grodno, where it was responsible for collecting, registering and reporting on the vast quantities war booty scattered throughout the region – a "special assignment" (*Sonderauftrag*) which had only angered and disappointed the general and his men.[428] After all, there was a war on, and they were missing out on it. One day in mid-July, General Studnitz learned from his operations officer that an artillery battery was quartered for the night in the same village as the general and his staff, whereupon the general decided to invite the battery chief, *Oberleutnant* Siegfried Knappe, to dine with him that evening. Long after the war, Knappe wrote about the encounter with his division commander:

> [The general] was in his middle 50s and a little on the heavy side. He was an impressive professional soldier who understood the art of warfare and was an

effective practitioner. He was an intellectual, a political and philosophical thinker, and an avid reader. He was highly respected by his men and subordinate officers.

"*Oberleutnant* Knappe, commander of 1st Battery, 187 Artillery Regiment, Herr General," I reported to him in his log house.

"Good evening, Knappe," he said, smiling broadly and offering his hand. "Have a seat." He motioned to a table, and waved to his orderly to pour wine for us. "How are things going for you?" he asked.

"Just fine, Herr General," I responded.

"How is the morale of your people?"

"Excellent. They are fine soldiers, and their attitude could not be better."

"How are your horses holding up?"

"They are doing well. As long as they get a day of rest now and then and are well cared for, they will do fine."

[The general] looked pensive for a moment. "How do you think the campaign has gone so far?" he asked.

"Great," I said enthusiastically. "Everything seems to be going according to plan."

He did not respond for a moment, his thoughts seemed to be far away. "I was in Russia during the last war," he said finally. "I have experienced the Russian winter. It is savage, like nothing we have ever experienced. It will come, and it will come soon. We are just in this little part of Russia. We have a vast empty country ahead of us, and if we do not take Moscow before the weather turns bitter cold. I worry about what will happen."

He was clearly not optimistic. I was amazed, because it could not have been easier up to now, but I knew he was intelligent, experienced, and capable, and I began to tone down my own optimism after that. If someone had overheard our conversation and reported it to the Nazi Party, it could have cost General von Studnitz his career.[429]

Of course, the sober thoughts of men such as Heusinger and Studnitz were not shared by most, yet they should have been. For the great victories achieved by the *Ostheer* were not quite what they seemed. To be sure, the German armies had registered impressive territorial gains, the armored spearheads of Guderian's panzer group alone logging an average daily advance of about 30 kilometers per day for the first 18 days of the campaign. Yet only in the central sector of the front had the *Wehrmacht* succeeded in smashing and annihilating the bulk of the Soviet first strategic echelon west of the Dvina-Dnepr Rivers in accordance with the mission assigned to it by the original *Barbarossa* directive.[430]

German losses, while a fraction of those sustained by the Red Army, had also been quite heavy. According to the pioneering analysis of key German wartime records made by historian Dr Ruediger Overmans in the late-1990s,[431] the Germans suffered 25,000 dead in the first nine days of the campaign alone (22-30 June), over 90 percent of which were incurred by the ground forces (Army and *Waffen*-SS); during July, fatal losses would accumulate at the rate of more than 2000 per day – more than double the rate of the six-week French Campaign of 1940. When the tens of thousands of wounded, sick and missing are added to these totals it becomes clear that the *Wehrmacht* in the east was already enmeshed in a brutal war of attrition.[432] Material losses, particularly those of the *Luftwaffe*, were also high. By 5 July, the German air fleets in Russia had lost a total of 491 aircraft (124 fighters, 196 bombers (and dive bombers), and 171 reconnaissance and transport aircraft), or more than 20 percent of their combat-ready strength of 2250 aircraft on 22 June;[433] hundreds more aircraft had been damaged. On 5 July, 8 Air Corps reported that fuel was running low, even though it had already scaled back its operational tempo.[434]

Far from totally destroyed, the Red Army was, by early July 1941, beginning to funnel new reserve armies into new lines of defense. With each passing day, the intelligence organs of German field formations were adding new units to the Soviet order of battle, while German aerial reconnaissance was reporting the ongoing movement of troop trains chugging west toward the front. The Soviets were also starting to function more effectively at both the strategic and tactical levels – if still far behind the Germans in the operational art of war – a state of affairs confirmed by many contemporary German accounts; among them, this report by 35 Panzer Regiment (4 Panzer Division) on 4 July 1941: "Impression of the enemy: a tough fighter and distinctly brave soldier, whose morale has yet to suffer."[435] The day before (3 July), Count Helmuth James von Moltke, a brilliant young lawyer serving in the *Abwehr* (German military intelligence) as legal advisor to OKW (and who would be executed in January 1945 for his role in the German Resistance) had confided in a letter to his wife:

> I still don't like the look of the Russian war; but today the big new attack begins [i.e., the advance toward the Dvina-Dnepr River lines], and perhaps it will have more decisive results than this first battle. – But the fighting morale and tactical leadership of the Russians far exceed all expectations and I'm coming to the conclusion that we were seriously misinformed about Russia; or at least I was.[436]

As July passed into August, Hitler and his military advisors would begin to recognize, and privately acknowledge, their catastrophic error of casually underestimating the fighting prowess and regenerative qualities of the Red Army in particular and the Soviet state in general. Gradually, the euphoria of the first days and weeks of the campaign would give way to a deep and abiding uneasiness about what the future of the war with Russia held in store for them.

ENDNOTES

1   Quoted in: H. Hoth, *Panzer-Operationen*, 110-11.
2   W. Kempowski (Hg.), *Das Echolot*, 174.
3   K.-R. Woche, *Zwischen Pflicht und Gewissen*, 105. The verse reads better in German: "*Rechts sind Russen, links sind Russen, vorn und hinten wird geschossen.*"
4   W. Kempowski (Hg.), *Das Echolot*, 223.
5   H. J. Schroeder, "*Erfahrungen deutscher Mannschaftssoldaten waehrend der ersten Phase des Russlandkrieges*," in: *Zwei Wege nach Moskau*, B. Wegner (Hg.), 313.
6   J. Keegan, *Second World War*, 186.
7   Incidents of the use of proscribed ammunition by the Soviets in the summer of 1941 (as well as the discovery of such ammunition on Red Army soldiers, or in captured Russian positions) were carefully catalogued by the *Wehrmacht* War Crimes Bureau (*Wehrmacht-Untersuchungsstelle fuer Verletzungen des Voelkerrechts*). See, BA-MA RW 2/v. 145, "*Kriegsverbrechen der russischen Wehrmacht 1941.*" For a detailed history of this neglected, albeit important, institution see, Alfred M. de Zayas, *The Wehrmacht War Crimes Bureau, 1939-45*. For details on the use of "dum-dum" bullets and explosive shells by the Red Army, see below, Chapter 9, Section 9.4.3: "Use of Proscribed Ammunition."
8   Attacks on German troops and supply columns by armed Soviet civilians – as well as by Red Army soldiers who had fled to the forests, shed their uniforms, and taken up partisan warfare – began on the first day of the war. About one such incident historian Timothy Mulligan writes: "Before nightfall on 22 June 1941 … 7 Panzer Division of the attacking Army Group Center encountered armed Soviet civilians who ambushed German vehicles and soldiers. During the first 48 hours of the invasion, at least two members of the division had been killed and several wounded, while 15 guerillas were shot in battle or summarily executed. The partisan war in the central USSR had claimed its first victims." T. P. Mulligan, "*Reckoning the Cost of People's War: The German Experience in the Central USSR*," in: *Russian History/Histoire Russe*, 9, Pt. 1, 27.

9   See Chapter 8, Section 8.3.3, "Fighting;" also, Chapter 9, Section 9.4, *Keine Kameraden*: Crimes of the Red Army."

10   W. Knecht, *Geschichte des Infanterie-Regiments 77*, 53-54.

11   K.-R. Woche, *Zwischen Pflicht und Gewissen*, 99-100.

12   W. Kempowski (Hg.), *Das Echolot*, 24-25.

13   E. Wagner, *Tage wie Jahre*, 27-28.

14   Ibid., 28-30.

15   Ibid., 30. For his role in the combat this day, Wagner was promoted to *Gefreiter*. Wagner survived the many crises of 23 June 1941, serving on the eastern front until the German capitulation in May 1945. He spent more than four years in Russian captivity.

16   *Tagebuch* Kreuter, 24./25.6.41. Kreuter also wrote: "Everywhere there is skirmishing, primarily at night. Russian vehicles often join our marching column. Whoever detects the presence of the other first tosses a hand grenade into their vehicle. On occasion, when we've challenged a Bolshevist vehicle, they answered: 'Don't shoot, we're transporting German wounded!'"

17   BA-MA RH 27-18/20, *KTB 18. Pz.-Div.*, 24.6.41; BA-MA RH 27-18/34, *"Eine Nacht auf dem Div.Gef. Stand einer Pz.Div."*

18   Describing the eventual German victory at Smolensk in early August 1941, Showalter's complete quote reads: "It was the climax of a series of virtuoso performances that combine to make a case that the relative tactical and operational superiority of the panzers over their opponents was never greater than in the first half of July 1941, on the high road to Moscow. Guderian spoke of attacks going in like training exercises." See, D. Showalter, *Hitler's Panzers*, 170-71.

19   E. Mawdsley, *Thunder in the East*, 60.

20   The decision cycle, or "OODA Loop," signifies the "process by which an entity (either an individual or an organization) reacts to an event. According to this idea, the key to victory is to be able to create situations wherein one can make appropriate decisions more quickly than one's opponent. The construct was originally developed out of Boyd's Energy-Maneuverability theory and his observations on air combat between MiGs and F-86s in Korea. Harry Hillaker (chief designer of the F-16) said of the OODA theory, 'Time is the dominant parameter. The pilot who goes through the OODA cycle in the shortest time prevails because his opponent is caught responding to situations that have already changed.' Boyd hypothesized that all intelligent organisms and organizations undergo a continuous cycle of interaction with their environment. Boyd breaks this cycle down to four interrelated and overlapping processes through which one cycles continuously: Observation: the collection of data by means of the senses; Orientation: the analysis and synthesis of data to form one's current mental perspective; Decision: the determination of a course of action based on one's current mental perspective; [and] Action: the physical playing-out of decisions ... This decision cycle is thus known as the OODA loop. Boyd emphasized that this decision cycle is the central mechanism enabling adaptation (apart from natural selection) and is therefore critical to survival." Internet site at: http://en.wikipedia.org/wiki/John_Boyd.

21   D. M. Glantz, *Barbarossa*, 40.

22   *GSWW*, Vol. IV, 527.

23   See the situation maps for 23-30 June 1941, depicting the advances made by the end of each day, in: K.-J. Thies, *Der Ostfeldzug – Ein Lageatlas*.

24   BA-MA RH 20-4/1199, *KTB AOK 4*, 23.6.41; J. Weal, *Jagdgeschwader 51 'Moelders,'* 58.

25   D. M. Glantz (ed.), *Initial Period of War on the Eastern Front*, 202.

26   BA-MA RH 27-18/20, *KTB 18. Pz.-Div.*, 23.6.41.

27   D. M. Glantz (ed.), *Initial Period of War on the Eastern Front*, 189-90.

28   BA-MA RH 20-4/199, *KTB AOK 4*, 23.6.41.

29   D. M. Glantz, *Zhukov's Greatest Defeat*, 31. For an excellent, and relatively recent (2001) biography of Model see, Marcel Stein, *Generalfeldmarschall Walter Model, Legende und Wirklichkeit*.

30   A town or village along Panzer Route 1, some 50 kilometers east of Kobrin. In the Thies atlas the town is designated as "Kartuska-Bereza." See, K.-J. Thies, *Der Ostfeldzug – Ein Lageatlas*, "Lage am 23.6.1941 abds., Heeresgruppe Mitte."

31   *Geschichte der 3. Panzer-Division*, Traditionsverband der Division (Hg.), 110-12. For an equally graphic account of the advance of 3 PD on this day see, H.-J. Roell, *Oberleutnant Albert Blaich, Als Panzerkommandant in Ost und West*, 45-48, 69-72.

32   *Geschichte der 3. Panzer-Division*, Traditionsverband der Division (Hg.), 112; Colonel H. Zobel (ret.), *"3rd Panzer Division Operations,"* in: *Initial Period of War on the Eastern Front*, 242. Recalls Zobel, at the time a young platoon leader in 6 Panzer Regiment: "During the first two days of combat, unarmored troops and rear echelons suffered considerable losses inflicted by hostile enemy troops cut off from their main bodies. They hid beside the march routes, opened fire by surprise, and could only be defeated in intense hand-to-hand combat. German troops had not previously experienced this type of war."

33   *Geschichte der 3. Panzer-Division*, Traditionsverband der Division (Hg.), 112.

34   Ibid., 112-13.

35   D. M. Glantz (ed.), *Initial Period of War on the Eastern Front*, 205.

36   C. von Luttichau, *Road to Moscow*, VI:39.

37   K.-J. Thies, *Der Ostfeldzug – Ein Lageatlas*, "Lage am 25.6.1941 abds., Heeresgruppe Mitte."

38   D. M. Glantz (ed.), *Initial Period of War on the Eastern Front*, 210.

39   Ibid., 210.

40   *Geschichte der 3. Panzer-Division*, Traditionsverband der Division (Hg.), 112.

41   H.-J. Roell, *Oberleutnant Albert Blaich. Als Panzerkommandant in Ost und West*, 73.

42   P. E. Schramm (Hg.), *Kriegstagebuch des OKW*, Bd. I, 420; K.-J. Thies, *Der Ostfeldzug – Ein Lageatlas*, "Lage am [26.-27.]6.1941 abds., Heeresgruppe Mitte;" R. Kirchubel, *Hitler's Panzer Armies*, 64; A. Seaton, *The Russo-German War*, 121.

43   BA-MA RH 21-2/927, *KTB Panzergruppe 2*, 28.6.41.

44   At one point, Kluge became so fed up with Guderian's inability to follow orders that he threatened the Panzer general with a court martial. See, R. A. Hart, *Guderian*, 74.

45   A. Seaton, *The Russo-German War*, 121; H. Hoth, *Panzer-Operationen*, 66; K.-J. Thies, *Der Ostfeldzug – Ein Lageatlas*, "Lage am 30.6.41 abds., Heeresgruppe Mitte."

46   Lead elements of 3 PD reached the outskirts of Bobruisk by 3.00 that morning. BA-MA RH 27-3/14, *KTB 3. Pz.-Div.*, 28.6.41; P. E. Schramm (Hg.), *Kriegstagebuch des OKW*, Bd. I, 422; K.-J. Thies, *Der Ostfeldzug – Ein Lageatlas*, "Lage am 28.6.41 abds., Heeresgruppe Mitte;" S. H. Newton, *Hitler's Commander. Field Marshal Walther Model*, 125.

47   BA-MA RH 27-3/14, *KTB 3. Pz.-Div.*, 29.6.41.

48   By 30 June 1941, 3 PD was on the move toward the Dnepr; two days later, lead elements were nearing Rogachev. M. Stein, *Generalfeldmarschall Walter Model*, 238.

49   D. M. Glantz (ed.), *Initial Period of War on the Eastern Front*, 217; P. E. Schramm (Hg.), *Kriegstagebuch des OKW*, Bd. I, 421-22.

50   C. Pleshakov, *Stalin's Folly*, 144-45.

51   W. Meyer-Detring, *Die 137. Infanterie-Division im Mittelabschnitt der Ostfront*, 32.

52   R. Kirchubel, *Hitler's Panzer Armies*, 64; P. E. Schramm (Hg.), *Kriegstagebuch des OKW*, Bd. I, 422; K.-J. Thies, *Der Ostfeldzug – Ein Lageatlas*, "Lage am 29.6.1941 abds., Heeresgruppe Mitte;" W. Paul, *Geschichte der 18. Panzer-Division*, 21.

53   Specifically, almost all of Soviet 3, 4 and 10 Armies, or at least their remnants, were inside the pockets, along with most of 13 Army. D. M. Glantz, *Barbarossa Derailed*, Vol. I, 32.

54   H. Guderian, *Panzer Leader*, 161.

55   Ibid., 160.

56   H. Guderian, *Panzer Leader*, 161; H. Hoth, *Panzer-Operationen*, 65-66.

57   H. Guderian, *Panzer Leader*, 160; *GSWW*, Vol. IV, 530; P. E. Schramm (Hg.), *Kriegstagebuch des OKW*, Bd. I, 423-24; H.-A. Jacobsen (Hg.), *Generaloberst Halder Kriegstagebuch*, Bd. III, 26-29. In his diary on 30 June 1941, Halder noted that aerial reconnaissance had detected tank traps being built in great haste between Vitebsk and Orsha.

58   H. Magenheimer, *Moskau 1941*, 40.

59   C. von Luttichau, *Road to Moscow*, VI:52-53.

60   BA-MA MSg 1/1147: *Tagebuch* Lemelsen, 1.7.41.

61   W. K. Nehring, "Die 18. Panzerdivision 1941," in: *Deutscher Soldatenkalender 1961*, 194-96. According to the war diary of 18 PD, the advance detachment included a tank battalion from 18 Panzer Regiment (II./PzRgt 18), one battalion from 52 Rifle Regiment (I./SR 52), two motorcycle companies, and a battery of 88 Artillery Regiment. BA-MA RH 27-18/20, *KTB 18. Pz.-Div.*, 1.7.41.

62   BA-MA RH 27-18/20, *KTB 18. Pz.-Div.*, 1.7.41; C. von Luttichau, *Road to Moscow*, VI:53.

63   BA-MA RH 27-18/20, *KTB 18. Pz.-Div.*, 1.7.41.

64   Ibid. See also, W. Paul, *Geschichte der 18. Pz.-Div.*, 23-26.

65   This change came into effect at 2400 hours on 23 June 1941; at the same time, 5 and 6 Army Corps, allotted to Hoth for the breakthrough operations on 22 June, reverted back to the control of Ninth Army. BA-MA RH 21-3/788, *KTB Panzergruppe 3*, 23.6.41.

66   H. Hoth, *Panzer-Operationen*, 56.

67   H. Hoth, *Panzer-Operationen*, 56; BA-MA RH 21-3/732, "*Gefechtsberichte Russland 1941/42*."

68   The *Luftwaffe* vehicles belonged to Lt.-Gen. von Richthofen's 8 Air Corps; they intermingled with the armor of 3 Panzer Group on the few available roadways. According to an official report of 3 Panzer Group, the column of *Luftwaffe* lorries comprised some 3000 vehicles. BA-MA RH 21-3/732, "*Gefechtsberichte Russland 1941/42*."

69   A. Seaton, *The Russo-German War*, 118. Of course, "fast," in this context, was very much a relative term!

70   BA-MA RH 27-7/46, *KTB 7. Pz.-Div.*, 23.6.41; BA-MA RH 21-3/732, "*Gefechtsberichte Russland 1941/42*;" H. Hoth, *Panzer-Operationen*, 58; R.H.S. Stolfi, *German Panzers on the Offensive*, 16-17; J. Erickson, *The Road to Stalingrad*, 134-35.

71   BA-MA RH 27-7/46, *KTB 7. Pz.-Div.*, 24.6.41; K.-R. Woche, *Zwischen Pflicht und Gewissen*, 102; H. Hoth, *Panzer-Operationen*, 60.

72   R. Hinze, *Hitze, Frost und Pulverdampf. Der Schicksalsweg der 20. Panzer-Division*, 28-29.

73   H. Martin, *Weit war der Weg*, 16-17.

74   D. M. Glantz, *Barbarossa*, 40.

75   D. M. Glantz, *Barbarossa*, 39-40; A. Seaton, *The Russo-German War*, 119-20.

76   W. Haupt, *Sturm auf Moskau 1941*, 25.

77   BA-MA RH 21-3/788, *KTB Panzergruppe 3*, 24.6.41.

78   *GSWW*, Vol. IV, 527; BA-MA RH 21-3/732, "*Gefechtsberichte Russland 1941/42*;" H. Hoth, *Panzer-Operationen*, 61-62; P. E. Schramm (Hg.), *Kriegstagebuch des OKW*, Bd. I, 418-19.

79   H. Hoth, *Panzer-Operationen*, 62.

80   H. Hoth, *Panzer-Operationen*, 62; C. von Luttichau, *Road to Moscow*, VI:30-31; H.-A. Jacobsen (Hg.), *Generaloberst Halder Kriegstagebuch*, Bd. III, 13.

81   C. von Luttichau, *Road to Moscow*, VI:34; K.-J. Thies, *Der Ostfeldzug – Ein Lageatlas*, "Lage am [24.-27.]6.1941 abds., Heeresgruppe Mitte;" BA-MA RH 21-3/732, "*Gefechtsberichte Russland 1941/42*."

82   BA-MA RH 27-7/46, *KTB 7. Pz.-Div.*, 26.6.41.

83   "*Der Luftkrieg im Osten gegen Russland 1941. (Aus einer Studie der 8. Abteilung 1943/1944.)*," KDC.

84   R.H.S. Stolfi, *German Panzers on the Offensive*, 17-18; BA-MA RH 27-7/46, *KTB 7. Pz.-Div.*, 25.6.41; BA-MA RH 21-3/732, "*Gefechtsberichte Russland 1941/42*;" H. v. Manteuffel, *Die 7. Panzer-Division*, 1935-1945, 54; K.-R. Woche, *Zwischen Pflicht und Gewissen*, 104; C. von Luttichau, *Road to Moscow*, VI:37.

85   C. von Luttichau, *Road to Moscow*, VI:37; D. M. Glantz (ed.), *Initial Period of War on the Eastern Front*, 215-16.

86   BA-MA RH 27-7/46, *KTB 7. Pz.-Div.*, 26.6.41.

87   For background on the Stalin Line see, Chapter 4, Section 4.4.

88   K.-R. Woche, *Zwischen Pflicht und Gewissen*, 104; BA-MA RH 21-3/788, *KTB Panzergruppe 3*, 28.6.41.

89   BA-MA RH 21-3/788, *KTB Panzergruppe 3*, 28.6.41.

90   K.-J. Thies, *Der Ostfeldzug – Ein Lageatlas*, "Lage am [26.-28.]6.1941 abds., Heeresgruppe Mitte."

91   In Minsk itself, elements of 12 Panzer Division battled against "*Terrorgruppen*" shortly after seizing the city; 20 Panzer Division, which entered the city after 12 PD, fought in or around Minsk against soldiers who had abandoned their uniforms for civilian clothing and against civilians as well. BA-MA RH 21-3/788, *KTB Panzergruppe 3*, 28.-29.6.41; R. Hinze, *Hitze, Frost und Pulverdampf. Der Schicksalsweg der 20. Panzer-Division*, 33.

92   BA-MA RH 21-3/788, *KTB Panzergruppe 3*, 28.6.41.

93   BA-MA RH 21-3/788, *KTB Panzergruppe 3*, 28.6.41; BA-MA RH 21-3/732, "*Gefechtsberichte Russland 1941/42*;" F. Kurowski (Hg.), *Hasso von Manteuffel*, 213. According to once unconfirmed source, Rothenburg had been wounded by an explosion from a burning armored train. His body was recovered the next day (29 June) by a German patrol.

94   R. Hinze, *Hitze, Frost und Pulverdampf. Der Schicksalsweg der 20. Panzer-Division*, 32.

95   BA-MA 21-3/788, *KTB Panzergruppe 3*, 30.6.41; P. E. Schramm (Hg.), *Kriegstagebuch des OKW*, Bd. I, 422.

96   BA-MA RH 21-3/732, "*Gefechtsberichte Russland 1941/42*;" C. von Luttichau, *Road to Moscow*, VI:49; K.-J. Thies, *Der Ostfeldzug – Ein Lageatlas*, "Lage am 28.6.1941 abds., Heeresgruppe Mitte."

97   K.-J. Thies, *Der Ostfeldzug – Ein Lageatlas*, "Lage am [29.6.-2.7.]1941 abds., Heeresgruppe Mitte."

98   Writes former U.S. Army colonel Robert Kirchubel: "The ostensible reason for their meeting was to coordinate how they would negotiate the Berezina River obstacle. However, the meeting took on the aspect of a conspiracy when, on their own initiative, the two agreed to renew eastward movement and to not brook any delays in their advance imposed by higher headquarters." R. Kirchubel, *Hitler's Panzer Armies*, 65; see also, R. A. Hart, *Guderian*, 74.

99   *GSWW*, Vol. IV, 527.

100 C. von Luttichau, *Road to Moscow*, VI:49; K.-J. Thies, *Der Ostfeldzug – Ein Lageatlas*, "Lage am 29.6.1941 abds., Heeresgruppe Mitte."

101 For example, a radio message from Army Group Center, arriving at 3 Panzer Group on the evening of 30 June, stated that the main task (*Hauptaufgabe*) for both panzer groups continued to be the tight encirclement of the enemy in close cooperation with the infantry armies. BA-MA RH 21-3/788, *KTB Panzergruppe 3*, 30.6.41.

102 S. H. Newton, *Hitler's Commander. Field Marshal Walther Model*, 124.

103 C. von Luttichau, *Road to Moscow*, VI:32; K.-J. Thies, *Der Ostfeldzug – Ein Lageatlas*, "Lage am 28.6.1941 abds., Heeresgruppe Mitte."

104 E. Mawdsley, *Thunder in the East*, 62; K.-J. Thies, *Der Ostfeldzug – Ein Lageatlas*, "Aufmarsch am 21.6.1941 abds., Heeresgruppe Mitte." See also, "Western Military District, Soviet Dispositions, 21 June 1941 [Map] 49," in: *D. M. Glantz, Atlas and Operational Summary. The Border Battles*.

105 See above (Section 7.1) for a German veteran's account of this action.

106 D. M. Glantz (ed.), *Initial Period of War on the Eastern Front*, 202-03; BA-MA RH 20-4/1199, *KTB AOK 4*, 23.6.41; K.-J. Thies, *Der Ostfeldzug – Ein Lageatlas*, "Lage am 23.6.1941 abds., Heeresgruppe Mitte."

107 On 23 June 1941, 6 ID was still controlled by Hoth's panzer group; at midnight, however, control reverted back to Ninth Army. BA-MA RH 21-3/788, *KTB Panzergruppe 3*, 23.6.41.

108 BA-MA RH 26-6/8, *KTB 6. Inf.-Div.*, 23.6.41; E.-M. Rhein, *Das Infanterie-Regiment 18*, 53. "VA" = *Vorausabteilung*.

109 *Tagebuch* Haape, 23.6.41.

110 *Tagebuch* Lierow, 23.6.41 (unpublished diary).

111 E.-M. Rhein, *Das Infanterie-Regiment 18*, 55.

112 *KTB 9 AOK*, quoted in: C. von Luttichau, *Road to Moscow*, VI:33.

113 K.-J. Thies, *Der Ostfeldzug – Ein Lageatlas*, "Lage am 24.6.1941 abds., Heeresgruppe Mitte."

114 D. M. Glantz (ed.), *Initial Period of War on the Eastern Front*, 191.

115 C. von Luttichau, *Road to Moscow*, VI:35; R. Kirchubel, *Operation Barbarossa 1941 (3), Army Group Center*, 36.

116 Elements of German 8 Army Corps were also drawn into the fighting. In his diary on 24 June 1941, Bock noted "heavy counterattacks near Grodno against [8 and 20] Army Corps;" the next day (25 June), he wrote of the "severe crisis facing the 20 and 8 Army Corps." K. Gerbet (ed.), *GFM Fedor von Bock, The War Diary*, 226-27.

117   C. von Luttichau, *Road to Moscow*, VI:35.
118   BA-MA RH 26-256/12, *KTB 256. Inf.-Div.*, 24.6.41.
119   The 129 ID was subordinated to 20 Army Corps at about 7.00 that morning. BA-MA RH 26-129/3, *KTB 129. Inf.-Div.*, 25.6.41.
120   C. von Luttichau, *Road to Moscow*, VI:36.
121   BA-MA RH 26-256/12, *KTB 256. Inf.-Div.*, 25.6.41.
122   A. Werth, *Russia at War*, 155.
123   D. M. Glantz, *Barbarossa*, 40; R. Kirchubel, *Operation Barbarossa 1941* (3), *Army Group Center*, 37; C. von Luttichau, *Road to Moscow*, VI:36-37.
124   C. von Luttichau, *Road to Moscow*, VI:36; A. Werth, *Russia at War*, 155.
125   D. M. Glantz (ed.), *Initial Period of War on the Eastern Front*, 217.
126   K.-J. Thies, *Der Ostfeldzug – Ein Lageatlas*, "Lage am 26.6.1941 abds., Heeresgruppe Mitte."
127   BA-MA RH 20-4/1199, *KTB AOK 4*, 25.6.41; P. E. Schramm (Hg.), *Kriegstagebuch des OKW*, Bd. I, 420.
128   BA-MA RH 20-4/1199, *KTB AOK 4*, 25.6.41.
129   C. von Luttichau, *Road to Moscow*, VI:41.
130   At 1850 hours, 25 June 1941, Army Group Center informed Fourth Army that OKH had ordered the "encirclement and annihilation of the strong enemy group around Belostok-Volkovysk by 4 and 9 Armies." Fourth Army was to drive vigorously (*scharf*) with its right flank across a line extending from west of Slonim to Volkovysk in the general direction of Mosty to link up with Strauss' Ninth Army. Kluge, it seems, through his general order issued at 1800 hours, had already anticipated the OKH directive. BA-MA RH 20-4/1199, *KTB AOK 4*, 25.6.41.
131   At midday, 27 June 1941, 12 Army Corps reverted to the control of Kluge's Fourth Army. BA-MA RH 21-2/927, *KTB Panzergruppe 2*, 27.6.41.
132   K.-J. Thies, *Der Ostfeldzug – Ein Lageatlas*, "Lage am 25.6.1941 abds., Heeresgruppe Mitte;" C. von Luttichau, *Road to Moscow*, VI:42; BA-MA RH 20-4/1199, *KTB AOK 4*, 25.6.41.
133   C. von Luttichau, *Road to Moscow*, VI:41; BA-MA RH 20-4/1199, *KTB AOK 4*, 30.6.41.
134   C. von Luttichau, *Road to Moscow*, VI:43.
135   K. Gerbet (ed.), *GFM Fedor von Bock, The War Diary*, 228.
136   Sold. S.K. (16 120 C), Collection BfZ.
137   Wm. Josef L. (22 633 C), Collection BfZ.
138   E.-M. Rhein, *Das Infanterie-Regiment 18*, 58.
139   Ibid., 58.
140   On 26 June 1941, 29 ID (mot.) was placed under Fourth Army control; two days later (28 June), Kluge was given control over elements of 10 PD. Both assignments were temporary. K. Gerbet (ed.), *GFM Fedor von Bock, The War Diary*, 228, 231.
141   BA-MA RH 20-4/1199, *KTB AOK 4*, 26.6.41.
142   C. von Luttichau, *Road to Moscow*, VI:43; K. Gerbet (ed.), *GFM Fedor von Bock, The War Diary*, 230.
143   BA-MA RH 20-4/1199, *KTB AOK 4*, 26.6.41.
144   BA-MA RH 20-4/1199, *KTB AOK 4*, 25.6.41; C. von Luttichau, *Road to Moscow*, VI:43-44.
145   As recorded in the war diary of Fourth Army: "The day was characterized by constant heavy Russian attacks against the Army's northern front." BA-MA RH 20-4/1199, *KTB AOK 4*, 27.6.41.
146   C. von Luttichau, *Road to Moscow*, VI:44.
147   BA-MA RH 20-4/1199, *KTB AOK 4*, 28.6.41.
148   K. Gerbet (ed.), *GFM Fedor von Bock, The War Diary*, 231.
149   C. Burdick & H.-A. Jacobsen (eds.), *The Halder Diary 1939-1942*, 426-32.
150   BA-MA RH 20-4/1199, *KTB AOK 4*, 28.6.41.
151   By 27 June 1941, Strauss' 20, 8 and 5 Army Corps (left to right) were all pushing south. Ninth Army's 6 Army Corps, on the far left flank east of Olita, did not participate in this movement. K.-J. Thies, *Der Ostfeldzug – Ein Lageatlas*, "Lage am 27.6.1941 abds., Heeresgruppe Mitte."
152   "*Tagesmeldungen der Operations-Abteilung des GenStdH*," in: P. E. Schramm (Hg.), *Kriegstagebuch des OKW*, Bd. I, 497; K.-J. Thies, *Der Ostfeldzug – Ein Lageatlas*, "Lage am 27.6.1941 abds., Heeresgruppe Mitte."
153   D. M. Glantz (ed.), *Initial Period of War on the Eastern Front*, 217.
154   P. E. Schramm (Hg.), *Kriegstagebuch des OKW*, Bd. I, 421; K.-J. Thies, *Der Ostfeldzug – Ein Lageatlas*, "Lage am 27.6.1941 abds., Heeresgruppe Mitte."
155   D. M. Glantz (ed.), *Initial Period of War on the Eastern Front*, 217-18; BA-MA RH 20-4/1199, *KTB AOK 4*, 26.6.41.
156   "*Tagesmeldungen der Operations-Abteilung des GenStdH*," in: P. E. Schramm (Hg.), *Kriegstagebuch des OKW*, Bd. I, 499.
157   BA-MA 26-137/4, *KTB 137. Inf.-Div.*, 28.6.41.
158   W. Meyer-Detring, *Die 137. Infanterie-Division im Mittelabschnitt der Ostfront*, 28.
159   In his diary on this day Halder wrote: "In the sector of [Army Group Center], the inner ring is now closing east of Belostok." C. Burdick & H.-A. Jacobsen (eds.), *The Halder Diary 1939-1942*, 430. According to Albert Seaton, "By nightfall on 28 June the marching infantry of Strauss' 9 and von Kluge's 4 German Armies had joined up in the shorter encirclement and completely cut off the [Belostok] pocket from the larger Novogrodek pocket to the east." A. Seaton, *The Russo-German War*, 123. However, as recorded in the daily report of the German Army Operations Branch, elements of Fourth and Ninth Armies did not join hands, effectively sealing the pocket, until the following day, 29 June. "*Tagesmeldungen der Operations-Abteilung des GenStdH*," in: P. E. Schramm (Hg.), *Kriegstagebuch des OKW*, Bd. I, 500.

160 D. M. Glantz (ed.), *Initial Period of War on the Eastern Front*, 222; B. Taylor, *Barbarossa to Berlin*, 51.

161 Without providing dates, Werner Haupt lists the following losses for several of the German infantry divisions taking part in liquidating the Belostok-Volkovysk pocket (losses in parentheses): 78 ID (340), 292 ID (550), 263 ID (650), 137 ID (700). W. Haupt, *Sturm auf Moskau 1941*, 31.

162 P. Carell, *Hitler Moves East*, 49; C. von Luttichau, *Road to Moscow*, VI:45; BA-MA RH 26-29/15, "*Bericht ueber die Gefechtshandlungen der 29. Div. (mot.) am 29. u. 30.6.41.*"

163 BA-MA RH 26-29/15, "*Feindnachrichtenblatt als Anlage zum Gefechtsbericht der 29. Division fuer 29./30.6.41.*"

164 Most of these details gleaned from, BA-MA RH 26-29/15, "*Bericht ueber die Gefechtshandlungen der 29. Div. (mot.) am 29. u. 30.6.41.*" This report was prepared by General von Boltenstern himself, and is dated 1 July 1941. For a virtually minute-by-minute account of the fighting from 27-29 June 1941 see, BA-MA RH 26-29/6, *KTB 29. Inf.-Div. (mot.)*, 27.-30.6.41.

165 C. von Luttichau, *Road to Moscow*, VI:46.

166 P. Carell, *Hitler Moves East*, 50.

167 Ibid., 50.

168 H. Guderian, *Panzer Leader*, 161.

169 The war diary of 29 ID (mot.) simply states that 47 officers were "lost" (*verloren*) in the fighting. BA-MA RH 26-29/6, *KTB 29. Inf.-Div. (mot.)*, 1.7.41. In his personal diary, General Lemelsen, (47 Panzer Corps) also recorded that 47 officers were among the "heavy losses" (*schwere Verluste*) sustained by the division in the defensive battles near Zelva. "It is a truly thankless task [*undankbare Aufgabe*]," he wrote bitterly on 1 July 1941, "to simply have to protect the flanks so that the panzer divisions can continue to advance." BA-MA MSg 1/1147: *Tagebuch* Lemelsen, 1.7.41.

170 C. von Luttichau, *Road to Moscow*, VI:46-47.

171 Ibid., VI:47-48.

172 Ibid., VI:48.

173 By this point, Kluge, determined to bring the time-consuming and costly operation to an end, had ordered his army corps to systematically sweep the forests and clear them of the enemy. See, BA-MA RH 20-4/1199, *KTB AOK 4*, 28.6.41.

174 P. E. Schramm (Hg.), *Kriegstagebuch des OKW*, Bd. I, 423.

175 D. M. Glantz (ed.), *Initial Period of War on the Eastern Front*, 223. For the overall situation along the front of Army Group Center on 30 June 1941 see, K.-J. Thies, *Der Ostfeldzug – Ein Lageatlas*, "Lage am 30.6.1941 abds., Heeresgruppe Mitte." For Soviet forces trapped inside the pockets stretching from Belostok to Minsk see, "Western Front Situation, 2300 hrs, 30 June 1941 [Map] 108," in: D. M. Glantz (ed.), *Atlas and Operational Summary. The Border Battles*.

176 C. von Luttichau, *Road to Moscow*, VI:48.

177 *Feldpost*, W. Heinemann, 25.6.41 (unpublished field post letter).

178 Ibid., 30.6.41.

179 Internet side at: http://www.lexikon-der-wehrmacht.de.

180 "*Abschrift aus dem Kriegstagebuch der AA 35*" (35 ID), quoted in: G. Bopp, *Kriegstagebuch*, 83.

181 R. Kirchubel, *Operation Barbarossa 1941* (3), *Army Group Center*, 44; BA-MA RH 20-4/192, "*Gefechtsbericht ueber die Wegnahme von Brest Litowsk.*"

182 R. J. Kershaw, *War Without Garlands*, 78; BA-MA RH 26-45/20, *KTB 45. Inf.-Div.*, 29.6.41; Dr R. Gschoepf, *Mein Weg mit der 45. Inf.-Div.*, 225.

183 Most of this paragraph was adapted from Robert J. Kershaw's *War Without Garlands*, 78; see also, BA-MA RH 26-45/20, *KTB 45. Inf.-Div.*, 29.6.41; and, Dr R. Gschoepf, *Mein Weg mit der 45. Inf.-Div.*, 225.

184 C. Bellamy, *Absolute War*, 187.

185 R. J. Kershaw, *War Without Garlands*, 78; BA-MA RH 20-4/192, "*Gefechtsbericht ueber die Wegnahme von Brest Litowsk.*"

186 The figures on German losses were gleaned from the after-action report of the division. BA-MA RH 20-4/192, "*Gefechtsbericht ueber die Wegnahme von Brest Litowsk.*" According to Dr Rudolf Gschoepf, division chaplain, by the end of June the division had lost 482 men killed and around 1000 wounded. Dr R. Gschoepf, *Mein Weg mit der 45. Inf.-Div.*, 225.

187 See, C. von Luttichau, *Road to Moscow*, VI:49.

188 Dr R. Gschoepf, *Mein Weg mit der 45. Inf.-Div.*, 225.

189 D. Irving, *Hitler's War*, 274; N. von Below, *At Hitler's Side*, 104-05; K.-J. Thies, *Der Ostfeldzug – Ein Lageatlas*, vii.

190 K.-J. Thies, *Der Ostfeldzug – Ein Lageatlas*, vii-ix; C. von Luttichau, *Road to Moscow*, VI:27; C. Schroeder, *Er war mein Chef*, 111.

191 E. F. Ziemke & M. E. Bauer, *Moscow to Stalingrad*, 4.

192 G. P. Megargee, *Inside Hitler's High Command*, 149.

193 Greiner's letter is dated 27 June 1941; it is quoted in: *Adolf Hitler: The Medical Diaries. The Private Diaries of Dr Theo Morell*, D. Irving (ed.), 81. Historian Geoffrey Megargee elaborates on Greiner's account: "Dampness was a special problem in the concrete bunkers where much of the work took place. The cramped rooms received little sunlight because of the thick pine forest and the bunkers' small windows. Additionally, the ventilation system set up a constant racket. For these reasons the staff officers much preferred to live and work in the compound's wooden barracks if they could." G. P. Megargee, *Inside Hitler's High Command*, 149.

194   C. Schroeder, *Er war mein Chef*, 111-112.

195   G. P. Megargee, *Inside Hitler's High Command*, 148-49.

196   C. von Luttichau, *Road to Moscow*, VI:27-28.

197   N. von Below, *At Hitler's Side*, 105.

198   Recalled Schroeder: "In the initial period of the Russian campaign Hitler was almost always in good humor [*gut gelaunt*] and inclined to making jokes." C. Schroeder, *Er war mein Chef*, 112.

199   G. L. Weinberg, *A World at Arms*, 264. In his diary, Goering's deputy, Field Marshal Erhard Milch, recorded the destruction of 1800 Soviet aircraft on 22 June, 800 on the 23rd, 557 on the 24th, 351 on the 25th, and 300 on 26 June 1941. W. Murray, *Strategy for Defeat*, 82.

200   I. Kershaw, *Hitler 1936-45: Nemesis*, 398.

201   D. Irving, *Hitler's War*, 282.

202   "*Sonderakte, 4. Juli 1941*," in: P. E. Schramm (Hg.), *Kriegstagebuch des OKW*, Bd. I, 1020.

203   D. Irving (ed.), *Adolf Hitler: The Medical Diaries. The Private Diaries of Dr Theo Morell*, 82.

204   H. Meier-Welcker, *Aufzeichnungen*, 19, 121. Meier-Welcker had served as a staff officer with Kluge's Fourth Army until May 1941, when he was transferred to 251 ID. The division was assigned to Army Group North.

205   Ibid., 19, 121.

206   A. Seaton, *The Russo-German War*, 122. See also, K. Gerbet (ed.), *GFM Fedor von Bock, The War Diary*, 226-27.

207   H.-A. Jacobsen (Hg.), *Generaloberst Halder Kriegstagebuch*, Bd. III, 9-15, 18-21, 24-30, 33-40.

208   G. Meyer, *Adolf Heusinger*, 151-52.

209   H.-A. Jacobsen (Hg.), *Generaloberst Halder Kriegstagebuch*, Bd. III, 11.

210   H.-A. Jacobsen (Hg.), *Generaloberst Halder Kriegstagebuch*, Bd. III, 23. The putative figures for total German Army losses in the east from 22-30 June 1941 are in Halder's diary entry on 3 July 1941. According to Halder, total casualties were 41,087; the dead were 524 officers and 8362 NCOs and men, while the wounded amounted to 966 officers and 28,528 NCOs and men (figures for men missing in action (MIA) are not provided, but according to Halder's calculations must have amounted to just under 3000). Ibid., 40. As Ruediger Overmans' exhaustive analysis has revealed, however, actual German losses had been much higher; in fact, through 30 June 1941, the Germans had sustained a total of 25,000 fatal losses in the east, over 90 percent of these in the *Ostheer* and more than double the number of dead in Halder's figures even if all 3000 MIA are considered among the fatal losses. R. Overmans, *Deutsche militaerische Verluste im Zweiten Weltkrieg*, 277.

211   *Wehrmachtbericht*, 2.7.41, quoted in: R. G. Reuth, *Hitler*, 524.

212   C. Burdick & H.-A. Jacobsen (eds.), *The Halder Diary 1939-1942*, 446-47.

213   *GSWW*, Vol. IV, 569; "*Sonderakte, 29. Juni 1941*," in: P. E. Schramm (Hg.), *Kriegstagebuch des OKW*, Bd. I, 1019-20.

214   In 1941, the Donbas (Donets Basin) was producing 60 percent of the USSR's coal and 75 percent of its coke; moreover, it was responsible for 30 percent of the total output of iron, and 20 percent of the country's steel production. A. Seaton, *The Russo-German War*, 193.

215   *GSWW*, Vol. IV, 569; "*Sonderakte, 4. Juli 1941*," in: P. E. Schramm (Hg.), *Kriegstagebuch des OKW*, Bd. I, 1020.

216   In a study published by the Army General Staff in May 1941, it was noted that "the best months for military operations are August and September." *Generalstab des Heeres, Militaergeographische Angaben ueber das Europaeische Russland, Zentral-Russland (ohne Moskau),*" quoted in: J. Piekalkiewicz, *Schlacht um Moskau*, 12.

217   H. S. Orenstein (ed.), *Soviet Documents on the Use of War Experience*, Vol. I, *The Initial Period of War 1941*, vii.

218   D. M. Glantz, *Barbarossa*, 74.

219   Ibid., 59.

220   D. Volkogonov, "*The German Attack, the Soviet Response, Sunday, 22 June 1941*," in: *Barbarossa, The Axis and the Allies*, J. Erickson & D. Dilks (eds.), 92.

221   R. Overy, *Russia's War*, 80.

222   B. S. Telpuchowski, *Die sowjetische Geschichte des Grossen Vaterlaendischen Krieges, 1941-1945*, 50-52; *History of the Great Patriotic War of the Soviet Union 1941-1945*, Vol. II, 230.

223   D. M. Glantz, *Barbarossa Derailed*, Vol. I, 579; *GSWW*, Vol. IV, 839; W. S. Dunn, Jr., *Stalin's Keys to Victory*, 63-75; D. M. Glantz, *Barbarossa*, 68.

224   W. Murray & A. R. Millett, *A War to be Won*, 125.

225   D. M. Glantz & J. House, *When Titans Clashed*, 67-68.

226   D. M. Glantz, *Red Army Ground Forces*, 36. "The mobilization system," maintains David Glantz, "and the forces it produced were severely flawed. The system produced the manpower which brought many existing formations near to full strength but failed to provide the equipment and support organs which new formations required to function effectively and survive in combat. Contrary to plan, the civilian economy failed to provide vehicular transport, tractors, and horses, and, as a consequence, force logistical units could not move heavy weaponry and supply formations with critical fuel, ammunition, and other provisions … Mobilization and transport difficulties fed … strategic reserves into the theater in piecemeal fashion. This, coupled with the rapid subsequent German advance, led to repeated defeats-in-detail of successive lines of defending Soviet strategic reserves. Numerous archival documents underscore the lack of preparedness of the initial reserve armies, which the *Stavka* committed to combat along the Dnepr River line." Ibid., 36.

227 Nearly 1.5 million freight cars were required to accomplish the evacuations. D. M. Glantz, *Barbarossa*, 72-73.

228 Ibid., 73.

229 By October 1941, 2500 locomotives and 200,000 railcars were required in the occupied territories to meet the exigencies of the front. K. Reinhardt, *Moscow – The Turning Point*, 147.

230 As noted by Klaus Reinhardt, "This impromptu shifting of the armaments industry, which took the Germans completely by surprise, was a decisive contributing factor to the inability of the German armaments industry to fulfill its orders, as a considerable share of the production for the new programs was to have been carried out in the conquered territories, to alleviate the bottlenecks in German industry." Ibid., 32.

231 D. M. Glantz, *Barbarossa*, 73-74; K. Reinhardt, *Moscow – The Turning Point*, 32.

232 D. M. Glantz, *Red Army Ground Forces*, 47.

233 D. M. Glantz, *Barbarossa*, 60. Writes Glantz: "[The *Stavka's*] responsibilities included evaluating political-military and strategic conditions, reaching strategic and operational-strategic decisions, creating force groupings and coordinating the operations of groups of *fronts*, *fronts*, field armies and partisan forces. The *Stavka* directed the formation and training of strategic reserves and material and technical support of the armed forces, and resolved all questions related to military operations."

234 S. M. Shtemenko, *The Soviet General Staff at War*, Book One, 37.

235 E. F. Ziemke & M. E. Bauer, *Moscow to Stalingrad*, 25.

236 E. F. Ziemke & M. E. Bauer, *Moscow to Stalingrad*, 30; *GSWW*, Vol. IV, 836-37.

237 G. Roberts, *Stalin's Wars*, 95.

238 Ibid., 95.

239 G. Roberts, *Stalin's Wars*, 95; D. M. Glantz, *Barbarossa*, 60.

240 The NKO was already in existence on 22 June 1941.

241 G. Roberts, *Stalin's Wars*, 95.

242 B. Taylor, *Barbarossa to Berlin*, 31-32.

243 G. Roberts, *Stalin's Wars*, 97; also, W. J. Spahr, *Zhukov*, 57; and, *GSWW*, Vol. IV, 836-37.

244 Quoted in: D. A. Volkogonov, "*Stalin as Supreme Commander*," in: *From Peace to War*, B. Wegner (ed.), 468.

245 For an insightful analysis of Stalin as a military leader see, Ibid., 463-478. For example, Volkogonov argues: "Stalin became used to manipulating human fates, often not considering the consequences of his decisions … They were the masses – he was the Leader. He was convinced that it had always been that way, throughout history, and would always remain so. I must have read through thousands of operational-level documents that Stalin had dictated or signed during the four years of war, but I did not find one where he specifically reduced the possible loss of life, avoided throwing his troops away in unprepared attacks, or worried about the lives of his fellow countrymen." (470) Nevertheless, Stalin "the military amateur did gradually learn the ropes – as early as after Stalingrad, as G. K. Zhukov wrote, 'he coped well with the larger strategic problems.'" (473)

246 According to Stepan A. Mikoyan, son of former Politburo and GKO member, A. I. Mikoyan, Stalin's "authority during the war was extraordinary." And despite his many military blunders, "the vast majority of the population did not associate him personally with the disasters and believed in him absolutely. It might be argued that the totalitarian political system of the country, reprehensible though it was, did furnish certain advantages in wartime." S. A. Mikoyan, "*Barbarossa and the Soviet Leadership*," in: *Barbarossa, The Axis and the Allies*, J. Erickson & D. Dilks (eds.), 128-29.

247 "The failure of communications in June 1941," avers Constantine Pleshakov, "proved truly lethal and probably explained the scope of the defeat as well as its absolute, instantaneous, and unmanageable nature." C. Pleshakov, *Stalin's Folly*, 215.

248 The reader will recall that, on the evening of 22 June 1941, Stalin had issued Directive No. 3, calling for a general counterattack across the entire front line. At this time, Stalin still hoped that once order had been restored along the front, he would succeed in conquering East Prussia and Poland. Ibid., 128-29.

249 *Congressional Record*, 84th Congress, 2nd sess., 4 June 1956, p. 9395, quoted in: E. F. Ziemke, *The Red Army 1918-1941*, 276.

250 E. Mawdsley, *Thunder in the East*, 63.

251 C. Pleshakov, *Stalin's Folly*, 155.

252 On 22 June, Stalin had ordered Zhukov to fly to Southwestern Front headquarters to help oversee and guide its operations. G. K. Zhukov, "*The Beginning of the War*," in: *Soviet Generals Recall World War II*, I. Vitukhin (ed.), 16.

253 E. F. Ziemke, *The Red Army 1918-1941*, 279. General Eremenko initially replaced Pavlov as commander of Western Front, only to be replaced himself by Marshal Timoshenko as front commander at the start of July 1941. W. J. Spahr, *Zhukov*, 54.

254 *Battles Hitler Lost and the Soviet Marshalls Who Won Them*, 44-45.

255 *Battles Hitler Lost and the Soviet Marshalls Who Won Them*, 45; C. Pleshakov, *Stalin's Folly*, 187-88.

256 C. Pleshakov, *Stalin's Folly*, 212.

257 Ibid., 212-13.

258 Ibid., 213-14.

259 E. Mawdsley, *Thunder in the East*, 64.

260 C. Pleshakov, *Stalin's Folly*, 219-20; E. Mawdsley, *Thunder in the East*, 63-64; C. Winchester, *Hitler's War on Russia*, 52; S. A. Mikoyan, "*Barbarossa and the Soviet Leadership*," in: *Barbarossa, The Axis and the Allies*, J. Erickson & D. Dilks (eds.), 127-28.

261   I. Kershaw, *Fateful Choices*, 288.

262   H. Magenheimer, *Hitler's War*, 101; D. Volkogonov, *Stalin*, 412-13; I. Kershaw, *Fateful Choices*, 288-89. Meeting with the Bulgarian ambassador, Ivan Stamenov, was the deputy chief of the NKVD's intelligence section, General Pavel Sudoplatov. The ambassador, perhaps simply telling the general what he thought he wanted to hear, said that Russian superiority would, in the long run, defeat Hitler; in any case, he passed on no message to the Germans.

263   D. M. Glantz, *Barbarossa Derailed*, Vol. I, 45.

264   W. J. Spahr, *Zhukov*, 54; E. Mawdsley, *Thunder in the East*, 60-61.

265   E. Mawdsley, *Thunder in the East*, 61.

266   J. Piekalkiewicz, *Die Schlacht um Moskau*, 84.

267   E. F. Ziemke, *The Red Army 1918-1941*, 280. See also, E. Mawdsley, *Thunder in the East*, 64. According to Mawdsley, Stalin's stressing of the importance of allies and friends, like Great Britain and the United States, signified "an extraordinary break from tradition."

268   C. Pleshakov, *Stalin's Folly*, 223-24.

269   Col.-Gen. G. F. Krivosheev (ed.), *Soviet Casualties and Combat Losses*, 111, 260.

270   D. M. Glantz, *Colossus Reborn*, 612-13.

271   E. F. Ziemke, *The Red Army 1918-1941*, 277. According to Ziemke, "the German air fleets and panzer groups overwhelmed the Red Army commands with a form of war for which they were wholly unprepared and mostly could not comprehend, a war which substituted mobility for mass to an extreme incomprehensible even to some of the German commanders until well after 22 June."

272   Quoted in: G. Roberts, *Stalin's Wars*, 93-94.

273   As early as 27 June 1941, the Soviet High Command had become aware of this flaw in the German advance and was preparing to exploit it. See, G. K. Zhukov, *"The Beginning of the War,"* in: *Soviet Generals Recall World War II*, I. Vitukhin (ed.), 26.-27.

274   D. M. Glantz, *Barbarossa Derailed*, Vol. I, 32.

275   D. M. Glantz, *Red Army Ground Forces*, 18.

276   S. M. Shtemenko, *The Soviet General Staff at War*, Book One, 37-38.

277   D. M. Glantz, *Red Army Ground Forces*, 18. While Glantz' comment pertains directly to the anecdote concerning 2 Rifle Corps, it is germane to the Shtemenko story as well.

278   E. F. Ziemke, *The Red Army 1918-1941*, 282.

279   D. M. Glantz, *Barbarossa Derailed*, Vol. I, 51.

280   *GSWW*, Vol. IV, 835-36.

281   D. M. Glantz, *Barbarossa Derailed*, Vol. I, 48.

282   E. Mawdsley, *Thunder in the East*, 64-65.

283   Ibid., 68.

284   E. F. Ziemke, *The Red Army 1918-1941*, 277.

285   On 1 July 1941, a doctor with 3 Panzer Division (24 Panzer Corps) at Bobruisk on the Berezina wrote: "Yesterday, at the edge of the forest, we again experienced many air attacks. They seemed to attack every 15 minutes. One could hardly catch a minute of sleep because of the racket. In our sector alone I saw 32 enemy planes shot down." *Assistenzarzt Dr H. Tuerk*, quoted in: W. Kempowski (Hg.), *Das Echolot*, 173. In late July 1941, the 3 PD, now in the Sozh River region, was exposed daily to attack by Soviet bombers, causing some losses. Of course, Model's division was one of the spearhead units and, as such, was singled out for attack by the Soviet Air Force. H.-J. Roell, *Oberleutnant Albert Blaich. Als Panzerkommandant in Ost und West*, 87.

286   Another factor contributing to the rapid recuperation of the VVS was that in the first days of war, "the numbers [of aircraft] destroyed on the ground were many times more than those shot down while airborne. One fact which should have been borne in mind, however, and which was not given enough attention by the German Command, was that in these circumstances Soviet losses in personnel were far smaller than in materiel. This explains in part the unexpectedly rapid recovery of the Soviet forces." Gen.-Lt. a.D. Walter Schwabedissen, *The Russian Air Force in the Eyes of German Commanders*, USAF Historical Studies: No. 175, 53-54.

287   *GSWW*, Vol. IV, 804.

288   R. Wagner (ed.), *The Soviet Air Force in World War II*, 44-45. While these numbers may be exaggerated, they are nevertheless an indication of Soviet air activity at the time.

289   Ibid., 45.

290   M. N. Kozhevnikov, *The Command and Staff of the Soviet Army Air Force in the Great Patriotic War 1941-1945*, 39.

291   H. von Luck, *Panzer Commander*, 66.

292   H.-A. Jacobsen (Hg.), *Generaloberst Halder Kriegstagebuch*, Bd. III, 34; K.-J. Thies, *Der Ostfeldzug – Ein Lageatlas*, "Lage am 2.7.1941 abds., Heeresgruppe Mitte."

293   C. von Luttichau, *Road to Moscow*, VI:57.

294   Ibid., VI:57.

295   According to Charles von Luttichau, "pacification of the rear areas began to worry von Bock as early as 1 July. The term 'partisans' appeared in German documents at the very time that Stalin had called for the forming of a partisan movement behind the German lines in his 3 July address. Thousands of Russian soldiers in small groups were roaming a no-man's land through which the armor had moved too fast to round them up. The slower infantry units had not yet caught up with the spearheads and could not clear

the gap in between. Bands of stragglers, many of them still armed and trying to work their way back toward the east, interrupted German supply movements and interfered with operations. The three security divisions Army Group Center had on hand to police the rear were not enough and regular divisions had to be diverted temporarily to perform security tasks." Ibid., XIII:26.

296   H. Spaeter, *Die Geschichte des Panzerkorps Grossdeutschland*, Bd. I, 267, quoted in: R. Kirchubel, *Hitler's Panzer Armies*, 65.

297   According to its records, Kluge's Fourth Army took 82,000 prisoners during the cauldron battles, while destroying or capturing 1285 tanks and 661 guns. BA-MA RH-20-4/337, *"Die Kaempfe der 4. Armee im ersten Kriegsjahr gegen die Sowjets."*

298   K. Gerbet (ed.), *GFM Fedor von Bock, The War Diary*, 243; K. Mehner (Hg.), *Geheime Tagesberichte*, Bd. 3, 179.

299   C. von Luttichau, *Road to Moscow*, VI:59; XIII:23. As discussed in Chapter 2 (Section 2.6), prior to the start of the campaign, OKH had reckoned fuel consumption at 282,000 cubic meters per month (more than 9000 cubic meters per day).

300   E. Mawdsley, *Thunder in the East*, 440, f.n. 7.

301   Col.-Gen. G. F. Krivosheev (ed.), *Soviet Casualties and Combat Losses*, 111.

302   Ibid., 260.

303   *"Sonderakte, 8. Juli 1941,"* in: P. E. Schramm (Hg.), *Kriegstagebuch des OKW*, Bd. I, 1021; C. Burdick & H.-A. Jacobsen (eds.), *The Halder Diary 1939-1942*, 457. In his personal diary on 7 July 1941, Karl-Wilhelm Thilo, a captain in the Operations Branch of the Army High Command, stated that 6100 Soviet tanks (out of German estimates of 10,000 total) had already been destroyed. BA-MA N 664/2, *Tagebuch* Thilo, 7.7.41.

304   C. Burdick & H.-A. Jacobsen (eds.), *The Halder Diary 1939-1942*, 457.

305   D. M. Glantz, *Barbarossa Derailed*, Vol. I, 51.

306   C. Burdick & H.-A. Jacobsen (eds.), *The Halder Diary 1939-1942*, 465.

307   R. Kirchubel, *Operation Barbarossa 1941 (3), Army Group Center*, 49.

308   Ltr, W. Vollmer to C. Luther, 9 Sep 07.

309   A. Seaton, *The Russo-German War*, 128.

310   K.-J. Thies, *Der Ostfeldzug – Ein Lageatlas*, "Lage am 2.7.1941 abds., Heeresgruppe Mitte."

311   In his study, Hoth described this broad front advance as an example of just how tank warfare should *not* be conducted. H. Hoth, *Panzer-Operationen*, 78.

312   *GSWW*, Vol. IV, 529; D. M. Glantz, *Barbarossa Derailed*, Vol. I, 43; A. Seaton, *The Russo-German War*, 126.

313   K. Mehner (Hg.), *Geheime Tagesberichte*, Bd. 3, 159; *"Tagesmeldungen der Operations-Abteilung des GenStdH,"* in: P. E. Schramm (Hg.), *Kriegstagebuch des OKW*, Bd. I, 505.

314   In fact, by the evening of 25 June, OKH had decided to put the two tank groups under the control of Kluge's Fourth Army headquarters, at a then undetermined time. H.-A. Jacobsen (Hg.), *Generaloberst Halder Kriegstagebuch*, Bd. III, 15.

315   R. Kirchubel, *Hitler's Panzer Armies*, 65.

316   Ibid., 65-66.

317   D. M. Glantz, *Barbarossa Derailed*, Vol. I, 42.

318   K.-J. Thies, *Der Ostfeldzug – Ein Lageatlas*, "Lage am 3.7.1941 abds., Heeresgruppe Mitte."

319   D. M. Glantz, *Barbarossa Derailed*, Vol. I, 42-43, 69; R. Kirchubel, *Hitler's Panzer Armies*, 66; K. Gerbet (ed.), *GFM Fedor von Bock, The War Diary*, 239.

320   S. H. Newton, *Hitler's Commander. Field Marshal Walther Model*, 125-26. On the primitive tracks of Belorussia the tanks also used up air filters at an "ungodly rate."

321   D. M. Glantz, *Barbarossa Derailed*, Vol. I, 68; *Geschichte der 3. Panzer-Division*, Traditionsverband der Division (Hg.), 123-24.

322   *Geschichte der 3. Panzer-Division*, Traditionsverband der Division (Hg.), 124.

323   The three Pz IVs belonged to the tank platoon led by *Oberfeldwebel* Albert Blaich, whom the reader has already encountered in this narrative. See, H.-J. Roell, *Oberleutnant Albert Blaich, Als Panzerkommandant in Ost und West*, 78-85.

324   According to David Glantz, the recent heavy rainfall (2/3 July 1941) had swelled the Dnepr to a width of 762 meters about Rogachev, seriously hampering German efforts to cross it. D. M. Glantz, *Barbarossa Derailed*, Vol. I, 68. Yet German accounts indicate that, at the specific point selected for the tank crossing, the river was only 80-100 meters in width, and four meters deep. The tanks required several minutes to navigate the river. H.-J. Roell, *Oberleutnant Albert Blaich, Als Panzerkommandant in Ost und West*, 82; also, *Geschichte der 3. Panzer-Division*, Traditionsverband der Division (Hg.), 125.

325   *Geschichte der 3. Panzer-Division*, Traditionsverband der Division (Hg.), 125.

326   R. Kirchubel, *Hitler's Panzer Armies*, 66.

327   *"After Action Report of Panzer-Regiment 35,"* in: *Knight's Cross Panzers*, H. Schaeufler (ed.), 78-79; *"Major von Lauchert, the First One at the Stalin Line,"* in: *Knight's Cross Panzers*, H. Schaeufler (ed.), 77-78.

328   S. H. Newton, *Hitler's Commander. Field Marshal Walther Model*, 126.

329   Ibid., 126-27.

330   Ibid., 127.

331   S. H. Newton, *Hitler's Commander. Field Marshal Walther Model*, 127; *Geschichte der 3. Panzer-Division*, Traditionsverband der Division (Hg.), 126.

332   *Geschichte der 3. Panzer-Division*, Traditionsverband der Division (Hg.), 126.

333   As noted in the war records of 3 PD, these tanks were T-34s. *"3. Pz. Div. Abt. Ia. Anl. Nr. 1 zum KTB Nr. 3, 6.7.41,"* quoted in: R. Steiger, *Armour Tactics in the Second World War*, 79.

334   *Geschichte der 3. Panzer-Division*, Traditionsverband der Division (Hg.), 127.

335   *Geschichte der 3. Panzer-Division*, Traditionsverband der Division (Hg.), 128-29; "*Tagesmeldungen der Operations-Abteilung des GenStdH*," In: P. E. Schramm (Hg.), *Kriegstagebuch des OKW*, Bd. I, 515; S. H. Newton, *Hitler's Commander. Field Marshal Walther Model*, 128; K.-J. Thies, *Der Ostfeldzug – Ein Lageatlas*, "Lage am 7.7.1941 abds., Heeresgruppe Mitte."

336   S. H. Newton, *Hitler's Commander. Field Marshal Walther Model*, 128; K.-J. Thies, *Der Ostfeldzug – Ein Lageatlas*, "Lage am 7.7.1941 abds., Heeresgruppe Mitte."

337   K.-J. Thies, *Der Ostfeldzug – Ein Lageatlas*, "Lage am 3.-7.7.1941 abds., Heeresgruppe Mitte;" D. M. Glantz, *Barbarossa Derailed*, 67.

338   According to Guderian, some of his units along the encirclement ring (among them 17 PD) did not receive their orders in time from Kluge directing them to remain where they were and not resume their march eastward until the Russians in the pocket had capitulated. Guderian also admitted, however, that the Army High Command (OKH) was "secretly hoping that the commanders of the panzer groups would continue to go for their original objectives, whether without orders or even against orders." Such was the Byzantine world in which Guderian and Hoth operated in the summer of 1941. See, H. Guderian, *Panzer Leader*, 166-67.

339   BA-MA MSg 1/1147: *Tagebuch* Lemelsen, 6.7.41.

340   In an after-action report submitted by *Leutnant* Kreuter on 11 July 1941, he referred to the tank he eventually neutralized as weighing 42 tons. "*Bericht, Kreuter, Lt. u. Kp.-Fuehrer, 11.7.41*," in: *Tagebuch* Kreuter.

341   *Tagebuch* Kreuter, 7.7.41. In his after-action report, Kreuter elaborated on the destruction of the heavy Russian tank: "With several others I attacked the tank with concentrated charges [*geballte Ladungen*]. But neither on the caterpillar tracks nor on the turret structure did they have any effect. We then fired into the slits with tracer ammunition to try to get the tank to catch fire, also without effect ... Only one possibility remained to put it out of action – a hand grenade in the barrel. Yet this was most difficult, because the barrel was slanting downward. My order to place a hand grenade in the barrel was carried out by *Gefreiter* Wendig of the anti-tank battalion ... The detonation of the hand grenade most likely ignited the loaded tank shell, whereupon the turret hatch cover was blown off. Two additional hand grenades down the turret finally ignited the tank." "*Bericht, Kreuter, Lt. u. Kp.-Fuehrer, 11.7.41*," in: *Tagebuch* Kreuter.

342   General Weber was the 17 PD's third commander since the start of the Russian campaign. Internet site at: http://www.lexikon-der-wehrmacht.

343   K.-J. Thies, *Der Ostfeldzug – Ein Lageatlas*, "Lage am 7.7.1941 abds., Heeresgruppe Mitte."

344   From his diary, it is clear that – at least in these early weeks of *Barbarossa* – Lemelsen was often underway by air in a *Fieseler Storch*.

345   BA-MA MSg 1/1147: *Tagebuch* Lemelsen, 10.7.41.

346   K.-J. Thies, *Der Ostfeldzug – Ein Lageatlas*, "Lage am 7.7.1941 abds., Heeresgruppe Mitte."

347   H. Guderian, *Panzer Leader*, 167.

348   K.-J. Thies, *Der Ostfeldzug – Ein Lageatlas*, "Lage am 7.7.1941 abds., Heeresgruppe Mitte."

349   As matters turned out, the infantry corps would begin to reach the Dnepr on a broad front by 15 July 1941. Ibid., 15.7.41.

350   H. Guderian, *Panzer Leader*, 167-68.

351   In his memoirs (*Panzer Leader*, 169) Guderian wrote that his headquarters was at Borisov on 9 July, "(to move on 10 July to Tolochino)." The *Lageost* map of the OKH Operations Branch places his command post at Tolochino (Tolotschin) by the evening of 9 July. K.-J. Thies, *Der Ostfeldzug – Ein Lageatlas*, "Lage am 9.7.1941 abds., Heeresgruppe Mitte."

352   H. Guderian, *Panzer Leader*, 168-69.

353   H. Guderian, *Panzer Leader*, 169; H. Guderian, *Erinnerungen eines Soldaten*, 153. According to David Glantz, this encounter with Kluge, described in such vivid terms by Guderian, never in fact took place. As Glantz notes – and GFM von Bock's diary confirms – Kluge was sick in bed on 9 July. Glantz states that it was not Kluge, but Colonel Blumentritt (Kluge's chief of staff) who visited Guderian's headquarters on that day, speaking with Guderian's chief of staff, Colonel von Liebenstein, while Guderian was away at the front. Whether or not the event recounted by Guderian actually took place (on 9 July, or perhaps a day or two before), it accurately reflects the disparate natures of the two men, their very different operational perspectives, and, certainly, their growing antipathy toward each other. See, D. M. Glantz, *Barbarossa Derailed*, Vol. I, 129, f.n. 4; K. Gerbet (ed.), *GFM Fedor von Bock, The War Diary*, 244.

354   At this time, the panzer group's 12 PD, 14 ID (mot.) and 20 ID (mot.) were still far to the rear. BA-MA RH 21-3/732, "*Gefechtsberichte Russland 1941/41*."

355   Apparently, Hoth believed that the continued advance of Army Group North's 4 Panzer Group, which had already breached the Dvina, would relieve the pressure on his front. D. M. Glantz, *Barbarossa Derailed*, Vol. I, 63.

356   Ibid., 63.

357   D. M. Glantz, *Barbarossa Derailed*, Vol. I, 63; R. Kirchubel, *Operation Barbarossa 1941 (3), Army Group Center*, 48; BA-MA RH 21-3/732, "*Gefechtsberichte Russland 1941/42*."

358   H.-A. Jacobsen (Hg.), *Generaloberst Halder Kriegstagebuch*, Bd. III, 40; K. Mehner (Hg.), *Geheime Tagesberichte*, Bd. 3, 165.

359   R. Hinze, *19 Infanterie- und Panzer-Division*, 140; K.-J. Thies, *Der Ostfeldzug – Ein Lageatlas*, "Lage am [3.-4.]7.1941 abds., Heeresgruppe Mitte."

360 *"Tagesmeldungen der Operations-Abteilung des GenStdH,"* in: P. E. Schramm (Hg.), *Kriegstagebuch des OKW,* Bd. I, 508; BA-MA RH 21-3/732, *"Gefechtsberichte Russland 1941/42;"* K.-J. Thies, *Der Ostfeldzug – Ein Lageatlas,* "Lage am 4.7.1941 abds., Heeresgruppe Mitte."

361 D. M. Glantz, *Barbarossa Derailed,* Vol. I, 64; BA-MA RH 21-3/732, *"Gefechtsberichte Russland 1941/42."*

362 R. Hinze, *Hitze, Frost und Pulverdampf. Der Schicksalsweg der 20. Panzer-Division,* 34-36.

363 *"Tagesmeldungen der Operations-Abteilung des GenStdH,"* in: P. E. Schramm (Hg.), *Kriegstagebuch des OKW,* Bd. I, 512; K.-J. Thies, *Der Ostfeldzug – Ein Lageatlas,* "Lage am 6.7.1941 abds., Heeresgruppe Mitte;" R. Kirchubel, *Operation Barbarossa 1941 (3), Army Group Center,* 49.

364 Quoted in: D. M. Glantz, *Barbarossa Derailed,* Vol. I, 70.

365 Ibid., 71-74.

366 K.-J. Thies, *Der Ostfeldzug – Ein Lageatlas,* "Lage am [6.-9.]7.1941 abds., Heeresgruppe Mitte."

367 D. M. Glantz, *Barbarossa Derailed,* Vol. I, 74.

368 Ibid., 74-75.

369 Ibid.., 70.

370 BA-MA MSg 1/1147: *Tagebuch* Lemelsen, 10.7.41.

371 D. M. Glantz, *Barbarossa Derailed,* Vol. I, 75, 78.

372 D. M. Glantz, *Barbarossa Derailed,* Vol. I, 78-79; R. Hinze, *Hitze, Frost und Pulverdampf. Der Schicksalsweg der 20. Panzer-Division,* 36-40; K.-R. Woche, *Zwischen Pflicht und Gewissen,* 111-12.

373 H. Boucsein, *Halten oder Sterben,* 27.

374 *"Tagesmeldungen der Operations-Abteilung des GenStdH,"* in: P. E. Schramm (Hg.), *Kriegstagebuch des OKW,* Bd. I, 516.

375 A. Seaton, *The Battle for Moscow,* 214.

376 Schmidt was one of the generals in the east who made a concerted effort to mollify the effects of the criminal orders which came from OKW or the *Fuehrerhauptquartier.* In September 1941, he would formally demand the repeal of the infamous Commissar Order, having also forbidden its implementation by his own troops. He also did whatever he could, under the circumstances, to mitigate the impact of the German occupation on the Russian people. For more details see, K.-R. Woche, *Zwischen Pflicht und Gewissen,* 10-11, 127-29, 150-51.

377 Ibid., 112-13.

378 General Wilhelm Josef Ritter von Thoma, quoted in: R. Steiger, *Armour Tactics in the Second World War,* 118.

379 J. Shay, *Achilles in Vietnam. Combat Trauma and the Undoing of Character,* 5.

380 K. Schueler, *"The Eastern Campaign as a Transportation and Supply Problem,"* in: *From Peace to War,* B. Wegner (ed.), 209. "The plan," writes Schueler, "was to execute the necessary supply movements with a combination of trucks and railway trains after the Dnepr-Dvina line had been crossed. In this, the railways were to be given the task of transporting the required supplies as far forward as possible to supply bases, where the trucks would take over the supplies and transport them to the units." That said, some of the territorial objectives assigned to the army groups for the first operational phase were beyond the calculated range of the motor transport columns; hence, "all deliberations and studies thus came to the same conclusion, namely that efficient railway operations must commence in the conquered Soviet territories as soon as possible in order decisively to relieve the burden on the motorized transportation capacity, to stock the supply bases for further advances, and to enable operations to develop unhindered."

381 R. L. DiNardo, *Germany's Panzer Arm in WWII,* 23.

382 Quoted in: R. Steiger, *Armour Tactics in the Second World War,* 113.

383 Ibid., 117.

384 M. van Creveld, *Supplying War,* 155; *GSWW,* Vol. IV, 1112.

385 *GSWW,* Vol. IV, 1113.

386 M. van Creveld, *Supplying War,* 157.

387 *GSWW,* Vol. IV, 1113-14.

388 Ibid., Vol. IV, 1113.

389 Ibid., Vol. IV, 1113.

390 Pz. AOK 3, Abt. Ia, *Tagesmeldung an AOK 9,* 23 June 1941, quoted in: R. Steiger, *Armour Tactics in the Second World War,* 119.

391 57. Pz. Korps Abt. Ia, *Fernspruch an Chef Pz. AOK 3,* 3 July 1941, quoted in: R. Steiger, *Armour Tactics in the Second World War,* 119. Concerning partisan activity Steiger writes: "Women and children had an important part in many partisan attacks … Small children often worked closely with Red Army units as scouts and agents, thus inflicting heavy losses upon German transportation companies." Ibid. 120.

392 10. Pz. Div. Abt. Ia, *Meldung an 46 Panzer Corps,* 16 July 1941, quoted in: R. Steiger, *Armour Tactics in the Second World War,* 125.

393 18. Pz. Div. Abt. Ia, *Zustandsbericht,* 20 July 1941, cited in: R. Steiger, *Armour Tactics in the Second World War,* 125-26.

394 C. von Luttichau, *Road to Moscow,* XIII:24.

395 B. H. Mueller-Hillebrand, *"German Tank Maintenance in World War II,"* CMH Publication 104-7, 2. According to Mueller-Hillebrand, who commanded a tank regiment in the east: "For the Russian campaign the Germans intended to apply a slightly modified, but essentially centralized system of tank maintenance. Most of the tank repairs were still to be performed in the zone of interior. On the other hand, each of the three army groups in the Russian theater was to have a spare-parts depot. Improved maintenance vehicles,

recovery vehicles, and better shop equipment were issued to the maintenance units in the field. No further planning was considered necessary because both the military and political leaders assumed that military operations would reach their climax during the autumn of 1941 and that most of the armored forces would return to Germany before the winter. Those remaining in the Russian theater would be withdrawn from action and rehabilitated in suitable areas during the winter months."

396   C. von Luttichau, *Road to Moscow*, XIII:24.

397   H.-A. Jacobsen (Hg.), *Generaloberst Halder Kriegstagebuch*, Bd. III, 32.

398   H.-A. Jacobsen (Hg.), *Generaloberst Halder Kriegstagebuch*, Bd. III, 32; C. von Luttichau, *Road to Moscow*, XIII:23.

399   *GSWW*, Vol. IV, 1112,

400   C. von Luttichau, *Road to Moscow*, XIII:23.

401   4. Pz. Div. Abt. Ia, Nr. 71/42 *geheim*, 12 March 1942, cited in: R. Steiger, *Armour Tactics in the Second World War*, 123.

402   KTB, Pz. AOK 2/O. Qu., 6 July 1941, cited in: *GSWW*, Vol. IV, 1112.

403   R. Steiger, *Armour Tactics in the Second World War*, 123.

404   57. Pz. Korps Abt. Ia, Anl. Nr. 429 zum KTB Nr. 1, 6 August 1941, cited in: R. Steiger, *Armour Tactics in the Second World War*, 124.

405   In March 1942, the OKH *Oberquartiermeister*, General Eduard Wagner, assessing ammunition consumption during the first nine months of *Barbarossa*, concluded: "Ammunition requirements were below the levels anticipated. At the start of operations particularly, the demands for the stockpiling of ammunition [*Munitionsbevorratung*] were much too excessive, yet they were carried out. As a result, transport capacity was, in this respect, overburdened, while numerous scattered stocks of ammunition were left in the field." G. Donat, *Der Munitionsverbrauch im Zweiten Weltkrieg*, 35.

406   Ibid., 6-8, 23, 31-35.

407   M. van Creveld, *Supplying War*, 157; *GSWW*, Vol. IV, 1114.

408   This was achieved by the end of 1942; by the end of 1941, more than 23,000 kilometers of track had been converted. K. Schueler, "*The Eastern Campaign as a Transportation and Supply Problem*," in: *From Peace to War*, B. Wegner (ed.), 210, f.n. 5.

409   New tools included a device known as the "*Schlagteller-Geissfuss*," which significantly increased the rate at which track could be dismantled and relaid. Gen.Lt. Hans v. Donat, a.D., "*Eisenbahn-Pioniere*," II., Part Two, in: *Deutsches Soldatenjahrbuch 1966*, 108; J. Piekalkiewicz, *Die Deutsche Reichsbahn im Zweiten Weltkrieg*, 35; E-Mail, C. Nehring to C. Luther, 17 Jan 12.

410   Soviet rail construction standards were poor. While German and most western rail bed construction methods embraced a multi-tiered rock and gravel foundation, Soviet rails were almost inevitably sitting on a bed of sand, perhaps covered with a layer of rocks to reduce the inevitable clouds of dust. Furthermore, the great majority of Soviet rail ties were made of untreated pine. The result was that the load-carrying capacity of Russian lines fell well below German railway norms. Soviet rail ties were also placed further apart than on German or American rail lines, and this, too, reduced the overall transportation capacity of Soviet railroads. See, "*Deutsche Reichsbahn*," at Internet site: www.feldgrau.com; also, H. Pottgiesser, *Die Deutsche Reichsbahn im Ostfeldzug*, 26-27.

411   M. van Creveld, *Supplying War*, 157-60; *GSWW*, Vol. IV, 1114; R. J. Kershaw, *War Without Garlands*, 167.

412   M. van Creveld, *Supplying War*, 153. For a series of fascinating and insightful photos of German repair and conversion efforts on Russian rail lines see, J. Piekalkiewicz, *Die Deutsche Reichsbahn im Zweiten Weltkrieg*, 38-46.

413   K. Gerbet (ed.), *GFM Fedor von Bock, The War Diary*, 237. As Bock also recorded on 3 July: "Talked the chief of field transport [Gercke] into converting the tracks from Baranovichi to Minsk to the German gauge, as we haven't captured any Russian tank cars and fuel can only be transported to the front in large quantities in German tank cars."

414   C. von Luttichau, *Road to Moscow*, XIII:23.

415   C. von Luttichau, *Road to Moscow*, XIII:23; M. van Creveld, *Supplying War*, 168.

416   *GSWW*, Vol. IV, 1125.

417   For the serious difficulties encountered in setting up these new supply depots see, *GSWW*, Vol. IV, 1125.

418   *GSWW*, Vol. IV, 1125-26.

419   *GSWW*, Vol. IV, 537-41; J. Keegan, *The Second World War*, 191; R. Kirchubel, *Hitler's Panzer Armies*, 136-37; "*Tagesmeldungen der Operations-Abteilung des GenStdH*," in: P. E. Schramm (Hg.), *Kriegstagebuch des OKW*, Bd. I, 515.

420   H. Magenheimer, *Moskau 1941*, 44-45; R. Kirchubel, *Hitler's Panzer Armies*, 19-24. See also, *GSWW*, Vol. IV, 546-66.

421   As of 2 July 1941, the greatest advances had been registered by Guderian's 2 Panzer Group: 24 Panzer Corps to the Berezina (450 km); 46 Panzer Corps to Dukora (450 km); and 47 Panzer Corps to Borisov (400 km). FMS P-190, R. Hofmann & A. Toppe, "*Verbrauchs- und Verschleisssaetze waehrend der Operationen der deutschen Heeresgruppe Mitte vom 22.6.41 – 31.12.41*," 14.

422   D. Stahel, *And the World held its Breath*, 175; J. Huerter, *Hitlers Heerfuehrer*, 280.

423   The German text reads as follows: "*Fuehrer betont grundsaetzlich, dass er Moskau und Leningrad dem Erdboden gleich machen wolle*." "*Sonderakte, 8. Juli 1941*," in: P. E. Schramm (Hg.), *Kriegstagebuch des OKW*, Bd. I, 1021.

424   C. Burdick & H.-A. Jacobsen (eds.), *The Halder Diary 1939-1942*, 458.

425   D. Irving, *Hitler's War*, 284.

426   R.-D. Mueller & G. R. Ueberschaer, *Hitler's War in the East. A Critical Assessment*, 89-90.

427   G. Meyer, *Adolf Heusinger*, 153.

428   H. Oehmichen & M. Mann, *Der Weg der 87. Infanterie-Division*, 79-81.

429   S. Knappe, *Soldat*, 211-12.

430   D. M. Glantz, *Barbarossa Derailed*, Vol. I, 33, 41.

431   Dr Overmans was the first to undertake a comprehensive analysis of the records of the *Wehrmacht's* Information Office for War Losses and Prisoners of War, or WASt, which during the war meticulously recorded German military casualties (dead, wounded, sick, missing). Today, this office is called the *Deutsche Dienstelle* (*WASt*) and is responsible for providing next-of-kin with information on *Wehrmacht* soldiers killed during the war. See, http://www.dd-wast.de.

432   R. Overmans, *Deutsche militaerische Verluste im Zweiten Weltkrieg*, 277. As Overmans' study makes clear, even Halder and the German General Staff were – astonishingly – unaware of the actual rate of the losses they were experiencing in the east. In his diary, Halder put the *Ostheer's* fatal losses up to 3 July 1941 at just 11,822 (724 officers), along with 3961 missing (66 officers). C. Burdick & H.-A. Jacobsen (eds.), *The Halder Diary 1939-1942*, 453-54. For the period 22 June to 31 July 1941, General Staff figures put total German Army dead in the east at 46,470 (along with 11,758 missing), when the actual number (as tallied by Overmans) was more than 80,000 dead. For German General Staff calculations see, "*Anlage 1 zu OKH/GenStdH/GenQu/Abt. I/Qu 2/III, Nr. I/58/42 g.Kdos. vom 5. Januar 1942*," in: P. E. Schramm (Hg.), *Kriegstagebuch des OKW*, Bd. I, 1120.

433   P. E. Schramm (Hg.), *Kriegstagebuch des OKW*, Bd. I, 1216. The *Luftwaffe* losses resulted primarily from the merciless wear and tear (*technischen Verschleiss*) to which the aircraft were subjected in the east, rather than from combat action. See, J. Prien, et al., *Die Jagdfliegerverbaende der Deutschen Luftwaffe*, Teil 6/I, *Unternehmen "Barbarossa*," 14.

434   W. Murray & A. R. Millet, *A War to be Won*, 127.

435   IfZ-Archiv, MA 1589: *Pz. Rgt. 35, Bericht an die 4. Pz. Div. vom 4.7.1941*, quoted in: C. Hartmann, *Wehrmacht im Ostkrieg*, 253, f.n. 44. Two days before (2 July), 4 PD had reported: "The Russians have begun to catch their stride again." BA-MA RH 27-4/109: 4. Pz. Div., Abt. Ic, *Taetigkeitsbericht vom 3.6.1941 – 31.3.1942, Eintrag vom 2.7.1941*, quoted in: C. Hartmann, *Wehrmacht im Ostkrieg*, 253, f.n. 45.

436   B. R. von Oppen (ed.), *Helmuth James von Moltke, Letters to Freya*, 12, 144. At the front, *Leutnant* Heinz Doell (18 PD) wrote on 1 July: "The fighting increased in intensity [*Haerte*] from day to day, as Red Army resistance began to coalesce. Even at night we had no peace. We formed hedgehog positions, whereby almost one-third of our battlegroup was always in combat readiness." (W. Kempowski (Hg.), *Das Echolot*, 174.) *Leutnant* Georg Kreuter (18 PD) recorded in his diary four days later (5 July): "At 2400 we continue the advance. The three large bridges along the Autobahn have been destroyed! The enemy is now doing a better job of organizing his resistance." (*Tagebuch* Kreuter, 5.7.41.) Accounts such as Hans-Joachim Roell's *Oberleutnant Albert Blaich* also illustrate how much more effective Soviet resistance at the tactical level rapidly became.

CHAPTER 8

The German Soldiers' Initial Experiences in the East –Panzermaenner, Infanterie, Luftwaffe

"This marching is more strenuous than action. An hour and a half's rest from 1:30 to 3:00 a.m. Later we marched with the moon behind us into a dark, threatening sky. It was like marching into a dark hole; the ghostly landscape was pale and bare. We slept like the dead for an hour and got up unsteadily with an awful pressure in the stomach. A delicate morning. Pale, fine colors. You wake up slowly, and at each stop you sleep. At any time during these advances you can see troops sleeping by the way-side, just as they have thrown themselves down. Sometimes they're doubled up like dead." (Helmut Pabst, Signal NCO, Army Group Center, n.d.)[1]

"My darling wife! My dear boy! We have fought in battle many days now and we have defeated the enemy wherever we have encountered him ... We only wait for our expected orders: Mount your tanks! Start your engines! Move out! Maedi, if you were only here and could see me – tanned by the sun, dusty and dirty, with eyes as clear as a falcon! Our losses have been minimal and our success great. This war will be over soon, because we are fighting against only fragmented opposition." (Karl Fuchs, 7 PD, 5 July 1941)[2]

"Since the initial reports of success reached us, with those incredible enemy losses with regards to manpower, materiel, and territory, we think the end of the campaign is already come and behave correspondingly recklessly. Some comrades slip out alone in the evening, "armed" only with cooking pots, to the outlying houses and villages, looking for milk. The Russians are hospitable and everything is always fine. Or at the guard posts, where we, arrogantly confident of victory, fail to recognize the threat of danger and behave as if we were on a campsite." ("Fritz" Belke, 6 ID, ca. July 1941)[3]

"We are in the midst of a struggle of the utmost pitilessness, there can be no illusion about this, despite the great extent of our successes. The days are filled with fighting which can only be endured with the aid of healthy nerves and every last ounce of physical and psychological strength. The theater of war is sober, dirty, unromantic, and the enemy facing us of a barbaric [asiatischen] brutality and determination; it is war in its most terrible, original form." (Heinrich Haape, 6 ID, 3 August 1941)[4]

This chapter represents a break from the battle narrative of the two preceding chapters; instead, an effort is made here to examine more deeply some of the defining experiences of the German *Landser* during the first six to eight weeks of the campaign – that is, through the month of August 1941. No attempt is made to do this in a comprehensive way; rather, a series of themes are explored which, it is hoped, provide deeper insight into the essential nature of war on the eastern front as it unfolded along the central axis of the German advance and shaped the bedrock experiences of the soldiers of Army Group Center.

Pursuing these objectives in a separate chapter enables this author to proceed in a manner that does not disrupt the cadence of the chapters in this book devoted to a more traditional battle narrative. While personal accounts of the soldiers have played an integral part throughout the preceding narrative, in this chapter the panzer crews, infantrymen and *Luftwaffe* pilots will be given an even fuller voice, as expressed through their field post letters, personal diaries, and post-war memoirs. As a result, a brief examination of the German World War II field post as a vital, albeit long neglected, source material is in order.

As noted in the preface to this book, unlike military historians in United States and other English-speaking countries, German scholars were slow to recognize the significant contribution ordinary soldiers could make to enlarge our understanding of 20th Century warfare. By the 1980s, however, tentative efforts were underway in Germany to evaluate the 1939-45 period from the "simple" soldier's perspective by marshalling a range of hitherto little used source materials, such as personal diaries and, more importantly, the tiny fragments of surviving field post which, during the war, flowed between the *Landser* at the front and their loved ones at home in enormous numbers. More recently, German scholars such as Klaus Latzel, Martin Humburg, Christian Hartmann and Johannes Huerter have sought to enhance our understanding of the experiences of German soldiers on the eastern front – from field marshals to rank-and-file – through their insightful analyses and use of field post letters.[5]

During the First World War, it is estimated that more than 28 billion letters, postcards, packages and telegrams circulated between the various German military fronts and the homeland; on average, 6.8 million pieces of mail made their way each day from the front back to Germany, while even more traveled from Germany to the front. Between 1939 and 1945, the aggregate figure climbed to 30 to 40 billion pieces of mail, with German soldiers at the front responsible for 7.5 to 10 billion of these mailings. Indeed, with more than 17,000,000 soldiers serving in the *Wehrmacht* during almost six years of war, *each* German soldier produced, on average, 430 to 570 letters throughout his wartime military service. Of this staggering correspondence, the tiniest of fractions, some 100,000 to 200,000 of the field post letters (*Feldpostbriefe*) of German soldiers, is known to still be in existence (as of 2005) – in German repositories, such as the Library of Contemporary History (Stuttgart), or in the hands of collectors. In addition, major collections of these letters most likely remain "unretrieved" in the homes of next of kin of *Wehrmacht* veterans.[6]

While it is beyond the scope of this narrative to delve too deeply into the nature and value of field post as historical source material, several key observations can nonetheless be adumbrated. In general, the field post provide a barometer for the morale (*Stimmung*) of the troops,[7] which explains why German military authorities attempted to screen and, in some cases, censor soldiers' letters. In particular, the letters from the front furnish myriad useful – and often thematic – insights into the "view from below" (*Blick nach unten*) that are not to be found in the largely impersonal and institutional unit war diaries, or gleaned from most other primary or secondary accounts. In this sense, the field post is indispensable to a fuller, and more human, comprehension of the war in the east. As Theodor Heuss, the first President of the Federal Republic of Germany after the Second World War, stated in 1946, "The innermost workings [*Innenseite*] of an epoch are, for the most part, recognizable only if one consults the intimate exchange of letters which it brings forth."[8]

As one German author observed in the mid-1980s, a personal letter (or a diary) of a soldier in wartime represents a historical document of "inestimable" value, for it enables us to:

• reconstruct the events of war in tangible, discrete snippets, at history's micro-level;

- grasp the interaction between the general and the personal levels, between micro- and macro-history;
- [and] check, augment or even correct the official historiography through the testimony of ordinary people.[9]

Of course, the fragmentary evidence gleaned from such intimate personal source materials as field post – or personal diaries, published memoirs and interviews for that matter – cannot begin to offer a complete picture of the experiences of the common soldier at the front. As noted, these letters were also subject to censor – both external and internal. External censor was carried out by the German military authorities; however, the censors were relatively few in number[10] and, for the most part, only managed to examine a small fraction of the outgoing German soldiers' mail. Moreover, this type of official censor was easy for the crafty soldier to circumvent: He simply handed his letter(s) to a comrade returning home on leave, who then saw that it got to its proper destination. While such behavior was officially forbidden, it was widely practiced in both the First and Second World Wars.[11]

Internal censor was that practiced by the soldiers themselves, and was the result of several overlapping factors. In the first place, letters from Russia – particularly during the opening phase of the campaign – often betray the palpable shock evoked by the barbarous nature of the fighting that, from the very start, was often characterized by reciprocal lawlessness and failure to observe traditional humanitarian principles. Quite often, however, the letter writer either refused, or was simply unable, to endow such pitiless personal experiences with words. This author's perusal of thousands of German field post confirms the observations of historian Wolfram Wette:

> Those of us who have read collections of battlefield letters cannot avoid the impression at times that many of the *Landser* were not capable of finding adequate words to describe the events swirling around them. They could not accurately describe what it was like to live on the borderline between life and death, in a chaos that shattered nerves and wore bodies to the bone. Yet it was by no means due to a lack of intelligence, or merely considerations for the feelings of the recipients of the letters, whom the soldiers did not want to alarm. Many enlisted men were simply struck dumb by the hideous reality of battle; what they were experiencing was an inferno that defied description.[12]

What does emerge quite clearly from the field post letters is the average *Lander's* close identification with, and support of, the goals of the Russian campaign as pursued by the German civilian and military leadership. Writes historian Stephen G. Fritz in his excellent work *Frontsoldaten*:

> The rank and file of the *Wehrmacht* were probably more thoroughly Nazified than has heretofore been acknowledged; indeed, average *Landers* were consistently among Hitler's strongest supporters. As a consequence, their letters and diaries disclose, there existed among the troops in Russia such a striking level of agreement with the Nazi regime's view of the Bolshevik enemy and the sort of treatment that should be dealt them that many soldiers willingly participated in murderous actions … Again, what made such letters remarkable was the widespread acceptance by average soldiers of these harsh and brutal measures, indeed the almost complete absence of any sense of moral or personal outrage.[13]

This is not to say – and it is not this author's contention – that the majority of German soldiers on the eastern front were guilty of criminal acts (a theme which will be explored in detail in Chapter 9 below); however, that they identified closely with the policies of the National Socialist regime is beyond dispute.[14]

A final point: As historian Klaus Latzel has noted, for German soldiers across the battlefields of Europe and North Africa – and, certainly, for the *Landser* marooned on the eastern front, far from wives, families, and friends – the reciprocal exchange of letters forged a lifeline of "existential value." Wrote one soldier:

> After weeks like that without post, you notice that field post is just as important as rations and ammunition, because it has to sustain and nourish our spirits, our emotions. And to sustain the soldier as a human being, to prevent him from becoming a raw, brutalized instrument of war, that is the higher task of the letter writer back home.[15]

8.1: Weather & Terrain

In scrutinizing the initial experiences of the soldiers of Army Group Center in the Russian campaign, it is appropriate to begin with the two factors which had a universal impact on man and beast – weather and terrain. As we have seen, the army group crossed the Soviet-German demarcation line on 22 June 1941 and advanced along a front of several hundred kilometers through the southernmost part of Lithuania and Soviet-occupied eastern Poland; within days, Bock's mobile formations had breached the 1939 Soviet frontier and struck out for Minsk, the sprawling capital city of the Belorussian Soviet Socialist Republic (SSR). However, because a large area of western Belorussia had been ceded to Poland at the end of the Polish-Soviet War in 1921 (Treaty of Riga), the German advance into Belorussia actually began in eastern Poland. The eastern borders of the Belorussian SSR reached beyond the Western Dvina River and almost as far as the city of Smolensk, which was part of the Russian Soviet Federated Socialist Republic (RSFSR).[16]

Oberleutnant Siegfried Knappe (87 Infantry Division) was one of more than one million soldiers of Army Group Center who took part in the march into central Russia in June and July 1941. In his post-war memoirs, he conveyed a colorful picture of the land – its flora, its fauna and, above all, its boundlessness – beyond the Russo-German frontier:

> As we marched through Russia, we began to acquire an appreciation for the vastness of the country. In some forested places, the earth was squeaky and springy beneath our boots. The leaves on the surface were light and brittle, but underneath them lay leaves that had withered many years before and created a brown spongy mass in which many tiny insects scurried. In other places, dead, brittle underbrush crumbled beneath our feet. The forest smelled musty with old leaves, and the trees were full of noisy birds. The living trees usually smelled fresh and damp, and the odor of the dead trees was dry and rich.
>
> In the open, the sun warmed the earth, as well as buttons, belt claps, harness rings, and anything made of metal. Yellow butterflies, blue-black beetles, and small brown ants were common. Grass snakes rustled through the grass, practically invisible. Grasshoppers were plentiful and could not seem to tell a moving soldier from a stationary tree, often hitching free rides. Swarms of gnats plagued us, and darting flies were everywhere.
>
> As we marched, low hills would emerge from the horizon ahead of us and then slowly sink back into the horizon behind us. It almost seemed that the same hill kept appearing in front of us, kilometer after kilometer. Everything seemed to blur into uniform gray because of the vastness and sameness of everything. We traversed treeless plateaus that extended as far as the eye could see, just one vast open field overgrown with tall grass. We encountered grainfields of unimaginable

vastness that sometimes concealed Russian infantry. Fields of sunflowers stretched for kilometer after kilometer after weary kilometer. In other places we encountered immense forests that were like jungles in the density of their tangled underbrush. We struggled through marshes in Belorussia that were as large as two German provinces. The rivers all seemed to run north and south, so we had to cross them, and they provided the retreating Russians with natural defensive positions.[17]

The further east the Germans marched, the greater the difficulties they had with the terrain. As Guenther Blumentritt, Fourth Army Chief of Staff in the summer of 1941, told Liddell Hart shortly after the war, beyond Minsk, the terrain was even more challenging, while the weather was no better:

> It was appallingly difficult country for tank movement – great virgin forests, widespread swamps, terrible roads, and bridges not strong enough to bear the weight of tanks. The resistance also became stiffer, and the Russians began to cover their front with minefields. It was easier for them to block the way because there were so few roads.
>
> The great motor highway leading from the frontier to Moscow was unfinished[18] – the one road a Westerner would call a "road." We were not prepared for what we found because our maps in no way corresponded to reality. On those maps all supposed main roads were marked in red, and there seemed to be many, but they often proved to be merely sandy tracks. The German intelligence service was fairly accurate about conditions in Russian-occupied Poland, but badly at fault about those beyond the original Russian border.
>
> Such country was bad enough for tanks but worse still for the transport accompanying them – carrying their fuel, their supplies, and all the auxiliary troops they needed. Nearly all this transport consisted of wheeled vehicles, which could not move off the roads, nor move on it if the sand turned into mud. An hour or two's rain reduced the panzer forces to stagnation. It was an extraordinary sight, with groups of tanks and transport strung out over a hundred-mile stretch, all stuck – until the sun came out and the ground dried.[19]

Blumentritt's post-war assessment of the gradually worsening impact of terrain on German tank forces was underscored during the campaign by General Hoth, Commander, 3 Panzer Group. On 13 July 1941, Hitler's chief Army adjutant, Colonel Schmundt, arrived at Hoth's headquarters outside Vitebsk. The panzer group commander told him that, while tank losses from combat had not been unduly large – in fact, no larger than those of the French campaign the year before – weather and terrain were causing high losses due to mechanical breakdowns.[20] Four days earlier (9 July), 3 Panzer Group had reported a total of 264 tanks awaiting repairs, nearly 30 percent of its marching out strength on 22 June.[21]

Belorussia, or "Ruthenia" as it was known to German occupational authorities, comprised an area of about 225,000 square kilometers.[22] The summer months in Belorussia are normally moderately warm, but in the summer of 1941, "virtually every witness took note of the hot, sunny weather and the immensely tall [fields of] wheat and rye."[23] The days were long and the nights short, with the first rays of sunlight rising above the horizon as early as 2.00 in the morning.[24] The long hours of daylight, and mostly clear weather, favored the attacking Germans, enabling them to conduct air and ground operations deep into the evening hours (ca. 2200). The summer of 1941 was also unusually dry, greatly reducing the levels of rivers and streams and making it easier for the German armor to find places to ford them.[25] Sudden thundershowers, however, could instantly reduce the region's unpaved roads and open terrain to rivers of mud, temporarily incapacitating both motor and horse-drawn vehicles.

The geography of Belorussia was, as illustrated by *Leutnant* Knappe, tediously monotonous and flat, with an average elevation of about 160 meters above sea level; it was also dissected by numerous rivers and streams, permeated by lakes, bogs and marshes, and covered with immense tracks of dense primeval forest. A series of modest ridgelines extended from the area around Grodno, across Minsk and Smolensk, to the Valdai Hills – the Desna, Dnepr, Western Dvina, Moscow and Volga Rivers all having their sources in this high ground, which in Belorussia reached its apex in the rolling hills north of Minsk (340-360 meters). A key terrain feature along this historic invasion route into Russia was the strategically vital "Smolensk gate." Stretching between Orsha and Vitebsk, where the upper reaches of the Western Dvina and Dnepr Rivers bent back sharply to the northeast, this landbridge formed a corridor 75 kilometers wide – enough space, according to General Hermann Hoth, for three armored divisions to maneuver. A German objective of paramount importance, the gate was protected along its western approaches by a broad belt of forests and swamps running north from the Pripiat' Marshes.[26]

Several major river lines, and their tributaries, crossed Army Group Center's route of advance. From west to east these included the Neman, Berezina, Dvina, Dnepr and Desna Rivers; indeed, in Belorussia alone the total length of the waterways amounted to 32,000 kilometers. Although these river lines posed a succession of potential natural obstacles, the German Army in 1941 was well-trained and equipped to conduct forced river crossings which, as one post-war study by former *Wehrmacht* officers put it, "belonged virtually to the daily bread of the German soldier."[27] As a result, all major river crossings in the summer of 1941 were successful, and many were carried out with surprising speed. In conducting such operations, the Germans enjoyed a considerable advantage due to a characteristic common to most all Russian rivers and streams: The west bank was higher than the east bank. Thus, whenever German forces approached a major, defended river barrier, they were on dominating ground. Also typical of most Russian rivers and streams were the extensive, swampy lowlands that lined one or both of their banks, posing serious challenges for an attacker. Crossing these lowlands, which afforded no cover at all, could consume a great deal of time and exact a high toll in casualties; moreover, this common terrain feature complicated the construction of bridges and approach roads after a river crossing had been completed.[28]

While in most parts of Europe marshlands had generally been drained or modified, those in Belorussia and throughout the Soviet Union remained, like most rivers and streams, in a mostly primitive, unregulated state.[29] The abundant marshlands, unless dried out by the summer heat, were largely untraversable for both motor and horse-drawn vehicles, forcing them to cling to the roadways. From the outset of the campaign, the marshy labyrinths became a favorite hiding place for Red Army stragglers and partisans, placing additional strain on the *Ostheer's* operations and lines of communication.[30] In areas of marshy terrain, it was, of course, the combat infantryman who bore the brunt of the fighting:

> The effect of artillery fire is largely nullified by swampy soil. Aerial bombs must be equipped with extension-rod fuzes (*Vorsatzzuender*) to produce any sort of result. Above all, however, combat in swamps puts the infantry to unusually severe physical tests. In summertime the men constantly live among dampness and moisture. Boots and uniforms begin to rot; myriads of mosquitoes never cease to make life miserable; drinking water is a rare and precious commodity; proper body hygiene is impossible; epidemics of diarrhea, dysentery, and typhoid spread like wildfire. Among the principal reason for the high casualty rates in swamp fighting is the impossibility of digging field fortifications. Every cut of the spade immediately fills up with water. Cover can only be built from logs, which frequently have to be hauled a long distance, and from sandbags.[31]

Another dominant topographical feature of central European Russia was the enormous tracks of woodlands – untamed thickets of spruce, oak, pine, and birch (and other types), which actually began in Poland and, as the former chief of staff of Army Group Center noted in a post-war study, "grow denser as one advances to the east."[32] In Belorussia, about one-third of the land was made up of wooded regions. Beginning on 22 June 1941, German panzer corps had to cross vast belts of forest at the frontier, stretching for almost 100 kilometers, before emerging into open country. Major forested areas also abounded in the regions of Gomel, Minsk, Borisov, Briansk, Orsha, Viaz'ma, Polotsk and Velikie Luki. The few tracks and roads which traversed these largely primitive forests canalized the movement of German formations and strung them out over great distances. The better roads, even fewer in number, were designated *Rollbahnen* and reserved for the tank and motorized units; however, due to the heavily vehicular traffic, these primary arteries were soon completely plowed up, severely limiting their usefulness and making repairs necessary.[33]

Advancing through these forests in the summer of 1941, German mobile and infantry columns were engulfed in clouds of dust and discomfited by the ubiquitous flies and mosquitoes, while water for men and horses was obtained only with difficulty. Forced to rely on wretched forest trails, the marching infantry were pushed to the point of exhaustion – and beyond – as they trudged on endlessly through the deep, powdery sand. Nearly all large tracks of forest also harbored extensive marshlands, and such areas were often chosen by the Russians – soldiers and partisans both – for their most determined efforts, as the marshy forest terrain (like marshlands in general) tended to limit German advantages in materiel. "Entirely new" to the Germans was the Soviet "use of forest fires as a hot weather weapon."

> In midsummer, when the trees were tinder-dry, the Russians attempted to delay German forces by putting forests to torch. Not only the physical, but the psychological impact of such fires was severe. The crackling of the burning trees, the acrid gray-black smoke, the increasingly unbearable heat, and the feeling of uncertainty put troops under a severe strain. Fleeing before towering sheets of flame, men would fight through mile after mile of burning forest only to be confronted by enemy bunkers and fortified positions. Ammunition dumps blew sky high and gave the impression that fierce battles were raging to the rear.[34]

Inexperienced in – and largely adverse to – combat in forests, the *Landser* suffered brutal casualties in their initial engagements in such areas; for this reason, "the very first day of the war saw the beginning of a search for new ways to support the [German] infantry in the unavoidable forest fighting."[35] (Note: The subject of forest fighting will be examined more closely in Section 8.3 below.)

Although the health of German soldiers was generally good throughout the summer of 1941, climate, terrain, and other factors contributed to certain health ailments, mostly of a minor nature. Recalled Panzer General Erhard Raus:

> During summer the woods and swamplands of Russia teem with mosquitoes, including malaria carriers, which for weeks scourge man and beast. Even mosquito nets do not furnish complete protection against bites on the head and neck. Flies torment men and animals in hot weather. Many of the wooden huts in the northern and central regions are infested with vermin such as bedbugs, fleas, head lice, and body lice.[36]

In his diary on 6 July 1941, Halder noted that the eastern armies had, by 3 July, suffered 54,000 "medical casualties," a figure he found "quite remarkable."[37] Stomach and bowel problems resulting from contaminated food or water, or the lack of proper hygiene, were not uncommon, while in marshy regions isolated cases of malaria occurred. The most common ailment was bacterial dysentery (*Ruhr*), which soon flared up in some units. *Oberleutnant* Kurt Kummer, an artillery officer in 18 Panzer Division, recorded in his diary on 24 August that half his battery was suffering from diarrhea, resulting in some hospitalizations.[38] Several days later (29 August), Dr Heinrich Haape (6 Infantry Division) observed:

> At the moment, dysentery is flourishing among our soldiers to a high degree, primarily transmitted through the millions of flies that do not leave us a single moment's peace. The flies are simply overwhelming. – I also have a small bout of dysentery behind me, but I was able to continue with all aspects of my duties.[39]

While rarely life threatening, dysentery could nonetheless temporarily incapacitate a soldier, as this account from *Obergefreiter* August Freitag (also 6 ID) illustrates all too graphically:

> During this time a sort of dysentery epidemic broke out, which was most likely transmitted by the many flies. On top of this was the fact that the first fresh potatoes were available in these days. Frequently, there were also yellow Russian peas at lunchtime, which, due to their peculiar qualities, we called 'crackers' [fireworks] because they encouraged diarrhea even more. I got sick one day, too. I must have had to step out 25 times in one day. But there was nothing but blood. So I lay there for four days, without sleeping, without eating anything. I was so listless and miserable that I could hardly walk.[40]

The editor of Freitag's war memoirs, Karl Sattler, contributes the following complementary details:

> Freitag was stricken with bacterial dysentery, which was by far the most common contagious disease among the German *Ostheer*. The symptom described here of frequent bowel movements, typically mixed with blood, can leave no doubt on that count. Since the western part of the Soviet Union was renowned for frequent outbreaks of dysentery, the common path of transmission – flies alighting on human excreta, then on food – explains why the soldiers were forbidden from accepting food and drink from the populace …
> The medical consultants of Army Group Center arrived at differing diagnoses in terms of how the very high numbers of diarrhea cases then appearing should be classified, which means that the validity of the available statistics is cast into doubt.[41]

Skin diseases became an "increasingly common affliction among tank crews in the summer of 1941,"[42] the result of water shortages, crowded conditions, dust laden with bacteria, and, of course, insects. As tank gunner Karl Fuchs (7 Panzer Division) complained in a field post letter to his wife on 3 August 1941:

> I've gotten some kind of a rash. I'm continually scratching my entire body. That's how bad it is. I'm blaming the Russian drinking water for it. The water is hardly good enough to wash with, so I guess I really shouldn't drink it. I can only tell you to be glad that you folks back home don't have to look at this "blessed" Soviet Russia.[43]

Before and during the eastern campaign, German soldiers received inoculations against dysentery, typhus, malaria and other potentially crippling maladies that were frequently encountered in European Russia. *Obergefreiter* Emil Bub (303 Flak Battalion) recorded in his diary (25 April 1941) the receipt of his fifth inoculation to date – this one against typhus.[44] In a collection of field post of *Landser* Wilhelm Buddenbohm (6 ID), recently self-published by the soldier's son, it is noted that while the health of the soldiers was "still relatively good" in August 1941, cases of intestinal illnesses were becoming more frequent, and that Buddenbohm received his third inoculation against dysentery at this time.[45]

8.2: *Panzermaenner*

In a staff report on 17 June 1941, 24 Panzer Corps observed that its great objective, the Soviet capital of Moscow, lay precisely 1040 kilometers to the east.[46] As the officers in this powerful, battle tested formation no doubt fully understood, a successful outcome to the campaign would hinge almost entirely on their ability – and that of the other panzer corps, which together made up the hard edge of the *Ostheer* – to successfully carry out the missions laid out for them in the *Barbarossa* directives. Hitherto, the panzer units of the *Wehrmacht* had enjoyed a rather good run. Harnessing mobility, firepower, radio communications and combined arms tactics – perhaps the most striking example of the "unparalleled profusion" of revolutions in military affairs (RMAs) originating in the interwar period between 1919-1939[47] – along with a leadership culture which, in the best traditions of the Elder Moltke, sought to push responsibility for critical decision-making on the battlefield down to the lower ranks (*Auftragstaktik*), the *Panzermaenner*, in their crisp, black uniforms, had shattered Germany's more conventional opponents in swift succession, from the plains of Poland, across the fields of France, to the rugged landscape of the Balkans. To be sure, Russia posed their greatest challenge yet; still, most were confident the campaign would progress no differently than those during the first 20 months of war.

In hindsight – if not to the OKH and their forces in the field in the spring of 1941[48] – it is all too apparent that Operation *Barbarossa*, and the key operational concept it embodied, signified a risk of immense proportion. Indeed, if one considers the relative paucity of operational and tactical intelligence on which the campaign was based, it becomes clear just how daring – perhaps foolhardy – was the mission assigned to the panzer corps: To push hundreds of kilometers beyond the frontier, deep into the enemy's hinterland, without regard for their flanks or rear, while encircling and destroying an enemy known to be much larger numerically. Nonetheless, as executed on 22 June, the concept seemed at first to work out brilliantly, the eastern blitzkrieg functioning, in the words of historian Christian Hartmann, with an "uncanny efficiency and speed."[49]

8.2.1: Characteristics of the Panzer *Vormarsch*

With permanent support from heavy weapons – assigned, yet not organic, to the panzer corps, including Flak artillery, medium and heavy motorized artillery battalions, assault gun units, *Nebelwerfer* rocket projector batteries, etc.[50] – and the bulk of *Luftwaffe* fighters, bombers, and dive bombers carving up the enemy before them, the tank and motorized divisions smashed through the Soviet frontier defenses and drove east toward their initial objectives. In his novel, *Moscow*, published shortly after the war, German writer Theodor Plievier captured the quintessence of the German armored advance into Soviet Russia:

> The stream of tanks thundered over the bridge. The infantry lying at the side of the road were covered with dust. When there was a halt the men of Gnotke's platoon could have a good look at the tanks. Only the driver sat inside, the crew sat on top – the commander on the edge of the turret with his headphones on, the others behind him.

"Look at that, they've got all their gear hanging on the outside." "Of course, everything goes bad in the heat with the stink of oil." Cooking utensils, drinking water, sacks of bread and rations – they all hung dangling on the walls of the tanks. Behind there were the gasoline tins, and no tank was without its boards and beams, its wooden matting to lay on soft patches. Then there were tanks with trailers.

"Like gypsies," remarked one of the infantrymen.

The column went on, there was a halt, and then it started again, rolling ahead at 10 miles an hour. An armored division had about 5000 vehicles; spaced out at the regulation interval with all the auxiliary units, it would cover more than a 100 miles ...[51]

There was no sign of the sun, which must be sinking, for all this rattling and roaring and whining and screeching that crept by blotted out the day. The long stream of armor and the long wake of thick dust it stirred up stretched as far back as the Bug and over the Bug far into the heart of Poland ... So it rolled on along the road through Brest-Litovsk, Minsk and Smolensk, rolled along the military highway to Moscow – the highway they had seized and would now irresistibly sweep clear.[52]

As outlined in Chapter 7, the greatest German successes developed on the central axis, where Army Group Center – unlike Army Groups North and South – had two tank groups at its disposal. Despite a negative correlation of forces of roughly 1:1.6 at the outset of the campaign (1800+ tanks of Army Group Center facing 2900 tanks of Soviet Western Front), the *Panzergruppen* of Hoth and Guderian again and again demonstrated their striking tactical superiority over the Red Army, which was patently overmatched by the new techniques of modern mobile warfare. A key point, however, all too often overlooked in accounts of the ostensibly unremitting chain of victories registered by German forces during the summer of 1941, is that their successes were as much the result of Soviet unpreparedness (shortfalls in training, weapons, ammunition, logistics, etc.) as they were the outcome of the training, experience, operational and tactical superiority of the *Ostheer*. For example, only 383 of Western Front's tanks were modern T-34 and KV models, the rest being older T-26 and BT light tanks.[53] In addition, many of the T-34 and KV tank crews had received little to no training prior to 22 June; on more than one occasion, groups of T-34s were driven inadvertently into swampy terrain, where they had to be abandoned by their crews. During their initial engagements, some German tank crews were astonished when Russian tanks failed to make use of their main armament (relying instead on machine gun fire). The conundrum was solved when several of the tanks were captured and found to have no shells on board.[54] The Red Army also lacked effective anti-tank weapons in June 1941, the majority of its 14,900 AT guns being underperforming 45mm weapons.[55]

Following the successful execution of the opening battles of encirclement at Belostok-Minsk in early July 1941, the tanks of Army Group Center breached the Dvina-Dnepr River lines – the crossing of the Dnepr by 24 Panzer Corps alone supported by 333 *Luftwaffe* aircraft.[56] Fighting and marching without surcease, the German mechanized units smashed division after enemy division; by 13 July, for example, 17 Panzer Division (47 Panzer Corps) – "this brave division," as Guderian called it – had knocked out 502 Russian tanks.[57]

What it was like to fight and die in a tank is described in exacting detail by former British Army Colonel Robert J. Kershaw in his fine account of Operation *Barbarossa*, *War Without Garlands*:

Panzer crewmen have a different battle perspective compared to infantry on their feet. Scenery, as a consequence of greater mobility, changes quickly and more often. Maps are read from a different vista in terms of time, distance and scale. Panzers quickly crossed maps. Infantrymen saw each horizon approaching through a veil of sweat and exhaustion ... A new horizon for the tank soldier meant an unknown and, very likely, a threatening situation. His was an impartial war, fought at distance. Technology separated him from direct enemy contact: he normally fought with standoff weapon systems at great range. When direct fighting did occur, it was all the more emotive for its suddenness and intensity ...

Little can be seen from the claustrophobic confines of a tank closed down for battle. Fighting was conducted peering through letterbox size – or smaller – vision blocks in a hot, restricted and crowded fighting compartment with barely room to move. Each report from the main armament or the chattering metallic burst of turret machine gun fire would deafen the crew and release noxious fumes into the cramped space. Tension inside would be high, magnified throughout by a prickling sense of vulnerability to incoming AT round strikes, anticipated at any time. These projectiles were easily seen flying about the battlefield as white-hot slugs, with the potential to screech through a fighting compartment and obliterate all in its path. The kinetic energy produced by the strike set off ammunition fires, searing the fighting compartment in a momentary flash, followed by an explosive pressure wave blasting outward through turret hatches, openings or lifting the entire turret into the air. An external strike by a high-explosive (HE) warhead would break off a metal "scab" inside; propelled by the shock of the explosion, this would ricochet around the cramped interior of the tank. The results were horrific. Flesh seared by the initial combustible flash was then lacerated by jagged white-hot shrapnel, which in turn set off multiple secondary explosions.

Tank crewmen were muffled to some extent from battle noises outside the turret, because the screams were dulled by the noise and vibration of the engine. Human senses were ceaselessly buffeted by violent knocks and lurches as the tank rapidly maneuvered into firing positions. Dust would well up inside upon halting, and petrol and oil smells would assail nostrils during momentary pauses.[58]

Gefreiter Erich Hager, a tank radio operator in 17 Panzer Division, experienced first-hand the horror of having the tank in which he was fighting destroyed in combat. During the initial days of the war, he took part in major tank versus tank combat and, despite some difficult moments, survived unscathed. On 28 June 1941, however, southwest of Minsk, Hager and his crew's good fortune finally ran out. In his diary, meticulously crafted in German *Sutterlin* script, using a Russian school notebook, Hager recorded the harrowing event:

28 June [1941]:
Everything keeps moving ... We get 60 liters of fuel from the half tracks and drive on through the line of bunkers. Receive fire and transmit okay. Get stuck in the mud, also ObLtn Zinschuetz. Our company commander pulls us out. We get in, get the shells, and get to the rendezvous point. Drive through the burning town which has been destroyed by *Stukas*. Outside the bunker there is Pak (anti-tank) artillery. We fire at everything and drive on. Once again, there is firing from the left and the right. The Russians are hiding and firing from an ambush. There has never been a war with so many snipers, civilians among them ...

We drive on in the lead and come to a village. Heavy firing there. We come to a corner and here it happened: Three shells from not more than 20-30 meters away struck our tank. Driver *Uffz*. Wedde is dead ... We bale out as the tank is already on fire. We get out with only what we have on us. It was so quick ...

Vormarsch of Army Group Center through Central Russia: Summer 1941

The Russo-German frontier. A Russian border patrol approaches (15 June 1941). (National Archives).

Barbed wire obstacles along the Russo-German frontier. (NA)

A medical company of 129 Infantry Division advances through West Prussia toward the Russo-German frontier (June 1941). (H. Boucsein)

Tanks of 17 Panzer Division departing Oldenburg station on their way to the east (March 1941). (D. Gardner & K. Andrew)

Tanks of 17 Panzer Division moving east on the German *Autobahn* (6 June 1941). (D. Gardner & K. Andrew)

22 June 1941: Elements of 25 Panzer Regiment (7 PD) on the march south of Kalvaria. (NA)

22 June 1941: German infantry cross the Bug River in pneumatic boats. (NA)

One of the dozens of Soviet tanks (here a T-34) destroyed by German armor near Olita (Alytus) on first day of the war, east of the Nemen River. (NA)

A Pz III rolls past marching German infantry. (R. Bender)

German assault guns on the move with mounted infantry. (R. Bender)

German infantry advance deeper into Russia (25 June 1941). (NA)

Outside town of Slonim – German tank crews of 17 Panzer Division make repairs to their Pz IV tanks. (D. Gardner & K. Andrew)

A German infantry column on the march (30 June 1941). (NA)

Exhausted *Landser* of 129 Infantry Division collapse by the side of a road after another long and arduous march. Daily marches of 30, 40, even 50 kilometers were common-place (June/July 1941). (H. Boucsein)

A German motorized column struggles to advance across a Russian "road" which has been transformed into a "sea of sand." (NA)

A German motorized column crosses an emergency bridge erected by German combat engineers. A clearly marked Red Cross vehicle is plainly evident in the foreground. (NA)

German infantry advances under cover of an assault gun (summer 1941).

An exhausted German motorcycle messenger takes a short nap (30 June 1941). (NA)

German artillery on the march (summer 1941). (NA)

German tanks advancing across the endless Russian steppe (summer 1941). (R. Bender)

Russian tanks destroyed by the *Luftwaffe* in eastern Poland (June 1941).

A battery of German 150mm medium field howitzers (s.F.H. 18) (29 June 1941). (NA)

Crew of a fire-ready 50mm AT gun digs in (24 June 1941). (NA)

German motorized column roars past a burning village – a common scene in the summer of 1941. (NA)

German infantry of 95 ID move past a village in flames. (K.-H. Hoyer)

Destruction inside the Soviet citadel of Brest-Litovsk. (NA)

Fortress of Brest-Litovsk following its destruction by German artillery fire and the *Luftwaffe*.

Graves of German soldiers at the German military cemetery at Brest-Litovsk (30 June 1941). (NA)

Panzer IV of *Gefreiter* Erich Hager (17 PD) at the gravesite of *Unteroffizier* Wedde, near Minsk. Wedde was killed on 28 June 1941. (D. Gardner & K. Andrew)

Panzer IV (17 PD) knocked out near Smolensk. Note the "G" on the rear of the tank, denoting that it belonged to Guderian's panzer group. (D. Gardner & K. Andrew)

A Pz III erupts into flames in Rozana (SW of Slonim). According to the caption of the propaganda company which snapped the photograph, it was a case of "spontaneous combustion" (30 June 1941). (NA)

German artillerists, wounded in an artillery assault, are later found mutilated and murdered by Red Army troops (July 1941). (NA)

German infantry on the attack (July 1941). (NA)

Crew of 37mm AT gun manhandles the weapon into position. (NA)

A destroyed Soviet KV-tank. (NA)

Tanks of 18 Panzer Division cross the Berezina bridge at Borisov as they advance toward Smolensk (3 July 1941). (NA)

German motorized troops leave their forest assembly area and advance on Lepel (4 July 1941). (NA)

Endless German columns cross the Nemen River carrying needed supplies of weapons, ammunition, and rations to the fighting troops (July 1941). (NA)

German forward artillery observers direct the fire of their battery.

Buildings in Minsk destroyed by German bombers. (NA)

A bridge in Minsk demolished by a German air raid. (NA)

The imposing building of the "House of Soviets" in Minsk; before it, a statue of Lenin. (NA)

Motorcycle troops stop to check their direction. They are on their way to Minsk (6 July 1941). (NA)

Only the church stands intact among the surrounding buildings destroyed by bombs in a town SW of Vitebsk (8 July 1941). (NA)

Pile of Russian rifles in a German salvage dump at Minsk (July 1941). (NA)

Section of Minsk leveled in first days of war by German bombers. (NA)

A motorized column of 18 PD on the highway between Minsk and Borisov (3 July 1941). (NA)

The *Ostheer's* advance into Russia was marked by the graves of its soldiers (somewhere in Russia, summer 1941). (NA)

A German military cemetery, near Vitebsk (July 1941). (NA)

Russian peasant women pose for a photograph (central Russia, summer 1941). (K.-H. Hoyer)

Russian children, barefoot and clad in rags – a picture of the relentless poverty inside the Soviet Union. (K.-H. Hoyer)

A simple Russian peasant dwelling, dominated by its large brick oven.

The church in Vitebsk (August 1941). The Germans reopened many churches in Russian towns and villages following their capture. (NA)

A Soviet partisan hangs from a tree.

A German artillery battery on the eastern front.

A heavy German howitzer in action.

A German 88mm Flak gun – in the summer of 1941 the only truly effective weapon against Soviet KV or T-34 tanks. (NA)

Mechanized artillery on the advance northeast of Smolensk (July 1941). (NA)

German motorized and horse-drawn troops advancing on the *Autobahn* between Minsk and Tolochino (13 July 1941). (NA)

Supply column of 106 Infantry Division (summer 1941).

German troops cross the Dvina River in pneumatic boats (7 July 1941). (NA)

A Soviet bunker of the "Stalin Line"
near Polotsk (July 1941). (NA)

German tanks and panzer grenadiers on the advance (July 1941). (BA-MA, Bild 1011-187-0230-22, Foto: Arthur Grimm)

Hitler meets with his soldiers in the east (probably August 1941).

Exhausted German troops seek shelter beneath an assault gun (date unknown).

Exhausted German infantry take a short rest by the Dvina River following a long march (July 1941). (NA)

Assembly area of Pz IV tanks of 17 Panzer Division (July 1941). (D. Gardner & K. Andrew)

Panzer III tank on the *Autobahn* Minsk-Moscow (July 1941). (NA)

Interdiction of railroad leading to the Smolensk region by the *Luftwaffe* (1941).

Russian guns of all calibers and other war materiel captured by Army Group Center in the Smolensk cauldron battle. (NA)

Disabled Soviet bomber (summer 1941). (W. Buddenbohm)

From left to right: GFM von Bock and Generals Hermann Hoth and Wolfram von Richthofen (summer 1941). (BA-MA, Bild 1011-265-0047A-34, Foto: Mossdorf)

General Guderian at headquarters of 292 Infantry Division. (R. Mobius)

Tanks of 2 Panzer Division on the advance (probably late summer 1941). (H. Wijers)

Motorized artillery of 2 PD (probably late summer 1941). (H. Wijers)

Destroyed T-34 tank (1941). (H. Wijers)

Shells struck the driver and just missed me. I can only speak of luck that I didn't get hurt. I'm so sorry about Wedde. He didn't make a sound. He must have been killed outright.[59]

Hager and the other survivors took refuge in a ditch, where they lay in the mud for three quarters of an hour, while the Russian fire continued. Pinned down, with hostile forces all about them, they were unable to get away: "We see our last hour coming." At the last moment, however, Hager and his comrades were rescued by a German infantry patrol. Having lost contact with their tank company, they stayed with the infantry the next day (29 June); outfitted by their hosts with helmets and rifles, they fought as infantry. On 30 June, they moved out to find their unit:

At 12.00 we find Sch ... (illegible) with his tank. We get on top and ride with him. All of a sudden *Uffz.* Hertlein comes up behind us with three pals. He turns completely pale. No one believed we were still alive. The whole company gathers together. We had been reported as dead and signed off by the boss. There is great joy.[60]

Still deeply affected by the tragic events of 28 June – the loss of a valued comrade – Hager returned to the site of his destroyed Panzer IV. Other knocked-out German tanks were also there, and he snapped photos of them. In his diary, he expressed shock at the damage sustained by his tank and the others – their armor plating stripped away by the impact of the shells. The driver, Wedde – "they found one good body part [of him]" – and the other dead panzer soldiers, were buried in simple, raised, rectangular graves, each one carefully adorned with the dead comrade's helmet, flowers, and a simple wooden cross.[61]

Racing on past the river barriers, the enveloping arms of 2 and 3 Panzer Groups linked up again, this time around Smolensk, some 600 kilometers from the frontier, forging a second spectacular battle of annihilation on the central front. On 16 July 1941, Guderian's motorized troops captured Smolensk; by 5 August 1941, some 300,000 more Soviet prisoners were marching into the POW pens. (Note: The Smolensk cauldron battle is addressed in detail in Chapter 10 below.)

The principal catalyst behind these extraordinary victories along the central axis was, of course, the panzer generals themselves – Guderian, Hoth, Schmidt, Geyr, Lemelsen, Model, Funck, Nehring, Harpe, et al. To a man they fully understood that victory hinged less on engaging the enemy in combat than on the rapidity of their movement. Immense distances needed to be overcome, and vital objectives secured, in a matter of weeks – while the weather was good and before the Russians were able to mobilize their enormous resources of men and materiel. As mentioned, on the eve of the campaign, Guderian had exhorted his tankers to be on the move day and night, without repose, without concern for threats to their flanks – to push on as far as their fuel would take them. "The main thing," he assured them, "is to advance far, and to shoot little."[62] An officer attached to 4 Panzer Division confided in his diary: "We shall be constantly on the march. There will be no stops. We will only rest during periods of refueling. We will take our meals either while on the march or during the short refueling pauses. There is only one objective – Moscow!"[63]

From 22 June onward, the pace of operations was remorseless, the panzer generals pushing their men, tanks and vehicles, and often themselves, to the limits of human endurance. An account by a veteran of 19 Panzer Division amplifies this point, while also punctuating other characteristics of the panzer *Vormarsch* – e.g., the Soviet tactic of slashing at the flanks of the German armored columns, which, advancing far ahead of the marching infantry, sometimes became temporarily cut off or outran their logistical support:

After a few days' marching, the march route of 19 PD swung from "P 1" (*Panzerstrasse 1*)[64] toward the south ... Here, the motorcycle riflemen marching at the front met stiff enemy resistance, and were also attacked from the flanks. A bridgehead which had been established over the river Gavia had to be temporarily abandoned. The remaining division elements were cut off from the elements located further forward by enemy units attacking from the flanks, so the [forward troops] could not at first receive support from heavy weapons. The platoon leader of one infantry gun platoon writes:

"Like an angel, an observer from the artillery suddenly turned up! A few moments later, the first shells exploded in the ranks of the enemy. Under the battery's fire cover, the platoons were able to withdraw to the near side river bank and to be immediately redeployed."

... The division then deployed in battle formation. Upon their arrival, the individual batteries immediately got themselves ready to fire. And with that ended the grueling, nerve-wracking, tension-laden, hot days of the first days of the advance. Up to that point, nobody had been either able or permitted to sleep a wink, which, however, would not have been bearable any longer.

A report on this:

"I had managed to keep myself awake for up to five days. Then my eyelids ineluctably dropped. Evidently there was a limit to the amount of sleep deprivation and desperate wakefulness which human beings could bear. The result was that we entered into our first action utterly exhausted, dripping with sweat, filthy, and otherwise provided with only meager rations."[65]

Despite the measures taken to make the mobile units largely self-sufficient for the first days of the campaign, the speed and depth of the advance meant that the panzer corps had soon left their support elements far behind. On occasion, fuel for tanks and vehicles had to be rushed forward in emergency airlifts, while soldiers often foraged for food to supplement their meager rations, an activity described in another anecdote involving 19 Panzer Division; like so many of the personal accounts in this narrative, it offers fascinating ancillary insights as well:

On one of these days, at the entrance to a Lithuanian village, *Oberleutnant* Lewerenz (7./AR 19) had commissioned me to take care of the necessary provisioning, because our field kitchen had not kept up. The "iron" rations were not to be touched. With a sidecar-motorcycle, I drove through the strung-out village and started by asking at the last house for bread, which was willingly given to me. After they had handed over the bread they had available, all the villagers directed me to the village grocer, who had built his wooden house in the shape of a rectangular fort with a courtyard. At my knock, a bearded, rather portly grocer in a black kaftan appeared, who declared in Yiddish: "I not have bread." Since he had been described by the other villagers as the wealthiest, but also the most miserly – which I found to be true – I shoved this fatso to one side and took a look at his warehouse, in which lay whole sacks of everything that our field kitchen could possibly need, just no baked bread. After loading the sidecar with round, strangely sour-tasting loaves of bread and eggs from the other villagers, I returned to our battery.[66]

Advancing mostly in ad hoc battlegroups – their columns strung out for 50 kilometers or more over the inadequate Russian road net – the German tank crews, motorized infantry and supporting combat units marched and fought for weeks on end, often without any badly needed breaks for rest, replenishment, or maintenance. By mid-August 1941, 24 Panzer Corps had yet to have a single day out of action, and despite its desperate need for rest and maintenance, and Guderian's pleas, OKH ordered its operations to continue.[67] No 21st Century "post-modern" western army would dare to even contemplate demanding of its soldiers what the Germans demanded of theirs (mobile troops and infantry alike) during the summer of 1941 in Russia.

8.2.2: German Panzer Generals led from the Front

Observes historian and former Swiss tank corps officer Rudolf Steiger: "When commanding armored units in particular, the situations change so rapidly, and the opportunities to make use of good luck pass so quickly that commanders should not confine themselves to posts far behind the lines."[68] As we have seen, German panzer generals led from the front. A glance at Guderian's memoirs accentuates this principle: The 53-year-old general was a whirlwind of purposeful activity, driving from one corps or divisional headquarters to the next, consulting with key subordinates, collecting information and issuing orders, and accompanying his troops at the point of the advance. In his recent biography of Guderian, historian Russell A. Hart succinctly outlines the general's command style:

> Despite the higher level of command [in France he had commanded a panzer corps] and the far greater scale of operations in Russia – with his forces stretched over hundreds of miles – Guderian continued to lead from the front as he had always done, irrespective of the tactical and operational limitations of this approach. His solution to the problem of distance was simply to drive himself, his chauffeurs, and his staff twice as hard. Repeatedly he came under direct enemy fire and on a number of occasions he had narrow escapes. But fortune continued to smile on him, at least for a while longer. Rapid deep penetrations bypassed large enemy forces that then tried to exfiltrate their way back through Guderian's forces to safety. The inability of the German infantry to keep up allowed many of these encircled forces to escape. Guderian blithely pressed ahead, indifferent to what went on behind him, where the situation rapidly became much more fraught. Guderian believed in safety through movement, a precept that was of little comfort to the much less mobile infantry.[69]

One of Guderian's narrow escapes occurred on the third day of the campaign (24 June). At 8.25 that morning, he drove toward the front at Slonin, where fighting was still in progress. On the way, he encountered Russian infantry that were sweeping the road with fire. A battery of artillery of 17 Panzer Division and dismounted motorcycle troops returned the enemy fire, albeit to no discernable effect. Guderian then joined in the action, firing the machine gun from his armored command vehicle. This succeeded in dislodging the enemy and he was able to drive on. At 1130 hours Guderian reached the CP of 17 Panzer Division on the western outskirts of Slonim. Here he found not only the division commander, Maj.-Gen. Hans-Juergen von Arnim, but the corps commander, General Lemelsen:

> While we were discussing the situation there was a sudden burst of lively rifle and machine gun fire in our rear; our view of the road from Belostok was blocked by a burning lorry, so that we were in ignorance of what was going on until two Russian tanks appeared from out of the smoke. They were attempting to force their way into Slonim, with cannons and machine guns blazing, and were pursued by German Panzer IV's that were also firing heavily. The Russian tanks noticed the group of officers, of which I was one, and we were immediately subjected to a rain

of shells, which, fired at such extremely close range, both deafened and blinded us for a few moments. Being old soldiers we had immediately thrown ourselves to the ground; only poor Lieutenant-Colonel Feller, who had come to us on a mission from the Commander of the Training Army, and who was unaccustomed to active service, was too slow and suffered a very painful wound as a consequence. Also, the commander of an anti-tank battalion, Lieutenant-Colonel Dallmer-Zerbe, received a severe wound from which, I regret to say, he died a few days later. The Russian tanks succeeded in forcing their way into the town where they were eventually put out of action.[70]

Having survived the encounter, Guderian visited the front line at Slonim, then took a Panzer IV straight through no-man's land to Nehring's 18 Panzer Division. By mid-afternoon, he was back in Slonim, from where he soon struck out for his panzer group command post at Pruzhany – a drive which took him directly across the path of a clutch of Russian infantry, who were dismounting from there vehicles on the outskirts of Slonim.

> I ordered my driver, who was next to me, to go full-speed ahead and we drove straight through the Russians; they were so surprised by this unexpected encounter that they did not even have time to fire their guns. All the same they must have recognized me, because the Russian press later announced my death; I felt bound to inform them of their mistake by means of the German wireless.[71]

Guderian, of course, was not the only German panzer general whose propensity to fight from the vanguard resulted in close scrapes, or even serious injury, in the summer of 1941. General von Arnim was wounded in late June 1941,[72] and forced to relinquish command of 17 Panzer Divison; General Model, the tempestuous commander of 3 Panzer Division – who "kept turning up, monocle in place and cursing, at every crisis point"[73] – had a close call on 24 June, when the armored car he had only just vacated was obliterated by Russian artillery fire.[74] General Schmidt, Commander, 39 Panzer Corps, barely escaped from a dangerous encounter caused by his own reckless behavior on the fourth day of the war. On 25 June, with his tanks advancing southeast from Vilnius toward Minsk, Schmidt personally led a terrain reconnaissance (*Erkundungsvorstoss*) at the head of his troops. In an article which appeared in a German newspaper several days later, Hans Hertel, an officer on the staff of the panzer corps, wrote about the incident:

> The troops had continued their attack the following morning at undiminished speed and boxed their way through the enemy resistance everywhere. But the rapid tempo was still not enough for the general of these troops [i.e., Schmidt]. He knew that speed was everything in this offensive. So he gave the order: forward, at any cost! [*Vorwaerts um jeden Preis!*] And then began an unprecedented chase. The general, accompanied by only a very few forces from a reconnaissance battalion and a few men from his staff, positioned himself personally at the spearhead, driving ahead in an open jeep in order to reconnoiter the best march routes.[75]

Yet the daring expedition into territory still teeming with Russians quickly turned sour. Schmidt and his small party were soon fighting for their lives, having been ambushed and surrounded by the Russians in a wooded area near Molodechno, with the general trapped in a ditch beside the road. Despite being assaulted from three sides by Soviet troops, collectively voicing their bone-chilling cries of "Urrah!," General Schmidt, keeping his composure, ordered his men to break out through the enemy lines. Under cover of darkness, Schmidt and his small party somehow managed to extricate themselves from their existential predicament and, early the next morning, linked up again with friendly troops.[76]

At the conclusion of his article, *Ordonnanzoffizier* Hertel praised the general for the example he had set for men. Schmidt's biographer, however, offers a rather different perspective on the general's behavior that day:

> Well, it's open to debate whether a reconnaissance foray by a corps commander is an encouraging example from a military point of view. If a general appears at the front with his troops, then he is providing his soldiers with a good example. However, if he ventures into the territory of enemy forces with only very weak cover, then in my opinion that's reckless and, in view of the unnecessary losses which could incur, irresponsible. After all, the corps could have lost its leader in that venture … Guderian's leadership principles – that a panzer general should lead from the front – were taken too far here. But even Guderian and other German generals had already exposed themselves to similar situations. It was, to be sure, in the mentality of the Prusso-German officer corps to lead their soldiers by example, and, in doing so, to occasionally disregard responsibility for their men and even themselves.[77]

Many months later Hertel would compose the following narrative, revealing the "method" in Schmidt's "madness:"

> By the onset of winter 1941, the officer corps of 39 Pz.Korps had, in percentage terms, suffered double the fatalities that the enlisted soldiers had. Such losses cannot be replaced in the long run, certainly not in terms of their quality: in view of the expected long duration of the war, they were not objectively justifiable, but they were the great secret for the exemplary discipline and admirable performance of the troops.
>
> At 39 Pz.Korps, the corps commander [Schmidt] is always right at the front, the chief of staff leads further back. The commander is always right there where the action is. He knows from the experiences of the First World War that a body of men only remains intact if the officers set a good example. On the first day of the Russia campaign, he crossed over the frontier with the combat engineer spearhead, during panzer attacks, he drives ahead of the panzers in an open command car. He gives no quarter to officers who fail, even in the slightest, to maintain their bearing and sends them straight home. This all gets round very quickly and all the soldiers have real trust in their "Papa" Schmidt. Yet he's not some sort of daredevil with a "sore throat" (this means a desire for medals to wear round the neck, e.g. the Knight's Cross and so on) or consumed by some sort of abnormal ambition. He certainly isn't some sort of chauvinist, more like a cosmopolitan, but really properly rooted in Germanness.[78]

There was an amusing postscript to this incident of 25 June 1941. From the shot-up and abandoned vehicles of Schmidt's reconnaissance party, the Soviets had salvaged a trove of documents. That evening, Moscow radio made a special announcement, declaring the complete destruction of German 39 Panzer Corps and the death in battle of General Schmidt. During the announcement, the names of all German officers ostensibly killed in the action – among them, Hans Hertel – were read out. The next morning, the same report was aired by the British Broadcasting Company's (BBC) German language broadcasts. At home, in Weimar, Germany, Frau Schmidt received a sympathy visit from an acquaintance, appropriately attired in a black suit and tophat. Even the C-in-C of the Army, Field

Marshal von Brauchitsch, was sufficiently alarmed by the foreign radio reports to place a telephone call to the staff of 39 Panzer Corps. To put the rumors to rest, special reports were promulgated by the German press, while General Schmidt was interviewed by a Dr Ernst from Radio Cologne (*Reichssender Koeln*) on the captured airfield at Molodechno.[79]

8.2.3: T-34s, KVs and "Stalin Organs"

While the T-34s and KVs were relatively few in number, and, for the most part, poorly led, they did force the Germans to take notice. On the first day of the war, 7 Panzer Division had been roughed up on its approach to Olita by T-34s fighting in hull-down positions; on 6 July, a tank battalion of 3 Panzer Division suffered heavy losses from a handful of well-concealed T-34s during combat along the Dnepr River line. Three days earlier (3 July), Nehring's 18 Panzer Division, advancing on Tolochino from its bridgehead over the Berezina at Borisov, had its first encounter with both T-34 and KV tanks. General Nehring recalled the event:

> The aerial reconnaissance of the division's flying squadron, which had always served us excellently, had, on 2 July, reported the approach of 100 tanks, including very large ones. So the division was prepared for new developments when the advance, in accordance with orders, was continued on 3 July along and to both sides of the highway toward Smolensk – Moscow ...
>
> The two tank spearheads collided at Lipki, east of Borisov. It was a tough battle, in which both T-34 and 52-ton tanks appeared for the first time, and whose armored plating our "little tank guns" [*Panzerkanoenchen*] were not able to penetrate – and certainly not the anti-tank guns we had then, of 37mm caliber, and not even the few available 50mm guns. Despite this, the Russians withdrew from the battlefield, leaving many heavy tanks behind – whether because of their poor leadership, or because of the fortitude of our own [tank and AT] crews, or because of our flexible tactical leadership, or thanks to our excellent gunnery. Our shells may not have penetrated – but they hit home! The writer [Nehring] saw immobilized 52-ton tanks with our 50mm shells buried up to the guiding ring in their armor plating, causing the crews to bail out ... In order to engage the heavy Russian tanks with some hope of success, 88mm Flak or 100mm long-barrel cannon of the divisional artillery were [subsequently] always brought right up front – a measure which really proved its worth on 7 July in the area of Tolochino (former quarters of Napoleon I).[80]

An officer in 18 PD's 18 Panzer Regiment also described the division's rude introduction to the T-34 at this time:

> Early morning 0700 hours, between Borisov and Tolochino, *Panzeralarm*. From the right comes a Russian tank battalion at "full speed" and attacks us. *Hauptmann* Kirn, with the 1st Battalion, fires furiously, but all hits simply slide off: the first T-34s. Horror grips us. Only a wet field separates us from the Russians. They drive at full throttle into the marshy ground and 11 T-34 tanks get stuck. The remaining tanks turn back, luckily for us. Now we wear the others down with our firing; they slowly climb out and we take 11 tank crews prisoner, with their commander and adjutants. The Russian commander is deeply impressed.[81]

In a diary entry on 25 July 1941, Major "S.," a tank battalion commander in 20 Panzer Division, vividly illuminated the visceral shock evoked by these early encounters with Soviet T-34 and KV tanks. On this day, Major "S." and his battalion took part in a harrowing engagement against a heavy Soviet tank brigade. After expending their armor piercing rounds on a KV-1, to no effect, the major and his crew discovered that their tank's engine would no longer turn over. Immobilized and out of shells, they abandoned their machine. Evading the Russian tank's machine gun fire in a desperate "cat and mouse" game, they managed their escape:

> Gradually, a reaction of nervous tension made itself felt amongst us. Somewhat exhausted, we went a little way back along the road, up to a street attendant's cottage, where we sat down on a bench to rest. From there we had a good overview of the battlefield in the sunken ground. We saw both our own and enemy tanks which had been put out of action, but none combat ready from either party. About 100 meters away from us stood a burning T-34 which, as was later ascertained, had been shot into flames by the commander of 6th Company. Half an hour later it blew sky high with a dull crack, flinging the turret 30 meters away. Further back at the forest edge we saw a T-34 which had rammed one of our Panzer IIs. It had even climbed up it and then not been able to free itself. From a distance it looked like the mating of two dinosaurs. This scene was later referred to in the regiment as the panzer wedding.
>
> Of course some of my men had suffered a shock, as they were taken completely by surprise and attacked right up close by an opponent clearly superior in terms of weapons and armor plating. And even more so when they discovered that they had hardly any impact with their own little tank guns [*Kanoenchen*]. Who could hold that against them? One non-commissioned officer drove back into the area of Combat Echelon B with his tank, which had been severely damaged in the fight. There, sinking down exhausted next to *Leutnant* K., he told the following about his experience:
>
> "*Herr Leutnant*, it was terrible! One [of the Russian tanks] just advances up to me, I'm firing and firing, armor piercing shells, high explosive shells, with the machine gun. Hit after hit, but he doesn't notice any of it. And he's coming ever closer, his shots missing us by a hair's breadth. Shoots again, the shot tears the track shield from my tank. I can calculate when he will have the next huge shell in his barrel, then he will hit home. I'm only 30 meters away from him, and then another tank comes at me from the side, its barrel pointed at me. That's when my driver puts his foot down and we drive off between the two of them with gusto. They are better armored, better armed, and faster, what else could we have done? Look how I'm shaking!"[82]

Echoing the account of General Nehring above, Major "S." explained how the German panzer crews not only survived but, more often than not, emerged victorious from such engagements during the summer of 1941:

> If the Russian tank soldiers had had good leadership and the proper conduct, the destruction of my battalion would have been unavoidable … To be precise, the difficult fighting of that day in a near hopeless situation was overcome by the fighting spirit, greater marksmanship, and quick responses of the German *Panzermaenner* of all ranks.[83]

In his post-war manuscript, Kurt Werner Andres, a motorcycle messenger in 21 Panzer Regiment (20 Panzer Division) added additional insight into the reasons behind the success of German panzer crews:

> The diary entries [of German tankers] show clearly on the one hand the surprise of the German panzer crews at the appearance of the first T-34s and KW-1s on the battlefield and, on the other hand, the better fighting spirit, the quicker

reactions, the mental flexibility in the midst of battle, and not least the [superior] marksmanship of the panzer crews. "Battle between Pak and tank, and tank and tank is like a dual, he who fires faster and more accurately will be the victor," so Major S. in his diary entry of 25 July 1941.

In the context of blitzkrieg warfare, it was of decisive importance to deploy panzer units *en masse* in accordance with the motto of *Generaloberst* Heinz Guderian (1888-1954): "Not in driblets but in mass!" [*Nicht kleckern sondern klotzen!*] In contrast, at the beginning of the campaign, the Soviet tank tactics stood out by allocating their tanks to the individual infantry companies. This was surprising, because following the capture of Minsk, on 30 June 1941, we found in some officers quarters a film projector and several rolls of film which showed, among other things, in the form of a training film, the German panzer tactics during the French campaign.

Oberleutnant K. in his diary entries of 27 July 1941: "The Russian leadership is not employing [its tanks] operationally in large masses, a tactical plan cannot be discerned, and so their use is being frittered away in individual actions. It is incomprehensible, but it has always been like this. We would hardly have survived these days if the Russian, who shows himself as an individual to be brave and determined, had been well led."[84]

Despite the obvious superiority of Soviet T-34 and KV tanks, they remained more of a novelty – albeit a sobering one! – than an existential threat to the panzer crews and their commanders in the summer of 1941. (Numerous photographs from the period show curious German soldiers closely examining, even crawling about, the tanks.) Nevertheless, it is a truism that soldiers in all armies, at all times, are badly shaken whenever confronted by the fact that their opponent possesses weapons of superior quality; as the accounts above illustrate, this was certainly true of the *Panzermaenner* in Russia. Not until early October 1941, however, at the start of Operation "Typhoon" (the final advance on Moscow), did the alarm bells go off, when 4 Panzer Division was badly mauled by large packs of well-led T-34s south of Mtsensk. "This was the first occasion," acknowledged Guderian, "on which the vast superiority of the Russian T-34 to our tanks became plainly apparent.

> The division suffered grievous casualties. The rapid advance on Tula which we had planned had therefore to be abandoned for the moment ... Descriptions of the quality and, above all, of the new tactical handling of the Russian tanks were very worrying. Our defensive weapons available at that period were only successful against the T-34 when the conditions were unusually favorable. The short-barrelled 75mm gun of the Panzer IV was only effective if the T-34 were attacked from the rear; even then a hit had to be scored on the grating above the engine to knock it out. It required very great skill to maneuver into a position from which such a shot was possible.[85]

(*Note*: Later in the fall of 1941, at Guderian's urging, a commission consisting of representatives of the Army Ordnance Office and tank designers was impaneled to examine the problems posed by the T-34 and begin the development of new tank designs to counter it. The commission arrived in Guderian's sector of the front in late November 1941.[86])

Another new Soviet weapon, the highly-secret BM-13 "*Katyusha*" solid fuel multiple rocket launcher, was first used in mid-July 1941 – against German forces fighting west of Smolensk. On 13 July, 17 Panzer Division captured the critical rail junction of Orsha, southwest of Smolensk.[87] The next day, the railroad station there was overflowing with *Wehrmacht* trains and supply transports; these were taken under fire by a battery of *Katyushas* in the first battlefield test of the weapon system. The battery fire began in mid-afternoon and lasted

15-20 minutes; about 100 132mm caliber rockets struck the rail yards, blowing up German ammunition trains and fuel tank cars, and turning the yards into a flaming inferno.[88]

On 15 July 1941, the *Katyusha* battery was again in action, this time against 12 Panzer Division at Rudnia,[89] midway between Smolensk and Vitebsk. About this action Soviet General A.I. Eremenko later wrote:

> We tried out this superb weapon at Rudnia, northwest of Smolensk. In the afternoon of 15 July, the earth shook with the unusual explosion of jet mines [rockets]. Like red-tailed comets, the mines were hurled into the air. The frequent and dazzling explosions, the like of which had never been seen, struck the imagination. The effect of the simultaneous explosion of dozens of these mines was terrific. The Germans fled in panic, and even our own troops near the points of the explosions, who for reasons of secrecy had not been warned that this new weapon would be used, rushed back from the front line.[90]

Despite the infernal racket made by multiple explosions, the Germans soon discovered that the rockets were not particularly accurate and the fragmentation effect was poor. The *Katyushas* were most effective as an area weapon – against troops caught in the open and lightly skinned vehicles. Against tanks the rockets had little effect, except for a rare and fortuitous direct hit. That the weapon could be extremely lethal, however, especially against troops unfamiliar with it, is beyond question. Recalled a former *Gefreiter* with the 14 Motorized Infantry Division:

> We weren't so afraid of ... the Stalin Organ. The casing was not thick, so the fragmentation effect was not great, but – large fragments, half shells lay around plentifully enough. A lot of earth was moved, but the deafening sound [*Krach*] was the biggest thing about it! You could see them approaching, but then, with time, we got wise to it: don't lie on the ground – like with artillery shells – stand ready, and then kick upward with the shifting sand or soil. In the beginning, we had too many losses to the Stalin Organ because everyone instinctively hit the ground inside their trench, and then they were buried by the soil movements and suffocated!
> Once, they shouted out over the trench loudspeaker: "Early tomorrow morning we will deploy the new 320mm rocket projector! None of you will survive the day tomorrow, so: Change sides tonight!" The 320s came and they came frequently after that – and I'm still alive today![91]

In the summer of 1941, the BM-13 multiple rocket-launcher saw only limited action. As many German war diaries and *Landser* accounts reveal, however, this would change dramatically in the fall of 1941, when the Red Army began to employ the weapon often, and to great effect, on the central front outside Moscow.

8.2.4: The Inevitable Outcome – Remorseless Attrition

In mid-July 1941, Lt.-Col. Smilo *Freiherr* von Luettwitz, Commander, 12 Rifle Regiment, took part in a commanders' conference on the outskirts of a village, somewhere beyond the Dnepr River. The regiment belonged to 4 Panzer Division, one of the most elite units of the *Wehrmacht*. The conferring officers were perched on several benches beneath a large apple tree in an orchard. It was a peaceful, idyllic scene. Suddenly, a shell from a heavy Russian gun burst atop the apple tree:

> [*Oberst* Dietrich von] Saucken and 4-5 others were critically injured, one of them died very soon after. Ecker and I, who sat right in the middle of all of them,

were thrown a long way clear by the air pressure, but not even scratched, an utter miracle! We immediately helped the severely wounded. I put pressure on the artery of an *Oberleutnant*, whose leg was ripped off, until the doctor eventually came. On the way back to the regiment, we washed off the blood in a puddle, great quantities of blood which plastered our entire uniforms.[92]

Scenes such as this were commonplace in Russia in the summer of 1941. Injury and death, when it came, was often sudden and unexpected.

In assessing the attrition of German mobile forces in the summer of 1941 it is instructive to begin with Clausewitz. Generally speaking, the debilitating effects of bad weather, terrain, poor roads, poor maps, tank and vehicle breakdowns, accidents, tactical errors, supply problems, human exhaustion and frailty, the unforeseen, and other phenomena too numerous to adumbrate, all fall under the rubric of friction, the "only concept," wrote Clausewitz, "that more or less corresponds to the factors that distinguish real war from war on paper."[93] The cumulative impact of such factors, coupled with inexorably hardening Russian resistance – by late July/August 1941, major, coordinated counterstrokes were underway across the central axis of the German advance – was to alarmingly attrit the panzer forces of both Hoth and Guderian while significantly slowing their pace of operations.

From the outset, the unexpected requirement to fight the cauldron battles to the bitter end – the result of tenacious Russian resistance – disrupted the advance of the panzer corps and caused serious casualties (29 Motorized Division, it will be recalled, alone losing 47 officers in late June 1941 while covering the sector of the Belostok-Minsk pocket west of Slonim).[94] As Robert J. Kershaw observes:

> The need to fight encirclements to annihilation had not happened before in [the Second World War]. It broke the tempo of Blitzkrieg. An ominous portent of the future had been the vicious battle for the citadel of Brest-Litovsk in the first days of the campaign … Encirclement battles at Minsk and Smolensk consecutively tied down more than 50% of the offensive potential of Army Group Center. In the west, creative General Staff planning had split and outmaneuvered the allied armies, which capitulated. The Russians doggedly fought on, whatever the cost. Inspired maneuver alone would not suffice to win battles on the new eastern front. The savaged opponent had first to be finished off, a time-consuming and costly affair. German "fast" motorized or panzer divisions were not configured for this development and were unpracticed in defense. They were badly mauled penning their fanatical opponents, waiting for the arrival of the infantry who were to administer the *coup de grace*.[95]

Racing rapidly eastward, the panzer corps were soon as much as 150-200 kilometers ahead of the marching infantry. Adeptly exploiting this vulnerability in the configuration of German forces – i.e., the ever-widening gap between the mechanized spearheads at the tip of the advance and the marching infantry bringing up the rear – the Russians tore repeatedly at the open flanks of 2 and 3 Panzer Groups. To counter their growing isolation, the armored combat teams improvised new defense and security measures – such as all-around defense (*Rundumverteidigung*) – which were often not even mentioned in German field manuals.[96] The further east the Germans advanced, the greater became the length of the front; because the front was often thinly held and far from contiguous, many gaps opened up, enabling Soviet forces, time and again, to attack and destroy rear area services and supply columns – missions also undertaken by Russian stragglers and partisans behind the front. In mid-July 1941, the diary of an officer in 18 Panzer Division recorded a Soviet ambush of the division's field hospital in Dobryn, resulting in heavy losses.[97]

Because the mobile units were constantly on the move at and beyond the forward edge of battle, sometimes becoming intermingled with, or even cut off, by Red Army forces, they were vulnerable to accidental attack by their own forces. In fact, such "friendly fire" incidents may well have contributed more to the attrition of the German armored forces than has been hitherto recognized. Recalled Kurt Werner Andres (20 Panzer Division): "Grievous [*bitter*] were the [friendly] losses resulting from the fire of our own weapons. In the excitement of the moment, it was not unusual for German tanks, mistaken for those of the enemy, to be knocked out [by friendly fire]."[98]

In modern warfare, with the antagonists normally separated by great distances, and employing horrifically destructive weaponry, getting killed or wounded by one's own troops with weapons intended for the enemy is an all too common occurrence.[99] In World War I, Adolf Hitler's own regiment, the Bavarian Reserve Infantry Regiment 16 (the so-called "List Regiment"), became a victim of "friendly fire" on its first day of combat in October 1914, during the First Battle of Ypres.[100] Paul Fussell, the late American cultural historian, discussing the large number of "friendly fire" incidents involving Anglo-American troops between 1939-45, saw in these and other types of deadly "blunders, errors, and accidents something very close to the essence of the Second World War."[101]

While several examples of such incidents among the troops of Army Group Center have been outlined in the preceding narrative, a few more will serve to reinforce this serious yet neglected theme. In his personal diary, *Leutnant* Georg Kreuter (18 Panzer Division) noted that a "high percentage" of his unit's losses on 22 June were the result of friendly artillery fire.[102] On 1 August, Guderian was caught in a *Luftwaffe* bombing attack, in which the "first bomb burst 5½ yards from my car;" the bombing caused "heavy casualties."[103] Several weeks later, as 2 Panzer Group drove south, into the Ukraine, the 2 SS Motorized Infantry Division *Das Reich* was set upon by more than two dozen *Stuka* dive bombers, whose bombing runs left 10 dead and more than 30 wounded *Waffen*-SS soldiers in their wake.[104]

The swift pace of the advance also meant that signal communications – radio and telephone – were becoming more difficult to maintain, while life sustaining lines of supply grew longer and more vulnerable. By the time of the Smolensk operation (July-August 1941) logistical problems were beginning to affect operations, in part because conversion of the rail lines from Russian broad gauge to European standard gauge was not proceeding with requisite dispatch. Shortages of spare parts were now appearing, as well as breakdowns in the delivery of supplies. Writes historian Kenneth Macksey:

> At this time in the German diaries, for example, that of the Chief of Staff of 2 Panzer Group, tales about the chaotic arrival of stores begin to appear. Mud shields arrived, but not vital parts for vehicles. On occasions concrete practice mortar rounds came forward instead of the real article. This was typical of what was happening.
> There was, therefore, a sort of steady decay: not total breakdown or anything like that, but things were not as good as they might have been, and this was beginning to restrict operations and make people more cautious. They looked over their shoulders, wondering whether tomorrow's supplies would arrive. Also, with the much more intense battles, ammunition expenditure was far higher than expected.[105]

Seriously exacerbating this slow, "steady decay" was the fact that the losses of the panzer groups (both personnel and materiel) were not being made whole. On 4 August 1941, when Guderian reported to Hitler at the headquarters of Army Group Center, in Borisov, he reminded his "Fuehrer" that only an "unbroken, steady stream" of new tanks, engines, and replacement parts – as well as aircraft – could keep the offensive going. Hitler replied that he needed all the new tanks and planes for "future tasks." Grudgingly, the dictator agreed to supply a month's production of new tank engines, nothing more.[106] Other than that, Guderian's panzer group and the rest of the tank forces would have to make do with what they had.

What they had, however, was, after six to eight weeks of continuous operations, markedly less than what had made up their orders of battle on 22 June 1941. Figures on tank and personnel strength for several of the panzer divisions of Army Group Center magnify this point:

- 3 Panzer Division, having entered the campaign with more than 200 tanks, had just 86 tanks in a combat-ready state on 30 July 1941 (with some 50 more in the workshops for repair).[107]
- 4 Panzer Division, by late July, had but 49 tanks ready for action (out of an initial complement of 177), with 83 more considered repairable. By mid-August, the division's motorized rifle companies had lost 50-70 percent of their combat strength, with many of "the best fighters" among the casualties.[108] By 31 August 1941, the division had suffered a total of 2325 casualties (dead, wounded, missing), while receiving only 528 replacements.[109]
- 7 Panzer Division, on 21 July 1941, reported a combat strength of 118 tanks, with 96 others under repair. To maintain its combat effectiveness, the division broke up one of its three tank battalions to keep the remaining two at effective strength. The division had begun *Barbarossa* with 265 tanks.[110]
- 10 Panzer Division, which had possessed 182 tanks on 22 June (including 45 Pz IIs, 105 Pz IIIs and 20 Pz IVs) had just five Panzer II and four Panzer III tanks fully combat-capable on 20 July 1941. An additional 25 Panzer IIs, 38 Panzer IIIs, and three Panzer IVs (many with minor engine damage due to a lack of oil) were considered capable of performing a defensive mission. Roughly 100 of the division's tanks required maintenance and repair.[111]
- 18 Panzer Division, which began the campaign with 218 tanks, had been reduced to 83 operational machines by 11 July – losses due, in part, to costly encounters with superior T-34 tanks. The division had also lost 2279 men, more than 13 percent of its manpower, in barely 20 days – an unsustainable loss rate of well over 100 men per day. By 28 July, 18 PD had suffered 765 dead (among them 63 officers) 1968 wounded, and 377 missing (including units temporarily under the division's control). Of its tanks, only 12 reached Smolensk in a combat-ready state. The division was so exhausted it was pulled out of the line for several weeks, undergoing rest and replenishment in the forests southeast of Smolensk.[112]
- 20 Panzer Division, by 26 July 1941, had incurred a total of 2085 casualties, for an average daily loss rate of 60. These losses embraced fully 35 percent of the division's officers, 19 percent of NCOs, and 11 percent of rank-and-file (compared to their respective marching out strengths).[113]

On 25 July 1941, General Lemelsen, Commander, 47 Panzer Corps, noted in his diary that his three divisions (17 PD, 18 PD, 29 ID (Mot.)) had sustained an average of 2200 casualties since the start of the campaign, while also losing up to 50 percent of their motor vehicles. "My divisions urgently require replenishment, but where it will come from no one knows," he wrote dejectedly.[114] Losses of officers, Lemelsen noted several days earlier, had been lamentably high:

16.7.[41]:
Yesterday evening, 29. [ID (mot.)] captured Smolensk despite fierce resistance. The 71 IR in particular distinguished itself here. House after house had to be taken with "cold steel" [*mit blanker Waffe*] and hand grenades, and in a city of 150,000 inhabitants, that's quite something.

The losses were considerable as a result. Many graves lined the road as I drove to Smolensk early this morning, including a large number of the most capable young active officers from 15 IR who had, until now, taken part in the entire war without injury. It's a real shame. *"Fallen for Greater Germany"* stands simply on the plain crosses. I even found the grave of *Leutnant* Keitel from 29 AR, the son of the Field Marshall, on that road today. Our best officers are dwindling away in this cruel war, which is so very different to that against Poland or even that in the west.[115]

The grinding attrition, particularly among officers (and NCOs), and the congealing Red Army resistance, were becoming growing concerns to the German Army High Command. Moreover, the first, quiet doubts about the future course of the campaign were beginning to emerge, as revealed by a diary entry of *Hauptmann* Georg Heino *Freiherr* von Muenchhausen, adjutant to Colonel Heusinger (Chief, OKH Operations Branch), in early August 1941:

The Russian has put up really strong forces opposite the eastern front of Army Group Center! And all those reserve armies behind them. Will we manage to smash him before Moscow? The supply problem is becoming increasingly difficult for us, the losses in the panzer groups due to the attrition of materiel will continue to rise, even after replenishment, and the troops are increasingly battle-weary [*abgekaempft*]. And above all the high number of losses among the officers![116]

By late July 1941, the panzer generals at the front, and many of their officers and men, were also starting to question how much longer they could endure the high attrition rates yet continue fight effectively. As General Nehring, Commander, 18 Panzer Division, recalled in an article published in 1961: "Four weeks of storming forth without pause, with their immense exertions and hardships, had their effect on both men and materiel. Very softly the question began to arise: 'How can this continue?'" (*Wie soll es weitergehen?*)[117] As early as 11 July 1941, Nehring, sounding the alarm on the dangerous attrition in his division, had warned that the high loss rates should not be allowed to continue, "if we do not intend to victor ourselves to death" (*wenn wir uns nicht totsiegen wollen*).[118] Weeks later, on 22 August, Army Group Center acknowledged in its war diary that "the armored units are so battle-weary and worn out that there can be no question of a mass operative mission until they have been completely replenished and repaired."[119] Yet despite the battle-weariness, major operations went on; not only the panzer corps of Army Group Center, but the *Ostheer* as a whole, continued to consume diminishing resources in constant marching and fighting – as the battle lines grew in length, the combat increased in intensity, and replacements of men, machines and materiel reached the front in insufficient increments.

Despite the heavy losses, and many unforeseen challenges, the morale of the panzer troops remained high. In a letter to his father, tank gunner and reserve officer candidate, Karl Fuchs (7 PD) gushed with pride about his and his unit's accomplishments during the opening weeks of the campaign:

24 July 1941:

Dear Father

… It's been quite a while since you wrote to me and informed me of your transfer. When I received your letter, we were already on the march against the enemy. The weather was incredibly hot, and dust and dirt were our constant companions. From the north of East Prussia we advanced over Kalvaria to Olita. There I was involved in the biggest tank battle in history! The enemy was thrown back with heavy losses. Immediately we pursued them. On the third day of the campaign we reached Vilnius. The Lithuanian civilians had staged an incredible reception for us. We were literally showered with flowers!

After a day's rest we continued in the direction of Minsk. I was always up front in my tank, creating gaps in the enemy lines. Special radio announcements reported our accomplishments. When we heard them outside of Minsk, we were overwhelmed. Our company was given special orders and we carried them out to everyone's satisfaction. For a week, during our attack of Lepel and further on in Vitebsk, I was always in the lead with my tank. I will never forget those battle experiences.

Now we are already on the other side of Smolensk ... For me the battle itself is the biggest adventure and experience. During our attack on Minsk I received the Tank Assault Medal and I have been recommended to receive the Iron Cross, Second Class. Yes, we're moving forward toward victory and peace.

I hope that you are in the best of health. I greet you with our old battle cry: Germany, Sieg Heil!

Your loyal son, Karl[120]

8.3: *Infanteristen*

War is cruel. War is particularly cruel when it creates situations characterized by pitiless irony, or cynically juxtaposes seemingly incompatible realities, producing tragic outcomes which even its most hardened practitioners find difficult – if not impossible – to comprehend. Such events, of course, are the bloody currency of all wars, yet they provide a poignant human marker to the fundamentally impersonal statistical aggregations of dead, wounded, and missing in wartime that fill our history books. In this context, two personal anecdotes – representative of thousands like them, and gleaned from the recollections of *Landser* in central Russia, in the summer of 1941 – begin this section on German infantry.

In his war memoirs, published in 2004, then 21-year-old *Gefreiter* Willi Loewer, an artillery gunner in 129 Artillery Regiment (129 Infantry Division) described a chance encounter in late-July 1941 with his brother, also a combat soldier in 129 ID. It would be their final meeting:

Calm in war is often deceptive; surprises were more often the rule than the exception. And so it was for us. The "Fury" war drew onward and we with it, to the east. On 25 July 1941, we reached the battle area of Smolensk, which was many square kilometers in size. During the march into this area I had a great surprise. As if through an act of providence, I met my brother Heinrich, who also served in 129 ID ... We had the same advance route and met often during those days. On the evening of 27 July, our battery was located in a beautiful valley, protected on all sides, in the area of Smolensk. We waited for our field kitchen to distribute food and rations. To my great joy, my brother Heinrich also came by. He had seen our tactical sign, and his company [2./IR 430] was bivouacking very close to us. In the meantime, our field kitchen had arrived and had brought a great many good things. There were noodles with goulash and rations for the following day, tea with rum to drink: a princely meal.

I asked my brother: "What do you have in your canteen?" "What else am I going to have? Black coffee," he replied. "Chuck it out, I'll give you some of our stuff," I said. I went to the [cook] with two bottles. He greeted me with "So one bottle isn't enough for you anymore, then?" I explained to him that my brother in the infantry was visiting us and they didn't have such delicacies. Without further ado, he filled both bottles. Heinrich was visibly delighted, and we sat together a while longer and talked. He told me as well that they would be attached to an assault party at dawn. It was getting dark by the time he eventually said goodbye. I felt almost compelled to look after him as he went. After a while he turned round and waved to me; neither of us knew that we would not see each other again.[121]

The next morning, at dawn, Loewer's battery of 150mm medium field howitzers opened fire in support of an infantry assault. Disgorging as many as eight shells per minute – although Army regulations limited the rate of fire to just four – the gun barrels became too hot to touch. Loewer's battery soon ran low on ammunition; yet despite heavy enemy counterbattery fire, replacement shells and cartridges were hustled forward with assistance from a nearby reserve infantry platoon:

> As I later discovered, our infantry had to repulse a tank assault, which was kept in check by us through observed and sustained fire.
> It went on. The Russians intended to break out of a huge cauldron near Smolensk in which they were trapped … They even succeeded in breaking through the encirclement in places. My brother's platoon was also deployed in these battles. Not one of them returned to the company. All the soldiers of that platoon have been missing to this day. To find not the slightest trace of 30 young soldiers, barely more than 20 years old, after combing the battlefield, was more than mysterious.[122]

One can only speculate as to the precise fate of Heinrich Loewer and the others in his platoon (and why their bodies were never found). In all likelihood, however, they were captured by the Russians and summarily executed – a grisly outcome at once suspected by Willi Loewer: "We had been told that the Russians did not take prisoners … I cursed the war, God and the world. I was for the moment no longer capable of fulfilling my role as a gunner. On orders from our platoon leader, our gun crew chief took over my position."[123]

About 25 July 1941, *Unteroffizier* Wilhelm Wessler (6 Infantry Division) and his company arrived in the area of Velizh, on the upper Dvina northeast of Vitebsk. From there, the strenuous marching went on, accompanied by heat, dust and thirst – the men pitching camp after a long march on 27 July on some rising ground adjacent to several houses. To the relief of Wessler and his comrades, the next day (28 July) was set aside as a rare day of rest for the company, a time normally used for cleaning weapons, doing maintenance on vehicles, resting overworked horses, and catching up on personal hygiene. Yet what began as a bucolic summer day, filled with coveted rest and recuperation, suddenly turned jarringly lethal:

> The company was woken at 0800 hours. Our orders for the day's duties were clothing and weapons maintenance. Comrades gave me monies to be sent home and, at 1200 hours, I handed them over to the paymaster.[124] As a thrifty person, I put RM 80 into my savings account. It was a glorious sunny day; dressed only in swimming trunks, every man relaxed in his own way.
> Shortly after 1400 hours it was my turn to have my hair cut by our company barber, Fritz Gauseweg. While having my hair cut, Russian bombers suddenly thundered along over us. I heard the whistling of bombs and dashed literally head first into a pit. This leap saved my life, because at that very moment, there was an explosion. One of the bombs struck only a few meters away from my pit, right next to an ammunition truck which immediately caught fire.

The Russian had done a pretty good job with those bomb drops; <u>the following result</u>:

The chair on which I had sat still stood there. Beside it lay Fritz Gauseweg, scissors and comb still in his hands. The bomb had ripped away the top of his skull.

<u>Those killed were</u>:

Schuetze Schmelzer (my batman),

Schuetze Specht,

Fritz Gauseweg – he lay so close to the ammo truck that his body had partially burned.

While the ammo truck burned, the ammunition blew up with a rattling crack. Everyone took to their heels, fearing a massive explosion …

Suddenly I hear a scream; Rudi Roethemeier (our company shoemaker) is lying close to the ammo truck. With a bound, I'm next to him, blood spurting from a vein in his leg like a fountain. How I got hold of some underwear and a piece of wood, I don't know any more. I fashioned a tourniquet on his leg with them. Although he had a small build, I only managed to get him away from the vicinity of the ammo truck with a great deal of effort.[125]

Along with three dead, and the destruction of the ammunition truck, all of the nearby combat wagons and infantry carts were destroyed by fire, along with the paraphernalia of the baggage train and several draft horses. Also lost was most of the men's clothing and equipment, along with Wessler's accountant's box and the 300 Reichsmarks it had contained. The men's rifles, neatly stacked in pyramids close to the burning ammunition truck, were oddly untouched.[126]

8.3.1: Equipping, Clothing, Feeding

While a relatively modest number of panzer and motorized divisions provided the *Barbarossa* invasion force with its cutting edge, the marching infantry remained the backbone and the "workhorse" (*Arbeitspferd*) of the *Wehrmacht*. Out of the 145 divisions (including OKH reserves) that comprised the *Ostheer*, more than two-thirds (103) were regular infantry divisions. Of Army Group Center's 50.5 divisions on 22 June 1941, 31 were infantry divisions – more than were available to either Army Group North or South (20 and 29, respectively). Yet Bock's army group had the lowest *percentage* of infantry divisions compared to other division types (armored, motorized, security, mountain) among the three army groups (just under 62 percent),[127] because it was the only one with two panzer groups.

The equipment and accoutrements of the German marching infantry in June 1941, while significantly updated, were not much different from what they had been at the turn of the century. Each enlisted man carried the Mauser 98K bolt-action rifle, a bayonet and hand grenades, while officers and NCOs were outfitted with machine pistols (normally the MP 40). The basic issue of rifle ammunition was 60 rounds, which were arranged in magazines of five bullets each and carried in black leather pouches attached to either side of the belt buckle in groups of three (six pouches in all, with two magazines to a pouch). In combat, the infantry soldier's standard field equipment (much of it organized in the so-called assault pack, or *Sturmgepaeck*)[128] included a canteen, cooking pot, bread bag, mess kit, poncho, tent square (*Zeltbahn*),[129] gas mask (often discarded, but its container used to carry other effects), blanket roll, and a hand spade (*Spaten*).[130] The latter item performed many vital functions and was one of the more critical pieces of standard equipment of the

German soldier. By the end of July 1941, when the *Vormarsch* of Army Group Center came to a temporary halt, the spade became the "weapon" of choice, as explained by a former *Landser* (6 ID):

> The construction of field positions is ordered – preparation of a *Hauptkampflinie*, a main battle line of defense. For the first time since the start of the campaign we are confronted with this term and with this activity. Until late into the night, we dig our foxholes in the hard, parched ground ... The only thing at hand for digging is the short infantry spade, the most important piece of equipment after the rifle. In the event of contact with the enemy, it's tucked behind the belt, close at hand; its steel plate functions like armor plating for the heart area. The sharpened edges work as a hatchet to chop away bushes and slender trees, even logs can be split into firewood with it. It is one of the close combat weapons.[131]

Fully laden (marching pack), the infantry soldier carried 25 to 30 kilograms of gear, to which might be added rations, extra ammunition (a crate of 300 MG shells weighed eight kilograms), and components for machine guns and mortars.[132] Recollected another former infantryman (26 ID):

> So we had a lot to cart around and that could only be achieved through hard training. Sometimes it got to be too much and I would dearly have loved to chuck the lot, but it couldn't be done and you just had to grit your teeth and bear it. So that the Machine Gunner 1 didn't have to bear the load of the machine gun alone ... we also helped, taking it in turns to carry the gun ...
>
> The demands were heavy, only a well-trained body could withstand that. That was why we had been drilled and toughened up for months beforehand. We were young, capable, and full of the ambition to fight as honorably for Germany as our fathers had done from 1914 to 1918.[133]

On the march into Russia – and, in many cases, even before the start of the campaign – soldiers readily discarded items considered extraneous, or turned them over to their baggage trains for safekeeping. The soldier's marching pack (*Tornister*), which remained to the rear during battle (minus the items which were also part of the assault pack), held, *inter alia*, a cooking pot, blanket, spare underwear, socks and shirts, cleaning utensils, a sewing kit, toiletries, and personal effects.[134] The helmet, weighing 1.4 kilograms, was not worn while marching, but attached by its chinstrap to the soldier's leather harness equipment or black leather belt. The rifle, weighing four kilograms, was normally slung over the shoulder while on the march, while the MG 34 was light enough to rest on the shoulder of an infantryman.[135] Each man was also provided with an oval identity disc, which hung on a string about his neck. The disc consisted of two separable aluminum halves, and was stamped with the soldier's name and the number of his field post or replacement troop. If the soldier was killed, one half of the disc was snapped off and provided to the burial officer or division chaplain.[136]

German uniforms of the period 1933-45 were "based on principles of simplicity and functionality," which had their origins in the Prussian Army of Frederick William of Brandenburg in the 17th Century. In fact, the uniforms worn by millions of *Wehrmacht* soldiers across the battlefields of Europe and North Africa were among the very best of any belligerent nation during the Second World War.[137] German uniforms and underclothing were made of both natural and synthetic fibers, with Germany's chemists during the 1930s leading the world in the development of rayon, a "highly versatile fiber matching the comfort standard of natural fibers" and helping to improve performance and economy.[138]

All soldiers who served with the infantry divisions wore the same basic gray-green (*Feldgrau*) field uniform. Its primary elements were long cloth trousers – tucked into the soldier's nail-studded jack boots – and a tunic (*Feldbluse*) made mostly of wool (the *Feldbluse* M-40 was 80 percent wool, 20 percent artificial fiber). Buttoned across the front, the tunic had a distinctive dark green collar, two shoulder flaps, and breast and side pockets; above the right breast pocket sat the Army emblem, "a spread-winged eagle, clutching in its talons a circular wreath containing a swastika."[139] The inner lining at the front of the tunic held a large packet of bandages, with a smaller one located in the right breast pocket. In the left breast pocket the soldier kept his record of service book that, in addition to his photograph, Army number, and address of next of kin, contained a rather detailed personal history (information on weapons training, inoculations, wounds, hospital stays, decorations, furloughs, etc.). In general, the soldier used his trouser and tunic pockets to stash important personal items, such as letters, photos, writing and eating implements, matches, paper, candles, string, pocketknife, can opener, smoking articles, and other paraphernalia.[140]

Other standard gear included a black leather belt, with a buckle emblazoned with the eagle emblem and the motto "*Gott mit uns*" (God with us); a field cap; collar bands (to reduce collar wear and provide the soldier with additional comfort by protecting his neck from the course fabric of the tunic); shirts and underclothing, made principally from a mixture of cotton and rayon; and socks, the most common types being webbed with wool and rayon material. The Russian system, which involved wrapping a flannel band (40 x 40 cm) around the feet, was quite popular with the troops, although it required some training to master.[141]

As a basic issue, each soldier received two sets of underwear, socks and foot wrappings, and was responsible for doing his own laundry;[142] however, as the campaign progressed, Russian women, or Russian volunteers serving with the German Army, often relieved the *Landser* of this duty. Although the troops regularly required new clothing, this was something of a luxury, given the enormous logistical demands, and more pressing requirements, of the armies in the east. In 12 Infantry Division, which fought with Army Group North during 1941, the men received a new pair of socks about every two months, a change of undergarments and a new shirt every six months, and a new uniform only once a year. As a result, "uniforms disintegrated in the field and, after heavy combat, many troops looked more like gypsies than soldiers."[143]

The German steel helmet (*Stahlhelm*), the dull gray or gray-green Model 35,[144] was a sophisticated piece of equipment which required a costly and laborious manufacturing process. Derived from the Model 1918 of World War I, the helmet was made from smooth sheet steel, 1.1 to 1.2 mm thick, and came in five sizes.[145] The excellent Model 35 was the helmet with which the German soldier went to war in September 1939; later models, however (e.g., Models 40 and 42), underwent a decline in quality. Nevertheless, the iconic German steel helmet of 1939-45 survives "as the trademark of the Nazi soldier to this day."[146]

The distinctive marching (jack) boot (*Marschstiefel*) was a uniform item harking back to the days of Otto von Bismarck's Prussia, or beyond; since the 1860s, it had been popularly characterized by the troops as the "dice shaker" (*Knobelbecher*). Worn by all German combat infantry in World War II, the boots were manufactured from high quality blackened cow leather; to enhance wear, the boots were fitted with doubled soles reinforced by 35 to 45 hobnails. The heels were reinforced by an indented iron plate along the outer rim.[147]

Yet as good as the clothing and accoutrements worn by the German soldier generally were, they were, nevertheless, in the assessment of one German general, "too heavy for summer. As a result, men perspired too easily, became very thirsty, and were soon caked with dirt."[148] Because commanders were intent on preserving tight discipline, during the initial days of the advance into Russia the troops were – in some cases at least – forbidden from unbuttoning even the top button on their tunic, despite the oppressive summer heat. For example, it was not until 4 July 1941 that the marching infantry of 9 Infantry Regiment (23

ID) were finally permitted to do so.[149] Yet as a former *Obergefreiter* in 77 Infantry Regiment (26 ID) recounted in his unpublished post-war memoirs, this tiny measure of mercy brought nary a scintilla of relief to the endlessly plodding infantry:

> We marched relentlessly onward in a blistering heat. Mariopol was stormed on 25.6.[41]. We were received rapturously by the populace. Everywhere in the villages, e.g. Swir, swastika flags were waved (heaven knows where they'd got hold of them so quickly) and we *Landser* were plied with food and drink.
>
> Then the march was continued in the mornings at 0500 hours until 1700-1800 hours. The sun burned mercilessly down from the sky. Since hardly any march relief was permitted – only the top button on the uniform jacket might be loosened – the sweat ran in streams down faces. With every step, we kicked up dust on the unsurfaced roads, and if we were overtaken by motorized vehicles, we all but disappeared in a dust cloud. In short: we were filthy from top to bottom, and the sweat congealed with the dust on our faces to form a gray mask. But we had to go on, even if our tongues were sticking to the roofs of our mouths. For, as the first infantry division following, we had to keep up with the motorized units.[150]

What did bring some relief was that many soldiers opted to set aside the heavy wool *Feldgrau* uniform in favor of their lightweight, olive green working or fatigue uniform (*Drillichanzug*). Every infantryman was issued a fatigue uniform during his basic training, using it for work details, cleaning weapons, and other duties likely to soil his clothing. The tunic was buttoned across the front (five buttons), had a closed collar, and two lower pockets without buttons. Both the tunic (*Drillichjacke*) and trousers (*Drillichhose*) were made of linen.[151]

The ration requirements of German forces in Russia were enormous. The daily ration of food for 6 Infantry Division, at full strength, amounted to some 30 tons; other divisions, no doubt, had similar needs.[152] Despite such colossal requirements, the pre-campaign planning of German logisticians envisaged the *Ostheer* subsisting off the land to the fullest extent possible (even if this meant a death sentence to millions of Russian civilians by starvation); as a result, each army group established special centers for storing and distributing captured supplies of all kinds.[153] Nonetheless, obtaining grains, livestock, foodstuffs, and forage for horses in requisite quantities from local sources often proved more challenging than anticipated.

Belorussia, which absorbed the full shock of Army Group Center's advance, was a poor agricultural region in Napoleon's time and still a primitive and backward land in 1941. In their diaries and field post, many *Landser* grumbled about the scarcity of fruits and vegetables along their route of march. On 29 August 1941, Dr Heinrich Haape (6 Infantry Division) complained to his diary: "Russia – A monotonous, uncultured and enslaved land! The only thing that is cultivated here is grain. No fruit, no vegetables – the people subsist under the most modest circumstances."[154] Another soldier of 6 ID recollected: "While in France the daily discussions were mostly about girls, in Russia we talked mostly about food."[155]

In fact, "vegetable cultivation was generally limited to small garden plots which barely covered needs of the civilian population," while "fruit was available only in the south, and then in limited quantities."[156] As a veteran of 14 ID (mot.) recalled, at a point several months into the campaign:

> The desire to eat some fruit or fresh vegetables for once turned our steps to the small gardens belonging to the houses. During the entire journey through Russia thus far I had not seen a single fruit tree, no cherries, strawberries, gooseberries, or blackcurrants in the summer, no apples, pears, or plums in the fall. The climate in [north central Russia] was probably unsuitable for cultivation. The population

cultivated only potatoes, cabbage, cucumbers, and onions in the little gardens around their huts, and only as much as would just last the winter. Nor did we come across different vegetables or fruit here either.[157]

Available stocks of food and forage were further diminished by Soviet scorched earth policies, the retreating Russians burning large quantities of grain and destroying many farm implements, while also taking with them some grain and most of the cattle from the collective farms. Despite such conditions, during the summer of 1941, the German invaders managed to secure much of their food supply from local sources, and to acquire part of the fodder for their horses in this manner as well.[158] A regular pastime of *Landser* across the eastern front was scouring the countryside and local villages – singly, or in small groups – for eggs, milk, poultry, livestock and other foodstuffs with which to supplement their often Spartan diet. The German soldiers even had a widely used slang term to describe these foraging expeditions – "to organize" (*organisieren*). In a telephone interview conducted on this author's behalf with Guenter Schulze – in the summer of 1941 aide-de-camp (*Ordonnanzoffizier*) to the commander of 18 Panzer Division, Walther K. Nehring – the interviewer summarized Schulze's recollections on the topic of provisioning the troops:

> The troops had lived primarily from the land during the advance: "We got everything from the civilian population." And rations were often extremely meager. (S. remembers, for example, soup made from boiled chicken bones, which he had got from the Russian civilian population and had only the slightest hint of flavor.) Frequently, not infrequently for over 3-4 days, there was hardly anything to eat at all. When you then received something to eat, you had to be extremely careful, because the body reacted very sensitively. Although there were still regular supplies of provisions, you "didn't notice them." The requisite provisions were generally "confiscated" from the countryside, "taken away from the civilian population."[159]

Although the invaders began the Russian campaign with strict orders not to accept food or drink from the local population – the acquisition of provisions was to be carried out by the proper military authorities – this was one regulation which was immediately flouted, as this account of 22 June underscores:

> As we continued onward, we saw the first German fatalities and also the first Russian prisoners. Further on, we went past a Russian provisions and clothing depot, from which we took some conserves, soap, towels, and blankets. Accepting food and drink offered by the civilian population was forbidden, and some civilians were offended by this …
>
> It was only in the evening that we caught up with [the rifle companies]. Everyone sank down exhausted for a brief rest in a meadow in the immediate vicinity of a large farmstead. We were thirsty, but our canteens had long been empty. What use is three-quarters of a liter of coffee for 24 hours under those exertions and in such great heat? We hadn't had lunch yet either. Here for the first time we violated the order and drank the proffered milk and water.[160]

German field rations included staples such as *ersatz* coffee and black bread. Food and beverages were generally prepared in bulk in horse-drawn, rolling field kitchens – their iron pots affectionately called "goulash-cannons" (*Gulaschkanonen*) in the idiom of the always famished troops – and then brought forward for distribution in insulated containers.[161] For all men, regardless of rank, the food was the same – "adequate but monotonous."[162] In his memoir, *Moscow Tram Stop*, Heinrich Haape repeatedly referred to the ubiquitous "goulash-cannon," the "huge iron pot" with the stew, which he and his comrades consumed daily in wearisome repetition. The special meal on 1 August 1941, however, was something to remember:

> [It] was a beautiful day – a day that had a holiday air about it. After breakfast we swam in the lake. There were few cases on sick parade and it was the first day of real relaxation since we marched from Suwalki for the attack on Russia.
>
> Our midday meal was special holiday food, too. For the first time we had not the one dish, churned round in the goulash-cannon, but three courses, served separately: goulash (we could hardly expect to miss that), potatoes and vegetables. It was a masterly performance on the part of the cook. Dehorn had another surprise for me after the meal. He had captured some eggs and had beaten them up with plenty of sugar. We had eaten nothing sweet for weeks and our systems craved sugar. While we greedily spooned the over-sweet egg flip into our mouths, I casually asked Dehorn: "Have you ever seen an opera?"[163]

(*Note*: By late October 1941, Haape and the men of his battalion would be eating horse meat in their goulash, the outcome of a sputtering supply system and the remorseless implementation of the Red Army's scorched earth policy.)[164]

In his fascinating and wonderfully illustrated history of the uniforms, equipment and personal items of the German *Landser*, Agustín Sáiz outlines the typical daily diet across the battlefields of Europe:

> Breakfast included bread – generally baked the day before or previously dried – marmalade, a solid honey substitute and some canned food, coffee, chicory or malt and margarine. Some animal fat and sometimes requisitioned butter completed the early morning meal.
>
> Lunch was the hot dish of the day. Pots and thermos flasks were filled with the "*Gulaschkanone*" stew, usually composed of potatoes, fat, legumes of some sort and anything of animal origin able to add color and taste to the whole … The usual ration of wheat bread, rye, barely or any other type of kneading cereal (even saw dust could be used) ranged between 250gr – 700gr and … included, in true German style, some fat to spread on it. Coffee, tea or other hot drinks along with some sort of dessert, a little cheese, fruit and some candies with added vitamins completed the soldier's main meal of the day.
>
> Dinner was a cold meal, generally consisting of canned meat or fish, margarine and a drink of some hot beverage that was deemed sufficient to keep a soldier alert during the long, sleepless nights.
>
> The monotony of the rations … was happily augmented by the arrival of a parcel from home or any extras that could be purchased at reasonable prices from the mobile canteen, which offered an ample choice of canned food, seasonings and some candies.
>
> Last but not least, under extreme conditions, alcohol was generally distributed. Many different kinds of liquor played a leading role in combating both the cold weather and harsh reality.[165]

In a letter to the author, Dr Walter Schaefer-Kehnert, a *Leutnant* in 11 Panzer Division in Russia in 1941, offered the unique insights of a former *Landser* into the victuals of the *Soldaten der Ostfront*:

> The "provisioning" of the troops was normally divided into three meals, of which one was "hot" from the field kitchen, e.g., a thick pea soup with bacon and pieces

of meat or goulash with potatoes and vegetables (for holidays). In the morning and evening, food was "cold," a base of ryebread (known as "*Kommissbrot*"), which would be cut into finger-thick slices, then spread with butter, margarine, or lard, and topped with sausage, ham, or cheese, or spread with jam.

During battle, hot rations were brought to the front by "ration carriers." During quiet periods, the soldiers would fetch their hot meals from the field kitchen in their own "mess kit." In contrast to the Russians, who had different food quality classifications for officers, non-commissioned officers, and enlisted men, in the German army all ranks received the same food from the field kitchen. In general, it was good and nutritious.

For cold meals there was so-called "*ersatz* coffee," known as *Muckefuck* by the *Landser*, which was made from roasted barley and chicory. To improve the flavor, a few "real" coffee beans were added in. There is a typical soldier joke: A group of *Landser* are discussing over their meal whether the warm liquid they happen to be drinking is coffee or tea, when the cook comes past with the jug and calls out: "Who wants more cocoa?"[166]

Of course, this "typical" diet was often unavailable to the soldier, particularly under the extreme conditions encountered in the Soviet Union. When normal rations were not forthcoming, the soldier fell back on his so-called iron rations (*eiserne Portion*). These consisted of a small bag with several hundred grams of hard zwieback (a biscuit, broken into small pieces) and a 200 gram can of meat; other items in the bag might include dried vegetables, coffee, or salt. These special rations were only to be eaten upon orders and "in cases of the most extreme need" – an intent which "soon proved to be unrealistic" due to the special hardships of the east.[167]

A few statistics will illustrate the enormous effort required to feed the German infantryman (or *Panzermann*, or *Luftwaffe* pilot) during the Russian campaign. From 22 June 1941 to 1 June 1942, the bakery company of 6 Infantry Division baked 2,380,000 loaves of bread, on average nearly 7000 loaves a day. The division's butcher company, with 20 butchers, slaughtered 4488 cattle, 928 sheep, and 2700 hogs over the same period. The reinforced 12 Infantry Division (Army Group North) had baked more than two million loaves of bread by the end of 1941 alone; it also slaughtered 3340 cattle, 1568 hogs and 190 sheep over the first six months of the campaign, providing its soldiers with 333,038 kilograms of beef, 124,818 kilograms of pork, 33,854 kilograms of fresh sausage, and 2489 kilograms of mutton.[168]

The requirements of an infantry division's horses were also immense, as historian R.L. DiNardo explains:

> All horses, whatever their breed, do share certain characteristics. The prime of these is a big appetite. Horses require an enormous amount of food. Even the hardiest horses need about 12 pounds of food per day. Larger horses proportionately require more food and water. A large cold blood can consume up to 20 pounds of food daily. In the absence of feed, horses can obtain sustenance by grazing on grass, but this would require about 8 hours daily.
>
> Horses can eat a wide range of foods. In the German Army, horse fodder consisted of a combination of oats, hay, and straw, with oats considered to be the best.[169]

With more than 5000 horses in the average 1941 German infantry division, the forage needs easily added up to 30 to 40 tons per day, per division. Of course, under the difficult conditions of the eastern front, such quantities often could not be had. Moreover, oats "were not widely sown in the Soviet Union," and while green fodder "was available in abundance," it could only be used under certain conditions.[170] In times of emergency (particularly during fall and winter of 1941/42), the horses were fed with straw from the thatched roofs of Russian peasant dwellings.[171] Something of the aggregate requirements of Army Group Center for horse fodder can be gauged from that fact that its two infantry armies, Fourth and Ninth Armies, began Operation *Barbarossa* with 129,000 and 87,000 horses, respectively.[172]

Any discussion of the German soldiers' diet would be incomplete without noting that cigarettes were often included in their rations, and were eagerly received in packages sent by loved ones from home. Enjoying a cigarette was, of course, a timeless ritual among soldiers of all nations, among other things helping to steady frazzled nerves before or after combat. As one former *Landser* observed, "Tobacco was also a comforter of the soul [*Seelentroester*] after many a difficult battle."[173] Recalled another eastern front veteran: "Although I only began to smoke near the end of the war (as our military situation turned more and more hopeless), the availability of cigarettes was surely significant for the combat strength (*Kampfkraft*) of the troops."[174]

On the eve of Operation *Barbarossa*, cigarettes and chocolates were distributed to troops across the eastern front. A careful reading of soldiers' field post and diaries makes clear that smoking, if not universal among the *Landser* in the east, was a commonly shared activity – a perspective supported by photographs of the period too many to count. Illustrative of the importance of cigarettes to the *Landser* are two *Feldpost* letters from the central front:

20 July 1941:
My dear parents! … Have also received the three little packages today and am truly grateful. Oh, German cigarettes are just too good. Just send cigarettes, tobacco, and cigarette papers. You have no idea how we crave cigarettes here. Buying cigarettes here in Russia is impossible. In any case, I haven't been able to spend any money at all since I set foot on Russian soil, at the most occasionally for milk, eggs, or chickens.[175]

3 August 1941:
My dear Parents [letter to his in-laws]: Yesterday I received your second package from Maierhofen. I really was pleased with the contents. I shared the excellent tobacco and quality cigarette paper with my comrades since that is the custom. No doubt you, dear father, remember this custom from the Great War. Cigarettes [seem] to be soldiers' bread and sometimes they are more important than the food we get. Russian cigarettes are for the birds![176]

When the "good" German cigarettes were unavailable, the soldiers made do with what they had. In August 1941, as 6 Infantry Division settled temporarily into positional warfare, many of the men began to smoke the local clover (*Kleeblumen*).[177] A more common alternative was a poor quality Russian tobacco, smoked by peasants and farmers, called *makhorka*. By all accounts, *makhorka*, with its high nicotine content, was nasty stuff. Horst Pagel, a 17-year-old *Luftwaffe* auxiliary (*Luftwaffenhelfer*) in 1945, who spent two years smoking *makhorka* in Russian captivity, offers this unflattering description of the tobacco:

American smokers would not even recognize this awful stuff as tobacco. For the average Russian of that time, it was the only tobacco … *Makhorka* … was a macho material … It was coarse in texture, chunky, it looked like dried out corn stalks chopped up into pieces, perhaps one quarter inch in length, one sixteenth to one eighth inch in diameter, gray-green in color ... To smoke it, it was manipulated into a kind of cigarette.[178]

Oberleutnant Siegfried Knappe (87 Infantry Division) recounted another characteristic of *makhorka* – one which, in this case at least, was useful in repelling a sudden Russian attack:

> The surrounded Russians, of whom we had not been aware, apparently had decided to try to break out under cover of darkness. They were attacking my battery, which apparently lay directly in their path, and my men were defending themselves and our guns and horses, although they had only rifles with which to do so. They could not see the Russians they were shooting at, but they could hear them – and they could smell them! The Russian soldiers smelled of *makhorka* tobacco, which had a very strong unpleasant odor. It was made of the stems of tobacco leaves instead of the leaves (only Russian officers were issued tobacco made of the leaves). This awful smell got into their thick uniforms and could be smelled for quite a distance.[179]

The Germans, it is noted parenthetically, often used Russian propaganda leaflets to roll their cigarettes (and as toilet paper).[180]

8.3.2: Marching

At 2200 hours on 23 June 1812, three companies of French light infantry slipped silently across the Neman in boats and fanned out onto the river's eastern bank.[181] So began the ill-fated march of Emperor Napoleon Bonaparte's *Grande Armée* into Czarist Russia, almost 129 years to the day before the start of Operation *Barbarossa*. In his magnificent novel, *War and Peace*, Leo Tolstoy brings to life the nature of the Russian retreat and the *Grande Armée's* advance:

> From Smolensk the troops continued to retreat. The enemy followed them ... The heat and drought had lasted more than three weeks. Every day curly clouds passed over the sky, rarely covering the sun; but toward evening the sky cleared again and the sun set in a glowing, red mist. But a heavy dew refreshed the earth at night. The wheat left in the fields was burnt up and dropping out of the ear. The marshes were dry. The cattle lowed from hunger, finding nothing to graze on in the sun-baked meadows. Only at night in the woods, as long as the dew lasted, it was cool. But on the road, on the high road along which the troops marched, there was no coolness even at night, not even where the road passed through the woods. The dew was imperceptible on the sandy dust of the road, more than a foot deep. As soon as it was daylight, the soldiers began to move. The transports and artillery moved noiselessly, buried up to their axles, and the infantry sank to their ankles in the soft, stifling, burning dust, that never got cool even at night. The sandy dust clung to their legs and to the wheels, rose in a cloud over their heads, and got into the eyes and hair and nostrils and lungs of the men and beasts that moved along the road. The higher the sun rose, the higher rose the cloud of dust, and through the fine, burning dust the sun in the cloudless sky looked like a purple ball, at which one could gaze with undazzled eyes. There was no wind, and the men gasped for breath in the stagnant atmosphere. They marched with handkerchiefs tied over their mouths and noses. When they reached the villages, there was a rush for the wells. They fought over the water and drank it down to the mud.[182]

The parallels between Tolstoy's historically accurate depiction of 1812, and the advance of Hitler's armies into Russia, are, of course, striking. Prior to the attack on the Soviet Union in June 1941, German generals and staff officers had carefully studied Napoleon's invasion of Russia and its catastrophic outcome. They were, of course, fully aware of the historic challenges posed by time and space in the Russian theater of war. In their cheerfully confident calculations, however, both problems – which had loomed so large in the *Grande Armée's* defeat – had been dramatically diminished by what was perhaps the seminal invention of the modern era – the internal combustion engine. Powered by the modern, fossil fuel driven engine – so their thinking went – the tanks, trucks, mobile artillery, and armored personnel carriers of the *Wehrmacht* would succeed where Napoleon had failed. There was, to be sure, a measure of logic in their calculus. Yet what the generals and their subalterns failed to fully appreciate was that three-quarters of Germany's mighty invasion force still marched at the same pace as Napoleon's foot soldiers in 1812 (or as the Roman legions some 2000 years before); that for the marching infantry, the realities of time and space – and their potential implications for success or failure – remained what they had always been.

As history informs us, perhaps with a certain irony, the *Grande Armée*, or what remained of it, actually made it to Moscow in September 1812; on the other hand, the modern armies of the *Wehrmacht*, or their remnants at least, collapsed in collective exhaustion on the city's outskirts in the fall of 1941.

The German infantry did two things in the summer of 1941 – they marched and they fought. After the initial frontier battles, however, they mostly marched, from dawn to dusk, until they caught up to the mobile units ranging far to the east. In the sector of Army Group Center, the infantry, after seemingly endless forced marches through the "vast oppressiveness of Belorussia,"[183] finally reached the forward edge of battle in mid- to late July 1941.[184] Typical were the experiences of *Gefreiter* Alois Scheuer (197 ID), as set forth in a letter to his wife:

Russia/26.7.41:

Dearest Friedchen!

  I finally have a chance again to write a letter to you after 10 days.

  I think we will march ourselves to death, we put 45 kilometers behind us nearly every day. We see and hear nothing of the enemy, the motorized units are always far ahead of us. Wherever we get through, the battles have always already taken place several days before. We march doggedly on, through destroyed villages, past fresh graves, always onward and onward.

  For the last few days I have had stomach problems for the first time, it must surely be because of the one-sided diet, because we're living very primitively. I also now have blisters and bleeding feet. Iodine and sticking plaster are the radical treatments for such troubles.[185]

A German training video, prepared for the Replacement Army (*Ersatzheer*), laid out the following guidelines for the marching troops:

• Everyone – Officers, NCOs and men – was responsible for maintaining good march discipline.
• Foot soldiers were to march on the left side of the road. The battalion commander was to ensure this. Load bearing and the manner in which weapons were carried was to be uniform. The muzzles of machine guns were to face to the back. Rifles were to be slung over the right shoulder.[186]

• Motorized columns were to keep to the right side of the road; vehicles to maintain uniform intervals.
• Rest areas had to provide opportunities for horses to drink. Drivers were to use rest periods for vehicle maintenance; men for cleaning weapons and equipment.
• Rifle squads were to be assembled off the roads during rest periods – keeping roads open for vehicle traffic.
• During the march, drivers of horse-drawn vehicles were to constantly check horses' harnesses and watch their gate. Axles were to be greased often.
• Sentries were always to be posted during rest stops, or stops for the day.
• Water was to be boiled before drinking; a handkerchief could serve as a filter.[187]

The brutal pace of the *Vormarsch*, the unholy trinity of heat, dust and thirst, forced the German *Landser*, particularly the marching infantry, into a daily existence that they often "found difficult if not impossible to accept."[188] Major Werner Heinemann (23 ID), in a field post letter to his wife, dramatically portrayed the rigors of the *Gewaltmaersche* (forced marches):

> 17.7.41:
> How can those back home even begin to fathom how many countless sacrifices and how much sweat and deathly exhaustion of the infantry soldier make up such pursuit marches as these? The apathy of man and horse is often <u>so</u> great, that not even a kind word helps … War is the toughest thing there is in life, and it is in the breathtaking tempo of our operations that the key to our rapid final victory lies. You have to have the courage to be tough, or else you can only conclude that you "can't go on!" Everything has to go on, and as fast as possible, but it's frequently bitterly difficult to have to demand everything and more, over and over again.[189]

What it was like to cover on foot 30, 40, 50 kilometers a day and more, often carrying a full pack, desperately short of sleep, hungry, thirsty, tormented by dust, heat and insects, pushed to the point of exhaustion and beyond, is encapsulated in a *Feldpostbrief* written by soldier Harald Henry on 4 July 1941:

> We're wet through all over, sweat is running down our faces in rivers, not just sweat but sometimes tears too, tears of helpless rage, desperation and pain, squeezed out of us by this inhuman effort. No one can tell me that someone who isn't an infantryman can possibly imagine what we're going through here.[190]

Each low hill seemed to be followed, in infinite succession, by another low hill, which looked exactly the same as the one before it. A German war correspondent wrote that, when a German infantryman told of his experiences in Russia, the first thing he noted was that, although the country was flat, all "roads go up hill irrespective of the direction in which they run."[191] Or so it seemed, in any case. The correspondent added that the German soldiers' "greatest efforts" did not come during battle, even though they fought tenaciously; rather, it was the "tremendous spiritual effort" the *Landser* had to make to overcome the virtually endless distances.[192] The boundless spaces disturbed, even depressed, the troops. "We had many soldiers," observed one veteran, "who became melancholy. Flat valleys, flat hills – flat valleys, flat hills, endless, endless. There was no limit. We could not see an end and it was so disconsolate."[193] Said another: "If the column comes off the road and moves on a compass bearing across fields, we look like lost world circumnavigators seeking new coasts beyond these oceans."[194] Writes military historian James Lucas:

Nothing within the experience of the German soldiers had prepared them for the size of the country through whose vastness they were marching. They passed fields of sunflowers or maize extending from one horizon to another; mile after boring mile of golden-yellow monotony – a monotony broken only when sniper fire came from the jungle of green stalks below those golden heads. The march snaked its way past woods of such dimension and of so primeval a growth that only token incursions could be made in pursuit of Red Army units who fled into them. The Army crossed unembanked rivers often half a mile in width and always fighting against an implacable, cunning enemy who might strike out of nowhere and then vanish completely.[195]

In a field post letter to his family on 24 June 1941, Lt.-Gen. Gotthard Heinrici, Commander, 43 Army Corps, offered his initial impressions of the *Vormarsch* into the Soviet Union:

Blistering heat, just like the last two days. The only available way of advancing is along the broad Russian sand tracks, through which we wade, ankle-deep in dust. Every step, every moving vehicle, churns up impenetrable clouds of dust. The advance routes are characterized by yellowy-brown clouds that stand out against the sky like long shrouds. Man and horse are suffering dreadfully from the heat. At every stop the soldiers fall to the ground like flies and sleep, lying right in the dust, in the little shade thrown by a vehicle. Faces aren't dusty, they're thoroughly encrusted with sand.

At 1000 hours I was with the Army in Kamieniec. *Feldmarschall* von Kluge gave us march objectives which were difficult to achieve under the weather conditions, and particularly with the inadequate supplies coming over the Bug bridges. Despite this, we reached them in the evening, though only by stretching our willpower to the utmost. In three days we have traversed the route from the Bug at Mielnik to the northeastern edge of the forest at Bialowieza. The advance detachments are already far ahead of that. It is an incredible achievement. And many troops still don't have their field kitchens with them and are living off their iron rations. However, the land also has to give up a lot to them. Chickens, pigs, and calves are giving up their lives in plentiful numbers. A bread shortage is beginning because it isn't possible to bring up provisions, since the paltry bridges built by the engineers are still choked with combat vehicles. The divisions are stretched out in depth up to 100 km.[196]

In a letter the next day (25 June), soldier Karl-Gottfried Vierkorn (23 ID) echoed the general's observations, while also revealing his towering sense of superiority over the beaten Russian enemy:

In the week we have behind us, we got barely any sleep, only marching, marching. In between times often in firing positions and being shot at with a vengeance. We only advance on sandy tracks. Man and animal are completely exhausted. We seem to have overestimated the Soviet Army – many prisoners, half ape-like and with shaved heads, poorly equipped and, so it would seem, on a low cultural level; many pass us by like that. The country has many charms: endless cornfields, vast forests, some of them primeval in appearance, now and then little farmsteads, and villages with typical wooden houses, draw wells, and cattle herds. The population seems helpful and friendly. Yesterday they showered us with flowers and put water and cool milk along the sides of the road against our infernal thirst and the dust.[197]

One of the worst constituents of the brutal forced marches was the sheer boredom: "The repetitive rhythm of the march had produced a mask of monotony on every face; a cigarette would dangle in the corner of the mouth. Smoke would not be inhaled, the aroma would simply waft around the marching soldier."[198] One veteran calculated that a single step covered 60 centimeters – "men took shorter or longer paces, but this was the average" – so 50 kilometers amounted to some 84,000 paces.[199] Conversations soon died down on the long marches, replaced by the "monotonous clatter of gas mask cases, field spades, bayonets and ammunition belts. The view of the marchers sank and remained fixed on the back of the man ahead."[200]

Along the route of advance, the marching infantry filed passed the residue of the battles which had preceded them: burnt out tanks and vehicles; demolished villages, their houses of wood and straw reduced to ash and cinder; homeless Russian civilians, old men, women and children, sifting through the remains for anything salvageable; dead horses, their bodies bloated by the merciless summer heat; and the ubiquitous, "simple and dignified birch bark crosses"[201] which marked the graves of fallen German soldiers. And above it all, observed one soldier, "there hung the stench of destruction: a disturbing mixture of the abattoir and putrefaction pervading the air with a stagnant decadence over our column."[202]

Men fell asleep while marching; others became victims of heat stroke or exhaustion; occasionally, a soldier crumpled and died. The physical toll was made worse by the inevitable damage to men's feet: "Feet already bruised by rutted roads began inexorably to rub on boots. Friction with each step produced blisters and calf-high boots became excruciatingly hot. Such discomfort stymies interest in all but the most immediate issues."[203]

In his diary, *Stabsarzt* Hans Lierow, a doctor in 37 Infantry Regiment (6 ID), depicted the rigors of the *Vormarsch*:

24.6.1941:
Six hours' sleep in the tent. It is 0630. Heavy gun and machine gun fire from the Neman wakes us. We're supposed to cross over today ... The sun shines down from a cloudless sky. From 1100 to 1200 hours crossing over the Neman with pneumatic boats. Bridge blown up by the Russians 20 minutes before arrival of German spearhead ... There are supposedly 130 Russians in the forest. Forests are, for the most part, fleetingly searched or not at all. Loss of time and unnecessary losses ...

March continues in the early evening. *Oberstleutnant* Hennicke brings the news that an enemy artillery battery is ahead of us, which is to be captured. The battalion marches toward it with weapons at the ready. 24-pound ammunition boxes on left and right shoulder straps, 15 km in 3 hours straight across very hilly countryside. I took the load from the last ammunition box carrier on one occasion. But I was soon drenched in sweat.

27.6.1941:
Already in the morning [there is] an awful heat and a lot of dust. The road leads south. Against expectations, there's soon a rest stop from 1200-1500 hours ... We're by a lake, a cool breeze refreshes us. Sweat and dust are washed off in high spirits.

28.6.1941:
There's more trampling on, the direction isn't consistent, sometimes to the east, or south, or even to the west. The first updates about the overall progress of the war so far gradually seep through. If we carry on like this, we'll soon have beaten Russia.

29.6.1941:

Sunday: We work our way through the deep, deep sand without stopping ... However, the passenger car now had to be pushed through the sand and that takes sweat. The marching is much more difficult than it generally was in France. It has rained, the dust is gone, but the sandy paths have become even more difficult.

3.-8.7.1941:

The last few days were filled with putting back around 25-30 km a day. The roads became more bearable ... Refreshing baths were taken at a bivouac location. In the afternoons we usually go to our quarters, wash, bathe, eat, drink, and sleep. We don't go into the shabby houses, with their thatched roofs, because of the horrendous number of fleas. We live in tents ... If it can be come by, the floor is lined first with straw, then with blankets. At any rate, we all sleep well, because we are dog tired.

I regularly visit the companies after the soldiers have rested for over 3-4 hours. I mostly find abrasion wounds on feet, as well as gastric troubles. The soldiers are permitted to sit up on ammunition and weapons wagons and armored vehicles ... The battalion transports 12-15 soldiers with march injuries in this manner. There are also a few who affect to have injuries and they are handled rather roughly and ruthlessly ... There has been no contact with the enemy. Individual Russians come out of the forests, are hungry, and come into the prisoners' camp. The populace is poor, very poor.

10.7.1941:

The heat is crazy. We march very early in the morning, setting out around 0300 hours. That means getting up at 0130 hours. But it's already hot at 0700 hours. We soon arrive at new quarters, then wash, eat, and sleep, as much as the mosquitoes and flies permit it ... My soldier's heart finds participating in the war as a doctor vulgar as well as unpleasant. Now I've got men with foot problems and weak hearts. I'm prohibiting unboiled water, and raw milk, bacon and ham as booty, and I'm still the man who can't make foot injuries better, or dyspeptics back to happy eaters fast enough.

11.7.1941:

I exchanged a few happy words today at midday with *Stabsmusikmeister* Koch, 58 years old, when he drove by in the car. His burial was this evening at 2000 hours. Heat stroke.[204]

To combat fatigue, the *Wehrmacht* made use of a stimulant called Pervitin. The drug, developed by a Berlin-based pharmaceutical company, had first been introduced in 1938, and quickly became popular among the German civilian population. In the military, the drug was first tested on Army drivers during the invasion of Poland; between April and July 1940, more than 35 million tablets of Pervitin and Isophan (a slightly modified derivative) were shipped to the German Army and *Luftwaffe*. According to a 2005 article at the German magazine *Der Spiegel's* internet site, the drug was widely used during the French campaign of 1940; and although Pervitin was classified as a restricted substance on 1 July 1941, 10 million tables were shipped to the troops in 1941. It is unclear, however, just how widespread use of the stimulant may have been during the Russian campaign. In his diary, Dr Hans Lierow (6 ID) stated he administered the drug to his battalion commander (in the winter of 1941), while Colonel Hans von Luck (7 PD) acknowledged using Pervitin (along with his driver) to stay awake during his long drive out of Russia in late January 1942, after Luck was transferred to Rommel's Africa Corps.[205]

Among the myriad hardships faced by the marching infantry was the paucity of drinking water, a serious problem recorded time and again in the letters, diaries, and post-war accounts of many *Landser*. "The water supply in European Russia," wrote Erhard Raus, "varies greatly from region to region. During the summer it is uniformly poor."[206] Every village in central Russia had one or two draw wells, but during the summer months "their water is scant and warm, and drinking water must be taken from books and rivers."[207] Observes David Glantz:

> One of the most serious problems for the [German] infantrymen was the lack of water since, although the shallow wells in the villages sustained the local population, they were wholly inadequate to quench the thirst of a million and a half men [of Army Group Center] and hundreds of thousands of horses. Nor was the water safe to drink without first boiling it and then purifying it with chlorine.[208]

In a letter to his wife (12 July 1941), *Gefreiter* Alois Scheuer (197 ID) noted a behavior which must have been all-too common, however unwholesome – drinking dirty water from a draw well:

> My dearest wife!
> We have now marched approx. 400 km to the east already, along dusty, cross-country dirt roads, through forests, swamps, and marshes, past places where bitter battles were fought, littered with the remains of all kinds of material and countless dead. But we go on without pause, and take turns to sit up on our vehicles. Many are extremely footsore, some fall to the ground with exhaustion. Many horses are also dropping out, because the lack of water and the extreme heat and dust are really testing us.
> We haven't yet had to go hungry, but we have to endure all the more thirst; there are neither wells nor a water supply system, we take all our water from cisterns (draw wells). It is often dirty, but we drink it; after all, we're not sensitive to it any more.[209]

Aggravating the problem was the fact that many wells were contaminated, or otherwise destroyed, by the withdrawing Red Army. In his post-war account, *Obergefreiter* August Freitag (6 ID) recalled the frustration caused by the inability to find drinking water during a rest stop in late July 1941, and the severe penalty levied for drinking from the wells without authorization:

> One day, it must have been the hottest and most oppressive of that summer, after hours of marching without stopping, we paused for a midday rest at the edge of a forest close to a small factory. A well was the only thing far and wide that could give us any water. This had long been inoperative and was heavily contaminated. So it was only used for the horses. Drawing water for the field kitchens was forbidden. Drinking water of that kind was always punished with five days strict detention. Two men stood guard at the well so that nobody would transgress this prohibition.
> As I drew up a bucketful for my horses, a *Landser* came up and asked me to let him drink a few mouthfuls. Before I could draw his attention to the fact that the water was really simply unfit for consumption, he had thrown himself at the bucket and was drinking in eager gulps. If I had put this water in front of my horses, even if they had worked the entire day, I don't believe they would have guzzled it.[210]

A major theme of this narrative has been the terrible toll taken by the primitive road infrastructure of European Russia on the armored fighting vehicles, trucks, prime movers, and automobiles of the *Ostheer* – a problem which not only affected the panzer and motorized units but the marching infantry as well. The horse-drawn field wagons issued by the German Army proved to be too heavy for conditions in Russia and often had to be replaced, either by captured Red Army vehicles or *Panje* wagons confiscated from local villages or collective farms.[211] Recalled Heinrich Haape (6 ID): "It had taken only 12 days of the campaign to show how completely unsuited was our transport to this type of country. The wagons were far too heavy for moving on these incredibly bad roads and tracks. Our beautiful well-bred horses were altogether too food-conscious and were not acclimatized."[212]

Only days after the start of the campaign, the small, tracked vehicles of French origin (*Chenillettes*) used by 137 Infantry Division to tow the guns of its anti-tank companies had broken down and were out of commission.[213] 129 Infantry Division, which had also outfitted its anti-tank companies with such vehicles, had, by 1 July, consigned 18 of them to the workshop for repair. The division's war diary noted the simple reason why they were so susceptible to breakdowns:

> The cause of the damage to the tractors can be found in their being overstressed during the first days of war. The French army had only intended the tractors for bridging short stretches of terrain, while under heavy enemy fire, and they were thus equipped with relatively weak engines, as was appropriate for their intended use.[214]

While the motor and horse-drawn vehicles of the German Army were beset by problems in Soviet Russia, the summer campaign of 1941 was "not ... exactly kind to the German Army's horses."[215] Simply put, the hot summer weather, coupled with the brutal demands placed upon the horses, resulted in the loss of large numbers of animals.[216] The most severely affected were the heavy draft horses, used primarily by the artillery battalions to haul their guns. The heavier artillery units were often unable to maintain the tempo of the advance, and thus fell behind. The horse-drawn columns of German formations were also vulnerable to attack from the air. On the third day of the campaign (24 June), 1 Cavalry Division (24 Panzer Corps) was struck twice by Soviet bombers, inflicting heavy losses of horses. The veterinarian of 21 Infantry Division (Army Group North) reported serious losses of animals from air attack on 25 June, a complaint echoed in a report by 23 Infantry Division on 4 August 1941.[217]

The infantry soldiers knew only too well how dependent they were upon their horses for what little mobility they had, and many of the men developed a palpable bond with their equine comrades. Wrote artillery soldier Willi Loewer (129 ID):

> It was a particularly happy moment when we discovered a Russian depot close to our position and filled with large supplies of hay, oats, and other types of feed. As soon as it was dark, our drivers came with their trucks and cleaned up. Feed for the horses was just as important as rations for the soldiers. After all, without our horses we were immobile. It was proven time and again just how valuable these patient and stoic animals were to us. That was no doubt why most comrades felt a close emotional bond with their "comrade" horse that is difficult to express in words. I did not feel any different.[218]

The diary of an artillerist in a 150mm medium field howitzer battery (s.FH 18) trenchantly evokes the endless torment of men and horses as they plodded eastward across the rutted roads of Belorussia, straining with every ounce of strength to propel the heavy guns and transport vehicles forward:

> The cannoneers of all the guns step up to the long ropes woven round the wheel hubs. "To the ropes!" – "Vehicle, maaarrrch!" – "Tooogether!" – After two, three attempts, the heavy unit finally moves. But if the cannoneers let up even slightly, the vehicle gets stuck again. It goes on like this for kilometers, until the layer of sand on the road gets a little thinner. Meanwhile, to the rear, vehicles have again become stuck. The gun crews march back with the long ropes and now pull the next unit ahead with a team consisting of up to 14 horses. The slapping of whips on exhausted horses' bodies – fly-covered, with sweat drenched flanks – crazy urging bellowing from hoarse throats, and amidst this, repeated commands: "Vehicle, march!" – "Together!" – and under the ropes the hunched bodies of the cannoneers giving their utmost with veins pulsing at their temples. That is the picture which is repeated all along the road the whole day. Meanwhile, the sun burns down from the sky, the heat wraps round us in the broad pine forests and glares back up into our faces from the light sand on the road. The dust covers us completely und parches our throats. On this day we lose a whole series of our best horses.[219]

Many *Landser* were deeply moved by the suffering of their horses – which the men could do little to ameliorate – as they struggled ceaselessly through the deep sand and the searing heat pulling the guns and the supply and ammunition wagons. In his unpublished "recollections" (*Erinnerungen*), Karl-Gottfried Vierkorn, also a veteran of a battalion of 150mm medium field howitzers (23 ID), poignantly portrayed the wretched fate of the horses:

> Every normal infantry division had an artillery regiment with 105mm howitzers (le.FH 18). In addition, [there was] a medium [*schwere*] battalion with 150mm caliber [howitzers] (s.FH 18), whose 4 guns per battery were driven or transported in 2 loads each (gun-barrel wagon + gun carriage),[220] harnessed with 12 … horses in total, the heaviest that there is! This is where my almost elegiac depiction now begins:
>
> After only 10-12 march days since 22 June 1941 … the near 100 percent sandy tracks on which our advance progressed had drained the strength of our poor horses to such an extent that tears rose in the eyes of most of us when we had to watch how they tried to pull – to the point of collapse … The so-called "drivers," one for every 2 horses, had got off long ago to lighten the load – the sight could not be borne!
>
> Our veterinarians spent all their time roaring up and down the march columns in their motorized vehicles to get the poor creatures back on their feet with fortifying injections – if it wasn't too late and the lives of these poor "war comrades" ended with a deep sigh.[221]

In the letter to his wife cited above, Major Werner Heinemann (23 ID) gave voice to the abiding appreciation the men had for their horses, as well as to their helplessness in the face of the animals' suffering:

> 17.7.41:
> The poor horses suffer the worst. What they have to do with those heavy vehicles on the sand-covered roads is unimaginable. It breaks your heart to see how

they fall away from day to day. Countless of them collapse while still in harness, patiently allow the pistol to be placed at their ear for a mercy shot, and line the roads of our advance.[222]

Acquiring replacements for the thousands of lost horses was often difficult. German infantry divisions began the Russian campaign with, at best, a reserve of only 150 horses. In addition, the Red Army's horses, while generally good, were not captured in large numbers. The 260 Infantry Division (Army Group Center), from 19 July to 11 September 1941, seized only 327 horses, not nearly enough to make good the losses sustained over that period.[223]

In response to such challenges, the Germans improvised. Where possible, Russian prime movers – captured from the Red Army or seized from the collective farms – were pressed into service to pull the heavier guns. As Karl-Gottfried Vierkorn (23 ID) recalled, "Without this solution, we would have never made it with our heavy guns to the northern suburbs of Moscow!"[224] In another instance, the medium field howitzer battalion of 137 Infantry Division repaired and put to work captured Soviet tractors to haul its 150mm guns.[225] The Germans were also quick to requisition many of the most common type of horses found in Russia, the *Panje* horses. These small animals – tough, "easy to feed, handle, and stable"[226] – were much better suited to the conditions in the east than were the heavier German and western European breeds. Recalled Dr Heinrich Haape (6 ID) with a certain wonder, "the *Panje* horses ate anything – old dry grass off the roofs, bark, dry twigs and garbage ..."[227] More importantly, "in all seasons and in all situations this horse proved outstanding for pack and draft use. It is *the* horse for European Russia."[228] Yet as the Germans soon found out, even the industrious little *Panje* horses could only do so much:

> The standard German artillery piece, a 105mm howitzer, when loaded with fodder, ammunition, and equipment (the gun and limber were driven as a single unit) weighed as much as four tons – a difficult task even for six well-fed draft horses. The heavy artillery gun, a 150mm piece, with gun and limber driven separately, required eight horses just to haul the reserve cart, which carried the ammunition. *Panje* horses were far too small and light for hauling artillery. They were also unsuited for hauling horse-drawn vehicles. The standard German Army horse-drawn vehicle was made of steel, which also proved too heavy for the small *Panje* horses. Here, however, the 200 Polish carts allocated to each infantry division before the invasion proved to be invaluable. Wooden vehicles were also obtained locally.[229]

Despite enormous obstacles, the distances covered by the infantry divisions of Army Group Center through July 1941, as they sought desperately to catch up to the panzer units at the forward edge of battle, were remarkable. After some six weeks of campaigning, the combat infantry of 6, 23 and 35 Infantry Divisions – to name but a few – had marched 750 to 1000 kilometers and more, averaging 25 to 30 kilometers per day.[230] During the first 20 days alone (by 11 July), 35 Infantry Division had covered an average of 37.5 kilometers per day, and a total of 750 kilometers.[231] From 8-18 July, 260 Infantry Division, brought by rail from France to eastern Poland (30 June to 3 July), conducted forced marches of 50 to 70 kilometers a day, until it finally went into action south of Bobruisk.[232] By 31 July 1941, the 40+ infantry divisions of Field Marshal von Bock's army group were mostly settling in along a now largely static front line some 700 kilometers in length, as Hitler and his Army High Command (OKH) debated the future course of the campaign. The line was anchored in the north on Velikie Luki, and in the south on the Dnepr, west of Gomel; between these two anchor posts, it stretched out far to the east, forming an enormous salient which extended beyond Smolensk (where a second major cauldron battle was reaching its climax) and reached its apex at El'nia, on the Desna River, pointed at Moscow.[233] But to reach this line deep inside Soviet Russia, the infantry had not only marched, they had fought.

8.3.3: Fighting

Infantry combat during the opening phase of Operation *Barbarossa* was diverse in scope, ranging from the bloody, chaotic, and often desperate engagements along the encirclement rings to the tedious task of clearing forests, swamps, villages, and farms of the omnipresent Red Army stragglers. Many infantry units also experienced their initial clashes with Soviet partisan groups. While the combat was often desultory in nature – days of unbroken marching, punctuated by brief but violent encounters – it could still be quite costly. While clearing terrain straddling its route of advance (*Vormarschstrasse*) of enemy stragglers, 18 Infantry Regiment (6 ID), lacking support from heavy weapons (still far to the rear), sustained "heavy losses" during the final days of June 1941.[234] In late July and August 1941, as the infantry divisions of Army Group Center transitioned to positional warfare, the attrition was often frightful.

The German infantry were stunned by the tenacity of their opponent in combat, while shocked and outraged by Soviet combat methods that the *Landser* considered underhanded and unsportsmanlike. In soldiers' letters and diaries, the term "*hinterlistig*" (deceitful) is often used to characterize the fighting technique of the Red Army. Soviet soldiers feigned surrender – then opened fire at point blank range on the Germans approaching to disarm them; they let the main German assault formations pass by – then fell savagely upon supply columns, administrative units, or military hospitals bringing up the rear, sometimes mutilating in the most bestial manner the unfortunate recipients of their rage. Russian troops regularly took German doctors, stretcherbearers and other medical personal under fire, despite clearly visible Red Cross markings. The *Landser* were astonished – and repulsed – to find themselves, on occasion, in bitter combat with Red Army female soldiers. And, of course, there were the ubiquitous enemy snipers, with their excellent automatic rifles, outfitted with telescopic sights, who could strike from anywhere, at any time, with lethal impact – picking off the drivers of supply vehicles, officers, and messengers on motorcycles.[235] As Major Werner Heinemann (23 Infantry Division) wrote to his wife on 11 July 1941: "Unfortunately, [Russian] snipers firing from concealed positions cause us endless problems. Two nights ago, a motor vehicle driver from my old 1st Company was murdered in the forest, as he tried to repair a flat tire. He was all alone."[236]

Typical of the attitude of German soldiers toward their Russian adversary are several field post letters of General Heinrici (43 Army Corps); the letters also lay bare the grim dialectic of the eastern front, as the *Landser* routinely reciprocated the gruesome tactics of their enemy:

23.6.41:
Yesterday, we had a Russian division in front of us, which completely scattered after being surprised. Everywhere in the huge forests, in countless farmsteads, there are lost soldiers who all too often ambush us from behind. The Russian is really conducting an underhanded war. In response, on several occasions our people have really cleaned up, without mercy.

24.6.41:
In general, the Russian seems to be withdrawing with his forces back to the east. But when he is forced to fight, he puts up a very determined fight. He is a much better soldier than the Frenchman. Extraordinarily tough, cunning, and deceitful [*hinterlistig*]. Many losses are caused because our people are shot at from behind.

The prisoners which have been taken, hitherto only a few hundred, are all kinds of peoples. Among them [are] people who look more like Chinese than like Russians.

4.7.41:
The war in Russia is enormously bloody [*ungeheuer blutig*]. The enemy has suffered the kind of losses which have not so far been seen anywhere in this war. The Russian soldiers have been told by their leaders that they would all be shot by us. Instead of giving themselves up, they now ambush and shoot at every German from behind. Of course, that demands tough countermeasures from us. So each party escalates the stakes in turn, with the result that hecatombs of human sacrifice are made. Then there's the complexity of the terrain: everywhere forest, swamp, high cornfields, in which the Russians can hide themselves, in short, it really isn't nice here.

6.7.41:
Our Russian who had been in front of us is now destroyed. The affair was incredibly bloody. In part no quarter was given. The Russian behaved with bestiality [*viehisch*] toward our wounded. So then our people struck down and shot dead everything running around in a brown uniform. But there are still large areas of forest full of stragglers and refugees – some with, some without weapons – which are a very great danger. You can send whole divisions through there and still tens of thousands will escape capture in these impenetrable areas.[237]

Few experiences rattled the German soldier more – or contributed more to his perception of the Soviet Union and its people as profoundly alien – than being forced into battle with female Red Army soldiers – a prospect which clearly offended the more conventional sensibilities of the average *Landser*. In the fighting around Velikie Luki in July 1941, Combat Engineer Battalion 253 (253 ID) resorted to flamethrowers to break the plucky resistance of a Red Army unit composed of women, as depicted by the following eyewitness account:

> Because they had again shot from ambush, these women were mown down with flamethrowers. They had jumped back into their trenches and so the whole operation was halted, and the engineers came forward with flamethrowers and forced the women out. They came out with burning hair, burning clothes. I saw that, of course, witnessed it … And these women, I think very few of them got out of there in one piece.[238]

In mid-July 1941, *Landser* Helmut Martin (14 ID (mot.)) had his first encounter with Soviet female soldiers, a jolting experience he recalled in his recently published account of his long trials on the eastern front:

> When we got onto the *Rollbahn*, we struck out again in the direction of Nevel … Ahead of us in the roadside ditch lay, in addition to several dead, two wounded *Flintenweiber*[239] and a seriously wounded commissar. One of them had a hole as large as a fist in her upper thigh, the other one had had the left side of her chest and left upper arm torn open by a shell. We bandaged up both of them. The commissar refused all help.
> I was confronted full on for the first time with the fact that the enemy was deploying women in the forwardmost line. For me, woman was the epitome of life, was its guardian and mother at the same time. Suddenly women in Russian uniforms lay in front of me in a roadside ditch, wounded, a breast torn open, there, where normally an infant would have been able to find sustenance. How cruel

must this state be if it expects a woman to do this, when her body, equipped with the finest organs, is riddled with bullets or torn up by razor sharp pieces of iron from exploded shells! Nobody can say: "C'est la guerre!" That's just not true!

Until now, soldiering had been a business for men only. And that was how it should have remained. What I saw here in the ditch in front of me was just the beginning. It all got a whole lot worse.[240]

In a fine history of the elite and tradition-rich 9 Infantry Regiment (23 ID), the author emphasizes the "otherness" of the experience of fighting against women soldiers, while also expressing astonishment over their martial prowess. The ensuing anecdote is from the summer of 1941:

A lot in this country was unfamiliar. The Slavic faces with their pronounced cheekbones and tanned by the sun, the near boundless expanses of the sparsely settled land, the heat, the dust, the headscarves which the women here wore.

There were even women in military uniform: Had not German soldiers been taught that women with weapons in their hands were "Flintenweiber"? Only, these women they now encountered in battle fought with amazing courage and unexpected tenacity! These Soviet women were somehow different in every way. A Soviet soldier with a stomach shot injury lay among the prisoners. It was clear to see that he was finished, a case where the doctor couldn't help any more. Then a new contingent of prisoners arrived with a Russian woman dressed in civilian clothes. She saw her dying countryman, kneeled down, kissed this soldier who was completely unknown to her, kissed his pale lips, caressed him, spoke a few words of comfort, incomprehensible to the German guards, to him. Where had this woman come from? Why did she do that?[241]

Much more common, of course, yet equally disturbing, was the Soviet tactic of attacking with large masses of infantry in repeated waves, despite the horrific casualties which, more often than not, were the result of the technique. The mass attacks took place frequently during the cauldron battles, as the Russians set about desperately to break free of encirclement by crushing the thin German lines of containment. From the *Landsers'* perspective, such a frightful squandering of human beings merely highlighted their enemy's contempt for human life and his deeply alien essence. The Soviets, however, viewed the matter differently: Short of tanks, artillery and other heavy weapons – following the immense losses in the opening stages of the war – they often had little choice but to resort to such tactics – for which the Russian Army (of both world wars) has been unfairly caricatured by western military historians as an army of mass, bereft of tactical skill or refinement. Regardless, the mass Red Army attacks often left those on the receiving end shaken and bewildered, the barrels of their machine guns veritably wilting under the strain:

For the soldiers deployed in Russia it was always an experience evoking horror when the Soviets sent infantrymen … forward to attack in terrific numbers, when they had them charge "wave after wave," so that it often seemed hopeless to try to "stop this unrelenting surging flood." … However crazy and "senseless" [such attacks] may often have seemed from a military perspective, they still spread horror, forced the German soldiers into such a distressing situation that it was not unusual for their nerve to fail them.[242]

The 106 ID, a division of the 12th wave formed in November 1940,[243] did not reach the forward edge of battle until late July 1941 (it began *Barbarossa* in OKH reserve).[244] In the weeks which followed, the division's 240 Infantry Regiment, defending positions on the Shidki Heights, about 100 kilometers northeast of Smolensk, was subjected to repeated Soviet human wave attacks – action described in a unit history prepared by the regimental commander, *Oberstleutnant* Ringenberg, in July 1942:

> The war immediately struck with terrific force against our gray lines. The Russian sacrificed his people wantonly and without regard! Day and night, they came sneaking up, catlike, trying again and again to intimidate the German *Landser* with their throaty "Urrah." But our eyes incessantly and coolly sought out the enemy. At night, tired eyes penetrated the darkness, and the ear heard the smallest sound of skulking reconnaissance patrols. The defensive battle raged. Timoshenko wanted to force a favorable result at any cost. The Bolsheviks pounded against our positions dozens of times, over and over again! Always without success! The German machine guns mowed the attackers down. No rest, no relief. The dark nights echoed again with the Russian "Urrah" of the storming Bolsheviks. In the morning, heaps of them lay in front of our trenches. Not a single one got through! What was here repeatedly charging against us, shooting and yelling wildly – those were no brave warriors, no soldiers: those were lifeless slaves, who, pumped up with vodka, were set against our lines over and again.[245]

Yet despite the requisite wartime bravado, Ringenberg readily admitted that his regiment also suffered terribly while repelling the mass Soviet attacks:

> Many of our comrades met a hero's death [*Heldentod*] here in the trenches, great was also the number of our wounded. The ranks became thinner. The Russian always had new manpower to deploy; with us, every loss left a gap. But even decimated like that, the regiment held the main battle line. The defensive battle raged on.[246]

In his study of combat trauma in Vietnam, psychiatrist Dr Jonathan Shay tells us that, in Vietnam,

> The enemy struck not only at the body but also at the most basic functions of the soldier's mind, attacking his perceptions by concealment; his cognitions by camouflage and deception; his intentions by surprise, anticipation, and ambush. These mind games have been part of war since time immemorial [but in Vietnam] American soldiers literally felt tortured by their Vietnamese enemy.[247]

While it may well be overstated to posit that the German *Landser* in Russia was "tortured" by the tactics of his enemy, it is, nevertheless, accurate to assert that he was palpably discomfited by methods of warfare that were, hitherto, beyond his frame of reference. The Red Army fighting man soon became an "object of fear"[248] for the German soldier – the psychological toll exacted by the "mind games" of the Russians evident from the following anecdote from the beginning of the campaign, gleaned from the memoirs of August Freitag (6 ID):

> In the evening we were to prepare to continue the march. A messenger brought us the news that a motorcycle messenger from the 14th Company, who had sat by a ryefield in a roadside ditch to spread a slice of bread, had been killed from behind by a Russian with the butt of his rifle. This happened only a few hundred meters from our resting spot, on the busy main route of advance. Caution was

ordered and we were forbidden to go anywhere alone. For the high cornfields and the many forests offered the Russian stragglers protection right up to the edge of the vehicles and the roads.

We didn't get far on this evening ... We bedded down in a clover field beneath a few trees. When the security detachments had taken up their positions, we lay down to sleep, one pressed up against the other, so that we didn't need to unpack as many blankets. At midnight – I was just standing guard – a bloodcurdling, gurgling cry rang out through the silence, emanating from the middle of our sleeping comrades. We rushed over in the belief that Ivan already had one of them by the throat. But everyone was sleeping peacefully, except for a few, who had been wakened by the cry and were staring at us questioningly. Somebody must have just had a not particularly nice dream. And that could only have come from the message [about the motorcycle messenger from the 14th Company]. So we knew that the devious warfare of the Russian stragglers lay heavy on all our minds.[249]

As this narrative has documented, however, the Russian soldier quickly became – begrudgingly, to be sure – an object of respect to the German soldier, who admired his adversary's toughness, resilience, and individual fighting qualities, while deploring the enemy's brutal methods. Moreover, the *Landser* were often astonished by the excellent quality of much of the Soviet arsenal of weapons and equipment.[250] In a letter on 2 July 1941, an unknown soldier in Army Group Center registered his surprise over the "splendid materiel" (*tadelloses Material*) of the Red Army,[251] while the next day (3 July), a *Gefreiter* in 23 Infantry Division wrote: "The equipment [*Armierung*] of the Russian troops is good. Every day we ask ourselves where the hundreds of tanks came from, which litter the roads everywhere. Gigantic, completely new types of guns, all of them drawn by tractors, have also been left behind."[252]

Like the panzer troops, the German infantry endured terrifying initial encounters with Soviet T-34 and KV tanks. *Leutnant* Erich Bunke (31 ID) and his *Panzerjaeger* (anti-tank) platoon first came up against the T-34 in late June 1941. His four 37mm Pak guns, along with the guns of another platoon (eight 37mm Pak in all), were in position outside Rozana, southwest of Slonim, awaiting Russian breakout attempts from the Belostok pocket. It did not take long until the first Soviet T-28 tanks, debouching from the forest and shooting wildly, headed straight for the German Pak front, which easily knocked out the medium (but obsolete) tanks at a range of about 800 meters. Further Russian attacks – massed infantry assaults, even a charge by 100-120 Red Army cavalry – were also beaten off successfully. Suddenly, as the day approached its end, and darkness embraced the battlefield – now blanketed by dead Soviet infantry, slaughtered horses, and knocked out Russian tanks – *Leutnant* Bunke and his *Panzerjaeger* troops detected a disturbingly foreign engine noise at the periphery of the forest, and it was heading straight toward them:

But then, what was that? ... A monster like we'd never seen before. It fired machine guns from the turret and from the bow side, and shot at us with a big long-barrel gun. We shot back with 8 Pak guns and watched as our shells, which had a thumb-sized illuminant charge [*Leuchtsatz*] at the back end of the shell, struck against the armored plating and bounced off. One shot after another bounced off and whirled through the air. A ghastly sight, especially for us.

We shot ceaselessly and sometimes had the impression that the tank was almost brought to a halt by the force of the impact of all those shells. It came ever closer, ever closer. Now it had reached our line and drove straight through to the rear, and there began to fire with a vengeance. Our limbers stood there. Our people took cover. Even the infantry staffs back there were threatened.

Trucks with mounted infantry on them, which had been following the tank, hadn't got far. They were burning and the Russian soldiers jumped down and took cover at both sides of the road. Behind us, this monstrous tank continued to tear about. It was driving all over the place and we didn't know what might happen. Then it came back to our line. The infantry who had jumped down from the trucks got up again and launched themselves at us with their Urrah. We held them back.

What was that? The tank had suddenly slumped forward. Its gun was stuck in the ground and the front part of the tank had sunk in deep. It had evidently driven itself to ground.[253]

Meanwhile, the desperate Soviet breakout attempts continued into the night – nourished by wave after wave of attacking infantry and a handful of T-28 tanks – only to be repeatedly crushed by Bunke's AT guns and the machine guns of the supporting German infantry. Finally, the fighting trailed off, and Bunke and his men were able to cautiously approach the now immobilized T-34:

We crept up to it and found that it had driven into a tank trap. This tank trap had evidently been laid out by the Russians. A pit with wood over it, and we hadn't even noticed it, it was hidden so well. But the tank had, thank God, stumbled into this pit and was stuck with its long barrel in the ground.[254]

Because the standard 37mm anti-tank gun was utterly useless – the 50mm Pak mostly so – against the T-34s and KVs, infantry units were forced to deploy their artillery well forward in a direct-fire role in an effort to stop them. If early reports sometimes made the T-34s and KVs out to be "invincible,"[255] the Germans immediately set about developing new methods to combat them, including the use of concentrated explosives (e.g., hand grenades bundled together into a single, powerful explosive charge), which would be secured to the tank, or placed in its path, by an intrepid – or perhaps suicidal! – soldier (or team of soldiers). Over time, the *Panzerschreck* (tank panic) subsided, and the *Landser* regained his confidence that T-34 and KV tanks could be confronted with a fair chance of success.

While Russian combat methods and weaponry took their toll on the German invaders, the fact remains that, like the panzer units, the German infantry – or "*Fusslatscher*" (foot sloggers) in *Landser* slang – used their superior training, experience, unit cohesion and morale to give much better than they got. To venture an educated guess, the casualty exchange rate (i.e., the ratio of losses inflicted by each side on the other) in the opening phase of the campaign fell somewhere between 3:1 and 10:1 in favor of German forces in most engagements.[256] Indeed, an overarching theme of combat along the eastern front in the summer of 1941 was the pronounced tactical superiority of German forces – both panzer and marching infantry – over their inexperience and ill-prepared Russian opponent.

A noteworthy example of the *Ostheer's* tactical superiority was an engagement involving the 137 Infantry Division (9 Army Corps) on 25 June 1941. The day before (24 June), an advance detachment of the division (*Vorausabteilung Wupper*), supported by elements of 263 Infantry Division, had, after a brief fight, captured the town of Bielsk, an important road junction some 50 kilometers beyond the frontier (and ca. 50 kilometers south of Belostok), thereby blocking a major line of retreat for Red Army forces. Advance Detachment Wupper then pushed on 10 kilometers to the east, establishing a bridgehead over the Orlanka and securing the right flank of the division. Although Wupper's group (anti-tank troops, combat engineers, and an artillery battery) was attacked by Soviet forces – including tanks and artillery – attempting to escape to the east, the bridgehead remained firmly in their hands.[257]

East of Bielsk, on 25 June, 137 Infantry Division's reconnaissance battalion was suddenly attacked by a Russian contingent of about 800 men, supported by tanks and artillery, which was also seeking to withdraw eastward. Although the reconnaissance battalion's bicycle troop (*Radfahrschwadron*) soon found itself in a delicate situation, reinforcements of infantry (II./ IR 448) and artillery arrived just in time to repel the Soviet attack with devastating results. As the battered Russian force staggered away in defeat, it was then struck by elements of 137 ID's two other infantry regiments (447 & 449 IR), which pivoted effortlessly out of their marching columns to the attack. Enveloped from the north, south, and west, the Russian force was systematically obliterated, the light field howitzers of I./AR 137 taking the enemy under direct fire (*im direkten Richten*) at 1600 meters:

> The gunners, who, from their gun positions, otherwise rarely saw their successes, were so excited that I had difficulty in getting them to cease fire. The whole thing was a rare scene for the artillery: the batteries in open firing position, the limbers 10 steps behind, the battery chief giving the commands to fire from atop his horse, it was like 1870.[258]

As Lt.-Col. Meyer-Detring, chief operations officer (Ia), 137 Infantry Division, recalled, the outcome was "a classic cauldron battle in microcosm,"[259] the enemy losing over 500 dead and 150 prisoners, while 18 tanks were destroyed and a gun battery captured. It was, he said, "a splendid success [*ein schoener Erfolg*] in which all the regiments had played a part."[260]

There were, however, several tactical situations in which the Germans were often at a distinct disadvantage; these were: fighting at night, close combat (*Nahkampf*) and, most significantly, fighting in forests (which, of course, also encompassed fighting at night and close combat). All of these tactical situations acted as force multipliers for the defense and were readily exploited by the Red Army, which conducted extensive training in all three areas. Conversely, the Germans tended to shun such tactics, relying more on firepower and mobility. As addressed in Chapter 2 of this narrative, German training in forest fighting prior to the start of the *Barbarossa* campaign was highly deficient – an oversight they soon came to regret.

Combat in forests has always been a costly form of warfare, and the Russo-German war was no exception to this rule: "The fact that the opponents clash in close terrain and come to grips in point-blank and hand-to-hand encounters leads by itself to numerous casualties."[261] As much as the Germans attempted to avoid combat in forests – seeking instead to give battle in open terrain, where they enjoyed distinct advantages – this was only possible to a limited extent, given the lack of open spaces and the Soviet tactic of withdrawing into, and fighting from, forested regions. The Germans soon discovered that their enemy was a master of forest fighting, and that the lethality of Russian troops in such areas was considerably amplified by their strong emphasis on concealment and camouflage.

Fighting in the dense undergrowth and tangled thickets of Russia's expansive forests was largely a task for the infantry, for the effectiveness of both tanks[262] and artillery,[263] was necessarily limited. Specific characteristics of combat in Russian forests during the Second World War are laid out in the following report:

> Combat in forests, whatever the size of the force originally committed, eventually assumes the characteristics of small unit actions. Dense wooded areas form a curtain between elements of any unit having a common objective and inevitably split them into smaller and smaller groups as the general situation becomes increasingly obscure.
>
> Terrain in which it is difficult to maintain contact and control makes great demands upon the mettle of troops and upon the effectiveness of their leadership.

The mental strain of forest combat is severe, particularly on inexperienced soldiers. The sound of every shell seems louder in wooded areas, and the prolonged periods of close combat inherent in forest fighting shatter the nerves and sap the strength of even well conditioned forces.

The German lack of experience in forest fighting was a great disadvantage in the Russian campaign. The German troops, trained to depend on the massed fire of all the combat arms, had to adapt themselves to terrain where the infantry had to carry the main burden. And even the infantry was limited to the use of the rifle, machine pistol, hand grenade, mortar, and the *Panzerfaust* [a recoilless anti-tank grenade and launcher, used in the latter period of the war]. The machine gun had but limited effect in dense woods, and suitable observation and firing positions for artillery in the forests of European Russia are rare.

The Russian, on the other hand, innately possessed characteristics that served him well in forest fighting. His physical strength, his ability to get along with few comforts, and his natural ability as a woodsman led him to seek combat in the forest as keenly as the German sought to avoid it.[264]

The heavy German losses in forest fighting resulted not only from their dearth of experience in such fighting, but from the superior tactics and cunning employed by the Russians. Red Army soldiers selected mutually supporting positions that were well camouflaged, made use of decoy positions, and carefully integrated natural obstacles into their defensive plan. Unlike the German infantry, which would defend positions on the forward edge of the tree line (or just inside it) to take advantage of wide fields of observation and fire, the Russians located their main defensive positions deep inside the forest, preferably behind swampy terrain. There were many reasons for doing this; for example, it hid their defensive positions from German aerial observation and air attack, while compelling the German infantry to use only short-range, direct fire, close combat techniques. In addition, there were few clearings which could be used by the attackers for setting up mortars and artillery, and it was harder for advancing German troops to maintain orientation and contact with neighboring units. Another noteworthy feature of Russian defensive positions in forested areas were infantry foxholes that could not be identified from the front; these only provided a field of fire to the rear, because their purpose was to pick off attacking enemy troops from behind after they had passed by. An easy way to create obstacles was by felling trees across forest roads and tracks, often interlocking their limbs toward the enemy. To make such obstacles less conspicuous to aerial observation, some trees might be left standing, and barbed wire and booby traps placed among the limbs.[265] Indicative of Soviet artfulness was the manner in which they cleared fields of fire:

> Whereas the German infantry would clear lanes of fire for themselves, if necessary by considerable felling of trees – which, of course, meant they were easily spotted from the air – the Russians worked like Red Indians. They would cut down the undergrowth only up to waist-height, creating tunnels of fire both forward and toward the sides. This gave them cover and a clear field of fire at the same time. The German divisions had to pay a heavy toll before they mastered this kind of fighting.[266]

Some of the costliest lessons were learned by 78 Infantry Division (13 Army Corps) in late June 1941, east of Bielsk, in the forest of Bialowieza. Advancing in three columns of march – 215 IR on the right, 195 IR on the left, and 238 IR to the rear, in echelon – contact was made with the remnants of several Soviet units (among them the remains of 4 Tank Division) outside the village of Popelevo. Bitter close quarter combat ensued, with hand grenades, pistols and bayonets the weapons of choice. The division's artillery was unable to intervene, as opposing forces were too closely intertwined. Only mortar fire proved useful:

> The afternoon of 29 June saw a massacre. The 3rd Battalion, 215 Infantry Regiment, succeeded in engaging the Russians in the flank and in the rear. Panic broke out. The Russians fled … Popelevo was again silent.
>
> On the following day the division was more careful. The gunners pounded each patch of forest before the companies moved in. "Infantry will enter platoon by platoon!" A white Very light meant: Germans here. Red meant: Enemy attack. Green meant: Artillery fire to be moved forward. Blue meant: Enemy tanks. Yes, tanks – even in the forest the Russians employed individual tanks for infantry support.
>
> By evening 78 Infantry Division was at last through that accursed forest of Bialowieza. The Russians had left behind some 600 dead. The regiments had taken 1140 prisoners. Some 3000 Soviet troops were being pushed toward the interception line of 17 Infantry Division. In its two days of fighting in the forest of Bialowieza the 78 Infantry Division lost 114 killed and 125 wounded.[267]

At the start of the campaign, 255 Infantry Division (53 Army Corps), later supported by 267 Infantry Division because of the enemy opposition, cleared Soviet forces from the forests around Maloryta, southeast of Brest-Litovsk, in a difficult and costly operation, whose purpose was to protect the highway (*Rollbahn*) against flanking attacks launched from the forests. The area of operations was an "old, uncultivated, high forest, with much underbrush … The operation developed out of a meeting engagement with an enemy division that was advancing on Maloryta from the southeast. No special measures of any kind for reconnaissance or security had been taken. A prearranged deployment was therefore impossible and German units went into action wherever they happened to encounter the enemy."[268]

The attacking Germans succeeded in trapping Soviet forces in the forest; these were then pounded by artillery. On the evening of 25 June, however, the enemy broke out toward Melniki, and, in a surprise attack, wiped out most of the gun crews of two batteries of 267 ID, which had entered the forest without taking proper security precautions. The next day (26 June), as enemy resistance appeared to ebb, a battalion of 455 Infantry Regiment (255 ID) was sent out from Lyakhovtse, on a broad front, to sweep the forest toward the north. Deep inside the forest, the battalion was suddenly set upon from all sides: "The Russians had permitted the leading German elements to pass, and then fired out of the trees. The battalion found itself in a critical situation and had to withdraw from the forest with very heavy losses."[269]

On 27 June, the entire forest was "systematically raked with strong artillery fire." The entire 475 Infantry Regiment (255 ID) was then committed to comb the forest from north to south. Enemy resistance finally collapsed. Several thousand prisoners were made and many guns and vehicles captured. The Maloryta operation had "required six days before it could be brought to a successful conclusion, and it was evident that a lesson had been learned."[270] Simply put, the pursuit of the enemy was to be carried no further into the forest than was necessary to protect the *Rollbahn*. As the commander of 53 Army Corps observed: "It is better to exercise discretion in the selection of objectives than to incur avoidable risks in forest fighting." This corps, at least, abandoned the technique of mopping up in forested regions, adopting instead the practice of sealing off such areas as a standing operating procedure. In the months ahead, this new tactic was "elaborated and refined" by 53 Army Corps.[271]

In a third action (25 June 1941), a battalion of 82 Infantry Regiment (31 Infantry Division, 12 Army Corps) sustained serious losses in forest fighting during its assault on the village of Michalin Stare, southwest of Slonim. As former regimental commander Friedrich Hossbach observed in a post-war study, an "exceptionally unpleasant" feature of this operation was the deadly fire from Russian snipers concealed in the trees (*Baumschuetzen*).[272] Supporting the battalion's attack was *Leutnant* Bunke and his platoon of anti-tank guns:

> Tactically, the Russians acted extraordinarily shrewdly here. They allowed the companies of the 2nd Battalion [82 IR] on the embankment and to both sides of it to march through a fair distance so that the first detachments reached the village of Michalin Stare. Then concentrated infantry fire broke out on the companies [of the regiment] on both sides of the embankment. It was only thanks to the intervention of 2 assault guns that the situation could be somewhat stabilized. The bridges were passable before darkness fell, and I received the mission to drive up on the embankment with my platoon so as to be able to intervene here with my Paks. Due to our exercises in Krotoszyn, we had some experience of using our armor-piercing shells in forest combat. These were – because of their ricocheting, rebounding all over the forest – an incredible weapon.[273]

Bunke and his platoon drove forward toward Michalin Stare, going into position in clearings in the woods. Because the infantry had incurred considerable casualties from flanking fire, Bunke's 37mm Pak pumped armor piercing rounds into the forest in rapid succession, with devastating effect:

> At first we received targeted fire back, which bounced off our protective shields. As the infantry of the 82nd later informed me, these armor-piercing shells, as ricochet shots, had … an uncanny effect … The enemy no longer carried out sudden concentrations of fire after that …
> According to the infantrymen … it was evidently snipers in the trees, who had sat a few meters up in the trees and shot effectively at the advancing infantry from above. After the armor-piercing shells – which did not just remain at ground level, but also whizzed up overhead – this kind of combat ceased, because the snipers no longer felt secure. The battalion commander thanked us for our efforts, because now a peace had finally descended which even held the entire night long.
> When, on the following morning, the sun slowly rose once more and it became lighter, there was no longer any resistance and the forest areas on both sides of the embankment were now systematically combed. The Russian had skedaddled. A very few of them were evidently not in possession of this order to retreat and were now taken prisoner. They were wiry "children of nature" [*Naturburschen*], who resembled the earth itself. Due to the brown uniforms and their unwashed, unkempt faces, they had been difficult to make out. They belonged to an active unit of the Red Army.[274]

On 26 June 1941, the Germans completed the capture of Michalin Stare, but only after more difficult fighting:

> Then we drove on toward Michalin Stare. There were only a few houses there. While searching the houses, again and again soldiers were suddenly shot at from an attic or some other place in the houses. This resistance from the houses by the Russians – it was a matter of only a few riflemen who had been left behind – was suicidal. We moved to setting the houses on fire. Only in this way could we defend ourselves against the dreadful risk of being suddenly ambushed from behind and shot dead.[275]

In the fighting in and around Michalin Stare, 2nd Battalion, 82 Infantry Regiment, suffered 28 dead and 50 wounded. "On a patch of high ground," recounted Friedrich Hossbach, "adjacent to Michalin Stare, we set up the first cemetery [*Ehrenfriedhof*] of 82 IR on Russian soil. Here we solemnly laid to rest the dead of the regiment on 26 June."[276]

Each of the engagements depicted above is an example of the steady, pounding attrition endured by Army Group Center's combat infantry in the summer of 1941 – a melting away of experienced and irreplaceable combat veterans – officers, NCOs and enlisted men – in an almost inexorable mathematical progression, to paraphrase Tolstoy. Through 31 August 1941, 134,000 men (of whom approximately 126,000, or 94 percent, belonged to the ground forces) had been killed in action (or died of other causes) across the entire eastern front,[277] or nearly 1900 per day. In a diary entry on 29 August 1941, General Halder, Chief of the Army General Staff, recorded a total of 389,924 casualties in the *Ostheer* as of 13 August – an average of 7357 per day for the initial 53 days of the campaign.[278] Assuming that the losses continued at this rate through the end of August, total casualties would have reached 522,350 after the first 10 weeks of the campaign. To make good these losses, only 217,000 replacements from the zone of interior (drawn from the Replacement Army's total of 300,000+ men) had reached the Russian theater of war by 31 August,[279] leaving a shortfall of about 305,000 men across the eastern front (less the fraction of slightly wounded and sick who had already returned to their units). Indeed, by the end of August 1941, 14 divisions were short more than 4000 men, 40 divisions more than 3000, 30 divisions more than 2000, and 58 divisions had personnel deficits of less than 2000 men.[280]

German casualties in Russia were shouldered disproportionately by the combat infantry and, as well, by Army Group Center, whose order of battle made up about 40 percent of the *Ostheer*.[281] If 40 percent of the Army's fatal losses through August 1941 are assigned to Field Marshal von Bock's forces, the figure comes to 50,400, or roughly 710 dead each day across the front of the army group, the majority of whom were infantry. The losses of 240 Infantry Regiment (106 ID) from 30 July to 30 August 1941 were not atypical of those sustained by infantry units defending the overextended front of Army Group Center after it had transitioned temporarily to positional warfare. The regiment's fatal losses during this four-week period amounted to 282 (among them eight officers), to which must be added a much larger number of wounded.[282] The point is that neither the army group, nor the *Ostheer* as a whole, could tolerate such losses indefinitely without eventually collapsing.

The average time an enlisted infantryman fought on the eastern front before being killed or wounded was perhaps two months.[283] According to one source, the life expectancy of a *Leutnant* was 18 days; that of a company commander 21 days; that of a battalion commander 32 days.[284] Whether or not these figures are accurate, what they do is highlight the fact that officers were becoming casualties at an alarming rate. "The fact is," Bock confided in his diary on 29 July 1941, "that our troops are tired and also are not exhibiting the required steadiness because of heavy officer casualties."[285] The losses of junior officers were "so bad that an infantry subaltern's chances of returning home in one piece from the Russian front compared unfavorably with those of a U-boat crewman or fighter pilot. Command of companies frequently devolved on non-commissioned officers. Even the NCOs, the backbone of the German Army, were disappearing much faster than they could be replaced."[286] During one day's combat (27 August 1941), two infantry battalions of 6 Infantry Division, defending along the Mezha River, northeast of Velizh, had both battalion commanders and all company chiefs killed or wounded, while the regimental commander (*Oberstleutnant* Hennicke, 37 Infantry Regiment) also perished in the fighting.[287] (For an account of this engagement on 27 August see, Chapter 10, Section 10.6.1.) Such losses among the *Ostheer's* experienced combat leaders were also unsustainable.

Impersonal statistics, however, such as those cited above, tell us nothing about the actual *experience* of fighting and dying on the eastern front during the summer of 1941. For this, we turn to the insightful study by Dr Karlheinz Schneider-Janessen, who answers the question, "how does a soldier die on the field of battle?" (*Woran stirbt ein Soldat "im Felde?"*):

> If, in this book, the war between Germany and Russia is described from the point of view of the physician, then that is why all those soldiers who had died on the battlefield itself remain outside its scope – in other words, those who were, as a rule, buried without a physician ever seeing them again ... Many laypersons imagine that their death came within only a few seconds. However, that was usually not the case ...
>
> In cases of bullet wounds to the throat, which damaged large blood vessels, the soldiers bled to death more or less quickly either externally or else internally into the windpipe. They then drowned, in the truest sense of the phrase, in their own blood ... In cases of injuries to the chest or stomach, which led to the death of the soldier while still on the battlefield, the wounded soldier usually bled to death, either relatively quickly in less than one minute or else took many hours. Victims of chest injuries suffocated, if the injury was such that both lungs had collapsed.
>
> Time and again, soldiers died on the battlefield from injury to a large artery in the arm or leg when there was no help at hand who might bind up the limb ... Based on observations from the First World War, estimates in the Second World War were that close to half of all soldiers [who died on the battlefield] bled to death. The soldiers who bled to death were then "white as a corpse." The anatomy of the stomach cavity especially is constructed in such a way that even damage to relatively small blood vessels can lead to death by exsanguination. This may well be the reason that limb shots are at the top of war medicine statistics: not because they were more common, but because soldiers wounded in this way on the battlefield survived more frequently ...
>
> The most rapid death was from a severe headshot wound, and it was – it is tempting to say: Thank God! – one of the commonest causes of death among soldiers who died on the battlefield itself. Severe injuries to the brain as good as always resulted in immediate loss of consciousness, even when death did not occur directly ... According to statistics from 1944, 43 percent of soldiers who died on the battlefield received headshots, followed by 22 percent with chest shots. 15 percent were from direct hits by shells, that is to say, these soldiers' bodies were either partially torn apart or were covered in shrapnel perforations. Only in fourth place, with 8 percent, were stomach shots. Arm and leg injuries together did not even amount to 4 percent of soldier deaths directly on the battlefield.[288]

Dr Schneider-Janessen goes on to quote from an account of a *Wehrmacht* doctor, somewhere in Russia, recalling the dreadful impact of a sudden and deadly artillery barrage on a German marching column. While the time and place are not given, the experience was universal:

> Scream after scream, howling, whimpering, groaning. Again and again, renewed salvos, and again and again, renewed screams, a satanic litany! And the sun shined high above the dust, smoke, putrefaction, and death, and sent its tolerant light earthward. Soon there were more prone than upright. The few who could still lift themselves up, staggered on. Go on through! On through! they cried. I took an outstretched arm as the starting post for my work. The hand was missing. It lay by the side, in the dirt, connected to the arm by only a few bloody threads. Two pointed, jagged bones protruded from the bloody mess. Shreds of skin and fleshy rags hung round it like brightly colored laundry. Showers of iron and dirt

repeatedly rained down. The deafening noise once again reached a crescendo. Wailing was all around, in a dreadful many-voiced choir. Earth and mud dashed against the open wounds. I crawled toward the next prone body. He lay face down in the earth; a white mess of brains had sprayed across his tunic. He had mercifully lost consciousness; his breathing was like a clogged motor, jerky and gurgling. His death throes made his limbs tense and twitch. Then that great calm came over him.

Through the force of the next detonations, I lost consciousness for a few moments. All at once, everything was dark and indistinct. I looked down at my limbs. They were still intact; my head was still on top. And as long as this was the case, the grim torment had to go on. The next victim had red foam at his lips. His chest heaving, he screamed and gurgled, and struggled for a mouthful of air. Big, bloody air bubbles spluttered up between his teeth and burst over his chin. I tore open his uniform and saw a grisly crater in his chest. The unfortunate man lay there with pleading eyes wide open, yellow face, half mad with torment. A fountain of blood shot out of this flesh crater with every draw of breath and sprayed, foaming, on the grass. A choking fear of death gripped his fluttering young heart. Only the morphine somewhat soothed the poor boy's convulsions of fear. Hour after hour passed by like this … When the shelling and screams had finally grown silent, only groaning, whimpering, cursing, praying, protests and invectives could be heard, along with the death rattles of the dying. They lay everywhere, among the meadows and sunflower fields – the dead and those who did not yet know whether they, too, were to die. A swarm of low-flying aircraft swept past and freed a few from this uncertainty.[289]

8.4: *Luftwaffe-Soldaten*

By the summer of 1941, the *Luftwaffe* was "at its zenith, fresh from the easy and spectacular victories in the Balkans and Crete, well-organized and experienced for battle as the result of operations in the west in 1940, and still with a strong bomber force after the winter's bombing offensive against Britain."[290] In Soviet Russia, the German fighter pilots, bomber and dive-bomber crews were pitted against an inexperienced and poorly trained adversary equipped for the most part with obsolete aircraft. Like the Army, the *Luftwaffe* was supremely confident that the war in the east would culminate in victory for the German Reich in a matter of weeks or, at most, a few months – a perspective buoyed by the spectacular results of the opening phase of the campaign. As early as 1 July 1941, Lt.-Gen. von Richthofen, Commander, 8 Air Corps, was convinced that the bulk of the Soviet Union's forces in western Russia had been eliminated; two weeks later (13 July), he confided to his diary that the road to Moscow lay open, and with no more military obstacles in the way – or so he thought – German forces could be in the Soviet capital in a mere eight days.[291]

Without doubt, the operations of the *Luftwaffe* were "one of the major reasons for the unprecedented success of German arms"[292] during the opening weeks and months of the Russian campaign: "Time and again, air power contributed materially to German success in the great encirclement battles of the summer and fall of 1941, achievements that convinced even skeptics that total victory over the Bolshevik colossus was imminent."[293] Avers air power historian Richard Muller:

> One can find little to criticize regarding the execution of the first phases of the *Luftwaffe's* war against the USSR. German bomber and fighter units exceeded the most optimistic hopes of their commanders when they virtually annihilated the Soviet Air Force during the first two days of the campaign … It is likely that this campaign against the VVS at the campaign's outset was the *Luftwaffe's*

major contribution to the course of the war. The momentous German advances of summer and early fall 1941 took place under conditions of general air supremacy; it is doubtful that they could have occurred otherwise.[294]

German ground forces came to rely increasingly upon air power to compensate for their shortages of artillery, anti-tank, and anti-aircraft weapons.[295] The mechanized units depended on support of the *Luftwaffe* to breach Red Army defenses and defend the outer encirclement rings, which were thinly manned by the panzer and motorized formations; in addition, transport aircraft were needed to deliver emergency supplies of fuel, oil, lubricants, and ammunition when the tanks outran their logistical support.[296] As one wartime *Luftwaffe* study noted, "it soon became apparent that the formations of the Army – against an opponent who always enjoyed a large numerical superiority and usually fought tenaciously – only made good progress when their attacks were effectively supported by the *Luftwaffe*."[297] As a result, ruthless demands were placed on German air and ground crews, and they were committed to a virtually seamless period of operations throughout the summer of 1941.

Within 48 hours of the start of the campaign – and, indeed, within 24 hours inside the battlespace of Army Group Center[298] – complete air supremacy (or at least superiority) had been achieved along the entire 1200+ kilometer front.[299] After 72 hours, Loerzer's 2 Air Corps of Kesselring's 2 Air Fleet was able to report that all Russian aircraft had been destroyed on airfields within a 300+ kilometer radius.[300] Thus was the *Luftwaffe* able to turn to what became its primary mission in the weeks and months that followed – direct and indirect support of operations of the ground forces. In the sector of Bock's army group, direct air support – the close air support, or CAS, mission – was performed mainly by Richthofen's 8 Air Corps, the only formation of the *Luftwaffe* specifically designed for the CAS role; yet even for this air corps, direct support of ground troops remained well down its list of priorities.[301]

Contrary to impressions conveyed by many post-war accounts, the great majority of the *Luftwaffe's* activities during 1941 were geared to *indirect* support of the *Ostheer*, and particularly of the armored forces. This mission embraced a large number of tasks, principal among them (in no particular order): destruction (interdiction) of lines of communication (rail lines, road junctions, bridges, etc.); isolation and destruction of Red Army headquarters and staffs; bombing and strafing Soviet troop, tank and vehicle concentrations; protecting the flanks of the armored forces; sealing off and isolating the battlefield; blunting Red Army counterattacks; and striking enemy rear area installations (supply depots, vehicle parks, etc.) These missions, to which the *Luftwaffe* committed the great bulk of its resources, were tactical in nature, with the "only operational-strategic" use of German air power in 1941 ("on orders from Hitler or the [OKW]") being the air raids on Moscow, which began in late July 1941.[302]

During the opening phases of the Russian campaign, German Air Force units encountered unusually large Soviet marching columns and troop concentrations all across the front; efforts to contest these critical targets, however, were seriously hampered by "unexpected technical difficulties." "The principal problem," recalled Paul Deichmann, former chief of staff of 2 Air Corps (1940-42), "was an insufficient supply of proper type bombs, which seriously reduced the effectiveness of bombing attacks during this most crucial period of the campaign in the east;" as a result, "the enemy had far stronger forces available during the critical phases of the battles before Moscow than would have been the case if properly effective types of bombs had been available to the German side in adequate quantities."[303]

Despite the impressive initial successes, events soon demonstrated that the *Luftwaffe* was simply too diminutive in size to suitably address the myriad demands placed upon it.

According to former *Luftwaffe* general Hermann Plocher:

> It was impossible for the *Luftwaffe* to perform simultaneously its two assigned missions, the achievement of air superiority and support of the ground forces, since the German air units in the east were numerically weak and the operational territory so vast. In attempts to perform both missions at the same time, the effectiveness of one effort or the other was found to diminish. Yet at the beginning of the Russian campaign the *Luftwaffe* successfully accomplished its primary mission of annihilating the Soviet air forces at hand and securing air superiority (almost air supremacy) ...
>
> The second mission (supporting the ground forces) which required all the air power available, began about 25 June. Sorties against Soviet air forces and their ground installations were then flown only occasionally and incidentally, and only when the steadily increasing Russian air activity became too bothersome for the German ground forces or caused them unbearable losses.[304]

The *Luftwaffe* began the Russian campaign with a total of only 2255 operational aircraft, several hundred fewer than had been available at the start of the French campaign in May 1940,[305] despite its vastly increased operational commitments. (Of these aircraft, 994 belonged to Field Marshal Kesselring's 2 Air Fleet, supporting Army Group Center.) That these forces were too few in number to achieve enduring results is illustrated by the following internal *Luftwaffe* study:

> During *Luftwaffe* operations it was soon clear that the units available were far from sufficient to win air superiority [*Luftueberlegenheit*] throughout the vast spaces of the eastern front, let alone air supremacy [*Luftherrschaft*], even though in terms of training standards, combat spirit, and quality of material, they were far superior to the Soviet units. Only by the sharp concentration of forces over the centers of gravity of ground operations was it possible to wrest total air supremacy from the enemy, and then only localized and temporarily.
>
> On other sectors of the front, which thus had to be stripped of their own fighter protection, the troops on the ground complained about Soviet air superiority, because the devastating blow against the Soviet Air Force carried out at the start of the war with such great success had gained the *Luftwaffe* air supremacy along the entire front for only a few weeks ...
>
> Conditions were similar in the battle against the railways, by which the German leadership, in view of the broad Soviet railway network, with its relatively few efficient stretches, had hoped to achieve an impact of operational scope. Yet here, too, the forces available proved far too weak for the size of the task in the broad Russian spaces. In the opening weeks of the war, the attacks on the railway network were undoubtedly extremely disruptive for the enemy, and in certain cases, particularly in the great battles of encirclement, even had fatal consequences. But the hoped for lasting success remained elusive. The impact of the battle against the railways remained localized and above all temporary, because the Soviets developed an entirely unexpected and quite astonishing ability to restore destroyed railway lines in an incredibly short space of time. Moreover, recognizing the enormous importance of an intact railway network for their conduct of the war, they soon began protecting all railway stations, including the smaller ones, with Flak, equipping all trains with light Flak guns, and deploying fighter planes along the railway lines, with the result that our own units soon encountered strong defenses in the battle for the railways ...

> The same ailment of insufficient forces ... was also suffered by aerial reconnaissance, above all long-range reconnaissance, whose focus lay in railway reconnaissance. Due to the lack of forces, it was not possible to thoroughly patrol the main railway lines twice a day across distances of several hundred kilometers and, at a minimum, to capture a daily aerial photograph of the railroad yards of the larger stations ...
>
> As a result of the inadequate forces, only a relatively modest partial segment of the enemy's extensive rail traffic could be ascertained, and whether the long-range reconnaissance missions brought results which might provide the leadership with significant insights into the enemy's intentions and actions was left more or less to chance.[306]

With too few resources, too many missions to perform, and too much airspace to patrol, the *Luftwaffe* saw the air superiority – and, in certain sectors, complete air supremacy – it had achieved so brilliantly in June and July 1941 rapidly attenuate. As this narrative has shown, the Soviet Air Force began to recover quickly from the devastating blows experienced in the first days of Operation *Barbarossa*, and while the Germans remained mostly in control of the air during the summer of 1941, as early as July some Army units were beginning to complain about the uncomfortable levels of Russian air activity. (See Chapter 7, Section 7.4.3.)

If the resources of the *Luftwaffe* in the east were modest to begin with, they also declined at an alarming pace due to attrition in combat, less than optimal operating conditions, and inadequate logistical support. As a general observation, German air units in Russia sustained serious attrition rates; yet unlike the French campaign of 1940 or the Battle of Britain, attrition during the Russian campaign of 1941 was characterized by lower loss rates coupled with sustained operations over an extended period. Still, the "cumulative effect of these small 'acceptable' losses was no less decisive in its impact than was the Battle of Britain."[307]

By 12 July 1941, while claiming the destruction of 6857 Soviet aircraft, the *Luftwaffe* had suffered 550 destroyed and 336 damaged planes, an average of 42 destroyed or damaged planes per day.[308] From 6-19 July 1941, air units in Russia lost 283 aircraft of all types destroyed (including 92 fighters and 82 bombers) and 194 damaged (77 fighters, 45 bombers), an average of 34 aircraft per day. As tabulated by the *Luftwaffe* General Staff, the total number of destroyed and damaged planes for the first four weeks of the campaign amounted to 1284, a figure equal to about 55 percent of the service's entire inventory of operational machines along the eastern front on 22 June 1941. Many of these aircraft losses were the result of effective Russian anti-aircraft fire against low-level German air attacks.[309]

At the end of August 1941, the number of Bf 109 E and F single engine fighters available in the east amounted to 626; yet of these, only 329 were reported as operational (*einsatzklar*), compared to 657 combat-ready machines on the first day of the campaign. In fact, by late August, many fighter *Gruppen* had been reduced to a dozen or fewer operational aircraft, barely the strength of a typical fighter squadron; at the same time, the first fighter groups were withdrawn from the front to be rebuilt.[310] All told, during the first four months of Operation *Barbarossa*, the German air fleets in Russia lost an average of 741 planes (destroyed or damaged) each month,[311] a figure equal to nearly one third of the total combat-ready strength on 22 June 1941. Over the same period, the *Luftwaffe* lost an average of 318 aircrew per month.[312]

Many of the aircraft destroyed or damaged in Russia were not lost in combat, but as a result of the primitive operating conditions across the front. Flying from dirt or grass airstrips, as was the norm, was often deadly; throughout all of 1941, on all fronts, the *Luftwaffe* incurred three aircraft losses due to non-combat causes for every four resulting from enemy action.[313] Compounding the problems of German air units in Russia was a system of supply and maintenance which rapidly deteriorated the deeper the Germans advanced inside the Soviet Union. Many aircraft (among them the large numbers of Bf 109s available in the east yet not operational at the end of August 1941) were lying about on forward airfields, inoperable due to breakdowns in deliveries of spare engines or parts. Because the *Luftwaffe* leadership – like the German political and military leadership as a whole – expected the campaign to be over in a matter of weeks, few replacement aircraft were available to replenish losses. Like the German ground forces, the air wings would have to fight and win the war largely with the resources available to them on 22 June.[314]

While operating conditions left much to be desired, German aircrews flew their missions under largely ideal climatic conditions throughout the summer of 1941. In July and August 1941, tactical air elements of Kesselring's 2 Air Fleet were favored by clear weather and good visibility, with cloud ceilings only infrequently below 1500 feet. Because of the limits imposed by early 1940s technology, which greatly restricted tactical air operations and target acquisition at night, 2 Air Fleet conducted the great majority of its missions in support of the ground armies during the daylight hours. Fortunately for the Germans, the days were long in central Russia at this time of year,[315] providing them with a significant tactical advantage:

> When [Army Group Center] advanced out of Poland ... on 22 June 1941, the German divisions in it had ... 17 hours of sunlight in which to fight, move, and navigate to the advantage of the sophisticated German mode of attack. The German armies, which fought the great battles of encirclement in the vicinities of Belostok, Minsk, and Smolensk ... were able to maintain the lines of encirclement successfully around the huge, trapped Soviet forces. The seldom discussed, natural geographic factor which favored the Germans was the presence of 17 hours of sunlight and the absence of full night conditions. The hard-pressed defending Soviet formations were forced to launch their counterattacks or attempt to infiltrate through the thin German lines of containment during a few hours of astronomical twilight.[316]

During the opening weeks of the campaign, the Messerschmitt Bf 109 "Emils" and the newer, swifter and more numerous "Friedrichs" of 2 Air Fleet's 27, 51, and 53 Fighter Wings flew multiple sorties each day in support of Army Group Center. In contrast to the air war over Great Britain, where the *Jagdflieger* often operated in group or squadron size units, in Russia the fighter formations tended to fly in small packages of four or five aircraft (*Schwarm*) and, as the campaign progressed, even in two-ship formations (*Rotte*). The reason for the change had less to do with any desired shift in tactics than with the need to cover the vast spaces of the eastern front; the use of such diminutive fighter packages was also dictated by the rapidly declining numbers of available aircraft. Even the fighter escort missions for bomber and *Stuka* units were conducted with considerably fewer assets than during the Battle of Britain. Of course, such arrangements were only practical so long as the *Luftwaffe* maintained its marked technical and tactical advantage over the Soviet Air Force.[317]

In addition to fighter escort duties, types of missions flown by the Bf 109 fighter force included: Sweeping the ground for targets, or the skies for enemy aircraft, an activity known in the idiom of the German fighter pilot as *"freie Jagd;"* patrolling the airspace above friendly ground forces; and conducting fighter-bomber and low-level attacks on airfields, concentrations of troops and vehicles, and rail targets. In another contrast to the aerial combat over England, which took place at greater and greater altitudes, the air battles in Russia generally occurred at altitudes up to just 3000 meters (10,000 feet), which placed the German fighters within the effective range of Soviet light and medium Flak artillery, for which the Bf 109 pilots soon developed an abiding respect. The low-level missions (*Tiefangriffen*) were particularly dangerous due to the robust Russian light Flak defenses and the collective fire from Soviet ground troops who, unlike the British and the French in 1940, were trained to open up with all available weapons on enemy aircraft. In fact, instead of taking cover when under low-level air attack, Soviet infantry often simply lay on their backs, peered skyward, and opened fire with their small arms. Particularly vulnerable to such fire was the Bf 109's radiator. Indeed, a fortuitous hit by a single rifle bullet was enough to drain the radiator fluid and force the pilot to make an emergency landing, with the daunting prospect of capture by the enemy if he were unable to reach his own lines.[318]

German pilots, of course, just like German ground troops, were quite fearful of becoming prisoners of war – a fear fueled by the unfortunate fate of a number of German fighter pilots in the first days of the war, who were captured and killed by often enraged Soviet troops or militia units. In general, pilots captured by either adversary were often mistreated or killed – a manifestation of the racism and visceral hatreds that affected the fighting forces of both sides. On the other hand, many cases were recorded in which downed German pilots were offered protection by local civilians and the opportunity to return safely to their own lines.[319] (If these helpful civilians viewed the arrival of the *Wehrmacht* as the beginning of their liberation from years of Soviet oppression, they would be bitterly disappointed.) For their part, Bf 109 fighter pilots could be less than particular when choosing their targets, often sending bursts of machine gun fire into the meandering columns of civilian refugees as they desperately sought their escape. As a rule, *Luftwaffe* aircrews indiscriminately bombed and strafed Russian soldiers and civilians alike. Writes Constantine Pleshakov:

> During air raids, mothers put buckets on their children's heads to protect them from shrapnel, and some, in desperation, used their purses for the same purpose. As soon as the *Luftwaffe* came in sight, people covered up girls wearing bright colors with coats and jackets, fearing that a red dress would certainly catch the eye of a German pilot.
>
> Mothers stuffed birth certificates and home addresses in little bags and tied them around the necks of younger children so they would have some chance of being identified if the mothers were killed – and many were, particularly during the air raids. One witness saw an infant sucking a dead mother's breast, another a group of children begging soldiers not to bury their mother and pleading with the dead woman to open her eyes. In a macabre twist, many highways were covered with scores of dolls that young girls had snatched up before fleeing and then lost to stampedes and death.[320]

Exploiting their superior training, experience, and tactics, as well as the pronounced technological edge of their machines, German fighter pilots registered astounding "kill" totals in the opening phases of the Russian campaign. (See, Chapter 3, Section 3.5.) The achievements of Lt.-Col. Werner Moelders' 51 Fighter Wing (51 JG) are instructive in this regard. On the first day of the war, the wing destroyed – on the ground and in the air – well over 100 Soviet planes, with Moelders himself registering four of the kills, including his 72nd overall, for which he was awarded the Swords to the Knight's Cross with Oak Leaves, becoming only the second *Wehrmacht* officer to receive this award. (The first award of this newly minted decoration had gone to Adolf Galland, 24 hours earlier, for his 69 kills in the west.)[321] The next day (23 June) the wing continued its low-level strikes, which resulted in only two enemy aircraft destroyed; however, in operations in support of Guderian's 2

Panzer Group, the wing's Bf 109s used their 20mm cannon to take out at least two dozen Soviet tanks near Pruzhany. On 24 June, the wing was credited with a further 82 kills – the majority, most likely, Soviet bombers, which were hurled in suicidal waves, and without fighter protection of their own, against the rampaging *Ostheer*. Twenty-four hours later (25 June), 51 JG was alone responsible for downing 83 Tupolev SB-2 bombers. On 28 June, the wing was again providing ground troops with much needed support, this time protecting 3 Panzer Division's small bridgehead over the Berezina at Bobruisk. On the final day of the month (30 June), the Soviets threw every bomber they could lay hands on against 3 Panzer's Berezina bridgehead, Moelders' fighters shooting down 110 of them![322] On 30 June it was also announced that 51 JG had become the first *Jagdgeschwader* since September 1939 to record 1000 victories.[323]

Because of the relatively "short legs" of the Bf 109s, the fighter bases were forced to change their operating locations repeatedly to keep pace with the German armored spearheads. When doing so, the components of the fighter *Gruppen* – advance parties (*Vorauskommandos*), main columns, equipment, personnel – often became widely separated as they struggled along the poor roadways toward their new destinations. As a result of the unavoidable breaks in the operations of affected units, air support of ground forces was intermittently disrupted for short periods of time. Between 29 June and 23 July 1941, elements of Richthofen's 8 Air Corps moved on six separate occasions until, in early August, the air corps and its *Gruppen* were transferred to Army Group North.[324]

The "heavy lifting" in support of the ground forces was performed by the *Luftwaffe's* bomber wings (*Kampfgeschwader*), which began the Russian campaign with 757 operational He 111H/P, Do 17Z and Ju-88A twin-engine medium bombers. Of these, 222 were assigned to 2, 3 and 53 Bomber Wings in 2 Air Fleet.[325] On 22 June 1941, bomber crews flew as many as eight missions apiece and, in the days that followed, the pace of operations was unrelenting. After the initial strikes against Soviet airfields, the bombers sought out tactical targets in support of the Army, dropping their loads on troop concentrations, transportation centers, bridges, roads and railway lines, and enemy strongpoints along the Army's three main axes of advance.[326] The Heinkel, Dornier and Junkers machines wreaked havoc with Russian troop movements and supply columns. Aerial photographs from this period, taken by *Luftwaffe* aircrews, often depict staggering scenes of death and destruction, with the twisted, charred remains of vehicles, tanks, artillery, men, horses and equipment littering the roadways leading away from the frontier.

In the area of Army Group Center, the bombers of 2 Air Fleet contributed greatly to the success of the German drive across Belorussia. For example, in late June 1941, bomber formations pounded Soviet forces encircled in the area of Belostok, Zelva and Grodno, which were attempting to slip through the forests and escape eastward. The bombers of Kesselring's air fleet also protected the vulnerable flanks of advancing German forces against Soviet counterattacks. In one action (24/25 June), bombers and dive bombers of 8 Air Corps contributed to the defeat of a Soviet tank attack on 8 and 20 Army Corps in the area of Kuznitsa, Odelsk, Grodno, and Dombrova by conducting relay attacks; in another, they halted an enemy counterstroke against the flank 3 Panzer Group near Lida until reinforcements arrived.[327] In addition, the bombers helped to prevent the breakout of Russian forces from the Belostok-Minsk pocket and, later, through early August 1941, from the Smolensk encirclement.

The *Kampfgeschwader* of 2 Air Fleet also struck roads and railway lines in an effort to seal off the battlefield and prevent the timely arrival of Soviet reinforcements. Among the rail lines targeted in the initial attacks were those at (or near) Minsk, Orsha, Gomel, Briansk, Smolensk, and Mogilev. On 14 July 1941, the rail link between Smolensk and Moscow was hit for the first time; and, at the end of July, the railway station at Orel was bombed, while 3 Bomber Wing (3 KG) conducted many "train busting" sorties.[328] The attacks on railway lines leading to the front continued in the weeks which followed; from the outset, however, they "were rather of a tactical-operational nature and their strategic effect was overestimated."[329]

The attrition experienced by the bomber forces was exceptional, amounting, on average, to 268 aircraft destroyed or damaged each month during the first four months of the campaign, along with the loss of many irreplaceable aircrews.[330] The physical and psychological toll exacted by the constant commitment to action – and the concomitant lack of rest and sleep – was considerable:

> The demands heaped upon the *Kampfgeschwadern* stretched them to, and often beyond, their limits. Crews made three to four sorties per day, each between four and five hours long, and most units remained operational for at least six months (some up to nine months) without a single day off since the start of the campaign. Unsurprisingly, medical officers of several units reported that extreme nervous exhaustion was widespread among aircrews. Relentless, long-range flights, constant mortal fear and the physiological stresses of dive-bombing severely degraded bodily and mental constitution. Men became fractious, a typical symptom of sleep deprivation, sometimes breaking into unprovoked weeping spasms. Air and ground crews alike were on the verge of a collective nervous breakdown. Some *Geschwaderkommodore* [wing commanders] were forced to implement timetables that at last made rest periods possible in rotation. Men seized the opportunity to sleep, sometimes for days at a time. Others resolved to get as far away as possible, as quickly as possible. Although rare and fleeting, a little peace had great restorative power upon a man's spirit. Returning mentally refreshed, he nevertheless began to sink back into the general state of nervousness within a few hours.[331]

While the bomber wings of 2 Air Fleet struck a number of Soviet cities during the first days of the war – among them, Smolensk, bombed by 32 planes of 2 Air Corps on the night of 28/29 June 1941, to "good effect," according to a *Luftwaffe* study later in the war[332] – the only concerted effort to mount a "strategic" air campaign were the raids against Moscow. These began on the night of 21/22 July 1941, when 127 bombers from several wings (mostly belonging to 2 Air Fleet) dropped 104 tons of high-explosive bombs (*Sprengbomben*) and 46,000 incendiaries (*Brandbomben*) on the Soviet capital.[333] The air campaign against Moscow will be examined in some detail in Chapter 10 (Section 10.3) of this book. Suffice it to note here that the raids on Moscow (along with several less significant attempts at strategic air war) signified "a steady and considerable drain on [the *Luftwaffe's*] ability to intervene decisively in the ground battle ... The raids were in violation of the principle of *Schwerpunktbildung* [concentration of effort] to which most *Luftwaffe* commands adhered during the first campaign year against the Soviet Union."[334]

Complementing the German bomber forces were the *Stukageschwader* – the terrifying symbol of the blitzkrieg through Poland and France – equipped with the Ju 87B single-engine dive-bomber. Of a total of 360 operational *Stukas* concentrated in the east (22 June 1941), 323 aircraft in 8 1/3 *Gruppen* were massed in 1, 2 and 77 *Stuka* Wings assigned to Kesselring's 2 Air Fleet.[335] Although the *Stuka's* "lack of adequate armored protection and corresponding vulnerability to small-arms fire made it a less than ideal close-support weapon,"[336] it was, nevertheless, the primary CAS asset in the *Luftwaffe* inventory. As noted in Chapter 3, a typical mode of attack for the Ju 87B was to strike its target in steep dive – that is, at an angle of ca. 70 degrees. In doing so, the *Stuka* crew could attain an accuracy of under 30 yards; while not precision bombing, it "was the most accurate [result] that technology could achieve at the time."[337] Tactical targets attacked by the *Stuka Gruppen* included bridges, rail lines, trains and rail installations, tanks, artillery, anti-aircraft sites, troop and vehicle concentrations, field fortifications and buildings.[338] (See also, Chapter 3, Section 3.5.)

Like the fighter and bomber forces, the *Stuka* squadrons maintained a furious pace of operations, resulting in an attrition rate of 60 aircraft destroyed or damaged on average each month for the first few months of the war, a figure equal to 20.5 percent of the total average monthly strength. Surprisingly, measured as a percentage of average monthly strength, *Stuka* loss rates were actually significantly less than those incurred by single-engine fighter and bomber units, whose average monthly losses (destroyed or damaged planes) amounted to 36.3 and 32.1 percent, respectively, of their average monthly strength.[339]

In this narrative, many examples have been given of the effective close air support furnished by *Stuka* formations, dispatched hither and thither to crisis points across the front of Army Group Center. Time and again, the dive-bombers helped to break enemy resistance along the forward edge of battle, creating opportunities for the panzer units of Hoth and Guderian to drive deeper and deeper into Soviet Russia, toward their ultimate objective of Moscow. As a result, the troops on the ground came to rely increasingly on the relief promised by the gull winged craft, as the following *Landser* accounts illustrate – the first from the diary of an officer in an infantry gun company, the second from a tanker's field post letters:

Leutnant Georg Kreuter (18 PD)   26 June 1941
I am in action for the first time at the bridge at Trakt. Two enemy divisions are reportedly ahead of us. But panzers from another corps are apparently already at their back! I lay with my observation post in some fine enemy artillery fire. *Stukas* are helping us a lot! … For three days now we have had nothing to eat or drink. We are finally permitted to consume our special rations. The "*Schokakola*"[340] tastes especially good. – We're attacking Baranovichi! – In the evening at 2100 hours I take up position under artillery fire behind a forested hill. From time to time, I think I see enemy tanks, but they're usually ours. There's still a lot of tank fright! [*Panzerschreck*] I frequently had to step in with other companies.

Leutnant Georg Kreuter (18 PD)   28 June 1941
I'm taking over the company! In the evening hours, the attack on the enemy in the forest intensifies. But he stays down in the darkness. Divisions allow themselves to be held up by 100 Reds with a few rifles, pistols, and mortars. It's a terrible shame to have to see the indecisiveness of our leadership. Without artillery and *Stukas*, absolutely nothing gets done.[341]

Klaus Fuchs (7 PD) 17 July 1941
Yesterday we moved past Smolensk on the city's northern fringe and are now heading toward Moscow. Russian opposition is weak and localized and wherever we meet them, they are forced to flee. Our Air Force, in particular the *Stuka* [dive] bombers, actively support our efforts. Our comrades from the Air Force are top-notch guys.

Klaus Fuchs (7 PD) 20 July 1941
Today is Sunday and for a change the sun is shining. It had rained heavily in the last couple of days, but now in clear weather our *Stuka* dive-bombers are once again on the prowl. These pilots are really something! Wherever they strike they create havoc and destruction.[342]

Flying several sorties each day, for days and weeks at a time, facing the constant prospect of sudden death or injury, while going without proper rest or sleep, *Stuka* pilots were exposed to enormous physical and psychological stress. In his memoirs, *Stuka* pilot Hans Rudel noted that, in the opening period of the campaign, crews in his squadron were flying missions as early as 3.00 in the morning and often not coming in "from our last landing" until 10.00 in the evening: "A good night's rest goes by the board. Every spare minute we stretch out underneath the aeroplane and instantly fall asleep. Then if a call comes from anywhere we hop to it without even knowing where it is from. We move as though in our dreams."[343]

The mission profile of a *Stuka* was highly demanding, the pilot, for example, subjected to uncomfortable G-force pressures of 4g to 12g for one to six seconds, depending on how he leveled out from his dive. Explained *Hauptmann* Robert Oleinic, a *Stuka* training instructor: "A dive speed of 480kph placed enormous strain on the system ... The pressure while leveling out was so intense that pilots occasionally experienced a temporary misting sensation that could last a few seconds. That meant for a moment he blacked out."[344] In addition, the infernal scream emitted by the dive-bomber's "Jericho Trumpet" siren could shatter an eardrum.

Hauptmann Herbert Pabst, squadron commander (later group commander) in a *Stuka* unit, operating in the sector of 2 Panzer Group, recorded his combat experiences during the summer of 1941, offering dramatic insights into the adventures of a *Stuka* pilot on the eastern front:

22.6.41:
Deblin ... in a barracks camouflaged as a farmhouse on a dreadfully dusty, but beautifully disguised advanced airstrip close to the Bug River.

It's time – the new special reports are coming. Early, at 0200 hours, I got up; at 0330 at first light, I started off into Russia for the first time. At 1900 hours, I've already flown 3 sorties and haven't yet had lunch. But I only noticed that at 1600 hours and it doesn't matter ... Over there – at first [we struck] bunker positions and batteries close to the Bug, then our tanks quickly moved forward, and we also flew further ahead.

A tank battle below – sort of rectangular little boxes crawling all over the fields followed by wafting billows of dust – ours? Enemy's? Constant flashes from below – here houses are burning, there smoke in the forest – there, a tank is burning and the ammunition goes up in bright flashes amid the red fire. Lower! It's our own panzers advancing there. Beyond the forest, columns are moving toward them – tanks, trucks, the roads and forests are full.

Attack! – The bomb is already flashing up behind me while I pull up, now another, then another – boom, that must have been an ammunition truck going up. A dazzling flash shoots up, black shards fly, leaving smoldering red fire in its place.

Attack with machine guns! One [plane] after another dives down behind me, putting constant bursts of fire into the motionless motor vehicles. There, one starts to burn. Even the Me 109s flitting round us are coming in low for the attack. Then I gather the *Bumas* [i.e., his *Stukas*] on the return flight. All nine there? Yes, all nine! ...

We land again soon after that ... The mechanics gather round us, eager for news, while the flight commanders report to me that all the machines have landed safely. A hasty meeting. Where were enemy, where friend, sighted? Impact of our attacks? Everything is very grave and hurried ... So! And now shirt off, a coffee, a cigarette.[345]

Between sorties, Pabst and his *Stuka* crews looked on in amazement as small groups of attacking Soviet bombers – one group stoically followed by the next, which was followed by yet another still – were pounced on and obliterated by the swift and nimble Bf 109s. All told, the men saw 21 of the ponderous enemy bombers go down in flames, with none escaping destruction. The Messerschmitts, rocking their wings in victory, returned to their bases.[346] His diary continues:

25.6.41:
1000 hours. Transfer to Pruzhany.

A lot going on, but the squadron and I are well. I have just got back (outside Brest-Litovsk) and am sitting with a good coffee together with Bumke, afterwards we're to go out again; but I have rest for the remainder of the day and this afternoon I'll get some good sleep. Lovely, sun, but a dreadful number of mosquitoes out there.

26.6.41:
Midday. Slutsk.

I was out again early today, but German tanks had already arrived where I was supposed to take out at Russian tanks. They rolled ahead at a sharp pace in dense columns. I flew onward, onward, along the huge road – it goes straight ahead endlessly, through forests and fields, miserable little settlements and vast swamps. Sometimes it was empty, then there were huge columns again – but when I began to come in closer for a look, they hurriedly fired light signals and rolled out flags – still Germans! Forward, forward. But eventually lack of fuel made me turn round …

Early yesterday a mission made me very happy, because it was very important. The evening before, we had crawled, dog tired, into a provisionally requisitioned farmhouse (most of my soldiers are in tents). Straw on the ground; after an hour of fruitless struggle with an army of mosquitoes, I gave up and curled up on the seat of my vehicle – but even there I had to fight another hour for sleep before I had finally got all the mosquitoes with the aid of the interior lighting.

27.6.41:[347]
Cauldron of Belostok outside Slonim.[348]

At first light: Alarm! The encircled Russians have broken through along the road of advance. 40 minutes later I was in the morning air with the squadron. But here, too, I saw a German column at the indicated spot. I go warily deeper to see better – there! Signal lights rise up, signs are hastily unfurled – hey, they are mightily afraid because of the threateningly circling *Stukas*. But you can rest assured – I'll look closer first. It is difficult to make out from above.[349]

There, a bit further ahead, two vehicles are burning – the road is otherwise empty – there, too, a shaky white signal light flares up. [Note: A white Very signal light always meant "German troops here!"] But from the forest edge, not far from the road, there is the occasional flash – muzzle flashes! Aha, so something is going on over there after all. I circle and look. Again, a signal light climbs into the air from the road: Be careful! It's us! But in the forest I can see vehicles hidden on a path, gathered densely at the side – nervous quiet, nothing moves. Only at the forest edge is there movement and shooting toward the road. "*Buma*-Attack!" The Germans on the road were probably scared shitless when we laid our eggs. Then there's a flash in the forest, huge columns of smoke shoot into the sky, boom, boom, again – there, a huge jet of flame, then something else exploded. Again and again we attack, bombs rain down into the little wood; as I pull up, I can see more vehicles in a field further away in the distance – I'm out of bombs, now the tracer of my machine gun leaps down in a slanting attack, and draws pale threads of smoke into the clear morning air.

Dense columns of our troops are again marching east even on this road today. We will no doubt soon follow.

Otherwise: food, vodka, cigarettes – everything there and everything's fine. I'm sitting bare-chested under shady trees, my radio playing gentle melodies, my trusty "culture hero," even in these distant ... vistas.

28.6.41:

2030 hours. Thank God, back on the straw in the farmer's cottage. I am utterly exhausted. Last night (I wasn't supposed to be awakened until 0430 hours, which was unusually late) at 0100 hours "alarm" – ... Russian stragglers are attacking from the forests! In the narrow corridor that we've driven between their armies, that's always a possibility. Everybody rushes to the berths, all machine guns are readied, we listen tensely into the night, but eventually it all turns out to be a latrine rumor, and I had woken all my men and hurried them to the machines for nothing.

I did manage to sleep a little in my car until dawn. From 0500 hours ready to go – and soon it was all go, right to the front of the panzer spearhead, which, having advanced far ahead, was threatened from the flank. Beastly weather on the way, I even wondered whether I should turn around, but then I made it after all, despite the clouds hanging almost as low as the crowns of the trees. Right at the front at Koydanov (outside Minsk), I saw them standing in a burning town, saw their signal lights and unfurled aerial recognition flags, and chucked a load on the heads of the enemy harassing them – again and again with bombs and machine guns. Landing to take on fuel on an airstrip (formerly Russian) way to the front where the ground was scattered with destroyed and burned out Soviet planes – a terrific number.

This afternoon I destroyed a bridge that would have been used by another Russian column heading laterally toward our route of advance. First bomb, 20 meters ahead of the bridge, square in the center of the road, which resulted in a huge crater, the second, a direct hit – the timbers went every which way and the bridge was gone; the other *Bumas* didn't need to drop anything at all ...

So now I lie, starved of sleep, on my straw, after my driver gave me something to eat. Now I've got back to my hot milk, cigarettes, letter, and the gentle music of my radio. (Further south, they're already at the Berezina! That makes me think of father.)

30.6.41:

I'm feeling splendid [*glaenzend*] and the squadron does, too.[350]

If, at the end of June 1941, the morale of the *Stukaflieger* was – in the idiom of *Hauptmann* Pabst – "splendid," over time, many would be pushed beyond the limits of their endurance; some would suffer nervous breakdowns. In a dramatic post-war interview conducted in the late-1970s, former *Stuka* pilot Karl Vogt recalled how he finally broke under the strain of multiple daily missions, for days on end, without surcease. From the nature of Vogt's responses, it is apparent that, more than 30 years after the war, he had yet to fully confront his traumatic wartime experiences. (Note: "L" and "S" are the interviewers.)

VOGT: I was with the *Luftwaffe* – I was also there at the start of the Russian campaign. And then I went into a hospital and wasn't allowed to fly anymore. I had gone off the rails. Nervous breakdown.
L.: Oh yes. How did that happen?
VOGT: Well, you try flying 10 to 12 missions every day.[351]

L.: Every day?

VOGT: Every day.

L.: Just for the nerves, that was too great a – and how did that show itself? You couldn't get into the plane anymore?

VOGT: No, I had got out of my plane when the adjutant came up and [said]: "There, your next machine." Then I hit him. If he'd had a gun, he'd have finished me. He didn't have one. They arrested me.

L.: And then they saw that what you had was an illness.

VOGT: And that's what they saw – I didn't react at all, didn't react any more. Was a bit too much.

L.: Were you virtually apathetic …

VOGT: There are still some of them in the loony bins, some of those who did it.[352]

S.: Who had to fly missions constantly?

VOGT: Constant missions. Nerves completely done in. And just, they became basket cases. They couldn't work it off like I did. I worked it off in that moment, when I hit out. Right there, I was in a situation where it hadn't gone too far, where I was still curable. I was *still* healthy.

S.: And those were always combat missions, too?

VOGT: Only combat missions. With the Ju 87. You know it?

S.: Oh, always nosedives?

FRAU VOGT: *Stuka*!

L.: The *Stuka*. Uuuuuuuoo …

VOGT: But that wasn't the awful thing.

L.: … it howls like that.

VOGT: Between the landing gear we had a siren, one-meter diameter …

L.: That's what I meant, yes.

VOGT: … and we would block that, so long as we were flying. When we began our dive, then the block would be removed: despite special flying caps,[353] the eardrum would rupture due to (- -). What do you think the effect on morale was for those below? For the people below?

L.: The machine spread dreadful fear among civilians.

VOGT: And it wore us down [*hat uns kaputt gemacht*].

S.: So the noise as well.

VOGT: Everything! And then see that: you fly [a mission]; and then you have to report – "what did you hit?" Back [in the air again], and then you see there the pieces flying all over the place. Of course then you have a real "sense of heroism," if you actually imagine yourself as a "hero." Let's drop it, it's better that way.[354]

ENDNOTES

1   H. Pabst, *The Outermost Frontier*, 12.

2   H. F. Richardson (ed.), *Your Loyal and Loving Son. The Letters of Tank Gunner Karl Fuchs, 1937-41*, 112.

3   F. Belke, *Infanterist*, 33.

4   *Tagebuch* Haape, 3.8.41.

5   German publications since the 1980s, which either address the analysis of World War II field post, or demonstrate how it can be used as a legitimate tool by historians, include: K. Latzel, "*Feldpostbriefe: Ueberlegungen zur Aussagekraft einer Quelle*," in: *Verbrechen der Wehrmacht*, C. Hartmann, et al., 171-81; H. J. Schroeder, "*Erfahrungen deutscher Mannschaftssoldaten waehrend der ersten Phase des Russlandkrieges*," in: *Zwei Wege nach Moskau*, B. Wegner (Hg.), 309-325; P. Knoch, "*Feldpost – eine unentdeckte historische Quellengattung*," in: *Geschichtsdidaktik*, Vol. 11, No. 2/86, 154-71; M. Humburg, *Das Gesicht des Krieges. Feldpostbriefe von Wehrmachtssoldaten aus der Sowjetunion 1941-44*; O. Buchbender & R. Sterz (Hg.), *Das*

andere Gesicht des Krieges. Deutsche Feldpost 1939-1945; H. Dollinger (Hg.), *Kain, wo ist dein Bruder?*; I. Hammer & S. zur Nieden (Hg.), *Sehr selten habe ich geweint. Briefe und Tagebuecher aus dem Zweiten Weltkrieg von Menschen aus Berlin*; C. Hartmann, *Wehrmacht im Ostkrieg*; J. Huerter, *Hitlers Heerfuehrer*. In Huerter's book, the personal diaries of German field marshals and generals, and their letters to wives and family members, are key source materials. For one of the very first publications in Germany of war letters from the Second World War (1952) see, W. Baehr, et al. (Hg.), *Kriegsbriefe Gefallener Studenten*.

6   K. Latzel, *Deutsche Soldaten – nationalsozialistischer Krieg?*, 26-27; K. Latzel, *"Feldpostbriefe: Ueberlegungen zur Aussagekraft einer Quelle,"* in: *Verbrechen der Wehrmacht*, C. Hartmann, et al., 171.

7   K. Latzel, *Deutsche Soldaten – nationalsozialistischer Krieg?*, 24; O. Buchbender & R. Sterz (Hg.), *Das andere Gesicht des Krieges*, 10.

8   O. Buchbender & R. Sterz (Hg.), *Das andere Gesicht des Krieges*, 9.

9   P. Knoch, *"Feldpost – eine unentdeckte historische Quellengattung,"* in: *Geschichtsdidaktik*, Vol. 11, No. 2 (1986), 156.

10   During the Second World War, the censor of German field post was the responsibility of so-called *Feldpost-Pruefstellen*, whose activities were regulated by an OKW service regulation of 12 March 1940. The OKW assigned one of these censor agencies to each field army, with a staff of about 5 officers and 19 NCOs. K. Latzel, *Deutsche Soldaten – nationalsozialistischer Krieg?*, 30.

11   Ibid., 30.

12   W. Wette, *The Wehrmacht*, 180.

13   S. G. Fritz, *Frontsoldaten. The German Soldier in World War II*, 55-57.

14   See also, J. Dollwet, *"Menschen im Krieg, Bejahung – und Widerstand?,"* in: *Jahrbuch fuer westdeutsche Landesgeschichte*, 13. Jahrgang, 1987, F. J. Heyen, et al. (Hg.), 281.

15   Quoted in: K. Latzel, *Deutsche Soldaten – nationalsozialistischer Krieg?*, 30.

16   "USSR: republics and selected administrative areas, 1941," in: *The Oxford Guide to World War II*, I.C.B. Dear (ed.), 954-55.

17   S. Knappe, *Soldat*, 213-14.

18   Private Otto Will, a driver in 5 Panzer Division, recalled an experience driving along this highway, between Minsk and Smolensk, in September 1941: "New deployment order for me. I am to go to Smolensk with *Oberleutnant* Jaskolla, and via the Minsk-Moscow highway no less, which is so familiar to me. It is similar to our highways, but it has no delineated traffic lanes. On the part of this route which is still unfamiliar to me I find that the asphalted, well-constructed sections become more infrequent, until finally they stop all together. Crude cobblestones or loose chippings are the usual road surface. This really compromises the manageable travel times considerably ... It is late in the afternoon when we leave the town of Smolensk. We drive back to Orsha ... I immediately get an abdominal bandage from the clothing truck so that I can better cope with the jolting during the journeys in my VW jeep with its rigid suspension." O. Will, *Tagebuch eines Ostfront-Kaempfers*, 11-12.

19   Quoted in: B. H. Liddell Hart, *The German Generals Talk*, 149.

20   A. Seaton, *The Battle for Moscow*, 46-47.

21   C. von Luttichau, *Road to Moscow*, XIII:24.

22   The area of the Belorussian SSR before the Molotov-Ribbentrop pact of August 1939 was 207,600 sq. km.; following the pact, and the Soviet occupation of eastern Poland, it was 225,700 sq. km., with a population of 10,528,000. *Belarus u Vialikai Aichynnai vaine, 1941-1945. Entsyklapedyia* [Belarus in the Great Patriotic War 1941-1945: An Encyclopedia] (Minsk: "Belaruskaia savetskaia entsyklapedyia imia Petrusia Brouki," 1990), 5. Special thanks to David Glantz for these data.

23   C. Pleshakov, *Stalin's Folly*, 199.

24   Dr E. Bunke, *Der Osten blieb unser Schicksal*, 298. In his personal diary on 22 August 1941, Dr Hans Lierow (6 ID) noted the start of a German assault (*Sturmangriff*) at dawn (4:00 a.m.). *Tagebuch* Lierow, 22.8.41.

25   C. Pleshakov, *Stalin's Folly*, 201.

26   R. Kirchubel, *Operation Barbarossa 1941 (3), Army Group Center*, 29; W. Haupt, *Army Group Center*, 10; H. Hoth, *Panzer-Operationen*, 45-47.

27   FMS T-34, K. Allmendinger, et al., *"Terrain Factors in the Russian Campaign,"* 30.

28   FMS T-34, K. Allmendinger, et al., *"Terrain Factors in the Russian Campaign,"* 30-31. For the German General Staff's own analysis of the waterways in central Russia prior to the start of the campaign see, *Militaergeographische Angaben ueber das Europaeische Russland, Zentral-Russland (ohne Moskau), abgeschlossen am 15. Mai 1941*, Generalstab des Heeres, Berlin 1941; quoted in: *Die Schlacht um Moskau*, J. Piekalkiewicz, 12-13.

29   The largest area of marshland in the Soviet Union was the Pripiat' Marshes, situated on the southern edge of Army Group Center's area of operations; for a brief description of these marshes see, Chapter 1, Section 1.6.

30   FMS P-052, H. von Greiffenberg, *"Combat in Forests and Swamps,"* 8-13; K. Uebe, *"Russian Reactions to German Airpower in World War II,"* USAF Historical Study No. 176, 11-12.

31   FMS T-34, K. Allmendinger, et al., *"Terrain Factors in the Russian Campaign,"* 72-75.

32   FMS P-052, H. von Greiffenberg, *"Combat in Forests and Swamps,"* 9. According to Albert Seaton, however, the "forests were thickest in the west near the old Polish frontier." See, A. Seaton, *The Battle for Moscow*, 44.

33   FMS T-34, K. Allmendinger, et al., *"Terrain Factors in the Russian Campaign,"* 51-52; A. Seaton, *The Battle for Moscow*, 44.

34   E. Raus, *"Effects of Climate on Combat in European Russia"* (DA Pamphlet No. 20-291), quoted in: *Fighting in Hell*, P. G. Tsouras (ed.), 225.

35   FMS T-34, K. Allmendinger, et al., *"Terrain Factors in the Russian Campaign,"* 52, 67.

36   E. Raus, *"Effects of Climate on Combat in European Russia"* (DA Pamphlet No. 20-291), quoted in: *Fighting in Hell*, P. G. Tsouras (ed.), 229.

37   C. Burdick & H.-A. Jacobsen (eds.), *The Halder Diary 1939-1942*, 454.

38   *Tagebuch* Kummer, 24.8.41 (unpublished diary).

39   *Tagebuch* Haape, 29.8.41.

40   A. Freitag, *Aufzeichnungen aus Krieg und Gefangenschaft*, 60.

41   Ibid., 60, f.n. 12.

42   H. F. Richardson (ed.), *Your Loyal and Loving Son. The Letters of Tank Gunner Karl Fuchs, 1937-41*, 112.

43   Ibid., 118.

44   E. Bub, *"Ein verlorenes Jahrzehnt. Tagebuchaufzeichnungen Emil Bub"* (unpublished diary).

45   W. Buddenbohm, *Das Leben des Soldaten Wilhelm Buddenbohm*, 60.

46   IfZ Archives, MA 1577: 24. Pz.K., Abt. Ic, Bericht, *"Die Rollbahn zwischen Brest-Litowsk und Moskau,"* 17.6.41, cited in: C. Hartmann, *Wehrmacht im Ostkrieg*, 251, f.n. 40.

47   W. Murray, "May 1940: Contingency and fragility of the German RMA," in: *The Dynamics of military revolution*, M. Knox & W. Murray (eds.), 154-55.

48   In his more "sober" moments, however, even such a prime mover of the Russian campaign as Franz Halder could be plagued by doubts. During Halder's front visit to 17 Army (Army Group South) on 24 May 1941, one officer observed how the Chief of the Army General Staff's "pronounced vigor" (*prononcierte Frische*) suddenly slackened "when the conversation trailed off. In moments when he thought he was not being observed his lips trembled incessantly." C. Hartmann, *Wehrmacht im Ostkrieg*, 250.

49   Ibid., 257.

50   For the *Heerestruppen* formations assigned to the three German army groups on the eve of *Barbarossa* see, OKH Gen St d H/Op.Abt. (III), *"Kriegsgliederung Barbarossa,"* Stand 18.6.41, in: K. Mehner (Hg.), *Geheime Tagesberichte*, Bd. 3.

51   According to Eddy Bauer's detailed study of German tank operations, the "typical" panzer division of 1941 possessed some 3500 motor vehicles, and, single file on a road, would have stretched for about 130 kilometers. E. Bauer, *Panzerkrieg*, 113.

52   T. Plievier, *Moscow*, 44-46.

53   D. M. Glantz (ed.), *Initial Period of War on the Eastern Front*, 35-37; E. Mawdsley, *Thunder in the East*, 196. Notes Mawdsley: "The Russians had lost the armored battles of 1941 mainly with the 11-ton T-26 and 14-ton BT light tanks."

54   K.-R. Woche, *Zwischen Pflicht und Gewissen*, 99.

55   E. Mawdsley, *Thunder in the East*, 194-95. Notes Mawdsley: "A major problem for the Red Army in the early war years had been the lack of effective anti-tank (AT) guns."

56   C. Hartmann, *Wehrmacht im Ostkrieg*, 257, f.n. 83.

57   H. Guderian, *Panzer Leader*, 174.

58   R. J. Kershaw, *War Without Garlands*, 72-74.

59   D. Garden & K. Andrew (eds.), *The War Diaries of a Panzer Soldier*, 33-34. (Note: To make the account more readable, this author has taken the liberty to slightly recast this translation of the original German *Sutterlin* script.)

60   Ibid., 35.

61   Ibid., 35-36.

62   Quoted in: J. Dinglreiter, *Die Vierziger. Chronik des Regiments*, 38.

63   BA-MA MSg 1/3268: Fritz Farnbacher, *Tagebuch*, 22.6.41, quoted in: C. Hartmann, *Wehrmacht im Ostkrieg*, 251.

64   Note: The reference here is to one of the panzer routes used by Hoth's 3 Panzer Group; thus, it is not to be confused with the Panzer Route 1 used by Guderian's group.

65   R. Hinze, *19. Infanterie- und Panzer-Division*, 133.

66   Ibid., 133-34.

67   H. Guderian, *Panzer Leader*, 195.

68   R. Steiger, *Armour Tactics in the Second World War*, 28.

69   R. A. Hart, *Guderian*, 72-73.

70   H. Guderian, *Panzer Leader*, 154-56.

71   Ibid., 156.

72   Internet site at: http://www.lexikon-der-wehrmacht.de.

73   S. H. Newton, *Hitler's Commander. Field Marshal Walther Model*, 133.

74   *Geschichte der 3. Panzer-Division*, Traditionsverband der Division (Hg.), 112.

75   Quoted in: K.-R. Woche, *Zwischen Pflicht und Gewissen*, 104.

76   Ibid., 105-06.

77   Ibid., 107.

78   Ibid., 107-08.

79   Ibid., 108.

80   W. K. Nehring, *"Die 18. Panzerdivision 1941,"* in: *Deutscher Soldatenkalender 1961*, 197.

81   *Leutnant* Pohl, quoted in: W. Paul, *Geschichte der 18. Panzer-Division*, 31.

82   *Tagebuch*, Major S., 25.7.41, quoted in: *"Panzersoldaten im Russlandfeldzug 1941 bis 1945. Tagebuchaufzeichnungen und Erlebnisberichte,"* 24-25 (unpublished manuscript; compiled by Kurt Werner Andres).

83   Ibid., 25.
84   K. W. Andres, *"Panzersoldaten im Russlandfeldzug 1941 bis 1945. Tagebuchaufzeichnungen und Erlebnisberichte,"* 22.
85   H. Guderian, *Panzer Leader*, 233-35.
86   Ibid., 237-38.
87   D. M. Glantz, *Barbarossa Derailed*, Vol. I, 101.
88   M. Foedrowitz, *Stalin Organs*, 11.
89   M. Foedrowitz, *Stalin Organs*, 11; D. M. Glantz, *Barbarossa Derailed*, Vol. I, 67. The German General Staff's *Lageost* map for 15 July 1941 indicates that the only German unit in the vicinity of Rudnia at this time was 12 PD. K.-J. Thies, *Der Ostfeldzug – Ein Lageatlas*, "Lage am 15.7.1941 abds., Heeresgruppe Mitte."
90   Quoted in: A. Werth, *Russia at War*, 172.
91   Ltr, R. Adler to C. Luther, 24 Nov 04.
92   BA-MA N 10/9: *Lebenserinnerungen Smilo Frbr. von Luettwitz*, Bl. 128, quoted in: C. Hartmann, *Wehrmacht im Ostkrieg*, 255.
93   P. Paret, *"Clausewitz,"* in: *Makers of Modern Strategy*, P. Paret (ed.), 202.
94   BA-MA RH 26-29/6, *KTB 29. Inf.-Div. (mot.)*, 1.7.41; BA-MA MSg 1/1147: *Tagebuch* Lemelsen, 1.7.41.
95   R. J. Kershaw, *War Without Garlands*, 238.
96   S. H. Newton (trans.), *Panzer Operations. The Eastern Front Memoir of General Raus, 1941-1945*, 8.
97   *Tagebuch* Kummer, 14.7.41.
98   K. W. Andres, *"Panzersoldaten im Russlandfeldzug 1941 bis 1945. Tagebuchaufzeichnungen und Erlebnisberichte."*
99   According to the late U.S. Army Colonel David Hackworth, 15 to 20 percent of American fatal casualties during the Vietnam War resulted from "friendly fire." J. Shay, *Achilles in Vietnam. Combat Trauma and the Undoing of Character*, 125. The percentage of soldiers on both sides killed by their own forces during World War II was undoubtedly higher, in part because communications between friendly forces were much more primitive.
100 Going into battle in their original gray cotton hats (instead of helmets), and only days before equipped with the standard German infantry rifle (*Gewehr* 98), which they had not been trained to use, the soldiers of the List Regiment were mistaken by other German units for British soldiers and, thus, fired upon, with devastating results. For a detailed account of this action see, Thomas Weber, *Hitler's First War*, 40-47.
101 P. Fussell, *Wartime. Understanding and Behavior in the Second World War*, 26.
102 *Tagebuch* Kreuter, 23.6.41. It is unclear whether Kreuter was referring to the losses of the division as a whole, or simply to those of his regiment.
103 H. Guderian, *Panzer Leader*, 186. Observed Guderian: "Insufficient training and a lack of combat experience on the part of the young aviators were the cause of this unfortunate occurrence; and this despite clear recognition signals on the part of the troops on the ground and very plain orders to the fliers concerning the roads that we would be using." In this case, the German unit affected by the bombing was 23 Infantry Division.
104 J. Lucas, *Das Reich*, 66.
105 K. Macksey, *"The Smolensk Operation 7 July – 7 August 1941,"* in: *Initial Period of War on the Eastern Front*, D. M. Glantz (ed.), 346.
106 C. Hartmann, *Wehrmacht im Ostkrieg*, 256; also, H. Guderian, *Panzer Leader*, 189-90.
107 H. Zobel, *"3rd Panzer Division Battles in the Smolensk Area,"* in: *Initial Period of War on the Eastern Front*, D. M. Glantz (ed.), 435-36.
108 IfZ-Archiv, MA 1578: 4. Pz. Div., Abt. Ia, *Meldung an das 24. Pz. Korps vom 22.7.1941*; BA-MA RH 24-24/88: 4. Pz. Div., Abt. Ia, *Meldung an das 24. Pz. Korps vom 15.8.1941*. Both cited in: C. Hartmann, *Wehrmacht im Ostkrieg*, 256, f.n. 70, and 255, f.n. 67. Writes Hartmann: "While the division was still operational, the six weeks of advancing [*Vormarsch*] had sufficed to deplete the core of its personnel and materiel strength."
109 J. Neumann, *Die 4. Panzer-Division 1938-1943*, 491.
110 H. F. Richardson (ed.), *Your Loyal and Loving Son. The Letters of Tank Gunner Karl Fuchs, 1937-41*, 115.
111 A. Schick, *Die Geschichte der 10. Panzer-Division*, 325.
112 W. Paul, *Panzer-General Walther K. Nehring*, 121; O. Bartov, *Hitler's Army*, 20; W. K. Nehring, *"Die 18. Panzerdivision 1941,"* in: *Deutscher Soldatenkalender 1961*, 198; R. J. Kershaw, *War Without Garlands*, 169. See also, K.-J. Thies, *Der Ostfeldzug – Ein Lageatlas*, for the period 28 July to 17 August 1941.
113 20. Pz. Div. Abt. Ia, *Zustandsmeldung an 57. Pz. Korps*, 27.7.41, cited in: R. Steiger, *Armour Tactics in the Second World War*, 30.
114 BA-MA MSg 1/1147: *Tagebuch* Lemelsen, 25.7.41.
115 Ibid., 16.7.41.
116 BA-MA N 813, *Tagebuch* Muenchhausen, Aug. 41.
117 W. K. Nehring, *"Die 18. Panzerdivision 1941,"* in: *Deutscher Soldatenkalender 1961*, 198.
118 BA-MA RH 27-18/17, 11.7.41, quoted in: R. J. Kershaw, *War Without Garlands*, 170; also, O. Bartov, *Hitler's Army*, 20.
119 H. Gr. Mitte, Abt. Ia, KTB Nr. 1, 22.8.41, quoted in: R. Steiger, *Armour Tactics in the Second World War*, 126.
120 H. F. Richardson (ed.), *Your Loyal and Loving Son. The Letters of Tank Gunner Karl Fuchs, 1937-41*, 117.
121 P. Tauber (Hg.), *Laeusejagd und Rohrkrepierer. Willi Loewer, an den Fronten des Zweiten Weltkrieges*, 42-43.
122 Ibid., 43-44.
123 Ibid., 44-45.

124   Wessler was the accountant and pay NCO (*Rechnungsfuehrer*) in his battalion.

125   *Tagebuch* Wilhelm Wessler, 28.7.41.

126   Ibid.

127   OKH Gen St d H/Op.Abt. (III), "*Kriegsgliederung Barbarossa*," Stand 18.6.41, in: K. Mehner (Hg.), *Geheime Tagesberichte*, Bd. 3. Counted among the total of 103 infantry divisions are the four light divisions assigned to Army Group South.

128   According to Agustín Sáiz, "the equipment of a German infantryman during the Second World War was divided between the '*Tornister*' (marching equipment) and the '*Sturmgepaeck*' (combat equipment). While in battle, the former remained with the rearguard, while the latter consisted of everything strictly necessary for combat (with emergency rations and little else as additional elements)." Some items – e.g., blankets, cooking pots – were included in both sets of equipment. A. Sáiz, *Deutsche Soldaten*, 121.

129   The tent square, weighing 1.27 kilograms, triangular in form (202 x 202 cm on the sides, 240 cm along the bottom) and made of waterproof fabric, was an essential piece of equipment. Four of the tent squares, combined with four tent poles and eight tent pegs, could be assembled into a tent for four men. Larger tents could also be made by using eight or more of the tent squares. This versatile equipment item could also be used to cover foxholes, or be worn by the soldier as protection against the elements. The tent square was also used as an improvised stretcher to carry wounded from the battlefield. A. Buchner, *German Infantry Handbook*, 20.

130   R. J. Kershaw, *War Without Garlands*, 90; A. Buchner, *German Infantry Handbook*, 19; see also, A. Sáiz, *Deutsche Soldaten*, 121-48.

131   F. Belke, *Infanterist*, 36.

132   R. J. Kershaw, *War Without Garlands*, 90; A. Sáiz, *Deutsche Soldaten*, 121; G. Barkhoff, *Ostfront 1941-1945. Ein Soldatenleben*, 17 (unpublished memoir).

133   G. Barkhoff, *Ostfront 1941-1945. Ein Soldatenleben*, 16-17.

134   R. J. Kershaw, *War Without Garlands*, 90; A. Sáiz, *Deutsche Soldaten*, 123-24.

135   *Frontschau Nr. 5/6*, in: *Die Frontschau*, distributed by International Historic Films. The MG 34, when used as a light machine gun (i.e., with a bipod mount), weighed about 12 kilograms (26.5 pounds); used as a heavy MG (tripod mount) it weighed 19 kilograms (42 pounds). *Handbook on German Military Forces*, U.S. War Department, 314.

136   R. J. Kershaw, *War Without Garlands*, 90; A. Buchner, *German Infantry Handbook*, 17.

137   A. Sáiz, *Deutsche Soldaten*, 27. According to Sáiz, German uniforms were possibly the "most evolved [of any nation] during the first half of the 20th Century and a true milestone that would greatly influence all other belligerent nations."

138   Ibid., 27. Rayon, notes Agustín Sáiz, "produced an almost perfect imitation of the tactility and texture of silk, cotton or linen, [it] could be dyed in many different colors and was smooth, fresh and absorbent. However, it retained body heat and tended to lose shape when soaked." The fabric was known as "viscose" in Europe; in September 1939, Germany was responsible for nearly 90 percent of the world's total output of rayon.

139   G. Forty, *German Infantryman at War 1939-1945*, 15.

140   A. Sáiz, *Deutsche Soldaten*, 33-34, 40; A. Buchner, *German Infantry Handbook*, 17-18; G. Forty, *German Infantryman at War 1939-1945*, 15.

141   A. Sáiz, *Deutsche Soldaten*, 28, 39, 53-59; A. Buchner, *German Infantry Handbook*, 18-19.

142   Ltr, K.-G. Vierkorn (23 ID) to C. Luther, Jan 04.

143   S. Hart, et al., *The German Soldier in World War II*, 16.

144   The prototype of the Model 35 was approved by the *Wehrmacht* in June 1935. A. Sáiz, *Deutsche Soldaten*, 15.

145   A. Sáiz, *Deutsche Soldaten*, 15; A. Buchner, *German Infantry Handbook*, 19.

146   A. Sáiz, *Deutsche Soldaten*, 15.

147   Ibid., 69-71.

148   E. Raus, "*Effects of Climate on Combat in European Russia*" (DA Pamphlet No. 20-291), quoted in: *Fighting in Hell*, P. G. Tsouras (ed.), 227.

149   M. Graf v. Nayhauss-Cormons, *Zwischen Gehorsam und Gewissen*, 167.

150   Dr W. Dicke, *Memoiren* (unpublished memoir).

151   A. Sáiz, *Deutsche Soldaten*, 46.

152   A. Buchner, *German Infantry Handbook*, 111.

153   G. Megargee, *Inside Hitler's High Command*, 124.

154   *Tagebuch* Haape, 29.8.41.

155   A. Freitag, *Aufzeichnungen aus Krieg und Gefangenschaft*, 91.

156   E. Raus, "*Effects of Climate on Combat in European Russia*" (DA Pamphlet No. 20-291), quoted in: *Fighting in Hell*, P. G. Tsouras (ed.), 228.

157   H. Martin, *Weit war der Weg*, 62-63.

158   E. Raus, "*Effects of Climate on Combat in European Russia*" (DA Pamphlet No. 20-291), cited in: *Fighting in Hell*, P. G. Tsouras (ed.), 228.

159   Telecom Intvw, F. Roemer with G. Schulze, 15 Dec 04.

160   A. Freitag, *Aufzeichnungen aus Krieg und Gefangenschaft*, 52-53.

161   For fascinating details on (and photos of) German field kitchens and their equipment see, *Handbook on German Military Forces*, U. S. War Department, 537-40.

162   G. Forty, *German Infantryman at War 1939-1945*, 64.

163 H. Haape, *Moscow Tram Stop*, 92. Haape's young fiancée, and future wife, was a professional opera singer.
164 Ibid., 146.
165 A. Sáiz, *Deutsche Soldaten*, 265; see also, A. Buchner, *German Infantry Handbook*, 110-11.
166 Ltr, Dr W. Schaefer-Kehnert to C. Luther, 10 Dec 03.
167 A. Buchner, *German Infantry Handbook*, 19; see also, D. Westwood, *German Infantryman (2) Eastern Front 1941-43*, 9.
168 A. Buchner, *German Infantry Handbook*, 113.
169 R. L., DiNardo, *Mechanized Juggernaut or Military Anachronism?*, 11.
170 Ibid., 43.
171 Ltr, H. Franze (263 ID) to C. Luther, 16 Feb 05. Using straw from the thatched roofs of Russian houses to feed German horses in the fall/winter of 1941/42 is widely acknowledged in many contemporary German accounts.
172 FMS P-190, R. Hofmann & A. Toppe, "*Verbrauchs- und Verschleisssaetze waehrend der Operationen der deutschen Heeresgruppe Mitte vom 22.6.41 – 31.12.41*," 65.
173 Ltr, K.-G. Vierkorn to C. Luther, Jan 04.
174 Ltr, Dr W. Schaefer-Kehnert to C. Luther, 10 Dec 03.
175 Quoted in: K. Latzel, *Deutsche Soldaten – nationalsozialistischer Krieg?*, 50.
176 H. F. Richardson (ed.), *Your Loyal and Loving Son. The Letters of Tank Gunner Karl Fuchs, 1937-41*, 119.
177 A. Freitag, *Aufzeichnungen aus Krieg und Gefangenschaft*, 60.
178 H. Pagel, "*From the Other Side. A Collection of Personal WW II Stories*" (unpublished manuscript).
179 S. Knappe, *Soldat*, 225.
180 H. C. Verton, *In the Fire of the Eastern Front*, 107.
181 D. Chandler, *The Campaigns of Napoleon*, 770; A. Zamoyski, *Moscow 1812*, 148.
182 L. Tolstoy, *War and Peace*, 799-800.
183 D. M. Glantz, *Barbarossa Derailed*, Vol. I, 62.
184 Situation maps of the German Army Operations Branch from 15-31 July 1941, in: K.-J. Thies, *Der Ostfeldzug – Ein Lageatlas*.
185 G. Scheuer (Hg.), *Briefe aus Russland. Feldpostbriefe des Gefreiten Alois Scheuer 1941-1942*, 26.
186 Photographs of the German *Vormarsch* into Russia, however, show that the soldiers did not always adhere to these requirements.
187 *Frontschau Nr. 3*, "*Vormarsch*," in: *Die Frontschau*, distributed by International Historic Films.
188 H. J. Schroeder, "*Erfahrungen deutscher Mannschaftssoldaten waehrend der ersten Phase des Russlandkrieges*," in: *Zwei Wege nach Moskau*, B. Wegner (Hg.), 312.
189 *Feldpost*, W. Heinemann, 17.7.41.
190 H. J. Schroeder, "*Erfahrungen deutscher Mannschaftssoldaten waehrend der ersten Phase des Russlandkrieges*," in: *Zwei Wege nach Moskau*, B. Wegner (Hg.), 312.
191 S. Hart, et al., *The German Soldier in World War II*, 28.
192 Ibid., 28.
193 D. Westwood, *German Infantryman (2) Eastern Front 1941-43*, 14.
194 Ibid., 14.
195 J. Lucas, *Das Reich*, 54.
196 J. Huerter, *Ein deutscher General an der Ostfront*, 63.
197 *Feldpost*, K.-G. Vierkorn, 25.6.41.
198 D. Westwood, *German Infantryman (2) Eastern Front 1941-43*, 13.
199 Ibid., 12.
200 M. Graf v. Nayhauss-Cormons, *Zwischen Gehorsam und Gewissen*, 148.
201 R. Schneider, *Siege. A Novel of the Eastern Front*, 137.
202 Quoted in: R. J. Kershaw, *War Without Garlands*, 92.
203 Ibid., 91.
204 *Tagebuch* Lierow, 24.6.-11.7.41.
205 A. Ulrich, "*Hitler's Drugged Soldiers*," in: *Spiegel Online*, 6 May 05; *Tagebuch* Lierow, ca. 24.12.41; H. von Luck, *Panzer Commander*, 83-84.
206 E. Raus, "*Effects of Climate on Combat in European Russia*" (DA Pamphlet No. 20-291), quoted in: *Fighting in Hell*, P. G. Tsouras (ed.), 216.
207 Ibid., 216.
208 D. M. Glantz, *Barbarossa Derailed*, Vol. I, 62.
209 G. Scheuer (Hg.), *Briefe aus Russland. Feldpostbriefe des Gefreiten Alois Scheuer 1941-1942*, 23.
210 A. Freitag, *Aufzeichnungen aus Krieg und Gefangenschaft*, 58-59.
211 W. Meyer-Detring, *Die 137. Infanterie-Division im Mittelabschnitt der Ostfront*, 31-32.
212 H. Haape, *Moscow Tram Stop*, 60-61.
213 W. Meyer-Detring, *Die 137. Infanterie-Division im Mittelabschnitt der Ostfront*, 31.
214 BA-MA RH 26-129/3, *KTB 129. Inf.-Div.*, 1.7.41.
215 R. L. DiNardo, *Mechanized Juggernaut or Military Anachronism?*, 41.
216 During his service in Russia between 1941 and 1944, *Gefreiter* Herbert Franze, a mounted messenger (*Meldereiter*) in 263 ID, lost a total of 85 horses to causes ranging from exhaustion and starvation to combat. Ltr, H. Franze to C. Luther, 16 Feb 05. From October 1941 through March 1942, the German Army in the east lost a total of about 200,000 horses, while receiving only 20,000 replacements. G. P. Megargee, *Inside Hitler's High Command*, 174.

217   R. L. DiNardo, *Mechanized Juggernaut or Military Anachronism?*, 44.

218   P. Tauber (Hg.), *Laeusejagd und Rohrkrepierer. Willi Loewer, an den Fronten des Zweiten Weltkrieges*, 51.

219   *Tagebuch* Wohlrab, quoted in: W. Meyer-Detring, *Die 137. Infanterie-Division im Mittelabschnitt der Ostfront*, 31.

220   Because of the heavy weight of the 150mm field howitzer, the gun's tube and breech were transported separately on a special four-wheeled wagon. See, H. Seidler, *Images of War, Operation Barbarossa*, 19.

221   K.-G. Vierkorn, "*Barbarossa – Feldzug gegen die Sowjet Union 1941. Meine Erinnerungen*," 16-17 (unpublished memoir).

222   *Feldpost*, W. Heinemann, 17.7.41.

223   R. L., DiNardo, *Mechanized Juggernaut or Military Anachronism?*, 45.

224   K.-G. Vierkorn, "*Barbarossa – Feldzug gegen die Sowjet Union 1941. Meine Erinnerungen*," 17.

225   W. Meyer-Detring, *Die 137. Infanterie-Division im Mittelabschnitt der Ostfront*, 31.

226   E. Raus, "*Effects of Climate on Combat in European Russia*" (DA Pamphlet No. 20-291), quoted in: *Fighting in Hell*, P. G. Tsouras (ed.), 229.

227   H. Haape, *Moscow Tram Stop*, 243.

228   E. Raus, "*Effects of Climate on Combat in European Russia*" (DA Pamphlet No. 20-291), quoted in: *Fighting in Hell*, P. G. Tsouras (ed.), 229.

229   R. L., DiNardo, *Mechanized Juggernaut or Military Anachronism?*, 46.

230   M. Graf v. Nayhauss-Cormons, *Zwischen Gehorsam und Gewissen*, 167; H. Grossmann, *Geschichte der 6. Infanterie-Division*, 55.

231   H. Baumann, *Die 35. Infanterie-Division, 1939-1945*, 82; I. Moebius, *Ueber Moskau ins Kurland. Ritterkreuztraeger Georg Bleher erzaehlt*, 54.

232   *Traditionsverband 260. I.D., e.V.* (Hg.), *Die 260. Infanterie-Division*, 54; see also, situation maps of the German Army Operations Branch from 8-18 July 1941, in: K.-J. Thies, *Der Ostfeldzug – Ein Lageatlas*.

233   K.-J. Thies, *Der Ostfeldzug – Ein Lageatlas*, "Lage am 31.7.1941 abds., Heeresgruppe Mitte;" "*The Battle of Smolensk – Situation, 2300, 31 July 1941*," in: D. M. Glantz, *Atlas of the Battle of Smolensk, 7 July – 10 September 1941*, 70.

234   E.-M. Rhein, *Das Infanterie-Regiment 18*, 58.

235   P. Carell, *Hitler Moves East*, 29.

236   *Feldpost*, W. Heinemann, 11.7.41.

237   J. Huerter, *Ein deutscher General an der Ostfront*, 62-65.

238   Quoted in: C. Rass, "*Menschenmaterial:*" *Deutsche Soldaten an der Ostfront*, 337.

239   A derogatory term to describe Soviet female soldiers or partisans. It was used by NS-propaganda as part of an effort to categorize the Russian enemy as sub-human. H. J. Schroeder, "*Erfahrungen deutscher Mannschaftssoldaten waehrend der ersten Phase des Russlandkrieges*," in: *Zwei Wege nach Moskau*, B. Wegner (Hg.), 315.

240   H. Martin, *Weit war der Weg*, 33-34.

241   M. Graf v. Nayhauss-Cormons, *Zwischen Gehorsam und Gewissen*, 164.

242   H. J. Schroeder, *Die gestohlenen Jahre*, 527.

243   G. F. Nafziger, *German Order of Battle – Infantry*, 147.

244   For the division's march route into Russia see, K.-J. Thies, *Der Ostfeldzug – Ein Lageatlas*, "Lage am 27.6.-30.7.1941 abds., Heeresgruppe Mitte."

245   Obstlt. Ringenberg, "*Der Kampf des Infanterie Regiments 240 im Osten.*"

246   Ibid.

247   J. Shay, *Achilles in Vietnam. Combat Trauma and the Undoing of Character*, 34.

248   R. J. Kershaw, *War Without Garlands*, 137.

249   A. Freitag, *Aufzeichnungen aus Krieg und Gefangenschaft*, 54.

250   For German perspectives on Soviet weapons see, Appendix 6: "*Ostfrontkaempfer*: German Assessments of Soviet Weapons."

251   W. Kempowski (Hg.), *Das Echolot*, 183.

252   Gefr. Heinz B. (05 854), Collection BfZ.

253   Dr E. Bunke, *Der Osten blieb unser Schicksal*, 257-63.

254   Ibid., 264.

255   See, for example, H. Haape, *Moscow Tram Stop*, 154. Wrote Haape: "A mighty juggernaut, the T-34 was said to be protected with impenetrable armor and early reports made it out to be invincible. Like wild-fire, tales of the T-34's exploits raced along the front."

256   Historian John Mosier posits an exchange rate for the entire war (1941-45) of 3.5:1 in favor of German forces; moreover, the Germans "continued to win the casualty exchange right up until the end of the war." J. Mosier, *Deathride*, 17-19. According to official German General Staff calculations, German Army losses in the east amounted to 830,905 by 31 December 1941; these included 173,722 dead, 35,875 missing, and 621,308 wounded. (See, *Anlage 1 zu OKH/GenStdH/GenQu/Abt. I/Qu 2/III, Nr. I/58/42 g.Kdos. vom 5. Januar 1942*," in: P. E. Schramm (Hg.), *Kriegstagebuch des OKW*, Bd. I, 1120.) If the missing – most of whom, no doubt, were already dead, including prisoners of war, as few Germans captured in 1941 survived – are added to the fatal losses, total Army dead for the first six months of the war comes to 209,597. This figure, however, is almost 100,000 short of the *total* German dead in Soviet Russia through 31 December 1941 – 302,000, of which approximately 90 percent were Army, the remainder *Waffen*-SS (four percent), *Luftwaffe* (four percent) and other – claimed by Ruediger Overmans in his comprehensive analysis of

German World War II losses. (See, R. Overmans, *Deutsche militaerische Verluste im Zweiten Weltkrieg*, 277). Accepting Overmann's figure, and assuming a similar ratio of wounded to dead as in the OKH calculations (i.e., just under 3:1), then total German losses in the east through December 1941 amounted to at least 1.1 million men. When one considers that the Red Army incurred just under 4.5 million losses (KIA, POWs, wounded, and non-combat losses) during 1941 (Col.-Gen. G. F. Krivosheev (ed.), *Soviet Casualties and Combat Losses*, 94), then the overall exchange rate for the first six months of the war was roughly 4:1 in the Germans favor. Even in the fighting against Anglo-American forces in western Europe the Germans, according to the detailed statistical analysis of the late U.S. Army Colonel Trevor N. Dupuy, "consistently outfought the far more numerous Allied armies that eventually defeated them ... On a man for man basis the German ground soldiers consistently inflicted casualties at about a 50 percent higher rate than they incurred from the opposing British and American troops under all circumstances. This was true when they were attacking and when they were defending, when they had a local numerical superiority and when, as was usually the case, they were outnumbered, when they had air superiority and when they did not, when they won and when they lost." Quoted in: M. van Creveld, *Fighting Power. German Military Performance, 1914-1945*, 4-9.

257 W. Meyer-Detring, *Die 137. Infanterie-Division im Mittelabschnitt der Ostfront*, 21-23.
258 *Tagebuch Hptm. d.R.* Meyer (Chef 3./AR 137), quoted in: W. Meyer-Detring, *Die 137. Infanterie-Division im Mittelabschnitt der Ostfront*, 23.
259 "*Eine klassische 'Kesselschlacht' im Kleinen!*" W. Meyer-Detring, *Die 137. Infanterie-Division im Mittelabschnitt der Ostfront*, 23.
260 Ibid., 23.
261 FMS T-34, K. Allmendinger, et al., "*Terrain Factors in the Russian Campaign*," 67.
262 In an anonymous article published in 1949, the author, merely identified as a "war participant" (*Kriegsteilnehmer*), wrote: "The tank is poorly suited to Russia's forests as a result of the difficult conditions of both roads and terrain, as well as the strong barriers of mines and anti-tank guns which the Russians employed along roads and in clearings." "*Der Waldkampf*," in: *Allgemeine Schweizerische Militaer Zeitschrift*, October 1949, 731.
263 Repeated experience in forest fighting informed the Germans that, "except in unusual circumstances, artillery in thick forests was just an impediment, and should be left behind. They much preferred heavy mortars such as the Russians used in large quantities and with great effect. These could be hand-carried over even the most difficult terrain and, being comparatively short-range weapons, they involved only minor problems in fire control." FMS T-34, K. Allmendinger, et al., "*Terrain Factors in the Russian Campaign*," 70; see also, "*Der Waldkampf*," in: *Allgemeine Schweizerische Militaer Zeitschrift*, October 1949, 730-31.
264 Department of the Army Pamphlet No. 20-269, "*Small Unit Actions during the German Campaign in Russia*," 236.
265 G. L. Rottman, *Soviet Field Fortifications 1941-45*, 58-60; P. Carell, *Hitler Moves East*, 69.
266 P. Carell, *Hitler Moves East*, 69.
267 P. Carell, *Hitler Moves East*, 69-70; also, K.-J. Thies, *Der Ostfeldzug – Ein Lageatlas*, "Lage am 30.6.1941 abds., Heeresgruppe Mitte."
268 FMS T-34, K. Allmendinger, et al., "*Terrain Factors in the Russian Campaign*," 57-58.
269 Ibid., 59.
270 Ibid., 59-60.
271 Ibid., 61-62.
272 F. Hossbach, *Infanterie im Ostfeldzug 1941/42*, 51.
273 Dr E. Bunke, *Der Osten blieb unser Schicksal*, 244-45.
274 Ibid., 245-46.
275 Ibid., 247.
276 F. Hossbach, *Infanterie im Ostfeldzug 1941/42*, 53.
277 R. Overmans, *Deutsche militaerische Verluste im Zweiten Weltkrieg*, 277.
278 According to Halder, the *Ostheer's* losses as of 13 August 1941 included 102,836 killed or missing, an average of 1940 per day. C. Burdick & H.-A. Jacobsen (eds.), *The Halder Diary 1939-1942*, 521. Halder's figures thus track closely with Overmans' definitive analysis. In contrast, an official compilation of the German General Staff in January 1942, which posited a total of 409,898 casualties through 31 August 1941 (including 87,489 killed and 19,588 missing), appears to have undercalculated the actual losses by about 20 percent. See, "*Anlage 1 zu OKH/GenStdH/GenQu/Abt. I/Qu 2/III, Nr. I/58/42 g.Kdos. vom 5. Januar 1942*," in: P. E. Schramm (Hg.), *Kriegstagebuch des OKW*, Bd. I, 1120.
279 G. E. Blau, *The German Campaign in Russia – Planning and Operations* (*1940-1942*,), Department of the Army Pamphlet No. 20-261a, 71; C. Burdick & H.-A. Jacobsen (eds.), *The Halder Diary 1939-1942*, 517. Of the total replacements, 79,000 had gone to Army Group South, 91,000 to Army Group Center, and 47,000 to Army Group North.
280 B. Mueller-Hillebrand, *Das Heer 1933-1945*, Bd. III, 19.
281 As noted, out of the 117 divisions in the first assault wave on 22 June 1941, 50.5 (including 31 infantry divisions) belonged to Army Group Center; by early July 1941, the army group had received a half dozen additional infantry divisions from the OKH reserve, bringing its total number of divisions to just under 60. The other army groups, of course, also received new divisions from the OKH reserve. *GSWW*, Vol. IV, 528-29; also, "*Opposing Orders of Battle*," in: D. M. Glantz, *Atlas of the Battle of Smolensk, 7 July – 10 September 1941*, 1-2, 6-7; K.-J. Thies, *Der Ostfeldzug – Ein Lageatlas*, "Lage am 4.7.1941 abds., Heeresgruppe Mitte."

282   Obstlt. Ringenberg, *"Der Kampf des Infanterie-Regiments 240 im Osten."*

283   Ltr, F. Belke to C. Luther, 30 Jul 05. According to Belke, a veteran of 6 Infantry Division, "the average time of an *Infanterist* on the *Ostfront* amounted to 10 weeks."

284   A. Naumann, *Freispruch fuer die Deutsche Wehrmacht*, 372.

285   K. Gerbet (ed.), *GFM Fedor von Bock, The War Diary*, 267.

286   C. D. Winchester, *Hitler's War on Russia*, 118.

287   H. Grossmann, *Geschichte der 6. Infanterie-Division*, 62. According to Hans Lierow, a doctor in 37 IR, 24 German officers became casualties on this day, nine of which were fatal. *Tagebuch* Lierow, 27.8.41.

288   K. Schneider-Janessen, *Arzt im Krieg*, 421-23.

289   Hansheinrich Grunert, *Der zerrissene Soldat*, quoted in: K. Schneider-Janessen, *Arzt im Krieg*, 423-24.

290   Air Ministry Pamphlet No. 248: *Rise and Fall of the German Air Force*, 166.

291   *GSWW*, Vol. IV, 766.

292   R. Muller, *The German Air War in Russia*, 51.

293   Ibid., 29.

294   Ibid., 28.

295   Observes Matthew Cooper in his study of the German Air Force: "The relative weakness of the German Army ... and its shortage of effective anti-tank guns and other weapons, meant that it had to call on the *Luftwaffe* to intervene on the battlefield with ever increasing frequency." M. Cooper, *The German Air Force*, 225.

296   C. D. Winchester, *Hitler's War on Russia*, 43.

297   *"Die Unterstuetzung des Heeres im Osten durch die deutsche Luftwaffe. (Aus einer Studie der 8. Abt./Chef Genst. d. Lw.),"* KDC.

298   *"Der Luftkrieg im Osten gegen Russland 1941. (Aus einer Studie der 8. Abteilung 1943/1944.),"* KDC.

299   *GSWW*, Vol. IV, 766.

300   M. Cooper, *The German Air Force*, 224. As a result, the Bf 110s of 2 Air Corps' 210 Fast Bomber Wing (*Schnellkampfgeschwader* 210) were able to conduct 1574 sorties from 22 June to 26 July 1941 at a cost of only 12 aircraft (i.e., one lost plane for every 131 sorties).

301   R. Muller, *The German Air War in Russia*, 45. For background on *Luftwaffe* development of its close air support mission see, Chapter 3, Section 3.5.

302   *GSWW*, Vol. IV, 805. For the *Luftwaffe's* Moscow raids see, Chapter 10 (Section 10.3).

303   P. Deichmann, *German Air Force Operations in Support of the Army*. USAF Historical Study No. 163, 109. For a fascinating and insightful discussion of *Luftwaffe* development and procurement of munitions for ground support see, Chapter II of this study (pp. 43-53). For example, Deichmann argued that it was "astonishing that the German command failed to realize the importance of very small bombs, to be scattered in very large numbers on targets. In the 1940 campaign in France the *Luftwaffe* had captured over one million of these 2.2-pound (1 kilogram) bombs to be delivered on targets in large drop containers. A special detonator caused the containers to open at a certain altitude above the ground and scattered the small bombs in a fairly regular pattern in the terrain. The bombs captured in France could have been used without any difficulty with the German bomb containers used for electron incendiary bombs, which were available in adequate quantities and which fitted into the German bomb clips. Without consulting the field forces, the *Luftwaffe* General Staff released the captured bombs for use as scrap metal, the idea being to salvage the small quantities of copper used in the detonators, since copper supplies were so very short in Germany. Too late, the importance of these bombs for use against live and dug-in targets was realized, and only then did production begin in Germany." Ibid., 44-45.

304   H. Plocher, *The German Air Force Versus Russia, 1941*. USAF Historical Study No. 153, 44.

305   On 10 May 1940, the *Luftwaffe* had 2589 combat-ready (*einsatzbereit*) fighters and bombers available for the campaign in the west. See, K.-H. Frieser, *"Die deutschen Blitzkriege: Operativer Triumph – strategische Traegodie,"* in: *Die Wehrmacht. Mythos und Realitaet*, R.-D. Mueller & H.-E. Volkmann (Hg.), 185.

306   *"Die Unterstuetzung des Heeres im Osten durch die deutsche Luftwaffe. (Aus einer Studie der 8. Abt./Chef Genst. d. Lw.),"* KDC.

307   W. Murray, *Strategy for Defeat*, 89.

308   *GSWW*, Vol. IV, 764.

309   *"Die deutschen Flugzeugverluste im ersten Monat (22.6.41-17.7.41) des Krieges gegen Russland. Nach einer Zusammenstellung der 6. Abteilung des Generalstabes der deutschen Luftwaffe,"* KDC.

310   J. Prien, et al., *Die Jagdfliegerverbaende der Deutschen Luftwaffe*, Teil 6/I, Unternehmen *"Barbarossa,"* 15, 28.

311   Average daily German aircraft losses actually fell off sharply after the first two weeks of the campaign, when the total number of destroyed or damaged planes had come to 807 – an average of just under 58 aircraft per day. *"Die deutschen Flugzeugverluste im ersten Monat (22.6.41-17.7.41) des Krieges gegen Russland. Nach einer Zusammenstellung der 6. Abteilung des Generalstabes der deutschen Luftwaffe,"* KDC.

312   W. Murray, *Strategy for Defeat*, 89.

313   Ibid., 93, 96.

314   W. Murray, *Strategy for Defeat*, 94; J. Prien, et al., *Die Jagdfliegerverbaende der Deutschen Luftwaffe*, Teil 6/I, Unternehmen *"Barbarossa,"* 14-15, 26.

315   On 15 July 1941, sunrise was at 0317 hours and sunset at 2021 hours (55 degrees north latitude). Russell H. S. Stolfi, *"Chance in History: The Russian Winter of 1941-1942,"* in: *History*, Vol. 65, No. 214, Jun 80, 224.

316   Ibid., 223.

317   J. Prien, et al., *Die Jagdfliegerverbaende der Deutschen Luftwaffe*, Teil 6/I, *Unternehmen "Barbarossa,"* 21-22. One *Gruppe* belonging to 52 JG was also part of 2 Air Fleet's single-seat fighter order of battle.

318   Ibid., 21-26.

319   Ibid., 23.

320   C. Pleshakov, *Stalin's Folly*, 135.

321   J. Weal, *Jagdgeschwader 51*, 59.

322   On 30 June 1941, the Soviets attacked the Germans' Berezina bridgehead at Bobruisk with "hundreds" of bombers; these included obsolete TB-3 four-engine bombers pulled off of training airfields in Central Russia. Approaching the target area at a suicidal 2000 meters in altitude, the Russian bombers "ran into a wall of fire from 10 Flak Regiment. Those aircraft that got through found their defensive formations torn apart, making them easy prey to the Bf 109s of *Oberst* Werner Moelders' 51 JG." A. Brookes, *Air War over Russia*, 40.

323   J. Weal, *Jagdgeschwader 51*, 58-61; "*Der Luftkrieg im Osten gegen Russland 1941. (Aus einer Studie der 8. Abteilung, 1943/1944),*" KDC.

324   J. Prien, et al., *Die Jagdfliegerverbaende der Deutschen Luftwaffe*, Teil 6/I, *Unternehmen "Barbarossa,"* 26; "*Gefechtsquartiere des VIII. Fliegerkorps im Russland-Feldzug 1941,*" compiled by Hans Wilhelm Deichmann, KDC.

325   *GSWW*, Vol. IV, 364; C. Bergström & A. Mikhailov, *Black Cross Red Star*, Vol. I, 264. In addition to staff elements, 3 and 53 KG each comprised three *Gruppen*, while 2 KG consisted of staff, one *Gruppe* and two additional squadrons. Additional He 111H, Do 17P/Z and Ju-88A aircraft were assigned to weather and long-range reconnaissance units.

326   J. Scutts, *Luftwaffe Bomber Units 1939-41*, 42.

327   *GSWW*, Vol. IV, 768.

328   *GSWW*, Vol. IV, 769-70, 806; J. Scutts, *Luftwaffe Bomber Units 1939-41*, 42.

329   *GSWW*, Vol. IV, 770.

330   W. Murray, *Strategy for Defeat*, 89; M. Griehl, *Luftwaffe at War. German Bombers Over Russia*, 6.

331   R. Stedman, *Kampfflieger*, 31-32.

332   "*Der Luftkrieg im Osten gegen Russland 1941. (Aus einer Studie der 8. Abteilung, 1943/1944),*" KDC.

333   Ibid.

334   R. Muller, *The German Air War in Russia*, 51-52.

335   *GSWW*, Vol. IV, 364-66; C. Bergström & A. Mikhailov, *Black Cross Red Star*, Vol. I, 264.

336   R. Muller, *The German Air War in Russia*, 32, 38.

337   R. J. Kershaw, *War Without Garlands*, 53.

338   Major F. Lang (a.D.), *Aufzeichnungen aus der Sturzkampffliegerei*, 6-7, 13-24.

339   W. Murray, *Strategy for Defeat*, 89.

340   *Schokakola* was a brand of German chocolate containing additional caffeine from cocoa, roasted coffee, and cola nuts; it helped to keep the user from falling asleep and to prevent fatigue. Internet site at: http://en.wikipedia.org; A. Sáiz, *Deutsche Soldaten*, 272.

341   *Tagebuch* Kreuter, 26./28.6.41.

342   H. F. Richardson (ed.), *Your Loyal and Loving Son. The Letters of Tank Gunner Karl Fuchs, 1937-41*, 115-16.

343   H. Rudel, *Stuka Pilot*, 16-17.

344   Quoted in, R. J. Kershaw, *War Without Garlands*, 53.

345   *Hauptmann* H. Pabst, "*Berichte aus Russland Sommer 1941,*" KDC.

346   Ibid.

347   Note: Unlike the earlier entries, no date is given here. From the context, however, it is most likely 27 June 1941.

348   The reader will recall that 29 Motorized Infantry Division was defending the sector west of Slonim from 27-30 June 1941 against furious Russian attempts to break out of the Belostok pocket. For details see, Chapter 7, Section 7.2.3.

349   From *Hauptmann* Pabst's account, it is easy to understand why "friendly fire" incidents involving aircraft and ground troops were so common.

350   *Hauptmann* H. Pabst, "*Berichte aus Russland Sommer 1941,*" KDC.

351   Vogt's recollection of flying 10-12 sorties per day is most likely an exaggeration; on the other hand, 5-6 sorties per day were surely a possibility.

352   It is possible that some *Stuka* crew members who suffered nervous breakdowns were murdered by the Nazi authorities in the course of various euthanasia actions. H. J. Schroeder, *Die gestohlenen Jahre*, 513, f.n. 56.

353   The German text – translated here as "special flying caps" – reads "*F.T. Haube.*" "*F.T.*" stands for "*Funktelegraphie,*" or radio telegraphy, while the word "*Haube*" means cap. A headset, along with a microphone, was built into the flying cap (*Fliegermuetze*) of a *Stuka* pilot, enabling him at all times to receive and send signals. From the context, Vogt seems to be saying that the cap and headset did little to protect him from the dreadful wail of the siren. Ibid., 513, f.n. 57.

354   Ibid., 512-13.

CHAPTER 9

Cultural Collisions & Crimes of War
on the Eastern Front

"The physical conditions of the population of Central Russia, which lives exceedingly primitively, are uniformly bad. By European standards, their housing displays an unparalleled meanness. The poverty of the populace, constantly living on the edge of starvation, is indescribable. The indifference to dirt and all kinds of vermin – especially lice and bedbugs, as well as flies – results in conditions that must, in some areas, be deemed catastrophic." ("Militaergeographische Angaben ueber das Europaeische Russland, Zentral-Russland (ohne Moskau)," Generalstab des Heeres, Berlin, May 1941)[1]

*"Bolshevism has undoubtedly been at work here and collectivized everything, i.e. the individual only has his house and his garden, everything else (fields, cattle, and agricultural machines) belongs to the village community ... The population is utterly stolid and opaque ... The people are unimaginably unambitious, and if they are not made to work, they do absolutely nothing ... Everything is incredibly crude and large and tastelessly primitive, but no doubt appropriate to this passive national character. It can be seen at every turn that, in this country, *every* individual manifestation of life has ceased completely."* (Major Werner Heinemann, 23 ID, 13 July 1941)[2]

"Hector, I'll have no talk of pacts with you, ... As between men and lions there are none, no concord between wolves and sheep, but all hold one another hateful through and through, so there can be no courtesy between us." (Achilles to Hector in Homer's *Iliad*)[3]

"They [Russian prisoners of war] slaughtered their own comrades. If a Russian couldn't carry on properly anymore, they murdered him and fed themselves off him." (Wehrmachtsoldat Heinz Niewerth)[4]

"The findings made by the Wehrmacht War Crimes Bureau ... in the first months of the war against the Soviet Union concerning the war crimes perpetrated ... against defenseless German soldiers ... surpassed even the worst fears and all imagination." (Wehrmacht War Crimes Bureau, November 1941)[5]

9.1: Encounters with People & Culture in the "Soviet Paradise"

On 22 June 1941, two to three million German soldiers poured into the Soviet Union with virtually no awareness of the country, its people, its culture, its history. "Before the start of the eastern campaign," recounted former panzer soldier Rolf Hinze, "the troops had no idea what to expect when they advanced into the territory of Soviet Russia. They knew nothing about the character [*Eigenart*] or life style of the population, about their ethnic makeup [*volkliche Zusammensetzung*], or about the different languages in the territories they occupied."[6]

Stalin's Russia was a hermetically sealed society, which actively sought to conceal both its strengths and weakness from the outside world, or to mislead political leaders and sympathetic leftist intellectuals and "literati" (such as George Bernard Shaw, in a well-known incident) in the capitalist West through propaganda and Potemkin-like props. (Perhaps the closest example of such a closed society in today's world would be Communist North Korea.) One is reminded of Winston Churchill's oft-quoted characterization of Soviet Russia, during a radio broadcast in October 1939, as a "riddle, wrapped in a mystery, inside an enigma." When one considers that the German political and military authorities were also largely ignorant of the Soviet Union – and the catastrophic outcome of that ignorance – it is hardly surprising that, to the average *Landser*, Russia was largely a blank slate.

On the other hand, through schooling, newspapers and other popular media, the typical German soldier was most likely aware of the more horrific chapters of Soviet history since the Bolshevik revolution of 1917; among them, the great famines of the early-1930s, the force collectivization of the countryside, the purges and the terror of the late 1930s, the infamous Gulags, the aggressive military adventures. His understanding of German history would have included knowledge of the advance of the Czarist armies into East Prussia in 1914, and the fear and terror they had spread through the population (a traumatic experience which still resonated with the people of East Prussia in 1941).[7] From Germany's more recent history he would have known about the abortive leftist/Communist attempt to take over Bavaria in 1918/19, or the years of bloody tumultuous street battles between Marxist/Communist groups (such as the Spartacus League) and right-wing nationalist outfits, like the Free Corps (*Freikorps*). In general, as a product of the cultural and political milieu of the inter-war period, he would have tended to negatively stereotype the average Russian citizen as backward, oppressed, and fundamentally alien, while Soviet Russia remained an object of fear and a palpable danger to his beloved Germany and all of Christian Europe.

These basic perceptions, however vague and inchoate, were strongly reinforced by years of National Socialist propaganda between 1933 and August 1939, which ended abruptly after the signing of the German-Soviet non-aggression pact. Nazi propaganda, exploiting generations of widespread and racially based apprehensions about the "Slavic threat" from the east, cunningly conflated Bolshevism with the putative danger posed by international Jewry to Germany's survival. As argued earlier in this narrative, the average German soldier in 1941, whether a party member or not, largely embraced the official National Socialist view of Soviet Russia as a pariah nation, dominated by Jews, and signifying an existential threat. In June 1941, he thus supported the Third Reich's objective of eliminating this threat through military action. "We were firmly convinced," recalled one former *Landser* in a letter to this author, "that we were fighting for a good, indeed, a necessary cause: To protect Germany and all of Europe from Bolshevism (with its untold millions of victims). The churches and the intelligentsia would have been the first victims."[8]

Whatever negative impressions the "average" German soldier held, *a priori*, of Soviet Russia – its culture and its people – these were typically reinforced by his initial experiences inside Russia. Recalled another veteran: "Observing daily the misery of the Russian people, and their primitive living conditions, we were convinced we were serving a just cause; and that through our efforts, we would be able to prevent an expansion of the Bolshevik world revolution into Europe."[9]

Marching across a depressing and monotonous landscape; through villages which looked "wretched and melancholy;"[10] exposed to an alien "race," whose customs he too often failed to comprehend; confronted by crushing scenes of poverty and human misery – the *Landser* was staggered by the overwhelming "otherness" of so much of what he saw and experienced. Helmut Martin, a soldier in 14 Motorized Infantry Division, recounted a personal experience near Minsk, in early July 1941, which deeply affected him: As evening rapidly approached, Martin and his comrades stopped in a clump of trees in a small wood to prepare their quarters for the night; before they settled in, however, they wandered across the road to an adjacent village, where stood a handful of modest wood peasant huts. Armed with their empty water canisters, they approached the draw wells of the huts looking for water. It was then that Martin came face to face with a disturbing local custom – one which was "hardly common" [*nicht ueblich*] at home:

> In the grass by the primitive picket fences, a large number of women lay or sat with bared breasts, which they proffered to their nursing infants to calm them. Such openness was unthinkable in our homeland, even though this was an entirely natural activity. But here it had something that filled our gaze with shame and repellent disgust, elicited by the physical condition of the women and their children. Their bodies and clothing were marked by dirt and squalidness, and the women's shapelessness and swollen corpulence was a particularly unfavorable aspect of this disagreeable sight. Their age could not be determined. They were not disturbed in the slightest by our appearance or when we stood still to look at them feeding. For me, 19 years old, this sight was something unusual, exciting, but mixed with this curiosity was also disgust, abhorrence.[11]

In their letters and diaries, many men described, often with palpable revulsion, what they perceived to be the impact of a generation of Bolshevik rule on the well being of the Russian people. Such nightmarish accounts – consciously or otherwise – functioned as a sort of cautionary tale to the *Landser* – what they, their families, and Christian Germany would surely have faced, had the cancer of Soviet Communism been left to metastasize unchecked. Once again, this narrative invokes the thought-provoking and insightful letters of Major Werner Heinemann (23 ID), which also betray his own stereotypical prejudices vis-à-vis the Russian people:

> 13.7.41:
> Unimaginable, that there should be water pipes anywhere in the world from which one could drink water, just like that, without contracting cholera! Bolshevism has undoubtedly been at work here and collectivized everything, i.e. the individual only has his house and his garden, everything else (fields, cattle, and agricultural machines) belongs to the village community. Even meals are taken by everyone together in the Party building.
>
> The population is utterly stolid and opaque, but, where the <u>lower</u> classes are concerned, appears to have led a relatively content life. The people are unimaginably unambitious, and if they are not made to work, they do absolutely nothing.
>
> In everything (e.g., road construction), you can somehow see the same general approach, which naturally should not be compared with our standards. Everything is incredibly crude and large and tastelessly primitive, but no doubt appropriate to this passive national character. It can be seen at every turn that, in this country, <u>every</u> individual manifestation of life has ceased completely.
>
> 26.8.41:
> What a desolate country this is here! The primitiveness and poverty of the population is, thanks to their exploitation by the Soviet authorities, so monstrous that it is not possible to conceive <u>how</u> the people can live at all. Yet the country is decidedly fertile, but then everything that they harvest is taken away from the people and out of the proceeds of the party organization the huge armaments, and the international propaganda are paid for.

So nothing remains but desolate, gray monotony in attitude, customs, clothing, and domestic economy, and, moreover, everyone is afraid of standing out from the rest of the colorless "human mass" in even the very slightest way (even if that is only by having a flower by the window or a neckerchief). The "commissars" keep the populace and military in constant fear for that little bit of miserable life in such unimaginable ways that any thought of protesting against this inhumane condition is extinguished right from the start.

That in such a country, across which, moreover, the war forged its bloody path, there was absolutely nothing more for us to obtain or buy in terms of goods should be evident. The term "to buy" is, in any case, utterly bourgeois, for that which the Soviet citizen "needs for life" is of course "allocated" to him by the state, and so a "shop" is nowhere to be seen. The pressure under which this country has been for the last 25 years still has an effect today where <u>we</u> are, and nothing is to be done with the population, either good or bad. Horrid![12]

As noted in several veterans' accounts in this narrative, the German invaders were often greeted as liberators as they pushed across the frontier and into the western border regions of the Soviet Union. These areas – eastern Poland, the Baltic States, portions of Romania – had been occupied by the Red Army between September 1939 and the summer of 1940 and, thereafter, subjected to brutal oppression. The jubilant reaction of many to the sudden arrival of the German Army contributed, no doubt, to the perception – eagerly embraced by many *Landser*, and fostered sedulously by National Socialist propaganda – that the *Wehrmacht* was conducting a virtuous crusade against Bolshevism on Europe's behalf. Such notions were also promoted by a basic ethnocentrism common to all peoples and their military institutions in times of war. Observes historian Dennis E. Showalter:

Contempt for alien ways seems virtually a universal characteristic of armies – particularly in the combat units, which are not usually manned by cosmopolitan intellectuals. For the *Wehrmacht's* rank and file, a vague, centuries-old sense of defending the West from Slavic barbarism was reinforced by direct experience of a culture that seemed at once incomprehensibly alien and overwhelmingly threatening to Germans whose provincialism had been fostered and reinforced by National Socialism.[13]

In soldiers' diaries, field post letters, and post-war narratives, descriptions abound of the almost preternatural poverty encountered inside the Soviet Union, particularly in the vast rural and agricultural regions. Whatever preconceptions were held by German soldiers as they advanced into Russia, they were shocked by the destitution, deprivation and human degradation they witnessed everywhere and attributed to the sinister and oppressive impact of Communist rule. Overtly sarcastic references to the "Soviet paradise" flourish in the soldiers' accounts. Hendrik C. Verton, a former *Waffen*-SS soldier and Dutch volunteer who deployed to Russia with his battalion in late 1941, later described the population in the town of Vinnitsa, in the Ukraine, where he and his unit were stationed for several weeks:

The population was passive and resigned, showing us no hostility. The reason for that undoubtedly was the social misery that they had had to endure under Stalin. One could not fail to see the utter poverty. You were not able to distinguish the men from the women on the streets. They all wore the same gray, ugly, wadded clothes, which they held together with strings or suchlike. There were no buttons and no shoes. Leather shoes and fur boots were seldom to be seen. Most wore the "local shoe," made from sailcloth or raffia. The poorest of the poor had bound a piece of an old car tyre to the soles of their feet. Those conditions were hardly the outcome of the first few months of the war. In a fatal light it illustrated a classless State and was in sharp contrast to the "Soviet paradise" as loudly proclaimed by the Russians.[14]

Poverty, the tragic side effects of the brutal forced collectivization, and declining sexual mores had resulted in large numbers of illegitimate or orphaned children, who roamed the countryside in rapacious bands. Verton's account continues:

> Year after year thousands of illegitimate children, in exploding numbers, without parents or state to look after them, gradually became a danger to the land and its people. We could assess it for ourselves. The picture was of orphans dressed in rags, without having washed or bathed for months on end, with boils, other skin infections and festering wounds. All of it made a mockery of everything and everyone who possessed a healthy, hygienic and normal standard of life.
>
> In large numbers, those bands of orphans wandered from town to town to beg, steal and rob, in order to keep themselves "above water." Already in 1941, the numbers could be assessed by non-Russian experts at some millions. The state that had caused the catastrophe, sought to solve the problem with a law that permitted youngsters from the age of 12 to be given the death sentence. As a result, the gangs armed themselves and then battled with the police. Such scenes made a very grave impression upon us. It confirmed to every one of us that Communism had to be repulsed at all costs. It also justified our presence in that land.[15]

While one may question Verton's figures (i.e., millions of destitute and peripatetic orphans as of 1941), the thrust of his account is genuine, corroborated in a number of soldiers' letters, diaries, and memoirs assembled by this author.

The poverty of the countryside was exemplified by the peasant villages, which had changed little, if at all, over the generations. Their primitive dwellings were built of wood with thatched or sod roofs in "varying stages of decay."[16] Most peasant huts consisted of nothing more than a single simple room, dominated by a large brick oven for cooking and furnishing warmth, and on top of which (or next to) the family slept during the long, arctic winters. "Adjoining the back of the house," recalled Heinrich Haape, "and separated by only a partition, there were always sheds for cows and pigs. They were kept close to the peasants so that all could share the warmth [in cold weather periods]."[17] Pigs and other livestock, it seems, were even kept inside the home with the family. Noted one *Landser* in a letter to his family in early fall 1941:

> We have a rest day and are in a Russian house. The Russians are eating just now. I can tell you, you wouldn't eat like this. It's so disgusting. I can't describe it to you at all. You'd have to see for yourselves.
>
> Utterly desolate, that is the Soviet paradise. Here, the people only have one room to live in; it has a large brick oven in it. On the oven there is space for four to five men to sleep. The pigs are in a pen in one corner. The cow has the stable in front of the living space.[18]

The huts thus tended to be filthy, reek fearfully, and were always overrun by insects. (As a rule, German soldiers, fearful of catching lice or contracting diseases, did not use peasant huts for quarters in the summer of 1941; this would change in the fall and winter, as the above letter illustrates.) Furniture, made by the peasant himself, was "sparse and wretched,"[19] the huts having earthenware pots and wooden tubs, with a wooden box normally serving as a small cupboard. Cradles for young children were suspended from the ceiling on ropes, while newspaper was often used as wallpaper. Electric lighting was unheard of, with illumination, if available, provided by kerosene lamps or paraffin candles (in poorer areas the peasants spent the hours between sundown and sunup in darkness). Toilets of any kind were unheard of[20] – family members doing their "business" outdoors, in outhouses or in the open, even in the depths of winter. The peasant homes, however, were always festooned with religious icons of various sorts, reflecting the Christian faith of a deeply devout people.[21]

Many *Landser* were repulsed by the primitive hygienic conditions common to rural areas of the Soviet Union. Heinrich Boucsein (129 ID), recalling an encounter with a Russian civilian in July 1941, wrote long after the war:

> A Russian, who had been in German captivity on a farm in Mecklenburg for four years in the First World War, complained that his children must go out begging and that "in Germany, the pig pen" had been better than his house here. Indeed, the hygienic conditions were hardly describable.[22]

Leutnant Joachim H. (131 ID), in a letter late in 1941, longed for the simplest, and most basic, appurtenance of modern life – a proper toilet:

> The Russian is a dogged fighter and would rather be hacked to pieces than submit, quite apart from their good weaponry, which meets modern standards in every way.
>
> In utter contrast to this stands the population's way of living, clothing, housing, etc. This primitiveness surpasses all description. There is no yardstick by which this might be measured. For us, it is a very strange feeling to hear dance music on the radio sometimes (provided we have the opportunity to do so). Then you remember, good Lord!, of course there is still music, dance, theater, clean homes, prettily dressed girls and women, but here ... only dirt and decay – that is the Soviet paradise. For over four months, we've been "going" by squatting. How we long to be able to use a clean toilet again or even to have a proper bath. Hopefully, the transportable field toilet with bathing facilities will soon be introduced into the Army.[23]

In a letter to this author in January 2006, former *Landser* Otto Will (5 PD) still expressed disbelief over the sanitary conditions in wartime Russia:

> I would like to tell you something general, and this applies to the entire time I spent in Russia, about the sanitary conditions [there], because I have not yet read anything in any publication – not even medical ones – about this (taboo?) topic. In the villages in the countryside, I myself did not come across a single house with a facility that might have been termed a toilet. And in the town, Viaz'ma, where I did stay for a time, I did not find any facility available which could – according to the ideas I was taught as a child – have been used as such. Believe me, it was dreadful! How and where the Russian folk did their own "business" has remained a puzzle to me to this day. When I was last in Russia, in 1993, I could not contain my amazement! Everything was there, even paper. Mind you, I wasn't "in the countryside" during that trip.[24]

The German soldiers in the east "processed" the poverty, deplorable conditions, and human misery they encountered in different ways. As a general observation, it can be stated that they developed highly ambivalent attitudes toward the Russian people and their predicament. For many, what they observed, or experienced directly, served only to reinforce deeply ingrained racial prejudices against the Slavic peoples as a less than fully human life form, an *Untermensch*. As *Oberleutnant* "K" (20 PD) recorded in his diary in July 1941:

> Expanse, never ending expanse, monotony in form and color, gray cottages, squat and isolated … It is a melancholy country, desolate for people from the West … The huts were most likely built in exactly the same way 1000 years ago as they are today. The only progress in this time is no doubt the glass windows. Gray on gray, impoverished and depressed, they stand there, far too tiny, incidentally, for the many children who grow up in them, but constructed with very clear proportions. In contrast to the few stone houses, usually party buildings in the towns, which are ugly and loveless constructions, these pitiful cottages are tasteful in the circumstances …
>
> The people live in pitiful conditions, unimaginably poor. They have nothing in their huts; they live with their many children in a single room … The Russians – if you listen to our men – then they are something between human and beast [*Mitteldinge zwischen Mensch und Tier*] – "You know, I don't think a peasant like that has even been to the cinema," was something I heard recently. The superior civilization of the West gives the simple man, and not only him, an arrogance without equal toward other life forms, and even more so toward other people who evidently don't want to know anything about all that technological stuff. That is, at a pinch, understandable, and yet we should see it differently. A nation of peasants lives as long as the earth has life. A nation that works between stone and asphalt can only use up its substances, but can't accumulate more.[25]

Despite such prejudice, some German soldiers responded compassionately to the poverty and human suffering which swirled about them. These men did what little they could to ease the burdens of the local peasant families, as this diary entry from Major "S" (20 PD) in August 1941 brings to light:

> The [peasant] houses are all built from tree trunks and, as a rule, contain one or two rooms. They all have a huge brick oven, which serves for both cooking and for heating … There are not usually beds or cots. The family sleeps on benches, which are grouped round the big oven at night. Sheep skins, more or less infested with lice, serve as blankets. There is no cutlery or plates, a wooden spoon must suffice, they eat straight from the cooking pot. By way of furniture, there is a crudely constructed table, and that is all. Some cut-out pictures from newspapers might be stuck to the walls; that's the only interior décor. They are poor, unfortunate people, these Soviet villagers. Their fields are usually as pitiful as they are miserably dressed. A consequence of the *kolkhoz* economy [*Kolchoswirtschaft*].
>
> Our *Landser* are deeply sympathetic to these unfortunate and lowly peasant farmers. They think with gratitude about their own culture, their home, Germany. Nobody takes even the slightest thing from these unfortunates. Anytime an exchange is made for an egg, a cucumber, a tomato, or similar, the little Soviet peasant is always the one to get the better deal.
>
> Seen as a whole, the people give an apathetic, joyless impression. After their bad experiences with the Soviet practices and their very dubious blessings, even the current war can no longer shock them.[26]

The soldiers of the *Ostheer*, with orders to live off the land to the fullest extent possible, were directly affected by the impoverishment of the vast regions that came under their control – an impoverishment exacerbated by the destruction of thousands of towns and villages, as well as by Soviet scorched earth and evacuation policies. In striking contrast to France in 1940, where goods of all kinds had been purchased or requisitioned from local sources – ranging from the products of regional wineries to toiletries and other necessities to replenish their basic kit – Russia offered up little in this regard. Compounding the problem was the growing inability of *Wehrmacht* supply lines to cover the basic requirements of the troops. As a result, the soldiers were compelled to turn more and more to their relations in Germany for such support. In a letter to his fiancée on 2 September 1941, Dr Heinrich Haape (6 ID) ended his remarks with a long "wish list" of needed items:

> We live here in such impoverished circumstances, you simply can't imagine it … No culture, not even the simplest facilities common to civilization can be found here …
>
> Please don't think that I'm moaning to you in writing this – if it came to it, I would gladly bear even more privations, but I want nothing more than sympathy for the wish list I'm going to write down now!
>
> There are no shops here, nothing to buy. Razor blades, comb, toothpaste, skin cream, soap, nail cleaner, writing paper, fountain pen, ink, *Frankfurter Zeitung*, *Koralle* [an illustrated magazine], card games, tobacco, all kinds of sweets, pocket handkerchiefs, etc.[27]

The preceding discussion begs the question of just how much contact the "typical" *Landser* actually had with Russian civilians during the months of the *Vormarsch* in 1941. Once again, there is no simple answer, for the degree of contact experienced by the soldiers varied considerably. (Unlike central Europe, the Soviet Union, despite a population of more than 170 million,[28] was a thinly settled land. Even in the Ukraine, where population density was the greatest, there were an average of only 69 people per square kilometer in 1939; in Belorussia the figure was only 44/sq.km.)[29] Whatever the extent of the contact between *Landser* and locals, however, it was often facilitated by the fact that some Russians were familiar with the German language. Recalled artillery soldier Willi Loewer (129 ID):

> And generally the relationship with the civilian population was uncomplicated. Many were very friendly toward us. We were usually received with bread and salt. The old men knew Germany in part from their captivity in the First World War. Many spoke at least a little German.[30]

For combat soldiers, who avoided villages and peasant dwellings as much as possible, contact with civilians in occupied areas tended to be infrequent and "fleeting" (*fluechtig*) in nature during the initial months of the campaign.[31] "We soldiers of the forwardmost line," remembered Otto Baese, then an infantryman in 110 Infantry Division, "seldom had contact with the civilian population; when we did, such as in Belorussia, the encounters were friendly ones. We were often greeted as liberators. During the advance, and also on the retreat from Moscow, the villages were mostly abandoned [*ausgestorben*], the civilians having disappeared without a trace."[32] Observed Heinrich Stockhoff (6 ID): "As the forward edge [*vordere Spitzen*] of the infantry we had very little contact with the civilian population."[33]

Conversely, men serving behind the front – e.g., in a bakery or butchery company, responsible for requisitioning foodstuffs or livestock – would, of necessity, have had more extensive dealings with farmers and other civilians. Commented veteran Aloys Gassmann (106 ID) in a letter to this author:

> As a bakery company, we had a lot of contact with the civilian population. If not officially, then unofficially, our underwear as well as our work clothes were washed by the Russian women. They did this gladly and were helpful. We usually secretly gave the women a 3-pound loaf of bread baked by us, and a piece of curd soap, and, in addition to that, candies, chocolate, and other sweets to the children from the Army stores supplies allocated to us. The fact that we were taking bread illicitly from the tent and giving it to the civilian population in return for their services was well known to the company command, and they did the same.
>
> As long as I was ever a soldier, and very often met with the Russian population, there was never any complaint against members of our company. Even harassment of a sexual nature toward women in general remained an "alien concept" to us.[34]

One may question just how enthusiastically Russian women provided their services to the Germans; that said, women were increasingly engaged by German soldiers to perform various menial tasks, such as washing clothing and assisting with food preparation. These women, like all civilians caught behind German lines, had little choice but to "weigh the options for [their] own survival;"[35] signifying, in effect, that they had little choice but to serve their temporary German masters. As one German veteran appositely put it, "An armed soldier always embodies power. The population was powerless and behaved accordingly."[36]

Although most likely not widespread, some genuinely close relationships developed between the German invaders and local Russian women. In other cases, no doubt out of desperation, women tendered sexual favors in exchange for food or protection. "Relationships between Russian girls and [German] soldiers were extremely rare," recalled Kurt Werner Andres (20 PD):

> In Orel, for example, where women only performed "favors" for the soldiers out of hunger, there was, to my knowledge, no brothel. However, I wrote to my then girlfriend, later my wife of 47 years, in a field post letter of 16 April 1943, among other things: "Yesterday I was in Orel with our regimental commander; as an officer candidate, you sometimes have to introduce yourself. I found out all sorts of gossip again, which will probably interest you, but will also astound you. At the army staff located in Orel, there have already been applications for permission to marry Russian women submitted by members of the German *Wehrmacht*, of course by members of the Flak, who have already been in Orel since October 1941. What do you say to that? Or another fact: in Orel, there are 900 illegitimate children by German *Landser*. No comment necessary."[37]

Numerous veterans' accounts underscore the fact that many German soldiers came to have great respect for the Russian women, admiring their strength, stoutness, and hard working ways. Again, K.W. Andres:

> We admired the women, who, in addition to their own households and their many children, had to work in jobs involving great physical demands, e.g., as tractor drivers, operators of machines of all shapes and sizes, miners, road and railroad construction workers. The second woman in the family was the *Babuschka*

(grandmother). Due to the working activities of the mother, the demands on her were high. Many families could hardly imagine a life without her. We often saw [the grandmothers] in the villages, supervising the children, and they made a patient and good-natured impression on us.[38]

Be that as it may, the soldiers of the *Ostheer* often used women – old men, even children – to perform forced labor of all kinds, at and behind the front. By the winter of 1941/42, civilians were being used to build trenches and bunkers and clear snow from roadways. To cite just one example, the use of civilian forced labor by 253 Infantry Division had, by 1943, become commonplace (*Alltag*), the division's work commandos (*Arbeitskommandos*) composed of women and men from 14 to 60 years of age.[39] These forced laborers were held in camps and made to construct objects of a military nature; their activities took place throughout the division's sector – that is, in rear areas and areas occupied by the fighting troops:

> By 1943/44, the [forced labor] work companies [within 253 ID] had reached the numbers of a decimated infantry regiment. At corps level, they numbered the equivalent of an infantry division. Meanwhile, the respective local population was set to work in agriculture and the local economic concerns under supervision of the *Wehrmacht*, or even used as living "mine detection equipment" [*Minensuchgeraete*], who had to walk or drive along the endangered roads, before they were used by German troops. Just as in previous years, when the location was changed, elements of the existing work commandos were routinely sent off to the *Reich*, new mobile work companies were formed from the population now to be deported, and the population found in the new operational sector was set to forced labor *in situ*.[40]

Even more devastating to Russian civilians was the massive requisitioning of provisions by German combat and rear area units. Almost from the outset of the campaign the *Ostheer's* logistical apparatus proved unequal to the task of supplying several million soldiers over the vast occupied territories of the Soviet Union, forcing the troops to live increasingly off the land to the great detriment of the civilian population. This is hardly surprising when one considers that the *Ostheer* began war with Russia with a stockpile of just 20 days' rations.[41] German forces often "ruthlessly plundered the villages through which they advanced, seizing meat, bread, wheat, livestock and milk."[42] In his relatively recent (2003) and exceptional social history of 253 Infantry Division,[43] German historian Christoph Rass describes how the process worked:

> The development of the German predatory practices can be reconstructed using the activity report of Department IVa [Rations] of 253 Infantry Division, which covers the period from April to December 1941. Even as early as 1 July [1941], barely a week after the start of the advance, basic provisions could no longer be obtained via the *Wehrmacht's* supply network.[44] Instead, the division's supply office [*Versorgungsamt*] began to search for stores of captured goods or to purchase scarce items. As long as the troops were located in the area of the Baltic States, payment for the items used was always carefully ensured. The sole exceptions were stocks of the Red Army and Jewish property, which were confiscated without compensation.
>
> After crossing over to Soviet territory, the conduct of the troops changed. Above all, it was the stocks of cattle that became a primary target for the requisition commandos. A pattern developed here, whereby the division's butchery company would follow the combat troops at irregular intervals, so that it could remain

stationary for several days at a time in a particular area, which, in this period, would be systematically exploited by the "collection of animals for slaughter from the surrounding area." As soon as the combat troops reached a critical distance for transport from the supply base, or when the accessible area had been stripped of all its foodstuffs, the relocation of the [base] toward the front followed. Where payments to the owners for their cattle were undertaken, then these were at an exchange rate of 1 RM to 10 rubles in *Reichskasse* credit notes, and at prices fixed by the *Wehrmacht*. In fact, there is reference to a payment on only the first procurement of cattle from a *kolkhoz* [collective farm] on 14 July 1941. The rule was most likely confiscation of the cattle in exchange for a requisition voucher.

Although the orders to the combat troops had forbidden them from procuring foodstuffs on their own account – because the requisitioned supplies were supposed to be delivered to a central distribution point by the supply units – it became normal for the advancing units to permit – parallel to the seizures made by the logistical services – the confiscation of supplies by their own commandos. Below these competing institutional levels, there were the individual raiding parties of *Wehrmacht* members. Some of these ended up in front of the divisional court and have thus been documented.

The civilian population in the conquered territories was thus exposed, in the shortest possible time, to three waves of robbery and plundering. First, the combat units helped themselves as they passed through; they were followed by the wide-ranging work of the supply services' commandos; and, in the shadow of this organized exploitation, there were also innumerable cases of looting by individual soldiers.[45]

By the fall of 1941, as a result of both German plundering and Red Army policies (i.e., scorched earth, evacuations of livestock and other supplies from cities, towns and collective farms), Russian civilians in captured German areas were experiencing "acute food shortages."[46] When German soldiers sought to help starving Russian civilians, the Army High Command intervened in an effort to put a stop to the practice.[47] For the sake of perspective, it should be noted that the exploitation of an occupied country's economic resources by the occupying power was fully recognized under international law;[48] hence, the soldiers of the *Ostheer* had a legal – and existential – right to conduct the requisitions, insofar as they did not overburden local resources. In other words, the crime was not the requisitions themselves, but their often ruthless scope and the manner in which they were carried out.[49]

The larger point, however, is that German policy at the highest levels not only accepted, but deliberately promoted, the starvation of the civilian population in the occupied territories. As Herbert Backe, State Secretary for Food and Agriculture and one of the prime movers behind this policy said shortly before *Barbarossa* began: "The Russian has put up with poverty, hunger and contentedness for hundreds of years. His stomach is elastic, so compassion is misplaced."[50] Although following the catastrophic "starvation winter" (*Hungerwinter*) of 1941/42 steps were taken to alleviate the plight of civilians – in some cases out of humanitarian concerns, but mostly because they were needed to keep the economy going and provide labor for the Germans – such efforts were tentative at best and, over the course of the war, hundreds of thousands, perhaps millions, perished from starvation.[51]

An additional factor, one that made the often brutal mistreatment of Russian civilians inevitable, was the budding partisan war which, for all its ambiguities and frustrations for the German soldier, was waged without mercy by both sides. (See, Section 9.3.4) In any case, the historiography of recent decades has fundamentally broadened our awareness of the *Wehrmacht's* behavior in the east, revealing that, from the beginning of the campaign, crimes against civilians were far from infrequent. After all, the objective of German forces in Russia was to crush the Soviet Union in a war envisaged by Hitler and his chief military advisers as a war of annihilation against the Soviet state and its people. Argues German historian Christian Hartmann:

> Even then [summer 1941], however, [German] rule very quickly showed its true face. In the highly-charged atmosphere of the first weeks in particular, the units at the front also committed excesses, not infrequently in cooperation with self-appointed native collaborators; victims were usually Jews, Communists, or guerillas, real or imagined. Details of such occurrences survive from, for example, Belostok, Brest-Litovsk, Dubno, Lemberg [Lviv], Liepaya, Mogilev, Zhitomir, and Tarnopol ... later from Kiev and Uman. The local military authorities reacted very differently: some encouraged these crimes; some tried to ignore them; some, however, were horrified by these excesses, and they succeeded in quickly putting a stop to them. Taken as a whole, the terror of the first weeks was limited to individual locations, especially in the Baltic and the Ukraine, meaning that the number of frontline soldiers who participated in it likely remained low.[52]

Yet even though the murderous policies pursued by Germany's political and military elites gave virtual license to the soldiers in the east to operate outside the laws of war, with immunity from prosecution, the results of new research (e.g., from Hartmann, discussed in Section 9.3.5 below) make a compelling case that a large majority of *Landser* were not guilty of war crimes against the civilian population (or against the Red Army for that matter) while fighting on Soviet soil from 1941 to 1944. This assertion certainly holds true for the first summer of the campaign, before the soldiers' relationship with Russian civilians was seriously complicated by the partisan movement and efforts to combat it. Reflected Dr Werner Dicke (26 ID): "Our approach toward the Russian civilian population changed fundamentally over the course of the war. As a messenger during the summer [1941], I could still go out to a farm alone without worry [*ohne Bedenken*] and ask for milk, which was then given to me in a friendly manner." As the *Partisanenkrieg* escalated, however, such casual behavior became much too dangerous: "We were no longer secure even in close proximity to our quarters. If, for example, one had to use the latrine, two men would accompany him, to make sure he didn't end up with a knife in his back [*abgestochen*]."[53]

Despite the lawlessness encouraged by Nazi occupational policies, serious transgressions against Soviet civilians – assault, robbery, rape, etc. – if often tolerated, were still prosecuted by German military authorities during the Russian campaign – the principal objective thereby being to uphold discipline in the fighting forces.[54] For as every officer from 2nd Lieutenant to field marshal knew full well, an army without discipline was little more than a dangerous rabble, and the officers leading the *Ostheer* were not about to let their soldiers behave like the *Landsknecht* of the 15th Century.[55] Furthermore, to argue a point which this author has yet to see advanced in the literature: Germany – despite National Socialist contempt for, and efforts to harass, the Protestant and Catholic Churches – remained a deeply Christian nation; many soldiers held sincere Christian beliefs, and most of them were fully aware of the difference between right and wrong, good and evil. Perforce, even if years of scurrilous National Socialist ideological training and propaganda had managed to blur basic moral boundaries, it only makes sense to conclude that Germany's bedrock Christian values functioned as a palpable break on the kinds of criminal actions promoted by Nazi policies in Soviet Russia. In other words, eight years of brutal dictatorship were not enough to fully expunge hundreds of years of inculcating Christian charity.

Following the capture of towns and cities, one of the initial acts of German military authorities was often to open the mostly orthodox Christian churches for use by the local population. These churches had been closed to the public for years and, in many cases, diverted by the Communists to other purposes (e.g., cinemas, market places, grain storage facilities, even breweries and horse stalls). In his "recollections," General (later Field Marshal) Maximilian von Weichs registered his disgust at the Soviet desecration of Christian churches, while also noting that a generation of Communism had failed to eradicate the deep faith of the Russian people. As Weichs also indicated, Hitler's decree governing use of churches in the east was, on occasion at least, flouted:

> Churches had been turned into storerooms, automobile workshops, [and] cinemas. Large churches, like the Smolensk cathedral [or] the church of the ... convent in Kiev, had become godless museums, containing despicable mockeries of the Christian faith. In B.[- - -], we removed the film projector equipment from a church, erected a large wreath of birch wood, and set up a table as an altar, so that we could hold religious services [*Feldgottesdienste*] here for both denominations [of troops].
>
> By the following morning, the local residents had already decorated the wreath and altar with flowers and icons. The locals, who were a mix of Orthodox and Roman Catholics in this area, thronged the soldiers' services, even the Protestant ones, of which they could, of course, understand nothing at all. So great was the demand for religious ceremonies – and so little success had Bolshevism had in destroying the deep faith of at least the older members of the population. Just as it was in B.[- - -], so it was everywhere we returned the churches to their original purpose ...
>
> The return of religious freedom could have been an important way of fostering a good relationship with the Russian population. Hitler, however, sought to limit these efforts. It was, by decree, permissible to open the churches for the use of local residents, but it was forbidden to use the churches for military services or to help the people in re-establishing the churches. Since the last mentioned activity had brought particularly good results, this proscription was not adhered to strictly. The population was grateful and filled the reclaimed places of worship. The old Russian church songs resounded in the church services. Often, masses of young people came to be baptized. But baptism of Polish or Russian people by German Army chaplains [*Feldgeistliche*] was forbidden by Hitler.[56]

While affecting a more cynical tone, Field Marshal von Bock also grasped the importance of giving religious freedom back to the Russian people. On 4 August 1941, he penned in his diary:

> Yesterday a number of churches that the Bolsheviks had converted, for the most part into cinemas or "godless exhibitions," were given back their vocation. The population had come, often from far away, cleaned the churches and decorated them with flowers. Many pictures of Christ and icons that had been hidden for decades were brought out. When the military services were over, the people – not just the old, but many young as well – streamed into the churches and kissed the holy objects – including the crosses around the necks of the armed forces chaplains – and often remained there praying until evening. This people would not be difficult to lead![57]

On 3 August, the field marshal had been touring the sectors of 5 and 8 Army Corps,[58] around Smolensk;[59] hence, it is possible that his observations included the reopening of the great cathedral there. The first mass in the cathedral in more than two decades was witnessed by *Panzer Offizier* Hans von Luck (7 PD):

> I obtained permission to go to Smolensk to see the old city. I took along my orderly officer and two men as guard. Here, there was, as yet, practically no German occupation since the pocket had formed more to the west of the city and was now being mopped up by the infantry.
>
> Smolensk looked as though it had been abandoned. Destruction in the industrial quarters and of the bridges over the Dnepr was immense. In the midst of the ruins, Smolensk cathedral pointed to the sky. It appeared largely unharmed. I followed the women and the old men and as I entered the cathedral, was deeply impressed by its beauty. It looked intact. The altar was adorned; burning candles and many icons richly embellished with gold bathed the interior in a festive light. As I went up to the altar with my companions, an old man, poorly dressed and with a flowing beard, spoke to me in broken German.
>
> "*Gospodin* officer, I am a pope who used to preach here before the Lenin-Stalin era; I have been in hiding now for many years, scraping a living as a shoemaker. Now you have liberated our city. May I say a first mass in this cathedral? ..." Without referring to HQ, I gave the pope permission to celebrate mass the next day, for which he wanted to bring in an additional pope.
>
> The following day, I went to Smolensk again, having informed the divisional commander in the meantime; as a precaution, I took along an armored patrol.
>
> The sight that met our eyes when we arrived was breathtaking. The square in front of the cathedral was full of people moving slowly toward the entrance. With my orderly officer, I jostled my way forward. Already, there was not a corner left in the cathedral in which people were not standing, sitting, or kneeling. We remained standing to one side to avoid disturbing the service by our presence.
>
> I was not familiar with the Russian Orthodox ritual, but the ceremony that now began drew me more and more under its spell. Invisible behind the altar, one of the two popes began with a monotone chant, which was answered by a choir of eight voices standing in front of the altar. The chanting of the precentor and the choir filled the vast space of the church. The acoustics gave the impression that the chanting came from above, from heaven. The people fell on their knees and prayed. All had tears in their eyes. For them, it was the first mass for more than 20 years. My companion and I were greatly moved. How deep must the faith have been of these poor, oppressed people; no ideology, no compulsion or terror had been able to take it from them. It was an experience I shall never forget.[60]

9.2: The Barbarization of Warfare on the Eastern Front

"In 1898," observed British historian Niall Ferguson in a 2006 article in *Foreign Affairs*, "H.G. Wells wrote The War of the Worlds, a novel that imagined the destruction of a great city and the extermination of its inhabitants by ruthless invaders.

> The invaders in Wells' story were, of course, Martians. But no aliens were needed to make such devastation a reality. In the decades that followed the book's publication, human beings repeatedly played the part of the inhuman marauders, devastating city after city in what may justly be regarded as a single hundred-year "war of the world."[61]

The 20th Century "was the bloodiest era in history." The First World War resulted in the deaths of nine to 10 million people (millions more if the influenza pandemic of 1918/19 is considered an outcome of the war). In the Second World War, an additional 59 million lives were lost. By one estimate, 16 conflicts throughout the last century each claimed more than one million lives; six more resulted in losses from 500,000 to a million; and 14 cost between 250,000 and 500,000 lives. In sum, between 167 and 188 million people were killed over the past century in acts of organized violence, or as many as one out of every 22 deaths during the period.[62]

In the Second World War, more than 4.0 million German soldiers lost their lives on the eastern front.[63] Irrecoverable Soviet military losses (i.e., those who died due to combat, sickness, or disease; perished in captivity; or went missing) amounted to just under 8.7 million, while the total number of Soviet citizens (soldiers and civilians) who died during the war is now estimated at 27 to 30 million or more.[64] Taking the lower estimate of 27 million Soviet dead, and adding to it the German figure of over 4.0 million dead, two stunning facts emerge: a) More than half of all fatal losses between 1939 and 1945 occurred in the Russo-German war; and, b) more than 15 percent of all deaths attributed to organized violence in the 20th Century took place in just 1418 days of warfare between the German Reich and Soviet Russia.[65]

These astonishing figures amplify the unparalleled savageness of the fighting and genocide, the incalculable suffering, which came to pass along the eastern front in the Second World War. The war was waged by two totalitarian states and was existential in its scope; it was, put simply, total war in its most extreme manifestation. The primary protagonists were tens of millions of common soldiers imbued with ideological and racial hatreds and commonly encouraged to violate the cannon of international law. That such a scrupulously toxic environment was highly conducive to criminal behaviors of all kinds is no surprise.

While major gaps remain in historians' knowledge and understanding of war crimes in the east, a consensus has been reached that the *Wehrmacht*, far from waging a "clean" war inside the Soviet Union – a perspective assiduously fostered by the memoirs of German generals like Manstein and Guderian in the early post-war period and, for decades, largely accepted at face value by many western historians – was deeply complicit in the murderous actions of the SS, police units, civilian occupational authorities, and other Nazi overlords inside Russia; as Christian Hartmann put it, "this Army long ago lost its innocence."[66] Historians are also learning more about the Red Army and its long catalogue of war crimes, even if these have often not received the same scrutiny from historians as the misdeeds of the *Wehrmacht*.[67]

In the narrative below (Sections 9.3 and 9.4), the purpose is to provide additional insight into violations of the body of international law governing armed conflict by the *Ostheer* – focusing, of course, on Army Group Center – and by the Red Army during the summer of 1941. While no attempt will be made at a comprehensive overview of war crimes on the eastern front, several major topics will be explored, such as the implementation of criminal directives by the German Army, the treatment of prisoners of war by both sides, and the disregard by the Soviets of Red Cross protections for German medical personnel. Among the sources assembled by this author are records of the *Wehrmacht* Office of Investigation for Violations of International Law (*Wehrmacht-Untersuchungsstelle fuer Verletzungen des Voelkerrechts*), an indispensable resource for Soviet war crimes (and one which has largely been neglected by historians); other official German records; memoirs and diaries of German soldiers; and key secondary published literature addressing the war crimes of both warring parties.

Before beginning, however, some general observations on the laws of war, as they existed in 1941, are in order. The international framework governing *how* wars were to be fought by combatants (*jus in bello*) was laid out in two sets of laws – The Hague Conventions of October 1907 and the Geneva Conventions of July 1929.[68] The Hague

Conventions (notably Convention IV, the *Laws and Customs of War on Land*) represented the "first general attempt to restrict the abuse of prisoners and wounded and to protect the civilian population by defining distinctions between combatants and non-combatants."[69] These were signed by Imperial Russia, which had played a significant role in bringing them about; as early as 1917/18, however, the new Soviet government refused to accept that Red Army soldiers would ever surrender to its "class enemies," and no longer considered itself as a signatory.[70]

On 27 July 1929, 43 parties signed the "Third Geneva Convention," which was actually two conventions covering military personnel who fell into an adversary's hands – one pertaining to POWs, the other to the care of wounded soldiers. Among the signatories were the United States, Germany, Italy, France and Great Britain (and its Dominions); Japan and the Soviet Union did not accede to the conventions. The USSR did sign the 1925 Geneva Protocol banning the use of poison gas and bacteriological warfare (ironic in view of German pre-*Barbarossa* fears about potential Red Army use of poison gas and other contaminants).[71]

The Geneva Conventions put in place significant protections for prisoners belonging to signatory nations. Yet because the Soviet Union had not signed the agreements, Germany felt it was under no obligation to adhere to them on the eastern front, and most likely would not have done so even had Russia been party to the conventions. The Red Army was the only army in the world that viewed being taken prisoner as an act of desertion and treason; thus, the Soviet government and military were totally disinterested in what became of their soldiers in captivity. German authorities also evinced little interest in the fate of their captured soldiers. In any case, neither belligerent had any intention of following either "the letter or the spirit" of the Geneva Conventions of 1929 (with its requirement, for example, for independent inspection of prison camps) or The Hague Conventions of 1907. In August 1941, the Soviet government indicated a desire to adhere to The Hague Conventions, "but the approach was tentative," and nothing came of the matter.[72]

Finally, it should be noted that armed civilians who participated in the fighting on the eastern front "came under the heading of irregulars according to the unambiguous terms of the [Hague Conventions], as well as the common usage of war;" as a result, they enjoyed no protections under international law. "This applies also," wrote the late German historian Joachim Hoffmann, "to Zoya Kosmodemyanskaya, executed by German troops on 29 November 1941 for arson; this young woman [was] presented as a shining example to the youth of the Soviet Union … Deplorable though the fate of the young Komsomol girl may have been, it should not be overlooked that it was inevitable under the merciless laws of war."[73]

9.3: *Keine Kameraden*: **Crimes of the *Ostheer***

In *The Afghan Campaign: A Novel*, former U.S. Marine Steven Pressfield provocatively recreates Alexander the Great's invasion of the Afghan kingdoms in the year 330 B.C. The great Persian Empire has fallen and "lies at Alexander's feet;" Darius, the great Persian leader, is dead. Now Alexander plans to march on "mythical India," but the road to it lies through Afghanistan, where the 28-year-old conqueror and his army will meet a new and very different foe. In one riveting passage, the fictional Alexander tells a group of replacements to prepare to fight "a different kind of war," against an enemy unlike any hitherto encountered:

> Understand: The actions we take in this campaign are as legitimate as those enacted in any other. This is not a conventional warfare. It is unconventional. And we must fight it in an unconventional way …
>
> [The enemy's] word to us is worthless. He routinely violates truces; he betrays the peace. When we defeat him, he will not accept our dominion. He comes

back again and again. He hates us with a passion whose depth is exceeded only by his patience and capacity for suffering. His boys and old men, even his women, fight us as combatants. They do not do this openly, however, but instead present themselves as innocents, even as victims, seeking our aid. When we show compassion, they strike with stealth. You have all seen what they do to us when they take us alive.[74]

Prior to the start of Operation *Barbarossa*, the propaganda branch of the German Armed Forces High Command (OKW), in collaboration with the Army High Command (OKH), worked out the "Guidelines for the Conduct of Troops in Russia" (*Richtlinien fuer das Verhalten der Truppe in Russland*). These were then passed on to the individual *Wehrmacht* commands on 19 May 1941, but were only to be distributed to the troops on the eve of the invasion (along with Hitler's order of the day).[75] The guidelines contained several key sentences:

> I. 1. *Bolshevism is the mortal enemy* [*Todfeind*] *of the National Socialist German people. Germany's struggle is aimed against that disruptive ideology and its exponents.*
> 2. That struggle demands ruthless and energetic action against *Bolshevik agitators, guerillas, saboteurs, Jews* and the complete liquidation of any active or passive resistance.
> II. 3. Extreme reserve and most alert vigilance are called for towards all members of the *Red Army* – even prisoners – as treacherous methods of fighting are to be expected. The *Asiatic soldiers* of the Red Army in particular are inscrutable, unpredictable, insidious, and unfeeling.
> 4. After the capture of units the *leaders* are to be *instantly separated* from the other ranks.[76]

Why the parallels are imperfect, the similarity in tone between Pressfield's Alexander and the *Ostheer's* guidelines is striking. In both cases, the troops are informed that their enemy is unconventional, even alien – a fanatic, who will strike without mercy, employing methods which are ruthless, insidious, and underhanded. In Alexander's speech the implication is that his men must meet fire with fire and employ equally uncompromising methods. In the *Barbarossa* guidelines the objective is to indoctrinate the troops and ensure implementation of key directives, such as the Commissar Order of 6 June 1941 that, in crass violation of international law, authorized the summary extrajudicial execution of captured Soviet political officers.[77] Indeed, the *Richtlinien* for the troops, by conflating "Bolshevik agitators, guerillas, saboteurs, [and] Jews," must have had "spectacular results for mishandling of prisoners, and for eliminating and alienating many people who might well otherwise have espoused the German cause. And there were many cases where the massacre of Jews was reported as 'anti-partisan operations.'"[78]

Orders such as the "Guidelines for the Conduct of Troops in Russia," the Commissar Order, and the Decree on Military Justice,[79] all drafted and promulgated by German military authorities in the weeks before the start of *Barbarossa*, reflect just how deeply the *Wehrmacht*, by 1941, had burrowed into the ideology and aspirations of the National Socialist state. Far from standing apart from – or above – the *NS Staat*, the German armed forces were deeply embedded in the political "culture" of Hitler's Third Reich, and shared, or were at least sympathetic to, its most basic objectives. Despite sporadic resistance, the synchronization (*Gleichschaltung*) of the German military with National Socialism had begun immediately after Hitler's seizure of power in 1933, with *Reichswehr* Minister General Werner von Blomberg promising his "Fuehrer" that Germany's soldiers would not only be trained to fight, but be educated to be conscious of their special racial characteristics (*Volkstum*).[80] In the years that followed, the Supreme Command (OKW/OKH) shaped the *Wehrmacht* into a powerful instrument, and a "compliant tool," of Hitler's imperialist and genocidal policies, among other things engulfing its soldiers in a veritable flood of propaganda depicting the "brutish [Russian] enemy" and the "Russian *Untermensch*."[81]

9.3.1: Soviet Prisoners of War

Most *Wehrmacht* soldiers, junior NCOs and many officers had come of age under Hitler and had few – if any – reservations about their mission in Russia; a significant minority – 29 percent according to one survey of three front-line German divisions – were also Nazi Party members.[82] Fuelled by anti-Bolshevik indoctrination, German troops often mistreated and murdered Soviet prisoners of war; in fact, "division and other records indicate that 'wild' and often indiscriminate shootings of Soviet POWs began during the very first days of the campaign."[83] Submits historian Omer Bartov:

> Having been told on the one hand that this was no ordinary war but a "*Weltanschauungskrieg*" in which there were "*keine Kameraden*," and on the other hand that "the Russian soldier has a right for decent treatment," they seem to have adopted the former, more brutal definition of the war, which also corresponded much better with their indoctrination in civilian life and in the army, as well as with the wishes of their Fuehrer and the general brutality of the fighting.[84]

Senior officers, concerned about the impact of such behavior on discipline, sometimes intervened in an effort to stop the killings, as did General Lemelsen (47 Panzer Corps), on 25 June 1941:

> I have observed that senseless shootings of both POWs and civilians have taken place. A Russian soldier who has been taken prisoner while wearing a uniform and after he put up a brave fight, has the right for a decent treatment. We want to free the civilian population from the yoke of Bolshevism and we need their labor force … This instruction does not change anything regarding the Fuehrer's order on the ruthless action to be taken against partisans and Bolshevik commissars.[85]

General Lemelsen's order, however, fell on deaf ears and, thus, he repeated it five days later (30 June):

> In spite of my instructions of 25.6.41 … still more shootings of POWs and deserters have been observed, conducted in an irresponsible, senseless and criminal manner. This is murder! The German *Wehrmacht* is waging this war against Bolshevism, not against the united Russian peoples. We want to bring back peace, calm and order to this land that has suffered terribly for many years from the oppression of a Jewish and criminal group. The instruction of the Fuehrer calls for ruthless action against Bolshevism (political commissars) and any kind of partisan! People who have been clearly identified as such should be taken aside and shot only by order of an officer … [descriptions] of the scenes of countless bodies of soldiers lying on the roads, having clearly been killed by a shot through the head at point blank range, without their weapons and with their hands raised, will quickly spread in the enemy's army.[86]

According to Bartov, Lemelsen's orders are "the best proof for the fact that acts of brutality and indiscriminate shootings [by German soldiers] began even before the brutalizing effect of the war could come into play."[87] This assertion of Bartov's, however, is, in part at least, incorrect. Numerous contemporaneous German accounts (see, Section 9.4 below) make all too clear that the murder (and, in many cases, horrific mutilation) of captured *Wehrmacht* soldiers by the Red Army took place all across the front from the opening hours of the campaign; shocked and enraged, German soldiers responded by administering their own summary justice (as many of their accounts also indicate). To turn Bartov's claim around, the criminal *Russian* behavior was thus also something other than simply a reaction to the "brutalizing effect of the war." What is indisputable as well is that criminal (or treacherous) behavior by one side begat more such behavior by the other; and that, from the very outset, a brutal dialectical logic of atrocity and reprisal resulted in a surging spiral of violence which dramatically accelerated the incidents of extrajudicial killings by both combatants.

How this dialectical tension played out on the battlefield was strikingly depicted by *Oberleutnant* Siegfried Knappe (87 ID), as he later recounted an event in the summer of 1941 at Orsha (between Minsk and Smolensk), where his division had to overcome a well-prepared defensive position:

> A prepared defensive line always consisted of several consecutive lines of trenches or foxholes, and when we attacked we had to overrun them all. The standard procedure in all combat until now was that when attacking infantry passed over the first line of trenches or foxholes, the enemy soldiers who had been overrun and were still alive and not badly wounded would stand and raise their hands in surrender to the soldiers advancing behind the first line of attacking troops. The captured enemy soldiers including the wounded, would then be collected and taken to the rear.
>
> While advancing in a large wooded area … we were spread out in a line. I was with the point company, in the center of the line. The Russian soldiers in the first line of defense were dug in so that only their heads were out of the foxholes, and they had branches over their heads, so they were very difficult to see. We received rifle fire from them, and we returned their fire and kept advancing. Then the fire became heavy. All around us were the crack of rifles, the boom of mortars, and the hollow chatter of machine guns.[88]

Knappe and the other attacking troops overran the first Soviet defensive line, and began to assault the enemy's second prepared position; suddenly, they realized they were being fired upon from behind as well as from in front – that German soldiers were being shot and killed from behind by Russian soldiers in the first line of trenches who were supposed to have surrendered. From Knappe's perspective, the enemy's behavior was highly treacherous, a violation of that "code of honor" which was the "combat infantry soldier's only hope of survival in a hopeless situation."

> If that hope was taken away, death was certain – and nobody *wanted* to die! In a combat situation, the soldier is under inhuman stress to begin with, and when he sees a friend he has been sharing his life with suddenly drop because he was shot in the back, it is too much. Men who share combat become brothers, and this brotherhood is so important to them that they would give their lives for one another. It is not just friendship, and it is stronger than flag and country.
>
> Our soldiers went berserk, and from that point on during the attack they took no prisoners and left no one alive in a trench or foxhole. I did not try to stop them, nor did any other officer, because they would have killed us too if we had. They were out of their minds with fury. If the Russian soldiers had put down their weapons and stood up with their hands raised, they would have been collected

and marched to the rear as had always occurred in the past. Their cause was lost; they could only be taken prisoner or die. As it was, they were all killed, without mercy or remorse.[89]

As discussed in Chapter 7 of this narrative, the forces of Army Group Center collected hundreds of thousands of prisoners during the opening phases of the fighting through July/August 1941. For example, in the sector of 12 Panzer Division, 52,000 Russians surrendered on a *single day* near the end of the Belostok-Minsk cauldron battles, while German Fourth Army reported taking a total of 82,000 prisoners by the end of these battles (see, Section 7.5). Artillery *Oberleutnant* Knappe was astonished by the enormous number of prisoners coming in: "We had started taking prisoners from the first day of the invasion. The infantry brought them in by the thousands, by the tens of thousands, and even by the hundreds of thousands … I wondered at first whether we were prepared to care for so many of them, and as the numbers continued to grow I was sure we were not."[90]

Most of the prisoners captured in 1941 were moved west, toward the POW pens which awaited them, in forced marches; these often continued for weeks, under catastrophic conditions over hundreds of kilometers, resulting in the deaths of tens of thousands along the roads leading to the camps. Due to chronic manpower shortages, the Germans would detail but a few companies of troops to look after tens of thousands of marching prisoners, forcing the guards, by necessity, to resort to brutal methods to drive the starving prisoners to the next poorly prepared rest area. While many of the prisoners were wounded, they only received minimal care, if any at all; an OKW order of 8 July 1941, addressing first aid for POWs, stipulated that "Russian medical personnel, doctors and medical supplies are to be used first," before the German. *Wehrmacht* transport was not to be utilized.[91] Exhausted, starving, and wounded prisoners, those who weakened and fell behind – thousands of them – were shot dead, even in large cities such as Minsk or Smolensk.[92]

Schuetze Benno Zeiser, serving in a special duty company, described his first encounter with a large column of marching Soviet prisoners – his account betraying both horror and a macabre fascination:

> We suddenly saw a broad, earth-brown crocodile slowly shuffling down the road toward us. From it came a subdued hum, like that from a beehive. Prisoners of war. Russians, six deep. We couldn't see the end of the column. As they drew near the terrible stench which met us made us quite sick …
>
> We made haste out of the way of the foul cloud that surrounded them, then what we saw transfixed us where we stood and we forgot our nausea. Were these really human beings, these gray-brown figures, these shadows lurching toward us, stumbling and staggering, moving shapes at their last gasp, creatures which only some last flicker of the will to live enabled to obey the order to march? All the misery in the world seemed to be concentrated there. There was also that gruesome barrage of shouts and wails, groans, lamentations and curses which combined with the cutting orders of the guards into a hideous accompaniment.
>
> We saw one man shuffle aside from the ranks, then a rifle butt crash between his shoulder blades and drive him gasping back into place. Another with a head wound lost in bloodstained bandages ran a few paces out with gestures almost ludicrous in their persuasiveness to beg one of the nearby local inhabitants for a scrap of bread. Then a leather thong fetched him a savage lash round his shoulders and yanked him, too, back into place …
>
> Stray dogs were legion, among them were the most unbelievable mongrels; the only thing they were all alike in was that they were thin … That was no hindrance to the prisoners. They were hungry, so why not eat roast dog? They were always

trying to catch the scary beasts. They would also beg us with gestures and *bow-wows* and *bang-bangs* to kill a dog for them. There it was, shoot it! And we almost always did; it was a bit of sport anyway, and at the same time it delighted those human skeletons ...

When we brought one down, there followed a performance that could make a man puke. Yelling like mad, the Russkies would fall on the animal and tear it in pieces with their bare hands, even before it was quite dead. The pluck they would stuff their pockets with, like tobacco, whenever they got hold of any of that – it made a sort of iron ration. Then they would light a fire, skewer shreds of the dog's meat on sticks and roast it. There were always fights over the bigger bits. The burnt flesh stank frightfully; there was almost no fat in it.[93]

Even before the campaign began, German military leaders had agreed that Soviet prisoners of war should receive "only those rations that are absolutely necessary."[94] Yet the rations actually provided were well below the minimum needed for survival. In 1941, during the westward marches, prisoners were often allocated daily rations such as "20 g millet and 100 g bread without meat," or "two potatoes."[95] By September 1941, the signs of an impending catastrophe "were already unmistakable. Documents exist showing that in a number of camps desperate prisoners were driven by hunger to eat grass, leaves, or tree bark. In some camps in the east, epidemics caused by hunger were already claiming thousands of lives."[96] Cases of cannibalism among the starving Russian soldiers in the camps were also recorded.

Typical of the harsh attitudes of many *Landser* toward the wretched conditions of Soviet POWs were those expressed by "Hans-Otto," a soldier in 268 Infantry Division, in a field post letter dated 20 November 1941:

Food for the prisoners is not a problem, if there's nothing there, the chaps don't get anything. But they find plenty of dead horses and potatoes, so it's only when there's a mass accumulation of prisoners that hunger appears. But in the end, these people are used to it, and it's their own fault, because their own oh-so-fine confederates carted off all the food. And few have to stand guard, though naturally with the use of very draconian measures. Luckily, we have nothing to do with that.[97]

The terrible plight of Red Army prisoners was well known to the German armies in the east, as it was to the command centrals in Berlin and Rastenburg, East Prussia. As *Hauptmann* Georg Heino *Freiherr* von Muenchhausen, adjutant to Colonel Heusinger in the OKH Operations Branch, confided to his diary in mid-August 1941, "The Ic [Intelligence Officer] of Army Group Center [Major Rudolf-Christoph von Gersdorff] reports that an enormous [*ungeheure*] number of prisoners are succumbing due to a lack of rations and ruthless treatment, while others are being shot. That contradicts our propaganda and it will get around; our troops will have to pay for it in battle."[98] Several weeks later he wrote: "The issue of prisoners is an ugly debacle. It's bad enough that all the commissars are being shot; and on top of that, the prisoners, left without shelter and provided the most meager rations for weeks on end. They're dropping like flies."[99] When, in mid-September 1941, Admiral Canaris, the Chief of Military Intelligence (*Abwehr*), protested the treatment of Soviet POWs and the ongoing liquidation of "politically undesirable" prisoners – both in crass violation of international law – he elicited a curt rebuke from the Chief of OKW, Field Marshal Keitel: "Your misgivings reflect the soldierly conceptions of a chivalrous war. At issue here is the annihilation of a *Weltanschauung*! For that reason I approve of the measures and support them."[100]

While individual front commanders – among them, Field Marshal Fedor von Bock – often condemned the brutal mistreatment and execution of POWs in orders giving vent to their outrage, they did nothing to address the causes; most likely because, with limited resources of their own, they were helpless to do so. As Bock acknowledged on 22 August 1941:

> Acts of brutality have occurred while prisoners are being shipped to the rear; I have objected strongly in a toughly worded letter to the armies. With the exhausted state of the prisoners and the impossibility of feeding them properly on long marches through vast, uninhabited regions, their removal remains an especially difficult problem.[101]

In a report on his trips to the front, Major von Gersdorff stated that "the shooting of Jews, prisoners and even commissars is repudiated by practically all the officers ... It is obvious that the full facts have been exposed and that the officers at the front are talking about it much more than was supposed."[102] While at least some of these officers petitioned their superiors to "alleviate the misery of prisoners" – and warned of the POWs' poor "state of health," and the rising "mortality rate in the prisoner-of-war camps, especially in prisoners' hospitals" – nothing was done to change this deplorable state of affairs.[103] Moreover, as Keitel's comments to Canaris reveal, at the highest levels, the Army leadership had accepted the brutal treatment of Soviet prisoners as a consequence of Germany's war of annihilation.

While the treatment of Soviet POWs by the Germans signified a dreadful violation of both The Hague and Geneva conventions, the question remains to what extent mass starvation and murder were the intended outcomes of German military policy. According to German historian Christian Streit, whose several-decades-old book on the subject remains a standard, the decimation of Soviet prisoners of war was part of a calculated program implemented by the German High Command.[104] Streit considered, *inter alia*, the cooperation of the *Wehrmacht* with the notorious SS Action Groups (*Einsatzgruppen*) in murdering Soviet prisoners of war. On the other hand, the sheer magnitude of the problem of feeding, housing and providing medical care to the several millions of Red Army soldiers taken prisoner by the end of 1941[105] unquestionably overwhelmed the logistical capabilities of the German armies in Russia; hence, the argument is also made (as it was by leaders of the German military indicted at Nuremberg, and is still today by German veterans' organizations and some historians) that the terrible plight of the POWs may have been less the outcome of deliberate policy than the result of an unavoidable crisis.[106] And, as British historian Chris Bellamy argues in his recent history of the Russo-German War:

> Even if the Germans had wanted to apply the generous provisions of the Geneva Conventions – that prisoners of war should be fed and accommodated to the same standard as one's own rear echelon troops – they were simply unworkable in these circumstances. The infrastructure in the western USSR was relatively primitive, and the Germans had their own very serious logistical problems. As for moving the prisoners back to Germany, the camps there could hold 790,000 prisoners, including those from countries who had signed the Geneva Conventions.[107]

According to historian and Holocaust researcher Leni Yahil, the vast numbers of Soviet prisoners taken in the first six months "stunned the Germans, including Hitler himself." Moreover, "the German Army's preparations to absorb prisoners were provisional and in no way adequate. Nor was the Army willing to allocate to its prisoners any of the food that was supplied to its own troops with great difficulty." As a result, the Germans concluded that the prisoner of war camps should be "purified," and, to this end, SS units were dispatched to the camps in the summer of 1941 to eliminate "intolerable" elements, among them Communist activists, officials and intellectuals, agitators, and all Jews. A directive to this effect was issued on 17 July 1941.[108]

Whether the fate of Soviet prisoners of war – a "second Holocaust," in effect, with as many as 3.3 million perishing in German captivity – was primarily the result of deliberate policy, or mainly due to an unavoidable crisis (and sublime indifference at the highest levels of command), some German authorities did what they could, under exceedingly difficult circumstances, to assuage the suffering of the prisoners. Historian Theo J. Schulte, in his study of *Korueck* 582,[109] the unit responsible for security in the hinterland of Ninth Army, points out that:

> Russian prisoners who escaped immediate execution often perished in transit on the long and arduous marches to the rear. So many corpses were lying in and around the town of Viaz'ma in November 1941 that *Korueck* 582 expressed serious concern that this would give succor to enemy propaganda. The most sinister dimension was that many prisoners had not died of hunger and exhaustion but at the hands of the German guard troops who summarily executed "stragglers." …
>
> This said, as with so much of [German] military policy, actual practice was often complex, not to say ambivalent and contradictory. At the same time as many troops were complying with higher command's draconian orders, *Korueck* 582 warned its men that charges would be brought against those who used sticks to beat Russian POWs, while those who were executing prisoners would be more severely punished.[110]

Schulte goes on to indicate that military court records of *Korueck* 582 offer no evidence that any soldiers were ever charged with such abuses. Yet this was "hardly surprising as the very same orders demanding proper treatment of the prisoners also warned of the dangers of too lenient an approach and the repercussions of allowing anyone to escape."[111] And while it is unclear if such calls for restraint had any impact, a "grim fate" still awaited those POWs who reached the camps:

> When *Korueck* 582 took over Army Prisoner Collection Point 7 [*Armee-Gefangenensammelstelle* 7] in Rzhev from AOK 9 at the end of November 1941, rations for the prisoners were at starvation levels. Inmates had defoliated the barbed wire enclosure, trees had been stripped of both leaves and bark, and the men were eating grass and nettles. As many as 450 prisoners at a time were crammed into unheated single-story huts, which measured no more than 12 meters by 24. Disease was rife because of malnutrition, lack of basic hygiene (there were two latrines for 11,000 prisoners), and exposure to the elements. Cases of cannibalism among the distraught inmates were not unknown. Some *Korueck* officials were more concerned about the dietary well being of the German perimeter guard dogs that received 50 times the rations of the captive Russians.[112]

Yet once again, posits Schulte, "There are exceptions to the rule. It should be recognized that much of the historical evidence used to demonstrate the degradation, abuse, and squalor is often drawn from reports by the few *Korueck* and POW camp commanders who made strenuous efforts to improve the lot of inmates, and entered into copious correspondence with higher authorities requesting increased resources."[113] In Army Prisoner Collection Point 8, the commander saw to it that gloves made out of old coats, and clogs from waste timber (the Russian prisoners' boots having been confiscated by German soldiers) were provided to POWs, while the local population was pressured to furnish food for the camp in order to dispense warm soup with horsemeat and bread three times daily. In addition, German guard units were prohibited from wielding clubs, while combat units were forbidden to commandeer work details unless they agreed to feed the prisoners. By late 1941, Ninth Army headquarters was also interested in taking positive steps to provide more humane treatment.[114]

In their memoirs, Dr Heinrich Haape (6 ID) and Bernard Haering – the latter a Catholic priest and army medic – cited many examples of the medical care they freely gave to captured wounded Russian soldiers.[115] Haering claimed that his regiment behaved honorably, not shooting prisoners and providing as much care as they could to Russian wounded, although their situation was soon complicated by the arrival of the *Waffen*-SS and, with it, the murderous policies of the *Vernichtungskrieg*, which stiffened Red Army resistance, gave impetus to the partisan movement and, in the end, consigned Germany to defeat:

> When we first entered the Ukraine at the beginning of the war against Russia, the population received us in a way that was not only friendly but almost triumphant, as if we were liberators. People were in the streets when we entered their villages, offering milk, bread, honey, strawberries, and other fine things to our exhausted men. Their excessive hopes had been kindled especially by the war prisoners of the First World War who had spent years in Germany, mostly as workers on farms. These ex-prisoners spoke well of Germans, and the people therefore expected all of us to be like those old German farmers of whom the veterans spoke so frequently and so favorably.
>
> During the first four weeks [of the campaign] our division did not suffer any great losses – although even our relatively small losses were dreadful. We treated the prisoners well, and the people's expectations rose even higher ... During those first weeks, doctors and medical helpers generally did what they were obliged to do by conscience and international agreements. We gave the wounded Russian soldiers as much care as the hurried movements of our army allowed.
>
> Then in the fourth week, two SS regiments were inserted into the same part of the front. These criminals soon began to kill their prisoners and to refuse any treatment to wounded Russian soldiers and civilians. Immediately, the attitude of the population toward us changed ...
>
> The message must have spread quickly among the Russian soldiers, for now they offered real resistance. Within one week we suffered more losses than in the previous four weeks, and the number of Russian prisoners dropped off sharply. Those who surrendered were frightened, and it took a lot of kindly talk to assure them that they would be treated as human beings. As far as our regiment was concerned, this was still true.[116]

9.3.2: The Commissar Order

Among the prisoners routinely liquidated following capture were the Soviet commissars. Although the commissars were political officers, they were also members of the Red Army and, as such, fully covered by the protections of the international laws of war;[117] their systematic elimination by units of the *Wehrmacht*, or by those of the *Waffen*-SS, SD (*Sicherheitsdienst*, or Security Service) and police, was a war crime of the first order. Nevertheless, Field Marshal Erich von Manstein's post-war judgment of the Soviet commissars, and their role in shaping the utterly remorseless character of combat on the eastern front, remains a valid one:

> They were, rather – without being soldiers – fanatical fighters, and, indeed, fighters whose activities could only be viewed as illegal in the traditional sense of warfare. Their task was not simply to safeguard the Soviet military leadership

politically, but rather to give the fight an extreme harshness [*Haerte*] and a character that utterly contradicted notions to date of soldierly warfare. In fact, it was even these commissars to whom those methods of fighting and treating prisoners were attributable which were in stark contrast to the provisions of the Hague convention.[118]

While precise figures on compliance with the Commissar Order will never be known, it is likely that most *Wehrmacht* combat units adhered to the order, often despite serious reservations. According to one recent source, "the evaluation of German documents has shown that the Commissar Order was carried out by more than 80 percent of German divisions."[119] In their general history of the Second World War, authors Williamson Murray and Allan R. Millett argue that, "the acceptance by most army authorities of the Commissar Order was direct and immediate."[120] On the other hand, Israeli author Marcel Stein offers a more nuanced perspective:

> It has not yet been possible to ascertain the scale on which this order was carried out. It is also highly unlikely that this will be possible in the future. The available archival documentation is incomplete in this regard and contradictory. The emergence of new documents may lead to isolated corrections, but will not give a final overall picture of the situation.
>
> What is certain is that a majority of *Wehrmacht* commanders [*Befehlshaber*] were hostile to the order, which contradicted all soldierly traditions, but that was not true of all of them … Since this was an order from the Fuehrer [*Fuehrerbefehl*], the commanders-in-chief had to pass it on down the chain of command to the divisions. However, the manner in which it was passed on was left to the commanders-in-chief, and a large number of them gave expression to their disapproval with the clear suggestion that they placed no value on the implementation of the order – so, for example, Field Marshal Ritter von Leeb [Commander, Army Group North]. The order was carried out, but not on the scale intended.[121]

Nevertheless, many German field commanders carried out the Commissar Order with enthusiasm, with General Lemelsen's directives of 25 and 30 June 1941 (see above) pertaining to the shooting of Red Army POWs providing one example. German records indicate that 4 Panzer Group (Army Group North), from 22 June to 19 July 1941, reported 172 commissars liquidated; by 24 July, Second Army had shot 177 of them; and, by the beginning of August 1941, 3 Panzer Group claimed 170 victims. These and other extrajudicial killings were encouraged by the OKW, whose decree of 17 July 1941 stated:

> The special situation of the eastern campaign therefore demands *special measures* that are to be executed free from bureaucratic … influence and with a willingness to accept responsibility. While so far the … orders concerning POWs were based solely on *military* considerations, now the *political* objective must be obtained which is to protect the German nation from Bolshevik invaders and forthwith take the occupied territory in hand.[122]

And yet, as noted in Chapter 2, Field Marshal von Bock had courageously – if unsuccessfully – protested the Commissar Order to the Army High Command (OKH) on the eve of *Barbarossa*, refusing as well to transmit the order to subordinate commands.[123] We also know that General Hans-Juergen von Arnim, who commanded 17 Panzer Division (47 Panzer Corps) until wounded several days after the start of the campaign, refused to implement the order.[124] On 17 September 1941, General Rudolf Schmidt, Commander, 39

Panzer Corps, demanded the order's immediate suspension, after expressly directing his subordinate commanders not to shoot captured commissars. As Schmidt told his troops: "As long as the commissars must defend themselves against certain death, they will stick together through thick and thin [*werden sie wie Pech und Schwefel zusammenhalten*] ... If, however, the individual commissar knows that his life will be spared should he desert, the cohesiveness of the [Red Army's] political leadership corps will collapse."[125]

In fact, by late August 1941, some German combat officers had begun to take initiatives in an effort to get the Commissar Order cancelled because of the negative effect it was having. Significantly, these initiatives came at a time when the German advance into Russia had begun to falter, as Soviet resistance – often led by fanatically fighting commissars, well aware of the fate that awaited them should they fall into German hands – noticeably stiffened and became more effective. While the OKH supported these initiatives, OKW (and Hitler) initially rejected them.[126] Not until 9 May 1942, did Hitler finally acquiesce to the growing demands of his officers at the front and terminate the notorious Commissar Order which, for the German war effort in the east, had proved so highly counterproductive.[127]

According to historian Geoffrey Roberts, "by the end of the eastern front war 160,000 captured 'commissars' had been killed by the Germans."[128] This figure, however, seems extraordinary large, particularly when considering the number of executions collectively recorded by 3 and 4 Panzer Groups and Second Army over the first four to six weeks of the campaign (519), when enforcement of the Commissar Order would have been at its most robust. In the sectors of two German armies, some 200,000 prisoners were taken by the end of 1941, but only 96 commissars reported as shot, leading German historian Franz W. Seidler to conclude that the *Kommissarbefehl* "had indeed been largely sabotaged" by German front commands; moreover, some front units padded their figures to feign compliance, while others counted commissars killed in combat as shot following their capture.[129]

As it was, by the spring of 1942, more than four million German soldiers (including replacements)[130] had seen service in Russia, the overwhelming majority of them assigned to formations of the regular Army. Assuming for the moment that Roberts' figure is correct, and that, theoretically, all 160,000 of the commissars had been liquidated by May 1942, and that all of them had been killed by soldiers of the Army – with no participation by SS, SD, or police units – on a one to one ratio (i.e., a separate soldier responsible for each commissar executed), then four to five percent of Army personnel would have taken part in the extrajudicial executions of Soviet commissars. Of course, the actual figure was but a tiny fraction of that.

Supporting this conclusion is the research of Marcel Stein for his biography of Field Marshal Walter Model. Among the Ic (Intelligence) records of Model's 3 Panzer Division, Stein discovered a *single case* of the shooting of a Soviet commissar. The order of the execution, handwritten on a slip of paper as a supplement (*Beilage*) to a report dated 28 July 1941, reads as follows:

3 Panzer Division, Lobkowicz, 28. VII Bl. 127

Prisoner Assembly Point Karachev

The two Jews (soldiers) are not [the word "not" is underlined twice] to be shot. Executions by shooting are only to be undertaken by special order of the division.
The commissar designated for execution by shooting is to be shot.
The other commissar discovered a few days ago is to be kept alive.
Prisoner Malow [name poorly legible] – report Mirski – is to be sent to the division immediately.

Signed: vom dem Knesebeck, *Leutnant.*[131]

"It is thus established," Stein concludes, "that in the [3 PD] one commissar was executed by shooting [*erschossen*].

Whether this occurred in the context of implementing the Commissar Order, or for other reasons, is not evident from the slip of paper. The document also contains the explicit instruction that the two Jews were not to be shot and that the execution order for a second commissar was to be suspended. From other Ic reports, it is clear that the Commissar Order was not systematically implemented by 3 Panzer Division – for example, in the interrogations of Oberst Odischarian, Division Commissar of 148 Rifle Division on 3 August 1941, and of Brigade Commissar Timofejew of 23 August 1941. The two commissars were not shot. The text of the reports shows that the interrogations were carried out correctly and according to international law.[132]

No reports of executed commissars can be found in the Ic reports of 41 Panzer Corps and Ninth Army; in contrast, one Ic report for the Ninth Army relates the capture of a NKVD Commissar Andruschew, who was accused of having taken part in illegal activities. When the accusations proved to be groundless, he was sent to a POW camp as a soldier by order of the Ic/AO.[133]

9.3.3: Support of Genocide against the Jews

Wehrmacht soldiers also participated in war crimes through their support of the notorious SS Action Groups (*Einsatzgruppen*). The mission of these groups had been clarified before the start of the Russian campaign in negotiations between SS-*Obergruppenfuehrer* (Lt.-Gen.) Reinhard Heydrich and Army Quartermaster Brig.-Gen. Eduard Wagner; the agreement they signed was ratified by the C-in-C of the Army, Field Marshal von Brauchitsch, on 28 April 1941.[134] Simply put, the SS was empowered to conduct certain activities in operational areas of the Army; its primary task, however, was to combat "anti-Reich tendencies" behind the front lines. Thus, the *Einsatzgruppen* were granted a "free hand" to operate in army and army group rear areas, in part to ensure that the *Wehrmacht* itself was not encumbered with the planned terror measures against Jews, Communist functionaries, the Soviet *intelligentsia*, and other "undesirables."[135] The action groups were to obtain their special "professional" orders from Heydrich, as head of the Security Police (*Sicherheitspolizei*) and the SD.[136] A liaison officer between the Army and the police was to be assigned to each of the three army groups.[137]

Four *Einsatzgruppen* ("A", "B," "C," and "D"), created from within the Security Police and the SD, were set up prior to the German attack on the Soviet Union. Each was commanded by an officer from the Reich Security Main Office, a major component of Himmler's SS empire, and composed of several commando units; these in, turn, were led chiefly by professional SS and Gestapo officers. The action groups numbered between 500 and 1000 men apiece,[138] their personnel including SS soldiers, members of the SD, Gestapo, police and local volunteers. (By comparison, a full-strength German infantry battalion numbered 700-800 men.) Each of the groups was attached to an army corps and acted in collaboration with it. Assigned to the sector of Army Group Center was *Einsatzgruppe B*, initially comprising 655 men and commanded by SS-*Brigadefuehrer* (Brig.-Gen.) Arthur Nebe.[139]

The advance of Army Group Center during the initial weeks of the campaign took it – and, in its wake, *Einsatzgruppe B* – through the former Pale of Settlement (*Cherta postayannoi yevreskoy osedlosti*), the region of Czarist Russia where residence of Jews was legally authorized. In 1897, about 4.9 million Jews (94 percent of the total Jewish population of Russia) had resided in the settlement area which, at the turn of the century, covered ca. one million square kilometers (386,000 square miles) from the Baltic to the Black

Sea, including Belorussian lands incorporated into the Pale upon their annexation by the Czars. Following the revolution of February 1917, the provisional government abolished the settlement area, and the Jews who remained there led a simple, poor existence. In June 1941, the Jews of Belorussia numbered about 850,000 (including those belonging to the eastern portions of Poland occupied by the USSR in September 1939), while the borders of the former Pale in the operational area of Bock's army group stretched beyond Vitebsk, Mogilev, and Gomel. The Jews of this area, having no access to foreign newspapers and denied information by the Soviet government (the result of its appeasement of Nazi Germany in the years before 1941), were poorly informed about the anti-Semitic policies of the Third Reich. Many, in fact, recalling the German occupation during World War I, at first greeted the Nazi invaders as liberators, a tragic behavior which only facilitated their elimination.[140]

Initially, all four *Einsatzgruppen* were tasked with killing able-bodied Jewish men; however, in an initiative reflecting the growing radicalization of the Russian campaign, Himmler, in August 1941, ordered the wholesale massacre of entire Jewish communities – of men, women, young, old, and sick. This ominous change in policy appears to have been related to the escalation of German anti-partisan tactics. As Geoffrey Roberts explains, there was an "intimate connection" between the German Army's anti-partisan policies and the genocidal campaign of the SS against the Jews: "All Jews were stigmatized as communists and partisans, and all partisans branded Jews. 'The Jew is a partisan. The partisan is a Jew.' 'A Jew is a Bolshevik is a partisan.' These were the German slogans that served the dual purpose of rationalizing the mass murder of Soviet Jews and legitimizing the harsh and indiscriminate anti-partisan measures."[141] As it was, through mid-November 1941, *Einsatzgruppe B* reported the liquidation of 45,467 Jews within its area of operations (Belorussia). Altogether, the four groups were responsible for murdering more than half a million Jews in the first wave of killings by the end of 1941.[142]

During the course of its operations, *Einsatzgruppe B* appears to have enjoyed – at least initially – a smooth working relationship with the formations of Army Group Center, SS-*Brigadefuehrer* Nebe reporting "no difficulties" with any of the commanders of the armies or the panzer groups.[143] On multiple occasions, in fact, small detachments from Nebe's group were attached to front line combat units, including units within 2 Panzer Group's (Guderian's) area of operations.[144] Support provided by the *Wehrmacht* – often by rear area commands, such as Rear Area, Army Group Center – included the registration and resettlement of Jews; the rounding up and assembly of Jews prior to their execution; the delivery of supplies, such as ammunition; and even the provision of combat engineers to help with the mass graves.[145]

Gradually, as the summer of 1941 dragged on and the struggle intensified, with no end in sight, German generals in the east began to consider the mass killings of Communists, Jews and others behind the front a key military objective. The conflation of the Russian Jew with the growing partisan threat led, in many cases, to an increased understanding of the escalation of genocidal actions against the Jews. On 22 September 1941, for example, Ninth Army headquarters issued an order, stating that, "the struggle against Bolshevism demands most of all ruthless and vigorous action against the Jews, the principal agents of Bolshevism." The entire Jewish population, the order went on, was "openly or secretly anti-German [*deutschfeindlich*] in its outlook." The order, which justified practically any action taken against Jews, was distributed by the headquarters of the forwardmost combat units to their troops on the eve of, and during, Operation "Typhoon," the advance on Moscow.[146]

Given these attitudes, it is understandable that units of the *Wehrmacht* were also involved in the killing actions. Among the worst offenders were the Secret Field Police (*Geheime Feldpolizei*)[147] and the second-line security divisions patrolling the vast spaces of the occupied interior; conversely, participation in such actions by regular combat units was much less common. In one instance, 354 Infantry Regiment collaborated in the round up and mass shooting of Jews in Minsk, which began on 7 July 1941.[148] The regiment belonged to 286 Security Division, one of three such divisions active at this time behind the front of Army Group Center; thus, it was not a front-line formation of the *Ostheer*.[149] On 6 October 1941, the regiment massacred about 1000 more Jews in the village of Krupka, 100 kilometers from Minsk; an activity followed by the shooting of a similarly large number of Jews in Kholoponichi several days later.[150]

The mass killings by *Einsatzgruppe B* often took place in the presence of German troops, and were photographed (and, occasionally, even filmed) by them. A particularly gruesome massacre occurred on 14 August 1941, in Vitebsk, where five SD men shot a large contingent of Jews with industry-like precision (*am laufenden Band*) just three kilometers outside the headquarters of General Adolf Strauss, Commander, Ninth Army.[151] Other actions, in July/August 1941, took place in the vicinity of Bock's headquarters at Borisov. Despite small signs of discomfort on the part of the *Generalitaet* – and despite a number of protests after the killings began to engulf women and children as well – no attempt was made to put a halt to the murderous activity. On the contrary, from the start of the campaign, Army Group Center gave the killing units great freedom of action.[152]

As for Field Marshal von Bock, he avoided taking a clear position on the systematic murder of Jews, and certainly did not intervene to stop it; only once, in November 1941, did he register a protest – when he learned that several trains from Germany, carrying Jews, were to be dispatched to the rear area of his army group, a move which threatened to tie up trains desperately needed for bringing supplies to the front and, hence, to interfere with military operations.[153] Bock, of course, had no illusions about *why* the Jews were to be sent there. In his harsh assessment of the field marshal, German historian Johannes Huerter writes:

> The highest-ranking officers … reacted at best defensively, helplessly, and with resignation to the start of systematic genocide in their command area. Among the Army leadership, this was the case for Brauchitsch and Halder, who remained reluctant to get mixed up in these political and ideological matters. And among the troop leadership, that also applied to the commander-in-chief of Army Group Center and his chief-of-staff …
>
> From [Bock's] entire conduct during this campaign, it is only possible to presume that, in the face of the "world-historical task" of defeating the Soviet arch enemy, this highest-ranking troop commander viewed the increasingly extreme persecution of the Jews as, at most, an admittedly very unpleasant, but unalterable marginal issue.[154]

The evidence of Army Group Center's deep complicity in the genocidal acts of the SS commandos and police units is indisputable; as is the record of the murderous behavior of its own security detachments and *Geheime Feldpolizei*. What also seems apparent, however, is that only a small fraction of the army group's front-line soldiers could ever have taken part in these crimes, willingly or otherwise. In the first place, as noted above, *Einsatzgruppe B* began the campaign with a roster of only 655 men, while both the police battalions[155] and Army security divisions were limited in number. The army group, on the other hand, began *Barbarossa* with more than 1.3 million soldiers under its command; realistically, few of them would have ever had an opportunity to come into contact with, much less collaborate with, the killing units; and simply serving in the *Wehrmacht*, as some contemporary observers would have us believe, is not *prima facie* evidence of being a war criminal.[156] Also exculpatory is the fact that most of the killing fields were located far behind the forward edge of battle, where the overwhelming majority of the *Landser* were fully absorbed in their legitimate combat duties. Such arguments are in no way meant to explain away the very real crimes committed by soldiers of Army Group Center (or by the *Ostheer* in general); rather, they serve to illustrate that the number of offenders was probably quite small, at least in terms of percentages. The question of the extent of the German soldiers' culpability in war crimes in the east will be explored in some detail below (see, Section 9.3.5).

9.3.4: *Bandenbekaempfung*: The Conduct of the Partisan War

Of the criminal orders promulgated by the German High Command prior to the start of *Barbarossa*, the one most germane to the conduct of partisan warfare was the "Decree on Military Justice," drafted by the OKW in May 1941. The decree stipulated that guerillas (*Freischaerler*) were to be "ruthlessly eliminated;" if the perpetrator of an offense could not be determined, collective measures were to be carried out against the civilian population. While such measures basically corresponded to existing laws and customs of war,[157] the decree's suspension of the force of prosecution (*Verfolgungszwang*) against *Wehrmacht* soldiers committing crimes against civilians (or even war crimes) did not. As Bock noted on 4 June 1941, the decree was "so worded that it virtually gives every soldier the right to shoot at from in front or behind any Russian he takes to be – or claims that he takes to be – a guerrilla." Although Bock considered the order "unacceptable," and "not compatible with discipline,"[158] he could do nothing to stop it. A supplemental order by the Army C-in-C, Field Marshal von Brauchitsch, issued on 24 May 1941 with the goal of ameliorating the decree, was simply designed to uphold discipline among the troops.[159]

Even before 22 June 1941, German military planners were acutely aware that the level of force allocated for pacification and security of rear areas was far from sufficient. Once again, as this narrative has sought repeatedly to emphasize, the resources made available for a key military objective of Operation *Barbarossa* were hopelessly inadequate. Ninth Army, for example, had only 300 men specifically dedicated to the mission of patrolling some 10,000 square kilometers behind its front lines.[160] The primary dedicated resources available to Army Group Center were its three security divisions (221, 286, 403) which, by the fall of 1941, were largely responsible for controlling some 150,000 square kilometers of territory in the army group's rear area.[161]

Each of these divisions, however, possessed but a single infantry regiment in its TOE (compared to three for a regular infantry division), was lightly equipped with artillery,[162] and was populated mostly by older men and older (and often reactivated) officers.[163] These soldiers were neither physically prepared, nor adequately trained, for the rigors of their mission. Only 10 days into the campaign (1 July 1941), Chief of the Army General Staff Halder recorded in his diary:

> Pacification of the rear area is causing serious concern. The character of our combat style [*Eigenart unserer Fechtweise*][164] has resulted in wide-reaching insecurity in the rear area due to dispersed enemy elements. The security divisions alone are not adequate for the huge areas. We have to release individual combat divisions for this.[165]

The Germans' answer to the serious shortfall in resources, and the emerging partisan threat (fueled in part by Red Army stragglers who, in many cases, formed a nucleus for the partisan bands) was typical: All resistance was to be broken through the application of massive and preventive force – that is, through the use of terror as a means of deterrence (*Abschreckung*). Writes historian Timm C. Richter:

> In securing the rear area, what mattered was to balance the unfavorable relationship between the area [to be covered] and the forces available for this by

[use of] deterrence. Hitler declared: "Of course, the police will keep their hands hovering just above their pistols." Anybody "who simply cast a crooked glance" [*der nur schief schaue*] was to be shot. The Chief of OKW, Keitel, promised his "Fuehrer" that anybody "who doesn't behave will be shot."[166]

In this context, Keitel's communication of 5 July 1941 with General Friedrich Fromm, Chief of the Replacement Army, is instructive:

> If this time the measures are very brutal indeed, this is because the Fuehrer sees serious dangers in the hinterland, in the immeasurable depth of the vast occupied zone, with its huge woodlands, as a result of a populace which has been totally incited by Bolshevism ... Pacification measures conducted solely with infantry combat methods are costly and time-consuming and lack a proper deterrent effect.[167]

Hitler clearly welcomed Stalin's exhortation to the occupied Soviet people, on 3 July 1941, to unleash a partisan war behind the German front. As the "Fuehrer" put it two weeks later (16 July), such a war offered an "opportunity to exterminate anyone who tries to resist us."[168] On 23 July 1941, Hitler encapsulated his pacification strategy in a supplement to Directive No. 33:

> The troops available for pacification of the occupied eastern areas will only be adequate, given the vastness of these areas, if all resistance is not dealt with through juridical punishment, but rather if the occupying power instills that sort of fear in [the population] which is the only way to remove any enthusiasm for insubordination ... Not by demanding additional security forces, but by using appropriately draconian measures, must the commanders find the means to maintain order in their security zones.[169]

Despite the call for "draconian measures," no significant partisan threat materialized during 1941 (although that would change by the spring of 1942).[170] As the eminent historian, the late Earl F. Ziemke, opined, "The impact of the rapid German advance and the apparent helplessness of the Soviet regime had made it difficult to kindle, even artificially, a spirit of resistance. Those partisan units that did appear were small, ineffective, usually isolated, and in constant danger of disintegrating."[171] According to Soviet estimates, the number of partisans operating in the dense forests of Belorussia in August 1941 was no more than about 12,000.[172] Moreover, because the movement was still in its infancy, the partisan units were "neither well led nor well coordinated ... Secondly, communications were still rudimentary and the main partisan headquarters in Moscow had yet to establish regular radio contact with more than a small number of guerilla units behind German lines. Thirdly, arms for the guerillas were insufficient and irregular."[173] According to one source, armaments available to the partisan bands in Belorussia in 1941 embraced: 30,750 grenades, 10,685 rifles, 133 machine guns, 389 machine pistols, and three artillery pieces. These were barely enough weapons to partially outfit one and a half Soviet rifle divisions.[174]

Nevertheless, Soviet partisans operating behind the front of Army Group Center in the summer of 1941 "were sufficient to cause concern and some actual losses to the German command."[175] On one occasion, on 25 July 1941, a partisan band operating west of Smolensk surprised a group of German cavalrymen bathing in a river, killing 20-25 of them; by its own records, this band claimed the killing of some 200 Germans by the end of September 1941.[176] Small partisan groups operating south of Minsk, and in areas such as Polotsk, Vitebsk, Orsha, Mogilev, Gomel, and Smolensk,[177] conducted their first attacks on German trains, rail lines, and rail installations – attacks that, in years to come, would cause desperate problems for the German Army. Among other actions, the partisans raided German command posts, ambushed individual soldiers and small units, sabotaged telephone lines, raided the collective farms, destroyed bridges and supply dumps, poisoned wells, and assassinated known collaborators. According to one estimate, Soviet partisans, despite their limited numbers, conducted 250 rail demolitions and destroyed 447 bridges in the rear areas of Army Group Center between 22 June and 16 September 1941.[178]

By way of contrast, German "anti-partisan" operations in the summer of 1941 – due to the paucity of actual partisans in the field – were often little more than hunting expeditions to find and eliminate putative enemies of the Reich, most notably, of course, Jews. A particularly gruesome illustration of this approach was the murderous rampage of the notorious SS Cavalry Brigade in its operations to "clear" the Pripiat' Marshes. Assigned to General Max von Schenckendorff, Commander, Rear Area, Army Group Center (*Befehlshaber Rueckwaertiges Heeresgebiet Mitte*), the brigade went into action on 27 July 1941, hunting down Red Army stragglers, partisans, and "plunderers." According to a special order of Himmler's, the latter term was used to describe Jews: "In most cases Jews are to be treated as plunderers. The only exceptions to this rule are particularly skilled workers, such as bakers, etc., and above all, doctors."[179] While these specialists were to be spared (at least for the moment), women and children were to be driven into the swamps. Following completion of the operation, the SS Cavalry Brigade, on 18 September 1941, issued its final report: "14,178 shot plunderers, 1001 shot partisans, 699 shot Red Army soldiers, and 830 prisoners."[180]

During the 1960s, a judicial inquiry was conducted against Franz Magill, commander of the 2 SS Cavalry Regiment, which, along with 1 SS Cavalry Regiment, made up the SS Cavalry Brigade. During the inquiry, former members of the regiment were questioned, in the process revealing that the "mopping up campaigns" in the Pripiat' region amounted to little more than the mass slaughter of Jews:

> Numbers 1 and 4 Troops were committed in Pinsk.[181] Here the population had been informed by means of placards that all Jewish men between 16 and 60 years of age were to report to the railway station to be put to work. From here the unwitting victims were taken to a place of execution outside the town by the SS Cavalry. They were forced to surrender items of value, take off their outer garments ("In my mind's eye I can still clearly see the mountain of shoes"),[182] and lie face down on the ground until it was their turn to step up to the trench to be shot. Children under 14 were shot separately. This sequence of events conforms exactly to the pattern of the usual mass-murder campaigns carried out by the Security Police, the SD, or other murder squads. During the second operation at Pinsk, SS units, led by the local militia, searched Jewish homes. Jews caught in this way were shot, as before, above outside the town.
>
> Similar events took place during the campaigns of 2, 3, and 4 Troops in the smaller towns and villages in the Pripiat' area … It was clear to all participants that they were not fighting any kind of enemy. The "enemy" was unarmed, and included women and children, and the population was not hostile to the German occupiers. The Jews did not even put up a fight in most cases, but were "simply taken out of their houses and shot." At the most they tried to escape … But, on the whole, the victims met their deaths with dignity. The SS men report how the Jews prayed while they were waiting at the mass graves and then "started to sing."[183]

In general, the Germans ratcheted up their murderous "deterrence" policies whenever confronted with new acts of resistance – real or perceived – from elements within the occupied territories. On 16 September 1941, Field Marshal Keitel, at OKW, issued a new reprisal policy, calling for the execution of 50 to 100 "Communists" for every German soldier killed behind the front; the deterrent effect of the new policy was to be enhanced by the style of the executions.[184] Through the application of such ruthless measures, Rear Area, Army Group Center, reported that, from 1 July 1941 to 30 May 1942, a total of 80,000 "partisans" were killed, with a German loss through 10 May 1942 of 1094 dead, 1862 wounded, and 328 missing. "Above all," affirms historian Timothy Mulligan, "[these statistics] demonstrate the failure of the German use of mass reprisals to break the guerillas."[185]

While estimates vary (and often considerably), by the end of 1941, the aggregate number of partisans on the eastern front was most likely 30,000 at a minimum; by the summer of 1942, the total had exploded to 150,000.[186] In Belorussia, according to Soviet figures, partisan strength climbed to 122,600 in November 1943, and 180,000 in March 1944. By the beginning of the Soviet offensive in the summer of 1944, which finally destroyed Army Group Center, more than a quarter of a million partisans were active in Belorussia.[187] Whatever the numbers, the growth of the movement was exponential, a phenomenon which – as the late, great German historian Andreas Hillgruber observed – can only be understood as a response to the war of annihilation waged by the German Reich's political and military elites, whose criminal policies were abundantly apparent to the Soviets within weeks of the start of the campaign.[188] The catastrophic impact of such policies, moreover, was soon apparent to more enlightened German officers, such as Georg Heino *Freiherr* von Muenchhausen, a captain in the OKH Operations Branch, who penned in his diary in early August 1941:

> In addition to that there's the danger of the partisan mischief and its threat to our rear area communications. If we make a mess of large parts of the country, and really turn the people against us as we do it, and let them starve on top of it all, then the problems will become <u>very serious</u>, if the population cooperates with the partisans. E.g., the people would like to have their fields back from the collective farms ... [But we can't] make clear decisions, even though things behind the front are already getting urgent because of the harvest; to begin with, the people should just be given the land for heaven's sake! [189]
>
> More church affairs, shootings, and all sorts of things! But the doctrine of the struggle against Bolshevism and the will (hate) to exterminate and, as much as possible, to destroy large parts of the Russian people has priority <u>above all</u> practical considerations and things that are <u>absolutely</u> necessary for the continuing war.[190]

Not only did the partisans refuse to be broken – when it came to dishing out punishment and acts of barbarism (meted out to German invaders and Russian civilians alike) they played "second fiddle" to no one. German soldiers unfortunate enough to be seized by partisans were routinely tortured to death, and often horrifically mutilated. Hendrik C. Verton, a Dutch volunteer fighting in the *Waffen*-SS, recounted how men captured by the partisan bands routinely had their eyes poked out, their tongues and ears cut off: "No one escaped those barbarians alive, and those who were shot in the back of the neck were the lucky ones."[191] Partisan bands derailed German hospital trains and burned the occupants alive with kerosene.[192] Russian villagers, whether or not suspected of collaboration with the enemy, were routinely terrorized by the partisans, plundered and murdered, the women raped. The result was that the villagers often feared the partisans as much as they did the Germans.[193]

In a study entitled *The German Soldier in World War II*, the authors describe an incident which, by its sheer depravity, encapsulates the almost unfathomable barbarism which characterized conduct of the partisan war on both sides:

> One German soldier in the Mogilev region recalled how a rumor reached them of hidden gold at a nearby state farm. With some comrades, the soldiers went to

the farm and tore the place to pieces looking for gold. The head of the settlement begged them to wait as he could get the gold in 24 hours and if the buildings were all destroyed, the peasants would have nowhere to spend the winter. At dusk the Germans left with the orders that the gold was to be produced the following day or the entire population of the farm would be placed under arrest. A detachment of four men was left behind, commanded by a soldier called Fisher. The next day there was no word from Fisher on the radio, and so a detachment returned to the farm in armored cars. They found the barn burned to the ground with only one building remaining. In it stood a very heavy leather box, *Gelb* (Gold) scrawled on it in white paint. On opening it, the Germans found the heads of Fisher and the three other German soldiers left behind.[194]

Once again, the question arises, just how deeply involved were the soldiers of Army Group Center in crimes of war – in this case, during the anti-partisan operations of the summer of 1941? And once again, the answer is – only marginally. As late as the end of September 1941, when the army group had massed some 70 divisions for Operation "Typhoon," the advance on Moscow, only six formations were assigned to General von Schenckendorff (Commander, Rear Area, Army Group Center) to secure its vast hinterland. These were: three security divisions (with a further security division in transfer from Army Group South), the SS Cavalry Brigade, and the 339 and 707 Infantry Divisions.[195] The 339 ID had been formed in December 1940 as a garrison (static) division, and, thus, was not fit for front-line duty; on 29 September, it was operating far behind the front, around Borisov.[196] The 707 ID had been activated in May 1941, as a division of the 15th wave, for occupation and security duties; by August 1941, it was fulfilling an anti-partisan role in Belorussia.[197] In other words, not a single *front-line* combat division of Army Group Center was, at this time, assigned to duties behind the battlefront.

The distinction is significant, and it underscores two key points: Firstly, "Despite the suggestion that the *Wehrmacht* was a single and consistent entity in terms of its military capacity and commitment to Nazism, the armed forces of the Third Reich did not constitute a homogeneous whole;"[198] and, secondly, in 1941, the German Army seldom committed regular *Wehrmacht* combat units to general security duties or fighting partisans, while the forces which were assigned such missions made up but a small fraction of the *Ostheer*. Across the eastern front, six regular divisions (in addition to the handful of security units) were active behind the lines in July 1941.[199] While this number is not insignificant – as German historian Ernst Klink correctly points out, "the use of partisans behind the German front proved to be tactically effective, as it tied down German forces that would otherwise have been available at the front itself or in other operations"[200] – it must be remembered that, by mid-July 1941, the armies in the east deployed some 145 divisions of all types.[201]

Just how little involvement most German combat units had in anti-partisan warfare in 1941 is reflected in the record of 253 Infantry Division. The division was activated in August 1939 (fourth wave),[202] and began Operation *Barbarossa* as a reserve unit attached to Army Group North; within weeks, it was shifted to Ninth Army, and deployed on the extreme left wing of Army Group Center. In early December 1941, 253 ID reported shooting a total of 230 Soviet partisans since the start of the campaign. Again, positing a theoretical relationship of one perpetrator to each victim (and leaving aside entirely the issue of whether the killings were, or were not, legally justified), just 1.5 percent of the division's ca. 15,400 soldiers would have taken part in killing Soviet partisans. Tasks of this nature, however, were generally handled by the *Feldgendarmerie*, or by special hunter-killer teams (*Jagdkommandos*).[203]

Although the regular army would often play a significant role in the large anti-partisan campaigns of 1942/44, the forces committed were, for the most part, negligible compared to those directly deployed along the forward edge of battle. Indeed, it could hardly have been otherwise – given the enormous length of the front; the chronic shortages of men, weapons, and materiel; and the inexorably growing strength of, and pressure applied by, the Red Army.

9.3.5: How Criminal was the *Wehrmacht*?

"*Wie verbrecherisch war die Wehrmacht?*" How criminal was the *Wehrmacht*? This is the question put by Christian Hartmann, a German military historian at the Institute for Contemporary History in Munich, who, in recent years, has written extensively, and persuasively, on the issue of war crimes and the *Wehrmacht*. The preceding examination of the complicity of Army Group Center in criminal acts during the opening phase of the Russian campaign has provided a foundation on which to build – with the support of insights from Dr Hartmann – a broader understanding of this complex and controversial issue, which, since the 1990s, has evoked a protracted, and often emotional, debate among German historians, as well as renewed interest among the German public in their recent military past.

To begin with, it is important to note what is *not* part of this debate – the complicity of the *Wehrmacht* as an *institution* in war crimes against the Red Army and the Soviet people. Decades of research – buttressed in recent years by unprecedented accessibility to the archives of the former Soviet Union and its eastern block allies – have revealed that, at the highest levels of command, the complicity of the *Wehrmacht* was indeed profound; no one, except perhaps the most egregious apologist, would contest this indisputable historical fact. Much more formidable, however, is the subject of *individual* guilt. How many of the 10 million or so German soldiers who fought on the Russian front between 1941 and 1944 took part in criminal acts? Depending on who you ask, the answers range from fewer than five percent, as German historian Rolf-Dieter Mueller has argued, to as many as 60-80 percent according to Hannes Heer, one of the principal architects of a relatively recent exhibit in Germany exploring war crimes of the *Wehrmacht* on the eastern front. Yet if these radically different, indeed unbridgeable, figures set the parameters of the debate, they also signify little more than metaphors for the concepts of "*viel*" and "*wenig*" (many and few).[204]

Historian Hannes Heer's striking figure of 60-80 percent requires further explanation. In March 1995, the traveling exhibit "War of Annihilation: Crimes of the *Wehrmacht* 1941 to 1944," opened in Hamburg. The exhibit was produced by the Hamburg Institute for Social Research (*Hamburger Institute fuer Sozialforschung*), a private organization founded and headed by Dr Jan Philipp Reemtsma. In a remarkable historical irony, Reemtsma had inherited the huge fortune of his father's tobacco company, which during the Second World War supplied the *Wehrmacht* with cigarettes.[205] It was Heer, however, a former Communist agitator, who was largely responsible for shaping the concept and content of the exhibit,[206] whose fundamental purpose could easily be construed as an attempt to achieve what not even the International Military Tribunal in Nuremberg had dared to do – to label the *Wehrmacht* a criminal organization, along with a majority of the 17 to 18 million soldiers who served in it.

The controversial exhibit was made up of written documents and more than 1400 photographs, most of them attributed to German soldiers; by the fall of 1999, it had been displayed in 33 cities across Germany and Austria and seen by more than 800,000 visitors.[207] Reaction to the exhibit culminated in the remarks of Michael Naumann, Minister of Cultural Affairs in Germany, who, in a February 1999 interview with the London "*Sunday Times*," opined that the *Wehrmacht* was nothing less than a "marching slaughterhouse" (*marschierendes Schlachthaus*).[208] Meanwhile, Polish historian Bogdan Musial, and Hungarian historian Krisztián Ungváry, among others, had been busy examining the exhibit's displays for authenticity and, in the process, discovered some disturbing irregularities. These included examples of improper or misleading captioning; or, in some cases, no captioning at all (yet always the insinuation that the photograph in question depicted a crime of the *Wehrmacht*). In an article published in October 1999, Musial outlined the results of his probe into the exhibit:

> Among these photographs there is also a series of images depicting German soldiers in front of heaps of corpses. These photographs are probably among the most expressive and shocking of the entire exhibit. In their context, they must undoubtedly awaken the impression that German soldiers had photographed themselves in front of the victims they had just shot, and then carried the photos around as souvenirs, like a kind of "war trophy."
>
> A closer inspection of these photos shows indications that these are pictures of exhumed corpses. If the assertions of the exhibitors are to be believed, then the *Wehrmacht* soldiers first killed these people, then buried them, and then exhumed them in order to make the questionable photographs. Nowhere in the history of the German crimes between the years 1939 and 1945 has such paradoxical behavior been documented.
>
> By contrast, closer inspection of a few other photographs indicates simply by the demeanor of the depicted soldiers (who are usually presented here unarmed), as well as by the presence of civilians (including women and children), that the members of the *Wehrmacht* shown here are observers, and not, however, perpetrators, as the exhibitors are trying to suggest.[209]

In his article, Musial posited that, at a minimum, nine of the exhibit photographs depicted crimes committed by Soviet secret police (NKVD), and not, as was at least inferred, by German soldiers; he then proceeded to assiduously deconstruct them. Furthermore, he identified another two dozen photographs that appeared highly suspicious. Musial went on to conclude:

> The "index of image sources" states that the majority of the image documentation comes from post-Soviet archives ... But can nine demonstrably, and around two dozen probably, or possibly, falsely attributed photographs cast an entire exhibit and its basic statements into doubt? After all, the catalogue shows, with passport photos, 801 images, and the exhibit shows 1433 photos. Yet the consequences for the exhibit are much graver than this quantitative analysis at first suggests.
>
> First, only a part of the photographs in the exhibit documents crimes as such (shootings, hangings), without even taking into account the complex problem of the legal situation at the time. Approximately half of the photos, in contrast, depict activities having nothing to do with war crimes, for example, marching soldiers or general acts of war, such as bombed out buildings.
>
> Second, the abovementioned images are extremely expressive photos, which are of great importance for the entire exhibit, as well as for the exhibit catalog.[210]

Because such criticism attacked the core of the exhibit's credibility,[211] it was suddenly withdrawn by Reemtsma in November 1999, and placed under a temporary moratorium. At the same time, he convened a commission of renowned historians – among them, Omer Bartov, Manfred Messerschmidt, and Christian Streit – to undertake a thorough review of the exhibit. A year later, on 15 November 2000, the commission released its findings to the public. Chief among them were: factual errors (*sachliche Fehler*), as well as inaccuracies and mistakes due to carelessness (*Ungenauigkeiten und Fluechtigkeiten*) in the use of the materials; most significantly, the nature of the presentation was often overly generalized and suggestive in tone. Conversely, the commission determined that fundamental statements in the exhibit about the *Wehrmacht* and its *Vernichtungskrieg* in Russia were accurate; and that it was beyond dispute that the German Army was deeply involved in – indeed, at times took a leading role in – a wide range of criminal actions, including genocide against the Jews, the liquidation of Soviet POWs, and crimes against civilians.[212] On the basis of the commission's recommendations, the exhibit was completely reworked, and reopened in Berlin on 28 November 2001. According to Christian Hartmann, the second iteration was "far better and more honest."[213] One might add that it also included fewer photographs.[214]

The controversy over the *Wehrmacht* exhibit (*Wehrmachtsausstellung*) manifests the dimensions, and often raw emotions, of the continuing controversy over the character of the German armed forces in the Second World War. It also reveals how ideological prejudices, and "political correctness," have helped to shape the debate and, regrettably, to distort historical reality. Which brings us to a brief discussion of the insightful and balanced analysis by Dr Hartmann.

In several recent publications,[215] Hartmann has critically explored the role of the *Wehrmacht* in war crimes in the east. Specifically, he identifies, and examines in detail, four major categories of criminal behavior (each of which has been addressed above for Army Group Center in 1941) in which German troops participated: the *Partisanenkrieg*, the systematic murder of Jews and other "undesirables," the mistreatment of Soviet POWs, and the exploitation (*Ausbeutung*) of the occupied Soviet territories. In doing so, Hartmann observes that the "German-Soviet war not only had a military topography, it also had a topography of terror."[216] A primary point of Hartmann's is that, while war crimes occurred throughout the occupied areas, the great majority took place well behind the front, not along the main battle line (*Hauptkampflinie*, or HKL). Yet it was along the HKL – the *Gefechtszone*, or forward edge of battle – that the great bulk of German troops were concentrated. Following the initial *Vormarsch* through western Russia, the HKL stretched from the primeval forests of Finland to the Black Sea, reaching its greatest extent, more than 2000 kilometers, by October 1942.[217] While the German *Hauptkampflinie* changed constantly with the ebb and flow of battle, it had two fairly stable characteristics: a) it rarely had a depth of more than 20 kilometers; and, b) it was, for the most part, not a contiguous line at all, but a thin band of strong points, trenches, bunkers and dugouts.[218]

Due to the Germans' chronic lack of forces in the east, every available man was stationed in this narrow combat zone, while areas behind it were much more thinly covered. Writes Hartmann:

> The *Ostheer* found itself in a fix from the very start, from June 1941, and not just from the time it began, more and more, to lose the initiative and could only react in desperation. From the outset, the Germans attempted against all reason to force a victory – against space, against time, against the climate, and above all against the enemy superiority. That was why every soldier who could in any way be made use of was sent forward, to the front! Despite this, the chronic lack of forces soon became characteristic of this most vulnerable area of the German reach of power [*Machtbereich*].[219]

In contrast to the U.S. Army, which during the Second World War had a "tooth to tail" ratio of about 57:43, in the German Army the ratio was 85:15, and thus much more heavily weighted toward combat troops (and against logistical units.)[220] In October 1943, for example, total German forces in the east amounted to 2.6 million men; of these, about two million were deployed on the main battle line. Directly behind them, to a maximum depth of about 70 kilometers, were half a million men, who directly supported the troops in the combat zone. Even further back, in the largest swath of territory controlled by the *Wehrmacht*, the rear areas of the army groups (*Rueckwaertiges Heeresgebiet*), there were only 100,000 troops.[221]

Because it was in these thinly occupied rear areas that most criminal acts took place, and because the further back a soldier was stationed the more likely he was to be involved in such activity, Hartmann posits an inverse relationship between the density of German troop deployments and incidents of criminal behavior for all four categories adumbrated above:

> Even if the hinterland has so far been distinctly better researched than the front, the extent and significance of the crimes committed in the hinterland still appear to have been considerably greater. This conveys the impression that the density of the German deployment and the density of crimes committed are in inverse relationship to each other. In the hinterland, the operational area of relatively few soldiers, the density of crimes was distinctly higher; here, the opportunities for criminial acts presented themselves much more frequently than in the narrow strip of the front, where most soldiers fought. Many have little and a few have much to answer for. To try to quantify this would be presumptuous. However, this inverse relationship seems to have been so marked that the hypothesis of Rolf-Dieter Mueller ... appears a great deal more realistic than that of Hannes Heer [i.e., that less than 5 percent of German soldiers in the east took part in criminal activities, versus Heer's much higher estimate of 60-80 percent]. Perhaps one should not rely too heavily on a few dry figures ... But it can be determined with considerable certainty that the proportion of truly criminal perpetrators in the *Ostheer* was relatively small.[222]

As Hartmann points out, however, even if the *percentage* of those who took part in war crimes was relatively small, when one considers the many millions of soldiers who fought in the east from 1941 to 1944, the *absolute numbers* of perpetrators still amounted to many hundreds of thousands:

> Assuming the estimated proportion of perpetrators of 5 percent is accurate, then this would mean that, with a total number of around 10 million soldiers who were deployed on the *Ostfront*, at least half a million had transgressed law and tradition. That is not just a few ... Moreover, these *relatively* few perpetrators had a big effect; that, too, is a structural characteristic of this war, this Army, and [the NS] political system. Even so: in the entire *Ostheer*, they were clearly in the minority.[223]

Hartmann makes two further points that require our attention. Firstly, he argues that, while the theaters of war in Russia, Italy, and the west (1944) signified distinct operational areas of the *Wehrmacht*, all evinced certain parallels, and particularly in the dynamic of criminal behavior. In each of these combat zones, maintains Hartmann, "Instead of a wholesale [*massenhaft*] participation in war crimes, it was generally a small number of specific units, commanders or headquarters which by far shouldered the greatest responsibility for all the injustice committed in Germany's name."[224] Secondly, in Soviet Russia, the opportunities for *Frontsoldaten* to engage in such activity were limited not only by their deployment along the HKL, but by their enormous casualty rates:

> The pronounced, if never entirely adequate, concentration of the *Ostheer* in the death zone [*Todeszone*] of the front was not its only structural characteristic. In addition, there were the extremely high losses, which were, understandably,

highest at the front. For the individual soldier, this meant two things: in his conduct he was, as a rule, as good as utterly absorbed by his military mission. And: his operational periods were often of short duration, or at least frequently interrupted. Even if these are the characteristics of many wars, the German-Soviet war was also an extreme case in this regard. This cannot be emphasized enough.[225]

In conclusion, this author quotes from his review of Hartmann's recent book (*Wehrmacht im Ostkrieg. Front und militaerisches Hinterland 1941/42*), in which Hartmann examines in painstaking detail the activities of five archetypal German formations on the eastern front in 1941/42 (one elite armored division, two infantry divisions, a rear area security division, and a rear area headquarters unit),[226] offering perhaps the most complete picture to date of the experiences of the "typical" German soldier who fought against the Soviet Union:

> So what then can be said about the German soldier in the east, particularly in relation to war crimes? [Hartmann] makes no attempt to quantify the number of those who committed such crimes, which he admits is hardly possible. He also avoids extreme positions that have often poisoned the debate over the *Wehrmacht*. What Hartmann does conclude is that the five divisions of his sample were, *institutionally* – like the *Ostheer* as a whole – responsible for a disturbing array of war crimes; however, the guilt of soldiers *individually* varied considerably, depending on such structural factors as unit assignment, function, and location. The latter factor – location – was critical, for most of the German Army's murderous activity took place *behind* the front, in its vast and thinly occupied hinterland.
>
> Yet it would be false, the author avers, to explain the actions of the "typical" German soldier through such factors alone. More significant were the intentions of his political and military leadership that, from the beginning, gave its soldiers in the east free reign to operate outside the canon of international law. Moreover, the fact that, on the eastern front, two totalitarian states fought each other with an intensity approaching "religious fervor," made the resulting "breach of civilization" appear – to German and Russian alike – as a virtually "normal" state of affairs. All things considered, however, the number of perpetrators, while significant, remained a distinct minority, for most German soldiers served directly at the front and were, perforce, fully absorbed in their legitimate combat duties.[227]

9.4: *Keine Kameraden*: Crimes of the Red Army

In Section 9.2, it was noted that, among the primary materials used to explore the war crimes issue – in this case, war crimes committed by soldiers of the Soviet Union – were the records of the *Wehrmacht* Office of Investigation for Violations of International Law (hereafter, cited simply as the *Wehrmacht* War Crimes Bureau). Established in September 1939, this agency was "not a special invention of Nazi Germany;"[228] rather, it was the direct successor to the Prussian Military Bureau of Investigation of Violations of the Laws of War, which had functioned during World War I as an organ of the Reich War Ministry. Both bureaus were responsible for documenting Allied violations of the laws of war and submitting reports to the German Foreign Office which, in turn, used the reports to lodge diplomatic protests against Allied nations. The members of both bureaus were military judges, "who either personally questioned the witnesses – mostly members of the armed forces – or delegated the taking of depositions to the competent military or civilian courts in the areas where the witnesses were stationed, hospitalized, or in residence."[229]

Originally published in 1979 in West Germany (and a decade later in the United States), the first (and, to date, only)[230] systematic evaluation of the records and activities of the *Wehrmacht* War Crimes Bureau was the work of Alfred M. de Zayas, a Harvard Law School graduate with a Ph.D. degree in history from the University of Goettingen. One of the first questions answered by de Zayas in his book was an obvious one: Were the reports prepared by an agency, which "operated within a highly unscrupulous system," really to be trusted? Did Propaganda Minister Joseph Goebbels order the faking of reports or photographs? Did the witnesses and judges referred to in the files, and whose signatures appear on the reports, actually exist? Put another way, what credibility, if any, was to be found in the tens of thousands of pages of surviving records of the bureau?[231] De Zayas' response to this question was unequivocal:

> The author first attempted to determine whether the files gave the impression of genuine investigations, whether the documents showed the various stages of every case, whether contradictions arose, whether there was any indication that evidence might have been fabricated or documents distorted for propaganda purposes.
>
> The next step was to establish whether the persons named in the documents – judges, witnesses, and victims – really existed, whether they were actually involved in the cases described, and whether they testified of their own volition or were forced to sign prepared statements. The author interviewed more than 300 judges, witnesses, and victims, and in every case they confirmed the correctness of the protocols ...
>
> The final effort consisted in verifying the events dealt with in the Bureau's documents by consulting other German record groups and also the relevant American, British, French, and Swiss files. In the Political Archives (German Foreign Office) ... , in the Public Record Office (Foreign Office, War Office, Air Ministry, Admiralty) in London, in the National Archives (State Department, War Department, SHAEF, Judge Advocate General) in Washington, and in the Swiss Federal Archives (Protecting Power papers) in Bern there are many documents that helped to complete the picture ...
>
> All in all, the coherency of the War Crimes Bureau files, the confirmation of persons involved, and the comparison with other historical sources justify the conclusion that the Bureau did function in a trustworthy manner, that its investigations were authentic and its documentation reliable. Though there is no guarantee that the depositions are correct in every detail, and though the files of course contain only the German view of the events, it is nevertheless evident that the Bureau was not a propaganda arm of the Nazi regime but a military investigative agency much like those that exist in the legal offices of the armed forces of many other nations.[232]

In his assessment of the agency, de Zayas also pointed out that the chief of the War Crimes Bureau, an "old lawyer" and judge by the name of Johannes Goldsche, had "no sympathy for the Nazis or their methods." Goldsche, in fact, despite his important post, was never a member of the National Socialist Party, "as was generally expected of senior civil servants under Hitler."[233]

In November 1941, in Berlin, the Bureau published the first detailed findings of its investigations of Soviet war crimes against soldiers of the *Wehrmacht* inside the Soviet Union. They began with a devastating indictment:

> The findings of the *Wehrmacht* War Crimes Bureau in the first months of the war against the Soviet Union concerning war crimes perpetrated by Russian troops against defenseless German soldiers, and with regard to attacks on medical formations, doctors, and medical orderlies, which are against international law,

surpass even the worst fears and all imagination. The Soviet Union has, through its behavior, abandoned all obligations pertaining to the laws of war which the cultural states drew up together in the Hague Convention and the Geneva Conventions, as well as in other agreements of international law, and, from the first day of the war on, brought brutal measures corresponding to its own internal methods of terrorization to bear on defenseless members of the German *Wehrmacht* who had fallen into their hands and against German medical formations.[234]

9.4.1: Disregard of the Red Cross & Attacks on German Medical Personnel

Assistenzarzt (2nd Lt., Medical) Heinrich Haape was born in 1910 in the Ruhr Valley, the son of a Lutheran minister. A man of impressive intellect, Haape studied at the universities of Bonn, Dusseldorf, and Kiel, obtaining doctorate degrees in medicine and philosophy and a diploma in psychology. In July 1939, while working as a doctor at Duisburg hospital, he was drafted into the military and transferred to the *Wehrmacht* medical corps.[235]

On the Russian front, Haape would become one of the most decorated doctors in the Army, garnering the German Cross in Gold, the Iron Cross (First and Second Class), the Infantry Assault Badge, the Wounded Badge, and a decoration for personally destroying two Russian tanks in close combat. As a doctor, "he never abandoned a single wounded man to the Russians [and] once went without sleep for 14 days."[236] Among the official documents of 6 Infantry Division, found in Haape's private papers, is one outlining his extraordinary achievements during the winter battles of 1941/42, and in the heavy fighting outside Rzhev in the summer of 1942: In December 1941, near Kalinin, Haape tended to 160 wounded men on a single day, often while under heavy enemy mortar fire; over a 20-day period in August 1942, working in the most primitive conditions, and often subjected to Russian artillery, tank, or infantry fire, he single-handedly cared for 521 wounded men. At times, Haape took an active role in the fighting, either to defend his dressing station or to prevent or seal off enemy breakthroughs.[237]

All of that, however, was in the not too distant and bloody future on 22 June 1941, when Haape, like thousands of other German soldiers, underwent his baptism of fire in Hitler's war of annihilation against the Soviet Union. It was a "strange war for a doctor, a war that was played without benefit of Geneva Convention rules, a war in which a front-line doctor very often operated with a scalpel in his hand and an automatic slung over his shoulders."[238] This was Haape's war – a war in which a Red Cross flag or armband, or a Red Cross symbol emblazoned on the side of an ambulance vehicle, offered no protection to German doctors or their medical staffs. Because Haape's experiences were typical, this section begins by recounting in detail the doctor's movements and activities on the first day of Operation *Barbarossa*.[239]

At 3:45 a.m., 40 minutes after the start of the opening bombardment, Haape's battalion (III./18 IR) received the order to advance; after hours of agonizing tension, the order came as a relief:

> We fall into position and move forward … I sit astride my horse with a tense grip on the reins. Lump [his horse] behaves restlessly and I try to relax … I wonder how I will acquit myself; and I have a dreadful fear that nervousness will rob my hand of its precision. I feel behind for my medical outfit, it is hanging from the saddle; everything is in order. Petermann, my groom, rides beside me, carrying two first-aid outfits. The motor ambulance is a few hundred yards in the rear with my medical team – Dehorn, Mueller, Wegener and a driver.

Almost immediately Haape and his medical team encountered their first wounded soldier – a superficial bullet wound in the arm. Haape removed the rubber tourniquet and the emergency bandage applied by a stretcher-bearer at the front; in their place he fixed a pressure bandage and put the arm in a sling. Haape then remounted Lump and galloped to the front of the column, where he met up with his battalion commander, Neuhoff, and the latter's adjutant, Hillemanns. Pointedly questioned by Neuhoff, Haape explained – to his superior's satisfaction – the measures he had put in place for evacuation and care of the wounded.

Shortly thereafter, Haape came upon the first dead officer of his battalion – it was the 21-year-old *Leutnant* Stock, who, like many German soldiers killed on this day, fell prey to a Russian sniper:

> His body was lying in a trampled cornfield. Two men from Kramer's 11th Company, to which Stock had belonged, were digging a grave in the soft earth. Watching them were four Russian soldiers, blood seeping through their fresh bandages. My lively little orderly, Dehorn, was giving one of them a drink from his waterbottle. But two Russians had not received medical attention, although one of them had a gaping leg wound. My medical N.C.O. Wegener was covering them with an automatic – evidently the one Stock had been carrying. My third medical orderly, *Gefreiter* Mueller, was watching them closely; he wore a puzzled frown.
>
> Wegener saluted, without lowering his automatic, and said: "We've treated these four men, Herr *Assistenzarzt*, but what shall we do with these two? They ambushed Herrn *Leutnant* Stock from behind this rye. Our men got them with a grenade. Do we have to give them first-aid, too?"
>
> "We're not the judges, Wegener," I said sharply. "Our job is to help the wounded – Germans and Russians alike, even if they have shot down one of our officers. Put that gun down."

Haape and his team had now passed beyond the burning customs house at the frontier and crossed into Lithuania, leaving behind the network of wire entanglements that snaked menacingly across meadows and cornfields. Civilians emerged from their hiding places, looking "helpless and confused," but Haape had no time to help them, or offer advice. Throughout the morning, as they advanced, they observed squadron after squadron of the *Luftwaffe* – bombers, fighters and *Stukas* – as they winged past in perfect order, on their way to distant objectives. They witnessed an attack by obsolete Russian dive-bombers – "they flew directly over our heads – we were not the target" – and gazed curiously at the first Russian prisoners.

From a farmhouse, came a shout for first-aid. With Dehorn and Wegener, Haape entered the house and found several civilians and wounded Russian soldiers. He quickly provided first aid, and moved on. Galloping through the cornfields along side the road, he overtook the marching column of troops and again joined up with Battalion Commander Neuhoff. Suddenly, shots rang out barely 50 feet in front from a field of rye. Both Neuhoff and Haape dismounted as a burst of enemy fire arced directly over their heads. Hillemanns, the adjutant, and several other men darted into the cornfield, firing their rifles and automatic weapons; a "mêlée" ensued in the tall corn, "a confusion of revolver shots, upraised rifle butts and screams.

> A tall infantryman from the H.Q. company brushed his way back through the rye. With his hands still gripping the barrel of his rifle, he shrugged and said: "Finished!" I noticed the butt of his rifle was splashed with blood. Neuhoff and I strode into the corn. A commissar and four Russian soldiers were lying on the trampled earth, their skulls battered into the soil, which had been freshly dug and thrown up into a mound for their suicidal ambush. The commissar's hands were still grasping uprooted cornstocks. Our casualties were negligible – one man with a bayonet wound in the arm, another man with a grazed calf. A little iodine, gauze and a couple of strips of adhesive plaster and they were ready to march on with the rest of us. Neuhoff, Hillemanns and I rode on together at the head of the column.

"I didn't expect that," said Neuhoff, rather shakily. "Sheer suicide, to attack a battalion at close quarters with five men." We were to learn that these small groups of Russians would constitute the greatest danger. The corn was high and made ideal cover for the small guerilla bands, which stayed behind as the main body of the Russian forces rolled back. As a rule they were fanatically led by Soviet commissars and we never knew when we should come under their fire.

The sun climbed and the day grew hot. The men marched on through the yellow dust, which clung to their uniforms, rifles, faces and hands; both men and vehicles "assumed ghostly outlines in the dust-laden air." At noon, they rested in a small wood, and looked on as a flight of eight Russian bombers – they "came toward us from the east, [and] circled to make sure of their target" – was methodically decimated by a clutch of Bf 109s. One of the downed bombers, however, had crashed into an artillery column, causing serious casualties. Haape galloped over to their aid, finding 15 of the artillerymen already dead and others seriously burned.[240] He did what he could to help, and sent a dispatch rider for an ambulance.

Having lost touch with his battalion, Haape, with his groom Petermann following, moved off to find it. Soon, he reached the road to Kalvaria, the immediate objective of his division. A steady stream of soldiers, vehicles and guns was drifting east along the road, and with it a baggage unit from Haape's battalion. Making his way past throngs of Russian prisoners heading to the rear, he came upon the commander of 10th Company, the "bull-like, genial" Stolze:

"Hey Doktor!" he shouted. "Work for you. See that farmhouse?" His horse jostled mine as his huge hand pointed out the place, about half a mile away across the fields. "There are some wounded men there."
"Yours?"
"No, thank God. But they need a doctor – there's only a stretcher-bearer with them at the moment."
"Thanks, Stolze – I'll go over there."

Taking along a couple of Stolze's men for protection, Haape set out for the farmhouse. For several hours now he had been out of contact with his medical team and ambulance; as a result, he sent back for another ambulance, which was soon rumbling down the dusty road toward the farmhouse, hooting its horn and scattering marching infantry as it went. Reaching the farmhouse with Petermann, Haape discovered five soldiers lying on the living-room floor; two of them were dead, their bodies still warm. The stretcher-bearer, "a quietly-spoken middle-aged man," who was clearly overwhelmed by his responsibility, reported: "It is terrible. For the first time in my life I've been really desperate, Herr *Assistenzarzt*. The theory – I know that. But real wounds knock the theory out of your head." He looked at Haape with "pleading eyes." "I hope it's not my fault the two men died. I tried –"

Haape offered reassuring words, insisting that the two dead soldiers would have died anyway, and that he, the stretcher-bearer, had done a fine job of attending to the three wounded men. Haape first turned his attention to the soldier with a stomach wound. The man's face was "ashen and drawn with pain and cold beads of sweat were on his forehead;" but he had a clean wound through the abdomen and Haape assured him that he would survive:

As his pain-racked face relaxed into a faint smile I closed both entry and exit holes of the wound with a plastic bandage, applied a covering of *Zellstoff* and with my scissors removed bits of blood stained clothing. The stretcher-bearer helped me to tie the man's knees up under his chin to ease the stomach. I gave him a sedative and an anti-tetanus injection, and had him wrapped warmly in a blanket and carried to the *Sankawagen* [ambulance], where a casualty-card was completed and hung round his neck.

Dr Haape attended to the two other badly wounded *Landser* – one, unconscious with a head wound ("I cleaned and bandaged the wound and he joined the stomach case in the ambulance"); the other, with a clean bullet wound through the upper thigh which, as it turned out, had not punctured the main artery ("otherwise there would have been little hope of saving his leg"). As Haape conversed with the latter wounded soldier, the stretcher-bearer interrupted: "Herr *Assistenzarzt*, the peasant woman here has made you a big can of coffee." He took the coffee gratefully, and glanced down at his watch – it was 3.15 in the afternoon: "We had been at war with Russia just 12 hours, but it was 18 hours since I had last eaten, or drunk anything but water. I had no appetite, but a great thirst."

Suddenly, there was a "crash of glass" in the back room. "That's been going on all day," remarked the old peasant woman. "Those Russians in the wood over there." On Haape's orders, one of the men from Stolze's company set up his light machine gun facing the wood. But before he could fire, "a bullet ripped through the roof of the ambulance." Haape told the driver to move his vehicle to a sheltered position behind the farmhouse; then he administered an anti-tetanus shot to the soldier with the leg wound and had him carried out to the ambulance on a stretcher. The ambulance then sped away, drawing a "hail of bullets" from the Russians in the wood. "I could only stand and watch with impotent rage," wrote Haape. "The prominent red cross was plainly visible in the bright afternoon sun. If a bullet found the engine and put the ambulance out of action, the stomach case would die – that was certain." Fortunately, "determined" machine gun fire from the front of the farmhouse now poured into the wood, temporarily quieting the Russian sniper fire.

At this point, the stretcher-bearer informed Dr Haape that six more bodies – one of them a doctor – were lying in a hollow about 100 yards from the farmhouse. Covered by the machine gun, and moving through a ditch that offered some concealment, Haape and the stretcher-bearer made a successful dash to the hollow, where a grisly discovery awaited them:

> Six bodies lay sprawled in the hollow. A stretcher-bearer lay on his back, arms flung wide, and four other soldiers lay close by just as they had fallen. And there was the doctor, lying face downward, Red Cross band on his sleeve, a bold Red Cross on the flag by his side. The contents of his medical pack were strewn around him.
>
> As if afraid of being overheard, the [stretcher-bearer] whispered: "A 100 yards from here – see there, behind those gorse bushes, the Russians were lying. The doctor had brought the wounded men into the hollow and was attending to them when the Russians started firing. I was watching from the farmhouse but could do nothing. The doctor stood up and waved his Red Cross flag, but they kept on firing at him. He fell, and they fired and fired until nothing more moved in the hollow. It was horrible … cold-blooded murder …" His voice broke and tears were in his eyes.

Haape and the stretcher-bearer crawled over to the doctor, gently rolling him over on to his back. The doctor's blond hair fell back from his brow, and Haape peered with horror into the lifeless eyes of his dear friend, Fritz:

> Without a word and without clearly realizing what I was doing I hoisted Fritz's body across my shoulders and trod heavily out of the hollow. There was silence now, both from the wood and from the house. The [stretcher-bearer] followed me.

I laid Fritz's body down in the orchard at the back of the farmhouse, and the two machine gunners and Petermann joined us. I opened the tunic and shirt. Both were red with Fritz's blood and torn by the savage volley of bullets that had smacked into him at close range. I broke his identity disc, and then emptied his pockets of pay book, photographs, matches and cigarette case. I wrapped them all in his handkerchief and handed the bundle to Petermann. "We'll send them back," I told him as we walked back to the house.

In a corner in the kitchen, they stacked the weapons of the dead and wounded. Shaken by his friend's death, Haape grasped an automatic weapon with a full magazine, and stuffed two extra magazines into his pockets; in his top tunic pockets he placed two light grenades. He then gave a rifle to Petermann, while the stretcher-bearer also picked up a rifle and flung it over his shoulder. Meanwhile, Haape became aware that one of Stolze's men had been watching him:

An amused smile played round the corners of [his] mouth and I noticed he was looking at my Red Cross armband, which was soaked with Fritz's blood. "You're right." I answered his unspoken question. Deliberately I slipped it off my sleeve, folded it carefully and put it into my pocket. "That doesn't go with guns. And in any case it means nothing to the Russians. There's no Geneva Convention here. I'm telling you … I'm a soldier like the rest of you now."

A short time later, Haape was informed that three of his regiment's stretcher-bearers had been "brutally shot down" while caring for wounded during fighting close by a concrete bunker on the frontier. "My heart hardened further toward the enemy," he later observed. In his diary, on the evening of 22 June 1941, he wrote: "Of the six doctors in the regiment [18 IR] one is dead (head shot) and one is wounded. In addition, four stretcher-bearers have been killed … I've had much to do, often dressing wounded comrades under heavy machine gun fire."[241]

From the outset, all along the eastern front, many incidents were recorded of Red Army units disregarding Red Cross markings and attacking German doctors, medical orderlies, other medical personnel, and wounded German troops under their protection. On 28 June 1941, Soviet soldiers in the Minsk region ambushed Motor Ambulance Platoon 127, which was clearly marked with Red Cross symbols, slaughtering most of the wounded and accompanying medical personnel.[242] In late June 1941, north of Minsk, Soviet stragglers repeatedly ambushed columns of 7 Panzer Division transporting wounded to the rear.[243] According to the diary of *Oberleutnant* Kurt Kummer, on 14 July 1941, the field hospital of 18 Panzer Division in Dobryn was attacked by Russian troops, resulting in heavy losses in men and materiel; this was followed three days later (17 July) by repeated low-level attacks of Soviet aircraft on a main dressing station (*Hauptverbandplatz*).[244] The diary of *Leutnant* Georg Kreuter (17 July) records that 18 Panzer's 2 Medical Company was ambushed and totally annihilated, while many German wounded were also killed.[245]

Several of the German eastern front veterans with whom this author corresponded also related stories of the murder and abuse of German medical personnel, including the rape (and, in some cases, mutilation) of Red Cross nurses.[246] Recalled Hans Schillke, a soldier with 8 Panzer Division (Army Group North): "From the beginning of the attack on Russia, our medical orderlies, although clearly recognizable by their white arm bands with the Red Cross symbol, were immediately shot dead when they attempted to care for the wounded."[247] While such personal stories could not be verified, the *Wehrmacht* War Crimes Bureau assembled indisputable case evidence of dozens of attacks on German field hospitals, dressing stations, field ambulances, doctors and other medical personnel, and wounded German soldiers.[248]

Because these attacks began in the very first hours of the German invasion, they cannot be construed as simply a response to the often ruthless behavior of the *Wehrmacht*.[249] Argues Franz W. Seidler:

> In the Second World War, all warring parties were guilty of transgressing against the [Geneva Convention for the Amelioration of the Condition of the Wounded and Sick in Armies in the Field] of 1929. The sign of the Red Cross was abused and ignored. German wounded, in particular, who fell into the hands of the Red Army, were at the mercy of the enemy's caprice. Members of the Red Army were not bound by any obligations of international law ... It was left to the personal morality of the individual to decide how he treated wounded enemies. Soldiers with religious convictions may, in individual cases, have recognized their brother in Christ in the helpless individual, but the majority of soldiers hewed to the propaganda slogans of the Party, which saw a canaille in every German.
>
> When the war began, the Soviet command ignored the sign of the Red Cross. Groups of German wounded and forward main dressing stations, which were marked with clearly visible Red Cross flags, attracted a particularly high degree of enemy artillery fire, until finally the flags were abandoned, as they provided no protection. Since the German field medics, who wore a Red Cross armband and were unarmed, were also being murdered along with the wounded if they were taken prisoner, they received a Pistol 38 to protect the wounded. Wearing the Red Cross armband was forbidden, in order to protect them from snipers, for whom they provided a clearly visible target.[250]

As Professor Seidler correctly submits, Soviet wartime propaganda, virtually unparalleled in its savagery – and including many stories of putative German atrocities (*Greuelpropaganda*) – played an integral part in encouraging all manner of war crimes by Red Army soldiers.[251] In addition, a generation of Soviet indoctrination in the principles of class hatred had instilled a deep antipathy in large segments of the Soviet population for Westerners and, in particular, for Germans. It was a toxic brew, and it is not too much to maintain, particularly in light of the Soviet Union's dismal human rights record (chillingly detailed in the *Black Book of Communism*),[252] that such crimes of war belonged to the very essence of the Soviet system.

(*Postscript*: The extrajudicial killing of German medical personnel and wounded German soldiers would continue throughout the war. Perhaps the most appalling example took place in late June 1944, only days after the beginning of Operation "Bagration," the gigantic Soviet offensive which finally destroyed Army Group Center, obliterating 28 of its divisions (out of 37 total) along with 350,000 men in about three weeks.[253] On 27 June 1944, Soviet troops stormed the "fortress" city of Bobruisk, on the Berezina. When German forces encircled there attempted to break out, they left behind more than 5000 badly wounded men scattered about the city's hospitals. These helpless soldiers were savagely butchered – not by partisans, but by regular troops of the Red Army. According to historian and eastern front veteran Rolf Hinze, only two survivors of this massacre were ever found.[254] Despite the monstrous nature of this crime, it has been largely ignored by western military historians.)

9.4.2: German Prisoners of War

According to authoritative sources, of the almost 3.2 million German soldiers imprisoned in Soviet POW camps between 1941 and 1956, an estimated 1.1 million, or about 35.2 percent, perished.[255] The death rate declined over the years, amounting to 90-95 percent in 1941/42, 60-70 percent in 1943, 30-40 percent in 1944, and 20-25 percent after 1945.[256]

Of course, an unknowable, albeit surely large, number of German prisoners of war (most likely, many hundreds of thousands)[257] were killed upon capture, or died of hunger, disease, wounds, or other causes, on the long treks to the camps. As indicated by de Zayas, those who ended up in the camps included 175,000 in 1941/42 (and as few as 26,000 in the initial months of the war), 220,000 in 1943, 560,000 in 1944, and 2,200,000 in 1945.[258]

Because the Soviets did, in fact, take prisoners, "one cannot speak of a uniform Soviet practice with respect to German prisoners of war."[259] In individual cases, Red Army units (up to divisional level) are known to have ordered the shooting of prisoners; moreover, orders to shoot certain *types* of prisoners – those belonging to particular units, or fighter pilots, for example – have also been verified. That said, it was not official policy of the Soviet government or military to execute German prisoners of war; furthermore, there are no indications the Red Army systematically sought to provide POWs with inadequate rations,[260] even if their undernourishment was, at times, inevitable in the harsh environment of the front (particularly during the periods of often headlong retreat in 1941/42).

A key document shaping Soviet policy with respect to the treatment of prisoners of war was the decree of the USSR Council of People's Commissars on the Position of Prisoners of War, of 1 July 1941. This decree was "entirely in line with the regulations of the Hague Convention,"[261] prohibiting, *inter alia*, the maltreatment of POWs, the use of force or threats to obtain information, and the robbing of personal belongings (uniforms, boots, medals and decorations, personal items, etc.). In practice, however, the decree often had little impact:

> Soviet military records, intercepted radio messages, and the testimony of countless Soviet prisoners of war indicate that Soviet commissars and soldiers largely ignored this [decree]. Moreover, certain captured documents show that higher Soviet authorities knew the [decree] was not being followed. One finds, for instance, many orders prohibiting the practice of killing prisoners before they could be sent to the rear for interrogation. In September 1941, two such documents were taken in the area occupied by German Second Army.[262]

Contributing to the general failure to adhere to the decree of 1 July 1941 were two primary factors. In the first place, Soviet propaganda undermined the acceptance of humanitarian principles by Red Army soldiers and lowered the threshold of restraint vis-à-vis their German adversary.[263] Secondly, various addresses of Stalin in the opening weeks and months of the war contributed to confusion about what was expected of the soldiers. As early as 3 July 1941, Stalin set the tone in his first address to the nation following the German attack: The enemy was "cruel and merciless," he said; the Soviet people should be "fearless in their struggle" and fight "selflessly" against the "Fascist enslavers," who were to be "smashed;" in the occupied regions, partisan units were to assemble, and the enemy was to be "persecuted and destroyed at every step."[264] While Stalin's remarks hardly amounted to an order to murder prisoners of war, more than a few soldiers interpreted them as such.

Later, however, Stalin appeared to go further. In his address of 6 November 1941, marking the 24th anniversary of the October Revolution, he "did not appear to discourage the practice" of killing German POWs. "From now on," he insisted, "it will be our task … to annihilate all Germans who have penetrated as occupiers, down to the last man." After "tumultuous applause," he went on: "No mercy to the German occupiers! Death to the German occupiers!" – remarks, of course, which were greeted by more "tumultuous applause."[265]

Egged on by anti-German propaganda, encouraged by the statements of Stalin himself, many Red Army commissars, officers, and soldiers enthusiastically embraced the killing of

German prisoners of war. German reconnaissance patrols were especially "hard hit, and many mutilated corpses were found by the troops that followed close behind."[266] Reports of mutilations of German soldiers had been "extremely rare in France, Belgium, and North Africa, but after the invasion of the Soviet Union on 22 June 1941, such reports arrived almost daily. As a result, the Army decreed on 27 August 1941 that additional experts in forensic medicine would be assigned to the eastern front 'to examine whatever wounds or injuries are caused by the Bolsheviks as are outside the scope of legal warfare.'"[267]

After the war, Hitler's *Luftwaffe* adjutant, Nicolaus von Below, stated that dispatches submitted by Army Group South in August 1941 contained the first accounts of atrocities by the Red Army. Apparently, these were "so appalling" that even Hitler had a hard time believing them; as a result, he sent von Below to Nikolayev to sort matters out with 16 Panzer Division:

> I spoke there with General Hube and a very good friend of mine, Udo von Alvensleben. They described to me the discovery of the corpses of more than 100 murdered soldiers of [6th Company, 79 Rifle Regiment] at Grigovo station. At another place German prisoners had been drawn and quartered alive. Our troops had responded accordingly. When I explained the facts to Hitler at *Wolfsschanze* he thought about it for some time and said finally that [the] General Staff ought to know: then they might take a different view of the sort of enemy we were fighting against.[268]

During the entire Russian campaign, reports of the torture, mutilation, and execution of captured German soldiers did not cease. As de Zayas observes, "the German aggression against the Soviet Union was met with vehement cruelty." Yet the behavior of the Red Army cannot be explained simply "as reprisals for German atrocities (although the latter undoubtedly account for many instances)," for "similar incidents occurred throughout the eastern theater of war and commenced immediately upon the outbreak of hostilities."[269] According to Joachim Hoffmann, "the murder of captured German soldiers and wounded began ... abruptly [*schlagartig*] on the first day of the war, 22 June 1941, and indeed along the entire front;" moreover, the killing began before the soldiers could have been influenced by efforts of Red Army propagandists to incite hatred against the German invaders.[270]

Examples of the "vehement cruelty" of *Rotarmisten* abound in the records of the War Crimes Bureau that, from 22 June 1941 on, received a flood or reports describing the murder of German prisoners; dozens of these reports cover Soviet crimes committed in the first week of the war. As a brief introduction to the records of the Bureau, several of its initial findings are provided below.

- At the end of June 1941, near Kernarava, northwest of Vilna, 14 German *Panzerjaeger* were bound up after capture by the Russians, and then, in their completely defenseless state, were murdered by blows to the head from a spade, by being stabbed with bayonets, or in other terrible ways.[271]
- On 27 or 28 June 1941, near the Skomorocchy fortress works, approximately 8-10 km north of Sokal on the Bug River, 5 German officers or non-commissioned officers and *Gefreite*, after being wounded in battle, were mutilated in gruesome fashion by Russian troops. *Major* Soehngen had his left eye gouged out, and his lower jaw was skeletonized by a smooth cut from ear to ear, so that lower and upper jawbones were separated. *Oberfeldwebel* Pelzer had his right eye gouged out, the left eye severely injured, and his left ear half removed by a semi-circular cut upwards, while his right humerus was shattered ... *Gefreiter* Schlaegers, too,

had his left eye gouged out, *Oberfeldwebel* Wegener the right eye ...

According to the report of the medical expert, the fact that in all these cases there was heavy bleeding from the eye sockets is evidence for the assumption that these mutilations had been inflicted before death.[272]

• On 28 June 1941, northeast of Belostok, at least 18 wounded German soldiers left behind were murdered by Russian troops through gunshots to the head, blows from rifle butts, or stabbing with their own bayonets.[273]

• On the Klewan-Broniki road on 30 June 1941, a large number of men from Infantry Regiment 35 fell into Russian captivity after a Russian attack close to the town of Rowne involving a huge superiority on the [enemy] side ... The prisoners were ordered to remove all their equipment and to take off their boots, field tunic, shirt, and (some of them) even their socks ... *Leutnant* Kroening reported his findings, which he came to after the Russian withdrawal, as follows: "I saw all the dead from 2nd Battalion in order to identify them. I ascertained the following particular atrocities and mutilations, and take my oath on their veracity: approximately 6 soldiers had had limbs, such as an arm or a leg, their head or half their head hewn off with sharp objects ... 12 to 14 soldiers had had their genitals cut off."[274]

• On 30 June 1941 on the Rozana – Slonim road, members of a signal detail in the midst of construction fell into Russian captivity after being deceived by Russian troops, who had outfitted themselves with German motorcycle coats and German helmets. A short time after that, 14 men from a signal detail were discovered with terrible mutilations: their arms were mutilated, throats slit, their faces smashed in.[275]

• Unheard of atrocities were revealed in the sworn testimony of *Leutnant* Woicke, as well as of *Unteroffizier* Sponholz and of *Gefreiter* Dr Tamme, of 10 September 1941. They describe the killing of 24 German soldiers in mid-August in a beet field near Jemtschicha, where the Russians were guilty of bestial mutilations. In two cases, they cut off their victim's genitals while he was still alive; in other cases, they slit open the stomach and gouged out the eyes of the defenseless wounded men; others had their throats cut, and the head of one of the wounded was hacked off.

Gefreiter Dr Tamme was a member of the burial commando. He had to stand guard over two corpses until they were picked up by the commando. He states that the sight of one of the dead in particular has etched itself indelibly in his mind. The arms of this dead man had been bent round backwards over his head, the eyes gouged out, the mouth wide open, frozen in a scream, the abdomen had been cut open with a long, vertical wound, his genitals were cut off. The position of arms and mouth indicated that the soldier had certainly been tortured and mutilated while alive and conscious.[276]

Of course, the incidents adduced above represent but a tiny fraction of the thousands of such accounts marshalled by the War Crimes Bureau. Numerous other examples of the killing of captured – and often wounded – German troops can also be found in the published literature, and in letters, diaries, and memoirs of German eastern front veterans. In his biography of General Rudolf Schmidt (39 Panzer Corps) Klaus R. Woche records the murder and plunder of at least 10 wounded German soldiers of 35 Reconnaissance Battalion (35 ID), near Rudnia, on 18 July 1941. During the fighting for the bridgehead over the Dvina at Disna, more than 100 men belonging to 14 Motorized Infantry Division were captured and brutally massacred.[277] In his diary on 20 July 1941, General Lemelsen (47 Panzer Corps) recorded the "bestial" murder – mostly by shots to the nape of the neck

(*Genickschuesse*) – of 18 captured soldiers of the corps signal battalion: "It was a massacre [*Abschlachten*]. The rage of our men knows no bounds. And still we treat our prisoners decently – that is the chivalrous way to fight, but the Russians don't have a clue."[278] In late July 1941, south of Velikie Luki, an entire infantry platoon of 77 Infantry Regiment (26 ID) was annihilated in close combat with an overwhelming Russian force; in their blood lust, the victorious *Rotarmisten* then set about to mutilate the bodies of the dead German soldiers, gouging out their eyes, cutting off their noses and genitals, and slicing open their abdomens.[279]

While one could go on endlessly with such grim tales, the crucial point is this: Thousands – many tens of thousands – of German soldiers met terrible ends like those described above. Which makes all too clear why the *Landser* fighting inside the Soviet Union – as corroborated by account after account – were utterly terrified of the thought of being captured. Even worse than being taken prisoner by Red Army soldiers, was falling in the hands of Soviet partisans. As former artilleryman Walter Vollmer (106 ID) stated in a letter to this author in 2006: "The partisans were blood-thirsty beasts, not even human. They received no quarter from our side."[280] It was the fear of capture, however, which helped to ensure that the retreat from Moscow in the winter of 1941/42 did not end in the collapse and disintegration of Army Group Center. In any case, the terrible crimes against captured German soldiers signify one of the defining characteristics of the total war waged on the eastern front – a fact which, all too often, is ignored by those who refuse to acknowledge that, while these soldiers were often perpetrators, they were also often victims.

9.4.3: Use of Proscribed Ammunition

Despite pre-*Barbarossa* fears, and a series of false alarms in the initial days of the campaign, there is no evidence that German forces were ever subjected to chemical or biological weapons by the Red Army; nor did the Germans resort to such deadly and outlawed agents. The Russians, however, did make more than infrequent use of so-called "dum-dum" and explosive bullets, both of which were proscribed under international law. In November 1941, at the request of the military court of German Sixth Army (Army Group South), the Forensic Medical Institute of the Military Medical Academy in Berlin examined the case of *Leutnant* Werner Fett (II./SR 93) to determine if his wounds had been caused by an illegal explosive bullet. The institute's final report (*Gutachten*), prepared by its director, *Oberstabsarzt* Dr Panning, concluded it was "highly probable" that the wounds had indeed been inflicted by such a projectile. The report also contained the following passages:

> By way of illegal infantry projectiles, the various forms of dum-dum bullets come into consideration, whose principle in general is for the lead core to be released when the casing at the tip is pierced. [The dum-dum bullet] operates by causing crude rupturing of human tissue, even in simple soft tissue shots, as it moves in the direction of the exit wound; this is explained by the bullet shattering, explosion-like, as the lead core exits the forward open end of the projectile.
>
> In addition, [on the eastern front], actual high explosive infantry projectiles [*Sprenggeschosse*] must also be considered, as they are, according to reliable findings, being used militarily by the Russians and are even being used against human targets. These are marked with red paint at the tip and cap, an ammunition type which has frequently been found deployed for military use by Russian units at the front. The Military Academy's collection of spent rounds already includes a large number of pieces of evidence, which were removed from German wounded during surgery.

The projectiles are filled with explosive material in the foremost third and with lead at the back. In between, there is an igniter with an iron firing pin, which moves forward when the tip is stopped by target object resistance and causes the explosive material to explode ... Their use in war and against human targets contravenes both the Petersburg Convention of 11 December 1868, which prohibits explosive charges for shells of less than 250g, and the clauses of the Hague Convention of 29 July 1899, according to which projectiles which "expand or flatten" inside the human body are prohibited.[281]

The use of dum-dum and explosive bullets by the Russians was reported by the Germans from the beginning of the invasion. In his unpublished war memoirs, Guenther Barkhoff (26 Infantry Division) relived his experiences of 22 June 1941, storming a Russian bunker position:

For me personally it was a strange feeling to be shot at by an enemy for the first time. I heard the whistling of the bullets and the "plop" of their impact in the ground. A shell tore into my map-case, carving in at the side and leaving a hole behind at the top. In the heat of battle, I only noticed that later. I still have the case with me today (Sept. 1996).

The Russians' rifle and machine gun ammunition were explosive bullets, which exploded on impact and tore open terrible wounds. Their field position was so strong that we could not take it; we lacked heavy weapons or an anti-tank gun.

This first little assault on "only" a field position had serious consequences. Our platoon leader, *Leutnant* Malina, only six weeks a lieutenant, was killed. The company chief, *Oberleutnant* Kockelkorn, had been shot through the thigh. *Schuetzen* Freddy Neuman and Leonhard received shots to the helmet and had little splinters from the explosive bullets in their scalps. After three days they were back with the company.[282]

In letters to this author, two veterans of 6 Infantry Division also described the use of explosive bullets by the Russians:

Heinrich Stockhoff (6 ID):
You ask about explosive ammunition. These were dangerous shells which caused serious wounds. During the assault by our 9./IR 37 on Upjerwitschi on 28 October 1941, soldier Hermann Klein was fatally wounded in the thigh by an explosive shell ... In the Gridino position, *Unteroffizier* Franz Lienkamp fell on 13.06.42, when an explosive shell ripped off the top of his skull. In my view, it was not permissible to fire with explosive ammunition. No countermeasures were taken on the German side ... The Russian also used explosive ammunition during the battles of Christmas 1941 in Sresnevo and Bukontovo, where our platoon leader, *Leutnant* S[- - -] fell, as well as during the assault on Gory-Kaseki on 5.8.42, during which 9./IR 37 lost 63 comrades – 8 dead, 8 missing, and 47 wounded.[283]

H. Stu[- - -] (6 ID):
These explosive projectiles were bullets from the Russian machine pistol. They exploded on impact and then always tore open large, dangerous wounds ... In our winter position 1941/42 in the village of Gridino, we were frequently shot at with this weapon. The Russian then simply shot randomly and without a particular target into the village of Gridino. It was rather like an artillery assault in miniature ... The village of Gridino was under constant fire during the day.

I experienced these explosive bullets for the first time on 21 December 1941. It must have been in the morning around 0600 hours, when this fire display really got going. I lay behind the protective shield of our Pak [*Panzerabwehrkanone*] with my comrade, Karl Ebert. It was a dreadful shoot-up. The bullets exploded in front of the shield. We fired a high explosive shell, but then the automatic breech mechanism would not open; it had frozen solid because of the sudden heat. It was below -30 degrees [Centigrade], even our machine guns had frozen up. We tried everything to get the breech to open, it was no use. With a machine pistol from *Unteroffizier* Konrad and 5 rifles, we were able to hold the Russians off for a short time. But then we ran out of ammunition and had to withdraw into the village. Our Pak gun was lost.

We then put in a counterattack, during which *Oberleutnant* Grupe and a few other comrades fell. These explosive bullets also played an important role in this counterattack. I saw one comrade, half his face had been ripped away by an explosive shell. He had no eyes any more and half his mouth and his nose were also torn off. A normal bullet would probably only have caused a graze wound [*Streifschuss*].[284]

While the veterans' accounts cannot, of course, be confirmed (it was not uncommon for German soldiers, who had been badly wounded by rifle or MG fire, to attribute their wounds to illegal projectiles), cases involving the use of such ammunition by the Russians were recorded by the War Crimes Bureau, along with the repeated seizure of dum-dum and explosive bullets by German units:

• At the end of June 1941, a member of a German division staff found entire bullet pouches filled with such ammunition in Russian positions near Sopockinie.
• In a Russian workshop shed at the train station in Dubno, approximately 30 Russian cartridges were found where the tips of the projectiles had had a few millimeters filed off. Beside the box containing these cartridges was another box with approximately 150 cartridges, which were evidently intended to be adapted in the same way. Both boxes stood close to each other on a workbench. Between the boxes was a vice; beside the vice lay various tools, mostly files. The situation left no room for doubt that the cartridges were clamped in the vice for filing in order to create a dum-dum effect.
• *Stabswachtmeister* Ollesch declared under oath that he had found cartridges on fallen Russian soldiers, where the tip of the shell had had approximately 1–1½ mm freshly filed off. He had also seen other shells there, which had <u>always</u> been tipless. This statement is confirmed under oath by *Oberleutnant* and company chief Walter Huebener. He adds that fallen German soldiers have had bullet wounds which could not be attributed to normal infantry or machine gun projectiles. The entry wounds were consistently as large as a five *Deutschmark* piece, and some of them were even larger.
• Cartridges of Czech origin were also found in mid-July 1941 in an outbuilding of the police station in Slawuta, which had been adapted by filing off the tips to make them into dum-dum bullets.
• Projectiles with an explosive effect were also used in many cases by the Russians against German troops. An infantry division reported on 13 July 1941 that during a low level attack by a Soviet plane on a German marching column, Russian ammunition – so-called "B ammunition" – with an explosive effect was used, which contains an explosive charge in the front part of the shell. The explosive charge is ignited upon impact, so that the bullet expands when it pierces the body, causing devastating wounds … An army headquarters reports similarly of such ammunition, which had caused remarkably severe injuries among Romanian troops.[285]

The War Crimes Bureau concluded its findings by noting that, "in all of these cases, the [explosive] projectiles were not used against aerial targets or tanks, or similar mobile or fixed ground targets, but against marching or fighting German troops in violation of international law."[286] The Bureau's findings do not indicate if the German government ever lodged a formal protest with the Soviet Union concerning the Red Army's use of dum-dum and explosive projectiles.

ENDNOTES

1   Quoted in: J. Piekalkiewicz, *Die Schlacht um Moskau*, 14.
2   *Feldpost*, W. Heinemann, 13.7.41.
3   Quoted in: J. Shay, *Achilles in Vietnam*, 83.
4   Quoted in: G. Knopp, *Die Wehrmacht. Eine Bilanz*, 109.
5   BA-MA RW 2/v. 145, *Wehrmacht-Untersuchungsstelle*, "*Kriegsverbrechen der russischen Wehrmacht 1941.*"
6   R. Hinze, *Das Ostfront-Drama 1944*, 17.
7   E-Mail, C. Nehring to C. Luther, 7 Aug 11.
8   Ltr, F. Belke to C. Luther, 30 Jul 05.
9   K. W. Andres, "*Panzersoldaten im Russlandfeldzug 1941 bis 1945. Tagebuchaufzeichnungen und Erlebnisberichte*," 17.
10   The words are those of a German general. Quoted in: B. H. Liddell Hart, *History of the Second World War*, 162.
11   H. Martin, *Weit war der Weg*, 20.
12   *Feldpost*, W. Heinemann, 13.7.41, 26.8.41.
13   Footnote by Dennis E. Showalter, in: H. F. Richardson (ed.), *Your Loyal and Loving Son. The Letters of Tank Gunner Karl Fuchs, 1937-41*, 121-22.
14   H. C. Verton, *In the Fire of the Eastern Front*, 79-80.
15   Ibid., 80
16   G. Blumentritt, *Moscow*, in: *The Fatal Decisions*, W. Richardson & S. Freidin (eds.), 37.
17   H. Haape, *Moscow Tram Stop*, 183.
18   *Feldpostbrief*, H. S., 9.10.41.
19   G. Blumentritt, *Moscow*, in: *The Fatal Decisions*, W. Richardson & S. Freidin (eds.), 37.
20   Recalled Bernard Haering, in 1941 a Catholic priest serving as a medic on the eastern front: "At that time in Russia, outside the cities there were no toilets in the houses. Even during the most severe winter, people had to go outdoors when nature called. The consequence was that after the long winters there was much cleaning to be done around the houses, and it was truly slavish work." B. Haering, *Embattled Witness*, 37.
21   S. Knappe, *Soldat*, 216-17; H. Haape, *Moscow Tram Stop*, 183.
22   H. Boucsein, *Halten oder Sterben*, 26.
23   Lt. Joachim H. (18 967), Collection BfZ.
24   Ltr, O. Will to C. Luther, 16 Jan 06.
25   *Tagebuch*, Oblt. K., quoted in: K. W. Andres, "*Panzersoldaten im Russlandfeldzug 1941 bis 1945. Tagebuchaufzeichnungen und Erlebnisberichte*," 7-9.
26   *Tagebuch*, Major S., quoted in: K. W. Andres, "*Panzersoldaten im Russlandfeldzug 1941 bis 1945. Tagebuchaufzeichnungen und Erlebnisberichte*," 10.
27   Ltr, H. Haape to fiancée, 2.9.41.
28   This is the "most widely accepted figure" for the population of the USSR in 1939. If the "spoils" of the non-aggression pact with Germany are considered – i.e., the occupation of the western Ukraine and western Belorussia in September 1939, and the formal incorporation of the Baltic States and parts of Romania in 1940 – the total population controlled by the Soviet Union in June 1941 was most likely more than 190 million. C. Bellamy, *Absolute War*, 8.
29   C. Hartmann, "*Verbrecherischer Krieg – verbrecherische Wehrmacht?*," in: *Vierteljahrshefte fuer Zeitgeschichte*, Sonderdruck, Heft 1/2004, 49-50. In the Russian Soviet Socialist Republic the figure was barely 6.5 people per square kilometer. In the German Reich, in 1933, the population density was 131/sq.km. Ibid., 50, f.n. 290.
30   P. Tauber (Hg.), *Laeusejagd und Rohrkrepierer. Willi Loewer, an den Fronten des Zweiten Weltkrieges*, 40.
31   C. Hartmann, "*Verbrecherischer Krieg – verbrecherische Wehrmacht?*," in: *Vierteljahrshefte fuer Zeitgeschichte*, Sonderdruck, Heft 1/2004, 50.
32   Ltr, O. Baese to C. Luther, 28 Feb 06.
33   Ltr, H. Stockhoff to C. Luther, 4 Apr 05.
34   Ltr, A. Gassmann to C. Luther, 7 Apr 06.
35   C. Merridale, *Ivan's War*, 143.
36   W. Wessler, "*Meine Erlebnisse mit der russischen Bevoelkerung in Rshew*" (unpublished manuscript).
37   K. W. Andres, "*Panzersoldaten im Russlandfeldzug 1941 bis 1945. Tagebuchaufzeichnungen und Erlebnisberichte*," 6.

38 Ibid., 5-6.

39 C. Rass, "*Verbrecherische Kriegfuebrung an der Front*," in: *Verbrechen der Wehrmacht*, C. Hartmann, et al. (Hg.), 84.

40 Ibid., 85.

41 C. Hartmann, *Unternehmen Barbarossa*, 76. Ultimately, the occupied eastern territories, ruthlessly exploited by German civilian and military authorities, were able to cover ca. 80 percent of the *Ostheer's* provisions. Ibid., 77.

42 S. Hart, et al., *The German Soldier*, 44. In November 1941 alone, 18 Panzer Division requisitioned 40 tons of meat from the local population.

43 The 253 ID began Operation *Barbarossa* as a reserve unit attached to Army Group North; by August 1941, it had been transferred to Ninth Army of Army Group Center. Internet site at: http://www.lexikon-der-wehrmacht.de.

44 By 1 July 1941, the responsible army supply depot was no longer able to furnish 253 ID with oats for its horses; the next day, the stocks of flour for baking bread were exhausted. C. Rass, "*Menschenmaterial:*" *Deutsche Soldaten an der Ostfront*, 343, f.n. 51.

45 Ibid., 343-44.

46 K. Reinhardt, *Moscow – The Turning Point*, 103-04.

47 Ibid., 124, f.n. 187. In November 1941, the OKH promulgated a secret order, which read in part: "In the fight against Bolshevism we are concerned with the survival or destruction of our people … The Soviet government has had all supplies transported away or destroyed. If the Russian people … are going hungry, their government alone must take the blame … German soldiers will be tempted to share their provisions with the people. They must, however, say to themselves: every gram of bread or other food, that I may give out of generosity to the population in the occupied territories, I am withholding from the German people and thus from my family … Had the Bolsheviks been able to carry out their plan to attack the German people … they would have proceeded mercilessly according to Bolshevik methods, even against our women and children … Therefore, in the face of starving women and children German soldiers must remain steadfast. If they refuse to do so they are endangering the nutrition of our people."

48 See, the Hague Conventions of 1907, Articles 47 and 52, cited in: C. Hartmann, "*Verbrecherischer Krieg – verbrecherische Wehrmacht?*," in: *Vierteljahrshefte fuer Zeitgeschichte*, Sonderdruck, Heft 1/2004, 36, f.n. 188.

49 Ibid., 36.

50 C. Hartmann, *Unternehmen Barbarossa*, 78.

51 Ibid., 78.

52 Hartmann, "*Verbrecherischer Krieg – verbrecherische Wehrmacht?*," in: *Vierteljahrshefte fuer Zeitgeschichte*, Sonderdruck, Heft 1/2004, 50-51.

53 Ltr, W. Dicke to C. Luther, 14 Apr 04.

54 For an example of the prosecution of soldiers' crimes by German military courts on the eastern front, see Christoph Rass' study of the 253 Infantry Division. Rass notes that the number of men sentenced by the division's court increased steadily over the final six months of 1941. During this period, the number of men charged with property crimes against civilians and rape also increased (the former markedly so), a fact which Rass attributes to the growing radicalization of soldiers continually directed by their superiors to wage war ruthlessly, and well beyond the bounds of convention. C. Rass, "*Menschenmaterial:*" *Deutsche Soldaten an der Ostfront*, 283-84, 345-46.

55 By 1944, *Wehrmacht* courts in all theaters of war had condemned a total of 5349 men for sexual offenses (*Sittlichkeitsvergehen*) against women, with sentences including imprisonment, transfer to a penal battalion, even death. Although on the eastern front such offenses could be handled with a certain insouciance – given an ideological template which classified most Soviet people as inferior human beings (*minderwertig*) – they were often adjudicated aggressively and serious sentences handed out; in some cases, men were convicted solely on evidence gleaned from victims of the assaults. Still, when one considers that during the Second World War German military courts administered ca. 1.5 million sentences, it is clear that prosecuting men for sexual assault was not a high priority. Of course, another interpretation – although it would surely fly in the face of Germany's contemporary anti-*Wehrmacht* hysteria – might be that such offenses were infrequent among the *Landser*. What is clear, however, is that incidents of sexual assault by soldiers of the *Wehrmacht* never reached the horrific dimensions seen, for example, with Japanese troops in China, or with the Red Army on German soil in 1944/45 (in Berlin alone estimates are that more than 100,000 women were raped by Soviet troops). Moreover, no evidence exists that German military leaders ever accepted, or sought to employ, the rape of women as a systematic terror weapon in the east or on any other front of the Second World War. J. Huerter, "*Keine Straffreiheit. Sexualverbrechen von Wehrmachtsangehoerigen 1939 bis 1945*," in: *Frankfurter Allgemeine Zeitung*, 13 Sep 05.

56 BA-MA N 19/9, *Nachlass von Weichs. Erinnerungen, Ost-Feldzug bis Fruehjahr 1942*. In the summer of 1941, Weichs commanded German Second Army.

57 K. Gerbet (ed.), *GFM Fedor von Bock, The War Diary*, 272-73.

58 Ibid., 271.

59 K.-J. Thies, *Der Ostfeldzug – Ein Lageatlas*, "Lage am 3.8.1941 abds., Heeresgruppe Mitte."

60 H. von Luck, *Panzer Commander*, 72-73.

61 N. Ferguson, "*The Next War of the World*," internet site at: http://www.foreignaffairs.org. (From *Foreign Affairs*, Sep/Oct 06.)

62   Ibid.
63   R. Overmans, *Deutsche militaerische Verluste im Zweiten Weltkrieg*, 265, 277. Overmans posits total German fatal losses in the east at just under 4.0 million, a figure which, by his calculations, includes several hundred thousand who perished in Soviet POW camps. Overmans' figure for POW losses, however, is quite low compared to other reliable sources, which estimate that 1.1 million German soldiers died in captivity in the Soviet Union. Using this latter figure for POW losses, and adding it to Overmans total of ca. 3.5 million German *combat* losses on the eastern front (including the final battles from the Oder River to Berlin), one arrives at a figure of approximately 4.6 million German dead attributable to the war in the east. For German losses in Soviet captivity see, F. W. Seidler (Hg.), *Verbrechen an der Wehrmacht*, 44; A. M. de Zayas, *The Wehrmacht War Crimes Bureau*, 305, f.n. 11; R. Traub, "*Versklavt und vernichtet*," in: *Der Zweite Weltkrieg*, S. Burgdorff & K. Wiegrefe (Hg.), 169.
64   Col.-Gen. G. F. Krivosheev (ed.), *Soviet Casualties and Combat Losses*, 4; C. Bellamy, *Absolute War*, 7-12, 15. The figure of 27 million is from Bellamy. The figure of 8.7 million for Soviet irrecoverable military losses does not include nearly three million Red Army soldiers who were "written off" during the war (e.g., taken prisoner) but later returned. When this latter group is added to the total, Russia's wartime "military-operational" irrecoverable losses come to almost 11.5 million.
65   The figure of 4.0+ million German soldiers killed in the east includes those who perished in Soviet POW camps. While a portion of the latter died during the years of captivity after 1945, their deaths were, of course, attributable to the war.
66   C. Luther, book review of C. Hartmann's *Wehrmacht im Ostkrieg. Front und militaerisches Hinterland 1941/42*, in: *The Journal of Military History*, Vol. 74, No. #1, Jan 10, 285. For an historical analysis of the myth of the "clean" *Wehrmacht* see, K. Naumann, "*The 'Unblemished' Wehrmacht. The Social History of a Myth*," in: *War of Extermination. The German Military in World War II*, H. Heer & K. Naumann (eds.), 417-29.
67   For an historiographical overview (and detailed bibliography) of the German Army's participation in Hitler's war of annihilation against Soviet Russia see, R.-D. Mueller & G. R. Ueberschaer, *Hitler's War in the East. A Critical Assessment*, particularly pp. 207-80.
68   F. W. Seidler (Hg.), *Verbrechen an der Wehrmacht*, 25.
69   C. Bellamy, *Absolute War*, 20.
70   Ibid., 20.
71   Ibid., 20.
72   C. Bellamy, *Absolute War*, 20-22; J. Keegan, *The Second World War*, 186.
73   *GSWW*, Vol. IV, 908.
74   S. Pressfield, *The Afghan Campaign*, 70-71.
75   K. Latzel, *Deutsche Soldaten – nationalsozialistischer Krieg?*, 48; C. Bellamy, *Absolute War*, 25; *GSWW*, Vol. IV, 514.
76   *GSWW*, Vol. IV, 514-15.
77   For details concerning origins and execution of the infamous Commissar Order see, M. Broszat, et al., *Anatomie des SS-Staates*, Bd. 2, 143-55.
78   C. Bellamy, *Absolute War*, 25.
79   Drafted by the legal branch of the OKW, the "Decree on Military Justice" (*Gerichtsbarkeitserlass*) of 13 May 1941 "withdrew crimes committed by enemy civilians in the east from the jurisdiction of military courts, required that partisans be 'brutally eliminated' and ordered that *Wehrmacht* soldiers committing crimes against the civilian population no longer needed to be prosecuted." B. Wegner, "*The Road to Defeat: The German Campaigns in Russia 1941-43*," in: *The Journal of Strategic Studies*, Vol. 13, No. 1, Mar 90, 108. The decree, in effect, stripped citizens of Soviet Russia of all legal protections, and functioned as a "preventive amnesty for crimes of soldiers against Soviet citizens in and out of uniform." J. Foerster, "*Wehrmacht, Krieg und Holocaust*," in: *Die Wehrmacht. Mythos und Realitaet*, R.-D. Mueller & H.-E. Volkmann (Hg.), 953.
80   Stefan Storz, "*Perfide Rechnung*," in: *Der Zweite Weltkrieg*, S. Burgdorff & K. Wiegrefe (Hg.), 314.
81   H. Heer, "*How Amorality Became Normality. Reflections on the Mentality of German Soldiers on the Eastern Front*," in: *War of Extermination. The German Military in World War II*, H. Heer & K. Naumann (eds.), 329, 333-34.
82   C. D. Winchester, *Hitler's War on Russia*, 55.
83   R. J. Kershaw, *War Without Garlands*, 141.
84   O. Bartov, *The Eastern Front, 1941-45, German Troops and the Barbarisation of Warfare*, 116.
85   BA-MA RH 27-18/24, 25.6.41, quoted in: O. Bartov, *The Eastern Front, 1941-45, German Troops and the Barbarisation of Warfare*, 116-17.
86   BA-MA RH 27-18/175, 30.6.41, quoted in: O. Bartov, *The Eastern Front, 1941-45, German Troops and the Barbarisation of Warfare*, 117.
87   O. Bartov, *The Eastern Front, 1941-45, German Troops and the Barbarisation of Warfare*, 116.
88   S. Knappe, *Soldat*, 219-20.
89   Ibid., 220-21.
90   Ibid., 210-11.
91   R. J. Kershaw, *War Without Garlands*, 140. 18 Panzer Division ordered that "in no circumstances" were wounded Soviet POWs to be cared for or transported alongside of German wounded; rather, they were to be transported in *Panje* wagons.
92   C. Streit, "*Soviet Prisoners of War in the Hands of the Wehrmacht*," in: *War of Extermination. The German Military in World War II*, H. Heer & K. Naumann (eds.), 83.

93   Quoted in: *The War 1939-1945*, D. Flower & J. Reeves (eds.), 213-14.

94   C. Streit, "*Soviet Prisoners of War in the Hands of the Wehrmacht*," in: *War of Extermination. The German Military in World War II*, H. Heer & K. Naumann (eds.), 82.

95   Ibid., 82.

96   Ibid., 82.

97   *Feldpostbrief*, "*Hans-Otto*," 20.11.41 (Courtesy of Konrad Distler).

98   BA-MA N 813, *Tagebuch* Muenchhausen, ca. 15.8.41.

99   Ibid., ca. Sep 41.

100 G. R. Ueberschaer & W. Wette (Hg.), "*Unternehmen Barbarossa*." *Der deutsche Ueberfall auf die Sowjetunion 1941*, 21.

101 K. Gerbet (ed.), *GFM Fedor von Bock, The War Diary*, 290.

102 K. Reinhardt, *Moscow – The Turning Point*, 264.

103 Ibid., 264.

104 See, C. Streit, *Keine Kameraden. Die Wehrmacht und die sowjetischen Kriegsgefangenen 1941-1945*, Stuttgart, 1978 (3rd revised edition, Bonn, 1991).

105 The number of Soviet prisoners of war collected by the Germans through 1941 remains somewhat in doubt. According to official OKH figures, 3,350,639 Soviet prisoners were taken by 20 December 1941. (*Anlage 5 zu OKH/GenStdH/GenQu/Abt. I* (*Qu 2/III*), *Nr. I/6562/41g.K. vom 25.12.1941*, cited in: P. E. Schramm (Hg.), *Kriegstagebuch des OKW*, Bd. I, 1106.) The late German historian Joachim Hoffmann posited a rather higher figure, stating that, by 31 December 1941, some 3.8 million Soviet servicemen and women had fallen into German hands. (*GSWW*, Vol. IV, 849.) Army Group Center alone claimed the capture of 1,912,376 Soviet prisoners in the first six months of the war. (*Heeresgruppe Mitte H 3/158 Gefangene und Beutemeldung*, 4.1.1942, cited in: *A. Seaton, The Russo-German War 1941-45*, 208, f.n. 53.) A Russian state commission in the 1990s, however, while acknowledging that precise data were lacking, suggested that some two million Red Army troops were captured in 1941, and more than four million over the course of the war. Figures on total Russians captured during the war range from about 4.1 to as many as 5.7 million. Regardless which figure is used, sources appear to agree that between 55 and 60 percent of Soviet POWs perished in captivity, or as many as 3.3 million if the higher figure for total captures (5.7 million) is accepted. E. Mawdsley, *Thunder in the East*, 103. See also, C. Streit, "*Soviet Prisoners of War in the Hands of the Wehrmacht*," in: *War of Extermination. The German Military in World War II*, H. Heer & K. Naumann (eds.), 80-81. Streit accepts the figure of 5.7 million Red Army soldiers captured.

106 Streit clearly rejects this position: "The entire design of the campaign meant that large numbers of prisoners were predictable, and feeding the prisoners was not an inherently impossible task. The more fundamental cause of the mass deaths was not the number of prisoners but the war aims that were pursued in the east. Those aims were formulated and the methods by which they were to be achieved were designed with the active participation of the command staffs of the *Wehrmacht*." (C. Streit, "*Soviet Prisoners of War in the Hands of the Wehrmacht*," in: *War of Extermination. The German Military in World War II*, H. Heer & K. Naumann (ed), 81.) Conversely, revisionist historian Heinz Magenheimer submits that it was not official German policy to starve POWs to death. About the treatment of the more than 650,000 prisoners taken at the start of Operation "Typhoon," the advance on Moscow in October 1941, he points out correctly that the area in which the fighting occurred had already been stripped bare (by both Germans and Russians), and that the Germans were suffering from serious food shortages, making it impossible to provide adequate nourishment to the prisoners. H. Magenheimer, *Moskau 1941*, 153-54.

107 C. Bellamy, *Absolute War*, 23.

108 L. Yahil, *The Holocaust*, 250-51.

109 *Korueck = Kommandant des rueckwaertigen Armeegebietes*, or Commander of the Army's Rear Area. Each army rear area unit was identified by a number; the term applied to both the unit and its commanding office. At its greatest extent, *Korueck* 582 covered an area of about 27,000 sq.km. T. J. Schulte, "*Korueck 582*," in: *War of Extermination. The German Military in World War II*, H. Heer & K. Naumann (eds.), 316, 325, f.n. 1.

110 Ibid., 318.

111 Ibid., 318.

112 Ibid., 318.

113 Ibid., 318-19.

114 Ibid., 319.

115 Haape was providing first-aid and other medical care to wounded Russian prisoners from the opening hours of the war. See, H. Haape, *Moscow Tram Stop*, 17-19.

116 B. Haering, *Embattled Witness*, 49-50.

117 Under both the Hague and Geneva Conventions, the commissars were recognized as prisoners of war in the same sense as doctors, veterinarians, administrative personnel, judges, etc., who served alongside the fighting troops. In German military circles, the preparation of the Commissar Order was significantly influenced by the Red Army's willful disregard of the Geneva protocols pertaining to POWs during the Russo-Finnish War of 1939/40; indeed, the 30 November 1939 request by the Finns that the Soviet Union adhere to these protocols had been ignored by the Soviet government. F. W. Seidler (Hg.), *Verbrechen an der Wehrmacht*, 18.

118 Quoted in: F. W. Seidler (Hg.), *Verbrechen an der Wehrmacht*, 19.

119 G. Knopp, *Die Wehrmacht. Eine Bilanz*, 11.

120   W. Murray & A. R. Millett, *A War to Be Won*, 140. Writes historian Klaus-Juergen Mueller, "How many political commissars and other 'politically suspected' POWs were executed by combat units or other units of the regular army, immediately after their capture or in the DULAGs (POW transit camp) cannot be ascertained correctly … For good reasons, one may assume that the application of the [criminal] directives varied widely, but available sources suggest that generally they were 'correctly' executed by the great majority of army units, at least during the first six months of the campaign." K.-J. Mueller, "*The Brutalization of Warfare, Nazi Crimes and the Wehrmacht*," in: *Barbarossa. The Axis and the Allies*, J. Erickson & D. Dilks (eds.), 230-31.

121   M. Stein, *Generalfeldmarschall Walter Model*, 252-53.

122   W. Murray & A. R. Millett, *A War to Be Won*, 140-41.

123   R. A. Hart, *Guderian*, 71. Whether or not Bock eventually transmitted the Commissar Order down his chain of command, as he was supposed to do, it is virtually certain that all of the top field commanders of Army Group Center (division and up) became privy to the order before the beginning of the Russian campaign.

124   K.-J. Mueller, "*The Brutalization of Warfare, Nazi Crimes and the Wehrmacht*," in: *Barbarossa. The Axis and the Allies*, J. Erickson & D. Dilks (eds.), 231. General von Arnim's position was an ironic one, given the enthusiastic backing of the Commissar Order by Lemelsen, his corps commander.

125   K.-R. Woche, *Zwischen Pflicht und Gewissen*, 127.

126   K.-J. Mueller, "*The Brutalization of Warfare, Nazi Crimes and the Wehrmacht*," in: *Barbarossa. The Axis and the Allies*, J. Erickson & D. Dilks (eds.), 231.

127   K.-R. Woche, *Zwischen Pflicht und Gewissen*, 127-28; M Stein, *Generalfeldmarschall Walter Model*, 253.

128   G. Roberts, *Stalin's Wars*, 85.

129   F. W. Seidler, *Verbrechen an der Wehrmacht*, 20.

130   The *Ostheer* had begun the Russian campaign with about 3.1 million soldiers, including first echelon forces and reserves. By the end of January 1942, the armies in the east had received some 500,000 replacements (including returning sick and wounded). Between February and April 1942, several hundred thousand additional replacements arrived (including 124,000 in February and 138,000 in March 1942), as well as new units transferred from Germany and other theaters of war. *DRZW*, Bd. 4, *Der Angriff auf die Sowjetunion*, 650; B. Mueller-Hillebrand, *Das Heer*, Bd. III, *Anlage 26*, "*Ab- und Zugaenge an Personal im Winter 1941/42 an der Ostfront*," 206.

131   BA-MA RH 27-3/167, quoted in: M. Stein, *Generalfeldmarschall Walter Model*, 253.

132   Ibid., 253-54.

133   BA-MA RH 19 IV/226, cited in: M. Stein, *Generalfeldmarschall Walter Model*, 254. Model became commander of 41 Panzer Corps on 26 October 1941; he was appointed C-in-C of Ninth Army on 16 January 1942. H. Grossmann, *Rshew. Eckpfeiler der Ostfront*, 130

134   J. Loeffler, *Walther von Brauchitsch*, 234; L. Yahil, *The Holocaust*, 249.

135   M. Broszat, et al., *Anatomie des SS-Staates*, Bd. 2, 145.

136   In addition to heading the Security Police, Heydrich was chief of the Reich Security Main Office (*Reichssicherheitshauptamt*, or RSHA). The RSHA included the SD, Gestapo and the Kripo (*Kriminalpolizei*), meaning that Heydrich was in complete control of Germany's secret police apparatus. In July 1941, Heydrich received orders from Goering to find a "total solution of the Jewish question." I.C.B. Dear (ed.), *The Oxford Companion to World War II*, 415.

137   L. Yahil, *The Holocaust*, 249.

138   M. Broszat, et al., *Anatomie des SS-Staates*, Bd. 2, 297.

139   J. Huerter, *Hitlers Heerfuehrer*, 549. According to Marcel Stein, each of the *Einsatzgruppen* was made up of 660 men. M. Stein, *Generalfeldmarschall Walter Model*, 237.

140   M. Stein, *Generalfeldmarschall Walter Model*, 241; Internet site at: http://www.jewishvirtuallibrary.org; A. J. Muñoz & O. V. Romanko, *Hitler's White Russians*, 91.

141   G. Roberts, *Stalin's Wars*, 67.

142   L. Yahil, *The Holocaust*, 255-56; M. Broszat, et al., *Anatomie des SS-Staates*, Bd. 2, 162.

143   R. A. Hart, *Guderian*, 72.

144   R. A. Hart, *Guderian*, 72; M. Stein, *Generalfeldmarschall Walter Model*, 242.

145   D. Pohl, "*Brutale Praxis*," in: *Der 2. Weltkrieg*, S. Burgdorff & K. Wiegrefe (Hg.), 139-40; H. Heer, "*Killing Fields. The Wehrmacht and the Holocaust in Belorussia, 1941-42*," in: *War of Extermination*, H. Heer & K. Naumann (eds.), 57-58.

146   J. Huerter, *Hitlers Heerfuehrer*, 561.

147   The Secret Field Police were attached to the armies, panzer groups, and security divisions behind the front: "According to agreements made between the SD and Army prior to the start of the Russian campaign, the role of the GFP units was only counterintelligence. [However], this limited role was soon expanded to include the elimination of anyone deemed a threat to the Nazi state." A. J. Muñoz & O. V. Romanko, *Hitler's White Russians*, 98, 159-160.

148   M. Stein, *Generalfeldmarschall Walter Model*, 242. The situation map of the OKH Operations Branch shows 286 SD operating around and east of Minsk as of 11 July 1941. K.-J. Thies, *Der Ostfeldzug – Ein Lageatlas*, "Lage am 11.7.1941 abds., Heeresgruppe Mitte."

149   G. F. Nafziger, *German Order of Battle – Infantry*, 503.

150   H. Heer, "*Killing Fields. The Wehrmacht and the Holocaust in Belorussia, 1941-42*," in: *War of Extermination*, H. Heer & K. Naumann (eds.), 61.

151   M. Stein, *Generalfeldmarschall Walter Model*, 249.

152 J. Huerter, *Hitlers Heerfuehrer*, 553. The first killing action to cause widespread alarm among the staff of Army Group Center was another massacre at Borisov, in October 1941, resulting in the murder of some 7000 Jews by the SS and by Belorussian militia. This also took place in the vicinity of the army group's headquarters and, in effect, assaulted the collective conscience of some of the younger officers on Bock's staff (von Tresckow, von Schlabrendorff, Gersdorff, etc.), pushing them irrevocably into the German Resistance against Hitler. Ibid., 563.

153 Ibid., 564-65.

154 Ibid., 564-65.

155 Police battalions operating in the rear of Army Group Center in 1941 included: 32, 131, 307, 309, 316, 317, 322 Police Battalions, 11 Reserve Police Battalion and *Polizei Regiment Mitte* (3 battalions). In sum, it appears that no more than about a dozen police battalions were active behind the front of the army group during the first six months of the campaign. See, J. Huerter, *Hitlers Heerfuehrer*, 550-51; A. J. Muñoz & O. V. Romanko, *Hitler's White Russians*, 107-08, 123, 154, 158.

156 Hannes Heer, for example, is one influential German historian who, in recent years, has consistently sought to indict not only the *Wehrmacht* as an institution, but the majority of the ca. 17,000,000 soldiers who served in it. Heer's propensity for facile generalization is underscored by the following comments in his article (originally published in 1995) on the Army's support of the Holocaust in Belorussia: "But both confirm that when it came to murdering Jews, one could count on the *Wehrmacht*;" and, "Aside from the fact that the troops had no problem with the Holocaust, but rather, as shown, liked to take matters into their own hands. . ." See, H. Heer, *"Killing Fields. The Wehrmacht and the Holocaust in Belorussia, 1941-42,"* in: *War of Extermination*, H. Heer & K. Naumann (eds.), 55, 65.

157 Argues Christian Hartmann: "Was the struggle of the German occupier against the Soviet partisans criminal? In principle it was not. It is legal under international law for an army of occupation to defend itself against irregular fighters, and can also be legitimate militarily. In this case, however, [German] practices looked rather different." (C. Hartmann, *Unternehmen Barbarossa*, 69.) It should also be noted that partisans operated outside of international law, under the terms of Article 1 of the Hague Conventions of 1907; moreover, the execution of guerillas was legal, as were harsh measures against the civilian population, if the perpetrators could not be found and a town or village was suspected of protecting them. See, F. W. Seidler (Hg.), *Verbrechen der Wehrmacht*, 10.

158 K. Gerbet (ed.), *GFM Fedor von Bock, The War Diary*, 217-18.

159 T. C. Richter, *"Die Wehrmacht und der Partisanenkrieg in den besetzten Gebieten der Sowjetunion,"* in: *Die Wehrmacht. Mythos und Realitaet*, R.-D. Mueller & H.-E. Volkmann (Hg.), 839-40.

160 Ibid., 849, f.n. 85.

161 G. P. Megargee, *War of Annihilation*, 124. At the time, the security divisions of Army Group Center were supported by two regular infantry divisions and the SS Cavalry Brigade, along with SS and police units and local auxiliaries. Yet this was hardly enough.

162 G. F. Nafziger, *German Order of Battle – Infantry*, 499, 503-4, 506. Each of the security divisions also possessed a regional defense regiment (*Landesschuetzen Regiment*), outfitted primarily with large numbers of light machine guns. These formations also consisted of older, poorly trained men. For example, *Landesschuetzbataillon* 738, which belonged to the rear-area formation of Ninth Army, was made up of officers between 40 and 50 years of age. The average age of junior officers in the battalion was just under 40 (in front-line units the average age of junior combat officers rarely exceeded 30), while the battalion commander was almost 60 years of age. There were also a significant number of men in the battalion with physical disabilities. T. J. Schulte, *"Korueck 582,"* in: *War of Extermination. The German Military in World War II*, H. Heer & K. Naumann (eds.), 317.

163 T. C. Richter, *"Die Wehrmacht und der Partisanenkrieg in den besetzten Gebieten der Sowjetunion,"* in: *Die Wehrmacht. Mythos und Realitaet*, R.-D. Mueller & H.-E. Volkmann (Hg.), 849. The commander of Rear Area, Army Group Center, Max von Schenckendorff, was born in 1875, and had retired from active service in 1930. Ibid., 849, f.n. 87.

164 Halder was referring to the rapid and deep advance of the panzer units, which had left hundreds of thousands of Red Army stragglers behind in the forests and swamps, where they threatened German lines of communication.

165 H.-A. Jacobsen (Hg.), *Generaloberst Halder Kriegstagebuch*, Bd. III, 32.

166 T. C. Richter, *"Die Wehrmacht und der Partisanenkrieg in den besetzten Gebieten der Sowjetunion,"* in: *Die Wehrmacht. Mythos und Realitaet*, R.-D. Mueller & H.-E. Volkmann (Hg.), 843.

167 *OKW/WFSt/Abt.1 Nr. 441148/41 g. Kdos. Chefs., an Chef Heeresruestung und Befehlshaber des Ersatzheeres, 5.7.1941, gez. Keitel*, quoted in: T. C. Richter, *"Die Wehrmacht und der Partisanenkrieg in den besetzten Gebieten der Sowjetunion,"* in: *Die Wehrmacht. Mythos und Realitaet*, R.-D. Mueller & H.-E. Volkmann (Hg.), 843.

168 Quoted in: C. Hartmann, *Unternehmen Barbarossa*, 70.

169 W. Hubatsch (Hg.), *Hitlers Weisungen fuer die Kriegfuehrung*, 144.

170 C. Hartmann, *Unternehmen Barbarossa*, 71.

171 E. F. Ziemke, *Stalingrad to Berlin*, 103. To this day, the Soviet partisan movement of World War II remains mired in mythology. After the war, greatly exaggerated claims as to its effectiveness were made by Soviet authorities; moreover, controversy has long existed among western historians as to the efficacy of the Soviet partisans.

172 U. Klussmann, *"Gegenwelt im Wald,"* in: *Der 2. Weltkrieg*, S. Burgdorff & K. Wiegrefe (Hg.), 134. According to Klussmann, Red Army stragglers provided the basis for the partisan units established in the summer of 1941.

173 A. J. Muñoz & O. V. Romanko, *Hitler's White Russians*, 18, 139-40. These authors also cite the figure of 12,000 for the number of Soviet partisans in Belorussia in August 1941.

174 Ibid., 140. Of these weapons, 750 grenades, 1125 rifles, all 133 machine guns, 124 machine pistols, and all three of the artillery pieces were captured from the Germans. The remainder was supplied by the concerned Soviet authorities.

175 Ibid., 140.

176 Ibid., 140.

177 Ibid., 162. In the fall of 1941, following the great encirclement battles of Viaz'ma and Briansk, partisan groupings also formed in the vast forest belts in these regions.

178 H. Heer, "*The Logic of the War of Extermination. The Wehrmacht and the Anti-Partisan War*," in: *War of Extermination. The German Military in World War II*, H. Heer & K. Naumann (eds.), 95; L. D. Grenkevich, *The Soviet Partisan Movement, 1941-1944*, 159.

179 H. Heer, "*The Logic of the War of Extermination. The Wehrmacht and the Anti-Partisan War*," in: *War of Extermination. The German Military in World War II*, H. Heer & K. Naumann (eds.),103.

180 *SS-Kav.Brig. Abschlussmeldung, 18.9.41*, quoted in: H. Heer, "*The Logic of the War of Extermination. The Wehrmacht and the Anti-Partisan War*," in: *War of Extermination. The German Military in World War II*, H. Heer & K. Naumann (eds.), 104. For a detailed and graphic account of the actions of the SS Cavalry Brigade's 2 Cavalry Regiment in the Pripiat' Marshes see, M. Cueppers, *Wegbereiter der Shoah*, 151-65.

181 Pinsk, a regional trade center with some 40,000 inhabitants, was the largest town in the region; it included a Jewish community rich in tradition. M. Cueppers, *Wegbereiter der Shoah*, 152.

182 A statement made by one of the participants in the massacre. R. B. Birn, "*Two Kinds of Reality. Case Studies on Anti-Partisan Warfare during the Eastern Campaign*," in: *From Peace to War*, B. Wegner (ed.), 279.

183 Ibid., 279-80. The singing was most likely of the "Shema Israel."

184 *Chef des OKW WFSt/Abt. L (IV/Qu), Nr. 002060/41 g. Kdos, 16.9.1941, Betr.: Kommunistische Aufstandsbewegung in den besetzten Gebieten*, in: P. E. Schramm (Hg.), *Kriegstagebuch des OKW*, Bd. I, 1068-69.

185 T. P. Mulligan, "*Reckoning the Cost of the People's War: The German Experience in the Central USSR*," in: *Russian History/Histoire Russe*, 9, Pt. 1 (1982), 32.

186 T. P. Mulligan, "*Reckoning the Cost of the People's War: The German Experience in the Central USSR*," in: *Russian History/Histoire Russe*, 9, Pt. 1 (1982), 32. A more recent Soviet source, with access to Soviet archives, estimates the total number of partisans in Army Group Center's rear area alone, prior to the winter of 1941/42, at up to 900 "detachments and groups" numbering 40,000 fighters. These figures may well be accurate, if the author is including those many thousands of trapped Red Army soldiers who melted into the forests following the immense encirclement battles of Viaz'ma and Briansk (on the approaches to Moscow in the fall of 1941) and ended up in partisan units. L. D. Grenkevich, *The Soviet Partisan Movement, 1941-1944*, 168.

187 U. Klussmann, "*Gegenwelt im Wald*," in: *Der 2. Weltkrieg*, S. Burgdorff & K. Wiegrefe (Hg.), 134; A. J. Muñoz & O. V. Romanko, *Hitler's White Russians*, 18, f.n. 18. Before the start of the Soviet summer offensive against Army Group Center on 22 June 1944, the now massive network of partisan groups, on the night of 19/20 June, set off at least 10,500 explosive charges on railroads, bridges, and other lines of communication in German rear areas, interrupting the army group's lines of supply for days. It was the greatest sabotage action of the Second World War. T. C. Richter, "*Die Wehrmacht und der Partisanenkrieg in den besetzten Gebieten der Sowjetunion*," in: *Die Wehrmacht. Mythos und Realitaet*, R.-D. Mueller & H.-E. Volkmann (Hg.), 837.

188 A. Hillgruber, "*Die weltpolitischen Entscheidungen vom 22. Juni 1941 bis 11. Dezember 1941*," in: *Der Zweite Weltkrieg 1939-1945*, A. Hillgruber, 79.

189 "The dearest hope of [the Russian] peasants," writes Catherine Merridale, "was for an end to Soviet power. In September 1941, though, they learned that the Germans had ordered that the collective farms should stay. Like the prewar Soviet authorities, the conquerors cared only for the ease with which the peasants' grain could be collected and shipped off. It was an irreversible mistake." C. Merridale, *Ivan's War*, 133-34.

190 BA-MA N 813, *Tagebuch* Muenchhausen, Aug. 41.

191 H. C. Verton, *In the Fire of the Eastern Front*, 111.

192 S. Hart, et al., *The German Soldier*, 133.

193 M. Stein, *Generalfeldmarschall Walter Model*, 141-42, f.n. 485. In his classic, albeit suspect, memoir of the eastern front, Guy Sajer maintained that German soldiers captured by the partisans had their faces smashed open with axes, so that the gold teeth could be pulled out; wounded men were tied with their heads inside the gaping entrails of dead comrades; other men had their genitals amputated. The authenticity of Sajer's account, however, is disputed by some historians, who, due to certain errors of fact, question if Sajer actually fought with the elite *Grossdeutschland* Division, as he said he did. G. Sajer, *The Forgotten Soldier*, 373.

194 S. Hart, et al., *The German Soldier*, 133. Gelb actually means yellow, but it was most likely as close to the word "Gold" the non-German speaking partisans could come.

195 *GSWW*, Vol. IV, 668.

196 G. F. Nafziger, *German Order of Battle – Infantry*, 522; K. E. Bonn, et al., *Slaughterhouse. The Encyclopedia of the Eastern Front*, 245; K.-J. Thies, *Der Ostfeldzug – Ein Lageatlas*, "Lage am 29.9.1941 abds., Heeresgruppe Mitte."

197 G. F. Nafziger, *German Order of Battle – Infantry*, 365-66; K. E. Bonn, et al., *Slaughterhouse. The Encyclopedia of the Eastern Front*, 255.

198   T. J. Schulte, "*Korueck 582*," in: *War of Extermination. The German Military in World War II*, H. Heer & K. Naumann (eds.), 315.

199   *GSWW*, Vol. IV, 583.

200   Ibid., 583.

201   A. Philippi & F. Heim, *Der Feldzug gegen Sowjetrussland*, 52.

202   G. F. Nafziger, *German Order of Battle – Infantry*, 238.

203   C. Hartmann, "*Wie verbrecherisch war die Wehrmacht?*," in: *Verbrechen der Wehrmacht*, C. Hartmann, et. al. (Hg.), 75. Argues Hartmann, "The majority [of the division's soldiers] would hardly have come into contact with the phenomenon of the partisan war [by December 1941]."

204   Ibid., 70.

205   A strong supporter of Hitler, Reemtsma senior had, by 1943, acquired what amounted to a virtual monopoly on the sale of cigarettes to the *Wehrmacht*. He also provided Goering with generous donations for the construction of Carinhall, Goering's opulent private estate. F. W. Seidler (Hg.), *Verbrechen der Wehrmacht*, 13.

206   Ibid., 9.

207   Internet site at: http://www.verbrechen-der-wehrmacht.de; "*Die neue Wehrmachtsausstellung*," internet site at: http://www.stern.de.

208   C. Hartmann, "*Verbrecherischer Krieg – verbrecherische Wehrmacht?*," in: *Vierteljahrshefte fuer Zeitgeschichte*, Sonderdruck, Heft 1/2004, 74, f.n. 416.

209   B. Musial, "*Bilder einer Ausstellung*," in: *Vierteljahrshefte fuer Zeitgeschichte*, 4. Heft, Oktober 1999, 563-64.

210   Ibid., 589.

211   According to Heinz Magenheimer, the organizers of the *Wehrmachtsausstellung* often accepted uncritically charges made during the Soviet show trials (*Schauprozessen*) against soldiers of the *Wehrmacht*. H. Magenheimer, *Moskau 1941*, 7.

212   Internet site at: http://www.verbrechen-der-wehrmacht.de; internet site at: http://en.wikipedia.org. For additional criticism of the exhibit see, F. W. Seidler (Hg.), *Verbrechen der Wehrmacht*, 8-14. As Seidler observes: "The attacks on the *Wehrmacht*, which from 1945 to 1990 occurred only sporadically and had to do with individuals, escalated into attacks [on the *Wehrmacht* as a whole] following the reunification of Germany." Seidler also points out that, by the end of 1996, in an on-going process, more than 5100 former German soldiers had been formally rehabilitated (*rehabilitiert*) by the current Russian justice system because they had been unjustly convicted of war crimes, or other criminal acts, and sentenced to Soviet POW camps. Ibid., 8, 14.

213   C. Hartmann, "*Verbrecherischer Krieg – verbrecherische Wehrmacht?*," in: *Vierteljahrshefte fuer Zeitgeschichte*, Sonderdruck, Heft 1/2004, 2.

214   "*Stichwort. Die neue Wehrmachtsausstellung*," internet site at: http://www.stern.de. (Note: After the commission had made its recommendations, the work of the exhibit team was supported by a second group, an advisory board (*Beirat*) of eleven scholars headed by German professor Hans Mommsen. The board, which first convened on 13 July 2001 in Hamburg, carefully vetted the content of the new exhibit to ensure accuracy. "*Neue Wehrmachtsausstellung zeigt Beteiligung der Truppen an Rasse- und Vernichtungskrieg*," internet site at: http://www.wissenschaft.de.; E-Mail, J. Foerster to C. Luther, 18 May 12.)

215   See, for example, C. Hartmann, *Wehrmacht im Ostkrieg. Front und militaerisches Hinterland 1941/42*, published in 2009. For my account of Hartmann's analysis, I have relied primarily on two of his articles: his long and detailed piece in the *Vierteljahrshefte fuer Zeitgeschichte*, cited often in this text; and on his much more abbreviated account, "*Wie verbrecherisch war die Wehrmacht?*," in: *Verbrechen der Wehrmacht*, C. Hartmann, et. al. (Hg.).

216   C. Hartmann, "*Verbrecherischer Krieg – verbrecherische Wehrmacht?*," in: *Vierteljahrshefte fuer Zeitgeschichte*, Sonderdruck, Heft 1/2004, 10.

217   By this time, the *Ostheer's* entire front line, from the Barents Sea to the Caucasus Mountains, stretched a distance of more than 3000 kilometers, while the main front of Germany and her Axis allies, from the Gulf of Finland west of Leningrad to the Caucasus, was just over 2000 kilometers in length. D. M. Glantz, *The Soviet-German War 1941-1945: Myths and Realities*, 5-6.

218   C. Hartmann, "*Verbrecherischer Krieg – verbrecherische Wehrmacht?*," in: *Vierteljahrshefte fuer Zeitgeschichte*, Sonderdruck, Heft 1/2004, 7.

219   C. Hartmann, "*Wie verbrecherisch war die Wehrmacht?*," in: *Verbrechen der Wehrmacht*, C. Hartmann, et. al. (Hg.), 71-72.

220   C. Hartmann, "*Verbrecherischer Krieg – verbrecherische Wehrmacht?*," in: *Vierteljahrshefte fuer Zeitgeschichte*, Sonderdruck, Heft 1/2004, 9.

221   Ibid., 8.

222   Ibid., 71.

223   Ibid., 71.

224   C. Hartmann, "*Wie verbrecherisch war die Wehrmacht?*," in: *Verbrechen der Wehrmacht*, C. Hartmann, et. al. (Hg.), 76.

225   Ibid., 72.

226   The formations studied by Hartmann all belonged to Army Group Center: the elite 4 Panzer Division, 45 Infantry Division, 296 Infantry Division, 221 Security Division, and *Korueck* 580 (the latter formation initially assigned to Fourth Army).

227   C. Luther, book review of C. Hartmann's *Wehrmacht im Ostkrieg. Front und militaerisches Hinterland 1941/42*, in: *The Journal of Military History*, Vol. 74, No. 1, Jan 10, 285-86.

228 A. M. de Zayas, *The Wehrmacht War Crimes Bureau*, xiv.

229 A. M. de Zayas, *The Wehrmacht War Crimes Bureau*, xiv, 13-14; see also, F. W. Seidler (Hg.), *Verbrechen der Wehrmacht*, 45-48.

230 German historian Franz W. Seidler's 1997 publication documenting over 300 separate Soviet war crimes, while gleaned from the records of the War Crimes Bureau, does not amount to a study of the Bureau itself. See, F. W. Seidler (Hg.), *Verbrechen der Wehrmacht*.

231 In April 1945, the surviving records of the Bureau were seized by the U.S. Army's records collection team and, eventually, dispatched to Washington D.C., where they remained for many years as classified documents. In the mid-1960s, the documents were declassified, put on microfilm, and made available to researchers at the Modern Military Branch of the U.S. National Archives. In 1968/69, the original documents (or, according to Franz Seidler, at least a portion of them) were returned to West Germany and deposited in the German Federal Military Archives in Freiburg (*Bundesarchiv-Militaerarchiv*, or BA-MA), where they were "provisionally bound" into 226 volumes (100 to 500 pages each) addressing some 8000 cases. The BA-MA placed no restrictions on their use. A. M. de Zayas, *The Wehrmacht War Crimes Bureau*, xiii-xiv; F. W. Seidler (Hg.), *Verbrechen der Wehrmacht*, 48, 55.

232 A. M. de Zayas, *The Wehrmacht War Crimes Bureau*, xvi-xvii.

233 Ibid., xvii.

234 BA-MA RW 2/v. 145, 3.

235 H. Haape, *Moscow Tram Stop*, 9.

236 Ibid., 10.

237 Ogfr. E. G. Schaefer, PK 612 (mot.), "*Der Arzt mit dem Deutschen Kreuz,*" 19.2.1943; "*Besonders ausgezeichnet hat sich Oberarzt Dr. Haape,*" n.d. (both in this author's possession as: *Nachlass Haape*). A typical evaluation of Haape's performance as a military doctor and soldier was that of his regimental commander in October 1942: "As a medical officer, soldier, and a man equally extraordinary [*gleich hervorragend*]. Rich in experience, practical in his thinking, independent, energetic and with his own ideas. Particularly dashing [*schneidig*] in the face of the enemy ... One could not wish for a better [military] doctor." "*Beurteilungen,*" in: *Nachlass* Haape.

238 H. Haape, *Moscow Tram Stop*, 10.

239 Unless otherwise indicated, this account of Haape's experiences on 22 June 1941 is derived from his war memoir, *Moscow Tram Stop*, 16-32.

240 Haape also recorded this tragic incident in his diary, stating only that six Russian "heavy bombers" were shot down, and that three men of the German artillery column "were immediately buried alive [by the impact of the burning Russian bomber] and completely carbonized [*verkohlten vollstaendig*], five others received the most severe burns." *Tagebuch* Haape, 23.6.41.

241 *Tagebuch* Haape, 22.6.41.

242 K.-R. Woche, *Zwischen Pflicht und Gewissen*, 203.

243 H. Hoth, *Panzer-Operationen*, 64.

244 *Tagebuch* Kummer, 14.7.41.

245 *Tagebuch* Kreuter, 17.7.41.

246 Intvw, Dr C. Luther with E.-M. Rhein, 8/9 Dec 06; Ltr, H. Schillke to C. Luther, 15 Mar 05; E. Wardin, "*Winterschlacht*" (unpublished memoir).

247 Ltr, H. Schillke to C. Luther, 15 Mar 05.

248 See, BA-MA RW 2/v. 145, 78-98; also, F. W. Seidler (Hg.), *Verbrechen an der Wehrmacht*, 279-327.

249 Of course, German ground and air forces were also guilty of attacking Soviet medical personnel, field hospitals, hospital trains, etc. However, from accounts by Haape and other German front doctors, it seems clear that such actions were not based on official policy. Germany was, after all, a signatory to both the Hague and Geneva Conventions, and Haape and other German military doctors did their best to abide by such protocols, as did many German soldiers.

250 F. W. Seidler (Hg.), *Verbrechen an der Wehrmacht*, 32. The Walther Pistol 38 was a 9mm, recoil-operated, semi-automatic pistol. *Handbook on German Military Forces*, U.S. War Department, March 1945, 309.

251 F. W. Seidler (Hg.), *Verbrechen an der Wehrmacht*, 35-43. Observes Seidler: "The hatred of the Soviet propagandists was characterized by a barbaric fury [*barbarischer Wildheit*]." Among the aspersions leveled at German soldiers by Soviet propagandists, such as Ilya Ehrenburg, were: "creatures," "thieves," "butchers," "mass murderers," "women killers," "criminals," "scoundrels," and "wild beasts."

252 S. Courtois, et al., *The Black Book of Communism. Crimes, Terror, Repression.* Harvard University Press, Cambridge, MA, 1999.

253 I. Kershaw, *Hitler 1936-45: Nemesis*, 647.

254 R. Hinze, *Ostfront Drama 1944*, 15.

255 See, F. W. Seidler (Hg.), *Verbrechen an der Wehrmacht*, 44; A. M. de Zayas, *The Wehrmacht War Crimes Bureau*, 305, f.n. 11; R. Traub, "*Versklavt und vernichtet,*" in: *Der Zweite Weltkrieg*, S. Burgdorff & K. Wiegrefe (Hg.), 169. According to official Soviet sources, however, only some 2.4 million Germans became POWs, of which 356,687 had died in captivity by 1956. A. Hilger, *Deutsche Kriegsgefangene in der Sowjetunion 1941-1956*, 71, 137.

256 A. M. de Zayas, *The Wehrmacht War Crimes Bureau*, 305, f.n. 11; F. W. Seidler (Hg.), *Verbrechen an der Wehrmacht*, 34; *GSWW*, Vol. IV, 914;

257 Between 22 June 1941 and 20 March 1945, 1.24 million German soldiers were listed as "missing in action." Many of these men, no doubt, were either killed upon capture, or perished before reaching the POW camps.

F. W. Seidler (Hg.), *Verbrechen an der Wehrmacht*, 44. "Often," states Chris Bellamy, "the [German] prisoners would be assembled and marched away from the front line areas, and were then shot 'en route.'" C. Bellamy, *Absolute War*, 29.

258   A. M. de Zayas, *The Wehrmacht War Crimes Bureau*, 165.

259   Ibid., 165.

260   A. Hilger, *Deutsche Kriegsgefangene in der Sowjetunion 1941-1956*, 57-62.

261   *GSWW*, Vol. IV, 914. For details on Soviet legal architecture pertaining to the handling of prisoners of war see, A. Hilger, *Deutsche Kriegsgefangene in der Sowjetunion 1941-1956*.

262   A. M. de Zayas, *The Wehrmacht War Crimes Bureau*, 169.

263   A. Hilger, *Deutsche Kriegsgefangene in der Sowjetunion 1941-1956*, 60.

264   A. Werth, *Russia at War*, 162-65.

265   C. Bellamy, *Absolute War*, 29.

266   A. M. de Zayas, *The Wehrmacht War Crimes Bureau*, 162.

267   Ibid., 64.

268   N. von Below, *At Hitler's Side*, 112.

269   A. M. de Zayas, *The Wehrmacht War Crimes Bureau*, 167-68.

270   J. Hoffmann, *Stalins Vernichtungskrieg 1941-1945*, 218. The "criminalization" of the German Army by Red Army propaganda organs began immediately after 22 June 1941. From the outset, the Germans were portrayed to Red Army soldiers as, *inter alia*, "fascist barbarians," "fascist beasts of prey," and "fascist reptiles." Ibid., 216.

271   BA-MA RW 2/v. 145, ca. 30.6.41.

272   Ibid., 27.-28.6.41.

273   Ibid., 28.6.41.

274   Ibid., 30.6.41.

275   Ibid., 30.6.41.

276   Ibid., ca. 15.8.41.

277   K.-R. Woche, *Zwischen Pflicht und Gewissen*, 128.

278   BA-MA MSg 1/1147: *Tagebuch* Lemelsen, 20.7.41.

279   W. Knecht, *Geschichte des Infanterie-Regiments 77*, 68-71; G. Barkhoff, *Ostfront 1941-1945, Ein Soldatenleben*, 22a.

280   Ltr, W. Vollmer to C. Luther, 1 Oct 06. This author, in the course of his research, asked dozens of German eastern front veterans for information and anecdotes pertaining to Red Army war crimes; several, however, responded with stories, or opinions, about the partisans, who, it seems, were often feared and hated more than the soldiers of the Red Army itself. As a veteran of 3 Panzer Division put it, "I still have a real reluctance to tell of the atrocities [*Abscheulichkeiten*] of the partisans. But there are plenty of books you can read to become fully informed about the horrific crimes they committed." Ltr, L. Bauer to C. Luther, 9 Nov 08.

281   Quoted in: F. W. Seidler (Hg.), *Verbrechen an der Wehrmacht*, 269.

282   G. Barkhoff, *Ostfront 1941-1945*, 17. *Ein Soldatenleben*, 18.

283   Ltr, H. Stockhoff to C. Luther, 12 Oct 07. In a field post letter dated 12 November 1941, Stockhoff also described the assault on Upjerwitschi, noting that "his best friend" in his rifle squad was killed in the attack. In the letter, however, he does not specifically mention the use of explosive bullets by the Russians. *Feldpost*, H. Stockhoff, 12.11.41.

284   Ltr, H. Stu[- - -] to C. Luther, 25 Oct 07. In a letter dated 16 February 1942, this soldier wrote: "At the moment, the Russians are shooting at us. I can hear hissing sounds of the bullets. The enemy is firing with explosive shells. That's a very dangerous thing." *Feldpost*, H. Stu[- - -], 16.2.42.

285   BA-MA RW 2/v. 145.

286   Ibid.

CHAPTER 10

Vormarsch II: The Encirclement Battle of Smolensk & Transition to Positional Warfare

(10 July – 5 August 1941)

"We have been speaking about a total victory … not simply of a battle won. Such a victory demands an enveloping attack or a battle with reversed fronts, either of which will always make the result decisive." (Carl von Clausewitz)[1]

"The material and moral consequences of any great battle are so far-reaching that they usually bring about a completely different situation, a new foundation for new measures. Everything depends on correctly grasping the situation of the moment." (The Elder Field Marshal von Moltke)[2]

"Guderian's attack has started and come through … the overall enemy situation indicates that hastily gathered elements are all the enemy can put up against us … Under these circumstances it is clear that the front, which also has no more reserves left, cannot hold much longer … The foe is making an effort to hold, but he is cracking in the attempt." (Chief of the Army General Staff Halder, 11 July 1941)[3]

"On all fronts the amount of enemy materiel and powers of resistance of the enemy have been underestimated. Fuehrer is very nervous due to the delay." (Karl-Wilhelm Thilo, OKH Operations Branch, 25 July 1941)[4]

"You will have heard about the fighting around Smolensk on the radio. Those were my proud soldiers who achieved the breakthrough, the flag raised in victory. We are standing just outside Moscow, all units welded together into an iron chain, the like of which the world has never before seen. Only a short while still, and then that great event of world history will take place." (Uffz. E.M., 17 PD, 28 July 1941)[5]

"What I have thought a lot about is the following: has anybody ever been a hero and a victor without battling and overcoming enemies, hostilities, malice, suffering, adversity? No! Without struggle there is no pride. The more difficult the battle, the more difficult the victory, and the more dogged, constant, and tough, and, if need be, the bloodier the effort to achieve it, the more brilliant, richer, and precious the happiness and pride in having done so. That is in no way limited to victory by arms, it also applies to the battles in life." (Stabsarzt Hans Lierow, 6 ID, 5 August 1941)[6]

For Adolf Hitler and the German High Command, Operation *Barbarossa* had begun in "spectacular fashion."[7] By 10 July 1941, the *Ostheer*, its four powerful panzer groups on the point, had plunged hundreds of kilometers into the western Soviet Union. Army Group South, after fending off fierce counterattacks by several Soviet mechanized corps, had penetrated to a depth of 350 kilometers; its 1 Panzer Group had punched through the

Stalin Line on the pre-1939 Soviet border, and, by 12 July, stood with two panzer divisions on the Irpen River, on the approaches to Kiev.[8] Moving even more rapidly, Army Group North had advanced as far as 500 kilometers, occupying Lithuania, Latvia, and most of Estonia in the process; on 10 July, its 4 Panzer Group began what was hoped to be the final drive on Leningrad and, within days, the panzer group's spearheads had built bridgeheads across the lower Luga River, barely 100 kilometers from the outskirts of the city.[9] In the middle of the front, the armies and panzer groups of Army Group Center had managed the most spectacular progress, thrusting up to 600 kilometers into Soviet Russia, swallowing up most of Belorussia, and reaching the Western Dvina and Dnepr Rivers.[10]

While carving out these territorial gains, the victorious *Wehrmacht* had smashed the Red Army's first strategic echelon. At least 28 Soviet divisions were totally destroyed, with a further 70 divisions losing more than half of their personnel, weapons, and equipment.[11] The operationally and tactically superior German forces had inflicted at least 747,870 casualties on the enemy (a figure equal to one sixth of the Red Army's pre-war strength) and removed 10,180 tanks and 3995 aircraft from the Red Army order of battle. "By any measure," avers David Glantz, the German victory was both "unprecedented and astounding."[12]

Over the next several days, on the central axis of the German advance, the tanks and mobile infantry of panzer generals Hoth and Guderian crushed the Red Army defenses along the Dvina-Dnepr River lines (Soviet second echelon forces) and raced eastward as far as 180 kilometers north and south of Smolensk. By 16 July, most of Smolensk was in German hands, while large Soviet forces were trapped in pockets north and west of the city.[13] This second major encirclement battle – which, the Germans hoped, would be decisive – had, by early August 1941, culminated in the destruction of several additional Soviet armies, as several hundred thousand more Red Army troops joined the POW pens of Army Group Center.

Euphoric over their stunning successes, Hitler and his leading military advisors were, by mid-July 1941, convinced the eastern campaign was already won. Certainly, Hitler's decision-making at the time reflects this viewpoint. On 14 July 1941, OKW issued a supplement to "Fuehrer Directive" No. 32 ("Preparations for the Period after *Barbarossa*," 11 June 1941), calling for a major reduction in the size of the Army (although the panzer forces were to be significantly increased) and a reorientation of the armaments program toward the *Luftwaffe* and the navy.[14] The more powerful air and naval forces resulting from this shift in priorities were to be used initially for direct attacks on England, upon its shipping in the Atlantic, and to threaten the British position in the Middle East. "This had been the intention," notes historian Gerhard L. Weinberg, "before the attack on Russia was launched; now seemed to be the time to begin implementing the projects designed to follow victory in the east."[15]

Among the projects contemplated by German military planners in the first flush of impending victory over the Soviet Union were: a.) a vast pincer movement through the Caucasus, and via Libya and Egypt, into the Middle East as far as Iran and Iraq, followed by the establishment of a base of operations in Afghanistan, from which to threaten India; b.) an advance through Spain and Gibraltar into Northwest Africa (Dakar), to build a bastion against America; and, c.) the capture of the Azores Islands in the North Atlantic, for use as an airbase from which launch long-range bomber's against America's eastern coastline. The objective of these and other initiatives, however fantastic, was to transform Hitler's continental European conflict into a "*Weltblitzkrieg*" against the Anglo-American block, resulting in final victory and Germany's attainment of uncontested global hegemony.[16]

On 15 July 1941, the OKH Operations Branch produced a memorandum that, *inter alia*, called for pulling most of the infantry divisions out of Russia beginning in early August, followed by the return of the first mechanized formations in September 1941. Only

56 divisions (34 infantry, 12 panzer, six motorized, and three mountain divisions, and one cavalry division) were to stay behind in the Soviet Union, to hold a line stretching from Astrakhan to Archangel and to conduct punitive raids into the Urals, including a potential panzer raid aimed at eliminating Soviet industry in the region. The OKH document also referred to an "*Operationsgruppe Kaukasus-Iran*," composed of two panzer, one motorized, and two mountain divisions – to be formed for a push into the Middle East.[17] In his personal diary on 15 July 1941, Captain Karl-Wilhelm Thilo (Operations Branch), no doubt addressing the same initiative, noted the planned assembly of an "*Operationsgruppe Ural*" (one panzer and one mountain corps) for a "thrust to Iraq."[18]

Hitler's overweening confidence was again on display on 21 July 1941, when he assured the Croatian Minister of Defense, Marshal Kvaternik, that the Soviet armies were largely destroyed, and that all serious resistance would cease within six weeks. When Kvaternik suggested that the Russians might then set up new armies beyond the Urals, Hitler could only laugh.[19] The "Fuehrer's" *Triumpfgefuehl* also explained his surprisingly candid remarks to Kvaternik about the ultimate fate he had in store for Europe's Jews. The Jews, so said Hitler, were "the scourge of humanity;" "if there were no more Jews in Europe, then the unity of the European states would no longer be disturbed." Ten days later, Air Marshal Goering, in Hitler's name, assigned SS-*Obergruppenfuehrer* Reinhard Heydrich the task of working out the preliminary measures to a "final solution" of the "Jewish question."[20]

If Hitler and the German High Command were not in doubt as to the outcome of the Russian campaign, at the battlefront, across the boundless forests, fields and steppe lands of western Russia, the mood was a more sober one. In a letter to his wife from Bobruisk, on 20 July 1941, General Heinrici, Commander, 43 Army Corps, offered a distinctly different perspective:

> The Russian is very strong and fights desperately, spurred on by his commissars. The forest battles are particularly bad. The Russian suddenly appears everywhere and shoots, ambushes columns, individual vehicles, dispatch riders, etc. The war here, at any rate, is very bad, and on top of that there are the huge road difficulties, the immense spaces, the endless forests, the difficulty of the language, etc. All campaigns up to now were child's play [*Kinderspiel*] compared to the current battles. The losses on our side are considerable, on the Russian side, very, very big.[21]

Two days later he amplified these remarks:

> No campaign to date can be compared to the current one ... Our people [are] physically utterly exhausted. Yesterday I found the drivers of the horse teams sleeping like the dead, lying in front of their horses. The immense marches, the scandalous state of the roads, of which no one in Germany can have even the slightest notion, the high nervous tension – not just because of the constantly changing situations, but also because of the danger to everyone of being ambushed – those are all things that are more than exhausting and that have not existed in a similar way in any other campaign so far. Moreover, not a soul knows how much longer this campaign will last. Because for the time being, there is no foreseeable end, despite all the successes achieved so far. Hopefully, one fine day Russian resistance will collapse, because the situations created here are no walk in the park for the Russian. Quite the contrary, he finds himself in a nasty situation ... But ... there is no sense that, in general, the Russian will to resist has been broken or that the nation wants to oust its Bolshevist leaders. For the time being, we get

the impression that the war will continue from somewhere in the depths of this never ending country, even if Moscow were to be occupied.[22]

The truth was, in fact, just as Hitler and his advisors were turning away from Russia to contemplate the conquest of the world, Soviet resistance was palpably stiffening, the German advance beginning to falter. Indeed, during the final two weeks of July 1941, the pace of the *Vormarsch* perceptively slowed along most of the eastern front.[23] Struggling through difficult terrain, Army Group North saw its advance toward Leningrad seriously hampered by the inexorable dispersal of its strength and resurgent Russian resistance. Army Group South, despite bottling up and destroying more than 20 Red Army divisions (and taking over 100,000 prisoners) at Uman in early August,[24] had failed to trap and annihilate the bulk of Soviet forces in the western Ukraine, and would not advance on Kiev for several more weeks. Army Group Center, during the third week of July, was surprised by yet another – a third – echelon of Soviet forces which, while much weaker than the previous two, "engaged the advancing German forces when they were most vulnerable, specifically, before the infantry caught up with the advancing panzer and motorized troops."[25] By late July, Bock's army group, its forward progress now stymied by mounting Soviet pressure across its entire front,[26] was still struggling to reduce the pocket at Smolensk, while beset by growing logistical problems and mounting casualties. As a result, the OKH ordered a halt to Army Group Center's advance on 30 July, to allow it to rest and refit. All told, the month of July 1941 cost the Germans 63,000 dead, more than any month in the Russian campaign until the fighting at Stalingrad in December 1942 and January 1943.[27]

As German operations in the east suddenly, albeit unexpectedly, started to sputter, Hitler and his chief advisors began to grow anxious and impatient about the direction of the campaign, which was no longer proceeding according to script. As a result, they now began to question basic assumptions they had made about the Red Army – its resources, fighting qualities, and regenerative powers. In this context, the letters of Colonel Adolf Heusinger (Chief, OKH Operations Branch) to his wife are instructive. As noted, in the opening days of the campaign, Heusinger had exulted over "fabulous" victories, and expressed his hope for a "rapid end to the campaign" (25 June); the battlefield successes, he confided, were "unimaginable," a fact he attributed to the "towering superiority" of German leadership over that of the Red Army (27 June). Everything was proceeding according to plan.[28]

By mid-July 1941, however, Heusinger was becoming concerned by the seemingly inexhaustible manpower of the Red Army. Shortly thereafter (22 July), he noted nervousness and agitation on the part of his superiors (e.g., Halder), as they battled "constant interference from the highest authority" (i.e., Hitler) and began to remonstrate with the "Fuehrer" over the future direction of the campaign. On 25 July, he was convinced that the moment had almost come, "when the Russians could no longer go on;" untrained men were being hurled into the battle as "sheer cannon fodder," and shot down by "thousands upon thousands," which could only go on for so long. Yet a few days later, Heusinger struck a decidedly different tone, admitting that an end to the war was "presently not in sight." On 31 July, he expressed the hope that "perhaps the next few weeks will provide us with a clear picture." He was, he told his wife, toiling harder than he "ever had in the entire war," for it was the "first time that a state had not directly collapsed" upon being attacked. Worst of all, he had to contend with the frayed nerves of his superiors. Halder, in particular, trying to get by on just four hours of sleep a night, was utterly worn out (*kaput*). As for Heusinger, he remained flummoxed by the unlimited reserves available to the enemy.[29]

Given that the mighty initial blows of Germany's eastern blitzkrieg had – against all expectations – failed to bring the Red Army and the Soviet political system to its knees, it is not surprising that the first strategic controversy of the campaign arose in mid-July 1941, highlighting disagreements between Hitler and his generals which had their origins in the pre-*Barbarossa* planning phase (see, Chapter 1, Section 1.6, "Military Preparations for the Russian Campaign (July – December 1940)"). Now deep inside Russia, but with victory still eluding their grasp, the German dictator and key military planners were at odds over which strategic path provided the way to final victory. The "Fuehrer," characteristically commingling political and economic factors with military ones, advocated (as he had done so consistently) seeking the decision on the flanks – in the north, by driving through the Baltic to Leningrad, and linking up with the Finns; in the south, by seizing the Ukraine, Donbas, and eventually, the Caucasus and its oil. Conversely, the capture of Moscow was still of secondary concern to Hitler. The Army General Staff, led by Brauchitsch and Halder – with the support of Bock, Guderian, and other front line generals – remained convinced that only the capture of Moscow, the political nerve center of the Soviet Union, as well as a major rail and industrial hub, would effectuate collapse. A direct advance on Moscow, they posited, was also to best way to annihilate what remained of the Red Army, which would be forced to commit most of its surviving resources to protect its capital.

The debate dragged on for weeks, Hitler issuing forth a flurry of, in part, contradictory directives from his dismal East Prussian compound, and not rendering a final decision until late August 1941. In the meantime, Army Group Center had hunkered down in positional warfare, while conducting several secondary operations along its southern flank. This was all in the future, however, on 10 July 1941, when Guderian's panzers sought to break out across the Dnepr River barrier and regain their operational freedom to the east – toward Moscow.

10.1: Guderian & Hoth Shatter Soviet River Line Defenses

10.1.1: 2 Panzer Group

At the start of July 1941, the initial probing operations of Guderian's 2 Panzer Group at and along the approaches to the Dnepr River had met with vigorous and effective Soviet opposition. Particularly the failure of 24 Panzer Corps at Rogachev – the fragile bridgehead of Model's 3 Panzer Division was abandoned on 7 July – had convinced Guderian of the need to regroup his forces and shift the *Schwerpunkt* of his efforts to breach the Red Army's river line defenses. By the evening of 9 July, with his three panzer corps settling into their assembly areas, he was poised to begin a second attempt. Because time was short – the approach of Soviet reinforcements had been reported by German aerial reconnaissance, and there was a "heavy enemy concentration" about Gomel – Guderian opted to conduct this "decisive" operation without waiting for the arrival of the infantry corps, which despite exhausting forced marches were still far behind the forward edge of battle.[30]

Guderian's intended river crossing was part of a larger operational plan devised by Halder[31] and approved by Hitler on 8 July 1941.[32] In an ambitious double envelopment spearheaded by 2 and 3 Panzer Groups – with Hoth forming the left, and Guderian the right wing – Army Group Center was to capture the strategically vital Vitebsk – Orsha – Smolensk triangle (i.e., the "Smolensk gate"), while encircling and annihilating the bulk of the remaining Soviet forces west of Moscow. With the enemy around Smolensk thus "finished off," "Hitler, and at this point presumably also Halder, assumed that ... they would be able to simply 'take over' the area all the way to the upper Volga without serious fighting."[33] Although Halder foresaw a difficult struggle with strong Soviet reserves, he was unaware that the Soviet High Command was hastening to assemble five fresh armies behind the Western Dvina and Dnepr river barriers to defend the area around Smolensk. The appearance of these armies would come as a major shock to the Germans, because "according to the assumptions of Plan *Barbarossa*, this was not supposed to occur."[34]

On 9 July, however, Timoshenko's Western Front forces were "fragmented at best,"[35] enabling Guderian to assemble his attacking forces at critical points for the crossing, which he planned to carry out in staggered fashion on 10/11 July 1941. Justifiably concerned about the condition of his mobile units, which had marched and fought without respite for 16 days, he "deliberately sacrificed the principle of concentration by attacking on two successive days without any main effort by either his panzer group or his subordinate [panzer] corps."[36] Guderian's ultimate objective was the narrow land bridge between El'nia on the Desna River and Dorogobuzh on the Dnepr, which offered the most direct route to Moscow by way of Viaz'ma and Mozhaisk. Resources available to Guderian included some 450 operational panzers[37] and the concentrated air power of Kesselring's 2 Air Fleet.

With the heavy howitzers and long-range artillery shepherded into position, and the tanks hunkered down in their staging areas, 2 Panzer Group's thrust across the Dnepr finally got underway at dawn on 10 July 1941. The assault groups of 4 Panzer Division and 10 Motorized Infantry Division (24 Panzer Corps) punched across the river at and north of Stary Bychov,[38] located some 40 kilometers south of Mogilev, supported by *Stukas* and the fighters of Moelders' 51 Fighter Wing. An officer in 4 Panzer Division described the beginning of the attack that morning:

10 July – 0500 Hours:
The artillery was firing with everything it had. A unique hissing emerged from the woods behind us. We threw ourselves flat on the ground. A howling – growing first stronger and then receding – went on for several minutes and deafened out all of the other sounds of war. Bundled tails of flame and smoke headed across the river. For the first time, we experienced the employment of a new weapon, the *Nebelwerfer*, which was also referred to as the *Do* gun. The rockets detonated on the far side among the enemy positions with a dull crash. Black mushroom clouds climbed skyward from the earth.

One wave of bombers after the other headed eastward. The Russian anti-aircraft guns bellowed in response. Bands of *Stukas* split apart above our heads and tipped over individually. They worked over the enemy field positions and the enemy batteries. The engineers ran at double time down to the riverbanks and threw their assault boats and pontoons into the tepid waters of the Dnepr. It was probably about 100 meters wide in this area.[39] The motors were turned on; the rudders heaved into position. Up to that point, not a rifle round had been fired.[40]

The combat engineers worked feverishly to anchor the pontoons in the river; within an hour, a footbridge was in place, which the first riflemen used to feel their way across. Ferries were built out of larger pontoons, and soon the first anti-tank and infantry guns had made it to the far bank of the river. By the time Russian artillery began to register on the crossing point, the first assault detachments were already disappearing into the woods beyond the river. After four hours of fighting, the troops of Langermann's 4 PD and Loeper's 10 ID (mot.) were in possession of a sizeable bridgehead.[41] The operation had gone off without a hitch.[42] By evening, the lead elements of Geyr's 24 Panzer Corps had pushed several kilometers beyond the Dnepr and cut the road leading from Mogilev to Gomel.[43]

The next day (11 July), the Soviet Dnepr line was punctured in two more places, this time between Orsha and Mogilev – at Kopys by 47 Panzer Corps, and at Shklov by 46 Panzer Corps.[44] At 6.10 in the morning, in "beautiful sunshine," Guderian departed his command post – now at Tolochino, less than 50 kilometers west of Orsha, and the site of Napoleon's headquarters in 1812 – and headed for Kopys to observe the crossing by Boltenstern's 29 Motorized Infantry Division; accompanying him was General Efisio

Marras, the Italian military attaché, who had arrived at Guderian's CP the night before:

> In view of the dense clouds of dust put up by our advancing columns the drive along the river bank was most unpleasant. This dust, endured now for weeks on end, was equally hard on men, weapons, and engines. In particular the cylinders of the tanks became so clogged that their efficiency was considerably affected. At the headquarters of the 29 Motorized Infantry Division, near Kopys, I found both the corps and divisional commanders and was briefed on the situation. Regiments 15 and 71 were already over the river and had reached the edge of the woods east of Kopys; we watched them advance against two enemy divisions … The enemy was laying down weak harassing fire on the area around the divisional headquarters, which was also mined. We had good observation of the advance of our infantry and of the bridge-building that was being carried on immediately beneath where we were standing.[45]

Following the departure of the Italian attaché, Guderian was ferried across the river in an assault boat in order to ensure the further progress of his forces. By mid-afternoon, Boltenstern's infantry, with the help of a battalion of assault guns, a Flak battery, Pak and pioneer units, had a bridgehead firmly in hand.[46] Meanwhile, efforts by General von Weber's 17 Panzer Division to get across the Dnepr directly south of Orsha had run into serious trouble. The division's assault troops had established a fragile foothold on the eastern bank in the face of withering enemy fire; seriously outgunned, the commander on the spot, *Oberst* Licht, decided to abandon the bridgehead and pull back across the river – an action strongly supported by Guderian.[47] In a history of 17 Panzer's 40 Rifle Regiment, self-published after the war by the regiment's veteran's organization, the abortive crossing attempt is recounted in detail:

> On the evening of the 10.7.[41], 2nd Battalion is standing in the area around Kochanovo, only about 30 km away from the Dnepr, the foremost battalion of *Kampfgruppe* Licht. During a rest stop in a patch of forest, 4 km east of Kochanovo, the regimental order comes in that the following day, so on 11.7., at dawn, the crossing of the Dnepr at Usstje is to be carried out. First, *Panzergruppe* Cuno has to clear the assembly area. What is more, the results of the reconnaissance by the regiment's motorcycle platoon have to arrive, so that II./SR 40 is only able to advance into the assembly area at 2100 hours. As a result of poor road conditions and several destroyed crossings, this goes forward only slowly. Ahead of II./SR 40, panzers and 17 Motorcycle Battalion move into the assembly area.
>
> On 11.7., at 0330 hours, elements of 2nd Battalion reach the patch of forest just west of Usstje. The rest of II./SR 40 only arrives around 0500 hours. The artillery is not yet ready to fire, which is why the attack will not begin as intended at 0600 hours, but only at 0730 hours, and even then still rather hastily. Terrain reconnaissance and observation have shown that the river is 50-60 meters wide at the crossing point, but that the far bank is very steep. The enemy has dug himself in securely in the forest opposite. In the area between the forest and the river, several machine gun positions and nests of riflemen are identified. In some areas, the enemy is still digging in. Available to 2nd Battalion for supporting the attack is: II./AR 27 with two batteries. I./SR 40 remains behind as reserve.[48]

At 7.30 that morning, the battalion put in its attack, advancing with 6th Company on the right and 7th Company on the left. The opposing Russians, strongly superior in artillery and heavy automatic weapons, inflicted punishing losses on the attackers from the outset, putting a number of pneumatic boats and their crews out of action before even reaching the river. Vigorous enemy flanking fire, from heavy weapons effectively positioned on the high ground overlooking the German assault troops, rapidly broke up the advance of 6th Company, which made it no closer than 100 meters to the river bank; moreover, the Germans lacked heavy weapons of their own with which to suppress the lethal Russian flanking fire. Despite these difficulties, the platoons of 7th Company, swept along by their valiant commander, carried the assault forward:[49]

> In doing so, *Leutnant* Rothenfusser, chief of 7th Company, proves his excellent military expertise and his fearlessness [*Unerschrockenheit*] once again. He crosses the river and forms a small bridgehead one-and-a-half platoons strong. The battle becomes increasingly intense. The enemy attempts to smash the core of the battalion with his vastly superior artillery by systematically shooting the village Usstje, which lies between the high ground and Dnepr, up in flames. This makes it increasingly difficult to maintain contact between the companies and to bring in reserves. The telephone links, as well as the radio connection, have already been disrupted several times, and several of the operating personnel are wounded …
>
> Despite the aforementioned initial successes, a crisis gradually grows, in which the futility of continuing the battle soon becomes clear. The artillery runs short of ammunition. It is not difficult for the enemy, whose weapons are far superior in numbers and caliber, to bring the battalion's attack to a standstill and inflict such losses on it that the continuation of the attack can no longer be justified. The battalion continues to fight on until the regiment orders the transition to defense. Since it is no longer possible to reinforce Rothenfusser's bridgehead, his detachment is pulled back to the west bank of the Dnepr to protect it from destruction. This, however, is only possible at night …
>
> In the course of the battle, the staffs and heavy weapons have had to bear severe losses. Even if the infantry battle is largely over by the evening, the enemy artillery stays active with undiminished fury until late into the night. An enemy air attack in the night of 11./12.7. inflicts one fatality and 11 wounded on the 8th Company. The riflemen and combat engineers on the far riverbank, in so far as they are unable to swim,[50] are brought back across the river by *Obergefreiter* Wagner and *Feldwebel* Waldner in fishing boats in several daring journeys. In spite of the shells striking all about, and raging machine gun fire, none of the men are lost.[51]

Among the many German dead of this failed action was the brave *Leutnant* Rothenfusser. Yet as the 17 Panzer Division's Order of the Day (*Tagesbefehl*) of 13 July made clear, his death was not without purpose:

> During his visit today, the commander of 2 Panzer Group, *Generaloberst* Guderian, expressed his greatest, unreserved appreciation and his particular thanks to the division for its accomplishments over the past few days … Through its ruthless attack, and particularly by the reinforced II./S.R. 40 across the Dnepr on the morning of 11.7., the division tied down a substantial number of enemy forces on its front and thus made the thrust by the reinforced 29 ID (mot.) at Kopys considerably easier … The sacrifices thus made had a truly great purpose! I am convinced that the division will also continue to fulfill its duties and obligations with the same devotion and initiative until the final victory has been achieved.
>
> Signed: von Weber[52]

While 29 ID (mot.) was conducting its operation, a successful crossing was also made by Vietinghoff's 46 Panzer Corps, immediately to the right of Lemelsen's 47 Panzer Corps. Although discomfited by heavy Russian artillery fire, and repeated aerial assault, Schaal's 10 Panzer Division, supported by the motorized infantry of the elite *Grossdeutschland* Regiment,[53] crossed the Dnepr at a point south of Shklov, and about 20 kilometers north of Mogilev. The activities of *Grossdeutschland* on the morning of 11 July are outlined in the following account:

> The night of 10./11.7.[41] is very cold. As it turns to day, the Infantry Regiment *Grossdeutschland* stands ready at its jump-off positions; pneumatic boats and ferries are brought forward, the division's artillery is ready to fire, but enemy artillery fire is also falling on the assembly areas.
>
> At 0500 hours, the *Stukas* appear over the Dnepr and toss their bombs on the identified targets. The artillery uses the *Stuka* attack to home in on its targets – ammunition already has to be rationed! – and begins its barrage punctually at 0515 hours. At 0520, the men from Infantry Regiment *Grossdeutschland* push their assault boats and pneumatic floats into the water. Despite the Russian defensive fire, the first wave is across to the other bank by 0535 hours, and 20 minutes later the message comes that the infantry has already pushed ahead around a kilometer.
>
> 1st Battalion, Infantry Regiment *Grossdeutschland*, has as its opponent the "Stalin Students," who fight fanatically. There are heavy losses on both sides, but the "*Grossdeutschen*" fight ahead with élan. By 0620 hours they have expanded their bridgehead to a depth of 2 km.[54]

Although heavy Russian artillery fire delayed the construction of pontoon ferries, and initially made it impossible to bring up bridging materials, the men of *Grossdeutschland* continued to widen their bridgehead. To buttress the German counterbattery fire, corps artillery assets (cannon and heavy howitzer batteries) added their weight to the artillery duel. Under cover of these protective fires, the regiment's heavy infantry weapons were ferried across the river.[55]

Directly to the north of *Grossdeutschland* and 10 Panzer Division, SS-*Gruppenfuehrer* Hausser's SS Motorized Infantry Division *Das Reich* launched its attack from the immediate vicinity of Shklov. However, before the SS grenadiers could begin with their crossing, they had first had to clear the Russians from their strongly fortified positions atop Hill 215, on the west bank of the Dnepr.[56] Not until midday, 11 July, was the division able to fight its way through and assemble for the river crossing. Despite such challenges, and despite the bridges in its sector having been damaged by air attack, the division successfully established its bridgehead. By day's end, the spearheads of 46 Panzer Corps were already 12 kilometers east of Shklov.[57]

Through his operations on 10/11 July 1941, Guderian had forged a series of bridgeheads across the Dnepr River between Orsha and Rogachev; in doing so, his assault forces had punctured the Stalin Line and split the seam between Soviet 13 and 20 Armies. In fact, Guderian "had rendered Timoshenko's defenses along the Dnepr River from Kopys southward to Mogilev and from Mogilev southward to Stary Bychov utterly superfluous. As a result, Timoshenko was losing control of the situation, a weakness Guderian was quick to exploit."[58]

Having conquered the Dnepr line, 2 Panzer Group rolled rapidly eastward, toward the open country south of Smolensk. On 13 July, 17 Panzer Division (47 Panzer Corps) captured Orsha; by 2400 hours, the corps' 29 Motorized, having burst out of its bridgehead at Kopys, was half way to Smolensk. Further south, 10 Panzer Division (46 Panzer Corps) captured Gorki and rumbled southeast toward the Sozh River, while 4 Panzer and 10

Motorized Divisions (24 Panzer Corps) debouched from Stary Bychov – the advance of the two panzer corps trapping major elements of Soviet 13 Army in and about Mogilev. The town of Mogilev, which 13 Army had transformed into an impregnable fortress, would continue to resist defiantly. As a result, Guderian wasted little time trying to subdue it – that task was better left to the infantry of General von Weichs' Second Army, which had now reached the Berezina and was rapidly advancing east by forced marches.[59] "Gallant Mogilev," as it turned out, would hold out for 17 days, until 27 July 1941.[60]

While these operations were underway, the tanks of Hoth's 3 Panzer Group had also been making progress on the northern wing of Army Group Center (see, Section 10.1.2); by nightfall, 13 July, the spearheads of 2 and 3 Panzer Groups – 29 Motorized and 7 Panzer Divisions, respectively – were only about 55 kilometers apart and rapidly converging on Smolensk from the south and north. The armies of Timoshenko's Western Front, their Dnepr line defenses having utterly collapsed, were now fighting for their very survival, threatened as they were with encirclement by the irresistibly advancing armada of German armor.[61]

In its daily report for 13 July, the Operations Branch of the German Army General Staff recorded "furious counterattacks" (*heftige Gegenangriffe*)[62] against Field Marshal von Kluge's Fourth Panzer Army which, since 3 July, had maintained uneasy control of both Hoth's and Guderian's panzer groups. The reference was to what Guderian would later call the "Timoshenko offensive," which began on this day and continued to 16 July. The Soviet marshal's intent was to cut off and destroy both 2 and 3 Panzer Groups, while restoring Western Front defenses along the Dnepr; yet "given the actual situation, no part of Timoshenko's plan was even remotely feasible."[63] Of the handful of armies taking part in the offensive, only 21 Army succeeded in carrying out its orders with any success at all, by pushing across the Dnepr and briefly threatening German communications at Bobruisk, on the Berezina. In addition, by evoking some confusion in German ranks, elements of Soviet 13 Army managed to extricate themselves from impending encirclement east of Mogilev. Despite these modest gains, and despite the unrelenting pressure applied by the *Stavka* (Soviet High Command), Timoshenko was unable to arrest the drive of the German armor on Smolensk.[64]

The irrepressible Guderian, meanwhile, now enjoying complete operational freedom, continued to press on eastward at a torrid pace, pushing men and machines ruthlessly, without concern for the open flanks of his panzer corps. By nightfall, 14 July, Boltenstern's 29 Motorized Division (47 Panzer Corps) was approaching Smolensk from the southwest, followed by the remaining tanks of Nehring's 18 Panzer Division. In addition, 10 Panzer Division (46 Panzer Corps) had almost reached the Sozh, its ultimate target being the strategically important town of El'nia, on the Desna, 75 kilometers southeast of Smolensk. On the far right flank, Geyr's 24 Panzer Corps screened the 2 Panzer Group advance.[65] German air activity was vigorous, with 2 Air Corps alone flying 885 sorties on 14 July;[66] the rail link between Smolensk and Moscow was also struck for the first time that day.[67]

Guderian's impetuous and highly demanding style of leadership, while understandable given that the stakes could not have been higher, sometimes placed his subordinates in perilous positions, as the following account, published by General Nehring in 1961, underscores:

> On 12 July, the crossing of the "wheeled elements" [*Radteile*] of [18 Panzer] Division began on a poorly constructed military bridge, while the panzer units had to cross on ferries. As a result of this and of enemy action, there were delays.
>
> The division's next objective was Krasnyi. The roads there were only sketchy, the terrain sandy, wet in the Rossosenka sector, the bridges not capable of heavy loads. Although 17 Panzer Division did not succeed, as our lefthand neighbor,

in crossing the Dnepr between Kopys and Orsha, and although ground and air reconnaissance reported a stronger enemy with tanks on what was thus our vulnerable flank, the corps ordered that no covering forces could be diverted. The principle of the rapid thrust into the depth [of the enemy front] went too far in this case and was carried out at the cost of tactical necessity. The consequence was that enemy tanks succeeded in destroying the majority of the division's supply services on 14 July near Dobryn, capturing the division's files, and coming close to capturing the divisional staff without the *Generalsstaffel*, which was located much further forward.

Nevertheless, the area around Krasnyi-Gusino is reached on 14 July, as ordered. The division's task here is to act as flank cover for the attack of 29 Motorized Division on Smolensk, which results in heavy, strength-sapping forest battles … Although the envisaged objectives are achieved, the troops are utterly battle-weary [*recht abgekaempft*]. Panzer and motorized vehicles have suffered a great deal on the poor roads and are in need of technical overhaul, for which the spare parts required for the multiplicity of vehicle types to be found in the division are lacking. On the whole, supplies across the great distance from the homeland to Smolensk are not yet secured.[68]

By evening, 15 July 1941, the assault units of the "magnificently led"[69] 29 Motorized Division – proudly referred to by its soldiers as the "Falcon" division – reached the southern outskirts of Smolensk,[70] where they would undergo a ferocious three-day fight to clear the city. Meanwhile, also on 15 July, the northern pincer of Army Group Center's vast encirclement movement, Hoth's 3 Panzer Group, reached Iartsevo, 50 kilometers northeast of Smolensk, severing the main road and rail links with the city.[71] Twenty (20) Soviet divisions – among them the remnants of two mechanized corps – were now trapped within the developing pocket, which extended westward from Smolensk toward Orsha.[72]

While another magnificent German "cauldron" battle was taking shape, the losses of Guderian's panzer group were mounting ominously. On 11 July 1941, a Colonel Ochsner, following a visit to both Hoth's and Guderian's panzer groups, reported back to Chief of the Army General Staff Halder, stating that the panzer troops had suffered serious losses in both men and materiel, and that the blistering operations tempo had made all the men tired.[73] By 12 July 1941, 3 Panzer Division (24 Panzer Corps) was so exhausted that its chief of staff asked for support from the corps reserve;[74] on 13 July, Geyr's other panzer division (4 PD) was down to about 25 operational tanks (although its situation would improve in the coming days, with the arrival of spare parts and replacement tanks);[75] only a few days later, 18 Panzer Division would have just 12 combat-ready tanks in its order of battle.[76] Despite the heavy losses of tanks and troops, few replacements were reaching the front. About this time, the divisional Catholic priest in 18 PD wrote:

Ambulances [*Sankas*] come and go, unload their sad cargo, and disappear again in the direction of the front. I go from room to room. All words fail here. Quiet whispering and groaning, usually silence, large, wide open eyes. Only here and there a tired smile. Behind the building, in a shady corner, the dead: officers and men. The numbers ever increasing. They are young people, barely come of age, for the division is, of course, comprised almost exclusively of active troops.[77]

Clearly, the armored forces of Army Group Center were declining rapidly in strength while, more generally, Bock's army group as a whole was beginning to suffer from a "debilitating lack of military resources" which, in the days and weeks ahead, would force "the juggling of units between crisis points and [give] rise to increasingly bitter disputes among commanders. There were simply not enough resources to meet the mushrooming demands of the war."[78]

10.1.2: 3 Panzer Group

By 10 July 1941, Hoth's 3 Panzer Group had advanced as far as 450 kilometers from the frontier and stood on the Western Dvina River. His two panzer corps had built secure bridgeheads across the river at Disna (57 Panzer Corps), on the panzer group's left wing, and at Ulla and Beshenkovichi (39 Panzer Corps), west of the city of Vitebsk, which was seized in a bold flanking maneuver on 9 July. As a result of these actions, Hoth had fatally compromised Timoshenko's defenses along the Dvina River. Over the next few days, the Soviets put in a vigorous attempt to wrestle back the Vitebsk region from the Germans, the *Rotarmisten* of Lt.-Gen. I.S. Konev's 19 Army counterattacking as they dismounted from their troop trains. Ably supported by Richthofen's 8 Air Corps, 39 Panzer Corps bloodily repulsed the Soviet attacks; by the end of 13 July, Konev's army had largely disintegrated.[79]

Despite their spectacular performance in the opening phase of the campaign, officers and men in 3 Panzer Group felt their efforts had not been fully acknowledged by higher headquarters, as this excerpt from a report by the panzer group makes clear. The report also reflects on Hoth's style of leadership:

> During the course of all operations, from as early as the Neman onward, the troops regretted that their achievements seemed not to receive full recognition in the Army Group and OKH situation reports. This appeared to be due in part to the nature of reporting in the *Panzergruppe*. It was always concerned to report the actual course of the battles, and its impression of the enemy, soberly and objectively, briefly and to the point. Only in this way can an accurate picture of the situation be conveyed to the higher-ranking leadership. If, however, exaggerated reports in flowery language arrive daily from other quarters, composed in superlatives about the "most difficult" battles, about an enemy who is always "superior," "strong," and these are adopted by higher headquarters, then, in the interests of the troops, everyone is gradually forced to adopt this new style without regard for the skewed picture which results. Every battle is difficult – reporting of "most difficult" battles should therefore only be done in exceptional circumstances.[80]

With well over 500 tanks at his disposal,[81] Hoth's primary mission after 10 July was to push eastward from Vitebsk with his most powerful grouping, Schmidt's 39 Panzer Corps,[82] capture the area north of Smolensk, and then wheel southeast with strong mobile forces to seize the *Autobahn* northeast of the city – a maneuver which, if successful, would bar the retreat of Red Army units fighting west and north of Smolensk.[83] So envisaged, the operation constituted the northern arm of Army Group Center's vast pincer movement – with Guderian's 2 Panzer Group providing the southern arm – to encircle and destroy most of the remaining Soviet forces along the central axis of the German advance. To carry out this mission, however, 3 Panzer Group would have to traverse terrain dominated by swamps, lakes and woods, and dotted with rolling hills extending down to Smolensk – a landscape far less favorable to the operations of tanks and motor vehicles than the region south of Smolensk.

Hoth's ancillary task (after 13 July), on the far left flank of his panzer group, was for Kuntzen's 57 Panzer Corps to drive from its Disna bridgehead toward the city of Nevel, a key communications hub on the boundary between Army Group North and Army Group Center. Conceived as part of a joint operation with Leeb's army group, the objective was to clear the inner flanks of the two army groups, while also trapping and annihilating large Soviet forces in the area. Yet by deflecting Kuntzen's panzer corps to Nevel, Hoth split his forces and propelled his two panzer corps along divergent axes. Ultimately, this ill-conceived operation would work to the detriment of Field Marshal von Bock's efforts to encircle and destroy Soviet forces in the Smolensk region. Still, it is important to note that the dispatch of 57 Panzer Corps to Nevel was the outcome of decision-making by Hitler and OKH, not Hoth.[84]

By 12 July, the tanks of 39 Panzer Corps were on the move, Stumpff's 20 Panzer Division driving northeast via Surazh toward Velizh, while Funck's 7 Panzer Division advanced due east toward Demidov. Both towns were reached the next day, following advances of ca. 60 and 70 kilometers, respectively,[85] as Schmidt's panzers "bypassed the left flank of F.A. Ershakov's 22 Army defending along the Western Dvina River and the right flank of P.A. Kurochkin's 20 Army south of Vitebsk, all the while driving the remnants of Konev's 19 Army toward the southeast, where M.F. Lukin's 16 Army was slowly assembling to defend Smolensk."[86] Early in its advance on Demidov, 7 Panzer engaged three full-strength rifle divisions of Soviet 25 Rifle Corps (19 Army), which had detrained at the town of Rudnia (less than 50 kilometers southwest of Demidov), and taken up defensive positions nine kilometers southeast of Vitebsk. According to a Russian account, when the German tanks approached, "25 Rifle Corps ran away and even did not join battle because of their fear of the enemy's artillery fire." The corps commander was captured along with his staff.[87]

By the evening of 14 July, lead elements of 7 Panzer were just 35 kilometers north of Smolensk, while 20 Panzer was approaching Bor, 75 kilometers beyond Velizh.[88] Passing up the opportunity to assault Smolensk from the north, Funck struck out even further to the east, capturing Dukhovshchina, 44 kilometers northeast of Smolensk, by midday, 15 July. Here, the division was fortunate to find a good "hard surfaced road," which it could exploit for the final push to its objective. Funck arranged his forces into a combined arms battlegroup consisting of a tank battalion, a battalion of motorized infantry, engineer, artillery and anti-aircraft forces, and sent them surging southward the final 24 kilometers to the town of Iartsevo:

> The *Kampfgruppe* captured the vital town, near where the highway and railroad to Moscow crossed the Vop' River, a tributary of the Dnepr River, at 2030 hours on 15 July and immediately blocked the main artery between Smolensk and Moscow by fire. Finding the highway clogged with traffic and all four of its lanes jammed with columns of troops and vehicles heading both eastward and westward, the *Kampfgruppe* repelled the first of many Soviet counterattacks and held its position. This was the 7 Panzer Division's finest hour. As Funck's panzers were entering Iartsevo, only hours behind, Boltenstern's 29 Motorized Division of Lemelsen's 47 Panzer Corps was entering the ancient city of Smolensk from the south, signaling Guderian's equally rapid advance. Thus, by day's end on 15 July, another grand encirclement was taking shape. An estimated, and later confirmed 300,000 Soviet soldiers of Timoshenko's 16, 19, and 20 Armies, most of whom were still fighting far to the west, were now falling into a deadly trap.[89]

While 7 Panzer Division blocked the *Autobahn* leading from Smolensk to Moscow, other mobile divisions operating with 39 Panzer Corps – 20 PD, 20 ID (mot.), 12 PD – began to form a cordon around the Soviet forces encircled west of Smolensk. By day's end, 15 July, Schmidt's divisions occupied an extended arc sweeping nearly 200 kilometers from just beyond Vitebsk to Iartsevo. Until the marching infantry divisions arrived from the west, however, the Smolensk pocket would remain fragile and vulnerable to penetration by Soviet forces; elements of both the Ninth and Second Armies (5 and 9 Army Corps, respectively) were approaching the western edge of the developing cauldron at this time.[90]

Meanwhile, debouching from its Disna bridgehead approximately 125 kilometers northwest of Vitebsk, Kuntzen's 57 Panzer Corps began its drive toward Nevel along the Polotsk – Nevel road on the morning of 14 July. Forming the spearhead was Knobelsdorff's 19 Panzer Division, strengthened by a regiment of 14 Motorized Division with supporting elements. Although the forward progress of 19 Panzer "suffered greatly throughout the day because of the indescribable road condition[s],"[91] the division struggled on toward the city; by nightfall, it was only 15 kilometers southwest of Nevel.[92] Taking part in the advance was 19 PD's motorized artillery regiment, which was soon in position to take the city under devastating fire:

> Following some skirmishes, progress continued in a northeasterly direction. An immense thunderstorm erupted and finally brought atmospheric relief, although with the disadvantage that the road completely churned up and the vehicles got stuck. II./AR 19, without its 4th Battery, fought with *Kampfgruppe* Schmidt (with 27 Panzer Regiment); 4./AR 19 with *Kampfgruppe* Iwandt (74 SR) led the advance through undulating terrain up to the bank of the Dryssa River. From a hill close to the city, there was a good overview of Nevel, which, however, was only accessible via a narrow isthmus between two large lakes. The Soviet artillery made itself heard. The German batteries, namely those of I. and III./AR 19, as well as 1./ Moerser Batallion 816, concentrated their fire, including observed fire, on the northwest and western parts of the city. As a result, there were flames everywhere (houses, vehicles, tanks). Some riflemen succeeded in taking the important bridge, which had been intended for demolition, intact in a *coup de main* …
>
> In Nevel, the burning houses gradually collapsed, so that the city subsequently made a thoroughly desolate impression.[93]

Dismantling the defenses of Soviet 62 Rifle Corps, Knobelsdorff's tanks and motorized infantry covered 68 kilometers in two days, reaching the outskirts of Nevel by evening, 15 July, and capturing it the next morning from the Soviet 48 Tank Division. By now, 12 Infantry Division (2 Army Corps), the vanguard of the German Sixteenth Army (Army Group North), was bearing down on Nevel from the northwest, poised to link up with 19 Panzer and form a pocket around Soviet Western Front's 22 Army west of the city.[94]

The German Army High Command hoped to effectuate the encirclement of Soviet 22 and 27 Armies (the latter, belonging to Soviet Northwestern Front, was also in the Nevel region) by concentric assaults using elements of Sixteenth Army, 57 Panzer Corps, and infantry of Strauss' Ninth Army (now reaching the Western Dvina between Drissa and Polotsk). If the operation were successful, it would eliminate the threat to Field Marshal von Leeb's right flank, as he turned north to capture Leningrad in cooperation with the Finns; perforce, "Nevel became a disproportionately important objective, a magnet attracting Hitler's and the OKH's attention, which required a portion of Hoth's 3 Panzer Group to resolve the problem."[95] From the perspective of Field Marshal von Bock, however, the "Nevel diversion" shifted badly needed resources (in particular, 57 Panzer Corps' 19 Panzer Division) away from the *Schwerpunkt* of Army Group Center's operations in the Smolensk area – a point of view also held by Panzer General Hoth.[96] As it was, the promising encirclement, which had so intrigued Hitler and OKH,[97] would fail to materialize, the two Soviet armies soon managing to slip from the developing trap.

On balance, however, the operations from 10-15 July 1941 had proceeded spectacularly for Hoth's panzer group; indeed, through its capture of Iartsevo on 15 July, Funck's 7 Panzer Division stood only 300 kilometers (186 miles) from Moscow a mere 24 days into the campaign.[98] Interestingly enough, Field Marshal von Kluge – in titular control, at least, of both Hoth's and Guderian's panzer groups through his command of Fourth Panzer Army, an arrangement favored by none of the field commanders – "appears to have exerted little influence as a coordinator of these operations."[99] About 15 July, Bock observed optimistically that "the situation at Smolensk appears to be causing difficulties for Timoshenko; the following radio message to the Russian general in command at Smolensk was intercepted this morning: 'Your silence is disgraceful, when will you finally understand? They are concerned about your health. Give your assessment of the overall situation at once.' This was immediately followed by a message that Smolensk was to be held at all costs!"[100]

Yet for Panzer General Hoth – as it was for his colleague Guderian to the south – the psychic and physical demands of the Russian campaign, the constant attrition of irreplaceable men and machines (resources which were hopelessly inadequate from the very outset of Operation *Barbarossa*), were taking an ever-increasing toll. Hoth's observations in his panzer group's war diary on 13 July 1941, posits historian David Stahel, "make clear the intractable predicament undercutting the German Army's apparent success.

> Assessing the advance to distant objectives Hoth bluntly observed: "The expenditure of strength is greater than the success." Yet with Soviet armies reeling in barely restrained chaos, there could be no question of a respite and so the motorized forces pressed on, mindful of their own dwindling strength, but unable to do anything about it. In substance, the Germans were damned it they stopped and damned if they did not, although Hoth was not yet drawing such an arrantly bleak conclusion. Instead the panzer general acknowledged the "heavy losses" of the campaign, but added that these were not in excess of those experienced in the previous western campaign. On the other hand, the physical strains he stated, "are very much greater," to which he highlighted the oppressive conditions created by the heat and dust. For the first time, Hoth also called into question the morale of his men, citing a multitude of factors beginning with the "barren expanses of the land and the doggedness of the enemy." Furthermore, Hoth remarked on the state of the roads and bridges,[101] as well as the fact that throughout the enormous operational area: "Everywhere the enemy is taking up arms." In conclusion the panzer general summed up the emerging frustration of his men, among whom there was "constantly the feeling, should the motorized troops have to do everything alone?"[102]

10.1.3: The Infantry Armies (Fortress Polotsk)

During the battles along the frontier – most prominently, the cauldron battles of Belostok-Minsk – the rapidly advancing panzer corps of Army Group Center had raced as far as 200 to 300 kilometers beyond the infantry of Fourth Army (after 3 July, Second Army)[103] and Ninth Army. Lacking infantry support, the tanks of Hoth and Guderian were forced to fight with dangerously exposed flanks and fragile lines of communication. As organized Red Army resistance inside the pocket flickered out at the beginning of July 1941, the infantry divisions sought to push eastward in a series of brutal forced marches to catch up to the hard-pressed panzer units, which were now racing to the Dvina-Dnepr River lines and beyond. To expedite their advance, the infantry divisions pooled their handful of motor vehicles into advance detachments, which then pushed on ahead of the main body of marching troops.

By 10 July 1941, advance detachments from several divisions of General Maximilian von Weichs' Second Army had made it as far as the Berezina River, between Borisov and Bobruisk, reducing the gap to Guderian's panzer group (now beginning its push across the Dnepr) to about 100 kilometers. The mass of the army's infantry, however, remained roughly 150-200 kilometers behind the front. On the left wing of Army Group Center, advance elements of Strauss' Ninth Army had reached the Dvina southeast and northwest of Polotsk (5 and 23 Army Corps, respectively), while the mass of Ninth Army closed on the river.[104]

The eastward migration of Second and Ninth Armies into mid-July 1941 was, for the most part, carried out with only limited combat engagements, although the task remained of clearing the ubiquitous Red Army stragglers from Belorussia's endless tracks of forest. In general, as recorded in the secret daily reports of the German High Command at this time, the advance of the marching infantry proceeded "according to plan" (*planmaessig*).[105] Nevertheless, the deliberate pace of the advance frustrated both the commanders of the panzer units – who eagerly awaited the promised relief – and the infantry alike. In a letter to his wife on 11 July, General Heinrici (43 Army Corps) gave vent to his frustrations, and offered a bold prediction for the post-war future of the German infantry:

> Put another 2 march days behind us. Both filled with blistering heat, unspeakable dust, and the greatest strains for the troops. One regiment walked 54 km yesterday, another 47 km. Doing that once, that's possible. But if there are several marches of 30-40 km before that particular achievement, and if there are more to follow, then it's monstrous. Moreover, nobody gets any nighttime sleep, instead you're off at 2 or 3 [a.m.], and go on long into the evening, sometimes 22[00 hours]. There may be a rest at midday, but usually without any water and in boiling sunshine. Anyone who stumbles across a stream for bathing is happy. Everyone tears their clothes from their bodies and gets into the water, even if it's filthy. Water is like gold.
>
> We are now in proper Russia, the nest today is called Kopyl … The Bolshevist is fighting along the Dnepr for the moment. At certain points, [our forces] have already crossed over. That means we have to march until our tongues are dropping, always marching, marching, marching. I think the infantry will be abolished after the war. The difference between motor and manpower is too great. Hartmut[106] is fighting on the Dnepr. May God protect him.[107]

By mid-July 1941, the 31 Infantry Division was approaching the Dnepr south of Mogilev. Fighting with the division was the young *Leutnant* and *Panzerjaeger* Erich Bunke. His post-war account offers insight into why the German infantry required so much time to reach the front:

> I had to hike along the route of advance all day long with the trucks. This entire road was a 100-meter wide section of terrain without any solid surface, on which man, horse, and motor toiled, in the truest sense of the word, along to the east. Wherever there were sections of river, there were hold-ups, sometimes even at entrances into forests, which were very narrow and where only single file [*Gaensemarsch*] was possible, vehicle behind vehicle. This was no advance, but rather a trudging along. The leadership had to realize that the infantry corps, for which they were clamoring, really could not advance any faster. Only fully motorized, cross-country vehicles could advance adequately here, but there were few of them, and the infantry had these heavy German Army wagons with them, which were simply a burden and held everything up. The horse-drawn artillery, and we only had them in the infantry divisions, had to double up the horses on the guns and the ammunition wagons at every hill and get one vehicle after another up the hill. And the gun crews were even setting to at the spokes to make everything go forwards.[108]

The reader of this narrative is fully aware of the trials and tribulations experienced by the German infantry as it slogged through the fields, forests and swamps of Belorussia, so they need not be recapitulated here. However, the example of the 45 Infantry Division is unique and merits additional scrutiny. The fighting for the fortress of Brest-Litovsk had ended on 29 June, and had cost the division over 1000 casualties, including more than 450 dead or missing. The next day (30 June), the division honored its dead in a solemn ceremony at the division's first Russian cemetery; shortly thereafter, a motorized advance detachment of 45 Infantry Division was heading east, followed by the main body of the division on 2 July. Initially, the troops marched on "relatively good" roads, without serious enemy contact, advancing by way of Kobrin and Antopol to Pinsk, where the division entered the northern rim of the Pripiat' Marshes (also called the Rokitno Marshes), the enormous natural barrier which separated the inner flanks of Army Groups Center and South. Modest Red Army forces had withdrawn from the frontier into the marshes, posing a threat to the flanks and rear of Bock's army group; hence, they needed to pursued and eliminated, a task initially allotted to 1 Cavalry Division[109] and now turned over to Maj.-Gen. Schlieper's 45 ID.[110]

The division's journey through the forbidding Pripiat' began about 6 July and continued for several weeks,[111] the men traversing the entire length of the marshes from west to east in a state of constant combat readiness. "The demands thereby placed on men, horses, engines and other materiel," recalled divisional Chaplain Rudolf Gschoepf in his history of 45 ID (first published in 1955), "can only be properly assessed by those who actually experienced them.[112]

> After only a few days in this perpetually damp and unhealthy air, you felt like you'd been shattered, unpleasant symptoms made themselves felt: pressure on the chest, breathing difficulties, sore throat; but the worst were the first cases of dysentery and malaria. With time, a kind of psychological apathy overcame us, a feeling of desolation, lack of a will to live and vitality. The dreadful plague of mosquitoes could have had a chapter to itself ... Mosquito nets may have been handed out, but they provided only scant protection.

> To speak of roads would be an overstatement. There were only a few poor roadways, which, at most, could withstand the light indigenous *Panje* wagons, but not the heavy columns of military movements. So it was not an "advance," but literally an agonizing plod through 40 to 50 centimeters of sand, through bottomless quagmires, through thick forests, and overgrown scrub. In places, long corduroy roads had to be built to move forward at all. The motorized vehicles experienced unimaginable wear and tear on their motors, because the fine sand got into everything and scratched pistons and cylinders; furthermore, they were built far too low in general for this terrain ...

> Horse-drawn artillery and horse-drawn columns could only plod through dust, swamp, and dirt on these run-down roads by putting the horses under extreme stress. A frighteningly large number of horses collapsed in their harnesses, because they were no longer capable of pulling guns, combat and supply wagons any further. The dead animals lay everywhere along the roads and formed a pitiful chain. It was a veritable mass dying of horses, the like of which we never really experienced again ...

> We came across only a few human settlements in this area; they were of a level of wretchedness that we had not been able to imagine until then. Men and women went around in filthy, home woven, primitive linen clothes; shoes and stockings seemed to be unknown ...

> Our movements mostly had to be carried out in darkness and in the first half of the day. The units and columns usually set off from their forest bivouac shortly after midnight and strove to reach their objectives before midday. The aim was, as much as possible, to avoid the most oppressive of the day's heat, as well as the Russian surveillance planes. That, incidentally, was when a new name for the 45

Division began to make the rounds: "45 SSS-Division," or "Schlieper's Swamp and Sand Division."[113]

On 8 July, at the former Polish-Soviet frontier, near Davidgrodek – Turov, the division's advance detachment clashed with a superior Soviet force and suffered significant losses, forcing it to adopt a "hedgehog" defense and await arrival of the main body of 45 ID. The division renewed its assault on the afternoon of 14 July, only to be stopped in its tracks by a powerful thunderstorm, which raged for several hours without respite, causing fatal casualties from lightening strikes and transfiguring the terrain into an impassable morass, abruptly halting all movement. Shortly after dawn the next day (15 July), the division attacked again; by midday, it had destroyed the Soviet positions west of Turov and occupied the town. The fighting in the area went on for another week, by which time the Russians had been successfully vanquished. In the vicinity of Davidgrodek, the division erected its second divisional cemetery of the Russian campaign – this one holding 36 of its dead.[114]

The infantry operations along the central axis of the German advance on the eve of the Battle of Smolensk culminated in the capture of the fortress of Polotsk by Strauss' Ninth Army on 15 July 1941. The fortress anchored the Polotsk Fortified Region – an integral component of the Stalin Line 112 kilometers in length and up to four kilometers in depth paralleling the Western Dvina River. Construction of the fortified region had begun in 1931 and, in 1939, the area was strengthened; its purpose was to "shield the land bridges between the upper reaches of the Western Dvina and Dnepr Rivers, block the Riga-Moscow railroad line, and protect the rail centers of Vitebsk, Orsha, and Smolensk."[115] The Polotsk Fortified Region consisted of about 200 concrete bunkers bristling with heavy weapons and machine guns; regular field positions, barbed wire obstacles and difficult terrain features – including lakes and marshy ground, adeptly integrated into the defenses by the Soviets – added to the strength of the position. In mid-July 1941, these fortifications furnished the final defensive bastion of Soviet 22 Army along the Dvina River.[116]

Cognizant of the formidable nature of the Soviet fortifications, Field Marshal von Bock had counseled caution, preferring to bypass Polotsk to spare lives and save precious time.[117] Strauss, however, was of a different mind, opting to assault the fortress and to do so in a big way with the divisions of two army corps: Foerster's 6 Army Corps was to attack from due west and south of the Dvina; Schubert's 23 Army Corps, already operating on the river's northern bank, was to move on Polotsk from the north. Although originally scheduled for 14 July, the assault was postponed for a day to allow more time for tactical reconnaissance.[118]

To soften up the Soviet positions, an impressive artillery preparation was to precede the assault. To supplement their organic light and medium howitzers, the divisions of 6 Army Corps (6 ID and 26 ID) were allotted general headquarters (GHQ) artillery (*Heeresartillerie*), including 210mm and 300mm heavy howitzers (*Moerser*); 88mm Flak batteries were also assigned to the attack. To suppress the enemy bunkers by means of direct fire, the heavy howitzers and 88mm Flak were positioned as far forward as possible. Finally, *Stukas* of Richthofen's 8 Air Corps would be available to provide air support.[119]

The night of 14/15 July was uncomfortably cool as the German infantry battalions, and the assault groups of the combat engineers, occupied their assembly areas. Shortly after dawn, 15 July, the German artillery opened fire. The Russians responded with counter fire of their own, which was rapidly suppressed by the heavy German guns. Just before 0600 hours, the Russian positions were smothered with smoke shells and, at precisely 0600 hours, the spearheads of Auleb's 6 Infantry and Weiss' 26 Infantry Divisions began to move forward.[120]

In the sector of 6 ID, the assault formations of 18 Infantry Regiment – some outfitted with flamethrowers – were led personally by *Oberst* Becker, the regimental commander;

the division's other attacking regiment (37 IR) advanced with two infantry companies of its 2nd Battalion and assault groups (*Stossgruppen*) of Combat Engineer Battalion 6. The combat teams of both regiments infiltrated the Russian fortifications and began to methodically reduce the bunker positions, effectively supported by the nimble German artillery, which poured down concentrated fire to suppress Soviet resistance wherever it flared.[121]

The diary of 2./Pi.-Btl. 6, recorded in graphic detail the role of the company's assault groups in support of 37 Infantry Regiment:

> For the attack on the bunker line, *Gruppe* Tatenhorst is subordinated to 6./ IR 37, which is advancing to the left, while *Gruppe* Sondermann is subordinated to 5./IR 37 … As they emerge from the forest, both companies receive heavy fire from enemy snipers in the trees and stay where they are. The first attempt by *Stossgruppe* Tatenhorst to approach Bunker "V" has to be abandoned due to heavy enemy fire. After renewed reconnaissance, and after successfully engaging the bunker with Flak (88mm), the group renews its attack at 0930 hours. To contest the enemy in the area between the bunkers, the platoon leader is reinforced by a heavy machine gun [s.MG] and *Infanteriegruppe* Rolfsmeier of 6./IR 37.
>
> The advance is well covered by high reeds, but is slowed down significantly by swampy terrain. During the *Stossgruppe's* approach, *Oberstleutnant* Sommer's infantry suppression group [*Infanteriebekaempfungsgruppe*] (two battalions of 6 AR and one battalion of 42 AR, less one battery) lays down heavy fire in front of the forest edge, in order to guard against enemy flanking fire. At the same time, neighboring bunkers are blinded. At 0950 hours, Bunker "V" is taken and destroyed. In the course of subduing enemy field positions on both sides of the bunker 49 prisoners are taken.
>
> *Stossgruppe* Sondermann, temporarily subordinated to 7./IR 37,[122] has a minor casualty thanks to a tree sniper … At 1015 hours, the group … is deployed against the heavily concreted Bunker "I," immediately to the right of the route of advance near Lessiny. Once again, the attack is preceded by heavy fire from 210mm heavy howitzers and 88mm Flak, then, at 1045 hours, the bunker's embrasures [*Scharten*] are sealed up with demolition charges and the bunker is cleared out.
>
> At 1050 hours, *Gruppe* Tatenhorst takes Bunker "X," located only a few hundred meters south of Bunker "I," and which during reconnaissance the previous day had not been identified and so was not shelled by the artillery. Embrasures and the bunker interior are destroyed by demolition charges. All bunkers are abandoned by the enemy at the approach of the *Stossgruppen*, and the bunker crews, so far as they are not destroyed … taken prisoner.[123]

Despite the Russian snipers, and difficulties due to inadequate maps,[124] by 1100 hours, the lead elements of both 18 and 37 Infantry Regiments had broken through the Russian bunker lines and begun to roll up the remaining enemy positions from the flanks and rear. Exploiting his success, *Oberstleutnant* Hennicke, Commander, 37 Infantry Regiment, improvised a small, motorized assault team that, by early afternoon, was racing through the woods toward Polotsk. In a coup-de-main, it seized the part of the town below the Dvina River; yet despite its bold and rapid advance, the assault team was unable to prevent destruction of the coveted Dvina bridges – the third, and final, bridge through Polotsk detonated by its defenders with the rapidly approaching Germans barely 200 meters away.[125]

Meanwhile, the initial advance of 26 Infantry Division (6 Army Corps) ran into heavy resistance from Soviet bunker positions, pinning down the attacking infantry. Seeking a way forward for his men, *Oberst* Hertzsch, Commander, 77 Infantry Regiment (26 ID), was caught in Russian artillery fire and severely wounded; he succumbed to his wounds on the way to the dressing station. To get the attack moving again, heavy weapons, artillery and 88mm Flak were rushed forward; soon the bunkers had been silenced and the infantry battalions of 77 IR were once more on the move, pursuing the defeated enemy.[126]

Beyond the Dvina, 86 Infantry Division (23 Army Corps) – whose advance elements had crossed the river at Disna on 9 July – stormed the northern part of Polotsk, capturing it by mid-afternoon.[127] One of the first to enter the burning city was the division commander, General Joachim Witthoeft, rolling into Polotsk in an armored fighting vehicle, its 20mm Flak gun spitting fire. In an order of the day, the commander of 23 Army Corps acknowledged his soldiers' achievement:

> Corps Command Post, 15.7.1941
>
> Through powerful blows and difficult individual battles against a tough and dogged enemy, you have beaten down the northwest front of the fortress and opened up the path to the enemy for our panzers.
>
> Over 60 bunkers of heavy, and heaviest, construction were stormed. Infantry, combat engineers, artillery, and Flak weapons of the Army all competed against each other in their boldness and bravery.
>
> When, on 15 July, our *Kameraden* south of the Dvina also began their assaults, the enemy's resistance collapsed completely. At 15 - - hours, the spearhead of 86 Division pushed into Polotsk.
>
> Soldiers, you have fulfilled the trust placed in you to the greatest degree. The fullest recognition of your Fuehrer and the thanks of the Fatherland are your due. I congratulate in particular 86 Division on their decisive breakthrough. Our sacrifices were not in vain. Polotsk is ours! Now it is time to make full use of our victory and put the defeated enemy to the sword.
>
> Forward to final victory! [*Vorwaerts zum Endsieg!*]
>
> Signed Schubert.[128]

The fall of Polotsk unhinged the southern wing of Ershakov's 22 Army and split the army in half, leaving four of its eight rifle divisions in danger of encirclement west of Nevel, and the other four cut off and isolated between Nevel and Polotsk.[129] The victory had resulted in relatively few casualties for Auleb's 6 Infantry Division (11 dead, 36 wounded), while *Oberstleutnant* Hennicke garnered the Knight's Cross for his special role in the operation.[130] With Polotsk firmly in German hands, 23 Army Corps took up pursuit of the defeated enemy beyond the Dvina; while 6 Army Corps, combing the forests west of the Polotsk, secured large quantities of Red Army weapons and huge stocks of ammunition.[131]

While Strauss' infantry routed the Soviets at Polotsk, other components of his Ninth Army – Ruoff's 5 and Materna's 20 Army Corps – hastened toward Vitebsk to reinforce the cordon Schmidt's 39 Panzer Corps was now building around the trapped Soviet armies north of Smolensk; on 15 July, a *Vorausabteilung* (advance detachment) of 5 Infantry Division (5 Army Corps) reached Vitebsk, while the division's main body was only 15 kilometers from the city.[132] Further south, in the large operational area of Weichs' Second Army, foremost elements of 53, 12, and 9 Army Corps had finally reached (from right to left) the Dnepr between Shlobin (south of Rogachev) and Orsha, while their main bodies approached the river and closed on Guderian's panzer corps. A second echelon of Second Army infantry – 43, 13, 7 Army Corps – was arriving at the Berezina River.[133]

By 15 July 1941, 35 Infantry Division (5 Army Corps) had reached the Smolensk gate, between Orsha and Vitebsk. *Gefreiter* Gerhard Bopp, a radio operator in the division's reconnaissance battalion (35 AA), marveled at the destruction the recent battles had left behind:

> Along the entire route of advance there are [destroyed and damaged] tanks, automobiles, and the like. Bomb craters, toppled trees, burnt-out underbrush – all bear witness to the destruction (our *Stukas!*). At midday we stop for a break, and begin our march again about 1700 hours. [Our route] always takes us through the forests. Some of our vehicles have to be towed through the deep sand, while the infantry simply passes us by.[134]

Still far from the front on 15 July, 23 Infantry Division (7 Army Corps) prepared to cross the Berezina at Borisov. Major Werner Heinemann, a battalion commander in the division, wrote a letter to his wife:

> For the first time today, storms and rain. It's off in the direction of Moscow via the Berezina and the Dnepr along totally Napoleonic roads. Area! Incredible! Unheard of exertions, of the 4 companies of the batallion, so many have fallen away that they make up an entire company. But we must keep at it and not give the Bolshevist any time to regroup.[135]

10.2: Encirclement Battle of Smolensk

The city of Smolensk, at the head of the navigable Dnepr River, was "pleasantly situated in a valley with hills and gentle, cultivated slopes."[136] Although once ethnically White Russian, Smolensk and its 170,000 inhabitants[137] lay just beyond the political borders of Belorussia in "dairy farming country and fields of corn and flax, studded with woodlands and orchards."[138] The ancient city, with its kremlin and fortress walls, was split into two parts by the Dnepr. South of the riverbank lay, according to one German account, a "lovely, romantic city,"[139] including the famous cathedral with its roots in the 12th Century. The newer sections of the city, including a railroad station and factories, were situated north of the river. With its long and bloody history – a "vital crossroads" fought over by Poles and Lithuanians in the Middle Ages; seized by the Russians in the 17th Century, and used by Peter the Great as a base of operations against Charles XII of Sweden; captured by Napoleon in August 1812 – Smolensk was a cherished historical symbol to all Russians.[140]

In July 1941, the city's location astride the most direct invasion route to Moscow – it formed one point of the strategic Vitebsk – Orsha – Smolensk triangle, the narrow landbridge between the Western Dvina and Dnepr Rivers – made it a highly coveted objective of Field Marshal von Bock's Army Group Center. Smolensk's vital significance was equally apparent to Joseph Stalin, who was resolved to defend the city to the last. As a result, the fighting throughout the Smolensk region in the weeks ahead was especially tenacious and unyielding, as both Russians and Germans were acutely aware that the battle could well determine the outcome of the war. As one German artillery soldier who fought in several theaters of war from 1939 to 1945 recalled: "The fighting around Smolensk in July and August [1941] was the heaviest and deadliest I saw during the war."[141] A German general inspecting the city shortly after its capture described it as a "smoking pile of ruins," dominated by the "wretched remains of burned-out houses."[142] An aerial photograph of the city, snapped by a German soldier in the spring of 1942, reveals a grotesque scene of unimaginable destruction, bearing witness to the savagery of the fighting there.[143]

During the three-week period from 16 July to 5 August 1941, the panzer groups of Hoth and Guderian both engaged in bitter combat on three axes: along the Smolensk encirclement ring (against the desperate breakout attempts of the trapped Soviet armies, until relieved by the marching infantry); across their "eastern fronts" beyond Smolensk and facing toward Moscow (against repeated Soviet counterattacks); and on their exposed and vulnerable flanks (particularly on the southern flank of 2 Panzer Group, from Roslavl to Krichev). Despite strong *Luftwaffe* support (an average of 575 sorties a day over the final three weeks of July),[144] unprecedented losses were sustained by both panzer groups – most significantly by the mobile infantry (panzer grenadiers) – as they strained to perform multiple missions in an environment increasingly characterized by overstretched (and progressively unresponsive) lines of supply, overextended combat frontages, and growing exhaustion of men and materiel. By late July 1941, appeals from units within the panzer groups to be pulled from the line and allowed to rest and refit were increasing in frequency.[145]

The period was also characterized by a series of violent Red Army counterstrokes, as the Soviets sought first to smash through the German mechanized groupings and recapture Smolensk and, when that failed, simply to extricate their trapped forces from impending annihilation and shepherd them eastward to safety. While these assaults were poorly coordinated and executed, they helped to stop Bock's blitzkrieg in its tracks and tie up his forces at Smolensk for much longer than he, Hitler, or the German High Command had anticipated. Moreover, the Red Army's aggressive operational approach revealed that Soviet forces were not nearly as exhausted as the Germans had imagined at the beginning of the Smolensk battles. By 5 August 1941, when Soviet resistance inside the Smolensk pocket finally collapsed, the Germans, despite having registered another impressive operational success, by crushing yet another large Red Army grouping, had failed to achieve their primary aim of tearing open the Soviet front and clearing the road to Moscow. Instead of following up their victory with a decisive push into the depths of Soviet Russia, the exhausted and badly crippled forces of Army Group Center suddenly found themselves ensnared in a strategic deadlock, as the German blitzkrieg congealed into the first stages of positional warfare.

In mid-July 1941, however, as the fighting at Smolensk began, the Germans radiated confidence. Oblivious to the fact that new Soviet reserve armies were massing behind the Soviet front, Foreign Armies East (*Fremde Heere Ost*, or FHO), the Army department responsible for evaluating military intelligence pertaining to Soviet Russia, produced a highly optimistic analysis about the threat posed by the remaining Red Army forces: Beyond the immediate front line of Army Group Center, FHO estimated that available Soviet forces consisted only of eight or nine Soviet infantry divisions and two or three tank divisions. Even if Chief of the Army General Staff Halder found this analysis, in part at least, "very optimistic," such intelligence only reinforced his unshakable faith in impending victory. Once the Red Army front was broken at Smolensk, he reasoned, given the paucity of Soviet reserves, Bock's forces would have the operational freedom to complete the march on Moscow.[146] As for Bock, his army group reported to OKH on 16 July that, although the Russians were still mounting stubborn – if sporadic – resistance against Fourth Panzer Army, the enemy no longer appeared capable of conducting a "coherent operation" against the panzer forces.[147]

10.2.1: 2 Panzer Group

On 16 July 1941, Guderian's 2 Panzer Group was advancing on a broad front more than 150 kilometers in length, pushing well beyond the Dnepr River in its pursuit of Timoshenko's beaten armies. On the panzer group's southern flank, the spearheads of Geyr's 24 Panzer Corps dashed northeast toward the town of Krichev, which a *Kampfgruppe* from Langermann's 4 Panzer Division seized the next day (17 July) against weak Russian resistance, although the enemy managed to blow the important bridges over the Sozh River.[148] On 17 July, Model's 3 Panzer Division, having extricated itself from the Mogilev encirclement ring, also reached the Sozh, above Krichev. Both of Geyr's panzer divisions would remain in this area until the end of July, screening the southern flank of 2 Panzer Group, often against violent Russian attacks.[149]

In the center of Guderian's group, on the morning of 14 July, motorcycle riflemen of Schaal's 10 Panzer Division (Vietinghoff's 46 Panzer Corps) had burst into Mstislavl (ca. 35 kilometers north of Krichev) on the Sozh River, the division's tanks arriving at the town an hour later;[150] two days later (16 July), the division was moving northeast along the Sozh, toward El'nia, still more than 75 kilometers distant, followed by the motorized infantry of Hausser's SS *Das Reich* Division. Frustrating the advance of Schaal's armor and panzer grenadiers, however, were the structurally weak bridges along the line of advance:

> The *Vormarsch* on 16.7.[41] did not then progress as easily as had been hoped. Instead of the panzers being able to set out at 0400 hours, they first, together with the riflemen and motorcycle riflemen, had to repel a Russian attack, which hit the German assembly area 10 minutes before the planned departure ...
>
> Then the panzer brigade began its advance, but a few of the panzers had barely rolled over the bridge at the east exit of Mstislavl when it collapsed. The panzers attempt to get across at the northwest exit, but the bridge there also collapses. Only one panzer company can be transported across via a ford. Finally, at 1030 hours, makeshift repairs to the bridge enable the motorcycle riflemen to cross over.
>
> In the meantime, all of I./Pz.Rgt. 7 has made it across the identified ford, so the panzer battalion can begin the march with the motorcycle riflemen ... In spite of this, more problems develop ahead of the division. Once again, bridges must be constructed along the *Vormarschstrasse*, because one after another simply collapses. The division commander, who is ahead in Mstislavl, orders the whole of Panzer Pionier Batallion 49 to be deployed to work on the bridges at Mstislavl and to repair the other bridges along the route of advance.[151]

On the northern wing of 2 Panzer Group, Ritter von Weber's 17 Panzer and Nehring's 18 Panzer Divisions had, by 16 July, occupied blocking positions on the southern rim of the Smolensk encirclement, along the Dnepr northeast of Orsha, between Dubrovno and Krasnyi (56 kilometers southwest of Smolensk).[152] Meanwhile, the lead elements of Boltenstern's 29 Motorized Infantry Division, despite stubborn Russian resistance causing a "perceptible number of casualties,"[153] had reached the southern edge of Smolensk late on 15 July. Guderian's panzer group, however, was still a good distance from Hoth's 7 Panzer Division (39 Panzer Corps) at Iartsevo, meaning that the Smolensk pocket was still far from being closed. In its diary late on 15 July, 3 Panzer Group registered its frustration: "Unfortunately, the link-up with 2 Panzer Group is lacking, just as at Minsk."[154]

The days ahead would bring even greater frustration, reaching all the way to Hitler's headquarters at Rastenburg, as Guderian, instead of wheeling northeast – as he could have done – with his 46 Panzer Corps to seal the gap, elected to continue its drive toward the high ground at El'nia,[155] fixated as he was on maintaining momentum toward Moscow. Unquestionably, the obstinate panzer leader's arbitrary decision to downgrade the encirclement front to a secondary priority for his panzer group meant that, in the Smolensk cauldron battles, tens of thousands of Russians would avoid death or capture and escape to fight another day. Guderian's willful action – taken in complete disregard of the operational imperatives of Field Marshal von Bock, Field Marshal von Kluge (Guderian's immediate superior), and General Hoth – would render the Smolensk *Kesselschlacht* an incomplete victory at best.

On the morning of 16 July, elements of Boltenstern's 29 Motorized Infantry Division attacked into Smolensk, seizing the golden-domed Uspenskii Cathedral and the vital railroad bridge over the Dnepr. Bock was gratified by the news. The next morning (17 July), the Japanese ambassador to Berlin, General Oshima, arrived at Bock's headquarters, located since 11 July in an abandoned sanatorium in the town of Borisov[156] on the Berezina River, about 80 kilometers northeast of Minsk. Oshima found the German field marshal "in an almost jubilant mood." Bock escorted his visitor on a tour of the battle front, culminating in a luncheon at Kluge's Fourth Panzer Army headquarters. Returning to his command post that evening, Bock ordered Weichs to move the infantry divisions of his Second Army across the Dnepr posthaste.[157]

By reaching Smolensk, Guderian's panzer group had now covered roughly 600 kilometers in 25 days since the start of the campaign, an average daily advance of 24 kilometers.[158] While the southern end of the city was rapidly secured, the northern bank was much more vigorously defended. As a result, Boltenstern's panzer grenadiers, eventually reinforced by tanks from Nehring's 18 Panzer Division, needed several days of savage and costly street fighting – often house by house, at close quarters with bayonets and hand grenades[159] – to pry the rest of the city loose of its defenders – 129 and 151 Rifle Divisions of Lukin's 16 Army. When the fighting was over, 18 Panzer had been reduced to 12 operational tanks – a reflection of the "ferocity of the fighting and the debilitating effect of it on German panzer forces when unsupported by infantry divisions."[160] Even after the Germans had captured Smolensk, skirmishing would go on in the city into late July.[161] Fully aware of the extreme pressures facing its mobile units, Army Group Center ordered the marching infantry divisions of Second and Ninth Armies to advance with utmost speed to their relief. Not until 25 July, however, did 137 Infantry Division (9 Army Corps) manage to relieve the 29 Motorized Division in Smolensk.[162]

On 17 July 1941, Guderian was awarded the Oak Leaves to the Knight's Cross, becoming only the fifth man in the Army, and 24th in the entire *Wehrmacht*, to receive the coveted decoration.[163] About the same time, Guderian paid a visit to the magestic Uspenskii Cathedral in Smolensk:

> [The cathedral] was undamaged. But on entering it the visitor was surprised to find that the entrance and the left half of the place of worship had been fitted up as an Atheistic Museum. At the door stood the figure of a beggar, carved in wax, asking for alms. Inside were life-size wax figures of the bourgeoisie, in exaggerated poses showing them engaged in maltreating and plundering the proletariat. It was not pretty. The right half of the church had been kept open for religious services.[164] An attempt had been made to bury the silver altar decorations and candles before our arrival, but there had apparently not been time. In any case this considerable treasure lay piled in the middle of the floor. I ordered a Russian found whom I could make responsible for the safeguarding of these valuable objects. The sacristan was brought to me, an old man with a full white beard. Through an interpreter I told him to take these precious objects under his care and remove them. The valuable gilded woodcarvings on the iconostasis were undamaged. What later happened to the church I do not know. At that time we took trouble to see it came to no harm.[165]

As mentioned, Russian forces encircled in the Smolensk region encompassed the bulk of 16, 19, and 20 Armies. Because the German infantry had yet to reach the forward edge of battle, the panzer and motorized infantry units of Army Group Center had assembled a cordon of tanks, half-tracks, and dismounted truck-borne infantry around the trapped Soviet armies. In the north, Schmidt's reinforced 39 Panzer Corps (3 Panzer Group) was able to forge a fairly solid front across the northern rim of the pocket; along its southern perimeter, however, Lemelsen's 47 Panzer Corps, locked in heavy combat, and holding a frontage of about 100 kilometers with just 10 battalions,[166] was unable to cover the final few kilometers to link up with Funck's 7 Panzer Division (39 Panzer Corps) northeast of Smolensk, near Iartsevo. This left open a narrow corridor along the swampy banks of the Dnepr, stretching eastward from the cauldron to the village of Solovevo (15 kilometers south of Iartsevo),[167] and through this corridor a stream of Soviet forces would exit the pocket to safety.

On 18 July, the infantry of Geyer's 9 Army Corps finally began to arrive at the southern edge of the encirclement ring. As a result, 17 Panzer Division was pulled from the line northeast of Orsha and shifted to an area south of Smolensk, where it was committed against Soviet forces attacking northward toward the city. During the ensuing combat, the commander of 17 Panzer, Ritter von Weber, was badly wounded by shell fragments on 19 July and died in a military hospital at Krasnyi the next day.[168] On 21 July, General Ritter von Thoma took command of the division; according to Guderian, von Thoma was "one of our most senior and experienced panzer officers; he had been famous for his icy calm and exceptional bravery both in the First World War and in Spain, and was now to prove his ability once again."[169]

While Ritter von Weber was being mortally wounded, the command post of Lemelsen's 47 Panzer Corps was suddenly attacked by Soviet forces advancing on Smolensk. Lemelsen described the harrowing event in his diary:

> Sunday, 20.7.[41]
>
> 4 weeks' battle!
> It was a very black day yesterday, which will remain unforgettable ... The enemy was attacking Smolensk from the south with one division and heavy artillery, and came upon our command post first. He exerted pressure on us from the south and, as it went on, also from the east. We were only very weakly protected by our security platoon and one Flak MG company, and thus ordered 29 [ID (mot.)] in Smolensk to provide support with one company of motorcycle riflemen. Despite this, the enemy approached ever closer and his Urrah! could be plainly heard. A *Kampfgruppe* of our corps' signal battalion, radio company, was ambushed by the Russians and butchered in an utterly bestial manner. 18 men were later found, among them the magnificent *Leutnant* Partschefeld, all murdered in the cruelest manner, most of them by shots to the back of the head.[170]

Meanwhile, Soviet forces trapped inside the pocket strained every nerve to break through the thin German picket lines, the daily report of the OKH Operations Branch on 18 July reporting "desperate breakout attempts."[171] The panzer divisions, however, perennially short of infantry, had never been intended to perform such a static defensive role, and they suffered as a result.[172] Writes historian Robert J. Kershaw (in 2000 a Colonel in the British Army):

> [Panzer] units not only lacked time when hastily organizing defensive pickets, but also lacked the expertise needed to produce the sort of coordinated defense in depth recommended in infantry training manuals. Motorized units skilled in the art of mobile warfare did not have the eye for the ground that experience conferred when selecting defensive positions ... In France or Poland motorized units had generally superimposed a hasty and *ad hoc* screen consisting of primarily security pickets around an encircled enemy force. It did not work in Russia ...
>
> Pockets were not only porous, they moved. As Red Army units continually sought to escape, German panzers had frequently to adjust positions to maintain

concentric pressure or bend as they soaked up attacks. "Wandering pockets" complicated the coordination of hasty defense and especially the reception of march-weary reinforcing infantry units moving up to form the inner ring.[173]

Pressure was now mounting on Guderian to slam the pocket shut; however, he was not about to do so at the cost of suspending his drive on El'nia and the crossings over the Desna River. On 18 July, Field Marshal von Bock stressed to Field Marshal von Kluge the vital importance of closing the trap near Iartsevo; the next morning (19 July), he telephoned Fourth Panzer Army headquarters and spoke to Kluge's chief of staff, Colonel Blumentritt, directing him to ask Guderian "whether or not he is in a position to carry out the order of three days ago to link up with 3 Panzer Group near Iartsevo. If not, I have to commit other forces to do so."[174] As described by Bock in his journal, the conversation then took an uncomfortable turn:

> I asked: "Is everything alright with the command there? Why, for example, is the Infantry Regiment *Grossdeutschland* still milling about far behind the front?" At this point Kluge jumped in and said that he had overheard the conversation and had to defend the panzer group against my accusation of poor command – which resulted in a brief argument."[175]

Guderian, in fact, had been making an effort to close the pocket, by marshalling forces for a drive toward Dorogobuzh, southeast of Iartsevo. On 18 July, he ordered Nehring's badly depleted 18 Panzer Division toward Dorogobuzh. The division had already lost the great majority of its tanks and almost half of its anti-tank guns; one regiment, which had begun the campaign with personnel strength of 2359, had lost 1000 of its men by 19 July.[176] When Kluge got wind of Guderian's intent – i.e., moving 18 Panzer from the southern rim of the cauldron before the infantry had arrived; "in essence ... attempting to close one hole by opening another"[177] – he immediately rescinded the order. And he did so without even informing Guderian, so strong had the antipathy between the two men become.[178]

Guderian made a second attempt on 20-21 July, dispatching elements of Hausser's *Das Reich* Division (46 Panzer Corps) northward toward Dorogobuzh, a battlegroup of the SS grenadiers reaching the banks of the upper Dnepr, barely 15 kilometers from 7 Panzer at Iartsevo.[179] Yet they got no closer to their objective, the attack breaking down due to difficult terrain and heavy Russian bombing attacks. On 23 July, Guderian visited *Das Reich's* forwardmost unit, motorcyclists under the command of *Hauptsturmfuehrer* (Captain) Klingenberg, to assess the situation. The visit convinced him of the need to postpone the attack. "All attempts to advance toward Dorogobuzh," he later acknowledged, "were a complete failure."[180] In any case, despite Guderian's rather disingenuous post-war assertion that he had been "very anxious" to help Hoth seal the pocket,[181] his actions proved otherwise, in particular his decision to direct 10 Panzer Division to El'nia, which was seized by Schaal's tanks and panzer grenadiers on 19/20 July (for details see, Section 10.6.2).[182]

By this point, containing the Smolensk pocket – in the face of mounting enemy pressure – had become something of an obsession for the army group commander. His patience wearing thin, Bock confided in his diary on 20 July 1941: "At the moment, there is only one pocket on the army group's front! And it has a hole! For so far we have unfortunately been unable to achieve the union of the inner wings of the two armored groups at and east of Smolensk which we have been striving for for many days."[183] Once again, he was critical of Kluge and his Fourth Panzer Army command, which he characterized as useless for failing to take a stronger stand with Guderian to ensure closure of the pocket. When 2 Panzer Group hailed the capture of El'nia as a great success, "which has to be exploited,"

Bock was dismissive. He immediately replied that the only thing that mattered was the "hermetic sealing of the Smolensk pocket while screening to the east." To reinforce his point, he dispatched a General Staff officer directly to 2 Panzer Group, bypassing Kluge's headquarters entirely, while also having Greiffenberg, his chief of staff, speak to Guderian by telephone to further underscore the army group's instructions.[184]

With the increasingly exhausted panzer and motorized units unable to seal the pocket, the *Luftwaffe* tried to do so from the air. *Stukas* lurked above the battlefield during the long hours of daylight, while bomber formations, in action both day and night, struck at Soviet troop columns and lines of communication behind the front and also flew close support missions.[185] Yet although the German fighter, fighter-bomber and bomber squadrons could strike by day with tremendous destructive power, precise target identification was virtually impossible at night due to the paucity of distinctive terrain features; simply put, the *Luftwaffe* "lacked the all-weather, round-the-clock capability to control ground on its own."[186] Indeed, as Field Marshal Kesselring acknowledged after the war, his 2 Air Fleet could only do so much:

> These battles led to the cauldron battle around Smolensk (from mid-July to the beginning of August), which was a great success (over 300,000 prisoners), but on the other hand provided nothing decisive, in other words just a "common victory" [*ordinaeren Sieg*]. It could have been decisive, if a gap located at the east of Smolensk could have been closed. My own requests for urgency and those of the Commander-in-Chief of the *Luftwaffe* failed in the execution. A narrow gap, a few kilometers wide, through the middle of which ran a small river valley with camouflaging ground cover, allowed a considerable number of the forces to leak out in the course of a few days, above all during the nights. While the close support planes were able to reduce much of this leakage during the day through unrelenting attacks, the Russians could still make use of the twilight and nighttime all the more successfully. The Russian soldiers who escaped to their rear in this way – I estimated this at over 100,000 men – became the skeleton of new Russian units.[187]

The fact that neither Guderian's nor Hoth's panzer group could cover the final patch of ground to plug the corridor near Iartsevo and seal the pocket speaks volumes to just how fatigued the mobile forces had become.[188] In 2 Panzer Group, the fact that a significant amount of infantry was being directed to the southern flank of the army group "engendered 'very bitter' resentment among the troops, who felt they were being abandoned after shouldering the heaviest fighting for 30 straight days."[189] The mental strain on the men was palpable, the result of physical exhaustion, inexorably mounting casualties, declining panzer support and growing concerns about shortages of artillery shells and other munitions desperately needed to hold the main battle line against ferocious Soviet counterattacks.

On 22 July, the quartermaster general's war diary (2 Panzer Group) stated that the munitions situation within the panzer group was "critical," especially for Geyr's 24 Panzer Corps; two days later (24 July), the stocks of shells available to Vietinghoff's 46 Panzer Corps were also considered "critical," while the situation of Lemelsen's 47 Panzer Corps was merely viewed as "tight."[190] What this meant for the troops at the front is perhaps best illustrated by Schaal's 10 Panzer Division at El'nia, for which ammunition had to be hauled by truck from supply depots over 400 kilometers to the rear.[191] On 21 July, the division's war diary stated that, "in spite of all efforts by the corps in the coming days there will be no oil for the panzers. The munitions situation is also strained … in particular artillery shells must be used sparingly."[192] As a consequence, drastic measures were implemented, such as allowing only sighted firing with artillery, which, in the face of constant enemy attacks, only added to the psychological burden of the troops.

The grinding attrition was also a growing factor. By 19 July 1941, Guderian's forces alone had sustained 830 officer casualties, with some units having lost fully half of their officers. In all, 2 Panzer Group's losses amounted to at least 15,228 men (dead, wounded, missing).[193] The losses of armored fighting vehicles had, by now, reached staggering proportions in some of the group's panzer divisions. The tank regiment of 4 Panzer Division possessed only 44 operational tanks on 22 July; fuel, ammunition, and rations – especially bread – were also in short supply.[194] On the same day, 10 Panzer Division had just nine tanks (5 Pz II, 4 Pz III) fully combat capable, with an additional 66 tanks (25 Pz II, 38 Pz III, 3 Pz IV), many with minor engine damage due to a lack of oil, able to perform limited defensive tasks.[195] As noted, Nehring's 18 Panzer Division, after the fall of Smolensk, was basically denuded of armor. Greatly inhibiting the rehabilitation of Guderian's tank forces was the fact that barely a trickle of new tanks and engines was reaching his panzer group, Hitler and OKH opting instead to allocate the great majority of new production to new divisions being created for post-*Barbarossa* tasks; for example, as of late July 1941, only 45 replacement tank engines were being provided on a monthly basis across the entire eastern front.[196]

Despite the burgeoning crises created by ongoing attrition of men and materiel, serious supply shortages, and the deepening physical and psychological strains on tank crews and panzer grenadiers, the combat went on with unabated fury across the battlefronts of Guderian's 2 Panzer Group. Still lacking infantry support (by 21 July, marching infantry was only starting to reach the panzer group),[197] the positions of Guderian's forces – along the southern rim of the Smolensk pocket (47 Panzer Corps), at El'nia (46 Panzer Corps), and in the south from Krichev to Propoisk (24 Panzer Corps) – remained for the most part extremely porous. Without the attached *Luftwaffe* Flak batteries, using their high-velocity 88mm guns in a ground support role, the predicament of his panzer corps would have been even worse.[198]

At El'nia, Schaal's 10 Panzer Division was bludgeoned daily, repeatedly, by unremitting Red Army attacks, supported by tanks, artillery and air power. Both Germans and Russians understood the strategic importance of the little town on the Desna River as a potential springboard for an attack on Moscow, thus the fighting there was some of the fiercest of the entire war. (Note: The fighting at El'nia in late July and early August 1941 is addressed in some detail below, Section 10.6., "*Stellungskrieg*: The Beginning of Positional Warfare.") While fighting flared along the El'nia salient, Infantry Regiment *Grossdeutschland* fought off powerful Soviet thrusts around Rudnia, less than 30 kilometers northwest of Roslavl, between 21 and 26 July. A wartime publication of *Grossdeutschland's* replacement brigade (*Ersatz-Brigade*), targeted at recruiting German youth, featured this heroic account of the fighting:

> On 11 July 1941, the Dnepr crossing was forced by Infantry Regiment *Grossdeutschland* … Then came the difficult days from 21 to 26 July, during which *Oberleutnant* Haenert earned the Knight's Cross. Infantry Regiment *Grossdeutschland* had to cover the south flank of [46 Panzer Corps near El'nia], and, at the same time, an important airfield, with two battalions. The enemy attacked the isolated 1st Batallion four or five times a day with its superior infantry and artillery forces, so that the wing had to be pulled back. However, *Oblt*. Haenert held the position despite the severe threat to the flank, and, at times, envelopment on both flanks, even standing in the forwardmost line. After several days, the attrition of equipment and ammunition for the heavy weapons had become acutely noticeable, and the width of the front line had shrunk down to 150 meters, while the enemy artillery fire had continually intensified. But *Oblt*. Haenert stood like an oak and, through his example, as well as through his excellent organization of

whatever was possible, compelled officers and men alike to hold out. The superior Russian forces were frequently only beaten down in close combat.

On the sixth day, it was hell for the defenders. The Soviet Russians destroyed any cover in the forward line with direct artillery fire at very close range, and, as a result, were able to occupy parts of the position. During the shelling, *Oblt.* Haenert leapt to the heavy weapons and the threatened remnants of the German defenders, and continued firing until he was wounded in the arm. Yet even now he did not yield. He kept at the enemy for another 6 hours, even though in the meantime he had received two bullets to the leg. The position was held, the enemy could not push forward.

For six long days, two Russian divisions, with their supporting artillery, had been beaten back with bloody losses for the enemy. As a result of this heroic struggle [*Heldenkampf*], the advance of the red masses across the airfield into the right flank of the panzer division advancing on El'nia,[199] and beyond that on Smolensk, was averted decisively. Three months later, after he had already received the Knight's Cross, *Oblt.* Karl Haenert fell at Briansk. His commander, in his recommendation for the award of the Knight's Cross, had described [Haenert] as a model German officer admired by all soldiers.[200]

On 23 July 1941, *Grossdeutschland* was joined by, and subordinated to, Nehring's 18 Panzer Division, which was finally being taken off the encirclement ring southwest of Smolensk.[201] The enemy pressure along 18 Panzer's front became so intense at times that even Guderian feared the division's complete collapse. On 25 July, 18 Panzer, defending against powerful Russian thrusts from the area of Roslavl, made the troubling observation: "[e]verywhere new enemy columns with artillery."[202] The next day (26 July), the division's war diary recorded: "constant heaviest artillery fire, of a kind the troops have seldom experienced."[203] The diary also questioned the morale of the men, while a battalion doctor diagnosed collective battle fatigue:

> A state of absolute exhaustion is noticeable … among all men of the battalion. The reason is … a far too great mental and nervous strain. The troops were under a powerful barrage of heavy artillery … The enemy charged them … penetrated their positions and was repulsed in hand-to-hand fighting … the men could not shut their eyes day and night. Food could be supplied only during the few hours of darkness. A large number of men, still serving with the troops at present, were buried alive by artillery fire. That the men were promised a few days of rest … but instead found themselves in an even worse situation … had a particularly grave effect. The men are indifferent and apathetic, are partly suffering from crying fits, and are not to be cheered up by this or that phrase. Food is being taken only in disproportionately small quantities.[204]

Despite the doctor's devastating diagnosis, Nehring's panzer grenadiers – ably supported by the *Luftwaffe* – held their ground until the arrival of the marching infantry brought welcome relief.[205] That they managed to do so in spite of such demonstrably adverse conditions accentuates the incomparable discipline and professionalism of the German Army of 1941.

With the arrival of 5, 8, and 9 Army Corps, all armored and motorized units of 2 Panzer Group (and most of Hoth's 3 Panzer Group) had been withdrawn from the encirclement ring by 25 July; hence, the ongoing task of compressing and breaking up the Smolensk pocket now fell to the follow-on infantry. Despite such progress, the gap east of Smolensk (and south of Iartsevo) was still open and hemorrhaging Soviet troops. On the evening of 24 July, a nervous and increasingly impatient Hitler telephoned Bock, asking about the "status of the hole in the pocket." The field marshal "briefed him on all the details, which he took in calmly." Hitler responded by offering suggestions of his own on how the cauldron might by closed. The next day (25 July), Field Marshal Keitel, Chief of OKW, arrived at Bock's command post to continue the dialogue. Hitler, it seems, still had "ideas on the subject," which Keitel was to convey.[206]

Despite Hitler's growing anxiety – and close attention to the problem – it was not until three days later that the narrow corridor east of Smolensk was finally closed. At 2015 hours on 28 July, Lemelsen's 47 Panzer Corps reported to Guderian's headquarters that its 17 Panzer Division and 3 Panzer Group's 20 Motorized Division – advancing from the south and north, respectively – had made contact at the village of Ratchino, on the Dnepr River 11 kilometers south of Solovevo, finally sealing the pocket.[207] That was the good news; the bad news for General von Thoma's 17 Panzer Division was that it was now once again on the encirclement ring – this time facing west, from positions due east of Smolensk. Moreover, the success would be shortlived, for the desperately fighting Soviets would manage to reopen the corridor several days later, to Field Marshal von Bock's unalloyed disgust.

The intense combat experienced by 18 Panzer and *Grossdeutschland* northwest of Roslavl was the result of the Red Army's first major counteroffensive in the Smolensk region, launched by its Western Front under Timoshenko's overall direction on 23 July. Responding to the Soviet High Command's (*Stavka's*) order of 20 July to "encircle and destroy the enemy's Smolensk grouping,"[208] and lift the siege of the city, Timoshenko assembled several large "operational groups" (each based on an army) in a wide arc extending from Toropets in the north to Roslavl in the south to mount a series of violent assaults toward Smolensk along converging axes. Although Timoshenko unleashed the bulk of this force against Hoth's 3 Panzer Group, considered the most immediate threat to Moscow, "Group Kachalov," the most powerful of the operational groups (based on Lt.-Gen. V.I. Kachalov's 28 Army, with 145 and 149 Rifle Divisions, 104 Tank Division, and supported by the 209 Assault Aviation and 239 Fighter Aviation Regiments) struck out northward from the Roslavl area toward Rudnia, Pochinok, and Smolensk early on 23 July.[209]

Although Kachalov's group consisted of poorly trained formations, lacking adequate artillery and armor support, its attack nevertheless threatened to envelop both flanks of Nehring's 18 Panzer Division, as well as the forward positions of Vietinghoff's 46 Panzer Corps in the El'nia salient. In response, Bock reinforced the threatened sector with two infantry divisions from Geyer's 9 Army Corps and, on 27 July, the German infantry, supported by 18 Panzer, was able to recapture Rudnia. The German *Kampfgruppen*, however, were too weak to push Kachalov's forces back toward Roslavl; by 29 July, 18 Panzer had retired into the forests southeast of Smolensk to lick its wounds; it would remain there refitting until mid-August 1941.[210]

Following consultations with OKH, Bock's solution to the "Kachalov problem" was to order an all-out assault with Guderian's southernmost panzer corps (24 Panzer Corps) against the base of the attacking Soviet group at Roslavl, a major road junction and communications node; Kachalov's group would then be encircled and annihilated, the serious threat to Guderian's right flank eliminated. On 27 July, Guderian, accompanied by his chief of staff, Lt.-Col. von Liebenstein, flew via Orsha to the headquarters of Army Group Center in Borisov; there, in the presence of Bock and the Army C-in-C, Brauchitsch, Guderian outlined his plan of attack, which Bock approved. Guderian requested, and was allotted, the additional forces he needed to conduct the offensive: 7 Army Corps with four infantry divisions. (9 Army Corps, in action north of Roslavl, had already been placed under Guderian's command.)[211] The significantly enlarged panzer group was now elevated in status to that of a full army group (*Armeegruppe* Guderian), while Kluge's Fourth Panzer Army headquarters, operative since 3 July, was unceremoniously dissolved. Once again, to his immense relief, Guderian would report directly to Field Marshal von Bock.[212]

In the days that followed, Guderian completed his preparations for the attack. "In particular," he later wrote, "the newly subordinated infantry corps, which up to then had scarcely been in action against the Russians,[213] had to be taught my methods of attacking. Since they had never worked in such close contact with tanks, problems arose which had to be cleared up."[214] Unfortunately, Guderian's supporting infantry would have but a modest number of tanks to work with, for by 25 July, total tanks available to 2 Panzer Group had sunk to just 286 (less than one third of the group's original strength of 930 tanks on 22 June); of these, four were Pz Is and 128 Pz IIs, both models long outdated. Subtracting the 19 command tanks left Guderian with just 97 Pz IIIs and 38 Pz IVs in his order of battle, shockingly low figures given the panzer group's proliferating responsibilities.[215]

The constant strain of combat – and the dawning awareness that the Red Army was still far from finished – was by now beginning to wear on the panzer general himself. On 31 July, he confided in a letter to his wife that, "the battle is harder than anything before ... it will take some time yet."[216] That evening, Guderian took a moment at his headquarters to award the Knight's Cross to generals Lemelsen (47 Panzer Corps) and Nehring (18 Panzer Division), and to *Oberstleutnant* Franz, the chief operations officer of 29 Motorized Division.[217] Two days before (29 July), Guderian himself had received his Oak Leaves to the Knight's Cross, personally delivered to the panzer general by Colonel Schmundt, Hitler's chief *Wehrmacht* adjutant.[218]

Guderian attacked the next morning, 1 August 1941. Before he did, however, the commander of 3 Panzer Division, General Model, also awarded Knight's Crosses to several deserving members of his command, among them *Oberfeldwebel* Albert Blaich, a young tank commander in Model's 6 Panzer Regiment:

> On the morning of 1 August, the division commander, *Generalleutnant* Model, came to the front. Almost the entire 6 Panzer Regiment had fallen in. A short while later, the commander of the 3rd Panzer Battalion, *Hauptmann* Schneider-Kostalski, *Feldwebel* Reinicke of the 2nd Company, to whom the Knight's Cross had been awarded on 9 July, and *Oberfeldwebel* Blaich stood before the division commander, who personally presented the three Knight's Crosses.
>
> After Model had presented the Knight's Crosses to Schneider-Kostalski and Reinicke, the slim general with the monocle approached the *Oberfeldwebel* at a brisk step, waited for him to make his report, and then stretched out his hand in greeting.
>
> "*Oberfeldwebel* Blaich," said Model, "it is a joy and an honor for me to present the Knight's Cross awarded to you on 24 July."
>
> General Model had his adjutant hand him a small box, removed from this the Knight's Cross with its broad black-white-red ribbon, and hung it round Blaich's neck, who was visibly both proud and nervous in equal measure. "I congratulate you. You are the 10th member of the Division permitted to wear this prestigious award."
>
> Then Model drove back to the division command post. This time there was no celebration. Together with the 4 Panzer Division, the division was to ... win the Krichev-Roslavl road beyond the Easter River and capture Roslavl.[219]

Shortly thereafter, 3 and 4 Panzer Divisions of Geyr's 24 Panzer Corps debouched from their bridgeheads over the Sozh River at Krichev, with the infantry of Fahrmbacher's 7 Army Corps advancing on the panzer corps' left flank. Supported by *Stukas* and other assets[220] of Loerzer's 2 Air Corps,[221] the initial strike of the two panzer divisions ripped a gaping hole in the defenses of Soviet 13 Army (on Kachalov's left flank), the German armor and infantry pouring through in a "veritable flood."[222] The tanks then wheeled northeast along the Roslavl road, 3 Panzer Division[223] taking up blocking positions on the road while 4 Panzer Division raced directly for Roslavl. At the same time, Fahrmbacher's infantry approached the city from the northwest, an advance detachment severing the railroad line from Roslavl to Rudnia.[224]

On 2 August, 9 Army Corps – with its 292 Infantry Division in the vanguard, strongly supported by artillery and devastating 150mm rocket projectors (*Nebelwerfer*)[225] – began its advance south toward Roslavl from the area around Rudnia. By the end of the day, the infantry of 9 and 7 Army Corps was bearing down on the city from the north and west, respectively, while the tanks and panzer grenadiers of Langermann's 4 Panzer Division were within striking distance, just eight kilometers southwest of Roslavl, despite having endured aggressive Russian aerial bombing.[226] Both Kachalov's right and left flanks were now turned, his group facing imminent encirclement.[227] Encouraged by the rapid progress, Bock remarked in his diary: "The attack on Roslavl is going well. The enemy troops there are poor, our losses are slight. It is a pity that we are at the end of our tether just now, and also that a thorough replenishing of the panzer divisions can no longer be postponed."[228]

The battle reached its climax the next morning (3 August). From positions just outside Roslavl, the *Landser* of 23 Infantry Division (7 Army Corps) watched in awe as Loerzer's *Stuka* squadrons pummelled the city in repeated attacking waves.[229] Brushing aside heavy anti-tank, anti-aircraft and artillery fire from the flank, 4 Panzer Division's *Gruppe Eberbach* (35 Panzer Regiment), having enveloped Roslavl from the south, stormed the city and captured it by 1045 hours. Due to the bold nature of the advance, the Germans also secured "a portion" of the bridges in the city (although the big bridge across the Easter River was destroyed).[230] Immediately exploiting its success, the spearhead of Langermann's 4 Panzer rumbled on to the northeast, linking up with forward elements of 292 ID (9 Army Corps) – which had struggled southward along muddy roads, the result of a sudden downpour[231] – at a destroyed bridge over the Ostrik River, east of the village of Kosaki and 17 kilometers beyond Roslavl, closing the trap around Kachalov's bewildered and overmatched forces.[232] Guderian, who had shuttled impetuously between the spearheads of his attacking corps, recounted the moment in his post-war recollections:

> The performance of 9 Army Corps during 2 August had not been very impressive.[233] I therefore decided to spend the next day, the 3rd, once again with this corps in order to hasten its advance and to ensure the success of the attack. I drove first to the headquarters of the 292 Infantry Division, near Kovali, and from there to the 507 Infantry Regiment. On the road I met the corps commander with whom I had a detailed conversation concerning the control of the battle. When I arrived at 507 Infantry Regiment I advanced on foot with the leading rifle company and thus ensured that there were no needless delays without having to waste many words to do so. Three kilometers before the great Moscow highroad was reached I recognized, through my glasses, tanks to the northeast of Roslavl. Everything immediately halted. I therefore told the assault gun, which was accompanying the infantry vanguard, to fire white signal shells, the agreed recognition signal for our troops: "Here I am!" Immediately I received a similar signal in answer from the Moscow road. They were my panzer troops from 35 Panzer Regiment of the 4 Panzer Division.[234]

One of the *Landser* taking part in the attack on Roslavl was Fritz Koehler, who described the memorable day in his diary:

> The start of the attack has been set for 0630 hours, and thus we go forward at that time. We advance along a broad front, a multitude of heavy weapons follows

us. After about an hour, we receive the first rifle fire, and a Russian artillery piece has already taken us under direct fire. Our artillery responds, and once our heavy infantry weapons have also joined in, the Russian gun is soon reduced to silence. But one of our panzers also comes to grief and is shot up in flames. We push further forward and take around 150 Russians prisoner. In addition, we capture 12 to 15 modern Flak guns (probably of American manufacture) ... In the meantime, we have reached the edge of Roslavl. White Very signal lights are flaring up to the right and left. Panzers and motorcycle riflemen have most likely already pushed into the enemy's flanks. We do not even experience any resistance and clean out the town. We find only isolated, scattered Russians. However, the Russians have set fire to the oil and gasoline supplies before they fled. Unfortunately, there is almost nothing to "organize" in this town. That sort of thing was better in France.[235]

Having observed the recognition signal from 4 Panzer Division, Guderian jumped in his command car and drove on to the tanks.

> The last Russians threw away their guns and took to their heels. On the Moscow road where the bridge over the Ostrik was blown, the men of the 2nd Company of 35 Panzer Regiment scrambled over beams and planks to greet me. This was the company which my elder son had until recently commanded. He had won the hearts of his men and their confidence and affection for him was extended to his father. Lieutenant Krause, who was now the company commander, described his experiences to me and I congratulated the whole company on their performance.[236]

With Kachalov's forces ("four divisions and armored formations")[237] now trapped directly north of Roslavl, the Germans systematically sealed off and liquidated the pocket over the next two days; 38,561 Russians were herded into captivity, the victorious German forces also capturing or destroying 250 tanks and tracked vehicles and 613 guns of all types – well over 80 percent of Group Kachalov's original force. General Kachalov himself died in the fighting near the village of Starinka, 16 kilometers north of Roslavl.[238] It was, recalled Guderian, "a considerable and highly satisfactory victory."[239] Offering a distinctly different perspective, more than 70 years after the long-forgotten battle, is historian David Stahel:

> Although the operation was clearly another painful Soviet defeat, the fact that it was the only offensive action Army Group Center could manage – and a small one at that – to redress the many trouble spots on its front, says much about Bock's strategic paralysis. Indeed, given the degree of pressure on Bock's extensive front and the absence of any substantive reserves, Halder judged Bock's decision to attack toward Roslavl as "downright careless." The operation was also instructive for its cost. Just two days after the start of the offensive 4 Panzer Division [which had been granted a rest period toward the end of July 1941, enabling it to build up its tank force] had lost almost a quarter of its tanks and Schweppenburg's corps (including 3 Panzer Division fighting further south) was reporting that its forces, "irrespective of the necessary reconditioning work, must also have a 4 day rest for the physical and mental strain." This, however, was impossible to achieve as local Soviet attacks continued ... While the battle for Roslavl remains an undisputed victory at the operational level, it is instructive of the limitations of the German Army in the east and a warning against the enduring optimism for a large-scale offensive solution to the still elusive German victory.[240]

While Guderian was preoccupied at Roslavl in the first days of August, the encirclement battles in the Smolensk region were drawing to a close, the Germans taking more than 300,000 prisoners at Smolensk, Mogilev, Roslavl and other locations along the central front in operations since crossing the Dnepr on 10/11 July 1941, while also capturing and destroying thousands of tanks and artillery pieces.[241] (*Note*: For a detailed discussion of the outcome of the Battle of Smolensk see, Section 10.2.3: "Conclusion of the Smolensk *Kesselschlacht*"). Farther north, along the Vop River, the tank crews and panzer grenadiers of Hoth's 3 Panzer Group were locked in a deadly struggle of their own. Indeed, on 1 August 1941, as recorded in the daily report of the OKH Operations Branch, the panzer group was only able to parry the relentless Soviet attacks by committing its final reserves.[242]

10.2.2: 3 Panzer Group

By mid-July 1941, Hermann Hoth's 3 Panzer Group had breached Soviet defenses along the Western Dvina River and was fanning out rapidly to the east along a broad front of roughly 200 kilometers. On the panzer group's right wing, Funck's 7 Panzer Division (39 Panzer Corps) had captured the town of Iartsevo late on 15 July, blocking the *Autobahn* leading from Smolensk to Moscow and, in conjunction with the drive of Guderian's 47 Panzer Corps from the south, creating the conditions for another great battle of encirclement. While Funck's tanks and panzer grenadiers, facing southwest toward Smolensk, occupied blocking positions covering Dukhovshchina and Iartsevo, other components of 39 Panzer Corps also moved into position along the *Kesselfront*, completing 3 Panzer Group's deployments along the northern perimeter of the pocket forming north and west of Smolensk.[243]

On 3 Panzer Group's left wing, far to the northwest, Kuntzen's weak 57 Panzer Corps (19 Panzer and 14 Motorized Infantry Divisions) covered the flank of Hoth's forces operating in the Smolensk region. On 14 July, Knobelsdorff's 19 Panzer Division (on orders from Halder at OKH) had begun to advance on Nevel, near the boundary with Army Group North, capturing the town on the morning of 16 July. The arrival of 19 Panzer at Nevel, coupled with the approach of infantry of Leeb's army group and Strauss' Ninth Army, which were converging on the town from the northwest and west, respectively, threatened Ershakov's 22 Army with encirclement and destruction west of Nevel.

Despite 3 Panzer Group's rapid progress, Red Army resistance began to grow stiffer beyond the Dvina River,[244] as Soviet conduct of the battle became more energetic, coherent, and effective. Moreover, with German aerial reconnaissance picking up new Red Army formations streaming westward in major road and rail movements, it soon became apparent to Hoth and his panzer group that the Russians intended to make a decisive stand in the Smolensk region – an intent confirmed by captured Soviet operational orders.[245] Unfortunately, with Kuntzen's corps far away to the northwest, Hoth's efforts to build a powerful *Schwerpunkt* along his primary (Smolensk) axis suffered correspondingly.

Compounding Hoth's many challenges was the difficult terrain – characterized by swamps, lakes, woods and rolling hills, with few good roads – in which his panzer group had to operate above Smolensk:

> The streets and roads in the area north of Smolensk had become, if possible, even worse than before. As a result, all movements were slowed enormously. The late arrival of fuel and ammunition impeded combat operations. High losses, which, however, were not heavier than in the west,[246] the physical strains on the troops through heat and dust, the psychological stress due to the vast, bleak countryside, and having to carry the battle almost alone as mobile troops without the majority of the Army, engendered in the troops the desire for refurbishment and a few days of rest.[247]

On the positive side, the tanks and motorized infantry of 3 Panzer Group were once again strongly supported by the Bf 109s, Bf 110s and Ju 87 *Stuka* dive-bombers of Lt.-Gen. Richthofen's 8 Air Corps. Patrolling the skies above the panzer group on the eve of the Battle of Smolensk, one *Gruppe* of 27 Fighter Wing registered 36 kills in a 48-hour period.[248] In his recent biography of Richthofen, airpower historian James S. Corum argues that the *Luftwaffe* general "performed brilliantly," while his airmen "played a key role in the grand victory" at Smolensk.[249]

Also in the panzer group's favor was the fact that morale, for the most part, remained intact, and confidence in final victory unshaken – despite remorseless attrition and the daily wear and tear on men's psyches and physical well-being. Typical of the attitudes of many *Landser* at this time is this letter from Karl Fuchs, a tank gunner in 7 Panzer Division, to his wife and baby boy:

15 July 1941

Dearest Darling, my dear little boy,

Finally another day of rest for men and machines![250] It feels good. You know, on a day like this, you can at least spend some time cleaning everything. For the first time in a long time I have had a chance to take a bath. That was a marvelous, refreshing feeling! My entire body felt like it had been reborn. Before that, however, we had to service our tank, clean it, repair some things, and get it back into tip-top shape. You can't imagine what this dust and dirt does to the machines and to the engines.

We are now positioned outside the city of Smolensk and have penetrated the highly acclaimed Stalin line. I would imagine that within eight to 10 days this campaign will be over. Yes, you can be proud of the German soldiers and the military accomplishments of our men.

The Russian prisoners all look emaciated. They haven't had anything to eat for days. They, too, are very happy that this war will be over soon. A fellow from the Ukraine was so happy to be taken captive that he almost crushed me while embracing me. I gave him a ride for a couple of miles.[251]

The capture of Nevel by 19 Panzer Division created two options to encircle and destroy large elements of Ershakov's 22 Army. Simply put, Knobelsdorff's tanks could have wheeled to the north (as Halder envisaged the operation) and encircled the Soviet army's 51 Rifle Corps in cooperation with Army Group North, or turned south to envelop its 62 Rifle Corps. Instead, Hoth opted to send 19 Panzer sweeping even further to the northeast to seize Velikie Luki, 52 kilometers beyond Nevel.[252] Velikie Luki possessed a clear strategic significance;[253] besides, Hoth was convinced that his 57 Panzer Corps could reach the area around Belyi – from where it would be able to participate directly in 3 Panzer Group's primary mission, the destruction of Soviet forces in the Smolensk region – more rapidly by advancing through Velikie Luki, rather than via Usviaty and Velizh, because, while longer, the route from Velikie Luki had better roads, which would save precious time.[254]

At Army Group Center, however, Bock strongly opposed the operation, concerned as he was that his panzer corps were now too weak ("because of the tremendous wear and tear on their equipment") to operate on their own.[255] The last thing the German field marshal wanted to see was, as he put it, 19 Panzer Division "tussling about uselessly" at Velikie Luki, and, thus, unnecessarily weakening his position around Nevel.[256] Unfortunately, Bock recorded this remark in his diary on 20 July 1941, by which time the raid to Velikie Luki had become a *fait accompli*. As it was, Bock blamed Kuntzen (57 Panzer Corps) for sending "his main fighting force" (19 Panzer) to Velikie Luki "against my wishes." Apparently, Bock was unaware that it was Hoth's panzer group that had ordered the operation.[257]

On 17 July 1941, 19 Panzer Division left the Nevel region for Velikie Luki, an important railway center. Among the many photographs in a pictorial history of the division is one of a dozen or so of its tanks in an assembly area before resuming their advance on the town – the two light tanks visible in the foreground festooned with heads of cabbage as camouflage.[258] In a narrative history of the division – by the same author, a former artillery soldier in 19 PD – the start of the operation is described from a distinctly human perspective common to all wars throughout the ages:

> An extraordinarily homelike landscape spread before the soldiers during the march: hilly, forested, with large and small lakes, green meadows, villages of wooden houses, with whitewashed churches. The advance went through this landscape on a paved road in the direction of Velikie Luki via Ssavino, Syenkovo, a light battery moving in unison with the advance detachment of the motorcycle riflemen. The remaining batteries followed with the mass of the forces.

> A diary report:
> "At the exit route out of Nevel there was a white-flecked hill to the right, a long stretch of poultry farm. Our riflemen 'helped themselves' admirably, as the continued advance to Velikie Luki showed. To the right and left of the *Rollbahn* the burning fire pits remained, over which the chickens were roasted. As soon as the march column moved on, the busy 'cooks' picked up their hub caps or steel helmets, which served as frying pans, and left the burning wood fires for those following behind, so they could continue the roasting activities. It fell to the vanguard to make fresh fires at each stop. The stretch to Velikie Luki was soon strewn with little white piles of feathers."[259]

By nightfall 17 July, the advance detachment of 19 Panzer was just 20 kilometers south of Velikie Luki, while the division had also made contact with 12 Infantry Division of Army Group North's 2 Army Corps northwest of Nevel;[260] efforts by Knobelsdorff's foremost elements to capture Velikie Luki the next day, however, were unsuccessful. By 19 July, the heavier German artillery batteries had arrived on the scene, and that morning they laid down a preparatory barrage to support a renewed attack. *Kampfgruppe* Schmidt, with elements of the division's 27 Panzer Regiment, was able to penetrate into the town of some 50,000 inhabitants, while *Kampfgruppe* Menkel reached the railroad freight station. The Germans cut the rail lines east of Velikie Luki and seized substantial stores of supplies, along with a trainload of new Soviet tanks, which were immediately pressed into service.[261]

Yet the German success at Velikie Luki was shortlived. On 18/19 July, infantry of Strauss' Ninth Army had gradually increased their pressure against the western and southern edges of the pocket west of Nevel; in doing so, they pushed the rifle divisions of Soviet 22 Army against the thin screen the panzer grenadiers of Fuerst's 14 Motorized Infantry Division had erected to cover the town. By the afternoon of 19 July, the "hapless" division – whose materiel was now "completely worn out" and widely dispersed – was anticipating massed Soviet attacks, against which, as noted in its war diary, it would not be able to hold.[262]

The attacks came during the night of 19/20 July, when, as Bock colorfully recorded in his diary, "hell was let loose."[263] Two to three Soviet rifle divisions struck the fragile picket lines of 14 Motorized Division; strongly supported by artillery, and 22 Army's remaining tanks, the Soviet infantry broke through the German defense perimeter at multiple points. Bitter fighting carried on throughout the night in the dense, dark forests; in the morning, Ershakov's trapped divisions broke out into no-man's land south of Velikie Luki. Because

Kuntzen's panzer corps had no other forces available, Hoth had no choice but to order 19 Panzer to send a battlegroup southward to intercept them – an initiative that failed due to stronger than expected Soviet resistance. Hours later, Red Army forces launched a powerful assault at Velikie Luki, compelling Knobelsdorff to abandon the town on 20/21 July. With the battered Soviet 22 Army having escaped encirclement, Hoth let loose the *Stukas* of Richthofen's 8 Air Corps in an effort to at least inflict some additional damage on the fleeing Soviet columns.[264]

Thus ended the ultimately pointless "expedition"[265] of Hoth's 3 Panzer Group to Nevel and Velikie Luki. Some *Landser* experienced a particularly peculiar frustration as they pulled out of Velikie Luki:

> On 20.7.[41], the evacuation of the city gradually got underway, while taking along the stores of provisions, above all the hard-cured sausages from the slaughter yard. "On every ammo-truck we had gramophones, aided by records 'procured' in all haste. These, however, to the disappointment of all, turned out not to be the wished for music records, but speeches by Stalin, numbered from 1 to 90."[266]

A month later, Army Group Center would have to recapture Velikie Luki all over again; in the interim, large Soviet forces would loom threateningly over Bock's left flank for another 30 days. In his post-war operational study, Hoth defended his decision to push on to Velikie Luki, even suggesting that the town could have been held.[267] Yet as historian David Stahel argues:

> Hoth's decision to attempt such an ill-fated move demonstrates how far removed even experienced field commanders were becoming from a pragmatic appraisal of what their forces could achieve. It was an archetypal example of what Clausewitz had warned against in the waning stages of an offensive. "The diminishing force of the attack," Clausewitz wrote, "is one of the strategist's main concerns. His awareness of it will determine the accuracy of his estimate in each case of the options open to him."[268]

According to David Glantz, the "Nevel diversion, which never should have occurred in the first place, resulted from poor planning by the OKH, which dispersed Leeb's and Bock's force at a time when no reserves were available to plug the inevitable gaps in so wide a front."[269] By driving 3 Panzer Group's 57 Panzer Corps so far north, in an abortive attempt to cooperate with Army Group North, Hoth was left with insufficient forces with which to conduct his operations along the Smolensk axis. Glantz concludes by stating that fighting in the Nevel region was "a serious mistake on the part of the German High Command, a mistake symptomatic of a growing nervousness and touchiness about open flanks. Although this syndrome was strongest in Hitler, the OKH was not immune to it either."[270]

After evacuating Velikie Luki, Hoth finally shifted 57 Panzer Corps (19 Panzer and 14 Motorized Divisions) eastward, via Usviaty and Velizh, toward the Belyi region, where, between 23-26 July, it began to occupy positions along the northern flank of Hoth's eastern front, facing toward Moscow.[271]

While the fighting on 3 Panzer Group's left flank was surely significant, it was in the center where Hoth had concentrated his main forces and where the battle in the Smolensk region would be decided. As Soviet forces streamed back toward Smolensk in disorder, Hoth began to tighten and compress the pocket north and west of the city with Harpe's 12 Panzer and Zorn's 20 Motorized Divisions (39 Panzer Corps), despite desperate Soviet breakout attempts;[272] on 17 July, infantry of 5 Army Corps (Ninth Army) made contact with 12 Panzer Division and began to occupy the northwestern corner of the cauldron,[273] bringing welcome relief to Hoth's panzer group. Meanwhile, 7 Panzer Division at Iartsevo held its ground against violent Soviet attacks from both inside and outside the pocket, as noted in this report of the division:

> On 18 July, the Russians attack against the division's positions in the afternoon with approximately 80 tanks, followed by strong infantry attacks. Our artillery fire causes the attack to collapse immediately to the front of the rifle regiment. In the evening a new attack by another 100 tanks or so, also halted by artillery. Thirty tanks remain burning. At the same time, in the dark we attack traffic on the highway and railroad. An enemy tank platoon is destroyed, detonations go on for two hours. The enemy continues to attack energetically against the division's northern flank, a section of 25 tanks remains in front of our positions.[274]

As in the sector of Guderian's 2 Panzer Group, air power played an integral part in the efforts of Hoth's panzer group to smash Soviet attempts to escape from the ineluctably tightening encirclement ring. For example, 8 Air Corps, using equipment capable of rapidly refueling nine aircraft simultaneously, conducted a series of attacks from 23 to 25 July, slowing breakout attempts near Iartsevo by enemy forces attempting to push across the Vop River west of Dorogobuzh – "a situation which endangered not only the Army units but also the command post of the air corps itself east of Dukhovshchina, as well as several of its airfields." Supporting the 8 Air Corps in these attacks was its 99 Flak Regiment.[275]

Despite its success in sealing off the Smolensk pocket from the north, Hoth's panzer group, like Guderian's forces to the south, was unable to plug the narrow gap south of Iartsevo, along the banks of the Dnepr River – through which large Red Army forces were slipping out of the pocket. In a report completed in early 1942, 3 Panzer Group explained why it had been unable to do so:

> 3 Panzer Group had not lacked the will to close this gap, even though it lay outside their sector, by 2 Panzer Group. It was impossible for 7 Panzer Division, which was first to advance as far as the *Autobahn*, to advance any further. It was in the middle of tough defensive battles to the west and east and could not make its defensive front any thinner by advancing further to the south. 20 Panzer Division initially lacked the fuel to be able to push from Frol to the south, later their forces were tied down repelling strong enemy attacks from the east and northeast. 20 ID (mot.) and 12 PD had to block the cauldron to the north on both sides of Demidov. 18 ID (mot.) had to deploy all its forces against the enemy at Belyi. So, however desirable it may have been to close the gap immediately, the entire forces of the *Panzergruppe* were committed and not available for this.[276]

With the arrival of the follow-on infantry of 5 and 8 Army Corps, 3 Panzer Group was finally able to extend its front to the south, below Iartsevo;[277] on 28 July 1941, Zorn's 20 Motorized Division linked up with 17 Panzer Division (2 Panzer Group) at Ratchino, closing the corridor east of Smolensk.[278] By 26 July, Harpe's 12 Panzer Division had been relieved from its blocking positions along the northern rim of the *Kesselfront* by 5 Army Corps; the pocket, moreover, still occupied by the remnants of Soviet 16, 19, and 20 Armies, had been systematically compressed by German infantry and mobile troops from every direction and reduced in size to a small area directly above Smolensk. The only formations of Hoth's panzer group still in action along the ring at this time (26 July) were 20 Motorized and 7 Panzer Divisions, both in position on the far northeastern corner of the cauldron.[279] The 20 Motorized Division would remain in place on the pocket to the end of the Smolensk *Kesselschlacht* in early August, defending against the final Soviet breakout attempts at that time.

From the start of the cauldron battle, Hoth had also sought to cobble together a cohesive "eastern front" northeast of Smolensk, a primary objective being to protect his northern encirclement arm against Soviet relief attacks from the outside. In forced marches, often through difficult terrain,[280] armored and motorized units of 3 Panzer Group gradually occupied screening positions extending roughly 150 kilometers – along the Vop River from Iartsevo to southwest of Belyi, and from there bending northwest to the Mezha River and the upper reaches of the Western Dvina. On 23 July 1941, the start date for Marshal Timoshenko's big offensive, which struck hard at 3 Panzer Group, the order of battle of Hoth's eastern front embraced (from right to left): 7 Panzer Division,[281] 12 Panzer Division, Instructional Brigade 900 (*Lehrbrigade* 900), 20 Panzer Division, 18 Motorized Division, and 19 Panzer Division. The 57 Panzer Corps' 14 Motorized Division, still hanging back between Usviaty and Velizh, would anchor the left wing of Hoth's eastern front by 25 July.[282]

While the battered Soviet armies inside the Smolensk pocket struggled to avert annihilation, Timoshenko, on orders from the *Stavka*, had assembled his forces in preparation for the Red Army's first major offensive of the war. Prior to the assault, Soviet Western Front was reinforced with the entire first echelon of the new Front of Reserve Armies (24, 28, 29, 30 Armies), which had been raised during the months of June and July 1941 and would furnish most of the forces for the offensive.[283] Having now assembled a strike force powerful enough to administer a major blow, General Zhukov, the Army Chief of Staff, devised a plan to conduct simultaneous concentric assaults against Army Group Center along a front of some 300 kilometers, extending from Toropets in the north via Iartsevo to Roslavl in the south. The attacks were to be conducted by five operational groups, all of them – with the exception of Group Kachalov, which, as previously discussed, attacked Guderian's 2 Panzer Group from Roslavl – striking the eastern front of Hoth's panzer group. As outlined in the *Stavka's* and Timoshenko's formal attack orders (the latter promulgated on 21 July), the four operational groups earmarked for the offensive against 3 Panzer Group evinced the following orders of battle (approximate):

- Group Maslennikov (29 Army: 243, 252, 256 Rifle Divisions, along with Armored Trains No. 53 and 82; supported by 31 Aviation Division) – to attack from the Toropets area (northeast of Velikie Luki);
- Group Khomenko (30 Army: 242, 250, 251 Rifle Divisions, supported by 190 Assault Aviation and 122 Fighter Aviation Regiments) – to make the main effort of the offensive, advancing toward Dukhovshchina;
- Group Rokossovsky (101 and 107 Tank Divisions,[284] plus 38 Rifle Division and 509 Anti-Tank Artillery Regiment) – to attack from the Iartsevo region, while cooperating with Group Khomenko;
- Group Kalinin (24 Army: 89, 91, 166 Rifle Divisions) – also to attack toward Dukhovshchina, while coordinating operations with Group Rokossovsky.[285]

While the attacking Soviet operational groups were to break through 3 Panzer Group's defenses and converge on Smolensk, the encircled Soviet armies, under overall command of Lt.-Gen. P.A. Kurochkin (20 Army), were to recapture the city and attack along the periphery of the cauldron in an effort to link up with advancing Western Front forces. Marshal Timoshenko, in overall control of the operation as commander of the new Western Direction (see Section 10.5 below), had "mixed feelings" about his prospects for success; Col.-Gen. A.I. Eremenko, who was to execute the counteroffensive as temporary commander of Western Front, later characterized the assault plans as "utterly unrealistic."[286]

Observes David Glantz:

> The most serious flaw in the *Stavka's* ambitious plan was the condition of the attacking forces. Hastily organized literally overnight, these new rifle and tank divisions consisted primarily of partially trained reservists and largely untrained conscripts strengthened by a cadre of NKVD officers and a leavening of former border guards. For the most part, other than Rokossovsky and Kachalov, the army (and group) commanders were senior NKVD officers. In addition to the poorly trained personnel, the divisions lacked the time necessary to conduct any sort of unit training at the platoon, company, and battalion level, much less at the level of regiment and division. Thus, the Western Front's divisions and regiments proved unable to employ specialized forces such as the artillery and engineers in concert with their infantry. Worst of all, the divisions utterly lacked cohesiveness at all levels of command.[287]

Timoshenko's counteroffensive got off to a slow and staggered start on 23 July 1941. Since his operational groups were unable to fully assemble prior to the attack, most began their advance (as is evident from the order of battle above) with just two or three divisions, instead of a complete army; thus, it was not until 25 July that the total strength of the forces involved (including Group Kachalov) climbed to 20 divisions. Furthermore, on 23 July, the *Stavka* reorganized its command and control of the armies operating along the Smolensk – Moscow axis, creating a Central Front from a portion of Western Front forces.[288]

Meanwhile, Knobelsdorff's 19 Panzer Division (57 Panzer Corps), advancing northeast from Velizh along hot dusty roads, reached the Dvina just beyond Ilino on 23 July,[289] despite unwelcome attention from Soviet bombers along its march route. Red Army troops, dug in on high ground along the river bank, were driven from their positions by the panzer grenadiers of 73 and 74 Rifle Regiments, supported by armor and the guns of the division's 19 Artillery Regiment.[290] No sooner had 19 Panzer registered this modest tactical success, than it was attacked by Russian cavalry:

> *Schwadronen* [troops] of Soviet cavalry (Cossacks) suddenly appeared at the right flank of the battery positions, evidently determined to drive right into them. This attack was not immediately observable from the firing positions, which had been selected for their cover. The guns had to be swung round. A platoon of medium infantry guns, which just happened to be changing position, immediately unlimbered onto the *Rollbahn* and fired right into the saber-swinging Cossacks, thereby aiding the batteries to swing round unhindered, so that they could do their bit in repelling the attack. Panzers also intervened, until the business ended in bloody losses for the enemy. The survivors galloped away in wild panic. According to prisoner statements, they had been told as they detrained that they were right at the German border; and that the tall objects which they saw ahead were not real, but fake, panzers.[291]

The next day (24 July) 19 Panzer was once more on the move, this time rolling southeast toward Bor – midway between Dukhovshchina and Belyi – which it reached on 26 July, despite ongoing Soviet air attacks. At Bor, the division wheeled to the northeast, and, by nightfall, its vanguard was in position along the eastern front of 3 Panzer Group, some 20 kilometers southwest of Belyi, with 20 Panzer on its right and 18 Motorized Division on its left.[292] To the soldiers of 19 Panzer, Moscow – the great prize – no longer seemed so distant, despite stiffening Red Army resistance:

The landscape changed once again. Light birch forests to the left and right of the *Rollbahn*, the routes sandy or even somewhat swampy. We pushed closer to Belyi, 250 km outside Moscow. Enemy resistance intensified: continuous aerial attacks, until finally Moelders' fighter wing reached us and made its presence known by dropping leaflets. From that moment on, no Russian plane made an appearance.[293]

In their positions outside Belyi, the tankers and panzer grenadiers of 19 Panzer helped to anchor Hoth's front against Timoshenko's unremitting attacks. 28 July was an especially difficult day for the division, which saw its own local thrust toward Belyi interrupted by a Soviet attack with horrific results:

Then began the advance on Belyi ... As enemy resistance arose, the batteries supported the continued advance, as necessary, with observed fire, each new action following "hot on the heels" of the last. After a few patches of forest had been secured in this manner, a big Soviet attack began, and just at the moment when only a battery of the advance guard was ready for action, with the others still on their way. As a result, the *Rotarmisten* reached a forward aid station [*vorgeschobenen Truppenverbandplatz*] and inflicted a dreadful blood bath there. They mutilated the wounded, gouged out their eyes, cut off their noses and ears. According to statements by prisoners caught later, it was a commissar who did all this.[294]

An account by a forward observer in 19 PD illustrates the indispensable contribution of the German artillery to holding together the often fragile front line:

In front of my observation post, which was positioned in the foremost line on an elevation, the swamp brush stretched out for kilometers. Beyond this, a ridge of hills rose up with villages and roads, the latter dominated by a lively enemy traffic. So I had a good backstage view of the Belyi offensive and I was able to make a number of useful observation reports.

Our assumption that the swamp was not traversable was disproved by deserters. But even so, serious attacks from this direction were not to be expected. So I first dedicated myself to combating the enemy supply traffic on the other side of the swamp ...

Of greater concern to us were the ongoing attempts by the Russians to break through on our right flank, which were doubtlessly initiated with the aim of blocking the large bend in the road west of us in order to destabilize the front at Belyi. On one morning, the Russians really did succeed in breaking through our front, which only consisted of individual strongpoints, and to penetrate into the forest between my observation post and my gun positions.

We only learned of the whole business when the bursts of MG fire began zipping about our ears and the Russians attempted to attack the gun positions. I was able to communicate by telephone with the battery officer, who reported the state of affairs to me. In direct fire, at a range of 100 meters, the battery shot the Russians to pieces. Then we sent assault troops into the forest on both flanks and cleaned up the last traces of this break through attempt. We brought back numerous prisoners and a lot of plunder. This was an entire battalion that we had finished off here.[295]

Also in action south of Belyi was Stumpff's 20 Panzer Division (57 Panzer Corps),[296] now short of tanks, combat infantry and irreplaceable experienced officers. During this period, the division engaged in desperate combat against Soviet T-34 and KV-1 tanks, against which its lighter tanks,[297] and 37mm and 50mm anti-tank guns, had little demonstrable effect. On the morning of 24 July, five T-34s broke through the 20 PD's thin screen of panzer grenadiers near Michailovshchina and burst into the rear area of its 21 Panzer Regiment:

> Great commotion, naturally: But as the daylight increased it was possible to intercept the tanks and take up the battle. Our men fired into the only weak point, the ventilation flaps, from a few meters' distance, thus setting the diesel engine on fire. Two tanks were finished off like this. In the case of the third, for some inexplicable reason, the crew climbed out and left their behemoth standing there, completely intact. The two other tanks bolted. However, this escapade also cost us three panzers.[298]

The next day (25 July), 20 Panzer demonstrated once again that, even a badly weakened German panzer division in 1941 remained tactically superior to just about anything the Soviets could throw at it. Under heavy assault by Soviet armor, the division destroyed 60 enemy tanks, many at very close range, including 18 "heavies" (*schwerste*) (T-34s, KV-1s).[299]

In the days that followed, 21 Panzer Regiment, or what remained of it, functioned as a kind of "fire brigade," repeatedly coming to the aid of hard-pressed elements of the widely dispersed division. Because the main battle line (*Hauptkampflinie*) was so thinly manned, small groups of Soviet riflemen, even individual tanks, managed to slip behind German lines and wreak havoc with supply columns and baggage trains. In one instance, a T-34 at the edge of a wooded area was destroyed by pouring gasoline over the engine compartment and setting it ablaze. Fighting to their front, flanks and rear, often in heavily wooded terrain superbly exploited by the *Rotarmisten*, the tankers and panzer grenadiers of 20 Panzer Division suddenly found themselves in a 360 degree war. The Soviet artillery was particularly lethal, leading the Germans to assume that its fire was being directed by enemy observers behind German lines. "The Russian artillery is never silent for a minute," complained Helmuth Dittri, an NCO in 20 Panzer, on 26 July.[300] The Soviet air force also made its presence felt; for example, by striking artillery and tank assembly areas.[301]

Yet if Stumpff's panzer division slowly bled to death, it also held its ground, denying the attacking Soviet forces any significant gains. In fact, by the end of July 1941, Timoshenko's offensive had registered but very limited gains across the entire front of Hoth's 3 Panzer Group, although the Soviet marshal, relentlessly pressured by the *Stavka*, had driven his attacks forward ruthlessly. Nevertheless, the ferocity of the Soviet assaults had further attrited the panzer group's ebbing strength, and, by 1 August, compelled Hoth (like Guderian) to commit his final reserves.[302] In the larger view, the Timoshenko counteroffensive, "as weak and uncoordinated as it was, brought Bock's offensive to a screeching halt in most sectors and inflicted far heavier than anticipated casualties on his forces, particularly among the panzer grenadiers assigned to his precious panzer and motorized formations."[303]

The heavy losses hitherto sustained by the mechanized units of Army Group Center are all too apparent from a brief glimpse of the status of 3 Panzer Group at this time. On 1 August, Hoth informed Army Group Center that his forces were becoming "weaker from day to day;"[304] and that the requirement to replace his badly depleted divisions with infantry had become "urgent."[305] On the same day, 20 Panzer Division noted in its war diary that its rifle regiments were "severely exhausted" as a result of the "unceasing battles," while officer casualties had reached 50 percent.[306] Just how badly the defensive fighting northeast of Smolensk had reduced the combat strength of 20 Panzer is evident from the fact that its motorcycle battalion had only 20 available motorcycle riflemen on 30 July 1941.[307] As of 21 July – that is, even before the start of Timoshenko's offensive – 19 Panzer Division had sustained personnel losses of 2045 men (including 445 dead and 1381 wounded).[308] In the divisions of Schmidt's 39 Panzer Corps, the strength in motorized infantry had plunged to as low as 30 to 40 percent of authorized strength.[309] What had begun on 22 June 1941 as a strategic war of movement had withered into a remorseless war of attrition.

The materiel situation of Hoth's panzer group was equally alarming.[310] As of 27 July, Schmidt's panzer corps possessed just 23 operational Panzer IVs, with its total tank strength at 40 percent of establishment; a week before (21 July) 7 Panzer Division had reported a strength of 118 tanks, having begun the Russian campaign with 265, more than any other panzer division in the *Ostheer*.[311] In a letter to General Paulus at OKH (29 July), Schmidt referred to the "very difficult battles" (*sehr harte Kaempfe*) of the preceding weeks, acknowledging that his divisions had suffered greatly, and that his materiel was now "totally run down" (*total auf den Hund*).[312] The situation in Kuntzen's 57 Panzer Corps was no better, with the panzer regiment of 20 Panzer Division reduced to 30 tanks by 31 July 1941, roughly equivalent to the authorized strength (*Sollstaerke*) of one-and-a-half tank companies.[313] On 26 July, Helmuth Dittri (20 PD) had scribbled in his journal: "On taking stock of our regiment [21 Panzer Regiment] we are driven to the sad conclusion that there is very little left of it ... There isn't enough to make a decent detachment."[314] (Note: For more details on the attrition of both Hoth's and Guderian's panzer groups see, Chapter 8, Section 8.2.4.)

The firepower available to Hoth's panzer group – and Bock's army group as a whole – was further diminished on 29 July, when orders arrived from Hitler's compound at Rastenburg withdrawing Richthofen's 8 Air Corps from Kesselring's 2 Air Fleet and transfering it to Army Group North to support its drive on Leningrad. The order, which went into effect immediately, left Loerzer's 2 Air Corps solely responsible for air support along Bock's elongated, bulging front of 700 kilometers. During the opening weeks of the campaign, Richthofen's *Stukas*, Bf 109s and Bf 110s had played a vital role in the headlong advance of Hoth's panzer corps. Needless to say, Bock was flummoxed by the decision:

> The fact is that our troops are tired and also are not exhibiting the required steadiness because of heavy officer casualties. – In this situation orders arrived to release the Richthofen Air Corps. When asked about this by Keitel, I had told him that it was highly undesirable at this moment and was, in the opinion of Kesselring, "impossible." The *Fuehrer* was supposedly told the opposite, a misunderstanding which I asked Jodl to clear up and report to Brauchitsch.[315]

Bock's objections, however, were futile; on 3 August, Richthofen's air corps departed for airfields behind the front of Field Marshal von Leeb's army group.[316] "The sector of Army Group North," writes historian Richard Muller, "was in dire need of air support, particularly since Hitler decreed the opening of a major offensive in the region on August 10."[317] The transfer of 8 Air Corps was simply one more example of how the Germans were forced to shuttle their insufficient resources about the eastern front to meet the operational exigencies of the moment – in this case, by robbing one army group ("Peter") to pay the other ("Paul").

Although Timoshenko's offensive had "clearly failed"[318] by 31 July, the Soviet Western Front's operational groups continued to hammer away at Bock's army group through the first week of August.[319] As indicated by the daily reports of the OKH Operations Branch, sharp Soviet assaults again struck the *Ostfront* of 3 Panzer Group on 2 and 3 August.[320] Once again, NCO Helmuth Dittri (20 PD) complained to his diary about the discomfiting effect of Soviet artillery fire:

1.8.41:
Strong Russian artillery fire.

2.8.41:
Strong Russian artillery fire.

5.8.41:
Russian artillery fire.

7.8.41:
We rejoined the remnants of our detachment located at our initial position a few miles behind our company. We were supposed to be relieved but we could not leave the spot as the Russians were sweeping the whole road with their blasted artillery.[321]

Fortunately, by late July, the infantry divisions of Strauss' Ninth Army had begun to reach the eastern front of 3 Panzer Group, where they would absorb more and more of the Soviet pressure. By 30 July, 6 and 106 Infantry Divisions were moving into place along Hoth's line, the former relieving elements of 14 Motorized Division on the far left flank of the panzer group (south of Toropets), and the latter occupying positions adjacent to 20 Panzer Division (south of Belyi).[322] As of 5 August, 5 and 8 Army Corps (Ninth Army) were beginning to relieve the formations of both 39 and 57 Panzer Corps.[323] In the days ahead, Hoth's panzer and motorized divisions would finally be pulled from the front to enjoy brief periods of technical refitting of tanks and vehicles and well-deserved rest for their men.

10.2.3: Conclusion of the Smolensk *Kesselschlacht*
One of the German infantry units which played a major role in reducing the Smolensk pocket was Brig.-Gen. Karl Allmendinger's 5 Infantry Division (5 Army Corps). In his diary, an unknown soldier serving in one of the division's artillery battalions recorded vivid impressions of the fighting there:

22.7.41:
There have been tough battles here. Our infantry has had a few losses and two batteries of 5 Artillery Regiment have been completely wiped out. Only 4 horses and a few men remain from one battery. The enemy is fighting here with all available means. Even women are fighting in the front line. The Russian infantry has dug itself in, and they are not coming out of their foxholes. Every meter of ground has to be won in close combat. Our infantry is even fighting with fixed bayonets. The dead are usually stabbed with bayonets. The Russians still keep to their foxholes and are stabbed to death there.

    You have to be very careful here. They may come out of one hole with their hands raised, while they shoot at you from another ... It's a great pity for every German soldier who falls victim here to this murdering gang. But, God willing, they will be exterminated in this war, and Europe will be freed from the blood lust of Bolshevism.[324]

23.7.41:
The first salutation of the day is fierce artillery fire. Our division attacks. We have to press forward. The enemy is thrown back a way. In a small area, the Russian has ca. 60 dead, so the infantry reports to me. But our losses are also high – 19 dead are taken away from the battlefield on a wagon. They are buried right next to our observation post. They are all from the 11./IR 56, including *Leutnant* Keller. Our infantry regiments have been seriously reduced in strength. One NCO from 75 Infantry Regiment reported to me that they had 83 fatalities and 240 wounded so far. The enemy on the opposing side is too strong. Our division is facing around 3 Russian divisions. The attack falters. We are now holding only the forward line.[325]

24.7.41:

Change of position! We are moving out, 28 [Infantry] Division is moving in. We are being pulled to the left. We march all day and half the night. Our route always goes around the cauldron; then when it got dark, you could see the infantry's white flares – i.e., "Here we are." In the meantime we find out what's up. The enemy has broken through here, and we are being pulled in here as reinforcements.[326]

26.7.41:

The cauldron has been sealed again since 0600 hours. Our division is continuing to attack to compress the enemy forces. Once again we are met by ferocious fire … The day goes by, and in the evening we are able to change positions. We receive fire again. While bringing in the limbers, we receive a direct hit. A driver and three gunners are severely wounded and two horses have been blown apart.[327]

27.7.41:

At our next gun position we don't need to fire. The infantry advances under its own steam. After a while it is time for another change of position. We pass some high ground, a place of horror. Death has held sway here. Heavy Flak and Pak were in combat with tanks here. The tanks were finished off, but our Flak and Pak, too, have lost guns and the brave heroes were buried behind their guns. That ridge has cost 300 dead in all. In our next position, all batteries are once again firing from all barrels, and in the evening, a firey glow lights up the nighttime sky.[328]

28.7.41:

The Russians are fighting with all available means, even with illegal means. A Russian fighter pilot was shot down today. He received a shot to the stomach and was taken to the main dressing station. His machine was a Russian one, but bore German insignia. The pilot himself was in the uniform of a German lieutenant and claimed to be from Vienna. After closer investigation, it turned out that he was a Russian after all.[329]

30.7.41:

Our division is still in the middle of a heavy attack. The artillery is so far forward that it even has to seek cover from infantry fire. We are to the left of the highway that leads to Moscow. Change of position at midday. We go across the highway and into position on the right of it.

In the meantime, we make a little detour. I enquire whether Smolensk is clear of the enemy and discover that the city has been in German hands for some time already. Smolensk lies another 10 km further left of the highway, and it is only a ¼ hour for our vehicle. We are there now, but it is simply not possible to describe how this city looks. It is a very large city, but not a single building is whole any more … Outside the city lies tank after tank, including German ones. Artillery and planes were deployed in huge numbers here, too. A lot of German blood has been spilled here, as the many graves testify. In the front garden of a larger building lie 60 soldiers of 7./IR 15 (mot.) [of the 29 Motorized Infantry Division].[330]

31.7.41:

Our battery is in position from 0500 hours. This must have been the worst gun position. It was close to the front line, and bursts of Russian machine gun fire and rifle bullets whistled out of the forest into our position. From time to time, we were even fired at by tanks. Despite this, everything went well, and we had no losses. We did not advance at all on this day. The Russian tried with all his strength to break through here. They stormed forward in huge numbers, but our infantry mowed them down, and in the night one could hear the loud screaming and groaning of the wounded.[331]

1.8.41:

The next morning, a strong attack was mounted. *Stukas* and destroyer aircraft intervened in the battle on the ground. The Russians had to fall back in haste, and we made good forward progress. A large number of Russians beat a path into captivity. Women and civilians are constantly among them. In the evening, change of position.[332]

2.8.41:

I do not want to describe in any more detail the images to be seen here on the battlefields and on the roads, because it is neither believable nor imaginable for somebody who has not seen or experienced it for themselves. Only now have we seen what a human being signifies. They lie around, in countless numbers. Body parts are torn away; some were only wounded, but then bled out as they dragged themselves forward a few meters in pools of their own blood. Others in turn are burned and charred. Horses are mutilated and full of holes, motor vehicles and tanks are burned down to their iron shells. With time, you get used to all these scenes; but the smell is unbearable and has such a powerful effect that one often has to put off meals.[333]

Although by 1 August 1941 the Smolensk *Kessel* had been dramatically compressed by the encircling German forces, it was "still proving a major thorn in the side of Army Group Center."[334] Field Marshal von Bock's growing frustration with the inability of his forces to bring their operations along the encirclement ring to a swift end was evident in his journal entry that day:

> The business at Smolensk is still not in order. We don't appear to be impressing the Russians there much either, for an intercepted radio message said that there was "little activity" by the Germans. I once again spoke by telephone with Strauss [Ninth Army] and with the Commanding General of 8 [Army] Corps [Heitz], in order to once again point out the strategic importance of the rapid winding-up of the pocket. Since the afternoon report by the Ninth Army suggests that it is already planning to withdraw three divisions from the pocket, I sent it a telex demanding "the total destruction of the enemy in the Smolensk pocket on 2 August."[335]

As of 1 August the dimensions of the pocket – which had gradually "wandered" to the region due east of Smolensk[336] – had been reduced to 20 kilometers from east to west, and 28 kilometers from north to south. Moving clockwise from the pocket's northeastern rim, the ring was held by 20 Motorized Division (39 Panzer Corps), 17 Panzer and 29 Motorized Divisions (47 Panzer Corps), and 28, 8, 5, 35, and 129 Infantry Divisions (Ninth Army).[337] Still fighting desperately inside the shrinking cauldron were remnants of some 15-20 Soviet divisions,[338] comprising fewer than 100,000 men; in addition, the Russian defenders were running short of fuel and ammunition. As indicated by a Soviet Western Front intelligence summary (1 August), these forces faced certain destruction if they remained inside the pocket.[339]

While the operational group under Rokossovsky (Group Iartsevo) had sought repeatedly to break through the front of 39 Panzer Corps and reopen a corridor to the trapped Soviet forces, it had hitherto failed to do so. Late on 1 August, however, the fragile German picket lines along the eastern periphery of the pocket finally gave way to the intense pressure of constant attacks from both east and west: Elements of the Soviet 44 Rifle Corps succeeded in recapturing the crossing over the Dnepr at the village of Ratchino, 11 kilometers south of Solovevo, from detachments of Zorn's 20 Motorized Division (although the crossing at Solovevo could not be retaken). Thus, only four days after the Germans had closed the pocket (on 28 July), the Soviets had once more opened up a small breach (just six kilometers wide), through which thousands of Red Army soldiers now struggled to escape to the safety of their lines to the east, as was reported by German aerial reconnaissance.[340]

By 2200 hours (1 August), 47 Panzer Corps had reported the mishap to its superiors at *Armeegruppe* Guderian: Early that evening, a scouting party of 17 Panzer Division, coming from the south, had been unable to make contact with 20 Motorized at Ratchino, instead stumbling upon enemy forces east of the village. "It appears," the panzer corps indicated, "as if [20 ID (mot.)] has evacuated Ratchino, and that the enemy is escaping from the pocket there."[341]

At midday, 2 August, the chief operations officer (Ia) at Army Group Center, Lt.-Col. von Tresckow, spoke with his counterpart (Lt.-Col. Bayerlein) at Guderian's command, requesting that 17 Panzer Division extend its defensive screen (*Sicherungen*) up to Ratchino to close the gap. Bayerlein responded by insisting that the village – where the Russians had built a bridge over the Dnepr – was outside the operational responsibility of Guderian's army group (i.e., in the sector of 3 Panzer Group's 20 ID (mot.)); besides, the difficult terrain made it "quite impossible" for 17 Panzer to carry out such an assignment. Bayerlein also observed, rather indelicately, that it was "incomprehensible" (*unverstaendlich*) that 20 Motorized Division had "given up" Ratchino in the first place; hence, it would have to deal with the problem.[342]

Bock, of course, thoroughly aghast that the pocket again had a hole in it, could not have cared less about whose operational sector Ratchino was in; he simply wanted the hole sealed up again. At 1400 hours (2 August), he shot off a pointed teletype message to Army Group Guderian:

> According to pilot reports, the Russian is streaming across the Dnepr to the east. It has not yet been possible to gain complete clarity concerning the sector in which this is occurring.
>
> I must make the commanders of 17 Panzer Division and of 20 Motorized Division personally responsible for seeing to it that, in their areas of command, even beyond the boundary lines, the escape of the Russians is put to a thorough stop.[343]

While the Germans bickered over who was responsible for closing the gap, Russian forces inside the pocket had finally received formal authority to breakout *en masse* to the east. Late on 1 August, the *Stavka* and Western Front "tacitly authorized" the breakout, which was to be assisted by attacks from the outside by Rokossovsky's Iartsevo Group. Although the withdrawal "was initially couched in terms of an 'attack' toward Dukhovshchina, in reality it was a fully sanctioned withdrawal." Simply put, after the failure of Timoshenko's grand offensive – and in light of the success at Ratchino – the only option remaining to the Soviet leadership was to attempt to extricate as many forces from the pocket as possible, so they could fight another day in the region beyond Smolensk.[344]

As the German infantry of 5 and 8 Army Corps continued to compress and dissect the pocket,[345] the breakout attempt of Red Army forces began "in earnest" on the night of 2-3 August 1941. Some of the retreating *Rotarmisten* sought to overwhelm the company-size strongpoints of 20 Motorized Division, deployed facing west along the Orleia River – from the village of Sushcheva (35 kilometers northeast of Smolensk) southeastward to the hamlet of Babeeva (two kilometers north of Ratchino and 35 kilometers east of Smolensk); others attempted to escape by pushing aside the pickets of 17 Panzer Division and "running a gauntlet" eastward through the corridor north of the Dnepr, before seeking to ford the river in places where it was quite shallow. As they did so, the Germans endeavored to smash the fleeing columns with repeated air strikes and artillery fire.[346] On 3 August, German NCO Karl Schoenfeld jotted down his impressions of the unequal battle in his diary:

> The *Kessel* at Smolensk is getting ever smaller, and for the Russians trapped there the situation is getting worse by the hour. This can be seen in the attacks up to Saturday morning, which 1st Company repelled. The Russian wants to cross the Dnepr and is throwing everything at it in an effort to establish a crossing point as an exit out of the *Kessel*. But artillery and *Stukas* are ensuring the contrary. In the late afternoon another attack. Nighttime Russian raid on the Pak (Heiss fallen).[347]

Because neither 20 Motorized nor 17 Panzer Division was able to push through to Ratchino, some Soviet forces were able to exploit the narrow opening between the two divisions and withdraw across the Dnepr. As noted in the diary of Army Group Guderian on the afternoon of 2 August, the efforts of 17 Panzer to reach the bridge just east of the village had failed due to marshy and heavily mined terrain. The next day (3 August) a battalion of infantry from Boltenstern's splendid 29 Motorized Division, supported by an artillery battery, managed to make it to within two kilometers of the Ratchino bridge, which they took under fire; they got no further, however.[348] That these German mobile units were unable to completely close the small hole – despite the fact that 20 Motorized Division in the north, and 29 Motorized Division in the south, were each within two kilometers of Ratchino – illustrates just how dramatically their offensive prowess had declined.

Battling fierce opposition to the very end, German forces did not complete the destruction of Soviet units inside the pocket until 5 August 1941. On this day, the daily report of the OKH Operations Branch stated laconically: "The Battle of Smolensk has ended. Enemy attacks have slackened along the entire eastern front of [Army Group Center] due to the exhaustion of the enemy."[349] The OKW lauded the victory in rather more flowery prose, declaring that the unprecedented spaces involved, the severity of the fighting, and the "relentless series of annihilating blows against the Bolshevik armed forces, give to the great Battle of Smolensk its historically unique character" (*geschichtlich einzigartige Gepraege*).[350] That evening, Field Marshal von Bock released an order of the day to commemorate the glorious German *Sieg*:

> With the destruction of the Russian divisions cut off at Smolensk, the three-week "Battle at the Dnepr and Dvina and of Smolensk" has concluded in another brilliant victory [*glaenzenden Sieg*] for German arms and German fulfillment of duty. Taken as booty were: 309,110 prisoners, 3205 captured or destroyed tanks, 3000 guns, 341 aircraft. The numbers are not yet complete. This deed of yours, too, has become part of history! It is with gratitude and pride that I look upon a force that is capable of such an accomplishment.
>
> Long live the Fuehrer!
>
> Signed: v. Bock
> *Generalfeldmarschall*[351]

While it is unknown precisely how many Soviet troops were able to extricate themselves from the Smolensk pocket, new documentary evidence reveals that, of the three Soviet armies trapped inside the pocket (16, 19, 20 Armies), as many as 170,000 men were killed or captured; since the pocket most likely had contained more than 220,000 men in mid-July 1941, this means that some 50,000 of them managed to escape – in organized units, in small groups, or even as individuals – over the three-week period of the Battle of Smolensk.[352] Yet the Red Army divisions which did manage to evade total annihilation had been reduced to one or two thousand men, and, in some cases, even fewer. Also devastating were the losses of tanks and artillery (even if they were most likely exaggerated by the Germans); in fact, by early August, the Soviets suffered from a serious shortfall of tanks, artillery, and other heavy weapons across the entire eastern front, having lost close to 6000 tanks (destroyed or captured) on the central front alone since the start of the campaign.[353]

From his command post in Borisov, Field Marshal von Bock viewed the outcome of the Smolensk *Kesselschlacht* with great satisfaction,[354] as underscored by his order of the day. Although it had taken longer than anticipated to bring the battle to a successful conclusion, and although the casualties of his forces had been higher than expected, Bock was firmly convinced that his Army Group Center had emerged from the fighting with a decisive victory; he had, he believed, now completed the difficult task of destroying most of Soviet Western Front; and, after his mobile formations were given a brief respite to rest and refit, he could resume his implacable march on Moscow, now barely 300 kilometers to the east.

Yet the outcome of three weeks of combat at Nevel, Smolensk, and Roslavl had "left entirely different impressions on Timoshenko and the *Stavka*."[355] While their forces had incurred horrific losses in men and materiel, they had salvaged parts of their encircled armies (16, 19, 20, 22) and rebuilt a cohesive defensive front extending from Velikie Luki in the north to the southeast beyond Smolensk, before curling southwest to the Dnepr River west of Gomel.[356] The Red Army had also inflicted serious attrition on the forces of Army Group Center, particularly upon the motorized infantry component of the panzer and motorized divisions.

Most significantly, while the Battle of Smolensk did not culminate in the victory heralded by Soviet propaganda, the Soviet military leadership had prevented the destruction of the bulk of their forces along the Smolensk – Moscow axis,[357] and, for the first time, blunted the momentum of the German blitzkrieg, temporarily denying Bock the operational freedom he so coveted in the direction of Moscow. As a result, the *Stavka* was convinced that its strategy of active defense, by mounting more and more powerful counteroffensives, was paying off:

> In light of its large number of uncommitted reserve armies and apparent increasing German weakness, the *Stavka* resolved to continue its determined war of attrition against Army Group Center in the firm belief its forces could ultimately halt and perhaps even destroy Bock's army group. Therefore, at the very moment the Germans were concluding the Battle for Smolensk was over, Stalin and his *Stavka* were busily preparing a massive new counteroffensive marking what they were convinced would be the battle's second and most decisive stage.[358]

10.3: The *Luftwaffe* Strikes at Moscow

10.3.1: Hitler Decides to Level Moscow

Only days after the start of the Russian campaign, Hitler declared that he wanted both Moscow and Leningrad to be annihilated by aerial attack – an intent he repeated on several occasions through mid-July 1941. As Halder recorded in his diary following the midday military conference at Rastenburg on 8 July 1941:

It is the Fuehrer's firm decision [*feststehender Entschluss*] to level Moscow and Leningrad, and make them uninhabitable, so as to relieve us of the necessity of having to feed the population through the winter. The cities will be annihilated by the *Luftwaffe*. Tanks must not be used for the purpose. "A national catastrophe [*Volkskatastrophe*] which will deprive not only Bolshevism, but also Muscovite nationalism, of their centers."[359]

Six days later (14 July), the German dictator spoke of the necessity to "bombard" (*bombardieren*) Moscow in order to "strike at the center of Bolshevik resistance and prevent the orderly evacuation of the Russian governmental apparatus."[360] Furthermore, the "Fuehrer" believed that an air campaign against the Soviet capital would help to counteract claims by Soviet propaganda that the German ground offensive in Russia was finally petering out.[361] Hitler's thoughts along these lines took concrete form in "Fuehrer Directive" No. 33 ("Continuation of the War in the East"), issued by the OKW on 19 July 1941, the pertinent section of which read: "3.) ... The attack on Moscow by bomber forces of 2 Air Fleet, temporarily reinforced by bomber units from the West, is to be carried out as soon as possible as "retribution [*Vergeltung*] for Soviet attacks on Bucharest and Helsinki."[362]

Hitler's decision to conduct terror raids on Moscow came at a time when the *Luftwaffe*, with its dwindling resources,[363] was finding it increasingly difficult to accomplish its primary mission of tactical support of the Army, while also continuing to contain Soviet air activity. In such a strained operational environment, the demands of a strategic air campaign against Moscow were well beyond the capabilities of the *Luftwaffe*; moreover, "the timing of the start of the attacks was clearly wrong, because in July [1941] the main task [as outlined in the original *Barbarossa* directive of 18 December 1940] was still to provide all-out support for the ground troops to help them reach their operational objectives."[364]

The top field commanders responded with scant enthusiasm to the impending new mission. On 20 July, Bock observed that he "would consider it more appropriate to commit the fighting strength of the *Luftwaffe* without any limitation to smash the enemy's reserves."[365] In his memoirs, Field Marshal Kesselring, Commander, 2 Air Fleet, stated that he considered any secondary tasks to be a "harmful dissipation" [*schaedliche Zersplitterung*] of limited air fleet resources, better put aside until the main goals had been accomplished.[366] Despite such doubts, Kesselring and his air fleet staff rapidly assembled the bomber wings for the offensive, along with the requisite ground equipment (e.g., radio beacons) and munitions.[367]

10.3.2: Moscow Prepares for Aerial Assault

While the *Luftwaffe* prepared for its terror raids, the Russians labored mightily to protect Moscow against possible attack from the air – a prospect which had, by mid-July 1941, with the German panzer spearheads already beyond the Dnepr and at Smolensk, become a virtual certainty. Moscow, in fact, had been blacked out since the first day of the war (the blackout remaining in effect until April 1945),[368] while municipal and military authorities had immediately begun to take all sorts of other precautionary measures. A keen observer of this determined activity – as well as of everyday life in the Soviet capital following the outbreak of war – was Alexander Werth, the Moscow correspondent of the London "*Sunday Times*," who had arrived in Moscow from London on 3 July via a circuitous route "only conceivable in wartime."

On the face of it, Moscow looked perfectly normal. The streets were crowded and the shops were still full of goods. There seemed no food shortage of any kind; in Maroseika Street, I walked that first day into a big food shop and was surprised by the enormous display of sweets and *pastila* and *marmelad*; people were still buying food freely without any coupons. In their summer clothes the young people of Moscow looked anything but shabby. Most of the girls wore white blouses, and the men white, yellow or blue sports shirts, or buttoned-up shirts with embroidered collars. Posters on the walls were being eagerly read, and there were certainly plenty of posters: a Russian tank crushing a giant crab with a Hitler moustache, a Red soldier ramming his bayonet down the throat of a giant Hitler-faced rat – *Razdavit' fascistskuyu gadinu*, it said: crush the Fascist vermin …

Everyone was being asked for papers on all kinds of occasions, and it was absolutely essential to have these in order, especially after the midnight curfew, when a special pass was required. Speaking anything but Russian aroused immediate suspicion.

Auxiliary militia-women were particularly keen. I remember walking with Jean Champenois[369] along Gorki Street at sunset, when suddenly a militia-woman pounced on him shouting: "Why are you smoking?" and ordered him to put out his cigarette at once; she thought he might be signalling to German aircraft!

All day long, soldiers were marching along the streets, usually singing. The *opolcheniye*[370] movement was in full swing; during those first days of July tens of thousands of men, many of them elderly, volunteered, appearing at assembly points – such as the one opposite the house I lived in, in Khokhlovsky Lane – by the hundred, all carrying small bundles or suitcases. After being sorted out – and partly rejected – they were sent to training camps.

Apart from that, the mood in Moscow still seemed reasonably calm. People could still be seen laughing and joking in the streets though, significantly, very few talked openly about the war …

For all that, Moscow was preparing for air raids. Already on 9 July, special trucks began to run along the tram-lines, distributing heaps of sand. That week I wrote an article on the London blitz and on British air raid precautions, and this was promptly published in *Izvestia*, was much talked about, and even produced some polemics on the pros and cons of pouring buckets of water over incendiaries, which I had declared to be wrong. My story of the London blitz was widely discussed, all the more so as during the Soviet-German Pact the Russian press had not dwelt very much on Britain's experiences of bombing.

The prospect of German air raids led, by the second week of July, to a large-scale evacuation of children from Moscow. Many women were also urged to leave and to work on *kolkhozes*. Railway stations were crowded with people who had permits to leave Moscow. Many of the women I saw at the Kursk Station on the night of 11 July, on their way to Gorki, were weeping; many thought they would not get back to Moscow for a long time, and perhaps, for all they knew, the Germans would come.[371]

Since the outbreak of hostilities with Germany, air defenses in and about Moscow – the responsibility of General M. S. Gromadin as head of the Moscow Air Defense District (*Moskovskaya Zona PVO*) – had been steadily improved.[372] These defenses were arranged in depth in a series of defensive rings. The outer ring, more than 200 kilometers from Moscow, comprised the men and women of the VNOS, the Air Observation, Warning and Communications Service, whose task it was to "observe all aircraft passing overhead day and night; identify their type, course and height; and convey that information to Moscow."[373] Their mission, however, was made more difficult by a serious shortage of binoculars, as well as by the observers' initial inability to reliably distinguish friendly from enemy aircraft.[374]

Behind the VNOS formations were the fighter regiments of Colonel Klimov's 6 Air Defense Corps, deployed about 125 kilometers outside Moscow. These consisted of 585 fighter aircraft, of which more than half (170 MiG-3s, 95 Yak-1s, 75 LaGG-3s)[375] were the most modern types; moreover, the modern twin-engine Pe-2 bomber would prove to be particularly adept as a night fighter, "stalking the raiders back to their bases and shooting them down as they landed."[376]

Defending the direct approaches to Moscow were roughly 800 anti-aircraft guns, many of them dug in and well-concealed in the clearings between the conifer and birch trees of the massive forest belts about the city.[377] Hundreds of large searchlights were set up in concentric circles around Moscow to enable the AA artillery and fighter aircraft to operate at night. Smaller searchlights, as well as anti-aircraft and machine guns, were also deployed within the city itself,[378] many of the guns atop buildings. Completing the layered air defenses of the Moscow Air Defense District were more than one hundred barrage balloons; every night the balloons were raised into the sky above the city, the objective being to compel the German bombers to fly higher and to disrupt their target acquisition.[379]

Finally, meticulous measures had been undertaken to camouflage the entire city, some of them "lavish and quite ingenious" and designed to deceive German reconnaissance crews during their flights over the Kremlin district of Moscow.[380] An observer, who witnessed the first days of the war in Moscow, described the camouflage measures implemented there by the Soviets:

> The walls of the Kremlin were painted over to resemble a row of dwelling houses. Lenin's mausoleum of red and black marble in Red Square was covered with sandbags and decorated as a village house. Mozhavaya Street was painted over with zigzag lines to present from above the appearance of a row of housetops. The Bolshoi theater was draped with canvas on which false entrances were painted. The facade of the palace in the Kremlin was covered with netting and decorated with green twigs. The five red stars usually illuminated on the highest towers of the Kremlin were hidden under cloaks of gray cloth. The golden domes of the Kremlin churches were boarded over with dark timber, and the brilliant green hue of the roofs of other large buildings was painted over with hideous blendings of blue and brown.
>
> Never had I witnessed anything similar in times of war, neither in Spain nor in France. However, I was convinced that this camouflage could deceive nobody. In the case of ground combat, it might have served its purpose, but surely it could never in the slightest degree mislead German bombers flying high above the city and moreover dazzled by searchlights and the flames of exploding shells.[381]

Factories, especially those turning out aircraft and other vital war equipment, were elaborately camouflaged; transportation centers and traffic-direction installations were also "covered by rather extensive camouflage constructions."[382] When all was said and done, however, Moscow remained "peculiarly hard to defend from aerial attack."[383] In spite of the major building program of the 1930s, 70 percent of residential structures inside the city were still made of wood; factory workshops were roofed with flammable rubberized material and tarred paper. Even in the center of the city, in places like Gorki Street, piles of firewood could be found, as well as wooden storehouses and other highly combustible buildings. Moscow, in effect, "was a tinderbox." Thus, a primary objective of the city's air defense organizations was to ensure that fires caused by air raids were held firmly in check. Significantly, the first decision taken by the State Defense Committee (GKO), following its creation on 30 June 1941, was to mandate an increase in the production of fire engines for Moscow's fire services.[384]

10.3.3: The Initial *Luftwaffe* Strikes

For the bomber offensive against Moscow, Kesselring's 2 Air Fleet had amassed the following bomber units by late July 1941: 2, 3, 53 KG (*Kampfgeschwader*, or bomber wings), all from Loerzer's 2 Air Corps; 4 KG, newly arrived from the west (and normally used to lay mines), from 1 Air Fleet (supporting Army Group North); 54 and 55 KG from 4 Air Fleet (supporting Army Group South); and 28 KG from 3 Air Fleet in the west, with its two pathfinder groups, *Kampfgruppe* 100 and III./KG 26. These eight bomber wings (or portions thereof) were composed of several hundred He 111H, Ju 88A, and Do 17Z twin-engine medium bombers; they were armed primarily with high explosive and incendiary bombs.[385]

The first raid on Moscow was flown on 21/22 July 1941; formations taking part in the attack included: 2, 3, and 53 Bomber Wings; elements of 4 and 55 Bomber Wings; and several He 111Hs of *Kampfgruppe* 100. That evening, 195 bombers lifted off from their forward airfields around Minsk, Orsha, Vitebsk and Chatalovska[386] – from where, in many cases, they could hear the sounds of the nearby encirclement Battle of Smolensk – and headed toward their destination 450 to 600 kilometers to the east. Because German aerial reconnaissance had detected heavy Russian Flak at Dorogobuzh, along the direct route to Moscow, the bomber formations dipped slightly to the south at that point to circumvent the threat.[387]

Flying at altitudes between 2000 and 4000 meters, the bomber crews enjoyed good visibility as they winged eastward. Thirty kilometers outside Moscow they were caught in the first searchlights, whose probing fingers of light punctured the darkness and illuminated individual aircraft for the Russian anti-aircraft guns, which now put up a curtain of fire.[388] A bomber of 53 *Kampfgeschwader*, struck by shrapnel from a nearby exploding shell, armed and jettisoned its bombs by emergency release, then dived earthward (down to 300 meters) to escape the searchlights and heavy Flak; having shaken off its tormentors, the bomber fled for home, safely reaching an airfield in Smolensk after a total flight time of five hours.[389]

Many of the bombers, however, made their way virtually unscathed to Moscow. Then, suddenly, the entire city was transformed into a "roaring volcano," as regiment upon regiment of light and heavy Flak opened up on the aerial intruders; adding to the chaos were the hundreds of searchlights, which blinded the bomber crews and made it difficult for them to locate their targets.[390] As one account indicated, "the [German] bomber crews encountered defenses which compared favorably with London at the time of the air battle over England" (*Luftschlacht um England*).[391]

On the ground, correspondent Alexander Werth observed the dazzling spectacle, which he recounted in his sweeping narrative, *Russia at War*:

> What was most impressive was the tremendous anti-aircraft barrage, with shrapnel from the anti-aircraft shells clattering down on to the streets like a hailstorm; and dozens of searchlights lighting the sky; I had never seen or heard anything like it in London. Fire-watching was organized on a vast scale. Later I heard that many of the fire-watchers had been badly injured by incendiary bombs, sometimes through inexperience but usually through sheer Russian foolhardiness. Youngsters would at first just pick up the bombs with their bare hands![392]

This first *Luftwaffe* raid lasted for five hours, the 127 bombers that managed to reach Moscow disgorging 104 tons of high explosive (HE) and 46,000 incendiary bombs on the city.[393] The results, however, were disappointing: Like all air forces in 1940/41, the German Air Force was unable to deliver bombs at night with any degree of concentration. In addition, the HE and incendiaries were not only scattered about the city, they were, in part at least, unsuited for their objectives. The wing commander of 55 KG, *Oberstleutnant* Kuehl, returned from the mission convinced that his crews had seriously damaged their primary target, the Kremlin. Although Kuehl proudly reported his success to the commander of 2 Air Corps, bomb damage photographs soon revealed that Kuehl's 35 He 111s had actually hit a sports stadium, whose contours closely resembled those of the Kremlin. Yet even had the wing's load of mostly incendiary bombs struck the Kremlin, they would have caused little damage, for its roofs were covered with so many layers of 17th Century tiles that the puny incendiaries would simply have bounced off the structure.[394] Clearly, in 1941, the science of matching weapons to targets was still very much in its infancy.

On the morning of 22 July, as the German bombers flew back to their bases, they left behind 130 dead, 241 severely injured, and 421 lightly injured Muscovites; their bombs and incendiaries had also demolished 37 buildings and started 1166 fires. Three incendiaries had landed on the British embassy and were extinguished by the fire brigade. "By the standards of the London blitz," avers author Rodric Braithwaite, the British ambassador to Moscow from 1988 to 1992, the raid "was a flea bite."[395] On the other hand, despite intense anti-aircraft fire and pesky Russian night fighters, the attacking *Luftwaffe* bomber wings lost but a single aircraft,[396] illustrating that "fighters and Flak blasting away indiscriminately were of limited utility."[397] Yet in the absence of effective radar tracking gear and radio communications, there was little else the Russian defenders could do.

The bombers with the black crosses emblazoned on their wings and fuselages sallied forth again on the nights of 22/23 and 23/24 July, on each occasion striking Moscow with more than 100 aircraft armed with high explosive and incendiary bombs. Once more, the results were disappointing for both parties: Minimal damage was achieved by the German bombers, while Soviet air defenses again shot down just one of the intruders on each of the raids. In his dairy on 24 July, Brig.-Gen. von Waldau, Chief of the *Luftwaffe* Operations Staff, expressed skepticism about the bomber offensive which, in his view, could hardly be decisive, given the relatively modest resources committed to it. "I hope [it] will soon be ended," he wrote.[398]

Still, the raids went on, and became even more challenging for German bomber crews as the Soviets continued to strengthen their air defenses.[399] In a history of 4 Bomber Wing, a former squadron chief in the *Kampfgeschwader* described the attack on the night of 26/27 July 1941:[400]

> The defenses here have been reinforced even more and have achieved a density and intensity seldom observed by the crews over London. Approximately 500 searchlights have been erected in a radius of 30 – 40 km around the city center, so that precise targeting is made very difficult due to the severe effects of dazzling. Flak batteries of all calibers are laying well-aimed concentrated anti-aircraft fire [*Planfeuer*]. Once more the bombs which are dropped are causing large fires and explosions in the urban area.[401]

In early August 1941, the *Luftwaffe* conducted its 14th and 15th raids on Moscow with 66 and 58 bombers, respectively; approaching at altitudes ranging from 1800 to 5800 meters, the bombers unloaded a combined total of 90 tons of high explosive and more than 80,000 incendiaries over a 48 hour period. A crew member in 55 KG captured the intensity of the missions:

> Just as we are flying along the edge of the Moscow cauldron, still rather hazy with cloud, dozens of powerful light sources flare up down below. Searchlights spin the Red capital into a gigantic net intended to ensnare our He 111. For several seconds, the white light, after restless searching, licks the belly of the bomber, but is unable to hang on to it.

> The Red gunners put up an iron curtain barricade from a multitude of Flak barrels. No matter! We penetrate it!
>
> Now we are above the city precincts. Moscow has already received heavy blows. Three large fields of fire are the result of the first contingent of high explosive and incendiary bombs which are to fall in their tens of thousands over the course of the night.
>
> In one of these fields, eight large fires are raging. That was where the first heavy caliber bombs struck. Direct hit to the center of the aircraft industry and to the support firms.
>
> We can orientate ourselves well by the two large loops of the Moskva River, which comes from the southwest and reaches right up to the edge of the city. We now know where the Kremlin is.
>
> So we circle, see barrage balloons like big, black ghost creatures swooping past us, lightning fast, observe the impact of incendiary and high explosive bombs from other bomber aircraft in the air space above Moscow, until *Oberleutnant* Mylius has his target directly in his sights. Now our heavy bomb is also falling and the incendiary bombs follow immediately afterwards, causing new destruction.
>
> We turn back on a homeward course, but have to break through the heavy Flak curtain again, which is directed at us, or perhaps even at the next wave of bombers.[402]

On 15/16 August 1941, the *Luftwaffe* flew its 20th mission over Moscow – this time, however, with just five bombers dropping 11 tons of high explosive.[403] Yet the raids were persistent enough that they were beginning to take a toll on the nerves of Moscow's citizens; moreover, the German bombers occasionally struck with devastating – albeit often indiscriminate – effect:

> MosGES, one of the main power stations in Moscow, was a prime target for the bombers, and the area around it was heavily damaged. The nearby Zatsepski Market was destroyed by incendiary bombs, and many apartment buildings round about were left damaged for months, their windows hanging loose, their interiors open to the public eye, the home of sparrows and stray cats. On 27 July a high-explosive bomb scored a direct hit on a newly built school in Zemskoi Lane, which was almost completely destroyed. More than 300 people were buried in the shelter beneath it. Despite the flames, the rescuers managed to get them out. A building opposite the Lenin Library was hit by a bomb which penetrated all four storeys and exploded on the roof of the cellar. Those sheltering inside were trapped by rubble as a fire broke out in the ruins above. With great difficulty the rescuers found a way through. It took them 13 hours to free the 30 survivors.
>
> On 5 August a 1000-kilo bomb landed opposite the monument to the distinguished agricultural scientist Timiryazev by the Nikitski Gates. It blew a crater 30 yards across and 10 yards deep, severely damaging the tramlines, the underground services and the nearby buildings. The statue was knocked down and shattered. A tram carrying sacks of flour had halted on the square when the alarm sounded. The flour was spread by the blast all over the square, which looked as if it was covered with snow …
>
> The staff and vehicles of Moscow's Central Ambulance Service were called out nearly 400 times during the raids in July, over 100 times in August and over 200 times in October.[404]

By 20 August 1941, having completed 23 missions over Moscow, the German bombing campaign came to a temporary halt; after a hiatus of several weeks, it resumed in early

September, albeit with numbers of aircraft so small as to be virtually insignificant. In fact, only the first three raids in late July had been carried out with more than 100 bombers; following a 63 plane raid on 10/11 August, the largest number of bombers committed to a single mission through 30 September 1941 was 16, while the average number of bombers taking part in the 12 raids in September was merely seven. In total, the Germans executed 35 raids between 21 July and 30 September 1941; of these, only nine involved 50 or more bombers, while 21 were conducted by less than 15 aircraft,[405] making the majority of the missions little more than nuisance attacks. Indeed, the sum total of high explosive dropped by the *Luftwaffe* in these three-dozen raids amounted to well under half of what Great Britain's Royal Air Force (RAF) deposited on average in a *single night* during its strategic bombing campaign over Germany in 1944.[406] About the best that can be said of the Moscow raids is that German bomber losses "remained within acceptable limits."[407]

The bombing campaign would continue into April 1942;[408] after the war, Kesselring offered a pessimistic assessment of its utility:

> The raids on Moscow ... caused me much anxiety. Crews which were shot down had to be considered written off [*erledigt*]; the effect of the Flak and the dazzling impact of the searchlights even impressed our airmen who had flown over England. Moreover, as time went on, the Russian defense fighters appeared in increasing numbers, fortunately only in the daytime. The results [of the bombing raids] did not entirely meet my expectations; in relation to the size of the target, our forces were quite weak [*recht schwach*], the effect of the searchlights disturbing, and the weight of the bombs which could be carried quite limited due to the increased fuel load.[409]

Although other attempts were made by the *Luftwaffe* in 1941 to wage strategic air war (e.g., through occasional attacks on aircraft factories and other industrial installations behind the front)[410] the only operation rising to the level of a *sustained* strategic campaign was the bombing offensive against Moscow.[411] Yet in light of the relatively small number of bombers committed to the effort, as well as the extremely limited capabilities of the *Luftwaffe's* two-engine bomber force in general, the obvious conclusion is that the strategic impact of the raids on Moscow was nil. German historian Horst Boog stresses the "frivolousness" and "lack of planning" with which these attacks were carried out, and he is surely right.[412]

Given the limited *Luftwaffe* bomber force, "there were more meaningful centers of gravity than Moscow in July 1941."[413] The entire Soviet logistical chain was initially vulnerable to attack, while the systematic destruction of aircraft and tank factories would have palpably eased pressure on German ground forces across the eastern front. Among other worthwhile targets for an independent strategic air campaign were: "the railway lines to and from Siberia, from the Arctic Ocean and the Caspian Sea to the interior of the country, the oil refineries in Tuapse and the oil pipelines in the Caucasus and from Guryev on the Caspian to Orsk, the cracking-plants for the production of aviation fuel in Ufa and Orsk, and the oilfields of Grozny and Baku."[414] Although professional airmen understood this, demands along these lines from *Luftwaffe* forces in the field were ignored at higher levels.

10.3.4: The Soviets Bomb Berlin

In response to the *Luftwaffe's* systematic air raids on Moscow (and, to a lesser extent, on Leningrad), the Soviet High Command undertook retaliatory raids of its own against Berlin. The mission was given initially to an air group of the 1 Mine-Torpedo Air Regiment of the Red Banner Baltic Fleet Air Force. Lifting off from Saaremaa Island off the coast of

Estonia, 13 DB-3 medium bombers of the air regiment struck Berlin on the night of 7/8 August 1941. According to one account, they "caught the Berlin air defenses off guard, and returned to their base without a loss. Damage to Berlin was slight."[415] Another author, however, offers a very different version, stating that, "only one bomber appears to have reached the German capital itself, where it was unceremoniously shot down."[416]

Several days later, Soviet Long-Range Bomber Aviation (*Dal'naya aviatsiya*, or DA) got into the act. On 11 August 1941, bombers belonging to its 81 Air Division, flying Il-4s and Pe-8s from an airfield at Pushkino, near Leningrad, headed out for Berlin in tight formation. This time the German air defenses were ready, and many of the attacking bombers were shot down; another was destroyed near Kronstadt by Soviet anti-aircraft fire and interceptors.[417]

Although it meant nothing more than a symbolic gesture of defiance, the Soviet night bombing of Berlin continued through early September 1941, by which time the advance of Army Group North had pushed the Russian air units beyond range of the German capital. The Soviets conducted a total of 10 raids on Berlin, dropping several hundred heavy high explosive bombs on military targets in the city.[418] The Soviet aircrews, however, had evinced little bombing proficiency, while their aircraft lacked range and payload capacity;[419] conversely, the Russian airmen deserve praise for their courage and willingness to fly into the teeth of Berlin's air defenses in 1941, and to do so without fighter cover.

In addition to the raids on Berlin, from 10 July to 30 September 1941, Soviet Long-Range Bomber Aviation and bombers of the Red Banner Baltic and Red Banner Black Sea fleets assailed enemy industrial facilities in Koenigsberg, Danzig, Helsinki, Warsaw, Ploesti, Bucharest, Sulina, and in other cities. From 10 to 30 July, pilots of the 4 Bomber Air Corps alone carried out eight raids against petroleum industry targets in Ploesti, Constanta, and Bucharest – attacks which, according to a primary Soviet source, reduced the productive capacity of the Romanian petroleum industry (at least temporarily) by 30 percent.[420]

10.4: Hitler & the German High Command

In his recent book, *Die Wehrmacht im NS-Staat*, German historian Juergen Foerster encapsulates the impact of the opening weeks of the Russian campaign on Hitler and the German High Command:

> The great operational successes after 22 June 1941 satisfied German expectations. They increased the *Wehrmacht*'s high level of self-esteem at all levels. After only two weeks, the Army and Hitler viewed the campaign in the east as already won. But only a few days later it became apparent that it had not been possible to destroy the "mass of the Russian army" west of the Dnepr-Dvina line, that the Bolshevist system continued to function, and that the Soviet adversary had been underestimated. Even the "intellectual elite" of the German General Staff had not been guided solely by "sober professionalism" in their operational planning. It was not just in Hitler, but also in this institution, "then highly respected throughout the world," that elements of "the unpredictable, even irrational," had been in evidence.[421] The actual situation at the front in July/August 1941 forced the abandonment of outdated assumptions, which were in part the result of an ideological view of the enemy. This process was – particularly after the euphoria of the first two weeks – painful for *all* involved, even if blame for the failure of the blitzkrieg was later placed solely at Hitler's door.[422]

As it slowly dawned on Hitler and his generals that their Russian blitzkrieg had failed to take down the Red colossus, they were suddenly confronted by the need to recalibrate their strategy for the next phase of the campaign. The issue, of course, was whether to continue Army Group Center's drive toward Moscow with the consolidated power of its two panzer groups, or to divert Bock's tanks and mechanized infantry to objectives on the flanks in support of Army Groups North and South – toward Leningrad and a linkup with the Finns in the north, and/or into the Ukraine, the industrial region of the Donbas, and the Caucasus in the south. The ensuing debate between Hitler and the OKH would lead to the first strategic crisis of the eastern campaign. To continue with Foerster's analysis:

> The severity of the argument over the *arcanum* of victory already reflected the growing recognition among the German leadership that their planning principles were flawed, that the blitzkrieg was not going to be won in 1941, and that the *Wehrmacht* would, in 1942, be "forced into an offensive against new Red forces which would cost more blood and time."[423] Yet still there was hope that it would be possible to bring the operations to a satisfactory end state before the winter broke. The newly available private sources[424] – as well as those sources already long known – from the Operations Branch of the General Staff of the Army, make manifest that it was not just Hitler who was really "very nervous" or appeared "extremely impatient" in view of the developments along the eastern front.[425]

10.4.1: Euphoria Gives Way to *Angst*

By late July 1941, the more perceptive officers in the OKH had begun to realize that, despite the *Ostheer's* impressive string of victories, the war against the Soviet Union remained far from over. Even General Paulus, Deputy Chief of Staff for Operations (OQu I) in OKH, and Halder's right hand man was, by now, beset by a "creeping disquiet," which tempered his initial optimism about the eventual outcome of the campaign. Moreover, the leading generals in the Army High Command were gradually gaining a healthy respect for their Russian adversary, who despite apparently ruinous setbacks, continued to fight fanatically while committing more and more new forces to the battle.[426]

General Paulus, it will be recalled, was the primary architect of Operation *Barbarossa*; on 22 June 1941, after reviewing the first optimistic reports from across the Russian front, he had predicted the blitzkrieg offensive would be over in six to eight weeks. To be sure, he had anticipated tough Russian resistance in the campaign's opening phase, but after that the Red Army would rapidly come apart as a result of the *Wehrmacht's* overwhelming blows. Now, however, Paulus was plagued by doubt. Meeting with his son Ernst, a *Leutnant* in the Army, outside Smolensk in July,[427] the father intimated that he was "deeply concerned" (*sehr besorgt*) by the strength of the Red Army in both numbers and equipment.[428] Observes Paulus' biographer Torsten Diedrich:

> [Paulus] had known about the problems which were still to come – the lengthening supply routes, the securing of sufficient technical and human replacements for ever increasing "combat wear and tear" [*Kriegsverschleiss*]. At the same time, however, he had been cautious about his fears, had not placed great emphasis on his concerns, but, as was his nature, had kept a low profile and upheld the general tone of the blitzkrieg prognosis, not least to avoid casting doubt on his own plans.[429]

At the OKH compound in the Mauerwald, 20 kilometers from Hitler's *Wolfsschanze* headquarters, Paulus, Heusinger, Halder and their military staffs worked tirelessly in an effort to meet the escalating and often unexpected challenges posed by the war against Soviet Russia:

> Barely a day went by on which the staff got to bed before midnight. A permanent high level of stress developed, which wore down the nerves and energy

of the General Staff officers. During these days Paulus was more than the usual extremely industrious and pedantic worker. He sat at his desk, so his adjutant recalls, from 0830 hours until late into the night, surrounded by his adjutant and the special-duties staff officer, neither of whom felt they were working to full capacity, because Paulus preferred to do everything himself. He wrote out plans in pencil in highly legible writing, methodically, weighing up every word; he frequently corrected himself, not, as he did later, by crossing something out, but rather by erasing and rewriting.

In such stressful phases this caused problems for Paulus' strained health. His delicate stomach forced him to eat a special diet. He had his meals prepared in his own kitchen by a cook. If this was not possible, then he kept to the strictest possible diet. As a result, his tall figure always appeared gaunt and haggard. The condition of his health, but also his own character, made him seem serious and reflective. In his calm temperament stress would manifest itself in greater absent-mindedness and, in times of greater psychological strain, in uncontrollable tics on one side of his face.[430]

By late July 1941, Paulus' boss, General Halder, was also recalibrating his assessment of the "Russian bear." On 8 July, Halder had reported to Hitler that only 46 of the 164 Russian rifle divisions hitherto identified by German intelligence were still active on the main fronts (89 of them "were totally or largely eliminated"), while only nine of 29 identified armored divisions were still combat capable.[431] On 23 July, however, he dramatically revised the Red Army's order of battle to show 93 divisions still capable of combat. The enemy, Halder opined, although "decisively weakened," was by no means "finally smashed." Because Soviet manpower reserves were thought to be inexhaustible, Halder argued "even more forcefully that the aim of further operations had to be the destruction of the areas of armaments production around Moscow."[432] Three days later (26 July), in a scene repeated all too often in the summer of 1941, Halder again revised his estimate upwards: "*Overall picture*: Enemy defense is becoming more aggressive; more tanks, more planes. In addition to 10 new divisions previously listed, 15 more new divisions have been reported."[433]

Although a much more sobering picture was beginning to emerge of the formidable task facing the *Wehrmacht* in the east, the German military leadership still clung, as best it could, to its increasingly tenuous conviction that the defeat of the Soviet Union remained imminent. In late July, the General Staff turned out studies addressing a panzer raid into the Urals and a fantastic expedition across the Caucasus Mountains to the borders of Iran and Iraq.[434] At the military conference on 23 July, Halder went so far as to assure Hitler that Moscow and Leningrad could be reached by late August, the Don and the Volga Rivers by the beginning of October, and Baku and Batum in the Caucasus oil region by 1 November 1941.[435] "In reality," asserts historian Geoffrey Megargee, "Halder's boast was an indication that he did not understand either the enemy's strength or his own logistical situation ... By mid-July the German thrusts had stalled almost exactly where the precampaign planning had forecast, but their preparations for the next phase progressed much more slowly than expected. In that light alone, Halder's goals fell in the realm of sheer fantasy."[436]

As for the "Fuehrer" himself, he was now seriously fretting over the predicament of his armies along the eastern front. The truly catastrophic failure of his military intelligence agencies to accurately assess size and strength of the Red Army "rattled" Hitler. An *Abwehr* (German Military Intelligence) colonel recorded apprehensively on 20 July 1941:

> C[anaris][437] has just returned from the Fuehrer's headquarters and describes the mood there as very jittery, as it is increasingly evident that the Russian campaign is not "going by the book." The signs are multiplying that this war will not bring

about the expected internal collapse, so much as the invigoration of Bolshevism. – C. warns in particular that attempts are being made to brand the *Abwehr* as the culprits, for not properly informing people about the true strength and fighting power of the Russian army. For example the Fuehrer is said to have remarked that had he known of the existence of the super-heavy Russian tanks he would not have waged this war.[438]

In his personal diary on 25 July, Captain Thilo, OKH Operations Branch, intimated that unexpected delays in military operations were making Hitler "very nervous."[439] On 28 July, during a short walk with his Army adjutant, Major Gerhard Engel, and his chief *Wehrmacht* adjutant, Colonel Rudolf Schmundt, Hitler confided that the situation in the east was causing him sleepless nights, as he wrestled with what course of action to take next.[440] At the end of the month, Hitler fell ill, as chronicled by his former *Luftwaffe* adjutant Nicolaus von Below:

> He failed to appear for meals and the daily situation conferences: it was quite obvious from his appearance how miserable he felt. Dr Morell said it was probably a slight apoplexy. Hitler's heart and circulation were not in good order, but within a short while he would return the Fuehrer to his former self. After a few days there was a noticeable improvement. We were ordered to observe the strictest silence about Hitler's condition. This was a health crisis with potentially serious consequences, however, and it worried me sufficiently to confide it to my brother on 30 July.[441]

The change in mood within the *Fuehrerhauptquartier*, in contrast to late June and early July, was also captured in the diary of Propaganda Minister Goebbels. On 1 August, he wrote: "One concedes openly, that the estimation of the Soviet military strength [*Kampfkraft*] was somewhat mistaken. The Bolsheviks are displaying stronger resistance than we expected and, above all, the material means available to them are greater than we had assumed."[442] (Three weeks before, on 9 July, Hitler had assured Goebbels that "the war in the east is essentially won. We will still have to fight a series of difficult battles, but the armed forces of Bolshevism will not be able to recover from defeats they've already suffered.")[443] Ten days later (10 August) Goebbels wrote: "It will still require very hard and bloody blows until the Soviet Union lies shattered [*zerschmettert*] on the ground."[444]

About the same time (early August), Captain von Muenchhausen, adjutant to Colonel Heusinger (Chief, OKH Operations Branch), summarized in his diary the new thinking which was rapidly taking hold within the Army High Command, as pressures of space and time began to inexorably intrude:

> It is often possible to doubt that we will manage to beat the Russians decisively and take possession of their main industrial regions in the <u>very brief</u> period up to the fall. Even at best, we won't make it to the Volga, and it is still highly probable that, with the aid of the industries in the Urals and in Siberia, new armies will emerge next spring! If these are dangerous, which may well be assumed, given the general nature of the Russians in this campaign, the resulting war on two fronts will have the worst consequences for the overall course of the war! Hopefully things will turn out differently!!![445]

Forty-year-old *Oberstleutnant* Hellmuth Stieff also served in the Army General Staff's Operations Branch in the summer of 1941. An intelligent and insightful officer who grasped the broader strategic picture, Stieff, who would later be executed for his role in the anti-

Nazi Resistance, had become increasingly bitter over the direction of military events and what he perceived as the growing corruption of the German General Staff. On Saturday, 2 August 1941, he penned a long missive to his wife; because of the profound insights it offers, the letter is quoted here at length:

My dear little Ling!

... Of overall developments it can be said in general that not all expectations have been met to the fullest extent hoped for – expectations, which, in my opinion, were unreasonably high in some areas. My opinion that this time we would be dealing with a struggle between two world views and new ideas, in which the severity of the struggle would acquire a completely different dimension, has been fully confirmed. Moreover, we have not only deceived ourselves about the military strength of our opponent, but also underestimated the abilities of his leadership. The forces which this life and death struggle has unleashed in this regard in our opponent are, in any case, quite considerable. With the exception of the double battle of Belostok-Minsk – where, using the element of surprise, the encirclement and destruction of considerable numbers of Russian forces led to the full achievement of our goal – the other battles, aside from localized successes, have only led to further frontal wrestling [*frontalen Abringen*]. We may have maintained the upper hand everywhere in this, and the enemy has suffered considerable losses in the process, but the big operational impact [*grosse operative Auswirkung*], which has been the objective, has not been forthcoming – there should be no illusions about this ...

Our operation has stalled in the center, less perhaps due to enemy counter actions than to the natural attrition of our mobile units, which, after all, have been in combat and advancing for 4 weeks without cessation, and are now in desperate need of a rest period to accomplish repairs on their vehicles and to replace personnel losses they have sustained of up to 30 percent. For this, they need to be relieved from the enemy, whose constant counterattacks do not let up, by the infantry divisions. This has already been implemented in part, but in part is only possible after clearing the Smolensk cauldron, where the enemy is holding on so tenaciously that he practically has to be killed one by one, because their fear of their commissars is still greater than their fear of us. For when commissars are no longer present, then our propaganda leaflets have a strong effect, and the people and their officers come over to us in their masses. Unfortunately, though, that is always an exception ...

You can imagine the nervousness at the highest level [i.e. Hitler]. If it were not so sad, you would laugh out loud about the strange effects that causes! ... [Whether], however, the ambitious goals can be reached this year may well remain anyone's guess. I fear that it will not be the case and we will have to advance once again with some elements of the Army in the coming year. Naturally, our situation is decisively worse as a result, and that gives the USA, despite all their concerns about the Japanese, the impetus either to enter into the war or to pull the kinds of dirty tricks [*Schweinereien*] like the one they did with Iceland,[446] which is already proving fateful for our conduct of the war in the Atlantic.

For the first time in this war, I have doubts as to whether we will be equal to the task. If our second strike in the east[447] does not positively galvanize developments there – and on this there is still some hope, since the Russian seems to still want to seek a decision with his last remaining forces, whereby we would be relieved of the concern of what effectively would be a war on two fronts – if, then, this hope is not fulfilled, then we will lose so much of our advantage in the other theaters of war that the outcome of this war really will be in doubt ...

One product of this nervousness at the highest level is the manner in which we report. In my view, it is bad. The *Wehrmacht* reports are no longer anything more than a medium of political propaganda, are drawn up only by him [i.e., Hitler] personally with no concern for the impact, impressed on him often enough, on the mood and expectations of the combat forces, for whom they are the only means of briefing on the overall progress of the battles. What is more, they exaggerate purported successes in such an abhorrent way and are anything but sober reports of the facts. Their truth content can justifiably be doubted. It is a shame that now even the last bastion of decency in this state is being sacrificed on the altar of a system led by corrupt or lunatic persons. I am bitter [*sehr verbittert*] like never before during this war and certainly like never before in the course of a campaign.[448]

The first formal "cracks in the High Command's confident façade"[449] appeared on 6 August 1941, when Brig.-Gen. Walter Warlimont, chief of the OKW's National Defense Branch (*Amt Landesverteidigung*) and General Alfred Jodl's deputy, produced a "Brief Strategic Overview on the Continuation of the War after the Campaign in the East." In the document, Warlimont stated that the military leadership must consider the fact that its armies in the east were not going to reach their operational objectives – a line from the Caucasus oil region in the south, to the Volga and northward to Archangel and Murmansk – in 1941; perforce, an open front would remain in existence during the coming year.[450]

While the deliberations of the OKW were hardly accessible to the German public, at least some civilians were also becoming acutely aware that the campaign in Russia was a very different one from those that had preceded it. On 8 August, *Frau* "K.B." wrote to a loved one at the front:

> Through the *Wochenschau* [weekly newsreel] we do get a small idea of what is going on in the east and, believe me, this snippet arouses so much horror in us that we would dearly love to close our eyes just to let some images roll by unseen. And the reality, what might that be like? I think we will never be able to imagine it. When I see our infantry marching past in the *Wochenschau*, then I always think that you also march ahead like that – ever onward through blazing sun and driving rain. It must have poured dreadfully out there recently, the roads have become absolute quagmires. And beltbuckles will also have to be fastened pretty tight – for there can't be anything to find in those Russian sinkholes. France provided a much greater array of delicacies in comparison.[451]

By 11 August, the distressing transformation in the Army General Staff's analysis of the Russian campaign was complete. "By and large," confided Halder to his journal that day, "no change along the entire front since yesterday …

> What we are now doing is the last desperate attempt to prevent our front line from becoming frozen in position warfare. The High Command is greatly handicapped in its capability for modifying the situation, as the army groups are separated by natural obstacles (marshes). Our last reserves have been committed. Any regrouping now is merely a shifting of forces on the baseline within individual army group sectors. This takes time and consumes the energy of men and machines. The upshot is impatience and irritation on the part of the High Command and an increasing tendency to interfere in trivial details …
>
> The whole situation makes it increasingly plain that we have underestimated the Russian colossus, who consistently prepared for war with that utterly ruthless

determination so characteristic of totalitarian states. This applies to organizational and economic resources, as well as the communications system and, most of all, to the strictly military potential. At the outset of the war we reckoned with about 200 enemy divisions. Now we have already counted 360. These divisions indeed are not armed and equipped according to our standards, and their tactical leadership is often poor. But they are there, and if we smash a dozen of them, the Russians simply put up another dozen. The time factor favors them, as they are near their own resources, while we are moving farther and farther away from ours. And so our troops, sprawled over an immense front line, without any depth, are subjected to the incessant attacks of the enemy. Sometimes these are successful, because too many gaps must be left open in these enormous spaces.[452]

Hitler, meanwhile, having sufficiently recovered from his brief illness, had visited the command post of Army Group Center at Borisov on 4 August to confer with his battlefield commanders. (For details of the Borisov conference see below, Section 10.4.3.) Back at the Wolf's Lair the next day, Hitler told his Army C-in-C, Field Marshal von Brauchitsch, that he feared the front was in danger of congealing into static warfare, just as it had in 1914.[453]

By 7 August, Hitler was ill again, this time seriously so with dysentery; for "three vital weeks," he was "weakened by diarrhea, stomach cramps, nausea, aching limbs, shivery feelings and fever."[454] No doubt the somber and oppressive atmosphere of his East Prussian compound, the daily situation conferences which dragged on for hours on end, sapping the strength of Hitler and his generals alike, and, most of all, the creeping uncertainty about the viability of the war with Russia, had all conspired to produce the serious downturn in his health; and this at a critical juncture in the eastern campaign, as Hitler remonstrated with his generals over the operational alternatives for the next phase of Operation *Barbarossa*.

10.4.2: Moscow or Leningrad & the Ukraine: Hitler vs. his Generals

By mid-July 1941, following the breach of the Dnepr River barrier and the start of a second series of encirclement battles, north and west of Smolensk, Hitler realized that the Army High Command had "set a definite course toward Moscow."[455] The "Fuehrer," however, abiding by his strategic vision – as initially laid out in the original *Barbarossa* directive of December 1940 – still considered the Soviet capital of secondary importance; as a result, and much to the dismay of Brauchitsch, Halder and the rest of the staff at OKH, the German dictator and warlord began to intervene "energetically" in the military planning process.[456]

On 19 July 1941, Hitler issued Directive No. 33, addressing the "Continuation of the War in the East;"[457] in it, he stipulated that the *Schwerpunkt* of future operations was to shift from the center to the wings, with Leningrad and the Ukraine, at least temporarily, receiving a higher priority than Moscow. As outlined in the directive, mobile units from Hoth's 3 Panzer Group, following destruction of the Soviet Smolensk grouping, were to "cut communications between Moscow and Leningrad," so as to cover the right flank of Leeb's Army Group North as it advanced on Leningrad.[458] In addition, strong elements of Guderian's 2 Panzer Group were to advance southeastward, into the Ukraine, to cooperate with Rundstedt's Army Group South. As for Bock's Army Group Center, after completion of mopping up operations around Smolensk – which, the directive advised, "will still require considerable time" – it was to continue the drive on Moscow with infantry forces alone.[459]

A supplement to Directive No. 33, promulgated on 23 July, not only "rammed [these points] home,"[460] it went further – calling for the temporary subordination of Hoth's panzers under Army Group North ("to surround the enemy in the Leningrad area"), and a joint advance by

Guderian's armor along with Kleist's 1 Panzer Group (Army Group South) to "occupy the Khar'kov industrial area and thrust forward across the Don to [the Caucasus]," while infantry formations seized the "Ukraine, the Crimea, and the area of Central Russia up to the Don."[461]

The new "Fuehrer" directives sent shock waves through the OKH, as the latent discord between Hitler and his Army General Staff over core operational concepts of the Russian campaign – reaching back to late 1940 – suddenly burst into the open, making indubitably evident that the original *Barbarossa* directive had signified "a superficial compromise between two fundamentally incompatible operational ideas."[462] Indeed, while Hitler sought to inform his decision-making through a sophisticated synthesis of political, economic and military factors – leading him to the conclusion that a decisive outcome could only be obtained by switching the weight of the German advance to the north (Leningrad and the Baltic) and south (Ukraine, Donbas, and Caucasus) – Moscow remained the *idée fixe* of his chief military advisors, convinced as they were that the Soviets were assembling their main forces along the approaches to the capital in an all-out effort to prevent its capture,[463] thus exposing them to destruction in a final great battle of annihilation. "The center of gravity of Russian strength," Halder wrote in a report prepared for the Allies shortly after the war, "was therefore in front of Army Group Center …

> The General Staff had been brought up with the idea that it must be the aim of an operation to defeat the military power of the enemy, and it therefore considered the next and most pressing task to be to defeat the forces of Timoshenko by concentrating all available forces at Army Group Center, to advance on Moscow, to take this nerve center of enemy resistance and to destroy the new enemy formations. The assembly for this attack had to be carried out as soon as possible because the season was advanced.[464]

On the evening of 23 July, Brauchitsch and Halder were given an opportunity to present their dissenting opinions to their commander in chief, the former World War I corporal, Adolf Hitler.[465] For the first time, Halder gave a presentation strongly recommending Moscow as the best choice for the continuation of the offensive.[466] Hitler, however, refused to be persuaded; in fact, when he spoke at the conclusion of Halder's presentation, "the break with the OKH was clearer than ever:"[467] Despite all the Chief of the Army General Staff and Brauchitsch had said, the German dictator remained adamant that, following the end of the Battle of Smolensk, the armor of both 2 and 3 Panzer Groups would be directed away from Army Group Center to objectives on the wings stipulated in Directive No. 33 (and the supplement).[468] Yet the failure of Brauchitsch and Halder on this day was hardly the end of the matter; rather, it was "the opening salvo in the now openly declared conflict that was to become a crisis of command that paralleled the rising crisis on the battlefield. As Halder wrote after the war, the OKH's open opposition to Hitler's plan was abhorred by the Fuehrer and 'the effect was explosive.'"[469]

When Hitler's new directives were passed down to the field commands, the impact was equally electrifying. Of course, it was Field Marshal von Bock's army group that was most directly affected by the new orders, and he responded with outright indignation, going so far as to suggest the abolition of his command (most likely, a veiled threat of resignation). In his journal, on 24 July, he gave vent his anger:

> During the morning the advance notice for a new directive arrived, which divides my army group into three parts: according to the instructions, I am to divert one group of forces, including Panzer Group Guderian, southeast to Army Group South, a group without tanks is to go toward Moscow, and Panzer Group Hoth is to be diverted north and subordinated to Army Group North.

> The army group commanders have been summoned by the Army High Command for tomorrow to discuss these new plans. I sent a report to Brauchitsch opposing the new operation and suggested that they remove the army group headquarters if they stick to the announced plan of action. Perhaps they will correctly construe that I am "piqued." That is rubbish! But if the army group is carved up into three parts there will be no need for the headquarters.[470]

The field marshal's "profound resentment"[471] of the new directives derived from two sources. In the first place, he fundamentally rejected any idea of shifting the *Schwerpunkt* of the German attack away from Moscow. During his convalescence in December 1940 from a serious stomach ailment, Bock had read a series of articles in the *New Zurich Times* entitled: "*How France Lost the War*," clearly impressed, Bock noted that, "I found Maurois' [the French journalist] view of the fall of Paris especially interesting. He wrote: 'At that moment it was clear to me that it was all over. After the loss of Paris, France became a body without a head. The war was lost!'"[472] Conceivably, Bock ascribed a similar significance to the capture of Moscow, only to suddenly see that hope slipping from his grasp. Also affecting Bock's attitude was the potential blow to his prestige. For all his soldierly acumen, the field marshal was a vain man: He had already endured the indignation of having to fulfill a secondary role in the French campaign of 1940; now, only 300 kilometers from Moscow, but with his panzer forces about to go to Leeb and Rundstedt, he faced an even greater outrage.

Visiting Bock's command post on 25 July, Field Marshal Keitel, Chief of OKW, reiterated Hitler's new operational plans. Leningrad, Keitel said, was to be rapidly sealed off (*abgeriegelt*), its population and Red Army defenders starved into submission (*ausgehungert*); to accomplish this objective, Hoth's 3 Panzer Group was to be sent northward. In the south, for the drive to Khar'kov and beyond, Guderian's 2 Panzer Group would be needed. Army Group Center, Keitel continued, was to advance on Moscow astride the *Autobahn* with its two infantry armies; the Soviet capital, like Leningrad, was not to be attacked directly, but encircled and starved out. At the same time, Bock's army group was to eliminate the enemy grouping on its southern flank, in the area around Gomel – Mozyr.[473]

Shortly thereafter, Brauchitsch and Halder, still quietly plotting to torpedo Hitler's recent directives, gained a new, and highly significant, convert to their cause – General Alfred Jodl, Chief, OKW Operations Staff (WFSt), and the "Fuehrer's" principal military advisor. This meant that the opposition to Hitler had now reached a veritable consensus embracing the central figures in OKW and OKH, as well as most all of the relevant field commanders (Bock, Guderian, Hoth, etc.). On 27 July, Jodl advised Hitler to launch an immediate assault on Moscow following the conclusion of the Smolensk battles; in doing so, Jodl, the trained artillery officer, based his arguments not on the importance of seizing the Soviet capital, but on his belief that it was only here, on the approaches to the city, where the bulk of the Red Army's remaining strength could be found and defeated.[474] Once again, Hitler was unmoved, regurgitating, *inter alia*, his now familiar arguments about the vital economic importance of the Ukraine and the Caucasus.[475] Given the level of opposition he now faced, it is remarkable that Hitler stuck by his convictions with such pertinacity.

From Halder's perspective, Hitler's constant and overbearing meddling[476] in matters that should have been the sole province of the Army *Generalstabschef*, and his trained military professionals, was infuriating. On 28 July, he noted that, "the operations ordered by the Fuehrer will lead to a scattering of forces and to stagnation in the decisive direction, Moscow. Bock will be so weak that he will not be able to attack."[477] He then aired his mounting frustration in a letter to his wife:

> He is playing warlord again and proposing such absurd ideas, that he is putting in question everything our splendid operations have won so far. The Russian won't

simply go away, like the French, when he has been operationally beaten. He has to be killed one at a time in a country that is half forest and marsh. This takes time and his nerves [Hitler's] won't stand it. Every few days I have to go there. Hours of empty talk with the result that there is only one man who knows how to wage wars. I am on the brink of despair, because I can predict exactly where this nonsense will end. If I didn't have my faith in God and my self-assurance, I'd be like Brauchitsch, who is at the end of his tether and hides behind his rank so as not to betray his inner helplessness.[478]

"Barely five weeks into a war," observes David Stahel, "that was supposed to be the decisive blitzkrieg campaign to secure hegemony in Europe against an inferior opponent, the demands of the conflict were overwhelming the Army, and the German command was expending as much energy fighting within itself as addressing the problems of the front."[479] On 29 July, Colonel Heusinger, Chief, OKH Operations Branch, noted that, together with Halder, he had "to fight against much resistance, particularly against the ideas of the Fuehrer."[480] It all "boded very ill for the outcome of the war, but like so many fundamental aspects of *Barbarossa*, the German command had to learn its lessons the hard way."[481]

At this point, disturbing new developments at the front, in particular the fierce and wide-ranging Soviet counterattacks against Army Group Center, which had started on 23 July, forced Hitler to temporarily adjust his plans. On 28 July, he informed Brauchitsch that he had decided to postpone the large-scale operations against Leningrad and in the south outlined in Directive No. 33a (the supplement to Directive No. 33). Instead, Hitler insisted, the "most urgent task" (*dringlichste Aufgabe*) was for Army Group Center to clear its southern flank by eliminating the enemy grouping about Gomel.[482] Hitler's abrupt change in plans was embodied in a new "Fuehrer Directive," No. 34, of 30 July 1941; it began thusly:

> The development of the situation in the last few days, the appearance of strong enemy forces on the front and to the flanks of Army Group Center, the supply position, and the need to give 2 and 3 Panzer Groups about 10 days to rehabilitate their units, makes it necessary to postpone for the moment[483] the further tasks and objectives laid down in Directive 33 of 19 July and in the supplement of 23 July.[484]

Directive No. 34 also specified that Army Group Center was to temporarily halt its eastward drive – which had already slowed to a crawl – and "go over to the defensive, taking advantage of suitable terrain;" its two panzer groups were to be pulled from the line for "quick rehabilitation as soon as the situation allows."[485] While no one, of course, could have predicted it at the time, the divisions of Bock's army group would not renew their drive on Moscow for two months.

As for Halder, still spearheading the generals' efforts to preserve the campaign's center of gravity along the high road to Moscow, he was encouraged by the new directive, for it at least put off Hitler's intention of withdrawing Hoth's and Guderian's armor from Army Group Center,[486] and this would buy the Chief of the Army General Staff more time to attempt to influence the "Fuehrer's" thinking. "This decision," Halder recorded in his diary, "frees every thinking soldier of the horrible vision obsessing us these last few days, since the Fuehrer's obstinacy made the final bogging down of the eastern campaign appear imminent. At long last we get a break!"[487] Halder's relief would be shortlived, however, as the massive and unexpected Soviet resistance east of Smolensk, coupled with mounting logistical problems, particularly in the central sector, would, in the end, only fortify Hitler's largely unshakable resolve that the *Ostheer* should switch its main effort to the wings.[488]

In adherence to Directive No. 34, both Guderian's panzer forces and Weichs' Second Army struck southward, toward Gomel and the region east of the city, in the second week of August 1941. The new operation promised to build on Guderian's recent success at Roslavl by reducing Soviet pressure on the deep right flank of Army Group Center, while also helping to close the widening gap between Bock's army group and Rundstedt's Army Group South.[489] Only days before, Hitler, as noted, had gone off to the eastern front, to Bock's headquarters, to talk to his generals and gain their perspectives on the future course of operations.

10.4.3: Hitler Visits Army Group Center (Borisov, 4 August 1941)

On the morning of 4 August, Hitler's personal pilot, Hans Baur, at the controls of "*Immelmann* III," a large Focke-Wulf Fw 200 "*Condor*" four-engine transport, flew the "Fuehrer," Field Marshal Keitel, General Jodl, and chief adjutant Schmundt to Army Group Center headquarters at Borisov.[490] Upon arrival they were greeted by Field Marshal von Bock; his chief of staff, Brig.-Gen. Hans von Greiffenberg; and his chief operations officer (Ia), Lt.-Col. Henning von Tresckow. Also present were Hoth, Guderian, and Colonel Heusinger – the colonel, no doubt, operating as the "eyes and ears" of General Halder.[491]

Hitler began by warmly congratulating Bock on the "unprecedented successes" of his armies in the east.[492] In an unusual move, Hitler then proceeded to question each of the generals – Bock, Hoth, Guderian – separately, in another room, enabling him to gauge their opinions individually and in such a manner that none of the men knew what the others had said. If the dictator was expecting any support for his line of reasoning, it was not forthcoming on this day, as each of the generals hewed closely to Halder's position on the vital significance of Moscow. Keitel, for one, was disgusted by the display, which he perceived as an "obvious sham orchestrated by the OKH."[493] Before his execution at Nuremberg, he recounted bitterly in his memoirs:

> [Hitler] came up against a blank wall of refusal … All three of them [Bock, Hoth and Guderian] were aware of the War Office's [OKH's] plan of attack and saw it as their panacea; any weakening of Army Group Center would jeopardize this plan, a plan which had electrified them all … The War Office, Army Group Center and the tank commanders had managed to put up a united front to their Fuehrer.[494]

Keitel went on – unfairly and inaccurately – to blame the generals for having "shipwrecked Hitler's great strategic master plan,"[495] while failing to acknowledge that both Bock and Hoth, and most likely Guderian, too, were arguing in favor of Moscow from strong personal conviction, and not merely parroting the desires of Halder and OKH. On the other hand, the absence of Field Marshal von Kluge from the meeting was at least suspicious:

> The only senior commander in Army Group Center to have openly endorsed the diversion of panzers to the south was Kluge;[496] however, his command had been recently made redundant by the disbandment of Fourth Panzer Army. As a Field Marshal, Kluge was the second highest ranking officer in Army Group Center and would be reinstated as an army commander. Even if the [OKH] had not expressly requested his attendance, Kluge had been involved in the campaign at the most senior level from the very beginning and would shortly resume his involvement, raising the question of whether there was a more devious agenda on the part of the OKH. Even if there [were] no active measures taken to exclude him, by ordering him to remain at his post, one wonders whether there was not a passive bias against him … In any case, there was no sympathetic ear for Hitler's preferred plans at Borisov.[497]

Following the generals' individual audiences with the "Fuehrer," the entire group was brought together and Hitler began to speak. What would determine the future course of operations, he avowed, was the requirement to occupy those regions deemed "essential" (*lebenswichtig*) to Soviet Russia's survival; in this context, he laid out three alternatives in order of priority. Once again, his top priority was Leningrad – with its "exclusive" factories for the production of heavy tanks (*alleinige Produktionsstaette fuer schwerste Panzer*) – along with seizure of the Baltic coast and elimination of the Soviet Baltic fleet; in addition, all of Estonia was to be occupied, as well as the islands in the Baltic Sea. In second place was the south of Russia, in particular the Donbas (Donets basin), south of Khar'kov, in the eastern Ukraine; this vital area, Hitler opined, made up the "entire basis of the Soviet economy," and its capture would precipitate the "sure collapse" of the Soviet Union's economy. To achieve this latter objective, Hitler was contemplating the dispatch of "strong elements" (*starke Teile*) of Bock's army group southward into the Ukraine.[498]

As for Moscow, it was still priority number three (*an dritter Stelle*) in the "Fuehrer's" calculations; thus, he said, it was probably appropriate, for the time being at least, to stay on the defensive on the central front. At this point, Bock countered that an immediate push toward Moscow would strike the main forces of the enemy, who was frantically assembling anything he could lay hands on before Army Group Center; hence, it could lead to a "decision of arms" (*Waffenentscheidung*). Hitler listened intently, yet refused to commit himself to a course of action.[499]

The conference then turned to other, "more detailed questions."[500] As Guderian wrote after the war, the decision was made not to evacuate the El'nia salient, "since it was not yet known whether this salient might not still be needed as a jumping-off point for an attack toward Moscow."[501] Both Hoth and Guderian seized the opportunity of Hitler's presence to lodge urgent pleas for the release of new tanks and replacement tank engines[502] (now "very worn as a result of the appalling dust")[503] from current production; without new engines, in particular, they insisted, "wide-ranging operations" would no longer be possible. Provided these requirements were met, and with a short period to rest and refit, Guderian predicted his panzer group could once more commence major operations by 15 August; Hoth, however, was more cautious, suggesting his group would be ready by 20 August.[504]

"Visibly impressed" (*sichtlich beeindruckt*) by the panzer generals' pleas, Hitler at once authorized release of 400 new tank engines (a month's production) to Hoth and Guderian from depots in Germany, along with a pitifully tiny number of new tanks, 35 in all.[505] Beyond that, Hitler would not budge; he also insisted that the two panzer divisions hitherto not committed in the east (2 and 5 PD) still needed to be held back in Germany in anticipation of potential English landings (for example, on the Iberian Peninsula, or in West Africa).[506] When Guderian protested that his command alone required 300 new tank engines, the dictator demurred. Soviet losses, he claimed, were now approaching those sustained by Imperial Russia in all of World War I, and this after just six weeks of combat;[507] moreover, "to Hitler's mind he had already been quite generous and, in any case, the success of operations rested mainly on adopting the correct strategic approach, not haggling over a few tanks or spare parts."[508] Thus, the diarist of 2 Panzer Group could only observe on 4 August 1941 – and, in retrospect, somewhat sheepishly – that even if the measures agreed to by the "Fuehrer" did not compensate for the wear and tear on the panzer units, they at least "gave the troops something of the feeling that they were not forgotten"[509] – a remarkable statement reflecting the dangerous degree to which the eastern front was being starved of new weapons and equipment, which Hitler was holding back for "future tasks."

After the conference, Heusinger made a detailed report to Halder, who noted with satisfaction that Hitler had agreed to release the new tank engines (for Pz IIIs), while also indicating that their release had, in fact, already been authorized by OKH, and without the "Fuehrer" being made aware of it! (The engines were to be shipped by air.)[510] On the other hand, Hitler's continuing inflexibility on the decisive question of how the campaign should go forward was a source of deep frustration and concern; indeed, the news that Moscow remained a tertiary priority for Hitler, behind Leningrad and the Ukraine, was a "bitter pill" for Halder, who was equally disturbed by the dictator's apparent inability to reach a final decision.[511]

Yet given the manifest continuity of Hitler's strategic outlook throughout this period, it may well be that, in his own mind, he had already come to a decision, and was simply being respectful and diplomatic when fielding the opinions of his top field commanders. In any event, with the Battle of Smolensk just winding down, and the panzer units of Army Group Center in dire need of rest and replenishment, a firm directive was, at the time, hardly urgent.

Two days later (August 6), Hitler flew to the command post of Army Group South, ensconced in a former Soviet military school in the "dreary Ukrainian town of Berdichev."[512] Among the "Fuehrer's" entourage was his diplomatic liaison officer, ambassador Walther Hewel, who recorded in his journal: "We strolled through Berdichev. Ruined monastery church. Opened coffins, execution, ghastly town. Many Jews, ancient cottages, fertile soil. Very hot. Three hours' flight back."[513] What Hewel apparently did not note was that Field Marshal von Rundstedt, the army group commander, had been equally unsuccessful in convincing Hitler of the need to advance on Moscow. Besides, the "Fuehrer's" meteorologists had assured him that the dry weather would hold longer in the center than in the south, providing yet another reason to strike south first, and leave Moscow for later.[514]

10.5: The "Other Side of the Hill"

From the very outset of Operation *Barbarossa*, the Soviet political and military leadership had executed a strategy based on three pillars in an effort to stop and hurl back Hitler's invading armies. In the first place, the *Stavka* (general headquarters) had responded vigorously to the initial German assault by ordering a series of counterstrokes and major counteroffensives and attempting to coordinate them with regard to timing, location, and objectives; these counterattacks commenced on the first day of the war and, over time, increased in intensity and effectiveness.[515] Unfortunately, the *Stavka* "woefully misunderstood the capabilities of its own forces and those of the *Wehrmacht* by congenitally overestimating the former and underestimating the latter. As a result, the *Stavka* assigned the Red Army utterly unrealistic missions with predictably disastrous results."[516]

On the other hand, the unexpected vigor of Soviet resistance at Smolensk – particularly Timoshenko's counteroffensive which began on 23 July – surprised the Germans, stalling the advance of Bock's Army Group Center and contributing to a "command crisis" at the highest levels of the German command structure. As Timoshenko told Comintern leader Dimitrov in early August 1941: "We gave the Germans a good beating. Smashed a few of their divisions. They do not come straight for me any more. They try to go around."[517] Despite the obvious hyperbole, there was more than a modicum of truth in Timoshenko's boast.

In late June 1941, after the shocking power of the German mechanized blitz had made all too apparent that the Red Army was not about to throw the invaders back across the frontier, General Zhukov, Chief of the Red Army General Staff, crafted the second pillar of the evolving Soviet strategy, which envisaged successive lines of defense (defense in depth) along the Moscow axis to further delay and attrit the attackers. By mid-July, six Soviet armies (24, 28, 29, 30, 31 and 32) were combined into a new Front of Reserve Armies, under NKVD Lt.-Gen. I. A. Bogdanov, and deployed in second echelon behind Western Front, their task being to secure a new strategic defensive line (roughly Ostashkov – Belyi – El'nia – Brianisk) against a possible German breakthrough toward

Moscow.[518] Several of these armies would eventually furnish most of the striking power for Timoshenko's counteroffensive.

Soviet defenses received another boost when, on 18 July, Stalin created the Front of the Mozhaisk Defense Line, under the command of NKVD General P. A. Artem'ev. Although anchored by the poorly trained and equipped divisions of 32 and 33 Armies, and by 34 Army, this new front, along the direct approaches to the capital, provided a third strategic line of defense. Finally, to further bolster these second and third defensive fronts, the *Stavka* ordered construction of three more lines of defense, some 300 kilometers in depth, centered on the Viaz'ma sector midway between Smolensk and Moscow.[519] The Germans, of course, were only dimly aware of these and other developments in Soviet defensive strategy, which would have such serious consequences for the attackers in the weeks and months ahead.

The third, and final, pillar of Soviet strategy – overlapping with and supporting the other two – was the mobilization and assembly of enormous new forces, first to slow the German advance, then to stop it for good in a decisive counteroffensive to be launched at a moment when the attackers were most vulnerable – their armies exhausted, deep inside Russia, at the end of fragile supply lines. Unlike the German High Command, the *Stavka*, having successfully halted the enemy advance at Smolensk, fully expected the war to go on into 1942 (although, as we have seen, the Germans were also beginning to doubt that the war would end in 1941); as a result, initial preparations were made at the end of July to assemble winter clothing and equipment drawn from the east of the country.[520] By August 1941, the Soviets, no longer fearing the collapse of their political system and the total defeat of their armies,[521] were already mobilizing and training the dozens of new divisions, rifle and tank brigades which, in December 1941, would conduct the decisive counterattack at the gates of Moscow.[522] (For more details on the Soviet mobilization effort see below, Section 10.5.2).

10.5.1: Changes to the Soviet Command Structure

Initial measures undertaken by the Soviet leadership to reorganize the machinery of their high command are described in Chapter 7 (Section 7.4.1) and need not be reexamined here. On 10 July 1941, on Stalin's orders, the Soviets set up three theater-level, multi-front strategic commands called High Commands of Directions (*Glavnye komandovaniia napravlenii*), whose purpose was "to provide unity of control over all *fronts* and other forces operating along a single strategic axis."[523] The Northwestern Direction, originally headed by K. E. Voroshilov, encompassed the Northern and Northwestern Fronts, as well as the Baltic and Northern Fleets; the Western Direction, under Timoshenko, included at first only Western Front (with other fronts added later); the Southwestern Direction, commanded by S. M. Budenny, embraced the Southwestern and Southern Fronts and the Black Sea Fleet.[524]

Although the new strategic directions were meant to be the "cornerstone of Stalin's new rationalized command and control system,"[525] in practice they would prove militarily ineffective. The commanders were, most prominently, politically trusted comrades with close personal connections to the Soviet dictator; as noted by historian Evan Mawdsley, "the appointment of Voroshilov, Timoshenko, and Budenny, to the [three strategic directions] was the last victory of the clique of veterans of the Civil War 1st Cavalry Army (*Konarmiia*) … None of the three would turn out to be a fully competent commander in the new war."[526] In any event, Stalin and the *Stavka* often bypassed the three directions and gave orders directly to front or army commanders. The directions would be disbanded in 1942.[527]

The *Stavka* of the Main Command was reorganized as the *Stavka* of the High Command on 10 July 1941, and placed directly under Stalin's control; four weeks later (8 August), it was recast again, this time as the *Stavka* of the Supreme Command (*Stavka Verkhovnogo*

Glavnokommandovaniia), with Stalin becoming the Supreme Commander of the Armed Forces. With authority over the Soviet General Staff, the *Stavka* remained "responsible for military strategy and for the planning, preparation and conduct of big operations."[528]

The Soviet General Staff also underwent "repeated restructuring"[529] during the opening period of the war. Operating on the basis of *Stavka* decisions, the General Staff "drafted directives to the troops, assigned operational and strategic tasks to the commanding generals of the 'fronts' and armies, verified the implementation of [*Stavka*] orders, assembled strategic reserves, and ensured that the lessons of war were learnt, that the troops were trained for wartime conditions, and that they were adequately supplied with weapons and equipment."[530] On 29 July, Stalin replaced Zhukov with the ailing Marshal Boris Shaposhnikov as Chief of the General Staff, after refusing to heed Zhukov's warnings of the impending encirclement of Southwestern Front in the Ukraine. The next day (30 July), Zhukov was made commander of the new Reserve Front, formed from the dissolution of Bogdanov's Front of Reserve Armies.[531]

Parallel to the developments outlined above, was the inexorable concentration of all authority in the hands of the Soviet dictator, a process consummated by the second week of August 1941. By this time, Stalin "occupied all the highest appointments in the Soviet state" – Chairman of the State Defense Committee (GKO), People's Commissar of Defense, and Supreme Commander – and "directly controlled all the rest."[532] (See also, Chapter 7, Section 7.4.1.) As celebrated English historian John Keegan explains, "this self-elevation entailed some risk. The odium of defeat now attached immediately to his person. However, so desperate was Russia's situation, after less than two months of war, that Stalin must have accepted he could not survive the consequences of further disaster. Victory alone could save him."[533]

Given the nature of the Soviet political system in 1941 – dominated as it was by abject fear following some fifteen years of Stalin's savagely brutal stewardship – it was arguably a rational decision to subordinate all sinews of power within the Soviet state, including the entire military command structure, to the will of the "man of steel." Upon the outbreak of war, there were few leaders, political or military, left within the Soviet Union with the courage to think or act independently, much less challenge Stalin directly; in such an environment, the Soviet dictator could at least be assured that his decisions would be carried out expeditiously and in complete accordance with his wishes. And even if Stalin's military decision-making sometimes proved calamitous in the summer of 1941 – for example, his tardy decision to withdraw his forces from Belorussia in late June, and his failure to abandon Kiev and much of the Ukraine in August – it at least avoided the paralysis and Byzantine politics which characterized the German command apparatus in July/August 1941, due to Hitler's inability to control his own refractory and disloyal General Staff.

10.5.2: Ongoing Red Army Mobilization & Force Generation

In the Soviet account of their Great Fatherland War, the Battle of Smolensk began on 10 July 1941, with the German push across the Dnepr River line and – in contrast to the German view, according to which the battle ended on 5 August, with the final clearing of the Smolensk pocket – only ended on 10 September, by which time the series of Soviet counterstrokes along the Moscow axis had finally petered out. Daily Soviet losses during this 63-day period opposite Army Group Center amounted to 12,063 men, 21 tanks, 147 artillery pieces and mortars, and 14 aircraft.[534] Across the entire eastern front, the Red Army sustained casualties of 2,744,765 men in the third quarter of 1941, an average of approximately 900,000 for each of the first three months of the war; of these losses, fully 75 percent (2,067,801) were irrecoverable losses (dead, POWs, and missing in action).[535] An astounding total of 97 Soviet divisions had been smashed by the victorious *Ostheer* by 30 September 1941.[536]

To plug the cavernous gaps ripped in the Red Army order of battle by such staggering losses, Soviet military authorities sought to funnel colossal quantities of new soldiers, weapons and equipment to the front on a continuous basis, and to do so in two ways: a.) through the transfer of active units from the eastern military districts (Far East, Siberia, Caucasus, etc.); and, b.) by mobilizing trained reservists and new military draftees. As we have seen (Chapter 7, Section 7.4.1) by 30 June 1941, 5.3 million trained reservists had been called up, with successive waves of mobilization ensuing in the weeks and months that followed.

Having mobilized and deployed eight new armies in late June, the *Stavka* raised an additional 13 armies in July, and 14 more in August. The number of new divisions established was equally remarkable. For example, in June/July 1941, 156 new divisions were formed, primarily by calling up reservists; these units were assigned to their armies in August and September and contributed to slowing the German advance.[537] In August, 78 more rifle divisions were created (along with 10 rifle brigades and 20 tank brigades), mostly from new recruits in the Caucasus, Ural, Volga, and Siberian military districts, as there were few reservists in these districts; most of these formations – better equipped than the divisions established in June and July and sent into battle immediately – would be given four months of training before being assigned to the armies which would counterattack and throw the Germans back from Moscow in December 1941.[538] In this manner, despite the ongoing heavy losses, the Red Army order of battle had expanded to 450 division equivalents by 31 August 1941, while aggregate personnel strength had climbed from approximately 5.4 million at the outset of the war to 6.9 million by this time.[539]

Of course, the newly mobilized divisions – at least those thrown into battle during the summer of 1941 – were greatly inferior in combat quality to the pre-war divisions crushed in the initial German onslaught. The most "daunting problem" now facing Soviet field commanders was the inadequate training received by many of the newly-mobilized soldiers – junior officers and enlisted personnel alike – which undermined the effectiveness of the formations to which they were assigned:

> Since most of these soldiers were partially-trained reservists or untrained conscripts, soldiers often did not know how to use even their most basic weapons, much less heavier and crew-served weapons in their units (regiments and brigades) and subunits (battalions, companies, platoons, and squads). Moreover, the military organizations to which they were assigned were neither effective nor durable in combat. This was the case because they lacked cohesion, which resulted only from weeks if not months of combat exercises and battle drills. Thus, these formations, units and subunits were not capable of performing the most basic combat functions, such as offensive, defensive, or other basic types of actions. Making matters worse, the new divisions did not have many of their authorized heavy weapons, such as heavy machine guns, 82mm mortars, anti-tank and anti-aircraft guns, engineer equipment, and radios.[540]

While these conditions applied to the first wave of new armies deployed along the Western Dvina and Dnepr Rivers (16, 19, 20, 21 and 22 Armies), they were even more germane to the 200-series rifle divisions formed in late June, July and August; these divisions were then assigned to the high-20s and 30-series armies, including 28, 29, 30, 31, 32, 33 and 34 Armies. Combat reports prepared by 29 and 30 Armies are illustrative of the wretched state of many of these armies. On 12 August, a report by 29 Army noted the condition of its artillery upon mobilization:

> The artillery of the 29 Army is woefully incomplete: there is no regimental artillery at all, a total of 50 percent of 45mm artillery, 33 percent of 122mm divisional

howitzers, and we have just received 4 152mm howitzers (1938 model). The corps artillery totals 12 152mm gun-howitzers (1937 models). Artillery personnel in army artillery units are especially young; the command personnel and staffs do not work [properly] and have received their first combat baptism in the past 10 days.[541]

The report went on to emphasize the inexperience of artillery staffs and their poor performance – in target acquisition, counter-battery fire, artillery maneuver, cooperation with other combat arms, camouflage, and in many other critical combat functions. Like other newly mobilized armies, 29 Army had no choice but to learn its trade in the crucible of combat, and, on this note, the report ended optimistically: "Army artillery and mortar units, on the whole lacking required training, are learning during the course of combat and to date have made considerable strides in mastering the equipment and the art of firing."[542]

On 27 July, Maj.-Gen. V. A. Khomenko, Commander, 30 Army, described the readiness of his forces in a report to Timoshenko's Western Direction Command; in it, he laid out many shortfalls, among them the constant failure of subordinate commanders and their staffs to properly transmit orders, poor march discipline, chaotic fire coordination and support, inefficient rear services, and command and staff violations of the most rudimentary combat staff procedures. In a detailed report submitted on 5 August, Khomenko informed Western Front of the many problems his command had encountered since mobilization. He outlined the disorganized process of assigning divisions to the army, as well as the confusing movement and assembly orders. The three rifle divisions assigned to 30 Army (242, 250, and 251) had to reach their concentration areas on foot and, according to the general, "were taken from their assembly points in the very midst of assembly and incomplete;" thus, "they did not approach being 'knocked together,' and went into battle unprepared for combat."[543]

To drive home his point, Khomenko described the case of 251 Rifle Division, which had formed up at the city of Kolomna. The division was dispatched to 30 Army on foot, understrength, and "totally lacking in cohesiveness." The state of the division upon arrival was as follows:

1.) The division was forced to arrive on foot, and it lacked a number of subunits (artillery, chemical company, etc.). It had no materiel support units, since the personnel of these subunits moved on three trains and arrived in the division's operational area only at the beginning of August. To date, some of them have still not arrived;

2.) The division has not succeeded in forming and putting together rear service organs;

3.) Party and Komsomol organizations have not been created in some units and subunits;

4.) An overwhelming number of divisional personnel were mobilized from the reserves. The entire division has only about 400 cadre soldiers from the NKVD;

5.) In the haste of formation, horses were improperly distributed. Artillery horses were left behind, and … for this reason, artillery horses were received as reinforcements only after the artillery regiment was loaded on trains;

6.) Haste of formation led to subunit commanders not knowing their subordinates and subordinates not knowing their commanders, and as a result there was poor discipline in divisional units;

These and a series of other instances, which related to the 251 Rifle Division, led to the fact that the division entered battle unprepared, badly fulfilled the missions assigned to it, and suffered heavy losses.[544]

250 Rifle Division, Khomenko added, was in a similar state, while 242 Rifle Division was but marginally more combat ready. He then catalogued all his army's deficiencies in detail.[545]

Such details merely serve to reinforce what by now should be abundantly evident: The Soviet system of mobilization and force generation, despite serious shortcomings, still succeeded in stamping out new armies, divisions, and brigades in simply mind-boggling numbers; these new formations, although ill-trained, ill-equipped, and often poorly led, learned their craft quickly and, by late July and early August 1941, helped to bring German Army Group Center – and, particularly, its tank and motorized units – to the brink of exhaustion. They achieved their success at a terrible price; yet as Halder had noted in exasperation on 11 August, if the Germans smashed a dozen new divisions, the Russians simply replaced them with a dozen more. And so the slow amputation of the *Ostheer* went on.

10.5.3: Red Army Reorganization

Beginning in July 1941, Stalin and the Soviet High Command also implemented a series of major reforms within the Red Army in an effort to enhance combat capability, provide more effective logistical support, and shore up flagging discipline and morale. Such measures were clearly needed, for while the *Rotarmisten* often fought heroically, their performance was, all too often, highly uneven; indeed, on many occasions they failed to meet the expectations of Stalin and his generals. As General Rokossovsky later admitted in his memoirs about the fighting in late July: "To my great regret, about which I have no right to be silent, I encountered a great number of instances of cowardice, panic, desertion, and self-mutilation to evade battle among the soldiers ... Self-mutilation occurred by agreement; a pair of soldiers would mutually shoot one another in the hands."[546]

As outlined by David Glantz, the *Stavka's* "wholesale reorganization of the Red Army simply validated the damage the *Wehrmacht* had already done to the Army's force structure by abolishing those elements the Germans had already largely destroyed or had proved ineffective during the German onslaught. The *Stavka* simply sought to create smaller and more effective forces that its still largely inexperienced commanders could more effectively control in combat."[547] Among the primary reforms implemented at this time were the following:

- On 15 July 1941, the *Stavka* issued a directive abolishing the large, unwieldy armies and replacing them with smaller, more manageable, field armies of a maximum of five to six divisions each;
- the directive also eliminated the large mechanized corps, formed only a year earlier, and replaced them with separate 100-series tank divisions of reduced size and earmarked for an infantry support role;[548] the motorized divisions were to be converted to regular rifle divisions;
- because the mobilization process was providing enough men to fill the new units, but not enough officers who were qualified to staff and command higher headquarters, all rifle corps headquarters were disbanded, leaving the armies in direct command of their divisions;[549]
- the 15 July directive also envisaged the formation of large numbers of highly-mobile, light cavalry units, capable of striking deep into the rear of German forces, disrupting command and control and attacking lines of supply;[550]
- finally, the *Stavka* reorganized and streamlined its badly truncated Air Force (VVS) by getting rid of its aviation corps headquarters, reducing the size of its aviation divisions to two regiments each, and halving the strength of each aviation regiment from 60 to 30 aircraft.[551]

It must be emphasized that these and other initiatives were simply temporary "stopgap measures," undertaken out of necessity, and, in many cases, to reduce the span of control exercised by Red Army commanders to more tolerable levels as they learned their leadership roles. By the spring of 1942, the Soviets had begun to undo these force structure changes and to rebuild a "heavier" Red Army.[552]

10.5.4: ULTRA & the Russians

ULTRA was the code-name for British signal intelligence derived from the decryption of intercepted German radio traffic enciphered in the high-grade cipher machine known as ENIGMA. The Germans, of course, were aware that their enemies were monitoring their signals; yet they placed absolute faith in ENIGMA, and were convinced that messages sent by the machines were undecipherable. By 1941, however, the British Government Code and Cipher School at Bletchley Park, 80 kilometers northwest of London, had made major strides in cracking certain ENIGMA keys, in particular, those associated with the *Luftwaffe*.[553]

In April 1941, the British, while careful not to reveal the source of the information, had begun to share ULTRA intelligence with the Russians in an attempt to warn them of a potential German attack; several additional warnings followed.[554] Despite the risks involved, they continued to furnish the Soviets with such intelligence after *Barbarossa* began. Churchill was a "prime mover" in the process, continually asking if certain decrypts had been passed on to the Russians and, if not, why not. As a rule, the information was first sent to the British Military Mission in Moscow and, from there, conveyed to the Soviets.[555]

In his comprehensive history of the Second World War, distinguished British historian Martin Gilbert cites several intriguing examples of ULTRA intelligence passed on to the Soviets in the first weeks of the Russian campaign:

- On 27 June, at Bletchley, British cryptographers broke the ENIGMA key being used by the German Army on the eastern front. Known as "Vulture," it provided daily readings of German military orders. On the following day, Churchill gave instructions that Stalin was to be given this precious intelligence, provided its source could remain a secret. An officer in British Military Intelligence, Cecil Barclay, who knew of the work at Bletchley, and who was then serving in the British Embassy in Moscow, was instructed to pass on warnings of German moves and intentions to the head of Soviet Military intelligence.[556]
- Early in July, British intelligence learned from the German Army's ENIGMA messages that the Germans were reading certain Russian Air Force codes[557] in the Leningrad area, as well as decrypting Russian naval messages in the Baltic. This information was passed on to the British Military Mission in Moscow on July 7, with the request that the Russians be alerted to this gap in their security.[558]
- Information was a key to survival; on 9 July a group of British cryptanalysts broke the ENIGMA key used by the German Army to direct its ground-air operations on the eastern front.[559]
- On [14 July] … British Military Intelligence sent a top secret message to the British Military Mission in Moscow, to pass on at once to the Russians details, culled from the German ENIGMA messages, of the dispositions and order of battle of the German forces. Two days later, at Churchill's specific request, the Military Mission in Moscow was sent an appreciation of German intentions in both the Smolensk and Gomel areas, together with the news, once again taken from the Germans' own most secret instructions, that the German Air Force had been ordered to prevent Russian withdrawals by attacks on the railways leading to the rear.[560]

- The German Army was finding itself confronted by much stiffer resistance than it had been led to expect. British intelligence learned from the German Army's own ENIGMA messages that this was so; that the Germans were disturbed by the scale of their own casualties, planned to slow down the advance, and could no longer provide adequate air protection either to the panzer formations at the front or to strategic positions at the rear. On 17 July, Churchill specifically requested that this information should be sent to Stalin.[561]
- On 9 September, British cryptologists at Bletchley decrypted the German orders for Operation Typhoon, for the attack on Moscow ... From London, with Churchill's authority, British Intelligence sent Stalin a series of warnings between 20-25 September, based upon the reading of the most secret German Vulture messages being sent to and from the eastern front, giving details of German intentions and movements on the Moscow front. These details included information on the location and strength of German air and ground concentrations in the Smolensk area.[562]

While such intelligence was, in theory at least, of inestimable value to the Russians, the reality was rather more complicated. In the first place, however enlightened Stalin and the *Stavka* may have been about German orders of battle and/or intentions, they were often helpless to counter German moves due to a lack of resources or the failings of their own forces. Secondly, given Stalin's deep and inveterate suspicions of Churchill and the English, he would, at least at first, have been disinclined to trust the information. And even assuming that Stalin fully trusted the intelligence, that does not mean that he acted on it, or even comprehended its implications.[563] Indeed, the Soviet dictator and his High Command were caught completely off guard by the beginning of Operation "Typhoon," the advance on Moscow, in the fall of 1941. In the final analysis, barring new revelations out of Soviet archives, we may never know what use, if any, Stalin and his High Command attempted to make of the ULTRA-derived intelligence they received in the summer of 1941.[564]

10.6: *Stellungskrieg*: The Transition to Positional Warfare

On 30 July 1941, with the promulgation of "Fuehrer Directive" No. 34, Army Group Center was ordered to halt its advance. As the clearing of the Smolensk cauldron approached its end, Bock's army group was holding an elongated front some 700 kilometers in length. The line stretched from just south of Velikie Luki in the north, eastward in a great bulging arc around Smolensk, until finally curling back in a southwesterly direction to the Dnepr (west of Rogachev – Shlobin) and, from there, to the northern edge of the Pripiat' Marshes. To hold this front, Bock now had about 60 divisions; of these, however, a half dozen (including three security divisions) were far to the rear, while another seven or eight divisions were still tied down along the Smolensk encirclement ring. In fact, only about 40 divisions were directly positioned along the army group's main front (with several more close behind), holding divisional frontages that averaged 15-20 kilometers and, in some cases, exceeded 20 kilometers in length.[565]

For the next two months, Bock's already weakened divisions were forced to wage an improvised defense – often on unfavorable terrain – with dangerously extended unit frontages and ineluctably declining resources. Given the chronic shortage of combat infantry, the German defenses typically consisted of a string of strongpoints, rather than a continuous front line held in depth.[566] While the German infantry were well trained, and would prove more than adept at holding the front together, they were often hamstrung by vehicles and equipment that proved deficient under the harsh conditions of the east. As a former officer in 4 Panzer Division recalled after the war: "The equipment, which had proved efficient in the previous campaigns, was not robust enough for battle under the conditions prevailing in Russia. Russian equipment seemed to be more robust and less sensitive. Therefore, whoever got hold of a Russian tommy-gun kept it."[567] An Italian officer, examining a Russian machine gun for the first time, commented: "I loved the simplicity, easy handling and firepower of this gun."[568] In contrast, German weapons, as a rule more sophisticated and finely tooled, tended to break down more often than their simpler Russian counterparts.

Under the conditions of positional (static) warfare now taking shape, the excellent Soviet artillery arm also began to make itself increasingly felt. During the first phase of the war, Soviet artillery had played a relatively insignificant role; as one German report (gleaned from the records of 6 Infantry Division) noted: "During the days of the war of movement [Bewegungskrieg] the Soviet artillery had a negligible impact [geringe Wirkung];" as a result, "sizeable losses did not occur."[569] In their foxholes and bunkers, however, the German Landser were now frequently outgunned by longer-range Soviet artillery with seemingly inexhaustible stockpiles of shells, leading the report to conclude that, "the powerful impact of artillery fire on our own troops is now becoming clear ... As a final judgment and consideration of the relative advantages and disadvantages [of German and Soviet artillery], it is clear that the German artillery is far superior [in every respect]. That said, with regard to the enemy's artillery, the German troops 'have also met their toughest opponent.'"[570]

Yet even if the Germans' artillery arm was better led and more technically proficient, that hardly mattered if their guns couldn't shoot. For it was during this period that the flow of munitions to the front, over the badly overstretched arteries of supply, often slowed to a trickle, denying German forces the ability to respond effectively to the hail of shells pouring down on them. Hermann Geyer, Commander, 9 Army Corps, noted that his 263 Infantry Division was, in late July, receiving at most 1000 shells per day for its 36 light field howitzers (and for other caliber weapons even fewer); collectively, this would allow for barely five minutes of fire each day at the guns' most rapid rate of fire, or for each gun to fire one shot a minute for 30 minutes a day. "We soon learned," Geyer wrote, "that in the defense it was not barrage fire or artillery duels ... but digging in quick and deep that was decisive and saved lives."[571]

In addition to the "appearance of stronger [Soviet] artillery on every front," reported Army Group Center on 30 July, there was the "reinforced activity of the enemy air force."[572] Indeed, the ongoing recrudescence of the Soviet Air Force (VVS) was yet another cause for alarm for officers and men of Bock's army group struggling to hold on to an overextended front against repeated battering by fresh Soviet armies up and down the main battle line (HKL). In this respect, the experiences of 6 Infantry Division were hardly atypical. During the initial weeks of war, the division had observed few signs of the Soviet Air Force; this was not surprising, however, as VVS units fortunate enough to have survived the bloodbath of the first 72 hours had focused their attention on the German armored spearheads. On 26 July, as 6 ID approached the front line northeast of Velizh, it encountered "lively" (lebhaft) enemy air activity for the "first time since the beginning of the campaign."[573] In subsequent days and weeks, 6 ID was struck repeatedly from the air, on occasion with telling effect. Furthermore, by early August 1941, the VVS had achieved air superiority on certain sectors of the central front.

Not to be overlooked among the many challenges now facing Army Group Center – and the Ostheer writ large – was the problem posed by new Soviet weapons, in particular the BM-13 "Katyusha" ("Little Kate") multiple rocket-launcher and the T-34 tank. The rocket-launcher made its debut in July 1941 (for a description see, Chapter 4, Section 4.3), opposite Army Group Center; in the months which followed, it would become a fixture in both attack and defense. As discussed at length in Chapter 8 (Section 8.2.3), the sudden appearance of the T-34 administered an adrenal shock to the collective German system. Different units made their acquaintance with the T-34 at different times. The SS Das Reich

Division first encountered the tank in late July, during the savage fighting along the El'nia salient; to their horror, the SS grenadiers discovered the virtual uselessness of their 37mm and 50mm anti-tank guns against the 30-ton steel behemoths; to destroy them, the men resorted to setting the tanks ablaze at point-blank range with Molotov cocktails.[574]

In light of prevailing conditions along the embattled front of Army Group Center in late July and August 1941, it is not surprising that attrition rates were high – at times even intolerable – or that the HKL could often only be held by throwing in the last modest reserves. With the battlefield immobilized, and Soviet artillery barrages reminding older German veterans of the First World War, the German divisions were bled white. The 137 Infantry Division (9 Army Corps) lost 850 men in the first three to four days upon reaching the front, while 263 ID lost 750 men and 292 ID 300 men.[575] By the time German forces withdrew from the El'nia bridgehead in early September 1941, several divisions had been wrecked, permanently diminishing the combat power of Bock's army group.[576]

To better illustrate the characteristics of the *Stellungskrieg* along the front of Army Group Center during the summer of 1941 – and the exorbitant attrition rates which accompanied these largely defensive battles, from which Bock's divisions never fully recovered – the author has selected two case studies. The first concerns Maj.-Gen. Helge Auleb's 6 Infantry Division of 6 Army Corps (Ninth Army), and its operations in the Mezha River sector on the northern wing of Bock's army group; the second – and much better known example – explores the bloody combat of Lt.-Gen. Heinrich-Gottfried von Vietinghoff's 46 Panzer Corps defending the strategically important El'nia bridgehead, 300 kilometers southwest of Moscow.

10.6.1: Case One – 6 Infantry Division in Mezha Sector

Following capture of the Soviet fortress of Polotsk (Section 10.1.3), 6 Infantry Division, on the morning of 18 July, had crossed the 154 meter-long *Kriegsbruecke* erected by the division's combat engineers 17 kilometers southeast of the fortress and continued its eastward advance.[577] Despite uncomfortably hot weather, and roads little more than deep, sandy tracks, the 15,000+ men of 6 ID marched through Gorodok (20 July), the largely obliterated town of Velizh (25 July), and beyond to the northeast. After the war, Dr Heinrich Haape (III./IR 18) described the *Vormarsch*, and the one, all-embracing desire which quickened the step of every *Landser*:

> We passed two burnt-out armored cars and four fresh graves – those of an *Oberleutnant* and three soldiers. Caterpillar tracks criss-crossed the roads and fields and in a small wood to the left of the road were about 60 Russian tanks, facing in all directions. Many were damaged, but others had been abandoned undamaged. It was a commonplace incident along the road to Moscow. A few graves, a few burnt-out vehicles and the silence in the woods were all that remained.
>
> Our marching column had little interest in the scene of battle: their eyes had become satiated with destruction. They wanted to get to Moscow. It was their only objective. They had been told it would be taken soon and to each man it meant the end of the march, rest, an organized life again, excitement, civilization, women, relaxation of discipline perhaps. Maybe, who knew, the end of the war! Victory! Every man looked to Moscow and looked no farther. It was the end of the road.
>
> On 28 July we reached the Schutsche Lake and camped for the evening 10 miles from the town of Belyi. We measured out on the map – 180 miles across country to Moscow! We had marched 600 miles from East Prussia, 600 miles in a little over five weeks. Three-quarters of the journey covered, a quarter still to go. We could do it in a fortnight at the most, even with resistance stiffening as we approached the capital … We could not fail to be in Moscow by the end of August.[578]

The next day (29 July), lead elements of 6 Infantry Division finally arrived at the Mezha River and the front of 3 Panzer Group.[579] Although the division had only encountered desultory resistance during its advance, two of its infantry regiments (37 and 58 IR) suffered serious losses on 29 July from enemy air attack.[580] A soldier in 58 Infantry Regiment recalled his company reaching the Mezha:

> At midday we cross over the roughly 100 meter long engineer bridge across the Mezha at Kanat. The provisionally last stage of 15 kilometers takes us through the "forest of corpses:" hundreds of bloated horse cadavers lie strewn through the forest, emitting the foulest stench of decay; the result of a battle between cavalry and tanks.
>
> We reach Katkovo, a small village, attractively located on a rise in rolling countryside with fields and meadows. To the right we can see a larger lake, the Putnoe Lake, and it is bounded by a large, dense forested area to the north and east.[581]

Upon reaching the front, 6 ID was to relieve the badly worn-out 14 Motorized Division (57 Panzer Corps); therefore, General Auleb's first act was to drive to the division's CP to confer with its commander. Because 14 Motorized was in a difficult situation, under intense enemy pressure, Auleb, via radio transmission, instructed his infantry to take over the line during the night of 29/30 July, a day earlier than had been ordered. The relief went off as planned.[582]

On 30 July, the men of 6 ID received the "incredible order" to dig in. To Dr Haape and his comrades, it came as a complete shock:

> During the next few days the whole of [Army Group Center] ground to a halt. A million men heard the order: "Prepare defensive positions." … Four hundred miles of front line became static. Panzers, motorized units, pioneers, artillery froze in their tracks and waited …
>
> We were not to find out the reason yet. We did not, in fact, know at the time that the order applied along the whole vast central front … Unbelievingly, we went about our tasks. Neuhoff [chief, III./IR 18] and Hillemanns [Neuhoff's adjutant] were away at a regimental officers' conference, and every man in the battalion was convinced that Neuhoff would return with the news that the order to prepare a defensive line was a mistake. For five weeks the daily order had been "March! March! March! Stick to it! We must follow the fleeing enemy and destroy him wherever he stops. He must not have time to regain his breath. The faster we advance, the faster he will have to run. Moscow is just beyond the horizon. Full speed ahead to Moscow!"
>
> And now … the order was given to prepare defensive positions. It did not make sense, even to the youngest recruit.
>
> Neuhoff and Hillemanns returned and all the officers assembled to learn the news, eagerly expecting to hear that someone had blundered. But Neuhoff offered no explanation. There had been no mistake. He went straight to a map and indicated the various sub-sectors of the defensive line that he was allocating to the individual company commanders.[583]

The front occupied by 6 Infantry Division extended for 40 kilometers,[584] a length which was considered "an impossibility at the time,"[585] at least from a pre-war perspective. (In Russia, however, in the years ahead, such vast defensive frontages would almost become commonplace.) The terrain posed an additional handicap – it was swampy and consisted almost exclusively of heavily forested areas. As a consequence, the division could only mount a series of strongpoints – anchored on villages like Vasilevo, Shishova and Kanat – while the intervening terrain was covered by patrols (*Spaehtrupps*) and a thin screen of outposts (*Feldwachen*).[586]

The division's 18 Infantry Regiment – along with supporting artillery, most of the reconnaissance battalion and a combat engineer company – occupied the right wing, stretching 25 kilometers in a northwesterly direction from Vasilevo into the area west of Stany and roughly paralleling the Mezha, which ran six to eight kilometers further east.[587] Of particular note is the fact that the regiment's 1st Battalion was dug in along a two-kilometer front shielding the village of Shishova, its positions buttressed by two artillery batteries. On the division's left stood 58 Infantry Regiment, whose line was also bolstered by artillery and a combat engineer company; on its far left flank, the regiment made contact with the neighboring 26 Infantry Division. Unavailable to the division was most of its 37 Infantry Regiment – held in reserve by 6 Army Corps 18 kilometers northwest of Lake Schutsche.[588] Simply put, the division's long and thinly held HKL, and the vast tracks of forest – in which Russian Cossacks were still hiding out – made the German defenders uneasy. "Not only too long – too many woods. Difficult country to defend," grumbled adjutant Hillemanns.[589] Still, the men dug in as best they could, as the following account reveals:

> Preparation of defensive positions is ordered. Construction of a HKL … We are confronted with this term, and with this activity, for the first time since the start of the campaign. We dig our foxhole in the hard, arid ground until late on into the night. Not funny, what is this all about? Ivan is finished, isn't he, the war is won!
>
> The HKL: The length of the front to be covered by the company is determined. Contact with our neighbors on the right and left is secured, the infantry squads are allocated their sectors. Next, every rifleman digs his foxhole, then crawl trenches are dug from hole to hole, and these are quickly expanded into communication trenches. A trench system under construction. For an infantryman, the digging never stops. The gun pits are refined. Machine gun emplacements are expanded.[590]

31 July witnessed vigorous patrolling by both German and Russian forces, while the positions of 6 ID's reconnaissance battalion (6 AA) received occasional harassing fire from a Russian armored train; attacks by combat-capable (*kampfkraeftig*) Russian patrols on a German outpost position of I./IR 18 at Kolenidova were beaten off. The next day (1 August), the outpost (*Feldwache* 5) was struck again, this time by two Russian cavalry squadrons, forcing the defenders to pull back to "Strongpoint Kisslova," having suffered several casualties. Total casualties for the division on this day were three dead, 10 wounded, one missing.[591]

The first major crisis for 6 Infantry Division in its defensive battles along the Mezha came on 2 August, as Russian forces facing the division – far superior numerically to their German counterparts – launched powerful attacks. Through intelligence gleaned from Soviet prisoners, the Germans were aware that, in the forests beyond the Mezha, opposite *Oberst* Becker's 18 Infantry Regiment, were several Soviet cavalry regiments (Cossacks). That morning, strong enemy cavalry formations made a successful surprise assault on *Feldwache* 3 (3./IR 18), holding a village five kilometers before the German main battle line. Concealed by dense, primeval forest, the Cossack cavalry enveloped the outpost and cut off its line of retreat. In the ensuing melee, 19 German soldiers became "victims of a merciless slaughter."[592] "The horde of horsemen," recalled Heinrich Haape, "had appeared as if from nowhere, shouting strange battle-cries. Mercilessly they had cut down the German soldiers with their flashing sabers, before most of them had time to use their guns. Many of our men had been split practically from crown to toe by the deadly swords; others had been decapitated."[593]

One of the few who escaped the massacre and made it back to German lines was *Obergefreiter* Matthias. Several days later, he put down his thoughts and feelings about the shattering experience in a letter:

> I am dreadfully shaken. In 1st Platoon we now have only 25 men instead of 40 ... We have lost the best comrades. In the meantime our patrols have found 11 of the missing comrades, all vilely mauled by the Soviets and killed by shots to the head. They were buried. We dug them up again and interred them with proper military honors. The [Catholic] divisional priest [*Freiherr* Geyr von Schweppenburg] held a speech. It was very sad for us ... Now only 6 comrades are missing and they have probably fallen into captivity. According to statements by the local populace, the Soviets took them away in chains.
>
> Yes, that is war! When the *Hauptfeldwebel* fell I was right next to him. Along with our medical NCO, I tried to bandage him up, but the Russians, who were armed with American manufactured magazine-fed carbines, were already within 15-20 meters of us. We were the last of the company. If there had been no scrubland, it would have been too late. While the bullets whistled by and over me, I collapsed 5 or 6 times, but always pulled myself together with the thought: "You must not fall into the hands of the Russians!" A happy fate preserved me from that! I am grateful to my maker ...
>
> Today we heard the special report [*Sondermeldung*] about Smolensk. It's wonderful! Hopefully the advance will continue soon![594]

Continuing their assaults on 18 Infantry Regiment, in the early afternoon Russian forces managed to elude the positions of 1st Battalion's 2nd Company at Kisslova and infiltrate southward. On his own initiative, *Hauptmann* Hoeke, in command of the reserve battalion (II./IR 18), dispatched his reinforced 7th Company against the enemy breakthrough. Advancing with élan, the German infantry threw back the attackers, recaptured the town of Stany, and restored the main battle line.[595]

In the late afternoon, however, the battle suddenly took a more ominous turn for the German defenders. "Massive" Soviet forces struck the 1st Battalion at "Strongpoint Shishova;" although failing to break through – in part due to the well-laid fire of the German artillery – portions of the attacking Soviet forces succeeded in slipping past the battalion's defenses northwest of the village and penetrating almost to the gun positions of the artillery regiment's 8th Battery (8./AR 6). Having run out of shells, the artillerists fought back as infantry in a desperate attempt to turn away the attackers, joined in their efforts by the CP of the 3rd Artillery Battalion, who fought for their lives with carbines, machine pistols, machine guns, and grenades. Arriving on the scene, General Auleb scraped together all rear area elements (*Trossteile*) he could lay hands on and personally flung them into the fight.[596]

The turning point in the battle came early that evening, when General Auleb ordered Cavalry Captain (*Rittmeister*) and Knight's Cross Holder Georg *Freiherr* von Boeselager to strike the enemy's flank with his mounted troop (*Reiterschwadron*). In the twilight, Boeselager's cavalry began its advance; the scene is vividly recounted by former 6 ID commander, Horst Grossmann, in his history of the division:

> At around 1930 hours, the troop started its attack in the faint evening light. It was agreed with III./AR 6 that the advance elements of the troop would continually identify themselves with Very signal lights fired vertically upwards. It

was an unforgettable sight – to watch those flares drifting slowly from right to left in front of I./IR 18 in the falling night, and ahead of them the impact of the shells from Artillery Battalion Krueger, now again firing vigorously. About 2200 hours the battle fell silent. The enemy had been thrown back. The troop bivouacked in a hedgehog position in front of I./IR 18.[597]

The Russian attacks on 2 August had been conducted by two cavalry divisions, each composed of three Cossack regiments heavily armed with automatic weapons (including heavy machine guns), 76mm cannons, and 45mm Pak;[598] as they withdrew, they left behind some 300 dead before the German lines.[599] As recorded in its war diary, 6 Infantry Division suffered 65 casualties on this bloody day, including 25 dead and missing.[600] One of the Germans who perished in the fighting was Boeselager's older brother; badly wounded in the purusit of the defeated enemy, he died soon after being brought to the medical company.[601]

That night, 2/3 August 1941, Dr Haape and his orderly Dehorn sheltered behind a low hill, at the 3rd Battalion command post, with a clutch of other soldiers, relatively secure from rifle and machine gun fire. While two of Haape's staff remained at a nearby farmhouse, the doctor and his orderly, having no time to pitch a tent, rolled up in their blankets and lay on the ground close to their Mercedes. "It was a perfect night," remembered Haape:

> A big moon sailed peacefully overhead and the fir trees cast their shadows over us. The noise of battle had died away until there was only an occasional staccato crackling of a machine gun. When the morning mist rose from the Schutsche Lake and the first birds began to twitter, we awoke from our doze, stiff and cold. Dehorn and I moved into the Mercedes for warmth, and sat silent, not trying to sleep any more. We were wondering what the new day would bring when ... the Russian artillery opened up.[602]

The first shells landed far behind them. Soon, however, they were dropping closer, but to the right. All at once, there was a "deafening crash," as a shell exploded in a huge tree not 12 meters away. The explosion split the tree asunder and showered soldiers sleeping in the area with shrapnel; many awoke screaming in pain. Haape and his orderly jumped from their vehicle and began to sprint toward the shouting men; they had barely moved when a second shell struck just five meters off. The physics of the explosion lifted Haape into the air – as if by a "mighty hand" – and deposited him back on the ground with terrific force.[603] In his journal, Haape recorded his close brush with death, and surveyed the havoc inflicted by the deadly barrage:

> I have never been so close to death as I was this morning at 7 hours 45 minutes. Except for a small shrapnel injury to the nose, which is so insignificant that I've not even put a dressing on it, I got away unscathed ...
>
> Dehorn's chest was torn open and his skull so smashed that his brain lay next to his head. (Dead immediately)
>
> *Leutnant* Jakobi lay on the ground with a shrapnel wound in his chest, a shell fragment through his stomach, a shattered right knee, and his left foot was as good as blown off. He lived for 1 hour and died.
>
> My car driver ... had both his legs smashed.
>
> Another four seriously injured and then another slightly injured. . .[604]

Haape was deeply affected by the sudden, tragic loss of Dehorn, his "lively little orderly."[605] A journal entry several days later reveals his attempt to come to grips with the untimely death of his good friend, whose makeshift gravesite offered an iconic image of the *Landser* in the *Russlandkrieg*:

> I also stood at the grave of my boy Dehorn again today. He was a good man; he died at my side in loyal fulfillment of his duties. It was like a stab through my heart to see him bleeding to death. He didn't speak a word; I had to take care of the other wounded. He was the dearest one to me of all those who die a soldier's death here.
>
> At a fork in the road, in the forest, stands a simple birch cross with a steel helmet. A friendly fence, made of the same wood, embraces the tranquil spot of that final peace, decorated by simple means. The flowers, always fresh, bear witness to the love and remembrance of his comrades. On the cross hangs inconspicuously the Iron Cross 2 [EK 2], which he received as an award for bravery and readiness for duty ...
>
> The sight of his grave evokes a long chain of memories – he was at my side at my every step. Christmas in France, shopping, packing boxes, experiences and work on the coast, then East Prussia, and the crazy war against Russia ... All these images are shared experiences. He was a good comrade, that little Dehorn![606]

On the afternoon of 3 August, elements of both 18 and 58 Infantry Regiments, supported by artillery, combat engineers with flamethrowers, five Pz III tanks and several armored scout cars,[607] set out to clear the forests of enemy up to the banks of the Mezha.[608] While the operation was largely successful, a platoon of 9./IR 58, holding an outpost in front of the main battle line, was shattered by a Russian assault on this day. Twenty-year-old *Oberschuetze* Fritz Belke belonged to one of two rifle squads (*Gruppen*) which had reinforced the outpost only hours before it was attacked and overrun. In his unpublished post-war account, he chronicled the disaster – made all the more catastrophic by the inexplicably insouciant behavior of the German troops – and the counterattack in which he participated:

> It is a very hot Sunday morning. We lie spread out in the tall grass and doze in the blazing sunshine. Nobody thinks of digging in, not even of constantly monitoring the enemy with a standing patrol, a patrol tailing the enemy – only one patrol on every second hour has been ordered. "What could Ivan possibly do to us – when he sees that we're lying here, he'll run away as fast as he can." But: Pride comes before a fall! Our comrades from 1st Platoon are also carefree; rifles and steel helmets lie in their foxholes, they themselves somewhere in the shade. Everything is so peaceful and quiet.
>
> At 1200 hours, the next patrol up goes off; it barely reaches the forest when Ivan goes on the attack with a bone-chilling cry of "Urrah" and heavy fire. He has worked his way forward entirely unnoticed and got into position – a masterful achievement! 1st Platoon and the anti-tank gun are immediately shot to pieces; the Russian breaks through. His attack focuses entirely on the positions of 1st Platoon. He has not noticed our two rifle squads at all. During the two hours of our presence here we lay flat on the ground, enjoyed doing sweet nothing, gazed into the blue sky, and recalled the exertions of the *Vormarsch* once more.
>
> Ahead of us nothing is happening, behind us hordes of Russians charge about, shooting wildly ... To try to defend against these numbers is senseless for us, we have no positions and a field of fire is only possible when standing! At the last minute we are able, benefitting somewhat from the lie of the land,

to pull back into the protection of the forest, sprinting through a hail of bullets. So we withdraw to the *Hauptkampflinie*, utterly demoralized and despondent: "German soldiers making a bolt for it before the Russians, impossible!" – we feel like wretched cowards and such is the reaction of our batallion commander, von Issendorff. The 2nd and 3rd Platoons from our company are immediately ordered to counterattack. Under the leadership of the batallion commander, one platoon advances to the left, the other to the right, of the road. On the road itself, two light infantry guns are dragged forward by a team of men. Immediately ahead of the outpost we come upon the Russians at very close range in dense underbrush. The fire fight begins!

The two infantry guns fire directly into the thick brush. The alien, tough Russian detachments, barely 30 meters ahead, and only in limited view, appear sinister to us, and the frightful roar of their weapons shows us we are faced with a great enemy superiority. The ricochets caused by the bushes zip past, if they strike home, they rip open large wounds; beside me *Gefreiter* Janssen has his left cheek torn off; his upper and lower jaw gape open.

Our losses increase! Platoon leader *Leutnant* Rolf Blase is shot in the arm; a short while later he is shot in the chest, but he refuses to be bandaged and sends the medical orderly over to attend to the other wounded. Neither does he go back; he wants to continue leading his platoon, until finally the third shot strikes him fatally.

Our squad leaders, *Unteroffizier* Broelhorst, and *Gefreiter* Liebender fall; platoon command group leader, *Feldwebel* Parmeier, is seriously wounded by a shot to the head; batallion commander von Issendorff is also wounded.

We now lie in this green hell virtually leaderless, can see little, but can hear the cries of the Russian wounded directly ahead of us and those of our own wounded next to us. They recognize the extreme helplessness of their situation, for the few orderlies are overstretched and their comrades cannot help – they have to keep firing or else the dam will break and bury everyone. Along with the pain and loss of blood which come with being wounded is the fear of those affected, usually incapable of walking, of falling into enemy hands and being massacred. Reports of inhuman treatment of prisoners, especially of the wounded, by the Russians, have become notorious.

To the right at the rear we can see Ivans, who have broken through our two platoons, running about. *Unteroffizier* Zillich gives the order to retreat. We strike a path in an arc to the left and reach the [HKL]; it is not possible to take the dead with us.

The losses in our 9th Company on this day: 18 dead, 14 wounded, 6 missing (dead or wounded who were left behind); in addition, seven light machine guns were lost …

Our severely damaged 9th Company, which is now comprised of only two weak platoons, now searches for suitable cover, from which it can be deployed as a reserve for counterattacking …

The right place for us is found after darkness falls. A few hundred meters behind the [HKL], well-situated on a slight reverse slope, we first construct foxholes for ourselves, connect these with communication trenches, then build MG and gun positions and bunkers.[609]

While *Oberschuetze* Belke's casualty figures for his 9th Company on this day could not be confirmed, according to Horst Grossmann, the 1st Platoon (9./IR 58) suffered 23 dead and wounded.[610] In the 6 ID war diary, the division's total losses on 3 August were recorded as

16 dead, 47 wounded, and 27 missing – many or most of the latter, no doubt, having also perished in the fighting.[611]

The days that followed brought little in the way of relief to the *Landser* of 6 Infantry Division. The Russians continued to strike at the division's outposts, often with numerically superior forces, while German assault parties (*Stosstrupps*) conducted vigorous actions of their own. "Almost every night there is an alarm," wrote Belke. "The Russian attacks again and again, and each time he is thrown back with heavy losses … Today [9 August 1941] the enemy attacked Katkovo four times, supported first by three, then by two tanks; two of the tanks are destroyed, and two badly damaged."[612] Deftly exploiting the forests and thick undergrowth as cover, Russian detachments slipped between the handful of German strongpoints and ambushed rear area service troops. Ammunition and rations for German troops had to be shepherded to the front along the handful of tracks which threaded their way through the dense forests; because of the omnipresent enemy threat, this activity mostly took place in partial darkness, under heavy guard.[613]

The Russian artillery became more active, as did the Red Air Force; in fact, with the *Luftwaffe* fully engaged on other fronts, the VVS soon enjoyed air superiority along the front of 6 Infantry Division.[614] The German artillery registered a major success when 3rd Battalion, 6 Artillery Regiment, was supplied with a special radio set (*Artillerieflieger-Funkgeraet*), enabling it to talk to an aerial artillery observer, with whose help the battalion smashed several Soviet batteries which had shelled areas around the battalion CP and the CP of 18 Infantry Regiment, causing a number of casualties.[615]

Among the enemy forces encountered by the division during this period of static warfare were many fanatical "Young Communists," members of the so-called "Stalin Guard." Cunning and tenacious fighters, they were supported by spies and partisans who were active behind German lines and sought to blend in with the inhabitants of local villages. "When coming upon civilians in no-man's land or behind the main battle line, one could never be sure if they were disguised soldiers or spies," recalled one veteran of 6 ID.[616] Therefore, the division, on 8/9 August, evacuated all civilians from the villages near the HKL. The effort was carried out by older, experienced NCOs, who moved the civilians to villages some 15 kilometers to the rear;[617] those evacuated "were allowed to take as many of their personal belongings as they could carry, either on their backs or on their *panje* wagons."[618]

"For more than 10 days now we've been in a war of position," observed Haape in his journal on 14 August. "We've build regular trenches and dugouts – and we've done that, we're told, for operational reasons. A new cauldron is going to be formed, then we'll storm eastward, on the heels of the enemy [*hart am Feind*]."[619] Haape, of course, and his fellow soldiers, would have to wait many weeks for the war of movement to get going again; in the meantime, the daily routine along the *Haupfkampflinie* was characterized by constant vigilance, inadequate rest and sleep, reduced rations (due to the long and tenuous supply lines), and little time for proper hygiene. "I sleep on a bed made of fir branches covered with a shelter half," wrote *Oberleutnant* Ernst-Martin Rhein, a company commander in 18 Infantry Regiment and future Knight's Cross holder, in a field post letter in mid-August; in his letter, Rhein indicated that the early morning hours had already become uncomfortably cool:

> In the early morning, so around 0300 hours, it usually gets so cold and damp that you end up passing the time in the short period until 0400 or 0500 hours by shivering and hopping from one foot to the other. We can't wash up, because we don't want to reveal ourselves to the enemy. My beard is flourishing nicely. As a result of the ongoing events and changing situations, as well as the constant battle readiness, my usual deep sleep has turned into a doze, from which I leap at the slightest sound …

> There was great joy just now. For the first time in two months there is margarine and *Plockwurst*. We'd just been living off canned meat and bread for the last few weeks.[620]

Despite the many hardships, there was also time to take in the enchanting countryside, and to gather one's thoughts, as this diary entry by *Stabsarzt* Hans Lierow, a doctor in II./ IR 37, reveals:

> We are lying close to the Schutsche Lake and are waiting on our deployment. The cornfields are ripe, the ears of rye are already shedding their grains. The harvesters will be organized from tomorrow morning. It would be a scandal if the harvest were to spoil. The meadows are blooming so magnificently, the clover a summery violet, the daisies white, the cornflowers blue, and the hemp a delicate, fragrant blue. The whole sunny day the air hums with the sound of busy bees ...
>
> A couple of [Russian] planes come during the night already. But they are only dropping very stupid propaganda leaflets, which cause nothing but hearty laughter among our soldiers ...
>
> There is a lot of time to think about all sorts of things. So I do that and think about my past, my marriage, think about Gisela and the good fortune of having children.[621]

On 14 August, 37 Infantry Regiment was subordinated to the hard-pressed 26 Infantry Division, 6 Infantry's neighbor to the northwest; the regiment occupied the main battle line on 26 ID's right flank.[622] In the days which followed, 37 IR saw difficult and costly defensive battles which seriously reduced its combat power. Beginning about 18 August, the Russians attacked daily in company or battalion strength, supported by tanks and artillery.[623]

For the *Landser* of 37 IR, 26 August turned out to be a conspicuously quiet day. Then began the day no one who fought with the regiment in Russia would ever forget – 27 August 1941. Two Russian cavalry divisions (243, 246), attacking without an artillery preparation – their approach hidden by thick sheets of ground fog – struck the regiment's overextended and sparsely-held line at about 2.30 that morning; exploiting their initial surprise, they rapidly broke through and advanced as far as the regimental command post. From the CP of the regiment's second battalion, Dr Lierow described how the attack unfolded:

> It is morning at 0200 hours. I cannot sleep and leave my dugout. The batallion commander is also awake. The night sky is cloudy. Lively aerial activity starts up. Bombs fall on the regiment's command post, the enemy machines fly very low and cannot be seen. That makes us edgy. A thick fog falls across the ground. Visibility is no more than 20 meters. The companies report that nothing particular is occurring in the enemy held forest except vehicle noise – and that everything is peaceful.
>
> Suddenly, the sound of shots and hand grenades to our right and a telephone call: "The enemy has broken through the neighbor batallion on the right." Wave after wave of Russian soldiers broke in. Alarm at our batallion command post. Everybody jumps into their fox holes. But there's utter chaos, because no one can recognize anyone else in the fog. The batallion commander, who is always there where the danger is greatest, gathers a platoon from 9th Company, which is subordinated to us, and tries to help our neighbor batallion with a counterattack. The "Urrah" of the Russians can be heard coming ever closer. And nothing can be

seen, even though morning is dawning … We strain to listen and look to the right in order to hear from the noise how far the batallion commander has got with his counterattack. Nothing precise can be heard. Only those hundreds of Urrahs out of the fog and machine gun fire. The German artillery shoots barrage fire. Nobody can ascertain the effect.

Suddenly a telephone call from 6th Company. The horror and cry for help from *Oberleutnant* Riehm can be clearly heard: "Enemy has just broken through by 6th Company." Complete helplessness among us, for nobody knows anything about the true situation. The fog prevents any kind of reconnaissance. The telephone line is destroyed. There is no response from there to radio monitoring. The artillery disgorges barrage fire again and again. Then our commander comes back. We don't see him, but we can hear him. Then he's visible, completely out of breath. His right arm hangs limply at his side. The counterattack was but a mere droplet against a sea of resistance. He had stood in the middle of a huge stream of Russians rushing on in waves. The crew of his machine gun, three men, was soon shot down. He managed to get back to us with the remnants [of the platoon]. Since the Russian could appear out of the fog in front of us at any moment, but nobody knows from which direction he might come, an all-round defensive position [*Igel*] is formed …

I help to move an anti-tank gun into position, then I bandage my commander. He has a clean shot through the shoulder. I have just finished bandaging when a shell explodes in our hollow. I receive a hefty blow to my left thigh. A small splinter has penetrated my trousers and grazed my skin. The fog *still* will not clear. The "Urrah" cries have swept past us and can be heard in the distance. There is no link to the regimental command post. The only means of communication is via the artillery …

We know that this is a battle for life or death; the Russians don't leave anybody alive, even the wounded are killed with rifle butts or bayonets. Still no contact with the regiment. It is now nearly 0700 hours and the fog still has not lifted … *Oberleutnant* Riehm has fallen. When he telephoned, the Russians were already on the threshold of his dugout. *Leutnant* Heldt is wounded, … *Unteroffizier* Hildebrand has fallen. No news from the regiment. The air is filled with the thunder of artillery, detonations; bullets from rifles and machine guns whistle above our heads, coming from unpredictable directions and going in other unpredictable directions. I fetch my secret orders, which are sealed, open them at the commander's order, and destroy them. These are rather the last measures which can be taken …

Hour after hour goes by … In the meantime, we receive the report that *Oberstleutnant* Hennicke, the regimental commander, has fallen. Only three days ago, he had been awarded the *Ritterkreuz* for Polotsk … *Leutnant* Borchelt has fallen. *Leutnant* Heimsoth has fallen. *Leutnant* Haardt is wounded. *Hauptmann* Prelle is badly wounded. *Oberleutnant* Ernstmann was also badly wounded; when he realized that he was surrounded by the Russians, he shot himself dead with his pistol.

Finally, also, the news that *Leutnant* Seehausen has fallen – a shot to the head.[624]

That afternoon, the tide of battle finally turned in the Germans' favor. Counterattacking with hastily assembled units of both 6 and 26 Infantry Divisions – including combat engineers, *Panzerjaeger,* and a self-propelled Flak company (1./Fla 46) equipped with twin-barreled 20mm guns, a simply devastating weapon – the Germans annihilated the attacking Russian forces or threw them back in disorder. The nature of the combat, and the skill of the Russians when finally pressed onto the defensive, is exemplified by this entry in the war diary of 6 ID:

> At 1700 hours, the enemy strongpoints are taken in an assault [*Sturmangriff*] involving flawless cooperation between 9./IR 58 and 3./Pi. 6 attacking from the east, with Pz.Jg. 6 and 1./Fla 46, before the corps order arrives to seize these locations. 120 prisoners are taken in Bol. Borck and over 150 Russian dead are confirmed. The enemy was able to create in only a few hours an extraordinarily strong position here, which put up tenacious resistance. In the tough battle for the place, losses for our own forces were unavoidable.[625]

By 1800 hours, the desperate German counterattacks had restored the original main battle line. Approximately 400 Russian dead blanketed the battlefield.[626] German losses were equally appalling, 37 Infantry Regiment alone sustaining 348 casualties: 10 officers and 162 NCOs and men killed; 13 officers and 127 NCOs and men wounded; and 36 NCOs and men missing in action.[627] When the Germans recovered their dead, many were found to have been diabolically mutilated – courtesy of an implacable foe who gave no quarter.[628]

In an order of the day, General Foerster, the corps commander, acknowledged the heavy sacrifice of his men:

> Soldiers of 6 Army Corps! Today a far superior enemy attacked under cover of thick ground fog … Staffs defended their command posts in close combat, batteries their gun positions … The performance of officers and men in these battles is beyond all praise … Soldiers of my corps! Today has shown what a brave force can achieve through loyalty and self-sacrifice.[629]

The general's ennobling words, however, could not conceal a simple immutable truth: Losses such as these, which eviscerated the *Ostheer's* combat strength, were simply catastrophic.

It rained that night. The survivors of the cruel day huddled in their trenches and dugouts, wondering what the next day might bring. Some, no doubt, killed time by playing the popular card games, *Skat* and *Doppelkopf*. Those fortunate enough to have a radio set might have been consoled by the mellifluous tones of cabaret singer Lale Andersen's sentimental soldiers' song, "Lili Marleen," now beamed nightly at precisely 9:57 p.m. by *Soldatensender Belgrade* (Armed Force Radio Belgrade) across the battlefronts of Europe and North Africa, just before signoff.[630] As a final thought in his diary, *Stabsarzt* Lierow wrote: "It was a tough day, the 27th of August. We all felt as if we were closer to death than life." In just 14 days of combat Lierow's battalion (II./IR 37) has been reduced to the size of a strong company.[631]

The dead of 37 Infantry Regiment were buried under a tall tree on the periphery of a local village, where the Germans had set up another military cemetery. At the foot of a tall birch cross, lay the grave of the regimental commander, *Oberstleutnant* Hennicke; alongside, the graves of his men. The dead were honored in a solemn Teutonic ceremony, a ritual which, by now, had become all too routine.[632]

10.6.2: Case Two – 46 Panzer Corps in El'nia Salient

In mid-July 1941, Guderian had made a fateful decision: After breaching the Dnepr River line, instead of wheeling to the northeast with his 46 Panzer Corps to meet the spearheads of Hoth's 3 Panzer Group beyond Smolensk, he had sent Vietinghoff's tanks and motorized infantry racing east to seize a bridgehead over the Desna River at El'nia, 300 kilometers west of Moscow. This was accomplished on 19/20 July, yet in doing so, the panzer general had forfeited an opportunity to forge a solid ring around the Soviet armies trapped north and northwest of Smolensk, enabling tens of thousands of Russian soldiers to slip from the incipient pocket and making the German victory there disappointingly incomplete.

Located 82 kilometers southeast of Smolensk, near the headwaters of the Desna River, El'nia was a "typical small town"[633] of western Russia. Typical it may have been, but it embodied several features which, no doubt, fired Guderian's imagination: A bridge over the Desna River, a rail station on a main east-west rail line, and, most significantly, high ground (due east of the town) which dominated the outermost approaches to Moscow. In other words, El'nia offered a vital foothold from which to continue the all-important drive on the Soviet capital.[634] Thus, for both Germans and Russians alike, El'nia and its environs was what Sun Tzu had called "desperate ground" – terrain that had to be defended or captured.

As soon became apparent, however, the German bridgehead at El'nia also evinced several serious tactical liabilities. The salient was surrounded on three sides by powerful – and continuously reinforcing – Russian forces, while its rearward communications were clogged with German units struggling to subdue the Smolensk cauldron; it was also some 450 kilometers from the closest German supply depots.[635] The mobile forces of 46 Panzer Corps which fought there in late July and early August 1941 – first 10 Panzer Division, soon joined by SS *Das Reich* and Infantry Regiment *Grossdeutschland* – did so at a distinct disadvantage. Both Schaal's 10 Panzer and "Papa" Hausser's *Das Reich* divisions were fatigued and below strength, while ammunition (particularly artillery shells) and fuel were in chronic short supply. In addition, the confining and difficult terrain within the salient – much of it what the Germans called *Kusselgelaende*, or low trees and brush which seriously hampered visibility – "nullified their mobility and shock effect."[636] Like all German tank units, 10 Panzer Division also suffered from a paucity of combat infantry and, thus, was poorly postured for the role of positional defense to which it was now committed.

Despite such challenges, the tanks and panzer grenadiers of 46 Panzer Corps would have to hold the salient against unremitting Soviet counterattacks – supported by armor, air power, and ample artillery – until finally relieved by marching infantry moving up from the rear. Nevertheless, the positions around El'nia were thought to be merely temporary, as most German commanders assumed they would resume their eastward drive as soon as the infantry had "tidied up" the Smolensk pocket and become available for other duties; however, as was so often the case during the summer campaign of 1941, this assumption was soon overtaken by events beyond the Germans' control. Indeed, at El'nia, Army Group Center would become inextricably ensnared in a brutal, eight-week bloodbath, which ultimately engulfed some 10 of its divisions in "a cauldron of fire and steel" unlike any the Germans Army had experienced since 1918.[637] That the Germans held out at all was, in part at least, due to effective close air support from the *Stukas* of Kesselring's 2 Air Fleet.[638]

Schaal's 10 Panzer Division had first received orders to capture El'nia at 0900 hours on 16 July 1941; delayed by thundershowers, bad roads and collapsed bridges, the attack did not begin until 19 July from positions east of Pochinok, a town at the intersection of the Smolensk-Roslavl and Mstislavl-El'nia roads.[639] At precisely 1312 hours, the division's artillery loosed a *Feuerschlag* on the Russian defensive positions; three minutes later, the tanks rolled out of their hiding places and advanced on El'nia. Despite encountering well-laid long-range artillery fire, and delays occasioned by a cavernous anti-tank trench (5 by 10 meters) across the Pochinok-El'nia road, the armor of the division's 7 Panzer Regiment was soon advancing astride the railroad tracks toward El'nia; by 1430 hours, the first tanks had reached the western and southern edge of the town under heavy enemy fire.[640]

Covered by the lead tanks, the first rifle squads of 10 Panzer's 69 Rifle Regiment pushed into the town. Bitter house-to-house fighting ensued with heavy losses to both attackers and defenders, the latter belonging to 19 Rifle Division of the Soviet 24 Army. Heavy artillery fire pummeled the advancing panzer grenadiers, and an intense struggle took place for the railroad station. Everywhere the German infantry came up against splendidly prepared field positions. At 1515 hours, General Schaal nourished his attack by committing his other rifle regiment (86 SR) to the battle; by 1800, it was closing on El'nia.[641]

The fighting surged back and forth, the Russians putting in a counterattack early that evening and recapturing some lost ground. Soon, however, 10 Motorcycle Battalion had cleared the eastern side of El'nia as far as the cemetery, 800 meters beyond the town limits; the church in the center of the town was also seized. Despite such progress, the division's 10 Rifle Brigade reported at 2000 hours that the attack was going forward very slowly: "Heavily mined, tough opponent!," it stated. Then, at 2230 hours, *Oberst* Fischer, the commander of the rifle brigade, reported that El'nia was finally in German hands.[642]

Yet the situation inside El'nia was still far from secure, much less stabilized. Again and again, Soviet infantry battalions sought to infiltrate back into the town, and the Russian artillery stayed active. About midnight, the defenders moved a battery into firing position directly before the lines of 10 Motorcycle Battalion, and pumped shells into the ruins of the houses. Meanwhile, an unbroken stream of vehicle columns shepherded Soviet reinforcements up to the town. The bloody day of battle had cost 2nd Battalion, 69 Rifle Regiment, 60 casualties; losses among the other rifle battalions, and the motorcycle battalion, were equally severe.[643]

Over the next two days (20/21 July), 10 Panzer Division sought to widen its bridgehead at El'nia under intense enemy pressure. In one Soviet attack on the morning of 20 July, the Germans destroyed 18 tanks, 10 of them knocked out by a single *Unteroffizier* in the division's *Panzerjaeger* battalion. Soviet prisoners revealed that the Russian leadership was bringing up any forces they could lay hands on to retake El'nia. As if to amplify their point, at midday, heavy Russian artillery fire, up to 210mm caliber, began once again to tear at the German lines, the shelling by mid-afternoon swelling to an enormous barrage (*Trommelfeuer*). This was followed by another Soviet attack strongly supported by armor, which was again repulsed, this time with the loss of 25 tanks. Undeterred, the Russians continued to press their assaults, only to be thrown back yet again by the beleaguered panzer grenadiers bolstered by 7 Panzer Regiment's handful of remaining tanks. Altogether, the Germans destroyed 50 Russian tanks and took 700 prisoners on this day.[644]

By now, a great majority of 10 Panzer Division's tanks were out of action. While some had become total losses in combat over the first four weeks of the campaign, most were now immobilized by lack of oil, spare parts, and replacement engines. During the actions on 20 July, a number of tanks had simply broken down on the battlefield, while the barrel recoils (*Rohrruecklauf*) on a few of the still battle-ready Panzer IVs had malfunctioned. The constant fighting had also resulted in the total exhaustion of the tank crews. On General Schaal's orders, at nightfall, the tanks were to be withdrawn for urgently needed maintenance and repair; only a reinforced company was to stay in action as a final reserve.[645]

The next morning (21 July), General Vietinghoff reported from 46 Panzer Corps headquarters that, despite the most strenuous efforts, 10 Panzer could not yet be supplied with oil or with shells for its artillery, which were also sorely needed; the oil, in fact, would not arrive for several days, leaving most of 7 Panzer Regiment out of action for an extended period.[646] As of 22 July, the regiment had just five Pz IIs and four Pz IIIs fully combat-capable; 66 panzers were deemed capable of limited action in a defensive role, and fully 100 in immediate need of refurbishment.[647] On a more positive note, by late 21 July, elements of the SS Motorized Division *Das Reich* were reaching the El'nia salient to shore up the hard-pressed 10 Panzer.[648] Hausser's SS grenadiers had been pushing from Baltutino toward the high ground at Dorogobuzh, another area Guderian had hoped to seize as a jump-off point for Moscow.[649] Yet because of the strong Russian pressure at El'nia, it was decided to redirect *Das Reich* into the salient to bolster German forces there.[650]

The nature of the fighting within the salient in the days which followed – and the almost perpetual state of crisis faced by 46 Panzer Corps – is vividly recorded in the war diary of Guderian's 2 Panzer Group:

22.7.41:
1040 hours: The supply situation for 46 Pz.K. has worsened due to the poor condition of the roads and fierce enemy attacks at El'nia, which are resulting in high consumption of ammunition. The corps reports:
1. A severe shortage of 100mm and 210mm howitzer [*Moerser*] ammunition.
2. A 100 cbm oil shortage …
1700 hours: … <u>46 Pz.K.</u> – Command post moving forward to Strigino … <u>10 Pz.-Div.</u> and <u>SS-Div. *Reich*</u> are attacking to extend the positions around El'nia. Details unknown …
2230 hours: … <u>10 Pz.-Div.</u> – The enemy attacked at El'nia from southeast and northeast in the morning hours in dense columns with heavy artillery fire. The attacks were repelled with bloody losses for the enemy.[651]

23.7.41:
1100 hours: <u>Report of 46 Pz.K.</u>:
The enemy is attacking from the east in divisional strength near El'nia. Our lack of artillery ammunition is becoming painfully acute …
1300 hours: … <u>10 Pz.-Div.</u> and <u>SS-Div. *Reich*</u> extended their positions around El'nia … The enemy is attacking especially fiercely from the south and southwest. Enemy assembly areas in the north are identified. The reconnaissance battalion of SS-Div. *Reich*, which was at Kaskova, had to be withdrawn via Garavitsa in the face of superior enemy forces to the railway station at Glinka (20 km northwest of El'nia).[652]

24.7.41:
1200 hours: <u>46 Pz.K.</u> reports:
The situation at El'nia is extremely tense, repeated enemy attacks on 3 sides, heavy enemy tanks from the southeast. Now the enemy is also attacking us from the direction of Dorogobuzh. The corps is urgently requesting the release of I.R. G.D. [Infantry Regiment *Grossdeutschland*]. If possible, at least 1 batallion [of the regiment] is to be supplied immediately.
To resolve the ammunition shortage, artillery ammunition is being requested from 17 Pz.-Div.

[End 46 Pz.K. report.]

The relief of I.R.G.D., and reinforcement of the front at El'nia, can only occur after elements of 18 Pz.-Div. still at Smolensk and M.G. Btn. 5 have been released and brought forward by Fourth Panzer Army …

1450 hours: <u>Report of 46 Pz.K.</u>:
The situation on the left flank at El'nia is critical. The enemy is pressing hard on Ushakova from the north. To stabilize the situation, the corps requests that either a battalion of I.R.G.D. is immediately made available, or that 17 Pz.-Div. takes over the sector Ushakova – Glinka railway station …
1700 hours: … <u>46 Pz.K.</u> – Command post 4 km west of El'nia … <u>10 Pz.-Div.</u> and <u>SS-Div. *Reich*</u> in battle with strong enemy, who is attacking from southeast, east, and now also from north. The enemy attacks are supported by heavy artillery and tanks.

The situation in this sector is critical. The left flank has to be moved back into the line south of Ushakova – Glinka railway station.[653]

25.7.41:
0600 hours: ... 46 Pz.K. ... SS-Div. *Reich* – Throughout the entire night heavy artillery fire on the division's sector. According to prisoner statements, the enemy is planning a large-scale attack today at 1100 hours.

[2 Panzer Group], however, cannot provide the corps with any reserves, since I.R.G.D. is still tied down [in another sector] ...

0825 hours: Report of 46 Pz.K.:
Since the delivery of artillery ammunition has been delayed by a day, and the last ammunition reserves have nearly all been used up in the course of the night and in the early morning, and as a result of the failure to deliver urgently required elements of I.R.G.D. and the lack artillery ammunition, the situation can only be considered extremely tense [*aeusserst gespannt*] ...
2300 hours:[654] ... 46 Pz.K. ... Renewed fierce enemy attack from the direction of Bogoroditskoe (12 km northeast of El'nia) and Ushakova on the sector around El'nia. Counterattack is underway.
In the battles around El'nia on 25.7., the corps destroyed 78 enemy tanks, including 8 heavy tanks, and 8 aircraft.[655]

26.7.41:
1350 hours: After the *Luftwaffe* reported an hour ago that enemy tanks were already gathering at Dadischtcheva (13 km northeast of El'nia), the *Flivo* [*Luftwaffe* liaison officer] is now reporting 40 enemy tanks at Kaskova advancing on El'nia.
1355 hours: To reinforce 46 Pz.K. against these enemy tanks, Pz.Jg.Abt. 611 (hitherto by 47 Pz.K.) is being subordinated to it ...
1535 hours: The situation in sector of 46 Pz.K. is becoming more critical. The enemy has succeeded in breaching the front of the rifle brigade of 10 Pz.-Div. south of El'nia. There are no reserves left to restore the situation ...
1730 hours: ... 46 Pz.K. – Corps command post unchanged.
The situation is especially critical in the battle around El'nia. The corps is attacked all day long by strongly superior forces with tanks and artillery.
At Lipnia, the enemy managed a penetration, which could not yet be sealed off.
During the enemy attacks south of the railway, 11 enemy batteries were identified.
Extremely heavy artillery fire is inflicting constant heavy losses on the troops. In addition, there is the constant impact of enemy bombers. Due to the artillery fire, evacuation of the many wounded is not possible at the moment. The attacks from the direction of Dorogobuzh resulted in a localized withdrawal of the front in the north.
Absolutely no reserves are available to the corps. The artillery ammunition is so depleted that no more shells can be used to contest the enemy's artillery [*Art.-Bekaempfung*].
10 Pz.-Div.'s panzer brigade has been immobilized for several days by lack of oil and fuel.
The corps might just succeed in holding its positions, but only amid severe bloody sacrifices.
Due to the delay in relieving I.R.G.D., no reserves can be delivered to the corps at this time.[656]

27.7.41:

0600 hours: … 46 Pz.K. – In sectors of 10 Pz.-Div. and SS-Div. *Reich* the night was quiet … The situation of the corps has somewhat eased, as during the night the first transports with ammunition and oil arrived, as did Pz.Jg.Abt. 611 and elements of I.R.G.D …

1700 hours: … 46 Pz.K. … Thanks to repeated attacks by the combined forces of *Nakafue* II [Close Air Support Leader II], delivery of artillery ammunition, and the bulk of I.R.G.D., the corps' situation at El'nia has eased.

The enemy attacks continue, but with somewhat decreased intensity. The enemy artillery fire is, as before, very uncomfortable [*sehr unangenehm*], and inflicts losses.[657]

29.7.41:

1035 hours: 46 Pz.K. inquires whether the supply of additional forces can be expected, since the corps had incurred considerable losses during the defensive battles.

A reinforcement of the corps, except with 268 ID, is not possible at the moment for *Armeegruppe* [Guderian], but a request has been lodged with [Army Group Center]. The 137 ID, now freed up at Smolensk, has to take over protection of 9 AK's east flank in the attack on Roslavl, and so cannot be deployed for relief in sector of 46 Pz.K …

1745 hours: … 46 Pz.K. … Lively patrol activity in the area around El'nia in sectors of 10 Pz.-Div., SS-Div. *Reich*, and I.R.G.D. The enemy was no longer attacking at this time, but resurgent artillery activity was detected to the north of El'nia.

268 ID – partly brought up to El'nia in trucks – in the evening hours begins with relief of 10 Pz.-Div.[658]

30.7.41:

0600 hours: … 46 Pz.K. 10 Pz.-Div. – IR 499 of 268 ID relieved elements of the division on its left flank …

I.R.G.D. has been fully deployed.

Since 0230 hours, along the entire corps sector, enemy attacks with tanks, artillery, and aircraft, some of which are still in progress …

1035 hours: Ic – *Armeegruppe* [Guderian] reports that a captured Russian flyer, an *Oberleutnant*, has stated the following:

By order of a higher Russian staff, El'nia is to be taken today. He himself was transferred with 170 bombers to Viaz'ma for this purpose.

Close Air Support Leader is being informed about this. The facts – attacks from 0230 hours on 46 Pz.K. – confirm the veracity of this statement …

1745 hours: … 46 Pz.K. … Several enemy attacks with artillery and tanks were repelled in the El'nia sector. Localized incursions were cleared up. Today the corps reports 13 enemy attacks and an increase in the number of batteries identified so far.

In the coming days, further attacks will have to be reckoned with, especially at the flanks of the El'nia salient.[659]

31.7.41:

0600 hours: … 46 Pz.K. – With the exception of localized artillery fire, the night was quiet by 268 ID, 10 Pz.-Div., and SS-Div. *Reich* …

1745 hours: … 46 Pz.K. … The enemy attacks again in the El'nia salient from the southeast and north with strong artillery and tanks. Enemy air attacks on headquarters staffs and the forward line …

2300 hours: … 46 Pz.K. – Corps command post 4 km west of El'nia. Since 0300 hours uninterrupted enemy attacks, which continue even now (2100 hours) in the south, southeast, northeast, north, in part with tanks amid heavy artillery fire. Our own artillery is severely handicapped by lack of ammunition.

Due to enemy artillery fire, there are continual losses of materiel and personnel. I.R.G.D. alone had 92 casualties from 28.-30.7. IR 499 of 268 ID had 82 casualties in the first 24 hours, among them 30 dead.

The relief [of 10 Pz.-Div.] by 268 ID comes to an end during the night of 31.7./1.8.[660]

The relief of 10 Panzer Division went off without a hitch. On 1 August, Schaal's panzer grenadiers occupied a security line (*Sicherungslinie*) south of El'nia, a quieter sector shielding the right flank of the salient. The line stretched some 30 kilometers – beginning on the bank of the Desna River at Stragina, along the southern rim of the town, then running northwest at the edge of an extensive marshland between the Desna and Striana Rivers, before turning south along the west bank of the Striana; the line's southernmost point was the village of Schmakovo, 30 kilometers S/SW of El'nia. The following day (2 August), on orders from 46 Panzer Corps, the division established an operational reserve (*Einsatzgruppe*), consisting of a rifle battalion, two tank companies, combat engineer and anti-tank companies; intended as the corps reserve, the *Einsatzgruppe* was to be ready to intervene at any crisis point along the salient within two hours of being notified. While both actions (security line and reserve force) were unavoidable, they disrupted efforts to refurbish the panzer regiment, whose tanks were still mostly out of action – awaiting oil, spare parts, new engines, and maintenance.[661] Meanwhile, Russian assaults up and down the embattled bridgehead went on with unabated fury. The 268 Infantry Division reported that Soviet soldiers were waving Red banners as they attacked; at 1745 hours, 2 August, 46 Panzer Corps reported that company strengths along the salient had been reduced to 60-70 men in some cases.[662]

The Soviet offensive at El'nia became the responsibility of General Zhukov on 30 July, with his appointment as commander of the Red Army's Reserve Front. His primary asset was Maj.-Gen. K. I. Rakutin's 24 Army, consisting of nine rifle, three mobile, and two militia divisions – the latter comprised largely of workers' militiamen from Moscow. Upon assuming the front command, Zhukov "sharply criticized" Rakutin's previous offensive operations and began to prepare a fresh assault against the German bridgehead.[663]

Although Red Army forces opposite the El'nia salient consisted mostly of recently mobilized, poorly trained, and often poorly equipped rifle divisions,[664] they were lavishly outfitted with artillery, providing the Soviets with a combat arm of tremendous lethality, as depicted by the 2 Panzer Group diary entries above. Further examples amplify this point: On 1 August, 46 Panzer Corps reported to Army Group Center that, in the average area of a company, as many as 200 shells landed in five minutes as the German infantry huddled helplessly in their foxholes; on 2 August, 268 ID reported 300-400 shells striking the sector of a battalion in one hour; and, on 3 August, during a Russian attack, Vietinghoff's corps was pounded by 1550 shells, the majority coming from heavy caliber 152mm guns. Barrages such as these had soon transfigured the 60 kilometer wide salient into a cratered wasteland.[665]

Made privy to such reports, Halder characterized the Russian artillery fire as "insufferable," and anxiously observed that, "the holding of this 'bridgehead' costs us much blood."[666] Much blood indeed – between 22 July and 3 August 1941, the units of 46 Panzer Corps suffered 3615 casualties defending the El'nia salient, most of them, no doubt, from unremitting artillery fire.[667] Casualties of close to 300 men per day were, of course, unsustainable in the long run. Nevertheless, "no one in the German command considered giving up the El'nia salient. Halder was still hoping to use it as springboard for further operations to the east and Hitler was, in general, opposed to any form of withdrawal, even if tactically advantageous."[668] And this despite the fact that, on 3

August, Bock informed Halder that, with his present resources, he could not guarantee against "catastrophe" at El'nia.[669] The same day, Guderian committed his final available reserve formation – the guard company of his group headquarters – to the fighting in the seething salient.[670]

The catastrophe feared by Bock was averted by the arrival of additional infantry units, and, by 8 August, the divisions of Materna's 20 Army Corps (15, 268, 292 ID) had replaced all of 46 Panzer Corps within the El'nia salient proper;[671] in addition, Flak batteries of the *Luftwaffe's* I Flak Corps, with their devastating 88mm guns, were brought up to bolster the defenses.[672] Following their "relief," SS *Das Reich* and Infantry Regiment *Grossdeutschland* were put right back in the line, this time in positions northwest of El'nia and covering the northern flank of the salient, replacing 17 Panzer Division and elements of 29 Motorized Division, both of Lemelsen's 47 Panzer Corps. Just prior to its relief, on 9 August, Thoma's 17 Panzer Division had been struck repeatedly by strong Russian forces, provoking a bloodbath clinically recorded by Lemelsen in his journal the next day:

> Moreover, yesterday *der Russe* attacked 17 Panzer Division the whole day with 2 divisions and strong artillery, powerful mass attacks in several waves one after another, which were scythed down by our machine guns and artillery fire. Mountains of corpses piled up. Naturally, incursions along the division's 35 km long front could not be avoided, but they were all ironed out by the counterattacks of our panzers, and the old line was entirely back in our hands yesterday evening.[673]

On 18/19 August 1941, both *Das Reich* and *Grossdeutschland* were, in turn, relieved from the front by units of 9 Army Corps and finally withdrawn for badly needed rest and refitting. Over the previous four weeks (through 15 August), the SS grenadiers of *Das Reich* had repelled 83 separate Soviet attacks while conducting 27 counterattacks of their own.[674]

By 23 August, all of 10 Panzer Division, having turned over its security line along the Striana, southwest of El'nia, to an infantry unit, had been withdrawn behind the front – into the area west of Pochinok, 40-50 kilometers south of Smolensk – to complete its refurbishment.[675] A week before (15 August), the commander of the division's panzer brigade, *Oberst* von Hauenschild, had issued a special order of the day; in it, he noted with pride that, through the combined efforts of the division's maintenance staff, Army supply services, the Organization Todt, the *Luftwaffe*, and the armaments industry in Germany, the division had increased its number of operational tanks to 160. "With this proud figure," the order read, "we now stand at the head of all panzer units on the eastern front. *Generaloberst* Guderian has asked me to convey to you his great joy and his special recognition."[676]

With the threat of collapse still hanging over the German front at El'nia – 20 Army Corps had a single battalion in reserve, and was suffering from ongoing shortages of artillery shells[677] – Guderian ordered both Vietinghoff and Materna to a meeting on 14 August. The evening before, the panzer general had discussed the prospect of abandoning the salient – and, thereby, shortening the German line – with the Army Group Center chief of staff, General von Greiffenberg. Guderian, however, was reluctant to do so: A withdrawal would hand the Soviets their first major victory of the war, which they would put to good use as propaganda.[678]

The emergency meeting on 14 August "was intended to decide the fate of the El'nia salient and sharply divergent opinions were exchanged."[679] General Materna (20 Army Corps) was convinced that the position had to be abandoned. (The evening before, he had "complained bitterly" – to Vietinghoff – that his 15 Infantry Division was particularly threatened, having lost 35 officers over the past two days alone, and that holding on to the current position was "pure insanity.") Materna pleaded for withdrawal, arguing that his badly emaciated infantry divisions could no longer hold against a determined enemy attack. Vietinghoff (46 Panzer Corps), however, was opposed to giving up the salient, pointing out that a withdrawal would simply encourage the enemy and lead him to step up his assaults. While Guderian was inclined to take Vietinghoff's position, in the absence of clear operational priorities (i.e., Hitler and his High Command were still at loggerheads over the future course of operations), he found it hard to reach a decision.[680]

As for the commander of Army Group Center, Field Marshal von Bock – he, too, was now unsure what to do. On 15 August he wrote: "It is difficult to decide whether holding the salient is right or wrong. If the Russians continue to attack, then holding is wrong; if they cease their attacks in the foreseeable future it is right, for El'nia is a springboard for a further advance [on Moscow!] and also offers a certain protection for the road and rail junction of Smolensk."[681] Bock had referred the matter to Brauchitsch the day before, and the Army C-in-C had promised to make a quick decision on "whether El'nia was to be abandoned or not." That evening (14 August), Bock received a response: "[His decision] contains many 'ifs' and 'buts' and turns responsibility over to me."[682] Bock, then, would have to decide on his own.

Most likely influenced by Halder, who warned Bock's chief of staff against abandoning the salient,[683] Bock eventually resolved to hold at El'nia; and this although Guderian had suddenly performed a *volte-face* and proposed that the salient be abandoned![684] When Bock asked Guderian what was required to hold the position there, the panzer general proposed a sizeable increase in the flow of munitions and the recommitment of "strong *Luftwaffe* forces" at El'nia. While the field marshal could not promise a major improvement in the delivery of munitions ("the utmost was already being done in that regard"), he did speak to Brauchitsch about shifting Kesselring's 2 Air Corps – which *Reichsmarschall* Goering, without consulting Bock, had abruptly assembled further south, in the sector of Second Army to protect the southern flank of the army group – back to the El'nia front. In this, however, Bock was not successful; the bulk of 2 Air Corps remained where it was.[685]

The decision to hold the salient signified that the fighting and dying there would go on for several more weeks. The *Landser*, of course, in their trenches and dugouts along the El'nia perimeter – the deepest eastward penetration hitherto made by the *Ostheer* on the entire eastern front – were hardly privy to the ongoing debates of their field commanders, or to the concerns and anxieties at the highest levels of command in Rastenburg and Berlin. Yet if the fighting had grown more bitter – the enemy tougher and more determined – the morale of the average *Landser* remained high, his faith in final victory unshaken.

On 15 August 1941, "Hans Otto," a soldier in 268 Infantry Division – since 1 August fully committed to the abattoir that was the El'nia salient – penned a field post letter to an unknown recipient:

> Our group can claim to have been the forwardmost boot of the German *Wehrmacht* for approximately 14 days. Since the end of last month we have been an irritating thorn in the pelt of the Russian bear, which he has been trying to attack with all his might. Despite all of his artillery, he does not succeed in removing this thorn, and his bloody infantry losses are unimaginable. The town I.,[686] which we surround, will one day be an important name in the history of this campaign.
>
> Yes, these battles are tough, and in our ranks, too, death tears a hole in the ranks of our best every day. But in these battles, the soldier has now learned to become tough, too, and shown that he is also equal to "storms of steel," just like his fathers in the World War. The grandeur of many an expression from that time now becomes clear. The incessant metallic hammering of the artillery, the crashing

explosions of the shells, and the zipping and humming of shrapnel makes its own music. And when that can be heard constantly from morning til night in any sector of the front, unending, without any indication that they are having to pause for breath over there, then you can put yourself in the position of the fighter in the World War.

But our guys have become tough in all this and have an admirable level of self-confidence, and if the Russian comes with infantry and tanks, then a bloody reception awaits him. And it matters not at all if one or two tanks break through the lines, because one of our Paks was destroyed and no other weapon can stop it. For then the infantryman leaps from his foxhole with hand grenade, molotov cocktail, and a concentrated charge, and finishes it off as matter of factly as if he were conducting a peacetime demonstration.

Our Ostmarkers have particularly proved themselves here, defending a commanding elevation (125.6), which the Russian attacks again and again. And here is laid bare the spirit of the fighter in the current war, he who knows for what he fights and, if necessary, dies, in contrast to the stupid cannon fodder which is only whipped forward over and again by the Reds' pack of lies and a pistol or a machine gun.[687]

ENDNOTES

1   Quoted in: H. Hoth, *Panzer-Operationen*, 110-11.

2   Quoted in: H. Hoth, *Panzer-Operationen*, 69.

3   C. Burdick & H.-A. Jacobsen (eds.), *The Halder Diary 1939-1942*, 465.

4   BA-MA N 664/3, *Tagebuch* Thilo, 25.7.41.

5   Quoted in: O. Buchbender & R. Sterz (Hg.), *Das Andere Gesicht des Krieges*, 75.

6   *Tagebuch* Lierow, 5.8.41.

7   D. M. Glantz, *Barbarossa*, 55.

8   *GSWW*, Vol. IV, 836; A. Seaton, *The Russo-German War*, 139, f.n. 20.

9   H. Magenheimer, *Moskau 1941*, 47; *DRZW*, Bd. 4, Beiheft, "*Frontveraenderungen der H.Gr. Mitte und Nord vom 6.7. bis 23.7.1941.*"

10   *GSWW*, Vol. IV, 836.

11   Ibid., 836.

12   D. M. Glantz, *Barbarossa*, 55. For a breakdown of Soviet losses by front see, Col.-Gen. G. F. Krivosheev (ed.), *Soviet Casualties and Combat Losses*, 110-13.

13   D. M. Glantz, *Barbarossa Derailed*, Vol. I, 248; K.-J. Thies, *Der Ostfeldzug – Ein Lageatlas*, "Lage am 16.7.1941 abds., Heeresgruppe Mitte."

14   See, W. Hubatsch (Hg.), *Hitlers Weisungen fuer die Kriegfuehrung*, 129-34, 136-39. As outlined in the supplement (32b), the *Luftwaffe* was allocated the highest production priority; it was to be "greatly strengthened." The *Kriegsmarine* was to continue to build more U-Boats, but not to develop a large surface fleet.

15   G. L. Weinberg, *A World at Arms*, 268.

16   A. Hillgruber, *Hitlers Strategie*, 541-43; A. Hillgruber, "*Die 'Endloesung' und das deutsche Ostimperium als Kernstueck des rassenideologischen Programms des Nationalsozialismus,*" in: *Hitler, Deutschland und die Maechte*, M. Funke (Hg.).

17   For more details see, "*Vortragsnotiz ueber die Besetzung und Sicherung des russischen Raumes und ueber den Umbau des Heeres nach Abschluss Barbarossa,*" in: P. E. Schramm (Hg.), *Kriegstagebuch des OKW*, Bd. I, 1022-25.

18   BA-MA N 664/2, *Tagebuch* Thilo, 15.7.41.

19   G. R. Ueberschaer & W. Wette (Hg.), "*Unternehmen Barbarossa." Der deutsche Ueberfall auf die Sowjetunion 1941*, 149.

20   A. Hillgruber, "*Die 'Endloesung' und das deutsche Ostimperium als Kernstueck des rassenideologischen Programms des Nationalsozialismus,*" in: *Hitler, Deutschland und die Maechte*, M. Funke (Hg.), 103.

21   J. Huerter, *Ein deutscher General an der Ostfront*, 69.

22   Ibid., 70.

23   The slowdown in the German advance was even apparent to the Americans. In late July 1941, General George C. Marshal observed, "The Germans seem to have stubbed a toe in Russia at present and their army

has been stalled for more than a week." On 5 August 1941, Laurence Steinhardt, the American ambassador in Moscow, cabled Secretary of State Cordell Hull, noting that "during the past two weeks or more the main German forces have not advanced appreciably toward either Leningrad or Moscow ... I find no evidence of any tendency toward a collapse of the Soviet defense." Quoted in: "*Operation Barbarossa and the American Controversy over Aid to the Soviet Union*," R. Kirchubel, 18-19.

24   C. Luther, "*German Armoured Operations in the Ukraine, 1941. The Encirclement Battle of Uman*," in: *The Army Quarterly and Defence Journal*, Vol. 108, No. 4, Oct 78, 464.

25   D. M. Glantz, *Barbarossa Derailed*, Vol. I, 248.

26   "*Tagesmeldungen der Operations-Abteilung des GenStdH*," in: P. E. Schramm (Hg.), *Kriegstagebuch des OKW*, Bd. I, 547; K.-J. Thies, *Der Ostfeldzug – Ein Lageatlas*, "Lage am 30.7.1941 abds., Heeresgruppe Mitte."

27   R. Overmans, *Deutsche militaerische Verluste im Zweiten Weltkrieg*, 277.

28   G. Meyer, *Adolf Heusinger*, 151-52.

29   Ibid., 153-54.

30   H. Guderian, *Panzer Leader*, 167-68.

31   Halder had contemplated this operation as early as 29 June 1941. See, H.-A. Jacobsen (Hg.), *Generaloberst Halder Kriegstagebuch*, Bd. III, 25-26.

32   H. Magenheimer, *Moskau 1941*, 48.

33   *GSWW*, Vol. IV, 533-34.

34   D. M. Glantz, *Barbarossa Derailed*, Vol. I, 128; also, H. Magenheimer, *Moskau 1941*, 49.

35   The divisions in Timoshenko's foremost line suffered from a paucity of artillery and armor, among other shortfalls. *GSWW*, Vol. IV, 865.

36   D. M. Glantz, *Barbarossa Derailed*, Vol. I, 92.

37   R. Kirchubel, *Operation Barbarossa 1941 (3), Army Group Center*, 54.

38   K.-J. Thies, *Der Ostfeldzug – Ein Lageatlas*, "Lage am 10.7.1941 abds., Heeresgruppe Mitte."

39   According to Glantz, the Dnepr "ranged in width from 250 to 300 feet at Bychov and was no obstacle, the only problem [Guderian] had to surmount was the swampy meadows and forests on the river's eastern bank." D. M. Glantz, *Barbarossa Derailed*, Vol. I, 93.

40   H. Schaeufler (ed.), *Knight's Cross Panzers*, 81.

41   D. M. Glantz, *Barbarossa Derailed*, Vol. I, 94. According to Glantz, Guderian had selected Stary Bychov "as his target over the more obvious choices of Orsha, Mogilev, or Rogachev because he had already failed to crack the Rogachev 'nut,' and he intended to either bypass the others or, if necessary, turn their flanks and encircle and reduce them later." Ibid., 93.

42   K. J. Walde, *Guderian*, 125.

43   "*Tagesmeldungen der Operations-Abteilung des GenStdH*," in: P. E. Schramm (Hg.), *Kriegstagebuch des OKW*, Bd. I, 518; K.-J. Thies, *Der Ostfeldzug – Ein Lageatlas*, "Lage am 10.7.1941 abds., Heeresgruppe Mitte."

44   K.-J. Thies, *Der Ostfeldzug – Ein Lageatlas*, "Lage am 11.7.1941 abds., Heeresgruppe Mitte."

45   H. Guderian, *Panzer Leader*, 171.

46   R. Kirchubel, *Hitler's Panzer Armies*, 67.

47   H. Guderian, *Panzer Leader*, 171.

48   J. Dinglreiter, *Die Vierziger. Chronik des Regiments*, 44-45.

49   Ibid., 45.

50   Note: The reference here is to the wounded German soldiers, who, of course, were in no condition to swim back across the river. All of the German pneumatic boats had been destroyed by the intense Soviet fire.

51   J. Dinglreiter, *Die Vierziger. Chronik des Regiments*, 45.

52   Ibid., 46.

53   The *Grossdeutschland* was a reinforced infantry regiment. It began the eastern campaign with 20 companies distributed among five battalions; heavy weapons included 400 Artillery Battalion with three batteries. H. Spaeter, *Die Geschichte des Panzerkorps "Grossdeutschland*," 248.

54   A. Schick, *Die Geschichte der 10. Panzer-Division*, 300-01.

55   Ibid., 301.

56   The fighting at Hill 215 apparently took place on the evening of 10 July. Ibid., 302.

57   H. Guderian, *Panzer Leader*, 172; "*Tagesmeldungen der Operations-Abteilung des GenStdH*," in: P. E. Schramm (Hg.), *Kriegstagebuch des OKW*, Bd. I, 519; K.-J. Thies, *Der Ostfeldzug – Ein Lageatlas*, "Lage am 11.7.1941 abds., Heeresgruppe Mitte;" also, A. Schick, *Die Geschichte der 10. Panzer-Division*, 302.

58   D. M. Glantz, *Barbarossa Derailed*, Vol. I, 99.

59   Advance detachments of Second Army were approaching Mogilev by 14 July 1941. K.-J. Thies, *Der Ostfeldzug – Ein Lageatlas*, "Lage am 14.7.1941 abds., Heeresgruppe Mitte."

60   R. Kirchubel, *Hitler's Panzer Armies*, 67. At Mogilev, Guderian encircled 13 Army's 61 Rifle and 20 Mechanized Corps.

61   D. M. Glantz, *Barbarossa Derailed*, Vol. I, 101; K.-J. Thies, *Der Ostfeldzug – Ein Lageatlas*, "Lage am 13.7.1941 abds., Heeresgruppe Mitte."

62   "*Tagesmeldungen der Operations-Abteilung des GenStdH*," in: P. E. Schramm (Hg.), *Kriegstagebuch des OKW*, Bd. I, 521.

63   D. M. Glantz, *Barbarossa Derailed*, Vol. I, 105.

64   D. M. Glantz, *Forgotten Battles*, Vol. I, 19.

65   K.-J. Thies, *Der Ostfeldzug – Ein Lageatlas*, "Lage am 14.7.1941 abds., Heeresgruppe Mitte."

66   R. Kirchubel, *Operation Barbarossa 1941 (3), Army Group Center*, 56.

67   *GSWW*, Vol. IV, 770. In mid-July 1941, Chief of the Army General Staff Halder seemed highly satisfied with the results of the *Luftwaffe's* interdiction campaign against Soviet rail lines. "[The] *Luftwaffe*," he wrote in his diary on 11 July, "now seems to have succeeded in wrecking Russian railroads also far to the rear of the enemy communications zone. The number of lines with immobilized railroad transport is growing most satisfactorily, and the good work is being continued." C. Burdick & H.-A. Jacobsen (eds.), *The Halder Diary 1939-1942*, 466.

68   W. K. Nehring, "*Die 18. Panzerdivision 1941*," in: *Deutscher Soldatenkalender 1961*, 197-98. The incident at Dobryn also resulted in a field hospital of 18 PD being attacked, causing serious casualties. See, Chapter 9 (Section 9.4.1).

69   H. Guderian, *Panzer Leader*, 174.

70   "*Tagesmeldungen der Operations-Abteilung des GenStdH*," in: P. E. Schramm (Hg.), *Kriegstagebuch des OKW*, Bd. I, 524.

71   R. Kirchubel, *Operation Barbarossa 1941 (3), Army Group Center*, 56; K.-J. Thies, *Der Ostfeldzug – Ein Lageatlas*, "Lage am 15.7.1941 abds., Heeresgruppe Mitte."

72   D. M. Glantz, *Barbarossa Derailed*, Vol. I, 121.

73   Colonel Ochsner also noted that the Red Army was well led and "fought fanatically and determinedly." D. Stahel, *And the World held its Breath*, 156.

74   BA-MA RH 27-3/14, *KTB 3. Pz.-Div.*, 12.7.41, cited in: D. Stahel, *And the World held its Breath*, 157.

75   R. Michulec, *4. Panzer-Division*, 4; BA-MA RH 27-4/27, *KTB 4. Pz.-Div.*, 13.7.41, cited in: D. Stahel, *And the World held its Breath*, 157. As Stahel points out, the Red Army "fought with a profound show of strength in artillery and anti-tank guns, exacting a great toll on the 4 Panzer Division's panzer regiment."

76   D. M. Glantz, *Barbarossa Derailed*, Vol. I, 121, 159.

77   S. Risse, "*Das IR 101 und der 2. Weltkrieg.*"

78   D. Stahel, *And the World held its Breath*, 179.

79   D. M. Glantz, *Barbarossa*, 79; RH 21-3/732, "*Gefechtsberichte Russland 1941/42*;" K.-J. Thies, *Der Ostfeldzug – Ein Lageatlas*, "Lage am 10.7.1941 abds., Heeresgruppe Mitte."

80   RH 21-3/732, "*Gefechtsberichte Russland 1941/42*." One can only speculate if the "exaggerated reports" referred to here emanated from Guderian's staff!

81   D. M. Glantz, *Barbarossa Derailed*, Vol. I, 113.

82   Schmidt's panzer corps, in addition to its 7 PD, 20 PD, and 20 ID (mot.), had been plumped up with 12 PD and 18 ID (mot.) as reinforcements. K.-R. Woche, *Zwischen Pflicht und Gewissen*, 111; also, RH 21-3/732, "*Gefechtsberichte Russland 1941/42*."

83   K.-R. Woche, *Zwischen Pflicht und Gewissen*, 112; K. Mehner (Hg.), *Geheime Tagesberichte*, Bd. 3, 176; RH 21-3/732, "*Gefechtsberichte Russland 1941/42*."

84   See, for example, RH 21-3/732, "*Gefechtsberichte Russland 1941/42*." According to this report, Field Marshal von Kluge, Commander, Fourth Panzer Army, had also insisted on the importance of the advance to Nevel.

85   *GSWW*, Vol. IV, 534-35; R. Hinze, *Hitze, Frost und Pulverdampf*, 46.

86   D. M. Glantz, *Barbarossa Derailed*, Vol. I, 113.

87   Ibid., 113.

88   K.-J. Thies, *Der Ostfeldzug – Ein Lageatlas*, "Lage am 14.7.1941 abds., Heeresgruppe Mitte."

89   D. M. Glantz, *Barbarossa Derailed*, Vol. I, 113-15.

90   D. M. Glantz, *Barbarossa Derailed*, Vol. I, 115; K.-J. Thies, *Der Ostfeldzug – Ein Lageatlas*, "Lage am 15.7.1941 abds., Heeresgruppe Mitte;" "*Tagesmeldungen der Operations-Abteilung des GenStdH*," in: P. E. Schramm (Hg.), *Kriegstagebuch des OKW*, Bd. I, 524.

91   BA-MA RH 24-57/2, *KTB 57. Pz.-Korps*, 14.7.41, quoted in: D. Stahel, *And the World held its Breath*, 165. On 14 July 1941, the war diary of 57 Panzer Corps also recorded that "in places the vehicles must be pulled or pushed separately through the deepest sand, which results in hold ups of hours on end." In view of such terrain problems, coupled with Soviet resistance, it is a wonder the division reached Nevel as rapidly as it did.

92   "*Tagesmeldungen der Operations-Abteilung des GenStdH*," in: P. E. Schramm (Hg.), *Kriegstagebuch des OKW*, Bd. I, 523; K.-J. Thies, *Der Ostfeldzug – Ein Lageatlas*, "Lage am 14.7.1941 abds., Heeresgruppe Mitte."

93   R. Hinze, *19. Infanterie- und Panzer-Division*, 152.

94   D. M. Glantz, *Barbarossa Derailed*, Vol. I, 116-17; K.-J. Thies, *Der Ostfeldzug – Ein Lageatlas*, "Lage am 15.7.1941 abds., Heeresgruppe Mitte."

95   D. M. Glantz, *Barbarossa Derailed*, Vol. I, 258.

96   See, RH 21-3/732, "*Gefechtsberichte Russland 1941/42*."

97   For perspectives of OKH and Halder on the Nevel operation see, C. Burdick & H.-A. Jacobsen (eds.), *The Halder Diary 1939-1942*, 467, 469-73. For example, on 13 July 1941, Halder noted in his diary: "This group [enemy forces in Nevel – Velikie Luki area] is strong, and it would pay to mount a special operation to destroy it for good."

98   R.H.S. Stolfi, *German Panzers on the Offensive*, 18. According to Stolfi, at the start of the Russian campaign, "the [7 Panzer Division] put together a series of advances more dramatic and effective than those of any other division in World War II." Ibid., 16.

99   A. Seaton, *The Russo-German War*, 129.

100   K. Gerbet (ed.), *GFM Fedor von Bock, The War Diary*, 252.

101   "The size and strength of bridges," states David Stahel, "was another critical weakness of Soviet infrastructure which had a detrimental effect on the swift movement of Bock's panzers." D. Stahel, *And the World held*

its Breath, 155. A post-war study by former German officers – making observations on southern Russia, yet germane to the entire Soviet Union – indicates that solidly constructed bridges were "scarce;" "in their place are found wooden bridges with limited capacities, or fords at small rivers and brooks. Wooden bridges can very easily be destroyed." Furthermore, before they could be used by tanks or other heavy tracked vehicles, wooden bridges, in most cases, had to be reinforced by combat engineers. FMS P-039, B. Mueller-Hillebrand, et al., *"March and Traffic Control of Panzer Divisions with Special Attention to Conditions in the Soviet Union and in Africa,"* 36.

102   D. Stahel, *And the World held its Breath*, 162; also, H. Hoth, *Panzer-Operationen*, 92-93.

103   The reader will recall that, on 3 July 1941, Field Marshal von Kluge's Fourth Army headquarters was redesignated as Fourth Panzer Army and placed in charge of 2 and 3 Panzer Groups. At the same time, most of Kluge's infantry divisions were turned over to General Maximilian *Freiherr* von Weichs and his Second Army headquarters.

104   *"Tagesmeldungen der Operations-Abteilung des GenStdH,"* in: P. E. Schramm (Hg.), *Kriegstagebuch des OKW*, Bd. I, 518; K.-J. Thies, *Der Ostfeldzug – Ein Lageatlas*, "Lage am 10.7.1941 abds., Heeresgruppe Mitte."

105   See, K. Mehner (Hg.), *Geheime Tagesberichte*, Bd. 3, 176-86.

106   Hartmut Heinrici (born in 1921), was wounded on 15 July 1941, during the capture of Smolensk; following recovery from his wounds, he returned to the front in late November 1941. J. Huerter, *Ein deutscher General an der Ostfront*, 177, f.n. 136.

107   Ibid., 67-68.

108   Dr E. Bunke, *Der Osten blieb unser Schicksal*, 289-90.

109   Commanded by Brig.-Gen. Kurt Feldt, 1 Cavalry Division operated as mounted infantry, rather than cavalry. According to Albert Seaton, the division "suffered from a lack of artillery ammunition and the difficulty, in the close country of the Pripiat' Marshes, of finding suitable artillery observation posts. Low cloud and the more important operations to the north deprived 1 Cavalry Division of air support and the battle might have gone badly for it, had not the enemy [attacking repeatedly in human waves] offered himself as an easy target to the cavalry carbine and machine gun." A. Seaton, *The Russo-German War*, 121. For a history of 1 Cavalry Division see, Dr F. M. v. Senger u. Etterlin jr., *Die 24. Panzer-Division vormals 1. Kavallerie-Division, 1939-1945*. For a fascinating personal account see, Hans Ludwig von Stockhausen, *Erinnerungen I: Ritter, Reiter, Russen*.

110   Dr R. Gschoepf, *Mein Weg mit der 45. Inf.-Div.*, 227-29. The 293 Infantry Division also took part in mopping up operations in the Pripiat' Marshes. Both 45 and 293 ID belonged to 35 Army Corps at this time. *GSWW*, Vol. IV, 529.

111   The motorized advance detachment of 45 ID, led by Lt.-Col. von Pannwitz, had reached Pinsk on 3 July, the main body arriving there on 6 July. By the latter date, Pannwitz' command had made contact with the left wing of Rundstedt's Army Group South (17 Army Corps of Sixth Army). K.-J. Thies, *Der Ostfeldzug – Ein Lageatlas*, "Lage am [3./6.]7.1941 abds., Heeresgruppe Mitte."

112   Dr R. Gschoepf, *Mein Weg mit der 45. Inf.-Div.*, 229.

113   Ibid., 229, 232-34.

114   Ibid., 234-37.

115   D. M. Glantz, *Barbarossa Derailed*, Vol. I, 131, f.n. 35.

116   D. M. Glantz, *Barbarossa Derailed*, Vol. I, 116, 131-32 (f.n. 35); H. Grossmann, *Geschichte der 6. Infanterie-Division*, 49; E.-M. Rhein, *Das Infanterie-Regiment 18*, 67.

117   In his diary on 14 July Bock wrote: "In the morning I talked with Strauss, who apparently intends to commit overly-strong forces for the capture of Polotsk. I warned him against this. If Polotsk is not overrun in the first assault, it will have to be sealed off with weaker forces and taken slowly, bunker by bunker, while everything else continues to advance past to the east. Strauss agreed with me." And the next day (15 July): "Strauss has gone ahead and committed four or five divisions against Polotsk. I called him again and told him the same as yesterday. He didn't back down quite as far. I therefore had to tell him that if the attack today did not succeed, he might only keep one division at Polotsk and everything else had to move past to the east." K. Gerbet (ed.), *GFM Fedor von Bock, The War Diary*, 248-49.

118   H. Grossmann, *Geschichte der 6. Infanterie-Division*, 50.

119   H. Grossmann, *Geschichte der 6. Infanterie-Division*, 50; W. Knecht, *Geschichte des Infanterie-Regiments 77*, 62.

120   H. Grossmann, *Geschichte der 6. Infanterie-Division*, 50; W. Knecht, *Geschichte des Infanterie-Regiments 77*, 62.

121   H. Grossmann, *Geschichte der 6. Infanterie-Division*, 51.

122   It appears 37 Infantry Regiment had, by now, committed a third infantry company of its 2nd Battalion to the fighting.

123   Quoted in: Dr H. Voss, *Das Pionier-Bataillon 6 im Feldzug gegen Russland 1941-1945*, 80-81 (unpublished manuscript).

124   W. Buddenbohm, *Das Leben des Soldaten Wilhelm Buddenbohm*, 55.

125   Dr H. Voss, *Das Pionier-Bataillon 6 im Feldzug gegen Russland 1941-1945*, 81; H. Grossmann, *Geschichte der 6. Infanterie-Division*, 51-52.

126   W. Knecht, *Geschichte des Infanterie-Regiments 77*, 62-67.

127   K.-J. Thies, *Der Ostfeldzug – Ein Lageatlas*, "Lage am 15.7.1941 abds., Heeresgruppe Mitte;" *"Tagesmeldungen der Operations-Abteilung des GenStdH,"* in: P. E. Schramm (Hg.), *Kriegstagebuch des OKW*, Bd. I, 524.

128   *"Der Ostfeldzug der 86. Rhein.-Westf. Inf.-Division, 28.6.41 – 4.11.43"* (unpublished manuscript).

129   D. M. Glantz, *Barbarossa Derailed*, Vol. I, 116. The 22 Army's 174 Rifle Division had been defending Polotsk.

130   H. Grossmann, *Geschichte der 6. Infanterie-Division*, 52.

131   K.-J. Thies, *Der Ostfeldzug – Ein Lageatlas*, "Lage am 16.7.1941 abds., Heeresgruppe Mitte."

132   "*Tagesmeldungen der Operations-Abteilung des GenStdH*," in: P. E. Schramm (Hg.), *Kriegstagebuch des OKW*, Bd. I, 524.

133   K.-J. Thies, *Der Ostfeldzug – Ein Lageatlas*, "Lage am 15.7.1941 abds., Heeresgruppe Mitte;" "*Tagesmeldungen der Operations-Abteilung des GenStdH*," in: P. E. Schramm (Hg.), *Kriegstagebuch des OKW*, Bd. I, 524.

134   G. Bopp, *Kriegstagebuch*, 90-91.

135   *Feldpost*, W. Heinemann, 15.7.41.

136   T. Plievier, *Moscow*, 226.

137   E. Mawdsley, *Thunder in the East*, 66.

138   A. Seaton, *The Battle for Moscow*, 45.

139   J. Dinglreiter, *Die Vierziger*, 47.

140   D. M. Glantz, *Barbarossa Derailed*, Vol. I, 60.

141   F. Frisch & W. D. Jones, Jr., *Condemned to Live*, 74.

142   BA-MA MSg 1/1147: *Tagebuch* Lemelsen, 21.7.41.

143   K. Knoblauch, *Zwischen Metz und Moskau*, 168.

144   From 10-31 July 1941, the *Luftwaffe* flew 12,653 sorties on the central front, many of them in an effort to interdict rail lines leading into Smolensk. R. Kirchubel, *Operation Barbarossa 1941* (3), *Army Group Center*, 57.

145   D. Stahel, *And the World held its Breath*, 186.

146   Ibid., 173.

147   "*Tagesmeldungen der Operations-Abteilung des GenStdH*," in: P. E. Schramm (Hg.), *Kriegstagebuch des OKW*, Bd. I, 525.

148   H. Schaeufler (ed.), *Knight's Cross Panzers*, 89-90.

149   K.-J. Thies, *Der Ostfeldzug – Ein Lageatlas*, "Lage am 17.7.1941 abds., Heeresgruppe Mitte;" "*Tagesmeldungen der Operations-Abteilung des GenStdH*," in: P. E. Schramm (Hg.), *Kriegstagebuch des OKW*, Bd. I, 527.

150   A. Schick, *Die Geschichte der 10. Panzer-Division*, 310.

151   Ibid., 312-13. Also inhibiting the advance of 10 PD were the wretched roads and the badly worn tank engines, which more than doubled fuel consumption. A typical unit of consumption (*Verbrauchssatz*) of gasoline, calculated for 100 kilometers under normal operating conditions, was only lasting for about 40 kilometers.

152   H. Guderian, *Panzer Leader*, 176-77; K.-J. Thies, *Der Ostfeldzug – Ein Lageatlas*, "Lage am 16.7.1941 abds., Heeresgruppe Mitte;" J. Dinglreiter, *Die Vierziger. Chronik des Regiments*, 47.

153   H. Guderian, *Panzer Leader*, 175-76.

154   BA-MA Microfilm 59054, *KTB Panzergruppe 3*, 15.7.41, quoted in: D. Stahel, *And the World held its Breath*, 174; also, BA-MA RH 21-3/732, "*Gefechtsberichte Russland 1941/42.*"

155   D. Stahel, *And the World held its Breath*, 174-75. "This fateful decision," opines Stahel, "illustrated yet again the inept capacity of the German generals to grasp the dangers of overextension."

156   K. Gerbet (ed.), *GFM Fedor von Bock, The War Diary*, 246; K.-J. Thies, *Der Ostfeldzug – Ein Lageatlas*, "Lage am [10.-11.]7.1941 abds., Heeresgruppe Mitte." Bock's CP was operational in the town of Borisov by 1200 hours, 11 July 1941. As Bock noted in his diary, "the new quarters are situated right beside an airfield; the staff was greeted by bombs. Our accomodations are in a sanatorium and are distinguished by having one wash basin for every 20 rooms!"

157   A. W. Turney, *Disaster at Moscow*, 65.

158   J. Piekalkiewicz, *Die Schlacht um Moskau*, 88.

159   BA-MA MSg 1/1147: *Tagebuch* Lemelsen, 16.7.41.

160   D. M. Glantz, *Barbarossa Derailed*, Vol. I, 121, 159.

161   According to Heinz Magenheimer, the Germans required 10 days to clear all the Russians from the city. H. Magenheimer, *Moskau 1941*, 50.

162   "*Tagesmeldungen der Operations-Abteilung des GenStdH*," in: P. E. Schramm (Hg.), *Kriegstagebuch des OKW*, Bd. I, 539; K.-J. Thies, *Der Ostfeldzug – Ein Lageatlas*, "Lage am 25.7.1941 abds., Heeresgruppe Mitte."

163   H. Guderian, *Panzer Leader*, 178.

164   It is unclear what Guderian meant by this. Perhaps the Communists had left part of the church open for some form of religious services. In his memoirs, Colonel Hans von Luck (7 Panzer Division) claimed that, in early August 1941, he attended the first orthodox mass in the church in over 20 years. In his diary, Field Marshal von Bock also indicated that "a number of churches" were "given back their vocation" at this time. (See above, Chapter 9, Section 9.1.)

165   H. Guderian, *Panzer Leader*, 180.

166   D. M. Glantz, *Barbarossa Derailed*, Vol. I, 249.

167   D. M. Glantz, *Barbarossa*, 82; D. M. Glantz, *Barbarossa Derailed*, Vol. I, 161.

168   Internet site at: http://www.lexikon-der-wehrmacht.de; J. Dinglreiter, *Die Vierziger. Chronik des Regiments*, 47.

169   H. Guderian, *Panzer Leader*, 178, 180.

170   BA-MA MSg 1/1147: *Tagebuch* Lemelsen, 20.7.41.

171   "*Tagesmeldungen der Operations-Abteilung des GenStdH*," in: P. E. Schramm (Hg.), *Kriegstagebuch des OKW*, Bd. I, 528.

172 A panzer operations manual, published just six months prior to the start of the Russian campaign, devoted 26 pages to the "Attack," while the topic of "Defense" was addressed in just two paragraphs. R. J. Kershaw, *War Without Garlands*, 95.

173 Ibid., 95.

174 K. Gerbet (ed.), *GFM Fedor von Bock, The War Diary*, 253-54.

175 Ibid., 254-55. Apparently, Kluge had not wanted to speak to Bock that morning, initially instructing Blumentritt to tell Bock that he, Kluge, had just driven away and was unavailable. When Kluge finally intervened in the conversation to defend Guderian, he was, no doubt, also defending himself against Bock's rather pointed line of questioning.

176 BA-MA RH 24-47/2, *KTB 47. Pz.-Korps*, 19.7.41, cited in: D. Stahel, *And the World held its Breath*, 177.

177 D. Stahel, *And the World held its Breath*, 177.

178 H. Guderian, *Panzer Leader*, 179.

179 "*Tagesmeldungen der Operations-Abteilung des GenStdH*," in: P. E. Schramm (Hg.), *Kriegstagebuch des OKW*, Bd. I, 531; K.-J. Thies, *Der Ostfeldzug – Ein Lageatlas*, "Lage am 20.7.1941 abds., Heeresgruppe Mitte."

180 H. Guderian, *Panzer Leader*, 181.

181 Ibid., 178-79.

182 "*Tagesmeldungen der Operations-Abteilung des GenStdH*," in: P. E. Schramm (Hg.), *Kriegstagebuch des OKW*, Bd. I, 531.

183 K. Gerbet (ed.), *GFM Fedor von Bock, The War Diary*, 256.

184 K. Gerbet (ed.), *GFM Fedor von Bock, The War Diary*, 255; D. Stahel, *And the World held its Breath*, 177-78.

185 C. Bergström & A. Mikhailov, *Black Cross Red Star*, Vol. I, 115.

186 A. Brookes, *Air War over Russia*, 42.

187 A. Kesselring, *Soldat Bis Zum Letzten Tag*, 123. Amplifying Kesselring's comments were these more generic post-war observations of *General der Flieger* Paul Deichmann, in the summer of 1941 chief of staff to 2 Air Corps: "[A major] air mission during the first year of the Russian campaign involved the support of ground operations during battles of envelopment … The mission of the German air forces in these battles … was to prevent the escape of the pocketed Russian forces thorough the German lines, and to frustrate attempts by Russian reserves to relieve the enveloped forces through attacks from the outside. In these operations the far sides of the pocket areas were closed initially only by small armored forces with their few motorized infantry elements, which had to prevent a Russian breakthough until the German infantry divisions advancing on foot could arrive. During the initial phases of a pocket, large gaps existed in the enveloping German lines, and if led by an energetic commander elements of the pocketed Russian forces could always find a point at which they could break out … The mission of preventing the escape of the Russian masses from the pockets thus fell to the German air forces. However, the *Luftwaffe* was only able to accomplish this mission very incompletely, since escape movements were often concealed against observation from the air by large wooded areas. Furthermore, it was impossible as a rule to take appropriate action at night, since no salient terrain features existed which could have served for orientation. As a result, large masses of Russian forces succeeded in escaping from the pockets." P. Deichmann, *German Air Force Operations in Support of the Army*. USAF Historical Study No. 163, 110.

188 In his post-war study of 3 Panzer Group's operations in the summer of 1941, Hoth blamed Guderian for the "snafu:" "For 2 Panzer Group, it was apparently more important to hold on to the heights at El'nia for the later continuation of the offensive toward the east than to close the pocket in its combat zone." H. Hoth, *Panzer Operationen*, 97.

189 D. Stahel, *And the World held its Breath*, 183.

190 BA-MA RH 21-2/819, *KTB der O.Qu.-Abt.*, 22.7.41, quoted in: D. Stahel, *And the World held its Breath*, 184.

191 H. Guderian, *Panzer Leader*, 181.

192 BA-MA RH 27-10/26a, *KTB 10. Pz.-Div.*, 21.7.41, quoted in: D. Stahel, *And the World held its Breath*, 184. In desperation, 10 PD considered using captured stocks of Russian oil, which turned out to be unsuitable. A. Schick, *Die Geschichte der 10. Panzer-Division*, 322.

193 BA-MA RH 21-2/757, "*Verlustmeldungen*," cited in: D. Stahel, *And the World held its Breath*, 183. By 25 July 1941, total casualties in Guderian's panzer group had increased to 20,271, making for an average daily loss of almost 600 men. The losses included 1023 officers (306 dead, 690 wounded, 27 missing). Over the same 34-day period 2 Panzer Group had received less than 10,000 replacements. BA-MA RH 21-2/928, *KTB Panzergruppe 2*, 29.7.41.

194 H. Schaeufler (ed.), *Knight's Cross Panzers*, 99.

195 A. Schick, *Die Geschichte der 10. Panzer-Division*, 325.

196 BA-MA RH 21-2/928, *KTB Panzergruppe 2*, 28.7.41.

197 Two infantry divisions (35 ID, 268 ID) were now holding down the southwestern edge of the encirclement ring, while the three divisions of Geyer's 9 Army Corps (137 ID, 263 ID, and 292 ID) were already east of Orsha. K.-J. Thies, *Der Ostfeldzug – Ein Lageatlas*, "Lage am 21.7.1941 abds., Heeresgruppe Mitte."

198 R. J. Kershaw, *War Without Garlands*, 97.

199 This is most likely a reference to General Ritter von Thoma's 17 Panzer Division, which had moved toward El'nia during this period. K.-J. Thies, *Der Ostfeldzug – Ein Lageatlas*, "Lage am 26.7.1941 abds., Heeresgruppe Mitte."

200 "*Der Kampf gegen den Bolschewismus*," in: *Infanterie Division (mot.) Grossdeutschland ruft die Jugend des Grossdeutschen Reiches*, 22.

201 K.-J. Thies, *Der Ostfeldzug – Ein Lageatlas*, "Lage am 23.7.1941 abds., Heeresgruppe Mitte."

202   BA-MA RH 27-18/20, *KTB 18. Pz.-Div.*, 25.7.41, quoted in: D. Stahel, *And the World held its Breath*, 204.

203   The underlining is in the original text. BA-MA RH 27-18/20, *KTB 18. Pz.-Div.*, 26.7.41, quoted in: D. Stahel, *And the World held its Breath*, 204.

204   BA-MA RH 27-18/26, 27.7.41, quoted in: O. Bartov, *Hitler's Army*, 21.

205   W. K. Nehring, "*Die 18. Panzerdivision 1941,*" in: *Deutscher Soldatenkalender 1961*, 198.

206   K. Gerbet (ed.), *GFM Fedor von Bock, The War Diary*, 261-62.

207   BA-MA RH 21-2/928, *KTB Panzergruppe 2*, 28.7.41. Without citing a source, the German quasi-official history of the Second World War states that the "hole" east of Smolensk "was not closed until 24 July." (*GSWW*, Vol. IV, 536.) The OKH Operations Branch reported that it was closed two days later, on 26 July. ("*Tagesmeldungen der Operations-Abteilung des GenStdH,*" in: P. E. Schramm (Hg.), *Kriegstagebuch des OKW*, Bd. I, 540-41.) Yet according to 2 Panzer Group – i.e., the command on the spot – Soviet forces were still escaping across the Dnepr River at Ratchino late on 27 July 1941. BA-MA RH 21-2/928, *KTB Panzergruppe 2*, 27.7.41.

208   E. Mawdsley, *Thunder in the East*, 69.

209   D. M. Glantz, *Forgotten Battles*, Vol. I, 47-51; R. Kirchubel, *Hitler's Panzer Armies*, 69.

210   D. M. Glantz, *Barbarossa Derailed*, Vol. I, 308; W. K. Nehring, "*Die 18. Panzerdivision 1941,*" in: *Deutscher Soldatenkalender 1961*, 198; K.-J. Thies, *Der Ostfeldzug – Ein Lageatlas*, "Lage am 29.7.1941 abds., Heeresgruppe Mitte."

211   H. Guderian, *Panzer Leader*, 182-83; K. J. Walde, *Guderian*, 126-27; K. Gerbet (ed.), *GFM Fedor von Bock, The War Diary*, 264. To relieve Vietinghoff's embattled 46 Panzer Corps in the El'nia salient, Guderian was also given 20 Army Corps, composed of two infantry divisions.

212   Guderian's direct subordination under Army Group Center went into effect at midday, 28 July 1941. BA-MA RH 21-2/928, *KTB Panzergruppe 2*, 28.7.41.

213   This is not an entirely fair judgment on Guderian's part, and is perhaps intended as a veiled criticism of the infantry forces. Guderian was critical of the performance of the marching infantry in the summer of 1941, and questioned its offensive spirit.

214   H. Guderian, *Panzer Leader*, 184.

215   BA-MA RH 21-2/928, *KTB Panzergruppe 2*, 29.7.41. In its war diary, 2 Panzer Group noted that the numbers of battle-ready tanks were "utterly negligible" (*aeusserst gering*) (underlining in original text), for they signified the entire available inventory of four panzer divisions (3, 4, 17, and 18 PD). The figures, however, do not include 10 Panzer Division; as of 25 July 1941, 10 PD's entire panzer brigade was out of action due to a lack of oil and spare parts.

216   Quoted in: K. Macksey, *Guderian*, 142.

217   BA-MA RH 21-2/928, *KTB Panzergruppe 2*, 31.7.41.

218   Ibid., 29.7.41.

219   H.-J. Roell, *Oberleutnant Albert Blaich. Als Panzerkommandant in Ost und West*, 87-88.

220   The first *Luftwaffe* strikes on Roslavl that morning encountered such robust enemy anti-aircraft fire that not a single plane returned to base without battle damage. BA-MA RH 21-2/928, *KTB Panzergruppe 2*, 1.8.41.

221   The *Luftwaffe* also contributed available Flak units to the offensive. A. Kesselring, *Soldat Bis Zum Letzten Tag*, 125; *GSWW*, Vol. IV, 773. In its war diary, 2 Panzer Group stated that three Flak battalions were loaned to Guderian from Second Army to support the attack. BA-MA RH 21-2/928, *KTB Panzergruppe 2*, 31.7.41.

222   D. M. Glantz, *Barbarossa Derailed*, Vol. I, 309-11.

223   3 Panzer Division began the drive on Roslavl with 103 operational tanks, making it perhaps the best equipped of Guderian's five panzer divisions at this time. H.-J. Roell, *Oberleutnant Albert Blaich. Als Panzerkommandant in Ost und West*, 88.

224   K.-J. Thies, *Der Ostfeldzug – Ein Lageatlas*, "Lage am 1.8.1941 abds., Heeresgruppe Mitte."

225   P. Carell, *Unternehmen Barbarossa*, 94.

226   "*Tagesmeldungen der Operations-Abteilung des GenStdH,*" in: P. E. Schramm (Hg.), *Kriegstagebuch des OKW*, Bd. I, 552; BA-MA RH 21-2/928, *KTB Panzergruppe 2*, 2.8.41.

227   K.-J. Thies, *Der Ostfeldzug – Ein Lageatlas*, "Lage am 2.8.1941 abds., Heeresgruppe Mitte;" "*The Battle of Smolensk – Situation, 2300, 2 August 1941,*" in: D. M. Glantz, *Atlas of the Battle of Smolensk, 7 July – 10 September 1941*, 79.

228   K. Gerbet (ed.), *GFM Fedor von Bock, The War Diary*, 271.

229   M. Graf v. Nayhauss-Cormons, *Zwischen Gehorsam und Gewissen*, 169.

230   At 1045 hours, Geyr's 24 Panzer Corps reported the capture of Roslavl. BA-MA RH 21-2/928, *KTB Panzergruppe 2*, 3.8.41; H. Schaeufler (ed.), *Knight's Cross Panzers*, 101.

231   In late July 1941, German movements on the central front had often been hampered by sudden downpours and thundershowers. For example, the daily reports of the Operations Branch of OKH recorded bad weather across the front of Army Group Center, or localized weather problems within the army group's area, from 21-26 July. Although less pronounced, occasional rainfall and thundershowers also took place in August 1941. "*Tagesmeldungen der Operations-Abteilung des GenStdH,*" in: P. E. Schramm (Hg.), *Kriegstagebuch des OKW*, Bd. I, 532-41; 550-603.

232   D. M. Glantz, *Barbarossa Derailed*, Vol. I, 316.

233   In his biography of Guderian (published in 1976), Karl J. Walde criticized this remark of the panzer general, insisting that it was "not justified" (*nicht gerecht*). Indeed, despite serious challenges, including difficult terrain, "[9 Army Corps] had done all that was humanly possible." See, K. J. Walde, *Guderian*, 127-28.

234   H. Guderian, *Panzer Leader*, 188.

235 Quoted in: H. Dollinger (Hg.), *Kain, wo ist dein Bruder?*, 92.

236 H. Guderian, *Panzer Leader*, 188.

237 *GSWW*, Vol. IV, 590.

238 D. M. Glantz, *Barbarossa Derailed*, Vol. I, 319, 326; "*Tagesmeldungen der Operations-Abteilung des GenStdH*," in: P. E. Schramm (Hg.), *Kriegstagebuch des OKW*, Bd. I, 561.

239 H. Guderian, *Panzer Leader*, 193.

240 D. Stahel, *And the World held its Breath*, 223-24.

241 BA-MA RH 20-4/337, *Die Kaempfe der 4. Armee im ersten Kriegsjahr gegen die Sowjets*; K. Gerbet (ed.), *GFM Fedor von Bock, The War Diary*, 273-74.

242 "*Tagesmeldungen der Operations-Abteilung des GenStdH*," in: P. E. Schramm (Hg.), *Kriegstagebuch des OKW*, Bd. I, 550.

243 K.-J. Thies, *Der Ostfeldzug – Ein Lageatlas*, "Lage am 16.7.1941 abds., Heeresgruppe Mitte."

244 G. Blumentritt, "*Moscow*," in: *The Fatal Decisions*, W. Richardson & S. Freidin (eds.), 50.

245 BA-MA RH 21-3/732, "*Gefechtsberichte Russland 1941/42*."

246 For example, by 13 July 1941, 19 PD and 14 ID (mot.) had, collectively, sustained losses of 163 officers and 3422 other ranks. H. Hoth, *Panzer-Operationen*, 92.

247 BA-MA RH 21-3/732, "*Gefechtsberichte Russland 1941/42*."

248 C. Bergström & A. Mikhailov, *Black Cross Red Star*, Vol. I, 90.

249 J. S. Corum, *Wolfram von Richthofen*, 269. From the opening days of the campaign, observes Corum, Richthofen's "Flivos [*Luftwaffe* liaison officers], operating with the infantry corps and each of 3 Panzer Group's divisions, were able to arrange effective *Stuka* support to reduce Soviet strong points. The response for requests for support to aircraft striking the target was about two hours – very impressive performance by 1941 standards. The advance of 3 Panzer Group was so rapid that the previous system of bomb lines was abandoned and the Army deployed signal panels, flares, and other signals to avoid friendly-fire incidents. Unfortunately, in the confusion of the rapid advance German units were often bombed by mistake by the *Luftwaffe*." The serious problem of bombing friendly German forces would remain a persistent one for the *Luftwaffe* during the Russian campaign. See, for example, "*Bombenwuerfe auf eigene Truppen. (Aus einem Bericht des Kommandierenden Generals des VIII. Fliegerkorps von 16.2.42 an die Heeresgruppe Mitte)*." KDC.

250 Fuchs' tank company must not have participated in 7 Panzer Division's dramatic drive to Iartsevo on this day.

251 H. F. Richardson (ed.), *Your Loyal and Loving Son. The Letters of Tank Gunner Karl Fuchs, 1937-41*, 114.

252 BA-MA Microfilm 59054, *KTB Panzergruppe 3*, 17.7.41, cited in: D. Stahel, *And the World held its Breath*, 172.

253 According to Hoth, the decision to push 57 Panzer Corps' 19 Panzer Division to Velikie Luki was predicated on the desire to intercept the "brisk rail traffic" (*lebhafter Zugverkehr*) reported there. H. Hoth, *Panzer-Operationen*, 99.

254 D. M. Glantz, *Barbarossa Derailed*, Vol. I, 262; BA-MA RH 21-3/732, "*Gefechtsberichte Russland 1941/42*."

255 K. Gerbet (ed.), *GFM Fedor von Bock, The War Diary*, 247.

256 Ibid., 255.

257 K. Gerbet (ed.), *GFM Fedor von Bock, The War Diary*, 255. Bock, it seems, had issued orders for 19 Panzer to hold at Nevel and only send reconnaissance to Velikie Luki. Due most likely to poor communications, however – not uncommon over the long distances on the eastern front – Bock's orders did not reach 19 Panzer until after it had begun its advance, routed Soviet forces in its path, and pursued them all the way to Velikie Luki. D. M. Glantz, *Barbarossa Derailed*, Vol. I, 262; BA-MA RH 21-3/732, "*Gefechtsberichte Russland 1941/42*."

258 R. Hinze, *Die 19. Panzer-Division. Bewaffnung, Einsaetze, Maenner*, 34.

259 R. Hinze, *19. Infanterie- und Panzer-Division*, 154-55.

260 "*Tagesmeldungen der Operations-Abteilung des GenStdH*," in: P. E. Schramm (Hg.), *Kriegstagebuch des OKW*, Bd. I, 527.

261 R. Hinze, *19. Infanterie- und Panzer-Division*, 155-56; D. M. Glantz, *Barbarossa Derailed*, Vol. I, 262; "*Tagesmeldungen der Operations-Abteilung des GenStdH*," in: P. E. Schramm (Hg.), *Kriegstagebuch des OKW*, Bd. I, 530.

262 BA-MA RH 26-14/10, *KTB 14. Inf.-Div. (mot.)*, 19.7.41, cited in: D. Stahel, *And the World held its Breath*, 172.

263 K. Gerbet (ed.), *GFM Fedor von Bock, The War Diary*, 255.

264 BA-MA RH 21-3/732, "*Gefechtsberichte Russland 1941/42*;" D. M. Glantz, *Barbarossa Derailed*, Vol. I, 264; "*Tagesmeldungen der Operations-Abteilung des GenStdH*," in: P. E. Schramm (Hg.), *Kriegstagebuch des OKW*, Bd. I, 531-33; K.-J. Thies, *Der Ostfeldzug – Ein Lageatlas*, "Lage am 21.7.1941 abds., Heeresgruppe Mitte."

265 *GSWW*, Vol. IV, 536.

266 R. Hinze, *19. Infanterie- und Panzer-Division*, 156.

267 H. Hoth, *Panzer-Operationen*, 99; also, D. Stahel, *And the World held its Breath*, 172.

268 D. Stahel, *And the World held its Breath*, 172.

269 D. M. Glantz, *Barbarossa Derailed*, Vol. I, 269.

270 Ibid., 269.

271 K.-J. Thies, *Der Ostfeldzug – Ein Lageatlas*, "Lage am [23.-26.]7.1941 abds., Heeresgruppe Mitte."

272 "*Tagesmeldungen der Operations-Abteilung des GenStdH*," in: P. E. Schramm (Hg.), *Kriegstagebuch des OKW*, Bd. I, 528-32.

273 *"Tagesmeldungen der Operations-Abteilung des GenStdH,"* in: P. E. Schramm (Hg.), *Kriegstagebuch des OKW*, Bd. I, 527; K.-J. Thies, *Der Ostfeldzug – Ein Lageatlas*, "Lage am 17.7.1941 abds., Heeresgruppe Mitte."

274 Quoted in: R. Kirchubel, *Hitler's Panzer Armies*, 101-02.

275 *GSWW*, Vol. IV, 770.

276 BA-MA RH 21-3/732, *"Gefechtsberichte Russland 1941/42."*

277 BA-MA RH 21-3/732, *"Gefechtsberichte Russland 1941/42;"* H. v. Manteuffel, *Die 7. Panzer-Division. Bewaffnung, Einsaetze, Manner*, 65.

278 BA-MA RH 21-2/928, *KTB Panzergruppe 2*, 28.7.41.

279 K.-J. Thies, *Der Ostfeldzug – Ein Lageatlas*, "Lage am 26.7.1941 abds., Heeresgruppe Mitte."

280 20 Panzer Division, for example, had reached the area north of Dukhovshchina on 15 July 1941, traversing difficult terrain which swallowed up gasoline; moreover, the many small wood bridges in the region collapsed under the weight of heavy vehicles and had to be rebuilt or replaced, causing significant delays. R. Hinze, *Hitze, Frost und Pulverdampf*, 45.

281 In addition to defending against the Smolensk pocket, 7 Panzer Division was also building a front facing east. *"The Battle of Smolensk – Situation, 2300, 23 July 1941,"* in: D. M. Glantz, *Atlas of the Battle of Smolensk, 7 July – 10 September 1941*, 45.

282 K.-J. Thies, *Der Ostfeldzug – Ein Lageatlas*, "Lage am [23.-25.]7.1941 abds., Heeresgruppe Mitte."

283 D. Stahel, *And the World held its Breath*, 178-79.

284 The 107 TD had been reassigned to Group Kalinin by 2000 hours on 23 July. D. M. Glantz, *Barbarossa Derailed*, Vol. I, 202.

285 Ibid., 196-204.

286 Ibid., 197.

287 Ibid., 196-97.

288 Ibid., 202.

289 *"Tagesmeldungen der Operations-Abteilung des GenStdH,"* in: P. E. Schramm (Hg.), *Kriegstagebuch des OKW*, Bd. I, 536.

290 R. Hinze, *19. Infanterie- und Panzer-Division*, 158.

291 Ibid., 159.

292 R. Hinze, *19. Infanterie- und Panzer-Division*, 160; K.-J. Thies, *Der Ostfeldzug – Ein Lageatlas*, "Lage am 26.7.1941 abds., Heeresgruppe Mitte."

293 R. Hinze, *19. Infanterie- und Panzer-Division*, 160, 162.

294 Ibid., 162.

295 Ibid., 163-64.

296 On 24 July 1941, 20 PD was transferred from Schmidt's 39 Panzer Corps to Kuntzen's 57 Panzer Corps. Internet site at: http://www.lexikon-der-wehrmacht.de.

297 The 20 PD had begun the Russian campaign with 229 tanks, but only 31 of these were medium Panzer IVs with the short-barreled 75mm gun (see Appendix 4). On 23 July 1941, however, the division had just a single operational Pz IV, the others having been lost in action or rendered *hors de combat* due to a lack of replacement engines and spare parts, such as bogie wheels. Yet even the Pz IV was hardly a match for the T-34 or KV-1. R. Hinze, *Hitze, Frost und Pulverdampf*, 49.

298 Ibid., 49.

299 K. Mehner (Hg.), *Geheime Tagesberichte*, Bd. 3, 215.

300 *True to Type. A Selection from Letters and Diaries of German Soldiers and Civilians collected on the Soviet-German Front*, 15. (Note: In the text, it states that Dittri was serving with 21 Panzer Division; this, however, was not possible, for 21 Panzer Division was not established until later in 1941, and then saw action in North Africa. The confusion most likely stems from the fact that Dittri was a member of 21 Panzer *Regiment*, a component of 20 Panzer Division.)

301 R. Hinze, *Hitze, Frost und Pulverdampf*, 52-55.

302 *"Tagesmeldungen der Operations-Abteilung des GenStdH,"* in: P. E. Schramm (Hg.), *Kriegstagebuch des OKW*, Bd. I, 550.

303 D. M. Glantz, *Barbarossa Derailed*, Vol. I, 222.

304 At OKH, Halder was also alarmed by the situation of 3 Panzer Group. On 1 August he confided in his diary that "the entire front of Hoth's armored group is uncomfortably thin. There is nothing behind it." C. Burdick & H.-A. Jacobsen (eds.), *The Halder Diary 1939-1942*, 491.

305 BA-MA RH 21-3/47, *Anlagen zum KTB*, quoted in: D. Stahel, *And the World held its Breath*, 218.

306 BA-MA RH 27-20/2, *KTB 20. Pz.-Div.*, 1.8.41, quoted in: D. Stahel, *And the World held its Breath*, 218.

307 R. Hinze, *Hitze, Frost und Pulverdampf*, 56.

308 R. Hinze, *19. Infanterie- und Panzer-Division*, 169.

309 D. M. Glantz, *Barbarossa Derailed*, Vol. I, 222.

310 In correspondence with GFM von Bock in late July, Hoth reported that ca. 60 percent of his panzer group's tanks were out of action; however, given 10 days to rest and refit, and the provision of replacement parts, Hoth was confident the number of available tanks could be brought to 60-70 percent of authorized strength. *"Anlage 6: Schreiben des Befehlshabers der Pz.Gr.3 an den O.B. der H.Gr.Mitte zwischen 22. und 26. Juli 1941,"* in: H. Hoth, *Panzer-Operationen*, 158.

311 R. J. Kershaw, *War Without Garlands*, 98. Fully 96 of the division's tanks, however, were under repair on 21 July 1941.

312 BA-MA N 372/22, *Schmidt an Paulus*, 29.7.41, quoted in: J. Huerter, *Hitlers Heerfuehrer*, 290.

313 R. Hinze, *Hitze, Frost und Pulverdampf*, 56.

314 *True to Type. A Selection from Letters and Diaries of German Soldiers and Civilians collected on the Soviet-German Front*, 16.

315 K. Gerbet (ed.), *GFM Fedor von Bock, The War Diary*, 267.

316 *GSWW*, Vol. IV, 771; "*Gefechtsquartiere des VIII. Fliegerkorps im Russland-Feldzug 1941*," compiled by Hans Wilhelm Deichmann, KDC.

317 R. Muller, *The German Air War in Russia*, 55.

318 D. M. Glantz, *Barbarossa Derailed*, Vol. I, 222. By 1 August, the Soviet operational groups, lacking sufficient artillery and armor, had only been able to register small gains – five to 10 kilometers in some areas. Ibid., 328.

319 The "Smolensk counteroffensive operation" had come to an end by 7 August 1941. D. M. Glantz, *Forgotten Battles*, Vol. I, 2, 47.

320 "*Tagesmeldungen der Operations-Abteilung des GenStdH*," in: P. E. Schramm (Hg.), *Kriegstagebuch des OKW*, Bd. I, 552-53.

321 *True to Type. A Selection from Letters and Diaries of German Soldiers and Civilians collected on the Soviet-German Front*, 16-17.

322 "*Tagesmeldungen der Operations-Abteilung des GenStdH*," in: P. E. Schramm (Hg.), *Kriegstagebuch des OKW*, Bd. I, 547; K.-J. Thies, *Der Ostfeldzug – Ein Lageatlas*, "Lage am 30.7.1941 abds., Heeresgruppe Mitte."

323 "*Tagesmeldungen der Operations-Abteilung des GenStdH*," in: P. E. Schramm (Hg.), *Kriegstagebuch des OKW*, Bd. I, 556; K.-J. Thies, *Der Ostfeldzug – Ein Lageatlas*, "Lage am 5.8.1941 abds., Heeresgruppe Mitte."

324 *Tagebuch* (author unknown), quoted in: *Gefallen! … und umsonst – Erlebnisberichte deutscher Soldaten im Russlandkrieg 1941-1943*, Dr H. Duesel (Hg.), 20 (self-published manuscript).

325 Ibid., 20.

326 Ibid., 21.

327 Ibid., 21.

328 Ibid., 21.

329 Ibid., 22.

330 Ibid., 22.

331 Ibid., 23.

332 Ibid., 23.

333 Ibid., 23-24.

334 D. Stahel, *And the World held its Breath*, 218.

335 K. Gerbet (ed.), *GFM Fedor von Bock, The War Diary*, 270. According to David Stahel, "the elimination of the Smolensk pocket was simply taking too long with Bock and Hoth becoming increasingly critical of the lack of vigor from the infantry in this sector. Halder too was losing patience." D. Stahel, *And the World held its Breath*, 218.

336 K.-J. Thies, *Der Ostfeldzug – Ein Lageatlas*, "Lage am 1.8.1941 abds., Heeresgruppe Mitte."

337 Ibid.

338 On 2 August, German intelligence estimated that 15 Soviet rifle divisions and six armored divisions were trapped inside the pocket. K.-J. Thies, *Der Ostfeldzug – Ein Lageatlas*, "Lage am 2.8.1941 abds., Heeresgruppe Mitte."

339 D. M. Glantz, *Barbarossa Derailed*, Vol. I, 331.

340 D. M. Glantz, *Barbarossa Derailed*, Vol. I, 334; D. Stahel, *And the World held its Breath*, 221; BA-MA RH 21-2/928, *KTB Panzergruppe 2*, 2.8.41.

341 BA-MA RH 21-2/928, *KTB Panzergruppe 2*, 1.8.41. Apparently, the village of Ratchino had been held by a single infantry company of 20 Motorized Division. Ibid., 2.8.41.

342 Ibid., 2.8.41.

343 Ibid., 2.8.41. The same message, no doubt, was also sent to Hoth's 3 Panzer Group and Strauss' Ninth Army.

344 D. M. Glantz, *Barbarossa Derailed*, Vol. I, 334.

345 On 2 August 1941, 8 and 5 Infantry Divisions pushed through the pocket along the Smolensk-Dorogobuzh road, splitting it into two smaller pockets. "*Tagesmeldungen der Operations-Abteilung des GenStdH*," in: P. E. Schramm (Hg.), *Kriegstagebuch des OKW*, Bd. I, 552.

346 D. M. Glantz, *Barbarossa Derailed*, Vol. I, 336-39, 345; "*Tagesmeldungen der Operations-Abteilung des GenStdH*," in: P. E. Schramm (Hg.), *Kriegstagebuch des OKW*, Bd. I, 552.

347 Quoted in: H. Dollinger (Hg.), *Kain, wo ist dein Bruder?*, 92.

348 BA-MA RH 21-2/928, *KTB Panzergruppe 2*, 2.-3.8.41.

349 "*Tagesmeldungen der Operations-Abteilung des GenStdH*," in: P. E. Schramm (Hg.), *Kriegstagebuch des OKW*, Bd. I, 556.

350 BA-MA RH 20-4/337, *Die Kaempfe der 4. Armee im ersten Kriegsjahr gegen die Soujets*.

351 BA-MA RH 21-2/928, *KTB Panzergruppe 2*, 5.8.41; K. Gerbet (ed.), *GFM Fedor von Bock, The War Diary*, 273-74.

352 D. M. Glantz, *Barbarossa Derailed*, Vol. I, 358-59.

353 H. Magenheimer, *Moskau 1941*, 52. According to the authoritative study by Russian Col.-Gen. G. F. Krivosheev, et al., published in the 1990s, only 1348 tanks – i.e., less than half the number claimed by Bock and the German High Command – were lost during the "Battle of Smolensk," the fighting along the central axis, which in the Soviet chronology of the war lasted from 10 July to 10 September 1941. Adding to this figure the 4799 tanks lost by Soviet Western Front during the 18-day battle of the frontier would bring total

Russian tank losses through 10 September 1941 opposite German Army Group Center to 6147. Col.-Gen. G. F. Krivosheev (ed.), *Soviet Casualties and Combat Losses*, 260.

354   Less enamored with the outcome at Smolensk was Brig.-Gen. von Waldau, Chief of the *Luftwaffe* Operations Staff, who recorded in his diary on 14 August 1941: "The 'encirclement battle' of Smolensk has not led to the destruction of [Soviet] forces to the extent expected." Waldau attributed this failure primarily to the "exceptional toughness of the Russian opponent, his tactically skillful leadership, and knowledge of the terrain," which enabled large numbers of Russian troops to escape from the pocket. BA-MA RL 200/17, Hoffmann von Waldau, *Tagebuch*, 14.8.41.

355   D. M. Glantz, *Barbarossa Derailed*, Vol. I, 361.

356   K.-J. Thies, *Der Ostfeldzug – Ein Lageatlas*, "Lage am 5.8.1941 abds., Heeresgruppe Mitte."

357   H. Magenheimer, *Moskau 1941*, 52.

358   D. M. Glantz, *Barbarossa Derailed*, Vol. I, 361.

359   C. Burdick & H.-A. Jacobsen (eds.), *The Halder Diary 1939-1942*, 458; "*Hitlers Absicht, mit der deutschen Luftwaffe die russischen Staedte Moskau und Leningrad zu vernichten*," (*Aus der Lagebesprechung am 8.7.41, 12.30 Uhr bei Hitler. Auszug aus dem Tagebuch Halder. . .*), Gen. a.D. Plocher Sammlung, 4.5.1955, KDC.

360   P. E. Schramm (Hg.), *Kriegstagebuch des OKW*, Bd. I, 1022.

361   C. Burdick & H.-A. Jacobsen (eds.), *The Halder Diary 1939-1942*, 470.

362   W. Hubatsch (Hg.), *Hitlers Weisungen fuer die Kriegfuehrung*, 141.

363   As addressed in Chapter 8 (Section 8.4), the total number of German aircraft destroyed or damaged during the first four weeks of Operation *Barbarossa* amounted to 1284. This figure was equal to roughly 55 percent of the *Luftwaffe's* inventory of operational aircraft across the entire eastern front on 22 June 1941. "*Die deutschen Flugzeugverluste im ersten Monat (22.6.41-17.7.41) des Krieges gegen Russland. Nach einer Zusammenstellung der 6. Abteilung des Generalstabes der deutschen Luftwaffe*," KDC.

364   *GSWW*, Vol. IV, 811.

365   K. Gerbet (ed.), *GFM Fedor von Bock, The War Diary*, 257.

366   A. Kesselring, *Soldat Bis Zum Letzten Tag*, 119.

367   Ibid., 127.

368   R. Braithwaite, *Moscow 1941*, 190. "Before the war," writes Braithwaite, "there were 26,000 street lights in Moscow (there are now 260,000). They were operated from so many different places that it could take an hour and a half to turn them on or off. The municipality therefore introduced a centralized system which made it possible to turn off all the city's street lights from one point … The roof of GUM, the department store on Red Square, was painted black, so effectively that the glass had to be replaced after the war … Special dampers were devised for blast furnaces which could not be closed down and which normally emitted a vivid glow at night. Traffic lights were masked so that they could only be seen from a short distance. Traffic moved very slowly and came to a halt whenever the air-raid alarm was sounded at night. All street lighting was shut off at the same time. The blackout was policed by duty officers in the factories, by PVO [home air defense organization] and self-defense units, and by mounted police and military patrols. The sound of horses' hooves on the deserted streets at night stuck in people's memories."

369   "The Agence Havas correspondent in Moscow who joined the Free French in 1941." A. Werth, *Russia at War*, 177.

370   Citizens' militia, or home guard.

371   A. Werth, *Russia at War*, 175-78.

372   Preparations to defend Moscow against air attack had begun in 1932, while the construction of air raid shelters began in 1933. Beginning in 1938, a "proportion of all new buildings and offices were designed with shelters incorporated." Despite such measures, "Moscow's air defenses remained inadequate. Colonel Sbytov's inspection in March 1941 and the fiasco over the flight to Moscow by the German Ju 52 in May, showed that much remained to be done." R. Braithwaite, *Moscow 1941*, 185-86.

373   Ibid., 186.

374   As a general observation, VNOS units "employed vision methods of aircraft detection and primitive means to determine the course and objectives of enemy aircraft." For excellent details on Soviet air defenses – including shortcomings in the VNOS units – on the eve of the German invasion see, D. M. Glantz, *Stumbling Colossus*, 168-74.

375   A. Brookes, *Air War over Russia*, 70-71.

376   R. Braithwaite, *Moscow 1941*, 186.

377   R. Braithwaite, *Moscow 1941*, 186; P. Gosztony, "*Die erste Entscheidungsschlacht des Russlandfeldzuges 1941/42 (II), Moskau in der Krise 1941 (I)*," in: *Oesterreichische Militaerische Zeitschrift*, Heft 2, 1967, p. 105. According to David Glantz, Moscow, part of the second PVO defensive belt, was protected by 137 anti-aircraft batteries. D. M. Glantz, *Stumbling Colossus*, 172.

378   According to Andrew Brookes, there were a total of 1044 pieces of anti-aircraft artillery and 336 machine guns situated in and about Moscow. A. Brookes, *Air War over Russia*, 71. German historian Horst Boog states that the anti-aircraft defenses of Moscow consisted of "approximately 1000 guns." *GSWW*, Vol. IV, 810.

379   R. Braithwaite, *Moscow 1941*, 186; P. Gosztony, "*Die erste Entscheidungsschlacht des Russlandfeldzuges 1941/42 (II), Moskau in der Krise 1941 (I)*," in: *Oesterreichische Militaerische Zeitschrift*, Heft 2, 1967, p. 105.

380   K. Uebe, *Russian Reactions to German Airpower in World War II*, USAF Historical Study No. 176, 39. Although these "schemes were quickly executed, the speed was not sufficient to prevent positive identification of the

capitol by German airmen, who saw the city during the various stages of camouflage construction." Ibid., 39.

381 Ibid., 39-40.

382 Ibid., 40.

383 R. Braithwaite, *Moscow 1941*, 187.

384 Ibid., 187.

385 Because the source material is highly contradictory, this order of battle must be considered approximate. Sources used to compile it include: *GSWW*, Vol. IV, 809-10; R. Muller, *The German Air War in Russia*, 51; A. Brookes, *Air War over Russia*, 70; C. Bekker, *The Luftwaffe War Diaries*, 224; C. Bergström & A. Mikhailov, *Black Cross Red Star*, Vol. I, 263-65; F. Kurowski, *Balkenkreuz und Roter Stern*, 98-99; U. Balke, *Kampfgeschwader* 100 "*Wiking*," 83; and, K. Gundelach, *Kampfgeschwader* "*General Wever*" 4, 145-46.

386 An exception was *Kampfgruppe* 100. Having just arrived from Chartres, France (where it had flown missions against England), it flew from its base at Terespol, close by Brest-Litovsk and near the extreme end of the He 111's range. On 19 July, only three of the bomber group's He 111H3's were combat ready, and they all took part in the attack. By 26 July, the group had increased its number of operational bombers to 10. U. Balke, *Kampfgeschwader* 100 "*Wiking*," 83.

387 C. Bekker, *The Luftwaffe War Diaries*, 223; U. Balke, *Kampfgeschwader* 100 "*Wiking*," 83-84; A. Brookes, *Air War over Russia*, 70.

388 C. Bekker, *The Luftwaffe War Diaries*, 224; "*Der Luftkrieg im Osten gegen Russland 1941. (Aus einer Studie der 8. Abteilung 1943/1944.*)," KDC.

389 F. Kurowski, *Balkenkreuz und Roter Stern*, 101.

390 C. Bekker, *The Luftwaffe War Diaries*, 224; U. Balke, *Kampfgeschwader* 100 "*Wiking*," 84; A. Brookes, *Air War over Russia*, 70.

391 U. Balke, *Kampfgeschwader* 100 "*Wiking*," 84. Of particular concern to 4 KG were the barrage balloons, which forced its aircrews to drop their bombs at altitudes above 4000 meters. K. Gundelach, *Kampfgeschwader* "*General Wever*" 4, 146.

392 A. Werth, *Russia at War*, 182.

393 *GSWW*, Vol. IV, 809; "*Der Luftkrieg im Osten gegen Russland 1941. (Aus einer Studie der 8. Abteilung 1943/1944.*)," KDC.

394 F. Kurowski, *Balkenkreuz und Roter Stern*, 100. After returning from the mission, Kuehl had listened incredulously as the chief operations officer (Ia) of 2 Air Corps, *Oberst* von Cramon – still unaware that Kuehl's bombers had badly missed their mark – explained that the incendiaries could have done little damage to the Kremlin. Cramon had served as an air attaché in Moscow, and was aware of the thick and sturdy layers of tile on the Kremlin's roofs; hence his justifiable skepticism.

395 R. Braithwaite, *Moscow 1941*, 195.

396 *GSWW*, Vol. IV, 810; "*Der Luftkrieg im Osten gegen Russland 1941. (Aus einer Studie der 8. Abteilung 1943/1944.*)," KDC.

397 A. Brookes, *Air War over Russia*, 71.

398 BA-MA RL 200/17, Hoffmann von Waldau, *Tagebuch*, 24.7.41.

399 "The night raids against Moscow were the most difficult missions that I carried out on the eastern front," recalled *Major* Hansgeorg Baetcher, pilot and *Staffelkapitaen* of 1st Squadron, *Kampfgruppe* 100. "The anti-aircraft fire was extremely intense, and the gunners fired with a frightening accuracy." Baetcher survived the war, having logged 658 bomber sorties (*Feindfluege*) between 1940 and 1945 (655 of them flying He 111s), more than any other German bomber pilot. Most of his missions were flown on the eastern front. C. Bergström & A. Mikhailov, *Black Cross Red Star*, Vol. I, 115; Ltr, H. Gaenshirt to C. Luther, 11 Jan 03.

400 A total of 65 bombers took part in the raid on 26/27 July, attacking at altitudes between 2400 and 5000 meters, and dropping 102 tons of HE and 7344 incendiaries. "*Einsatz gegen Moskau im Jahre 1941*," compiled by H. Plocher, KDC.

401 K. Gundelach, *Kampfgeschwader* "*General Wever*" 4, 146.

402 Quoted in: F. Kurowski, *Balkenkreuz und Roter Stern*, 102-03.

403 "*Einsatz gegen Moskau im Jahre 1941*," compiled by H. Plocher, KDC.

404 R. Braithwaite, *Moscow 1941*, 195-96.

405 "*Einsatz gegen Moskau im Jahre 1941*," compiled by H. Plocher, KDC.

406 *GSWW*, Vol. IV, 810.

407 *GSWW*, Vol. IV, 810. Soviet sources, whose reliability may be suspect, contend the Moscow raids cost the Germans 173 aircraft through 1 October 1941 – 110 destroyed by Soviet fighters, 60 by anti-aircraft fire, and three planes lost in collisions with the steel wires of the barrage balloons. C. Bergström & A. Mikhailov, *Black Cross Red Star*, Vol. I, 121.

408 A total of 87 missions (76 night and 11 day raids) were flown against Moscow, with the final attack conducted on 5 April 1942. According to Soviet figures, 1088 persons were killed by the German bombing campaign. *GSWW*, Vol. IV, 810; "*Der Luftkrieg im Osten gegen Russland 1941. (Aus einer Studie der 8. Abteilung 1943/1944.*)," KDC.

409 A. Kesselring, *Soldat Bis Zum Letzten Tag*, 128.

410 For example, in September 1941, 2 Air Fleet launched attacks on the aircraft factory at Voronezh, while also striking factories in or near Briansk, Tula, Aleksin, and Kaluga. In October, the air fleet again struck the factory at Voronezh, industrial targets in Aleksin, Kashira, Balabanova, Narafominsk, and a chemical plant in Tula. November 1941 brought attacks on the tank factory at Gorki; and, in December, the *Luftwaffe* in the

central sector bombed the aircraft factory at Rybinsk and open oil storage facilities near Rybinsk. *GSWW*, Vol. IV, 807-08.

411   The only "caveat" here is whether or not to also consider the aerial bombing of Leningrad as part of a sustained strategic air campaign. In any case, beginning in late September 1941, as the siege of Leningrad got underway, 1 Air Fleet "repeatedly" attacked "targets of military importance" in the city with "good results." See, H. Plocher, *The German Air Force Versus Russia, 1941*, 150; also, *GSWW*, Vol. IV, 777, 790.

412   *GSWW*, Vol. IV, 811.

413   A. Brookes, *Air War over Russia*, 71.

414   *GSWW*, Vol. IV, 813.

415   V. Hardesty, *Red Phoenix*, 26.

416   A. Brookes, *Air War over Russia*, 46. Unfortunately, while a major Soviet account confirms the 7/8 August raid – as well as the air unit and the type of aircraft involved – it offers no additional details. See, M. N. Kozhevnikov, *The Command and Staff of the Soviet Army Air Force in the Great Patriotic War*, 1941-1945, 50.

417   V. Hardesty, *Red Phoenix*, 26; M. N. Kozhevnikov, *The Command and Staff of the Soviet Army Air Force in the Great Patriotic War*, 1941-1945, 50.

418   M. N. Kozhevnikov, *The Command and Staff of the Soviet Army Air Force in the Great Patriotic War*, 1941-1945, 50.

419   V. Hardesty, *Red Phoenix*, 27.

420   M. N. Kozhevnikov, *The Command and Staff of the Soviet Army Air Force in the Great Patriotic War*, 1941-1945, 50.

421   Thus had German historian Karl-Heinz Frieser characterized the difference between Hitler and his general staff in May 1940. See, K.-H. Frieser, *Blitzkrieg-Legende*, 321.

422   J. Foerster, *Die Wehrmacht im NS-Staat*, 173-74.

423   BA-MA N 664/3, *Tagebuch* Thilo, 24.8.41.

424   The reference here is to the diaries of Captains Thilo and Muenchhausen, both of which are used in this section of the text.

425   J. Foerster, *Die Wehrmacht im NS-Staat*, 174.

426   T. Diedrich, *Paulus*, 182.

427   Although a precise date is not given, the meeting most likely took place sometime after mid-July, as Smolensk was not reached by the Germans until 15/16 July 1941.

428   T. Diedrich, *Paulus*, 183.

429   Ibid., 183.

430   Ibid., 187.

431   C. Burdick & H.-A. Jacobsen (eds.), *The Halder Diary 1939-1942*, 457.

432   I. Kershaw, *Hitler 1936-45: Nemesis*, 409.

433   C. Burdick & H.-A. Jacobsen (eds.), *The Halder Diary 1939-1942*, 485.

434   For example see, "*Erlaeuterung zur Karte 'Kraefteansatz fuer Unternehmen gegen Industrie-Gebiet am Ural;'*" and, "*Operation aus Nordkaukasien ueber den Kaukasus und Nordwestiran zur Inbesitznahme der Paesse Rewanduz und Khanaqin an der iranisch-irakischen Grenze,*" in: P. E. Schramm (Hg.), *Kriegstagebuch des OKW*, Bd. I, 1037-40. The first document is dated 27 July 1941; the second appears to belong to the same time period.

435   BA-MA N 664/3, *Tagebuch* Thilo, 25.7.41; G. P. Megargee, *Inside Hitler's High Command*, 132. There is some question, however, as to just how sincere Halder's projections were, given that, at the time, he was pulling out all stops in an effort to convince the "Fuehrer" to maintain the *Schwerpunkt* of the German assault along the road to Moscow. Argues historian David Stahel: "Halder was purposefully trying to sway Hitler by indulging his delusional fantasies of grandeur ... Later that day, when Hitler restated these same goals, Halder took a disdainfully cynical tone and mocked him in his diary. 'Apparently he [Hitler] believes that the motorized units alone can make it to the Volga and into the Caucasus as we head into the wet autumn.'" D. Stahel, *And the World held its Breath*, 182.

436   G. P. Megargee, *Inside Hitler's High Command*, 132-33.

437   Admiral Wilhelm Canaris, Chief of the *Abwehr*.

438   Quoted in: D. Irving, *Hitler's War*, 286.

439   BA-MA N 664/3, *Tagebuch* Thilo, 25.7.41.

440   H. von Kotze (Hg.), *Heeresadjutant bei Hitler 1938-1943. Aufzeichnungen des Majors Engel*, 107.

441   N. von Below, *At Hitler's Side*, 109.

442   R. G. Reuth (Hg.), *Joseph Goebbels Tagebuecher*, Bd. 4, 1645.

443   Ibid., 1627.

444   Quoted in: B. Musial, *Kampfplatz Deutschland*, 458.

445   BA-MA N 813, *Tagebuch* Muenchhausen, Aug 41.

446   American troops had landed on Iceland on 7 July 1941. H. Muehleisen (Hg.), *Hellmuth Stieff. Briefe*, 221.

447   The reference here is to "Fuehrer Directive" No. 33 ("Continuation of the War in the East"), of 19 July 1941. See, Section 10.4.2.

448   H. Muehleisen (Hg.), *Hellmuth Stieff. Briefe*, 113-15. Under Keitel at OKW a special office, headed by a colonel, was responsible for preparing the daily *Wehrmacht* reports. While Stieff's assertion that Hitler personally prepared the reports is highly doubtful – although Hitler, no doubt, must have intervened from time to time in their preparation – his damning critique of the reports is clearly accurate. E-Mail, C. Nehring to C. Luther, 30 May 12.

449   G. P. Megargee, *Inside Hitler's High Command*, 133.

450   Ibid., 133.

451   O. Buchbender & R. Sterz (Hg.), *Das andere Gesicht des Krieges*, 76-77.

452   C. Burdick & H.-A. Jacobsen (eds.), *The Halder Diary 1939-1942*, 505-06.

453   Ibid., 497.

454   D. Irving (ed.), *Adolf Hitler: The Medical Diaries. The Private Diaries of Dr Theo Morell*, 82. In his diary on 7 August Morell wrote: "At Fuehrer's headquarters. Saw Fuehrer at 1:30 p.m. in map room. Said he'd been sitting down when he suddenly felt dizzy, with attacks of nausea and retching. Had flown to Berdichev yesterday [in the Ukraine, to meet with Army Group South], three hours out and three hours back. Of late he's been looking pretty bad all the time, and pale ... This bunker atmosphere has been getting him down for five or six weeks now." Ibid., 84.

455   *GSWW*, Vol. IV, 571.

456   Ibid., 571.

457   For the text of the directive in English see, H.R. Trevor-Roper (ed.), *Hitler's War Directives 1939-1945*, 85-88; for the original German text see, W. Hubatsch (Hg.), *Hitlers Weisungen fuer die Kriegfuehrung 1939-1945*, 140-42.

458   On 17 July, Hitler, "in view of the situation by Army Group North," had "again taken up the idea" of dispatching 3 Panzer Group northeast into the sector of Leeb's army group. The panzer group's mission would be threefold: cut lines of communication between Leningrad and Moscow, destroy enemy forces before the front of Army Group North (in cooperation with Leeb's forces), and support the encirclement of Leningrad. "*Fuehrererwaegung am 17. Juli 1941*," in: P. E. Schramm (Hg.), *Kriegstagebuch des OKW*, Bd. I, 1029.

459   H.R. Trevor-Roper (ed.), *Hitler's War Directives 1939-1945*, 85-87.

460   J. Keegan, *The Second World War*, 193.

461   H.R. Trevor-Roper (ed.), *Hitler's War Directives 1939-1945*, 89.

462   B. Wegner, "*The Road to Defeat: The German Campaigns in Russia 1941-43*," in: *The Journal of Strategic Studies*, Vol. 13, No. 1, Mar 90, 111.

463   In the weeks ahead, German aerial reconnaissance would vindicate this view, as the Soviets assembled strong forces between Smolensk and Moscow. J. Loeffler, *Walther von Brauchitsch*, 248.

464   Quoted in: W. L. Shirer, *The Rise and Fall of the Third Reich*, 856.

465   P. E. Schramm (Hg.), *Kriegstagebuch des OKW*, Bd. I, 1034-35.

466   For details of Halder's presentation see, *GSWW*, Vol. IV, 574-75; also, P. E. Schramm (Hg.), *Kriegstagebuch des OKW*, Bd. I, 1030-31.

467   D. Stahel, *And the World held its Breath*, 182.

468   *GSWW*, Vol. IV, 574-75; P. E. Schramm (Hg.), *Kriegstagebuch des OKW*, Bd. I, 1031.

469   D. Stahel, *And the World held its Breath*, 183.

470   K. Gerbet (ed.), *GFM Fedor von Bock, The War Diary*, 261.

471   The words are David Stahel's. D. Stahel, *And the World held its Breath*, 193.

472   K. Gerbet (ed.), *GFM Fedor von Bock, The War Diary*, 195.

473   "*Besprechung des Chefs OKW mit Oberbefehlshaber der Heeresgruppe Mitte am 25. Juli 1941*," in: P. E. Schramm (Hg.), *Kriegstagebuch des OKW*, Bd. I, 1035-36.

474   B. Fugate & L. Dvoretsky, *Thunder on the Dnepr*, 317-18. According to the authors, Jodl had hitherto favored sending armor from Army Group Center northward to cooperate with Army Group North following the capture of Smolensk; however, most likely after learning of Paulus' visit to Leeb's headquarters on 26 July – where panzer generals Hoepner, Manstein and Reinhardt had all indicated that the approaches to Leningrad from the south were in no way suitable for armor due to the difficult terrain (many lakes, swamps, and thick forests), with Manstein going so far as to propose turning Army Group North's tanks away from Leningrad toward Moscow – Jodl changed his mind.

475   Ibid., 317.

476   As Halder recalled after the war: "What had been comparatively infrequent in previous campaigns now became a daily occurrence. [Hitler] interfered in the detailed conduct of operations." F. Halder, *Hitler as War Lord*, 43.

477   Quoted in: K. Assmann, "*The Battle for Moscow, Turning Point of the War*," in: *Foreign Affairs*, Jan 50, 315.

478   Quoted in: D. Stahel, *And the World held its Breath*, 198.

479   Ibid., 198.

480   G. Meyer, *Adolf Heusinger*, 154.

481   D. Stahel, *And the World held its Breath*, 198.

482   B. Fugate & L. Dvoretsky, *Thunder on the Dnepr*, 318; "*Erwaegungen und Anordnungen des Fuehrers am 28. Juli 1941*," in: P. E. Schramm (Hg.), *Kriegstagebuch des OKW*, Bd. I, 1040-41.

483   In the Trevor-Roper translation of Directive No. 34, the words "for the moment" are italicized; in the original German, the word "*vorerst*" is not. See, W. Hubatsch (Hg.), *Hitlers Weisungen fuer die Kriegfuehrung 1939-1945*, 145.

484   H.R. Trevor-Roper (ed.), *Hitler's War Directives 1939-1945*," 91.

485   Ibid., 91.

486   J. Loeffler, *Walther von Brauchitsch*, 248.

487   C. Burdick & H.-A. Jacobsen (eds.), *The Halder Diary 1939-1942*, 490.

488   During visits to the headquarters of all three army groups – on 21 July (Army Group North), on 4 August (Center), and on 6 August (South) – Hitler, in each case, reaffirmed his decision to shift the weight of the

eastern offensive to Leningrad and the south before continuing the push on Moscow, thus affirming the continuity of his strategic outlook. G. R. Ueberschaer & W. Wette (Hg.), *"Unternehmen Barbarossa." Der deutsche Ueberfall auf die Sowjetunion 1941*, 153.

489   D. M. Glantz, *Barbarossa Derailed*, Vol. I, 326-28, 385-87; K.-J. Thies, *Der Ostfeldzug – Ein Lageatlas*, "Lage am [8.-21.] 8.1941 abds., Heeresgruppe Mitte."

490   C. G. Sweeting, *Hitler's Personal Pilot*, 166.

491   *"Besprechung gelegentlich Anwesenheit des Fuehrers und Obersten Befehlshabers der Wehrmacht bei Heeresgruppe Mitte am 4. August 1941,"* in: P. E. Schramm (Hg.), *Kriegstagebuch des OKW*, Bd. I, 1041.

492   As Bock noted in his diary: "[Hitler] repeatedly congratulated me in a very friendly way on the 'unprecedented successes.'" K. Gerbet (ed.), *GFM Fedor von Bock, The War Diary*, 272.

493   The words are David Stahel's. D. Stahel, *And the World held its Breath*, 230. For Guderian's take on the meeting see, H. Guderian, *Panzer Leader*, 189-90.

494   W. Gorlitz (ed.), *The Memoirs of Field-Marshal Wilhelm Keitel*, 150-51.

495   Ibid., 151.

496   According to GFM von Kluge's chief of staff, Guenther Blumentritt, the field marshal "was inclined to prefer Hitler's strategic concept." See, G. Blumentritt, *"Moscow,"* in: *The Fatal Decisions*, W. Richardson & S. Freidin (eds.), 51.

497   D. Stahel, *And the World held its Breath*, 230.

498   *"Besprechung gelegentlich Anwesenheit des Fuehrers und Obersten Befehlshabers der Wehrmacht bei Heeresgruppe Mitte am 4. August 1941,"* in: P. E. Schramm (Hg.), *Kriegstagebuch des OKW*, Bd. I, 1042-43.

499   Ibid., 1043.

500   H. Guderian, *Panzer Leader*, 190.

501   Ibid., 190.

502   As David Glantz correctly observes, the fact that Hoth and Guderian had to plead with Hitler for new engines and tanks illustrates the alarming extent of the "Fuehrer's" "micro-management" of the war. D. M. Glantz, *Barbarossa*, 84.

503   H. Guderian, *Panzer Leader*, 190.

504   *"Besprechung gelegentlich Anwesenheit des Fuehrers und Obersten Befehlshabers der Wehrmacht bei Heeresgruppe Mitte am 4. August 1941,"* in: P. E. Schramm (Hg.), *Kriegstagebuch des OKW*, Bd. I, 1043; H. Guderian, *Panzer Leader*, 190; H. Hoth, *Panzer-Operationen*, 117. As David Glantz has pointed out, however, both Guderian's and Hoth's estimates were "wildly over-optimistic," given the losses hitherto sustained and Army Group Center's growing logistical problems. D. Glantz, *Barbarossa Derailed*, Vol. I, 306.

505   BA-MA RH 21-2/928, *KTB Panzergruppe 2*, 4.8.41; *"Besprechung gelegentlich Anwesenheit des Fuehrers und Obersten Befehlshabers der Wehrmacht bei Heeresgruppe Mitte am 4. August 1941,"* in: P. E. Schramm (Hg.), *Kriegstagebuch des OKW*, Bd. I, 1042. After the war, both Hoth and Guderian claimed to have received no new tanks; however, the diary of Guderian's panzer group states otherwise, indicating that the 35 tanks were indeed delivered to the front. More importantly, Army Group Center would receive several hundred replacement tanks from Army depots in the weeks prior to the start of Operation "Typhoon," the advance on Moscow. (See, Chapter 11, Section 11.4.1.)

506   *"Besprechung gelegentlich Anwesenheit des Fuehrers und Obersten Befehlshabers der Wehrmacht bei Heeresgruppe Mitte am 4. August 1941,"* in: P. E. Schramm (Hg.), *Kriegstagebuch des OKW*, Bd. I, 1041-42.

507   Ibid., 1042.

508   D. Stahel, *And the World held its Breath*, 231.

509   BA-MA RH 21-2/928, *KTB Panzergruppe 2*, 4.8.41.

510   C. Burdick & H.-A. Jacobsen (eds.), *The Halder Diary 1939-1942*, 495.

511   D. Stahel, *And the World held its Breath*, 231.

512   D. Irving, *Hitler's War*, 298.

513   Quoted in: D. Irving, *Hitler's War*, 298, f.n. 1.

514   D. Irving, *Hitler's War*, 298; *GSWW*, Vol. IV, 584; FMS T-6, A. Heusinger, *"Eastern Campaign, 1941-1942 (Strategic Survey),"* 82-83. In David Irving's view, when Hitler visited Bock's headquarters on 4 August, he "had not yet made up his mind on how to fight the next phase of the campaign." However, Irving argues that, by 6 August (visiting Rundstedt at Army Group South), "Hitler's mind was all but made up. He would make his main push southeastward toward the oil fields, while the northern advance on Leningrad from the Luga bridgeheads began. Moscow would be left for last."

515   Observes historian Dennis Showalter: "Recently available archival evidence shows that, far from collapsing in disorganized panic, from *Barbarossa's* beginning the Red Army conducted a spectrum of counterattacks in a coherent attempt to implement pre-war plans for an active defense ending in a decisive counteroffensive." D. Showalter, *Hitler's Panzers*, 162-63.

516   D. M. Glantz, *The Soviet-German War: Myths and Realities*, 18.

517   E. Mawdsley, *Thunder in the East*, 69.

518   *GSWW*, Vol. IV, 865-66.

519   *GSWW*, Vol., IV, 866; D. M. Glantz, *Barbarossa Derailed*, Vol. I, 151-53.

520   K. Reinhardt, *Moscow – The Turning Point*, 72.

521   Ibid., 72.

522   W. S. Dunn, Jr., *Stalin's Keys to Victory*, 74-80.

523   D. M. Glantz, *Barbarossa*, 61-62.

524   Ibid., 62.

Battle of Moscow & Winter Battles
October 1941 — March 1942

German infantry prepare to advance. (K.-F. Hoyer)

A 150mm medium howitzer in action on 2 October 1941, as Army Group Center begins its advance on Moscow. (H. Sohn)

A German artillery piece supports start of Operation "Typhoon," the drive on Moscow (2 October 1941). (H. Sohn)

Ju 87 *Stuka* dive bombers head east at start of "Typhoon" (2 October 1941). (H. Sohn)

Russian bunker position near the Desna River, some 33 km northeast of Roslavl, captured by 197 Infantry Division (2 October 1941). (NA)

Tanks and infantry advancing on Moscow (early October 1941). (H. Wijers)

Reserve infantry unit marching through abandoned Red Army positions after start of Operation "Typhoon." (H. Boucsein)

The village of Kasilovo burns (7 October 1941). (H. Sohn)

A German assault gun and other vehicles on the *Rollbahn* near Viaz'ma (14 October 1941). (H. Sohn)

Rollbahn near Viaz'ma (14 October 1941). (H. Sohn)

Shortly after the capture of Kalinin in mid-October 1941, the local German commander opens the churches to the inhabitants for religious services. (H. Boucsein)

A motorized column of 5 Panzer Division struggles to inch its way forward during the Russian rainy season – the so-called *Rasputitsa* (literally, the "time without roads") (October 1941). (O. Will)

Merklovo (20 October 1941): It takes a massive team of horses to pull this heavy German artillery piece across the rain-softened road. (H. Sohn)

In snake-like fashion this floating bridge crosses the Dnepr River (October 1941). (NA)

German draft horses suffered terribly during the Russian rainy season, with many collapsing and dying in their harnesses (fall 1941). (K.-F. Hoyer)

German supply truck stuck in the mud (fall 1941). (H. Wijers)

Attempting to tow a passenger vehicle out of the mud (fall 1941). (R. Mobius)

Supply column of 5 Panzer Division (fall 1941). (O. Will)

150mm medium field howitzer battery in position on the Nara River (October 1941). (R. Mobius).

Near a village 69 km southwest of Moscow – a German *Nebelwerfer* rocket projector in a covered position (November 1941). (NA)

A German regimental staff on the central front (October 1941). (NA)

Russian obstacles and defensive positions in front of Malojaroslavets, 108 km southwest of Moscow (late October 1941). (NA)

The burning town of Orel (November 1941). (D. Garden & K. Andrew)

A German heavy MG position (fall 1941). (BA-MA, Bild 1011-268-0181-10, Foto: Vorpahl)

Elements of 427 Infantry Regiment (129 ID) advancing in open order toward the Volga reservoir in -15° C. temperatures and without winter clothing (15 November 1941). (H. Boucsein)

German panzers advancing from the Kalinin region southward toward Moscow (fall 1941). (H. Boucsein)

Tank assembly point (17 PD) (winter 1941/42). (D. Garden & K. Andrew)

A battery of 35 Artillery Regiment (35 ID) in firing position northwest of Moscow (2 December 1941).

A column of 35 Infantry Division during the retreat; in the distance the village of Gorki (12 December 1941).
(H. Sohn)

German tanks on the move on central front (14 December 1941). (H. Sohn)

Outside village of Stepankovo – column of 35 Infantry Division (16 December 1941). (H. Sohn)

Remnants of a decimated infantry battalion of 6 Infantry Division retreat from Moscow (December 1941). (H. Bruenger)

German infantry column retreating from Moscow (December 1941). (H. Bruenger)

Elements of 35 Infantry Division retreating near Volokolamsk (19 December 1941). (H. Sohn)

A signal unit of 35 ID retreating near Volokolamsk (19 December 1941). (H. Sohn)

Vehicles of the 292 Signal Battalion (292 ID) near Alenkino (22 December 1941). (R. Mobius)

Horsedrawn elements of 129 Infantry Division thread their way onto the *Rollbahn* during the retreat from Moscow. The motorized vehicles have the right of way (December 1941). (H. Boucsein)

Dead soldiers of 427 Infantry Regiment (129 ID) in the church at Romanovo; because the ground was frozen hard as cement, a proper burial was not possible (winter 1941/42). (H. Boucsein)

A German military cemetery of 129 Infantry Division east of Papino (winter 1941/42). (H. Boucsein)

A German military cemetery in central Russia (winter 1941/42). (K.-F. Hoyer)

German motorized artillery struggles to advance through snow and ice.

German artillery in position behind a snow wall (winter 1941/42). (H. Wijers)

The bloody outcome of a Russian mass attack with infantry and tanks somewhere on the eastern front.

The German Rusa-position west of Moscow (January 1942).

Elements of 17 Panzer Division counterattack toward Bolchov (north of Orel) in January 1942.
(D. Garden & K. Andrew)

A "supply route" on the central front in winter 1941/42; by January 1942, the walls were 1.8 meters high. (A. v. Garn)

German heavy machine gun securing the *Rollbahn* 81 km west of Kaluga (February 1942). (NA)

Soldiers in winter camouflage near Orel. On the right, two soldiers aiming with captured Soviet machine pistols (winter 1941/42). (BA-MA, Bild 1011-287-0885-29A, Foto: Karl Mueller)

A young platoon leader in an assault gun unit – somewhere on the eastern front.

Artillerie im Osten – somewhere on the eastern front.

The remnants of an anti-tank platoon (originally 30 men) of 38 *Panzerjaeger* Batalion (2 PD) after the end of the winter battles. (H. E. Braun)

Photo Supplement

The author with Herrn Walter Vollmer, former artillerist with 106 Infantry Division, and member of the *Kuratorium Rshew*, at the German "soldiers' cemetery" (*Soldatenfriedhof*) in Rzhev, Russia (May 2005). The *Kuratorium* was established in 1992 by veterans of 18 Infantry Regiment (6 ID), with the objective of seeking reconciliation with the former Russian enemy. A delegation from the *Kuratorium* has visited Rzhev every year since 1993, meeting with Russian veterans and providing generous humanitarian and financial assistance to the people of Rzhev.

The remains of more than 600 German soldiers, who perished in the fighting around Rzhev from December 1941 to March 1943, are finally laid to rest in the German soldiers' cemetery at Rzhev in 2006. The culmination of years of work by the *Kuratorium Rshew*, the cemetery was dedicated in September 2002.

On the highway, just outside Moscow, one finds this imposing monument dedicated to the Soviet victory before Moscow in 1941.

Gravesites of German and Russian soldiers still dot the landscape about Rzhev – here the remains of *Landser* who perished in the winter of 1941/42. Many of these sites have been dug up and vandalized by Russian grave robbers, looking for "dog tags" and other items of value.

The highway from Rzhev to Moscow; picture taken in late May 2005.

Typical of the dense, almost primeval, underbrush in the forested regions outside Moscow, which witnessed such bitter and costly fighting.

From this recent photograph of the monastery church outside the town of Staritza, on the Volga River roughly 175 km NW of Moscow, one can see why so many German *Landser* were inspired by Russia's great natural beauty. Staritza was captured by the Germans in October 1941, at the start of Operation "Typhoon," and abandoned during the retreat from Moscow.

525   Ibid., 61.
526   E. Mawdsley, *Thunder in the East*, 66. Budenny had commanded the *Konarmiia* as a whole, while Voroshilov had served as the main commissar and Timoshenko had commanded one of the army's divisions.
527   E. Mawdsley, *Thunder in the East*, 66; D. M. Glantz & J. House, *When Titans Clashed*, 63; W. J. Spahr, *Zhukov*, 61. According to Spahr, "Stalin's professional military advisors opposed [formation of the strategic directions]."
528   R. Roberts, *Stalin's Wars*, 95. According to John Keegan, the Soviet General Staff, "extended to oversee all branches of the armed forces," was not formally subordinated to the *Stavka* until this time (8 Aug 41). J. Keegan, *The Second World War*, 190.
529   *GSWW*, Vol. IV, 837.
530   Ibid., 837.
531   *GSWW*, Vol. IV, 837; G. L. Weinberg, *A World at Arms*, 280.
532   J. Keegan, *The Second World War*, 190.
533   Ibid., 190.
534   Col.-Gen. G. F. Krivosheev (ed.), *Soviet Casualties and Combat Losses*, 116; 260.
535   Ibid., 101. Figures for the third quarter also include 22-30 June 1941.
536   W. S. Dunn, Jr., *Stalin's Keys to Victory*, 63.
537   Ibid., 63.
538   Ibid., 74, 77-80.
539   D. M. Glantz, *Barbarossa*, 68. For a list of all the new armies created from June to December 1941 see, "Table 1, Red Army Wartime Mobilization, 1941," 69.
540   D. M. Glantz, *Barbarossa Derailed*, Vol. I, 143.
541   D. M. Glantz, *Red Army Ground Forces*, 39.
542   Ibid., 40.
543   Ibid., 40.
544   Ibid., 40-41.
545   Ibid., 41.
546   Quoted in: D. M. Glantz, *Barbarossa Derailed*, Vol. I, 281.
547   Ibid., 142.
548   Because tanks became so scarce in the Red Army in the summer and fall of 1941, tank brigades were the largest new tank units formed during this period, their large-scale establishment beginning in August 1941. Some of these tank brigades were outfitted with as few as 50 newly manufactured tanks, with minimal maintenance and other support units. W. S. Dunn, Jr., *Stalin's Keys to Victory*, 77; D. M. Glantz, *Barbarossa*, 65.
549   The catastrophic losses of the summer of 1941 also led to reductions in the rifle divisions' table of organization, particularly of automatic weapons. For example, the number of machine pistols in a rifle division was dramatically reduced from 1200 to 171, machine guns from 558 to 270. At the same time, authorized manpower was reduced to 10,859 (from 14,483). The individual rifle company was left with only six machine pistols and six light MGs, while the howitzer regiment was eliminated from the rifle division to furnish army artillery. W. S. Dunn, Jr., *Stalin's Keys to Victory*, 91.
550   As noted in the directive: "Our army has somewhat underestimated the significance of cavalry. Given the present situation at the front, where the enemy's rear is spread out over several hundred kilometers in wooded locations and has not been at all secured against major diversionary action by our side, raids by Red cavalrymen against the extended rear of the enemy might play a decisive role in disorganizing the administration and supply of the German forces, and in consequence, in bringing about the defeat of the German forces." Quoted in: E. Mawdsley, *Thunder in the East*, 64.
551   These bullet points gleaned from: D. M. Glantz, *Barbarossa Derailed*, Vol. I, 142-43; G. Roberts, *Stalin's Wars*, 97; E. F. Ziemke & M. E. Bauer, *Moscow to Stalingrad*, 31; E. Mawdsley, *Thunder in the East*, 64-65.
552   D. M. Glantz, *Barbarossa*, 64.
553   I. C. B. Dear (ed.), *The Oxford Companion to World War II*, 108, 910.
554   For more details on British attempts – using intelligence gained from ULTRA – to alert the Russians about Operation *Barbarossa*, see comments by John Somerville (Wells, England) in: J. Rohwer & E. Jaeckel (Hg.), *Kriegswende Dezember 1941*, 220-21.
555   Ibid., 221.
556   M. Gilbert, *Second World War*, 203.
557   From decrypts of *Luftwaffe* ENIGMA traffic, the British discovered that the Germans had broken "a number" of Soviet codes and methods of encryption. J. Rohwer & E. Jaeckel (Hg.), *Kriegswende Dezember 1941*, 221.
558   M. Gilbert, *Second World War*, 208.
559   Ibid., 209.
560   Ibid., 210.
561   Ibid., 213.
562   Ibid., 232, 237.
563   In this context, it should be pointed out that even Anglo-American commanders who had been fully briefed on the source of the information they were receiving, did not always trust, or make good use of, the ULTRA intelligence.
564   In the years ahead, Stalin would continue to receive ULTRA intelligence from the British. "Under carefully controlled conditions," writes English historian Paul Johnson, "Stalin was fed in spectacular detail knowledge

of German dispositions and plans on the eastern front acquired through the Enigma/Ultra intelligence system. This had a major direct bearing on the campaign from 1942 onwards and helped to make possible Stalin's spectacular victories in 1943-4, for which he has been given credit." P. Johnson, *Modern Times*, 386.

565   K.-J. Thies, *Der Ostfeldzug – Ein Lageatlas*, "Lage am 30.7.1941 abds., Heeresgruppe Mitte."

566   T. Wray, *Standing Fast: German Defensive Doctrine on the Russian Front*, 42.

567   Quoted in: *D. Stahel, And the World held its Breath*, 199.

568   Ibid., 199.

569   For a detailed report on the Germans' initial experiences with Soviet artillery see, BA-MA RH 26-6/16, "*Erfahrungsbericht ueber russische Artillerie*," Artillerie Regiment 78, 29.8.1941, in: *Anlagenband 1 zum KTB Nr. 5 der 6. Inf.-Div., Ia.*

570   Ibid.

571   H. Geyer, *Das IX. Armeekorps im Ostfeldzug 1941*, 98-99.

572   "*Tagesmeldungen der Operations-Abteilung des GenStdH*," in: P. E. Schramm (Hg.), *Kriegstagebuch des OKW*, Bd. I, 547.

573   H. Grossmann, *Geschichte der 6. Infanterie-Division*, 54.

574   D. Stahel, *And the World held its Breath*, 203.

575   H. Geyer, *Das IX. Armeekorps im Ostfeldzug 1941*, 95, 97.

576   W. Murray & A. R. Millett, *A War to Be Won*, 128; T. Wray, *Standing Fast: German Defensive Doctrine on the Russian Front*, 47.

577   H. Grossmann, *Geschichte der 6. Infanterie-Division*, 53-54.

578   H. Haape, *Moscow Tram Stop*, 87-88. (Note: On 28 July 1941, 6 ID was actually some 75 kilometers west of Belyi. See, K.-J. Thies, *Der Ostfeldzug – Ein Lageatlas*, "Lage am 28.7.1941 abds., Heeresgruppe Mitte." The division, however, had indeed marched 1000 kilometers from the Russo-German frontier by this time.)

579   H. Grossmann, *Geschichte der 6. Infanterie-Division*, 55; K.-J. Thies, *Der Ostfeldzug – Ein Lageatlas*, "Lage am 29.7.1941 abds., Heeresgruppe Mitte."

580   The diary of doctor Hans Lierow states that 37 IR suffered six dead and 15 wounded from an aerial attack on 29 July. A post-war account notes that an infantry company in 58 IR sustained four dead and 18 wounded on this day, while also losing 15 horses and seeing most of its weapons and vehicles either destroyed or damaged. These figures, however, could not be confirmed. *Tagebuch* Lierow, 29.7.41; F. Belke, *Infanterist*, 35.

581   F. Belke, *Infanterist*, 35.

582   BA-MA RH 26-6/8, *KTB 6. Inf.-Div.*, 29.7.41; H. Grossmann, *Geschichte der 6. Infanterie-Division*, 55-56; "*Tagesmeldungen der Operations-Abteilung des GenStdH*," in: P. E. Schramm (Hg.), *Kriegstagebuch des OKW*, Bd. I, 547.

583   H. Haape, *Moscow Tram Stop*, 89-90.

584   BA-MA RH 26-6/8, *KTB 6. Inf.-Div.*, 30.7.41.

585   H. Grossmann, *Geschichte der 6. Infanterie-Division*, 56.

586   BA-MA RH 26-6/8, *KTB 6. Inf.-Div.*, 30.7.41; H. Grossmann, *Geschichte der 6. Infanterie-Division*, 56; E.-M. Rhein, *Das Infanterie-Regiment 18*, 75.

587   E.-M. Rhein, *Das Infanterie-Regiment 18*, 75.

588   H. Grossmann, *Geschichte der 6. Infanterie-Division*, 56-57.

589   H. Haape, *Moscow Tram Stop*, 94.

590   F. Belke, *Infanterist*, 35-36.

591   BA-MA RH 26-6/8, *KTB 6. Inf.-Div.*, 31.7.-1.8.41; H. Grossmann, *Geschichte der 6. Infanterie-Division*, 56-57; E.-M. Rhein, *Das Infanterie-Regiment 18*, 75; "*Der Marsch- und Einsatzweg der III./AR 6 vom 23.3.1941 bis 18.1.1942*," compiled in Summer 1942 by Lt. Kleine, III./AR 6.

592   E.-M. Rhein, *Das Infanterie-Regiment 18*, 75.

593   H. Haape, *Moscow Tram Stop*, 96.

594   Quoted in: E.-M. Rhein, *Das Infanterie-Regiment 18*, 75-76.

595   Ibid., 76.

596   BA-MA RH 26-6/8, *KTB 6. Inf.-Div.*, 2.8.41; E.-M. Rhein, *Das Infanterie-Regiment 18*, 76; H. Grossmann, *Geschichte der 6. Infanterie-Division*, 57; H.-J. Dismer, *Artillerie-Offizier im II. Weltkrieg*, 47; "*Der Marsch- und Einsatzweg der III./AR 6 vom 23.3.1941 bis 18.1.1942*," compiled in Summer 1942 by Lt. Kleine, III./ AR 6.

597   H. Grossmann, *Geschichte der 6. Infanterie-Division*, 58. Also participating in the fighting at Shishova on 2 August 1941 were elements of 6 ID's anti-tank battalion, combat engineer troops, and III./IR 18. BA-MA RH 26-6/8, *KTB 6. Inf.-Div.*, 2.8.41.

598   BA-MA RH 26-6/8, *KTB 6. Inf.-Div.*, 2.8.41. According to the war diary of 6 ID, the attacking enemy forces belonged to the Russian 50 and 53 Cavalry Divisions.

599   H. Grossmann, *Geschichte der 6. Infanterie-Division*, 58.

600   BA-MA RH 26-6/8, *KTB 6. Inf.-Div.*, 2.8.41.

601   H. Haape, *Moscow Tram Stop*, 97. *Rittmeister* Boeselager's brother, a lieutenant, was the only fatality suffered by the German mounted troop in its successful counterstroke. BA-MA RH 26-6/8, *KTB 6. Inf.-Div.*, 2.8.41.

602   H. Haape, *Moscow Tram Stop*, 97-98.

603   H. Haape, *Moscow Tram Stop*, 98; *Tagebuch* Haape, 3.8.41.

604   *Tagebuch* Haape, 3.8.41.

605   H. Haape, *Moscow Tram Stop*, 17.

606   *Tagebuch* Haape, 14.8.41.
607   General Auleb had borrowed the five tanks from the 19 Panzer Division of 57 Panzer Corps; three of the tanks were assigned to 18 Infantry Regiment, two to 58 Infantry Regiment. BA-MA RH 26-6/8, *KTB 6. Inf.-Div.*, 2.-3.8.41.
608   H. Grossmann, *Geschichte der 6. Infanterie-Division*, 58; "*Der Marsch- und Einsatzweg der III./AR 6 vom 23.3.1941 bis 18.1.1942*," compiled in Summer 1942 by Lt. Kleine, III./AR 6.
609   F. Belke, *Infanterist*, 36-37.
610   H. Grossmann, *Geschichte der 6. Infanterie-Division*, 58.
611   BA-MA RH 26-6/8, *KTB 6. Inf.-Div.*, 3.8.41.
612   F. Belke, *Infanterist*, 37.
613   H. Grossmann, *Geschichte der 6. Infanterie-Division*, 58; E.-M. Rhein, *Das Infanterie-Regiment 18*, 77.
614   In fact, by 11 August 1941, the Russians had gained air superiority across the entire front of German Ninth Army. "*Tagesmeldungen der Operations-Abteilung des GenStdH*," in: P. E. Schramm (Hg.), *Kriegstagebuch des OKW*, Bd. I, 565.
615   H. Grossmann, *Geschichte der 6. Infanterie-Division*, 60; "*Der Marsch- und Einsatzweg der III./AR 6 vom 23.3.1941 bis 18.1.1942*," compiled in Summer 1942 by Lt. Kleine, III./AR 6; H.-J. Dismer, *Artillerie-Offizier im II. Weltkrieg*, 48.
616   E.-M. Rhein, *Das Infanterie-Regiment 18*, 77.
617   E.-M. Rhein, *Das Infanterie-Regiment 18*, 77; "*Der Marsch- und Einsatzweg der III./AR 6 vom 23.3.1941 bis 18.1.1942*," compiled in Summer 1942 by Lt. Kleine, III./AR 6; H. Haape, *Moscow Tram Stop*, 91.
618   H. Haape, *Moscow Tram Stop*, 91.
619   *Tagebuch* Haape, 14.8.41.
620   E.-M. Rhein, *Das Infanterie-Regiment 18*, 79-80.
621   *Tagebuch* Lierow, 5.8.41.
622   H. Grossmann, *Geschichte der 6. Infanterie-Division*, 59.
623   W. Buddenbohm, *Das Leben des Soldaten Wilhelm Buddenbohm*, 59.
624   *Tagebuch* Lierow, 27.8.41.
625   BA-MA RH 26-6/8, *KTB 6. Inf.-Div.*, 27.8.41.
626   H. Grossmann, *Geschichte der 6. Infanterie-Division*, 62-63; Dr H. Voss, *Das Pionier-Bataillon 6 im Feldzug gegen Russland 1941-1945*, 116; F. Belke, *Infanterist*, 39.
627   BA-MA RH 26-6/8, *KTB 6. Inf.-Div.*, 27.8.41.
628   H. Grossmann, *Geschichte der 6. Infanterie-Division*, 63; F. Belke, *Infanterist*, 39.
629   F. Belke, *Infanterist*, 40.
630   Dr E. Bunke, *Der Osten blieb unser Schicksal*, 619. In his memoirs, Heinrich Haape claimed to have first heard the song on 1 August 1941: "'Lili Marlene' came into our lives that evening. The battalion officers were sitting comfortably together listening to the radio. It was a new set and we had tuned in to Belgrade. Our conversation ceased as [Lale Andersen] sang her nostalgic soldiers' tune." H. Haape, *Moscow Tram Stop*, 93.
631   *Tagebuch* Lierow, 27.8.41.
632   H. Grossmann, *Geschichte der 6. Infanterie-Division*, 63.
633   J. Lucas, *Das Reich*, 60.
634   R. Kirchubel, *Hitler's Panzer Armies*, 70; T. Wray, *Standing Fast: German Defensive Doctrine on the Russian Front*, 39.
635   H. Guderian, *Panzer Leader*, 181. Because stocks at the "advanced" supply depots were so low, German motorized convoys often had to travel back to the nearest railhead, which was fully 750 kilometers from the El'nia salient. *GSWW*, Vol. IV, 1126.
636   T. Wray, *Standing Fast: German Defensive Doctrine on the Russian Front*, 40.
637   B. Fugate & L. Dvoretsky, *Thunder on the Dnepr*, 170-71. Many older German officers compared their experiences at El'nia to those at Verdun in 1916.
638   D. Glantz, *Barbarossa Derailed*, 407. See also, H. Plocher, *The German Air Force Versus Russia, 1941*, 108-110.
639   By nightfall, 18 July, the advance detachment of 10 PD was just 10 kilometers west of El'nia. "*Tagesmeldungen der Operations-Abteilung des GenStdH*," in: P. E. Schramm (Hg.), *Kriegstagebuch des OKW*, Bd. I, 528; K.-J. Thies, *Der Ostfeldzug – Ein Lageatlas*, "Lage am 18.7.1941 abds., Heeresgruppe Mitte."
640   B. Fugate & L. Dvoretsky, *Thunder on the Dnepr*, 168-69; A. Schick, *Die Geschichte der 10. Panzer-Division*, 317-18.
641   B. Fugate & L. Dvoretsky, *Thunder on the Dnepr*, 168-69; A. Schick, *Die Geschichte der 10. Panzer-Division*, 318-19.
642   B. Fugate & L. Dvoretsky, *Thunder on the Dnepr*, 169; A. Schick, *Die Geschichte der 10. Panzer-Division*, 319-20.
643   A. Schick, *Die Geschichte der 10. Panzer-Division*, 320. On 22 July, the war diary of 10 PD noted that the "lack of aerial reconnaissance [the result of poor weather] had greatly hampered the attack on El'nia, as neither the enemy movements nor the enemy fortifications [*Befestigungen*] were discovered in a timely fashion." Quoted in A. Schick, 325.
644   "*Tagesmeldungen der Operations-Abteilung des GenStdH*," in: P. E. Schramm (Hg.), *Kriegstagebuch des OKW*, Bd. I, 532; A. Schick, *Die Geschichte der 10. Panzer-Division*, 320-22.
645   A. Schick, *Die Geschichte der 10. Panzer-Division*, 321.
646   Astoundingly, as of 2 August, the urgently needed oil (approximately 7000 liters) had still not arrived. Ibid., 334.

647   Ibid., 325.

648   A. Schick, *Die Geschichte der 10. Panzer-Division*, 323; K.-J. Thies, *Der Ostfeldzug – Ein Lageatlas*, "Lage am 21.7.1941 abds., Heeresgruppe Mitte."

649   B. Fugate & L. Dvoretsky, *Thunder on the Dnepr*, 168-69. As discussed in Section 10.2.1, Guderian had dispatched portions of *Das Reich* toward Dorogobuzh in an abortive attempt to help seal the Smolensk pocket; perhaps more importantly, at least from Guderian's perspective, capture of the town would have also supported a drive on Moscow.

650   B. Fugate & L. Dvoretsky, *Thunder on the Dnepr*, 170; K.-J. Thies, *Der Ostfeldzug – Ein Lageatlas*, "Lage am [20.-21.7.]1941 abds., Heeresgruppe Mitte."

651   BA-MA RH 21-2/928, *KTB Panzergruppe 2*, 22.7.41.

652   Ibid., 23.7.41.

653   Ibid., 24.7.41.

654   The final general situation report of the day, providing the latest status updates of all subordinated army and panzer corps, was normally logged into the war diary of Guderian's 2 Panzer Group between 2200 and 2400 hours.

655   BA-MA RH 21-2/928, *KTB Panzergruppe 2*, 25.7.41.

656   Ibid., 26.7.41. All entries from "1730 hours" onward reflect the 46 Panzer Corps situation report for that time only (1730 hours).

657   Ibid., 27.7.41.

658   Ibid., 29.7.41. The reader will recall that, at this time, Guderian's panzer group had been temporarily redesignated as *Armeegruppe* Guderian.

659   Ibid., 30.7.41.

660   Ibid., 31.7.41.

661   A. Schick, *Die Geschichte der 10. Panzer-Division*, 333-38; K.-J. Thies, *Der Ostfeldzug – Ein Lageatlas*, "Lage am 1.8.1941 abds., Heeresgruppe Mitte."

662   A. Schick, *Die Geschichte der 10. Panzer-Division*, 334; BA-MA 21-2/928, *KTB Panzergruppe 2*, 2.8.41. (Note: On 2 August 1941, Wolfgang Fischer, hitherto commander of the division's 10 Rifle Brigade, replaced Schaal as commander of 10 PD.)

663   D. M. Glantz, *Barbarossa Derailed*, Vol. I, 535.

664   Ibid., 535.

665   D. Stahel, *And the World held its Breath*, 223.

666   Ibid., 223.

667   BA-MA RH 21-2/928, *KTB Panzergruppe 2*, 5.8.41.

668   D. Stahel, *And the World held its Breath*, 223.

669   T. Wray, *Standing Fast: German Defensive Doctrine on the Russian Front*, 40.

670   H. Guderian, *Panzer Leader*, 189.

671   K.-J. Thies, *Der Ostfeldzug – Ein Lageatlas*, "Lage am 8.8.1941 abds., Heeresgruppe Mitte." On the morning of 6 August, Guderian's headquarters issued *Gruppenbefehl No. 10*, assigning 20 Army Corps its sectors within the salient. BA-MA RH 21-2/928, *Panzergruppe 2*, 6.8.41.

672   H. Plocher, *The German Air Force Versus Russia, 1941*, 116; *GSWW*, Vol. IV, 774-75. According to Plocher, a former *Luftwaffe* general, "in the severe fighting in the El'nia salient, the batteries of the I Flak Corps were the strong backbone of the defense of all the ground forces there for more than four long weeks."

673   BA-MA MSg 1/1147: *Tagebuch* Lemelsen, 10.8.41.

674   D. M. Glantz, *Barbarossa Derailed*, Vol. I, 539-42; K.-J. Thies, *Der Ostfeldzug – Ein Lageatlas*, "Lage am 19.8.1941 abds., Heeresgruppe Mitte;" O. Weidinger, *Das Reich III*, 7.

675   A. Schick, *Die Geschichte der 10. Panzer-Division*, 343-45; K.-J. Thies, *Der Ostfeldzug – Ein Lageatlas*, "Lage am 23.8.1941 abds., Heeresgruppe Mitte."

676   A. Schick, *Die Geschichte der 10. Panzer-Division*, 342-43.

677   K. Gerbet (ed.), *GFM Fedor von Bock, The War Diary*, 281. As noted in the war diary of Guderian's panzer group, as long as artillery shells remained in such short supply, the *Stukas* of Kesselring's 2 Air Fleet functioned as flying artillery for both 20 Army Corps and 46 Panzer Corps. BA-MA RH 21-2/928, *Panzergruppe 2*, 13.8.41.

678   BA-MA RH 21-2/928, *Panzergruppe 2*, 13.8.41.

679   D. Stahel, *And the World held its Breath*, 261.

680   D. Stahel, *And the World held its Breath*, 261; BA-MA RH 21-2/928, *Panzergruppe 2*, 14.8.41.

681   K. Gerbet (ed.), *GFM Fedor von Bock, The War Diary*, 283.

682   Ibid., 282.

683   C. Burdick & H.-A. Jacobsen (eds.), *The Halder Diary 1939-1942*, 508. On 14 August, Halder recorded in his diary: "I warned him [Greiffenberg] against abandoning El'nia. No matter how badly off our troops are, it is worse even for the enemy."

684   H. Guderian, *Panzer Leader*, 195. "Up to this point," recalled Guderian, "all the steps taken by the Panzer Group had been based on the belief that both the Army Group and the OKH regarded the operations toward Moscow as the decisive move. Despite the [Borisov] conference of 4 August, I had not given up hope that Hitler would agree with this point of view which – to me at least – seemed the natural and obvious one. On 11 August I was disillusioned on this score. My plan of attack, with point of main effort through Roslavl toward Viaz'ma, was turned down by the OKH and described as 'unsatisfactory.'" With his plan rejected, Guderian, by 15 August, had concluded that the salient at El'nia no longer had any purpose,

and had simply become "a continual source of casualties." Yet here, too, Guderian was overruled. Ibid., 194-95.

685 K. Gerbet (ed.), *GFM Fedor von Bock, The War Diary*, 281-82; T. Wray, *Standing Fast: German Defensive Doctrine on the Russian Front*, 40; H. Plocher, *The German Air Force Versus Russia, 1941*, 107-11. In Plocher's view, Goering's decision was the proper one: "A concentrated commitment of the 2 Air Corps in the El'nia salient would at best have been able to achieve only a tactical defensive victory on a relatively small sector of the front ... In contrast, the concentrated employment of *Luftwaffe* forces in front of the Second Army and the 2 Panzer Group in and east of the Gomel area enabled the right wing of Army Group Center, which was behind the others, to advance and thereby eliminated the deep Soviet wedge between Army Groups South and Center."

686 Most likely, this is a reference to El'nia, which the Germans normally spelled "*Jelnja.*" "Hans-Otto" may have simply been unaware of the proper spelling.

687 *Feldpostbrief*, "*Hans-Otto,*" 15.8.41.

CHAPTER 11

Barbarossa Denied – The Collapse
of the Eastern Blitzkrieg

(*August – December 1941*)

"*He who comes to Russia with a sword, shall die by the sword.*" (Alexander Nevsky, 13th Century)

"*Few wars are rooted in dispassionate analysis. Self-delusion sparks most such catastrophies.*" (Lt.-Col. Ralph Peters, U.S. Army, retired)[1]

"*[Hitler's] armies in Russia enjoyed swift and stunning success against the ill-prepared Russian troops deployed on the frontier … Then the offensive stalled out, partly as a result of stout Soviet resistance but mainly due to the inherent limitations of the Wehrmacht.*" (Max Boot)[2]

"*To paraphrase Clausewitz' comments on Napoleon's critics, a plan which succeeds is bold and one which fails is reckless … [Hitler] clearly hoped that the destruction of the Red Army in western Russia would lead to the collapse of Stalin's regime. His major miscalculation – but one which seemed to be supported by the upheavals in Russia in the mid-1930s – was, like Napoleon's, political.*" (Theodor Ropp)[3]

"*We're slowly going crazy here. Oh, you just cannot imagine (in fact, nobody who was not or is not here can imagine) the conditions prevailing here. You can't get anything here. And then everything's so filthy. Yes, that's what it's like here.*" ("Hans Olte," Corps Signal Battalion 52, 12 Army Corps, 9 September 1941)[4]

"*This war is dreadful, but we will be victorious, even though the road is long and hard! – Not that, among all the difficult things we must experience, the thought ever arises: why are we at war with Russia?! – The war with R. had to come and we must be grateful that it has now come; it is the only way to success! This dreadful war is the fate of our Volk!*" (Heinrich Haape, 6 ID, 11 September 1941)[5]

11.1: *Armeegruppe* Guderian & Second Army – Krichev & Gomel

As the bloody war of attrition raged across the El'nia salient, and across the entire eastern front of Field Marshal von Bock's Army Group Center, Guderian's army group (*Armeegruppe* Guderian) continued the "southward tilt" it had begun during the first days of August 1941 with its victory at Roslavl (Section 10.2.1). While the destruction of Group Kachalov (28 Army) at Roslavl had eased the pressure on Guderian's southern flank, it had not solved all of the panzer general's problems; to have truly open flanks for the planned drive on Moscow, he would first have to eliminate the Soviet concentration around Krichev, southwest of Roslavl, where strong forces of the new Soviet Central Front were firmly dug in.[6]

After briefly resting the three mobile divisions of Geyr's 24 Panzer Corps (3 PD, 4 PD, 10 ID (mot.)), Guderian was ready to strike by the end of the first week in August. In conjunction with the assault by *Armeegruppe* Guderian, Weichs' Second Army – manning positions west of the Dnepr River opposite and south of Rogachev, then eastward to the Sozh, from there northeastward along the Sozh to Krichev – was to conduct an even larger offensive to capture Gomel. In accomplishing these objectives, Guderian and Weichs would satisfy one of the primary requirements of Hitler's Directive No. 34 (30 July 1941) by destroying the large enemy forces threatening the right wing of Bock's army group. The combined offensive would also help to move Bock's heavily refused right wing forward, closing the growing gap to the left wing of Rundstedt's Army Group South.[7]

Despite delays due to muddy roads, which complicated movement into their assembly areas, Model's 3 Panzer and Langermann's 4 Panzer Division (24 Panzer Corps) began their assault southward from positions east of Krichev on the morning of 9 August, while infantry of Fahrmbacher's 7 Army Corps protected the panzer corps' left flank. Despite tough enemy opposition (including counterattacks), and "particularly poor road conditions"[8] caused by bad weather, the tanks and panzer grenadiers of 3 Panzer Division wheeled rapidly westward and, the next day (10 August), seized the town of Klimovichi, encircling several divisions of Lt.-Gen. K. D. Golubev's 13 Army in a pocket southeast of Krichev.[9]

During the next 48-72 hours, Model's panzer division, now supported by 7 Infantry Division[10] and elements of 10 Motorized Division, carved up the small pocket; southeast of Krichev, 4 Panzer Division erected a defensive screen above the town of Kommunary to thwart any attempts by the Russians to rescue their trapped divisions. By 13 August the battle was over: Despite repeated breakout attempts, the encircled forces of Golubev's 13 Army were eliminated; 16,000 *Rotarmisten* marched into captivity, while the Germans also captured or destroyed 76 guns, 15 tanks, and one armored train (shot up by tanks of 4 Panzer Division).[11]

The modest victory also took a palpable toll on the attacking forces of Geyr's panzer corps. On 11 August, 4 Panzer Division had reported it was down to 64 available tanks, of which only 25 were Pz IIIs and eight Pz IVs.[12] Only days later, on the evening of 14 August, the panzer division's war diarist observed that the most recent fighting had been "very costly, also in materiel;" moreover, the men were "tired," the division "increasingly more worn out." The Russian tanks, he acknowledged, "especially the <u>heavy</u> ones, are good."[13]

Meanwhile, Weichs' Second Army had launched its drive on Gomel; to support the army's advance, on 15 August OKH ordered Guderian to continue to push southward with 24 Panzer Corps to slip in behind the Soviet 21 Army defending the city. At this time, the panzer forces of Geyr's corps, milling about in the area of Klimovichi and Kommunary, were roughly midway between Roslavl and Gomel, and some 60 kilometers north of Unecha, a key railroad junction astride the vital Gomel – Briansk – Moscow railroad line.[14]

Events continued to unfold rapidly. The next day (16 August), the advance detachment of Model's 3 Panzer Division seized the road junction at Mglin, 30 kilometers north of Unecha; on 17 August, Model's splendid tankers and grenadiers, meeting only weak opposition, captured Unecha and cut the key railroad line. By now, Guderian had committed Lemelsen's 47 Panzer Corps to the operation, dispatching its 29 Motorized Division toward Briansk to screen his army group's flank along the Desna River, and its 17 Panzer Division to strengthen the advance of 3 Panzer Division southward from Unecha; by nightfall, 17 August, lead elements of Ritter von Thoma's 17 Panzer Division were approaching Pochep, 50 kilometers east of Unecha. Continuing their southward plunge, by 21 August the two panzer corps had reached the line (running east-west) Pochep (17 PD) – Starodub (3 PD) – Klintsy (10 ID (mot.)) – Surazh (10 ID (mot.)).[15] In this manner, Guderian's swift advance had "carved a 115-kilometer-wide and 120-kilometer-deep salient south of the Sozh River between Eremenko's Briansk Front and Efremov's Central Front and threatened the latter with isolation and encirclement in the Gomel region."[16]

In his diary on 22 August, General Lemelsen, no doubt deeply gratified by the fine showing of his men, put down his thoughts on the superiority of the German soldier vis-à-vis his gritty Russian opponent:

> In general, the superiority of the German soldier over the Soviet forces is becoming increasingly noticeable, especially since the divisions now appearing are mostly newly activated units of poorly trained soldiers who have little combat value; they fight only out of fear of their commissars.

> From the division's command post I drove in my vehicle through the most amazing dust to Pochep and Russaka to the church tower there, which provided a view deep into enemy territory. The church was a gruesome sight, utterly ravaged and abused, and in it, as in Smolensk, an anti-Christian museum with the nastiest of pictures.[17]

Farther west, Weichs' Second Army – its offensive having been repeatedly postponed due to a lack of forces, bad weather, muddy roads, a shortage of artillery ammunition, and, perhaps, by a "lack of nerve"[18] – had finally gotten underway on 12 August. From the perspective of Bock, an operation to seize Gomel had become a "virtual necessity" from the moment Soviet 21 Army had struck his army group's right wing in mid-July, recapturing Shlobin and Rogachev along the Dnepr River and briefly threatening Bobruisk with a cavalry corps. Hence, when Guderian commenced his advance south on 8 August, Bock seized the opportunity to eliminate, once and for all, Red Army forces between the Sozh and Dnepr Rivers by conducting an ambitious envelopment maneuver against Gomel – Guderian pressing in from the northeast and Weichs from the northwest and west.[19]

Weichs' assault began shortly after dawn (12 August), when his left wing (12 and 13 Army Corps) – supported by a powerful preparatory artillery barrage, *Stukas* and bomber units – advanced southward between the Sozh and Dnepr Rivers, making good progress on this first day. The next day (13 August) Second Army's right wing, Gotthard Heinrici's 43 Army Corps, joined the assault, forging several bridgeheads on the eastern bank of the Dnepr, northwest of Gomel; with the Soviet defenders managing only "local resistance" (*oertlichen Widerstand*), by nightfall Weichs' attacking army corps had broken through along the entire enemy front. The success of the attackers, however, was dampened by the death of Brig.-Gen. Kurt Kalmukoff, Commander, 31 Infantry Division (12 Army Corps); driving out to visit his regiments, his vehicle struck a Russian mine, instantly killing the general and his adjutant.[20]

By 14 August, Weichs' infantry had surrounded the bulk of Lt.-Gen. V. M. Gordov's 21 Army's 63 and 67 Rifle Corps (a total of at least six rifle divisions) in a *Kessel* on the eastern bank of the Dnepr southeast of Rogachev. The Soviets sought to breakout to the south and southeast, toward Gomel, compelling Weichs to commit strong forces to contain the pocket; by 17/18 August, the encircled Russian units, hammered by repeated German blows along their perimeter, had either been destroyed or surrendered, with only small groups of soldiers making their escape. During the fighting, the commander of Soviet 63 Rifle Corps, Maj.-Gen. L.G. Petrovsky, perished outside the village of Skepnia. In recognition of his "gallant defense," the Germans buried their brave adversary with full military honors, erecting "a cross over his grave with an inscription attesting to his bravery" – an act of chivalry seldom seen in the east.[21]

With the elimination of the pocket, Weichs' Second Army had cleared all enemy forces from between the Sozh and Dnepr Rivers, satisfying (as noted above) a key objective of Field Marshal von Bock. In a letter to his family on 18 August, General Heinrici, whose 43

Army Corps had played a large part in the victory, outlined the results of the battle with satisfaction; the parallels to Lemelsen's diary entry cited above, in terms of an appraisal of the Russian forces, are clearly evident, while Heinrici's observations on the peculiar characteristics of the eastern front – as well as the death of the commander of Soviet 63 Rifle Corps – are also of interest:

> [The defeat near Gomel] is a very heavy blow for the Russian, who is now fighting only with pieced-together units, possesses barely any cohesive divisions, and who had to abandon an as yet unknown amount of artillery and vehicles in the forests. Operationally, this means the collapse of the southern half of his central front and is causing far-reaching consequences. We can, therefore, look back on the past 10-12 days with satisfaction.
>
> For me personally, they were not easy. We had to overcome very critical situations and sometimes the strain was ratcheted up to the maximum. It is also not particularly pleasant to drive through the countryside alone time and again, with only a paltry escort, through kilometer-long forests, always with the possibility of running into Russians. For the fronts are so far stretched, and so permeable, that friend and foe are often mixed up together.
>
> At a critical point 8 days ago, I personally took over the command of a battalion, where everything was chaos, and two days ago the Russian used 2 heavy batteries to shoot up our command post to such an extent that it's a marvel we only suffered 7 wounded. We were all given plenty to contend with, and we can only be grateful that everything has gone well so far. The possibility that it could have gone differently lay before us often enough …
>
> My first adversary, the Russian commanding general of 66 [Rifle] Corps, was sent before a military tribunal at the beginning of August, as we learned from a captured enemy order. The [commanding general] of 63 [Rifle] Corps was shot along with both his commissars by our people during a large-scale breakout attempt, when they refused to give themselves up.
>
> There's a severe crisis looming over there. The collapse is beginning to gather pace.[22]

Supported by the *Stukas* and bombers of 2 Air Corps, Second Army now struck out rapidly for Gomel; with Group Behlendorff and Schroth's 12 Army Corps protecting the army's left flank, infantry of Felber's 13 Army Corps quickly reached the northern outskirts of Gomel. In a desperate, yet futile, attempt to defend the city, Gordov threw workers' battalions – according to Bock, armed with little more than shotguns – into the house fighting; at 1500 hours, 19 August, Second Army reported the capture of the city.[23]

The loss of Gomel forced the surviving elements of Soviet 21 Army to withdraw toward the east and southeast; as they did, they were intercepted by the tanks and panzer grenadiers of Geyr's 24 and Lemelsen's 47 Panzer Corps, which had established strong blocking positions in two parallel north-south lines – the first extending from Surazh to Klintsy (10 ID (Mot.)); the second, further east, running from Mglin to Starodub (3 and 4 PD, elements of 17 PD).[24]

With the seizure of Gomel, the Germans could look back with satisfaction on the results of the previous two weeks' fighting. From 9-21 August, the combined victories at Krichev and Gomel had brought in 78,000 Russian prisoners, and resulted in the capture or destruction of 144 tanks, 700 guns, 38 aircraft, and two armored trains.[25] In the process, Soviet 13 and 21 Armies – and, with them, Soviet Central Front – had been routed and largely destroyed. On 20 August, Weichs issued a resounding order of the day from his headquarters:

Soldiers of the Second Army!

The battle in the Rogachev – Gomel region is ended.

Over several days of dogged struggle, the Russian 21 Army was successfully encircled and almost entirely destroyed. In an uninterrupted attack over several days, [Second Army] breached the enemy front and pursued the remnants of his divisions to the south.

Despite many hardships, commanders and troops once again displayed a combat spirit capable of breaking any resistance. Thanks to [your] tenacious will to resist, numerous enemy attempts to break through were repelled both day and night.

More than 50,000 prisoners, 400 guns, and an immeasurable amount of war material are the proud result of this *Kesselschlacht*, not to mention the incredibly high, bloody losses for the enemy …

My thanks and my special appreciation go to the commanders and troops.

My thoughts are with all those *Kameraden* who fell before the enemy for this decisive victory.

I am proud in the knowledge of the heroic devotion of every soldier to their Fuehrer and Fatherland.

signed Frhr. v. Weichs.[26]

The consequences of the capture of Gomel were indeed "far reaching:" Along with eliminating the persistent threat to Army Group Center's southern flank, it "helped precipitate the collapse of the entire Soviet defensive system west of the Dnepr and Desna Rivers."[27] For example, the loss of Gomel was at least partly responsible for major withdrawals conducted by Col.-Gen. Kirponos' Southwestern Front in the Ukraine, particularly of the front's 5 Army from its positions west of the Dnepr around Korosten, where its obstinate resistance had delayed the advance of Army Group South on Kiev for several weeks. As a result, Kleist's 1 Panzer Group was able to cross the Dnepr at several points in late August.[28]

As for Bock, he was ebullient over his recent successes, and felt that conditions for a resumption of the advance on Moscow were now falling into place. On 19 August, the field marshal recorded his thoughts in his diary: "In the evening I once again made Weichs aware that no time must be lost! For now it might come to pass that, after Second Army's victory, and after the success of the planned attack on Velikie Luki on Ninth Army's northern wing, which is imminent, the entire army group can attack to the east!"[29]

Less enthusiastic was General Heinrici, who despite his optimistic assessment of recent battles in his letter of 18 August, now struck a more somber tone in a letter to his wife five days later (23 August):

Despite all the defeats, the Russian has shown extraordinary resilience. Yesterday, I read the statement of a captured Russian army commander, who claimed that they would continue fighting, even if Moscow were lost. I am inclined to think that, too. A change will only come if the system in Russia is brought to collapse from within. Whether the conditions for that have already been created seems doubtful to me …

Now we have been deployed in another sector of our army, also with other divisions. We're now nearly 200 km deeper inside Russia. The towns are all *completely* burned out. We camp – you can't say we live – in desolate villages. Today I'm residing in a school classroom, because the schools are usually still the cleanest. All the houses are in a squalid state. According to the inhabitants, the idea is to make everything as ugly and impoverished as possible, so as not to be persecuted as people of property …

The war here is proving very costly for us. Was it really necessary?[30]

11.2: 3 Panzer Group Recaptures Velikie Luki

The Germans' second attempt to take and hold the strategically important town of Velikie Luki began on 22 August 1941; once again, the attack was spearheaded by Kuntzen's 57 Panzer Corps – the only mobile corps Hoth had available following the sudden and unexpected transfer of Schmidt's 39 Panzer Corps to Field Marshal von Leeb's Army Group North. On 14 August, Leeb had reported a dangerous concentration of Red Army forces on his southern flank – a major Soviet offensive south of Staraia Russa had penetrated the overextended front of 10 Army Corps – which threatened to further delay the encirclement of Leningrad. The development "so alarmed Hitler"[31] that he immediately intervened, ordering the transfer of significant mobile units (one panzer and two motorized divisions) from Army Group Center to Army Group North. In response, on 16 August, Schmidt's 39 Panzer Corps (12 PD, 18 ID (mot.) and 20 ID (mot.)) began to move north from its rest areas between Smolensk and Dukhovshchina, arriving in the area of Leeb's army group by 24 August.[32]

Hitler's decision to remove an entire panzer corps from Army Group Center was met with dismay and anger by both Halder at OKH and Bock, coming as it did at a time when both men were hoping to assemble as much strength as possible for a resumption of the advance on Moscow. In his diary, Halder vented bitterly about disproportionate reactions "to all pinpricks" which "frustrates any planning on an operational scale and prevents concentration of our forces."[33] When the order arrived at Bock's headquarters, informing the field marshal that he would have to relinquish three of his precious mobile divisions, despite the burgeoning pressures along his sprawling 700 kilometer front, he was "stirred to a frantic outburst of dismay."[34] In a telephone call with Halder, Bock sharply attacked the decision, insisting that the reassignment of the three divisions – which, parenthetically, had yet to complete their refitting – would probably so weaken his army group as to render major offensive action impossible.[35] As for Halder, he, too, was reduced to despair: All that Army Group Center had "accomplished to date," he noted mordantly in his journal, "is wasted;"[36] and, like Bock, he feared that the army group was "probably now unalterably stalled."[37]

"The implications of Bock and Halder's conclusions," avers historian David Stahel, "spelled unmitigated disaster for German operations in the east.

> By mid-August 1941, it had already become exceedingly difficult to move the front forward and yet it was also impossible to maintain a sustainable, long term defense. German resources were simply overtaxed and grossly inadequate for their assigned tasks, especially with more Soviet offensives being planned … The rigors of long marches and heavy fighting had exhausted the Army, leaving too many units badly worn-out, insufficiently supplied and sprawled out over the vast expanse of the Soviet hinterland. Added to this was the wayward strategic direction of the campaign that had become so haphazard that it was now being improvised on a day to day basis, without any semblance of inter-command agreement or joint long term objectives.[38]

It is intriguing to note that, prior to Schmidt's panzer corps leaving the sector of Army Group Center, it was stripped of all its *Korpstruppen* (corps artillery, combat engineers, etc.) – an action which, quite naturally, incensed Schmidt, who appealed to Colonel

Schmundt, Hitler's chief *Wehrmacht* adjutant, that these vital units be returned at once to his command.[39] One can only wonder if the confiscation of these units signified an act of defiance by either Halder or Bock (or both). Regardless, both men clearly had more urgent matters at hand, such as planning and executing a new offensive on the army group's northern wing on Hitler's explicit orders.

For Hitler, the Soviet strongholds at Velikie Luki and Toropets, and the large Soviet groupings there, posed a very real threat to the left flank of Hoth's 3 Panzer Group and of Strauss' Ninth Army (since 5 August temporarily commanded by Hoth, as Strauss had fallen ill).[40] In a supplement to Directive No. 34, on 12 August 1941, he ordered that the enemy on the northern flank of Army Group Center "must be defeated as soon as possible by the employment of mobile forces west of Toropets."[41] After this had been accomplished, the left wing of the army group was to be pushed "as far northward as is necessary" to relieve the pressure on the right flank of Army Group North and enable Leeb to shift additional infantry divisions to the drive on Leningrad (still a major priority of Hitler's).[42]

Like his "Fuehrer," Bock was also worried by the precarious situation on his army group's extreme left flank; moreover, both Bock and Halder ultimately supported Hitler's decision to launch an attack through Velikie Luki to Toropets with *schnelle Truppen* of 3 Panzer Group,[43] if for rather different reasons. Simply put, both men realized that such an offensive, by concentrating powerful forces on the left wing of Army Group Center, would support a resumption of a general eastward advance by the army group; indeed, an OKH memorandum of 18 August, laying out the General Staff's plans for the attack toward Moscow, envisaged a large group of forces beginning an ambitious encircling maneuver from the area about Toropets.[44]

In any event, efforts to implement Hitler's supplement to Directive 34 proceeded rapidly. By 20 August 1941, Bock had regrouped 19 and 20 Panzer Divisions (57 Panzer Corps) from their rest areas behind the front of Ninth Army (west of Belyi) into assembly areas northeast of Usviaty. There, the two panzer divisions were combined with several infantry divisions to form a special composite group under 40 Panzer Corps headquarters, commanded by General Georg Stumme.[45] The plan of attack was for 19 and 20 Panzer Divisions – protected on the left by Ninth Army's 23 Army Corps and supported by the infantry divisions of the composite group – to envelop the town of Velikie Luki from the east; encircle and destroy Ershakov's 22 Army; and, finally, push Maslennikov's 29 Army eastward while securing the region around Toropets. "If successful, in addition to clearing Soviet forces from Army Group Center's left flank, the offensive would align the advance in the north with the front lines of Army Group Center's forces struggling east of Smolensk."[46]

Although the attack on Velikie Luki was scheduled to start on the morning of 21 August, inclement weather, which softened roadways and made *Luftwaffe* support questionable, resulted in a postponement of 24 hours.[47] At 0430 hours the next day (22 August), the German artillery opened fire; 10 minutes later, the fearsome *Nebelwerfer* rocket launchers joined the deadly cacophony, followed by screaming *Stuka* dive bombers and sleek Bf 109 fighters. The German attack caught the Russians by complete surprise, and came just after their 22 Army had begun a major assault of its own; deployed for attack and not for defense, the Soviets were ill-prepared to resist the steel hurricane which now descended upon them.[48]

As the lead divisions of Ershakov's 62 and 29 Rifle Corps attempted to attack southward from southeast of Velikie Luki, they ran straight into multiple German tank wedges rumbling northward supported by *Stukas* bombing and strafing out front of the advancing panzers. Both 19 and 20 Panzer Divisions, supported by infantry, made rapid progress; within hours, their blitzkrieg in miniature had "paralyzed and shattered" 22 Army's main assault groups. As darkness fell, 22 Army "was in a state of shock," the powerful German blows having also disrupted communications between Ershakov's main command post and his army's three rifle corps, while severing the railroad line from Velikie Luki to Rzhev.[49]

Building on their success, on 23 August, Knobelsdorff's 19 and Stumpff's 20 Panzer Divisions raced toward Velikie Luki from the east, while 86 and 253 Infantry Divisions (23 Army Corps) began to invest the town from the south and west; by nightfall, the panzer spearheads were less than 10 kilometers from Velikie Luki and a pocket had been formed around Soviet forces southeast of the town. Further to the east, Stumme's 110, 102 and 256 Infantry Divisions smashed remnants of Soviet 62 Rifle Corps and moved slowly eastward behind the front of Maslennikov's 29 Army and toward Toropets, an advance detachment pushing to within 20 kilometers of the city.[50]

Throughout 24 August, the tanks, panzer grenadiers and infantry of *Gruppe Stumme* continued to compress the pocket from the east, while 23 Army Corps did the same from the west; at the same time, the eastern wing of the attacking German forces pushed on toward Toropets. The trapped Soviet forces, fortified with alcohol and bellowing "Urrah," launched repeated attempts to break through the Germans' iron ring, albeit with little success. The grenadiers of 59 Rifle Regiment (20 PD), dug in on Hill 166, repulsed numerous breakout attempts; breaches in the German line were quickly patched up by counterattacks. In a noteworthy coup, the railroad bridge across the Lovat, southwest of Velikie Luki, was seized intact. Speaking by telephone with *Oberst* Weckmann, Ninth Army chief of staff, Bock was informed that "the battle is proceeding like a map exercise!"[51]

For the *Landser* of 19 Panzer Division, the night of 24/25 August was one to remember; in fact, it would enter divisional lore as the "night of the long knives" (*Nacht der langen Messer*)[52] – a night of often confusing and chaotic fighting as the Russians persevered in their frenzied breakout attempts. An artillerist with the panzer division recalled the deadly tumult in a brief yet graphic report:

> All at once, from up ahead, cries of "Urrah" from drunken throats were heard, grimly resounding through the night. A radio link between the forward observer and the gun position could not be established, because the old two-part "*Berta*" radio devices were disrupted at night by ultraviolet rays. The gunners waited in vain for a signal to unleash their barrage fire. Very signal lights went up and threw ghostly silhouettes! Despite this, even though the forward observers could not have requested it, the batteries let off barrage fire, because they had to assume that the attacking Russians would be located somewhere in the barrage fire areas.
>
> Everyone had the impression that a huge melee at close quarters was raging up ahead, but could not make out anything precise. The cries of "Urrah" eventually ended.[53]

Military historian Rolf Hinze, who fought with 19 Panzer's artillery regiment (19 AR) on the eastern front, offered his own account of the night of 24/25 August, which included the following passages:

> The hours until that long-awaited dawn were rather eerie for the battery gun crews, because nobody knew where the boundary lay between friend and foe. From time to time a flare went up, making silhouettes of forms visible, yet not identifiable. Groups of *Rotarmisten* had penetrated between the positions or they ducked into depressions in the ground. Only when the self-propelled Flak cleared out the remaining enemy troops at dawn was a clear picture of the enemy established again.
>
> It could not be determined just how many members of the Soviet 22 Army were able to get through. Apparently, only a few, after making it past the line of gun positions, had been able to march further in a northeasterly direction, perhaps

because of a lack of orientation and leadership. Some of them were subsequently caught by tank fire and decimated.

The riflemen moved into their old positions at dawn and were able to improve them somewhat ... In the morning light of 25 [August] one could see the signs of the night before on the battlefield. Dead and wounded lay scattered about the battlefield ahead of the foremost positions and between these and the artillery positions, some lying on top of one another, women and youths among them. The wounded and dead had to be recovered, the latter buried ... After the experiences of the previous night, the combat zone was laid out in greater depth, with reserve forces.[54]

During the ensuing 36-48 hours, German artillery and 2 Air Corps *Stukas* continued to pulverize elements of Ershakov's 22 Army as they sought to escape from the shrinking pocket. Meanwhile, the task of completing liquidation of the cauldron fell to the infantry divisions of 23 Army Corps, while the tanks and panzer grenadiers of 19 and 20 Panzer Divisions occupied blocking positions immediately to the east and southeast of Velikie Luki.[55]

By 26 August, 253 Infantry Division (23 Army Corps) had captured Velikie Luki from the west[56] and resistance in the pocket had flickered out. A *Wehrmachtbericht* the next day proclaimed the results of the operation: "After several days of difficult battles the mass of the Soviet 22 Army was encircled and destroyed east of Velikie Luki. More than 30,000 prisoners were taken and 400 guns captured. That the losses of the enemy were unusually high is confirmed by the identification of more than 40,000 dead."[57] The war diarist of Ninth Army exulted that the results "greatly surpass our expectations ... One can indeed declare without exaggeration, that this victory is unique [*einzigartig*] in both the dispatch with which it occurred and in its completeness." Contributing decisively to the outcome was the "immortal spirit of attack [*unsterbliche Angriffsgeist*] of the German soldier."[58]

A crushing defeat had indeed been inflicted on Soviet 22 Army, ripping a gaping hole in the right wing of the Red Army's Western Front. "Hitler's successful gambit with Group Stumme," argues David Glantz, "seriously undermined the pervasive 'air of unrequited optimism' in Moscow and in the Western Front's headquarters as well. At the same time, it also materially damaged some aspects of Stalin's and Timoshenko's 'grandiose plans.' In addition to surprising both Soviet leaders, it forced them to alter their planned counteroffensive significantly just as the climax of the battle for Smolensk was approaching."[59] Having completed its mission, Group Stumme was disbanded on 26 August.[60] Three days later (29 August), Germans troops battled their way into Toropets.[61]

In his diary on 26 August, Field Marshal von Bock also recorded the results of the successful cauldron battle of Velikie Luki, noting as well that, since the start of the Russian campaign, "the numbers for my army group ... have thus risen to more than 800,000 prisoners, 6870 tanks, about 6500 guns and 774 aircraft!"[62] Yet while the German victory was significant, Bock was well aware that such limited offensives – be they at Velikie Luki, Krichev or Gomel – were not going to achieve his objective of destroying the bulk Red Army forces before him, along the Smolensk – Moscow axis. Furthermore, they did not succeed in adequately reducing Soviet pressure along his army group's enormous front, for within days Bock was complaining to Halder that, if the Russians continued their assaults, the defensive front of Ninth Army would, "in the long run," surely fail to hold.[63]

On 24 August 1941, as the Velikie Luki operation approached its climax, Bock had glumly observed: "This is the seventh or eight time in this campaign that the army group has succeeded in encircling the enemy. But I'm not really happy about it, because the objective to which I devoted all my thoughts, the destruction of the main strength of the enemy army, has been dropped."[64] What had been "dropped" were any and all plans of the

OKH and Bock's Army Group Center for an attack on Moscow, for after weeks of apparent indecision, Hitler had finally rendered his verdict on the future course of the *Ostheer's* operations.

11.3: Strategic "Crisis" Resolved – Hitler Triumphs over his Generals

As the dispute between Hitler and his generals over strategy for the eastern campaign dragged on deeper into August 1941, Halder redoubled his efforts to win the "Fuehrer's" support for a swift resumption of the advance of Army Group Center on Moscow. Once again, he could count on a key ally in General Alfred Jodl, Chief, OKW Operations Staff (WFSt). Simply put, the arguments put forth to Hitler by his generals[65] were essentially as follows: a.) the bulk of the Red Army was concentrated around Moscow in anticipation of the impending German thrust; b.) the destruction of these forces and capture of the Soviet capital – the political center of the Soviet Union, as well as its key railroad hub and a major armaments center – would decisively influence the outcome of the campaign; and c.) Army Groups North and South were strong enough to secure their objectives on their own, without help from Army Group Center (meaning that Bock could assemble every man, gun and tank he could lay hands on for the decisive thrust). In marshalling their arguments, both Halder and Jodl sought to tailor them to Hitler's "assumed mental state;" for example, they agreed to soft pedal the significance of the strong forces of Soviet Southwestern Front concentrated north of Kiev (off the southern flank of Army Group Center).[66]

Yet while the generals schemed to influence Hitler's thinking by plying him with "subtly controlled information"[67] which buttressed their position, they also managed to mislead themselves. On 8 August, Halder stated in his journal that the Soviet Union had only "limited forces left" to support future operations – an assessment based (predictably) on inaccurate intelligence from the Army General Staff's Foreign Armies East; moreover, the Chief of the Army General Staff confidently asserted that the Russians had just about reached the limits of their human reserves; hence, "we need not anticipate any further large-scale activations."[68] According to German intelligence, Red Army forces along the entire eastern front possessed a fighting value of just 60-65 divisions, along with, at best, 10 armored divisions. Behind the front, some 40 divisions were thought to be organizing, albeit with inadequate leadership, weapons, and equipment. Soviet morale and the value of Red Army units were considered to be in decline – problems exacerbated by logistical shortcomings, inadequate nutrition, and feelings of inferiority vis-à-vis the *Wehrmacht*.[69]

11.3.1: Hitler Comes to a Decision (12-21 August 1941)

Spurred to action by the generals' lobbying, Hitler finally issued a supplement to his Directive No. 34 (30 July) on 12 August 1941. With Directive No. 34a, Hitler now stated categorically for the first time[70] that Moscow, as the Soviet Union's "government, armament, and traffic center," was to be captured "before the coming of winter."[71] However, whatever solace Halder, Jodl and other proponents of the Moscow alternative may have derived from their "Fuehrer's" sudden interest in the Soviet capital was tempered by the dictator's carefully attached conditions. Once again, Hitler made clear that, before any new attack along the Moscow axis could begin, operations against Leningrad were to be brought to a satisfactory conclusion; in other words, Leningrad, the Baltic, and linking up with the Finns remained a higher priority. Furthermore, the "most important task" for Army Group Center was to clear its flanks of dangerous enemy groupings – a task already underway along the army group's southern flank since the start of August, when Guderian had advanced on Roslavl. In fact, "only after these threats to our flanks have been entirely overcome and armored formations have been rehabilitated will it be possible to continue the offensive, on a wide front and with echeloning of both flanks, against the strong enemy forces which have been concentrated for the defense of Moscow."[72]

Thus, while Directive 34a had raised the tantalizing prospect of a direct advance on Moscow, it had fallen "well short of ordering it,"[73] a situation which could only have compounded the frustration and anxiety felt by Brauchitsch, Halder, Heusinger and others at OKH, as they struggled to set their eastern armies on a path to victory while, at the same time, beset by nagging doubts as to whether such a victory was still even possible. The climate of crisis which now enveloped the Army High Command's Mauerwald compound (outside Rastenburg), and the growing strains on the combat troops, were subjects of a letter from *Oberstleutnant* Hellmuth Stieff (OKH Operations Branch) to his wife on 12 August 1941:

> Sweetheart, you complain – and no doubt rightly so – that I write so little. But I am simply not in the mood for writing. This campaign is so utterly *different* to all the previous ones. A kind of tenseness and nervousness like never before hangs over all of us, such that you want to avoid everyone if you possibly can. It may in part have to do with the length of the war, which *everyone* is more than sick of. But the main thing is probably the oppressive feeling that, despite all the seemingly lovely successes, we're in the middle of a very acute crisis of which outsiders are, of course, unaware. The time up to the start of winter (start of October) is really preying on our minds, and we haven't yet achieved even half of what we need to in order not to end up in a war on two fronts.
>
> The difficult battles and exertions of the first 6 weeks have, however, not only led to severe physical exhaustion and weakening of the troops, which thus makes an operational break absolutely necessary – but which will, in its turn, benefit the enemy – but, as a further dangerous consequence, they have also led to serious fatigue among all command authorities right up to the army groups. The result has been that good opportunities have been missed and many things have been tackled only half-heartedly.
>
> A further unpleasant consequence has arisen in a mutual over-sensitivity among the personalities in the leadership, extending right down to the divisions and regiments, which is slowly developing into a free-for-all, so that instructions and orders are often simply not being carried out any more, as everyone thinks they're smarter than the next man, to the great detriment of the whole business. It just about makes me sick.
>
> All these conditions, which we see and experience day in, day out – it all starts right here at the top! [i.e., at the OKH headquarters in the Mauerwald near Angerburg in East Prussia] – slowly create a state of resentment in you, so that you would really rather withdraw into your own shell. If some sort of change does not occur shortly in all this, there'll be a catastrophe. Having to watch this go on is awful.[74]

Three days later (15 August), at a conference attended by Brauchitsch and Jodl, Hitler reaffirmed the priority of Leningrad, dictating that an attack on Moscow could not be considered until the successful conclusion of the operations of Army Group North; in the interim, Bock was forbidden to conduct any attacks at all in the direction of the Soviet capital.[75] At the same time, Hitler ordered the dispatch of a panzer corps from Hoth's 3 Panzer Group to Army Group North. The proximate cause of this tactical measure was, as noted, a local crisis south of Staraia Russa; that said, the transfer of the panzer corps to Leeb's army group was "entirely in consonance" with the dictator's basic strategic conceptions.[76] As discussed above (Section 11.2), Hitler's impulsive decision to remove the three mobile divisions from Army Group Center was met by both OKH and the army group with anger and despair.

Hitler's order of 15 August galvanized Halder to take decisive action, for both the transfer of the panzer forces to Army Group North and the abandonment of operations by Bock's army group to improve its jump-off positions for an advance on Moscow were "incompatible with his plans."[77] As a result, he directed Colonel Heusinger, Chief, OKH Operations Branch, to prepare a memorandum marshalling all arguments for an immediate resumption of the attack toward Moscow. Sent by Brauchitsch to the "Fuehrer" on 18 August, the memorandum "expressed more clearly than all previous ideas and drafts Halder's strategy,"[78] its basic thrust being that the annihilation of the Red Army around Moscow and the conquest of industrial resources in the region had to remain the primary objective of German military operations before the onset of poor weather in October. Once again, Halder argued that the two other army groups (North and South) were strong enough to achieve their goals without the support of Army Group Center, which, the memorandum stated, would be able to assemble 42 infantry divisions, 13 mechanized divisions, and one cavalry division in time to begin the offensive in early September.[79]

The OKH memorandum was supported by a similar document completed the same day (18 August) by General Jodl's deputy at the OKW, Brig.-Gen. Walter Warlimont (Chief, National Defense Branch). This "Assessment of the Situation in the East" (*Beurteilung der Ostlage*), which, for the most part, recapitulated the arguments made by the OKH,[80] ended by insisting that:

> The *Ostheer* is strong enough to entrust Army Groups North and South with the fulfillment of their missions by their own forces, while simultaneously conducting the decisive thrust on Moscow with Army Group Center. A key condition is that inviting partial successes (e.g., the southeastward thrust of 2 Panzer Group) be dispensed with, and that, if necessary, local crises be accepted for the sake of the overall success.[81]

Meanwhile, on 18 August, Goebbels had paid a visit to Hitler at the *Wolfsschanze* outside Rastenburg. The German propaganda minister was stunned by the state in which he found his beloved "Fuehrer," who was not only suffering from badly frayed nerves – the result of the increasing stresses and strains of the eastern campaign – but for almost two weeks had been tormented by a serious case of dysentery. Hitler appeared "strained and sickly" (*angegriffen und kraenklich*),[82] and Goebbels was aghast to hear him contemplating the prospect of accepting peace terms from Stalin, even going so far as to posit that Bolshevism, once the Red Army was neutralized, would no longer pose a threat to Germany.[83] At the same time, Hitler fully recognized the grave seriousness of Germany's strategic situation, for only four days before, the promulgation of the Atlantic Charter had made unmistakably clear that the entry of America into the war was inching inexorably closer.[84]

Most likely it was Hitler's poor health – at a time when he was astonished by the realization that German intelligence had grossly underestimated the true scope of Soviet forces – which temporarily weakened his resolve to continue the Russian campaign,[85] while also impairing his ability to overrule his fractious generals and levy a definitive decision about future operational objectives. In any case, as Jodl told Heusinger on 20 August, Hitler's stubborn reluctance to move on Moscow was due, in part, to deep-seated psychological motives. As Jodl framed it, the "Fuehrer" "instinctively recoiled from taking the same path as Napoleon;" furthermore, Moscow gave him a "sinister feeling" (*etwas Unheimliches*), and he feared an attack on the city could result in a "life and death struggle with Bolshevism."[86] Yet as historian David Stahel incisively observes, if Hitler was "skeptical of treading this path," it was not simply because of historical parallels with Napoleon:

> Bock's powerful forces had twice lunged in this direction, destroying large Soviet armies, but bringing no result and entangling themselves in long, fierce

battles ... The fact remained that the Red Army had not, as intended, been destroyed in the initial battles and a renewed thrust on Moscow, as the OKH advocated, seemed too much like reinforcing failure having already failed twice to achieve the desired result. Hitler also saw no war-winning potential in seizing Moscow. To the south, however, he saw the prospect of an immediate success over the Soviet Southwestern Front and the opening of the resource rich eastern Ukraine to his forces.[87]

On 21 August 1941, five weeks of open conflict between Hitler and his generals, and uncertainty about the direction of future operations, came to abrupt end; on this day, the dictator responded to the OKH memorandum by issuing new orders (drafted on his instructions by Jodl) charting a clear course for the next phase of the campaign. Addressed to Field Marshal von Brauchitsch, as C-in-C of the Army, they once and for all levelled the opposition of the Army High Command; indeed, they began by stating that "the Army's proposal for the continuation of operations in the east, of 18 August, does not conform with my intentions. I order the following:

> 1. The most important objective to be achieved before the onset of winter is not the capture of Moscow, but the occupation of the Crimea[88] and the industrial and coal region of the Donets [Donbas], together with the isolation of the the Russian oil regions in the Caucasus. In the north, [it is] the encirclement of Leningrad and union with the Finns.[89]

In the next paragraph, the document stated that the "uniquely favorable operational situation" resulting from Army Group Center reaching the line Gomel – Pochep was to be immediately exploited by a "concentric operation," involving the inner wings of both Army Groups Center and South, to effect the encirclement of Soviet 5 Army in the area east of Kiev; this would free Rundstedt's army group to push eastward, beyond the Dnepr, to secure the vital industrial centers of Rostov and Khar'kov.[90] One is struck by the palpable irony of this operational scheme: The advance of the right wing of Bock's army group (Second Army and *Armeegruppe* Guderian) southward during the first three weeks of August had been undertaken to clear its southern flank and secure jump-off positions for the drive on Moscow; and yet the success of these very maneuvers, coupled with the deplorable set up of Soviet Southwestern Front, opposite Army Group South, had also created a unique opportunity for a dramatic German victory in the Ukraine – an opportunity Hitler was now quick to seize.

11.3.2: The Army High Command Responds

Hitler's new orders arrived at OKH late that evening, where they struck, in the vernacular of Heusinger, "like a bomb" (*wie eine Bombe*).[91] For Halder, the "Fuehrer directive" of 21 August was "decisive for the outcome of this campaign"[92] – decisive in the sense that it meant – or so he thought – the end to his plans and hopes for bringing the war to a successful conclusion in 1941. To Hitler's army adjutant, Major Engel, it simply signified "a black day for the Army."[93]

It was not until early the next morning (1:30 a.m.) that Colonel Heusinger's adjutant in the Operations Branch, *Hauptmann Freiherr* von Muenchhausen – relaxing in the officers' mess with several other OKH officers – was handed a copy of Hitler's directive. He recorded his reaction – and that of his fellow officers – in his personal diary:

> We read it and were outraged, because we immediately saw its decisive importance and knew what disappointment it would cause. It was signed personally by A.H ...

This clearly means that an attack on Moscow this year will now probably no longer be possible! As *Generaloberst* Halder writes in a marginal note to the directive: "This order means that the majority of the German Army will remain bound up in Russia during Winter 41/42, and it will not be possible to carry out the planned operational intentions of the Army (and most likely of the *Luftwaffe* as well)." ... Everyone is simply outraged. "That could mean losing the war!"[94]

Yet for the Army High Command, Hitler's profoundly disappointing directive of 21 August was but the initial blow in a devastating "one-two punch" administered by the Nazi potentate in a sudden flurry of purposeful activity after weeks of inaction. For the following day (22 August) brought an even more pointed rebuff of OKH when a second document arrived – this one personally dictated by the "Fuehrer" himself. In a detailed and rambling "study" "bursting with personal spite,"[95] Hitler proceeded to lecture his generals on the "fundamentals" (*das Grundsaetzliche*) of the eastern campaign. While the particulars need not concern us, it should be noted that the document "included a scathing attack on the leadership of the Army, citing poor management and a failure to provide adequate direction which, by contrast, was being superbly exhibited by Goering in command of the *Luftwaffe*."[96]

At OKH Halder reacted with unreserved fury. After the "crushing setback" of Hitler's first directive, the "arrival of Hitler's study effectively blaming the OKH for all the Army's woes, was simply too much."[97] Turning again to his diary, Halder recorded his most private and painful thoughts:

> I regard the situation created by the Fuehrer's interference unendurable for OKH. No other but the Fuehrer himself is to blame for the zigzag course caused by his successive orders, nor can the present OKH, which now is in its fourth victorious campaign, tarnish its good name with these latest orders. Moreover, the way ObdH [Brauchitsch] is being treated is absolutely outrageous. I have proposed to ObdH to request his relief together with mine.[98]

Neither Halder nor Brauchitsch, however, would resign their posts. After all, as Brauchitsch counseled his distraught colleague, Hitler would not, in any case, accept their resignations, thus nothing would be changed; besides, the last thing the Army needed at such a critical juncture in the war was chaos within its high command.[99] Yet although he elected to stay on, Brauchitsch refused to confront Hitler over his directive of 21 August (and again push for the Moscow alternative), despite repeated attempts by both Halder and Heusinger to persuade him to do so.[100] The Army C-in-C's acquiescence in the face of Hitler's new orders bitterly disappointed Halder, who saw in Brauchitsch's failure to act an act of betrayal.[101] Brauchitsch, however, an increasingly weak and ineffectual commander-in-chief, had by now become an easy target of Hitler's growing contempt for his General Staff; hence, it is hardly surprising that he lacked the will to confront the dictator directly.

The first news of Hitler's new directive reached the command post of Army Group Center on 22 August, just as Bock was preparing to send out orders to his armies for a resumption of the "attack to the east by the entire army group."[102] Astonished by the "Fuehrer's" decision, he telephoned Halder, informing him that he, Bock, considered the new operation "unfortunate, above all because it placed the attack to the east in question." In his diary, the field marshal described the impending turn south (to cooperate with Rundstedt's army group) – to be carried out by "strong elements" of Weichs' Second Army and Guderian's group – as nothing more than a "secondary operation." "I want to smash the enemy army and the bulk of this army is opposite my front!," he jotted in his journal in obvious despair.[103]

The next day (23 August) Halder flew to Bock's CP at Borisov, arriving there in the afternoon. Bock also summoned Guderian to attend the conference, whose ostensible purpose was to discuss execution of Hitler's new attack orders. The three generals, however, also had a more urgent task in mind, namely the hatching of a "plot" in a final desperate attempt to convince Hitler to support the operational planning of the Army for an attack on Moscow. During the conference, Guderian recalled in his memoirs, "We discussed at length what could still be done to alter Hitler's 'unalterable resolve.' We were all agreed that this new plan to move on Kiev must result in a winter campaign: this in its turn would lead to all those difficulties which the OKH had very good reasons for wishing to avoid."[104] Guderian went on to explain to his "co-conspirators" why the turn south was untenable for his forces, among other things mentioning the "road and supply problems" which would inevitably accompany such a move, while also pointing out the exhausted state of his 24 Panzer Corps, which had been in almost continuous action since the beginning of the campaign. In fact, the mercurial panzer general went so far as to dismiss the proposed operation as a "crime."[105]

After "a great deal of chopping and changing,"[106] Bock suggested that Guderian accompany Halder back to the *Fuehrerhauptquartier*, where he would make a last ditch effort to change Hitler's mind – the thinking being that Guderian, as a general from the front, "could lay the relevant facts immediately before Hitler" in a uniquely powerful and persuasive way. The field marshal then placed a telephone call to Schmundt at the *Wolfsschanze*, requesting that Guderian be permitted to speak to the "Fuehrer." Later that afternoon, Guderian set off with Halder on his return flight, arriving at Loetzen airfield in East Prussia as darkness fell.[107]

The details of Guderian's suspenseful encounter with Hitler at his evening conference on 23 August are well known, and need not be reexamined at length. Simply put, when granted an opening, Guderian launched into an "impassioned plea for sustaining the drive on Moscow."[108] Hitler, who had a special regard for the panzer pioneer, heard Guderian out; when he was finished, the "Fuehrer" took to the offensive. He spoke of the absolute necessity of seizing the raw materials and agricultural production of the Ukraine for the future prosecution of the war, and of the importance of capturing the Crimea ("that Soviet aircraft carrier for attacking the Romanian oil fields"). It was at this point that Hitler rendered his notorious rebuke: "My generals know nothing about the economic aspects of war."[109]

Guderian listened in silence, refraining from opposition. After all, Hitler was surrounded by the usual cast of OKW officers – Keitel, Jodl, Schmundt, etc. – all nodding their approval of everything their "Fuehrer" said. (The "Fuehrer myth" was still very much in evidence at this point in the war.) Moreover, neither Brauchitsch nor Halder had accompanied Guderian to the conference. The panzer general later justified his lack of opposition to Hitler's sharply opposing viewpoints by stating, "I did not then think it would be right to make an angry scene with the head of the German state when he was surrounded by his advisors."[110] Nevertheless, Guderian did manage to extract at least one concession from Hitler: His panzer forces were to be committed in their entirety to support Rundstedt's operations in the south, and allowed to rejoin the Moscow axis after the battle east of Kiev had been won. In the final analysis, however, Guderian was "simply overawed in Hitler's company and the result finally spelled defeat for Halder's cherished plans."[111]

The next morning (24 August), Guderian reported to Halder, informing the Chief of the Army General Staff of his failure to convince Hitler, and that the push into the Ukraine by Army Group Center would have to be carried out. Enraged by Guderian's apparent capitulation when confronted by the "Fuehrer" first hand, Halder heaped abuse on his colleague and, Guderian claimed, "suffered a complete nervous collapse."[112] Halder, apparently, was particularly put out by Guderian's effort to ensure that the new operation was conducted from the start with adequate strength (i.e., with all of his armored forces);

moreover, he was bewildered by Guderian's *volte-face* after he had so sharply criticized Hitler's new plans during the conference in Borisov. The two men parted "without having reached agreement," their relationship having suffered a blow from which it would never recover.[113] Guderian flew back to his headquarters with orders to begin the drive toward Kiev on 25 August.[114]

Meanwhile, from his "perch" inside the OKH Operations Branch, Hellmuth Stieff had continued to monitor the activities of the Army General Staff, as well as events at the front, growing increasingly appalled by the direction of the war, his own participation in it, and what his astute and incisive mind regarded as absolute moral failure. On 23 August, under the immediate influence of Hitler's new war directive, he again penned a long letter to his wife:

My dear little Sweetheart!

Thank you very much for both your dear letters of 16 and 17 [August], likewise for the little package with the lovely cake. All the men in the group particularly enjoyed the latter at their usual afternoon tea …

Your words did me real good, and I think you are right. I am just not as hopeful as you anymore. However, that has less to do with developments in the war situation than with conditions in general. Sometimes I utterly despair of everything and carry within me a real hatred for so many things which just can't be expressed in words in a letter. We are thus placed helplessly at the mercy of a fate which must, as a consequence, necessarily result in a decline of all our values, and yet this is ignored!

When you told me it would be good for me to see everything from another vantage point, I had already thought of doing that myself. So I'm going to go over to a panzer corps for a little while – 2-3 weeks – at the beginning of September. I already have Heusinger's agreement.[115] It seems doubtful to me that it will really help, because I have lost my faith in the business and my readiness to devote myself unconditionally to my utmost to it, however sad that may sound. However, not a single day now goes by here in which the general rejection of this increasingly megalomaniacal lout [i.e., Hitler] does not increase. Only just yesterday, we received another written sample of this,[116] the tone of which was *so* ill-advised that I can only say that anybody who lets that kind of thing go by without comment deserves whatever's coming to them. And the other side will, with time, *of course* be persuaded that they can do anything they like if everybody just swallows it all without protest. My respect for certain people has sunk deeply, at any rate. Sweetheart – it is simply vile and dishonorable!

The overall situation hasn't been doing at all badly in the last few weeks … In the center the Gomel operation to remove the threat to the south flank of Army Group Bock ended quickly and successfully. But the conclusion [drawn from Gomel operation], again forced by an intervention [i.e., by Hitler], is failing to exploit this success against our most dangerous opponent, in order to remove him and thus really bring about an end to the campaign before the onset of winter. In a complete misunderstanding of the limits of time and space, these forces are now advancing in a pointless direction, chasing another little victory anywhere they can, a victory which falls to us anyway as a result of the pursuit north of Kiev …

This bloody dilletantism, which is even supported by such illustrious representatives as K[eitel] and J[odl], could, God knows, cost us this war. Because for us, the issue is now not to lose any more time, and especially to hold our already badly worn out forces together, not to wilfully decimate them. Our bloody losses already amount to over 300,000 men after all,[117] and combat strengths have sunk to half or less. But replacements can only be brought out after several weeks, because the still rather inefficient rail lines are already operating at full capacity loaded up with supplies of fuel, ammunition, and rations. That gives you an idea of what sort of worrisome thoughts won't let go of me! Don't let the days get too lonely for you, and do at least have some fun, insofar as that is possible.[118]

Hauptmann Karl-Wilhelm Thilo, who served in the same OKH department as *Oberstleutnant* Stieff, also agonized over Hitler's conduct of the campaign – his alarming (and growing) interference in operational and tactical details – and the collective failure of the OKW and OKH leadership to take effective action against the "Fuehrer's" decision-making. His diary entry of 24 August included frank observations on Hitler's increasing domination of the German officer corps, as well as on Germany's deteriorating strategic outlook:

> Yesterday the Fuehrer, contrary to objections by OKH, released an order, which could (like his order before Dunkirk to halt the panzer units) have disastrous consequences for the <u>entire</u> campaign ... According to this, 2 infantry corps and 2 Panzer, 2 motorized divisions are to deploy from Gomel under Guderian, with the right flank at Chernigov, to envelop the Red 5 Army ...
>
> At the start of the war we underestimated the Russian; today we are overestimating him; every gap is causing serious jitters [*Nervenkrisen*] at OKW.
>
> What is deplorable is that nobody from the Fuehrer's circle – C-in-C of the Army [Brauchitsch] certainly not – can resist any more. He [Hitler] is far too autocratic, even the old people ... are frustrated (Goering recently just left the HQ for 14 days for this very reason!).
>
> If Moscow is not taken this year, then this winter we'll have the positional warfare [*Stellungskrieg*] our enemy wants, which will give him time and materiel (from the Moscow industrial region) for replenishment. Large elements of the *Luftwaffe* and the Army are committed to the east, while, without sufficient defenses in place, the English are able to bomb western and northern Germany. In the spring we'll be forced to attack once more against new Red forces, costing more blood and time.[119]

If younger General Staff officers at OKH like Stieff and Thilo were deeply disillusioned by the turn of events – and by the conspicuous lack of courage displayed by their superiors[120] – the German soldiers at the front, not privy of course to the inner workings of the High Command, reacted in a less complicated fashion to the sudden and surprising shift in strategy. For the men of Army Group Center, Moscow was *the* objective, and most were convinced its capture would bring a victorious end to the war. The *Landsers'* fixation on Stalin's capital city was reflected in their habit throughout the summer of 1941 of hanging signposts reading "TO MOSCOW" along the route of advance, as recounted by Guderian:

> On 13 August I visited the Desna front, to the east of Roslavl, on either side of the Moscow highway. With a heavy heart I saw how my soldiers, confident that they would soon be advancing straight toward the Russian capital, had put up many signposts marked 'TO MOSCOW.' The soldiers of the 137 Infantry Division, with whom I spoke at the front, would talk only of a rapid resumption of the move to the east.[121]

According to Field Marshal von Bock, his soldiers asked only one question: "When will we march to Moscow? We don't want to get stuck here in winter."[122] As one junior officer observed, "We were counting the kilometers, we were counting the days – when would

Moscow lie before us?"[123] And the reader may recall the fervent hopes of Heinrich Haape (Section 10.6.1): "Our marching column ... wanted to get to Moscow. It was their only objective ... the end of the road."[124] Yet for the moment at least, the *Vormarsch auf Moskau* had been officially cancelled, and the troops responded with disappointment and confusion, even anger; after all, they had already covered more than two-thirds of the distance to the Soviet capital, and even if the fighting had been tougher than anticipated – their ranks winnowed by grinding attrition – they remained steadfastly confident in the superiority of the *Wehrmacht* and their ability to finish what they had begun. Soldier Erich Mende noted that his men were "agitated" and could not understand why they were not marching on Moscow:

> Moscow was only 280 kilometers away. The troops hoped that we would be in the Soviet capital in August or latest September and then the resistance of the Red Army would probably be broken. We were very angry that the panzer divisions were pulled out and sent to the Ukraine to fight at Kiev. We saw this as a completely wrong strategy.[125]

Artilleryman Werner Adamczyk, learning in late July 1941 that his unit was about to be shifted northward, toward Leningrad, sensed that the Russian campaign might have hit a serious snag. As he explained in his war memoirs:

> I had a chance to look at a map of Russia. It showed the distance between Smolensk and Leningrad to be about 600 kilometers. On the other hand, the distance from where we were to Moscow was less than 400 kilometers. And we were really making progress – prisoners from the Smolensk encirclement were still passing by every day. Definitely, the Russians confronting us on our way to Moscow had been beaten. And now it seemed we were to turn away from our greatest chance to get to Moscow and bring the war to an end. My instinct told me that something was very wrong. I never understood this change in plans.[126]

It hardly bears mention that Adamczyk's instincts were good. Yet in light of the serious crisis which now confronted the *Wehrmacht* in the east, one can also posit that Hitler's decision-making of late August 1941 also reflected superior instincts, at least in comparison to his General Staff.

11.3.3: Analysis of the 21 August "Fuehrer Directive"

The five-week strategic crisis which had dominated German command authorities in July and August 1941 had ended with Hitler emerging as the "undisputed victor."[127] He had not only once again prevailed against the "spirit of Zossen" (*Geist von Zossen*)[128] – that is, the Army High Command – he had as well, in the opinion of this author, opted for an alternative which, from both an operational and a broader strategic perspective, signified a sounder course of action. Operationally, several points can be made in favor of Hitler's momentous decision:

• Despite the tactical successes at Krichev, Gomel and Velikie Luki, the flanks of Army Group Center remained vulnerable to attack from both the north and the south; thus, Hitler was correct to seek to eliminate these threats before resuming a general advance on Moscow.[129] Particularly in the Ukraine the powerful Soviet Southwestern Front posed a serious danger to the already elongated southern wing of Bock's army group – a danger that would be banished in dramatic fashion by the Kiev operation ordered by Hitler in his 21 August directive.[130]

• A drive on Moscow in either late August or early September 1941 would not only have been conducted with Bock's flanks vulnerable to attack, it would have marshalled far fewer forces (ca. 56 divisions) compared to the actual operation ("Typhoon") which began on 2 October 1941 with 78 divisions in Army Group Center's expanded order of battle. In addition, the Soviet armies defending Moscow were much stronger in August than they were by the end of September, having "shot their bolts" in offensives north and south of Smolensk.[131]

• In late August 1941, the logistical situation of Army Group Center was badly strained (see, Section 11.4) and would not have sustained an attack on Moscow. The prodigious requirement for munitions – in particular, artillery shells – to hold the army group's eastern front against the furious Soviet counterattacks had significantly slowed the buildup of stockpiles to support a renewed offensive; only after these counterattacks had ended (in the second week of September) were requisite stockpiles laboriously rebuilt – a process not completed until late in the month. On the other hand, the push of Guderian's panzers toward Kiev *was* logistically feasible, in large part due to the German railhead reaching Gomel by late August.[132]

• The precarious forward deployment of the Soviet Southwestern Front (including its 5 Army)[133] – the result of Stalin's stubborn refusal to abandon Kiev – coupled with the tilt southward of Bock's southern wing and the advance of Kleist's 1 Panzer Group to the Dnepr, had created the operational preconditions for another great *Kesselschlacht* – this time in the eastern Ukraine through a joint operation of Army Groups Center and South. Beyond Guderian's group and Weichs' Second Army, Bock's forces would not take part in the operation, which "in view of [the army group's] logistical situation was just as well."[134]

From the perspective of (grand) strategy, Hitler was also on firmer ground than his Army General Staff, which, as it was, had been trained to think operationally and not to cogitate on the larger issues of war and peace; to wit:

• Unlike Brauchitsch, Halder and Heusinger at OKH, Hitler had come to the sobering realization that the war in the east could no longer be ended successfully in 1941, making him a "more realistic judge of the situation" than his General Staff.[135] If his strategic insights ultimately fell short, it was not because they were wrong, but because they could hardly overcome the fact that, by late August 1941, the war in Russia was probably already lost.

• To prosecute a war which had gone from a blitzkrieg to a protracted "slugfest" – with Great Britain still undefeated and the prospect of an American entry into the conflict looming – Hitler realized that resources had become vital. What mattered now was securing the industrial regions about Leningrad, the grain of the Ukraine, the coal and other minerals of the Donbas, and the oil of the Caucasus region, while depriving the Soviet Union of them.[136]

• To obtain these economic objectives, Hitler needed to speed up, and provide additional support for, operations in both the north and south. The German dictator, in fact, with his superior strategic insight, was "probably the first to realize the entire campaign was in jeopardy because Army Groups North and South were not strong enough to achieve their missions and would thus require assistance," which could only be provided by diverting elements of Army Group Center's mobile forces.[137]

To be sure, other military historians have come to a very different conclusion about Hitler's decision of 21 August 1941, and its implications for the outcome of Operation

Barbarossa. According to this view, while execution of the "Fuehrer Directive" culminated in a spectacular victory in mid-September in the Kiev cauldron battle (resulting in the capture of more than 650,000 Soviet soldiers,[138] more than double the number of prisoners taken in the victories at Belostok-Minsk and Smolensk combined), the concomitant failure to move against Moscow in August 1941 cost the German Reich its only conceivable chance of emerging victorious from the war with Russia. As former *Bundeswehr* officer and historian Dieter Ose argues, Hitler's decision "not to capture the most obvious, politically and militarily important objective of Moscow," resulting operationally in a "weakening of the area of main effort, [and a] scattering of forces toward the flanks," meant that the goal of bringing the campaign to a successful conclusion before the onset of winter "was lost sight of," a catastrophic mistake which ultimately doomed *Barbarossa* to defeat.[139] Indeed, according to the late historian Theodore Ropp, Hitler's "August postponement of the drive on Moscow cannot be defended."[140]

Perhaps the most outspoken exponent of the Moscow alternative is the late R.H.S. Stolfi, former professor emeritus at the U.S. Naval Postgraduate School in Monterey, California. In his book (2011), *Hitler, Beyond Evil and Tyranny*, he repeats his long-held conviction that "had the Germans taken Moscow in August 1941, they would have won the campaign and war.

> Almost as surely, when Hitler delayed the final strike for Moscow until October, the Germans had little chance of winning ... Adolf Hitler ... intruded on history to sign the Fuehrer Directive of August 21, the single most significant political-military document of the 20th Century ... Hitler's decision as embodied in the brief, five-paragraph document marked Germany's irretrievable loss of World War II, literally, on August 22, the day that OKH ... began to execute [the directive].[141]

Stolfi also insists that only Hitler's directive, and "no action taken by the Red Army," had halted the advance of Army Group Center along the Moscow axis; and that the capture of the Soviet capital would have brought the "inescapable result of total defeat," because the "Russian peasant masses could not be expected to support an oppressive, crushing government incapable of defending its own capital."[142] Neither assertion, however, holds up under closer examination.

In the first place, it was not Hitler's operational edicts which brought the hitherto swift advance of Bock's army group to an abrupt and protracted halt east of Smolensk; rather, it was: a.) the exhausted state of his forces (particularly of the mobile units, and their need to rest and refit);[143] b.) the serious strains to a logistical apparatus which, even when functioning normally, was increasingly incapable of meeting the requirements at hand; and, c.) the series of violent counterattacks unleashed against Army Group Center in late July and persisting through early September 1941. As far as "c" is concerned, Stolfi is hardly alone among historians in underestimating the efforts of Stalin, Zhukov and Timoshenko to halt the German drive at Smolensk, even if they failed to destroy Bock's forces in the process; that said, it was the surprisingly stiff Soviet resistance about and east of this city which ultimately dashed the hopes of Halder and his OKH colleagues – by reinforcing Hitler's desire to adhere to his original plan of seeking a decision on the wings of the eastern front.[144]

Secondly, one must seriously question the assumption that the capture of Moscow would have precipitated the "total defeat" of the Soviet Union.[145] Although Hitler and his generals had begun the campaign confident that the – in their view – highly fragile Soviet state would collapse in a matter of weeks, this had failed to occur despite the series of devastating blows administered by the *Wehrmacht*. Unlike France in 1940, the Soviet state, its people and its armed forces, simply refused to acknowledge defeat, no matter how many blows they endured – a remarkable fact which not only underscored the collective will of the Soviet people, but the enormous strategic depth of a country which could absorb such catastrophic blows and survive. Thus, it is difficult to see how the Russians would have quit following the loss of their capital, particularly in light of Germany's genocidal occupation policies, which, by late summer 1941, were well-known to all Russians and steeling their will to resist. And even if Bock had taken Moscow (either in September or in the fall), it is doubtful he could have held on to it through the arctic winter of 1941/42 (for which his forces were utterly unprepared), given the exhausted and overextended condition of his troops.[146]

Finally, in evaluating Hitler's decision-making during this critical period, two intriguing questions demand our attention: Was Hitler truly paralyzed by indecision in the several weeks prior to promulgation of his 21 August directive? If so, what impact, if any, did this have on the outcome of the 1941 campaign? In his comprehensive account of the Russo-German war, the late Albert Seaton included a chapter entitled, "The Fuehrer Vacillates,"[147] while eminent British historian John Keegan observed more recently that the "'19-day interregnum' (4-24 August), which may well have spared Stalin defeat in 1941, was characterized not only by slow German progress on all fronts but also by a succession of changes of mind."[148] According to David Glantz, "for almost the first time in his life, Hitler did not know what to do."[149]

Surely, during the protracted dispute with his generals, Hitler was, at times, beset by doubts concerning the proper path forward, and his indecision, however far it may have gone, can be partially explained by his poor health during this period. Yet it is also true that delays and postponements are frequently encountered during military campaigns, and thus "should be regarded as part of the inevitable friction of war."[150] In this context, it is intriguing to observe that Hitler managed to reach a final decision just as Weichs' Second Army and Guderian's panzer forces were winding up their victory at Gomel; in other words, at the very moment these forces became available for future operations, the "Fuehrer's" "vacillation" came to an end.[151] On the other hand, the timing may have simply been coincidental; and, in any case, Hitler needed to respond promptly to the OKH memorandum of 18 August, which signified a direct challenge to his plan of campaign.

More fundamentally, even a cursory examination of Hitler's recorded statements, orders and directives – reaching back to 5 December 1940, when he was first informed in detail of the OKH's operational planning for the Russian campaign – reveals that his strategic ideas remained remarkably consistent; for example, he never really deviated from the concept of the campaign as laid out in the original *Barbarossa* directive of 18 December 1940, which called for Army Group Center to pause at Smolensk and shift strong mobile forces northward to support the drive on Leningrad and the destruction of enemy forces in the Baltic.[152] Repeatedly, Hitler made clear to his generals that, for him, Moscow remained but a secondary – even tertiary – objective, behind Leningrad and the Baltic, the Ukraine and the Donbas, etc. Hence, instead of debilitating indecisiveness, this author sees an almost seamless continuity in Hitler's thought processes throughout the summer campaign of 1941. And again, at the first opportunity to convert his intentions to action – that is, after the panzer and motorized units of Army Group Center had at least partially refitted, and the operations along Bock's southern flank had ended – the dictator acted and did so decisively.

In the final analysis, the historical weightiness of both Hitler's putative vacillation, and the decisions he eventually handed down, has been vastly overblown in much of the historiography of the Russo-German war. This is understandable, however, for in the immediate post-war period, former German generals such as Halder, Guderian, Manstein and Blumentritt, had sedulously fostered the myth that, first, Hitler's "wobbling" at a critical time, and, second, his decision to send Bock's panzers into the Ukraine, instead of against

Moscow, forfeited the campaign and the war for Germany. These patently biased and self-serving perspectives were first conveyed to British military historian Liddell Hart in the late 1940s;[153] thereafter, they successfully made their way into the mainstream of western historiography.

As far as Halder goes, the general's biographer, Christian Hartmann, argues that, however much the Army *Generalstabschef* sought his own rehabilitation (and that of the German officer corps writ large) by unloading all blame onto Hitler, he gradually convinced himself of what he said:

> With regard to the protracted and occasionally tortuous course of this ... tug-of-war between Hitler and OKH, one should not lose sight of that important question which lay at the very heart of the argument. At issue is not to speculate further about the advantages or disadvantages of the two operational conceptions; far more important is the consideration that this dispute – in its significance as well as its consequences – was greatly overstated by most of the German military.[154]
>
> It is precisely in the case of Halder that we can establish the – psychologically extremely illuminating – process, whereby his gradual realization of the glaring misjudgment of the Soviet military potential, and thus of the fundamentally misguided conception of an eastern campaign, directly preceded this dispute or even overlapped with it. It is remarkable how muted Halder's self-criticism appeared in this regard, and how, instead, he increasingly tended to shift all the blame onto Hitler.
>
> In later years, when the dreadful consequences of this war were finally revealed in full, this notion had taken hold of Halder so completely that he was now actually convinced it was not until Hitler's decision of 21 August 1941 that the catastrophe had been triggered.[155]

As a sober alternative to the dubious narrative first advanced by Hitler's generals, some scholars have gradually put forth a more realistic appraisal of the strategic crisis between Hitler and his generals in the summer of 1941, in large part by revealing the seriously weakened condition of Army Group Center by late August, as well as the deplorable state of its logistics, which, as it was, would not have permitted a resumption of the Moscow offensive before the latter half of September at the earliest. Indeed, as Martin van Creveld observes in his perceptive analysis of *Barbarossa's* logistics, any postponement of the attack on Moscow, "if there was one, can hardly have amounted to more than a week or two, at the very most."[156] And the outcome of Hitler's attack on Russia hardly hinged on "a week or two."[157]

11.4: The Status of Army Group Center (August – September 1941)
As early as 7 August 1941, Field Marshal von Bock had expressed serious doubts about future prospects of his army group:

> The extreme right wing continues to be a source of worry ... On the rest of the army group's front small-scale attacks at the hot spots, otherwise quiet enough that the withdrawal of armored and motorized divisions from the front can continue.
>
> The situation is nevertheless extremely tense. If I want to create a reserve and try to pull out a division to do so, it is declared "impossible," if a division deployed in the rear army area arrives at the front it is snatched from my hands! I therefore wrote to the commanders of the armies and armored groups, made them aware of the results of such a blinkered policy, and asked them to be reasonable on this point.

I don't exactly know how a new operation is to take place out of this situation and with the slowly sinking fighting strength of our constantly attacking forces – but things are undoubtedly even worse for the Russians![158]

11.4.1: Ongoing Attrition & Partial Regeneration

The losses of Army Group Center had certainly been high, and the blood letting was to go on unabated. Bock's divisions were, collectively, sustaining about 3000 casualties per day (ca. 40 percent of the more than 7300 casualties incurred daily on the entire eastern front),[159] including some 700 dead. Officer losses had been alarmingly high, averaging roughly 80 per day through August 1941 (out of slightly more than 200 per day along the entire front during this period).[160] In sum, by 31 August, the army group had suffered about 50,000 dead out of approximately 126,000 fatalities across the *Ostheer*,[161] whose total losses (dead, wounded, missing) had climbed to roughly half a million men. Combat strength of the infantry divisions in the east had plunged on average by 40 percent; that of the panzer units by fully 50 percent.[162]

Reserve manpower (*Marschbataillone*) from the Replacement Army was now reaching the front,[163] but their numbers were far from sufficient to cover all losses; by the end of the month, the eastern armies as a whole suffered from a deficit of more than a quarter of a million men. And the outlook for the future was bleak: As Halder recorded on 26 August, "After 1 Oct. we shall have exhausted practically all our replacements."[164] Only days later (1 September), OKH acknowledged that, "at the moment there is such a shortage of men that it is no longer possible to offset casualties."[165] On 5 September, *Oberstleutnant* Stieff noted in a letter to his wife ("*Mein liebes Linglein!*") that the losses would soon "require the disbandment [*Aufloesung*] of about 15 divisions to bring the others back up to strength."[166] Even more portentously, the Army High Command was running out of reserve divisions, having committed 21 (out of 28) reserve divisions across the eastern front by 31 August – 10 divisions to Army Group South (nine infantry, one motorized division), eight infantry divisions to Army Group Center, and three infantry divisions to Army Group North.[167]

According to Ruediger Overmans definitive analysis, German fatalities in the east (all combat arms) were even higher in September (51,033) than they had been in August (46,066), bringing the aggregate figure through 30 September 1941 to 185,198; of these, an overwhelming majority, about 174,000 (94 percent), must be attributed to the ground forces – Army (90 percent) and *Waffen*-SS (four percent). Once again, factoring 40 percent of these fatal losses to Army Group Center (the largest of the three army groups), indicates that, through the first 101 days of the campaign, Bock's divisions had sustained approximately 70,000 dead – grievous losses that fell disproportionately on the combat infantry.[168]

Yet if the infantry bore the brunt of the personnel losses, the panzer divisions of Bock's 2 and 3 Panzer Groups had seen their tank fighting strength continue to decline dangerously. During August, both Hoth and Guderian attempted to pull their exhausted divisions out of the line to rest and refit; the results, however, were far from satisfactory. In the first place, the refitting process was disrupted by the heavy demands of the front, which often delayed the withdrawal of tank and motorized units and sorely limited their time for rest and recuperation. Moreover, frustrating delays in the delivery of spare parts, and particularly the urgently needed spare engines, 400 of which Hitler had promised the two panzer generals at the conference at Borisov on 4 August (a number which Guderian, at the time, had characterized as "totally inadequate"),[169] posed an additional handicap. It was at this point (mid-August), in fact, that Army Group Center revealed that only 150 tank engines were now anticipated for both 2 and 3 Panzer Groups,[170] and these had yet to be delivered.[171] Given this dismal state of affairs, on 22 August the army group concluded that, "The armored units are so battle-weary and worn-out that there can be no question of a mass operative mission until they have been completely replenished and repaired."[172]

Under such trying circumstances the panzer and motorized units did what they could to complete their technical refitting; despite their efforts, as of 4 September, only 34 percent of the tanks within Army Group Center were considered combat-ready, and this at a time when Guderian had already begun his advance south into the Ukraine. Specifically, Hoth's group reported 41 percent of its tanks, and Guderian's group just 25 percent of its armored fighting vehicles as operational.[173] Hoth's three panzer divisions had a total of 320 available tanks – 7 PD (130), 19 PD (102), and 20 PD (88) – with 196 still under repair. By comparison, Guderian's four panzer divisions possessed just 190 battle-ready tanks between them: 3 PD (41), 4 PD (49), 17 PD (38), 18 PD (62).[174] This total of 510 tanks stands in stark contrast to the 1800+ panzers with which the two groups had begun Operation *Barbarossa* on 22 June 1941.

Stunningly indicative of how tenaciously Hitler had starved his eastern armies after the start of the Russian campaign is the fact that, while the *Ostheer's* four panzer groups had, by 31 August 1941, lost a total of 1488 armored fighting vehicles, they had received just 96 replacement tanks from a new production of 815 tanks between June and August.[175] Before the beginning of Operation "Typhoon," however, 316 additional tanks (more than the total production for September 1941) were made available from Army depots,[176] while 2 and 5 Panzer Divisions with 450 tanks between them were assigned to Army Group Center from the OKH reserve.[177] As a result of this major accretion of combat power, as well as the arrival of additional armored units from Army Groups North and South, and furious ongoing repair work by the maintenance shops of the panzer divisions, Army Group Center would resume its push toward Moscow with a sizeable tank contingent.[178]

Before moving on to a discussion of logistics, the *Luftwaffe's* ongoing support of Army Group Center should be briefly addressed. During the late summer of 1941, this support was provided solely by Loerzer's 2 Air Corps of Field Marshal Kesselring's 2 Air Fleet which, on 6 September, comprised just 240 operational combat aircraft (141 bombers, 55 dive bombers, 44 fighters).[179] Of course, a single, modestly resourced air corps was utterly incapable of covering the 700 kilometer front of Bock's army group; perforce, it concentrated its efforts at the *Schwerpunkt* of army group operations – first along the southern wing (Gomel region), and then in support of Guderian's headlong drive into the Ukraine in late August and September.[180] This left Bock's eastern front largely devoid of air cover, leading Ninth Army to complain on several occasions in mid-August that the Soviet Air Force had gained complete air superiority in the army's entire area of responsibility.[181] Not until late September did Richthofen's 8 Air Corps – its forces now "tired and depleted" – return from the sector of Army Group North to support Operation "Typhoon."[182]

Like the ground forces, the *Luftwaffe* sustained frightful attrition rates across the eastern front throughout the summer of 1941. By 6 September, the number of operational aircraft in the three air fleets in the east had dropped to just 960 (440 bombers, 186 dive bombers, 295 fighters, 39 long-range fighters).[183] This compared with a front-line strength on 22 June 1941 of almost 2300 combat-ready planes, nearly 1000 of them in Kesselring's 2 Air Fleet alone. In his letter of 5 September, *Oberstleutnant* Stieff had decried the serious diminution of German air power, telling his wife that, "the eastern campaign has already consumed so much of the *Luftwaffe* that at the moment we no longer have air superiority anywhere in the east; on the other hand, even at some decisive points, this is now entirely in the hands of the Russians."[184] While Stieff may have exaggerated the current plight of the *Luftwaffe*, his basic point was well taken: Alarming attrition, coupled with the ceaseless and growing demands of an ever-expanding front, had remorselessly reduced the *Luftwaffe's* combat strength.

11.4.2: The Strained Logistical Situation

As Army Group Center pushed deeper into the Soviet Union, German logisticians had shifted the supply depots of the Dnepr Supply District (*Versorgungsbezirk Dnepr*)[185] forward in several bounds behind the advancing spearheads. By mid-July 1941, the string of depots (*Stuetzpunkte*) had been extended as far to the east as Polotsk – Lepel – Borisov – Bobruisk; by the end of July, a depot was established at Orsha and, by the beginning of August, at Smolensk – both along the main route toward Moscow. On the southern flank, a major supply center was built up at Gomel, following its capture in mid-August; in the north, the depots were pushed forward to Nevel, Vitebsk and Toropets by September 1941. Supply bases were also established at Mogilev and at Roslavl, the latter close behind the front.[186]

Setting up the new depots was one thing; stocking them with the enormous quantities of ammunition, POL (petroleum, oil, and lubricants) and spare parts needed not only to cover running requirements but to build stockpiles for future operations, was quite another. Although the initial leap of German forces to the Dvina-Dnepr River lines in early July 1941 had been largely (and effectively) supported by Army Group Center's *Grosstransportraum* (its organic truck-borne hauling capacity), the sustainment of operations beyond that point would depend in large measure on the handful of rail lines behind the front. In this context, German logisticians made two surprisingly facile assumptions: a.) operations beyond the Dvina-Dnepr Rivers would primarily entail the mopping up of residual Red Army forces which had escaped encirclement and annihilation west of the river lines; and, b.) to support these operations they would be able to rely heavily on captured Soviet rail lines, locomotives, and rolling stock (thus greatly limiting the need to convert the lines from Soviet to European standard gauge). Both assumptions proved hopelessly false.

As the course of operations rapidly revealed, not only did the Soviets succeed in maintaining large, intact (and constantly nourished) fighting forces, they were also able to destroy rail lines and key rail installations as they withdrew, while evacuating most of their locomotives and rolling stock;[187] thus, the invaders were compelled to undertake a major effort to re-lay the lines and restore them to operating condition.[188] Efforts to advance the railheads went forward deliberately, albeit much too deliberately to alleviate the Army's growing shortages. By 16 August 1941, German railroad troops (*Eisenbahntruppen*) had converted the railway gauge from Orsha to Smolensk; in late August, the German railway reached Gomel in the south, and was soon extended eastward to Roslavl; in the north, a standard gauge track was pushed through Vitebsk to Toropets by September.[189]

Although the advance of the rail lines somewhat improved the supply situation, the daily throughput of trains remained well below what was required to satisfy all the needs of the army group. In August, Field Marshal von Bock required 24 supply trains per day to meet existing requirements, and six more to build stockpiles for a resumption of the advance (30 trains in all); the Chief of *Wehrmacht* Transport, however, could promise him only 24, and, in practice, the army group seldom received more than 18 trains per day during the month.[190] In September, too, the "transportation capacity of the railways was unable to meet requirements."[191] Contributing to the shortfall was the nascent, yet growing, partisan movement, which was beginning to destroy rail lines, installations and trains with alarming frequency. In its war diary on 7 September, German Ninth Army recorded its growing frustration with Soviet partisan operations:

> The partisan threat has now also reached an alarming level in the area of Ninth Army. Thus not a day goes by in which ambushes against isolated drivers or columns, acts of sabotage of all kinds (cutting telephone lines) are not reported. But of most concern are the constantly increasing railway disruptions, which threaten the continuation of operations ... The army leadership recognizes this threat and is determined to take drastic measures [*ist zu durchgreifende Massnahmen entschlossen*].[192]

Bridging the gap between the railheads and the troops at the front was the motorized transport of the *Grosstransportraum*, which, at the start of the Russian campaign, had amounted to 25,000 tons of hauling capacity in Army Group Center. From the very beginning, however, the incessant demands made upon these truck transport regiments and battalions had resulted in alarming and unsustainable loss rates. The "ruthless utilization of engines" on the appalling roadways led to "rapid deterioration" of the vehicles;[193] the consumption of both fuel and oil was well above pre-war calculations, while spare parts (particularly tires) were difficult to obtain. Under such conditions, actual hauling capacity rapidly dipped well below expectations; in fact, after only a few weeks of fighting the army group had lost one third or more of its trucks – a situation exacerbated by the fact that facilities for making major repairs were not brought forward but remained behind in Poland, or even in the Reich itself.[194] Furthermore, despite the hopes of OKH that the advance on Moscow would prove decisive, insufficient effort was made to concentrate all available truck transport behind Army Group Center; in late August, 5000 tons of hauling capacity were even withdrawn and transferred to Army Group South to help build up its base of supply.[195]

By August/September 1941, the formations of Army Group Center (and, certainly, the *Ostheer* as a whole) were running short of a "laundry list" of items essential for the conduct of modern, mechanized warfare; even the most basic items of a soldier's personal kit were now often in short supply, as illustrated by the example of 98 Infantry Division which, as of late September, was under strength by nearly 4000 men:

> On 14 September [the division] was off again, leaving the Pripiat' Marshes and von Reichenau's Sixth Army of Army Group South behind it, on its long march northeast following in Guderian's wake to Army Group Center, ready for the thrust on Moscow. At first the men were relieved to be away from the mud and the marshes, and the sight of a motor vehicle actually moving made them feel quite European again. Their elation was moderated, however, by the 25-mile a day marches over the deep sandy tracks, the difficulty of which defied description, and the sobering sight of the many foundering horses[196] and the frequent jettisoning of vehicle loads. It was still only September, but soon there was incessant rain and a cold northeast wind, and any night shelter, squalid and bug-ridden though it usually was, had all been occupied by motorized troops before the worn-out infantry arrived. Anything during the day was bearable provided a night's shelter and warmth was to be had, but when this was denied, the troops plumbed the depths of wretchedness.
>
> Gradually the most simple necessities were missing, razor blades, soap, tooth paste, shoe materials, needles and thread. On 23 September came the first hoar frost. The rain, cold and lack of rest increased the sickness, which in normal events would have admitted the men to hospital. With the lack of transport all, even the sick, had to march and there could be no question of leaving anyone behind as the area was notorious for banditry. One day followed like another and the great chain of men moved forward in the slashing rain, obedient and silent with nothing to be heard but the snorting of horses and the creak of the wagons and the everlasting roar of the wind in the firs on either side of the track.[197]

Yet however missed the "simple necessities" may have been, what truly troubled the *Landser* of Army Group Center were far more serious shortages of both ammunition and POL. The daily requirements of Bock's divisions for artillery shells and mortar rounds were enormous[198] and, during the heavy defensive fighting from late July to September 1941, they were well above the average.[199] These defensive battles had hardly begun when, on

1 August, Bock complained in a telephone conversation with the Army Quartermaster General that the shortages of munitions previously described as "serious" were, following a week with no improvement, "gradually becoming a crisis."[200] In early August, *Hauptmann* Muenchhausen (OKH Operations Branch) noted in his journal that the "supply problem is becoming more and more difficult … [the Russians] also have plenty of artillery and a lot of shells, which we can't manage to move up."[201] A few days later he commented on the "constant shortage" of artillery shells in the El'nia salient, while the Russian forces attacking there were "extravagantly" (*verschwenderisch*) supplied.[202]

Simply put, the shortages of artillery shells prevented Bock from compensating for the absence of strategic reserves, and the ongoing attrition of his forces, with adequate firepower.[203] The situation of 26 Infantry Division was probably typical. In a post-war study of the division's artillery regiment (26 AR), a former German general recalled the frustrations created by the shortages:

> Our ammunition supply was insufficient. During pre-war maneuvers the expenditure of ammunition had been calculated as one unit of fire per day of major operations.[204] For the regiment, that meant 8100 rounds for light howitzers, and 1800 rounds for medium howitzers.[205] Nevertheless, when our light howitzers fired only 3000 rounds, and our medium howitzers only 600 rounds – i.e., about one-third of a unit of fire – during critical days like 22 and 27 August, we experienced serious difficulties.
>
> The shortage of ammunition forced us to conduct our artillery operations in far too passive a manner. There was hardly enough ammunition for satisfying requests from the infantry for direct fire support and for neutralizing definitely identified assemblies of enemy forces, particularly in view of the fact that requests from the badly and constantly pressed infantry were very numerous.
>
> For an active conduct of fire that would seek out and crush the enemy in his rear area, his probable bivouac sites, his headquarters, and similar installations, we lacked the necessary ammunition. An active conduct of fire along those lines would have been highly desirable especially in that situation. Moreover, we had all the signal and survey facilities needed for such a conduct of fire … The ammunition shortage … completely prevented … the translation into practice of the modern principles of leadership set forth in the German instruction manual D-201[206] and taught in the artillery schools. We were forced to revert to artillery tactics of days long past.[207]

It did not help matters that desperately needed ammunition trains were becoming "lost" in the Warsaw supply catchment area, with days often elapsing until they were once again discovered and sent on their way.[208] Nor did it help matters that, on 10 September, Ninth Army was informed that only 15 trainloads of shells for the 150mm medium field howitzers (s.F.H.) were still available for the entire eastern front; and not until the middle of October was a normal resupply of the shells expected to resume. As a result, Ninth Army at once issued orders calling for the "greatest economy" in expenditure of the shells, "so that sufficient quantities can be stocked for coming operations."[209] The shortsighted decision of German military authorities in the period preceding the start of the Russian campaign to drastically throttle back ammunition production was finally coming home to roost with a vengeance.[210]

To address the inchoate ammunition crisis, priority had been given to ammunition supply at the beginning of August; this, however, could only be accomplished by making "drastic" cuts to the supply of fuel and rations.[211] On 21 August, Bock was informed that Guderian, "for reasons of materiel and fuel," could advance no farther toward Gomel.[212]

During a conference on 30 August, General Wagner, Quartermaster General of the Army, explained that both Army Groups Center and South had a "critical fuel shortage," and that replenishment would be impossible due to the serious problems with the railways.[213] Yet replenishment was critically required, for the difficult terrain (and, increasingly, the poor weather) had raised fuel consumption well above the previously calculated fuel quotas, meaning that more fuel trains were needed than originally envisaged by German logisticians; in September 1941 alone, however, 120 approved fuel trains were unable to reach the front because of transport problems on the railway.[214] It is hardly a wonder that in mid-September, Field Marshal von Kluge, Commander, Fourth Army, wrote: "The Army lives from hand to mouth, especially as regards the fuel situation."[215]

Due to the debilitating interplay between the tenacious and repeated Soviet counterattacks, and the growing deficiencies of German rail and motorized transport, the buildup of supplies for the renewed push on Moscow proceeded at a frustratingly deliberate pace; in addition, stockpiles, as far as they went, could only be accumulated by cutting back on subsistence, forcing the troops to live increasingly off the land.[216] In mid-August, both Second and Ninth Armies reported that ammunition stocks were still falling, instead of rising in preparation for a new attack; furthermore, POL supplies remained thoroughly inadequate.[217] It was not until 15 September that Second Army characterized its supply situation as secure; and even then the slow accretion of stocks rendered any resumption of major offensive operations impossible before the beginning of October. At the same time, both Fourth and Ninth Armies described the transport capacity as insufficient to meet existing requirements while also stocking depots for the planned general offensive.[218] As it was, in September and October 1941, major supply dumps – e.g., Smolensk, Gomel, Roslavl and Vitebsk – would be fortunate on any given day to receive even two-thirds of the supplies needed to maintain Operation "Typhoon" at full strength.[219]

The immense burden on Army Group Center's creaking logistics was partially lifted in the second week of September, as Bock's eastern front settled down after weeks of Red Army counterstrokes. On 29 September, Wagner reported to Halder that supplies for the new offensive were "satisfactory" (*zufriedenstellend*) and that all was "ready for the jump off" (*zum Absprung … bereit*).[220] In a letter to his wife, Elisabeth, he radiated confidence that his weeks of exhaustive preparation would bring Army Group Center to Moscow "forthwith" (*ohne weiteres*).[221] Beyond that, however, "he dared not think,"[222] merely noting that by then, "the winter will be here and, hopefully, the war will come to an end."[223]

Wagner's confidence was, of course, unwarranted. For example, as late as 26 September (four days before the start of the attack) the arrival of fuel trains was "considerably in arrears,"[224] even though the reinforced army group now had three panzer groups and three armies to supply (nearly 80 divisions in all); in fact, the stocks of fuel were barely enough to move Bock's armor another 300 kilometers – that is, at best as far as the "gates of Moscow."[225] According to German historian Rolf-Dieter Mueller:

> Wagner was playing a dangerous game with his readiness to take any risk in the conduct of operations, and his tendency always to give an optimistic answer to any question about the range of supply despite "some nerves." Though all the signs indicated that Army Group Center was not strong enough to achieve its operational goals, Halder was vociferous in advocating the advance on Moscow. Wagner was not the type of man to oppose him because of concern for the management of supply. Should a crisis arise, the railway was always a good scapegoat, particularly as it was not under the control of Army High Command.[226]

While a detailed discussion of logistical preparations for Operation "Typhoon" is outside the purview of this narrative,[227] the key point is this: The logistical apparatus of Army

Group Center was totally inadequate to meet the exigencies of the coming offensive.[228] Yet the situation was even worse than that, for as this narrative has demonstrated, the logistics of the army group had begun to fail after just a few short weeks of campaigning; as a result, Bock had been unable to project his offensive strength much beyond Smolensk during the July-September period. Indeed, as early as mid-July 1941, ammunition and fuel requirements, as well as the stark realities of the rail and road network, had made an immediate advance to Moscow logistically impossible; hence, the discussions among Halder, Bock, Hoth and Guderian regarding the impending capture of the city were "purely an academic exercise.

> Logistical constraints dictated Bock's infantry armies would have to halt east of Smolensk, and only a portion of his panzer forces were able to go farther forward and even then at great risk. Without any doubt, these realities reflected the most dangerous weakness in Plan *Barbarossa*, specifically, its calculations regarding logistical support necessary to sustain the campaign, whose explosive impact, which had previously been almost contemptuously ignored, was now being felt.[229]

11.5: The *Stellungskrieg* Continues East of Smolensk

In the second half of August 1941, the front of Army Group Center beyond Smolensk was anchored by Adolf Strauss' Ninth Army and Hans von Kluge's newly reactivated Fourth Army;[230] both armies, however, following Hitler's decision to send Hoth's 3 Panzer Group northward, and to continue Guderian's drive past Gomel into the Ukraine, were left to contend with the ongoing Red Army counterstrokes with completely inadequate mobile reserves.[231] Moreover, the migration of the panzer units away from Ninth and Fourth Armies did not go unnoticed by the Soviet High Command, which saw in it another incentive to keep up their intense pressure along Bock's embattled eastern front.

The growing scarcity of air assets available to Army Group Center was also exploited by the Soviets, who, as noted above (Section 11.4.1), were able to garner air superiority over much of the front – a reflection of the incipient revival of the Soviet Air Force (VVS). About this time, the Germans were introduced to a new weapon by the VVS – a nasty surprise which 241 Infantry Regiment (106 ID) first encountered during combat southwest of Belyi:

> The nighttime aerial attacks were unpleasant. The units became acquainted with phosphorus bombs for the first time. The command post of 1st Batallion experienced an aggressive attack of this kind. The forest lit up everywhere and hardly anyone knew how this phosphorus might be combatted. No water was available; wouldn't have done any good anyway. So there was nothing left to do but the dangerous work of smothering the burning or smouldering phosphorus with earth.[232]

With the Soviets becoming more active in the air, the Germans suddenly found themselves on the receiving end of terrifying aerial assaults, as experienced by *Leutnant* Soeffker (6 ID) in September 1941:

> This morning at 0800 hours I was riding with 2 non-commissioned officers and 2 men to reconnoiter the road … As I'm riding my bicycle on the return journey through Prechistaya, I run into a Russian low-level attack. 3 bombers and 2 fighters are flying at lowest altitude over the road. The bombers drop ca. 20 fragmentation bombs, while the fighters blanket the march route with machine gun fire. I leap from my bicycle and seek cover behind a house. There's a lot

of confusion. The drivers shamefully and irresponsibly leave their vehicles and horses in the lurch. Horses run whinnying all over the road. Motor vehicle drivers leap from their vehicles and abandon them with engines still running.

To my right, 6 bombs land in a garden. The shrapnel whizzes over the road, smashing window panes and house roofs. Some houses immediately go up in flames. The civilian population suffers considerable losses. Several severely injured Russians are carried out of one house, some of them are missing arms and legs. Beside me, a sobbing woman carries a small, naked child covered in blood out of the house. I myself have been enormously lucky, that was the first proper low-level attack [*Tiefangriff*] that I have ever experienced. Now I can finally picture what it must be like when German fighters and bombers attack Russian march columns.[233]

Holding dangerously diluted positions, the German infantry divisions normally defended their overextended lines[234] with all three infantry regiments forward, backed up by whatever local reserves could be scraped together. Defenses consisted of a clutch of platoon and company strongpoints, the most durable of which were anchored in and around villages and interlaced with bunkers and communications trenches. Gaps between the strongpoints were – in theory at least – protected by pre-planned and on-call interlocking artillery and mortar fire.[235]

Under the prevailing conditions of static warfare, and the dominating role played by the artillery, the *Landser* were often struck by similarities to their fathers' experiences in the Great War of 1914-18;[236] moreover, as the hardships of the front ineluctably multiplied, comparisons to their fathers became more common. In late August 1941, the war diary of Ninth Army observed that, from the grim ordeal of the weeks-long defensive battles, a "type of German fighter" (*deutscher Kaempfertyp*) was emerging "who embodies the toughness and feelings of superiority of that glorious German *Weltkriegskaempfer*. He lets the enemy tanks simply roll on by and then overcomes the trailing *Rotarmisten* in close combat."[237] Such heroic language was in the best tradition of Ernst Juenger, who had glorified his experiences as a German soldier on the western front in World War I in his 1920 book *Storm of Steel* (*In Stahlgewittern*).

As the weeks past, the men dug deeper into the ground to improve their chances of survival. The weather grew colder and insects began to torment the men, while the pressures of the front left little time to tend to basic human needs, such as personal hygiene. Gradually, the men began to take on a peculiarly primitive existence. On 18 August, 21-year-old Harald Henry, a soldier in Army Group Center, wrote: "It would hardly be an overstatement to say that 'not even a dog could go on living like this,' because no animal could possibly stoop to live any lower or more primitively than us. All day long we hunker down below the ground, crammed into tight holes, helplessly exposed to sun and rain and try to sleep."[238]

Two days later (20 August), *Gefreiter* Alois Scheuer (197 ID) wrote to his wife from the defensive positions of his unit along the Desna River:

My dearest, beloved wife!

Right now, it's 10 o'clock in the morning. The sun is shining really warmly again and our stuff, soaked through in a heavy storm-filled night, is drying again. For several days now we have been in position on an elevation in the middle of a cornfield. For the moment, we've settled into defensive positions … The hours go past slowly, we lie in our foxholes and wait for further orders, wait for post from home. Now and then the silence of these hours is interrupted by the iron greetings of Russian artillery. If the impacts get dangerously close, we press our noses a bit deeper into the dirt. The spade has often proved itself to be a true lifesaver in such situations.

Our mode of life is extremely primitive. It is not at all unusual if we haven't washed or shaved for days. But the most unpleasant thing is that our rations are not completely adequate. Despite the turnips and carrots which we get from the gardens, we can't get rid of that constant sensation of hunger. We've even tried new potatoes, but they aren't ripe yet and our stomachs start to churn …

I've met several comrades from St. Ingbert recently … Each looks as scruffy as the next, and every one of them has only one desire: to get out of this country as fast as possible. There's many a loud-mouth still back home I'd like to see here just for 14 days, I think they'd soon be cured of that.[239]

On 22 August 1941, *Unteroffizier* "W.F.," a soldier attached to the staff of 459 Infantry Regiment (251 ID), just west of Velikie Luki, echoed Scheuer's sentiments in a field post to an unnamed recipient.

I've already had it up to here with this much-vaunted Soviet Union! The conditions here are prehistoric. Our propaganda definitely didn't exaggerate, more like didn't go far enough. At the moment, we're stuck outside a town between Petersburg and Moscow and are keeping the Russians occupied. The losses in our regiment are pretty high, although in my unit they're normal. We're suffering a lot from artillery fire here, and we have to live day and night in foxholes for protection from shrapnel. The holes are full of water. Lice and other vermin creep in, too.[240]

At the beginning of September, *Obergefreiter* Matthias (6 ID), wrote home to his family; like most all of the *Landser*, he was disappointed by the slowdown of the war, and longed for the front to be in motion again:

A trench war has developed here, with communication trenches, "fox burrows," bunkers (in the earth), etc. It's bitterly cold and rainy. There's water in our positions, all the walls are collapsing, and the bunkers have become damp. Hopefully we'll be able to move on soon, too. The best thing would be a swift attack! To our right and left, the panzers have already pushed ahead and soon another cauldron will be complete. Leningrad is already encircled as well. According to rumors [*Latrinenparolen*], the same fate awaits Moscow, but I don't believe it, since nothing official has been announced about it. At any rate, the trap has to be sprung in September now or else it will soon be winter and the war will be up s… creek![241]

Despite the many factors which made the war in the east so monstrously cruel, the soldiers of both sides sometimes found ways to mutually ease the burdens of life in the trenches, as the soldiers of 241 Infantry Regiment (106 ID) discovered during September 1941:

A deceptive calm held sway at the front. The enemies lay only a few meters away from each other. The companies of 241 Infantry Regiment and the Russians were sometimes only separated by a potato field. And potatoes were important, because they had become the primary foodstuff during these weeks in September. The reason: the field bakery had burned down and there was hardly any bread – usually, though, none. But besides the potatoes, there were onions and cucumbers for "free delivery to your door."

There was an unspoken agreement between the Russian soldiers and our *Landser*. If a Russian soldier dared to wander onto the potato field, our guns stayed quiet. In return, if a German soldier went onto the potato field, then, too, nothing would happen on the Russian side. But our soldiers were careful. Just before setting foot on the potato field, a steel helmet would be placed at the top of a carbine and briefly held over the edge of the trench. If the coast was clear, then they could safely go onto the field.[242]

11.5.1: Soviet "Dukhovshchina Offensive"

On 17 August 1941, Timoshenko's Western Front had launched another major counteroffensive ("Dukhovshchina Offensive"). On 21 August, Zhukov expanded the front's mission to include the capture of Velizh, Demidov and Smolensk; by month's end, the offensive had grown to embrace the entire Western Front sector from Toropets to Iartsevo.[243] Fortunately for Bock's weakened divisions, the piecemeal fashion in which the Soviet attack developed diminished its overall punch, as did the fact that many of the attacking enemy formations were weak in armor, heavy weapons and machine guns; nevertheless, in the days ahead, the Red Army would score "unprecedented tactical victories," and "genuinely hurt" Army Group Center.[244]

The intense and unremitting pressure the Soviet Dukhovshchina Offensive put on the front of German Ninth Army is evident from the brief daily summaries in the OKW war diary:

17.8.41:
On the eastern front of the Army Group [Center] there are isolated enemy attacks against the … Ninth Army, which are being repelled. An attack in division strength against 161 ID could only be parried through commitment of the last of the local reserves. The HKL is being taken back a little there.

18.8.41:
On the eastern front … of Ninth Army, the enemy is attacking at several points in company to regimental strength. The northern flank of the 8 AK (161 ID) had to be withdrawn in the face of a superior assault to a prepared covering position [*Aufnahmestellung*].

19.8.41:
Numerous superior enemy attacks on Ninth Army, against the front of 8, 5, and 6 AK, have led to localized incursions, which for the most part have been cleared up again in counterattacks.

20.8.41:
The tense situation in the area of Ninth Army continues, especially at the northern flank of 8 AK and in front of 5 AK. Enemy continues his attacks, which lead once again to several localized incursions. However, they can be neutralized again in the course of the fighting. In order to relieve the northern flank of 161 ID, which had been pushed back the previous day, 7 PD struck from the area southwest of Frol into the northern flank of the encroaching enemy. The attack pushes through as far as southwest of Makovya, but has to be broken off due to nightfall.

21.8.41:
The enemy offensive activity continues in sector of Ninth Army. The situation continues to be tense. The counterattack carried out by 7 PD against the northern flank of the enemy, which had broken through at the northern flank of 161 Infantry Division, has brought some relief, but cost the division considerable losses …

In front of 5 and 6 AK heavy artillery fire and enemy attacks, which are beaten back in counterattacks with severe losses for the enemy. Our own losses are also high.

22.8.41:
The enemy attacks around Ninth Army have become less intense. An enemy attack of around 2 divisions, led in close formation and directed at the junction of 6 ID and 26 ID, is driven back by 6 ID with heavy losses for the enemy; the battles are still ongoing in 26 ID's sector. In the area of 161 ID there is further enemy offensive activity.

23.8.41:
Enemy attacks persist for the entire day on Ninth Army. At the left flank of 8 AK the HKL is successfully won back through the deployment of 14 ID (mot.) in a counterattack.

In the areas of 5 and 6 AK, the enemy offensive activity continues. Strong enemy attacks, supported by artillery and tanks, are repelled or cleared up in counterattacks. The enemy suffers heavy damage through bloody losses and losses of tanks.

25.8.41:
There are repeated enemy attacks against … Ninth Army's front. At individual front sectors of Ninth Army, the HKL is being systematically moved back to more advantageous terrain for defense.

27.8.41:
The enemy attacks at several locations along … Ninth Army's eastern front and directs an intense assault against 6 AK with at least 1 division, which leads to a deep incursion at 26 ID. The situation can be cleared up with the deployment of the last reserves and the HKL restored. The lack of sufficient reserves, especially in this sector of Ninth Army, however, means the situation continues to appear tense.[245]

On 28 August, the furious Soviet assaults against Ninth Army temporarily ebbed; yet the damage done had been considerable. For example, the battalions of Maj.-Gen. Hermann Wilck's 161 Infantry Division had been decimated during the initial days of the fighting by I. S. Konev's 19 Army; by nightfall, 19 August, the division's combat strength had plummeted to roughly 25 percent of initial strength,[246] eliciting the remark from Bock that the division was at the "end of its tether. It almost looks," Bock mused in his diary, "as if the Russians noticed the departure of the motorized divisions behind Ninth Army's front."[247] And indeed they had.

As the OKW daily summaries reveal, the Germans responded to Timoshenko's new offensive by counterattacking as often and aggressively as their limited resources allowed to patch up holes in the HKL. Such was standard German practice, and while the practice was effective, it could also be costly. The 20 August counterstroke by Funck's reinforced 7 Panzer Division, whose objective was to rout Soviet 19 Army, immediately lapsed into a two-day slugging match, during which the panzers were ensnared in a "deadly web of dug-in tanks, interlocking infantry and anti-tank strongholds and under a hail of Soviet artillery and mortar fire."[248] About two-thirds of 7 Panzer's tanks were destroyed by Konev's forces, and the remainder forced to withdraw. The Russian victory signified the *first time in the war* that they had stopped a major German armored thrust, and stopped it dead in its tracks.[249]

Although the German lines had held (despite minor adjustments), and attacking Red Army forces had suffered prohibitive losses, the total casualties incurred by Ninth Army were also enormous. In fact, over a somewhat longer period (6-28 August 1941), the army's

5 and 8 Army Corps (seven divisions in all) collectively sustained casualties of 271 officers, 8075 NCOs and men; of these, 56 officers, 2019 NCOs and men were fatal losses, while three officers and 366 NCOs and men went missing. Over the same three-week period, the two corps made 4350 prisoners, while destroying or capturing 182 Soviet tanks.[250]

11.5.2: The Red Army Recaptures El'nia

In late August 1941, Kluge's Fourth Army (7, 9, 12, 20 Army Corps) covered some 250 kilometers of Army Group Center's front. The army's positions ran southeast from the area east Smolensk (northern front), embraced the El'nia salient, then turned south along and eventually west of the Desna River as far as Pochep, some 60 kilometers southwest of Briansk.[251] By now, some of Fourth Army's divisions were so diminished in strength that combat engineers, although desperately needed behind the front to build roads, were being used as infantry by Geyer's 9 Army Corps covering the northern flank of the El'nia salient; the corps' 137 Infantry Division lost over 50 men per day in local actions between 20-30 August, while the adjacent 263 Infantry Division sustained 1200 casualties between 20-27 August.[252]

Kluge's men, like those of Ninth Army to the north, were well aware that the normal campaigning season in Russia was approaching its end, and they were also itching to get moving again. In an early morning missive (1:00 a.m.) to his wife on 30 August, Major Werner Heinemann (23 ID) captured the longing of every soldier in Fourth Army at this time; his thoughts, however, betrayed a growing uneasiness about the future direction of the campaign:

> When we, here at the position of the front projecting furthest to the east, will begin to advance again, nobody knows. Only that it must be, that we <u>have</u> to have Moscow this year, that's certain. The Russian is certainly shaken to his very core, but an increasing tenacity remains (he, after all, is fighting for "Russia," not for Bolshevism any more) and an absurd number of men. Defectors arrive daily, but still he makes life most difficult for us, and the commissars above all know their trade, keeping the masses under pressure.[253]

The major's observations were, of course, spot on. After a brief respite of several days, Soviet assaults against Fourth Army picked up again that very day (30 August). In the sector of Heinemann's 23 Infantry Division (7 Army Corps), along the Desna River, the attackers managed to break through, punching a hole 8-10 kilometers deep in the division's front; a counterthrust by 10 Panzer Division, supported by infantry, restored the situation the following day.[254]

More significantly, on 30 August, the Soviets began their final push to capture the El'nia salient from the infantry of Materna's 20 Army Corps, which had defended the position for several weeks at great cost against relentless Red Army attacks;[255] indeed, in an early post-war study for the U.S. Army, former Army Group Center Chief of Staff, General Hans von Greiffenberg, characterized the fighting there as "particularly grim."[256] Zhukov's Reserve Front once again unleashed Rakutin's 24 Army, recently reinforced by three additional divisions, bringing its total strength to 10 divisions (including 102 and 105 Tank and 103 Motorized Divisions).[257] Rakutin struck with two assault groups – one north, one south of the salient – supported by 800 guns, mortars, and multiple rocket launchers; moreover, his assault was coordinated with simultaneous offensives by Western Front in the north (at Dukhovshchina) and Briansk Front in the south (Roslavl – Novozybkov).[258]

The German defenders were ill prepared for the Soviet onslaught. Because of the chronic shortage of combat infantry, their defenses normally consisted of little more than a single trench line, instead of a multizone, elastic defense in depth, as prescribed by German doctrine. The lack of troops also prohibited the establishment of advanced positions or outposts in front of the main battle line; without adequate forward security, many units had no choice but to abandon the preferred reverse-slope defensive positions, which offered protection from enemy observation and fire.[259] When Kluge's Fourth Army assumed control of the El'nia sector from Guderian's headquarters on 22 August, the conditions there had appalled Colonel Guenther Blumentritt, the army's chief of staff. As he wrote after the war: "When I say that our lines were thin, this is an understatement. Divisions were assigned sectors almost 20 miles wide. Furthermore, in view of the heavy casualties already suffered in the course of the campaign, these divisions were usually understrength and tactical reserves were non-existent."[260] In his fine study of German defensive doctrine for the U.S. Army Combat Studies Institute, Timothy Wray, then a U.S. Army major, underscored Blumentritt's observations using the example of 78 Infantry Division (20 Army Corps):

> During a forward reconnaissance on 19 August, while preparing to relieve another division at El'nia, officers of the 78 Infantry Division discovered that the German front consisted mostly of a thin line of disconnected rifle pits. No rearward positions had been prepared, and due to a shortage of mines and barbed wire, only a handful of obstacles stood in the way of any Soviet attack. The German lines were poorly sited, being almost entirely exposed to enemy positions on higher ground. As a result, any daylight movement within the German lines invited a rain of enemy artillery and mortar shells. In fact, the Soviet fire was so dominant that German casualties had to remain in their foxholes until after dark before they could be evacuated.
>
> Despite good intentions, leaders of the 78 Infantry Division found it virtually impossible to improve the defensive situation after occupying their sector on 22 August. A battalion commander in the 238 Infantry Regiment noted that the strength and accuracy of Soviet fire precluded all efforts to extend German entrenchments by day, while the necessity of guarding against Soviet infiltration at night prevented the formation of nocturnal work parties. Also, adequate reserves could not be found to reinforce threatened sectors; after manning its 12-mile-wide sector, the entire 78 Infantry Division held less than one full battalion in reserve.[261]

The powerful offensive by Soviet 24 Army rapidly succeeded in penetrating German forward defenses; by 4 September, despite desperate and repeated German counterattacks, both Rakutin's northern and southern shock groups had deeply enveloped the defenders, threatening them with encirclement. Complicating the defense of the salient was the fact that, because of the intense fighting now raging up and down the front of Army Group Center, the Germans were unable to reinforce the beleaguered defenders within the bridgehead.[262]

Two days before (2 September), Field Marshal von Bock had noted that his divisions within the El'nia salient were simply being "bled white;" and, after several conversations with Kluge, he decided the time had finally come to abandon it. As always, his eyes were riveted on Moscow, and he explained his decision by noting that "the attack to the east cannot begin until the last third of September at the earliest! Until then it is vital to preserve and save our strength, for only two fresh divisions … are being sent to the army group from the rear."[263]

Bock's decision was greeted with relief by the *Landser* fighting and dying inside the bloody inferno at El'nia. In a letter on 2 September, *Obergefreiter* "M. H." (268 ID), described conditions there:

> We're experiencing grim times and heavy losses. We've been stuck in the same place for five weeks now and we're badly and constantly tormented by the Russian artillery. I just don't know how much longer our nerves can stand up to this … I think we've already made enough heavy sacrifices. We're also constantly being promised that we'll be going back home, but it always comes to nothing.[264]

Ordered to conduct a fighting withdrawal, Materna's infantry divisions methodically pulled back from the salient to prepared positions along the Ustrom and Striana Rivers, where they halted any further Soviet advance.[265] To the northwest, 137 Infantry Division (9 Army Corps), which had helped to shield the salient's northern flank, was temporarily withdrawn to a well-deserved rest area southeast of Smolensk, despite a driving rain which transformed the roads into a gooey mass, posing major challenges to the movement of men, horses, vehicles and artillery.[266] After the withdrawal was complete, Maj.-Gen. Friedrich Bergmann, Commander, 137 ID, issued a divisional order on 7 September; it began with an extraordinary accounting of the division's recent experiences:

> Soldiers of the 137 [Infantry] Division!
> Nearly three weeks of the toughest combat are behind us. In 19 days defending the El'nia bend along an entire front of 21 km in the righthand sector, the operations of all units and weapon types repelled:
> Approximately 10-15 attacks daily up to company strength for six days under moderate enemy artillery fire.
> Approximately 20 attacks daily up to regiment strength, repeated as many as four times at the same location, for eight days under heavy fire from ca. 15 batteries.
> Continuous attacks [*zusammenhaengende Angriffe*] along the entire front from dawn to dusk, as well as several nighttime attacks, for five days under the heaviest fire from ca. 30 batteries.[267]

The 19 days of fighting had taken a heavy toll on Bergmann's troops; altogether, the division suffered 1900 combat casualties, an average of 100 per day and an irreplaceable contraction of its fighting strength.[268]

Meanwhile, after more heavy fighting, the Soviet 19 Rifle Division penetrated into the battered town of El'nia on 5 September; with the help of several additional rifle divisions, it seized the town the next day. For the Russians, the victory at El'nia signified their first real victory of the war, modest though it was; in fact, it was the "first occasion when Soviet forces successfully penetrated prepared German defenses and regained a sizeable chunk of occupied territory."[269] From the German perspective, the "operational withdrawal from El'nia was the first imposed on the German Army in World War II."[270] Yet for the Russians the cost had been "excessive:" Of the total of 103,200 men committed to the operation, they lost 31,853 – 10,701 killed, captured or missing, and 21,152 wounded. For having distinguished themselves in the fighting, four Red Army rifle divisions (100, 127, 153, 161) became the first to be redesignated as "guards" divisions.[271]

As noted above, the Soviet El'nia operation was but part of a general offensive which engulfed most of Army Group Center's front. On 1 September, Timoshenko had renewed his Western Front offensive at Dukhovshchina, unleashing a combined assault with three armies (16, 19 and 20). Two days before (30 August), the Soviet Briansk Front,[272] commanded by General Eremenko (known to his peers as the "Soviet Guderian"), had begun its operations, with the objective of attacking "into the very teeth of General Guderian's advance"[273] toward Kiev, while also striking the southern flank of Fourth Army. Thus began a renewed period of crisis for Bock's army group, as the Soviet attacks once more placed immense pressure on the brittle German main battle lines. In his journal, the field marshal observed with a certain insouciance: "Against the Ninth Army the enemy is attacking east of Smolensk and further north at his old favorite places."[274] The next day (2 September), however, he registered a distinctly more serious tone: "Today the enemy attacked the extreme southern wing of the [Fourth] Army[275] at Pochep and due north of it, there for the first time. If he keeps at it, we could end up in a fine mess!"[276] On 3 September, in response to a breakthrough by Soviet tanks ("in considerable depth") on Fourth Army's southern wing (12 Army Corps), Bock placed his sole reserve division in the sector, Brig.-Gen. Lothar Rendulic's 52 Infantry Division, at Kluge's disposal, with the injunction that it be committed "only if it is really necessary."[277]

On 5 September 1941, from the Army High Command compound in East Prussia, Hellmuth Stieff commented darkly on the increasingly precarious predicament of Bock's army group:

> The eastern front of [Army Group Center] has been involved in the heaviest defensive fighting on the scale of the World War (up to 300 enemy batteries in a single corps sector) for days, even weeks, during which there have been serious daily breaches [of the HKL] and in the course of which the combat strength of our divisions has melted away like snow in the sun. The tragic thing in all this is that our troops are suffering chronic ammunition shortages due to transport issues. The situation there is on the razor's edge, because we have no more reserves. Hopefully the Russian will run out of steam first, otherwise there's the distinct danger of losing Smolensk.[278]

11.5.3: The Heavy Fighting Subsides & Germans Prepare "Typhoon"

As matters turned out, Stieff and his fellow staff officers were soon able to breathe at least a temporary sigh of relief, for the Red Army offensives did indeed "run out of steam." On 10 September, at Zhukov's request, the *Stavka* permitted Western and Reserve Fronts to suspend their offensives along the Dukhovshchina and El'nia axes, respectively. Both fronts had incurred enormous losses of men and materiel, while further south Guderian's panzers were dismantling the attacking forces of Eremenko's Briansk Front, whose offensive ground to a halt two days later.[279]

While the Soviet offensives of late August and early September had badly pressed Bock's forces, they had also drained the attacking Red Army fronts of much of their combat power for either attack or defense. For example, in addition to the heavy losses suffered by Zhukov's Reserve Front at El'nia, the Briansk Front had sustained about 100,000 casualties and lost 140 tanks – figures equal to nearly 40 percent of the men (261,696) and more than half of the tanks (259) committed to its Roslavl-Novozybkov operation.[280] More generally, the average strength of many Soviet rifle divisions was now down to about 3000 men.[281] Such losses, which seriously reduced the Red Army order of battle just as the Germans were gearing up to strike out again toward Moscow, would contribute to the catastrophic defeats endured by the Russians in October 1941, during the first phase of Army Group Center's Operation "Typhoon."[282]

With the many weeks of heavy combat finally drawing to a close,[283] the soldiers on both sides returned to the less eventful routines that characterized quieter periods of static warfare. The men engaged in regular patrolling, conducted occasional local assaults, and reinforced their rifle pits and bunkers to escape sudden bursts of artillery fire or attack from the air. For the first time in weeks, the *Landser* had time to clean weapons and equipment, tend to personal hygiene, catch up on letters to loved ones at home, and, most vitally, get some rest and sleep.

Yet as the increasingly cool September days slipped away, a tangible sense of excitement began to grip the battle-hardened veterans of Army Group Center, as once again the front was jolted by bursts of purposeful activity. New units, weapons and equipment were now arriving and rumors began to fill the air. Among those caught up in the sudden tumult were the men of 241 Infantry Regiment (106 ID):

> There was something in the air, but nobody could say what it was. A kind of feverish bustle pervaded the troops and the command posts. There were secret orders and there was extensive reconnaissance. The digging of trenches or improvement of the positions were largely ignored. Only the most essential was done to the positions.
>
> The troops pricked up their ears when suddenly new cipher documents for radio traffic were distributed. Then it became clear to many that it could only mean an attack in an eastward direction.[284]

On 6 September 1941, Adolf Hitler, satisfied that operations in the north (Leningrad) and south (Ukraine) were proceeding according to plan, had issued Directive No. 35, ordering the attack of Army Group Center toward Moscow to begin "at the earliest possible moment (end of September)."[285] Ten days later (16 September), Bock issued his "Typhoon" operations order for the three panzer groups under his command (Guderian's group would return from the south, and 4 Panzer Group was on its way from Army Group North).[286] On 24 September, at his command post in Smolensk, he conferred with his army and panzer group commanders one last time, and together they pored over operational plans and objectives.[287] ("It is time!" Bock exclaimed in his diary that day.)[288] On 26 September, he issued the general attack order for the offensive.[289] (It began: "Following a long period of waiting, the army group once again is moving to the attack.") On 27 September, the field marshal set the time for launch of the main attack at 5.30 a.m., 2 October.[290] ("Somewhat hurried," he wrote in his diary, "but we have no time to lose.")[291] By then, nearly two million men, arrayed in 78 divisions, supported by hundreds of tanks and aircraft and thousands of guns, would be assembled for an operation of world historical moment – and operation, they fervently hoped, which would knock Russia out of the war and bring them all home.

By 24 September 1941, 6 Infantry Division had been relieved from its positions west of Belyi and shifted slightly southward, as the Ninth Army regrouped for the impending attack.[292] Yet while the division completed its preparations for the renewed advance to the east, the war of position continued unabated, as Heinrich Haape observed in his journal on 27 September:

> The *Stellungskrieg* has reached its zenith! In some places, our trenches lie 80 meters away from the Russian positions. Everybody has dug themselves into the ground. Rations, ammunition, and other necessities are only delivered at night. So we're living the life of proper military moles here [*ein rechtes kriegerisches Maulwurfsleben*]. The impacts of the shells beat down around our little self-made dugouts the entire day. A medical bunker has been built next to my sleeping bunker, where I can accommodate the day's wounded and provide medical attention for them; they're transported back to the main dressing station at night. Our quite justifiable hope is that this dreary and yet dangerous mess will soon come to an end.[293]

On 29 September, the division's combat engineer battalion (6 Pi.B.) began the treacherous task of clearing the German minefields before the main battle line. Heavy weapons were hauled into position. At the end of the month, 6 ID received its attack order for "Typhoon."[294] In his diary, *Leutnant* Soeffker captured the mood of virtually every man in the division:

> Our Army Group Center is on the verge of great, decisive operations. In a few days the major offensive on Moscow will begin for us. Until now, our march

direction was always Moscow. Our greatest wish is to hold to this direction and to be there when Moscow is stormed. We have been here on the defensive for weeks. This has caused an unfair internal readjustment for our men, but soon what will count for us is that word again: Attack![295]

On the eve of the assault, *Unteroffizier* Helmut Pabst, a soldier in Ninth Army, observed the mighty buildup of forces with obvious wonder:

> What news there is we piece together like bits of a mosaic. Somebody has seen the tanks, the yellow ones which were meant for Africa.[296] Now they've turned up here. Someone else has seen assault guns. And a man from the *Nebelwerfers* appeared by mistake. All kinds of special weapons – lots of them – guns of every caliber; they are all being concentrated in this sector. It's piling up inexorably like a thunderstorm. It is the sword above the calm – the drawing of breath for a stroke which may be bigger than any we have seen yet.[297]

"We don't know when it will start," Pabst went on, "We only feel the veil over the calm getting thinner, the atmosphere gathering tension, the approach of the hour when it will only need a word to let loose hell, when all this concentrated force will spring forward."[298]

11.6: Operations on the Flanks, "Typhoon" & the Defeat of Operation *Barbarossa*

Following Hitler's decision of 21 August 1941, the *Schwerpunkt* of German operations shifted temporarily to the flanks of the eastern front (that is, to the areas of operation of Army Groups North and South), bringing a "degree of strategic clarity ... which had been absent for many weeks.

> Still, the grueling effects of the long period of indecision and internal wrangling left its mark on the higher command with frayed nerves and bitter personal animosity reflective of an Army that had suffered a major reversal. The daily business of directing the war, of course, went on, but it was no longer a Blitzkrieg campaign, now it was a war of endurance – and in such a war the Soviet Union, backed by its allies in the west, was already in a favored position.[299]

11.6.1: Leningrad & the Kiev Cauldron

Already on 10 August, after significant delays, Field Marshal Ritter von Leeb's Army Group North had begun a general attack on Leningrad, effectively supported by the *Stukas* and medium bombers of Richthofen's 8 Air Corps.[300] Despite tough Soviet resistance, panzer units broke out into the open country beyond the line of the Luga River – Leningrad's outermost defensive line some 100 kilometers from the city. On 20 August, Leeb's right wing reached Chudovo, severing the main rail line running southeast from Leningrad to Moscow; on 31 August, the attackers cut the last rail link from Leningrad to the east at Mga.[301]

By now, the lead elements of Schmidt's 39 Panzer Corps were barely 25 kilometers from Leningrad.[302] Desperate to employ every possible armament in the defense of the city, the Soviets brought the naval guns of the Neva Squadron into action against the Germans; many naval guns were removed from their ships and mounted on land, and "even the gun batteries of the 40-year-old cruiser *Aurora*, which had fired blanks at the Winter Palace in November 1917, frightening the remnants of the Provisional Government into surrendering to the Bolsheviks, were dismounted, and placed in position on the Pulkovo heights."[303]

On 3 September, German long-range heavy artillery (240mm) opened fire on Leningrad for the first time.[304] In savage fighting, panzer and motorized units battled their way through extensive and concentric lines of defense (1000 kilometers of earthworks, 645km of anti-tank ditches, 600km of barbed wire, and some 5000 pillboxes and fire-points),[305] Reinhardt's 41 Panzer Corps reaching the city's suburbs by 5 September.[306] Three days later (8 September) the Germans seized Shlisselburg, on the shore of Lake Ladoga, depriving Leningrad of its last land link with the rest of the Soviet Union.[307] On 9 September, the *Luftwaffe* began to pound the city with around-the-clock bombing missions.[308] On 10 September, the badly understrength 1 Panzer Division penetrated Russian defenses on the Dudergof height, barely 10 kilometers southeast of Leningrad. From this tactically vital patch of ground, the Germans could see the city spread out before them, with its gleaming golden cupolas and towers; warships were visible in the port, lobbing shells on German targets to their rear.[309]

But the attackers would get no further. Hitler had already decreed that most of Leeb's armor was to be transferred to Army Group Center, to support the assault on Moscow; soon Hoepner's 4 Panzer Group headquarters, three panzer corps headquarters, and several panzer divisions were on the move to join Bock's army group.[310] The "Fuehrer," moreover, had decided not to capture Leningrad, but to surround it, starve out its inhabitants, and obliterate every building and structure with a massive aerial and artillery bombardment.[311] As Halder recorded in his diary on 5 September, following the afternoon "Fuehrer conference:" "*Leningrad*: Our objective has been achieved. Will now become a 'subsidary theater of operations.'"[312] And so began the terrible 900-day siege of the city with its population of nearly three million.[313]

In the Ukraine, meanwhile, Field Marshal Gerd von Rundstedt's Army Group South had also been advancing. Following the reduction of a large Soviet pocket at Uman where, by 8 August, Kleist's 1 Panzer Group had destroyed over 20 Soviet divisions and netted 103,000 prisoners (along with 858 guns and 317 tanks),[314] the tank units drove on toward Kirovo and Krivoi Rog – the iron ore center of European Russia – capturing the latter on 14 August.[315] Exploiting Kleist's success, Rundstedt moved to clear Red Army forces from the entire western bank of the Dnepr River. Although the Soviet salient at Kiev held firm, by 1 September, Army Group South had secured bridgeheads across the river above Kiev (Sixth Army), at Dnepropetrovsk (1 Panzer Group), at Berislav (Eleventh Army), and Kremenchug (Seventeenth Army).[316]

While Rundstedt's forces widened their Dnepr bridgeheads, Guderian's 2 Panzer Group, by 25 August, had begun its advance southward from northeast of Kiev with its 24 and 47 Panzer Corps.[317] By early September, the operations of both Rundstedt's army group and Guderian's panzers were threatening Col.-Gen. M. P. Kirponos' Southwestern Front with encirclement and destruction. Aware of the imminent danger, on 9 September, Marshal S. M. Budenny, Commander, Southwestern Direction (in overall control of Southwestern and Southern Fronts), asked Stalin for permission to abandon Kiev and pull back to less exposed positions. Stalin refused. Two days later (11 September), Budenny appealed again to Stalin to begin "a general withdrawal" from Kiev; hours later, Budenny was dismissed.[318] Determined to defend the city, the Soviet dictator telegraphed Kirponos: "Kiev is not to be given up and the bridges are not to be blown without *Stavka* authority. Kiev was, is and will be – Soviet. No withdrawal is allowed. Stay and hold, and if necessary die! Out!"[319]

On 9 September, Geyr's 24 Panzer Corps crossed the Seim River; the next day, the corps' (and Guderian's) vanguard, Model's brilliant 3 Panzer Division, seized the town of Romny – along with its two bridges over the Romen River – deep in the Soviet rear behind Kiev.[320] The Soviets, however, despite the valiant efforts of Eremenko's Briansk Front, and repeated attacks from the air against Model's forces, strung out along muddy roads, could do little to impede the German advance. On 12 September, 1 Panzer Group, after assembling the requisite supplies and building a suitable bridge, advanced northward out of Seventeenth Army's bridgehead at Kremenchug with its 48 Panzer Corps.[321] The same day, at the request of Army Group South, Bock instructed Guderian to drive for the town of Lokhvitsa (ca. 45 kilometers southwest of Romny) and to link up there with the tanks of Kleist's panzer group. On the cusp of another exhilarating victory, the tension at Bock's command post was palpable: "At noon came the news that the enemy is streaming east out of the more than 200-kilometer-wide gap between Kremenchug and Romny in dense columns. Immediately afterward, three telephone calls were received from Army Group South within a half hour, asking if Lokhvitsa had been reached yet!"[322]

Over the next two days, the converging spearheads of Guderian's and Kleist's panzer groups fought their way toward each other. On the morning of 14 September, Model launched a small battlegroup (2 officers and 45 men) on a daring raid to the south;[323] hours later, white Very lights, which always signified a German presence, were exchanged between the battlegroup of 3 Panzer Division and a company of combat engineers of Kleist's 16 Panzer Division. Shortly thereafter, Guderian's CP received a brief radio message: "14 Sep 1941, 1820 hours, *Panzergruppen* 1 and 2 establish contact." The next morning, 3 Panzer Division established "conclusive physical contact" with 1 Panzer Group's 9 Panzer Division at Lokhvitsa in the central Ukraine.[324] Trapped inside their armored jaws, and facing certain destruction, was the entire Soviet Southwestern Front. "The 'Battle of Kiev,'" Bock proclaimed triumphantly, "has thus become a dazzling success."[325]

At 2340 hours, 17 September, the *Stavka* signaled Kirponos that Stalin had finally authorized a withdrawal from Kiev,[326] but it was already too late for the Soviet armies trapped inside the bulging pocket. On 19 September, Kiev fell to elements of Field Marshal Walter von Reichenau's Sixth Army, German troops hoisting the Reich battle flag (*Reichskriegsflagge*) above the citadel within the city.[327] In the days which followed, the tankers and panzer grenadiers of 1 and 2 Panzer Groups compressed the gigantic pocket[328] from the east, while the infantry of the Seventeenth, Sixth and Second Armies did so from the south, west and north, respectively; overhead, the fighters, dive bombers and bombers of the *Luftwaffe* decimated Soviet troop and vehicle columns inside the *Kessel*, while systematically interdicting rail lines leading into the pocket to block the arrival of reinforcements and disrupt lines of retreat.[329]

By 24 September, the fighting in the pocket was over. A doctor with 3 Panzer Division surveying the battlefield reported his impressions:

> A chaotic scene remained. Hundreds of lorries and troop carriers with tanks in between are strewn across the landscape. Those sitting inside were often caught by the flames as they attempted to dismount, and were burned, hanging from turrets like black mummies. Around the vehicles lay thousands of dead.[330]

Six Soviet armies (5, 21, 26, 27, 38, 40) were either wholly or partially annihilated in the immense cauldron battle, eliminating 50 Soviet divisions from the Red Army order of battle.[331] In sum, the Germans claimed to have captured 665,212 prisoners, while seizing 824 tanks and 3018 guns, in the operations of Army Groups Center and South since late August 1941 – the large majority of the POWs, more than half a million, attributed directly to the Kiev *Kesselschlacht*.[332] Among the *Rotarmisten* who perished in the pocket was Kirponos himself: At dawn, 20 September, about 12 kilometers southwest of Lokhvitsa, the general's column, about 1000 strong, was "ambushed and encircled; in the evening, already wounded in the leg, Kirponos was hit by mine splinters in the head and chest. He died in less than two minutes."[333] Of course, the fighting had been far from one sided, as many German units also incurred heavy casualties attempting to hold in check the furious Russian breakout attempts. The 45 Infantry Division, which had suffered such horrendous losses at Brest-Litovsk in the opening days of the campaign, lost another 40 officers and 1200 NCOs and men in the combat east of Kiev;[334] by 15 September, the panzer regiment of Model's 3 Panzer Division had been reduced to 10 serviceable tanks (1 Pz IV, 3 Pz III, 6 Pz II).[335]

11.6.2: Operation "Typhoon" – The Advance on Moscow

Despite the great victories at Leningrad and in the Ukraine, for the Army High Command, and Bock at Army Group Center, the actions on the wings of the eastern front were merely sideshows. On 2 October 1941, after weeks of frustrating inactivity, the "main event" finally got underway: At first light, Bock's massive strike force – ca. 1.75 million men (72+ divisions) and 1400 tanks, supported by nearly 4000 guns[336] – lurched out of its assembly areas and advanced along a 600 kilometer front; overhead, the squadron's of Kesselring's 2 Air Fleet flew repeated sorties, striking the forward enemy lines and key targets behind the front.[337] An unknown soldier with 5 Infantry Division described the start of the assault in his diary:

> A few minutes more and the hands of the watch read 0600 [hours]. Now it's time. All at once, the entire front roars. It's as if all hell has been let loose. You can't hear yourself think any more. But the thunder rolls on from thousands of barrels. It doesn't stop. Then the planes come, which we've not seen in such a long time. In groups of up to 30 airplanes, the *Stukas* soar over and above us, heavily laden with bombs. They'll soon show the Russians what's what. The first ones are already coming back, while the others fly over. Our fighters are patrolling the entire air space. There's no sight of any Russian airplane and no shells come down on us ... An hour has gone past. Our artillery slacks off. Some batteries are already changing position, while others stay in position and guard the advance ... The *Stukas* have a lot to do today, because they are still heading out to the enemy in squadrons.[338]

Operation "Typhoon" had begun. As doctor Hans Lierow (6 ID) jotted in his journal, it was "the most beautiful, sunny, fall day,"[339] and the men were thrilled to once again be on the move. *Unteroffizier* Helmut Pabst watched the assault go in along the front of Strauss' Ninth Army:

> 0600. I jump on top of a dugout. There are the tanks! Giants rolling slowly toward the enemy. And the planes. One squadron after another, unloading their bombs across the way. Army Group Center has launched its attack.
> 0610. The first *Nebelwerfer* salvo. Dammit, it's really something worth seeing; the rockets leave a black trail, a dirty cloud which drifts slowly away. The second salvo goes off! Red and black fire, then the projectile emerges from the cone of smoke. You can see it clearly as soon as the rocket burns off: the things fly straight as arrows through the morning air. None of us have seen it before. Reconnaissance planes come flying back low over the lines. Fighters are circling overhead.
> 0645. Machine gun fire ahead of us. It's the infantry's turn.
> 0820. Tanks roll by, close to the gun position. A hundred have gone by already, and they're still coming on. Where there was a field 15 minutes ago there's now a road. Five hundred yards to our right assault guns and motorized infantry come on without a pause.[340]

Enjoying large local superiorities at their breakthrough points, the German panzer units tore large gaps in the Soviet front and raced on toward their objectives further to the east – Panzer Groups 3 and 4 aiming for Viaz'ma, while 2 Panzer Group struck out for Briansk and Orel.[341] Buoyed by the initial success, Hitler traveled to Berlin the next day

(3 October) in his special train. After lunching with his staff at the Reich Chancellery, he drove through throngs of cheering Berliners to the *Sportpalast*, where he gave an inspired speech to open the annual Winter Aid (*Winterhilfswerk*) campaign. It was, in fact, "one of the most stirring speeches of his life," delivered "wholly *ex tempore*."[342] Of the *Wehrmacht's* accomplishments in Russia he exclaimed: "If people now talk of lightning [*Blitz*] wars, then it is these soldiers who are responsible for it; their achievements are like lightning, because never in history have there been advances like these."[343] To rapturous applause he declared that, "the enemy is already broken and will never rise again."[344] Within an hour, the "Fuehrer's" train was bearing him back to his East Prussia compound. Victory in the east appeared certain.

As the powerful armored prongs of Bock's spearheads pushed deeper into the Soviet hinterland, they rapidly enveloped the defending forces of the Red Army's Western, Reserve, and Briansk Fronts. On 4 October, Halder observed with satisfaction that the offensive was "developing on a truly classic pattern."[345] Two days later, on Army Group Center's southern wing, tanks of Guderian's 2 Panzer Army[346] seized the headquarters of Eremenko's Briansk Front (but not Eremenko himself, who managed his escape), while also capturing the town of Briansk and its bridges over the Desna; continuing its advance, by 8 October, Guderian's armor had linked up with Weichs' Second Army near Zhizdra (northeast of Briansk), entrapping the shocked defenders of three Soviet armies.[347] Meanwhile, to the north, on the morning of 7 October, lead elements of Reinhardt's[348] 3 Panzer Group and Hoepner's 4 Panzer Group – 7 and 10 Panzer Divisions, respectively – joined hands at Viaz'ma, encircling another four Soviet armies and parts of a fifth.[349]

In less than a week's time, Bock's infantry armies and panzer forces had ripped a 300 kilometer-wide breach in the Soviet central front. Elated by their success, on 7 October, the Army High Command ordered Bock to begin the pursuit of the beaten enemy toward Moscow. So caught up was Hitler in the unfolding drama that he did not eat that day, which Jodl characterized as the "most crucial day of the whole Russian war," comparing it with Koeniggraetz, the decisive battle of the Austro-Prussian War in 1866. The next day (8 October) Jodl "repeated his triumphant verdict: 'We have finally and without any exaggeration won this war.'"[350] On 9 October, the Reich Press Chief, Dr Otto Dietrich – and, to be sure, not without Hitler's imprimatur – proclaimed to the world that, with the "smashing" (*Zertruemmerung*) of the Red Army before Moscow, "the campaign in the east has been decided."[351]

The autumn rains began on 6 October along the southern sector of Army Group Center, and, that night, the first gentle snow fell, though it did "not lie for long."[352] Over the next two days, the rains spread across the remainder of the army group's front, turning the unpaved roads to mud and "noticeably slowing down the offensive."[353] On 9 October, Bock's war diarist noted that, "the movement of panzer units off the main roads is at the moment not possible as a result of the bottomless, bad roads, due to bad weather, which is also causing problems with fuel supplies."[354] Because of the dangers posed by icing, poor visibility and soggy runways, *Luftwaffe* sorties plunged precipitously, from 1400 on 6/7 October to just 139 on 9 October.[355] The bad weather also disrupted movement of supplies and evacuation of wounded to the rear.

Yet the advance continued, if at a slower pace, for the most devastating consequences of the Russian rainy season, the "Rasputitsa" (literally, the "time without roads"),[356] had yet to make itself felt. On 10 October, the vanguard of Hoepner's 4 Panzer Group reached the western edge of the Red Army's Mozhaisk Defense Line, meeting only desultory resistance.[357] The most robust of the several concentric layers of defense embracing the Soviet capital, the Mozhaisk Line – bristling with gun positions, anti-tank obstacles, dragon's teeth and barbed wire – ran north-south for several hundred kilometers, covering the towns of Volokolamsk, Mozhaisk and Kaluga.[358] On 5 October, Stalin had ordered a withdrawal to this line, yet with most of his armies trapped at Viaz'ma and Briansk, all he could do initially was attempt to secure its most vital points with officer cadets, "destroyer" battalions, People's Militia, and NKVD and police units.[359]

Fighting their way into the belts of fortifications, German forces captured Medyn on 11 October and Kaluga the following day; by 13 October, the Mozhaisk Line had been punctured at several points. This was followed by savage and costly fighting on the historic Napoleonic battlefield around Borodino (part of the Mozhaisk Line), as the spearheads of 4 Panzer Group – SS *Das Reich* and 10 Panzer Division – systematically dislodged the determined defenders from their trenches and concrete bunkers, which were protected by an array of formidable obstacles, including automatic flamethrowers.[360] On the army group's northern wing, Strauss' Ninth Army captured Rzhev, on the banks of the Volga River, while the tanks and panzer grenadiers of Reinhardt's 3 Panzer Group seized Kalinin – the primary river port on the upper Volga, a major industrial city of nearly a quarter million people, and, barely 150 kilometers northwest of Moscow, a key anchor of the Soviet position – after difficult fighting (both by 15 October).[361] In the south (12 October), Guderian's 24 Panzer Corps reached Mtsensk, while his panzer army's right wing closed on Kursk.[362]

It was now mid-October 1941, and, after the splendid initial successes, Moscow appeared ripe for the taking; indeed, Zhukov, whom Stalin had recalled from the Leningrad front to take over the defenses of Moscow, would later call the period from 10-20 October the most dangerous moment for the Red Army, for this was the period when the road to the capital lay wide open.[363] Three overlapping factors, however, would conspire to break the momentum of the German advance and thwart their plans to seize the Soviet capital. In the first place, after formation of the pockets at Viaz'ma and Briansk, the Army High Command, confident that little in the way of enemy forces now stood between Bock's army group and Moscow, had diverted Ninth Army and 3 Panzer Group northward (toward Rzhev and Kalinin, as noted above), an eccentric maneuver which palpably weakened the main drive on Moscow; in the south, the elements of 2 Panzer Army making for Kursk offered no support whatsoever to the main advance. Secondly, Soviet resistance within the pockets was tenacious, tying down dozens of German divisions and delaying their release for the conduct of pursuit operations.[364] Russian escape attempts caused heavy German casualties among some of the encircling units; in a letter to Bock on 18 October, the commander of 7 Panzer Division informed the field marshal that, on 11/12 October, his division had lost 1000 men; and that an entire battalion had been "literally … wiped out" in its positions north of Viaz'ma.[365] The desperate nature of the fighting in the Viaz'ma pocket is graphically depicted in a letter written a few days later (27 October) by *Major* Werner Heinemann, a battalion commander in 23 Infantry Division:

> The recent events of 10-15 October in the encirclement of Viaz'ma were the worst strain on the nerves. On 10 [October] my battalion struck a withdrawing Russian division; we took 7000 prisoners on this one day alone. But to float around quite literally like tiny little islands in the rear area of a hundred-fold superior enemy army, cut off from all supplies and communications, surrounded on all sides in the immense forests by desperately fighting Russians – those were bitter days.
>
> We really breathed down their neck … but for us leaders, left to rely entirely on ourselves, that was a dreadful strain; I stood alone with my battalion for 6 days, for days at a time without any radio link to my regiment. And back home they were all rubbing their hands and saying: "Great! 6 armies in a cauldron and over half a million prisoners!" What do they know about what that means! Because each [Russian] has a weapon in his hand and wants, come what may, to get out of the

cauldron, to get back to <u>his</u> home. Our slender ring gave way here and there on dozens of occasions, and <u>we</u> were the ones encircled. My God, those nights in the forests, icy nights in biting frost and snow![366]

Yet the factor most responsible for the German failure to capture Moscow was the dramatic change in the weather. By mid-October, the impact of the *Rasputitsa* had assumed catastrophic proportions, and the movements of Bock's panzer and motorized divisions slowed to a crawl. On 12 October, Guderian's panzer army complained of unimaginable difficulties, as its columns were now advancing at the rate of one kilometer per hour.[367] In his journal on 16 October, Bock observed that Kluge's Fourth Army had "gained little ground on bottomless roads."[368] As supply lines broke down under the strain, desperately needed fuel and ammunition had to be flown in by air. Tanks were withdrawn from the line to pull guns and ammunition trucks out of the axle-deep mud. Soldiers' uniforms, and footwear, rapidly deteriorated; some troops went for days without bread and were forced to live off the land and from such local food supplies as the Russians had not destroyed.[369] Horses also suffered terribly, and many collapsed and died under the strain; "in some cases," Bock noted with obvious stupefaction, "24 horses are required to move a single artillery piece" through the muck and the mud.[370]

On 16 October, General Lemelsen (47 Panzer Corps) recorded his impressions of the travails of the marching infantry; the deep admiration he felt for these overburdened "foot sloggers" (*Fusslatscher*), who bore their burgeoning hardships stoically, was universal within the *Ostheer*:

> In flurries of snow, interspersed with rain, we then went back to Karachev on this dreadfully rutted route, through deep holes and ruts with standing water. On the way, we encountered the companies of the foot [infantry] divisions, who were also participating in this cauldron. The poor men tramped wearily through the mire with shelter halfs hung round their shoulders, on which fell the snow and rain. And then they take up their position, dig their foxholes in the wet forest ground, and camp in them, freezing in the icy cold and wet night. It really is a silent heroism exhibited here by the German soldiers in addition to their achievements in marching and combat. And all of that after they've marched over 1000 km from Warsaw, day in, day out. The demands which are made on the physical capabilities of our soldiers exceed even those of the World War. I was thoroughly ashamed of myself when, as darkness fell, I returned to my quarters completely frozen through, and was able to dry myself both outside and inside in a warm room with the help of a vodka.[371]

With the Germans deprived "of their dearest advantage, mobility," the Red Army was able to "fight more equal battles with the bogged down German tanks and infantry."[372] More importantly, the sudden standstill of Bock's offensive gave Zhukov precious time to begin to rebuild a cohesive defensive front along the approaches to the Soviet capital. In mid-October, Zhukov began to concentrate any formation or detachment he could lay hands on along the tottering Mozhaisk Line; initially, these forces amounted to no more than 14 rifle divisions, 16 tank brigades, and 40 rifle regiments – some 90,000 men in all.[373] In the days ahead, however, additional forces were gradually shepherded into the area, and the "unsuspecting Germans soon encountered the first driblets of what would become a significant flood of reinforcements from the vast Red Army strategic reserve."[374]

On 20 October, Soviet resistance in the Viaz'ma pocket came to an end;[375] several days later (23 October), the fighting at Briansk was over.[376] The encirclement battles basically destroyed Western and Reserve Fronts, while badly damaging the Briansk Front. According to David Glantz, the three fronts lost 7 of their 15 armies, 64 of 95 divisions, 11 of 15 tank brigades, and 50 of 62 attached artillery regiments; equipment losses amounted to 6000 guns and mortars and 830 tanks. Most significantly, roughly one million Red Army troops were lost in these battles, of which 688,000 were taken prisoner by the Germans. "By any measure, the results were truly catastrophic."[377] In an order of the day (*Tagesbefehl*), Bock registered the results of the Viaz'ma-Briansk cauldron battles, and offered up praise to his men: "This difficult battle, too, you have come through with honor, and, in doing so, completed the greatest feat of arms of the campaign! [*groesste Waffentat des Feldzuges!*]."[378]

During the final days of October 1941, the exhausted formations of Army Group Center struggled on against intensifying Russian resistance, mounting supply problems, and brutal climatic conditions. Operations of the *Luftwaffe* were seriously hampered by low-hanging clouds, snowshowers, and the danger of icing; on 26 October, Richthofen's 8 Air Corps was grounded due to the bad weather.[379] On 27 October, infantry of 5 Army Corps (Fourth Army) captured Volokolamsk, slightly more than 100 kilometers northwest of Moscow;[380] by 29 October, Guderian's lead tanks were just four kilometers from Tula, a major arms manufacturing center approximately 160 kilometers south of the Soviet capital. Attempts to take Tula in a *coup de main*, however, failed as a result of the Russians' strong anti-tank and anti-aircraft defenses.[381] The same day, General Heinrici, Commander, 43 Army Corps, informed Guderian of the "bad condition of his troops' supplies: among other things, there had been no issue of bread since 20 October."[382]

By the end of October, Army Group Center had come to a temporary halt along and east of the Mozhaisk Defense Line, its positions running from Kalinin through Volokolamsk, Naro-Fominsk, Aleksin (on the Oka River) to the outskirts of Tula. Since the start of "Typhoon," Bock's divisions had advanced 230-260 kilometers closer to Moscow,[383] while units of Fourth Army and 4 Panzer Group were little more than 50-75 kilometers from the Soviet capital.[384] On 31 October, Bock acknowledged that his army group's losses had become "quite considerable;" officer losses were such that more than 20 battalions were now commanded by lieutenants.[385] The next day (1 November), he gave vent to his frustration:

> Kluge spoke once again about the possibilities of attacking.[386] He said that if he drove his forces forward now there might be a gain of a few kilometers then that would be it again because artillery and motorized weapons became stuck. I told him that we would gain nothing by that. Naturally we must stay alert to any weakening by the enemy and strike there immediately. But in general the army has to, as per orders, make thorough preparations for an attack as soon as the cold sets in. This time benefits the enemy but unfortunately there is no other solution.
>
> The situation is enough to drive one to despair and filled with envy I look to the Crimea, where we are advancing vigorously in the sunshine over the dry ground of the steppe and the Russians are scattering to the four winds. It could be the same here if we weren't stuck up to our knees in mud …
>
> The Army High Command was again briefed on our desperate situation by Greiffenberg.[387]

With the momentum of "Typhoon" broken, and Bock's thoroughly emaciated divisions[388] dangling at the end of an increasingly tenuous supply line almost 1000 kilometers in length, the culmination point of Operation *Barbarossa* had been reached. On 7 November, recalled Guderian, "we suffered our first severe cases of frostbite;"[389] by mid-November, Army Group Center's casualties resulting from frostbite had climbed to 400 a day.[390] Adding to the army group's growing list of difficulties was the fact that Kesselring's 2 Air Fleet headquarters, along with much of his air fleet, was now withdrawn from Army Group

Center and transferred to the Mediterranean theater of war, leaving Bock almost entirely dependent on Richthofen's understrength 8 Air Corps for air support.[391] The time had thus clearly come to suspend operations, establish a strong winter defensive line, and build up strength to support a resumption of offensive operations in the spring. Instead, following a rather perfunctory debate, the Germans decided to make one final lunge for Moscow after stocks of ammunition and fuel were rebuilt and a permanent frost set in (freezing the roads and making them once again traversable).

The prime movers behind the badly ill-advised decision to renew the offensive were Bock at Army Group Center and Halder at OKH;[392] moreover, the Chief of the Army General Staff, still obstinately convinced the Red Army was on the verge of collapse, was, as late as the second week of November, still contemplating objectives hundreds of kilometers beyond Moscow.[393] Surprisingly, Hitler had little to do with the decision-making at this time; in fact, during October and November 1941, the dictator hardly intervened at all in the operational decisions of OKH, assuming instead an "astonishingly passive" role.[394] Argues British historian Ian Kershaw in his insightful Hitler biography: "Had Hitler been more assertive at this stage in rejecting Halder's proposals, the disasters of the coming weeks might have been avoided. As it was, Hitler's uncertainty, hesitancy, and lack of clarity allowed Army High Command the scope for catastrophic errors of judgment."[395]

The accumulation of stocks by Army Group Center proceeded at an agonizing pace. "The armies," observed Bock on 14 November, "are all complaining about serious supply difficulties in all areas – rations, munitions, fuel and winter clothing. With the limited number of trains in use it is impossible to do anything about it. Naturally this has significantly complicated the attack preparations."[396] While Bock fretted, Zhukov was busy shoring up his defenses in the woods and hamlets along the approaches to Moscow. Fortifications were expanded and laid out in depth; in the first two weeks of November, Soviet forces around the capital received an additional 100,000 men, 300 tanks, 2000 guns and more anti-tank guns. (Army Group Center, by comparison, received no reinforcements at all during this period.) In addition, 1138 aircraft, the majority of them new models, were stationed on airfields close to Moscow;[397] and unlike the primitive frontline airstrips available to the *Luftwaffe*, most Soviet squadrons were able to operate from well-equipped permanent airfields.

On the "raw and misty morning" of 15 November 1941, with the "sun dim and red"[398] above the fields and woods, Army Group Center began the final phase of Operation "Typhoon." The operational plan envisaged a two-pronged armored envelopment of Moscow, 2 Panzer Army forming the southern and 3 and 4 Panzer Groups the northern wings of the attack. At first Bock's tanks – painted white to blend with the landscape, now blanketed by a light dry snow – made surprisingly good progress, even if the shortened days, low hanging clouds and occasional snow flurries restricted their air cover; and if the troops were unaccustomed to temperatures 10 to 20 degrees below freezing, at least the armor could now move cross-country over the frozen ground. But this, "the Germans were uneasily aware, was not the real Russian winter. Fighting then would be altogether different."[399] And still their stocks of winter clothing languished in depots between Warsaw and Smolensk.

In the area of Ninth Army, the armor of 3 and 4 Panzer Groups broke through south of the Volga Reservoir on 18 November, opening the way for an assault on Klin and Solnechnogorsk on the Moscow – Kalinin – Leningrad railway line; as the fighting developed, the prospects for a breakthrough on a broad front north of the Smolensk – Moscow highway appeared to be good. On the right wing, Guderian's panzers pushed past Tula and advanced on Kashira and Kolomna.[400] After these initial successes, both Halder and Bock became "profoundly convinced that one last great effort would destroy the enemy facing them and that 'victory will go to the side that sticks it out longer.'"[401] On 21

November, Bock committed his only reserve division to the fighting, influenced, it seems, by his recollections of the Battle of the Marne in 1914, when – in the German mythology of the Great War – the younger Moltke had seen victory torn from his grasp by his failure to commit his final battalions to battle.[402]

Yet however "convinced" Bock might have been of impending victory, at other moments during these difficult days he was gripped by serious doubts about what the immediate future might bring. Certainly, he could not ignore the fact that his divisions were crumbling before his very eyes. On 21 November, he described the deplorable state of his armies in a long journal entry:

> Drove from Gzhatsk to 7 Army Corps.[403] The Commanding General has been visibly affected by the heavy fighting and described the pitiful state of his divisions, whose strength is spent.
>
> Losses among the officers, in particular, are making themselves felt. Many second lieutenants are leading battalions, one first lieutenant leads a regiment, regimental combat strengths of 250 men, also the cold and inadequate shelter, in short: in his opinion the corps can do no more. I gave him a word of encouragement and said that I wasn't demanding major combat operations from him at present …
>
> The whole attack is too thin and has no depth. Based on the number of divisions, as seen from the green table, the ratio of forces is no more unfavorable than before. In practice the reduced combat strengths – some companies have only 20 and 30 men left – the heavy officer losses and the overexertion of the units in conjunction with the cold give a quite different picture. Still, in spite of everything we might succeed in cutting off several enemy divisions west of the Istra reservoir. But it is doubtful if we can go any farther.[404]

Along with eviscerating personnel losses – which, from the start of "Typhoon" through 15 November 1941, amounted to 87,455 men[405] – the losses of precious panzers continued to accumulate as well. For example, the figure for operational tanks available to 2 Panzer Army had plunged from 248 on 16 October to just 38 on 23 November; over the same time period, 3 Panzer Group had seen its numbers drop from 259 to 77.[406] The attacking German forces were also undergoing serious punishment at the hands of the Soviet Air Force, whose air superiority was now complete. On 24 November the war diary of 2 Panzer Army read thusly: "Intense enemy air activity. Attacks by bombers and low-flying aircraft occasioning casualties. The troops regret the absence of our own aircraft."[407]

And still the infantry, tanks and panzer grenadiers of Army Group Center – at least what was left of them – trundled on, battling and scraping their way forward – across the next stream or river line; through the dark, dense forests; into the towns and villages draped with freshly fallen snow. On the afternoon of 23 November, after a hard fight, 7 Panzer Division (3 Panzer Group) captured Klin; on its right flank, 2 Panzer Division (4 Panzer Group) seized Solnechnogorsk.[408] At the town of Istra, less than 40 kilometers from Moscow, fighting raged for several days against a Siberian division and other Soviet troops recently arrived from the Far East; furious combat engulfed the Istra cathedral (west of the Istra River) and a surrounding aggregation of six large ecclesiastical buildings ringed by a robust 5-meter high wall – until the town was finally secured by SS *Das Reich* and 10 Panzer Division (26 November).[409] In a daring raid during the early morning hours of 28 November, a battlegroup of 7 Panzer Division seized a bridgehead over the Moscow-Volga Canal at Iakhroma (less than 35 kilometers from the Kremlin), only to have to abandon it the next day due to furious counterattacks by the new Soviet 1 Shock Army. Directly to the south, by 30 November, the remaining tanks and panzer grenadiers of 2 Panzer Division captured the town of Krasnaia Poliana, within artillery range of Moscow. Meanwhile, on the southern flank of Bock's army group, elements of Guderian's panzer army had almost encircled Tula and, pushing north, were barely 15 kilometers from Kashira.[410]

By the end of November, Army Group's Center's losses had increased to 120,996 men since the start of "Typhoon."[411] Even Halder, in a moment of sober reflection, was forced to admit that Germany would never again possess an Army as magnificent as the *Ostheer* of June 1941.[412] On 1 December, Bock dispatched a gloomy teletype message to OKH, outlining the desperate state of his army group; in it, he noted that his forces no longer had the strength for "large-scale encirclement movements" – hence, his attacks were now, for the most part, "being conducted frontally, taking advantage of every tactical opportunity." Further attacks, he insisted, would only lead to more "bloody combat," and "will scarcely have a strategic effect;" moreover, "as the fighting over the past 14 days has shown, the notion that the enemy in front of the army group 'is collapsing,' was a fantasy [*Traumbild*] … The attack thus appears to be without sense or purpose [*ohne Sinn und Ziel*], especially since the time is approaching when the strength of the units will be exhausted." The field marshal, who was now suffering from severe stomach cramps, proposed that his attack be broken off, and the army group withdrawn to a shorter, more defensible line.[413]

Neither Hitler nor OKH, however, were as yet prepared to take such a momentous step, which would have signified the final failure of Operation *Barbarossa*; more to the point, they persisted in underestimating the difficulties of Army Group Center while overestimating those of their adversary. So the offensive went on, although by now it had largely been reduced to a series of disjointed tactical actions wholly devoid of operational effect. The final attack of any potential strategic value began on the morning of 1 December, when Kluge's Fourth Army, operating at the very center of the Soviet defenses covering Moscow, advanced across the Nara River on both sides of Naro Fominsk; its objective was the Minsk – Moscow highway, the shortest route to the Soviet capital. Fourth Army's assault breached the front of Soviet 33 Army north of Naro Fominsk, and sought to encircle 5 Army to the north. Reacting promptly to the danger, Zhukov threw every available reserve into the battle. In the arctic cold, with German infantry "screaming in the snow that they could not go on,"[414] swarms of Soviet T-34s shot it out with German assault guns in the villages. Once again, losses were heavy, with many resulting from exhaustion or frostbite, due to exposure; one German infantry regiment (15 ID) lost eight company commanders and 160 men on a single day.[415] On 2-3 December, Kluge's attack stalled in the forest belt near the railway town of Golizno; on his own initiative, the field marshal, fearing encirclement of his own forces, ordered them back behind the Nara.[416]

5 December 1941 – At Guderian's forward CP south of Tula, on Count Leo Tolstoy's estate, the temperature suddenly plummeted to -35 Centigrade.[417] Vehicles no longer started; engines froze while they ran; the breaches of artillery pieces froze shut; tank turrets froze solid; machine guns jammed; artillery fire became irregular (the gunpowder seemed to burn differently); radios quit functioning.[418] With Army Group Center immobilized by the frost, and having reached the very end of its combat strength, the entire offensive was suspended, Bock's shattered divisions going over to the defensive in the positions they had attained.[419] Since 15 November, they had advanced 80-110 kilometers, reaching the "very threshold of the Soviet capital."[420] Reinhardt's 3 and Hoepner's 4 Panzer Groups were barely 25-30 kilometers from the outskirts of Moscow, astride the Leningrad, Piatitskoe and Volokolamsk roads; in the center, Fourth Army was within 40 kilometers of the capital. In the south, Guderian's advance had been halted just south of Kashira by fierce Soviet counterattacks,[421] while he had also failed in his bid to capture Tula (even though the panzer general had personally marched with his infantry to share their hardships);[422] his handful of surviving tanks were practically out of fuel.[423]

The "Situation East" (*Lageost*) map of the Army High Command's Operations Branch illustrates just how close the Germans had come: Some two dozen of Bock's divisions had gotten to within 75 kilometers of the Soviet capital; and many of these, much closer.[424] German officers nearest to Moscow could actually see the spires of the city through their field glasses, or watch as the city's searchlights and anti-aircraft guns engaged the small packets of *Luftwaffe* bombers which sometimes circled overhead. Yet after five and one-half months of uninterrupted combat, the crippled *Ostheer* no longer had the strength to advance another kilometer. Operation *Barbarossa* had ended in failure.

Two days before (3 December), *Unteroffizier* "Karl R.," a soldier in 5 Panzer Division, had written a letter home to Germany:

> It's increasingly winter here, it's already very cold, and there's more and more snow. I think soon we won't be able to do anything more with the panzers, because it's very difficult for us in this downright forested area. We don't even *have* that many panzers any more. We are now 25 km away from Moscow; the closer we get, the tougher it gets. The Russians have deployed the absolute elite here [and have] superbly constructed positions. We come across a lot of English tanks, but they're not as dangerous as the heavy Russian ones, which are superior to ours in both their armor and, especially, their weaponry. Well, I guess it's enough if the newspapers say we have the best weapons in the world. We can't do a thing against these heavy [tanks], and we only rarely have any heavy Flak, the only thing which can help at all. We've been told again today that we'll be getting reinforcements of mountain troops and infantry – that'd be pretty good – because there aren't that many of our riflemen left.[425]

11.6.3: The Red Army Counteroffensive & the German Retreat from Moscow

German plans to spend a relatively quiet winter in their shelters and dugouts – while rebuilding their armies to resume the advance in the spring – were abruptly upended on 5/6 December 1941, when the Red Army counterattacked the dangerously exposed flanks of Army Group Center in weather of -30 Centigrade and below.[426] Caught by complete surprise – German intelligence had failed to detect the build up of substantial Soviet reserves[427] – the depleted German divisions began to withdraw in a frantic effort to secure vital lines of communication, avoid encirclement and certain annihilation. After more than five months of ceaseless combat, infantry divisions could often muster no more than 20-25 fighting men per rifle company, while the panzer divisions had disintegrated to a handful of tanks and retained little mobility. The overburdened logistical system now collapsed completely, meaning that little in the way of food, fuel, weapons and munitions reached the front.

By mid-December 1941, fighting had flared up along the entire front of Army Group Center, as Stalin and his generals expanded the scope of the offensive, their threatened flanks now free of the most immediate German threat to Moscow. Paralleling the arrival of the most severe winter weather in memory,[428] combat across the front took on new characteristics. The Germans no longer held a cohesive line; rather, they began to cling – fortress-like – to key towns and villages, and to defend the handful of roadways and rail lines that were the sole arteries for major movements of troops and supplies. Masters of infiltration tactics, Soviet ski troops slipped between the German strong points, which often became surrounded, and streamed into the snow-covered landscape behind what was left of the German front. As noted, the arctic conditions played havoc with German weapons, which, for the most part, were more finely machined than those of their adversary and not designed to function in such extreme cold. Frostbite began to cause more casualties than action in battle, while sicknesses associated with the terrible cold, exhaustion and lack of food took an increasing toll. Wounded German soldiers died from the shock of even minor wounds, while others froze to death on the way to rear area dressing stations. A crisis of confidence spread across the front, as the *Landser* looked to their generals for leadership yet found them wanting.

Photos and newsreels from this period offer shocking images of the retreating *Landser*, who, in their outward appearance, were unrecognizable compared to the proud warriors who had stormed confidently across the German-Soviet frontier on 22 June 1941; having received little in the way of proper winter gear, clad from head to toe in whatever clothing or rags – man's or woman's – they could lay hands on, they more closely resembled bands of marauding gypsies. Dr Heinrich Haape recounted the terrible retreat of remnants of 6 Infantry Division in late December 1941, as they withdrew southwest of Kalinin:

> The retreating [troops] marched against a backdrop of flames. Special "scorched-earth commandos" were organized to carry out Hitler's adaptation of Stalin's earlier policy. But our men carried it out more thoroughly than ever the Russians had done. The night shone red as buildings, whole villages, broken-down vehicles, everything of any conceivable value to the enemy, went up in flames. Nothing had to be left to the Red Army – and nothing was left. We marched with the flames licking our footsteps, marched day and night, with only short halts, for we well knew that we were the rearguard of the army that had fallen back from Kalinin; there were no troops between us and the pursuing Russians.
>
> On the evening of 29 December we had crossed the Volga at Terpilovo; we marched the whole of that night, right through the next day and the next night, with the Russians on our heels. But if our spur was the enemy, the whip that flayed us as we marched was the unholy cold. Like mummies we padded along, only our eyes visible, but the cold relentlessly crept into our bodies, our blood, our brains. Even the sun seemed to radiate a steely cold and at night the blood-red skies above the burning villages merely hinted a mockery of warmth.
>
> For long periods at a stretch each man was conscious only of the man who walked in front of him as the shrunken gray column marched ceaselessly toward Staritsa.[429]

At dusk, on 31 December, Haape and his marching column reached Staritsa, and found it already in flames – "a sign that our 'scorched earth squads' were already at work and that the city was in the process of being evacuated."[430] Discovering hundreds of wounded German soldiers left behind in the city, Haape at once set about organizing their evacuation, while his regimental commander, *Oberst* Becker, deployed a thin screen of troops to cover the approaches to Staritsa:

> By the light of the blazing buildings of Staritsa, we commandeered every vehicle that could be found in the doomed city. When some of the few remaining units refused to hand over their vehicles, we took them at pistol point. Panic was abroad that night as these [rear-area] units felt the breath of the Red Army on their backs for the first time and took to flight. Every lorry, sledge, even artillery and infantry gun carriages, were packed with wounded. Cases whom we would normally have been afraid to touch were quite prepared to allow themselves to be wrapped in blankets and placed on jolting artillery limber-wagons. Wounded with broken bones sat on *panje* wagons or rode on the backs of the unsaddled draught horses. We shot morphia into the worst of the cases, improvised seats and stretchers, but the wounded men were only too happy to take their chance – anything to avoid falling into the hands of the Reds. By 11:00 o'clock that night only 200 light casualties still remained at the casualty assembly area; all the others were on their way to Rzhev. The 200 who were left could, if the Russians made a

surprise attack, be taken along with us and if necessary many of them could be made to march. Not a single man needed to be abandoned to the Russians.

Meanwhile *Oberst* Becker's calmness had put a stop to the panic in the city and the remaining [rear-area] units carried on with the evacuation of Staritsa secure in the knowledge that a thin line of German troops stood between them and the advancing Russians. Had they known how thin was the line their panic would probably have returned 10-fold.[431]

The pursuing Russians, however, had their own challenges with which to contend. While their offensive slowly ground its way forward,[432] problems of poor leadership, inelegant tactics, and shoddy operational control became immediately apparent. Many of the attacking armies were made up of poorly trained and equipped reservists, while after the catastrophic personnel and equipment losses of the summer and fall, heavy weapons, such as artillery and tanks, were in short supply.[433] Conversely, the Red Army offensive received a major boost from the Soviet Air Force, which enjoyed complete superiority over the battlefield and behind the German front. Legend has it that the Germans were only stopped outside Moscow, and then pushed back, due to the sudden arrival of elite Red Army units from Central Asia, the Transcaucasus region and the Far East, after it became apparent that Imperial Japan had decided to strike into southeast Asia and the Pacific, and not against the vulnerable Soviet rear in Manchuria in support of Operation *Barbarossa*. In truth, however, while these elite forces did make a difference from the fall of 1941 onward, they were always too few in number to fundamentally alter the calculus of the battlefield.

The initial turning points in this titanic winter struggle came in mid-December 1941 – firstly, when, on 16 December, Hitler issued his famous, albeit still controversial, "Halt Order,"[434] forcing the tottering formations of Army Group Center to stand fast where they were and retreat no further,[435] even when threatened by encirclement; secondly, when, three days later (19 December), Hitler accepted the resignation of Field Marshal Walther von Brauchitsch, the sick, exhausted, and utterly demoralized C-in-C of the Army, and himself assumed its operational command; and, thirdly, when, from this time forward, he began to relieve tired, sick and worn out general officers at the front – Guderian among them[436] – and fill their posts with more effective commanders.[437] Simply put, these bold initiatives – one and all a reflection of Hitler's iron will and determination to take direct control of operations in the east[438] – began to raise morale and fill the vacuum in leadership, helping to prevent the disintegration of the embattled remnants of Army Group Center.

Joseph Stalin, buoyed by the initial success of his counteroffensive on the central front, now decided to dramatically escalate operations by launching a general offensive from Lake Ladoga in the north to the Black Sea in the south. In other words, the Soviet High Command – against its better judgment – was ordered to pursue an overly ambitious and unrealistic plan of attack because Stalin, in his mounting impatience, had decided that the enemy could now be brought to collapse along the *entire* eastern front of more than 2000 kilometers. The plan was implemented in early January 1942; the inevitable outcome was a fatal dissipation of effort, instead of amassing Red Army resources on the decisive central axis to complete the encirclement and destruction of the German armies outside Moscow.

For Army Group Center, now led by Field Marshal Hans von Kluge,[439] the crisis appeared to reach its apex in mid- to late January 1942, as the Red Army's enveloping pincers along the two primary axes, north and the south of Moscow, supported by airborne troops and partisans operating in the vast forested regions behind German lines, sought to close on the ancient little town of Viaz'ma, a major railroad junction far to the rear of Army Group Center's main line of resistance and more than 150 kilometers west/southwest of Moscow. Operations of both Red Army and German forces were severely hampered by the arctic cold and deep snow, with a mean temperature in January 1942 in the area northwest of Moscow of -32 Fahrenheit. On 26 January 1942 this same area experienced the lowest recorded temperature of the entire Russian campaign: -63 Fahrenheit.[440]

On 15 January 1942, due to increasing Soviet pressure, Hitler had finally acceded to the repeated pleas of Halder and Kluge and given permission for the army group to withdraw its Fourth Army, along with 3 and 4 Panzer Armies,[441] to winter positions along the line Iukhnov – Gzhatsk – Zubtsov – Rzhev, 150 kilometers and more west of Moscow, the objective being to shorten the German line and release forces for the creation of desperately needed reserves.[442] *Feldwebel* Peter Stahl, a Ju 88 pilot, described the desperate plight of the retreating *Landser* observed by *Luftwaffe* crews as they flew above the snow-draped battlefield on 17 January 1942:

> We are offered a sorrowful view: long columns of our own soldiers strenuously stumbling back. Everywhere one can see abandoned vehicles, some half-covered with snow, and others just recently abandoned. As we fly past the columns and small groups of soldiers at low altitude, it is evident that they are half unconscious out of fatigue. They pay no attention to us. We pass by burning villages. The enemy won't be able to use them as living quarters when he pursues our troops. The entire horizon is filled with columns of black smoke. It is a merciless war.[443]

By the end of January, however, even though several armies of Army Group Center were now practically enclosed in a great pocket, the Soviet pincers had failed to snap shut. Kluge, moreover, had begun to counterattack at critical points, in the process encircling – and eventually destroying – several Soviet armies and operational groups that had broken through into rear areas of the German front. Reinforcements from Germany, France and other areas were also finally reaching the front,[444] while the *Luftwaffe* was again becoming active. Meanwhile, the Red Army consistently failed to crack major German strong points in key cities and towns, and was unable to interrupt primary road and rail communications for more than short periods of time, enabling essential supplies of food, fuel and ammunition – and, eventually, winter clothing – to trickle through to the German defenders.

By February 1942, Army Group Center – and the *Ostheer* as a whole – had essentially weathered the storm, even if much difficult and bloody fighting, and many a local crisis, still remained ahead. On 12 February 1942, with the eastern front beginning to stabilize, the German Army High Command (OKH) issued a major directive addressing the conduct of operations after the winter, in which it acknowledged that "thanks to the incomparable achievements and toughness of the troops" the worst of the crisis had past – the Red Army had been stopped (*zum Stehen gebracht*).[445] Indeed, despite pushing back German forces some 150 to 400 kilometers to the west,[446] as well as liberating 60 cities and hundreds of towns and villages, Stalin's counteroffensive had failed to achieve any of its primary objectives. Contributing decisively to the defensive victory of *Ostheer* were: a.) the handful of surviving low-ranking officers and NCOs, whose toughness, experience, combat skill and, when required, ruthlessness in the face of human weakness, held the remnants of their exhausted units together and made them fight;[447] and, b.) the remaining heavy weapons – artillery, Flak, tanks, assault guns – deployed at pivotal sectors of the front and exercising an influence on tactical events well beyond their all too modest numbers.

Yet despite its remarkable defensive success, the *Wehrmacht* never recovered from the losses sustained in the failed Russian campaign of 1941. Nor did Hitler's Germany recover from this failure. Hitler and his generals had risked all on smashing the Soviet Union with a single overpowering blow – a "blitzkrieg" – before it could bring to bear its superior resources in manpower and weapons production. By mid-December 1941, with Russia undefeated and resurgent, and America now in the war, Germany found herself mired in a war of attrition against an Allied coalition that marshalled some 75 percent of the world's human and material resources.[448]

11.7: *Barbarossa* Denied – Why did Hitler's Russian Blitzkrieg Fail?

The *Wehrmacht's* 1941 campaign against the Soviet Union was unparalleled in terms of its scope, objectives, and tactical and operational brilliance. Along the central axis of advance, after little more than three weeks of fighting, the largest of the three German army groups, Army Group Center, had reached Smolensk – more than 600 kilometers from the frontier – establishing a record that not even U.S. forces advancing on Baghdad in 2003 could equal.[449] By late November 1941, the *Ostheer* had "accomplished one of the greatest sustained offensives in military history,"[450] driving nearly 1000 kilometers to the gates of Moscow, encircling Leningrad and capturing Rostov, the gateway to the Caucasus, while inflicting several millions of casualties and destroying tens of thousands of tanks, guns and aircraft. Equally impressive, Hitler's armies had deprived the Soviet Union of approximately 40 percent of its population and 35 percent of its productive capacity.[451]

Yet despite such historically unprecedented achievements, Operation *Barbarossa* ended in failure, with the attacking German forces unable to secure a single one of their primary objectives. At the peak of their training, experience and prowess in June 1941, after five months of unremitting battle the armies of the *Ostheer* had been reduced to mere fragments of their original combat strength. By the end of 1941, the Germans (Army, Waffen-SS and *Luftwaffe*) had incurred 302,000 fatal casualties in the east,[452] along with two to three times as many wounded – losses from which they never fully recovered. To be sure, the *Wehrmacht* remained a highly lethal instrument and, following its partial recovery in the spring of 1942, once again resumed the offensive; in its weakened state, however, this was only possible in the southern theater of operations. Yet the outcome was strikingly similar – overextension and defeat, this time among the bloody ruins of Stalingrad.

Why did the *Wehrmacht* fail in Russia? Was the line separating victory from defeat indeed a slender one – as more than one military historian has argued[453] – or was the German conviction that Russia could be irretrievably smashed in a "blitz" campaign of short duration – the only conceivable path to victory – illusory at its core? Following more than a decade of intensive historical research, this author has concluded that, despite the great operational successes achieved by the Germans in the summer and fall of 1941, Operation *Barbarossa* was, from the outset, an enterprise doomed to failure.

As this account has repeatedly emphasized, the German attack on the Soviet Union was fatally underpowered. Carelessly – and arrogantly – underestimating the unprecedented challenges of a war with Russia, German military planners, from the outset, failed to equip the *Ostheer* with the resources it needed to succeed; after the campaign began, the eastern armies received but a trickle of reserves and replacements (both men and materiel), as Hitler and his High Command, convinced of impending victory, prepared for the next stage along the Reich's path to world domination. One can only speculate what might have been if German industry – still operating well below capacity under a largely peacetime economy – had produced a mere 50-60 more medium tanks a month during the period from July 1940 to June 1941. An additional 600-720 tanks could have outfitted the *Ostheer* with a fifth panzer group, thereby obviating many of the operational dilemmas faced by the Germans in the summer of 1941. Instead, production limped along at a rate of barely 200 units per month.[454] And this is simply one example of how the Germans – in what may well have been their greatest blunder – forfeited the opportunity to seriously ramp up for war in the east.

Two further themes addressed at some length in this narrative are the crippling shortcomings of both the German Army's logistical system and intelligence gathering apparatus. Although the supply and transporation challenges which had to be overcome staggered the imagination,[455] German logisticians, led by the Army Quartermaster-General, consistently fell back on facile and overoptimistic assumptions about what could be accomplished in this realm. From the start, however, it was apparent that the Army's supply system would be incapable of adequately sustaining an advance into the Soviet Union of more than 500 kilometers – but no matter, for the campaign would be over, so it was thought, before supply became an issue. Yet as we have seen, Army Group Center began to suffer from serious logistical shortfalls by August 1941, barely six weeks into the campaign; in the weeks and months which followed, the supply problems only multiplied, until the system collapsed altogether. Certainly, the crucial failures of German logistics in the summer/fall of 1941 were a proximate – and still not fully appreciated – cause of the failure of Operation *Barbarossa*.

Much of the pre-war intelligence product of OKH's Foreign Armies East (FHO), pertaining to Red Army numbers and capabilities, would prove wholly inaccurate, as became alarmingly apparent to many German officers in Russia only days after the invasion began; moreover, the agency's inaccurate forecasts continued right through the end of the year. Focused largely on operational concerns, and evincing a distinct, if subtle, institutional bias against the intelligence function itself,[456] the German General Staff devoted insufficient resources to intelligence gathering (both human and material); furthermore, what they did know – or thought they knew – was often badly distorted by racial and ideological prejudices. In any case, "the upper echelons of the German military were not interested in information that did not match their plans and preconceptions."[457] One of the "victims" of such cultural biases was Hitler himself, who, as we have seen, was soon tormented by what the fighting revealed about the true size and scope of the Red Army.

A major cause of Germany's eventual defeat in *Barbarossa* was the overriding obsession of the campaign's principal architects and executioners with operational issues and solutions. Indeed, the Army General Staff, led by Halder, often acted as if the key to victory was simply a matter of determining the correct operational approach without proper regard for firepower, logistics, friction, or other vital components which together comprise the calculus of battle. Through their study of Clausewitz, and, more to the point, of Schlieffen, German officers had come to rely on concepts of maneuver and encirclement, culminating in a "battle of annihilation" (*Vernichtungsschlacht*), as the only conceivable solution to Germany's political-military problems. There is, perhaps, no better illustration of the inadequacy of such doctrinal thinking than the fact that the great encirclement victories of 1941 – Belostok-Minsk, Smolensk, Kiev, Viaz'ma-Briansk, etc. – fell far short of destroying the Red Army, or causing the ostensibly brittle Soviet state to crumble apart. Put another way, the cumulative failure of these – admittedly brilliant – operational successes to bring victory underscores the conceptual bankruptcy of the *Barbarossa* blueprint, with its fixation on crushing the Soviet Union in a series of ambitious operational encirclements.

What the Russian campaign of 1941 revealed, much to the Germans' dismay, was that to defeat Soviet Russia, something was clearly needed beyond operational acumen on the battlefield, particularly in light of the country's, and its military's, astonishing strength, resiliency, and regenerative powers. By the end of 1941, dozens of Soviet armies – more than 200 divisions! – had been smashed by the rampaging *Wehrmacht*, the Red Army sustaining a total of nearly 4.5 million casualties, including three million irrecoverable losses (dead, captured, or missing).[458] Yet despite its virtually inconceivable losses, by 31 December 1941, the Red Army's line strength had risen to 592 division equivalents (compared to 401 division equivalents on 1 August, and 450 on 1 September), while its total personnel strength had climbed from about 5.4 million on 22 June to 6.9 million on 31 August, and 8 million by 31 December 1941. These astounding increases were the result of the Soviet Union's admittedly cumbersome, yet extraordinarily prolific mobilization system, which, from June to December 1941, generated more than 50 new field armies and a total of approximately 285 rifle divisions, 88 cavalry divisions, 12 re-formed tank divisions, 174 rifle brigades, and 93 tank brigades.[459] According to historian Walter S. Dunn, Jr.:

> While other countries had surrendered after losing one army, let alone two, the Soviets came back with a third that sent the Germans reeling to the rear ... Soviet divisions, not cold weather, stopped the Germans. The actual reason the Soviets were able to stop the Germans in late 1941 was an unbelievable mobilization of men and weapons beginning in September 41, which created a new Red Army. The Soviets formed and sent into combat in a few months more new divisions than the United States formed in the entire war.[460]

Indeed, as the late German historian Andreas Hillgruber observed almost 30 years ago, what was "decisive" (*entscheidend*),[461] from a military perspective, was the ability of the Soviet Union to make good its enormous losses by mobilizing and committing to battle millions of trained reservists in the final six months of 1941. In the 1930s, Stalin, through his five-year plans and the total mobilization of Soviet society, had transformed the Soviet state into a "militarized juggernaut;"[462] and it is this historical fact, more than any other, which accounts for the Red Army's ability to first halt, then defeat, the German blitzkrieg of 1941.[463] Beginning in 1942, the ongoing shipment of war materiel and supplies to Russia from England and America would further tip the balance in the Soviet Union's favor.[464]

Yet the unprecedented military mobilization undertaken by the Soviet Union in 1941 was simply a reflection of an even more significant phenomenon underlying the Red Army's ultimate ability to stop the Germans at the gates of Moscow – a phenomenon which might best be described as a fundamental asymmetry of effort between Hitler's Reich and Stalin's Russia. Simply put, the Russian people simply fought harder, in the largest sense of the idea. Unlike the German dictator, Stalin was able to extract "the last drop [of] their potential" from his people:

> [T]he Germans only talked of total war until late in 1943. From the very beginning, Russia demanded incredible sacrifices from its people. Fourteen-year-old boys, women, and invalids were employed in factories working 10-hour shifts six or seven days a week to replace men in the army. Every possible ounce of human and industrial capacity was devoted to winning the war, stripping the civilian economy of all but the barest essentials. In contrast until the very end the Germans still had the highest ratio of personal maids of any country in World War II. German women were not employed in industry to any appreciable extent and factories worked only one shift. Some teenagers served part time in anti-aircraft units, but the high schools remained open. On the other hand, the Germans continued to manufacture luxuries such as furniture and other civilian goods and obtained more nonessential products from the occupied countries.[465]

At the front, Soviet soldiers enjoyed few luxuries and were subjected to brutal discipline. When weapons were in short supply, they were made to attack without them (ready to pick up a discarded rifle or machine gun from a comrade who had been killed or wounded); behind the attacking soldiers stood Red Army commissars, prepared to gun down any "Ivan" who lost courage and attempted to retreat. Stalin summarily dismissed and, occasionally, even executed generals who failed at the front; furthermore, as the "*vozhd*" soon decreed, any soldier captured by the enemy was to be treated as a traitor by the Soviet state.

Stalin could enforce such policies, and make such demands, on soldiers and civilians alike, because, by 1941, he dominated the Soviet state (and its people) so thoroughly that it functioned as a single-minded manifestation of his individual will. "In Stalin's USSR," opines historian Constantine Pleshakov, "state brutality compensated for everything – impassable roads, broken tanks, ignorant generals, inadequate food. As long as the dictatorship was able to manipulate its own people, it *was* efficient and could sustain almost any challenge, despite a faltering economy and jamming guns. June 22 and the 10 days that followed offer gruesome proof of that."[466] In a manner that Hitler could only have admired, Stalin ruthlessly lashed his soldiers – his people, his nation – on to victory, in the process sparing them no indignity or sacrifice.[467]

The foregoing analysis merits an intriguing question: Is it possible to pinpoint the precise moment when Operation *Barbarossa* was defeated – when the opportunity, however slim, to crush Soviet Russia was, in all likelihood, gone forever? In this author's view, the question can be answered in the affirmative: The critical turning point came in August 1941, with the disruption of Army Group Center's advance on Moscow during the three-week Battle of Smolensk. For it was then that the seemingly unstoppable momentum of the German blitzkrieg was first broken by the Red Army's increasingly effective resistance; thereafter, the Soviet armed forces, the Soviet state, began slowly to stabilize, rendering the prospects of an eventual collapse exceedingly small. "After Smolensk," concludes Jacob Kipp in his study of the Battle of Smolensk, "it was clear that this would be a long war, not a blitzkrieg."[468] And such a war would be a war of attrition, dominated not by tactical or operational ingenuity – and certainly not by battlefield courage – but by the cruel calculus of production, industrial capacity, and material and manpower reserves.[469]

When the Germans attacked the Soviet Union, they knew they had but a "short window of opportunity to strike down the Soviet colossus;"[470] by mid-August 1941, however, following the failure of the initial German blows to effect a decision, the window had slammed shut. From that point forward, the *Ostheer*, marooned deep inside Soviet Russia and bleeding from a thousand cuts, was consigned to inevitable defeat at the hands of a numerically far superior opponent, soon to be fighting alongside the United States with its enormous industrial and military power. "When the hoped for lightning victory against the Soviet Union proved beyond the *Wehrmacht's* strength," observes David Stahel, "a longer term war-winning solution was all that remained open to Germany, but the prospects of success for this option can be immediately dismissed."[471] Simply put, in a strategic environment dominated by sheer numbers of men, tanks, and planes, Germany could not hope to compete.

"Raw statistics" exemplify this point: During 1941, German industry produced an aggregate of 5200 tanks, 11,776 aircraft, and 7000 artillery pieces (37mm and above). By comparison, in the first half of 1941, the Soviet Union produced 1800 modern tanks, 3950 aircraft, and 15,600 artillery pieces and mortars. Yet astoundingly, Soviet production actually rose, and did so significantly, in the second half of 1941, despite the loss of vital production centers and the massive relocation of industry to the east; indeed, during this period, Soviet workers turned out an additional 4740 tanks, 8000 aircraft, and 55,500 artillery pieces and mortars. In other words, the Soviet Union actually out-performed Germany in all major armament categories even during the first – and, for Russia, most catastrophic – year of the war. Of course, the disparities increase dramatically when one also considers the industrial output of Great Britain and the United States.[472]

Finally, in the popular realm of "what if" history, one may ask – Was there any conceivable way for Germany to have emerged victorious from its Russian campaign in the summer of 1941? What Clausewitz understood from his own experience in 1812 was that Russia could only be subdued "by its own weakness, and by the effects of internal dissention."[473] Thus, "what if" the Germans had abolished the hated collective farms and returned the land to the Soviet peasantry? During the initial weeks of the German invasion there had been "many willing collaborators," but by autumn the mood was rapidly turning against the invaders:

> [*Politruk*] Moskvin observed the same shift in the peasants' mood. In late August 1941, the *politruk* [had come] close to absolute despair. The shooting of Jews would not have troubled his peasant hosts, he realized, for they blamed them for most of the troubles Communism had brought. Their antisemitism went hand in hand with a "fanatical belief in God," a faith that the invading Germans wisely indulged everywhere. Some even volunteered to become Fascism's local agents – *politzei* – but at heart it was not politics but survival that impelled them. "After each battle," Moskvin noted, "they rush to the field to loot the corpses for whatever they can find." The dearest hope of these peasants was for an end to Soviet power. In September 1941, though, they learned that the Germans had ordered that the collective farms should stay. Like the prewar Soviet authorities, the conquerors cared only for the ease with which the peasants' grain could be collected and shipped off. It was an irreversible mistake. "The mood of the local population has changed sharply," Moskvin wrote on 30 September. His heart still sickened at the news that reached him from the front. Like everyone around him, he was desperate for advice. But he was no longer in danger of cheap betrayal.[474]

Blinded by hubris and racism, Hitler and his eastern satraps sought only – as the "Fuehrer" expressed it in a notorious policy meeting on 16 July 1941 – to divvy up the "giant cake" that was Soviet Russia, so as first to "rule" it, second to "administer" it, and third to "exploit" it.[475] And the *Ostheer*'s generals rarely complained, even though Germany's murderous occupation policies only stirred up resistance and put additional strain on their already overburdened armies.

To bring our story full circle it was, in the final analysis, the dutiful German soldier – the *Landser* of the Russian front – who also suffered, and died, because of the inability of Adolf Hitler and his military leadership to conceive the limits of their own mortality. "Wise commanders," avers scholar Frederick W. Kagan, "design plans that can be executed by ordinary soldiers.

> They know that if they expect every soldier to be a hero and every commander a genius, they will inevitably be disappointed. Wars are never neat. The unexpected happens. The enemy gets a vote in determining how things go. Sound planning therefore builds in a margin of error: attacking with more force than necessary; maintaining large reserves; expecting greater friction; and preparing for stronger enemy resistance.[476]

Kagan was addressing, quite critically, U.S. military policy in 2006. Yet his words encapsulate the fatal errors of Adolf Hitler and the German General Staff in their abortive *Barbarossa* adventure in the summer of 1941; as such, they stand as a fitting epitaph for its outcome.

ENDNOTES

1   R. Peters, "*Does Iran want War*," at: http://www.nypost.com, 9 Apr 06.
2   M. Boot, *War Made New*, 236.
3   T. Ropp, *War in the Modern World*, 333.

4   Quoted in: K. Latzel, *Deutsche Soldaten – nationalsozialistischer Krieg?*, 53.

5   *Tagebuch* Haape, 11.9.41.

6   The *Stavka* had established the new Central Front on 23 July 1941. Commanded by Col.-Gen. F. I. Kuznetsov, the front comprised 13 and 21 Armies, whose purpose was to protect Gomel and the Sozh River sectors. On 7 August 1941, Kuznetsov was replaced by Lt.-Gen. M. G. Efremov as Central Front commander. D. M. Glantz, *Barbarossa*, 85-86.

7   D. M. Glantz, *Barbarossa Derailed*, Vol. I, 384-85; K.-J. Thies, *Der Ostfeldzug – Ein Lageatlas*, "Lage am [6.-8.]8.1941 abds., Heeresgruppe Mitte."

8   The bad roads increased fuel consumption by as much as 75 percent, straining 24 Panzer Corps' fuel supply. BA-MA RH 21-2/928, *KTB Panzergruppe 2*, 9.8.41.

9   BA-MA RH 21-2/928, *KTB Panzergruppe 2*, 9.-10.8.41; D. M. Glantz, *Barbarossa Derailed*, Vol. I, 387; K.-J. Thies, *Der Ostfeldzug – Ein Lageatlas*, "Lage am [9.-10.]8.1941 abds., Heeresgruppe Mitte;" "*Tagesmeldungen der Operations-Abteilung des GenStdH*," in: P. E. Schramm (Hg.), *Kriegstagebuch des OKW*, Bd. I, 562-64.

10   7 Infantry Division had been detached from 7 Army Corps and assigned to 24 Panzer Corps on 31 July 1941. Internet site at: http://www.lexikon-der-wehrmacht.de.

11   BA-MA RH 21-2/928, *KTB Panzergruppe 2*, 13.8.41; "*Tagesmeldungen der Operations-Abteilung des GenStdH*," in: P. E. Schramm (Hg.), *Kriegstagebuch des OKW*, Bd. I, 565-68; K.-J. Thies, *Der Ostfeldzug – Ein Lageatlas*, "Lage am 12.8.1941 abds., Heeresgruppe Mitte."

12   BA-MA RH 27-4/10, *KTB 4. Pz.-Div.*, 11.8.41, cited in: D. Stahel, *And the World held its Breath*, 257-58.

13   Ibid., 258.

14   P. Carell, *Hitler Moves East*, 108; "*Tagesmeldungen der Operations-Abteilung des GenStdH*," in: P. E. Schramm (Hg.), *Kriegstagebuch des OKW*, Bd. I, 572; K.-J. Thies, *Der Ostfeldzug – Ein Lageatlas*, "Lage am 15.8.1941 abds., Heeresgruppe Mitte."

15   P. Carell, *Hitler Moves East*, 108; "*Tagesmeldungen der Operations-Abteilung des GenStdH*," in: P. E. Schramm (Hg.), *Kriegstagebuch des OKW*, Bd. I, 573-83; K.-J. Thies, *Der Ostfeldzug – Ein Lageatlas*, "Lage am [15.-21.]8.1941 abds., Heeresgruppe Mitte."

16   D. M. Glantz, *Barbarossa Derailed*, Vol. I, 397.

17   BA-MA MSg 1/1147: *Tagebuch* Lemelsen, 22.8.41.

18   D. M. Glantz, *Barbarossa Derailed*, Vol. I, 385.

19   Ibid., 387.

20   A. Bollmann & H. Floerke, *Das Infanterie-Regiment 12*, 101; "*Tagesmeldungen der Operations-Abteilung des GenStdH*," in: P. E. Schramm (Hg.), *Kriegstagebuch des OKW*, Bd. I, 567-69; K.-J. Thies, *Der Ostfeldzug – Ein Lageatlas*, "Lage am 13.8.1941 abds., Heeresgruppe Mitte."

21   D. M. Glantz, *Barbarossa Derailed*, Vol. I, 390; "*Tagesmeldungen der Operations-Abteilung des GenStdH*," in: P. E. Schramm (Hg.), *Kriegstagebuch des OKW*, Bd. I, 575; K.-J. Thies, *Der Ostfeldzug – Ein Lageatlas*, "Lage am 14.8.1941 abds., Heeresgruppe Mitte;" A. Bollmann & H. Floerke, *Das Infanterie-Regiment 12*, 102.

22   J. Huerter, *Ein deutscher General an der Ostfront*, 74-75.

23   "*Tagesmeldungen der Operations-Abteilung des GenStdH*," in: P. E. Schramm (Hg.), *Kriegstagebuch des OKW*, Bd. I, 579; K.-J. Thies, *Der Ostfeldzug – Ein Lageatlas*, "Lage am 19.8.1941 abds., Heeresgruppe Mitte;" K. Gerbet (ed.), *GFM Fedor von Bock, The War Diary*, 286.

24   K.-J. Thies, *Der Ostfeldzug – Ein Lageatlas*, "Lage am 20.8.1941 abds., Heeresgruppe Mitte;" D. M. Glantz, *Barbarossa Derailed*, Vol. I, 399-401; also, BA-MA RH 21-2/928, *KTB Panzergruppe 2*, 19.-20.8.41.

25   K. Mehner (Hg.), *Geheime Tagesberichte*, Bd. 3, 288; K. Gerbet (ed.), *GFM Fedor von Bock, The War Diary*, 287.

26   A. Bollmann & H. Floerke, *Das Infanterie-Regiment 12*, 102-03.

27   D. M. Glantz, *Barbarossa Derailed*, Vol., I, 401-03.

28   Ibid., 403, 548.

29   K. Gerbet (ed.), *GFM Fedor von Bock, The War Diary*, 287.

30   J. Huerter, *Ein deutscher General an der Ostfront*, 76.

31   *GSWW*, Vol. IV, 590.

32   *GSWW*, Vol. IV, 590; K.-R. Woche, *Zwischen Pflicht und Gewissen*, 116; D. Stahel, *And the World held its Breath*, 263; *OKW Nr. 441 386/41 g.K. Chefs. WFSt/L (I Op.)*, 15.8.41, in: P. E. Schramm (Hg.), *Kriegstagebuch des OKW*, Bd. I, 1045; K.-J. Thies, *Der Ostfeldzug – Ein Lageatlas*, "Lage am 15.8.1941 abds., Heeresgruppe Mitte."

33   C. Burdick & H.-A. Jacobsen (eds.), *The Halder Diary 1939-1942*, 508. While Halder initially considered the incident south of Staraia Russa to be "inconsequential," it was hardly so for Leeb's 10 Army Corps, and Halder soon learned that the corps had been struck by about a dozen Soviet divisions, including several cavalry divisions. Nevertheless, he still considered the transfer of 39 Panzer Corps to be a "grave mistake for which we will have to pay heavily." Ibid., 510-11.

34   D. Stahel, *And the World held its Breath*, 263.

35   K. Gerbet (ed.), *GFM Fedor von Bock, The War Diary*, 283-84; D. Stahel, *And the World held its Breath*, 263.

36   C. Burdick & H.-A. Jacobsen (eds.), *The Halder Diary 1939-1942*, 510.

37   The words are David Stahel's. D. Stahel, *And the World held its Breath*, 264.

38   Ibid., 264.

39   N. von Below, *Als Hitlers Adjutant*, 289. The outcome of Schmidt's appeal is unknown.

40   H. Hoth, *Panzer-Operationen*, 118.

41   H. R. Trevor-Roper (ed.), *Hitler's War Directives 1939-1945*," 94.

42   Ibid., 94.

43   *DRZW*, Bd. 4, 503-04.

44 See, "*Vorschlag fuer Fortfuehrung der Operationen der Heeresgruppe Mitte im Zusammenhang mit den Operationen der Heeresgruppe Sued und Nord*," ObdH, H.Qu. OKH, 18.8.41, in: P. E. Schramm (Hg.), *Kriegstagebuch des OKW*, Bd. I, 1055-59.

45 57 Panzer Corps was subordinated to Stumme's headquarters on 18 August 1941. "*Tagesmeldungen der Operations-Abteilung des GenStdH*," in: P. E. Schramm (Hg.), *Kriegstagebuch des OKW*, Bd. I, 577; K.-J. Thies, *Der Ostfeldzug – Ein Lageatlas*, "Lage am 20.8.1941 abds., Heeresgruppe Mitte;" D. M. Glantz, *Barbarossa Derailed*, Vol. I, 551.

46 D. M. Glantz, *Barbarossa Derailed*, Vol. IV, 551.

47 R. Hinze, *Hitze, Frost und Pulverdampf*, 61.

48 Ibid., 61.

49 D. M. Glantz, *Barbarossa Derailed*, Vol. IV, 556-57; R. Hinze, *Hitze, Frost und Pulverdampf*, 61-62; "*Tagesmeldungen der Operations-Abteilung des GenStdH*," in: P. E. Schramm (Hg.), *Kriegstagebuch des OKW*, Bd. I, 585.

50 "*Tagesmeldungen der Operations-Abteilung des GenStdH*," in: P. E. Schramm (Hg.), *Kriegstagebuch des OKW*, Bd. I, 586-87; K.-J. Thies, *Der Ostfeldzug – Ein Lageatlas*, "Lage am 23.8.1941 abds., Heeresgruppe Mitte;" D. M. Glantz, *Barbarossa Derailed*, Vol. I, 559.

51 "*Tagesmeldungen der Operations-Abteilung des GenStdH*," in: P. E. Schramm (Hg.), *Kriegstagebuch des OKW*, Bd. I, 588-89; R. Hinze, *Hitze, Frost und Pulverdampf*, 63-64; K. Gerbet (ed.), *GFM Fedor von Bock, The War Diary*, 292.

52 R. Hinze, *19. Infanterie- und Panzer-Division*, 180.

53 Quoted in: R. Hinze, *19. Infanterie- und Panzer-Division*, 178.

54 Ibid., 182-83.

55 D. M. Glantz, *Barbarossa Derailed*, Vol. I, 572; "*Tagesmeldungen der Operations-Abteilung des GenStdH*," in: P. E. Schramm (Hg.), *Kriegstagebuch des OKW*, Bd. I, 591.

56 K. Mehner (Hg.), *Geheime Tagesberichte*, Bd. 3, 300.

57 Quoted in: R. Hinze, *19. Infanterie- und Panzer-Division*, 185.

58 BA-MA RH 20-9/16, *KTB AOK 9*, 26.8.41.

59 D. M. Glantz, *Barbarossa Derailed*, Vol. I, 573. (Note: In the Soviet understanding of their "Great Patriotic War," the Battle of Smolensk lasted for an entire two months – from 10 July through 10 September 1941.)

60 "*Tagesmeldungen der Operations-Abteilung des GenStdH*," in: P. E. Schramm (Hg.), *Kriegstagebuch des OKW*, Bd. I, 591.

61 Ibid., 599.

62 K. Gerbet (ed.), *GFM Fedor von Bock, The War Diary*, 294.

63 Ibid., 295.

64 Ibid., 292.

65 On 10 August 1941, at Halder's urging, Jodl reported to Hitler in an effort to bring the dictator around to the OKH's operational objectives. Jodl's "talking points" had been carefully influenced beforehand by Halder. *GSWW*, Vol. IV, 585. See also, "*Lagebeurteilung zur Lagenkarte vom 10.8. abends durch OKW/WFSt. Abt. L*," in: P. E. Schramm (Hg.), *Kriegstagebuch des OKW*, Bd. I, 1043-44; and, C. Burdick & H.-A. Jacobsen (eds.), *The Halder Diary 1939-1942*, 500.

66 *GSWW*, Vol. IV, 585-88.

67 D. Stahel, *And the World held its Breath*, 253.

68 C. Burdick & H.-A. Jacobsen (eds.), *The Halder Diary 1939-1942*, 503.

69 *GSWW*, Vol. IV, 586.

70 I. Kershaw, *Hitler 1936-45: Nemesis*, 411.

71 H.R. Trevor-Roper (ed.), *Hitler's War Directives 1939-1945*," 94.

72 Ibid., 94.

73 D. Stahel, *And the World held its Breath*, 267.

74 H. Muehleisen (Hg.), *Hellmuth Stieff. Briefe*, 119.

75 *OKW Nr. 441 386/41 g.K. Chefs, WFSt/L (I Op.)*, 15.8.41, in: P. E. Schramm (Hg.), *Kriegstagebuch des OKW*, Bd. I, 1045.

76 K. Assmann, "*The Battle for Moscow, Turning Point of the War*," in: *Foreign Affairs*, Jan 50, 316.

77 *GSWW*, Vol. IV, 590.

78 Ibid., 591.

79 Both assumptions, however, were highly questionable, given the *Ostheer's* strained supply situation and rapidly diminishing combat strength. "*Vorschlag fuer Fortfuehrung der Operation der Heeresgruppe Mitte im Zusammenhang mit den Operationen der Heeresgruppe Sued und Nord*," ObdH, H.Qu. OKH, 18.8.41, in: P. E. Schramm (Hg.), *Kriegstagebuch des OKW*, Bd. I, 1055-59; J. Loeffler, *Walther von Brauchitsch*, 248-49; *GSWW*, Vol. IV, 591; I. Kershaw, *Hitler 1936-45: Nemesis*, 412.

80 As Heusinger wrote shortly after the war, Warlimont's estimate of the situation for Jodl's Armed Forces Operations Staff "fully endorsed" the memorandum by the OKH. FMS T-6, A. Heusinger, "*Eastern Campaign, 1941-1942 (Strategic Survey)*," 92.

81 "*Beurteilung der Ostlage durch OKW/WFSt/Abt. L am 18. August 1941*," in: P. E. Schramm (Hg.), *Kriegstagebuch des OKW*, Bd. I, 1054-55.

82 R. G. Reuth, *Hitler. Eine politische Biographie*, 532.

83 I. Kershaw, *Hitler 1936-45: Nemesis*, 411-12.

84   R. G. Reuth, *Hitler. Eine politische Biographie*, 532.

85   Writes Ian Kershaw: "Despite mounting hypochondria, [Hitler] had, in fact, over the past years enjoyed remarkably good health – perhaps surprisingly so, given his eating habits and lifestyle. But he had now been laid low at a vital time." Moreover, electrocardiograms taken during this period indicated that the dictator suffered from "rapidly progressive coronary sclerosis." I. Kershaw, *Hitler 1936-45: Nemesis*, 411-12.

86   A. Heusinger, *Befehl im Widerstreit*, 133.

87   D. Stahel, *And the World held its Breath*, 253-54.

88   The occupation of the Crimean Peninsula had long been a paramount objective of Hitler's, fearing as he did its potential use by the Soviet Air Force as a staging area to bomb the Romanian oil fields, which were vital to Germany's prosecution of the war.

89   "*Wehrmachts-Fuehrungsstab/L, Nr. 441412/41 g.Kdos. Chef, 21. August 1941*," in: P. E. Schramm (Hg.), *Kriegstagebuch des OKW*, Bd. I, 1062-63.

90   Ibid., 1062.

91   G. Meyer, *Adolf Heusinger*, 156. According to British historian David Irving, Halder "literally wept … as he believed that Hitler was throwing away the year's main chance. Brauchitsch suffered his first mild heart attack. For many nights his adjutant heard him arguing with Hitler in his sleep." D. Irving, *Hitler's War*, 306.

92   C. Burdick & H.-A. Jacobsen (eds.), *The Halder Diary 1939-1942*, 514.

93   H. von Kotze (Hg.), *Heeresadjutant bei Hitler 1938-1943. Aufzeichnungen des Majors Engel*, 110.

94   BA-MA N 813, *Tagebuch* Muenchhausen, ca. 22.8.41. In his diary, Muenchhausen also stated that the new directive "struck like a bomb."

95   F. Halder, *Hitler as War Lord*, 46.

96   D. Stahel, *And the World held its Breath*, 284. For the text of Hitler's "study" see, "*Studie, FHQu, den 22. August 1941*," in: P. E. Schramm (Hg.), *Kriegstagebuch des OKW*, Bd. I, 1063-68.

97   D. Stahel, *And the World held its Breath*, 284.

98   C. Burdick & H.-A. Jacobsen (eds.), *The Halder Diary 1939-1942*, 515.

99   C. Burdick & H.-A. Jacobsen (eds.), *The Halder Diary 1939-1942*, 515; J. Loeffler, *Walther von Brauchitsch*, 249; G. R. Ueberschaer, *Generaloberst Franz Halder*, 66.

100   In his diary, *Hauptmann* Muenchhausen stated that, "the entire day [22 August] Halder and Heusinger worked on Brauchitsch to once again verbally, and unmistakably, bring the divergent opinion of OKH to the Fuehrer's attention." Their efforts were in vain, for the field marshal refused to act. As he said to Heusinger, "What is the purpose of expressing everything to the Fuehrer again?" To which a frustrated Heusinger replied: "God, must we arrange our whole life as if all we do has to have a purpose?" BA-MA N 813, *Tagebuch* Muenchhausen, ca. 22.8.41.

101   D. Stahel, *And the World held its Breath*, 285. For an analysis of Halder's behavior at this time see also, C. Hartmann, *Halder. Generalstabschef Hitlers 1938-1942*, 282-84.

102   K. Gerbet (ed.), *GFM Fedor von Bock, The War Diary*, 288.

103   Ibid., 289.

104   H. Guderian, *Panzer Leader*, 198.

105   H. Guderian, *Panzer Leader*, 198; K. Gerbet (ed.), *GFM Fedor von Bock, The War Diary*, 291.

106   H. Guderian, *Panzer Leader*, 198.

107   H. Guderian, *Panzer Leader*, 198-99; K. Gerbet (ed.), *GFM Fedor von Bock, The War Diary*, 291.

108   J. Keegan, *The Second World War*, 195. Keegan provides a concise and accurate account of Guderian's encounter with Hitler on 23 August 1941.

109   H. Guderian, *Panzer Leader*, 199-200.

110   Ibid., 200.

111   D. Stahel, *And the World held its Breath*, 289.

112   H. Guderian, *Panzer Leader*, 202.

113   R. A. Hart, *Guderian*, 75.

114   H. Guderian, *Panzer Leader*, 202. There is, however, another explanation for Guderian's reluctance to confront Hitler during the 23 August conference at the *Wolfsschanze*. In August 1941, Guderian was being quietly considered as a replacement for the ineffective Brauchitsch as the Army Commander-in-Chief; when approached by a group of senior officers at that time, Guderian had expressed his willingness to accept the position. Hence, his accommodating behavior opposite the "Fuehrer" becomes more understandable. K. Macksey, *Guderian*, 145; R. A. Hart, *Guderian*, 76.

115   As it turned out, on 24 September 1941, Stieff was transferred to Fourth Army to serve as its chief operations officer (Ia). H. Muehleisen (Hg.), *Hellmuth Stieff. Briefe*, 23.

116   This is certainly a reference to Hitler's "study" of 22 August 1941.

117   Once again, the German High Command was seriously undercounting its losses. By 31 August 1941, German fatal casualties alone on the eastern front amounted to 134,165 (more than 90 percent belonging to the ground forces), while the ratio of wounded men to fatalities was most likely close to 3:1. R. Overmans, *Deutsche militaerische Verluste im Zweiten Weltkrieg*, 277.

118   H. Muehleisen (Hg.), *Hellmuth Stieff. Briefe*, 121-23.

119   BA-MA N 664/3, *Tagebuch* Thilo, 24.8.41.

120   As *Hauptmann* Muenchhausen exclaimed in his diary with obvious disgust, "The courage of one's convictions [*Zivilcourage*] is precisely what these folks lack!" BA-MA N 813, *Tagebuch* Muenchhausen, ca. 22.8.41.

121   H. Guderian, *Panzer Leader*, 195. Panzer artilleryman Franz Frisch recalled, "seeing with amusement several signs raised by *Panzer* tank troops along the roads leading from Smolensk that read, 'To Moscow.'" F. Frisch & W. D. Jones, Jr., *Condemned to Live*, 74.

122 BA-MA RH 19II/386, *KTB H.Gr.Mitte*, 23.8.41, quoted in: D. Stahel, *And the World held its Breath*, 286.

123 A. Stahlberg, *Bounden Duty*, 169.

124 H. Haape, *Moscow Tram Stop*, 88.

125 Quoted in: D. Stahel, *And the World held its Breath*, 287.

126 W. Adamczyk, *FEUER! An Artilleryman's Life on the Eastern Front*, 143.

127 D. Stahel, *And the World held its Breath*, 291.

128 G. Meyer, *Adolf Heusinger*, 157.

129 Austrian historian Heinz Magenheimer supports this viewpoint, arguing that Hitler's "controversial directives of July and August 1941 cannot, therefore, actually be described as blunders." H. Magenheimer, *Hitler's War*, 89.

130 As noted by German historian Klaus Reinhardt, had Bock resumed his offensive in late August, the Soviet High Command clearly intended to "press the flank" of Army Group Center with the large forces of their Southwestern Front. K. Reinhardt, *Moscow – The Turning Point*, 76, f.n. 19.

131 D. M. Glantz, *Barbarossa*, 135.

132 M. van Creveld, *Supplying War*, 169-70.

133 As correctly noted by van Creveld, the Germans insisted on referring to the enemy concentration in the Kiev region as 5 Army, when, in fact, Red Army forces there numbered half a dozen armies belonging to the Southwestern Front. M. van Creveld, *Supplying War*, 169. See also, A. Seaton, *The Russo-German War*, 147.

134 M. van Creveld, *Supplying War*, 169.

135 *GSWW*, Vol. IV, 1252; G. Meyer, *Adolf Heusinger*, 157.

136 E. Mawdsley, *Thunder in the East*, 70. As Mawdsley observes, "if the war was to be won in 1941, then Russian resources did not matter." Obviously, Hitler, by late August 1941, had come to a very different conclusion.

137 D. M. Glantz, *Barbarossa Derailed*, Vol. I, 138-39.

138 *GSWW*, Vol. IV, 604, f.n. 252.

139 D. Ose, "*Smolensk: Reflections on a Battle*," in: *Initial Period of War on the Eastern Front*, D. M. Glantz (ed.), 352-53.

140 T. Ropp, *War in the Modern World*, 338. Ropp also characterized Hitler's Kiev *Kesselschlacht* as "Hitler's greatest single victory and, perhaps, his greatest blunder." Ibid., 335.

141 R.H.S. Stolfi, *Hitler. Beyond Evil and Tyranny*, 445.

142 Ibid., 444-48.

143 In his analysis, Stolfi does go on to state that Bock's drive on Moscow was also halted by the requirement to refurbish his panzer divisions. Ibid., 448.

144 As discussed in Chapter 1 (Section 1.6), Halder had gambled on the assumption that the unstoppable momentum of Army Group Center along the Minsk – Smolensk axis would override Hitler's intent to stop Bock's advance at Smolensk and direct his armor away from the center, to the north and south. Halder's plan collapsed when Bock's momentum was broken.

145 As Marshal Timoshenko assured the Supreme Defense Council: "If Germany succeeds in taking Moscow that is obviously a grave disappointment for us, but it by no means disrupts our grand strategy; that alone will not win [them] the war." Quoted in: R. Kirchubel, *Operation Barbarossa 1941* (3), *Army Group Center*, 90.

146 See, for example, A. Seaton, *The Battle of Moscow*, 287.

147 See, A. Seaton, *The Russo-German War 1941-45*, Chapter 9.

148 J. Keegan, *The Second World War*, 194. Keegan also accused the OKH, Bock and Guderian of "continuing to prevaricate."

149 D. M. Glantz, *Barbarossa Derailed*, Vol. I, 306.

150 T. Ropp, *War in the Modern World*, 338.

151 The reader will recall that, in late July 1941, Hitler had insisted that the "most urgent task" of Army Group Center was to secure its southern flank by eliminating the strong enemy forces around Gomel (see, Section 10.4.2); as he fully understood, doing so was a vital prerequisite to a push by Guderian southward into the Ukraine.

152 As discussed in this narrative, on 15 August 1941, Hitler had sent 3 Panzer Group's 39 Panzer Corps to support the drive on Leningrad; by early September, the group's other panzer corps (57 Panzer Corps) was also operating with Army Group North. "*Tagesmeldungen der Operations-Abteilung des GenStdH*," in: P. E. Schramm (Hg.), *Kriegstagebuch des OKW*, Bd. I, 612.

153 Liddell Hart, no doubt influenced by his discussions with former German generals, concluded that, "Hitler's gamble in Russia failed because he was not bold enough. He wobbled for weeks at the critical phase, losing time he could never regain … Hitler had counted on destroying the bulk of the Red Army before reaching the Dnepr. When he missed his mark – by a hair's breadth [!] – he could not make up his mind what to do. When at last he decided to drive on Moscow it was too late to win before the winter." B. H. Liddell Hart, *The German Generals Talk*, 139.

154 Halder, for example, in his brief study of Hitler's military acumen (or want thereof), observed that Hitler's directive of 21 August 1941, "marked the final turning point of the eastern campaign. Hitler's decision forced the Army Command to abandon the clear line which it had hitherto followed of aiming at the central point of Russian power, and to take on in its place an operation of minor importance which at best could do no more than hasten the collapse of an already yielding secondary front. This success, however, would have to be bought at the cost of irreplaceable time and strength … After the 'Battle of Kiev' had been fought with reckless disregard for the demands which it made on the already overdriven engines, Hitler gave orders for an attack in the direction of Moscow … But now it was too late – the engines were all but finished." F. Halder, *Hitler as War Lord*, 47.

155   C. Hartmann, *Halder Generalstabschef Hitlers*, 284.

156   M. van Creveld, *Supplying War*, 176.

157   In his account of the Battle of Moscow, Heinz Magenheimer insists that, had Operation "Typhoon" commenced just one week earlier (ca. 25 Sep 41), the German armored spearheads would have succeeded in encircling Moscow before the advent of the Russian rainy season, which brought their forward progress to a sudden halt; moreover, he characterizes the loss of this week as "fatal" to the outcome of the battle, and also implies that the capture of the Soviet capital might very well have won the war for Germany. (See, H. Magenheimer, *Moskau 1941*, 227-28) Yet while it is true that, given an extra week of good weather, Bock's tanks would most likely have completed the encirclement of Moscow, such an operational triumph would not have altered the underlying conditions which consigned *Barbarossa* – and, thus, Hitler's war against Russia – to failure.

158   K. Gerbet (ed.), *GFM Fedor von Bock, The War Diary*, 275-76.

159   Figure on total losses/day derived from Halder's diary. See, C. Burdick & H.-A. Jacobsen (eds.), *The Halder Diary 1939-1942*, 521; also, K. Assmann, "*The Battle for Moscow, Turning Point of the War,*" in: *Foreign Affairs*, Jan 50, 325.

160   FMS P-190, R. Hofmann & A. Toppe, "*Verbrauchs- und Verschleisssaetze waehrend der Operationen der deutschen Heeresgruppe Mitte vom 22.6.41 – 31.12.41,*" 73. By 31 August 1941, more than 14,000 officers had become casualties. The daily losses of slightly more than 200 officers were equal to almost 40 percent of the 518 officers in the organization table of a typical German infantry division. R. J. Kershaw, *War Without Garlands*, 172.

161   The 126,000 figure is derived from the analysis by Ruediger Overmans. See, R. Overmans, *Deutsche militaerische Verluste im Zweiten Weltkrieg*, 277.

162   D. Stahel, *And the World held its Breath*, 279.

163   The march battalions each consisted of about 1000 soldiers. Army Group Center would receive 154 of these battalions, beginning in mid-August and ending in October 1941, by which time the trained manpower of the Replacement Army had been exhausted. FMS P-190, R. Hofmann & A. Toppe, "*Verbrauchs- und Verschleisssaetze waehrend der Operationen der deutschen Heeresgruppe Mitte vom 22.6.41 – 31.12.41,*" 68-69.

164   Quoted in: K. Reinhardt, *Moscow – The Turning Point*, 67, f.n. 26.

165   Ibid., 67-68, f.n. 26.

166   H. Muehleisen (Hg.), *Hellmuth Stieff. Briefe*, 126-27. In the letter Stieff also told his wife that, "our overall situation – and not only in my view – has turned so decisively to our disadvantage that, while we certainly won't lose the war, we can also no longer win it."

167   G. E. Blau, *The German Campaign in Russia – Planning and Operations (1940-1942,)*, Department of the Army Pamphlet No. 20-261a, 71-72. According to Blau, there were only 24 divisions in the OKH reserve at the start of *Barbarossa*; however, the official OKH order of battle on the eve of the campaign lists 28 divisions. See, OKH Gen St d H/Op.Abt. (III), "*Kriegsgliederung Barbarossa,*" Stand 18.6.41, in: K. Mehner (Hg.), *Geheime Tagesberichte*, Bd. 3; also, P. E. Schramm (Hg.), *Kriegstagebuch des OKW*, Bd. I (foldout at back of volume).

168   R. Overmans, *Deutsche militaerische Verluste im Zweiten Weltkrieg*, 277.

169   H. Guderian, *Panzer Leader*, 190. In his memoirs, Guderian stated – erroneously – that Hitler had promised 300 engines for the entire eastern front; the actual figure was 400, and they were to go exclusively to Hoth and Guderian.

170   By 22 August 1941, the designation *Armeegruppe* Guderian had been dropped, and Guderian's command again became "2 Panzer Group." "*Tagesmeldungen der Operations-Abteilung des GenStdH,*" in: P. E. Schramm (Hg.), *Kriegstagebuch des OKW*, Bd. I, 585.

171   D. Stahel, *And the World held its Breath*, 259.

172   BA-MA RH 19II/386, *KTB H.Gr.Mitte*, 22.8.41, quoted in: D. Stahel, *And the World held its Breath*, 279.

173   These figures compared to 53 percent combat-ready tanks for 1 Panzer Group (Army Group South), and 70 percent for 4 Panzer Group (Army Group North). B. Mueller-Hillebrand, *Das Heer 1933-1945*, Bd. III, 20. While the panzer groups were without question badly run down by early September 1941, one must bear in mind that, "it would certainly have been unrealistic to expect the front-line troops to submit precise reports of losses and actions during the fighting. A tank which was initially regarded as a write-off might be repaired shortly after, and would then appear as a loss for the second time when it broke down again … [T]here must often have been a temptation to manipulate the figures on losses, repairs, and combat-readiness, in order to secure as large a share of supplies as possible." *GSWW*, Vol. IV, 1128-30.

174   Figures on tanks under repair were not available for 2 Panzer Group. At the time, 10 Panzer Division (previously assigned to the panzer group's 46 Panzer Corps) had been temporarily subordinated to Field Marshal von Kluge's Fourth Army; it boasted 159 operational tanks. B. Mueller-Hillebrand, *Das Heer 1933-1945*, Bd. III, 205.

175   *GSWW*, Vol. IV, 1127.

176   While it is not clear that *all* of these tanks went to Bock's army group, at a minimum, the vast majority of them would have. Ibid., 1131.

177   *GSWW*, Vol. IV, 1131. According to Thomas L. Jentz, on 12 September 1941, there were 126 tanks (including 71 Pz IIIs) in the "OKH Reserve Sagen" (Orsha/Duenaburg) "ready to be issued as replacements." The Army High Command also requested release of another 181 tanks (including 95 Pz IIIs) from the ordnance depots in Magdeburg and Vienna. These replacements reached the front in September-October 1941. T. L. Jentz (ed.) *Panzer Truppen*, 205.

178   By the start of Operation "Typhoon," the three panzer groups assigned to Army Group Center for the general offensive toward Moscow had lifted their percentages of operational tanks to 50 percent for 2 Panzer Group, 70-80 percent for 3 Panzer Group, and 100 percent for 4 Panzer Group. B. Mueller-Hillebrand, *Das Heer 1933-1945*, Bd. III, 20.

179   C. Burdick & H.-A. Jacobsen (eds.), *The Halder Diary 1939-1942*, 529.

180   2 Air Corps also took part in the attacks on the northern wing of Army Group Center, in the region of Velikie Luki, in late August 1941. *GSWW*, Vol. IV, 773-74, 783-85.

181   "*Tagesmeldungen der Operations-Abteilung des GenStdH*," in: P. E. Schramm (Hg.), *Kriegstagebuch des OKW*, Bd. I, 565-68.

182   J. S. Corum, *Wolfram von Richthofen*, 274.

183   C. Burdick & H.-A. Jacobsen (eds.), *The Halder Diary 1939-1942*, 529.

184   H. Muehleisen (Hg.), *Hellmuth Stieff. Briefe*, 127.

185   The Dnepr Supply District had been set up by mid-July 1941, and was intended to support the advance of the panzer units as far as Moscow. *GSWW*, Vol. IV, 1125-26; FMS P-190, R. Hofmann & A. Toppe, "*Verbrauchs- und Verschleisssaetze waehrend der Operationen der deutschen Heeresgruppe Mitte vom 22.6.41 – 31.12.41*," 84-85.

186   *GSWW*, Vol. IV, 1126-31; FMS P-190, R. Hofmann & A. Toppe, "*Verbrauchs- und Verschleisssaetze waehrend der Operationen der deutschen Heeresgruppe Mitte vom 22.6.41 – 31.12.41*," 85-87; also, R. Kirchubel, *Operation Barbarossa 1941 (3), Army Group Center*, 68.

187   On 2 August, Gercke, Chief of *Wehrmacht* Transport, informed Halder that the "numerical scarcity" of captured Soviet locomotives and rolling stock was seriously complicating the supply of the Army in the east. D. Stahel, *And the World held its Breath*, 226.

188   See, Chapter 7, Section 7.7, for more details on this topic.

189   R. J. Kershaw, *War without Garlands*, 168; M. van Creveld, *Supplying War*, 170; A. Seaton, *The Russo-German War*, 175; K. Reinhardt, *Moscow – The Turning Point*, 62.

190   *GSWW*, Vol. IV, 1130.

191   K. Schueler, "*The Eastern Campaign as a Transportation and Supply Problem*," in: *From Peace to War*, B. Wegner (ed.), 213. The problem, of course, did not only apply to Army Group Center. Instead of the required minimum of 18 supply trains per day, Army Group North was receiving an average of only 15 in September 1941; Army Group South, which needed at least 24 trains per day, was getting only 14 on average. Ibid., 213, f.n. 8.

192   BA-MA RH 20-9/16, *KTB AOK 9*, 7.9.41. The impact of Soviet partisan activities is also apparent in the notes of *Generalmajor* Windisch, chief logistician of Ninth Army. On 1 September 1941 he wrote: "Partisans. The most recent demolitions of rail lines had caused delays of more than a day and a half. Sweeping measures must be taken. Either use an infantry division to conduct sweeps or bring in special forces from the homeland. Things will only get better after we've taken Moscow, for then the head will be missing. But half measures accomplish nothing." FMS P-201, *Generalmajor* Windisch, "*Personal Diary Notes of the G-4 of the German 9th Army*," 38.

193   M. van Creveld, *Supplying War*, 157.

194   Ibid., 155.

195   *GSWW*, Vol. IV, 1130.

196   By 27 September, 98 ID had lost 1320 horses. The division had been transferred from France, and did not experience its first combat in Russia until the end of July 1941. M. Gareis, *Kampf und Ende der 98. Infanterie-Division*, 128.

197   A. Seaton, *The Russo-German War*, 174. See also, M. Gareis, *Kampf und Ende der 98. Infanterie-Division*, 125-30.

198   From 22 June to 31 December 1941, Army Group Center expended 207,500 tons of ammunition of all types and calibers, an average of 1075 tons per day. According to an authoritative German primary source, expenditures of shells would have been about 25 percent higher during this period had the supply and transport system functioned more effectively. FMS P-190, R. Hofmann & A. Toppe, "*Verbrauchs- und Verschleisssaetze waehrend der Operationen der deutschen Heeresgruppe Mitte vom 22.6.41 – 31.12.41*," 96-97.

199   According to the precise figures of Gerhard Donat, who served in the Army General Staff as the special-missions staff officer (*Ordonnanzoffizier*) to the Quartermaster General in 1944/45, expenditure rates of artillery shells were, in most cases, higher in the defense than during attack. For example, during the summer of 1941, average monthly consumption rates for light and heavy field howitzers (measured by full initial loads) were 2.2 and 2.0, respectively, in attack, and 2.0-2.5 and 2.25-2.75 in defense; rates for 210mm howitzers (*Moerser*) were 1.9 in attack and 2.0-5.0 in defense. G. Donat, *Der Munitionsverbrauch im Zweiten Weltkrieg*, 33-34.

200   BA-MA RH 19II/386, *KTB H.Gr.Mitte*, 1.8.41, quoted in: D. Stahel, *And the World held its Breath*, 226.

201   BA-MA N 813, *Tagebuch* Muenchhausen, ca. early Aug 41.

202   BA-MA N 813, *Tagebuch* Muenchhausen, 12.-15.8.41. In a discussion with Bock on the morning of 14 August, Guderian informed his superior that, in his view, a key prerequisite for continuing to hold the El'nia salient was to greatly increase the flow of munitions. K. Gerbet (ed.), *GFM Fedor von Bock, The War Diary*, 281.

203   D. Stahel, *And the World held its Breath*, 226.

204   The original German text was not available; hence, it is unclear if the author's reference here is to an initial load of ammunition (*Erstausstattung*), which, under normal circumstances, was expected to last for 4-5 days. FMS P-190, R. Hofmann & A. Toppe, "*Verbrauchs- und Verschleisssaetze waehrend der Operationen der deutschen Heeresgruppe Mitte vom 22.6.41 – 31.12.41*," 94.

205 A German infantry division had 36 light (l.F.H.) and 12 medium (s.F.H.) howitzers in its table of organization. See, Chapter 3, Section 3.2, for more details.

206 *"Studie ueber Gliederung und Feuerleitung starker Artillerie,"* 1 Jan 1939. (Berlin: *Reichsdruckerei*: 1941).

207 FMS D-221, G. Grassmann, *"An Artillery Regiment on the Road to Moscow (22 June to December 1941),"* 14-15.

208 *GSWW*, Vol. IV, 1126.

209 FMS P-201, *Generalmajor* Windisch, *"Personal Diary Notes of the G-4 of the German 9th Army,"* 59. By late August 1941, wear and tear on the medium field pieces was also taking a toll, the army noting an increased incidence of barrels bursting when firing (*Rohrkrepierer*). Ibid., 20.

210 See, Chapter 3, Section 3.1. The maximum production of artillery ammunition in 1941 was reached in February, with outlays of 69.1 million *Reichsmarks*; not until the spring of 1942 would production again reach this level. G. Donat, *Der Munitionsverbrauch im Zweiten Weltkrieg*, 7.

211 *GSWW*, Vol. IV, 1126.

212 K. Gerbet (ed.), *GFM Fedor von Bock, The War Diary*, 288.

213 Wagner also declared, however, that the stocks of fuel required to complete operations in 1941 could be provided if more extensive cutbacks were made by industry, the home army and in the occupied territories; at the same time, he also came to the conclusion that, by January 1942, supplies would be depleted and "new oilfields would have to be captured." Hitler's eventual decision to strike south in 1942, to seize the oilfields of the Caucasus, was no doubt influenced by such thinking. K. Reinhardt, *Moscow – The Turning Point*, 151.

214 Ibid., 152.

215 M. van Creveld, *Supplying War*, 170-71. According to van Creveld, motor oil was also in short supply; in fact, it signified the "bottleneck of the entire transportation system."

216 Ibid., 171.

217 Ibid., 168-69.

218 *GSWW*, Vol. IV, 1130.

219 A. Tooze, *The Wages of Destruction*, 492.

220 K. Schueler, *Logistik im Russlandfeldzug*, 408.

221 E. Wagner (Hg.), *Der General-Quartiermeister*, 203.

222 *GSWW*, Vol. IV, 1132.

223 E. Wagner (Hg.), *Der General-Quartiermeister*, 203.

224 *GSWW*, Vol. IV, 1132. The arrival of fuel trains was not only limited by the insufficient throughput of the railroads, but by the growing partisan activity as well. See, K. Schueler, *Logistik im Russlandfeldzug*, 406-07.

225 *GSWW*, Vol. IV, 1132.

226 Ibid., 1132-33.

227 For terrific insights into the enormous logistical preparations required for the launch of "Typhoon" see, FMS P-201, *Generalmajor* Windisch, *"Personal Diary Notes of the G-4 of the German 9th Army."* For example, on 30 September 1941, Windisch noted the distribution of 400 machine pistols, 250 machine guns, 80 light and 50 medium mortars, 35 Pak 37mm, and 13 Pak 50mm to the divisions of Ninth Army to cover existing shortfalls in weaponry. Equipment for protection against attack by gas was also delivered to the troops. Ibid., 94.

228 According to Klaus Schueler, "At the start of Operation 'Typhoon,' Army Group Center did not have at its disposal a basis of supply which corresponded to the requirements of the new offensive, as the transportation system [*Transportwesen*] was not up to the task under the given circumstances." K. Schueler, *Logistik im Russlandfeldzug*, 403.

229 D. M. Glantz, *Barbarossa Derailed*, Vol. I, 141.

230 At 12:00 noon, 22 August, Fourth Army was reactivated under Field Marshal von Kluge and given control of 7, 9 and 20 Army Corps; by 26 August, Kluge's span of control also included 12 Army Corps. *"Tagesmeldungen der Operations-Abteilung des GenStdH,"* in: P. E. Schramm (Hg.), *Kriegstagebuch des OKW*, Bd. I, 584, 593.

231 See, for example, K.-J. Thies, *Der Ostfeldzug – Ein Lageatlas*, "Lage am 22.8.1941 abds., Heeresgruppe Mitte."

232 A. Meyer, *Infanterie-Regiment 241*, 11. Another incident of the Soviet use of phosphorus bombs is recorded in the diary of an officer in 6 Infantry Division in late September 1941. *"KTB Soeffker,"* 23.9.41, in: *Rundbrief Nr. 50, Traditionsverband Inf.Rgt. 37*, Dec. 93, 15.

233 *"KTB Soeffker,"* 27.9.41, in: *Rundbrief Nr. 50, Traditionsverband Inf.Rgt. 37*, Dec. 93, 18.

234 The divisional frontages of Ninth Army often exceeded 20 kilometers in length. T. Wray, *Standing Fast: German Defensive Doctrine on the Russian Front*, 42.

235 D. M. Glantz, *Barbarossa Derailed*, Vol. I, 437-38. For an insightful study of the defensive operations of Army Group Center during the July-September 1941 timeframe see, T. Wray, *Standing Fast: German Defensive Doctrine on the Russian Front*, 39-48. For example, Wray notes that, "from 11 August onward, Soviet attacks created local crises along the Ninth Army front on an almost daily basis;" and that, "the improvised methods that German units were compelled to use in the central front battles resulted in heavy casualties." Ibid., 42, 47.

236 In early September 1941, Ninth Army noted that massed Soviet artillery fire had become stronger as time went on. As the army's war diarist put it, "On the entire eastern front of the army [enemy artillery] hammers our lines day and night with an intensity which only has its counterpart in the drumfire of the World War." Unfortunately, the Germans' ability to counter the Soviet artillery with "the most effective means" – air power – was rendered virtually impossible due to the "pronounced Russian air superiority." BA-MA RH 20-9/16, *KTB AOK 9*, 9.9.41.

237 Ibid., 27.8.41.

238 W. Baehr, *et al.* (Hg.), *Kriegsbriefe Gefallener Studenten*, 74. Henry was killed on 22 December 1941, northwest of Moscow. Ibid., 68.

239 G. Scheuer (Hg.), *Briefe aus Russland. Feldpostbriefe des Gefreiten Alois Scheuer 1941-1942*, 32-33. For weeks, Scheuer had been deeply concerned about the impending birth of his second child. As he also wrote in this letter to his wife: "Dear Friedchen, the time of your great and difficult hour draws ever nearer. As regrettable as it is, and as sorry as I am, we must simply accept the fact that I will not yet be home with you by that time. Thus I worry about you all the more, and want to do anything I can, to somehow ease your burden. I pray each day to our Lord God for you – that you stay healthy and that we receive a healthy child." Ibid., 33.

240 Quoted in: O. Buchbender & R. Sterz (Hg.), *Das andere Gesicht des Krieges*, 79.

241 Quoted in: E.-M. Rhein, *Das Infanterie-Regiment 18*, 82-83.

242 A. Meyer, *Infanterie-Regiment 241*, 14-16.

243 D. M. Glantz, *Forgotten Battles*, Vol. I, 77.

244 D. M. Glantz, *Barbarossa Derailed*, Vol. I, 579.

245 P. E. Schramm (Hg.), *Kriegstagebuch des OKW*, Bd. I, 469-79. The Soviet attack on 27 August, which also decimated 37 Infantry Regiment of 6 Infantry Division, is addressed in some detail in Chapter 10, Section 10.6.1.

246 D. M. Glantz, *Barbarossa Derailed*, Vol. I, 481-82. By 19 August, 161 ID had also lost nine light and six medium howitzers to the Soviet assault. FMS P-201, *Generalmajor* Windisch, "*Personal Diary Notes of the G-4 of the German 9th Army*," 18.

247 K. Gerbet (ed.), *GFM Fedor von Bock, The War Diary*, 287.

248 D. M. Glantz, *Barbarossa Derailed*, Vol. I, 485.

249 Ibid., 528.

250 K. Mehner (Hg.), *Geheime Tagesberichte*, Bd. 3, 314.

251 K.-J. Thies, *Der Ostfeldzug – Ein Lageatlas*, "Lage am 31.8.1941 abds., Heeresgruppe Mitte."

252 H. Geyer, *Das IX. Armeekorps im Ostfeldzug 1941*, 122.

253 *Feldpost*, W. Heinemann, 30.8.41.

254 "*Tagesmeldungen der Operations-Abteilung des GenStdH*," in: P. E. Schramm (Hg.), *Kriegstagebuch des OKW*, Bd. I, 601; K.-J. Thies, *Der Ostfeldzug – Ein Lageatlas*, "Lage am 31.8.1941 abds., Heeresgruppe Mitte." While this Soviet attack occurred well south (ca. 20-25 km) of the El'nia salient, it was, no doubt, tactically related to the simultaneous Red Army assault there.

255 Directly within the salient on 30 August 1941 were – front right to left – 268, 292, and 78 Infantry Divisions of 20 Army Corps. K.-J. Thies, *Der Ostfeldzug – Ein Lageatlas*, "Lage am 30.8.1941 abds., Heeresgruppe Mitte."

256 FMS T-28, H. v. Greiffenberg, *Battle of Moscow (1941-1942)*, 7.

257 D. M. Glantz, *Barbarossa*, 89. As noted above (Chapter 10, Section 10.6.2), Rakutin's army had consisted of 14 divisions (9 rifle, 3 mobile, and 2 militia divisions) on 30 July 1941. However, during the month of August 1941, its composition, like that of many Soviet armies, had undergone appreciable changes. E-Mail, D. Glantz to C. Luther, 6 Jun 12.

258 D. Stahel, *And the World held its Breath*, 274.

259 T. Wray, *Standing Fast: German Defensive Doctrine on the Russian Front*, 44. In this 1986 study for the U.S. Army, Wray explored in detail the development and implementation of German defensive doctrine from World War I through early 1943 in Russia. According to Wray, "in 1941, the German Army's doctrine for defensive operations was nearly identical to that used by the old Imperial German Army in the final years of World War I. The doctrinal practice of German units on the Western Front in 1917 and 1918 – the doctrine of elastic defense in depth – had been only slightly amended and updated by the beginning of Operation *Barbarossa*." Ibid., 1.

260 G. Blumentritt, "*Moscow*," in: *The Fatal Decisions*, W. Richardson & S. Freidin (eds.), 52.

261 T. Wray, *Standing Fast: German Defensive Doctrine on the Russian Front*, 44-45.

262 D. M. Glantz, *Barbarossa*, 89.

263 K. Gerbet (ed.), *GFM Fedor von Bock, The War Diary*, 302.

264 Quoted in: O. Buchbender & R. Sterz (Hg.), *Das andere Gesicht des Krieges*, 79-80.

265 D. M. Glantz, *Barbarossa*, 89. According to the daily report of the OKH Operations Branch for 5 September 1941, the withdrawal of 20 AK, and the right wing of 9 AK, was proceeding "according to plan" (*planmaessig*). "*Tagesmeldungen der Operations-Abteilung des GenStdH*," in: P. E. Schramm (Hg.), *Kriegstagebuch des OKW*, Bd. I, 614.

266 W. Meyer-Detring, *137. Infanterie-Division im Mittelabschnitt der Ostfront*, 75.

267 Ibid., 63.

268 Ibid., 73.

269 D. M. Glantz, *Barbarossa*, 90.

270 T. Wray, *Standing Fast: German Defensive Doctrine on the Russian Front*, 47.

271 E. Mawdsley, *Thunder in the East*, 72. The four divisions were redesignated as 1, 2, 3, and 4 Guards Rifle Divisions.

272 The new Soviet Briansk Front had been established on 14 August 1941 to fill the gap between the Reserve and Central Fronts; its mission was to stop Guderian's southward advance. On 26 August, the *Stavka* abolished the Central Front and assigned its armies to Briansk Front, which now comprised 3, 13, 21, and 50 Armies. D. M. Glantz, *Barbarossa Derailed*, Vol. I, 393; D. M. Glantz, *Forgotten Battles*, Vol. I, 89.

273 D. M. Glantz, *Forgotten Battles*, Vol. I, 88.

274 K. Gerbet (ed.), *GFM Fedor von Bock, The War Diary*, 300.

275 Note: In his diary, Bock wrongly referred to the Ninth Army; however, he clearly meant Kluge's Fourth Army. See also, "*Tagesmeldungen der Operations-Abteilung des GenStdH*," in: P. E. Schramm (Hg.), *Kriegstagebuch des OKW*, Bd. I, 607.

276   K. Gerbet (ed.), *GFM Fedor von Bock, The War Diary*, 301.

277   Ibid., 302.

278   H. Muehleisen (Hg.), *Hellmuth Stieff. Briefe*, 128.

279   D. M. Glantz, *Barbarossa*, 89, 94.

280   Ibid., 95.

281   R. Kirchubel, *Operation Barbarossa 1941 (3), Army Group Center*, 54.

282   According to official Russian figures, between 10 July and 10 September (in the Russian version of the war the period of the "Battle of Smolensk"), the four Soviet fronts in action along the central axis (Western, Central, Reserve, Briansk) sustained a total of 759,974 casualties, of which 486,171 were irrecoverable losses (the majority having been taken prisoner in the Smolensk pocket and other pocket battles). Between them, the Soviet fronts also lost 1348 tanks, 9290 guns and mortars, and 903 aircraft. Col.-Gen. G. F. Krivosheev (ed.), *Soviet Casualties and Combat Losses*, 116, 260.

283   On 11 September, for example, the war diary of Ninth Army observed that a "certain relaxation" had set in along the front; on 14 September, it reported that a "conspicuous calm" was continuing in the army's sector. BA-MA RH 20-9/16, *KTB AOK 9*, 11./14.9.41.

284   A. Meyer, *Infanterie-Regiment 241*, 14.

285   H.R. Trevor-Roper (ed.), *Hitler's War Directives 1939-1945*, 96-98.

286   R. Kirchubel, *Operation Barbarossa 1941 (3), Army Group Center*, 66.

287   Brauchitsch, Halder and Kesselring (2 Air Fleet) were also present at the 24 September 1941 meeting. K. Gerbet (ed.), *GFM Fedor von Bock, The War Diary*, 317-18; K. Reinhardt, *Moscow – The Turning Point*, 58-59.

288   K. Gerbet (ed.), *GFM Fedor von Bock, The War Diary*, 318.

289   G. R. Ueberschaer & W. Wette (Hg.), *"Unternehmen Barbarossa." Der deutsche Ueberfall auf die Sowjetunion 1941*, 155; K. Reinhardt, *Moscow – The Turning Point*, 59; K. Gerbet (ed.), *GFM Fedor von Bock, The War Diary*, 319.

290   Guderian's 2 Panzer Group was to begin its assault two days earlier, on 30 September. K. Reinhardt, *Moscow – The Turning Point*, 59.

291   K. Gerbet (ed.), *GFM Fedor von Bock, The War Diary*, 319. By this point, it was clear to the Germans that, with bad weather just around the corner, they were running out of time. On the same day, *Hauptmann* Thilo (OKH Operations Branch) noted in his diary: "[For Army Group Center] and South it has now become a race with the winter, whose precursor, 'bad weather,' will smother all operations in mud for 6-8 weeks." (BA-MA N 664/3, *Tagebuch* Thilo, 27.9.41.) German Ninth Army had already gotten a foretaste of what the impending "bad weather" (i.e., the fall rainy season – the so-called "Rasputitsa") held in store, when in late August and early September a period of heavy rains disrupted operations and exercised an "almost crippling" effect on the morale of both officers and men. "For the first time," the army's war diary noted, "we became fully conscious just how much operations under the impracticable conditions in Russia depend upon the weather." BA-MA RH 20-9/16, *KTB AOK 9*, 2.9.41.

292   *KTB 6. Inf.-Div.*, 22.-24.9.41, cited in: *Rundbrief Nr. 50, Traditionsverband Inf.Rgt. 37*, Dec. 93, 14-17; also, K.-J. Thies, *Der Ostfeldzug – Ein Lageatlas*, "Lage am [22./24.]9.1941 abds., Heeresgruppe Mitte."

293   *Tagebuch* Haape, 27.9.41.

294   H. Grossmann, *Geschichte der 6. Infanterie-Division*, 66-67.

295   *"KTB Soeffker,"* 23.9.41, in: *Rundbrief Nr. 50, Traditionsverband Inf.Rgt. 37*, Dec. 93, 15-16.

296   This is a reference to 5 Panzer Division; part of the OKH reserve, it had been destined for North Africa until assigned to "Typhoon." Internet site at: www.lexikon-der-wehrmacht.de.

297   H. Pabst, *The Outermost Frontier*, 26.

298   Ibid., 26.

299   D. Stahel, *And the World held its Breath*, 290.

300   *GSWW*, Vol. IV, 635.

301   *GSWW*, Vol. IV, 636-37; E. Mawdsley, *Thunder in the East*, 84.

302   K. Mehner (Hg.), *Geheime Tagesberichte*, Bd. 3, 310.

303   M. Gilbert, *Second World War*, 228.

304   P. E. Schramm (Hg.), *Kriegstagebuch des OKW*, Bd. I, 612.

305   R. J. Kershaw, *War Without Garlands*, 124; J. Erickson, *The Road to Stalingrad*, 192.

306   E. Bauer, *Der Panzerkrieg*, 130.

307   *GSWW*, Vol. IV, 641; J. Erickson, *The Road to Stalingrad*, 191.

308   D. Irving, *Hitler's War*, 313.

309   R. J. Kershaw, *War Without Garlands*, 124-25.

310   H. Guderian, *Panzer Leader*, 220.

311   In his diary, Richthofen (8 Air Corps) wrote: "Colonel Schmundt came this afternoon to lecture the higher echelons of the army on how the Fuehrer sees things … Over [Leningrad] the 'plow shall pass!'" Quoted in: D. Irving, *Hitler's War*, 313.

312   C. Burdick & H.-A. Jacobsen (eds.), *The Halder Diary 1939-1942*, 524.

313   Murray & A. R. Millett, *A War to Be Won*, 130.

314   *"Tagesmeldungen der Operations-Abteilung des GenStdH,"* in: P. E. Schramm (Hg.), *Kriegstagebuch des OKW*, Bd. I, 560.

315   *"Tagesmeldungen der Operations-Abteilung des GenStdH,"* in: P. E. Schramm (Hg.), *Kriegstagebuch des OKW*, Bd. I, 570; E. M. Howell, *The Soviet Partisan Movement* (Department of the Army Pamphlet 20-244), 29.

316   *"Tagesmeldungen der Operations-Abteilung des GenStdH,"* in: P. E. Schramm (Hg.), *Kriegstagebuch des OKW*, Bd. I, 589-605; *GSWW*, Vol. IV, 597-601.

317 The reader will recall that, at their meeting at the *Wolfsschanze* on 23 August, Hitler had assured Guderian that he could advance south with his entire panzer group; nevertheless, 46 Panzer Corps was withdrawn from Guderian's command and put in reserve behind Kluge's Fourth Army in the area Roslavl-Smolensk. In his memoirs, the panzer leader called this decision a "grievous disappointment." H. Guderian, *Panzer Leader*, 203.

318 M. Gilbert, *Second World War*, 232-33.

319 R. J. Kershaw, *War Without Garlands*, 155.

320 H. Guderian, *Panzer Leader*, 213-14; "*Tagesmeldungen der Operations-Abteilung des GenStdH*," in: P. E. Schramm (Hg.), *Kriegstagebuch des OKW*, Bd. I, 625.

321 *GSWW*, Vol. IV, 602.

322 K. Gerbet (ed.), *GFM Fedor von Bock, The War Diary*, 310-11.

323 W. Haupt, *Army Group Center*, 74.

324 R. J. Kershaw, *War Without Garlands*, 157.

325 K. Gerbet (ed.), *GFM Fedor von Bock, The War Diary*, 313.

326 J. Erickson, *The Road to Stalingrad*, 209.

327 "*Tagesmeldungen der Operations-Abteilung des GenStdH*," in: P. E. Schramm (Hg.), *Kriegstagebuch des OKW*, Bd. I, 646. According to one observer inside Hitler's East Prussian headquarters, the capture of Kiev elicited "immense joy" [*riesige Begeisterung*] within the *Wolfsschanze*. M. Vogt (Hg.), *Herbst 1941 im "Fuehrerhauptquartier*," 29.

328 The pocket represented "a huge triangle with sides 500km long encompassing an area of 135,500 sq.km." R. J. Kershaw, *War Without Garlands*, 157.

329 A. Kesselring, *Soldat Bis Zum Letzten Tag*, 126-27.

330 Quoted in: R. J. Kershaw, *War Without Garlands*, 162.

331 Ibid., 162.

332 "*Tagesmeldungen der Operations-Abteilung des GenStdH*," in: P. E. Schramm (Hg.), *Kriegstagebuch des OKW*, Bd. I, 661.

333 J. Erickson, *Road to Stalingrad*, 209-10.

334 Dr R. Gschoepf, *Mein Weg mit der 45. Inf.-Div.*, 264.

335 H. Guderian, *Panzer Leader*, 219.

336 H. Magenheimer, *Moskau 1941*, 120. After the buildup for "Typhoon," Army Group Center comprised some 78 divisions (among them, 14 armored and 8 motorized divisions); of these, however, four security and two infantry divisions operated in the army group's hinterland. For Bock's complete order of battle see, BA-MA RH 19 II/120, *KTB H.Gr.Mitte*, 2.10.41; also, *GSWW*, Vol. IV, 668-69.

337 Richthofen's 8 Air Corps had been transferred back to Army Group Center to support "Typhoon." The air corps' squadrons flew an average of four, and as many as six, sorties on this day. BA-MA RL 8/49, "*VIII. Fl.K., Einsatz Russland*," 2.10.41.

338 *Tagebuch* (author unknown), quoted in: *Gefallen! … und umsonst – Erlebnisberichte deutscher Soldaten im Russlandkrieg 1941-1943*, Dr H. Duesel (Hg.), 39.

339 *Tagebuch* Lierow, 2.10.41.

340 H. Pabst, *The Outermost Frontier*, 27.

341 As stated, while the general advance began on 2 October, 2 Panzer Group, at Guderian's request, had attacked two days earlier (30 September): "In the area across which 2 Panzer Group would now be attacking there were no metalled roads available and I wished to make full use of the limited period of fine weather which we might still expect in order to reach the good roads around Orel before the mud set in and to secure the transverse Orel-Briansk road so that I might have a decent supply route." H. Guderian, *Panzer Leader*, 224-25.

342 D. Irving, *Hitler's War*, 319.

343 Quoted in: D. Irving, *Hitler's War*, 320. For the complete text of Hitler's speech see, M. Domarus, *Hitler – Reden und Proklamationen 1932-1945*, Bd. II, 1758-67.

344 "*Dieser Gegner ist bereits gebrochen und wird sich nie mehr erheben*." H.-A. Jacobsen, *Der Zweite Weltkrieg in Chronik*, 38.

345 C. Burdick & H.-A. Jacobsen (eds.), *The Halder Diary 1939-1942*, 546.

346 On 6 October 1941, Guderian's headquarters was promoted from panzer "group" to 2 Panzer Army. "*Tagesmeldungen der Operations-Abteilung des GenStdH*," in: P. E. Schramm (Hg.), *Kriegstagebuch des OKW*, Bd. I, 682.

347 D. M. Glantz, *Barbarossa*, 148-49; H. Guderian, *Panzer Leader*, 233.

348 Lt.-Gen. Georg-Hans Reinhardt, hitherto commanding 41 Panzer Corps, had taken over at 3 Panzer Group on 5 October 1941; Hoth was transferred to Army Group South, to take command of Seventeeth Army. Internet site at: http://www.lexikon-der-wehrmacht.de.

349 K.-J. Thies, *Der Ostfeldzug – Ein Lageatlas*, "Lage am 6.10.1941 abds., Heeresgruppe Mitte;" "*Tagesmeldungen der Operations-Abteilung des GenStdH*," in: P. E. Schramm (Hg.), *Kriegstagebuch des OKW*, Bd. I, 684; D. M. Glantz, *Barbarossa*, 149.

350 Quoted in: D. Irving, *Hitler's War*, 321-22.

351 M. Domarus, *Hitler – Reden und Proklamationen 1932-1945*, Bd. II, 1767. The euphoria at the Wolf's Lair at this time (8/9 Oct 41) is captured in the detailed report prepared by Werner Koeppen, Alfred Rosenberg's personal representative at Hitler's East Prussian headquarters. In July 1941, Hitler had appointed Rosenberg to head the Reich Ministry for the Occupied Eastern Territories. See, M. Vogt (Hg.), *Herbst 1941 im "Fuehrerhauptquartier*," 69-71.

352 H. Guderian, *Panzer Leader*, 233.

353 K. Reinhardt, *Moscow – The Turning Point*, 88.

354 BA-MA RH 19 II/120, *KTB H.Gr.Mitte*, 9.10.41.

355 R. Kirchubel, *Operation Barbarossa 1941* (3), *Army Group Center*, 75; K. Reinhardt, *Moscow – The Turning Point*, 88. For an excellent account of German air support of Operation "Typhoon" see, H. Plocher, *The German Air Force Versus Russia, 1941*, 225-48.

356 R. Overy, *Russia's War*, 113.

357 E. Mawdsley, *Thunder in the East*, 96.

358 For a description of the defensive lines covering Moscow see, H. Magenheimer, *Moskau 1941*, 126-27. The Soviets had begun work on the Mozhaisk Line as early as July 1941; by mid-October 1941, however, it was only 40-50 percent complete.

359 E. Mawdsley, *Thunder in the East*, 95.

360 R. J. Kershaw, *War Without Garlands*, 189-90.

361 K. Reinhardt, *Moscow – The Turning Point*, 91; "*Tagesmeldungen der Operations-Abteilung des GenStdH*," in: P. E. Schramm (Hg.), *Kriegstagebuch des OKW*, Bd. I, 695-702; K.-J. Thies, *Der Ostfeldzug – Ein Lageatlas*, "Lage am 13.10.1941 abds., Heeresgruppe Mitte;" A. Seaton, *The Battle for Moscow*, 107. Soviet forces were not completely cleared out of Kalinin until 17 October; in the weeks which followed, the Soviets sought repeatedly, albeit unsuccessfully, to recapture the city. Over a 36-day period in October/November 1941, 36 ID (mot.), defending in and about Kalinin, alone repelled three Soviet attacks in regimental strength, 16 in battalion strength, 28 in company strength, and five tank attacks. The city was finally recaptured in December 1941 during the course of the Soviet counteroffensive against Army Group Center. "*Vorstoss und Kampf um Kalinin der 36. Inf.Div. (mot.)*," bearbeitet durch 36. Inf.Div. (mot.), Abteilung Ic, Nov 41.

362 *GSWW*, Vol. IV, 677.

363 E. Mawdsley, *Thunder in the East*, 105. It was on 5 October 1941 that Stalin had ordered Zhukov back to Moscow. Ibid., 95.

364 According to Glantz, Bock was forced to commit 48 divisions – well over half his total divisions – for a period of 7-14 days to break Red Army resistance in the twin encirclements, thus "losing the opportunity to exploit the empty defenses west of Moscow." D. M. Glantz, *Barbarossa*, 158.

365 K. Reinhardt, *Moscow – The Turning Point*, 110-11, f.n. 45.

366 *Feldpost*, W. Heinemann, 27.10.41.

367 *GSWW*, Vol. IV, 676-77.

368 K. Gerbet (ed.), *GFM Fedor von Bock, The War Diary*, 334. German movements on the *Autobahn* between Smolensk and Viaz'ma were also frequently disrupted by the withdrawing Russians, who planted large numbers of heavy artillery shells with delayed action fuzes [*Zeitzuender*] on the highway; the resulting explosions tore massive craters measuring 8-10 meters in depth, and up to 25 meters in diameter. M. Vogt (Hg.), *Herbst 1941 im "Fuehrerhauptquartier*," 88.

369 CMH Publication 104-6: "*Effects of Climate on Combat in European Russia*," 36-37.

370 K. Gerbet (ed.), *GFM Fedor von Bock, The War Diary*, 340.

371 BA-MA MSg 1/1148: *Tagebuch* Lemelsen, 16.10.41.

372 D. M. Glantz, *Barbarossa*, 158.

373 A. Seaton, *The Russo-German War*, 184-85.

374 D. M. Glantz, *Barbarossa*, 158. According to the late German historian Joachim Hoffmann, by the end of October 1941, "it had proved possible to integrate into the front west of Moscow at least 13 rifle divisions and 5 armored brigades from the interior of the country," helping to temporarily stabilize the Russian lines. *GSWW*, Vol. IV, 893.

375 *GSWW*, Vol. IV, 891.

376 K. Reinhardt, *Moscow – The Turning Point*, 108, f.n. 16.

377 D. M. Glantz, *Barbarossa*, 153.

378 BA-MA RH 19 II/120, *KTB H.Gr.Mitte*, 19.10.41; also, K. Gerbet (ed.), *GFM Fedor von Bock, The War Diary*, 336. Bock pegged Soviet losses at 8 Russian armies with 73 rifle and cavalry divisions, 13 tank divisions and brigades, and "strong army artillery." According to German estimates, total booty amounted to: 673,098 prisoners, 1277 tanks, 4378 artillery pieces, 1009 anti-tank and anti-aircraft guns, and 87 aircraft.

379 BA-MA RL 8/49, "*VIII. Fl.K., Einsatz Russland*," 26.10.41. On 30 October, 8 Air Corps operations were thwarted by "sleet! – totally devastating weather … Only *Stukas* were flying, due to the most extreme urgency, at an altitude of about 100 meters in order to parry a Russian counterstroke with tanks against the flank of 110 ID." Ibid., 30.10.41.

380 "*Tagesmeldungen der Operations-Abteilung des GenStdH*," in: P. E. Schramm (Hg.), *Kriegstagebuch des OKW*, Bd. I, 727.

381 H. Guderian, *Panzer Leader*, 244.

382 Ibid., 244.

383 R. J. Kershaw, *War Without Garlands*, 195. From 2-15 Oct. 41, Army Group Center advanced at an average pace of 16 km./day; the average pace of 3 Panzer Group from 11-15 Oct. 41 was 30 km./day, and that of 2 Panzer Group from 30 Sep.-2 Oct. 41 as much as 60 km./day. During the second half of October, however, the average pace of the advance plunged to 5.3 km./day. K. Reinhardt, *Moscow – The Turning Point*, 132, f.n. 1.

384 K.-J. Thies, *Der Ostfeldzug – Ein Lageatlas*, "Lage am 2.11.1941 abds., Heeresgruppe Mitte."

385 K. Gerbet (ed.), *GFM Fedor von Bock, The War Diary*, 347.

386 Because of heavy enemy pressure, leading in some cases to local breaches of its front, Kluge's Fourth Army had largely suspended its advance by 26 October. "*Tagesmeldungen der Operations-Abteilung des GenStdH*," in: P. E. Schramm (Hg.), *Kriegstagebuch des OKW*, Bd. I, 725.

387 K. Gerbet (ed.), *GFM Fedor von Bock, The War Diary*, 347-48.

388 From 1-17 October 1941, Army Group Center suffered ca. 50,000 casualties. Tank losses had also been heavy. For example, on 16 October, no panzer division in 2 Panzer Army had more than 82 tanks (3 PD), while 4 PD, which had sustained heavy losses in fighting with Soviet T-34s at Mtsensk, had been reduced to just 38 combat-ready vehicles. The panzer army's 9 PD had just 23 operational tanks on this day. K. Reinhardt, *Moscow – The Turning Point*, 92; also, BA-MA RH 19II/123, "*Zahl der bei den Panzer-Divisionen vorhandenen Panzer*," 16.10.41.

389 H. Guderian, *Panzer Leader*, 246.

390 A. Seaton, *The Battle for Moscow*, 201.

391 W. Murray, *Strategy for Defeat*, 87.

392 German historian Johannes Huerter argues that the "catastrophe" for Germany did not begin with the Soviet winter offensive in December 1941; rather, it was the "fatal decision" to resume "Typhoon" in November. Writes Huerter: "The recklessness with which the final offensive on Moscow was ordered is incomprehensible, and the responsibility belongs not only to Halder, but even more to Bock, because this most important commander of the *Ostheer* was much closer to the reality of the front than was the Chief of the General Staff." J. Huerter, *Hitlers Heerfuehrer*, 302, 307.

393 For example, at a top-level conference at Orsha, on 13 November, in weather of -8 degrees Fahrenheit, Halder attempted to assign Guderian's panzer army the objective of capturing Gorki, roughly 400 kilometers east of Moscow, to cut off the Soviet capital from its eastward communications. Opposition to Halder's plans, however, resulted in the decision to limit a renewed offensive to a direct assault on Moscow. "This was pushed through," writes Ian Kershaw, "in full recognition of the insoluble logistical problems and immense dangers of an advance in near-arctic conditions without any possibility of securing supplies." I. Kershaw, *Hitler 1936-45: Nemesis*, 437-38.

394 J. Huerter, *Hitlers Heerfuehrer*, 315. According to Huerter, instead of intervening in the OKH conduct of operations, which was driven by Halder, Hitler had "fatalistically" awaited the outcome of operations in the east. Only after the local reverse suffered by Army Group South at Rostov (30 Nov 41), did Hitler begin again to intervene energetically. Ibid., 310.

395 I. Kershaw, *Hitler 1936-45: Nemesis*, 438.

396 K. Gerbet (ed.), *GFM Fedor von Bock, The War Diary*, 357.

397 *GSWW*, Vol. IV, 893-94.

398 J. Erickson, *Road to Stalingrad*, 257.

399 E. F. Ziemke & M. E. Bauer, *Moscow to Stalingrad*, 51.

400 *GSWW*, Vol. IV, 693.

401 Ibid., 695.

402 *GSWW*, Vol. IV, 696; K. Gerbet (ed.), *GFM Fedor von Bock, The War Diary*, 366.

403 Fahrmbacher's 7 Army Corps was fighting astride the Smolensk – Moscow *Autobahn*, east of Mozhaisk, about 50 kilometers from the outskirts of Moscow. K.-J. Thies, *Der Ostfeldzug – Ein Lageatlas*, "Lage am 23.11.1941 abds., Heeresgruppe Mitte."

404 K. Gerbet (ed.), *GFM Fedor von Bock, The War Diary*, 366.

405 K. Reinhardt, *Moscow – The Turning Point*, 203, f.n. 19.

406 W. Haupt, *Sturm auf Moskau*, 223.

407 Quoted in: K. Reinhardt, *Moscow – The Turning Point*, 234-35, f.n. 84.

408 "*Tagesmeldungen der Operations-Abteilung des GenStdH*," in: P. E. Schramm (Hg.), *Kriegstagebuch des OKW*, Bd. I, 773; K.-J. Thies, *Der Ostfeldzug – Ein Lageatlas*, "Lage am 23.11.1941 abds., Heeresgruppe Mitte."

409 R. J. Kershaw, *War Without Garlands*, 210.

410 R. J. Kershaw, *War Without Garlands*, 206-07; D. M. Glantz, *Barbarossa*, 172; H. v. Manteuffel, *Die 7. Panzer-Division. Bewaffnung, Einsaetze, Maenner*, 89; "*Tagesmeldungen der Operations-Abteilung des GenStdH*," in: P. E. Schramm (Hg.), *Kriegstagebuch des OKW*, Bd. I, 785; K.-J. Thies, *Der Ostfeldzug – Ein Lageatlas*, "Lage am 28.11.1941 abds., Heeresgruppe Mitte."

411 K. Reinhardt, *Moscow – The Turning Point*, 249, f.n. 2.

412 C. Burdick & H.-A. Jacobsen (eds.), *The Halder Diary 1939-1942*, 562.

413 K. Gerbet (ed.), *GFM Fedor von Bock, The War Diary*, 375-76. German text of Bock's teletype in: R. Hofmann, "*Die Schlacht von Moskau 1941*," in: *Entscheidungsschlachten des zweiten Weltkrieges*, H.-A. Jacobsen & J. Rohwer (Hg.), 163.

414 J. Erickson, *Road to Stalingrad*, 266.

415 "*Tagesmeldungen der Operations-Abteilung des GenStdH*," in: P. E. Schramm (Hg.), *Kriegstagebuch des OKW*, Bd. I, 790.

416 J. Erickson, *Road to Stalingrad*, 266-67; A. Seaton, *The Russo-German War*, 207-08; G. Blumentritt, "*Die Ueberwindung der Krise vor Moskau im Winter 1941-42, dargestellt an der 4. Armee*," in: *Wehr-Wissenschaftliche Rundschau*, Mar. 54, 109.

417 BA-MA RH 21-2/244, *KTB Panzer AOK 2*, 5.12.41.

418 BA-MA RH 21-2/244, *KTB Panzer AOK 2*, 5.12.41; D. Irving, *Hitler's War*, 350.

419 K. Reinhardt, *Moscow – The Turning Point*, 228.

420 D. M. Glantz, *Barbarossa*, 177.

421 *GSWW*, Vol. IV, 698.

422 R. Kirchubel, *Hitler's Panzer Armies*, 81.

423 BA-MA RH 21-2/244, *KTB Panzer AOK 2*, 4.-5.12.41. At the end of November 1941, Guderian's 4 PD had just 21 operational tanks and 18 artillery pieces; by 3 December, his 10 ID (mot.) was reduced to 7 artillery pieces. R. Kirchubel, *Hitler's Panzer Armies*, 81; BA-MA RH 21-2/244, *KTB Panzer AOK 2*, 5.12.41.

424   K.-J. Thies, *Der Ostfeldzug – Ein Lageatlas*, "Lage am 6.12.1941 abds., Heeresgruppe Mitte."

425   *Uffz.* Karl R. (35 672), Collection BfZ.

426   Argues Guderian biographer Russell A. Hart: "Racially and ideologically dismissive of Soviet capabilities, Guderian and the other senior German generals underestimated the scale, scope, and savagery of the Soviet winter counteroffensive." R. A. Hart, *Guderian*, 77.

427   On 4 December 1941, the intelligence estimate of Foreign Armies East (FHO) had concluded that Soviet forces facing Army Group Center were, "at present," unable to mount a large-scale attack without significant reinforcements. *GSWW*, Vol. IV, 702.

428   The winter of 1941/42, states R.H.S. Stolfi, was the "coldest winter in the east in possibly a quarter of a millennium." R.H.S. Stolfi, "*Chance in History: The Russian Winter of 1941-1942*," in: *History*, Jun. 80, 222.

429   H. Haape, *Moscow Tram Stop*, 286

430   Ibid., 287-88.

431   Ibid., 289.

432   The average daily rate of advance of the Red Army's Western Front ranged from 4 to 15 kilometers per day between 6 and 25 December 1941. H. S. Orenstein (trans.), *Soviet Documents on Use of War Experience*, Vol. III, 15.

433   The Red Army had begun the war with 33,200 artillery pieces, and had lost 24,440 of them in six months. E. Mawdsley, *Thunder in the East*, 194.

434   According to David Irving, Hitler's "Halt Order was dictated to Bock over the telephone by Halder at 12:10 p.m." D. Irving, *Hitler's War*, 357.

435   Many front-line generals, such as Guderian, were opposed to the Halt Order, instead favoring retrograde maneuver. Yet as Guderian biographer Russell A. Hart argues, "given the immobility of the German Army – owing to lack of transport and minimal winter equipment – the only viable action was to stand fast in fortified village hedgehog defenses and weather the Soviet storm as Hitler demanded. Any time German forces had fought delaying withdrawals they had found it difficult to disengage from the enemy – who were better equipped for winter warfare – without suffering appreciable losses, particularly heavy weapons that had to be abandoned for lack of transport and fuel." (R. A. Hart, *Guderian*, 80.) In his post-war study of the German tank arm, former panzer general Walther K. Nehring wrote: "Through Hitler's intervention, a panic and disintegration of the Army was most likely avoided." W. K. Nehring, *Die Geschichte der deutschen Panzerwaffe*, 238.

436   Clearly worn out, his nerves frayed, Guderian, in accordance with his own wishes, was formally relieved of his command on 26 December 1941. In the weeks leading up to his relief, Guderian had "proved too prone to retrograde movement with forces incapable of such action … Moreover, [he] was simply not a very effective defensive commander. He had not trained for or studied defense and considered it to be by far the inferior posture." R. A. Hart, *Guderian*, 79.

437   For example, some three dozen corps and divisional commanders were dismissed by Hitler during the winter of 1941/42. J. Keegan, *The Second World War*, 206.

438   On 20 February 1942, Goebbels wrote in his diary: "The Fuehrer tells me that he has just put three weeks of the most barbaric work [*drei Wochen barbarischster Arbeit*] behind him. On most days, he has stood in the map room, from early morning to late at night, which has caused his feet to swell up." R. G. Reuth (Hg.), *Joseph Goebbels Tagebuecher*, Bd. IV, 1735.

439   Worn out and again sick, Field Marshal von Bock asked for, and was granted, a temporary leave of absence. He departed Army Group Center on the morning of 19 December 1941. K. Gerbet (ed.), *GFM Fedor von Bock, The War Diary*, 397-99.

440   Peter G. Tsouras (ed.), *Fighting in Hell*, 172.

441   On 1 January 1942, 3 and 4 Panzer Groups were redesignated as panzer armies. *GSWW*, Vol. IV, 726, f.n. 630.

442   H. Magenheimer, *Moskau 1941*, 219; *GSWW*, Vol. IV, 728-29.

443   Quoted in: C. Bergström & A. Mikhailov, *Black Cross Red Star*, Vol. II, 45-46.

444   While Army Group Center received no new divisions in December 1941, it did receive some infantry battalions flown in by troop transports. In January 1942, the army group received four new divisions; in February 1942, five new divisions. During the same period of time, the Red Army was massively reinforced. R. Hofmann, "*Schlacht von Moskau 1941*," in: *Entscheidungsschlachten des zweiten Weltkrieges*, H.-A. Jacobsen & J. Rohwer (Hg.), 181.

445   OKH GenStdH/Op.Abt. (Ia), Nr 420053/42 g.Kdos./Chefs, "*Weisung fuer die Kampffuehrung im Osten nach Abschluss des Winters*," in: P. E. Schramm (Hg.), *KTB OKW*, Bd. I., 1093. On the same day, Kluge submitted his first situation report in weeks in which he had no impending disaster to report. Ziemke & Bauer, *Moscow to Stalingrad*, 171-72.

446   A. S. Knjaz'kov, "*Die sowjetische Strategie im Jahre 1942*," in: *Stalingrad. Ereignis – Wirkung – Symbol*, J. Foerster (Hg.), 39.

447   And remnants they were! In one battalion of 18 Infantry Regiment (6 ID), by the end of the winter only 28 men remained of the original 800 or so who had marched confidently into Russia in June 1941. Such losses were hardly uncommon. H. Haape, *Moscow Tram Stop*, 359.

448   H.-A. Jacobsen (Hg.), *Halder Kriegstagebuch*, Bd. III, vii.

449   M. van Creveld, *The Changing Face of War*, 130-31.

450   R. E. Dupuy & T. N. Dupuy, *The Encyclopedia of Military History*, 1080.

451   D. M. Glantz, *Barbarossa*, 210.

452   R. Overmans, *Deutsche militaerische Verluste im Zweiten Weltkrieg*, 277.

453 See, for example, R.H.S. Stolfi, *Hitler's Panzers East – World War II Reinterpreted.*

454 D. Stahel, *And the World held its Breath,* 81; E. Bauer, *Der Panzerkrieg,* 113.

455 As Rolf-Dieter Mueller put it: "The supply task which had to be mastered outstripped all historical precedents." *GSWW,* Vol. IV, 1107.

456 For an insightful discussion of this problem – and the German intelligence apparatus in general – see, G.P. Megargee, *Inside Hitler's High Command,* 102-16.

457 Ibid., 115-16.

458 Col.-Gen. G. F. Krivosheev (ed.), *Soviet Casualties and Combat Losses,* 101; D. M. Glantz, *Barbarossa,* 68, 210.

459 D. M. Glantz, *Barbarossa,* 68.

460 W. S. Dunn, Jr., *Stalin's Keys to Victory,* 4.

461 A. Hillgruber, *"Die weltpolitischen Entscheidungen vom 22. Juni 1941 bis 11. Dezember 1941,"* in: *Nationalsozialistische Diktatur 1933-1945,* K. D. Bracher, *et al.,* (Hg.), 441-42.

462 D. Stahel, *And the World held its Breath,* 297.

463 When one considers that the German Army High Command began *Barbarossa* with just 28 divisions in reserve – along with some 300,000+ replacements in its Replacement Army – it is perhaps surprising that the *Ostheer* did as well as it did in 1941 against the unending flood of new Soviet armies encountered along all three axes of its advance through European Russia.

464 By the end of 1941, a total of 360,700 tons of aid – weapons, equipment, raw materials – had been dispatched from the western hemisphere (i.e., the United States, Canada, Latin America) to the Soviet Union. Of this total, 3.7 percent went through the Persian Gulf (Iran), 53.6 percent via the Far East (Vladivostok), and 42.7 percent by way of Northern Russia (Murmansk & Archangel). Additional aid was sent from Great Britain. R. Kirchubel, *"Operation Barbarossa and the American Controversy over Aid to the Soviet Union,"* 28. By the fall of 1941, references to American and British weaponry – tanks, aircraft, etc. – began to turn up in the letters and diaries of German soldiers on the eastern front.

465 W. S. Dunn, Jr., *Hitler's Nemesis,* xvii-xviii.

466 C. Pleshakov, *Stalin's Folly,* 273.

467 "Throughout the entire period [1941]," states David Glantz, "Stalin 'turned the screws' on Red Army troops, issuing directives that demanded absolute obedience to orders under threat of censure, arrest and even execution." D. M. Glantz, *Barbarossa,* 209.

468 Quoted in: D. Stahel, *And the World held its Breath,* 292.

469 For Germany, another negative outcome of the Battle of Smolensk may have been its impact on Japan's strategic decision-making. The abrupt slowdown in Army Group Center's advance may have influenced Japan's ultimate decision not to intervene in Germany's war with Russia, but to strike out into the Pacific and Southeast Asia. In any case, by 9 August 1941, Japan had definitively decided not to join Operation *Barbarossa.* For a detailed discussion of this intriguing issue see, A. Hillgruber, *"Die Bedeutung der Schlacht von Smolensk in der Zweiten Julihaelfte 1941 fuer den Ausgang des Ostkrieges,"* in: A. Hillgruber, *Die Zerstoerung Europas,* 296-312.

470 D. Stahel, *And the World held its Breath,* 280.

471 Ibid., 293.

472 Ibid., 293.

473 T. Ropp, *War in the Modern World,* 333. According to Ropp, Hitler's "major miscalculation – but one which seemed to be supported by the upheavals in Russia in the mid-1930s – was, like Napoleon's, political."

474 C. Merridale, *Ivan's War,* 133-34.

475 I. Kershaw, *Hitler 1936-45: Nemesis,* 405.

476 F. W. Kagan, *"A Strategy for Heroes – What's wrong with the 2006 Quadrennial Defense Review,"* in: *The Weekly Standard,* 20 Feb 06.

APPENDIX 1

Comparative Military Ranks

(German/American)[1]

OFFICER RANKS

Generalfeldmarschall	Field Marshal
Generaloberst	General
General (der Infanterie, etc.)	Lieutenant General
Generalleutnant	Major General
Generalmajor	Brigadier General
Oberst	Colonel
Oberstleutnant	Lieutenant Colonel
Major	Major
Hauptmann or Rittmeister	Captain
Oberleutnant	First Lieutenant
Leutnant	Second Lieutenant

NON-COMMISSIONED OFFICERS

Stabsfeldwebel	Sergeant Major
Oberfeldwebel	Master Sergeant
Feldwebel	Technical Sergeant
Unterfeldwebel	Staff Sergeant
Unteroffizier	Non-Commissioned Officer

ENLISTED MEN

Stabsgefreiter	Administrative Corporal
Obergefreiter	Corporal
Gefreiter	Lance Corporal
Obersoldat	Private 1st Class
Soldat (Schuetze)	Private (Rifleman)

MEDICAL RANKS

Oberstarzt	Colonel (med.)
Oberfeldarzt	Lt.Col (med.)
Oberstabsarzt	Major (med.)
Stabsarzt	Captain (med.)
Oberarzt	First Lt. (med.)
Assistenzarzt	Second Lt. (med.)
Unterarzt	NCO (med.)

ENDNOTES

1   G. P. Megargee, *Inside Hitler's High Command*, 238; *Handbook on German Military Forces*, U.S. War Department, March 1945, 5-7; A. Buchner, *The German Infantry Handbook 1939-1945*, 6; Internet site at: http://www.feldgrau.com.

APPENDIX 2
Army Group Center Order of Battle

(21 June 1941)[1]

Heeresgruppe Mitte
Ob.Bfh.:   Gen.Feldm. v. Bock
Chef d.St.:   Gen.Maj. v. Greiffenberg
Ia: Obstlt.i.G. v. Tresckow

Heeresgruppe Reserve
53. Armeekorps
Kom. Gen.:   Gen.d.Inf. Weisenberger
Chef d.St.:   Oberst i.G. Waeger

293. ID:[2]   Gen.Lt. v. Obernitz

Rueckwaertiges Heeresgebiet (R.H.G.) 102[3]
Bfh.:   Gen.d.Inf. v. Schenckendorff
Chef d.St.   Obstlt.i.G. Ruebesamen

Panzergruppe 2 (AOK 4 unterstellt)[4]
Bfh.:   Gen.Oberst Guderian
Chef d.St.:   Obstlt.i.G. Frhr. v. Liebenstein
Ia: Obstlt.i.G. Bayerlein

46. Panzerkorps[5]
Kom. Gen.:   Gen.d.Pz.Tr. v. Vietinghoff
                gen. Scheel
Chef d.St.:   Obstlt.i.G. v.d. Burg

SS-Div. "R" (mot.): SS-Gruppenfuehrer Hausser
10. PD: Gen.Lt. Schaal
Inf.-Rgt. "G.D." (mot.): Oberst v. Stockhausen

47. Panzerkorps
Kom. Gen.:   Gen.d.Art. Lemelsen
Chef d. St.:   Oberst i.G. Bamler

18. PD: Gen.Maj. Nehring
17. PD: Gen.Lt. v. Arnim
29. ID (mot.): Gen.Maj. v. Boltenstern
167. ID: Gen.Lt. Schoenhaerl

12. Armeekorps
Kom.Gen.:   Gen.d.Inf. Schroth
Chef d.St.:   Obstlt.i.G. v. Waldenburg

34. ID: Gen.Lt. Behlendorff
45. ID: Gen.Maj. Schlieper
31. ID: Gen.Maj. Kalmukoff

24. Panzerkorps
Kom. Gen.:   Gen.d.Kav. Frhr. Geyr v.
Schweppenburg
Chef d. St.:   Oberst i.G. Schilling

1. Kav.-Div.:   Gen.Maj. Feldt
267. ID: Gen.Maj. v. Wachter
4. PD: Gen.Maj. Frhr. v. Langermann
                u. Erlenkamp
3. PD: Gen.Lt. Model
10. ID (mot.): Gen.Lt. v. Loeper

zur Verfuegung der Panzergruppe:[6]
255. ID: Gen.Lt. Wetzel

Armeeoberkommando 4
Ob.Bfh.:   Gen.Feldm. v. Kluge
Chef d.St.:   Oberst i.G. Blumentritt
Ia: Obstlt. i.G. Zitzewitz

13. Armeekorps
Kom. Gen.:   Gen.d.Inf. Felber
Chef d. St.:   Oberst i.G. Hofmann

78. ID: Gen.Lt. Gallenkamp
17. ID: Gen.Lt. Loch

7. Armeekorps
Kom. Gen.:   Gen.d.Art. Fahrmbacher
Chef d. St.:   Oberst i.G. Krebs

7. ID: Gen.Lt. Frhr. v. Gablenz
258. ID: Gen.Maj. Dr. Henrici
268. ID: Gen.Maj. Straube
23. ID: Gen.Maj. Hellmich
221. SD:[7]   Gen.Lt. Pflugbeil

9. Armeekorps
Kom. Gen.:   Gen.d.Inf. Geyer
Chef d. St.:   Obstlt. i.G. v. Linstow

292. ID: Gen.Maj. Dehmel
137. ID: Gen.Lt. Bergmann
263. ID: Gen.Maj. Haeckel

43. Armeekorps
Kom. Gen.:   Gen.d.Inf. Heinrici
Chef d. St.:   Oberst i.G. Schulz (Fr.)

131. ID: Gen.Maj. Meyer-Buerdorf
134. ID: Gen.Lt. v. Cochenhausen
252. ID: Gen.Lt. v. Boehm-Bezing

zur Verfuegung der Armee:
286. SD: Gen.Lt. Mueller (Kurt)

Armeeoberkommando 9
Ob.Bfh.:   Gen.Oberst Strauss
Chef d. St.:   Oberst i.G. Weckmann
Ia: Obstlt. i.G. Blaurock

8. Armeekorps
Kom. Gen.:   Gen.d.Art. Heitz
Chef d. St.:   Oberst i.G. Steinmetz

8. ID: Gen.Maj. Hoehne
28. ID: Gen.Lt. Sinnhuber
161. ID: Gen.Maj. Wilck

20. Armeekorps
Kom. Gen.:   Gen.d.I. Materna
Chef d. St.:   Oberst i.G. Vogel

162. ID: Gen.Lt. Franke
256. ID: Gen.Lt. Kauffmann

42. Armeekorps (spaeter OKH-Reserve)
Kom. Gen.:   Gen.d.Pi. Kuntze
Chef d. St.:   Oberst i.G. Ziegler

87. ID: Gen.Lt. v. Studnitz
102. ID: Gen.Maj. Ansat
129. ID: Gen.Maj. Rittau

zur Verfuegung der Armee:
403. SD: Gen.Maj. v. Ditfurth

Panzergruppe 3 (AOK 9 unterstellt)[8]
Bfh.:   Gen.Oberst Hoth
Chef d. St.:   Obstlt. i.G. v. Huenersdorff
Ia: Major i.G. Wagener

6. Armeekorps
Kom. Gen.:   Gen.d.Pi. Foerster
Chef d. St.:   Obstlt. i.G. Degen

6. ID: Gen.Lt. Auleb
26. ID: Gen.Maj. Weiss

39. Panzerkorps
Kom. Gen.:   Gen.d.Pz.Tr. Schmidt
Chef d. St.:   Oberst i.G. Hildebrand

7. PD: Gen.Maj. Frhr. v. Funck
20. PD: Gen.Lt. Stumpff
20. ID (mot.):   Gen.Maj. Zorn
14. ID (mot.):   Gen.Maj. Fuerst

5. Armeekorps
Kom. Gen.:   Gen.d.Inf. Ruoff
Chef d. St.:   Oberst i.G. Schmidt

5. ID: Gen.Maj. Allmendinger
35. ID: Gen.Lt. Fischer v. Weikersthal

57. Panzerkorps
Kom. Gen.:   Gen.d.Pz.Tr. Kuntzen
Chef d. St.:   Obstlt. i.G. Fangohr

12. PD: Gen.Maj. Harpe
19. PD: Gen.Lt. v. Knobelsdorff
18. ID (mot.):   Gen.Maj. Herrlein

ENDNOTES

1   Compiled from: W. Keilig, *Das Deutsche Heer*, Bd. I, Abschnitt 34, S. 7-13; *K. Mehner* (Hg.), *Geheime Tagesberichte*, Bd. 3.
2   For all divisions only the division commander is given.
3   This unit was responsible for security in the army group's rear areas.
4   Guderian's tank group was subordinated to Fourth Army for the initial attack.
5   As of June 1941, the panzer corps were still officially designated as motorized army corps (although some units were already employing the term "panzer corps"). In other words, 46 Panzer Corps = 46 Army Corps (mot.). Shortly after the start of the Russian campaign, the designation was officially changed to "panzer corps."
6   Apparently, this division was available to 2 Panzer Group, if needed, but was not directly subordinated to it.
7   *Sicherungs-Division* – i.e., a division intended for rear area security.
8   Hoth's tank group was subordinated to Ninth Army for the initial attack.

APPENDIX 3[1]

292 Infantry Division
(Organization, Personnel, Weapons & Equipment)

(21 June 1941)

Note: Details on the 292 Infantry Division are provided here as an example of a "typical" German infantry division on the eve of Operation *Barbarossa*. The division was mobilized in the 8th Wave and formed in February 1940 on the Troop Training Grounds (*Truppenuebungsplatz*) Gross-Born, in Military District II (*Wehrkreis* II); it was considered to be fully combat capable. At the beginning of the eastern campaign, 292 ID was assigned to 9 Army Corps in Field Marshal von Kluge's Fourth Army. During the summer and fall of 1941, it would see major action in the central sector of the eastern front, including in the fierce defensive fighting at El'nia, east of Smolensk. The division also took part in Operation "Typhoon," the assault on Moscow. The 292 ID would see continuous action on the eastern front into early 1945, when it was finally destroyed in the cauldron battle at Heiligenbeil. The remnants of the division were distributed among other units.

Combat Strength (*Gefechtsstaerken*):[2]
Officers: 269
Civilian Officials:[3]7
NCOs:[4] 1553
Enlisted Personnel: 9712

Ration Strength (*Verpflegungsstaerken*):[5]
Officers: 358
Civilian Officials: 85
NCOs: 2196
Enlisted Personnel: 12.510
Horses: 5729

Organization
292 Mapping Detachment (mot.)

507 Infantry Regiment
1 Signal Platoon
1 Pioneer Platoon (3 l.M.G.)
1 Regimental Band
3 Infantry Battalions, each with
3 Rifle Companies (9 l.M.G., 2 s.M.G. & 3 l.Gr.W. each)
1 Hvy Company (8 s.M.G. & 6 s.Gr.W.)
13 Infantry Gun Company (2 s.I.G. & 6 l.I.G.)
14 *Panzerjaeger* (AT) Company (mot.) (12 l.Pak & 4 l.M.G.)
1 Mounted (horse) Reconnaissance Platoon
1 Light Infantry Supply Column

508 Infantry Regiment
(same as 507 IR)

509 Infantry Regiment
(same as 507 IR, but no regimental band)

292 *Panzerjaeger* (AT) Battalion
1 Signal Platoon (mot.)
3 *Panzerjaeger* Companies (mot.) (12 l.Pak & 6 l.M.G. each)

292 Bicycle Squadron
1 Bicycle Squadron (12 l.M.G.)
1 *Panzerjaeger* Platoon (3 l.Pak & 1 l.M.G.)

292 Artillery Regiment
3 Battalions (1, 2, and 3), each with 3 Batteries (4 l.F.H. & 2 l.M.G. each)
4. Battalion with 3 Batteries (4 s.F.H. & 2 l.M.G. each)

292 Replacement Battalion (*Feldersatz-Bataillon*)
3 Companies

292 Signal Battalion
1 Radio Company (mot.)
1 Telephone Company (mot.)
1 Signal Supply Company (mot.)

292 Pioneer (Combat Engineer) Battalion
2 Pioneer Companies (9 l.M.G. each)
1 Pioneer Company (mot.) (9 l.M.G.)
1 Bridging Column "B" (mot.) (*Brueko "B"*)
1 Engineer Supply Column (mot.)

292 Divisional Supply Troops
Several Light Columns (mot.)
Light Fuel Column (mot.)
Maintenance Platoon (mot.)
Supply Company
Divisional Administration
Field Bakery
Butcher Detachment (mot.)
Medical Company
Medical Company (mot.)
Field Hospital
Ambulance Companies (2)
Veterinary Company
Military Police Troop (mot.)
Field Post Office (mot.)

Total Available Weapons (*"Verwendungsbereite Waffen"***)**[6]

(included following):

l.M.G.   384

s.M.G.   108

Pz.B.   93

l.Gr.W.   79

s.Gr.W.   53

l.I.G.   18

s.I.G.   6

l.Pak   43

m.Pak   6

l.F.H.   36

s.F.H.   12

Definitions

l.M.G. = light machine gun

s.M.G. = heavy machine gun

Pz.B. = light AT rifles (*Panzerbuechse*)

l.Gr.W. = light mortar (50mm)

s.Gr.W. = medium mortar (81mm)

l.I.G. =   light infantry gun (75mm)

s.I.G =   medium infantry gun (150mm)

l.Pak =   37mm AT gun

m.Pak = 50mm AT gun (or French 47mm AT gun)

l.F.H. = light field howitzer (105mm)

s.F.H. = medium field howitzer (150mm)

ENDNOTES

1   Sources for this appendix include: BA-MA finding guide (292 ID); BA-MA 26-292/7, *"Gefechts- und Verpflegungsstaerken, 292. Inf. Division;"* W. Haupt, *Die deutschen Infanterie-Divisionen*, 27-28; G. F. Nafziger, *The German Order of Battle. Infantry in World War II*, 279-80; *German Military Dictionary*, originally published by U.S. War Department, 1944.

2   Figures for "combat strength" exclude rear area services, medical personnel, and personnel belonging to the divisional baggage trains.

3   Civilian officials of the armed forces (*Wehrmachtbeamte*) had nominal rank and wore uniforms; they were classified as combatants.

4   NCOs = *Unteroffiziere* and sergeants.

5   Figures for "ration strength" include all *Wehrmacht* personnel, and horses, provisioned by the division on the 1st, 11th and 21st of every month.

6   These figures are gleaned directly from the division's war diary. Figures provided by G. F. Nafziger differ in some cases. According to Nafziger, the division also boasted 2300 pistols, 800 machine pistols, and 13,541 98K rifles.

APPENDIX 4[1]

Tank Strength of Panzer Divisions in Army Group Center Order of Battle

(21 June 1941)

Note: For Operation Barbarossa, the German Army assembled about 3350 tanks (and 250 assault guns). Of these, over 1900 tanks, well over half the total, were assigned to the 9 panzer divisions in Field Marshal von Bock's Army Group Center. Five panzer divisions (13 tank battalions) were assigned to General Heinz Guderian's 2 Panzer Group, while 4 divisions (12 tank battalions) belonged to General Hermann Hoth's 3 Panzer Group. Bock's Army Group also boasted 6 of the 11 assault gun battalions committed to the attack on Russia. Below is a breakdown of the tanks in both of the panzer groups.

2 Panzer Group
Total Personnel & Tanks

205,000 personnel[2]
994 tanks (including 57 command tanks)
5 Panzer Divisions
13 Tank Battalions

3 Panzer Division
(6 Pz. Rgt.)

58 Pz II
29 Pz III (37mm)
81 Pz III (50mm)
32 Pz IV
15 Pz.Bef.[3]
———
215

4 Panzer Division
(35 Pz. Rgt.)

44 Pz II
31 Pz III (37)
74 Pz III (50)
20 Pz IV
8 Pz.Bef.
———
177

10 Panzer Division
(7 Pz. Rgt.)

45 Pz II
105 Pz III (50)
20 Pz IV
12 Pz.Bef.
———
182

17 Panzer Division
(39 Pz. Rgt.)

12 Pz I
44 Pz II
106 Pz III (50)
30 Pz IV
10 Pz.Bef.
———
202

18 Panzer Division[4]
(18 Pz. Rgt.)

6 Pz I
50 Pz II
99 Pz III (37)
15 Pz III (50)
36 Pz IV
12 Pz.Bef.
———
218

3 Panzer Group
Total Personnel & Tanks

150,000 personnel[5]
942 tanks (including 36 command tanks)
4 Panzer Divisions
12 Tank Battalions

7 Panzer Division
(25 Pz. Rgt.)

53 Pz II
167 Pz 38(t)
30 Pz IV
15 Pz.Bef.
———
265

12 Panzer Division
(29 Pz. Rgt.)

40 Pz I
33 Pz II
109 Pz 38(t)
30 Pz IV
8 Pz.Bef.

_____

220

19 Panzer Division
(27 Pz. Rgt.)

42 Pz I
35 Pz II
110 Pz 38(t)
30 Pz IV
11 Pz.Bef.

_____

228

20 Panzer Division
(21 Pz. Rgt.)

44 Pz I
31 Pz II
121 Pz 38(t)
31 Pz IV
2 Pz.Bef.

_____

229

ENDNOTES

1   Sources: G. F. Nafziger, *The German Order of Battle. Panzers and Artillery*; T. L. Jentz, *Panzer Truppen*; BA-MA RH 19 II/123, *Anlagen zum KTB H.Gr.Mitte*; W. Paul, *Geschichte der 18. Panzer Division*.

2   Includes assigned *Luftwaffe* and Army troops. Figure is for "*Kopfstaerke*," literally "head strength," thus it must include all personnel – both combat and support – permanently or temporarily assigned to the panzer group.

3   *Panzer Befehlswagen* = command tanks. These vehicles were outfitted with communications equipment and did not carry any main armament.

4   The 1st Battalion, 18 Panzer Division, was outfitted with 80 special "underwater" tanks for wading the Bug River at the start of the invasion. The division also possessed a battalion of flamethrower tanks (*Panzer-Flammabteilung 100*).

5   Same as above for 2 Panzer Group.

APPENDIX 5

Soviet Western Front Order of Battle

(22 June 1941)[1]

General D. G. Pavlov
Commander

Soviet 3 Army
Lt.-Gen. V. I. Kuznetsov

4 Rifle Corps
27 RD[2]
56 RD
85 RD

68 Fortified Region (Grodno)
7 Anti-Tank Artillery Brigade
152, 444 Corps Artillery Regiments
16 Separate Anti-Aircraft Artillery Battalion

11 Mechanized Corps (414 tanks)
Maj.-Gen. D. K. Mostovenko
29 TD
33 TD
204 MD
16 Motorcycle Regiment

Soviet 4 Army
Lt.-Gen. A. A. Korobkov

28 Rifle Corps
Maj.-Gen. V. S. Popov
6 RD
42 RD
49 RD
75 RD

62 Fortified Region (Brest-Litovsk)
447, 445, 462 Corps Artillery Regiments
120 High-Power Howitzer Artillery Regiment
12 Separate Anti-Aircraft Artillery Regiment

14 Mechanized Corps (518 tanks)
Maj.-Gen. S.I. Oborin
22 TD
30 TD
205 MD
20 Motorcycle Regiment

Soviet 10 Army
Lt.-Gen. K.D. Golubev

1 Rifle Corps

Maj.-Gen. F.D. Rubsev
2 RD
8 RD

5 Rifle Corps
Maj.-Gen. A.V. Gamov
13 RD
85 RD
113 RD

6 Cavalry Corps
Maj.-Gen. I.S. Nikitin
6 CD
36 CD
155 RD

66 Fortified Region (Osovets)
6 Anti-Tank Artillery Brigade
130, 156, 262, 315 Corps Artillery Regiments
311 Gun Artillery Regiment
124, 375 Howitzer Artillery Regiments
38, 71 Separate Anti-Aircraft Artillery Battalions

6 Mechanized Corps (1131 tanks)
Maj.-Gen. M.G. Khatskilevich
4 TD
7 TD
29 MD
4 Motorcycle Regiment

13 Mechanized Corps (282 tanks)
Maj.-Gen. P.N. Akhliustin
25 TD
31 TD
208 MD
18 Motorcycle Regiment

Soviet 13 Army
Lt.-Gen. P.M. Filatov
(Rear Field Headquarters only)

Front Units

2 Rifle Corps
Maj.-Gen. A.N. Ermakov
100 RD
161 RD

21 Rifle Corps
Maj.-Gen. V.B. Borisov
17 RD
24 RD
37 RD

44 Rifle Corps
Maj.-Gen. V.A. Yushkevich
64 RD
108 RD

47 Rifle Corps
Maj.-Gen. S.I. Povetkin
50 RD
55 RD
121 RD
143 RD

4 Airborne Corps
Maj.-Gen. A.S. Zhadov
7 AB
8 AB
214 AB

17 Mechanized Corps (63 tanks)
Maj.-Gen. M.P. Petrov
27 TD
36 TD
209 MD
22 Motorcycle Regiment

20 Mechanized Corps (94 tanks)

Maj.-Gen. A.G. Nikitin
26 TD
38 TD
210 MD
24 Motorcycle Regiment

58 Fortified Region (Sebezh)
61 Fortified Region (Polotsk)
63 Fortified Region (Minsk-Slutsk)
64 Fortified Region (Zambrov)
65 Fortified Region (Mozyr)
8 Anti-Tank Artillery Brigade
293, 611 Gun Artillery Regiments
360 Howitzer Artillery Regiment
5, 318, 612 High-Power Howitzer Artillery
    Regiments
29, 49, 56, 151, 467, 587 Corps Artillery
    Regiments
32 Separate Special-Power Artillery Battalion
24 Separate Mortar Battalion
86 Separate Anti-Aircraft Artillery Battalion
4, 7 PVO Brigades[3]
Baranovichi, Kobrin, Gomel, Vitebsk and
    Smolensk PVO Brigade Regions
10, 23, 33 Engineer Regiments
34, 35 Pontoon-Bridge Regiments
275 Separate Sapper Battalion
43 Fighter Aviation Division
59, 60 Fighter Aviation Divisions (both forming)
12, 13 Bomber Aviation Divisions
9, 10, 11 Mixed Aviation Divisions
184 Fighter Aviation Regiment
313, 314 Reconnaissance Aviation Regiments

ENDNOTES

1   Sources: D. M. Glantz, *Barbarossa*, 247; D. M. Glantz, *Red Army Ground Forces*, 21, 51; D. M. Glantz
     (ed.), *Atlas and Operational Summary. The Border Battles*, 32-33; H. Seidler, *Images of War. Operation
     Barbarossa*, 172-73. For numbers of tanks in the mechanized corps, I have used the detailed table in Glantz'
     Red Army Ground Forces, 21. Figures in other sources (including some of Glantz' own) are often slightly
     different.
2   RD = Rifle Division. TD = Tank Division. MD = Motorized Division. CD = Cavalry Division. AB = Airborne
     Brigade.
3   PVO = air defense units. An NKO order (14 February 1941) had established a new national air defense
     system in the Soviet Union. D. M. Glantz, *Red Army Ground Forces*, 33.

APPENDIX 6

Ostfrontkaempfer: German Assessments of Soviet Weapons

Note: Throughout my decade of research into German military operations along the central part of the eastern front in 1941/42, I asked many questions of the dozens of German veterans who graciously supported my efforts. One of my questions was this: "With regard to the weapons of the enemy which, in your opinion, were the most effective." (*Im Hinblick auf die Waffen des Feindes, welche besassen Ihrer Meinung nach die allergroesste Wirkung?*) While this hardly made for a scientific survey, it nevertheless offered a unique opportunity to query a large group of surviving veterans about the primary weapons of their tenacious Russian adversary. A sampling of their responses is provided below. Hopefully, it will offer the casual reader, as well as the serious researcher, useful insights into the nature of the fighting along the eastern front during the Second World War.

Of course, the veterans were in their 80s – and even their 90s – when responding to my query, and time and age take their toll on mental acuity. Conversely, as noted in the preface to this book, "Some people's memories dim and others ... remain crystal bright for a lifetime ... Tragedies and humiliations seem to be etched most sharply, often with the most unbearable exactitude."[1] Be that as it may, the responses of the former *Ostfrontkaempfer* offer fascinating perspectives on the deadly "tool box" of the Soviet armed forces; and while certain themes emerged from their responses, I was struck by their diverse, even contradictory, opinions about the efficacy of Red Army weaponry. Sadly, a large number of those few surviving veterans, whose support I was so honored to receive, are now gone, as the opportunity to ask such questions, and gain such insights, slips irretrievably away.

Veterans' Responses[2]

R. Adler (14 ID (mot.)): The greatest threat of all from them was their artillery, of which they always had enough! We weren't so afraid of the Stalin Organ, whose caliber increased all the time.[3] The casing was not thick, so the fragmentation effect was not great, but – large fragments, half shells lay around plentifully enough. A lot of earth was moved, but the deafening sound [*Krach*] was the biggest thing about it! You could see them approaching, but then, with time, we got wise to it: don't lie on the ground – like with artillery shells – stand ready, and then kick upward with the shifting sand or soil. In the beginning, we had too many losses to the Stalin Organ because everyone instinctively hit the ground inside their trench, and then they were buried by the soil movements and suffocated![4]

O. Baese (110 ID): I did come across the Stalin organ, too. Its impact was very inaccurate and so it wasn't particularly feared. So far as I can remember, I came across it only rarely.[5]

L. Bauer (3 PD): Naturally the first appearance of the T-34 was a great surprise, above all because back then our cannon on the Pz III and IV had little or no effect against them. Back then, on the Pz III, we still had the 50mm gun with a short barrel. Direct hits at distances greater than 250/300 meters had as good as no discernible success rate. From the beginning of 1942 we started receiving the so-called *Panzergranate* 41, with very high velocity. In the spring of 1942, when we received the new Pz III with its extended barrel on the 50mm gun, we were able to knock out the T-34 from a distance of up to 500 meters. Yet even here there were sometimes tank battles which took place at very close range. It was in such a battle, tank against tank, that I and my Pz III were rammed several times by a Russian KV-1 and then shot up. Later on, with the Pz IV and the long 75mm gun (L48), all our problems were solved. A T-34 could always be put out of action from a distance of up to 800/1000 meters. At first, it did take a bit of time before our soldiers were sure that this was the case, because the T-34 had such an extraordinary mystique [*Nimbus*] surrounding it. The Stalin Organ was less dangerous for the panzers. Only a chance hit could put a panzer out of action. Many a time, though, when fire was highly concentrated, it had a disheartening effect on the infantry.[6]

K. Beimdieke (2 PD): We did not think that the *Stalinorgel* was dangerous, we could get away from it … But the Russian infantry was a dangerous opponent indeed.[7]

F. Belke (6 ID): A strong and good artillery with a high level of ammunition consumption. A lot of mortars in the foremost line. They had little effect on the infantryman in his foxholes (for anti-tank defense), or in a trench – a direct hit was rare. As a rule, the artillery shot over and beyond the HKL. Maybe they thought strong reserves or our leaders were back there? But there was nobody there. The "Stalin Organ," with its countless impacts, usually fizzled out [*verpuffte meist*]. It didn't have any effect on morale (for "old" soldiers in their third year of war). The German infantryman was less afraid of death than of falling, wounded, into enemy hands, being stabbed, beaten, massacred. For the infantryman, the infantry rifle, the targeted shot, had the greatest effect.[8]

W. Bergelt (56 ID): The Stalin Organs were feared weapons, and the 5 or 6 different mortars, as well as the versatile T-34.[9]

W. Dicke (26 ID): The effects [of Soviet weapons] were different in each case. During a heavy barrage fire [*Trommelfeuer*], for example, the infernal roar of the Stalin Organ put a nervous strain on many of the soldiers. The T-34 was feared at first. Later, the tanks were just allowed to drive on through, the accompanying infantry were then stopped or shot down; many of the tanks which had broken through were destroyed with the aid of anti-tank guns, the rest drove back again.[10]

W. Dowe (86 ID): In particular as an anti-tank unit, we became familiar with the KV-1 and the T-34. Both tanks had 76.2mm guns with a long barrel. The T-34 was particularly feared … The Stalin Organ was, according to my observations, without significance in winter 41/42 during the battles outside Moscow and around Rzhev. It was only in 1943/44, during the combat operations around Orel and Kursk, and along the rest of the central front, that we found that the Stalin Organ, with its rapid rate of fire … exhibited a major impact.[11]

H. Effing (26 ID): The T-34 tank with its 76mm cannon was a nigh on invulnerable tank for the German 37mm Pak. The Stalin Organ, however, was an even more unpleasant surprise. Its 32 howling rockets could rattle even the best soldier.[12]

P. Folger (252 ID): Elite troops were very well armed, their machine pistols were even operational when dirty, which could not be said of ours. Their [machine gun], however, still reliant on water cooling, as in World War I, was a primitive combat weapon. The Stalin Organ was vile [*gemein*], if you can put it that way, because it could fire off a huge number of rockets; on top of that, there was the unpleasant howling, and it covered a wide area. In the winter outside Moscow, it made the life of the frontline soldier hell.[13]

H. Franze (263 ID): The Stalin Organ worked with its repeated loud cracks, its explosive and fragmentation effect was not great … I frequently lay in the impact zone without harm! Tanks were less dangerous for us infantry – unless there were soldiers on them; but then we fired tracers with the machine gun, and the infantrymen would flee. Outside Moscow, we dealt with tanks less – usually T-34s – [and] our Pak and the 88mm Flak were very successful there. In January 1942, I took out a T-34 with a magnetic hollow charge [*Hafthohlladung*]. The artillery, 172mm caliber, was dangerous; it had a sinister fragmentation effect. Even the 120mm caliber mortars and the "Ratsch-Bum[m]" – I don't know the caliber – they were effective in direct fire. I lost many horses that way.[14]

A. von Garn (252 ID): Stalin Organ: First appeared for us at the end of November 1941. No formidable effect as such, except on morale. You never knew whether the first rocket which detonated would be the furthest or shortest detonation from the rocket launcher, or if you lay in the middle of the salvo. The fragmentation effect was still negligible in 1944. The T-34 tank, or before that the KV-1 and 2, were considerably more disagreeable.[15]

A. Gassmann (106 ID): It's true to say that, at the beginning of the battles in our sector, almost every other Russian was armed with a mortar – while we inexcusably had to ration ammunition, especially artillery ammunition; even though there were opportunities to lay some severe blows on the Russians, for the reasons mentioned, we had to pass them up. Yet from dawn to dusk we were subjected to artillery fire, but mainly mortar fire. At night trees had to be felled … to provide cover for our makeshift bunkers.[16]

R. Grimm (58 ID): The Russians' weapons were far superior to ours. The T-34 disabled our panzers with just a few shots … The only weapon which the T-34 feared was our 88mm Flak gun. But this [gun] was so heavy that it could not be used on anything other than solid roads … The Stalin Organ had more of an effect on morale. Its accuracy was mediocre. The machine guns were outstanding; they seemed always to work, while ours constantly jammed in the cold. Even the Russian trucks always seemed to work [in sub-freezing temperatures]. We had to start up [our vehicles] every two hours at night and let them warm up, and even then they often didn't spring into life the next morning … The [Russian] mortars, which were quite mobile, were very unpleasant; they could already be firing from another position by the time our artillery let off their first defensive fire.[17]

A. Gutenkunst (35 ID): The Stalin Organ in November [1941] and the T-34 in December/January [1941/42] were a great danger for us, above all because we had no weapon which could stand against them. For the T-34 only the 88mm Flak, which, however, the infantry divisions as good as never had.[18]

K. Hempel (258 ID): We feared the first "Stalin Organs" (launchers) which came into use because of their effect. Later, however (December 1941), the Siberian troops with ski equipment and machine pistols were overwhelmingly and rapidly superior to us. Their winter equipment (coats, felt boots, gloves, fur hats) and their frost impervious weapons stood the test of sub-zero temperatures as low as 40 degrees [Centigrade].[19]

W. Kunz (87 ID): The Stalin Organ was horrible [*grausam*]. Not least because the [German] soldiers had always been told – we had the best weapons.[20]

K.H. Mayer (30 ID): At that time [1941] we had not yet come into contact with the Russian T-34 tank, and I had not yet (as I was later) been confronted with the Stalin Organ in my sector of the front. The Russian divisional cannon – caliber 76.2 mm, the so-called "Ratsch-Bumm" – was dangerous. We soldiers called it this because – in contrast to 105mm, 125mm, and 150mm artillery – there wasn't a single moment between firing and impact, which is why you could hardly take cover.[21]

A. Meyer (106 ID): Among the weaponry of the [Russian] troops was, in addition to the machine-gun, also the small mortar. The rumor spread among the Russians that every other German soldier had received the Iron Cross, but that every other Russian had a small mortar … The effect of the Stalin Organ was contradictory. It had more of an effect on morale than an explosive effect, because the sheer number of rockets in the attacks was demoralizing. For example, the rockets during an attack at the Donetz River caused hardly any damage to the igloos constructed by our soldiers.[22]

R. Moebius (292 ID): The Stalin Organ had more of an impact on morale. At first simply with fear … The actual effect itself was not so great in my opinion – but when up to 36 rockets landed in your immediate area, then of course you were stressed. Advantage: After getting used to it, you could roughly estimate the impact area when the rockets were fired and take cover appropriately. The *Panzerschreck* [tank fright] was rather more disagreeable and, at first, struck terror in entire units … The Russian machine gun was superior up to a point: It wasn't at all as precise as our MG, but as a result it was simpler, because it wasn't so sensitive to getting dirty. Our MGs immediately jammed if the belt was pulled through the sand.[23]

H. Moennich (12 Flak Rgt.): Stalin Organ had a terrific effect, the effect on morale in particular was very great. It wasn't just the power [*Gewalt*] of the weapon which was impressive, but also its sounds: when Stalin Organs fired, "hell's gates opened." [Moennich] has, however, no recollection of the so-called "Ratsch-Bumm." M. did come into contact with Soviet T-34 and did take part in battles against these tanks with the Flak guns in his unit. However, he no longer has a more detailed memory of these battles. M. can merely recall that the T-34s were viewed as "strange [*unheimlich*] because they were so primitive."[24]

G. Mueller-Wolfram (71 Flak Abtl.): The Red Army soldiers' weaponry was poor, they had only simple (machine) guns, but in winter at least, these had the advantage over the German weapons of simpler and thus easier operation. [M.-W.'s] unit was only confronted with the T-34 or Stalin Organ for the first time from summer 1942 … [M.-W.] now also tells of the use [from 1943] of Flak against Soviet aircraft, primarily against the Il-2, which were used as ground attack aircraft, but which were, for the German Flak, "nearly impossible to bring down."[25] … [M.-W.] now also compares the successes of the Flak against aircraft and tanks in operations in France (where he was previously deployed) with that on the eastern front in general. In France more tanks were destroyed than aircraft, in the east, by contrast, more aircraft, because the 20mm gun didn't stand a chance, especially against the T-34.[26]

H.W. Niermann (6 PD): Only experienced Stalin Organ fire 2-3 times. Rockets [were] loud but fragmentation effect [was] not great. You were protected [from Stalin Organ fire] inside a building. T-34s sometimes fired individually into houses in which our soldiers had withdrawn to seek shelter from the cold [in winter 1941/42]. Serious losses as a result. [Russians had] great success through shelling from mortars.[27]

E.M. Rhein (6 ID): T-34: ideal for Russian conditions. Concentration of Soviet artillery. Stalin Organ: Covered large area; not very accurate. If troops adequately sheltered, they had little to fear from the weapon.[28]

W. Schaefer-Kehnert (11 PD): We came under fire from "Stalin Organs" for the first time outside Moscow. Their impact was equivalent to that of our "*Nebelwerfer*." … I have written to you before that, in the night of 5/6 December 1941, we fired on the Kremlin with one of our 105mm cannon (which had a range of 20km). The response to that was a sudden barrage the next morning from Stalin Organs. These were a feared weapon due to their great firepower. After that they accompanied us throughout the entire war in Russia.[29]

H. Schillke (8 PD): With regard to the dangerousness of the weapons, I must say that they were all dangerous and represented a great threat. I repeatedly lay within the dispersion zone [*Streubereich*] of the Stalin Organ. This had a broad shrapnel dispersion zone of about 50 meters in diameter. Roughly 50 small rockets, which were similar to our mortars, would land in this dispersion area, and cost many wounded and also fatalities. Once, in my case, for example, at my back, my canteen, cooking utensils, tarpaulin, and even my tunic were riddled with holes from shrapnel, just like with artillery ... The T-34, which was deployed by the Russian throughout the war in huge numbers in increasingly improved versions, was a weapon truly feared by us, because it had enormous fire power, good cross-country mobility, and could even traverse swampy terrain.[30]

H. Stockhoff (6 ID): The greatest danger came from the Stalin Organ and the T-34 tanks, above all due to their effect on morale, even with the tanks. During the advance, contact with the Stalin Organ and [T-34] was minimal. There was more during the defensive battles.[31]

F. Strienitz (7 MG Btl.): The impact on morale through the commitment by the enemy of new weapons like the Stalin Organ, T-34, was, at the time of our deployment (first quarter of 1942), not significant. It was different in other front sectors nearby. Hand grenades, the bayonet, and primarily the sniper dominated in our sector.[32]

H. S. (6 ID): ... the "Stalin Organ" was a dangerous weapon. As a motorcycle messenger, I found myself in the thick of it several times, along with *Feldwebel* Hanheide. Were we lucky that nothing happened? I think that the merciful God held his protecting hand over us, or else that a holy guardian angel was with us in dicey situations and guided us ... The armor-piercing shells [*Panzergranaten*] from our 37mm Pak did not penetrate [the T-34 tank]. We received new ammunition – this shell was loaded at the front of the barrel and fired with a powerful cartridge. We destroyed many a tank in Gridino with that back then ... The "Ratsch-Bumm" was also a dangerous weapon. The discharge of the gun could only be heard after the impact of the shell. Hence the name "Ratsch-Bumm." At the end of the winter [1941/42], we received the 75mm Pak. We could handle any tank with that gun.[33]

O. Trotsch (5 PD): The greatest danger in terms of armor plating and gun was the T-34. We had nothing to counter it. The Stalin Organ had more of an effect on morale than a destructive effect. You got used to it. The Russian drum machine pistol was also better.[34]

K.-G. Vierkorn (23 ID): [I experienced the Stalin Organ] now and then, but rather more rarely! Very effective psychologically due to the huge noise generation, less so materially, since often imprecise target acquisition. The *Landser*, I recall, once said: "Much ado about nothing" [*viel Laerm um nichts*] (what had been a famous title for a very popular musical in Germany at this time).[35]

W. Vollmer (106 ID): On two occasions I lay in the middle of Stalin Organ fire. Impact on morale. The T-34s were a surprise and our artillery destroyed a great many. The Russian mortars were a powerful weapon.[36]

W. Werner (252 ID): Here I should mention the T-34 tank in particular. The "Stalin Organ" had a huge impact on morale. The shells made a racket in the air as if several shelves of shoeboxes had suddenly fallen over. On the ground they had rather more of an area effect [*Flaechenwirkung*] than a pentrating one [*durchschlagende*].[37]

H. Wexel (31 ID): As a member of an anti-tank unit, I ascribe decisive importance to the role of the T-34 in the eventual Russian victory. The Stalin Organ was not without danger – I have often experienced its effect myself – but it was, compared to the effect of the Russian artillery, not terribly impressive.[38]

E. Willich (112 ID): Snipers, Stalin Organ.[39]

ENDNOTES

1   J. Foer, *"Remember This,"* in: *National Geographic*, 44, 53.
2   Unless otherwise indicated in the endnotes, all entries are direct translations of responses received by the author from German eastern front veterans. The great majority of the responses are from German veterans who served with Army Group Center in 1941/42.
3   In an early post-war study, the former chief of staff of Army Group Center, General Hans von Greiffenberg, stated that the "value" of this multi-barrel rocket launcher was "very confined to [its] morale effect." See, FMS T-28, H. v. Greiffenberg, *Battle of Moscow (1941-1942)*, 11. As the veterans' responses reveal, however, their perspectives on the weapon varied significantly.
4   Ltr, 24 Nov 04.
5   Ltr, 28 Feb 06.
6   Ltr, 9 Nov 08.
7   Ltr, 11 Apr 07.
8   Ltr, 30 Jul 05.
9   Ltr, 16 Feb 03.
10   Ltr, 14 Apr 04.
11   Ltr, 4 May 04.
12   Ltr, 14 Jan 06.
13   Ltr, 9 Nov 02.
14   Ltr, 8 Mar 05. "Ratsch-Bumm" was *Landser* slang for the excellent Soviet 76.2mm field piece; it fired a high-velocity, flat trajectory shell, which "was so fast (1000 m/s) that the German soldier heard the impact before the discharge of the gun." A. von Kageneck, *La guerre à l'Est*, 60. According to Dutch Waffen-SS volunteer, Hendrik C. Verton, this Soviet weapon "put the fear of God into us." H. C. Verton, *In the Fire of the Eastern Front*, 101. See also, entries for K. H. Mayer and "H. S." in this appendix.
15   Ltr, 17 Oct 02.
16   Ltr, 7 Apr 06. (Note: Gassmann is describing his experiences from late July to late September 1941 along a stationary division front – *Stellungskrieg*.)
17   E-Mail, 26 Jan 05 and 6 Feb 05. Grimm's division belonged to Army Group North.
18   Ltr, 28 Jul 04.
19   Ltr, n.d.
20   Ltr, 3 Nov 04.
21   Ltr, 29 Jul 04.
22   Ltr, n.d.
23   Ltr, n.d.
24   *"Unheimlich"* might also be translated as "sinister." E-Mail with atch, P. Steinkamp to C. Luther, 8 Feb 05. (Note: This E-Mail summarizes the interview with Herrn Moennich conducted on this author's behalf by Peter Steinkamp.)
25   G. Mueller-Wolfram served in a Flak unit equipped with 20mm Flak guns.
26   Telephone Intvw, P. Steinkamp with G. Mueller-Wolfram, 9 Nov 04. (Note: Interview conducted on this author's behalf by Peter Steinkamp.)
27   Ltr, 3 Dec 02.
28   Intvw, Dr C. Luther with E.-M. Rhein, 8/9 Dec 06.
29   Ltr, 10 Dec 03.
30   Ltr, 15 Mar 05. Herr Schillke fought with Army Group North.
31   Ltr, 4 Apr 05.
32   Ltr, 26 Feb 07.
33   Ltr, n.d.
34   Ltr, 12 Jan 09.
35   Ltr, Jan 04.
36   Ltr, n.d.
37   Ltr, 28 Nov 02.
38   Ltr, 8 Feb 06.
39   Ltr, 17 Jan 06.

Select Bibliography

Archival Materials

1. Air Force Historical Research Agency (AFHRA) (Maxwell AFB):

A. Karlsruhe Document Collection (KDC):[1]
"Angriff auf Brest-Litovsk am 28.6.1941." Aus Lagebericht Nr. 660 vom 30.6.41 des Ob.d.L. Fuehrungsstab Ic."
"Berichte aus Russland Sommer 1941." (Hauptmann Herbert Pabst. Staffelkapitaen und Gruppenkommandeur in einer Sturzkampfgruppe) (KDC: G/VI/3d).
"Bombenwuerfe auf eigene Truppen." (Aus einem Bericht des Kommandierenden Generals des VIII. Fliegerkorps von 16.2.42 an die Heeresgruppe Mitte).
"Die deutschen Flugzeugverluste im ersten Monat (22.6.41 – 17.7.41) des Krieges gegen Russland." Nach einer Zusammenstellung der 6. Abteilung des Generalstabes der deutschen Luftwaffe. (KDC: G/VI/3a).
"Der Luftkrieg im Osten gegen Russland 1941." Aus einer Studie der 8. Abteilung. 1943/1944. (KDC: G/VI/3a).
"Die Unterstuetzung des Heeres im Osten 1941 durch die deutsche Luftwaffe." Aus einer Studie der 8. Abt./Chef Genst. d. Lw. (KDC: G/VI/3d).
"Das II. Fliegerkorps im Einsatz gegen Russland vom 22.6.41 – 15.11.41." (KDC: G/VI/3b).
"Einsatz gegen Moskau im Jahre 1941." Zusammengestellt von Gen.a.D. Hermann Plocher.
"Erste Kaempfe vom 22.6. bis ca. 3.7.41." (Lothar v. Heinemann, Oberst i.G.a.D.).
"Gefechtsquartiere des VIII. Fliegerkorps im Russland-Feldzug 1941." Aufgestellt von Hans Wilhelm Deichmann.
"Generalkommando VIII. Fliegerkorps. Operationsabschnitt: Erste Kaempfe vom 22.6. bis ca. 3.7.1941 (Doppelschlacht von Bialystok und Minsk)." (Lothar v. Heinemann, Oberst i.G.a.D.) (KDC: G/VI/3a).
"Hitlers Absicht, mit der deutschen Luftwaffe die russischen Staedte Moskau und Leningrad zu vernichten," (Aus der Lagebesprechung am 8.7.41, 12.30 Uhr bei Hitler. Auszug aus dem Tagebuch Halder. . .) (Gen. a.D. Plocher Sammlung).
"Ueberblick ueber den deutschen Luftkrieg gegen Russland." (KDC).

B. USAF Historical Studies:
Deichmann, Paul. *German Air Force Operations in Support of the Army* (No. 163, 1962).
Plocher, Hermann. *The German Air Force Versus Russia, 1941* (No. 153, 1965).
Schwabedissen, Walter. *The Russian Air Force in the Eyes of German Commanders* (No. 175, 1960).
Suchenwirth, Richard. *Command and Leadership in the German Air Force* (No. 174, 1969).
—. *Historical Turning Points in the German Air Force War Effort* (No. 189).
Uebe, Klaus. *Russian Reactions to German Airpower in World War II* (No. 176, 1964).

2. Bibliothek fuer Zeitgeschichte (BfZ) (Stuttgart):
Field post letters (*Feldpostbriefe*) of German soldiers assigned to Army Group Center in summer/fall 1941, including:
Gefr. Heinz B. (05 854) (23 ID)
Sold. S.K. (16 120 C) (78 ID)
Wm. Josef L. (22 633 C) (129 ID)
Lt. Joachim H. (18 967) (131 ID)
Hptm. Herbert S. (00 401) (292 ID)

Slg. Sterz (04 650) (296 ID)
Uffz. Karl R. (35 672) (5 PD)
Oblt. Richard D. (35 232) (7 PD)

3. Bundesarchiv-Militaerarchiv (BA-MA) (Freiburg):

MSg 1/1147 & 1/1148: Tagebuch Gen. Lemelsen ("Russlandfeldzug" Band I: 6. Jun – 8. Okt 41 & Band II: 10. Okt 41 – 24. Apr 42)

N 19/9: Nachlass Maximilian *Freiherr* von Weichs (Ostfeldzug 1941/42)

N 664/2/3: Tagebuch Karl-Wilhelm Thilo (Op.Abt. des Heeres)

N 813: Tagebuch Georg Heino *Freiherr* von Muenchhausen 1941 (Op.Abt. des Heeres)

RH 19 II/120: KTB Hr.Gr.Mitte (Okt 41)

RH 19 II/123: Anlagen zum KTB H.Gr.Mitte

RH 19 II/128: Anlagen zum KTB H.Gr.Mitte

RH 20-4/188: "Die Kaempfe der 4. Armee."

RH 20-4/192: "Gefechtsbericht ueber die Wegnahme von Brest Litowsk."

RH 20-4/337: "Kaempfe der 4. Armee im ersten Kriegsjahr gegen den Sowjet Union" (22.6.41-22.6.42)

RH 20-4/1199: KTB AOK 4 (22.6.-1.7.41)[2]

RH 20-9/16: KTB AOK 9 (25.8.-17.9.41)

RH 21-2/244: KTB Pz.AOK 2 (Dez 41)

RH 21-2/927: KTB Pz.AOK 2 (22.6.41- 1.7.41)

RH 21-2/928: KTB Pz.AOK 2 / Pz.Gr. 2 (22.7.-20.8.41)

RH 21-3/788: KTB Pz.Gr. 3 (22.6.-1.7.41)

RH 21-3/43,732: Anlagen zum KTB Pz.AOK 3 (22.6.-1.7.41 & Gefechtsberichte Russland 41/42)

RH 26-6/8: KTB 6. ID (22.6.-1.7.41) (29.7-27.8.41)

RH 26-6/16: Anlagenband 1 zum KTB Nr. 5 der 6. Inf.-Div., Ia.

RH 26-29/6: KTB 29. ID (mot.) (22.6.-1.7.41)

RH 26-29/15: Anlagen zum KTB 29. ID (mot.) (22.6.-1.7.41)

RH 26-45/20: KTB 45. ID (22.6.-1.7.41)

RH 26-78/26: KTB 78. ID (22.6.-1.7.41)

RH 26-129/3: KTB 129. ID (22.6.-1.7.41)

RH 26-137/4: KTB 137. ID (22.6.-1.7.41)

RH 26-137/5: Anlagen zum KTB 137. ID (22.6.-1.7.41)

RH 26-256/12: KTB 256. ID (22.6.-1.7.41)

RH 26-292/7: KTB 292. ID (22.6.-1.7.41)

RH 27-3/14: KTB 3. PD (22.6.-1.7.41)

RH 27-7/46: KTB 7. PD (22.6.-1.7.41)

RH 27-18/20: KTB 18. PD (22.6.-1.7.41)

RH 27-18/34: Anlagen zum KTB 18. PD (22.6.-1.7.41)

RH 27-18/69: Gefechts- u. Kampfstaerken (10.41-3.42); *Gefechtskalendar* (18. PD) (20.10-13.12.41)

RL 2/1185: "Verluste lt. Meldungen des GQM, 6. Abt."

RL 8/49: "VIII. Fl.K., Einsatz Russland – Mittelabschnitt," (Sep 41–Jan 42) (H.W. Deichmann)

RL 200/17: Tagebuch General von Waldau (Jun – Dez 41)

RW 2/ v. 145,149,153: Wehrmacht-Untersuchungsstelle: "Kriegsverbrechen der russischen Wehrmacht 1941/42"

4. Feldpost-Archiv Berlin:

Becker, Klaus (Flak Einheit / Hr.Gr.Mitte)
Neuser, Uffz Walter (AR 59/23. ID)
Sartorio, H. (Pz.Pion.Btl. 98/18. PD)

5. The Hoover Library (Stanford University):

Die Sowjet-Union. Gegebenheiten und Moeglichkeiten des Ostraumes. Tornisterschrift des OKW (Berlin, 1943, Heft 72).

Diewerge, Wolfgang (Hg.). *Deutsche Soldaten sehen die Sowjet-Union. Feldpostbriefe aus dem Osten* (Berlin, 1941).

Wittek, Erhard (Hg.). *Die Soldatische Tat. Berichte von Mitkaempfern des Heeres. Der Kampf im Osten 1941/42* (Berlin, 1943).

6. Staats- u. Personenstandsarchiv Detmold:

D 107/56 Nr. 4: "Aus Briefen des Adjutanten Inf.Rgt. 18, Oberleutnant Juerg von Kalckreuth." (6 ID).

7. Institut fuer Zeitgeschichte (IfZ) (Munich / Berlin):

MS 506: "Feldzug gegen Russland im Rahmen der 2. Panzer-Armee, 20.6.-4.12.1941." Feldpostbriefe und Tagebuchnotizen Uffz. Robert Rupp.

8. National Archives & Records Administration (NARA):

Record Group 242-GAP-286B-4: "German troops in Russia, 1941" (photographs).

9. U.S. Army Military History Institute, Carlisle Barracks:

Foreign Military Studies (FMS) prepared by former *Wehrmacht* officers in late 1940s and 1950s for the U.S. Army in Europe:

D-034: "Diseases of Men and Horses Experienced by the Troops in Russia." Dr Erich Rendulic. 1947.

D-035: "The effect of extreme cold on weapons, wheeled vehicles and track vehicles." Dr Erich Rendulic. 1947.

D-098: "Horse Diseases during the Eastern Campaign (1941-45)." Dr Maximilian Betzler. 1947.

D-187: "The Capture of Smolensk by the 71st Motorized Infantry Regiment on 15 July 1941." Genlt. Wilh. Thomas. 1947.

D-221: "An Artillery Regiment on the Road to Moscow (22 June to December 1941)." Genmaj. Gerhard Grassmann. 1947.

D-247: "German Preparations for the Attack against Russia (The German Build-up East of Warsaw)." Genlt. Curt Cuno. 1947.

P-039: "March and Traffic Control of Panzer Divisions with Special Attention to Conditions in the Soviet Union and in Africa." Genmaj. Burkhart Mueller-Hillebrand, et al. 1949.

P-052: "Combat in Russian Forests and Swamps." Gen. Hans von Greiffenberg. 1951.

P-190: "Verbrauchs- u. Verschleisssaetze waehrend der Operationen der deutschen Heeresgruppe Mitte vom 22.6.41 – 31.12.41." Gen. Rudolf Hofmann & Genmaj. Alfred Toppe. 1953.

P-201: "Personal Diary Notes of the G-4 of the German Ninth Army, 1 Aug 1941 to 31 Jan 1942." Genmaj. Josef Windisch. 1953.

T-6: "Eastern Campaign, 1941-42. (Strategic Survey)." Genlt. Adolf Heusinger. 1947.

T-28: "Battle of Moscow (1941-1942)." Gen. Hans von Greiffenberg, et al., n.d.

T-34: "Terrain Factors in the Russian Campaign." Gen. Karl Allmendinger, et al. 1950.

Primary Sources (Books, Unpublished Memoirs/Manuscripts, Misc.)

Adamczyk, Werner. *Feuer! An Artilleryman's Life on the Eastern Front* (Wilmington, 1992).

Alvermann, H.-G., "*Erlebnisbericht*," in: "*Jahresbrief 2007*," *Traditions-Verband der 110. Infanterie-Division* (courtesy of Horst Paul).

Andres, Kurt Werner. "*Panzersoldaten im Russlandfeldzug 1941 bis 1945. Tagebuchaufzeichnungen und Erlebnisberichte*" (unpublished manuscript; courtesy of author).

Assmann, Kurt. *Deutsche Schicksalsjahre. Historische Bilder aus dem zweiten Weltkrieg und seiner Vorgeschichte* (Wiesbaden, 1951).

Baehr, Walter, and Hans W. Baehr (Hg.). *Kriegsbriefe Gefallener Studenten, 1939-1945* (Tuebingen & Stuttgart, 1952).

Balke, Ulf. *Kampfgeschwader 100 "Wiking"* (Stuttgart, 1981).

Barkhoff, Guenther. *Ostfront 1941-1945. Ein Soldatenleben* (unpublished memoir; courtesy of author).

Baumann, Hans. *Die 35. Infanterie-Division im 2. Weltkrieg 1939-1945* (Karlsruhe, 1964).

Baur, Hans. *Mit Maechtigen zwischen Himmel und Erde* (Oldendorf, 1971).

Beinhauer, Oblt. Eugen (Hg.). *Artillerie im Osten* (Berlin, 1943).

Belke, Friedrich-August. *Infanterist* (unpublished memoir; courtesy of author).

Below, Nicolaus von. *At Hitler's Side. The Memoirs of Hitler's Luftwaffe Adjutant 1937-1945* (London, 2001).

Bidermann, Gottlob Herbert. *In Deadly Combat. A German Soldier's Memoir of the Eastern Front.* Translated and edited by Derek S. Zumbro (Lawrence, 2000).

Boeselager, Philipp *Freiherr* von. *Valkyrie. The Story of the Plot to Kill Hitler, by its Last Member* (New York, 2009).

Bollmann, Albert, and Hermann Floerke. *Das Infanterie-Regiment 12 (3. Folge von 1933-1945). Sein Kriegsschicksal im Verbande der 31. (Loewen-) Division* (Goettingen, 1975).

Bopp, Gerhard. *Kriegstagebuch. Aufzeichnungen waehrend des II. Weltkrieges, 1940-1943* (Hamburg, 2005).

Boucsein, Heinrich. *Halten oder Sterben. Die hessisch-thueringische 129. Infanterie-Division im Russlandfeldzug und Ostpreussen 1941-1945* (Potsdam, 1999).

Bub, Emil. "*Ein verlorenes Jahrzehnt. Tagebuchaufzeichnungen Emil Bub*" (unpublished diary; courtesy of R. Gehrmann).

Buchbender, Ortwin, and Reinhold Sterz (Hg.). *Das andere Gesicht des Krieges. Deutsche Feldpostbriefe 1939-1945* (Munich, 1982).

Buddenbohm, Wilfried. *Das Leben des Soldaten Wilhelm Buddenbohm und der Weg des Osnabruecker Infanterieregimentes I.R. 37 von 1939 bis 1943* (self-published, ca. 2004).

Buecheler Heinrich. *Hoepner. Ein deutsches Soldatenschicksal des Zwanzigsten Jahrhunderts* (Herford, 1980).

Bunke, Dr Erich. *Der Osten blieb unser Schicksal 1939-1944. Panzerjaeger im 2. Weltkrieg* (self-published, 1991; courtesy of author).

Burdick, Charles, and Hans-Adolf Jacobsen (eds.). *The Halder Diary 1939-1942* (Novato, 1988).

Chertok, Boris. *Rockets and People*, Vol. I (Washington D.C., 2005).

"*Conversations with a Stuka Pilot.*" Conference Featuring Paul-Werner Hozzel, Brig.-General (Ret.), German Air Force, at the National War College, Nov 78. Battelle Columbus Laboratories, Columbus, Ohio.

Deck, Josef. *Der Weg der 1000 Toten. Ein Leben in Krieg und Frieden* (Karlsruhe, 1978).

"*Der Marsch- und Einsatzweg der III./AR 6 vom 23.3.1941 bis 18.1.1942*," compiled in Summer 1942 by Lt. Kleine, III./AR 6 (courtesy of H.-J. Dismer).

"*Der Ostfeldzug der 86. Rhein.-Westf. Inf.-Division, 28.6.41 – 4.11.43, dargestellt aufgrund von Tagebuchnotizen, Karten, Fotos, Briefen und unvergessenen und unvergesslichen Eindruecken und Erlebnissen*" (unpublished manuscript, ca. 1962, author(s) unknown; courtesy of Ernst Meinecke)

Dicke, Dr Werner. *Memoiren* (unpublished memoir; courtesy of author).

Dinglreiter, Obstlt. a.D. Joseph. *Die Vierziger. Chronik des Regiments*. Kameradschaft Regiment 40 (Hg.) (Augsburg, n.d.).

Dismer, Hans-Joachim. *Artillerie-Offizier im II. Weltkrieg. Vom Beobachter bis zur Kriegsakademie* (self-published, 1992).

Dollinger, Hans (Hg.). *Kain, wo ist dein Bruder? Was der Mensch im Zweiten Weltkrieg erleiden musste – dokumentiert in Tagebuechern und Briefen* (Munich, 1983).

Domarus, Max. *Hitler. Reden und Proklamationen 1932-1945*, Bd. II: *Untergang (1939-1945)* (Wuerzburg, 1963).

Drabkin, Artem, and Oleg Sheremet. *T-34 in Action. Soviet Tank Troops in WWII* (Mechanicsburg, 2006).

Duesel, Dr Hans H. (Hg.). *Gefallen! … und umsonst – Erlebnisberichte deutscher Soldaten im Russlandkrieg 1941-1945* (self-published; Bad Aibling, 1993).

Flannery, Harry W. *Assignment to Berlin* (New York, 1942).

Franze, Herbert. *Kriegskamerad Pferd. Sie dienten treu, litten und starben – wofuer?* (Berlin, 2001).

Freitag, August. *Aufzeichnungen aus Krieg und Gefangenschaft (1941-1949)*. Eingeleitet und annotiert von Karl Sattler (Bochum, 1997).

Freter, Hermann. *Fla nach Vorn*, Bd. I (Eigenverlag der Fla-Kameradschaft, 1971).

Frisch, Franz A.P., and Wilbur D. Jones, Jr. *Condemned to Live. A Panzer Artilleryman's Five-Front War* (Shippensburg, 2000).

Frontschau Nr. 2, "*Russischer Stellungsbau*," in: *Die Frontschau* (distributed by International Historic Films).

Frontschau Nr. 3, "*Vormarsch*," in: *Die Frontschau* (distributed by International Historic Films).

Frontschau Nr. 5/6, in: *Die Frontschau* (distributed by International Historic Films).

Garden, David, and Kenneth Andrew (eds.). *The War Diaries of a Panzer Soldier. Erich Hager with the 17th Panzer Division on the Russian Front 1941-1945* (Atglen, 2010).

Gareis, Martin. *Kampf und Ende der Fraenkisch – Sudetendeutschen 98. Infanterie-Division* (Doerfler Zeitgeschichte, n.d.; first published, 1956).

Gerbet, Klaus (ed.). *Generalfeldmarschall Fedor von Bock. The War Diary 1939-1945* (Atglen, 1996).

German Infantry Weapons. Special Series, No 14 MIS 461, Military Intelligence Service, U.S. War Dept., 25 May 43.

Gersdorff, Rudolf-Christoph Frhr. v. *Soldat im Untergang* (Frankfurt, 1977).

Geschichte der 3. Panzer-Division Berlin-Brandenburg 1935-1945. Traditionsverband der Division (Hg.) (Berlin, 1967).

Geschichte einer Transportflieger-Gruppe im II. Weltkrieg. Kameradschaft ehemaliger Transportflieger (Hg.) (1989).

Geyer, Hermann. *Das IX. Armeekorps im Ostfeldzug 1941* (Neckargemuend, 1969).

Gorbachevsky, Boris. *Through the Maelstrom. A Red Army Soldier's War on the Eastern Front, 1942-1945*. Translated and edited by Stuart Britton. (Lawrence, 2008).

Gorlitz, Walter (ed.). *The Memoirs of Field-Marshal Wilhelm Keitel. Chief of the German High Command 1938-1945* (New York, 1966).

Grossmann, Horst. *Die Geschichte der rheinisch-westfaelischen 6. Infanterie-Division 1939-1945* (Doerfler Zeitgeschichte, n.d.; first published, 1958).

—. *Rshew. Eckpfeiler der Ostfront* (Bad Nauheim, 1962).

Gschoepf, Dr Rudolf. *Mein Weg mit der 45. Inf.-Div.* (Nuernberg, 2002; first published, 1955).

Guderian, Heinz. *Erinnerungen eines Soldaten* (Heidelberg, 1951).

—. *Panzer Leader* (New York, 1952).

—. *Achtung-Panzer! The Development of Armoured Forces, Their Tactics and Operational Potential.* (C. Duffy, trans.) (London, 1992).

Guenther, Helmut. *Hot Motors, Cold Feet. A Memoir of Service with the Motorcycle Battalion of SS-Division "Reich" 1940-1941* (Winnipeg, 2004).

Gundelach, Karl. *Kampfgeschwader "General Wever" 4* (Stuttgart, 1978).

Gutenkunst, Alfred. *Geschichte der 3. Kompanie des Infanterie-Regiments 109 im Krieg 1939-1945* (self-published, 1985, 1991).

Haape, Heinrich. *Nachlass. Tagebuch, Feldpostbriefe*, and other personal items (courtesy of his son, Johannes Haape).

Haape, Heinrich (in association with Dennis Henshaw). *Moscow Tram Stop. A Doctor's Experiences with the German Spearhead in Russia* (London, 1957).

Haering, Bernard. *Embattled Witness. Memories of a Time of War* (New York, 1976).

Hahn, Lt. Jochen. *"Feldzug gegen Russland"* (collection of field post letters; courtesy of R. Mobius).

Halder, Franz. *Hitler as War Lord* (London, 1950).

Hammer, Ingrid, and Susanne zur Nieden (Hg.). *Sehr selten habe ich geweint. Briefe und Tagebuecher aus dem Zweiten Weltkrieg von Menschen aus Berlin* (Zurich, 1992).

Handbook on German Military Forces (1990, Baton Rouge). Originally published by U.S. War Department as TM-E 30-451 (March 1945).

Heinemann, Werner. *Pflicht und Schuldigkeit. Betrachtungen eines Frontoffiziers im Zweiten Weltkrieg* (Berlin, 2010).

—. *Feldpostbriefe* (collection of unpublished field post letters; courtesy of his daughter, Birgit Heinemann).

Heusinger, Adolf. *Befehl im Widerstreit. Schicksalsstunden der deutschen Armee 1923-1945* (Tuebingen, 1950).

Hinze, Rolf. *Die 19. Panzer-Division. Bewaffnung, Einsaetze, Maenner. Einsatz 1941-1945 in Russland* (Doerfler Zeitgeschichte, n.d.).

— *19. Infanterie- und Panzer-Division. Divisionsgeschichte aus der Sicht eines Artilleristen.* (6. Auflage, Dusseldorf, 1997).

—. *Hitze, Frost und Pulverdampf. Der Schicksalsweg der 20. Panzer-Division* (6. Auflage, 1996).

History of the Great Patriotic War of the Soviet Union 1941-1945. Vol. II: *Repulse by the Soviet People of the Treacherous Attack by Fascist Germany on the USSR, Creating Conditions for a Radical Turn in the War* (*June 1941 – November 1942*) (Moscow, 1961) (Note: Unedited translation distributed by the Office of the Chief of Military History, United States Army, Washington D.C.).

Hossbach, Friedrich. *Infanterie im Ostfeldzug 1941/42* (Osterode, 1951).

Hoth, Hermann. *Panzer-Operationen. Die Panzergruppe 3 und der operative Gedanke der deutschen Fuehrung Sommer 1941* (Heidelberg, 1956).

Hubatsch, Walther. *Hitlers Weisungen fuer die Kriegsfuehrung 1939-1945* (Frankfurt, 1962).

Huerter, Johannes. *Ein deutscher General an der Ostfront. Die Briefe und Tagebuecher des Gotthard Heinrici 1941/42* (Erfurt, 2001).

Humburg, Martin. *Das Gesicht des Krieges. Feldpostbriefe von Wehrmachtssoldaten aus der Sowjetunion 1941-1944* (Wiesbaden, 1998).

Irving, David (ed.). *Adolf Hitler: The Medical Diaries. The Private Diaries of Dr Theo Morell* (London, 1983).

Jacobsen, Hans-Adolf (Hg.). *1939-1945. Der Zweite Weltkrieg in Chronik und Dokumenten* (Darmstadt, 1959).

—, (Hg.). *Generaloberst Halder Kriegstagebuch. Taegliche Aufzeichnungen des Chefs des Generalstabes des Heeres 1939-1942*, Bd. II: *Von der geplanten Landung in England bis zum Beginn des Ostfeldzuges (1.7.1940 – 21.6.1941)* (Stuttgart, 1963).

—, (Hg.). *Generaloberst Halder Kriegstagebuch. Taegliche Aufzeichnungen des Chefs des Generalstabes des Heeres 1939-1942*, Bd. III: *Der Russlandfeldzug bis zum Marsch auf Stalingrad (22.6.1941 – 24.9.1942)* (Stuttgart, 1964).

Jakubowski, Ofw., *Tagebuch I./I.R. 509 – I./I.R. 507* (courtesy of R. Moebius).

Kageneck, August von, *La guerre à l'Est. Histoire d'un régiment allemand 1941-1944* (1998, 2002).

Keilig, Wolf. *Das Deutsche Heer 1939-1945*, Bd. I & II (Bad Nauheim, from 1956).

Kempowski, Walter. *Das Echolot. Barbarossa '41. Ein kollektives Tagebuch* (Munich, 2002).

Kesselring, Albert. *Soldat Bis Zum Letzten Tag* (Bonn, 1953).

—. *The Memoirs of Field-Marshal Kesselring* (Novato, 1989).

Knappe, Siegfried (with Ted Brusaw). *Soldat. Reflections of a German Soldier, 1936-1949* (New York, 1992).

Knecht, Wolfgang. *Geschichte des Infanterie-Regiments 77 1936-1945* (1964).

Knoblauch, Karl. *Zwischen Metz und Moskau. Als Soldat der 95. Infanteriedivision in Frankreich und als Fernaufklaerer mit der 4. (F)/14 in Russland* (Wuerzburg, 2007).

—. *Kampf und Untergang der 95. Infanteriedivision. Chronik einer Infanteriedivision von 1939-1945 in Frankreich und an der Ostfront* (Wuerzburg, 2008).

Knoke, Heinz. *I flew for the Fuehrer* (1953).

Kotze, Hildegard von (Hg.). *Heeresadjutant bei Hitler 1938-1943. Aufzeichnungen des Major Engel* (Stuttgart, 1974).

Kozhevnikov, M.N. *The Command and Staff of the Soviet Army Air Force in the Great Patriotic War 1941-1945* (Moscow, 1977).

Krehl, Eberhard. *Erinnerungen eines 85 Jahre alten Mannes. Unteroffizier beim Stab Ari.-Kdr. 121 der Panzertruppen* (self-published, 1997; courtesy of author).

Kreuter, Lt. Georg. *Persoenliches Tagebuch* (unpublished diary; courtesy of Klaus Schumann).

Kuhnert, Max. *Will We See Tomorrow? A German Cavalryman at War, 1939-1942* (London, 1993).

Kummer, Oblt. Kurt, *Tagebuch* (unpublished diary; courtesy of C. Nehring).

Lang, Major a.D. Friedrich. *Aufzeichnungen aus der Sturzkampffliegerei*. Christian Heine (Hg.) (2002.)

Lierow, Dr Hans. *Persoenliches Tagebuch* (unpublished diary; courtesy of his son, Dr Med. Konrad Lierow-Mueller).

Luck, Hans von. *Panzer Commander. The Memoirs of Colonel Hans von Luck* (New York, 1989).

Manteuffel, Hasso von. *Die 7. Panzer-Division 1935-1945. Die "Gespenster-Division"* (Friedberg, 1978).

—. *Die 7. Panzer-Division. Bewaffnung, Einsaetze, Maenner* (Doerfler Zeitgeschichte, n.d.).

Martin, Helmut. *Weit war der Weg. An der Rollbahn 1941-1945* (Munich, 2002).

Mehner, Kurt (Hg.). *Die Geheimen Tagesberichte der Deutschen Wehrmachtfuehrung im Zweiten Weltkrieg 1939-1945*, Bd. 3: *1. Maerz 1941 – 31. Oktober 1941* (Osnabrueck, 1992).

Meier-Welcker, Hans. *Aufzeichnungen eines Generalstabsoffiziers 1939-1942* (Freiburg, 1982).

Mellenthin, F.W. von. *German Generals of World War II* (Norman, 1977).

Meyer, August. *Infanterie-Regiment Grenadier-Regiment 241, 1940-1944* (Bonn-Beuel, 1999).

Meyer-Detring, Wilhelm. *Die 137. Infanterie-Division im Mittelabschnitt der Ostfront* (Doerfler Zeitgeschichte, n.d.; first published, Verlag der Kameradschaft 137. I.D., 1962)

Miethe, Marianne. *Memoiren 1921-1945* (unpublished memoir; courtesy of author).

Moebius, Ingo (unter Mitarbeit von Christian Konrad). *Ueber Moskau ins Kurland. Ritterkreuztraeger Georg Bleher erzaehlt* (self-published by I. Moebius; Chemnitz, 2008).

Moeller, Johannes. *Gratwanderung am Rande des Geschehens 1937-1945* (self-published, ca. 1991).

Moltke, Helmuth James von. *Letters to Freya 1939-1945*. Edited and translated by Beate Ruhm von Oppen. (New York, 1990).

Mueller-Hillebrand, Burkhart. *Das Heer 1933-1945*, Bd. II: *Die Blitzfeldzuege 1939-1941. Das Heer im Kriege bis zum Beginn des Feldzuges gegen die Sowjetunion im Juni 1941* (Frankfurt, 1956).

—. *Das Heer 1933-1945*, Bd. III: *Der Zweifrontenkrieg. Das Heer vom Beginn des Feldzuges gegen die Sowjetunion bis zum Kriegsende* (Frankfurt, 1969).

Mueller-Hillebrand, Burkhart, et al. *"German Tank Maintenance in World War II."* CMH Publication 104-7 (1982).

Muehleisen, Horst (Hg.). *Hellmuth Stieff Briefe* (Berlin, 1991).

Mulcahy, Robert. *The Experiences of a World War II German Panzer Commander O.H. 2314 (Rolf Hertenstein)* (Cal State U. Fullerton, Oral History Program, Feb 92).

Nebe, Friedrich. *Erinnerungen* (self-published by Karlfriedrich Nebe, 2006).

Nehring, Walther K. *Die Geschichte der deutschen Panzerwaffe 1916-1945* (Stuttgart, 2000).

Neumann, Joachim. *Die 4. Panzer-Division 1938-1943. Bericht und Betrachtung zu zwei Blitzfeldzuegen und zwei Jahren Krieg in Russland* (self-published, Bonn, 1985).

Nitz, Guenther. *Die 292. Infanterie-Division* (Berlin, 1957).

Oehmichen, Hermann, and Martin Mann. *Der Weg der 87. Infanterie-Division* (self-published by division, 1969).

Orenstein, Harold S. (trans.). *Soviet Documents on the Use of War Experience*, Vol. I: *The Initial Period of the War 1941* (London, 1991).

—, (trans.). *Soviet Documents on the Use of War Experience*, Vol. 3: *Military Operations 1941 and 1942* (London, 1993).

Pabst, Helmut. *The Outermost Frontier* (London, 1958).

Pagel, Horst. *From the Other Side. A Collection of Personal WW II Stories* (unpublished manuscript; courtesy of author).

Peeters, Dieter. *Vermisst in Stalingrad. Als einfacher Soldat ueberlebte ich Kessel und Todeslager 1941-1949* (Berlin, 2005).

Perau, Josef. *Priester im Heere Hitlers. Erinnerungen 1940-1945* (Essen, 1962).

Prueller, Wilhelm. *Diary of a German Soldier* (New York, 1963).

Raus, Erhard. *Panzer Operations. The Eastern Front Memoir of General Raus, 1941-1945*. Edited and translated by Steven H. Newton. (2003).

Reuth, Ralf Georg (Hg.). *Joseph Goebbels. Tagebuecher 1924-1945*, Bd. 4: 1940-1942 (Munich, 1992).

Rhein, Ernst-Martin. *Das Rheinisch-Westfaelische Infanterie-/Grenadier-Regiment 18 1921-1945* (self-published, 1993).

Richardson, Horst Fuchs (ed. & trans.). *Your Loyal and Loving Son. The Letters of Tank Gunner Karl Fuchs, 1937-41* (Washington D.C., 1987).

Risse, S. *"Das IR 101 und der 2. Weltkrieg"* (unpublished report; courtesy of Klaus Schumann).

Rudel, Hans Ulrich. *Stuka Pilot* (Bantam edition, New York, 1979).

Rundbrief No. 50, Traditionsverband Inf.Rgt. 37/184/474 (Osnabrueck, December 1993; courtesy of G. Wegmann).

Sajer, Guy. *The Forgotten Soldier* (Washington D.C., 1971).

Schaeufler, Hans (ed.). *Knight's Cross Panzers. The German 35th Panzer Regiment in WWII* (Mechanicsburg, 2010).

Scheuer, Guenter (Hg.). *Briefe aus Russland. Feldpostbriefe des Gefreiten Alois Scheuer 1941-1942* (St. Ingbert, n.d.).

Scheurig, Bodo. *Henning von Tresckow. Ein Preusse gegen Hitler* (Frankfurt, 1987).

Schlabrendorff, Fabian von. *Offiziere gegen Hitler* (Frankfurt, 1959).

Schramm, Percy E. (Hg.). *Kriegstagebuch des Oberkommandos der Wehrmacht (Wehrmachtfuehrungsstab) 1940-1945*, Bd. I: 1. August 1940 – 31. December 1941, zusammengestellt und erlaeutert von Hans-Adolf Jacobsen (Frankfurt, 1965).

—. *Hitler als militaerischer Fuehrer. Erkenntnisse und Erfahrungen aus dem Kriegstagebuch des Oberkommandos der Wehrmacht* (Frankfurt, 1962).

Schrodek, Gustav W. *Die 11. Panzer-Division. "Gespenster-Division" 1940-1945* (Doerfler Zeitgeschichte, n.d.).

Schroeder, Christa. *Er war mein Chef. Aus dem Nachlass der Sekretaerin von Adolf Hitler* (Munich, 1985).

Schulze, Guenter A. *"General der Panzertruppe a.D. Walther K. Nehring. Der persoenliche Ordonnanzoffizier berichtet von der Vormarschzeit in Russland 1941-1942"* (unpublished manuscript; courtesy of author).

Selder, Emanuel, *Der Krieg der Infanterie. Dargestellt in der Chronik des Infanterie-Regiments 62 (7. Infanterie-Division) 1935-1945. Teil IV: Unternehmen Barbarossa – Der Russlandkrieg und Teil V: Angriff auf Moskau – ab 1.10.1941* (Landshut, 1985).

Shtemenko, S. M. *The Soviet General Staff at War 1941-1945*, Book One (Moscow, 1985).

"*Small Unit Actions during the German Campaign in Russia*," Dept. of Army Pamphlet No. 20-269 (Washington D.C., 1953).

Spaeter, Helmuth. *Die Geschichte des Panzerkorps Grossdeutschland*, Bd. I (Duisburg-Ruhrort, 1958).

Speer, Albert. *Erinnerungen* (Berlin, 1969).

Stahlberg, Alexander. *Bounden Duty. The Memoirs of a German Officer 1932-45* (London, 1990).

Steinhoff, Johannes, and Peter Pechel and Dennis Showalter. *Voices from the Third Reich. An Oral History* (Washington D.C., 1989).

Tauber, Peter (Hg.). *Laeusejagd und Rohrkrepierer. Willi Loewer, an den Fronten des Zweiten Weltkrieges* (Norderstedt, 2004).

Thies, Klaus-Juergen. *Der Zweite Weltkrieg im Kartenbild*, Bd. 5: Teil 1.1: *Der Ostfeldzug Heeresgruppe Mitte 21.6.1941 – 6.12.1941. Ein Lageatlas der Operationsabteilung des Generalstabes des Heeres* (Bissendorf, 2001).

Trevor-Roper, H. R. *Hitler's War Directives 1939-1945* (London, 1964).

True to Type. A selection from Letters and Diaries of German Soldiers and Civilians (London). No reference to an editor or date of publication.

Tsouras, Peter G. (ed.). *Fighting in Hell. The German Ordeal on the Eastern Front* (New York, 1995).

Vassiltchikov, Marie. *Berlin Diaries, 1940-1945* (New York, 1987).

Verton, Hendrik C. *In the Fire of the Eastern Front. The Experiences of a Dutch Waffen-SS Volunteer on the Eastern Front 1941-45* (Great Britain, 2007).

Vetter, Fritz. *Die 78. Infanterie- und Sturm-Division 1938-1945* (Doerfler Zeitgeschichte, n.d.).

Vierkorn, Karl-Gottfried. "*Barbarossa – Feldzug gegen die Sowjet Union 1941. Meine Erinnerungen*," 16-17 (unpublished memoir; courtesy of author).

—. *Feldpostbriefe* (unpublished field post letters; courtesy of author).

Vogt, Martin (Hg.). *Herbst 1941 im "Fuehrerhauptquartier." Berichte Werner Koeppens an seinen Minister Alfred Rosenberg* (Koblenz, 2002).

"*Vorstoss und Kampf um Kalinin der 36. Inf.Div. (mot.)*," bearbeitet durch 36. Inf.Div. (mot.) Abteilung Ic, Nov 41 (courtesy of Juergen Foerster).

Voss, Dr Hellmuth. *Das Pionier-Bataillon 6 im Feldzug gegen Russland 1941-1945* (unpublished manuscript).

Wagner, Elisabeth (Hg.). *Der General-Quartiermeister. Briefe und Tagebuchaufzeichnungen des Generalquartiermeisters des Heeres General der Artillerie Eduard Wagner* (Munich, 1963).

Wagner, Erwin. *Tage wie Jahre. Vom Westwall bis Moskau 1939-1949* (Munich, 1997).

Wagner, Ray (ed.). *The Soviet Air Force in World War II*. (The Official History, originally published by the Ministry of Defense of the USSR.) Translated by Leland Fetzer (Garden City, 1973).

Wardin, Eberhard, "*Winterschlacht*" (unpublished memoir; courtesy of author).

Warlimont, Walter. *Inside Hitler's Headquarters 1939-45* (New York, 1964).

Weidinger, Otto. *Das Reich III 1941-1943. 2 SS Panzer Division Das Reich* (Winnipeg, 2002).

Werth, Alexander. *Russia at War 1941-1945* (New York, 1964).

Wessler, Wilhelm. "*Meine Erlebnisse mit der russischen Bevoelkerung in Rshew*" (unpublished manuscript; courtesy of author).

—. *Tagebuch* (unpublished diary; courtesy of author).

Wijers, Hans (Hg.). *Chronik der Sturmgeschuetzabteilung 210. Tagebuchaufzeichnungen und Erinnerungen von ehem. Angehoerigen* (1997, 2003).

Will, Otto. *Tagebuch eines Ostfront-Kaempfers. Mit der 5. Panzerdivision im Einsatz 1941-1945* (Selent, 2010).

Zhukov, Georgi K., et al. *Battles Hitler Lost and the Soviet Marshalls who Won them* (New York, 1986).

Zirk, Georg. *Red Griffins over Russia. World War II over Russia – as seen from the cockpit of a Heinkel 111 bomber, 1941-1945* (Mesa, 1987).

Secondary Sources (Books)

Aaken, Wolf van. *Hexenkessel Ostfront. Von Smolensk nach Breslau* (Rastatt, 1964).

Axell, Albert. *Russia's Heroes 1941-45* (New York, 2001).

Barker, Lt.-Col. A. J. *Stuka Ju-87* (Englewood Cliffs, 1983).

Barnett, Correlli (ed.). *Hitler's Generals* (New York, 1989).

Bartov, Omer. *Hitler's Army. Soldiers, Nazis, and War in the Third Reich* (New York, 1991).

—. *The Eastern Front, 1941-45, German Troops and the Barbarisation of Warfare* (New York, 1985).

Battistelli, Pier Paolo. *Panzer Divisions: The Eastern Front 1941-43* (Oxford, 2008).

Bauer, Eddy. *Der Panzerkrieg. Die wichtigsten Panzeroperationen des zweiten Weltkrieges in Europa und Afrika*, Bd. I: *Vorstoss und Rueckzug der deutschen Panzerverbaende* (Bonn, 1965).

Beevor, Antony. *The Mystery of Olga Chekhova* (New York, 2004).

Bekker, Cajus. *The Luftwaffe War Diaries* (London, 1966).

Bellamy, Chris. *Absolute War. Soviet Russia in the Second World War* (New York, 2007).

Bergström, Christer, and Andrey Mikhailov. *Black Cross Red Star. Air War over the Eastern Front.* Vol. I: *Operation Barbarossa 1941* (Pacifica, 2000).

Besymenski, Lew. *Die Schlacht um Moskau 1941* (Cologne, 1981)

Blau, George E. *The German Campaign in Russia – Planning and Operations (1940-1942)* (Washington D.C., 1955).

Boatner, Mark M. *Biographical Dictionary of World War II* (Novato, 1996).

Boog, Horst, et al. *Germany and the Second World War*, Vol. IV: *The Attack on the Soviet Union* (Oxford, 1998).

Boog, Horst, et al. *Das Deutsche Reich und der Zweite Weltkrieg*, Bd. 4: *Der Angriff auf die Sowjetunion* (Stuttgart, 1983).

Boot, Max. *War Made New. Technology, Warfare, and the Course of History, 1500 to Today* (New York, 2006).

Braithwaite, Rodric. *Moscow 1941. A City and its People at War* (London, 2006).

Brookes, Andrew. *Air War over Russia* (Great Britain, 2003).

Broszat, Martin, and Hans-Adolf Jacobsen and Helmut Krausnick. *Anatomie des SS-Staates*, Bd. 2 (Freiburg, 1965).

Brown, Captain Eric. *Wings of the Luftwaffe. Flying German Aircraft of the Second World War.* Edited by William Green and Gordon Swanborough. (London, 1977).

Buchner, Alex. *The German Infantry Handbook 1939-1945. Organization, Uniforms, Weapons, Equipment, Operations* (Atglen, 1991).

Burgdorff, Stephan, and Klaus Wiegrefe (Hg.). *Der 2. Weltkrieg. Wendepunkt der deutschen Geschichte* (Munich, 2005).

Byers, Michael. *War Law. Understanding International Law and Armed Conflict* (New York, 2005).

Calvocoressi, Peter, and Guy Wint. *Total War. Causes and Courses of the Second World War* (New York, 1972).

Carell, Paul. *Hitler Moves East 1941-1943* (Boston, 1964).

—. *Unternehmen Barbarossa. Der Marsch nach Russland* (Berlin, 1963).

Chandler, David G. *The Campaigns of Napoleon. The Mind and Method of History's Greatest Soldier* (New York, 1966).

Citino, Robert M. *The German Way of War. From the Thirty Years' War to the Third Reich* (Lawrence, 2005).

Cooper, Matthew. *The German Air Force 1933-1945. An Anatomy of Failure* (London, 1981).

Corum, James S. *Wolfram von Richthofen. Master of the German Air War* (Lawrence, 2008).

Courtois, Stéphane, et al. *The Black Book of Communism. Crimes, Terror, Repression* (Cambridge, 1999).

Creveld, Martin van. *Supplying War. Logistics from Wallenstein to Patton* (Cambridge, 1977).

—. *The Changing Face of War. Lessons of Combat from the Marne to Iraq* (New York, 2006).

—. *Fighting Power. German Military Performance, 1914-1945.* Submitted to: Office of Net Assessment, Department of Defense (Washington D.C., 1980).

Cueppers, Martin. *Wegbereiter der Shoah. Die Waffen-SS, der Kommandostab Reichsfuehrer SS und die Judenvernichtung 1939-1945* (Darmstadt, 2005).

Dahm, Volker, et al. (Hg.). *Die toedliche Utopie. Bilder, Texte, Dokumente, Daten zum Dritten Reich* (Munich, 2008).

Dear, I.C.B. (ed.). *The Oxford Guide to World War II* (Oxford, 1995).

—, (ed.). *The Oxford Companion to World War II* (New York, 2001).

de Zayas, Alfred M. *The Wehrmacht War Crimes Bureau, 1939-1945* (Lincoln, 1989).

Diedrich, Torsten. *Paulus. Das Trauma von Stalingrad. Eine Biographie* (Paderhorn, 2008).

DiNardo, R. L. *Germany's Panzer Arm in WWII* (Mechanicsburg, 1997).

—. *Mechanized Juggernaut or Military Anachronism? Horses and the German Army of World War II* (New York, 1991).

Donat, Gerhard. *Der Munitionsverbrauch im Zweiten Weltkrieg im operativen und taktischen Rahmen* (Osnabruck, 1992).

Dunn, Walter S., Jr. *Hitler's Nemesis. The Red Army, 1930-45* (Mechanicsburg, 1994).

—. *Stalin's Keys to Victory. The Rebirth of the Red Army* (Westport, 2006).

Dupuy, R. Ernest, and Trevor N. Dupuy. *The Encyclopedia of Military History – from 3500 B.C. to the present* (New York, 1986).

Erickson, John. *The Road to Stalingrad. Stalin's War with Germany* (New Haven, 1975).

Erickson, John, and David Dilks, (eds.). *Barbarossa. The Axis and the Allies* (Edinburgh, 1994).

Faerber, Mathias. *Zweiter Weltkrieg in Bildern* (Munich, 1988).

Ferguson, Niall. *The War of the World. Twentieth-Century Conflict and the Descent of the West* (New York, 2006).

Foedrowitz, Michael. *Stalin Organs. Russian Rocket Launchers* (Atglen, 1994).

Foerster, Juergen (Hg.). *Stalingrad. Ereignis – Wirkung – Symbol* (Munich, 1992).

—. *Die Wehrmacht im NS-Staat. Eine strukturgeschichtliche Analyse* (Munich, 2007).

Forty, George. *German Infantryman at War 1939-1945* (Great Britain, 2002).

Fritz, Stephen G. *Frontsoldaten. The German Soldier in World War II* (Lexington, 1995).

Fugate, Bryan, and Lev Dvoretsky. *Thunder on the Dnepr. Zhukov – Stalin and the Defeat of Hitler's Blitzkrieg* (Novato, 1997).

Funke, Manfred (Hg.). *Hitler, Deutschland und die Maechte. Materialien zur Aussenpolitik des Dritten Reiches* (Duesseldorf, 1978).

Fussell, Paul. *Wartime. Understanding and Behavior in the Second World War* (New York, 1989).

Gilbert, Martin. *Second World War* (Toronto, 1989).

Glantz, David M. *Barbarossa. Hitler's Invasion of Russia 1941* (Charleston, 2001).

—. *Barbarossa Derailed. The Battle for Smolensk 10 July – 10 September 1941*, Vol. I: *The German Advance to Smolensk, the Encirclement Battle, and the First and Second Soviet Counteroffensives, 10 July – 24 August 1941* (Solihull, England, 2010).

—. *Stumbling Colossus. The Red Army on the Eve of World War* (Lawrence, 1998).

—. *Zhukov's Greatest Defeat. The Red Army's Epic Disaster in Operation Mars, 1942* (Lawrence, 1999).

—. *Red Army Ground Forces in June 1941* (self-published, 1997).

—. *Forgotten Battles of the Soviet-German War (1941-1945)*. Vol. I: *The Summer-Fall Campaign (22 June – 4 December 1941)* (self-published, 1999).

—. *Atlas and Operational Summary. The Border Battles 22 June – 1 July 1941* (self-published, 2003).

—. *Atlas of the Battle of Smolensk 7 July – 10 September 1941* (self-published, 2001).

—. *Red Army Weapons and Equipment (1941-1945)* (self-published, 2004).

—. *The Soviet-German War 1941-1945: Myths and Realities: A Survey Essay* (self-published, n.d.).

—. *Colossus Reborn. The Red Army at War, 1941-1943* (Lawrence, 2005).

—. *The Military Strategy of the Soviet Union. A History* (London, 1992).

—, (ed.). *The Initial Period of War on the Eastern Front 22 June – August 1941* (London, 1993).

Glantz, David M., and Jonathan House. *When Titans Clashed. How the Red Army Stopped Hitler* (Lawrence, 1995).

Goette, Franz, and Herbert Peiler. *Die 29. Falke-Division 1936-1945* (Doerfler Zeitgeschichte, n.d.)

Gorodetsky, Gabriel. *Grand Delusion. Stalin and the German Invasion of Russia* (New Haven, 1999).

Green, William. *War Planes of the Second World War. Fighters*, Vol. I (Garden City, 1960).

Grenkevich, Leonid D. *The Soviet Partisan Movement 1941-1944* (London, 1999).

Griehl, Manfred. *German Bombers over Russia* (London, 2000).

Hardesty, Von. *Red Phoenix. The Rise of Soviet Air Power, 1941-1945* (Washington D.C., 1982).

Hart, B.H. Liddell. *The German Generals Talk* (New York, 1948).

Hart, Russell A. *Guderian. Panzer Pioneer or Myth Maker?* (Washington D.C., 2006).

Hart, Dr S., and Dr R. Hart and Dr M. Hughes. *The German Soldier in World War II* (Osceola, 2000).

Hartmann, Christian. *Halder. Generalstabschef Hitlers 1938-1942* (Paderborn, 1991).

—. *Wehrmacht im Ostkrieg. Front und militaerisches Hinterland 1941/42* (Munich, 2009).

—. *Unternehmen Barbarossa. Der deutsche Krieg im Osten 1941-1945* (Munich, 2011).

Hartmann, Christian, and Johannes Huerter and Ulrike Jureit (Hg.). *Verbrechen der Wehrmacht, Bilanz einer Debatte* (Munich, 2005).

Haupt, Werner, *Die deutschen Infanterie-Divisionen 1-50. Infanterie-, Jaeger-, Volksgrenadier-Divisionen 1921-1945* (Doerfler Zeitgeschichte, n.d.; first published, 1991).

—. *Sturm auf Moskau 1941. Der Angriff – Die Schlacht – Der Rueckschlag* (Friedberg, 1990).

—. *Army Group Center. The Wehrmacht in Russia 1941-1945* (Atglen, 1997).

Heer, Hannes, and Klaus Naumann. *War of Extermination. The German Military in World War II, 1941-1944* (New York, 2000).

Higham, Robin, and Stephen J. Harris (eds.). *Why Air Forces Fail. The Anatomy of Defeat* (Lexington, 2006).

Hilger, Andreas. *Deutsche Kriegsgefangene in der Sowjetunion 1941-1956. Kriegsgefangenenpolitik, Lageralltag und Erinnerung* (Essen, 2000).

Hillgruber, Andreas. *Deutsche Grossmacht- und Weltpolitik im 19. und 20. Jahrhundert* (Duesseldorf, 1977).

—. *Hitlers Strategie. Politik und Kriegfuehrung 1940-1941* (Munich, 1982).

—. *Der Zweite Weltkrieg 1939-1945. Kriegsziele und Strategie der grossen Maechte* (Stuttgart, 1982).

Hinterhuber, Hans H. *Wettbewerbsstrategie* (Berlin, 1990).

Hinze, Rolf. *Der Zusammenbruch der Heeresgruppe Mitte im Osten 1944* (Stuttgart, 1980).

—. *Das Ostfront-Drama 1944. Rueckzugskaempfe Heeresgruppe Mitte* (Stuttgart, 1997).

Hoffmann, Joachim. *Stalins Vernichtungskrieg 1941-1945* (Munich, 1996).

Hoffmann, Peter. *The History of the German Resistance 1933-1945* (Cambridge, 1977).

Hogg, Ian V. *Armoured Fighting Vehicles* (2000).

Howell, Edgar M. *The Soviet Partisan Movement: 1941-44*. Dept. of Army Pamphlet 20-244. (Washington D.C., 1956).

Hoyt, Edwin P. *Stalin's War. Tragedy and Triumph 1941-1945* (New York, 2003).

Hubatsch, Walther. *Deutschland im Weltkrieg 1914-1918* (Frankfurt, 1966).

Huerter, Johannes. *Hitlers Heerfuehrer. Die deutschen Oberbefehlshaber im Krieg gegen die Sowjetunion 1941/42* (Munich, 2006).

Irving, David. *Hitler's War* (New York, 1977).

Jentz, Thomas L. (ed.). *Panzer Truppen. The Complete Guide to the Creation & Combat Employment of Germany's Tank Force 1933-1942* (Atglen, 1996).

Johnson, Aaron L. *Hitler's Military Headquarters. Organization, Structures, Security and Personnel* (San Jose, 1999).

Johnson, Paul. *Modern Times. The World from the Twenties to the Nineties* (New York, 1991).

Keegan, John. *The Second World War* (New York, 1989).

Kershaw, Ian. *Hitler 1936-1945: Nemesis* (New York, 2000).

—. *Fateful Choices. Ten Decisions that Changed the World, 1940-1941* (New York, 2007).

Kershaw, Robert J. *War Without Garlands. Operation Barbarossa 1941/42* (New York, 2000).

Kirchubel, Robert. *Operation Barbarossa 1941 (3). Army Group Center* (New York, 2007).

—. *Hitler's Panzer Armies on the Eastern Front* (Great Britain, 2009).

Knopp, Guido. *Die Wehrmacht. Eine Bilanz* (Munich, 2007).

Kohl, Paul. *"Ich wundere mich, dass ich noch lebe." Sowjetische Augenzeugen berichten* (Guetersloh, 1990).

Krier, Leon (ed.). *Albert Speer. Architecture 1932-1942* (1985).

Krivoshecv, Col.-Gen. G. F. (ed.). *Soviet Casualties and Combat Losses in the Twentieth Century* (London, 1997).

Kurowski, Franz. *Balkenkreuz und Roter Stern. Der Luftkrieg ueber Russland 1941 – 1944* (Friedberg, 1984).

—, (Hg.). *Hasso von Manteuffel. Panzerkampf im Zweiten Weltkrieg* (Schnellbach, 2005).

Latzel, Klaus. *Deutsche Soldaten – nationalsozialistischer Krieg? Kriegserlebnis – Kriegserfahrung 1939-1945* (Paderborn, 1998).

Leach, Barry A. *German Strategy Against Russia 1939-1941* (Oxford, 1973).

Lewis, S. J. *Forgotten Legions. German Army Infantry Policy 1918-1941* (New York, 1985).

Loeffler, Juergen. *Walther von Brauchitsch (1881-1948). Eine politische Biographie* (Frankfurt, 2001).

Lucas, James. *War on the Eastern Front. The German Soldier in Russia, 1941-1945* (London, 1979).

—. *Hitler's Enforcers. Leaders of the German War Machine 1939-1945* (London, 1996).

—. *Das Reich. The Military Role of the 2nd SS Division* (London, 1991).

Luther, Craig, and Hugh Page Taylor, (eds.). *For Germany. The Otto Skorzeny Memoirs* (San Jose, 2005).

Luttichau, Charles v. P. *The Road to Moscow. The Campaign in Russia – 1941* (unpublished manuscript).

Luttwak, Edward N. *Strategy. The Logic of War and Peace* (Cambridge, 2001).

Macksey, Kenneth. *Guderian. Panzer General* (London, 1975).

Magenheimer, Heinz. *Moskau 1941. Entscheidungsschlacht im Osten* (Selent, 2009).

—. *Hitler's War. Germany's Key Strategic Decisions 1940-1945* (New York, 1998).

Mason, Chris. *Personal Effects of the German Soldier in World War II* (Atglen, 2006).

Mawdsley, Evan. *Thunder in the East. The Nazi-Soviet War 1941-1945* (London, 2005).

Megargee, Geoffrey P. *Inside Hitler's High Command* (Lawrence, 2000).

—. *War of Annihilation. Combat and Genocide on the Eastern Front, 1941* (Lanham, 2006).

Merridale, Catherine. *Ivan's War. Life and Death in the Red Army, 1939-1945* (New York, 2006).

Meyer, Georg. *Adolf Heusinger. Dienst eines deutschen Soldaten 1915 bis 1964* (Hamburg, 2001).

Michulec, Robert. *4. Panzer-Division on the Eastern Front (1) 1941-1943* (Hong Kong, 1999).

Mitcham, Samuel W., Jr. *Hitler's Field Marshals and Their Battles* (New York, 2001).

Mitcham, Samuel W., Jr., and Gene Mueller. *Hitler's Commanders. Officers of the Wehrmacht, the Luftwaffe, the Kriegsmarine, and the Waffen-SS* (New York, 2000).

Montefiore, Simon Sebag. *Stalin. The Court of the Red Tsar* (New York, 2004).

Moorhouse, Roger. *Berlin at War* (New York, 2010).

Mosier, John. *Cross of Iron. The Rise and Fall of the German War Machine, 1918-1945* (New York, 2006).

—. *Deathride. Hitler vs. Stalin: The Eastern Front, 1941-1945* (New York, 2010).

Mueller, Rolf-Dieter. *Der letzte deutsche Krieg 1939-1945* (Stuttgart, 2005).

Mueller, Rolf-Dieter, and Gerd R. Ueberschaer. *Hitler's War in the East. A Critical Assessment* (New York, 2002).

Muller, Richard. *The German Air War in Russia* (Baltimore, 1992).

Muñoz, Antonio J., and Dr Oleg V. Romanko. *Hitler's White Russians: Collaboration, Extermination and Anti-Partisan Warfare in Byelorussia, 1941-1944* (Bayside, 2003).

Murray, Williamson. *Strategy for Defeat. The Luftwaffe 1933-1945* (Maxwell Air Force Base, 1983).

Musial, Bogdan. *Kampfplatz Deutschland. Stalins Kriegsplaene gegen den Westen* (Berlin, 2008).

Nafziger, George F. *The German Order of Battle. Infantry in World War II* (London, 2000).

—. *The German Order of Battle. Panzers and Artillery in World War II* (London, 1995).

Naumann, Andreas. *Freispruch fuer die Deutsche Wehrmacht. "Unternehmen Barbarossa" erneut auf dem Pruefstand* (Tuebingen, 2005).

Nayhauss-Cormons, Mainhardt Graf von. *Zwischen Gehorsam und Gewissen. Richard von Weizsaecker und das Infanterie-Regiment 9* (Bergisch Gladbach, 1994).

Necker, Wilhelm. *The German Army of Today* (Reprinted in Great Britain, 1973; first published in London, 1943).

Newton, Steven H. *Hitler's Commander. Field Marshal Walther Model – Hitler's Favorite General* (2006).

Overmans, Ruediger. *Deutsche militaerische Verluste im Zweiten Weltkrieg* (Munich, 2004).

Overy, Richard. *Russia's War. Blood Upon the Snow* (New York, 1997).

Paret, Peter (ed.). *Makers of Modern Strategy. From Machiavelli to the Nuclear Age* (Princeton, 1986).

Paul, Wolfgang. *Panzer-General Walther K. Nehring. Eine Biographie* (Stuttgart, 2002).

—. *Geschichte der 18. Panzer Division 1940-1943. Streiflichter aus 4 Kriegsjahren* (ca. 1975).

Philippi, Alfred, and Ferdinand Heim. *Der Feldzug gegen Sowjetrussland 1941 bis 1945. Ein operativer Ueberblick* (Stuttgart, 1962).

Piekalkiewicz, Janusz. *Die Schlacht um Moskau. Die erfrorene Offensive* (Augsburg, 1998).

—. *Die Deutsche Reichsbahn im Zweiten Weltkrieg* (Stuttgart, 1979).

Pleshakov, Constantine. *Stalin's Folly. The Tragic first Ten Days of World War II on the Eastern Front* (Boston, 2005).

Plievier, Theodor. *Moscow* (New York, 1953).

Pottgiesser, Hans. *Die Deutsche Reichsbahn im Ostfeldzug 1939-1944* (Neckargemuend, 1960).

Pressfield, Steven. *The Afghan Campaign* (New York, 2006).

Prien, Jochen, et al. *Die Jagdfliegerverbaende der Deutschen Luftwaffe 1934 bis 1945*, Teil 6/1: *Unternehmen "Barbarossa," Einsatz im Osten 22.6. bis 5.12.1941* (2003).

Putney, Diane T. (ed.). *ULTRA and the Army Air Forces in World War II. An Interview with Associate Justice of the U.S. Supreme Court Lewis F. Powell, Jr.* (Washington D.C., 1987).

Rass, Christoph. *"Menschenmaterial:" Deutsche Soldaten an der Ostfront. Innenansichten einer Infanteriedivision 1939-1945* (Paderborn, 2003).

Reinhardt, Klaus. *Moscow – The Turning Point. The Failure of Hitler's Strategy in the Winter of 1941-42* (Oxford, 1992).

—. *Die Wende vor Moskau. Das Scheitern der Strategie Hitlers im Winter 1941/42* (Stuttgart, 1972).

Reuth, Ralf Georg. *Goebbels. Eine Biographie* (Munich, 1990).

—. *Hitler. Eine politische Biographie* (Munich, 2003).

Roberts, Geoffrey. *Stalin's Wars. From World War to Cold War, 1939-1953* (New Haven, 2006).

Roell, Hans-Joachim. *Oberleutnant Albert Blaich. Als Panzerkommandant in Ost und West* (Wuerzburg, 2009).

Rohwer, Juergen, and Eberhard Jaeckel (Hg.). *Kriegswende Dezember 1941. Referate und Diskussionsbeitraege des internationalen historischen Symposiums in Stuttgart vom 17. bis 19. September 1981* (Koblenz, 1984).

Ropp, Theodore. *War in the Modern World* (New York, 1959).

Rottman, Gordon L. *Soviet Field Fortifications 1941-45* (New York, 2007).

Sáiz, Agustín. *Deutsche Soldaten. Uniforms, Equipment & Personal Items of the German Soldier 1939-45* (Philadelphia, 2008).

Schick, Albert. *Die 10. Panzer-Division 1939-1943* (Cologne, 1993).

Schneider, Russ. *Siege: A Novel of the Eastern Front, 1942* (Garden City, 2003).

Schneider, Wolfgang. *Panzer Tactics. German Small-Unit Armor Tactics in World War II* (Mechanicsburg, 2000).

Schneider-Janessen, Karlheinz. *Arzt im Krieg. Wie deutsche und russische Aerzte den zweiten Weltkrieg erlebten* (Frankfurt, 1993).

Schroeder, Hans Joachim. *Die gestohlenen Jahre. Erzaehlgeschichten und Geschichtserzaehlung im Interview: Der Zweite Weltkrieg aus der Sicht ehemaliger Mannschaftssoldaten* (Tuebingen, 1992).

Schueler, Klaus A. Friedrich. *Logistik im Russlandfeldzug. Die Rolle der Eisenbahn bei Planung, Vorbereitung und Durchfuehrung des deutschen Angriffs auf die Sowjetunion bis zur Krise vor Moskau im Winter 1941/42* (Frankfurt, 1987).

Scutts, Jerry. *Luftwaffe Bomber Units 1939-41* (London, 1978).

Seaton, Albert. *The Russo-German War 1941-1945* (London, 1971).

—. *The Battle for Moscow 1941-1942* (New York, 1971).

—. *The German Army 1933-45* (New York, 1982).

Seidler, Franz W. (Hg.). *Verbrechen an der Wehrmacht. Kriegsgreuel der Roten Armee 1941/42* (Selent, 1997).

Seidler, Hans. *Images of War. Operation Barbarossa. Hitler's Invasion of Russia. Rare Photographs from Wartime Archives* (Great Britain, 2010).

Shay, Jonathan. *Achilles in Vietnam. Combat Trauma and the Undoing of Character* (New York, 1994).

—. *Odysseus in America. Combat Trauma and the Trials of Homecoming* (New York, 2002).

Shirer, William L. *The Rise and Fall of the Third Reich. A History of Nazi Germany* (New York, 1960).

Shores, Christopher. *Luftwaffe Fighter Units Russia 1941-45* (London, 1978).

Showalter, Dennis. *Hitler's Panzers. The Lightning Attacks that Revolutionized Warfare* (New York, 2009).

Slaughterhouse. The Encyclopedia of the Eastern Front (Garden City, 2002).

Snyder, Louis L. *Encyclopedia of the Third Reich* (Great Britain, 1998).

Spahr, William J. *Zhukov. The Rise & Fall of a Great Captain* (Novato, 1993).

Stahel, David. *And the World held its Breath. The German Strategic Crisis in the Summer of 1941 and the Failure of Operation Barbarossa.* Manuscript published under the title of *Operation Barbarossa and Germany's Defeat in the East* (Cambridge, 2009).

Stedman, Robert. *Kampfflieger: Bomber Crewmen of the Luftwaffe 1939-45* (New York, 2005).

Steiger, Rudolf. *Armour Tactics in the Second World War. Panzer Army Campaigns of 1939-41 in German War Diaries* (New York, 1990).

Stein, Marcel. *Generalfeldmarschall Walter Model. Legende und Wirklichkeit* (Bissendorf, 2001).

Stolfi, R.H.S. *German Panzers on the Offensive. Russian Front, North Africa 1941-1942* (Atglen, 2003).

—. *Hitler. Beyond Evil and Tyranny* (Amherst, 2011).

Sweeting, C. G. *Hitler's Personal Pilot. The Life and Times of Hans Baur* (Washington D.C., 2000).

Taylor, Brian. *Barbarossa to Berlin. A Chronology of the Campaigns on the Eastern Front 1941 to 1945. Vol. I: The Long Drive East, 22 June 1941 to 18 November 1942* (Staplehurst, 2003).

Telpuchowski, Boris S. *Die sowjetische Geschichte des Grossen Vaterlaendischen Krieges, 1941-1945* (Frankfurt, 1961).

Tessin, Georg. *Verbaende und Truppen der deutschen Wehrmacht und Waffen-SS im Zweiten Weltkrieg 1939-1945*, Bd. I: *Die Waffengattungen – Gesamtuebersicht* (Osnabrueck, 1977).

—. *Verbaende und Truppen der deutschen Wehrmacht und Waffen-SS im Zweiten Weltkrieg 1939-1945*, Bd. II: *Die Landstreitkraefte 1-5* (Osnabrueck, 1973).

The Rise and Fall of the German Air Force 1933-1945 (Public Record Office, 2001) (Reproduction of Air Ministry Pamphlet No. 248, 1948).

Tolstoy, Leo. *War and Peace.* Translated by Constance Garnett. (Modern Library Paperback Edition, New York, 2002).

Tooze, Adam. *The Wages of Destruction. The Making and Breaking of the Nazi Economy* (New York, 2006).

Turney, Alfred W. *Disaster at Moscow: Von Bock's Campaigns 1941-1942* (1970).

Ueberschaer, Gerd R. *Generaloberst Franz Halder. Generalstabschef, Gegner und Gefangener Hitlers* (Goettingen, 1991).

—, (Hg.). *Hitlers militaerische Elite*, Bd. 2: *Vom Kriegsbeginn bis zum Weltkriegsende* (Darmstadt, 1998).

Ueberschaer, Gerd R., and Wolfram Wette (Hg.). *"Unternehmen Barbarossa." Der deutsche Ueberfall auf die Sowjetunion 1941* (Paderborn, 1984).

Volkogonov, Dmitri. *Stalin. Triumph and Tragedy* (New York, 1988).

Walde, Karl J. *Guderian* (Frankfurt, 1976).

Wallach, Jehuda L. *The Dogma of the Battle of Annihilation. The Theories of Clausewitz and Schlieffen and Their Impact on the German Conduct of Two World Wars* (Westport, 1986).

Weal, John. *Bf 109 Aces of the Russian Front* (Oxford, 2001).

—. *Jagdgeschwader 51 "Moelders"* (Oxford, 2006).

Weber, Thomas. *Hitler's First War. Adolf Hitler, the Men of the List Regiment, and the First World War* (Oxford, 2010).

Wegner, Bernd (Hg.). *Zwei Wege nach Moskau. Vom Hitler-Stalin-Pakt zum "Unternehmen Barbarossa"* (Munich, 1991).

—, (ed.). *From Peace to War. Germany, Soviet Russia and the World, 1939-1941* (Providence, 1997).

Weinberg, Gerhard L. *A World at Arms. A Global History of World War II* (Cambridge, 1994).

Weiss, Hermann (Hg.). *Biographisches Lexikon zum Dritten Reich* (Frankfurt, 2002).

Westwood, David. *German Infantryman (2) Eastern Front 1941-43* (Oxford, 2003).

Westwood, J. N. *A History of Russian Railways* (London, 1964).

Wette, Wolfram. *The Wehrmacht. History, Myth, Reality* (Cambridge, 2006).

Wetzig, Sonja. *Die Stalin-Linie 1941. Bollwerk aus Beton und Stahl* (Doerfler Zeitgeschichte, n.d.).

Winchester, Charles D. *Hitler's War on Russia* (New York, 2007).

Woche, Klaus-R. *Zwischen Pflicht und Gewissen. Generaloberst Rudolf Schmidt 1886-1957* (Berlin-Potsdam, 2002).

Wray, Major Timothy A. *Standing Fast: German Defensive Doctrine on the Russian Front during World War II. Prewar to March 1943* (Fort Leavenworth, 1986).

Wright, Jonathan. *Germany and the Origins of the Second World War* (New York, 2007).

Yahil, Leni. *The Holocaust. The Fate of European Jewry, 1932-1945* (Oxford, 1990).

Zabecki, David T. (ed.). *World War II in Europe. An Encyclopedia* (New York, 1999).

Zamoyski, Adam. *Moscow 1812. Napoleon's Fatal March* (New York, 2004).

Ziemke, Earl F. *The Red Army, 1918-1941: From Vanguard of World Revolution to US Ally* (London, 2004).

—. *Stalingrad to Berlin: The German Defeat in the East* (New York, 1985).

Ziemke, Earl F., and Magna E. Bauer. *Moscow to Stalingrad: Decision in the East* (New York, 1988).

Articles & Essays

Arazi, Doron. *"Sigint and 'Blitzkrieg.' German Military Radio Intelligence in Operation 'Barbarossa,'"* in: *From Peace to War. Germany, Soviet Russia and the World, 1939-1941.* Edited by Bernd Wegner (Providence, 1997).

Assmann, Vice Admiral Kurt. *"The Battle for Moscow. The Turning Point of the War,"* in: *Foreign Affairs*, Jan 50.

Bartov, Omer. *"A View from Below. Survival, Cohesion, and Brutality on the Eastern Front,"* in: *From Peace to War. Germany, Soviet Russia and the World, 1939-1941.* Edited by Bernd Wegner (Providence, 1997).

—. *"Von unten betrachtet: Ueberleben, Zusammenhalt und Brutalitaet an der Ostfront,"* in: *Zwei Wege nach Moskau, Vom Hitler-Stalin-Pakt zum "Unternehmen Barbarossa."* Bernd Wegner (Hg.) (Munich, 1991).

Birn, Ruth Bettina. *"Two Kinds of Reality? Case Studies on Anti-Partisan Warfare during the Eastern Campaign,"* in: *From Peace to War. Germany, Soviet Russia and the World, 1939-1941.* Edited by Bernd Wegner (Providence, 1997).

Boog, Horst. *"Higher Command and Leadership in the German Luftwaffe, 1935-1945,"* in: *Air Power and Warfare. The Proceedings of the 8th Military History Symposium USAF Academy 18-20 October 1978.* Edited by Col. Alfred F. Hurley and Robert C. Ehrhart (1979).

Blumentritt, Guenther. *"Moscow,"* in: *The Fatal Decisions.* Edited by William Richardson and Seymour Freidin (London, 1956).

—. *"Die Ueberwindung der Krise vor Moskau im Winter 1941-42, dargestellt an der 4. Armee,"* in: *Wehr-Wissenschaftliche Rundschau,* 4. Jahrgang, Mar 54.

Corum, James S. *"The Luftwaffe's Army Support Doctrine, 1918-1941,"* in: *The Journal of Military History* 59 (Jan 95).

"Der Waldkampf," in: *Allgemeine Schweizerische Militaer Zeitschrift,* Okt 49 (Heft 10), Nov 49 (Heft 11) (No author listed).

Dollwet, Joachim. *"Menschen im Krieg, Bejahung – und Widerstand? Eindruecke und Auszuege aus der Sammlung von Feldpostbriefen des Zweiten Weltkrieges im Landeshauptarchiv Koblenz,"* in: *Jahrbuch fuer westdeutsche Landesgeschichte,"* 13. Jahrgang, 1987. F. J. Heyen, et al. (Hg.) (Koblenz, 1987).

Donat, Hans v. *"Eisenbahn-Pioniere,"* II., abschliessender Teil, in: *Deutsches Soldatenjahrbuch 1966* (Munich, 1966).

Erickson, John. *"Barbarossa June 1941: Who Attacked Whom?"* in: *History Today,* July 2001.

Foer, Joshua. *"Remember This. In the Archives of the Brain, Our Lives Linger or Disappear,"* in: *National Geographic,* Nov 07.

Foerster, Juergen, and Evan Mawdsley. *"Hitler and Stalin in Perspective: Secret Speeches on the Eve of Barbarossa,"* in: *War in History,* 2004 11 (1).

Frieser, Karl-Heinz. *"Die deutschen Blitzkriege: Operativer Triumph – strategische Tragoedie,"* in: *Die Wehrmacht. Mythos und Realitaet.* Rolf-Dieter Mueller & Hans-Erich Volkmann (Hg.) (Munich 1999).

Gorodetsky, Gabriel. *"Stalin and Hitler's Attack on the Soviet Union,"* in: *From Peace to War. Germany, Soviet Russia and the World, 1939-1941.* Edited by Bernd Wegner (Providence, 1997).

Gosztony, Peter. *"Die erste Entscheidungsschlacht des Russlandfeldzuges 1941/42 (II), Moskau in der Krise 1941 (I),"* in: *Oesterreichische Militaerische Zeitschrift,* Heft 2, 1967.

Hartmann, Christian. *"Verbrecherischer Krieg – verbrecherische Wehrmacht?,"* in: *Vierteljahrshefte fuer Zeitgeschichte,* Sonderdruck aus Heft 1/2004.

Heer, Hannes. *"The Logic of the War of Extermination. The Wehrmacht and the Anti-Partisan War,"* in: *War of Extermination. The German Military in World War II, 1941-1944.* Edited by Hannes Heer and Klaus Naumann (New York, 2000).

—. *"Killing Fields. The Wehrmacht and the Holocaust in Belorussia, 1941-42,"* in: *War of Extermination. The German Military in World War II, 1941-1944.* Edited by Hannes Heer and Klaus Naumann (New York, 2000).

Hillgruber, Andreas. *"Die Bedeutung der Schlacht von Smolensk in der Zweiten Julihaelfte 1941 fuer den Ausgang des Ostkrieges,"* in: *Die Zerstoerung Europas. Beitraege zur Weltkriegsepoche 1914 bis 1945,* Hillgruber, Andreas (Frankfurt, 1988).

—. *"Die weltpolitischen Entscheidungen vom 22. Juni 1941 bis 11. Dezember 1941,"* in: *Der Zweite Weltkrieg 1939-1945. Kriegsziele und Strategie der grossen Maechte,* Hillgruber, Andreas (Stuttgart, 1982).

—. *"Das Russland-Bild der fuehrenden deutschen Militaers vor Beginn des Angriffs auf die Sowjetunion,"* in: *Die Zerstoerung Europas. Beitraege zur Weltkriegsepoche 1914 bis 1945,* Hillgruber, Andreas (Frankfurt, 1988).

—. *"Die 'Endloesung' und das deutsche Ostimperium als Kernstueck des rassenideologischen Programms des Nationalsozialismus,"* in: *Hitler, Deutschland und die Maechte. Materialien zur Aussenpolitik des Dritten Reiches.* Manfred Funke (Hg.) (Duesseldorf, 1978).

—. *"Der Faktor Amerika in Hitlers Strategie 1938-1941,"* in: *Deutsche Grossmacht- und Weltpolitik im 19. und 20. Jahrhundert,* Hillgruber, Andreas (Duesseldorf, 1977).

Hoffmann, Joachim. *"The Soviet Union's Offensive Preparations in 1941,"* in: *From Peace to War. Germany, Soviet Russia and the World, 1939-1941.* Edited by Bernd Wegner (Providence, 1997).

Hofmann, Rudolf. *"Die Schlacht von Moskau 1941,"* in: *Entscheidungsschlachten des zweiten Weltkrieges.* Hans-Adolf Jacobsen & Juergen Rohwer (Hg.) (Frankfurt, 1960).

Holborn, Hajo. *"The Prusso-German School: Moltke and the Rise of the General Staff,"* in: *Makers of*

Modern Strategy from Machiavelli to the Nuclear Age. Edited by Peter Paret (Princeton, 1986).

Huerter, Johannes. *"Keine Straffreiheit. Sexualverbrechen von Wehrmachtsangehoerigen 1939 bis 1945,"* in: *Frankfurter Allgemeine Zeitung*, 13 Sep 05.

"Infanterie Division (mot.) Grossdeutschland ruft die Jugend des Grossdeutschen Reiches!" (Cottbus, ca. 1942).

Kagan, Frederick W. *"A Strategy for Heroes – What's wrong with the 2006 Quadrennial Defense Review,"* in: *The Weekly Standard*, 20 Feb 06.

Kirchubel, Robert. *"Operation Barbarossa and the American Controversy over aid to the Soviet Union"* (unpublished research paper, n.d.; courtesy of author).

Kirŝin, Jurij J. *"Die sowjetischen Streitkraefte am Vorabend des Grossen Vaterlaendischen Krieges,"* in: *Zwei Wege nach Moskau, Vom Hitler-Stalin-Pakt zum "Unternehmen Barbarossa."* Bernd Wegner (Hg.) (Munich, 1991).

Knoch, Peter. *"Feldpost – eine unentdeckte historische Quellengattung,"* in: *Geschichtsdidaktik*, Vol. 11, No. 2 (1986).

Kroener, Bernhard R. *"The 'Frozen Blitzkrieg.' German Strategic Planning against the Soviet Union and the Causes of its Failure,"* in: *From Peace to War. Germany, Soviet Russia and the World, 1939-1941.* Edited by Bernd Wegner (Providence, 1997).

Latzel, Klaus. *"Feldpostbriefe: Ueberlegungen zur Aussagekraft einer Quelle,"* in: *Verbrechen der Wehrmacht, Bilanz einer Debatte.* Christian Hartmann, Johannes Huerter & Ulrike Jureit (Hg.) (Munich, 2005).

Loganathan, Maj. *"Failure of Logistics in 'Operation Barbarossa' and its Relevance Today,"* in: *Pointer. Journal of the Singapore Armed Forces*, Vol. 24, Apr-Jun 98.

Luther, Craig. *"German Armoured Operations in the Ukraine 1941. The Encirclement Battle of Uman,"* in: *The Army Quarterly and Defence Journal*, Vol. 108, Oct 78.

Magenheimer, Heinz. *"Krieg zweier Angreifer,"* in: *Junge Freiheit*, 20 Jun 08.

Mawdsley, Evan. *"Crossing the Rubicon: Soviet Plans for Offensive War in 1940-1941,"* in: *The International History Review*, xxv, 4: Dec 03.

Mikoyan, S. A., *"Barbarossa and the Soviet Leadership,"* in: *Barbarossa, The Axis and the Allies.* Edited by John Erickson and David Dilks (Edinburgh, 1994).

Mulligan, Timothy P. *"Reckoning the Cost of People's War: The German Experience in the Central USSR,"* in: *Russian History/Histoire Russe*, 9, Pt. 1, 1982.

Murray, Williamson. *"May 1940: Contingency and fragility of the German RMA,"* in: *The dynamics of military revolution 1300-2050.* Edited by MacGregor Knox and Williamson Murray (Cambridge, 2001).

Musial, Bogdan. *"Bilder einer Ausstellung. Kritische Anmerkungen zur Wanderausstellung 'Vernichtungskrieg. Verbrechen der Wehrmacht 1941 bis 1944,'"* in: *Vierteljahrshefte fuer Zeitgeschichte*, 47. Jahrgang, Okt 99.

Naumann, Klaus. *"The 'Unblemished' Wehrmacht. The Social History of a Myth,"* in: *War of Extermination. The German Military in World War II, 1941-1944.* Edited by Hannes Heer and Klaus Naumann (New York, 2000).

Nehring, Walther K. *"Die 18. Panzerdivision 1941 im Rahmen der Panzergruppe Guderian,"* in: *Deutscher Soldatenkalender 1961* (Munich-Lochhausen).

Opitz, Alfred. *"Die Stimmung in der Truppe am Vorabend des Ueberfalls auf die Sowjetunion,"* in: *Der Krieg des kleinen Mannes. Eine Militaergeschichte von unten.* Wolfram Wette (Hg.) (Munich, 1992).

Paret, Peter. *"Clausewitz,"* in: *Makers of Modern Strategy. From Machiavelli to the Nuclear Age.* Edited by Peter Paret (Princeton, 1986).

Ratley, Major Lonnie O. *"A Lesson of History: The Luftwaffe and Barbarossa,"* in: *Air University Review*, Mar-Apr 83.

Record, Jeffrey. *"Appeasement Reconsidered: Investigating the Mythology of the 1930s,"* internet site at: www.StrategicStudiesInstitute.army.mil., Aug 05.

Reinhardt, Klaus. *"Das Scheitern des deutschen Blitzkriegskonzepts vor Moskau,"* in: *Kriegswende Dezember 1941. Referate und Diskussionsbeitraege des internationalen historischen Symposiums in Stuttgart vom 17. bis 19. September 1981.* Juergen Rohwer & Eberhard Jaeckel (Hg.) (Koblenz, 1984).

Richter, Timm C. *"Die Wehrmacht und der Partisanenkrieg in den besetzten Gebieten der Sowjetunion,"* in: *Die Wehrmacht. Mythos und Realitaet.* Rolf-Dieter Mueller & Hans-Erich Volkmann (Hg.) (Munich, 1999).

Rothenberg, Gunther E. *"Moltke, Schlieffen, and the Doctrine of Strategic Envelopment,"* in: *Makers of Modern Strategy from Machiavelli to the Nuclear Age.* Edited by Peter Paret (Princeton, 1986).

Schroeder, Hans Joachim. *"Erfahrungen deutscher Mannschaftssoldaten waehrend der ersten*

Phase des Russlandkrieges," in: *Zwei Wege nach Moskau, Vom Hitler-Stalin-Pakt zum "Unternehmen Barbarossa."* Bernd Wegner (Hg.) (Munich, 1991).

Schueler, Klaus. *"The Eastern Campaign as a Transportation and Supply Problem,"* in: *From Peace to War. Germany, Soviet Russia and the World, 1939-1941.* Edited by Bernd Wegner (Providence, 1997).

Schulte, Theo J. *"Korueck 582,"* in: *War of Extermination. The German Military in World War II, 1941-1944.* Edited by Hannes Heer and Klaus Naumann (New York, 2000).

Seidler, Franz W. *"Hilfstruppen. Von russischen Hiwis zu den Ostlegionen,"* in: *Deutsche Militaerzeitschrift,* Nr. 37.

Showalter, Dennis E. *"The Prusso-German RMA, 1840-1871,"* in: *The dynamics of military revolution 1300-2050.* Edited by MacGregor Knox and Williamson Murray (Cambridge, 2001).

"Snapshots from History. Logistics Vignettes," in: *Air Force Journal of Logistics,* Vol. XXXIV, 2010.

Stolfi, Russell H.S. *"Chance in History: The Russian Winter of 1941-1942,"* in: *History,* Vol. 65, No. 214, Jun 80.

Streit, Christian. *"Soviet Prisoners of War in the Hands of the Wehrmacht,"* in: *War of Extermination. The German Military in World War II, 1941-1944.* Edited by Hannes Heer and Klaus Naumann (New York, 2000).

Thomas, David. *"Foreign Armies East and German Military Intelligence in Russia 1941-45,"* in: *Journal of Contemporary History,* Vol. 22 (1987).

Ulrich, Andreas. *"Hitler's Drugged Soldiers,"* in: *Spiegel Online,* May 05.

Volkogonov, Dmitri. *"The German Attack, the Soviet Response, Sunday, 22 June 1941,"* in: *Barbarossa. The Axis and the Allies.* Edited by John Erickson and David Dilks (Edinburgh, 1994).

—. *"Stalin as Supreme Commander,"* in: *From Peace to War. Germany, Soviet Russia and the World, 1939-1941.* Edited by Bernd Wegner (Providence, 1997).

Wegner, Bernd. *"The Road to Defeat: The German Campaigns in Russia 1941-43,"* in: *The Journal of Strategic Studies,* Vol. 13, No. 1, Mar 90.

Wildermuth, David. *"Handlungsspielraeume im Vernichtungskrieg."* Research paper presented at the German Studies Association (GSA) Conference, Oct 07.

Yingling, Lt.-Col. Paul. *"A failure of Generalship,"* in: *Armed Forces Journal,* May 07.

Zhukov, Georgi K. *"The War Begins: June 22, 1941,"* in: *Battles Hitler Lost and the Soviet Marshalls who Won them* (New York, 1986).

—. *"The Beginning of the War,"* in: *Soviet Generals Recall World War II.* Edited by Igor Vitukhin (New York, 1981).

Support from German Veterans[3]
List of German veterans who saw combat on the Russian front[4] during 1941/42, and who – directly or indirectly – provided materials to this author during the preparation of the book. These materials included: completed questionnaires, field post, personal diaries, unit histories, photographs and other items of historical interest.

H.-O. (268 ID)
H. S. (6 ID)
R. Adler (14 ID (mot.))
K. Andres (20 PD)
O. Baese (110 ID)
H. Baetcher, (K.Gr. 100)
G. Barkhoff (26 ID)
L. Bauer (3 PD)
K. Beimdieke (2 PD)
F.-A. Belke (6 ID)
W. Bergelt (56 ID)
P. F. Boeselager (86 ID)
H. Boucsein (129 ID)
H. Bruenger (86 ID)
E. Bub (Flak Abtl. 303)
Dr E. Bunke (31 ID)
Dr W. Dicke (26 ID)
H.-J. Dismer (6 ID)
W. Dowe (86 ID)
H. Effing (26 ID)
P. Folger (252 ID)
H. Franze (263 ID)
E. Fritze (6 PD)
A. von Garn (252 ID)
A. Gassmann (106 ID)
R. Grimm (58 ID)
A. Gutenkunst (35 ID)
H. Haape (6 ID)
J. Hahn (292 ID)
W. Heinemann (23 ID)
K. Hempel (258 ID)
L. Hoyer (95 ID)
Ofw. Jakubowski (292 ID)
E. Krehl (ARKO 121)
G. Kreuter (18 PD)
E. Krombholz (3.(H)/21(Pz))
K. Kummer (18 PD)
W. Kunz (87 ID)
H. Lierow (6 ID)
W. Loewer (129 ID)
K. H. Mayer (30 ID)
E. Meinecke (86 ID)
A. Meyer (106 ID)
R. Moebius (292 ID)
H. Moennich (12 Flak Rgt.)
G. Mueller-Wolfram (71 Flak Abtl.)
E. Nebe (6 ID)
H. W. Niermann (6 PD)
H. Pagel (RAD/Flak)
E.-M. Rhein (6 ID)
G. Richter (2 PD)
Obstlt. Ringenberg (6 ID)

S. Risse (18 PD)
W. Schaefer-Kehnert (11 PD)
H. Schillke (8 PD)
G. Schulze (18 PD)
H. Stockhoff (6 ID)
F. Strienitz (7 MG Btl.)
O. Trotsch (5 PD)
K.-G. Vierkorn (23 ID)
W. Vollmer (106 ID)
H. Voss (6 ID)
E. Wagemann (23 ID)
E. Wardin (9./537 HNR)
W. Werner (252 ID)
W. Wessler (6 ID)
H. Wexel (31 ID)
O. Will (5 PD)
E. Willich (112 ID)
G. Zirk (4 & 55 KG)

Internet Sites
http://www.dd-wast.de.
http://www.feldgrau.com
http://www.foreignaffairs.org
http://hco.hagen.de/barbarossa
http://www.history.army.mil
http://www.iremember.ru
http://www.jewishvirtuallibrary.org
http://www.lexikon-der-wehrmacht.de
http://www.lonesentry.com
http://www.nypost.com
http://www.redstate.com
http://www.shtetlinks.jewishgen.org/
http://www.stern.de.
www.StrategicStudiesInstitute.army.mil.
http://www.verbrechen-der-wehrmacht.de
http://en.wikipedia.org/
www.WorldRailFans.org

ENDNOTES

1   These studies were prepared by the *Luftwaffe* during the war, or by former *Luftwaffe* officers on behalf of the U.S. Air Force in the mid-1950s.

2   Note: Inclusive dates cited for war diaries (KTB) of armies, panzer groups and divisions denote the portions of these texts consulted by this author, not the total time periods covered by the diaries themselves, which in most cases are much greater.

3   Note: Many of the more significant items provided by the veterans (or their family members) are listed among the "Primary Sources."

4   Note: The great majority of these men fought with Army Group Center during 1941/42.

Index of Names

Index of German and Soviet Military Formations
(Divisions and above)

GERMAN FORMATIONS: